MW00826712

Victory Roll

Victory Roll

The American Fighter Pilot and Aircraft in World War II

Dr. William Wolf

Schiffer Military History
Atglen, PA

Dedication

I wish to dedicate this book to my wife, Nancy, and my good friend, partner, and fellow historian, Jim Lansdale. But most of all I wish to dedicate it to the brave men of VMF-323, who gave up precious years of their youth—and sometimes their lives—to defend America.

Book Design by Ian Robertson.

Copyright © 2001 by Dr. William Wolf.
Library of Congress Catalog Number: 2001096126

Printed in China.
ISBN: 0-7643-1458-0

We are interested in hearing from authors with book ideas on related topics.

Published by Schiffer Publishing Ltd.
4880 Lower Valley Road
Atglen, PA 19310
Phone: (610) 593-1777
FAX: (610) 593-2002
E-mail: Schifferbk@aol.com.
Visit our web site at: www.schifferbooks.com
Please write for a free catalog.
This book may be purchased from the publisher.
Please include $3.95 postage.
Try your bookstore first.

In Europe, Schiffer books are distributed by:
Bushwood Books
6 Marksbury Avenue
Kew Gardens
Surrey TW9 4JF
England
Phone: 44 (0) 20 8392-8585
FAX: 44 (0) 20 8392-9876
E-mail: Bushwd@aol.com.
Free postage in the UK. Europe: air mail at cost.
Try your bookstore first.

Contents

Acknowledgments 7

Preface 8

Foreword 9

Chapter 1: U.S. Pilot Training

USAAF 10

USN 21

Training Aircraft 25

Chapter 2: Building a Fighter

Introduction 30

Engines 32

Armament and Accessories 38

Pilot Protection 46

Chapter 3: Fighter Combat Tactics 51

Chapter 4: Fighter Missions

ETO 56

Carrier 64

Pacific 70

Chapter 5: Ace Races and Victory Credits

Victory Credits 74

European Ace Races 76

Pacific Aces Races 82

Chronologies 90

Chapter 6: First American Victories (Service/Theater) 96

Chapter 7: First American Aces (Service/Theater) 103

Chapter 8: USAAF Fighters: First Victories, First Aces, and Top-Scorers

ETO, MTO, CBI, PTO/Flying the Fighter

P-40 (Includes AVG) 108

P-38 124

P-47 141

P-51 (A-36 and F-6) 155

P-39 (P-400) 177

Spitfire 183

Miscellaneous (P-26, P-35, P-36 P-43 and Liaison) 188

USAAF Fighter Aircraft Comparative Strengths 192

Chapter 9: USN/USMC Fighters: First Victories, First Aces, and Top Scorers

By Theater/Flying the Fighter

F4F (FM-2) 194

F6F 209

F4U 221

F2A 233

Miscellaneous (SBD, TBF/TBM) 237

Chapter 10: Night Fighters

Background/Training/Tactics 241

P-61 242

F6F(N) 250

Miscellaneous (F4U, P-38, PV-1, Beaufighter, Mosquito, P-70) 254

Chapter 11: Aces in Multiple Aircraft
      Two Aircraft 264
      Three Aircraft 264
      Four Aircraft 268
Chapter 12: Multiple-War Aces
      Spanish Civil War/WWII 276
      WWII/Korea 277
      Three Decade 280
Chapter 13: Victories Over Axis Powers 282
Chapter 14: Aces in a Day 290
Chapter 15: Fighter Bombers & TAC R, and Photo Reconnaissance Units 310
Chapter 16: Pistons vs. Jets (Vs. Me-262, Me-163, Ar-234, V-1, and Ohka) 329
Chapter 17: Lasts (Victories, aces, battles etc.) 337
Chapter 18: Top Fighter Squadrons and Groups (USAAF, USN, USMC) 345
Chapter 19: Aircraft Vulnerability and Personnel Losses 352
Chapter 20: Americans in Foreign Service, Foreigners in American Service And Others
      Americans in the RAF 368
      Poles in the USAAF 372
      Chinese American Composite Wing 374
      African Americans in the USAAF 377
Chapter 21: Aces Personal Markings 379
Chapter 22: Some Miscellany
      All in the Family (Father-son, brothers, etc.) 404
      Gray Beard, No Beard (Oldest, youngest) 407
      Movie Star Ace 412
      Aces Attack the Sound Barrier 412
      U.S. WWII Air Decorations 415
      Service Academy Aces 422
Chapter 23: Appendices
      USMC aces list 423
      USN aces list 425
      USAAF aces list 433
      Ace's Victory by Fighter Type 449
      Equivalent Ranks 450
      Japanese Aircraft Codes 451
      Glossary and Abbreviations 452

      Index 455

Acknowledgments

My lifelong hobby has been WWII aerial combat, and over the years I have collected over 14,000 books and magazines, along with hundreds of reels of microfilm on the subject. I have probably nearly every book written on WWII combat aviation and complete collections of every combat aviation magazine published since 1939. Also included in my collection are many hundreds of aviation unit and aircraft pilot's histories, parts, and maintenance manuals. My microfilm collection includes vintage intelligence reports, USAF, USMC, and USN group and squadron histories, complete Japanese Monograph and U.S. Strategic Bombing Survey series, as well as USAF Historical Studies. Over the years I have been fortunate in meeting many fighter aces, pilots, and aviation buffs who have shared stories and photographs with me (I have 5,000+ photos of aces alone). I have made many multi-day expeditions to various military libraries, museums, and photo depositories with my copy machine and photocopy stand, collecting literally reams of material and 1,000s of photographs. I also have had a dark room where I developed 1,000s of rare photos from microfilm negatives.

The author wishes that every person who contributed over the past quarter century could be personally mentioned. A bibliography is impossible, as this book has been a work in progress for many years. Initially, information was collected piecemeal for magazine articles and for personal reference. As the information accumulated on discs and in files in my computer, I decided that I would add to it and compile it into this book. Special thanks go to the many aces who have written the "To Fly" accounts of their aircraft,

or who have given me personal recollections of the combats which made them remarkable as fighter pilots. The cornerstone of historical accuracy that this book is based on are the monumental research works by Dr. Frank Olynyck. His meticulous multi-volume *Credits for the Destruction of Enemy Aircraft in Air-to-Air Combat, WWII* series and *Stars & Bars, A Tribute to the American Fighter Ace* are undoubtedly the "Bible" for any serious researcher of WWII combat history. Again, thanks, Dr. Olynyck, for spending countless hours researching and compiling an enormous amount of source material and then sharing it with us.

Over the years the origin of the 1,000s of photos I have been lent to copy and those I have copied and collected myself have become obscured. Most are from military and government sources, but many also are from private individuals. I apologize if some photos which are credited as from the "author's collection" or otherwise are in fact from individuals who were kind enough to have given or lent me these photographs. Also, some of the photos are not of the best quality because of their age and source, but were used because of their one-of-a-kind significance.

Thanks to J.W. "Rocky" Gooch for the use of his aircraft drawings used in various parts of this book. Mr. Gooch may be contacted at www.warbirdresourcegroup.org. Also, thanks to Gary Velsaco, who researches and reproduces wonderful nose art panels and can be contacted at www.flyingcolors.com.

Thanks go to my persevering wife, Nancy, who has seen her car parked outside in the hot Arizona sun as my WWII library luxuriates in the remodeled, air-conditioned three-car garage.

Author, Bill Wolf, in his library holding a replica victory art panel from a VMF-323 Corsair. Wolf has another book, *Death Rattlers: Marine Squadron VMF-323 Over Okinawa*, also published by Schiffer Publishing. (Author)

Preface

The American fighter pilot cadet was an intelligent young man in his late teens or early twenties from all walks of life, just starting his life, and often leaving his first years of college. He was selected from the cream of American youth, with admission standards much more restrictive than any other branch of the military. The hastily trained cadet became the pilot who, early in the war, flew inferior aircraft (the P-39, F2A, and F4F) against a better trained and more experienced enemy pilot who flew superior equipment. These early American pilots knowingly flew against great odds and held the line until American know-how and can do attitude allowed its massive industrial base to meet its potential. Their sacrifice allowed new pilots time to enter a training scheme that produced superior, well-trained pilots, and American industry to develop and produce superior new designs, such as the F4U, F6F, P-47, P-38, and finally, the P-51. Well-trained pilots flying superior new fighter aircraft against an enemy, losing its best pilots and unable to afford the luxury of extended training, brought about the inevitable defeat of the Axis air forces. After the war these young men, America's "best and brightest," took a leading place in American society and industry.

Foreword

Throughout my career in the Marine Corps, I have been very fortunate to have been presented opportunities that most pilots only have dreamed of. I have had the opportunity to fly over 260 types of aircraft, including over 30 X-planes, for over 14,000 hours in the air in both combat and as a test pilot. I flew combat with VMF-221 over Midway—where I got my first victory—and over Guadalcanal, where I became the Marine Corps' first ace and got 15 1/2 victories there. As a test pilot after the war I held world speed and altitude records and test flew numerous X-planes.

In combat over Guadalcanal we were lucky to be able to encounter the Japanese almost every day and run up our victory totals. But, during the war there were many excellent pilots who never saw an enemy or fired a shot in their entire combat tours. This was a time when we were trying to hold the line against the Japanese, who had a superior fighter in the Zero, and which was flown by experienced pilots. I understood the strengths and limitations of my Grumman F4F Wildcat fighter and exploited them. I was able to press aggressive attacks, as I had full confidence in my wingmen to protect me while I concentrated on my firing run. I was lucky, but I was also confident and well-trained, and just knew I was better than the Jap pilot. When the war ended, American aircraft and equipment were the finest in the world, and her pilots were the best trained and most proficient.

Maj. Gen. Marion Carl (Ret. USMC)

Maj.Gen. Marion Carl. (Author/Carl)

CHAPTER 1

U.S. Pilot Training in WWII

USAAF Pilot Training in WWII

Introduction

Aerial combat at the outbreak of WWII quickly demonstrated that the day of the lone wolf pilot had passed. The transformation of aerial strategy from individual to group coordination and tactics, in which pilots worked together toward an objective, forever altered the pilot's status. The pilot had become only one part of a functioning unit, and although he received the lion's share of the headlines, he was, nonetheless, subordinated to the group and mission.

Procurement

At Pearl Harbor the annual manpower goal for the Air Force was 30,000 pilots, but by October 1942, the requirement had risen to 50,000. Pre-war experience had shown that of all applicants only 20% were able to meet the rigid physical and mental standards required, and that of these no more than 40 to 50% would graduate. Therefore, to graduate 50,000 pilots annually, 500,000 applicants would be needed to qualify 100,000 entering students. Early in the war college attendance was required to become a Flying Cadet, but due to the vast, aforementioned manpower requirements, this prerequisite was found too restrictive by Brig.Gen. Carl Spaatz, Air Staff Chief. He felt college requirement placed too much emphasis on formal education and did not utilize the numerous young men who did not have the opportunity for a college education, but possessed the native intelligence and background to meet the requirements for flight training.

The Aviation Cadet Examining Board was established to give a two-part (physical and mental) examination. These boards were located in the Post Office or Federal building of large cities and on most Air Force bases. To be eligible several general conditions had to be met. The applicant must have reached his 18th birthday, but could not be older than 27. A 17-year old applicant could, with written parental permission, enlist in the Air Corps Enlisted Reserve. The applicant could be married or single. He had to be a citizen for ten years with proof of place of birth or citizenship (a non-citizen from an Allied nation could request a waiver of the ten year requirement from the Adjutant General). An enlisted man in the Army, with the required qualifications, could apply for Aviation Cadet Training, and if he was found physically and mentally qualified he could be transferred in grade (post 1943) to the Air Corps, unassigned. However, in practice this proved difficult, as few Army unit commanders wished to part with the type of man who could qualify for pilot training. Also, prior to 1943, a transferee would lose dependency allowances and often suffered reductions in pay until he was allowed to transfer in grade.

The physical requirements for an Aviation Cadet candidate were the same as those prescribed for appointment and call to active duty as a Reserve Officer in any branch of the Army. However, duty as a flying officer required some special physical standards. Visual acuity, color perception, and hearing had to be normal. A flying officer—except for a fighter pilot—had to stand between 5 feet and 6 foot 4 inches and weigh 105 to 200 pounds. A fighter pilot had to

Classes 40E and 40F at Randolph Field, Texas, May 1940. (USAF)

Ground school class Randolph Field. (USAF)

measure 5'4" to 5'10" and weigh 114 to 160 pounds. Physical standards were not changed, but the definition of the qualifications was eased by the use of waivers so that disqualifications decreased from 73% in 1939 to 50% in 1941. Later, when excess manpower was available the use of waivers was decreased.

The mental test was designed to measure the types of proficiency in comprehension and in problem solving which were typical of those required in training. The examination was of a multiple-choice, short answer variety designed to give a picture of the general field of knowledge possessed by each candidate. It was felt that the test had wide enough latitude that a candidate with above average intelligence but possessing only average academic background could achieve a passing grade.

Pay for an applicant accepted for Aviation Cadet Training through voluntary induction was that of a private at $50 per month. After appointment as an Aviation Cadet and while training in that grade, he received $75 per month and $1 per day ration allowance. He was also furnished quarters, medical care, uniforms, and other clothing and equipment. He was given a $10,000 Government Life Insurance policy at government expense while undergoing actual flying training. After his graduation and while on flying status, this life insurance had to be continued at his own expense. An enlisted man of the Army who transferred in grade to the Air Corps, unassigned, for Aviation Cadet training, received the pay and allowances of his enlisted grade while undergoing the pre-flight training prior to his appointment as an Aviation Cadet.

Pre-Flight Training

Basic Training: Before 1943, Basic Training was considered a weak link in the training program. The lack of experienced personnel to administer the program and the urgency to send recruits on to flight training and specialized schools, along with the lack of facilities contributed to these deficiencies. Reports from combat indicated that graduates lacked sufficient training required for combat survival, particularly marksmanship (increased to 15 hours) and bivouac, survival (increased to 29 hours), and health measures (increased to 20 hours). As the imperative of war subsided the pre-

flight course was increased from four to five weeks. Of course, the legendary drilling (73 hours), physical training (15 hours), and military procedure (13 hours) were ever present. A period of 18 (usually) to 26 days after the beginning of basic training saw the candidate undergo a series of exhaustive medical, psychological, and mental/psychomotor tests to determine his fitness for advancement into the flight program.

Medical and psychological tests usually were administered during the first five days, while aptitude and psychomotor tests followed in the next five to seven days. An example of these psychomotor (coordination between eyes, hands, and feet) tests was the use of a turret lathe. A turret lathe operates completely opposite the standard lathe. A stylist was held in each hand and held on rotating dime-sized discs, which rotated in opposite directions. This test was not unlike rubbing one's stomach while patting one's head.

The aptitude tests were of a multiple-choice type. They were designed to measure speed and accuracy of perception, the ability to read and understand technical information, and measure logic and judgment, along with determining general knowledge in mathematics, general information, and mechanical principles.

In making aircrew assignment three factors were considered in order of priority: 1) aptitude; 2) individual preference; and 3) quota availability. However, in late 1943, when quotas were progressively smaller the order of priority shifted to 1) quota availability, 2) aptitude, and 3) individual preference. Candidates eliminated from the program were informed of alternate types of training available to them. Generally, the eliminee was sent to a BTC for reassignment to gunnery or to technical training.

Pre-Flight School: The objective of pre-flight training was stated in March 1942 by Brig.Gen. W.W. Welsh, Deputy Chief of Staff Training Command:

Academic preparation will include such subjects as will prepare the trainee for the flight and ground school instruction which he will receive in the Air Corps Flying Schools. Military indoctrination, military customs and regulations, and infantry drill. Physi-

Meteorology Class at Randolph Field, Spring 1942. (USAF)

cal training will fit trainees to absorb future intensive training without undue fatigue or ill effects.

Until early 1942, pre-flight school was a four-week course, after which a nine-week course was inaugurated. In May 1944, another week was added. There were separate curricula for pilot and non-pilot trainees, with pilot training stressing math, physics, map reading, meteorology, and recognition of the aircraft and shipping. Until 1943, each pre-flight school exercised broad latitude in its cadet instruction. This lack of uniformity was shown to be detrimental in later stages of training, and a single curriculum was instituted in April 1943.

Because primary training—the next stage of the cadet's training—was to be given at civilian contract schools, the purpose of the pre-flight school was to make certain the cadet would receive military indoctrination. Also, cadets who could not adapt to military regimen could be eliminated in pre-flight school before too much time and money were invested in their training. In summer 1943, it was estimated that 80% of cadets who successfully completed pre-flight school would become pilots.

Pre-flight school was probably the most taxing period of training for a cadet. The two-class system gave upper class students the right to discipline the incoming lower class, so upper class cadets who five weeks earlier were forced to awake at 4 am to drill in double time could now require the same of the lower class cadets. Hazing was allowed until May 1943, when public outcry led to its official abolishment. However, in practice officers unofficially encouraged hazing. The dining room was the favorite area for hazing. Lower classmen had to sit at attention at the dining table on the front two to three inches of their chairs, sometimes with a cracker between their stomach and the table. In the "square meal" ritual the cadet had to make all eating motions in a square pattern, eyes staring horizontally ahead. Not only did this make finding the plate and food difficult, but also the mouth.

A widespread rumor in pre-flight (and primary) training was that some cadets had been placed in each class to spy on other cadets in order to report the cadets who were troublemakers and chronic complainers. This accusation cannot be substantiated, but persisted throughout the war.

Despite the Code of Honor, cheating on examinations was widespread and instructors had to proctor the tests. Cadets set a low value on ground school subjects and felt to be eliminated because of failure in a subject such as physics, which was considered to be of no practical value in actual flying, was unfair and, therefore, justified cheating.

Weather permitting, full-dress parade and inspection was held every Saturday before open post. Dress parades required absolute stance at attention. Cadets soon learned tricks, such as wetting their white gloves to keep their hands and wrists cool while standing at attention in the heat. Wriggling of the toes kept the circulation moving but, nonetheless, infrequently a cadet would faint and was not allowed to be assisted by other cadets. Cadets were allowed to answer officers in one of three responses: "Yes, Sir"; "No, Sir"; and "No excuse, Sir."

Probably the most impressive ritual was "drumming out." At midnight, the P.A. system would sound with drum rolls, indicating that the entire cadet corps, sometimes numbering several thousand, had five minutes to change into full dress uniform. Late arrivals would incur five tours (a tour was a one hour march in full dress uniform). Once in formation, cadet officers with swords drawn would inspect the entire cadet corps, "gigging" for the smallest infraction. Then the name of the offending cadet would be read only once, and thereafter he would be referred to by his serial number. To the beating of drums the details of the offense (usually a breach of honor) was read, and the cadet was "drummed out" to the words: "Henceforth, it is decreed, his name shall not be named at (such and such) Field and is to be stricken from the rolls, never to be mentioned or recalled again." These dramatics, undoubtedly, had great psychological effect on the cadet corps.

Pre-flight school served as a remedial academic and "spit and polish" military phase of a cadet's training. The average day for a pre-flight school cadet (c.1942) was as follows:

0515: Shower	1400-1500: Athletics
0530: Shave	1500: Shower/change
0545: Clean room	1515-1615: Free: Study, personal
0600: Reveille formation	1615: Prepare to parade
(laundry, barber, repair equipment)	1630: Fall out for parade
0615: Back to room special instruction	1645: March to parade
0630: Form/march to breakfast	1700: Parade
0645-0715: Breakfast	1730: March to barracks
0715: March back to barracks	1745: Free
0730: Free	1800: Fall out & march to mess
0745: March to class	1815-1845: Dinner
0800-1115: Classes	1845: March to barracks
Code, physics, math & map reading	1900: Free: Study, visit/socialize
1130: Free	1930-2130: Call to Quarters
1145: Fall in for lunch	2130: Prepare for bed
March to lunch (study)	2200: Taps
1200-1230: Lunch	
1230: March back to barracks	
1245: Prepare & fall out for drill	
1300-1345: Drill & prepare for athletics	

"Tootsie," "Pluto," and "Zombie" were cockpit mock-up trainers arranged on rollers to give the pitch and roll feeling of flying. Scott Field, East St. Louis, IL. (USAF)

College or Pre-Flight Preparatory Training

During 1942, the AAC had recruited aviation cadets in excess of its immediate needs. These recruits were held in Air Corps Enlisted Reserve (ACER), because Air Force facilities for processing and housing them were inadequate. By the end of 1942, 93,000 men were awaiting classification and instruction. The War Manpower Commission and Selective Service looked upon this large excess of manpower disapprovingly. At this time America's colleges were financially troubled due to the loss of students to the armed services. The colleges, of course, had the necessary facilities available to feed, house, and instruct cadets. Consequently, Gen. H.H. Arnold recommended to the Secretary of War that these men be called to active duty and be given a period of remedial training. A directive was issued enrolling 70,000 men in over 150 colleges by April 1943.

An Aviation Cadet Educational Exam (AC 20A) was prepared to be given to pre-aviation cadets to ascertain individual deficiencies. This test determined the number of weeks of college training that was to be given to each man (85% required some additional training, while 60% required the entire 20 week curriculum).

Since the program was a personal rather than a true training scheme, the AAF never established a definite educational objective. Academic subjects, including math, physics, English, history, and geography were taught and tested. Failure meant re-examination and tours. The officers of each detachment emphasized military indoctrination, drill, and discipline. Military indoctrination and physical training rather than academics were considered the most useful aspect of the college program, as these prepared the student for the regimen of service life and training. Initially, the program was directed to a college level, but as the program progressed, its quality regressed to a high school level.

Many colleges offered a ten-hour flight-training program in conjunction with the Civil Aeronautics Administration and civilian contract flying schools. This flying indoctrination, usually in a Cub J-3, was rudimentary at best, and was criticized as "riding around." Nonetheless, it certainly was a great morale booster for cadets who had been waiting to fly.

By late 1943, a full quota of men in training, along with a small backlog of inactive recruits caused the Air Training Command (ATC) to reduce cadet college admission by half. By spring 1944, a general manpower shortage in the non-flying Army forced the AAF to return to Army Ground Forces and Army Service Forces all personnel recruited from those forces that were not yet in pre-flight training. This order caused the withdrawal of many students and the Secretary of War to terminate the program in July 1944, after 254,000 men had been enrolled.

Flight Training

Introduction: In the 1930s, the extent of the Air Corps training scheme was the 300 pilots it graduated annually from Randolph Field. By mid-1940, three regional training centers were established, and in January 1941, the training program was coordinated and supervised by the newly formed Flying Training Command (FTC), with three regions designated as subcommands: 1) Eastern FTC; 2) Central FTC; and 3) Western FTC. On the outset, FTC was segmented into flight training, ground training, technical training, etc.

In mid-1943, the Technical Training Command merged the three regional FTCs to form the AAF Training Command (AAFTC).

The key figure in the FTC was a 1907 classmate of Gen. Arnold, Lt.Gen. Barton K. Yount. Yount was called to Washington from his post as Commandant of the Air Corps Training Center to head the FTC in January 1942. In his book *Global Mission*, Gen. Arnold lavishly praised Gen. Yount's immeasurable contribution to AAF training: "He did a grand job. From then on, I knew it would function in accordance with the general directive it had received."

Generally, the four stages of flight training were:
1) Primary: the student learned to fly a light and stable aircraft of low horsepower.
2) Basic: the student progressed to a heavier and more complex aircraft containing instruments.
3) Advanced: the student learned to fly a trainer whose characteristics were similar to combat aircraft.
4) Transitional: the student learned to fly combat aircraft.

Primary Flight Training

In late 1938, with war clouds gathering in Europe, planners at the Office of the Chief of the Air Corps (OCAC) reported that existing training facilities were inadequate and that expansion was necessary, but without affecting the quality of the training. The course of new construction and expansion would require time and personnel, which were both at a premium. Gen. Arnold hoped to transfer the primary training responsibility to free Air Corps resources for later stages of training. In October, Arnold called the operators of the nation's three best civilian flying schools to meet him in Washington. Among those present were Theopholis Lee of the Boeing School of Aeronautics, Oakland, California; Oliver Parks of Park's Air College, East St. Louis, Illinois; and C.C. Moseley of Curtiss-Wright Technical Institute, Glendale, California. Gen. Arnold proposed each school establish and expand facilities to train and accommodate Army Flying Cadets. At the time Arnold did not have any Congressional appropriations or any official sanctions, however, Arnold persuasively assured the school operators that Congress would soon allot the necessary moneys. Also, certain laws restricting the number of Army personnel who could be trained in non-military schools had to be redrafted and revised. The War Department and Congress then had to approve the proposed program. Public Law No. 18 accomplished this on 3 April 1939, but only by a scant two votes. In May 1939, nine civilian schools were contracted to initiate primary training in July.

Early civilian contract primary training programs lasted 12 weeks, with new classed beginning every six weeks. But by early 1942, with the pressure of war, the program was reduced to two weeks with new classes beginning every five weeks. This reduction was at the expense of ground training, which was reduced from 225 hours to 94 hours by transferring this ground study time to pre-flight training. The ground, or academic phase, of primary training was a continuation of pre-flight study, with navigation, weather and aircraft, and aero-equipment added. Still later, primary training was further reduced to eight weeks, but often cadets were posted for additional training due to the excess number of trainees being processed.

The quality of a civilian flying school was directly correlated to the quality of its instructors. When the program was initiated, instructor proficiency levels were high, but as the programs expanded to accommodate more trainees, more instructors were required and were of a lesser quality. Also, the aviation manpower demand of the Navy/Marines, Ferrying Command, airlines, and Selective Service Boards claimed many civilian school instructors. These groups were asked to voluntarily refrain from taking instructors, which by and large they did, except for the Navy, whose recruiting officers could not resist tempting civilian instructors.

A study by the Training Command found that civilian schools were able to train cadets for about $1.75 per hour less than could military bases. However, the study felt that military schools furnished higher quality trainees and provided better health care and morale. Many cadets who graduated from civilian schools would tend to disagree with the lower morale claim, as civilian schools provided plush accommodations and less military discipline. Training officers in Basic Flight Training often complained that it was difficult to rid the new primary graduates of the "country club" attitude they acquired at the civilian schools.

By May 1943, fifty-six primary civilian contract schools existed, but by 1944 contract schools were phased out. Of course, by this time the war was being won and many pilots had been graduated. The extra air bases and facilities available to AAFTC could easily handle the diminished number of cadets which were then required. Plainly, the vast numbers of cadets could not have been trained so quickly without the aid of the civilian contract schools.

Primary school flight training consisted of four phases, with the following basic teaching techniques used in each phase:
a) Description of each technique by the instructor.
b) Demonstration of the technique by the instructor.
c) Student execution of the technique under the instructor's direct supervisor
d) Critique of the student's execution of the technique.
e) Practice of the technique.

Pre-solo Phase: The student was familiarized in fundamental light aircraft handling, usually by observing and feeling from the rear cockpit the instructor's manipulation of the various controls through a linked set of controls. Every day was spent in the air, and after a while the instructor did not touch the controls as the cadet practiced take offs, landings, and spin and stall recovery. One thing most student-pilots remember of their first flights was the gosport helmet, which was officially described as: "the instructor's means of verbal communication with the cadet while in flight." However, the gosport was a one-way communications system: instructor to cadet only. A particularly poor execution of a maneuver by a "Dodo," or novice student, often solicited a rather impious tirade from the instructor through the gosport tube, giving it the nickname "profanity filter." A favorite trick of the cadets was to stuff the instructor's end of the tube with cotton.

Intermediate Phase: The student received pre-solo and precision instruction utilizing elementary aerobatic maneuvers, such as the various eight patterns and chandelles (climbing turns). Finally,

about the third week, the student had gained enough experience and confidence to solo. After the first solo flight, solo practice of take offs, landings, and prescribed flight maneuvers were carried out. The instructor occasionally flew along to further demonstrate elementary maneuvers and spot landings. During this phase the Link Trainer was utilized. The Link Trainer was essentially an opaque cockpit connected to a series of electrically driven pumps and gyroscopes which simulated attitudes of flight. The student sat in the totally enclosed opaque cockpit and received directions from an instructor for practice in navigation and instrument flying. The student's responses to the instructor's directions were recorded and graphed so that an assessment of his skill and progress could be determined.

Accuracy Phase: The student gained proficiency in landings (e.g. 90 degree cross-wind, spot, short run, etc.). On crosswind landings each student had to be scored on ten landings, and often it became a race to be first to complete the ten. A favorite method used to accomplish this was to toe the brakes hard, rev up the engine, and pull the stick back against the stomach, and when the starter waved his flag, snap release the brakes, along with some forward stick, thus causing the light trainer to literally leap into the air. Often in flight the instructor would suddenly stop the engine in an area with power lines, trees, and other obstructions. The cadet was to find a place to land by gliding and turning. Just at touchdown the instructor would start the engine and have the student repeat the procedure—unexpectedly—later. Besides scaring the cadet, the procedure did develop judgment of ground terrain and distance.

Aerobatic Phase: The student in duel and solo practice became accomplished in 180-degree overhead approaches, pylon and lazy eights, chandelles, advanced aerobatics, and night flying. Often there were advanced and transitional training fields in the same area, and it was not uncommon for a P-40 or P-39 to bounce an unsuspecting primary cadet in the midst of a chandelle or Immelmann. The poor cadet, earnestly concentrating on his aerobatic maneuver, would become unnerved at the appearance of such an intimidating aircraft. By the final weeks of primary training the cadet would become pretty cocky about his skills, and buzzing pretty country girls and cattle became a favorite activity. The girls were often impressed, but the cows were not. Often the farmers would complain to the base commander that their cows had stopped giving milk. Orders were invariably issued to every class to stop buzzing or be washed out. Buzzing usually stopped, as there always was the threat of an Inspector General's staff officer being present in the area.

Various aircraft were tried in the primary phase, but generally the Stearman PT-17, Fairchild PT-19, and the Ryan PT-22 and their variants were utilized by virtue of their ease of handling and rugged construction.

Basic Flight Training
Since Basic Schools were to make military pilots from Primary School graduates, this phase of training was almost entirely directed by the Air Force. Cadets trained in the "country club" atmosphere

of the Primary Civilian Contract Schools had a rude awakening upon graduating to the austere, regimented Basic School surroundings. It was often necessary for Basic Training officers to "reorient" newly arrived civilian contract cadets.

Basic ground school stressed the principles of weather, navigation, code, and instrument flying. The chief feature of Basic ground school development during the war was the decreased emphasis on code, the continued importance of weather, and the increased emphasis on navigation and instrument flying.

In this phase, 70 flying hours and 15 hours in the Link Trainer were given. Night flying and instrument flying were stressed. The cadet was introduced to a trainer of greater power, weight, and complexity, with the accent on the mastery of precision and smoothness in flying technique. Instrument training was probably the greatest challenge to most cadets. The Vultee BT-13 Valiant was the standard basic trainer until 1943, when the North American AT-6 Texan replaced it.

From 1942 to 1944, nine weeks were allotted to Basic schooling, but this was to expand to ten weeks, as combat studies demonstrated that more time was required for instrument flying. Selection of pilots for single and twin engine aircraft in the Advanced Schools was the responsibility of the Basic Schools. Students who failed were usually reassigned to various branches of the AAF, such as bombardier or navigator schools, if qualified, or else, gunnery or mechanical training schools. Later, Basic Schools would assign students to one of five Advanced School categories: 1) single engine fighter; 2) twin engine fighter; 3) medium bombardment; 4) multi-engine heavy bombardment; and 5) twin engine standard. The student indicated his first three preferences, while his instructor would recommend the student for three categories.

Advanced Flight Training

Advanced Training was divided into single engine and twin-engine training. These categories themselves were divided into ground and flight schools. Single and twin engine ground training were similar and included advanced weather instruction, further training in instrument flying, and flight planning, along with the study of aircraft attack and defense. The major differences in the two ground courses were in the aircraft equipment course, as twin-engine aircraft were more complex. Also, single engine students received gunnery and armament instruction, which was not required of twin-engine students. Both courses consisted of 60 hours of ground school.

Single engine flight training consisted of 70 hours of flying instruction divided into five stages: 1) transition; 2) instrument; 3) navigation; 4) formation flying; and 5) aerobatics. Combat experience had established that increased formation flying training was required. Also, gunnery results in combat were unsatisfactory, resulting in the separation of gunnery training in Transitional Schools 1944. Since single engine school pilots would graduate to become fighter pilots, emphasis was placed on gaining expert control in fast, maneuverable training aircraft.

Transitional Flight Training

As the word "transitional" indicates, the cadet pilot, now awarded his wings and appointed as a flight officer or commissioned as a second lieutenant, was transitioned from training to combat status. The majority of pilots were given transitional training in either Flying Training Command (FTC) or the domestic Air Forces. A few other agencies, whose primary function was not training but utilized tactical aircraft, also carried out some transitional training, particularly early in the war. Transition procedures conducted by all agencies were generally similar, each having its individual approach to the training program and, therefore, each having its particular difficulties.

Fighter transitional ground and air training attempted to give the pilot total familiarization with instrumentation, controls, engine accessories, flying characteristics, and performance of combat aircraft. Because the pilot's flights were to be necessarily solo, prior intensive ground indoctrination was essential. When possible, an hour's check in a specially modified duo-place fighter was completed to demonstrate the student's proficiency in take offs, climbing turns, medium and steep turns, chandelles, stalls, gliding turns, and landings. In a progressive series of five to eight flights the student was instructed on what to do, how to do it, and what to look for in aircraft performance and engine operation. At the end of each flight the student was questioned and tutored upon the various phases of the flight. Gunnery training was initially given in the AT-6. Cadets initially made dry run passes under supervision and then fired live ammunition at towed target sleeves. These sleeves were long

Learning the function of the joystick. (USAF)

cloth tubes attached by a trailing wire to the tow plane. The bullets of each cadet AT-6 were color-coded so that each man's hits could be identified and assessed. Strafing was not stressed, as it was felt that a competent pilot could use his tracers to hit a target. When proficiency was attained the student was transferred to an obsolete combat fighter, such as the P-39 or P-40. Generally, fighter transition throughout Flying Training Command encountered few problems, with few changes in instructional methods except to improve on safety.

Twin-engine graduates were sent to separate schools according to the type of combat bomber they were to eventually fly. FTC administered medium and heavy bomber transition, while the Third Air Force conducted light bomber transition as part of Operational Training Units (OUT). Until late 1942, one year's flying experience was required to enter bomber transitional school, but the demands of war allowed the acceptance of advanced school graduates. However, transitional training was then doubled to ten weeks with 100 hours of flying. Ground school bomber pilot trainees received more intensive instruction in weather, radio communication, aircraft handling, bombing tactics (e.g. aircraft weight and balance, bombing procedures, target identification), and leadership/teamwork concepts. Commonly, four engine schools emphasized instrument, formation, and high altitude flying, while two engine schools emphasized formation flying.

Operational Training
Basically, the AAF copied the RAF's operational training system. Certain groups, referred to as "parent groups," with authorized over strength, were to provide a nuclei of experienced officers for the training of newly activated groups called Operational Training Units (OTU). Recently graduated students from transitional schools manned the OTUs. Once trained these new groups would return to the parent group, restoring its over strength, and again the cycle would be repeated. A nine-week bomber or twelve week fighter period was usually needed to complete the formation, organization, and training of a new group before it returned to the parent group. In the operational training scheme of 1943, certain elements from the parent group were sent to 30 days of instruction at the AAF School of Applied Tactics at Orlando, Florida. This course was divided about equally between academic and practical phases. The academic phase stressed command, intelligence, and operations in connection with the particular function the new group was to execute. Meanwhile, the practical phase consisted of operations and the flying of simulated missions. Upon completion of instruction these men would be assigned to a newly formed OTU group to initiate training as instructor-officers in the new group.

In mid-1942, Replacement Training Units (RTU) were established to replace crews and crew members lost in combat or returned home after their combat tour was completed. Initially, experienced men or crews were withdrawn from U.S.-based regular units and sent to combat theaters. But this procedure jeopardized OTU training, so the AAF decided to authorize certain units as training units to be maintained at over strength to fill combat losses. By February 1944, the formation of new combat groups was virtually (90%) completed, therefore phasing out OTU and leaving RTU as the primary operational training organization. The RTU course was shorter than OUT, with less emphasis on group training, since RTU graduates, as individuals or crews, were sent to established combat units.

The First and Fourth (Domestic) Air Forces were the chief fighter pilot teaching organization in the operational training phase. Since crew teamwork was not necessary in single place fighter aircraft, training stressed the attainment of individual proficiency and squadron/unit coordination. The basic objectives of operational training to be accomplished were to teach the pilot to have the aircraft become an extension of himself and to aim and fire his armament accurately. Pilots were familiarized in obsolete combat fighter types, such as the P-39 or P-40. After complete familiarization with the mechanical and handling aspects of the aircraft, specified aerobatic, bombing, gunnery and, later, rocket exercises were practiced, along with simulated combat. Actual combat experience demonstrated the need in training for increased high-altitude flying, navigation, instrument and night flying, take off and assembly, group landing, and tactical training. The prohibitive losses suffered by Eighth Air

Bracing was a punishment of standing at attention. (Author)

Force heavy bombers on unescorted missions over France and the subsequent development of long-range escort fighters necessitated the inclusion of fighter/bomber cooperation into training programs. As the war progressed the amount of training flying time increased from 40 hours at the end of 1942 to 70 hours at the end of 1944. This increase in training time was due to more emphasis on gunnery, navigation, instrument flying, and formation flying.

After the pilot had completed operational training, being assimilated into unit (fighters) and crew and unit (bombers), the final phase was modification to meet the requirements of the theater of operations. These alterations were rendered in each theater at a combat replacement center. Here, two purposes were served. First, individual deficiencies were detected and corrected. Second, the procedures and problems of the theater of war were learned. After this the pilot or crew was eased into actual combat operations. In late 1943 the Fighter Training Groups were established as the 495th (26 October) and the 496th (11 December) to train newly arrived replacement pilots from the U.S. in operational procedures and gunnery in specific aircraft. Each FTG had two component squadrons; the 495FTG had the 551FS and 552FS, while the 496FTG had the 554FS and 556FS. The 495FTG trained in the P-47C & D and P-38H & J, while the 496FTG trained in the P-38 (until August 1944) and the P-51.

In November 1944, pilots coming to combat theaters from training in the U.S. bypassed the 495/496FTGs and went directly to the fighter groups with who they would fly. Veteran pilots administered these "Clobber Colleges," as they were to be known. The value of this program was soon realized, in that the new arrivals quickly became enthusiastic students learning the latest combat tactics and the operation and procedures of the group. The new pilots immediately felt they were part of the group and were anxious to fly. The 495/496FTGs continued to furnish conversion and refresher courses and also to train 9AF replacements.

Washout Procedures

A total of almost 132,000, or 39% of all pilot candidates failed to complete the primary, basic, or advanced stages of pilot instruction. A number of factors decided the number of failures. Of course, the individual skill and motivation of the cadet, along with the attitude and quality of the instructor determined the elimination standards and therefore the rates at a given base and time. Since the judgment of flying skill is subjective, rather than an objective measurement, this provides an explanation for the variations in washout rates.

Officially, there was no quota system for washouts, but the training scheme was perceptive to the exigencies of the times and ebb and flow in the attitude of the higher echelons. Whenever large backlogs of pilot trainees occurred and the manpower requirements of combat stabilized, headquarters would accent firm adherence to training standards. Consequently, if, because of the above policy, the failure rate climbed to exorbitant levels, headquarters would remind the training bases of their manpower wastage.

So as not to expend manpower needlessly, it is not surprising that 67% of all washouts occurred in primary schools, usually during the first eight hours of dual instruction. During these eight hours

the instructor could usually determine whether the cadet had the "makings" to become a pilot. The major reasons for failure were a lack of coordination, poor judgment, and a general lack of ability. When a cadet received two consecutive "pink slips" from an instructor (in any school: primary, basic, or advanced) he would be sent to "group." Group consisted of two check pilots who would test the student and determine his future. It the two check pilots concurred with the pink slips then the cadet was washed out. If there was a split decision or two approvals by the check pilots, the student was put on probation and allowed to continue under a more capable instructor.

Nearly 67% of all eliminations occurred in primary school, while 21.8% occurred in basic, 5.5% in advanced, and 5.7% in transitional. More qualified washouts were usually sent to bombardier or navigator school, which actually required more intelligence than pilot training, but of course was not as glamorous. Less qualified washouts were utilized as gunners or mechanics.

Safety and Accidents

Safety was stressed throughout all phases of the training scheme. Training accidents were usually attributed to cadet flying inexperience or "pilot error," which in most cases amounted to "fooling around." Very rarely did aircraft mechanical failure cause an accident. Particular idiosyncrasies of an individual aircraft were noted (Form A-1) so that the pilot would be aware of them beforehand.

If a cadet was guilty of a flying violation he was made to wear the "dumb bell award" around his neck for a number of days to be determined by the seriousness of the violation and the adroitness of his explanation for it to his instructor.

Primary schools, probably because of more dual flying and closer supervision, had the lowest fatal accident rate at 4 deaths/100 accidents and 2.6 deaths/100,000 flying hours. Basic school had the highest fatality rate at almost 17 deaths/100 accidents, but only 6.5 deaths/100,000 flying hours. The average for *all* aviation in the U.S. during a comparable time was 11.5 deaths/100 acci-

An obvious PR photo of cadets learning air tactics. (USAF)

dents and 6 deaths/100,000 flying hours. Primary and Advanced schools approximated the U.S. average of 55 accidents/100,000 flying hours with 48 and 55/100,000, respectively. However, Basic schools showed a rate of only 27 accidents/100,000 flying hours. Basically, Primary, Basic, and Advanced schools had fewer accidents than the average rate for all American aviation, which is a tribute to the personnel and hardware employed in these training programs.

Comparisons and Conclusions

The ultimate factor in aerial combat is the man piloting the aircraft and firing its weapons or delivering its ordnance. A very obvious maxim is that the amount and quality of pilot training is directly proportional to the success of the air force.

The Japanese strategy of a quick, decisive war affected their training programs, which were geared to supply the limited num-

AAF Training Fatalities & Eliminees by Type of Course

Course	Number	%
Primary	88,279	66.9
Basic	28,798	21.8
Advanced	7315	5.5
SE	4631	
TE	2684	
Transition	7474	5.7
SE (fighter)	797	
SE (misc)	1681	
TE (fighter)	6	
Bombers	3754	
Others	1236	
Total	131,866	100.0

USAAF PILOT TRAINING PROGRAM-1944

WEEKS>>>	10	20	30	40	50	60
BASIC LTRAINING (5)	PRE FLIGHT (10) TRAINING	PRIMARY FLIGHT (10) SCHOOL	BASIC FLIGHT (10) SCHOOL	ADVANCED SINGLE ENGINE SCHOOL (10)	ADV. SINGLE ENGINE SCHOOL (5)	Operational Training (1AF & 4AF) (12)
					AIR TRANSPORT TROOP CARRIER (1TCC) (13-20)	
				ADVANCED TWIN ENGINE SCHOOL (10)	INSTRUCTOR (8)	
					HEAVY BOMBER TRANSITIONAL (10)	HEAVY BOMBER OPERATIONAL (2AF) (9)
					MEDIUM BOMBER TRANSITIONAL (10)	MEDIUM BOMBER OPERATIONAL (3AF) (9)
					LIGHT BOMBER TRANSITIONAL (12)	
					AIR TRANSPORT TROOP CARRIER (13-20)	
					INSTRUCTOR (10)	

( ) = Weeks

COURSE OUTLINE PILOT TRAINING PROGRAM-1944

BASIC TRAINING SCHOOL		PRE-FLIGHT FLIGHT SCHOOL		PRIMARY FLIGHT SCHOOL		BASIC FLIGHT SCHOOL		ADVANCED	
Hrs.	Course	Hrs.	Course	Hrs.	Course	Hrs.	Course	Hrs.	Course
73	Drill	48	Code	94	Ground School	94	Ground School	70	Flight School
15	Physical Ed.	30	Sea/Air	70	Flight School	70	Flight Training	60	Ground School
13	Mil. Procedure		Recognition	54	Military	47	Military Training	19	Military Training
12	Sanitation	24	Physics		Training				
8	First Aid	20	Math						
5	Clothing & Equipment Care	18	Map& chart Reading						
4	Map & Photo interpretation	Plus:Daily physical & military training							
4	Air Attack Defense								

ber of pilots that would be required to attain this strategic objective. Therefore, these limited training programs were never able to expand rapidly enough to supply the appetite of the long war of attrition that beset Japan and consumed large numbers of pilots.

Early in the war the training requirements were high, especially in the Japanese Naval Air Force, as its pilots were selected

Cadet completing flight log in the cockpit of a BT-14 (USAF)

from the best young officer manpower. Japanese Army Air Force training never reached the level of the JNAF and was particularly deficient in over water and night flying capabilities, which were important in the far-flung areas of Japanese conquest.

As the war evolved, the lack of qualified pilot material, along with an inadequate fuel supply, training aircraft, and qualified instructors further diminished the quality of pilot training. It is well documented that Kamikaze pilots were given only the rudiments of flight training and had to be led to the place of attack due to their utter lack of navigational training.

The Luftwaffe was continually forced to modify its training programs to meet the requirements of a changing strategy in a changing war. German air strategy was initially geared for a short (Blitzkrieg) offensive war. At the commencement of the war, 40% of the Luftwaffe consisted of bomber, 35% of transport, reconnaissance, and training aircraft, and only 25% fighter aircraft. As the war developed into a prolonged defensive struggle for Germany this fighter imbalance had to be redressed.

Initial modifications in the training program due to the effective exploitation of training facilities and personnel doubled single seat pilot numbers and increased night fighter pilot numbers five fold, with only a slight diminution of pilot quality. But by 1942, the quality of Luftwaffe training was beginning to show signs of deterioration. The major factor in this deterioration was the loss of many instructor pilots and aircraft from the training program for use in the aerial supply of the surrounded Sixth Army at Stalingrad.

By late 1943, the constant use of instructors and aircraft as stopgaps in the various crises which faced the hard-pressed Third Reich led to an instructor and operational training aircraft shortage. Also, the increasing Allied bombing and strafing attacks caused damage to training facilities and interrupted training. Improvisation and reduction in training time, though yielding sufficient numbers of replacement pilots, had a telling effect on the quality of new Luftwaffe trainees. New pilots were more concerned with the nuts and bolts of flying their aircraft than concentrating on gunnery and tactics. This was to manifest itself operationally, as many experienced German pilots were lost while trying to watch over these poorly trained pilots who were assigned to them as wingmen.

By mid and late 1944, Allied bombing attacks on German fuel sources left the training program without adequate quantities for flight training. Also, by this time good weather training areas in Southern France and Italy had fallen to the Allied ground forces and forced training to be conducted in areas of poor weather, which limited the number of days available for training. The Luftwaffe thus became caught in a vicious cycle: because of poor pilot training and the lack of fuel she was unable to defend her fuel production from attack and therefore could not spare sufficient fuel for training. This predicament nullified Armament Minister Albert Speer's gargantuan efforts in increasing aircraft production. Aircraft cannot fly without fuel.

America, because of her vast manufacturing and manpower capabilities—which were protected from enemy attack by the ex-

Colonel: Commanded a Group and the station, or served in a higher echelon above Group level. He was assigned his own aircraft, vehicle, and the best quarters, food, and liquor.

Lt. Colonel: Commanded a Group, or served on a Group Staff as Ops Officer, Exec Deputy Group Commander, or Station Commander. He had his own aircraft and vehicle.

Major: Commanded a squadron, or served as Group Ops Officer, Tactical Inspector, etc. He had his own aircraft.

Captain: Led a section or flight, and often a squadron in combat. His ground duties were squadron Op Officer or Assistant Ops Officer, or lesser Group Staff assignments. He had his own aircraft, but others could use it if he gave permission.

1st/2nd Lieutenants: Led elements (2 a/c), sections (4 a/c), flights

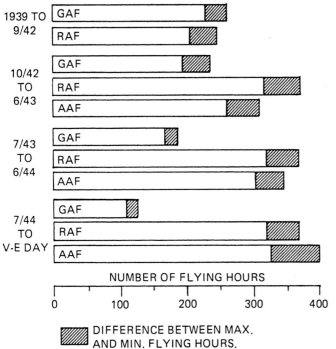

COMPARISON OF TOTAL TRAINING HOURS
LUFTWAFFE, RAF, AND AAF

NUMBER OF FLYING HOURS

DIFFERENCE BETWEEN MAX. AND MIN. FLYING HOURS.

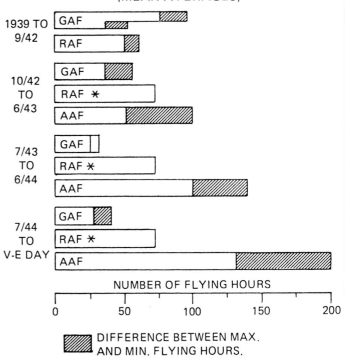

COMPARISON OF FLYING TRAINING HOURS IN
OPERATIONAL TYPE AIRCRAFT
(MEAN AVERAGES)

NUMBER OF FLYING HOURS

DIFFERENCE BETWEEN MAX. AND MIN. FLYING HOURS.

* AFTER 9/42 RAF TRAINING LARGELY DONE IN THE COMMONWEALTH; EACH HAVING ITS OWN STANDARDS BUT ALWAYS COMPLING WITH MINIMUM STANDARDS.

panse of two oceans—was able to increase pilot quality without a reduction in quality in her training programs. AAF pilot training was physically and mentally arduous throughout. There were no second chances; the cadet had to succeed or washout. When AAF cadets earned their wings they were undoubtedly the world's best.

Duties of USAAF Officer Ranks
Once the cadet received his wings he became a 2Lt. and then worked his way up the ranks. The duties of the various ranks were:

(8 a/c), and rarely squadrons (16 a/c). His non-flying duties could include Gunnery officer, Historian, Oxygen Officer, etc. He had a regularly assigned aircraft that he shared when he was not scheduled to fly a mission. The senior officer would paint his personal markings and art on his aircraft.

Flight Officer (F/O): Warrant Officer equivalent, who flew combat as a wingman to other ranks. Initially, he had no assigned aircraft until he gained seniority, after which he would share one.

Officer Pay Rates

Rank USN	Rank AAF USMC	$ Annual Base	$ Monthly Base	$ Monthly Long	$ RSA Dep.	$ RSA W/O	$ RA Dep.	$ RA W/O
Capt	Col	4000	333.33	16.67	42	21	120	105
Cdr	LtCol	3500	291.67	14.58	63	21	120	105
LtCdr	Maj	3000	250.00	12.50	63	21	105	90
Lt	Capt	2400	200.00	10.00	42	21	90	75
Lt(jg)	1Lt	2000	166.67	8.32	42	21	75	60
Ens	2Lt/FO	1800	150.00	7.50	42	21	60	45

Long.=Longevity   RSA=Ration   Subsistence Allowance
Dep.=Dependents   W/O=Without dependents   RA=Rental Allowance

Typical Flying Officer Pay Scales

Rank USN	Capt	Cdr	LCdr	Lt	Lt(jg)	Ens
Rank AAF/USMC	Col	LCol	Maj	Capt	1Lt	2Lt/FO
Typical years of service	12	9	6	>3	>3	>3
Monthly base $	333.33	291.67	250.00	200.00	166.67	150.00
Longevity $ (1)	66.67	43.74	25.00	10.00	8.33	7.50
Ration subsistence $	42.00	63.00	63.00	42.00	42.00	42.00
Rental allowance $	120.00	120.00	105.00	90.00	75.00	60.00
Flight pay $ (2)	200.00	167.70	137.50	105.00	87.50	78.75
Overseas pay $ (3)	53.33	45.94	38.75	30.50	25.42	22.88
Monthly pay $	815.33	732.05	619.05	477.50	404.92	361.13
Annual pay $	9784	8785	7431	5730	4859	4334

(1) 5% for every 3 years service
(2) 50% of the sum of base pay + longevity pay
(3) 10% of the sum of base pay + flight pay

Dependent pay:
(1) $22/month was deducted from pay, but the government contributed the remainder.
(2) A wife with no children received $50/month.

(3) A mother with one child received $80/month, plus $20/month per each additional child.

Death Allowance:
Six months pay, including longevity and flight pay, but not rental or other subsistence allowances.
Allotments: Personnel could specify portions of their pay to be deducted and sent to designated payees to insure regular payments (e.g. to relatives, insurance premiums, etc.) even if a POW or MIA.

U.S. Navy Pilot Training in WWII

Introduction
As Japanese bombs destroyed the U.S. Fleet at Pearl Harbor they also created the impetus for what would become the greatest naval air force in the world. After years of Depression-impeded growth, pilot training, the first step in building U.S. Naval air power, had to be given priority. An initial program for 27,000 aircraft and 30,000 pilots was authorized, and the early months of the war saw a training program become developed and standardized, allowing it to be modified to meet changing wartime tactics and conditions.

Procurement
Just as the Air Force found that the pool of aviation manpower was not unlimited, the Navy found that only a small percentage of all applicants were able to qualify and then pass the stringent training process. The applicant was required to be 18 to 26 years old, an American citizen, a high school graduate (or qualified and recommended high school senior), and able to pass the standard flight physical. The would-be ace applied to the Naval Aviation Cadet Selection Board, which passed qualified applicants on to the Armed Forces Recruiting and Induction Center. A favorable review by the Center would assign the applicant to the Navy. The Marine Corps applicants were also assigned to the Navy program for training. Although the supply of cadet material was limited, it was larger than what could be processed by the embryonic training program. To reserve their recruited manpower, the Navy instituted the deferred enlistment program, which placed the recruit on inactive duty

Cadets study Bakelite resin models that were placed inside the wooden shadow boxes on table. The ship or aircraft models were viewed for a few seconds in varying situations and lighting conditions for identification. (USN)

Pre-flight Training

As the name implies, the cadet did not receive any flight training in this phase, which emphasized physical and then academic training. To determine his physical suitability and ability as a team player, sports, especially football, were stressed. The cadet also found that the Navy was synonymous with swimming, and spent hours in the pool. The academic phase introduced the rudiments of Naval aviation, recognition, navigation, communications, first aid, and gunnery. Four pre-flight schools (the universities of Georgia, North Carolina, Iowa, and St. Marys (CA)) were opened in February 1942, with a fifth, Del Monte (CA), being added in later that year. In early 1943, the Flight Preparation Program was added, utilizing 20 colleges, which were happy to accept the program due to low student enrollment during the war. The 12 week training course took up the backlog of AVCADS (aviation cadets). Civilian professors taught academics, while discipline, physical education, and drill were administered by the Navy. By March 1943, 12,000 men were enrolled. Besides taking up the backlog, it lessened the work covered in ground school later.

Primary Flight Training

The next training stage was called primary flight training, and the cadet was finally in the real Navy. The three-month course was at first conducted at Pensacola NAS, but was soon transferred to all 16 naval reserve stations in the U.S. Aviation candidates from the Regular Navy reported for training at this point, skipping pre-flight. Course content was divided approximately equally between ground and flight schools. Ground school expanded on the academics of pre-flight training (e.g. navigation, recognition, and communications/code, along with the ever-present and ever-lasting drilling and fitness regimens). Flight training consisted of 85 hours in the Stearman N2S and/or the Naval Air Factory's N3N-3 primary trainers. Take offs and landings, airmanship and aerobatics, and precision and formation flying were stressed. The future of the cadet depended on the competence and quality of his instructors and check pilots. Boards of Evaluation judged reports of poor performance,

until called to active duty. This program, called V-5, removed the applicant from the draft and assured him of becoming a commissioned pilot in the Naval Reserve if he could pass the examinations. If the applicant was a college student he was allowed to complete the school year before being called up.

Another program (V-1), initiated somewhat later in 1942, enabled college sophomores and freshmen to finish their two years of college. At the end of the sophomore year the recruit could either shift to the V-5 program for aviation training or apply to the V-7 program, which allowed the student to complete his education and then train as a deck officer. These "V-programs" were eventually consolidated into the BV-12 program, which was comparable to the Air Force's Special Training Program. In the V-1 and V-5 programs students were civilians sworn into the Naval Reserve going to school without pay, while in the V-12 program, the recruit was active Navy, being paid and uniformed. During the war more and more V-12 candidates were selected from the Navy enlisted ranks. Only the V-5 program was designed for aviation recruits, while the V-1 and V-12 programs were for all Naval officer material.

Like the Air Force, the Navy utilized the civilian Pilot Training Program in 1941, continuing after Pearl Harbor. In July 1942, its name was changed to the War Training Service (WTS), and the program was stepped up to accommodate 20,000 pilots per year trained in 92 schools and colleges. A three month, six day a week, physical and academic curriculum trained V-1 and V-5 reservists, saving the Navy time by culling out the unsuitable. This curriculum, called Flight Preparatory training, was equivalent to basic training and concentrated on physical training. The next step saw the reservist sent to elementary and secondary flight training, which was managed by the Civil Aeronautics Administration at 250 War Training Service Centers. The elementary stage gave 35-40 hours of flight training in light civilian aircraft. About a quarter of the students received the 40-50 hours of secondary training. In 1942, the Navy standardized its training programs into four segments.

Tactical problems and aircraft ID were taught in intermediate flight training. (USN)

Naval cadets at the Link Trainer. (USN)

Control tower at NAS Corpus Christi, Texas. Note the Stearman PT-17s (N2S-2) which were nicknamed "Yellow Perils" as they were painted all-over chrome yellow and flown by inexperienced pilots. (USN)

and after two "down checks" decided whether to give the cadet further instruction. Three to six hours of extra instruction were assigned. If the cadet continued to underachieve he faced the Naval Air Station Commandant, who would be the final arbitrator. Marion Carl, Marine ace with 18 1/2 victories, related this story about his time as an instructor before the war. After graduating from Pensacola in December 1939 and serving at Quantico, he was transferred to Training Command as an instructor. Carl became proficient in aerobatics, which he enjoyed very much. One day, while flying a Stearman, he decided he would show a student what it was like to do some "real" aerobatics and really "wrung out" the biplane trainer. Upon landing the student, green in the gills, got out of the trainer and promptly threw up. The student pilot, Joe Foss, later would become the Marine's top ace with 26 victories.

Intermediate Training

The outbreak of WWII separated Primary and Intermediate Training. Primary training was distributed to 16 Naval Air Stations around the U.S., while Intermediate training was completed at Pensacola and Corpus Christi Naval Air training Centers. Before the War, Naval flight training centered on Pensacola, which was known as the "Annapolis of the Air." While Pensacola was developed over several decades, Corpus Christi was a product of wartime need. Construction began in 1940, and at war's end it would become the largest naval aviation training facility in the world.

The final stage of aviation training was the 14-week intermediate phase, which was divided into Basic and Advanced which, in turn, was broken down into specialized training sections that were dictated by the Navy's pilot requirement at the time and availabil-

Standing by for morning flight assignments at Corpus Christi. PT-17s stand awaiting the cadets in the background. (USN)

Cadet (in the rear) and his instructor takeoff in a BT-13 (USN)

ity of equipment. In Basic the cadet flew the SNJ, the Vultee Valiant, or, as it was more familiarly known, the "Vibrator." In the "Bee Tee" the cadet received dual instruction (10 hours) and soloed (22 hours). After soloing he learned day and night formation flying. After this the cadet indicated his future specialization: multi-engine bombers/flying boats or single engine observation/carrier-based fighter aircraft. The Navy had the final decision, but 75% were usually assigned to the coveted carrier fighter training.

From Basic the cadets were sent to an Instrument Squadron. Instrument flying was stressed, initially in the Link Trainer and other simulators and then in the air. In air blind flying instrument instruction was flown under a hood with a front seat instructor. This was probably the most anxious phase of flight training. But after 15 flights totaling 22 hours, the cadet would enter Advanced Training.

Here the cadet flew the North American SNJ ("Texan"/AT-6), which was heavier, faster, and more intricate than previous trainers. The flight syllabus was arduous, consisting of 75 flights totaling 100 hours: 14 hours of dual and 86 hours of solo. The cadet had to learn equipment use, such as landing gear, flaps, and engine adjustments, along with flying techniques, such as precise take offs and landings. Navigation, night flying, and cross-country flying were practiced. Formation flying and aerobatics were practiced as employed in combat. Aerial gunnery was practiced, first with supervised dry runs and then firing color-coded bullets at towed sleeves with live ammunition. Dive-bombing was practiced, with small practice bombs aimed at 100-foot target circles. Cadets soon discovered that minor deviations in their dive angle or air speed and wind speed and direction caused problems in accuracy.

In late 1944, Pre-operational training was added to the curriculum in order to familiarize the future carrier fighter with a "combat" aircraft. Unfortunately, the "combat" aircraft was the venerable SBD Dauntless dive-bomber, which was in surplus at Corpus Christi. After five flights (7 1/2 hours) the cadet was ready for his commission and leave.

Upon passing through the intermediate phase, successful students were designated naval aviators (officers) or naval aviation pilots (enlisted men), winning their wings and commission as an ensign in the Navy or as a first lieutenant in the Marine Corps. At this point, Marine flyers went on to their own operational course at Cherry Point, NC, and bases on the west coast. They concentrated on tactics utilized by the "Flying Leathernecks," especially close air support in amphibious operations, along with strafing and bombing tactics.

Operational Training

Before the war, squadrons attached to the fleet had conducted Operational training. After Pearl Harbor the Fleet went on operations, and Operational training was obliged to become land-based. The first Operational Training Command was established at Jacksonville, and soon included bases along the east coast of Florida and southern Georgia. Training squadrons stationed at these bases were specialized: VO-VCS (squadron/battleship and cruiser aviation) or VP (squadron/patrol aviation); or the most coveted, CV (squadron/carrier aviation). Early in its existence the OTC experienced shortages in aircraft, as the newest types went into combat, but as production caught up this problem was overcome.

The purpose of Operational training was to prepare the pilot for combat. After the pilot familiarized himself with the faster, heavier, and more powerful "warbird," he began a demanding regimen to prepare him for combat. Section and division combat tactics, as well as individual combat tactics were taught. Gunnery and bombing techniques to be utilized in these phases were also included. Combat veterans imparted their experience, stressing teamwork and leadership.

Of all the new experiences in Operational training, Carrier Qualification (CQ) was the most exhilarating. Initial CQ, called Field Carrier Landing Practice (FCLP), began flying the SNJ on "land carriers"; short runways set up to simulate a carrier deck. Low and slow was the fundamental precept in carrier landings, and the pilots flew at just above stalling speed and landed under the direction of the Landing Signals Officer (LSO), who waved paddles to indicate "too low," "too fast," "cut," and, worst of all, "wave off," or go around. When the LSO felt the pilot was ready, the pilot was authorized for CQ. Before the war CQ was made on Fleet carriers off the East or West coasts, but as the fleet became operational other CQ provisions were made. Two Great Lakes side-wheel steamers USS *Wolverine* and USS *Sable* were converted into carriers, and carried out much of the carrier qualifications out of Great Lakes NAS, Chicago. The *Wolverine* was built in 1913 as the *Seeandbee* and converted to a training carrier and commissioned on 12 August 1942. The *Sable* was built in 1924 as the *Greater Buffalo* and commissioned on 8 May 1943. Training carriers, such as the *Charger* and *Ranger*, were stationed out of Norfolk or Jacksonville. Later in the war new escort carriers coming out of the shipyards no longer needed to be rushed into battle, and new squadrons could take their operational training on these carriers' shakedown cruises. CQ was the last stage of Operational training, from which they were assigned to an Air Group—usually on the West Coast—to be assigned to the Fleet or sent as replacement pilots to Pearl Harbor.

Flexibility of the Naval Training Program

The training program achieved its maximum development in 1943, after which modifications and cutbacks took place. In August 1943,

USN Dual Instruction form used by instructors to grade cadets. (Author Collection/USN)

Then Learn To Hit The Sleeve EVERY Time

A page from the 1942 USN Training Division booklet, "There's No Substitute for Marksmanship." (Author collection)

The *USS Wolverine* was built in 1913 as the side-wheel steamer, *Seeandbee*, and converted and commissioned in August 1942 for carrier qualifications out of Great Lakes NAS, Chicago. The side-wheel steamer, *USS Sable*, built in 1924 was commissioned in May 1943. (USN)

the training division was transferred from the Bureau of Aeronautics to the new Deputy Chief of Naval Operations for Air (DCNO/Air). All primary, intermediate, and operational training was coordinated under the new chief of Naval Training. At this time the Navy had 31,500 aircraft and needed to convert its Miami and Jacksonville intermediate bases into operational programs. As described previously, the flight preparatory schools were established in early 1943 to take up the personnel backlog.

By March 1944, the first cutbacks took place, decreasing the pilot requirement from 25,000 to 20,000. With these cutbacks there was a concurrent reduction in training facilities: six primary stations; one intermediate; and one pre-flight (Del Monte). The Navy decreased the number of trainees by 7,000 by offering these "De-Selectees" several choices: 1) become a civilian (and probably be drafted); 2) transfer to the personnel-short aircrew man program (unglamorous to the pilot hopeful); and 3) transfer to other sections of the naval program (again an unattractive alternative). The 20 colleges and universities in the flight preparatory phase were eliminated. The pre-flight schools reduced their emphasis on physical education, and the academics were extended from 11 to 26 weeks. The V-12 program was extended, allowing students to get three college semesters instead of two. The total training scheme was expanded to 70 weeks.

By the end of 1944, the large naval air battles around the Philippines had led to casualties and attrition. It was also found that two combat tours were the maximum for efficiency. These factors and the cutbacks of that year led to a pilot shortage, and the "Deselectees" were allowed to reapply for flight training. Four thousand reapplied, and with the new carrier-qualified Marine Corps pilots the deficit was filled. As the tactical emphasis changed in 1945, more bombing and rocket training was given to the fighter pilot, along with coordination between the fighter and its carrier or ground control units, the Combat Information Center (CIC).

Conclusion

The Navy's training program, like the Air Force's, was notable in its flexibility, especially moving from quantity to quality. The program eliminated redundancy and de-emphasized physical training for the academic. The result was the best naval pilots in the world, who scored lopsided kill ratios in the last year and a half of the war.

Training Aircraft

Stearman PT-13, 17, 18

The Stearman was the most numerous primary trainer, numbering 10,345, including equivalent spare parts, 8,588 actual aircraft, and 4,693 for the AAF. Though officially designated the Boeing "Kaydet" in 1941, as part of the government's promotion for popular aircraft names the trainer was called "Stearman" by all who flew it. The Stearman Aircraft Company bought the original model 203 design from Boeing in 1931. In 1934 the company became a

Boeing PT-17 Stearman/Kaydet of the Confederate Air Force/Arizona Wing. (Author/CAF-AZ Wing)

PT-17 Dual cockpit (Author/CAF-AZ Wing)

Fairchild PT-19 Cornell (USAF)

Boeing subsidiary, finally becoming the Boeing Wichita Division in 1939. The Stearman (model 73), the first military training version, was purchased by the Navy in 1934, which designated them the NS-1. The Army bought 26 Lycoming-powered model 75 Stearmans in 1935, designating it the PT-13. All succeeding AAC Stearmans were similar, except for the engine and minor equipment changes (e.g. the PT-17 of 1940 was fitted with a 220hp Continental engine, while the PT-18 was powered by a 225hp Jacobs engine). The AAC Stearmans were painted with a blue fuselage and yellow wings and tails until spring 1942, when all silver models replaced them. Throughout the war the USN Stearmans were painted all over chrome yellow, and were nicknamed the "Yellow Perils" because of their color and inexperienced pilots at the controls.

This biplane was considered ideal for teaching basic flying maneuvers, aerobatics, and takeoffs. Taxiing was easy due to the steerable tail wheel, but S-turns were necessary due to the large engine. Takeoff acceleration was only fair, and the tail took time to rise. Once in the air it cruised between 70 and 90mph and maxed at 125mph. It was considered an honest aircraft to fly, but heavier on the controls and less docile than its primary-training contemporaries. Stalls were a non-event, and simple aerobatics were easy, but

the constant altitude loss needed to be observed during these maneuvers. However, it could give inexperienced, low hour cadets difficulties on landings. Fishtailing, ground loops, and landing prangs were not uncommon. Generally, cadets taught with the Stearman were considered to become more accomplished Basic Cadets than their counterparts who learned in more forgiving Primary machines.

Fairchild PT-19, 23

Another trainer used extensively in primary training was the PT-19, designed and developed by the Fairchild Aircraft Company of Hagerstown, MD, as the M-62 "Cornell." After the AAF placed its first order in 1940 it designated it the PT-19. The aircraft filled a deficit in the pilot training program, not only in the U.S., but also in Canada, where it also was built.

The PT-19 (270 built) was a low mono wing aircraft of welded tubular steel frame construction covered with fabric, and the wings and tail group were fabricated of plywood. It was powered by the 175hp Ranger engine, which left the trainer under-powered. The PT-19A version was fitted with a 200hp Ranger engine. This -19A version was the most numerous built, with 3,181 built by Fairchild, 477 by Aeronca, and 44 in St. Louis. The PT-19B, of which 917

Ryan PT-22 Recruit (USAF)

Vultee BT-13 Bee-Tee/Vibrator/Valiant (USAF)

were built by Fairchild and Aeronca, was similar to the -19As, except for being equipped for blind flying. Due to the shortage of Ranger engines, 776 PT-23s were built with 220hp Continental engines, but were otherwise identical to the PT-19.

The only faults the aircraft suffered from was difficult rudder control, and if landed too hard the fixed leg cantilever landing gear could be pushed through the top surface of the wing. Even with engine upgrades it was somewhat under powered, which made it the "sweetest" handling trainer, easy to fly and easy to land. However, this virtue was also its biggest vice. It was felt that pilots trained in the docile PT-19s tended to have much more difficulty adjusting to the BT-13 and AT-6 later.

Ryan PT-20, 21, 22

The third most numerous primary trainer was the PT-20-21-22 series manufactured by the Ryan Aeronautical Company of San Diego, CA. Ryan developed it from its S-T-A Sport Trainer, which first flew in mid-1934. In June 1939 the Army placed a $96,000 order for 15 XPT-16 trainers—the military version of the S-T-A—which made it the first low-wing monoplane trainer in the Army's inventory.

The XPT-16 was powered by a 125hp Menasco engine, while a 1940 order called for 40 similarly powered aircraft but with a larger cockpit that was designated the PT-20. The PT-20A was built with a 132hp Kinnner engine, while 100 PT-21s were built with 132hp radial engines, both of which were greatly under powered. Also, its wheel and tail wheel fairings were removed, as they were vulnerable to the wear and tear of cadet landings. The need for more powerful engines brought about the most numerous (1,032) version, the PT-22, which was equipped with the 165hp Kinner engine. The "22" went into service at CPT (Civilian Pilot Training) schools, particularly in California and Arizona. Because of its small engine that sounded a lot like a washing machine, the PT-22 was called the "Maytag Messerschmitt."

The aircraft was considered a "hot" trainer, causing the cadet to be alert on takeoff and landing. It was fast and had a great rate of roll. Aerobatics, both inside and out, could be easily accomplished, while stalls and spins could be recovered from simply and predictably. Until the cadet mastered the manipulation of the brakes the first several landings could be rather hairy. Cadets transitioning to Basic trainers usually had no problems after flying the "22."

Vultee BT-13, 15

The Vultee Valiant BT-13 was the standard basic trainer until 1943, when the North American AT-6 Texan replaced it. The "Bee Tee," or "Vibrator," was a two seat, low-wing cantilever monoplane that was first ordered by the AAC in 1939. By the time production ceased in mid-1944, 11,537 were manufactured for the services (2,012 to the USN as the SNV). The BT-13 variants differed mainly in matters of equipment. The difference between the BT-13 and BT-15 series was that the former was powered by a 450hp Pratt & Whitney, while the latter was engined by a 450hp Wright. There were 300 BT-13s, 6,407 BT-13As, 1,125 BT-13Bs, and 1,693 BT-15s built.

The "Bee Tees" introduced the cadet to the closed cockpit, controllable pitch propeller, two-way radio, and wing flaps, and was

basically similar to the advanced trainers. Except for landing gear retraction and gunnery apparatus, the cockpit and the instrument panel were similar to the advanced trainer. It was nicknamed the "Vibrator" due to the extreme noise created by the propeller pitch, which could be set only at full low pitch for takeoff and climb and high pitch for cruise. Takeoff high RPMs caused a deafening prop noise, and to further add to the din was a canopy vibration during spins and rolls.

Pilot reflections on the BT in training were generally negative, with nearly everyone experiencing some harrowing escapade in the aircraft. The BT's reputation as a "killer" seems to be more of a product of the training scheme rather than as a basic fault of the aircraft. The transition from the relatively docile aircraft of Primary Flight Training and the underlying overconfidence of the newly passed cadets led to a large number of accidents in this aircraft. Many of these accidents took place in bad weather, cross-country and night flying exercises, low altitude aerobatics, and just plain "showing off." The BT was under powered for its size and weight, and thus under performed going up, down, or in between. Its controls were well harmonized, but somewhat sluggish, and if smoothness and coordination were maintained, the BT could be flown safely through any maneuvers at any altitude. The BT was not a forgiving aircraft, and any lapse in coordination by the fledgling pilot near the ground could result in tragedy. The BT had a bad but deserved reputation for unforgiving stalls. The aircraft gave more than ample warning of an approaching stall, and the "slight buffeting and vibration" referred to in the pilot's handbook was much more than that, with the entire aircraft shaking and the canopy shaking off its tracks. Quick and prudent light use of coordinated aileron and rudder would bring the plane out of the spin. Due to its extreme weight (4,500lbs loaded), the aircraft with full flaps and throttle would want to climb and then stall on landing approach. Experience (easing the throttle, reversing the nose high trim, and easing up the flaps) would rectify this tendency, and the trainer was considered stable and easy to land. By the end of Basic Flight Training, however, the cadets usually gained the necessary experience in the trainer to confidently master its idiosyncrasies.

By mid-1943, the BT-13 was considered inadequate for Basic Flight Training, as the transition between the Primary Trainers (Stearman), the BT-13, and the AT-6 of Advanced Flight Training

North American AT-6/SNJ/Texan of the Confederate Air Force/Arizona Wing. (Author/CAF-AZ Wing)

were not sufficient to warrant continuation of production, especially in light of the problems inexperienced cadets encountered. The BT was supplanted by the AT-6, which was already in use as an Advanced trainer.

North American AT-6 Texan

The standard advanced single-engine trainer was the AT-6 built by North American Aircraft Company of Inglewood, CA. By those who flew it the trainer was called the "AT-6" by the AAF, the "SNJ" by the Navy and Marine Corps, the "Harvard" by the Canadians and British, and the "T-6" by the post war cadets and reservists. It was only called the "Texan" by the media and PR types. The aircraft was derived from the BT-9 (NJ-1/USN) designed by James Kindelberger in 1935, which became the standard trainer for the AAC and USN. The BT-9 evolved into the NA-16, then the NA-26, which became the BC-1, and the NA-36 that became the BC-1I, a fixed undercarriage basic combat trainer that was manufactured in 1937. The design was modified to include a retractable undercarriage in 1938. In 1939 the AAC ordered 94 to be utilized as transitional trainers between the BT-9 and BT-14 then in use. The USN also was interested in the BC-1 and ordered 16 as the SNJ-1. North American had taken the basic NA-16 design and added a 550hp

Major training aircraft (top-bottom): PT-17, BT-13, AT-6 and P-40 (USAF)

Pratt & Whitney engine, a flush retracting landing gear, provision for armament, a two-way radio, and advanced instrumentation, and by 1938 it was designated as the BC-1A. When the Army re-evaluated its Basic Combat category the BC-1A became the AT-6. When war came to Europe in 1939, the British and Canadians ordered the aircraft in large numbers as the Harvard. By the time the U.S. entered the war the "Texan" had established itself as the standard advanced trainer, and in late 1943 it replaced the BT-13 as the standard Basic trainer (although it continued to carry the AT rather than the BT designation).

The various subtypes of the AT-6 models differed principally in internal equipment. The 550hp P&W engine remained standard throughout the 15,000 odd manufactured: 8,732 for the AAF; 2,761 as the SNJ for the USN; and the remainder as the Harvard for the RAF and RCAF. The aircraft was universally considered one of the best trainers ever built, as its numbers and longevity in service (1958) attest.

The AT-6 could takeoff in 900 feet and had an initial climb rate of 1,150fpm. Normal cruise was 180mph, and economical cruise was at 140mph, giving it a range of 500+ miles at a fuel consumption of 35mpg with a fuel capacity of 110 gallons. It had a maximum speed of 210mph and could land in 700 feet.

The Texan had a very reliable engine, strong airframe, and was easy to maintain. It was constructed and handled like a combat fighter, and while it was easy to fly, it was fast enough to be demanding on the reflexes. It was tough to taxi and land, easy to fly, and very noisy in all its versions. On takeoff the pilot advanced the throttle smoothly, kept the aircraft aligned on the runway by increasing right rudder to compensate for torque, raised the tail slightly, pulled back lightly on the stick, and let the plane fly itself off the ground at about 85-90mph. Once in the air the cadet tapped the brake to stop the wheels from rotating and then retracted the landing gear. The cadet would bring the stick back to maintain cruise-climb airspeed and climb to altitude. It was stable, smooth, and a positive aircraft to handle. It was responsive on the controls, particularly the ailerons, and was a good aerobatic aircraft. It had poor high speed stall characteristics, which were sharp but manageable. It was difficult to recover from a spin, and quick, firm recovery procedures needed to be taken. Due to the narrow undercarriage and high center of gravity, the aircraft had poor directional control on landing, and landing was considered the most demanding and remembered element of flying the Texan. Wing tips were the most prevalent replacement part, as the plane would ground loop if the cadet lost concentration for only an instant on landing. It was not unusual for a cadet to be congratulating himself for a good landing, only to find himself in a ground loop on the roll out! The cadet needed to stay alert and keep the stick back until the aircraft was parked and the engine shut down.

The AT-6 could be considered one of the most important aircraft of WWII, as its adaptable design allowed it to be utilized in various training capacities. It was to prove to be the ideal trainer to transition from the Primary and Basic trainers and prepared the cadet to fly the Mustang, Thunderbolt, Hellcat, or Corsair in combat.

	Mfg. Company	AAF Name	Nickname	Top Speed	Cruise Speed	Land Speed	Range	Service Ceiling	Engine & (HP)	# Built
P r i m a r y	Boeing	PT-17	Stearman Kaydet (Co.)	125	50	105	440	11700	Lycoming Continental (200 HP)	4693
	Ryan	PT-22	"22" Recruit	130	55	115	325	14800	Kinner (132 HP) a Menasco (125 HP) b Kinner (165 HP) c	1217
	Fairchild 1 Aeronca 2 St. Louis 3	PT-19	Cornell (Co.)	130	60	100	450	15000	Ranger (175 HP) d Ranger (200 HP) e	4889
B a s i c	Vultee	BT-13	Bee-Tee Vibrator Valiant (Co.)	180	55	165	740	21000	P & W (450 HP)	9525
*	North American	AT-6	Texan (Co.)	210	65	170	750	24000	P & W (600 HP)	8732

a-PT16A, 20A, 21 1-86.4%
b-PT-20. 21 2-12.7%
c-PT-22, 22A 3-0.9%
d-PT-19
e-PT-19A, 19B

* Served as advanced and then basic and advanced in late 1943

Payday (*see table p. 21*). (USAF)

CHAPTER 2

Building a Fighter

From the beginning of July 1940 to the end of August 1945, American industry produced approximately 300,000 military aircraft, of which nearly 100,000 were fighters: 62,889 for the Air Force and 31,344 for the Navy and Marines. Fighter acceptances were: 1,162 in 1940; 4,416 in 1941; 10,769 in 1942; 23,988 in 1943; 38,873 in 1944; 20,742 in 1945, thus demonstrating the great productivity of the American war machine.

Fighter Acceptances

A/C	USAAF # A/C	A/C	USN/MC # A/C
P-47	15,579	F6F	12,210
P-51	14,490	F4U	11.236
P-40	13,700	F4F	7898*
P-39	9585		
P-38	9535		
Total	62,889	Total	31,344

* Includes FM-2s

A total of 802,161 engines were produced for all aircraft: 653,647 (81%) for the USAAF and 148,514 (19%) for the USN/USMC. Wright produced 218,632 (27.2%), Pratt & Whitney 393,795 (49.0%), and 189,544 (23.8%) were by other manufacturers (especially Packard and Allison).

Fighter aircraft were not only produced in quantity and types, but also in time frames dictated by changing strategic demands of the war. Generally, prewar designs languished until war clouds appeared, whereupon production accelerated due to American industrial know-how and capacity.

Fighter Design Evolution

A/C	Design Begun	Prototype First Flown	First Production	500th Acceptance	Years to Mass Prod.
P-39	06/1936	04/1939	09/1940	10/1941	5.33
P-40	03/1937	10/1939	05/1940	11/1941	3.50
P-38	06/1937	01/1938	09/1940	04/1942	4.75
P-51	05/1940	10/1941	08/1941	05/1942	2.00
P-47	07/1940	05/1941	12/1941	12/1942	2.50
F4F	07/1936	09/1937	02/1940	07/1941	5.00
F4U	05/1938	05/1940	10/1942	05/1943	5.00
F6F	06/1941	06/1942	10/1942	06/1943	2.00
					Avg. 3.75

During the war the cost of the American aircraft program was $45 billion. From 1940 to 1945, the air services received better aircraft for less money, despite the fact that material costs increased, along with a 50% increase in hourly aircraft workers' wages.

Aircraft Costs ($)

A/C	1939-41	1942	1943	1944	1945
P-26	16,567	——	——	——	——
P-35	22,500	——	——	——	——
P-36	23,000	——	——	——	——
P-38	134,280	120,408	105,567	97,147	——
P-39	77,159	69,537	63,000	50,666	——
P-40	60,562	59,444	49,449	44,892	——
P-47	113,246	105,594	104,258	85,578	83,001
P-51	——	58,698	58,824	51,572	50,985
P-63	——	——	——	48,000	*****
F4F+	*****	*****	*****	50,000	——
F4U	*****	*****	*****	75,000	*****
F6F	——	*****	*****	63,000	*****
Spit	*****	*****	45,000	——	——
P-61	——	*****	*****	170,000	*****

+ = FM-2   ***** = only figures available

The steady decrease in aircraft costs was due to volume production. The cost decrease would have been greater if it were not for numerous changes and modifications during actual production as dictated by combat experience. New models became larger and more complex, as more communication equipment, armament, armor, and fuel tanks were added. The military aircraft could not be mass produced in the way an automobile could because of its complexity. The typical fighter could utilize 10,000 or more parts, 10,000 feet of wiring, 3,000 feet of hydraulic tubing, and 36,000 rivets (which had to be hand-driven).

Breakdown of Representative Fighter Costs

A/C	M	Cost ($)	Model	Cost ($)	GFE cost	Total cost
P-38	K	86,645	V-1710-81	23,733	30,111	140,489
P-47	D	65,308	R-2800-21	24,762	25,364	115,434
P-51	D	26,600	V-1650-7	15,423	16,523	58,546
P-63	A	29,413	V-1710	14,608	21,989	66,010
	M = model		GFE = Government furnished equipment			

The united effort of American industry and the American air forces changed the United States from a nation deploying obsolete fighters at Pearl Harbor to a nation with the world's dominant Air Force.

North American P-51 production line at Inglewood, CA. Some 15,367 Mustangs were built with the P-51D the most numerous at 7,956 with the identical B and C models accounting for 3749 (1,999 Bs and 1,750 Cs). (North American)

Lockheed P-38 production line in San Diego, CA. A total of 9923 P-38s of which 3810 were the L-model and 2970 the J-version. (Lockheed)

USAAF Fighter Factory Acceptances

A/C *	Total	1940	1941	1942	1943	1944	1945**
Fighters	68,193	1422	3784	9042	17,687	24,138	12,120
P-38	9536	1	205	1265	2213	4186	1666
P-39	9588	13	926	1973	4947	1729	———
P-40	13,738	778	2246	4454	4258	2002	———
P-47	15,585	———	1	532	4428	7065	3559
P-51	14,501	———	138	634	1710	6908	5111
P-61	682	———	———	———	34	449	199
P-63	3273	———	———	———	31	1786	1456
P-70	60	———	———	———	60		———
P-80	115			———	———	5	110
Others	1115	630	268	184	6	8	19
Recon	1117	65	203	223	284	95	247
F-2	55	13	———	———	———	20	22
F-4/F-5	500	———	2	214	284	———	
F-6	299	———	———	———	———	74	225
Others	263	52	201	9	———	1	———

* Includes: Experimental and U.S. financed Canadian production
** January to August 1945

Factory Acceptances USAAF Fighter and Reconnaissance Aircraft

A/C *	Total	1940	1941	1942	1943	1944	1945 **
Fighter	100,554	1689	4421	10,780	24,005	38,895	20,764
Recon	3981	123	727	1468	734	261	668
Trainer	58,568	2731	9376	17,632	19,942	7578	1309

* Includes: Experimental and U.S. financed Canadian production
** January to August 1945

The Grumman Beth Page factory, Long Island, NY. Plant 2 had over 61 acres under roof. (Grumman)

Right: With many men in the military, women, symbolized by "Rosie, the Riveter," were a vital cog on the production line. By the end of 1944, 19 million or one third of the American work force were women. The Boeing Seattle factory employees were one half women. (Author)

ENGINES

The WWII aircraft engine was a reciprocating engine. Reciprocating described the movement of the engine's pistons, as they provided power by moving up and down in the cylinders. The piston movement was converted to rotary motion to move the propeller via the connecting rods and crankshaft. Aircraft engine manufacturers were constantly looking for ways to increase power, and the way to accomplish this was to increase the number of cylinders. The increase in cylinder number also had the advantage of providing a smoother power supply and increased number of power strokes per revolution of the crankshaft. To accommodate a number of cylinders in an engine there were several different engine designs. The standard method of classifying engines is by their cylinder arrangement.

During WWI the rotary and in-line engines powered aircraft, as the radial engine was still under development. As the war ended the rotary was phased out, and the in-line was the engine of choice.

Right: Frederick Rentschler established Pratt & Whitney in 1925 and developed the R-1830 Twin Wasp and then the R-2800. This engine was arguably the most important American aircraft engine, as it supplied 49% of all horsepower in U.S. fighters and bombers. (Pratt & Whitney)

Radial development proceeded rapidly, and soon the in-line vs. radial controversy developed and continued into WWII. The controversy centered on their cooling systems: air-cooled radial vs. liquid-cooled in-line.

The internal combustion engine converts heat into mechanical energy. An efficient engine only converts 30-35% of generated heat into mechanical energy. About 40% is expelled on the piston's exhaust stroke, while another 5-10% is lost through friction. This means another 20-25% must be released to continue efficient operation and prevent damage. A cooling system dissipates this excess heat. To prevent the generation of even more heat, all moving parts require lubrication to reduce friction, prevent deterioration of engine parts that rub together, and increase efficiency. There are two ways to cool an engine: air-cooled (radial) and liquid-cooled (in-line).

Radial Engine

The radial engine had its cylinders arranged in a circle around the crankshaft, like spokes on a wheel. All the connecting rods were connected to a single master rod on the crankshaft. The engine could have only one row of cylinders, or they could be arranged in two or more banks. Each bank had its own master connecting rod. Radial engines always had an odd number of cylinders, usually seven or nine in each bank. The cylinders usually exhausted into an exhaust collector ring with one or two outlets.

Radial engines were air-cooled. This made this engine more lightweight, because no radiator and its associated plumbing were required, but they necessitated a large frontal area. Radial twin-row, or "twin-bank" engines were developed to gain more power without increasing frontal area. The two rows of seven or nine cylinders each were mounted on an elongated crankcase, like two engines, one behind the other. In the twin row version the problem was to get enough cooling air to the rear cylinders. The rear cylinders were placed behind the openings behind each pair of front cylinders to increase cooling. Baffle plates kept the hot air from coming off the front cylinders away from the back cylinders, and also slowed down the circulating air to its best cooling speed. Cooling was also accomplished by cast or machined cooling fins on the cylinder heads and along the cylinder barrel. The improvement of design and manufacturing procedures and of materials yielded an increase in cooling area as horsepower per cylinder increased due to higher cylinder head temperatures. Air coming through the cowling from the outside swept away the heat of combustion. Cowling flaps were controlled by the pilot, who could open or close them according to conditions and engine temperatures. On the ground these flaps were opened, as only the propeller provided air for cooling. At high altitudes the air is very cold, and more air is provided over the engine through forward motion, so the engine could possibly run too cold for efficient operation. Airflow could be further increased by an augmenter tube that created a pressure differential between air inlet and outlet that caused a suction, speeding airflow when necessary (venturi effect).

The radial engine was shorter, lighter, and more compact than the in-line engine per cubic inch displacement. The radial, however, was not lighter for equivalent horsepower. The installation was larger in diameter than the in-line and increased drag. Radial fighters, such as the Navy Grummans and the Thunderbolt, were pug-nosed when compared to the sleek in-line Mustangs and Spitfires.

Pratt & Whitney Double Wasp R-2800 (Pratt & Whitney)

Left: Pratt & Whitney Twin Wasp R-1830 (Pratt & Whitney)

Pratt & Whitney R-2800 installation in the F4U Corsair. (USMC)

Engine change on a 373FG P-47. (USAF)

Pratt & Whitney

Frederick Rentschler, who had resigned as president of Wright Aeronautical, established Pratt & Whitney in Hartford, CT, in 1925. Rentschler had set up his new aircraft engine company in an unused factory owned by machine tool company Pratt & Whitney, from which his company received its name. His first engine was the venerable nine cylinder air-cooled Wasp radial.

The R-1830 Twin Wasp, two-row radial, was designed in 1931 by a team headed by Luke Hobbs. The 14 cylinder was the largest aircraft engine being built in the United States in the 1930s. Produced in the greatest numbers of any U.S. piston engine in WWII, a total of 178,000 of this great engine were built, not only by P&W, but also by Buick and Chevrolet. Most of these engines powered the 19,000 B-24s, along with PBYs and C-47s. Almost all (98%) of American transport aircraft were powered by P&W engines. The engine was fitted in the Seversky P-35, Curtiss P-36, and Republic P-43 fighters, but the Grumman F4F Wildcat and later FM-1 were the most famous of the R-1830 powered fighters. The R-1830-76 was the world's first two-stage supercharged engine. However, as a fighter power plant it lacked the necessary horsepower and displacement to match Japanese aircraft, but for American bombers and transports it was the perfect engine.

Arguably the most important American engine of WWII was the P&W R-2800 Double Wasp. The R-2800 was a development of the 1936 R-2600 and was ready for production in 1940. P&W built a manufacturing plant in Kansas City to build the R-2800 C-series. Chevrolet and Nash also built the R-2800, but Ford was the biggest sub-contractor. In fact, Ford built an exact duplicate of P&W's Hartford plant in Dearborn to manufacture the R-2800 B model. During its long production life the engine saw extensive development and increase in power. The 18 (air-cooled) cylinder, two row, geared drive supercharged, 4-cycle engine digressed from earlier P&W twin radial engine design. The crankshafts and cylinder heads were not only of a unique design, but required the development of new manufacturing methods. The R-2800 was not a world-beater in any one area of performance, but the dependable engine was powerful, relatively small and of low weight, had low fuel con-

sumption, and was extremely tough and could sustain enormous battle damage and return to base. The supercharger was constantly improved, and toward the end of the war became almost as large as the engine itself. Water/methanol injection for war emergency power (WEP) gave the engine significant increases in power for a recommended maximum of five minutes, although this was often exceeded in combat.

The major drawback of the radial engine was, being air cooled, it required an extensive baffle system. The cylinder/baffle pictured here is from a Wright Cyclone R-1820 G-series. (Author)

Besides the Douglas A-26 and Martin B-26 bombers, the R-2800 powered America's great fighters of the Second World War, including the Grumman F6F Hellcat, Chance-Vought F4U, Northrop P-61 Black Widow, and the Republic P-47 Thunderbolt, which was the epitome of radial-powered WWII fighters.

In-line Engines

An in-line engine had all its cylinders in a straight line in either a vertical or inverted position. The family automobile has an in-line engine. The V in-line engine had two straight lines, or banks, of cylinders set like the letter V. The V-engine was compact and had the advantage of being easily streamlined, because it had little frontal area. An upright V in-line engine had its cylinders located above the crankshaft. The inverted V in-line engine had the crankshaft above the cylinders. The opposed engine had its cylinders arranged in two parallel rows, one row on each side of the crankcase. The opposed type was most frequently used on low-powered four or six cylinder engines.

In-line engines were more efficiently cooled with liquids, because air could not be easily directed over all cylinder heads, espe-

James A. Allison founded his aircraft engine company in 1915 building 20,000 V-12 Liberty engines in WW-1. When he died in 1929 the company was bought by General Motors which developed the Allison V-1710 in-line engine. (General Motors)

cially the ones in the rear. Liquid systems cooled more evenly and could be built with less frontal area opposing the air stream. They were heavier, more expensive to manufacture, difficult to maintain, and in combat were more vulnerable to damage from enemy fire. Liquid-cooled engines actually had a significant problem of the cooling agent actually freezing in the cold of high altitudes.

Since in-line engines were liquid-cooled, radiator construction and placement were always the preeminent design considerations for cooling. The internal cores of the radiator improved in the 1930s, and as war broke out automobile radiator producers, with no automobiles being manufactured, turned their attention to aircraft radiators. Fin and tube cores were developed that reduced drag and weight, and were much more efficient and less expensive to manufacture. Also, advances in coolant development with 30-50% glycol to water were finally being used. Radiator placement varied with the aircraft: the P-51, British Hurricane, and Japanese Ki-61 in an aerodynamic duct in the fuselage belly; the P-40, Typhoon, and Tempest under the engine; the Spitfire and Me-109 under the wing; and the Mosquito on the wing leading edge.

Even though they were longer, in-line engines had much less frontal area than radials with equivalent displacement. Because of its better cooling, the horsepower (weight per horsepower) of the in-line was higher, and high and war emergency power could also be sustained longer. Liquid-cooled were notably more vulnerable to battle damage. One bullet penetrating a radiator would mean loss of coolant, and the engine would rapidly overheat and seize. Stories abound of entire cylinder heads of radial engines being shot off and the engine continuing to run for hours.

Allison

During WWII only one American company, Allison, a division of General Motors, produced an American designed liquid-cooled aircraft engine. James A. Allison founded the company in 1915 in Indianapolis, IN. During WWI the company designed and produced 20,000 water-cooled V-12 Liberty engines. The Liberty was a poor design and suffered through numerous problems, and the post-war reduction in demand meant lean years for Allison. After Allison suddenly died in 1929, Fischer & Co. of Detroit purchased the company. After three months the Fischer sold the company to General Motors, which kept the company going during the Depression by supplying dirigible and blimp engines.

In 1928 the company looked into the development of the family aircraft business. The Depression killed the idea, but its six-cylinder engine became the basis in 1930 for the 12 cylinder V-1710 that was to be known as the 1710, or "Allison." The design was a combination of the conventional and the innovative, and thus suffered developmental and production problems, which were not resolved until the late 1930s and early 1940s. The major criticism leveled against the engine was its lack of high altitude performance, as it was only driven by a single-stage, engine-driven supercharger. The AAC insisted that all Allisons utilize the General Electric supercharger that was to be succeeded by the GE turbo-supercharger. Because tooling was in place for mass production of the V-1710, trade-offs needed to be made so as not to disrupt vital production at this critical stage of the war. So the addition of the turbo-super-

Allison V-1710-F. (North American)

charger was neglected, as the engine continued to suffer developmental and production problems that needed to be resolved first to meet contract demands. When Rolls Royce developed its superior two-speed, two-stage inter-cooled/after-cooled supercharger, Allison did not add it to the V-1710.

The lack of altitude performance was to penalize Allison's bottom line. The Allison-powered P-51A was to be re-engined with the Rolls Royce Merlin licensed to Packard. The P-38 would have also been re-equipped with the Merlin, but for persuasive lobbying by General Motors. Royal Air Force orders for the P-40, P-38, and P-39 may also have continued at a higher level. The P-38 suffered many problems serving with the Eighth Air Force, where missions were flown at high altitudes, and by October 1944 the Eighth abandoned the Lightning. Fortunately, the Pacific, with its milder climate and lower operational altitudes, proved to be more suited to the P-38's attributes.

Among the fighter aircraft powered by the Allison were the P-39, P-40, P-38, P-51A, and P-63. The P-40, P-39, and Allison P-51s served America well early in the war. All were sold as export models to augment the RAF early in the war. The unwanted P-39 and P-63 were given to a desperate Soviet Union throughout the war. The Allison success story was the P-38, which was the top USAAF scorer in the Pacific and boasted America's two top aces, Dick Bong (40v.) and Tom Maguire (38v.).

Rolls Royce

Before his death in 1933, Sir Henry Royce initiated an engine design to replace the aging Kestrel. Rolls Royce was forced to develop the new engine, the PV-12 (PV = private venture), without government funding. When the government funded the project the engine was named the Merlin, after a bird of prey, as were most RR engines. The design was similar to the Kestrel, being a 60 degree, V-12 mono-block, pressure water-cooled, gear driven, supercharged 4-cycle. Like the Allison, it suffered many design and developmental problems. But, unlike the Allison, RR was able to constantly resolve problems and improve the design throughout the late 1930s and during the war. The development of the Supermarine Spitfire and the Merlin were synonymous. The Spitfire's success and that of the Hawker Hurricane led the RAF to try the two-stage Merlin in

the North American Aviation Company's Mustang I (P-51A). The Mustang II (P-51B) was the first Merlin-powered Mustang. The result was perhaps the war's best fighter aircraft. Because the Merlin was more fuel economical, yielding more miles per gallon, and the fighter was able to carry auxiliary fuel tanks it was able to escort bombers deep into Germany. The Merlin was a flexible engine design, and changes doubled its power output over the years without increasing bore or stroke size. The frontal area stayed the same, and the length increased only a matter of a few inches. The two-speed, two-stage inter-cooler/after-cooler supercharger gave the fighter superior altitude capabilities for escort and interceptor duty. This supercharger was the cornerstone of RR Merlin performance.

At VJ-Day Pratt & Whitney and its licensees had manufactured 49% of all horsepower (fighter and bomber) used by combined American air forces and a significant portion of England's air power. Wright Aeronautical and its licensees provided 27% (mostly bomber), and the remaining 24% was divided between Packard as the Rolls Royce Merlin licensee and Allison.

Superchargers

The need to increase power output at high altitudes where atmospheric pressure is lower led to the development of the supercharger. At sea level the weight of the earth's atmosphere is 14.7 pounds per square inch, but at 25,000 feet it decreases to 5.5 pounds. The greater

Factory V-1710 engine installation in P-38. (Lockheed)

Before he died in 1933, Sir Henry Royce initiated the design that was to become the Merlin, which would transform the P-51 Mustang into a superlative fighter aircraft. (Author)

Packard Rolls Royce V-1650-7. (Packard)

of air from the outside to keep the weight flow of air from decreasing. By using a supercharger the weight of airflow can be maintained at the rated power output of the aircraft. This is done mechanically by pumping air into the engine carburetor at the required pressure, causing the carburetor to add more fuel to keep the air/fuel mixture at the proper ratio. This increased amount of fuel and air, under greater than normal pressure, goes through the intake manifold and provides a greater charge to the cylinder, thus increasing the force of the piston's power stroke. The mean effective pressure in the cylinder determines horsepower. There are two types of superchargers: external and internal.

Internal Supercharger
The internal supercharger is one that is located between the carburetor and the intake manifold and forces a charged mixture into the cylinder. The internal supercharger provides a uniform distribution of the fuel/air charge to the cylinder and increases the density of the charge. It is built into the engine and obtains its power by being geared to the crankshaft.

the air pressure the greater the air weight (density = pounds per cubic foot), and vice versa. As an aircraft flies higher the pressure becomes less and the density becomes less. If an engine is to maintain its power at higher altitudes, it has to take in a higher volume

Engines

Manufacturer	Allison	Rolls Royce/Packard	Pratt & Whitney
Model	V-1710	Merlin	R-2800
Type	In-line V/60 Degrees	In-line V/60 Degrees	Radial/2 Row
Cylinders	12	12	18
Cooling	Ethylene glycol	Pressure water	Air
Displacement (cu.in.)	1710	1649	2804
Width (in.)	29.3	29.8	52.5 (diameter)
Height (in.)	37.6	41.2	52.5 (diameter)
Length (in.)	85.8	70.6	88.5
Frontal Area (sq.ft.)	6.1	5.8	15.0
Weight (lbs.)	1395	1450	2480
Wt./hp (lb/hp)	0.95	0.98	1.24
Fuel Consumption (lbs./hp/hr.)	0.54	0.52	0.48
Max. HP	1475	1480	2000
Normal HP	1100	1210	1675
Supercharger	Gear driven/1-speed	Gear driven/2-speed	Gear driven/2-stage

External Supercharger

The external supercharger is one that is located between the outside air and the carburetor and forces an increased amount of air or compressed air into the carburetor. The external supercharger is a turbine (turbosupercharger) which is turned by the engine's exhaust gases.

Intercoolers and Aftercoolers

In using a supercharger with sufficient compression capacity to provide the full weight of air at high altitudes it is necessary to cool off the air or mixture after it has been compressed. This is accomplished by using special radiators, called intercoolers or aftercoolers, depending on their location in relation to the carburetor. Both methods, with their large radiator equipment, not only increase weight and drag, but increase aircraft vulnerability, as it adds another vital system which could be hit by enemy fire.

Packard RR V-1650 installation in the P-51 Mustang. (USAF)

FIGHTER ARMAMENT AND ACCESSORIES

Machine Guns

The American air services adopted the .50 caliber M2 Browning Machine Gun derived from the .50 caliber ground service heavy machine gun as its standard fighter weapon during WWII. It was a recoil-operated, air-cooled, belt-fed gun that weighed 52 pounds and was 57 inches long (barrel 36 inches). Its rate of automatic fire (shots per second) averaged 700 to 750 rounds per minute, depending on attachments, such as a flash suppresser or muzzle booster. Its muzzle velocity was 2,700 to 2,850 feet per second. Its extreme range (extent of forward travel) was 20,000 to 21,500 feet, and its effective range (round able to penetrate airframe or engine to cause damage) was 3,400 to 3,500 feet. All of the above performance figures varied in the field due to internal (e.g. age and condition of

the mechanism and barrel, age of the ammunition, feed, and type) and external (e.g. temperature) conditions.

The M2 was either engine, nose, or wing-mounted. When engine-mounted it was synchronized to fire through the propeller by a mechanical trigger motor attached to the gun receiver, causing the gun to fire semi-automatically. When the gun was wing-mounted, firing was attained through a remote control solenoid attached to the receiver, causing it to fire automatically. To assure that a fighter's gunfire would exact the maximum damage to an enemy aircraft, the guns were harmonized so that their fire would converge at the optimum combat range. Harmonization range was often the personal preference of the individual pilot, but it is well known that most aces preferred very short ranges.

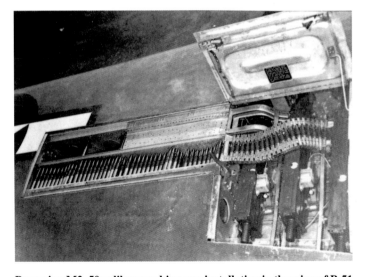

Browning M2 .50 caliber machine gun installation in the wing of P-51 was the standard American aircraft weapon in WW-2. It was a recoil-operated, air-cooled, belt-fed gun. It fired at 700 to 750 rounds per minute at 2700 to 2850 feet per second at an effective range of 3400 to 3500 feet. The P-51 carried four to six M2s with 400 rounds per gun. (USAF)

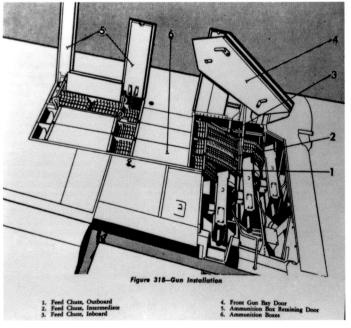

Figure 318–Gun Installation

1. Feed Chute, Outboard
2. Feed Chute, Intermediate
3. Feed Chute, Inboard
4. Front Gun Bay Door
5. Ammunition Box Retaining Door
6. Ammunition Boxes

.50 cal. M2 installation in the P-47. (Author: P-47 Parts Manual)

Though the .50 caliber bullet lacked the punch of a 20mm cannon shell, the concentrated firepower from six or eight machine guns had a devastating effect. There were four basic types of .50 caliber ammunition: armor piercing (distinguished by a painted black tip); tracer (red tip); incendiary (blue); and armor piercing incendiary (silver). The bullet weighed about 1.6 ounces and was about 5.5 inches long. Between 267 and 500 rounds of ammunition could be stowed per gun (rpg). The P-47 carried eight guns with 425 rpg, the F6F and F4U mounted six guns with 400 rpg, and the P-51 carried four or six guns with 400 rpg. The expression "the whole nine yards" is attributed to Dick Bong. The ammunition belts of the P-38's .50 caliber machine guns measured 27 feet when laid out full length. As he pre-flighted his P-38, he made sure it was topped with fuel, oil, and had the "full nine yards" of ammo.

Cannon

The U.S. dabbled with cannon armament in early fighters. The P-39 Aircobra was equipped with a 30 round Oldsmobile 37mm T-9 or M-4 cannon. Because of its inherent inaccuracy and low rate of fire it was abandoned in favor of the .50 caliber machine gun. The P-38 carried the Hispano-Suiza 20mm cannon, and late in the war several fighter-bombers were fitted with 20mm cannon, as was the P-61 night fighter. But because no Axis fighter could withstand the

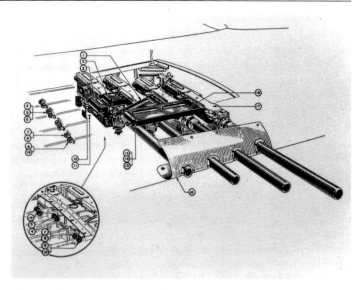

.50 cal. M2 installation in the F4U. (Author: F4U Parts Manual)

pounding of multiple .50s, the cannon was reserved for special purposes.

The Machine Gun vs. Cannon Controversy

The difference between a machine gun and cannon was that a machine gun fired a solid slug, while a cannon fired rounds called shells that could be solid, but were often hollow and filled with detonation or incendiary material. The solid machine gun round did its damage through kinetic energy, which is the function of projectile weight times its velocity squared. The .50 caliber slug weighed about 1.6 ounces, while the 20-mm projectile weighed 4.6 ounces and the 37-mm projectile weighed almost 17.6 ounces. The machine gun had a somewhat higher muzzle velocity, which is the speed at which the projectile leaves the barrel. Thus, the machine gun round's kinetic energy was higher, as its higher muzzle velocity was squared. It also had a higher rate of fire than the cannon, which means it could fire more rounds per minute, or more correctly, per second to do damage. The muzzle velocity affects the round's kinetic energy and the flight time to the target. The shorter the time to the target gave the target less time to maneuver. Guns with higher muzzle velocities are more likely to hit a target, can be fired at longer ranges, and cause more damage.

A cannon shell, depending on its design, will explode on contact, or penetrate and then explode or set a fire. A solid machine gun slug will penetrate and depend on its kinetic energy to cause damage. The aircraft cannon was a more deadly weapon due to their heavier explosive shells. But they were heavier than a machine gun, often weighing more each than two machine guns, depending on the caliber (a 37mm cannon weighed 135lbs. and a 20mm cannon weighed 118lbs. vs. a .50 cal. machine gun that weighed 52lbs. and a .30 cal. machine gun that weighed 24lbs.). Therefore, the equal weight of two machine guns could fire many more rounds per second than a cannon. Also, cannon shells weighed more and were larger than machine gun rounds, so a cannon-equipped fighter could carry far fewer rounds than a machine gun-equipped fighter could. The 37mm gun (P-39) could carry 30rpg, the 20mm (P-38)

Armorers loading .50 belts into the ammunition bays on Gabby Gabreski's P-47. (USAF)

The P-38 was armed with four Browning .50 cal. M2 machine guns and a 20mm Hispano-Suiza cannon. (USAF)

The P-39 was equipped with a 30 round Oldsmobile 37mm T-9 or M-4 cannon which was fired through the propeller hub. The inaccurate cannon had a low rate of fire and was abandoned for the .50 machine gun. (USAF)

American aircraft ammunition: .50 caliber belted AP (top), .30 caliber belted tracer (left center), 37mm cannon (right center) and 20mm cannon (bottom) (from Author's equipment collection).

150rpg, the .50 cal. (P-47 or P-51) between 400-450rpg, and the .30 caliber (P-39) 1,000rpg. Fewer cannon shells meant a shorter firing time at a lower rate of fire. The 30 rounds of 37mm shells fired by a P-39 had a duration of fire of 11.8 seconds, while its four .30 cal. machines with 1,000rpg fired for 67 seconds per gun. The P-38's 20mm cannon fired 150 rounds at 11.2 rounds per second in 13.4 seconds. The .50 cal. machine gun fired 12 rounds per second for a duration of 35 seconds (425 rounds). A cannon shell caused more damage per hit, but there were less potential hits when compared to the higher rate of fire and more rounds found in machine gun equipped fighters. Many British and Luftwaffe fighters carried a combination of machine guns and cannon, with the machine guns being used to find range and attain hits and the cannon to deliver the lethal blow. The RAF replaced its Browning .303 caliber machine guns with the Hispano-Suiza 20mm cannon, as one 20mm shell did much more damage than four .303 hits, which were ineffective against armor plate and self-sealing fuel tanks. The 20mm cannon, with its explosive shell, would leave a large hole upon impact. The American fighter aircraft .30 cal. machine gun was replaced with the .50 cal. Both projectiles left small, clean entrance holes in the metal fuselage surface, but after they hit they would be deflected and begin to tumble end over end. The larger .50 cal. slug would cause a substantially larger exit, or secondary, hole than the .30 cal.

The American fighter carried six or eight .50 cal. machine guns that concentrated enough firepower to cope with Axis fighters, especially against the fragile Japanese fighters in the Pacific and particularly when using the API round. Also, the major Axis bombers (He-111, Do-17, and G4M3 Betty) were usually of medium bomber size and not well armed or armored. Thus, the six or eight machine guns mounted in the superior P-51, P-47, P-38, or F4U and F6F gave the American fighter pilot a good chance of achieving a high probability shot, firing out the most number of rounds in the shortest amount of time.

Harmonization

Harmonization—commonly called bore sighting—was aligning the path of the rounds fired from all guns. It was accomplished by one of two methods. One was to converge the four, six, or eight machine guns to a point 250 to 300 yards ahead of the fighter. At a three mil gunsight setting the convergence pattern at 300 yards was about three feet in diameter, which was difficult for the average pilot/marksman and resulted in excessive dispersion at most ranges. A remedy to gain wider bullet dispersion was to boresight each gun at different ranges, generally 250, 300, and 350 yards for outboard, middle, and inboard guns, respectively. Called "pattern harmonization," it was innately less damaging than a tighter cone of fire, but the greater dispersion of bullets made the probability of obtaining a hit more likely. Against Japanese aircraft, which lacked pilot armor protection and self-sealing fuel tanks, a few hits could be lethal.

American Aircraft Guns

GUN/AMMO	Gun Weight (lbs.)	Muzzle Velocity (ft./sec.)	Rounds per Gun	Projectile Weight (lbs.)	Rate of Fire (rps)	Duration of Fire (sec.)	Weight of Fire (lbs/sec)
Browning .30 cal. Machine Gun	24	2600	1000	0.025	15.0	66.5	0.40
Browning .50 cal. Machine Gun	52	2800	425	0.100	10.2	19.6	0.90
Hispano-Suiza 20mm Cannon	118	2800	150	0.290	11.2	13.4	3.20
American Armament 37mm Cannon	135	1800	30	1.100	1.5	11.8	1.65

Types of Ammunition

Type	Use	Color of Tip	How It Works
Ball	Against personnel and light material targets	Unpainted; plain copper	The outer jacket point contains a lead and antimony filler that covers the tip of the underlying steel core. When the projectile hits a target, the soft outer jacket and filler smears, giving the steel core a grip. The core then penetrates the surface instead of being turned aside.
Armor-Piercing	Against armored aircraft and vehicles, concrete shelters and other bullet-resisting targets	Black	The projectile is the same as the ball cartridge, except that the core is made of very hard tungsten-chrome steel to give it greater penetrating power.
Tracer	For observing fire, it makes a streak of light easily seen at night and usually is visible in daylight	Red	Inside the outer metal jacket is a slug of lead and antimony. Behind it is a pocket of tracer composition that is set afire by the propelling charge as the projectile leaves the cartridge case.
Incendiary	Used to set fire to explosive or very inflammable targets	Light blue	In front of the jacket is an incendiary composition that is sealed by plugs of an alloy that easily melts. As the bullet goes through the barrel, the heat melts the plugs and the incendiary composition is set on fire as it meets the air.
Dummy	Training	Unpainted (hole in side of case)	Has no priming or propelling charge.
Armor-Piercing Incendiary	Used to set fire to armor-plated inflammable objects.	Black with small blue tip on the nose.	Similar to the armor-piercing projectile, except that there is incendiary compound behind the steel core.

Harmonization, commonly called bore sighting, aligned the path of rounds fired from all guns. Here armorers of the 41FS/39FG set up boresighting apparatus 1000 inches in front of a P-51D at Clark Field, Philippines late in the war. P-51 guns, gun cameras and gun sights were generally harmonized at 300 yards. (USAF)

size of the enemy wingspan. The pilot would fly the fighter so that the target appeared in the gyro reticle circle and rotate a throttle twist grip until the diameter of the gyro reticle circle. The gyro apparatus in the sight produced the correct deflection for the range and rate of turn corresponding to the target size. The pilot would frame the target with the twist grip as the range changed, track the target for at least one second, and then would fire. Initially, it was not well-received because of its size and apparent intricacy, but soon earned the nickname "No Miss Um." It allowed shooting at twice the previous maximum range, and more importantly greatly improved deflection shooting, which with the N-9/MK VIII sights were a combination of guesswork and individual ability. The K-14 made even 90 degree deflection as easy as that from dead astern. Though the new sight required some additional manual coordination, it greatly increased the number of kills at long range (500+ yards) and at large deflection angles (45+ degrees).

Gun Sights

The simple ring and bead gun sight of the interwar years was no longer sufficient with the increasing performance and combat ranges seen in the newer monoplane fighters of the mid-1930s.

The N-2, N3A, L3-B, N-9, and MK VIII series of reflector sights were basically a refined ring and bead sight, of which the latter two eventually became the standard. They were characterized by a center dot, or "pipper" (bead), surrounded by 50- and 100- mil radii rings, which aided in the calculation of deflection. The retile image of this sight, although it was only a few inches from the pilot's eye, was made to look as if it were at a distance in front of the fighter. There was no need to readjust focus, the sight could be viewed with both eyes open, and the pilot could move his head without changing the alignment of the target. The image of the ring(s) and pipper was superimposed onto a special glass in front of the pilot's eyes in such a way that they were visible only if the pilot were looking along the longitudinal axis of the fighter (convergence of the guns). The pilot had only to track the target and get it into the center of the sight. The sight was accurate when closing on an enemy at the same speed and course, but deflection shooting ("lead-shooting," e.g. bird hunting) continued to be the province of the gifted pilot.

The AAF K-14 series and Navy Mark 18 were introduced in July 1944 and were a development of the British gyroscopic Mk IIC and Mk IID sights. It was originally developed for bomber turrets, but engineers adapted it as the standard U.S. fighter gunsight. The new sight provided much improved deflection shooting from the average pilot, as it computed the correct lead angle for a target crossing speed at ranges of 200 to 800 yards. The K-14 was based on the reflector sight, but was combined with a gyroscope. Below the reflecting glass was a panel with a control calibrated to the wingspan of the intended victim. The pilot dialed in the enemy's wingspan (pre-marked on the controls as Me-109, FW-190, etc.), and the sighting reticle on the reflector glass then adjusted itself to the

Navy MK-8 Illuminated Optical Reflector Sight. The pilot leaned forward and looked into the glass with both eyes open to superimpose the sight and target and then fired. Note protective pad under glass. (Author's equipment collection)

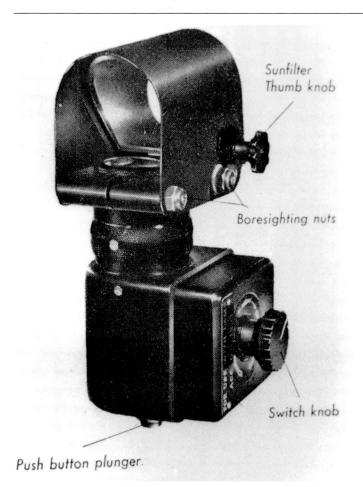

Sunfilter
Thumb knob

Boresighting nuts

Switch knob

Push button plunger.

Navy MK-9 Gunsight succeeded the ring and bead sights. They were characterized by a center dot or "pipper" surrounded by 50 and 100 mil radii rings which aided in calculating deflection shots but required a combination of guesswork and individual ability. (USN)

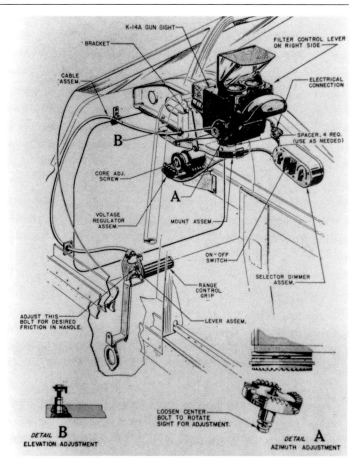

K-14A installation in the P-51 D/K. (Author: P-51 Parts Manual)

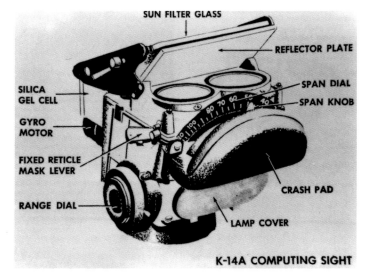

SUN FILTER GLASS

REFLECTOR PLATE

SPAN DIAL

SPAN KNOB

SILICA GEL CELL

GYRO MOTOR

FIXED RETICLE MASK LEVER

RANGE DIAL

CRASH PAD

LAMP COVER

K-14A COMPUTING SIGHT

K-14A/AAF P-51. Although it did require some additional manual co-ordination the K-14 made even a 90-degree deflection shot as easy as that from one astern. (USAF)

Gun Cameras

The utilization of the Type N-4 or N-6 gun camera greatly aided in authenticated victory claims. The gun camera, officially titled the Gun Sight Aiming Point Camera, was manufactured by the Fairchild Camera and Instrument Company of Jamaica, NY, and the Morse Instrument Company of Hudson, OH. The gun camera was mounted in the leading edge of the inboard port wing or inside the leading edge of the starboard outer wing panel behind curved laminated glass faired into the wing. It was accessible for loading and adjustment from the wheel well. A small, spring-loaded metal plate covered the camera aperture in the wing, remained open during flight, and was closed by a mechanical cable linkage when the landing gear was extended, protecting the lens from blown sand and pebbles. A small, self-contained heater warmed the camera bay. The electrically operated 16mm camera could be set for 16, 32, or 64 frames per second. The diaphragm stops were marked "B" (bright), "H" (hazy), and "D" (dull) to allow for various light conditions. But in practice the camera was unable to adjust to light conditions, and footage was lost or would be inconclusive. Each unit did its own

MK-18 Gunsight. The Navy MK-18 and Air Force K-14 were intro-duced in July 1944 and were a development of the British gyroscopic MK 11C and MK 11D Models. (USN)

Sperry K-13 Gyroscopic Lead-Computing Optical Sight (LCOS). (Author's equipment collection)

Type N-6, 16mm gun camera manufactured by Morse Instrument Co. The camera contained 50 feet of film in a magazine and had a 35mm ƒ3.5 plane lens. (Author's equipment collection)

Gun camera film frame of a Me-109 under attack. (USAF)

evaluation of combat film and would forward conclusive film to higher echelons for confirmation.

Guns and camera were controlled by a three-way toggle switch (guns, camera, and sight). The camera was focused on the convergence point by the boresight adapter. When the trigger on the stick was pressed the guns fired, and the cameras operated if the toggle was in the gun position. The camera and sight positions on the toggle took motion pictures when the trigger was pressed but did not fire the guns. The camera was sighted a little below the gun sight line so that the camera remained on the target for a longer period after the pullout from the gunnery run.

Drop Tanks

Of the developments which affected the course of the war, the jettisonable auxiliary fuel tank was one of the most consequential. The "belly," or "drop" tank gave the fighter extended range to allow it to provide continuous escort to bomber formations or reach deeper into enemy territory on fighter-bomber missions. During 1942 it became evident that the P-47 did not have sufficient range for bomber escort duties. Various wing-mounted tanks were tried, from two 75-gallon steel tanks to two 108-gallon metal or composition paper tanks, to two 150-gallon steel tanks. Single centerline fuselage paper or steel 108 gallon tanks, steel 150 gallon tank, and paper or steel 200 gallon tanks were used. The P-51, which had very good range without tanks, used two wing-mounted 108-gallon paper tanks, nicknamed "babies," as more or less the standard drop tank. These large tanks were equipped with external sway braces to keep them from swinging and breaking loose in flight. Steel bands were wrapped around the middle of the tank for added strength. These paper tanks had flat, reinforced indentations where fuel and air connections and filler caps were located. At high altitudes the drop tanks needed to be pressurized by a vacuum pump so that the fuel could be drawn. The P-38 generally used two 165-gallon steel tanks. The 110-gallon metal tank produced in 1944 was a development of the 75-gallon metal tank and was mostly used in the Pacific and Italy, with a few going to the ETO.

The lighter paper tanks were preferred to steel tanks by ground crews because they were easier to manhandle, and by pilots because they had less effect on flight characteristics. The auxiliary tank was attached behind the center of gravity, or in tandem under each wing, which affected handling characteristics. To remedy this situation, after using the main wing tank for takeoff the pilot switched to the fuselage tank and used it until there were about 30 gallons remaining. He then switched to and alternated between the external drop tanks, changing from one to another about every three quarters of an hour to an hour, and when empty jettisoned them. The routine for jettisoning the drop tanks was to switch to internal fuel first so as not to interrupt the flow of fuel to the engine. Upon entering combat the pilot jettisoned his drop tanks, but in the excitement more than a few pilots forgot to switch over to internal fuel and found their engine would stop in mid-dive. After jettison the pilot had the 30 gallons of fuselage fuel and a large amount of wing tank fuel left for combat and/or to return to base. But, if a drop tank did not deliver fuel to the engine or did not release, the sortie needed to

"Baby," the 108 U.S. gallon plastic-pressed paper tank which was manufactured by Bowater in England is being lofted by a 78FG pilot at Duxford. (USAF)

355FG armorer removing gun camera film magazine for processing from its heated compartment on the leading edge of a P-47 wing. The 16mm-film magazine can seen in his right hand. The Plexiglas covered window is above the access panel. (USAF)

The 110-gallon metal tank was used mainly in the Pacific and Italian campaigns. (USAF)

be aborted, not only for the troubled fighter, but also for another pilot to escort him back to base. Thousands of drop tanks were jettisoned over the European countryside by both the Allies and Luftwaffe.

There were some unusual aerial victories recorded using a drop tank. On 11 November 1943, over Rabaul, Lt(jg) George Blair of VF-9 hit a Kate bomber when he dropped his auxiliary belly tank on it. On 22 June 1945, 1Lt. John Leaper of VMF-314 had shot down a Betty carrying a Baka bomb and an escorting Zeke, but his F4U suffered a shattered windshield from a bullet. He looked up and saw another Zeke diving from 10 o'clock high on his wingman, 1Lt William Milne, who had destroyed a Zeke and Betty. Leaper fired his last rounds but missed, and climbed until he was just under the Zeke. He tried to chew off the Jap's tail with his prop but missed. He climbed above the Zeke and succeeded in digging his prop into the Jap's nose forward of the cockpit. His right pylon fuel tank hit the Zeke and exploded, tearing off his right wing, but also

taking down the Zeke. Leaper managed to bail out despite a violent spin, but split his parachute and broke two shroud lines. On the way down another Zeke started to make a pass on him, so he collapsed his chute and fell like a rock for 3,000-4,000 feet before his chute reopened. He spent an hour and a half in the water before the *Cheyenne* picked him up.

PILOT PROTECTION AND SAFTEY
Armor
Theoretically, the ideal means to protect the pilot would be to armor the entire aircraft so that there would be no vulnerable areas. Of course, this aircraft probably would be so heavy that it would be unable to fly. So aircraft designers attempted to find a compromise between the "maximum protection/minimum weight" formula in their designs. The ever-increasing speeds of the fighter during the war meant that the 400 mph+ fighter flew so fast as compared to rate of fire of machine guns and cannon that bullet holes were four inches or more apart. So, unless the pilot or a vital area of the fighter were hit, the wide dispersal of bullet strikes gave the aircraft a protection to hits. Aircraft speed not only dispersed the hits, but also brought about changes in the angles the bullets hit the rapidly moving aircraft. Knowing the angles from which enemy attack was most probable, designers were able to locate the armor plate most strategically. Stopping and deflecting the bullet were two ways to protect a pilot. To stop frontal bullets a heavy armored plate was placed behind the propeller hub. Another plate was placed in front of the cockpit to stop bullets not stopped by the engine and hub plate, and a heavy armored bulkhead was placed behind the pilot's seat to stop bullets from the rear. When ground strafing became more prevalent a floor plate was fitted. To save weight, these bulkheads were placed as close to the pilot as possible so he could hide directly behind them, and thus they could be made smaller than if they were placed further away. This armor plate was a nickel-alloy steel known as X-7440, and was either face-hardened or homogeneous. Face-hardened, as its name indicates, had the front face of the plate hardened, while the homogeneous was uniformly hard throughout. The

Classic photo of a 375FS/361FG crew chief at Bottisham waiting for "his" Mustang to return from a mission on D-Day. The two tanks on the ground on the right are 108-gallon paper while the others are 75-gallon steel tanks. (USAF)

The pilot seat armor on a P-51A. The armor, designated X-7440, was manufactured from a nickel-alloy steel and was either face-hardened or homogeneous. (Author)

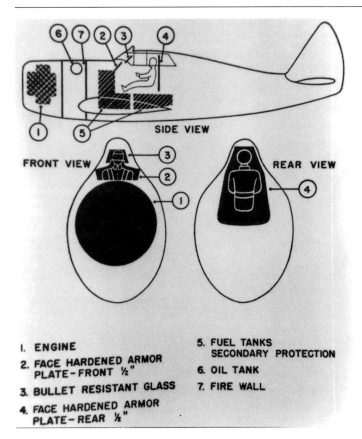

1. ENGINE
2. FACE HARDENED ARMOR PLATE – FRONT ½"
3. BULLET RESISTANT GLASS
4. FACE HARDENED ARMOR PLATE – REAR ½"
5. FUEL TANKS SECONDARY PROTECTION
6. OIL TANK
7. FIRE WALL

Armor protection arrangement on the F4U. (Author: F4U Parts Manual)

face-hardened plate was preferred, as when a bullet struck it only a small coin-sized piece fell off the plate, while the homogeneous tended to shatter. Also, in plate thicker than $3/8^{th}$'s of an inch, face-hardened was lighter and had a higher ballistic limit (e.g. bullet resistance). But face-hardened was less adaptable to mass production methods and required complex heat treatment, and therefore cost more.

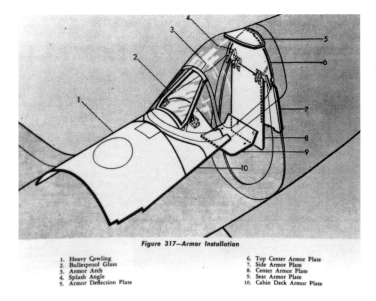

Figure 317—Armor Installation

1. Heavy Cowling
2. Bulletproof Glass
3. Armor Arch
4. Splash Angle
5. Armor Deflection Plate
6. Top Center Armor Plate
7. Side Armor Plate
8. Center Armor Plate
9. Seat Armor Plate
10. Cabin Deck Armor Plate

Armor protection arrangement on a P-47. (Author: P-47 Parts Manual)

Another method of protecting the pilot while reducing weight was to fit the fighter with aluminum alloy deflector plates to protect the cockpit and engine. The engine was protected by curved aluminum plates on top and under the cowling to protect the engine and pilot from bullets from a head on attack. Deflector plates were placed at the left and right sides of the cockpit to deflect bullets fired at angles from the rear. All armor needed to be accessible and was bolted for easy removal and repair in case of hits.

Windscreens presented a particular problem, because laminated glass needed to be very thick and thus heavy because of its low ballistic limit. A one-foot piece, 1 1/2 inches thick, weighed 30 pounds. This thickness stopped the penetration of a .30 caliber bullet, while twice that thickness was required to stop a .50 bullet (1/2 inch of armor plate could do the same). Armored glass was manufactured by taking sections of highly polished glass and sandwiching them between sheets of transparent plastic and bonding them under very high heat and pressure. Because laminated glass does not resist bullets at right angles it was set at deflection angles as close as possible to the pilot's eyes. Armored glass stopped a bullet by breaking it up and absorbing the pieces between the layers of glass. At the point of impact the glass powdered, starred, and cracked three inches around impact.

Self-sealing Fuel Tanks
The fuel cell was constructed of hard, thick formed rubber in two layers. A gel-like substance was sandwiched between the inner and outer layers of rubber. The gel expanded when it contacted gasoline, so when a bullet penetrated the tank, gasoline leaked into the gel, which expanded to close the hole. When the fighter returned to base the hole could be easily repaired by placing a piece of rubber in the hole.

G-Suit
Dog-fighting fighter pilots often found that tight high-speed turns or pullouts would cause a sequence of symptoms called "pulling Gs." The "Gs," or G-force, was the force of gravity exerting itself on the pilot as a feeling of increased weight as acceleration was increased. Acceleration forces created a pressure on the body's circulatory system, which became greater than blood pressure, causing the symptoms. The flow of blood was reduced to parts of the body, especially the eyes and brain. Prolonged exposure to G-forces of ten to thirty seconds or more forced venous blood from the chest into the lower body. This caused a drop in blood pressure as the heart was deprived of blood to pump, preventing blood from reaching the eyes and brain. As cerebral tissues retained oxygen, no effects would be felt for several seconds into a maneuver. As the maneuver became more extreme and prolonged (ten seconds plus) the G-forces became higher, causing a sequence of G symptoms. These symptoms ranged from: feeling pressed into the seat at two Gs; unable to move the body and difficulty in moving the arms at three Gs; "gray out" (dimmed vision) at three to four Gs; "black out" (loss of vision) at four to five Gs; and unconsciousness at five to six Gs. It was obvious that the development of a pressure suit to prevent blackout would allow the fighter pilot to have the tactical advantage of being able to make tighter turns in combat than the

enemy.

The basic premise of the G-suit was to girdle the abdomen and legs to restrict the downward flow of blood. In 1939, at the University of Toronto, W/C William Franks of the RCAF developed an effective pressure suit. The bulky 18-pound waist-high rubber suit was pressurized by water. The "Franks" suit never gained acceptance due to its size and weight, warmth, and restriction of movement.

In 1940, the Berger Brothers Company of New Haven, CT—a manufacturer of corsets—worked with the Navy and Mayo Clinic in developing a pressure suit. The result was the G-1 gradient pressure suit, a ten-pound wrap around, overall-style, three-piece pressure suit with a girdle containing 17 air bladders. The suit's bladders were inflated automatically when centrifugal force during maneuvers reached 2 1/2 Gs. Bladder pressure was exerted against the abdomen, thighs, and calves to keep blood from pooling in the lower extremities. The G-1 proved to be too complicated and uncomfortable; being heavy, bulky, and hot. It gave way to the G-2, which resembled its predecessor. It was a single pressure type containing five bladders instead of 17 and weighed 6 1/2 pounds. After 3,500 G-2s were tested by the 8th and 9th Air Forces in the summer of 1944, it was found unsatisfactory for the same reasons as the G-

Armored glass stopped a bullet by breaking it up and absorbing the pieces between the layers of glass. As seen on the P-47 windscreen, the glass powdered, starred and cracked three inches around the point of impact. (USAF)

1. David Clark of the David Clark Company and Dr. D. E. Wood of the Mayo Clinic refined the G-2 into the G-3. It weighed 2 1/2 pounds and was cooler and smaller, covering only the parts of the body actually pressurized. The G-3 was standardized in mid-August 1944 and accepted for use by the AAF in November 1944. Improved versions were quickly introduced, with the G-3A standardized in March 1945 and used by the Air Force for several years after the war. The Navy chose the comfortable Z-1 manufactured by the David Clark Company. It was similar to the ordinary summer flying suit, being made of light, porous rayon, and was available in nine sizes. It was a step-in type closed by an abdominal and two leg zippers. A single piece bladder system inflated against the abdomen and legs. Late in the war the AAF received the Z-1/G-4, which was a tropical version. With modifications the Z-1/G-4 saw service during the Korean War.

The G-suit increased the individual's ability to withstand centrifuge Gs by 1 to 1 1/2 times, as they were able to pull 8 to 9 Gs without even experiencing gray out. In actual combat there was an increased resistance to G forces over those experienced in tests in the centrifuge. The apparent reason for this was the natural adrenaline-producing tension of combat, which further increased G-resistance. There was unanimous approval of the G-suit, especially in the ETO. Its tactical advantage was not only in one-to-one dog fighting, particularly when making sustained circling deflection maneuvers in tight formation, but also in taking evasive action during low-level strafing and dive bombing, especially when trying to avoid flak. The G-suit allowed the pilot to sit up and look to the side or rear without fear of blackout. The ability to keep the enemy in sight while having an increased capacity to out turn him was the fighter pilot's ace-in-the-hole against the enemy.

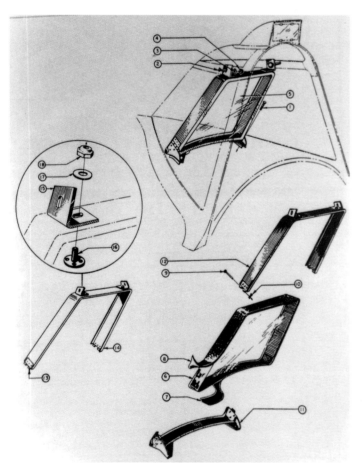

Armored windscreen installation on a P-47. Manufactured by taking sections of highly polished glass and sandwiching them between sheets of transparent plastic and then bonding them under high heat and pressure. (USAF)

Parachutes

The standard U.S. fighter parachute was the Type S-1, or AN6510 seat type with cushion. The ripcord handle was located on the left side. It had snap fasteners for the three-point harness release, one on the chest and one on each leg strap. The Type S-1 had a 24-foot nylon canopy, while the S-2 with a 28-foot nylon canopy was designed for pilots weighing over 180 pounds. The harness was constructed of flexible or nylon webbing. The primary element was the main lift web, which passed from the connector links at the hips in slings around each leg and connecting to the shoulder straps, which were secured by a fastener across the chest and criss-crossed the back. The rip cord assembly was a 31 inch metal cord that attached to a "D" ring. The S-1 was replaced by the AN6510 and the S-2 by the AN6511 in mid-June 1942, and were almost identical to their predecessors except for minor differences in cushions, chest straps, and fasteners. The B-7 was standardized in October 1940 and fea-tured the standard 24-foot canopy, with a three-point harness release and a waistband to hold it close to the body. In June 1942 the B-7 was standardized for Army/Navy use as the AN6512. The AN prefix designated **A**rmy**N**avy. P-47 pilots wore the S-1, or AN6510, with the C-type dinghy backpack, while P-51 pilots wore the B-8 backpack parachute and the dinghy pack as the cushion. Navy and Marine F4U, F6F, and F4F pilots used S-1, or AN6510 seat packs, with attached C-type dinghy. The pilots carried a sheafed ankle knife to cut away the heavy parachute/dinghy pack in case it was necessary, such as in a ditching.

One Man Dinghy

The AN6520-1 one man parachute type pneumatic life raft was widely used by Army and Navy fighter pilots. The raft fit into a parachute pack, which was stowed on the pilot's seat or fastened to his parachute harness by snap rings. Its weight with accessories

Self-sealing Fuel Tanks. The fuel cell was constructed of hard, thick formed rubber in two layers. A gel-like substance was sandwiched between the inner and outer layers of rubber. The gel expanded when it contacted gasoline so when a bullet penetrated the tank, gasoline leaked into the gel which expanded to close the hole. When the fighter returned to base the hole could be easily repaired by placing a piece of rubber in the hole. (Author/USAF)

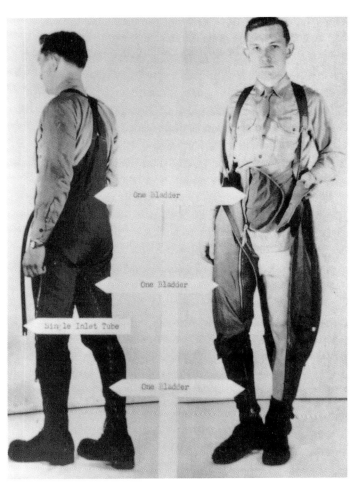

Dog-fighting pilots often found that tight high-speed turns or pull outs would caused sequence of symptoms called "pulling Gs" which included various stages of unconsciousness. Shown is the G-3 suit manufactured by the David Clark Company, The G-suit contained inflating bladders which exerted pressure on the lower extremities and abdomen to prevent blood from pooling there and keep it the head. (USAF)

S-1 AN6510 backpack parachute was used by P-47, F4F, F6F and F4U pilots. The AN designation indicated A=Army and N=Navy. (USAF)

was 16 pounds, and inflated dimensions were 66x40x12 inches. The accessory pack contained a CO_2 cylinder, sail, sea anchor, bailing cup, pair of hand paddles, can of drinking water, first aid kit, repair kit, bullet hole plugs, three cotton cords, and a can of sea marker. The VIII FC widely used the RAF one man K type dinghy in a C type pack until the AN6520-1 was available.

Life Vests

The B-3 and B-4 life vest was dubbed the "Mae West" by the British after the buxom 1930s Hollywood star. It was constructed from rubber and bright yellow canvas and worn over all flight clothing. Two small CO_2 cylinders inflated each of the two inflatable bladders in the chest compartments and were supplemented by mouth tubes to each bladder. The vest weighed about four pounds. In early 1944, the B-4 was designated as AN6519-1.

B-4 (AN6519) life vest was dubbed the "Mae West" by the English after buxom 1930s Hollywood film star. Nine victory ace Capt. Virgil Merony of the 352FG is shown here. (USAF)

CHAPTER 3

Fighter Combat Tactics

Role of the Fighter Aircraft and Pilot in Air Combat

An ace can be defined as a talented pilot being in the right place at the right time to encounter enemy aircraft. Then, possessing the physical and mental characteristics which gave him the ability to fly and shoot better than the enemy and employing skill and superior tactics—often helped by luck—he was able to shoot down five or more enemy aircraft. The higher-scoring ace by nature was an aggressive and determined pilot who was in the right place because he sought out the enemy and went in for the kill, often without regard for personal safety.

Where does the fighter aircraft fit into this definition? All external factors being equal, a pilot in a superior aircraft *should* be able to outfight a pilot in an inferior aircraft. Many American pilots early in the Pacific War had extensive pre-war flying experience, but were shot down in obsolete fighters, such as the F2A Buffalo or the P-39 Airacobra, by the Jap Zero, which early in the war was also flown by experienced pilots. With the introduction of the F6F Hellcat and F4U Corsair, the average American could more than hold his own against the same Zero, flown by increasingly less experienced pilots. Of course, utilizing the superior characteristics of an aircraft while not allowing the enemy to utilize his aircraft's strong points was the key to achieving success. General Claire Chennault's "no dogfighting—dive in, fire, dive away" edict to his Flying Tigers when flying their hard diving P-40s against the maneuverable Zero is the prime example of this philosophy. The AVG totaled a phenomenal 11:1 kill to loss ratio over better Japanese pilots flying a better fighter in greater numbers. Therefore tactical

doctrine entered the equation, and strict adherence to its tenants gave the pilot who understood the limitations and strengths of his aircraft command of a situation. For this reason Marine pilots like Joe Foss (26 victories), John Smith (19), and Marion Carl (15 1/2), flying the F4F Wildcat over Guadalcanal, were able to combine ability and aircraft with tactics to shoot down the superior Zero, piloted by above average Japanese pilots, or evade them to get at the bombers they were escorting.

Most air combats did not result in an aerial victory, and the true measure of victory of any encounter with the enemy was the ability to return to base safely. Thus, the ruggedness and dependability of the fighter came into play. The Japanese fighter aircraft sacrificed pilot protection (armor plate and self-sealing fuel tanks) for quickness and maneuverability. American aircraft, particularly the P-47 and the Grumman-built Navy fighters, were renown for the ruggedness of their airframes and engines, and ability to return to base heavily damaged.

A change in a fighter can transform it from an ordinary to extraordinary aircraft. An outstanding example is the replacement of the Allison engine with the Rolls Royce in the P-51 Mustang, which made it arguably the best fighter in World War II. Other more subtle modifications in a fighter can give it an advantage in combat, albeit often temporary, as it usually was not long before the enemy made similar changes or developed new innovations, which were copied in turn. The introduction of superchargers and water-methanol power boosters, the bubble canopy, better communications, and the gyroscopic K-14 (USAAF) and Mark 18 (USN) gunsights all made for

Classic depiction of the "finger 4" fighter formation which was composed of two elements with each element consisting of a leader and wingman. The "wingman system" allowed the leader to concentrate on his attack while the wingman protected him from attacks from the rear. (USAF)

better aircraft and, in turn, better pilots.

There were two types of fighter pilots: those whose priority was to fight the war, and those who only looked to survive the war. No matter how much faster, more powerful, and hard hitting a fighter became, it depended on a combination of the skill and aggressiveness of its pilot to be effective. This appears to be the bottom line of air combat.

The views presented in this book by the top American aces of their individual fighter aircraft are their reflections and opinions after fifty years and are not to be considered as a flight syllabus. It will be seen that many of the impressions of different aces flying the same fighter are similar, but also there are differences predicated on model, theater of war, and time frame in the war. An ace was one with his aircraft; he strapped it on like a gunfighter and his six gun.

When fighter aces were questioned about the most important factors that made them successful, two, luck and surprise, were mentioned most frequently. Luck, or being in the right place at the right time, was something the pilot had no control over. Undoubtedly, many excellent pilots never became aces or even scored a

victory simply because they never had the luck to encounter an enemy aircraft. Conversely, many average pilots, utilizing surprise in their encounters with enemy aircraft, were successful.

The single-most important controllable factor in successful air combat was surprise. It could be achieved by:
1) Gaining the altitude advantage, as altitude controlled the combat.
2) Attacking directly out of the sun (the most used means of surprise).
3) Attacking from the darker part of the sky, as aircraft in the brighter part become silhouetted and more visible and the attacker less visible.
4) Attacking in the early morning or evening when lighting was problematical.
5) Making use of clouds, both offensively and defensively. When the enemy used the clouds, the vulnerable pilot had to try to establish where the enemy aircraft were likely to emerge.
6) Making use of haze banks in summer, as aircraft approaching on the same level are difficult to see if they attack from the side opposite the sun.

Other factors mentioned were more of a defensive, stay alive nature:
1) Awareness at all times was essential: Jim Flatley, "Eternal vigilance or eternal rest." The importance of developing a "rubber neck" was stressed. Before take off or landing, when an aircraft was most vulnerable, a search of the sky for enemy aircraft was essential. Watch your tail. Keep the sky under constant surveillance. Do not let the enemy slip out of the sun to get at you. See the enemy first, identify him as an enemy, and report him to the rest of the flight.
2) Altitude, altitude, altitude: roll out and dive to escape when caught in a surprise bounce. This tactic was the credo of Gen. Claire Chennault when the P-40s of his AVG were outclassed and outmaneuvered by the nimble Japanese Zero. It was nescessary to always maintain an airspeed of at least 250 mph and enough altitude so that if trouble developed there was enough height to dive and escape. Never be jumped on deck. Altitude advantage was a great asset, as it could be turned into airspeed and surprise at the pilot's choosing.
3) Turn into an attacking enemy aircraft if he were seen in time. Turning into an attack shortened his approach and made him turn more rapidly and be forced to break away. Don Blakeslee stressed to his pilots that if attacked they should immediately turn into the enemy and meet him head on, and then under no circumstance break from this course. When asked by a young pilot "What if the German doesn't break, either?" Blakeslee answered, "Well, then you earned your hazardous duty pay!"
4) When being chased, attempt to tighten a turn to gain the advantage and get into a position behind the enemy.
5) The wingman system, the basic tenant of faith in the American fighter combat doctrine, allowed the element leader to concentrate on the attack with the confidence he was being covered from attack by his wingman.

LtCdr. James Flatley preached "Eternal vigilance or eternal rest" as a tenant for pilot survival. (USN)

Once an enemy aircraft was seen and closed on there was one common axiom for the attacking pilot, "Get in so close that you can't miss." Do not waste ammo at long range. Dive, hit hard, hit fast, and get out. Haul the stick back into your lap and use your excess speed to regain the altitude advantage.

Individual traits, such as excellent eyesight, natural judgment of height and distances, quick reflexes, and the aggressor mentality were essential. Sharp eyesight was the fighter pilot's most important faculty, as the essential factor in all air combat was to see your enemy first and then continue to keep him under observation. It was often demanding and tiring to be continually observant with the sunlight dazzling through the canopy and goggles for hours on end.

Master tactician Hub Zemke felt that to be successful, the fighter pilot must at all times have the inner desire to go into combat. Pilot attitude—being the hunter and not the hunted—not only made the pilot confident, but also increased his survivability. The survival rate of the aggressive pilot was greater than that of the cautious pilot.

But also important was that the pilot have an understanding of the performance and handling capabilities and limitations of his fighter and those of the opposing enemy aircraft.

Fighter Formations

The principal motive for a fighter formation was management and discipline. In the interwar years the United States favored the conventional fighter formation organized into elements of three aircraft in a V formation that was favored by bombers. The V was discarded as soon as America entered the war, and the British leader/wingman two-plane system was adopted. The RAF experience in the Battle of France and Battle of Britain caused the British, in turn, to be influenced by the successful Luftwaffe fighter formation techniques used against them there. The Luftwaffe had developed the "Rotte," or pair technique, during the Spanish Civil War. The Rotte, a leader and wingman, would fly 200 yards apart, the wingman slightly below and to the rear so that the two could cover each other effectively. Two Rotte would form a Schwarm, which

was to become the fundamental fighter formation in WWII. Later in WWII, the Luftwaffe also used the line abreast, or "wall" formation. The Japanese generally flew the *shotai*, a division of three fighters arranged in vics, in echelons, or in a loose, staggered trail formation. The two wingmen would weave in loose formation behind their leader. When engaged the *shotai* could stay together, fall into trail, or break, with each aircraft fighting independently, the latter the most common result. The Japanese suffered from a lack of teamwork, preferring individual dogfights that were successful early in the war when the Zero and their numbers were superior.

The fundamental fighter unit was two fighters, a leader and wingman ("No.2" in RAF parlance), known as an element. The leader's duty was to attack, while the wingman was to protect his leader from interception from the rear throughout the mission. This technique was known as the "Wingman System," and was the key to survival and used with great success by American Air Forces. The two-plane element was the basic unit of all larger combat formations.

A flight was composed of two elements and was led by the leader of one of the elements. It was considered the most effective fighter combat formation for attack and defense. It was adaptable to various combat situations, as each element was easily able to assist the other. This formation was referred to as the "Finger Four," because from above the four fighters were in the position correlating to the finger tips when one looks down at the top of one's right hand. The element Leader, No.1 (middle finger), was about 100 feet in front and to the right of his wingman, No.2 (first finger), while the second element Leader No. 3 (ring finger) was about 150 feet behind and to the right of the element leader No.1, and his wingman No.4 (pinkie finger) was about a 100 feet behind and to the right of him. The No.2 wingman could fly to the left or right of the Leader, 100 feet behind and stepped slightly down for maneuverability. The second element flew 150 feet to the rear of the Flight Leader and crossed underneath with his wingman on all turns. During the war group tacticians, such as Don Blakeslee and Hub Zemke, were encouraged to develop and experiment with new formations, but the Finger Four continued as the fundamental combat tactical formation.

Two flights made up a section and was the usual component for bomber escort and support. Two sections made up the typical squadron of 16 fighters (that initially were organized into three 4-plane flights). Although there were variations in section and squadron tactics, the Finger Four remained the basis of all larger formations.

Fighter Flight Maneuvers

Barrel Roll: A complete rolling circle around a longitudinal axis of the aircraft performed without the use of the rudder. The direction of flight remains the same, but the aircraft rolls around at the same distance from the line of flight, as around the outside of a barrel laying on its side. (Also called an Aileron Roll).

LtCdr. John "Jimmy" Thach was one of the Navy's master tacticians and was the developer of the "Thach Weave." (USN)

Col. Don Blakeslee, leader of the 4FG, stressed turning into the enemy's attack and to meet him head on. (USAF)

Col. Hub Zemke, CO of "Zemke's Wolfpack", the 56FG, believed that pilot attitude, being the hunter, not the hunted, made the aggressive pilot the surviving pilot in a combat. (USAF)

Chandelle: An abrupt, climbing turn to almost a stall, in which the momentum of the aircraft is used to obtain a higher rate of climb than would be possible in unaccelerated flight. The purpose is to gain altitude at the same time that the direction of flight is changed.

Falling Leaf: In a stall the aircraft starts to spin on one side and then is forced to spin in the opposite direction, simulating the motion of a falling leaf.

Glide: Controlled flight without the use of power, necessarily descending at a speed greater than stalling.

Figure Eight: A training maneuver in which the pattern of the number eight was flown. The lazy eight was flown while gliding, while the pylon eight was flown under power around two ground markers.

High Side Attack: Beginning at a higher altitude, the aggressor begins a smooth, nose high turn and then drops his nose to keep the E/A/C in sight, and begins to bank in the opposite direction to reverse the turn, making sure to fire ahead of his target.

Immelmann: A maneuver made by completing the first half of a normal loop; from an inverted position at the top of the loop, half rolling the aircraft to the level position, attaining a 180-degree change in direction simultaneously with a gain in altitude. Named after German WWI ace Max Immelmann.

Loop: A maneuver in which the aircraft follows a closed curve approximately through a vertical circle, then returning to its original flight path.

Lufbery: Aircraft formation in which two or more aircraft follow each other in a vertical spiral or a horizontal circle in order to protect one another, and also to be in a position to face attacking aircraft. Named after WWI ace Raoul Lufbery.

Roll: Maneuver in which a complete revolution about a longitudinal axis is made, with the horizontal direction of flight maintained.

Side slipping: Motion in which the aircraft moves inward of its intended direction of flight as the nose is held too high during a turn. It is the opposite of skidding.

Skidding: Sliding sideways away from the center of the direction of intended direction of flight in a turn. It is caused by not banking enough (aileron use) and is the opposite of side slipping.

Slow Roll: A circling maneuver along the aircraft's line of flight coordinating both the rudder and aileron.

Snap roll: A roll done by a quick movement of the controls, in which a complete revolution is made. This tactic was used when attacked from behind by a fast closing enemy, who would overshoot while the aircraft being attacked was in his revolution.

Spin: A maneuver in which an aircraft descends in a small spiral around a longitudinal axis pitch, nose first. On a normal spin the pilot is on the inside of the rotation, while on an outside spin he is on the outside of the aircraft's plane of rotation.

Split-S: High-speed maneuver in which the aircraft makes a half roll onto its back (upside down) and then dives groundward, leveling off going in the opposite direction at a much lower altitude.

Stall: The aircraft loses lift and drops because its flying speed is too low, or excessive climb and level flight can not be maintained. If lateral equilibrium is not continued the aircraft will go into a spin.

Thach Weave; In a two-plane section, lead and wingman maintain sufficient lateral separation to be able to watch each other's tail and turn in toward each other if attacked, which gave one fighter a head-on shot at the attacker. Named after U.S. Navy ace and tactician, James Thach.

Wingover: From a normal flying attitude the aircraft nose is pulled up until stalling speed is reached, and the aircraft then is allowed to fall off into a 180 degree turn, with flying speed being regained as the nose drops.

CHAPTER 4

Fighter Missions

ETO Fighter Mission

The afternoon sun glinted off the bare metallic finish of the sleek Eighth Air Force Mustang fighter as it taxied off the runway towards its revetment. The P-51's Crew Chief noticed its gun tapes were broken; the pilot had seen combat. But, like all crew chiefs his first question was, "How was the plane?" and then, "How many did you get?" The pilot answered, "What a great plane! Got a Focke Wulf and pieces off a 109." The CC will have to stencil another Swastika under the plane's cockpit.

There were three brotherhoods involved in the mission: the "Brass," who planned the mission and gave the orders; the ground crews, who got the aircraft ready; and the pilots, who carried out the orders.

The planning phase began at Eighth Air Force Headquarters days before, when it was decided that a bombing mission to a specified target in Germany would be escorted by fighters of the VIII Fighter Command. The Eighth Fighter Command was informed of the mission, and a Field Order (FO) was formulated and teletyped to the Combat Operations Staffs of its Fighter Wings and Groups. The FO included the basics on the routes, check points, mission size, and target. On escort missions the fighter groups provided "Little Friend" protection for their bomber "Big Friends" during penetration, over target, and during withdrawal. Which phase of the mission the group would be assigned to depended on its aircraft and experience. The range of the group's fighter type (P-51, P-47, or P-38) and the availability of auxiliary fuel tanks determined its place in the mission. Before the P-51 came on-line, the bombers had to be left unprotected before reaching deep-penetration targets by their short-ranged P-47 and P-38 escorts. The more seasoned squadrons were sent to areas of expected Luftwaffe activity, while green squadrons were sent out on the more benign withdrawal phase, when enemy action was likely to be less. With the group's selection information on hand, the mission was detailed by 8AF HQ and new information was sent on to VIII FC to draft a finalized FO to be forwarded to its Fighter Wing and Group HQs. The mission passed from intangible to tangible, from the unseen administrators to the men who would carry out the orders, enduring hardships and risking their lives.

Outside the mission, these men had needs and feelings. Compared to their contemporaries in other theaters, the England-based fighter pilot lived in relative comfort. A lucky few fighter groups inherited bases built in the 1930s by the RAF. They were equipped with permanent buildings, usually centrally heated, and definitely more comfortable than the accommodations of the newly-built airbases, which were of the Nissen-type or other temporary-type buildings (e.g. Liang, Thorne, Janes). The Nissan hut was a generic term referring to a basic pre-fabricated building design: a long semi-

circle of khaki-green double-corrugated steel sheet attached to a steel frame anchored to a concrete slab, whose ends were constructed of brick or wood. Two windows and a door stood at one or both ends, but larger Nissens had windows along their sides. The original design could be Nissen, Quonsett, Iris, or Romney, and could house four to 40 men. A coke-burning stove stood at its center, but did little against the damp English weather that pervaded everything and everywhere. The stove took forever to heat up and required constant and skillful attention to supply its inadequate output of heat. Forced by the North Sea winds blowing across the fens and moors, the dampness seeped into the quarters, making them cold and dank. Nonetheless, compared to the tent-lodging of the MTO and Pacific the English airbase was preferred. The comforts of these lodgings would be lost for many groups in the Winter of 1944-45, when they transferred to newly captured bases on the Continent and were billeted in cold tents. On base, the center of the pilot's social life was the officer's club, where he could have a warm English beer, play cards, cribbage, or darts, read, or write a letter home. The PX was the source of the pilot's weekly rations: cigarettes; candy bars; chewing gum; and soap and razor blades. Mail was more regular in the ETO, and R&R was closer at hand and more entertaining. Bicycle riding became a major diversion, and local English villages were invaded daily.

The American air groups intruded and changed the way of life of many East Anglican villages. The changes were both physical and psychological. Land was procured and cleared, and quarters were requisitioned and occupied. While some new USAAF bases

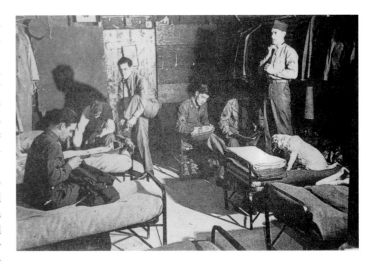

Pilots in the ETO lived in Nissan huts which was a generic term referring to a basic pre-fabricated building design: a long semi-circle of khaki-green double corrugated steel sheet attached to a metal frame which was anchored to a concrete slab, whose ends were constructed of brick or wood. (USAF)

The Glenn Miller band was ever popular. (USAF)

The ubiquitous bicycle was the way to get around in gasoline-rationed England. (USAF)

were former RAF bases, their colorful new occupants displayed novel eccentricities and were often called "over-sexed, overpaid, and over here." Most villagers enjoyed the company of the Yanks. The Pub was the center of English social life, and often the only local diversion available to the Americans, who were found to be unique, friendly, and generous. After a long mission, the pub was a place for the pilot to lift a pint of ale or cider with his friends. Occasionally, a local family would invite an airman to dinner. "A Yank for Christmas" was often the start of a lifelong friendship. Each was a foreigner to the other, and the best in the guest and host was brought to bear, cementing grassroots Allied alliances. All in all, the English overlooked the inconvenience and the occasional unpleasant incident in exchange for the ultimate result.

"48s," a two-day pass, came every two or three weeks. They usually involved a cold, drafty train ride to London, standing for a foot-numbing three hours to a wartime soiree. Still, it was a good place to make female acquaintances, especially if one were lucky enough to get to sit in the snug compartments. Piccadilly was the destination, with its pubs, cafes, theaters, nude shows, and dance

"48s," a two-day pass was issued every two to three weeks. Since most air bases were located in southern England, London was the destination. Here a MP checks a pass. (USAF)

The ground crews consisted of three mechanics, the Crew Chief (CC), and Assistant Crew Chief and an armorer who was shared. Here 56FG ace, Robert Johnson discusses his P-47 with his Crew Chief, S/Sgt. J. C. Penrod. (Author/Johnson)

Usual wake up call for fighter pilots was 5am but the pilots were often awakened by the drone of B-17s leaving early. The 45 minute breakfast consisted of powdered eggs, greasy bacon or fried Spam and toast and, of course, the staple, coffee. (USAF)

Briefing today's target. The S-2 reviews mission times, rendezvous points, the bomber group to be escorted, its route, strength and target; plus group withdrawal and return routes and times. (USAF)

halls. Dance halls, the converted Covent Garden Opera House, and the most famous of all, Hammersmith Palais, featured American-style swing bands, with everyone dancing English-style in a large circle. There was "the Vic," Victoria Hall, which highlighted dancing to the records of Glenn Miller, Artie Shaw, and Jimmy Dorsey. Pub-crawling led to many a splitting headache bequeathed by the English boilermaker: Beefeaters and Guinness. Here the American was introduced to fish and chips, served in a newspaper by a street vendor. Nightclubs, such as the American Eagle Club and The Nuthouse were available, but expensive. Visit the Mecca for the homesick American G.I., the Red Cross' Rainbow Corner, where dunking doughnuts in coffee became a tradition. During the day the American could play tourist, visiting Big Ben, Parliament, and Westminster Abbey. Female companionship and romantic attachments needed to be instantaneous. Women, young and old, virtuous and not, were available for drinks, dinner, dancing, and romance. "Piccadilly Lilies" were obtainable for romance, as well. "How much is two pounds worth in dollars? Two dollars, more? It's only money." Forty-eight hours goes by quickly. Can't spend money over Germany. Back at base the next mission has been selected.

Four hours before takeoff, the CQ (Charge of Quarters) woke the ground crews, the Engineering Section. Each fighter had its own ground crew. The crews usually consisted of three mechanics, the Crew Chief (CC) and Assistant Crew Chief, and an armorer who was shared by two other crews. For every four aircraft there was a maintenance coordinator, the flight chief. Two hangar crews, each working a 12 hour shift, took care of maintenance which could not be accomplished on the line, such as engine changes and repair of battle damage. At many bases, ground crews lived a mile or two from the base and bicycles, jeeps, or truck were their transportation to the hardstand. To provide refuge from the fickle English weather,

most crews set up tents or constructed more elaborate shelters from wooden drop tank crates near their aircraft. The tour of duty of a ground crew was usually for the duration. They were assigned the responsibility for a single fighter during its service life. The importance of the ground crew to the pilot was seen by the frequency their names were stenciled below the pilot's name on the cockpit.

Right: The well-dressed fighter pilot. Here Dave Schilling of the 56FG climbs into his P-47. The A-12 demand-type oxygen mask and S-type seat pack parachute with C-type dinghy back pack can be readily seen. (USAF)

Crew Chiefs were usually "older" men, being in their mid to late twenties, while their assistant CCs were youngsters in their late teens or early twenties. They often filled in on other aircraft that were shorthanded due to illness or leave.

Some Crew Chiefs of the aces were:

S/Sgt. George Baltimore	Jerry Johnson
S/Sgt. Ralph Safford	Gabby Gabreski
S/Sgt. Lew Lunn	George Preddy
S/Sgt. Jack Holleman	Dave Schilling
S/Sgt. J. Barnes	Bud Mahurin
S/Sgt. H. Bush	Walt Beckham
S/Sgt. Ernest Gould	Robert Johnson
S/Sgt. J.C. Penrod	Robert (Sam) Johnson

(note: Robert Johnson, second in the ETO with 27 victories, recognized his CC by naming his P-47 "Penrod and Sam")

After wake up, often one of the two crew would head to the aircraft, while the other went to breakfast. That way someone would be present to remove the covers from the Plexiglas and engine air intakes and begin the pre-flight inspection. An external walk around visual inspection was done, checking the canopy, gun camera, panel fastenings, control surfaces, undercarriage, and tire inflation. Any puddles developing under the fighter overnight were given the taste test. Coolant had a very bitter taste. The propeller was pulled through five or six blades to clear the cylinder of accumulated oil or gasoline. The battery cart was connected, and the CC climbed into the cockpit to prime and start the engine and run it up to high power. The damp English weather played havoc with the spark plugs and electrical system. A thorough pre-takeoff check of oil pressure, fuel, hydraulics, temperature, and mag drop were made. The fuel selector was switched to the right and left tanks to draw fuel into the lines.

Once the CC shut down the engine, the armorer took over. At this time, his was essentially an inspection, as the majority of his duties were done after the previous mission. If the guns had been fired on that mission he removed them from their bays and took

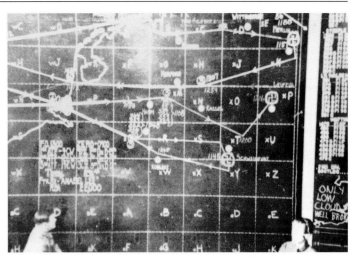

As the mission flew to its target, its progress was followed back at base on the mission plotting board. (USAF)

them to the armament hut for cleaning and inspection for wear and damage. If more than 25 rounds had been fired, all the rounds were changed to avoid mixing two ammunition issue lots. All ammo drawn from the dump, even if it were new, was run through the repositioning machine to insure it would be correctly aligned in the metal clipbelts. The number of rounds for each gun varied on group requirements, but usually were set at the maximum. As a warning to the pilot that he was running low on ammo, five rounds of tracers were belted before the final 25 rounds. The magazine bays were filled with the help of the CC so that the belt (linked rounds) would stay in alignment. To complete the armorer's post-mission work, the gun muzzles were retaped to keep out dirt and moisture on the ground and in the air. On the morning of the next mission, he did a pre-flight inspection of two or three fighters. The inspection included gunsight, gunmount seating, opening of the gun bay doors to check ammo feeds and chutes, solenoid and firing circuit testing, and finally, gun charging. The armorers and radiomen remained on call in case of last minute problems.

The fuel service tanker, or "gas wagon," arrived to fill the external drop tanks and top off the internal fuel tanks, which were diminished somewhat during the CC's pre-flight check. The ground crew checked fuel leaks, especially on the drop tanks. Ground members chewed gum, and if a drop tank had a small leak it could be sealed with a piece of gum. After fueling, the jeep-drawn oxygen cart delivered new oxygen bottles to be installed in the fuselage behind the cockpit. This concluded the ground crew's work, but usually the CC stayed until the pilot arrived, taking care of last minute details, such as polishing the last smudges off the windshield and canopy. Soon the pilots would arrive.

On the morning of the mission, the CQ's wake up call was often unnecessary, as nerves made it difficult to sleep, and the drone of the lumbering B-17s, leaving early, roused the light sleepers. The group leaders had already been up for half an hour, going over the mission details one more time. The few lucky pilots not scheduled to fly turned over in their beds and tried to ignore the commo-

The squadron was airborne in four or five minutes and the entire 48 plane group in 12 to 15 minutes. After a single orbit over the base the lead squadron climbed toward the English coast with two squadrons on either side in stepped down V-formation and continued to climb to an altitude of 18,000 feet. (USAF)

Big Friend, Little Friend. (USAF)

tion. It was 5 AM, and an hour before briefing. Socks were put on to walk to the cold, damp central latrine to brush teeth and take a quick shower and shave, if that had not been done the night before. The pilots dressed in OD pants and shirts, long underwear, silk scarf, leather jacket, and, perhaps, a knife secreted in the top of a boot. Half an hour later, a truck came by for transport to the mess hall. Coffee was always a staple, followed by powdered eggs—though sometimes fresh eggs would be a surprise—greasy bacon or fried Spam, and toast. Forty-five minutes later, after a last cup of coffee, the men would walk to the briefing room and take their designated seats. The flight leader sat in the front row, with his wingman (number 2) directly behind him. The element leader (number 3) sat behind number 2, while "tail-end Charlie" (number 4) sat behind number 3. The 15-20 minute briefing was conducted by the Duty Intelligence Officer (S-2), the Weather Officer, and the mission leader. The briefing hut, made famous in numerous Hollywood movies, contained rows of wooden folding chairs facing a raised wooden platform capped by a podium. There were maps, charts, and recog-

nition posters on the walls. However, the room was both physically and psychologically dominated by a large curtain-covered wall map. After everyone was seated the Duty Officer stepped up to onto the platform and opened the curtain to reveal the day's target. High drama, just like in the movies. A red string marked the route from the base to the rendezvous point, and then to the bomber's target…"Oh, God, Berlin." The string zigzags to avoid flak concentrations on route. Whispers, nervous rustling, and the S-2 began to speak. He reviewed the mission times, rendezvous points, the bomber group to be escorted, its route, strength, and target; plus group withdrawal and return routes and times. German fighter strengths and tactics and anti-aircraft concentrations and how to deal with them were discussed. Call signs and bomber group recognition were reviewed. The Weather Officer, usually the butt of light-hearted ribbing, took over next. Updated weather expectations were read; wind and cloud conditions on route, visibility, icing conditions, and the temperatures and altitudes which caused revealing condensation trails were discussed. The mission leader concluded the briefing by abstracting the Field Order (FO). During all briefings certain phrases were repeated and predominated:

"Expect heavy and determined opposition."

"Maximum effort."

"Heavy flak."

"Stay with your wingman."

"Cut down on the radio chatter."

Questions were fielded. Times were repeated: engine start times; takeoff times; bomber-rendezvous times; and target times. The briefing finished with GI wristwatch synchronization countdown to the exact time, marked by the word "Hack." Sometimes a chaplain blessed the men, or short services or communion were offered directly after the briefing.

Following the briefing the pilots left for the squadron ready room, either by foot or transport, depending on the distance. Either way, there was the automatic stop at the local "six-holer," as pilots learned early on to be regular. In the ready room the pilots gave the S-2 or sergeant their personal possessions, as orders stated that nothing could be taken into combat which might be helpful to the enemy in case of capture. From their flight locker the pilots got out the following equipment:

(1) Flying Helmet was a matter of choice, but the A-11 was the most popular and standard after 1943. The AN-H-15 was also in wide use.

(2) Goggles were also a matter of choice, but the Army all-purpose goggle, often called "gunner's goggles," was the most popular.

(3) Oxygen mask- type A-12 demand type.

(4) Flight Suit A-4 coveralls with an A-2 leather jacket were popular, and in April 1944, the A-11/B-15 intermediate flying suit was standard.

(5) Mae West B-4 life jacket.

(6) Gloves were a matter of choice, but the B-3 summer flying glove was a favorite.

(7) Boots: the A-6 were standard, but the RAF boot was preferred, as they did not have the tendency to come off during bailout.

Just like in the Hollywood war films the ground crews and Brass waited at the control tower for the first sight of the returning fighters. (USAF)

(8) Parachute—the S-type-seat pack was worn with a C-type dinghy back pack and was used in the P-47, while in the P-51 the dinghy was used as the seat cushion and the B-8 back pack parachute was worn.

(9) G-Suits—the Berger G-3 anti-gravity suit prevented blackouts in dives and sharp turns.

The S-2 distributed maps, course check cards, and escape kits (consisting of money—francs or marks—waterproof maps printed on linen, candy bars, and concentrated foods). Every pilot had to wear his dog tag ID. After dressing, the pilots tried to relax, studying their course check cards, or writing important times on the back of their left hand for future reference. About 20 minutes before engine start the pilots drifted toward the doors to be picked up and transported to various dispersal areas and their aircraft.

On arrival to the hardstand, the pilot was supposed to inspect the fighter, but chatted with the CC instead, having the utmost confidence in his ability. Once the pilot had been with the squadron for a while, he was assigned a personal aircraft and crew. A personal aircraft gave the pilot assurance in its maintenance, and like a race car driver, special knowledge of all its idiosyncrasies and characteristics. It was "his" aircraft, and no other pilot would mistreat it. However, by 1945 many senior pilots rotated out or were shot down, captured, or killed, but many more replacement pilots continually arrived. So it was that only aces and senior pilots were equipped with their own aircraft. But even these personal aircraft had to be shared, depending on the number of serviceable aircraft available to the squadron and who was scheduled to fly. Before climbing into his aircraft the pilot relieved himself on the taxiway one last time. Doing so, perhaps he could avoid using the clumsy, inelegant relief tube located in the cockpit. The tube was connected to a plastic funnel and could be used once, because the urine froze in the tube at high altitudes. A second use would fill the ice-clogged funnel, and the pilot would have to fly with his right hand and hold the funnel in his left hand until the urine froze and he could put it down. Or, he could just dump it on the cockpit floor and hope not to get into an inverted combat until it froze!

Before entering the cockpit the pilot got the seat pack parachute from the CC and attached it to the dinghy pack, and either put them both on or placed them on the seat and then adjusted the straps. With the CC standing on the wing, he helped the seated pilot adjust the seat belt and shoulder harness. The pilot put on his helmet, jacked in the mask microphones and earphones, and attached the oxygen tube to the harness, plugged it into the supply, and tested it. He then carried out the required list of interior checks: instruments; controls; gunsight; radio; oxygen; landing gear; and brakes. Gun heaters were switched on to prevent moisture from freezing in the colder high altitudes. Once the check was completed, the CC jumped off the wing, grabbed a fire extinguisher, and stood by the engine to supervise the start. The position of the tail wheel was checked so it would not swing the aircraft around at the start of the taxi. The pilot checked the start time written on the back of his hand. When it was time to start the engine the ground crew removed the wheel chocks and the pilot applied the brakes. The pilot "cleared," and the CC acknowledged with "clear." The canopy was closed. The pilot

flipped on the master switch, held down the spring-loaded primer switch for a few seconds, turned on the ignition switches, and held the starter switch. The inertial starter built up speed to turn the engine over, the prop blades turned over a few revolutions, and the engine gave several preliminary spurts, then a puff of black smoke signaled the steady roar of the smoothly running engine. The engine warmed up for several minutes, and the pilot taxied toward the row of fighters waiting at the hardstand exit to enter the taxiway. The pilot looked at the back of his hand for the ID code letters of the plane he was supposed to follow. When that aircraft passed the taxiway, the pilot pulled out behind him. Usually there were long lines of idling fighters on the taxiway waiting to reach the take-off end of the runway. The pilot rechecked his instruments, had to ratchet in more right rudder trim to accommodate the very high torque at low speed and high power, lower the flaps ten degrees for the heavy take-off weight, and check the fuel selector valve on the left main. The pilot, with his wingman on his right, moved up to the flagger, holding his orange and white checkered flag. The brakes were applied, and the engine revved 25%. The flag man circled his flag over his head to signal to increase engine revs and then dropped it to signal brake release. The two fighters started to move, and the power was slowly advanced and they lifted off the ground. The pilot signaled "landing gear up" to his wingman, and when sufficient airspeed was reached, he signaled "flaps up." The position of the two fighters ahead was noted, so when they entered the usual English morning overcast, a slight course change was made to prevent running into their prop wash while on instruments. The squadron was airborne in four or five minutes, and the entire 48 plane group in 12 to 15 minutes. A single orbit of the base, and the lead squadron climbed toward the English coast, with the other two squadrons on either side in stepped down V-formation, continuing to climb to an altitude of 18,000 feet over the North Sea. A major problem in the ETO was the weather, and probably half of the time flying to the Continent was done in instrument conditions. The weather was considered the other enemy. It was not unusual for

After five or six hours in the air, the squadron approached base, flying over it, following the line of the runway to be used in landing. At the end of the runway engine power was reduced and each pilot fanned off in a tight left climbing turn, lowering flaps and landing gear. (USAF)

missions to be flown without seeing land between take off and landing, and strong winds could cause a drift from the correct heading. It was necessary that all pilots be proficient at instrument and close formation flying until the overcast was breached. In a P-51, using the main fuel tank, the aft fuel tank selector was switched on to burn about half its fuel out to ease the tail-heavy state before switching to the external drop tanks. In the P-38 and P-47, the drop tanks were switched to from the main. Oxygen was automatically started at 10,000 feet through the face mask, which was buttoned to the helmet.

Once above the "soup" the formation spread out to permit the pilots to look for enemy interceptors and navigate without having to concentrate on flying close formation. The fighter formation continued to climb to 20-25,000 feet as it reached the Continent. It was vital that flight schedules be adhered to as closely as possible, as rendezvous with the bombers was to be made at a specific time and location. It was imperative that early combat with the enemy be avoided, so that the drop tanks would not have to be dropped prematurely, reducing the escort's range and duration. Any enemy attack was met solely by a high squadron, while the remaining squadrons stayed with the bombers. It was stressed that the drop tanks be held as long as possible. The only way to protect the bombers was to conserve fuel on the way in, so the fighter would be there when he was needed and not headed home, low on fuel because he had jettisoned his drop tanks early. About 45 minutes to an hour later the rendezvous time and point was about to be reached, and in good visibility, visual contact could be made at 25 miles. Soon the long east-bound bomber stream was approached by the fighter escort. A fighter was chosen to leave formation and close in on the bomber formation to determine the assigned group to escort. Care had to be taken not to be shot at by the nervous B-17 gunners. A P-51 could look like a Me-109, while a P-47 looked much like a FW-190. There was no excuse for them to shoot at the uniquely configured twin-boom P-38. The bombers were ID'd by the numbers and letters on their vertical tail surfaces. The radio was used to locate the bomber group only if really necessary. Once identified, one fighter group,

After landing, off to the debriefing hut. The Intelligence Officer informally debriefed each flight of four pilots at one time while the pilots snacked on coffee, hot chocolate, sandwiches and donuts. (USAF)

made up of three squadrons, was assigned to protect each bomber wing combat box. One squadron would place itself in two sections above the bomber box, one directly above and the other several miles ahead. The second squadron also split into two sections, each a mile out, slightly above on either side. The third squadron was assigned top cover in two sections, one about a mile directly above and the other ten miles ahead. These definite assigned positions in relation to the bombers made it easier to keep the squadron together after a combat when aircraft became separated. Everyone knew his assigned position and returned to it. Because of the speed difference between the bombers and escorts, the fighters had to weave or circle, throttling back and regulating fuel mixtures. The external fuel tanks had to be switched from one to the other to keep them balanced until they were jettisoned. Escort was continued until relieved by another relay group, or until the "limit of endurance" of the group. The relay system granted the bombers a 150 to 200 mile escort from each succeeding fighter group, with a built-in overlap contingency to allow for inevitable delays. If there were inadequate fighter units available for the mission then the area support concept was utilized. Fighter groups would patrol a designated area on the bomber route while the bombers passed through.

The escort mission required continual attention by the pilot and his being in the proper position. Major George Preddy, 26 5/6 victory P-47 ace, said, "It is impossible to see everything, but each pilot must keep his head moving and look to find." Anything suspicious or an enemy attack was reported over the radio using designated call signs. Each group and squadron was identified by a word, while flights were ID'd by a color, and each fighter in that flight by a number (leader, 2, 3, 4). Using this method, any pilot immediately knew the location of the aircraft making the call by its position in relation to the bomber box. Before 1944, fighter escorts were ordered to remain with the bombers, and their response to an enemy attack was to send out a flight of four and keep the second flight as top cover for these counter-attackers. The remainder of the group was to remain with the bombers. The counter-attackers were to drive away the Germans and then return to the bombers; there was to be no pursuit. Fighting close to the bomber box had its hazards. The bomber gunners had trouble identifying the rapidly moving combatants flashing past and fired at everything flying, so SOP was to stay out of their range. When they returned to formation the escorts would pull up abreast, out of firing range, so the gunners could ID their profile as a "Little Friend."

In early 1944 HQ decided to put pressure on the Luftwaffe, and some units were allowed to leave the bomber formation and pursue the enemy away from the formation. They were to leave adequate protection for the bombers and pursue only if not outnumbered. The methods for protecting the bombers were many and varied. Many factors affected the method used, such as the number of bombers to protect (in case an escort squadron or group did not rendezvous), the bomber formation becoming spread out, bombers being late, etc. Thus, it was the responsibility of the group leader to determine how to use his group and deal with each situation. Group or squadron leaders let it be known beforehand that they would "take the bounce" first, supposedly to avoid confusion and indecision: the "follow me" attitude. In actual practice, however, usually the bounce was made by who saw it first and who was closest. Too many E/A got away, waiting for the flight leader to come on the scene. As 1944 wore on and Luftwaffe resources were stretched, the flights were allowed to range farther from the bombers. By ranging ten miles or more, they could prevent the Germans from even reaching the bombers. Attackers were to be pursued until victory was achieved, if necessary (and it usually was) by chasing the German down to the deck. The best offense was to stay together and be aggressive. The best defense was also to stay together and try and disperse and disorganize the enemy before he could reach the bombers.

In January 1944, after a fighter group was relieved from escort duty and had sufficient fuel remaining (e.g. had not engaged the enemy), the group was allowed to hunt enemy aircraft and strafe airfields and transport. Gun camera films extol the exhilarating high-speed, low-level strafing run. Locomotives belching steam through their perforated boilers, their ammunition-laden cars violently exploding, and the fighter pulling up abruptly to escape the billowing fireball. Luftwaffe aircraft, sitting on airfields for lack of fuel, were sitting ducks. To encourage strafing the 8th AF decided to credit ground victories towards total victories. Attacking German airbases was tempting, entertaining, and dangerous. As the Allies closed in on Germany, the Luftwaffe concentrated more AA guns on a shrinking number of bases. Their gunners were on constant alert for the inevitable strafer, who had few air targets and a lot of ammunition. Without the element of surprise, strafing losses mounted. Although this mandate greatly disrupted the Luftwaffe and German transport, more American aircraft were lost in strafing missions than in air-to-air combat. The list of aces lost on strafing mission sounds like an ace's who's who: Gabreski; Beeson; Gerald Johnson; Godfrey; Goodson; and Beckham. George Preddy, 26 5/6 victory ace, was shot down by "friendly" flak while flying low over an American base. Elwyn Righetti, the top-scoring strafing ace with 27 ground victories, was shot down by flak over an airfield near Dresden. He crash-landed and was murdered by angry civilians. During a 1980s post-war symposium, former strafing POW Walter Beckham, tongue-in-cheek, summed it up: "strafing was great fun, but I'm not going to do it anymore, it's too dangerous!"

When the bombers headed in on their bombing run, the fighters backed off, unwilling to share the vicious flak barrages usually found defending the target. They picked them up again, escorted them to the Dutch border, and were then allowed to strafe and pursue targets of opportunity if they had sufficient fuel. After air combat and strafing, groups, squadrons, flights, sections, and individual fighters became widely separated and were forced to return to base individually, or joined to other units or their fragments. The one instrument watched by all pilots was the fuel gauge. Once the mission entered Germany it was half over. At that point the fighter pilot prayed that he would not see or be attacked by enemy fighters. Dogfights, or opening the throttle to escape guzzled huge amounts of fuel. Stories of fighters landing in England on fumes were legion. Compass headings were used until a radio fix could be picked up. Two course headings were always remembered: the course home from Berlin was 270, while from Munich it was 310. The fighters climbed to 15,000 feet to avoid the light ground fire and AA over

Holland. Of all the hazards faced by fighter and bomber pilots, flak caused the most anxiety. The harmless-looking puffs, almost beautiful, were often deadly. The mission planners routed the formations around the thickest concentrations. But once encountered there was nothing to be done to elude it, only get out of its range and try not to think about it. If the unit remained intact, or a number of separated fighters joined together they flew a loose in-trail formation which made for easy flying. For cosmetic effect this formation was tightened up near base. Any straggling bombers were escorted out of harm's way. Once over the North Sea altitude was lost so that the uncomfortable oxygen mask and its throat drying gas could be removed. If a ditched bomber or fighter was spotted the returning fighter was to orbit over it. The fighter was to continue to orbit, not so much for protection, but an orbiting fighter was easier to spot than a life raft on the water. Finally, a cigarette could be lit and an "in-flight lunch" of candy bars eaten.

Many missions ended in poor weather and 100% cloud cover. In bad weather many pilots favored coming in low over the deck over the English Channel. Descending through the cloud cover onto England meant confronting 100s of bombers doing the same thing.

After the mission, the day was over for the pilots but the ground crews began their two-hour post mission duties no matter the weather. (USAF)

The trick to descending through cloud cover was not to suffer vertigo and become disoriented once in the clouds. The pilot had to believe the instrument panel, not the pressure in his ears. Coming in on deck meant the pilot could see the descending aircraft and search for home base, taking care not to hit a barrage balloon or the White Cliffs of Dover. Nonetheless, it was not unusual for fighters to land on the wrong airfield.

Finally, after five to six hours in the air, the squadron approached the base, flying over it and following the line of the runway to be used in landing. The lead flight, in a tight-echelon right formation, approached a mile out from the runway at 250 mph and 40 feet. At the end of the runway, power was reduced and each pilot fanned off in a tight left climbing turn, lowering flaps and landing gear. Each pilot delayed his turn slightly so that all four planes were evenly spaced to land in tandem at 15 second intervals.

The fighter taxied to its hardstand. The first thing the CC looked for was to see if the gun muzzle tapes were broken. If so, then the CC knew that the pilot had seen action, and he took a concerned survey for bullet holes and battle damage on their fighter. After five or more hours of flying, the stiff pilot often had to be helped out of the cockpit. Two vital immediate concerns were, in order, relieving oneself and lighting a cigarette. The CC handed the pilot Form 1, which was to report any mechanical problems during the mission that needed to be corrected before the next mission. Soon transport took the pilots to the locker room to deposit their equipment, and then to mission debriefing. The flight surgeon greeted each pilot with a shot of "mission whiskey." The Intelligence Officer informally debriefed each flight of four pilots at one time. The pilots snacked on coffee, hot chocolate, sandwiches, and doughnuts, while questions were asked on what was seen, when it was seen, and what happened to it. Enemy fighters, their tactics and markings. American aircraft damaged or shot down. Strafing enemy airfields, aircraft on them, damage done. Strafing enemy transport, disposition of transport and troops, damage done. Air-to-air combat claims required encounter reports. The claims were dictated and typed for the signature of the pilot and witnesses. The claims were checked against the gun camera film, which the armorers had removed and sent to Wing HQ, which in turn forwarded it to Kodak for processing. Five copies of these claims were sent to various headquarters for review and the pilot received one. After debriefing, the Intelligence Officer telephoned a detailed report to Group Intelligence, which in turn prepared a report for Wing HQ.

At 1500, after debriefing pilots walked over to the squadron operations building to check the mission board to see who was flying again the next day. Most pilots returned to their barracks to clean up and grab a nap before supper at 1730. There were always a hyper few who went to the officer's club to unwind and refly the mission.

The day was over for the pilot, but the ground crew began its usual two hour post-mission duties, which could take longer if the 50 or 100 hour inspection was due, or if the tires or spark plugs needed to be changed. Spark plugs were a chronic headache, as they required replacement every 15 to 20 hours of flying time. The exhaust plugs were easy to replace, but the intake plugs were difficult, because it took a long time for the engine, which had been running for five or six hours, to cool down. If the previous drop tanks were jettisoned in combat then new tanks were installed. Three men were needed for this job, so the armorer helped out. As described earlier, after the previous mission the armorer inspected the gun bays and removed the gun camera film magazine for processing and replaced it. The eight machine guns were removed and transported to the armory for cleaning and inspection. The belts and ammo were also removed and replaced. The cleaned and inspected guns were remounted in the aircraft and the ammo replenished. The gasoline service crew filled the main tanks so moisture would not accumulate inside them and the fighter would be ready if needed. The oxygen system was checked and radio specialists tested the radio. The Plexiglas and air intakes were covered. The fighter, their personal weapon against the Germans, was ready for immediate availability. The ground crew returned to their quarters to wash up before dinner.

At 8AF headquarters a new FO was being drafted.

Thanks to Jerry Johnson, 16 1/2 victory P-47 ace, for his input and corrections.

Carrier Mission PTO

Early in the war the imagination of the American public was stirred by English newsreels of the Battle of Britain. R.A.F. Hurricane and Spitfire pilots in full flight gear were seen lounging, reading, and smoking near their fighters in the August 1940 summer sun. The word "scramble" put the pilots in motion to engage incoming Heinkels and Messerschmitts. When America entered the war a new facet of the air war, the aircraft carrier, was seen in such motion pictures as Twentieth Century-Fox's "A Wing and a Prayer" and "The Fighting Lady." In these films the camera panned in on com-

LtGen. Gerald Johnson at an American Fighter Aces Association convention. (Author)

bat-dressed Navy pilots waiting in the carrier's ready room when the battle call, "Pilots, man your planes," blared from speakers. The excitement of the seeming confusion of a carrier launch again captured the public's imagination.

The majestic *Essex*-class aircraft carriers were the envy of the rest of the Navy, which considered them veritable cruise ships. Perhaps they were when compared to other ships of the line. And just as the crews of the Navy's lesser ships were envious of the carrier's crews, members of the carrier's crew coveted the life of the carrier aviator. Fliers received extra pay, had lighter duties, and spent most of their time lounging in the reclining chairs of the air-conditioned ready room. Off-duty, the ready room was much like a college fraternity house; a place to study, to read, to write letters home, to play cards, and a place to "B.S." But on-duty, it was a waiting area in which pilots, dressed in full flying gear, spent long, nervous hours waiting to man their fighters. Combat carriers were invariably overcrowded, and Naval airmen received no dispensations in their lodging. Hot rooms designed for two quartered four. Junior flying officers often slept in bunkrooms with their equipment hanging from cable-supported bunks. Clean beds and daily showers were some compensation, but the ready room was ever-inviting. LCdr. John Thach emphasized the importance of the carrier fighter pilot after the Battle of Midway: "Only fighters can keep our aircraft carriers afloat."

Two or three sittings in a hot wardroom mess were frequent, but this inconvenience was more than offset by coffee available at any hour and the fact that the Navy was traditionally known for its quality meals. A typical combat zone carrier breakfast consisted of tomato or fruit juices, eggs any way, and bacon, all often supplemented by pancakes and toast and, of course, coffee. Because the carrier war was frequently fought in the tropics and because daily duties and combat occurred in the daylight, lunch would consist of bread, rolls, cold cuts, cheese, potato salad, and iced tea. Dinner was the highlight of the day. It offered beef, pork, or ham; a potato, rice, or beans, and a vegetable—all in copious quantities. Desserts were cakes, pies, or ice cream. Hot or iced coffee, tea, milk (powdered), or water were the drink choices. In the wardroom, soft drinks and snacks were generally available, along with the inevitable coffee.

Inactivity and boredom were the pilot's second enemy, attacking his free time, which was plentiful while at anchor or on extended cruises to and from battle zones. Playing card games, such as poker, rummy, acey-deuce, cribbage, or solitaire was popular, and for some, a profitable pass time. The carrier or squadron library was well-stocked and widely used, especially early in the war when many pilots had attended or graduated from college. Movies, though old and often seen previously, were a weekly event for many. Radio broadcasts from Hawaii or the West Coast were aired into

A F6F is on the elevator as it is being moved from the hangar deck to the flight deck. Once on the flight deck it will be moved aft by plane pushers for spotting for the next mission. (USN)

Left: Two or three sittings in the hot wardroom mess were frequent, but this inconvenience was more than offset by the fact that the Navy was traditionally known for its quality meals. (USN)

The ready room was located close to the flight deck. Squadron COs and their men, dressed for battle, reviewed today's mission and noted pertinent data on their plotting boards. Here pilots of VF-9 are seen on the *Lexington* before their February 1945 raid on Tokyo. (USN)

The Plane Captain helps his pilot clip into his parachute harness, radio and oxygen apparatus. (USN)

the wardrooms, as was the amusing Japanese propaganda and good music of "Tokyo Rose." Letter writing, though complicated by censorship controls and long periods away from mailing points, was conscientiously indulged, often serving as a daily diary. The infre-

"Pilots, man your aircraft." (USN)

quent mail calls were awaited with high anticipation, but could be a great disappointment if none arrived, or if it brought bad or worrisome news. Bull sessions, sports discussions, and friendly arguments on every topic filled bunk rooms, wardrooms, and mess halls at all hours of the day.

Fliers' duties were routine and relatively mundane. Lectures were attended, and each pilot took his turn as the squadron's duty officer. As the carrier entered the combat zone, CAP and anti-submarine patrols were flown more frequently. Long hours in full flight gear were spent in the ready room or on CAP. Anxieties built up, as uneventful days in the combat zone were followed by more uneventful days, but everyone knew that the Task force was approaching its objective.

On the day of the scheduled operation, pilots arose early and took breakfast. The CO would confer with his AGC (Air Group Commander) and squadron leaders to discuss organizing the attack, utilizing the most recent information gathered by Intelligence. The launch times, routes of various elements to the target, the target, the attack time and, most importantly, the element's function in the mission were coordinated.

The squadron commanders joined their men in the squadron's ready room, which was situated close to the flight deck. From the blackboard, notes on tactics were reviewed. Information from surrounding dials, which recorded wind direction and force and the ship's course and speed, were noted on the pilot's plotting boards. A divided bulletin board was checked. On one side, Japanese composition and disposition was entered, while on the other, Task Force data was entered. Pilots again noted pertinent data on their plotting boards. The mission was discussed, coffee drunk, and cigarettes smoked.

If the squadron was assigned CAP, its duties were reviewed and emphasized: preventing enemy aircraft from reaching the re-

Classic photo of Adm. Marc Mitscher on the Lexington bridge during the Marianas Turkey Shoot on 19 June 1944. Seen on deck are the F6F Hellcats of VF-16. (USN)

A gun camera frame of a F6F Hellcat attacking a Zero. (USN)

lease point and keeping the carrier within sight. If the squadron were to escort torpedo and dive bombers, its duty was to make sure the bombers got safely to the target without interference from enemy interceptors. Strafing duties on enemy shipping entailed destroying and disrupting enemy anti-aircraft gunners so that the vulnerable dive and torpedo bombers could make unopposed runs on their targets.

Each step of the pre-launch procedure had to be carried out as promptly as safety and accuracy permitted. In preparation to launch, the carrier turned into the wind on a steady course, which left it vulnerable to torpedo attack. The loud speaker announcement "Pi-

"Prepare to launch planes." F6F Hellcats were first in line for takeoff because they were smaller and took up less deck space and required less room for their takeoff run. Here the LO (Launch Officer) is ready to lower his checkered flag as the pilot waited to takeoff with brakes on, his fighter at max RPMs, flaps lowered for maximum lift and prop at flat pitch. Pictured is the new *Yorktown*. (USN)

lots, man your aircraft" put the pilots into action, collecting their data-filled plotting boards, automatic pistols, jungle kits, yellow dye markers, Mae West life vests, parachute harnesses, goggles, and helmets with attached oxygen masks. Leaving the ready rooms, the pilots double-timed starboard along dim, narrow catwalks, passing through the hangar deck and moving towards hatches opening near the ship's island. The island superstructure, rising on the right of the flight deck, was the control tower for flight operations.

The wooden teak decks became even more confused as the pilots converged on their assigned aircraft. The pilot greeted his plane captain, getting assurances that the plane was ready to go. The pilot climbed into his plane, with the PC helping him settle in the cockpit. The pilot's comfort came first, and he adjusted the seat height, rudder pedal length, shoulder harness, and rear view mirror. The parachute was already there, and all buckles were put in place, but were not connected until the plane was airborne. To spread the folded wings of the Hellcat with the engine shut down, the hydraulic system had to be hand pumped and wings moved manually into place and locked by pins. The pilot determined, checked and adjusted settings, switches, and controls for prompt action on the order "Start your engines." The crew turned the prop through 12 or 15 blades to be sure there was no residual fuel or oil in the engine's lower cylinders. Pre-start settings, fire up, warm up, rev up the engine one last time to clear it, and check out and adjust all takeoff settings. Give thumbs up if the plane is OK for take off. The take off was controlled from the island bridge wing, where the ship's Captain ordered the Air Officer to "prepare to launch planes." The Watch Deck Controlman hand-signaled the pilot that the tie-downs were released. Yellow-clad plane directors pushed the aircraft, while the pilot followed the WDC's directions to the takeoff spot. Here the pilot was turned over to the Launch Officer, "Fly One," who was given a thumbs up. The Air Officer had two flags with which he signaled the LO. He relayed the "prepare to launch" order with a red flag, while a white flag soon thereafter signaled the "commence launching" order from the Captain.

F6F Hellcats were first in line for takeoff because they were smaller, took up less deck space, and required less room for their takeoff run. Next came the TBM Avengers and the SB2C Helldivers with their folded wings. A CV with 800 feet of deck accommodated these three types of aircraft, while the smaller 600 foot decks of the CVLs took only Hellcats and Avengers. Ordnance men dressed in red removed the safety wires from the torpedos and bomb fuses from the bombers. Catapult crews dressed in green were on hand in case the wind was not strong enough for unassisted deck launch. Firefighters in white asbestos suits were on alert. The non-working carrier crew, or "audience," was increasingly deafened by the crescendo of noise. The inertial starter's high-pitched whine and the shotgun blasts of cartridge starters initiated the roar of 60 or more aircraft engines. Wheel chocks were removed and brakes applied.

The Captain issued the "Commence launch" order, which his Air Officer relayed with his white flag to "Fly One" (Launch Officer), who was armed with a small white wand or black and white checkered flag. The color-coded deck crews were gone, except for the catapult crews and fire fighters. Standing at the fighter's starboard wing, "Fly One" rapidly circled his flag overhead, signaling the waiting pilot to taxi onto the takeoff spot. Taxiing was usually simple, except in a cross wind, when the tail wheel needed to be locked. The pilot held the brakes on, and when he saw the LO circling his flag, he revved the engine to maximum RPMs, lowered flaps for maximum lift, put the prop in flat pitch, and again waited for the LO. "Fly One" checked that all was clear and waited for the carrier's bow to begin its rise in an ocean swell. When the signal flag came down and forward, the pilot released the brakes and the fighter began to roll. The pilot had to remember to keep the nose-heavy Hellcat's tail down and wheels on the deck until there was no more deck under the fighter. The last several feet of the deck slanted downward, and the aircraft became airborne at this point. Takeoff speed was about 85 mph, and the wheels were retracted as soon as possible to build up air speed more rapidly. Level flight was maintained for around a quarter mile in order to gain enough airspeed to prevent a stall in the first turn. This turn, slightly to the left, enabled the pilot to get out of the carrier's path. The pilot regained his heading, climbing into the wind. The entire launch sequence took about 30 seconds, versus one minute for a catapult launch.

At "Fly Two"—the section of flight deck which was forward of the aft elevator—"Fly Two," the deck officer, was stationed. Assisted by plane-handling crews, he waited for the prop wash of the launched aircraft to subside and then directed the waiting pilot from his parked position to takeoff position. In the rear, torpedo aircraft with folded wings rolled forward as more aircraft were launched. As more space became available, their wings were dropped and locked. After a short time 10 or 12 bombers could move into the takeoff area at once. The deckmen, clothing whipped by the prop wash, were constantly alert to avoid the whirling props and swinging wings.

After takeoff it took a quarter hour for the Hellcats to pair up into sections and then become four aircraft divisions. The torpedo bombers flew in three and four plane divisions. The mission was led by Air Group Commanders, who rotated with three other AGCs of the Task Force, which was usually comprised of two *Essex* and two *Independence*-class carriers.

In the two years after the Battle of the Coral Sea, U.S. naval tactics and formations had greatly improved. Fighters flew in sections of four instead of three, and to increase upward visibility flew in "stepped up" rather than "stepped down" formation. The four plane sections flew in the "Thatch Weave," in which the two plane element, when under attack, flew toward the other friendly element, putting the attacker in jeopardy.

Missions usually lasted four or five hours and were flown over 200-250 miles of open water, which made navigation difficult. If the enemy was engaged, air combat would consume huge quantities of fuel, and the return leg to the carrier required the pilot to

Landings required close cooperation between the Landing Signals Officer (LSO) or "batman" and the pilot. A set of 13 basic signals were relayed by a set of ping-pong shaped paddles called "bats". Here renown, *Yorktown* LSO, Dick Tripp, gives the "cut" signal to a pilot whose landing approach was satisfactory. (USN)

conserve fuel. Trim and throttle were set for fuel economy, and manifold pressures increased, RPMs lowered, and fuel mixtures leaned. The pilot referred to the pilot's manual to determine the best settings to achieve maximum range under various loading conditions. Fly at the lowest possible altitude and speed to attain the maximum range endurance. The pilot turned his ZB radio receiver to the carrier's YE radio transmitter, listening for the Morse code "homing" letter in each 15 degree compass segment. In about an hour the Task Force's wake was spotted, and the carrier rendezvous was reached. Squadrons circled in the day's recognition turns, awaiting their turn to land.

Landings required close cooperation between the Landing Signal Officer (LSO) and the pilot. The LSOs, known as "Batmen," wore various brightly colored outfits for high visibility and were located on a small platform extending from the after port side of the flight deck. A canvas screen behind the platform made the LSO easier to be seen by the incoming pilot. A set of 13 basic signals were relayed by two large ping-pong shaped paddles, called "bats," which were also strung with bunting to increase visibility. Ten signals warned of pilot error, such as improper speed, height, approach, aircraft attitude, etc., or wheels or tailhook not down, etc. Three signals were final commands: (1) "roger" (everything OK); (2) "cut" (cut engine and land); (3) "wave off" (no good, go around again).

After landing, a pilot would return to the ready room or an adjoining area for debriefing by the ACIO (Air Combat Information Officer). (USN)

The carrier would be headed into the wind as the fighter squadron separated into divisions, circling in 40 second intervals for landing. The pilot opened the canopy and locked it in case he had to get out of the cockpit quickly. He adjusted the seat belt and shoulder harness, set the fuel to auto rich, switched to the most filled internal fuel tank, and set the prop in low pitch. The tailhook was lowered electrically, the undercarriage lowered hydraulically, and the tail wheel was locked. With the flaps lowered, the final approach was made at about 90 mph, usually in a curving approach to get a better view of the deck and LSO. If the LSO held his paddles straight out from each shoulder, the approach was satisfactory. As the fighter was just above the deck, the LSO would quickly drop his left paddle to his side and draw the right paddle below his chin. This signaled the pilot to chop his throttle as late as possible (to prevent nose drop), to pull the stick back, and stall in; trying to touch the main wheels first. The tail hook would engage the arresting wires, and with screeching tires the fighter would snap to a quick halt.

If the landing approach was unsatisfactory, the LSO would wave off the fighter by crossing the paddles above his head. Even if the approach were perfect, the aircraft could still be waved off due to a barrier crash, enemy attack, etc., which would be unknown to the pilot. The pilot, under all circumstances—even in a damaged plane or low on fuel—was obligated to go around. Crash photographers were on hand to film likely problem landings, and often caught some of the most spectacular combat footage of the war.

Steel cables, supported by five foot uprights, were installed immediately after the last arresting wire to prevent a plane that failed to hook from crashing into plane-servicing personnel and aircraft parked in "Fly Two." At the end of the landing run the wing flaps were immediately raised, and cowl flaps opened to their widest position to prevent overheating. Once a fighter came to a stop, plane-handling crews immediately pounced on it from behind protective netting. Each crew wore its own numbered and colored T-shirt. The tailhook man released the hook from the landing wire and returned it to its retracted position in the tail. The wingmen positioned themselves at each wingtip, while the tailman took his position; all three ready to guide the aircraft. The crew's leader motioned the pilot to rev up the engine and taxi forward to park and shut down the engine. With the wing flaps already in the raised position, the wing-locking pins were disengaged, and the wing was folded back and locked. With the wing folded, it could be difficult for the pilot to get out of the cockpit, as the wing laid very close to it. The deck crew would then retreat behind the protective netting, waiting its turn to retrieve another landed aircraft.

The deck was divided into zones, which were controlled by a traffic signalman who would take over the direction of each aircraft moving into his territory. They also wore colored T-shirts or caps which indicated their function. The aircraft was directed port or starboard, according to its flight deck stowage arrangements. The heavy torpedo bombers were stowed astern, the dive bombers next, and the fighters forward. This arrangement allowed the fighters to be stationed close to the bow for takeoff in defense of the carrier in case of enemy attack, or to fly CAP duties. Also, the heavier bombers needed the longer takeoff runs which became available once the fighters left. Aircraft requiring repair or overhaul were

Cdr. Alex Vraciu with the author at an American Fighter Aces Association convention. (Author)

Pilots on Henderson Field gather for the day's briefing. (USMC)

taken down the elevators to the hangar deck for servicing. Heavily damaged aircraft were frequently dumped overboard to make room for replacement aircraft, which were hung from the ceiling of the hangar deck. Carrier aircraft serviceability needed to be high because of the limited number of aircraft available. Each squadron had its own maintenance crew of about 30 men under the direction of the Squadron Engineering Officer, who was a senior pilot. The Materiel Officer directed the various chief petty officers, who were specialists in airframes, electronics, ordnance, and aircraft engines. The Hellcat airframe was easily maintained, but the Pratt & Whitney R-2800 Double Wasp radial was a highly-engineered engine. While regular maintenance on it could be carried out onboard, some engines were chronically troublesome. As the war progressed these engines, along with their attached fighters, were dumped overboard. This was possible because of a large number of replacement aircraft readily available to be flown in from nearby island depots.

After leaving his fighter, a pilot would return to the ready room or adjoining area for debriefing by the ACIO (Air Combat Information Officer). After the mission a pilot would return to his quarters to wash up, have a smoke and coffee, and nap and rest. He would get ready for the next meal, which usually was dinner, as carrier missions departed in the morning, continued through lunch, and ended in the afternoon. However, frequently a second and even third mission could be flown during a day. But at the day's end, a good dinner, good friends, and a second helping of dessert made the war go away, at least until the next "Pilots, man your plane" order came across the speakers.

Thanks to Alex Vraciu, 19 victory ace, for his input, corrections, and deletions.

Fighter Mission Pacific

It could not be a nightmare, because the Marine pilots never really slept. Who could sleep in a hot, humid tent in the middle of the jungle? The cots were hard and uncomfortable. The mosquitoes relentless. Clothes were not changed, and for good reason. "Louie the Louse" was making his midnight visitation. He came nearly every night. Only a small two-place Japanese floatplane. Its annoy-

ingly unsynchronized engine was a signal for the pilot to leave the tent and run to the nearby foxholes and slit trenches. What would these sanctuaries harbor tonight? A snake, rat, or spider? Would yesterday's rain still be standing in a puddle on the bottom? No time to think about that. Get up, and run before the bombs start falling. For an hour or two "Louie" would fly back and forth, occasionally dropping a bomb. Finally he was gone, but sometimes he came back. "Gotta get some sleep."

Of all American pilots in WWII, those in the Pacific suffered the worst conditions in any combat theater. The grand strategy of the Pacific war was "Island Hopping," the invasion, capture, and securing of a succession of Japanese-held islands, each closer to the Japanese homeland. The objective was to procure bases—particularly air bases—to be used to attack the next island. These islands laid south of the equator. They were as large as New Guinea, or only a few square miles of coral atoll, such as Tarawa. Their elevations could range from the 9,000 foot peaks of New Guinea's Owen Stanley Mountains to the low hills of the Palaus Group, whose Jap-infested, honeycombed ridges took the lives of many Marines.

On Guadalcanal, an abandoned Japanese building, nicknamed the Pagoda was the Air Operations Center for the "Cactus Air Force." (USMC)

The islands of the Central Pacific were small, low, tropical coral atolls covered with coconut palms and sandy coral ridges washed by cooling sea breezes. The ground battles for possession of these island were short but bloody, and the first airmen were often greeted by sniper fire. The islands of the Southwest Pacific were covered with dense jungle and kunai grass, and marked by oppressively hot, rainy days with periods of sweltering sun and temperatures and humidity in the 90s. The ground battles for these islands generally took months, and the sounds of the battle could often be heard by the flyers on the newly captured air strips.

The early war jungle island airbases of the Southwest Pacific were embodied by Henderson Field on Guadalcanal, Dobodura on New Guinea, and Torokina on Bougainville. Once an island was declared "secure," the SeeBees (Naval construction crews) moved in to repair and enlarge the newly captured Japanese air fields. These fields were fairly primitive, being hacked out of coconut planta-

Food on Guadalcanal was of poor quality and in short supply and was supplemented from captured Japanese food. However, by April 1945, during the Okinawa campaign the supply system improved markedly. Sol Meyer, master mess chef for VMF-323, became a legend for his culinary expertise on the island. He was a consummate Japanese souvenir collector and traded Japanese flags and swords to the Navy ships offshore for food stores. (Author/Brandon)

tions. These plantations had provided the Japanese easier clearing than the jungle, along with fresh water and some roads and buildings. They usually afforded access to the sea for coral to use as a foundation for the runway and to receive supplies. When the Americans took over they found that all their air and naval bombardment did little real damage. The bomb craters were quickly filled with dredged live coral, rolled flat, wetted, and re-rolled until it formed a hard, rough-textured flat surface. In addition to its strength and durability, coral provided excellent traction when either wet or dry. Being white, it had a high light reflectivity that aided night takeoffs and landings. In soft or sandy areas where coral was not readily available, Marston matting, an interlocking, pierced steel planking, was laid down. While better than landing on a soft runway, the matting made a deafening racket that pilots likened to a succession of car crashes. Landing at high speeds could be interesting on the Marston, because braking was minimal, especially when it was wet.

As soon as the construction crews finished a runway the Marine pilots would arrive. Usually the fighters were the first arrivals, in order to defend against Japanese attacks from nearby airbases. The pilots crammed all their worldly possessions into their fighters and flew ahead to wait on their ground crews and auxiliary personnel, who would arrive by transport ship.

Because most of the Japanese airbase facilities were destroyed in the battle, the airmen were billeted in tents. The new base would be a Japanese target, so the Marines needed to disperse and conceal, or camouflage their aircraft, living quarters, mess, and alert shack. Slit trenches and foxholes were dug nearby to dive into in case of attack. When putting up the tent, the new supporting ropes were never tightened, as the rains would soon take care of that. The tents had only the ground for a floor, and were chronically damp from the seepage of the daily rains. Cots and sleeping mats sunk into the mud, and within days everything in the tent was damp and covered with mildew. Sometimes local "Fuzzy Wuzzies" would build thatched huts, which kept out the rain and sun but not the bugs. Which mosquito bite would cause malaria? Ammunition, bombs, and gasoline were concealed and stored away from personnel. The operations tent, located near the airstrip, was the social center of the base. The chairs and tables were occupied by fatigued card players. Bridge, acey-deucey, and poker were played with little enthusiasm. There were also the Monopoly players, whose endless game was often interrupted by the Japanese. Off by themselves were the letter writers, readers, solitaire players, and involuntary nodders. The Air Operations center on Guadalcanal was an abandoned Japanese building, nicknamed the "Pagoda." The operations desk, with its field phones, notebooks, and blackboard was located here. The mess tent was also floorless, with long tables and uncomfortable benches. But here the pilots could always count on a cup of coffee, maybe not always freshly brewed and sometimes tasting like kerosene, but coffee nevertheless. The dreadful food was plopped on stainless steel plates, which did not make it any more palatable. Most everything was either canned or dehydrated. Canned Spam, hash, sausages, and butter. Dehydrated potatoes, vegetables, and fruits. Much of the daily diet was not compatible with the rampant dysentery circulating among the men. Who needed reconstituted prunes or cereal roughage? Since there was no PX, none of the

Conditions on the newly won Pacific islands were primitive, at best. The few permanent buildings were destroyed in the pre-invasion softening up process or ensuing battles. Tents, like these on Henderson Field, were the standard billets and heavy tropical rains made jungle living very uncomfortable. Damp clothing and bedding were prevalent and led to a high occurrence of fungal diseases and skin infections. (USMC)

little pleasures of life were available. No cigarettes, no candy, no gum, no beer. Only the necessities were available—bombs, ammo, and fuel—and even they could be in short supply. Sometimes someone discovered some cigarettes and alcohol that the Japs left behind. Mail came infrequently. Sometimes radio broadcasts from Hawaii or the West Coast were picked up and informed the pilots how well everything was going out there in the South Pacific. Supply transports arrived under the duress of Japanese attack, and war material had the priority, so even necessities were lacking. No soap, no fresh clothing, and no insect repellent. However, there was no shortage of insects, rain, mud, and Japs.

Appalling living conditions and aerial combat induced a pervasive debilitating physical and mental fatigue which could not be shaken and chronically deepened. Nature and combat conspiring against man. At first there was the Japanese shelling and snipers, and then "Louie the Louse." And sometimes the "Tokyo Express" would come down the "Slot" at night and shell. Sometimes the flashes and rumblings of great sea battles could be seen and heard in the distance. There was a reason it was called "Iron Bottom Sound." Regularly scheduled daily air raids by the elite of the Japanese Air Force meant scrambling into air combat. Pilots were not trained to live like front-line infantry men and to fly combat; that's not what the recruiter promised. Air combat was scanning the sky for an oncoming Zero at 20,000 feet and sucking oxygen that dried the nose and throat. Nervous excitement quickly and relentlessly drained already depleted energy reserves. Just survive this mission. Survive the next day, the next week, then a month. Maybe malaria or dysentery would mean R&R back in Australia. Thirty day survivors—shaking, sleepless human wreckage—were relieved by naive, fresh-faced replacements. These surrogates would find improved conditions. Ground and air superiority. Combat supplies had given way to human supplies. The replacements would wonder why these guys looked so bad and never really would know.

Air combat took two forms. Japanese bombers and escorts would attack the American base, and Marine fighters would scramble to intercept them. Or Marine fighters would escort bombers to attack Jap bases, and their fighters would scramble to intercept. In either case the Japanese planes, especially the Zeros and even the Betty bombers, were superior to the Grumman F4F-4 Wildcat, but the later introduction of the F4U Corsair more than equalized matters. But more important than this initial qualitative advantage was the Japanese quantitative superiority in reserves of pilots, aircraft, and material. The Marines could not afford to lose any planes or pilots.

The Japanese Air Force was based on Rabaul, which was almost four flying hours away, so they could be expected to hit Henderson on a pre-determined schedule. In order for the Japs to takeoff and land in the daylight, they were expected to arrive between 1130 and 1430. There were coast watchers on Bougainville who reported their formations shortly after takeoff and then, three quarters of an hour out of Henderson, coast watchers on New Georgia reported in. Primitive radar was in place at Henderson, pulsing with peculiar blips that usually turned out to be thunderstorms.

When Air Ops in the Pagoda confirmed that the Japanese were on their way, a captured Rising Sun flag was run up the flag pole in front of the building to warn the pilots that "Tojo time" had arrived. The aircraft were widely dispersed to lessen losses to Jap bombs, so there was a mad dash in every direction. Some pilots were on foot, while others were clinging to the fender of a jeep, dropping off as they passed their aircraft. All zipping their raggedy flying suits over their undershirts and homemade khaki cutoff shorts. Some wore a rusting .45 in a shoulder holster, just in case, but then what? Reaching their stubby Wildcat fighters, they would be met on its wing by their Crew Chief, who threw the life vest over the pilot's head and pulled the strap under his crotch and snapped it into place. The helmet and goggles were hung over the stick. Settle into the cockpit. Wiggle into the shoulder straps. Helmet on, goggles up, connect the radio and oxygen. Swipe the switches on. The CC knew to clear ASAP, warned by the audio/visual signal of the shotgun starter firing out a belch of black smoke. After a few convulsive

PR photo of a scramble. "Pappy" Boyington (left) leads a VMF-124 "Black Sheep" flight to their Corsairs on Espiritu Santo in September 1943. (USMC)

coughs the engine would turn over and then even out into a continuous roar. The fighter would be rolling toward the end of the field, often enshrouded by a white mist caused by the propeller cutting through the high humidity of the jungle air. With Wildcats converging from every revetment, who had time to check mag or pitch settings? The Wildcats would pair off at the end of the runway. Spaced by twenty second intervals; two, four, six, eight stubby blue fighters crawled full throttle into the air. Once airborne and wheels up, pilots finished snapping snaps, buckling buckles, and tried to wiggle and squirm into a comfortable position. Instruments and controls were more carefully checked and set. Oxygen masks were pulled on and checked. Climbing to altitude took 15 minutes of straining from the Pratt & Whitney engine. An inattentive pilot could be jolted into the present when he wandered into someone's prop wash, quickly dropping a wing and finding the pit of his stomach in his throat. Looking below, dominating the scene was a long channel separating the islands of the Solomons. The Slot was the aerial and naval battleground of the Guadalcanal campaign. It was the coffin for Japanese and American ships and planes, and their seamen and airmen.

Marine air combat tactics were based on two-plane sections and four plane divisions which had been developed by the Luftwaffe. With the early warning the Marines were able to climb to a 5,000 foot height advantage before the Japanese formations arrived. Once

at altitude, the Marines would try to position themselves ahead and off to the side of the ponderous V formations flown by the Japanese. When they were far enough ahead, they would turn 180 and head directly toward the Japanese Betty bombers. The CO, with his throat mike twin disks pressing against his Adam's Apple, announced, "Bogies, at six o'clock ahead." Diving vertically and coming across the Japanese formation from right to left, the F4Fs got into premier firing position at 300 yards, while staying out of the Betty bomber's formidable defensive fire. After the maneuver ("overhead run") was completed, the pilots would pull out of their dives and climb left to avoid collisions. If the Zero escorts had not arrived then another run on the bombers would be initiated. But if the Zeros had come on the scene then Wildcats would ingloriously dive back toward Henderson or bank into the nearest cloud. The Marine air mission was to break up today's enemy bomber attack and be around for tomorrow's. A Wildcat could not dogfight against a Zero, and its only hope to continue combat was a surprise hit and run attack. A long, shallow dive, howling with speed, took the pilot out of danger. The Zero was handicapped by its fuel-consuming eight hour round trip back to Rabaul. With their belly drop tanks attached, the Japanese pilot was reluctant to chase after the fleeing Wildcats because he could lose it under full throttle maneuvering. With the drop tanks, the Zero had only a few minutes of combat, so the Japanese pilot often did not engage the Marines and broke off, also to fight another day.

The Wildcat pilots got into their landing traffic patterns. Sweat running everywhere, open the flight suit, look to see if the cooling vents were open. Light up a cigarette if the plane had not been hit. Swing around the field before landing to make sure there were no wrecks, new bomb craters, or another plane in your pattern. Touch down, slowdown, open the canopy, look out for other planes and fire trucks, and pull into your revetment. The Crew Chief would be there to guide the Wildcat like a philharmonic conductor, and with two fingers across his throat he signaled the end of the scramble.

Thanks to Marine aces Marion Carl (18 1/2 victories) and George Hollowell (8 victories) for information they supplied.

Because of their huge Pratt & Whitney radials, visibility for taxiing the F4U was difficult. A VF-17 crewman sits on the wingtip and directs a pilot to the runway on Bougainville for a raid on Rabaul, February 1944. (USN)

MGen. Marion Carl with the author at his Roseburg, OR, home. (Author)

CHAPTER 5

Ace Races and Victory Credits

Victory Credits

Air victory claims procedure has always been a controversial system. In WWI, the U.S. Air Service victory credits were given upon confirmation by a balloon observer, or if the wreckage was found. Sometimes confirmation by three disinterested observers would be accepted as evidence of a claim.

Early in the Second World War it was obvious that many claims were exaggerated, or in the case of the Luftwaffe seemed to be exaggerated. It is often asserted that early American claims in the Pacific were also exaggerated, which they probably were, but many genuine victories were also lost due to lack of proper verification or claims procedure. On 7 May 1943, the War Department announced a claims policy patterned after the RAF system:

There are only three circumstances in which an enemy plane is definitely counted as lost. These are:

1 If the plane is seen descending completely enveloped in flames.
2 If the plane is seen to disintegrate in the air, or if a complete wing or tail assembly is seen to be shot away from the fuselage.
3 If the plane is a single seater and the pilot is seen to bail out.

Enemy aircraft are not counted as having been destroyed on the basis of the fact that flames are licking out from the engine or wheel, or if some other similar part of the plane is seen to be shot away.

After each combat mission, every fighter pilot and member of a bombardment crew is interrogated by intelligence officers. When any crewmember or pilot claims to having shot down or damaged an enemy plane, he is questioned about pertinent details. He is questioned also about the claims of other crewmembers or pilots. After the debriefing is completed, the intelligence officers make a complete breakdown, and their official reports are to be on the conservative side.

Taken into consideration by the commanding and intelligence officers are the following:

1 The number and type of enemy planes attacking.
2 The direction and angle of attack.
3 The range at which the gunner or pilot is believed to have opened fire, and the distance at which he destroys the plane.
4 The rounds fired and results.
5 The time, place, and altitude of our planes and their positions relative to other factors.

A plane is counted as having been probably destroyed if it is sufficiently in flames to preclude the chance of extinguishing the fire, or when damaged to the extent where it is believed it must have crashed but where there is not 100% certainty. A plane is counted as having been damaged when parts are seen to be shot away. The commanding and intelligence officers, in analyzing the claims, are cognizant that as long as the enemy has a plane in the air, some skeptics will doubt the accuracy of the claims of the enemy planes destroyed. Consequently, the first thought of the officers is to eliminate duplicate claims. They do so whenever there is any doubt.

Although this stated policy for establishing claims gave pilots a set of stringent guidelines it remained imperfect. In the heat of combat, excitement and fear stimulated the imagination and events tended to become confused, especially during multiple combats. Witnesses, usually a wingman, verified a claim to the Fighter Victory Credit Board.

The Intelligence Officer (IO) conducted a thorough post mission debriefing, which went into a detailed discussion of any claims made. An Encounter Report was filed listing the date, unit, hour, area, weather condition, enemy a/c encountered, and result. This was followed by a first hand account by the pilot describing the combat and result in detail. The claim was to be validated by gun camera footage and witnesses. After the gun camera film was developed a written report was made. It listed the length of attack in seconds, the target position in yards, and angle of attack and the results of the attack and film quality. The official AAF name for gun camera footage was GASP (Gun Alignment and Spotting Photography), but was never in common use.

At the start of the war the USN and USMC had no standard method of evaluating or crediting victories. In the ETO USAAF fighter squadrons and groups sent claims to the Victory Evaluation Board, but in the PTO USN/USMC units were either on carriers or

Top Luftwaffe ace, Erich Hartmann (L), needed 1405 missions which resulted in 825 combats to score 352 victories while Gerd Barkhorn (R) needed 1104 missions to score 301 victories. Top U.S. ace, Dick Bong, scored 40 in 200 missions. (Author/West)

remote islands, and therefore each unit adopted its own method of reporting and evaluating claims. Claims were taken at the pilot's word and were initially exaggerated. As pilots became more experienced and saw real claims they became more accurate in assessing their own claims. Later in the war gun camera evidence and witness collaboration was utilized.

Close But No Victory

A probable combat claim is "A plane believed to be sufficiently in flames to preclude the chance of extinguishing the fire, or when damaged to the extent where it is believed it must have crashed but there is no 100% certainty."

Top American ace Dick Bong, with 40 victories, also had the most probable claims with eight, high for the AAF. Ray Wetmore (AAF-17 victories) followed with six probables. Donald Aldrich (USMC-20 victories) had six probables, while Tom Blackburn (USN-11 victories), David McCampbell (USN-34 victories), and James Rigg (USN-11 victories) each had five probables, and were high for their branch of service.

Maj. Eugene Roberts of the 84FS/78FG led the early ETO ace race, helped by scoring the first ETO triple victory in a day on 30 July 1943 and then a double (shown here) on 24 August to become an ace. (Author/Roberts)

A damaged aircraft is "A plane which is seen to have parts shot away." Air Force ace Don Beerbower (15 1/2 victories) had 11.33 damaged, while aces Glenn Eagleston (10 1/2 victories) and Steven Gerrick (5 victories) each damaged nine enemy aircraft, followed by Gerald Tyler (11 victories) and Hampton Boggs (9 victories) with eight, and Bong with seven. For the Navy, Howard Hudson (5 victories) and Rigg each had five damaged. For the Marines, Francis Terrill (6 victories) and Franklin Thomas (9 victories) each had four damaged credits.

Really Shared Victories

Frequently, pilots shared victories for shooting down the same enemy aircraft. However, there were occasions when sharing a claim bordered on the ridiculous.

Covering the Task Force after Christmas Day 1943 raid on Kavieng Harbor, New Ireland, no less than eight F6F Hellcat pilots of Sam Silber's VF-18 off the *Intrepid* subdued an incoming Japanese Betty bomber to gain 1/8th victory apiece.

The Air Force's 97FS, 82FG saw seven of its P-38 pilots down a He-111 bomber towing a Gotha 242 Glider near Kivolak on 1 January 1944 for 1/7th victories apiece.

Six Marine Corps F4U pilots of VMF-321 destroyed a Zeke fighter east of Cape Gazelle, Bougainville, to share 1/6th victory each on 18 January 1944.

Cdr. Daniel "Dog" Smith claimed a wartime total of 6 and 1/12th victories while flying Hellcats for VF-20 off the *Enterprise* in late 1944 and early 1945. Besides downing three Zekes on 17 October and a Tony on 14 November, Smith had five claims involving shared victories. He had three claims for half victories, one claim with two other pilots, and a Frances with three other pilots. These fractional scores (1/2+1/2+1/2+1/3+1/4) totaled 2 and 1/12th victories.

VBF-85 had the most shared victories of any USN unit. It had a total of 10 victories by 14 pilots and only three solo.

Four Navy pilots came within a .50 caliber shell hit on a Jap of becoming an ace, ending their tours with 4 and 5/6th victories:

Haas, Lt(jg)Walter F4F VF-42 & VF-3 *Yorktown*
Kerr, Lt(jg) Leslie F6F VF-23 *Langley*
Sedaker, Lt. Thomas F6F VC-84 *Bunker Hill*
Swisher, Ens. Lee F6F VF-47 *Bataan*

American Victory Claims

The top two American and British aces each scored 40 victories (Richard Bong and Marmaduke "Pat" Pattle), and the two runners up scored 38 victories (Thomas McGuire and Johnny Johnson). Fifteen Luftwaffe pilots scored over 200 victories, five claimed over 250, and two (Erich Hartmann 352 and Gerd Barkhorn 301) scored over 300. The top five Luftwaffe aces were credited with 1,453 victories (the equivalent of 58 USAAF fighter squadrons!), while the top five American aces could muster only 167.

So, why didn't American aces run up such high totals? After the initial early war crises the American pilot supply increased and the RAF system of operational duty tours was introduced. After a specified number of missions were completed the pilot was assigned non-operational duties. The aces were assigned to OTUs (Opera-

The 56FG dominated ETO scoring. Shown here are (L-R standing) "Gabby" Gabreski (28 victories), Robert Johnson (27 v.), "Bud" Mahurin (19 3/4 v.) and Robert Landry (1 v.) (L-R wing) Walter Cook (6 v.) and Dave Schilling (22 1/2 v.). (USAF)

tional Training Units) to give students the benefit of their combat experience, and thus perpetuating the pool of well-trained pilots. This stricture obviously deprived U.S. aces from gaining higher totals. Leading ETO ace Francis Gabreski had 28 victories in 168 missions, while American Ace of Aces Richard Bong had 40 victories flying just over 200 missions. In fighting an offensive war, American pilots in damaged aircraft either had to bail out or crash land in enemy territory, and were consequently taken prisoner. During the last year of the war the Luftwaffe and Japanese had all but disappeared from the skies in many areas. Many American fliers could complete an entire combat tour without encountering an enemy aircraft.

RAF aces Johnny Johnson got 38 victories in 515 missions and Pierre Closterman 33 in 420 missions, but Ginger Lacy got 28 in just 80 missions. Top Allied ace and Soviet pilot Ivan Kozhedub downed 62 Luftwaffe aircraft in 330 missions (120 combats), while second ranked ace Alexander Pokryshkin got 59 victories in 600 missions (156 combats) and third ranked Allied ace Gregori Rechkalov downed 58 enemy aircraft in 609 missions (122 combats).

Longevity and experience were key to the Luftwaffe's astronomical victory totals. German pilots who survived their initial missions soon flew in a realm of experience and ability that few pilots ever approach. With each mission—and some Luftwaffe pilots flew combat for five years—their combat and survival skills became sharper. Flying and fighting close to the front or over the constantly attacked Fatherland, they met the enemy every day and often several times a day. Multiple daily missions were the rule for the Luftwaffe. There were no long-standing patrols or long range escort five or six hour missions without sighting the enemy. German (and Japanese pilots) scrambled knowing they were going to engage in combat in a matter of minutes. If their aircraft were damaged they could bail out and fight again. The World's Ace of Aces, Erich Hartmann, scored 352 victories in 1,405 missions, 825 of

which resulted in dogfights, but he was shot down only two times. His unit, JG-52, was the Luftwaffe's most successful fighter unit, scoring over 10,000 victories during the war on the Eastern Front. Gerd Barkhorn, also of JG-52, was the second highest scoring ace. He did not achieve the first of his 301 victories until his 120th mission and was shot down nine times during the war and flew 1,104 missions. Gunther Rall scored 275 victories in 621 missions but was shot down five times, and Otto Kittle, fourth ranked ace scored 267 victories in 583 missions. During the course of his 222 victory career Erich Rudorfer was shot down 16 times in 1,000 missions, bailing out nine times and crash landing seven, and escaping capture each time. During a 17-day period beginning in late April 1942, Herman Graf scored 72 victories and then added 75 more in September. Probably the most phenomenal record was achieved by Kurt Welter, who scored 33 victories in just 40 missions (21 four engine and seven difficult Mosquito kills). What makes his record even more unbelievable was that he was shot down nine times! Eastern Front Luftwaffe aces acknowledge that their victories were easily gained, but the conditions that prevailed there were much more arduous than anywhere in the war: freezing winters; muddy springs and autumns; and dusty summers. Their airfields were primitive, while logistics and maintenance was a nightmare in a war of constant retreat. As the war progressed their Russian opponents became more skilled.

The closest American approximation to this kind of fighting came during the campaigns in the Solomons, where Marine pilots engaged the attacking Japanese nearly every day. Between 14 and 30 January 1944, 1Lt. Robert Hanson (VMF-215) scored 20 victories in six missions over the North Solomons, but was KIA on his only unsuccessful mission on 3 February 1944. Capt. Joseph Foss (VMF-121) scored 23 victories over Guadalcanal between 13 October and 15 November 1942 (he was shot down on 3 November and returned to base three days later). On 19 November the squadron was relieved, but Foss returned to combat in January 1944 and got three more victories to tie Eddie Rickenbacker's WWI record before he returned to the States to receive the CMH and sell War Bonds.

European Ace Races (ETO/MTO)

The European air war saw no American Air Force fighter pilot score a victory for over nine months after Pearl Harbor, nor did it have an American ace until the end of July 1943. In the Pacific, U.S. fighter aircraft and warships were the Allies' frontline of defense, single-handedly holding off the advance of the onrushing Japanese war machine towards Australia. Similarly, the Royal Navy and Air Force contained Germany after the fall of Continental Europe. Churchill's "Few," flying Spitfires and Hurricanes, held the Luftwaffe at bay during the Battle of Britain. Their valor prevented Hitler from launching "Operation Sealion," his amphibious invasion of England, causing him to turn his sights on Russia with the eventual disastrous consequences.

By the end of 1942, one year into the war, the AAF in Europe had scored just 156 aerial victories (14 in the ETO and 142 in the MTO). During the same period the American Air Forces in the Pacific had claimed 1,275 enemy aircraft (475 by the Marines, 406 by the Navy, and 394 by the Air Force). By the end of 1943, the 8th Air Force in Europe had only scored 456 victories. The 12th and 15th Air Forces and North African Air Force (NAAF) had scored a great number of victories over the active battlefields of North Africa, Sicily, and Italy, but none of the contending aces would come out of the MTO. So, in 1942, the media turned to the Pacific to give the public heroes, such as the Navy's "Butch" O'Hare and John Thach and Marine Guadalcanal aces John Smith (19 victories), Marion Carl (15 1/2), and Joe Foss (23). When Foss tied Eddie Rickenbacker's all time American record of 26 established in WW-I, he was awarded the Congressional Medal of Honor by F.D.R., and his national PR tour was given extensive coverage. But by the autumn of 1943, the 8AF had its personnel and equipment on station in England. The Germans had been driven out of North Africa and Sicily, and the 8AF bomber offensive was getting into high gear. The bombers required escorts, and the Luftwaffe was hunted in sweeps, heating up the European air war. By August the 8AF had its first ace, Charles London of the 78th Fighter Group, and by mid-November its first double ace (ten victories), Walker Mahurin of the 56th Fighter Group. From this time on the air war in the ETO received more attention than that in the Pacific. In Europe air bases were concentrated in southeastern Britain, where reporters comfortably domiciled and had good communications with London and then America. The Pacific air bases were aircraft carriers or were spread out on primitive Pacific islands, both of which were inhospitable to reporters and out of easy communication with far-away Australia.

Newsmen covering European air forces generally had a much easier time than their counterparts in the Pacific. Stationed in London, they could easily drive out to a fighter group for a story or interview. The rule of thumb was the closer to London the plusher the base, and the more news space the unit would receive in the dailys. The 4FG "Eagles," based at nearby Debden, throughout the war was a favorite of reporters because of its amenities, especially the availability of American food, and so was often referred to as the "Pearl of the ETO." Of course, its popularity stemmed from being one of the top-scoring Groups with 550 victories, boasting such aces as Don Gentile (19 7/8), Duane Beeson (17 1/3 victories), John Godfrey (16 1/3), Kid Hofer (15), Jim Goodson (12), et al. The 56FG "Wolf Pack" was in constant competition with the 4th, with the most aerial victories at 664. They were based further east from London and were not so luxurious as Debden. Even though they were possibly slighted by the media, they did receive their share of print because of its many and colorful aces: "Gabby" Gabreski (28 victories, tops in the ETO); Robert Johnson (27); Dave Schilling (22 1/2); Fred Christensen (21); Walker Mahurin (19 1/2); Gerald Johnson (16 1/2); and its great leader, "Hub" Zemke (17 1/2). The 352FG, with 504 1/2 victories, received less attention, despite aces such as Gerald Preddy (26 7/8), John Meyer (24), and Bill Whisner (15 1/2). The 353rd FG, which scored 328 victories, had aces Glenn Duncan (19 1/2) and Walt Beckham (18), but received even less coverage than the 352nd.

The first victory scored by American forces was a shared credit by 2Lt. Elza Shahan in a P-38 of the 27FS and 2Lt. Joseph Shaffer of the 33FS flying a P-39. In the late morning of 14 August 1942,

the two lieutenants combined to down a prowling FW-200 recon bomber off the coast of Iceland. Five days later, 2Lt. Samuel Junkin of the 31FG, in a Spitfire VI, was flying air cover for the British and Canadian commando raid on Dieppe. Junkin shot down a FW-190, and in the same air battle two future 8AF aces who were flying with the RAF 133rd "Eagle Squadron" scored victories. Flt/Lt. Don Blakeslee (4 victories RAF and 11 1/2 8AF) and P/O Don Gentile (2 victories RAF and 19 7/8 8AF) each claimed a FW-190.

1Lt. Stanley Anderson, flying Spitfires for the 334and 335FS/4FG, led the ETO victory race for over five months when he scored his second victory (14 January 1943) and third victory (22 January 1943). He was tied by Capt. Charles London on 29 June 1943 and lost the lead to 1Lt. Duane Beeson on 28 July 1943. But most of the air action would take place in North Africa for the time being.

Hitler's desire to capture the Suez Canal and ultimately link up with his forces coming through Russia into the Middle East changed

Walker Mahurin (L) and Walt Beckham (R) dueled for the victory lead for five months between November 1943 and March 1944 and between 9 and 19 victories. Both were shot down, with Beckham becoming a POW and Mahurin evading and returned to be removed from action, to put an end to their victory aspirations. (USAF)

the focus of the war. The deployment of the Afrika Korps and Luftwaffe to North Africa saw the 12th and 15th Air Forces have the opportunity to fatten their victory totals. The first ace of the MTO was either 1Lt. Virgil Lusk of the 49FS//14FG, who shot down five Italian SM transports on 24 November 1942, or 1Lt. Virgil Smith of the 94FS/14FG, who shot down a FW-190 while flying a P-38 on 12 December 1942. (See P-38, First MTO Ace). The first ace over Europe was Capt. Charles London of the 83 FS/78 FG, nine months later on 30 July 1943. While flying his P-47 on a bomber escort mission over Haldern, Germany, London added two Me-109s to the three victories he got in June. After the magic fifth, the affable London and Gene Roberts of the 84FS, who got the ETO's first triple (3 victories in a day), led a rousing celebration well attended by the press and reported in the States. London was rotated Stateside to do public relations. Before London became an ace, Maj. Levi Chase of the 60FS/33FG had become the first American double ace, scoring his tenth victory some four months earlier on 5 April 1943. Chase got nine Germans and an Italian Mc-202 fighter in his combat tour (December 1942 to April 1943) over Tunisia. Chase later led a P-51 unit in Burma, and subsequently commanded a fighter-bomber unit in Korea.

By the end of June 1943 1Lt. Sylvan Feld of the 4FS/52FG had become the leading Spitfire ace by downing nine Luftwaffe fighters over Tunisia. There were 12 USAAF Spitfire aces in the MTO. This theater was an aerial patchwork, with pilots flying the dated P-40s and "borrowed" Spitfires. However, a number of P-38s were diverted from England and sent to equip the 14FG/15AF and 82FS/12AF. The top P-38 ace over North Africa was 1Lt. William Sloan of the 96FS/82FG, who was credited with 12 victories and five damaged between January and August 1943. As the Afrika Korps surrendered in North Africa and the air action in the MTO wound down, Sloan was to remain the top ace in this theater for eight months. In seven weeks over Italy in July/August 1944, another P-38 pilot, 1Lt. Michael Brezas of the 48FS/14FG, also got 12 victories.

The next top MTO ace was Maj. Herschel Green, who flew a variety of fighters for the 31FS/325FG. In his first tour he flew P-40s over the Mediterranean, shooting down three Me-109s in May/June 1943. On 30 January 1944, Green had a great day when he became an instant ace. P-47s of Green's Group were assigned to precede bomber groups in their attacks on Luftwaffe air bases near Udine, in order to catch the German fighters while they were taking off. Green's unit intercepted a formation of 15 Ju-52s at 1,000 feet. Diving out of the sun at the strung out transports he was able to fire at several in each firing run and destroyed four. He continued the mission and destroyed a Macchi 202 fighter and a Dornier 217 to finish the day with six victories. Green led the MTO aces with 15 victories, but was briefly caught by Maj. Sam Brown of the 307FS/31FG on 26 June 1944. On that day Brown broke up a formation of fifty or more Luftwaffe fighters that were attacking American bombers. In the combat Brown destroyed four and damaged two. Green, now flying P-51s, regained the MTO victory lead, getting victories number 16 and 17 on the 9th and 14th of July, respectively. On 4 August, Capt. James Varnell of the 2FS/52FG briefly took over the MTO lead when he shot down a Rumanian Ju-52 for

his 17th and last victory. Green regained the lead on 23 August when he shot down a FW-190 for his 18th and last victory. The highest scorer in the MTO was Capt. John Voll of the 308FS/31FG. The 31FG was the top Fighter Group in the MTO, with its three squadrons (307-308-309) scoring 560 aerial victories and producing 36 aces while flying Spitfires and P-51s over North Africa and Italy/ Austria/ Rumania. Voll flew as a wingman for 20 missions before he was promoted to element leader. He scored his first victory on 23 June 1944 on the return leg of an escort mission to Ploesti. In the next five months Voll was to roll up victory after victory. Voll's biggest day came on his last mission, one that was to make him the MTO leader, on 16 November 1944. Becoming separated from his group over Northern Italy, he dove on a Ju-88 and destroyed it. He was immediately bounced by a mixed group of 12 Luftwaffe fighters from above. In the unequal, desperate combat Voll claimed two FW-190s and a Me-109 destroyed, along with a FW-190 and Me-109 probable and two Me-109s damaged. The day's four victories gave him 21 total, not only to lead all American aces in the MTO, but also to edge out Australian G/C Clive Caldwell of the RAF's 250th and 112th Squadrons, who had 20 1/2 (Caldwell later scored an additional eight victories in the Pacific). But Voll's rapid victory total never was a challenge to the ETO leadership, which had peaked at 28 in May and June 1944.

There was a lull in air action in the ETO until October 1943, but in the nine-month period from October 1943 to July 1944, the top ace slot changed hands no less than ten times in the ETO, a major reason being that its leaders were shot down and being taken prisoner.

After getting the first ETO triple in one day on 30 July 1943, Maj. Eugene Roberts of the 84FS/78FG shot down a Me-110 on the Schweinfurt bombing raid on 17 August while flying his P-47 *Spokane Chief.* Roberts scored a double on 24 August to tie London at five and take the lead at six to become the ETO's second ace.

Capt. Walker Mahurin of the 63FS/56FG was a PR man's dream: handsome, in the Hollywood leading man fashion, and stereotypical of a WWII fighter ace. On 4 October 1943, Mahurin had a big day when he destroyed three Me-110s on an escort mission

Bob Johnson (L) and Gabby Gabreski (R) ended the war as co-top scorers in the ETO with 28, but after the war a victory was removed from Johnson's total. (USAF)

east of Suren. He would figure prominently in the next several months, as he tied Roberts' six victories among press photos and hoopla for the feat.

The next challenger was a former RAF American Eagle (133 Sq.) volunteer from Boise, Idaho. Meticulous and handsome in a Dana Andrews sort of way, 1Lt. Duane Beeson also was the archetypal fighter ace. Flying his P-47 "*Boise Bee*" for the 334FS/4FG, Beeson scored his fifth and sixth victories to tie Roberts and Mahurin on 8 October when he got two Me-109s and damaged another over Holland. By April 1944, the now Lt.Col. Beeson had fallen behind in the ETO race, but was battling Don Gentile for top 4FG ace, leading 17 1/3 to 16. On 5 April, while strafing a Luftwaffe airdrome near Berlin, Beeson was shot down by flak and spent the final 13 months of the war in Stalag Luft I POW camp.

The five-day period 10-14 October 1943 saw challengers and lead changes. Roberts regained the lead from his Beeson/Mahurin tie by downing a Me-110 and 210 at noon on 10 October for his eighth victory. That day a new challenger appeared in the ace race; the first Johnson, Gerald W., who flew P-47s for the 61FS/56FG. There is often a confusion of the "Johnson" aces in the war. Gerald R. flew P-38s for the 5th Air Force in the Pacific, counting 22 Japanese victims. This Johnson was killed in a transport crash, heroically giving up his parachute during a typhoon immediately after the Pacific war. He is often confused with Gerald W., and Gerald W. is sometimes confused with yet another prominent 56FG ace, Robert S. Gerald W. got his 5 1/2 to 7 1/2 victories during this time to come within a half victory of Roberts. Gerald W. went off ops soon after and would return to combat later, out of the ace race, and getting a total of 16 1/2 before being shot down strafing trains at the end of March 1944 and taken prisoner. Also, the 10th of October saw three men become aces: Dave Schilling; Robert S. Johnson; and the next challenger and leader, Capt. Walter "Turk" Beckham of the 351FS/353FG.

Beckham's early combat career had been relegated to the backwaters, "protecting" Ecuador and the Panama Canal Zone. He was finally shipped to England with the newly formed 353FG. Beckham started off combat slowly, not scoring until he discovered that it was his luxuriant mustache which jinxed him! Now barefaced, Beckham, an expert gunner, went on to score 18 victories. On 10 October Beckham, in his P-47 "*Little Demon*," was leading his flight to rendezvous with outward-bound bombers over Holland that were being harassed by the Luftwaffe. Beckham dove on a Me-210, destroying it, but picked up another Me-110 on his tail. A skillful diving turn reversed the tactical situation, and Beckham got to his attacker. Returning to the bomber formation, he was ambushed by two more Me-110s. He emptied his guns on one and then, defenseless, turned into his attacker, deceiving it to break off the attack. On the way back to base Beckham had to evade several more enemy fighters and almost ran out of gas before landing. The three victories made him an ace. On 11 November his victory over a FW-190 would tie him for the lead with Roberts at nine. He would lose the lead two weeks later to Mahurin, but would regain it at 16 on 3 February 1944. That morning Mahurin got his 14 1/2, but several minutes later Beckham got a Me-109 and FW-190 south of Oldenburg for numbers 15 and 16. Five days later he got another

Me-109/FW-190 parlay over Belgium for numbers 17 and 18. On 22 February, he was strafing Ju-88s on the ground at Osfheim. His flight followed Glenn Duncan's flight in, and the alerted German AA gunners were able to take bead and hit Beckham's engine, which caught fire. He literally ejected himself out of the burning cockpit and bailed out into captivity. He spent the rest of the war as a POW at Stalag I until liberated by Patton in April 1945.

Beckham and Mahurin were center stage in the battle for top gun for four months, November '43 to March '44. Mahurin had become the first double ace over Europe on 26 November. The 8th bomber Command put up 633 heavies to bomb multiple targets. Mahurin's group escorted a formation homeward after it had bombed Bremen, and the leader got two Me-110s and a probable. In his autobiography *Honest John* (Putnam, N.Y. 1962), Mahurin often mentions the competition between the aces and fighter groups, especially his 56th and the 4th. After moving into the lead he states: "the shoot'em down bug had really bitten him." He was intent on scoring victories, so much so that on 3 February 1944, his zeal almost got him court-martialed. While flying escort for the withdrawal of B-24s over Wilhelmslaven, he and his wingman broke

Herschel Green of the 317FS/325FG flew three fighter types on his way to leading the MTO most of 1944 with 18 victories. (Author/Green)

off escort to attack and dispatch a lone Me-109. They lost their bomber formation and rejoined another, which was under attack by rocket-lobbing Me-110s. Mahurin got behind one and exploded it. When he returned to base, instead of congratulations Mahurin drew the wrath of CO Hub Zemke. It was a gross tactical transgression to leave group formation, and Zemke flew down to initiate court martial proceedings with Gen. William Kepner. The General told Zemke to go ahead, but he was going to award Mahurin the DSC for the same action!

After losing his lead to Beckham at 14 1/2, Mahurin caught up after Beckham was taken prisoner. The 63FS was flying top cover for 8BC bombers over the VFK Ball Bearing Works near Berlin on 8 March. Mahurin shot down two FW-190s and a Ju-88 near Wessendorf airfield to put him at 19 1/2 victories, and to give him a lead he would only hold for a week. On 15 March, Maj. Robert S. Johnson, a flight training classmate of Mahurin, fellow 56 FG squadron commander, and friend got a triple for victories 20-22. On 27 March, the tail gunner of a German bomber hit Mahurin's *"Spirit of Atlantic City,"* causing him to bail out. He was an evader for six

Capt. John Voll 308FS/31FG became the MTO's top scorer on his last mission of the war, when he downed 4 German aircraft on 16 November 1944 to take the lead from Herschel Green. (Author/Voll)

weeks until the French Underground helped him in his return to England, and then back to the States in June. By that time both Johnson and Gabreski, another 56th squadron commander and ace, had been credited with 28 victories. While he was in Washington, DC, Mahurin managed to pull some strings to get himself assigned to the 3 Air Commando Group operating with Gen. Orde Wingate's British Chindits in Burma. He got a waiver bypassing the regulation prohibiting combat pilots from returning to combat duty sooner than one year. He was credited with only one victory in the Pacific, but flew many ground support missions. In Korea he was the Group Commander of the 4FIG, where he scored 3 1/2 MiG-15 victories. He was shot down, captured, and tortured by the North Koreans before being released.

During this time a controversy arose in the ace race, as in May 1943 Gen. "Hap" Arnold released figures on the performance of the Air Force. His figure of 23,838 enemy aircraft destroyed since Pearl Harbor included 3,664 enemy aircraft destroyed on the ground. This tabulation seemed to indicate the relative importance of ground and air victories. Accordingly, the 8AF and 14AF in the CBI accepted ground victories into total claims.

Don Gentile, another former 133 Eagle Squadron veteran, was posted with the 336FS/4FG. The group flew Spitfires until 1943, when they received the P-47, which they never liked. When they re-equipped with the P-51 Mustang, Gentile began to score in earnest. Coupled with wingman John Godfrey, the two probably formed the most famous and effective duo in the war. Gentile got 16 5/6 quick victories in March 1944. When he scored three victories on 8 April he also scored seven ground victories to surpass Rickenbacker's record of 26, which the press noted aided by PR releases from the 8AF. Despite the inherent dangers and losses sustained in ground strafing, the media and public continued to consider only aerial victories as a means to acedom.

If Beeson and Mahurin were a Hollywood preconception of the dashing, stereotypical ace, then Robert Johnson filled the media's need to give the public the All-American boy next door. Johnson was blond and blue-eyed, possessing modesty, intelligence, and a good sense of humor. Flying for Zemke's "Wolf Pack," Johnson was a slow starter in the ace race, not scoring until his eleventh mission. In fact, Johnson's squadron mates thought he would be the 56th's most likely to be shot down because of his Lone Wolf propensities. His first victory was scored by making a bounce, unprotected, as he left formation without permission or his wingman. Despite the victory he was reprimanded by Gerald W. Johnson for his violation of doctrine. G.W. Johnson, Gabreski, and Zemke were chronically on Johnson's case in these early days, but it made him a better, more cautious pilot. It was not until his 43rd mission on 10 October that he became an ace, destroying a FW-190 and Me-110. The 61FS was covering the homeward leg for B-17s returning from Munster. A large, mixed group of Luftwaffe fighters attacked and also made G.W. Johnson and Dave Schilling aces that day. Initially not a good shot, Johnson improved as he gained experience and self-discipline. Once he got into the scoring groove, the next seven months saw him score 23 victories and become the first ETO pilot to break Eddie Rickenbacker's WWI record of 26 aerial victories. In his autobiography *Thunderbolt!* (Holt, Rinehart and Winston,

N.Y. 1959), Johnson counts off each of his victories after becoming an ace, and then counts down to Rickenbacker's record. After his triple on 15 March to give him 22, Johnson had nearly expended the 200 hours of combat time needed to rotate home. Zemke readily granted Johnson's request for a 25-hour extension, as he wanted the 56th to claim the honor of breaking Rickenbacker's Air Force record. At this time Richard Bong had 23 in the Pacific, and Marine Joe Foss already had tied the record over Guadalcanal in November 1942. So with the promise of good weather and bomber escort missions on tap, Johnson had a good chance to break the record with five more victories. But during the next 2 1/2 weeks victories eluded him. The Luftwaffe opposition was half-hearted, and Johnson could not score. During this time Bong had the same dilemma, and on the morning of 3 April the score stood at Bong 23 and Johnson 22. On 3 April both pilots scored victories to make it Bong 24 and Johnson 23. But then Johnson was hit by another frustrating drought, as was Bong. On 13 April, on a bomber escort mission to Munich, the Luftwaffe finally decided to intercept in mass. Johnson got a FW-190 and then dove on a hedgehopping FW-190. Wanting to get a sure shot Johnson waited too long, and the German pilot evaded with a steep chandelle to the right. Now Johnson was at a disadvantage, as the P-47 was strictly a high altitude fighter. The German fighter made a head-on attack and rolled left to break. Johnson kicked left rudder and fired a hail of .50 caliber bullets into the cockpit and wing roots for victory number 25 to close in on the record. But word came in the next day that Bong had scored three victories the previous day to break Rickenbacker's record. So now Johnson concentrated on becoming the first ETO ace to do so. But the Luftwaffe continued to stay on the ground, frustrating Johnson, whose tour extension was running out. Finally, on 8 May, on his last mission—a bomber escort to Berlin—Johnson became so discouraged when the Germans failed to appear, he considered claiming engine failure so he could abort the mission. But at last, Messerschmitts flashed through the bomber formation, and he dove on a "Me-209" (his log book designation) and destroyed it. To protect Johnson, the three other members of his flight had refrained from engaging in the combat and stayed on top cover. Soon a group of FW-190s were spotted below heading towards the clouds. Johnson raced after the leader and claimed #27. Upon landing, Brass, reporters, and photographers were waiting. Johnson flashed a two-finger V as flashbulbs went off.

Johnson was flown home, and like Richard Bong was overwhelmed, meeting the President, the Pentagon, the press, and on and on. At the Pentagon he met Bong, who had come home before Johnson. Bong told Johnson that he was fed up with the PR: "It was worse than having a Zero on your tail!" Johnson saw no more combat, but did see a lot more PR.

In June 1944, Johnson had been officially credited with 28 victories when his damaged credit on 15 March was upgraded. The "official" post war USAF Historical Study #85 credits him with 27 victories. The diligent research of Frank Olynyk found that the 8th Fighter Command Final Assessment credited two victories by R. (Ralph) A. Johnson (another Johnson!) to R.S. Johnson, but also gave credit for only one victory on 30 December 1943 instead of two (28 minus 2 plus 1 equals 27).

The top ace of the ETO was a bandy, blue-eyed, square-jawed son of Polish immigrants named Francis Stanley Gabreski, known as "Gabby." The Oil City, Pennsylvania, resident was never very academically-minded, but decided to follow his brother in pre-med at Notre Dame. He soon left the home of the Fighting Irish to become a fighting Pole and entered flight school. Winning his wings, he was stationed at Honolulu at the time of the Pearl Harbor attack. Although he did not get into combat there, he did shuttle aircraft to safety.

He was ordered to England and assigned to the RAF's 315 Polish Squadron. He flew 13 missions without result before being transferred to Hub Zemke's 56FG in February 1943. Like Johnson, Gabreski was also a slow starter after beginning his combat tour in April 1943. He got his first victory, a FW-190, on 24 August, after damaging a FW-190 in mid-May. He did not become an ace until 26 November, when he claimed a double on Me-110s near Oldenburg. Once he became an ace his score mounted steadily.

On 29 November Gabreski's flight, escorting B-17s over Bremen, encountered a large number of Me-110s that were salvoing rockets at the bomber boxes. He quickly dove on a Me-110 and fired, blowing it to pieces, some of which entered his cockpit through the heater vents. The debris damaged both wings and tore open the canopy. Despite the damage, Gabreski took his P-47 back to altitude to cover the bombers. He spotted another German about to attack and dove to destroy it. For this action he received the DSC and his second and third victory.

On his next mission, 11 December, the 61FS picked up a mixed group of B-17s and B-24s in route to Emden. After flying through heavy cloud and then chasing and finally destroying a Me-110, Gabreski found himself in a vulnerable predicament, low on fuel and alone. A Me-109 bounced and hit the P-47, causing it to go into a spiral which Gabreski allowed to continue, hoping to trick the German into thinking he had the victory and breaking off. Pulling out of the dangerous spin, Gabreski ducked into a cloud and nursed his crippled fighter back to Debden to be written off.

Gabreski's biggest day occurred on 22 May 1944, when he observed a group of FW-190s in a landing pattern at Hopenhofer. His first run was driven off by heavy AA fire protecting the field. The fuel-starved German aircraft were forced to land, and the ground fire ceased. Gabreski easily shot down three aircraft like ducks in a shooting gallery for victory numbers 20, 21, and 22.

Gabreski was flying but awaiting orders to be sent back home on leave to marry Kay Cochrane, whom he met during his Hawaiian tour. On D-Day he got a FW-190 and Me-109, and got another double five days later to tie Rickenbacker's record (too late) and move within one of Robert Johnson's ETO lead of 27. On 27 June, he got #27, and on 5 July he added a Me-109 for #28.

Gabreski's tour was over; all he had to do was get a seat home. But on 20 July, he decided to go on one more mission. On a strafing run over a Luftwaffe airfield west of Frankfurt, he burned several parked He-111s on his first run. Circling around, he flew "Little Miss Kay" at ground level when his prop hit a rise and he crashlanded at high speed. Wriggling out of his jammed canopy, he managed to evade the Germans for five days before being captured and spending the war in Stalag Luft I.

After the war, Gabreski spent time as a test pilot, and then was relieved from active duty. He went to work in private industry for a short time and went back to active duty in 1947. When the Korean War broke out he got two victories with the 4th Fighter Interceptor Wing, and then got 4 1/2 more with the 51FIW to give him 34 1/2 career victories and become one of seven WWII aces to become aces in Korea.

The month of July put an end to the ETO ace race. Gabreski joined contender Col. Glenn Duncan of the 353FG, who had 19 1/2 victories but was shot down and captured two weeks earlier on 7 July. Fred Christensen, another 56FG ace, scored six victories on 7 July when his flight intercepted a dozen Ju-88s to give him 21 1/2 victories, but he was rotated home and out of the race. David Schilling with 13 victories was home selling war bonds, and did not return until late August. Hub Zemke had 15 victories, but curtailed his flying, as he left the 56th to assume command of the 479FG, which was the last fighter group to become operational in the 8AF. On 30 October his P-51 was caught in a violent storm and he was forced to bail out, becoming a POW with 17 1/2 victories.

At this time, Maj. George Preddy was an 11 victory ace with the 487FS/352FG. Preddy won his wings just after Pearl Harbor, and by mid-January was on his way to Australia with 49FG. He flew combat and claimed two "damaged" before being returned to the States to recuperate from serious injuries suffered in a mid-air collision. By July 1943, he was in England flying P-47s for the 352FG. Preddy, too, was a slow starter, not getting his first victory until 1 December 1943 when he claimed a Me-109. On 29 January he downed a FW-190, but was hit by flak and forced to bail out over the English Channel. His wingman, Bill Whisner, led a RAF Walrus amphibian to Preddy to pick him up.

It seemed when the 352nd converted to the P-51 Mustang that Preddy began to score. This long-ranged fighter was able to penetrate deeper into Germany and take on large groups of Luftwaffe fighters waiting there. On 13 May he became an ace in his Mustang *"Cripes a Mighty"* with a double over Me-109s. Preddy recorded his best day of the war on 6 August, when he shot down six Me-109s. Of his combat tactics that day he said: "I just kept shooting and they kept falling." With 22 7/8 victories, Preddy was sent home as the leading active ETO ace.

He returned to combat with the 352nd in November, scoring two destroyed, one probable, and one damaged during the month. When the German Wehrmacht launched their Ardennes Campaign ("The Battle of the Bulge") in late December, the 352nd was moved to advanced bases in Belgium. On Christmas Day he tallied two Me-109s southwest of Koblenz. A FW-190 was seen coming in on deck, and Preddy dove after it. As he closed, friendly American AA batteries opened fire on the Focke-Wulf. Preddy flew into the fire and went into a desperate chandelle to clear the area. Part way through the maneuver Preddy's canopy blew off and his fighter plunged into the ground, killing its pilot with 26 7/8 victories, another challenger down.

Upon Preddy's death and the turn of the year Dave Schilling was back in the States after getting five victories (three Me-109s and two FW-190s) on 23 December to run his total to 22 1/2. Of the active aces at the time John Meyer, Preddy's stable mate at the 352nd, had 21 victories, and Ray Wetmore of the 370FS/359FG had 16 victories.

Meyer went on to down two German fighters on 1 January when the Luftwaffe launched "Operation Bodenplatte" against Allied airfields in Belgium. Several days later, Meyer was seriously injured in an automobile accident outside Paris. The mishap almost cost Meyer his leg and cut short his WWII combat flying. Remaining in the Air Force, he flew combat in the early Korean War as commander of the 4FIW, running his career total to 26 with two MiG-15 victories.

Wetmore downed a German during "Bodenplatte" and got 4 1/2 FW-190s on 14 January 1945. His final claim was a Me-163 rocket fighter on 15 March to run his total to 21 1/2. But there was little opportunity to increase victory totals, as the Luftwaffe was almost absent from the skies toward the end of the war.

By the time the war ended, Gabreski continued to hold the his lead at 28, and Robert Johnson would join him with the "damaged" upgrade, only to be demoted to 27 some years later into second place.

Debates will forever rage over the quality of the enemy in the Pacific and Europe. Politically and tactically the Allied strategy was to defeat Germany first, as she was considered the more dangerous enemy. The Japanese only needed to be contained short of Australia, and then a "bunch of islands held by inferior Orientals" could be liberated after Germany was subdued. The Luftwaffe was a quality force in men, materiel, and tactics until the later stages of the war in 1945. The Luftwaffe pilots in 1944 were certainly better pilots than the Japanese pilots, who were slaughtered in mass during the "Marianas Turkey Shoot," the Battle of Leyte Gulf, and then over Formosa and the Philippines. To beat the Luftwaffe was to beat the best.

Pacific Ace Races (USMC/USN/USAAF)

Part of the American psyche is its desire to rate the best; an inclination which is particularly evident on its sport's scene: baseball's batting and pitching leaders; football's running and passing heroes; and basketball's top-scorers and rebounders. This penchant extends beyond sports; witness the continual barrage of top ten lists, rating the most popular movies and recordings. So, in a time when heroes were needed, the veneration of the air ace was a natural extension of the number one nation's personality. The fighter pilot was an all American boy, fighting a chivalrous man-to-man war, and became the new star to the American public, who were accustomed to voluminous coverage of the famous.

The Pacific Theater air race began on the first day of the war when the Army Air Corps' 1Lt. George Welch of the 47th Pursuit Group quickly jumped into the lead by scoring four victories defending Pearl Harbor. Nine days later, on the other side of the Pacific, another AAC pilot, 1Lt. Boyd "Buzz" Wagner of the 17th Pursuit Group of the 5th Interceptor Command, became the first American ace when he destroyed a Japanese fighter taking off from a Philippines airdrome. Perhaps other victories and aces were made in these early days of the war, but they were lost in the general chaos and marginal communications of the times.

It was not until two months later on 20 February 1942, that America's second ace appeared, one whose spectacular "instant ace" feat could be savored by the American public. Navy 1Lt. Edward "Butch" O'Hare was credited with saving the carrier *Lexington* by intercepting the determined attack of eight Japanese bombers and single-handedly downing five of them. In April, O'Hare was returned to the States as a celebrated hero, who the media pursued across the country as he traveled to Washington to receive the Congressional Medal of Honor. His awarding of the medal was widely publicized, as his wife draped the ribbon around his neck in the presence of President Roosevelt. The hype surrounding O'Hare created the ace charisma that was to carry through the war.

It was only five days after O'Hare's victories (24 February) that 1Lt. George Kiser of the 17PS tied Wagner and O'Hare with five victories. Subsequently Kiser, flying P-40s over Java, destroyed three more enemy aircraft over the next two months to lead the ace race with eight.

"Buzz" Wagner, now a Major and Director of Fighters of the Fifth Fighter Command flying P-39s out of Port Moresby, got three victories, his last of the war, on 30 April 1942 to tie Kiser with eight.

In the skies over Guadalcanal, the Marine VMF's took on the superior Japanese Air Force that appeared every day. Maj. John Smith (L) of VMF-223 left as America's top scorer with 19 victories after battling squadronmate, Capt. Marion Carl (R) who ended with 16 1/2. In the center is 13 victory VMF-224 ace, Maj. Robert Galer who was awarded the CMH for his action there. (Author/Carl)

On 16 June, there was a new leader with nine victories—2Lt. Andrew Jackson Reynolds of the 49FG. Reynolds, who had flown in George Kiser's unit over Java, was flying P-40s for the 9FS out of Darwin, Australia, when his squadron intercepted 27 bombers escorted by 15 Zeros. Leading his flight, Reynolds found the enemy 30 miles west over Point Charles at 23,000 feet. Making diving attacks, he hit the #1 and #3 bombers, setting them on fire but only getting a "confirmed" on one. An errant bullet hit Reynolds' engine, damaging the lubricating and coolant systems. Reynolds was able to make a crash-landing on an auxiliary strip near Darwin.

The war and the ace race heated up as the Marines went ashore at Guadalcanal on 17 August 1942. There was no shortage of air targets for the beleaguered "Cactus Air Force," as it was dubbed ("Cactus" was the code for Guadalcanal). The Japanese dispatched land-based bombers, escorted by fighters, from its bastion at Rabaul some 600 miles to the northwest. To meet the Japanese threat, Marine Squadron VMF-223 was launched from the carrier *Long Island* to reinforce Henderson Field on 20 August. The group had recently exchanged its deficient F2A Brewster Buffalos for the chubby F4F Grumman Wildcat. The –223 CO was an "old" veteran of 27 years; John L. Smith, who was a former Army artillery man-cum-dive bomber pilot. Smith, newly promoted Major, was assessed (probably rightly so) as an ambitious, arrogant, and generally difficult individual. Joining Smith was an easy-going Oregonian, Marion Carl, who had served with VMF-221 at Midway, where he scored his first victory, and Montanan 2Lt. Eugene Trowbridge. The squadron had been at Henderson Field for less than 24 hours when they scrambled to meet six Zeros over Iron Bottom Sound. In the air battle, Smith got one Zero, while Trowbridge got two confirmed. The next day Trowbridge added another Jap to his total. On 24 August, VMF-223 got into the carrier battles between the *Saratoga* and *Enterprise* and the Japanese carrier *Ryujo*, which was escorting transport-carrying reinforcements. In the skirmish, Carl got two Kate bombers and two Zeros to make him the Marine Corps' first ace. Trowbridge got two Japanese (unconfirmed) to become an unconfirmed ace. In the next 15 days Carl got eight more victories to become the war's first double ace, totaling 13. During this time both Smith and Trowbridge became double aces with ten victories each. The big day in this period was 30 August, when 18 experienced Japanese Naval pilots from the carriers *Shokaku* and *Zuikaku* headed toward Cactus. The scrambled Wildcats gained the altitude advantage on the Hamps, which enabled Smith to shoot down four while Carl got three. The good hunting continued for Smith, as during the four days from 10-13 September he got four bombers and a fighter to put him in the ace race lead with a triple ace total of 16. Marion Carl was shot down on 9 September when an unnoticed Zero set his F4F on fire and forced him to bail out. Carl missed five days of combat getting back to base, and in the process allowed Smith to gain the lead. When Brig.Gen. Roy Geiger was told that Carl was safe, he asked to meet the young ace. During the meeting, in jest, Geiger informed Carl that Smith now had 16 victories to his 13 and asked, "What are you going to do about that?" Without hesitation, Carl replied, "Damn it, General, ground Smitty for five days." But Carl was never able to catch Smith, even though Smith, too, was shot down. On 2 September Smith was bounced by three Zeros. He managed to flame one, but the odds forced Smith to make a forced dead stick landing. After months of difficult times on the ground and in the air, the final ace standing was Smith 19, Carl 16 1/2. Carl subsequently returned to combat in December 1943, flying F4U Corsairs over New Britain and adding two more victories. When VMF-223 was rotated out of combat in mid-October from Guadalcanal, only six of the original twenty pilots who left Hawaii in July remained. Upon their departure on 12 October, the squadron claimed 110 victories, including 47 Zeros. Smith and Carl, with eight and ten bomber victories, respectively, shot down more multi-engine bombers than any other Marine pilots. The VMF-223 roster showed eight aces in its ranks. Smith was awarded the Congressional Medal of Honor for his tactical skills and leadership qualities.

VMF-223 was replaced by VMF-121, which was commanded by Maj. "Duke" Davis and his XO, another old man at 27 years old named Joseph Jacob Foss, who was to succeed Smith as the top ace. The initial meeting between Smith and the 20 new pilots of VMF-121 was inauspicious, to say the least. The ever-sardonic Smith met the group as they landed at Henderson and sarcastically apprised them of the fact that they had landed at the wrong field! The Marine fighter strip was over there. So VMF-121, which would become the top Marine unit of the war, humbly got back into their Wildcats and flew another 1/2 mile to begin their war.

The scope of the Pacific war had narrowed to Guadalcanal, and the media people had congregated there. It was easier to interview a flier over a beer at Henderson Field behind the lines than brave the dangers and discomforts of a foxhole. Besides, fliers made good copy, as generally most were intelligent, loquacious, and exuded an aura of dash and bravura. The affable Foss, a graduate of the state university of his native South Dakota, made good copy. But his skills in the F4F Wildcat spoke for him. He shot down 26 Japanese aircraft, 20 of which were the maneuverable Zeros, which were still flown by experienced pilots. His rapid assault on Eddie Rickenbacker's WWI American record of 26 enemies (which included five balloons, two tethered) took only three months, and the record, once tied, made Foss a national hero. A marksman from his hunting days as a farm boy carried over to his aerial gunnery expertise, both as an instructor at Pensacola and as a fighter pilot. Foss' first 23 victories were compressed into 33 days, scoring daily victories at first and then scoring multiple daily victories seven times during his first tour. He also crash landed six times, but credited the rugged F4F and his protecting wingman, Lt. Thomas Furlow, for his survival.

Foss' first sortie was almost his last. During the afternoon of 30 October, while leading three divisions of Wildcats against 15 incoming Betty bombers, Foss suddenly found himself left alone when his fellow VMF-121 pilots dove to evade Jap Zeros diving from above. The first eager Zero pilot overshot Foss and presented himself as an easy target as Foss' first victory. In the battle Foss' P & W engine was hit and lost oil, causing Foss to sweat out reaching Henderson safely. The mission earned Foss the nickname "Swivel Neck Joe"; Foss learned the hard way that a fighter pilot must constantly look out for bounces. Foss became an ace in less than a week when he got two Zeros and a bomber on 18 October. His

biggest days came on the 23rd when he downed four Zeros, and on the 25th when he became the first Marine Corps pilot to become an ace in a day. On the 25th on his morning mission, as his flight was climbing after takeoff it was bounced by diving Zeros. By skillful flying the Marines escaped and Foss got two Zeros. On his afternoon mission he got three more Japanese to give five victories for the day and 16 in 13 days. On 7 November, he downed a Zero and two float planes that were covering a Japanese convoy 120 miles NW of Henderson. These victories tied Foss with John Smith for top gun in the Pacific with 19. But the celebration had to wait, as Foss ran out of gas while getting lost in a thunder squall. He ditched off Malaita and spent the night with a coast watcher before boarding a PBY bound for Cactus the next morning.

On 12 November, the Japanese made earnest attempts to bloody the American reinforcement of Guadalcanal by Adm. Kelly Turner's troop transports. Flying CAP at 29,000 feet, Foss and six other VMF-121 pilots spotted approximately 20 torpedo-carrying Bettys running in on Turner's vulnerable transports, which were unloading off Kukum Point. Going into power dives from their high altitude,

Capt. Joe Foss (VMF-121) left Guadalcanal with the Medal of Honor and as America's leading ace having tied Eddie Rickenbacker's WW-1 record of 26. ((USMC)

Foss' men found their windscreens frosted over. To make matters worse for Foss, the increased pressure of his dive blew his canopy off. The Bettys were closing on the transports, and the Wildcats, abetted by some Army P-400s, were desperately trying to catch them from astern. Wind howling around him, Foss fired within 100 yards of a bomber, hitting its starboard engine and causing it to crash into the sea. The determined American pilots disrupted the harried Japanese attack, and little damage was done to the transports. While chasing a fleeing bomber, Foss was bounced by a Zero. He quickly turned into the attack, and the surprised Jap became the victim of an expert snap deflection shot. Foss returned to the fray, flaming his previous interrupted target. This three victory mission made Foss the first American to score 20 victories in the war. The next day he got a Pete float plane for victim #23. As were most – 121 personnel, Foss was racked by malaria and dysentery, dropping his weight from 197 to 160 lbs. The squadron was sent on a well-earned R & R to New Caledonia and Sydney.

Upon recuperating, Foss, three victories short of Rickenbacker's 26, returned to a secured Guadalcanal. The crisis had passed, and the American Air Forces would become the hunters. In the afternoon of 3 January 1943, Foss' outfit and a few Army P-39s escorted Dauntless dive bombers, which were to finish off a Japanese destroyer force near New Georgia. Upon approaching the enemy warships, three Wildcats led by Bill Marontate dove on Zeros that were on CAP, while Foss and three others circled at altitude. The air battle moved upwards, as Foss fired a short burst, missing a fleeing Zero. He turned to help Oscar Bate shake some Zeros off his tail. As Foss turned, a Jap fighter dove in front of him and was dispatched in an explosion, as Foss' .50 caliber bullets hit him. Quickly another Zero on the tail of another Wildcat dove in front of Foss, who snapped off a few hasty but highly effective rounds that sent the enemy into a flaming spin. Bate's persistent attacker was only a 100 yards astern and lining up a fatal firing run. Foss dove and began desperately firing at the Jap at long range, persuading him to break off his attack on Bate. The Zero then pulled up and came head on at Foss. Both pilots fired and missed, passed each other, and both again turned into each other, with Foss above and the Jap below. Both adversaries were on a nerve-racking head on firing run when the Jap gave in and broke right, allowing Foss to put machine gun rounds into his cockpit area. The tenacious Jap broke into a dive, circling back toward Foss, who was being menaced by approaching Zeros. Foss broke off and headed for the safety of nearby clouds. Just as he entered the clouds Foss saw his wounded Jap burst into flames and head down. Foss had gotten his 26th victory to tie Rickenbacker's record of 25 years.

On 26 January 1943, VMF-121 left Guadalcanal and flew island hopping to New Zealand. The squadron sailed for America on 25 March and landed in San Diego on 19 April. On the long voyage Foss almost died of his on-going malaria, and was in poor physical condition to meet the hectic schedule that was awaiting him. After initial appearances in Washington and New York, the Marine Corps had scheduled a nationwide tour for him. The exhausting, well-publicized tour was interrupted by a visit to his Sioux Falls home, and on 18 May by the presentation of the Congressional Medal of Honor. Accompanied by his mother and wife, June, Foss was per-

sonally awarded the medal by F.D.R. Twice, in fact, so the photographers could get all their pictures. The frantic agenda continued, as Foss was to remain the top ace for nearly 15 months. But even before he left the Solomons, new and superior American fighters were appearing over the battlefront. The Army Air Force's twin-boomed Lockheed P-38 Lightning had arrived in the Solomons and New Guinea. It would not be too long before Foss would be reading in his morning newspaper of the exploits of such new aces as Tommy Lynch, Neel Kearby, and a young, unassuming midwesterner named Richard Ira Bong.

P-38s were shipped to the SWPA in late summer 1942, but numerous mechanical problems postponed combat duty. Finally, at mid-day on 27 December 1942, 12 P-38s of the 39FS under Capt. Thomas Lynch left 14 Mile Drome, New Guinea, to meet a formation of more than two dozen Japanese bombers and escorts heading toward Buna Mission. Lynch destroyed two Ki-43 Oscar escorts to become an ace. Previously, Lynch had bagged three Zeros while flying the P-400 (export P-39) in May 1942 over New Guinea. Also scoring a double that day was Dick Bong, who was on temporary duty from the 9FS. Thus began another ace derby, but one which appeared as though it might be rather one sided. On 31 December, Bong fired on six Japanese aircraft, gaining only one "probable" and a large amount of expended ammunition. Bong became an ace on an anti-shipping attack on Lae Harbor on 8 January 1943 when he splashed an Oscar in a diving attack. During this time Bong flew on Lynch's wing and the two developed a close rivalry based on their friendship. Lynch excelled as a combat pilot and leader, and was genuinely admired by his men. Bong was modest and reserved on the ground, but was a Mr. Hyde in the air. He came to the Pacific with a flying attitude which bordered on undisciplined. Lynch's influence put restraints on Bong's enthusiasm and directed them into life-preserving aerial tactics.

The next combat for the two occurred in March when the group escorted B-17s against well-protected Japanese shipping in Huon Harbor. It was during this time that Bong surpassed Lynch in victories. By mid-April Bong had scored his tenth victory to become the AAF's first double ace in the Pacific: Bong 10 and Lynch 9. Lynch tied Bong on 8 May and went ahead again on 10 June (11 to 10) by downing a bomber. Then Bong tied him two days later when he got an Oscar. On 26 August, Bong had the biggest single day of his career when he encountered 20 enemy fighters over Markham Valley, south of Lae. In 20 minutes Bong had two Tonys and two Zeros to register his 16th victory and collected a few bullet holes and the DSC.

Bong went on leave to Brisbane, Australia, in August. When he returned, his missions in September were unfruitful, and his victory total remained at 16. Meanwhile, Lynch, losing weight and becoming exhausted from the effects of Dengue Fever, managed to score five single daily victories to creep into to a tie with Bong. Lynch was sent back to his Pennsylvania home and wife, Rosemary, to recuperate. The long leave put him out of the race for the time being, as he did not return to combat until early January 1944. While Lynch was gone Bong found slim pickings and only scored five victories to increase his total to 21. This total made him America's third ranking ace, behind the Marine Corps' Foss with

26 and Pappy Boyington with 25. There is some controversy over Boyington's career total, as during his tour with the AVG Flying Tigers he was credited with six victories. But later inquiries found that four of those victories were on ground targets, which were accepted and bonused by Chennault as victories.

Bong also was sent on leave, so both of America's leading aces were on the home front. Bong did extensive PR work, which was well covered by the media. While back home in Poplar, Wisconsin, Bong was asked to crown the Home-Coming Queen of Wisconsin State Teacher's College, Marjorie Vattendahl, and it was love at first sight. When he returned to combat, the infatuated Bong's P-38 would bear the name "*Marge*."

During the months that Lynch and Bong were gone, a Marine Lieutenant would make one of the most spectacular and concentrated victory runs of the war. In 17 days and only six missions, 1Lt. Robert Hanson would earn his nickname "Butcher Bob." In January 1944, he tallied an incredible 20 Japanese aircraft to threaten Foss, Bong, and Rickenbacker. Hanson was born in Lucknow, India, of missionary parents. After Pearl Harbor he left Hamline College in Minnesota to enter Navy flight training in May 1942, and

Cdr. David McCampbell of VF-15 had a 9 victory and 7 victory day on his way to becoming the Navy's top scorer and the third ranking American ace with 34 victories. (Author/McCampbell)

earned his wings in mid-February 1943. In June he was flying F4U Corsairs for Marine Squadron VMF-215 in the northern Solomons. Hanson was credited with only five victories in his first two combat tours in 1943.

On 1 November 1943, the American landings on Bougainville were taking place, and Hanson was flying CAP for Lt.Col. Herbert Williamson's VMF-215. He spotted six torpedo-carrying Kates heading low over Empress Augusta Bay toward the American fleet. Hanson dove through the formation, getting two and breaking up the attack. A Japanese rear-gunner hit Hanson's Corsair, forcing a ditching. The wet Marine spent several hours floating on a life raft before a destroyer picked him up.

Hanson's next big day occurred on 14 January 1944. He and his wingman, 2Lt. Richard Bowman, were escorting Navy TBF Avenger torpedo bombers over Simpson Harbor, Rabaul. Spotting 60-70 Japanese Zeros, Hanson's group went into a swirling, cloud-to-cloud dogfight. Hanson became separated from Bowman and got five enemy fighters in the clash, making him a double ace and earning him the sobriquet "Master of Individual Combat." On his next two sorties over Rabaul (20 and 22 January) he got one and three victories to total 14. On the 24th, he again became separated from his squadron and was surrounded by Zeros. Aggressive tactics saved his life and added four more victories and a probable to his total. On the 26th he got three, and on the 30th four more to give him 25, 20 of them over Rabaul.

On 3 January, the day before his 24th birthday and near the end of his tour, Hanson took off on an escort and strafing mission to New Ireland, north of Rabaul. On a strafing run on gun emplacements on Cape St. George, apparently ground fire killed him, as his guns ceased firing. His Corsair crossed the target area, slowly lost altitude, and crashed into the sea with 25 Jap flags under its cockpit. On 24 January, Maj.Gen. Lewis G. Merritt presented the Congressional Medal of Honor to Hanson's mother for his actions on 1 November 1943. Hanson was the third Corsair pilot to win the CMH (with Greg Boyington and Ken Walsh), and was the top-scoring Corsair pilot (Boyington 22, Walsh 21, and Don Aldrich 20).

Hanson was not the only pilot to take advantage of Bong and Lynch during their R&R. A 32-year-old Texan, Col. Neel Kearby, CO of the 348 FG, ran his total up to 20 victories in four months. The 348th, a P-47 Thunderbolt group, was slated to go to Europe, but Gen. George Kenney, commander of the 5AF, used his influence to divert them to his command. The seven-ton P-47 was an unproven entity in the Pacific, being considered too big and heavy to successfully engage the light and maneuverable Zero. It was fitted with the most powerful aircraft engine in the world, the 2,000hp Pratt & Whitney R-2800 radial, which gave it a high operational ceiling and a great diving speed. Its rugged construction and heavy armament could be used to advantage, but the P-38 remained the favorite in the theater. The 348th shared the Dobodura airfield with the 9FS and their P-38s. Constant speculation and arguments broke out over the relative merits of each aircraft. Shortly before Bong went on leave, Kearby scheduled several mock dogfights, pitting his P-47s against the seasoned P-38 pilots. But the results were mixed, perhaps with the edge going to the P-38, and only fueled the controversy.

On 1 October 1943, Kearby distinguished himself and the P-47 by destroying six Japanese aircraft in one mission. Flying "*Fiery Ginger*" in a sweep over Jap airfields at Borum, Kearby destroyed two Zekes, two Tonys, and two Haps. These victories, when added to his previous three made him an ace plus. For this action Kearby was awarded the Congressional Medal of Honor, which he personally received from Gen. MacArthur in Brisbane, Australia, on 24 January 1944. By that time he had achieved 21 victories to tie Bong, despite heavy staff duties at 5AF HQ. When Kenney queried Kearby on his combat ambitions, the ace set 50 as his goal. On 5 March, while shooting down a Nell bomber, Kearby neglected to watch his tail and was shot down by an Oscar. Kearby's total ended at 22 to supposedly tie Bong, but Kearby never knew that Bong had scored two victories two days previously to bring his total to 24.

Throughout the years accusations of favoritism have arisen concerning Gen. Kenney's treatment of Bong. Kenney's sugary biography *Dick Bong, Ace of Aces*, written in 1960, tends to confirm these allegations, as did the 5AF commander's book *General Kenney Reports* (Duell, Sloan, Pearce, NY, 1949). It is filled with references to the Bong-Lynch-Kearby and the later Bong-McGuire ace races. For instance, in December 1942 Kenney commented to Brig. Gen. Gus Whitehead: "Watch that boy Bong. There is the top American ace of aces of this war. He just started to work today." Throughout the book Kenney mentions the ace races and which pilots were closing in on Bong. Kenney went so far as to have a diver confirm Bong's "probable" of 12 April 1944, which had gone into the water off Hollandia. This victory was the Oscar that gave him #28 of his triple when he broke Rickenbacker's record. Kenney refers to Bong as a "tow-headed cherub." Kenney also had an evident fondness for Tommy Lynch, but neutrality toward the hard-working, business-like Kearby. When Lynch and Bong returned to combat Kenney had his three top aces—Bong, Lynch, and Kearby—assigned to the V Fighter Command in HQ positions. Kenney allowed Lynch and Bong to fly as a duo, which they christened the "Flying Circus." Unlike Kearby, their deskwork was limited, and they were allowed to fly missions at their discretion. They could accompany other squadrons on bomber escort missions or fly sweeps as a team. They were assigned personal P-38s, stripped down for combat. Bong named his fighter "*Marge*," while Lynch's carried no personal markings. Kenney was very PR conscious, as he felt that the Pacific Army Air Forces were being treated as the war's stepchild when compared to the 8AF in Europe. He gave both Lynch and Bong free rein so that their victory totals would keep his command in the public eye. This was especially evident as Rickenbacker's record was coming into reach. The "Flying Circus" scored its first victory on 10 February on a sweep of Tadji airfields when Lynch got a Lily bomber. The two aces continued to score victories, with Bong closing in on Rickenbacker with 24 and Lynch with 20. After celebrating Lynch's promotion to light Colonel the previous evening, the morning of 8 March saw the two sweep the New Guinea coast looking for targets. While strafing luggers and barges, Lynch's P-38 was hit by small arms fire at wave top level. With the aircraft's nose damaged and right engine on fire, Lynch attempted to bail out at 100 feet, but his parachute failed to open completely and he fell to his death. In three days Kenney had lost two-thirds (Lynch and

Kearby) of his ace race. He ordered Bong to Australia to ferry a new P-38 back to New Guinea, but more importantly to compose himself after the death of two of his boys. Bong flew eight missions before obeying the order at the end of March.

Returning to combat on 3 April, Bong got an Oscar in two firing passes over Sentani Lake to give him his 25th. Joe Foss and Pappy Boyington were tied with Rickenbacker with 26. Again, Boyington had 20 victories with the 5AF and six with the AVG (later downgraded down to two). Boyington's three victories on 3 January 1944 were unknown at this time, as both he and his wingman were shot down, and confirmation would not be made until after the war, when Boyington was released from a Jap POW camp. Earlier on a visit to the 5 AF Rickenbacker promised a case of whiskey to the first pilot to break his record. But now Bong, a non-drinker, was the only challenger.

On 12 April, 20 P-38s of the crack 80FS "Headhunters" were flying escort for B-24s over Hollandia. Flying without a wingman and free-lancing like the pilots of WWI, Bong attached himself to Capt. C.M. Smith's flight as a "tail end Charlie." Bong was flying a loaner aircraft "*Down Beat*" when his flight arrived over the target area at 1145 and was intercepted by 12 to 15 Jap fighters in groups of three or four. In the next 45 minutes Bong destroyed three Oscars to give him the record. He knew he had several eyewitness confirmations of at least two of the victories, but became worried upon landing when he found he had set his gun cameras wrong. By the next morning, two official victory confirmations were received, with the third Oscar listed as a "probable." This probable was later confirmed as a victory by Kenney, who dispatched a diver to the area to find the wreck. Kenney immediately promoted Bong to major, and also grounded him to be sent back to the States as a celebrity, being heralded in the newspapers, radio, and newsreels. Much of Bong's five-month leave was filled with public relation and war bond sales appearances. He flew a P-38 over towns and cities, meeting dignitaries, making uncomfortable speeches, and

Joe Foss (VMF-121) had tied Eddie Rickenbacker's American WWI record of 26 victories on 15 January 1943. Richard Bong (R) is shown here with Rickenbacker after he broke the record on 12 April 1944. (USAF)

attending breakfasts, luncheons, and dinners. Also during the time Bong, a self-confessed poor shot (27 victories in 25 combats, indicating few multiple victories), attended gunnery school. The leave time was made easier by his visits with his family and his engagement to Marge. Bong feared he, like Foss, would be pulled from combat forever. But at gunnery school Bong heard of Kenney's intention to have him learn and then serve as a gunnery instructor and "observer" in combat areas, and be allowed only to shoot in "self-defense."

At the time Bong broke the record the next challenger, a Navy flier, had not yet flown a mission! In fact, for naval aviators, the opportunities to score against the Japanese had been scarce. The large early naval battles at Midway and the Coral Sea, unlike the later great battles, did not pit vast numbers of aircraft against aircraft. During the Guadalcanal campaign, the Navy needed to be prudent in exposing its few remaining carriers and their aircraft to superior Japanese forces. The high scorer for the Navy at the end of January 1944 was Lt. Stanley Vejtasa of VF-10 with only 10 1/2 victories. Vejtasa scored seven of these victories in one day, way back on 26 October 1942 during the Battle of Santa Cruz. He was the first of six aces to score seven victories in one day. Flying a Wildcat for VF-10 (the "Grim Reapers") off the carrier *Enterprise*, Vejtasa joined his CO, the redoubtable Jim Flatley, on CAP when a large wave of Japanese torpedo bombers attached the U.S. fleet. In the battle Vejtasa destroyed two Aichi Val dive-bombers and five Nakajima Kate torpedo bombers. Previously, Vejtasa had three victories while flying a Dauntless dive-bomber, and these victories made him the leading Navy ace for 15 months.

It was not until early 1944 that Vejtasa was challenged. In October 1943 VF-17, called "Blackburn's Irregulars" after their commander, Tommy Blackburn, landed their F4U Corsairs at Ondonga, New Georgia. Their assignment was to protect Navy shipping and attack enemy land and maritime targets. On 11 November 1943, Ens. Ira Kepford was flying top cover for a task force which included two carriers, *Essex* and *Bunker Hill*. A mixed group of 30 Japanese dive and torpedo bombers attacked the carriers in Empress Augusta Bay, off Bougainville in the Solomons. Diving through intense AA fire, Kepford destroyed three Vals and a Kate and damaged another to win the Navy Cross. It was not until 27 January 1944 that he became an ace when he got two Zeros on an escort mission on Tobaro airbase, Rabaul. In the next 24 days Kepford would score 12 victories, including four on his next mission on 29 January. Kepford scored 16 quick victories before he was shipped back to the States as the Navy's leading ace.

The Navy's next top ace was Lt. Alexander Vraciu, the son of Rumanian immigrants. He gained his first victory on 5 October 1943 during the raid on Wake Island. He was an element leader in one-time leading Navy ace Butch O'Hare's Fighting Six when he got a Zero. The carrier raids on the Gilberts in November and Kwajalein in January 1944 netted him four Betty bombers to make him an ace. The carrier strike on the Carolines on 17 February got him four more victories to give him nine. VF-6 headed home, but Vraciu managed to transfer to VF-16 aboard the *Lexington*. He scored three victories before his biggest career day during the "Great Mariana's Turkey Shoot" on 19 June 1944. That day he destroyed

six Judy dive-bombers in eight minutes. The next afternoon he claimed a Zeke for his 19th and last victory to lead the Navy.

During the "Turkey Shoot" when Vraciu scored his six, another Navy pilot got seven. He was Cdr. David McCampbell, another "old man" at 34. The Annapolis graduate from Alabama was the AGC of VF-15 on the carrier *Essex*. The "Fabled 15" was to be in almost continuous combat for five months (mid-June to mid-November 1944), participating in the greatest air-sea battles in history: the Battle of the Philippines Sea (Turkey Shoot) and Battle of Leyte Gulf. In these massive air battles McCampbell was able to grab victories in large chunks. During two missions during the Turkey Shoot (19 June) he destroyed five Judys in the morning and then got two Zekes in the afternoon to make him an ace with nine victories. On 12 September he got four, the next day he got three, and by the 24th he had tied Vraciu with 19. The evening of 24 October 1944 would see the end of the greatest victory in naval aviation history: a total of 270 Japanese aircraft had been destroyed, and nine Navy fliers had scored five or more victories in a single day.

One of these aces in a day was McCampbell, who would get credit for five Zekes, two Oscars, two Hamps, and two probables, while his wingman, Roy Rushing, would get six. These nine victo-

The race for "Ace of Aces" boiled down to two contenders, Dick Bong (L) and Tommy McGuire (R). Bong would leave the theater with 40 victories and McGuire would lose his life in his quest to beat Bong with 38 victories. (USAF)

ries would give him 30 to tie him with Bong. Since so many victories came so fast for McCampbell, and since Bong regained the lead three days later, the tie was never publicized, and it is virtually unknown even today. In November McCampbell got four more victories to give him a career 34 and the Congressional Medal of Honor. But Bong had 36 at the time, and McCampbell was headed back to the States. In any event, the press, which created and perpetuated the ace race, was more interested in a new, brash, and self-proclaimed pretender to Bong's title: Capt. Thomas McGuire of the 475FG/5AF.

While Bong was on his five month leave from April to October 1944, McGuire, whose trade mark was his old, beat up officer's dress hat, was closing in on Bong's 28 with 21 of his own. McGuire made his intentions known that he was out to pass Bong. McGuire's flying skills were unquestioned, but his contemporaries almost unanimously disliked the man. He was variously described as a "pain in the ass," "self-centered," "abrasive," "constantly pulling rank," "certainly no intellectual," and "constantly running off at the mouth." Perhaps something can be read into the man's personality by the name painted on the nose of his P-38, "Pudgy," an intimate nickname for his wife, Marilyn.

When Bong returned he continued to fly "observation missions" to oversee the results of his gunnery lectures. In "self-defense" he managed to shoot down enough Japs to always keep McGuire's total about ten behind:

October 1944	Bong 5 (33)	McGuire 3 (24)
November 1944	Bong 3 (36)	McGuire 3 (27)
December 1944	Bong 4 (40)	McGuire 3 (30)

Bong flew only nine missions in November and December, as Kenney was afraid he would lose his Ace of Aces. On 28 November Capt. John Davis, while flying Bong's P-38, had its engine catch fire and crashed on take off, killing the pilot. At first it was thought Bong was in the aircraft, but the incident caused Kenney to resolve to remove Bong from combat after his 40th victory.

As McGuire often publicly asserted his intention to pass Bong, it was surprising that Bong chose McGuire's 431FG as his next assignment, and then chose to room with McGuire! On 7 December, McGuire was leading a flight, which had Bong leading the second element over Ormac Bay. McGuire came back with two victories but gained no ground on Bong, as he matched that deuce. On 12 December, Bong was away receiving the Congressional Medal of Honor from MacArthur and McGuire was chattering away to the press after he narrowed Bong's lead to eight with a victory over a Jack fighter on the 13th. Bong returned to down an Oscar on the 15th.

On the 17th Bong logged his 40th and last victory. He left Delag airstrip at 1450, climbing to 9,000 feet and leading a sweep over the Mindoro beachhead. At 1615 he spotted two incoming Oscars at 12 o'clock and dropped his auxiliary fuel tanks to climb towards the Japs, who were fleeing north toward home. The chase lasted ten minutes, as Bong closed astern on the frantically evading Jap. Bong fired and flamed the Jap, who crashed into the jungle. Kenney immediately ordered Bong to go off operations. On 29 December, he boarded an Air Transport Command C-54, heading home for marriage and a career as a jet test pilot. McGuire was the leading active ace with 32 victories.

Now unopposed and no longer frustrated by matching victories, McGuire became almost obsessed with the record. On Christmas morning, McGuire led a volunteer mission escorting B-24s that were to bomb Mobalcat. McGuire got three Zeros before his guns malfunctioned. Despite being virtually defenseless, the frustrated McGuire continued to attack enemy fighters, supposedly "forcing them into his wingman's line of fire." The next day, he volunteered again for a B-24 escort mission over Clark Field. He lured three Zeros off a crippled B-24, and with remarkable flying skill and marksmanship he got two to run his score to 38. Eager to fly, McGuire was upset by Kenney's order not to fly any more missions until further notified that Bong had arrived in the States and had completed the planned ceremonies to honor him as the Ace of Aces. Kenney did not want Bong to be second before reaching America. The impatient McGuire, beset with malaria and incipient battle fatigue, was forced to remain inactive until 7 January, when Kenney lifted the ban. ASAP, McGuire led a four-ship element from Dulag in marginal weather for a sweep over Japanese airfields at Fabrica and Manapla on the Los Negros Islands. Flying under the low overcast at 1,400 feet, McGuire's wingman, Capt. Edwin Weaver, spotted a solitary Ki-84 Oscar returning to Fabrica below the P-38s. McGuire pulled around, but the experienced Jap pilot turned into the American formation. The Oscar fired on McGuire's #3, Lt. Douglas Thropp. McGuire ordered the unit not to release their drop tanks, which was a violation of combat doctrine for the situation. Perhaps, McGuire felt he could score an easy victory over the lone Oscar and save fuel to resume further combat. The aggressive Oscar continued his concerted attack, closing in on the inexperienced Weaver. McGuire turned to catch the enemy, putting his Lightning on the verge of a stall to help his wingman. The added stress on the wing tanks caused the P-38 to go into a full stall, snap rolling, inverting at 200 feet, and diving into the jungle. At 0708, 7 January 1945, the American WWII Ace Race was over, marked by a huge fireball in the Philippine jungle and several footnotes. There were no serious challengers in Europe. The challengers either were rotated home or were POWs. The Luftwaffe posed no threat and gave the replacements no opportunity. In the Pacific the Japanese air forces had expended their frontline pilots and fighters, and only the kamikazes over Okinawa would provide targets, but not in sufficient numbers. David McCampbell flew no further combat. Dick Bong married Marge on 10 February 1945 and was killed testing the P-80 jet fighter on 6 August 1945, just days before the dropping of the Atomic Bomb and the end of the war. Thomas McGuire was awarded the Congressional Medal of Honor on 7 March 1945.

Victory #	Pilot Name and Rank	Total	A/C	Unit	Date
0.5	Shahan, 2Lt. Elza	1/2	P-38	27FS/1FG	8/14/42
0.5	Shaffer, 2Lt. Joseph	1/2	P-39	33FS/IAC	8/14/42
1	Junkin, 2lt. Samuel	1	Spit.	309FS/31FG	8/19/42
1.5	Shaffer, 2Lt. Joseph	1.5	P-39	33FS/IAC	10/18/42
2	Anderson, 1Lt. Stanley	3	Spit.	334FS/4FG	1/14/43
3	Anderson, 1Lt. Stanley	3	Spit.	334FS/4FG	1/22/43
3	London, Capt. Charles	5	P-47	83FS/78FG	6/29/43
4	Beeson, 1Lt. Duane	17.33	P-47	334FS/4FG	7/28/43
4-5	London, Capt. Charles	5	P-47	83FS/78FG	7/30/43
5-6	Roberts, Maj. Eugene	9	P-47	84FS/78FG	8/24/43
6	Mahurin, Capt. Walker *	19.75	P-47	63FS/56FG	10/4/43
6	Beeson, 1Lt. Duane	17.33	P-47	334FS/4FG	10/8/43
7-8	Roberts, Maj. Eugene	9	P-47	84FS/78FG	10/10/43
9	Roberts, Maj. Eugene	9	P-47	84FS/78FG	10/20/43
9	Beckham, Capt. Walter	18	P-47	351FS/352FG	11/11/43
10-10.5	Mahurin, Capt. Walker	19.75	P-47	63FS/56FG	11/26/43
11.5	Mahurin, Capt. Walker	19.75	P-47	63FS/56FG	11/29/43
12.5-13.5	Mahurin, Capt. Walker	19.75	P-47	63FS/56FG	12/22/43
14.5	Mahurin, Capt. Walker	19.75	P-47	63FS/56FG	1/30/44
15-16	Beckham, Capt. Walter	18	P-47	351FS/352FG	2/3/44
17-18	Beckham, Capt. Walter	18	P-47	351FS/352FG	2/8/44
18.5-19.5	Mahurin, Capt. Walker	19.75	P-47	63FS/56FG	3/8/44
20-22	Johnson, 1Lt. Robert	27	P-47	61FS/56FG	3/15/44
23	Johnson, 1Lt. Robert	27	P-47	61FS/56FG	4/9/44
24-25	Johnson, 1Lt. Robert	27	P-47	61FS/56FG	4/13/44
26-27	Johnson, Capt. Robert	27	P-47	61FS/56FG	5/8/44
27	Gabreski, Lt.Col. Francis	28	P-47	61FS/56FG	6/27/44
28	Johnson, Capt. Robert	27	P-47	61FS/56FG	6/44 **
28	Gabreski, Lt.Col. Francis	28	P-47	61FS/56FG	7/5/44

*Mahurin's PTO victory not included.

**15 March 44, "damaged" upgraded to destroyed in June 1944, but post-war Johnson's total was downgraded to 27.

MTO Victory Chronology

Victory #	Pilot Name and Rank	Total	A/C	Unit	Date
1	Mount, 1Lt. William	1	P-40	64FS/57FG	10/9/42
2	Whittaker, 1Lt. Roy	7	P-40	65FS/57FG	10/2742
2	Wymond, 1Lt. Gilbert	3	P-40	65FS/57FG	10/27/42
3	Middleditch, 1Lt. Lyman	5	P-40	64FS/57FG	10/27/42
4-5*	Lusk, 1Lt. Virgil	6	P-38	49FS/14FG	11/24/42
	or Smith, 1Lt. Virgil	5	P-38	94FS/14FG	12/12/42
5.5	Ilfrey, 1Lt. Jack	5.5	P-38	94FS/1FG	3/3/43
6	Chase, Maj. Levi	10	P-40	60FS/33FG	3/30/43
7-8	Momyer, Lt.Col. William	8	P-40	33FG/HQ	3/31/43
9-10	Chase, Maj. Levi	10	P-40	60FS/33FG	4/5/43
11	Sloan, 1Lt. William	12	P-38	96FS/82FG	7/10/43
12	Sloan. 1Lt. William	12	P-38	96FS/82FG	7/22/43
13	Green, Maj. Herschel	18	P-47	317FS/325FG	4/7/44
14	Green, Maj. Herschel	18	P-47	317FS/325FG	6/13/44
15	Green, Maj. Herschel	18	P-51	317FS/325FG	6/23/44
15	Brown, Maj. Samuel	15.5	P-51	307FS/31FG	6/26/44
16	Green, Maj. Herschel	18	P-51	317FS/325FG	7/9/44
17	Green, Maj. Herschel	18	P-51	317FS/325FG	7/14/44
17	Varnell, Capt. James	17	P-51	2FS/52FG	8/4/44
18	Green, Maj. Herschel	18	P-51	317FS/325FG	8/23/44
19-21	Voll, Capt. John	21	P-51	308FS/31FG	11/16/44

*In question: See P-38 First MTO Ace

Pacific Ace Race Chronology

Victory #	Pilot Name and Rank	A/C	Service	Unit	Date
1-4	Welch, 2Lt. George	P-40	USAAC	47PS	12/7/41
5	Wagner, 1Lt. Boyd	P-40	USAAC	17PS	12/16/41
5	O'Hare, Lt. Edward	F4F	USN	VF-3	2/20/42
5	Kiser, 1Lt. George	P-40	USAAC	17PS	2/24/42
6-8	Kiser, 1Lt. George	P-40	USAAC	17PS	4/27/42
8	Wagner, Maj. Boyd	P-39	USAAC	5FC	4/30/42
9	Reynolds, 2Lt. Andrew	P-40	USAAC	9FS	7/30/42
9-11	Carl, Capt. Marion	F4F	USMC	VMF-223	8/30/42
12-13	Carl, Capt. Marion	F4F	USMC	VMF-223	9/9/42
13-14	Smith, Maj. John	F4F	USMC	VMF-223	9/11/42
15-19	Smith, Maj. John	F4F	USMC	VMF-223	9/12-10/10/42
19	Foss, Capt. Joseph	F4F	USMC	VMF-121	11/7/42
19-26	Foss, Capt. Joseph	F4F	USMC	VMF-121	11/12/42-1/15/43
26-28	Bong, Maj. Richard	P-38	USAAF	5FC	4/12/44
29-30	Bong, Maj. Richard	P-38	USAAF	5FC	10/10/44
30	McCampbell, Cdr. David	F6F	USN	VF-15	10/24/44
31-36	Bong, Maj. Richard	P-38	USAAF	5FC	10/24 –11/11/44
40	Bong. Maj. Richard	P-38	USAAF	5FC	11/11-12/17/44

USAAF Victory Chronology PTO

Victory #	Pilot Name and Rank	A/C	Total	Unit	Date
1-4	Welch, 2Lt. George	P-40	16	47PS	12/7/41
5	Wagner, 1Lt. Boyd	P-40	8	17PS	12/16/41
5	Kiser. 1Lt. George	P-40	9	8PS	2/24/42
6-8	Kiser, 1Lt. George	P-40	9	8PS	To 4/27/42
8	Wagner, Maj. Boyd	P-39	8	5FC	4/30/42
9	Reynolds, 2Lt. Andrew	P-40	9.3	9FS	7/30/42
10	Bong, 1Lt. Richard	P-38	40	9FS	4/14/43
11	Lynch, Capt. Thomas	P-38	22	39FS	6/10/43
11	Bong, 1Lt. Richard	P-38	40	5FC	6/12/43
12-15	Bong, 1Lt. Richard	P-38	40	5FC	7/26/43
16	Bong, 1Lt. Richard	P-38	40	5FC	7/28/43
16	Lynch, Capt. Thomas	P-38	22	5FC	9/16/43
17-21	Bong, Capt. Richard	P-38	40	5FC	To 11/5/43
21	Kearby, Col. Neel	P-47	22	5FC	1/9/44
22-25	Bong, Maj. Richard	P-38	40	5FC	To 4/3/44
26-28	Bong, Maj. Richard	P-38	40	5FC	4/12/44
29-30	Bong, Maj. Richard	P-38	40	5FC	10/10/44
35-36	Bong, Maj. Richard	P-38	40	5FC	To 11/11/44
37-38	Bong, Maj. Richard	P-38	40	5FC	12/7/44
39	Bong, Maj. Richard	P-38	40	5FC	12/15/44
40	Bong, Maj. Richard	P-38	40	5FC	12/17/44

USMC Victory Chronology

Victory #/*	Pilot Name and Rank	Total	Unit	Date
1-2	Elrod, Capt. Henry	2	VMF-211	12/10/41
2	Kunz, 2Lt. Charles	8	VMF-221	6/4/42
2	Trowbridge, 2Lt. Eugene	11	VMF-223	8/21/42
3	Trowbridge, 2Lt. Eugene	11	VMF-223	8/22/42
4-5	Carl, Capt. Marion	18.5	VMF-223	8/24/42
5	Trowbridge, 2Lt. Eugene	11	VMF-223	8/24/42
6-7	Carl, Capt. Marion	18.5	VMF-223	8/26/42
8	Carl, Capt. Marion	18.5	VMF-223	8/29/42
9-11	Carl, Capt. Marion	18.5	VMF-223	8/30/42
12-13	Carl, Capt. Marion	18.5	VMF-223	9/9/42
13-14	Smith, Maj. John	19	VMF-223	9/11/42
15	Smith, Maj. John	19	VMF-223	9/12/42
16-19	Smith, Maj. John	19	VMF-223	9/13 to 10/10
19	Foss, Capt. Joseph	26	VMF-121	11/7/42
20-22	Foss, Capt. Joseph	26	VMF-121	11/12/42
23	Foss, Capt. Joseph	26	VMF-121	11/15/42
24-26	Foss. Capt. Joseph	26	VMF-121	1/15/43

*All victories were scored in the F4F Wildcat

USN Victory Chronology

Victory #	Pilot Name and Rank	A/C	Total	Unit	Date
1	Dickenson, Lt. Clarence	SBD	1	VS-6	12/7/41
	Miller, Arm/1c. E. William	SBD	1	VS-6	12/7/41
2	Gray, Lt. James	F4F	6	VF-6	2/1/42
3	Thach, Lt.Cdr. John	F4F	6	VF-3	2/20/42
4-5	O'Hare, Lt (jg). Edward	F4F	7	VF-3	2/20/42
6	Thach, Lt. Cdr. John	F4F	6	VF-3	6/4/42
6	McCusky, Lt(jg). E. Scott	F4F	13.5	VF-3	6/4/42
7-8	Runyon, Mach. Donald	F4F	11	VF-6	8/24/42
9-10	Vejtasa, Lt. Stanley	F4F	10	VF-10	10/26/42
11-12	Kepford, Lt(jg). Ira	F4U	16	VF-17	1/30/44
13	Kepford, Lt(jg). Ira	F4U	16	VF-17	2/3/44
14-16	Kepford, Lt(jg) Ira	F4U	16	VF-17	2/19/44
17-18	Vraciu, Lt(jg). Alexander	F6F	19	VF-16	6/19/44
19	Vraciu, Lt(jg). Alexander	F6F	19	VF-16	6/20/44
20-21	McCampbell, Cdr. David	F6F	34	VF-15	10/21/44
22-30	McCampbell, Cdr. David	F6F	34	VF-15	10/24/44
31-32	McCampbell, Cdr. David	F6F	34	VF-15	11/5/44
33	McCampbell, Cdr. David	F6F	34	VF-15	11/11/44
34	McCampbell, Cdr. David	F6F	34	VF-15	11/14/44

Ace's Role in WWII
Aces Share of Total Victories in WWII

Service	Victories	Probable	Damaged	# Aces	Victories	% V.
USN/PTO	6826	780	830	381	2727.6	39.9
USMC/PTO	2696	154	64	123	992.6	36.8
AVG/CBI	231	43	33	18	134.7	58.3
USAAF	16257	2239	5179	754*	5776	35.5
CBI	1273	444	754	60	384	30.2
PTO	3716	537	425	183	1447	38.9
ETO	7504	681	2535	330	2698	35.9
MTO	3764	577	1465	164	1140	30.2
TOTALS	26010	3216	6106	1276*	9630.9	37.0

*17 aces scored victories in 2 theaters (107 victories total)

Ace's Victories by Fighter Type by Theater
Aces Victories by Fighter Type

USAAF AIRCRAFT	ETO	MTO	PTO	CBI	Total in type	# Aces V.	Aces
P-51	4053	991	279	343	5666	268	2082
A-36	——	67	——	2	69	1	5
F-6	186	5	18	——	209	5	33.5
P-51 TOTAL	4239	1063	297	345	5944	274	2114.5
P-38	497	1431	1700	157	3785	172	1259.33
P-47	2685.5	263	696.67	16	3661.16	114	930.16
P-40	——	592	660.5	741	2225.5	73	578.83
(AVG)				232		18	134.67
Spitfire	15	364	——	——	379	12	71.83
P-39	2.5	25	243	5	275.5	1	5
P-400	——	——	45	——	45		
P-61	59	——	63.5	5	127.5	4	22
Beaufighter	6	25	——	——	31	——	——
P-43	——	——	3	3	6	——	——
P-36	——	——	3	——	3	——	——
P-70	——	——	2	——	2	——	——
P-26	——	——	2	——	2	——	——
P-35	——	——	1	——	1	——	——
Mosquito	——	1	——	——	1	——	——
TOTALS	7504	3764	3716.67	1504	16488.67	668	5015.83

USN/USMC AIRCRAFT	ETO	MTO	PTO	Total	# Aces in Type	Aces V.
F6F USN	8	——	5064	5168	311	2194
USMC	——	——	96		1	6
F4U USN	——	——	519	2140	24	178.5
USMC			1621		75	582.5
F4F USN	——	26	497	1012	26	200
USMC	——	——	489		34	292
FM-2 USN	——	——	422	422	5	30.5
SBD USN	——	——	138	138	——	——
TBF/TBM USN	——	——	98	98	——	——
F2A USN			10	10	——	——
TOTALS	8	26	8954	8988	476	3483.5
USN	8	26	6748		366	2603
USMC	——	——	2206		110	880.5

Note: Aces in type does not include 99 aces scoring 546 victories in two of more aircraft types (71/393 AAF, 15/83 USN and 13/70 USMC) but does include: 10 AAF, 4 USN and 1 USMC pilots who were aces in two a/c types.

American citizens who were aces in the RAF and RCAF by a/c: Spitfire 12 (7 Eagle and 5 RAF); Hurricane 5; Mosquito 3; and Tempest 1

USAAF and USN/USMC Fighters vs. the Axis

Claims By Services

Service	Victories	Probable	Damaged	Total Claims
USN	6826	780	830	8436
%	80.9	9.2	9.8	
USMC	2696	154	64	2914
%	92.5	5.3	2.2	
AVG	231	43	33	307
%	75.5	13.7	10.8	
USAAF	16257	2239	5179	23675
%	68.7	9.4	21.9	
Totals	26010	3216	6106	35332
Avg.	73.6	9.1	17.3	100.0

Claims By Theater of Operations

Theater	Victories	Probable	Damaged	Total Claims
CBI	1504	487	787	2778
%	54.1	17.5	28.3	
PTO	13238	1471	1319	16028
%	82.6	9.2	8.2	
ETO	7504	681	2535	10720
%	70.0	6.4	23.6	
MTO	3764	577	1465	5806
%	64.8	9.9	25.2	
Totals	26010	3216	6106	35322
Avg.	73.6	9.1	17.3	100.0

Enemy Aircraft Destroyed by the USAAF by Theater and in the Air or on the Ground

Enemy Aircraft Destroyed Theater/Cause of Loss	Total	1942	1943	1944	1945
ETO	*			*	
Total Losses	14,218	7	451	7977	5783
In the Air	7422	7	451	5602	1362
On the Ground	6796	——	——	2375	4421
MTO	**			**	
Total Losses	4664	92	1459	2845	268
In the Air	3300	81	1270	1760	189
On the Ground	1364	11	89	1085	79
PTO+	***			***	
Total Losses	3556	245	1284	1315	712
In the Air	3113	211	1252	1158	492
On the Ground	443	34	32	157	220
CBI	****			****	
Total Losses	1467	52	325	729	361
In the Air	847	52	288	418	89
On the Ground	620	——	37	311	272

*August-December 1942 & January-May 1945
**June-December 1942 & January-May 1945
***January-December 1942 & January-August 1945
****April-December 1942 & January-August 1945
+PTO includes Pacific Ocean Area, Far East AF and Alaska

CHAPTER 6

First American Victories of WWII

First USAAC and USN Victories/Pearl Harbor

The Pearl Harbor attack remains as the classic example of a tragic result of a nation's unpreparedness. The popular historical emphasis on the destruction of the Pacific Fleet battleships and the general chaos of the event has led to confusion and neglect in the chronicling of the American air response to the Japanese attack. The Japanese strike plan initially attacked all air bases, so that American air interference with Japanese sorties over Battleship Row was nullified. The Japanese strategy was so successful that only token aerial resistance was met, rendering their carriers and returning aircraft safe from counterattack.

The Japanese launched 355 aircraft (two aborted on takeoff) in two attack forces from six carriers (*Akagi, Kaga, Soryu, Hiryu, Shokaku,* and *Zuikaku*). The first attack wave, led by LCdr. Mitsuo Fuchida, consisted of 185 aircraft, of which 89 were to attack the U.S. Pacific Fleet, while the remainder was to attack the airfields. Forty-five A6M2 Zeros fighter of the "Air Control Force" under LCdr. Shigeru Itaya were to gain air superiority and then strafe the airfields: Ford Island (USN); Wheeler (USAAC); Hickham (USAAC); Kaneohe (USN); Ewa (USMC); and Bellows (USAAC). The Zeros were followed by 51 Type 99 Aichi D3A1 Val dive-bombers under LCdr. Kakuichi Takahashi. Each Val was to drop a single 550-pound bomb on hangars and aircraft on the ground at Ford Island (17 Vals), Hickham (9), and Wheeler (25).

The Japanese aerial armada passed off Kahuku Point, north of Oahu, at 0740, proceeding over the Army airfield at Haleiwa at 0750. Japanese intelligence had overlooked this auxiliary field on the northern coast. The 47PS, 15FG from Wheeler Field was using the field for gunnery practice and had P-40s, P-36s, and a few obsolete P-26s there. At 0755-0800, the six U.S. airbases were attacked with devastating results. Kaneohe was the first base attacked; the nine Zeros destroyed 26 aircraft and damaged a PBY Catalina patrol bomber (three were out on patrol and spared). At Ford Island, 10 Zeros and 17 Vals damaged or destroyed 33 of 70 aircraft and rendered the runways inoperable. At Ewa (pronounced Ev-va) the 49 Marine aircraft were parked wingtip-to-wingtip to protect against sabotage, and were instead easy targets for the strafing Zeros, which came in over the mountains to destroy 33 aircraft and again damaged the runways. At Hickham, 10 Zeros and 9 Vals attacked from different quadrants, first attacking the parked aircraft and knocking out 18 of 30, and then attacking the hangar line. Wheeler was strafed by eight Zeros, and then by 25 Vals, which dropped 250kg bombs from 200-250 feet. A total of 43 of 83 aircraft were destroyed and 29 others damaged. At 0830 a single Zero strafed Bellows, destroying three of 12 fighters there.

Meanwhile, Cdr. Howard "Brigham" Young of VS-6 "Scouting Six" took off from the carrier *Enterprise* at 0615 in a SBD Daunt-

less. LCdr. Bromfield Nichol, riding in the rear seat, carried a highly classified radio transmitter. Young and his wingman, Ens. Perry Teaff, proceeded to Ford Island, followed by 16 other SBDs of VS-6 led by LCdr. Hallsted Hopping from the *Enterprise* at 0615. Young and his wingman arrived off Barber's Point at 0820 and assumed the circling aircraft over Ewa were U.S. Army fighters, until they were attacked by them. The two VS-6 SBDs quickly landed at Ford Island.

Ens. Manuel Gonzalez of VS-6 was probably the first Japanese aerial victory of the war and the first American casualty. Upon approaching Oahu, Gonzalez's last radio transmission warned "Please don't shoot! Don't shoot. This is an American plane." Then to his rear gunner "We're on fire, bail out." Gonzalez and his gunner were lost without a trace. Ens. John Vogt, also of VS-6, was probably shot down over Ewa, as he was last seen being engaged by several Zeros while trying to reach Ford Island.

Lt(jg.) C.E. Dickinson and wingman Ens. J.R. McCarthy were alerted by the smoke and AA bursts over Ford Island, but were nonetheless surprised by Zero fighters. Dickinson has described the action in his book *The Flying Guns "6"*. McCarthy flew into Zero bullets intended for Dickinson. His dive-bomber burst into flame, slowly descending. McCarty climbed out of his cockpit, but hit the tail assembly in his jump and broke his leg. Fortunately, his

The first American aerial victories were scored over Pearl Harbor. 2Lts. Ken Taylor (left) and George Welch flew P-40s for 47PS and met the first waves of Japanese Kate bombers. Welch is given credit for the first victory but Taylor stated in a post-war interview that Welch was an upper classman, 41A to 41C, and had a "rather strong personality" so was given the credit. Welch went on to score 16 victories in WW-2 and Taylor four. Taylor also was credited with two probable victories at Pearl Harbor. (Author/Taylor)

parachute opened and he landed safely, but was hospitalized for many months afterward. McCarthy's rear gunner was unable to get clear of the encumbering rear seat/machine gun area and perished in the crash. Meantime, Dickinson found four or five Zeros on his tail. His rear gunner, Arm.1/c William Miller, downed an attacker, expending all his six ammo drums. Miller's victory was confirmed by a Marine on the ground at Ewa. Miller was wounded in the initial attack and was mortally wounded in the subsequent Zero attacks. Dickinson bailed out at low altitude and landed at Ewa about 0825. Thus, Dickinson and Miller, in an SBD dive-bomber, appear to have scored the first USN victory of WWII.

Ens. E.T. Deacon and his rear gunner expended all their ammo and, defenseless, were riddled with bullets. Despite being wounded in the leg, Deacon was able to make a safe water landing. The remaining 12 SBDs of VS-6 were able to land at Ford Island despite intense USN AA fire.

Early the previous evening, 2Lts. George Welch and Kenneth Taylor were dressed in tuxedos to attend the weekly Saturday dance at Schofield Barracks, Wheeler Field. Since their unit had scored poorly on Squadron gunnery tests it was exiled to Haleiwa, on the northwest coast of Oahu, for further practice. After the dance the two pilots played in an all night poker game. Popular histories have Welch and Taylor deciding whether to sleep at Wheeler or go for a swim back at Haleiwa when the Japanese attacked. Taylor confirmed to me in an interview that they were sleeping at Wheeler and were awakened by the bombs. Taylor telephoned Haleiwa and instructed the ground crews to fuel and arm two P-40s. The two lieutenants got into Taylor's car and raced the ten miles back to base, being unsuccessfully strafed by a Japanese fighter along the way. Arriving at Haleiwa, they found that squadron CO Major Austin was deer hunting, and acting CO Robert Rogers was unavailable. So without authorization and dressed in their tuxedo shirts, the two pilots skipped flight pre-check and climbed into their awaiting P-40Bs, which were armed with four rifle-caliber .30 machine guns. The tandem headed toward Barber's Point on the southwest tip of Oahu, where they spotted 10-12 enemy Kate dive-bombers that were flying near the Marine base at Ewa. Each man broke off to attack the bombers. Welch got astern of a bomber and scored hits despite having one gun jam, and set the Kate on fire. Probably simultaneously, Taylor also downed a Jap dive-bomber, and on his turn spotted another one heading out to sea. He fired, hitting the rear gunner; the Kate flew into a cloud, came out, lost altitude rapidly, and crashed into the sea. Meanwhile, Welch's P-40 had been hit in the baggage compartment by an incendiary shell fired by his victim's rear gunner, and Welch broke away into cloud-cover to check the damage. Finding no loss of performance, Welch saw a Jap bomber headed out to sea off Barber's Point and shot it down. Welch flew into Wheeler to rearm. Taylor followed a third Kate out to sea, firing on it and causing smoke and damage before he ran out of ammo and returned to Wheeler. Both men had to dodge intense friendly AA fire in their landing approach, which was necessarily short and rapid.

Welch is generally given credit for scoring America's first victory of WWII in this sortie. Though this distinction could go just as well to Taylor, Welch has been described as a "rather strong per-

Pearl Harbor victors (L-R): 2Lt. Harry Brown (2v.), 1Lt. Philip Rasmussen (1v.), 2Lt. Ken Taylor (2v.), 2Lt. George Welch (4v.) and 1Lt. Lewis Sanders (1v.). Brown went on to score five more victories in the Pacific. (Author/Taylor)

sonality" and was an upper classman to Taylor, 41A to 41 C. After the war Taylor maintained: "George and I agreed we would never know which one of us got the first Jap, so we agreed the survivor would claim the honor." They both survived the war.

2Lts. Harry W. Brown and John Dains of the 47PS were on weekend leaves from Wheeler when the attack began. After picking up Bob Rogers they drove to Haleiwa, avoiding strafing to arrive just as Welch and Taylor took off. At 0830, Brown took off in an obsolescent Curtiss P-36 fighter whose synchronization of its .50 caliber machine guns was defective. Brown got airborne and headed toward Wheeler at 1,000 feet. He spotted a low-wing fighter, which turned out to be another P-36 piloted by acting squadron CO Bob Rogers, who had taken off after Brown from Haleiwa. Due to his gun defect Brown followed Rogers, and both unsuccessfully attacked a Kate dive-bomber. Over Kaneohe Point, they intercepted two Vals and each pilot attacked one. Brown shot his Val down, while Rogers damaged his, but suffered hits from the rear gunner and was forced to land. Brown Immelmanned out of combat, flying through 10-15 surprised Japanese who did not have time to fire. Brown then joined another P-36 from Wheeler piloted by 2Lt. Malcomb "Mike" Moore of the 46PS, and the two chased a straggling Zero. Moore scored hits, but ran out of ammo, returning to Wheeler at 0930. Brown followed the Zero out to sea, firing his last ammo and starting a fire, for which he was awarded a probable.

2Lts., John J. Webster and John Dains also took off from Haleiwa about 0835. Webster attacked two Japanese aircraft, but was wounded and forced to land. Dains was unable to make contact with the Japanese and landed at Wheeler to refuel.

At 0855, the 170 aircraft Second Attack Force, led by LCdr. Shigekazu Shimazaki, arrived over Oahu. This force consisted of 54 Kate, Nakajima Type 97 B5N2 horizontal/torpedo bombers, 80 Vals, and 36 Zeros. The Kates, led by Shimazaki, were divided: 27 to attack Hickham; 18 to attack Ford Island; and nine to Kaneohe. The Air Control Force of 36 Zeros under Lt. Suburo Shindo was to maintain air superiority, then strafe Ford, Hickham, Wheeler, and Kaneohe air fields.

At 0850, five pilots under 1Lt. Lewis Sanders, CO of the 46PS, were able to take off from Wheeler after the first Japanese attack

Lt(jg) Clarence Dickinson (left) and his gunner, Arm1/c William Miller (right), were flying a SBD dive-bomber for VS-6 off the *Lexington* to Ford Island when they were attacked by Zeros in the Pearl Harbor attack. Miller expended all six of his ammo drums and got a Zero but was mortally wounded and Dickinson bailed out to safety. (USN)

and before the second wave arrived. Fortuitously, the previous day Sanders had dispersed his P-36s to the east end of Wheeler, where they were spared as they were hidden by the dense smoke. 2Lt. Philip M. Rasmussen, 1Lt. John M. Thacker, 1Lt. Mike Moore, and 1Lt. Norris were selected by Sanders to accompany him. However, when Norris went back to the parachute truck for a smaller chute, 2Lt. Gordon M. Sterling, standing nearby in chute and life vest, quickly climbed into Norris' P-36. He handed the crew chief his wristwatch with the instructions to send it to his mother, as he would not be coming back. Warned not to take off due to the intense friendly AA fire, the five ignored the warning, took off safely, and climbed to 8,000 feet, heading south towards Diamond Head. They spotted 11 Zeros and dove at maximum throttle, leveling off over bellows Field to attack. Sanders hit the Japanese leader in the fuselage with tracers, scoring a victory. Rasmussen also scored a victory over Kaneohe Point. Thacker's guns jammed as he was attacked by a persistent Zero that caused him to force land at Wheeler, badly damaged. As previously described, Moore joined Brown and damaged a Zero. Sanders reported he saw three aircraft in a steep, near vertical dive towards the ocean. The lead plane was a Zero that was being fired upon by Sterling's P-36, which in turn was being followed by another Zero which was firing on Sterling. Sterling and his victim were unable to pull out and crashed into the sea. Sterling's premonition had come true.

Sanders, Rasmussen, Thacker, and Moore landed at Wheeler as the Japanese attack ended at 0930. Again, "friendly" AA and ground fire was so intense over Wheeler that reports claimed Rasmussen's P-36 had 544 holes of various sizes, including the multiple holes caused by the two Zeros which plagued him throughout his mission.

Over at Bellow's Field—the P-40 base for the 44PS—ground crews fueled and rearmed three P-40s about one hour after the first attack. 2Lt. George A. Whiteman, 2Lt. Hans Christiansen, and 1Lt. Sam W. Bishop were ready for take off when six Zeros (probably those attacked by Sanders' group) approached to strafe. Whiteman was killed on his taxiing run. Christiansen was hit while on the runway, and his P-40 plunged into the underbrush at the end of the runway, exploding and killing him. Bishop was able to get airborne, but had his controls shot out at 400 feet. Bishop struggled with his damaged fighter and crashed into the sea off Oahu, but managed to swim ashore despite a leg wound. The Japanese proceeded to destroy four of the remaining six P-40s at Bellows (10 of 12 total).

Welch and Taylor dodged their own AA and ground fire and landed at Wheeler at 0840. Two ground crewmen ran into a burning hangar to get ammo boxes and belts. Just as refueling was completed, the second wave of Japanese attacked Wheeler from the south. Welch took off first, flying directly into the enemy formation, and sustained damage. Taylor was delayed in rearming and took off from the south, firing on the Kates as they passed his nose. He struggled to gain altitude and was immediately picked up astern by a Japanese fighter. Welch, seeing Taylor's predicament, swung behind Taylor's attacker and scored a long burst from his three working machine guns, exploding the Zero somewhere between Wahlawa and Haleiwa. Taylor was wounded in the left arm and had some fragments in his legs, but continued to chase the Vals, scoring a probable before running out of ammunition. He landed his damaged P-40 at Wheeler. Welch was hit by the rear gunner of a Japanese bomber, causing damage to his prop, engine block, and cowling. He continued flying, intercepting a Val bomber near Ewa. He pursued it for five miles offshore, destroying it for his fourth victory of the day.

At the 45ᵗʰ Squadron hangar, Lt. Bill Haney was headed for the hangar basement when the first Vals and Zeros struck Wheeler. Haney ran to the flight line to a P-36 that was being armed with some difficulty by three soldiers, including a cook! With bombs bursting nearby and the struggle to install the .50 caliber machine guns into the cramped P-36 nose, Haney jumped into the cockpit as is, armed only with two .30 caliber guns. He headed towards Pearl Harbor from Wheeler. His engine was hit by AA fire from the USS *San Francisco*, causing him to make a dead-stick landing back at Wheeler. Haney, with his chute still on, ran over to another P-36 and immediately took off and headed back towards Pearl. Skirting the main harbor, he saw a line of cruisers leaving the Harbor. Un-

fortunately, the cruisers saw him, also, and again his engine was hit and he was forced to glide back to Wheeler, shot down twice by the U.S. Navy in less than an hour!

At 0905, Rogers, Brown, and Dains took off in their P-36s from Wheeler. They were unable to make enemy contact, and all shortly returned safely to Wheeler despite its heavy AA fire.

After landing again at Wheeler to refuel and rearm, Welch took off at 0930 with a new wingman, John Dains. Both pilots were making their third sortie of the day. The AA fire was more intense than ever, panicked and indiscriminate. While flying over Schofield Barracks (Wheeler) Dains was shot down and killed. Welch was lucky to dodge this AA fire, but then was fired upon by AA defending Pearl Harbor. By this time the Japanese attack was concluded, and Welch returned safely to Wheeler.

Thus ended the American air response to the Japanese attack. Japanese aerial losses for the day were: 11-destroyed/4 probables/1 damaged.

PEARL HARBOR ATTACK
Chronology of American Aerial Action

Time	Pilot Name	Base	A/C	Unit	Result	Action
0745	Gonzalez	Enterprise	SBD	VS-6	————	KIA
0815	Welch					
	Taylor	Haleiwa	P-40	47PS	2 Kates	Return & Rearm/refuel
					2 Kates	
					1 probable	
0825?	Dickinson/Miller	Enterprise	SBD	VS-6	1 Zero	A/C lost/Miller KIA
	Vogt/?				————	Crew KIA
	McCarthy/?					A/C lost & gunner KIA
	Deacon/?					A/C lost & crew OK
0830	Brown	Haleiwa	P-36	47PS	1 Val/1 Zero	Return & Rearm/refuel
0835	Rogers	Haleiwa	P-36	47PS	1 probable	Return: A/C damaged
	Dains				————	Return & Refuel
	Webster					Return: A/C damaged/wounded
0850	Sanders	Wheeler	P-36	46PS	1 Zero	Return: attack ended
	Rasmussen				1 Zero	Return: A/C damaged/wounded
	Sterling				1 Zero	KIA
	Thacker				1 damaged	Return: A/C damaged
	Moore					Return: attack ended
0855	Haney	Wheeler	P-36	45PS	————	A/C lost: friendly AA fire
0855	Whiteman	Bellows	P-40	44PS	————	KIA (take off)
	Christiansen					KIA (take off)
	Bishop					A/C lost/wounded
0900	Welch				1 probable	Return & Rearm/refuel
	Taylor	Wheeler	P-40	47PS	1 Val/1Zero	Return: A/C damaged/wounded
0905	Dains	Wheeler	P-36	47PS		Return & Refuel
	Rogers					Return: attack ended
	Brown					Return: attack ended
0920	Haney	Wheeler	P-36	45PS	————	A/C lost friendly AA
0930	Welch	Wheeler	P-40	47PS		Return: attack ended
	Dains					KIA: friendly AA

Destroyed:
4   Kates (Welch 2, Taylor 2)
5   Zeros (Dickinson, Sanders, Rasmussen, Sterling, Welch)
2   Vals (Brown, Welch)

At surrender 15 August 1945, the Japanese admitted losses at Pearl Harbor to all causes:

First wave: 9 A/C (3 Zeros, 1 Val, 5 Kates)
Second wave: 20 A/C (6 Zeros, 14 Vals)

American aerial losses included 10 aircraft:
5   SBDs of VS-6 (Gonzalez, McCarthy, Dickinson, Deacon, Vogt)
2   P-36s (Sterling, Dains)
3   P-40s (Whiteman, Christiansen, Bishop)
6   damaged (Rogers, Webster, Rasmussen, Thacker, Taylor, Welch)

The destruction of American aircraft on the ground was devastating:

USN   92 destroyed/31 damaged
USAAC   96 destroyed/128 damaged

Postscript:
For their part in the Pearl Harbor attack Taylor and Sterling (posthumously) were awarded the DSC (Distinguished Service Cross) in January 1942. Welch was awarded both the DSC and DFC (Distinguished Flying Cross). A request for the Congressional Medal of Honor for Welch was rejected because he had taken off without orders!

Clarence Dickinson won the Navy Cross for making a 175-mile search flight after he returned from his crash landing. He subsequently won two gold stars in lieu of his second and third Navy Crosses, and then won an Air Medal.

The Silver Star was awarded to Bishop, Brown, Christiansen, Dains, Moore, Rogers, Rasmussen, Sterling, Thacker, Webster, and Whiteman.

During the remainder of the war the participants scored the following:

Thacker, Bishop, and Webster scored no further.

Moore scored one damaged and Rogers scored a probable.

Rasmussen scored one victory (12/31/43- an Oscar) and one damaged in further air combat.

Haney went on to score eight victories in 252 sorties with the 49FG in the Pacific.

Taylor was transferred to Guadalcanal in October 1942; flying P-40s , he scored two more Zero kills with the 44FG. His next victory was scored on 7 December 1943. After the war the Inspector General credited Taylor victories for the two probables he claimed on his first (Kate) and second (Val) sorties. These victories would make him an ace with six victories, but the USAF Historical Study 85 does not recognize these victories.

From Hawaii Welch was posted to Australia with the 80FS/8FG, then on to Port Moresby, New Guinea. On 7 December 1942, Welch, now a 1Lt., led a flight of four P-39s intercepting nine escorting Zeros. Welch shot down a Zero and then two Vals to become an ace with seven victories. As a Captain in New Guinea flying P-38s he scored nine more victories to finish the war with 16. By scoring four victories in the P-40, three in the P-39, and nine in the P-38 he became one of the few aces to score victories in three different fighters. He was killed in a flying accident on 12 October 1954 while test flying a F-100 Super Sabre over Edwards AFB.

Brown scored five more victories in the Pacific. Flying a P-38 for the 9FS/49FG, he destroyed an Oscar and damaged another in the Battle of the Bismarck Sea, 3 March 1943. He became an ace on 16 August as a captain with the 431FS/475FG when he scored the group's first three kills (all Zekes) over Watut Valley. He scored his last victory over a Zeke near Rabaul on 24 October 1943.

Francis "Gabby" Gabreski, top ETO ace with 28 victories, was assigned to the 45PS at Wheeler after receiving his wings in March. He was awakened to explosions, and drove to the base and had to physically pull the P-36s from burning hangars, with ammunition cooking off around him. He took off in a lone P-36 and was joined by several P-40s, and they headed towards Pearl Harbor but had to skirt the area because of he heavy AA fire. The makeshift squadron patrolled without making enemy contact until they almost ran out of fuel.

Six months later, the Japanese carriers *Akagi*, *Kaga*, *Soryu*, and *Hiryu* were sunk in the Battle of Midway, taking many of the Japanese heroes of Pearl Harbor with them.

First Aerial Victory ETO
Pilots: 2Lt. Joseph D. Shaffer 33FS/P-39
          2Lt. Elisa E. Shahan 27FS/P-38
Time: 14 August 1942/10:30
Place: Icelandic Coast, approximately eight miles NE Keflavik and 10 SW of Reykjavik
Action: In mid-1942, the Luftwaffe's Norwegian-based, long range four engine Focke Wulf 200 Kurier flew recon sorties across the North Atlantic. Their mission was to spot Allied convoys for the lurking U-boat wolf packs, and they were virtually unopposed. In mid-June the 8AF ordered P-38s of its 1st and 14th Fighter Groups to deploy to England. An element of four Lightnings, led by a B-17, made the 2,965 mile trip in four stages. Leaving Presque Isle on the extreme northwest tip of Maine, the route led to Goose Bay, Labrador, then to Bluie West 1 on the southwest tip of Greenland, then onto Reykjavik, Iceland, and finally to Prestwick, Scotland.

The Icelandic base command was responsible for defending the area, but their P-39s and P-40s did not have sufficient range for the extended patrols required to search out the FW-200s or U-boats. For this reason, the P-38s of the 27FS were ordered to remain in Iceland. The Squadron was stationed in Keflavik and its air control in Reykjavik.

In mid-morning 14 August, Maj. John Weltman, CO of the 27th, and his wingman, 2Lt. Elisa Shahan, were in the alert shack. Maj.

Woody Korgas of Reykjavik control called, informing the two of an unidentified aircraft off the coast. Initially it was thought to be a lost B-17. Weltman and Shahan took off in 2,000 foot overcast, with Korgas radioing that the aircraft was not a lost B-17, but a German recon bomber, identified as a FW-200.

Heading north from Keflavik, Weltman and Shahan spotted the Kurier heading north, just below the clouds off the south shore of Reykjavik. The two set up gunnery runs, with Weltman attacking first and Shahan standing off. Weltman fired short bursts, but on his third pass the German gunners hit Weltman's P-38, causing his guns to stop and his right engine to run very rough. He feathered the engine and returned to nearby Reykjavik to get another fighter.

Meanwhile, 2Lt. Joseph Shaffer of the 33FS of Icelandic Base Command, flying a P-39 Airacobra, also contacted the German bomber, joining Shahan in the attack. Shahan dove on the Focke Wulf, firing at close range and hitting it in the fuselage. Shaffer fired 37 mm cannon shells through the P-39's propeller hub, also hitting the enemy, whose engine flamed. The wounded bomber exploded and crashed into the water. There were no survivors, and only small pieces of debris remained afloat and were recovered later.

When Weltman landed he found he was short about five inches off one of his props, and an armor-piercing bullet had jammed the P-38's nose-mounted guns. The bullet was the first to hit an American aircraft flown by an American pilot in the ETO. The bullet is on display at the Air Force Museum at Wright-Patterson, Ohio.

Both Shaffer and Shahan were awarded one-half victory, the first for the Air Force in the ETO. Joseph Shaffer scored another victory over a Ju-88 on 18 October over Iceland. Elisa (name change to Michael in 1948) Shahan also scored another victory over North Africa for which he was not officially credited.

Various popular sources, such as Roger Freeman's *Mighty Eighth* and Gerritt Zijistra's *Diary of an Air War* perpetuate the myth of Weltman's and Shahan's P-38s engaging in mock combat with Shaffer's "P-40" when the Focke Wulf flew onto the scene and into its destruction. However, Weltman and Shahan have both confirmed the above account to me.

First USAAC Aerial Victory over Europe

Pilot: 2Lt. Samuel Junkin
Unit: 309FS/31FG/8AF
Time: 19 August 1942/approx. 0800-0830
Place: Dieppe
A/C: Spitfire/FW-190
Action: Early in the morning of 19 August 1942, British Commandos and Canadian troops initiated "Operation Jubilee," a "reconnaissance in force" on the French coastal town of Dieppe. What ensued in the next 16 hours was the largest air battle of the war until that time.

The 309FS of the 31FG under Maj. Harrison Thyng flew out of West Hampnett to the beaches that morning. This unit, flying borrowed Spitfire VIs, intercepted German Focke Wulf 190s. 2Lt. Samuel Junkin of Natchez, MS, shot down a FW to score the first American victory over Continental Europe. Moments later, Junkin was jumped by a German fighter and was slightly wounded. He managed to bail out and was rescued from the English Channel. He later received the DFC for this action.

Maj. Thyng scored a probable over a FW-190, while Capt. J.E. Thorsen damaged a Do-217. The 31st lost three aircraft with one pilot lost and two rescued.

It is interesting to note that two Americans who later became top 8AF aces flew with the RAF 133 Squadron and the "Eagle Squadron" that day over Dieppe. F/L Don Blakeslee destroyed one

2Lt. Elisa Shahan (shown at left), flying a P-38 for the 27FS, joined 2Lt. Joseph Shaffer flying a P-39 for the 33FS and shared the First American victory in the ETO when they shot down a FW-200 four engine patrol bomber off the coast of Iceland on 14 August 1942. (Author/Shahan)

2Lt. Samuel Junkin (center) destroyed the first German aircraft over Europe while flying a Spitfire for the 309FS/31FG. He downed a FW-190 over Dieppe on 19 August 1942.

and damaged two Fw-190s, while P/O Don Gentile scored a victory over another Focke Wulf. These men would end the war with 15 1/2 and 19 7/8 victories, respectively.

First USMC Victory
Pilots: 2Lt. David D. Kliewer
          T/Sgt. William J. Hamilton
Unit: VMF-211
Time: 9 December 1941/1145
Place: Wake Island, SE over Peacock Point
A/C: F4F-3 Wildcat
Action: On 4 December 1941 VMF-211, commanded by Maj. Paul A. Putnam, flew off the carrier *Enterprise* to reinforce the Wake Island garrison. Eleven pilots of VMF-211 had recently been introduced to their Grumman F4F-3 Wildcats, converting from F3F biplanes. Upon arriving at Wake, the squadron had less than 30 hours on type, with no gunnery or bombing practice. To make matters worse, pilot and maintenance manuals were destroyed during the first Japanese surprise raids of 8 December. This devastating air attack destroyed seven of 12 Wildcats, and three pilots were killed and four wounded.

At sunrise, four Wildcats took off to scout the area south of Wake, looking for an anticipated Japanese invasion fleet. Later that morning 2Lt. David Kliewer and T/Sgt. Bill Hamilton, an enlisted pilot, took off for CAP duty. At 1145, 27 Mitsubishi GM3 Bettys approached at 13,000 feet. Kliewer and Hamilton attacked the flanks of the Jap bomber formation, hoping to break it up before it reached the island. Each pilot attacked the same bomber, sending it down in flames to share a victory credit. The two Marine pilots had to terminate their pursuit of the remainder of the formation due to bursts of friendly 3-inch AA fire from the batteries on Peacock Point.

Maj. William Weltman, CO of the 27FS of the Icelandic Base Command, led the first American victory attack, but was hit by the first Luftwaffe bullets when a gunner on a FW-200 hit his P-38's prop and gun cowling. (USAF)

Neither pilot scored again during the heroic struggle for Wake. On 11 December at 1600, Kliewer claimed to have sunk a surfaced Japanese submarine that was suspected to have been directing Japanese air attacks on the island. Hamilton did yeoman's work, salvaging damaged aircraft and putting them back into combat. VMF-211 lost only two F4Fs in actual combat while claiming eight victories. With no aircraft available, Kliewer and other grounded pilots held out, fighting valiantly until surrender on 23 December when they were taken prisoner. The POWs were evacuated from Wake on 12 January after enduring harsh treatment and hard labor. They were transferred to China and Japan and were repatriated after surrender in August 1945.

CHAPTER 7

First American Aces

First USAAC and American Ace/PTO

Pilot: Lt. Col. Boyd "Buzz" Wagner
Unit: 17PS/5th Interceptor Command
Time: 16 December 1941
A/C: P-40 E

Action: The first day of the war was almost as devastating for the Americans in the Philippines as it had been at Pearl Harbor. The Japanese air raids of 8 December destroyed over half of the Far East Air Force's aircraft, including a devastating three-quarters of the front line P-40s. By 11 December, only 30 pursuit aircraft were available, and of these eight were the outclassed P-35 Severskys. The fighter situation was so desperate that the FEAF ordered fighters to engage in recon or observation sorties and to avoid combat.

Pennsylvanian Boyd Wagner joined the Air Corps in 1938 after graduating with an aeronautical engineering degree. The 25-year-old first lieutenant was shipped to the Philippines in late 1940, where he took command of 18 P-40Es of the 17PS stationed at Clark Field, Luzon. His nickname, "Buzz," came from his sometimes-annoying practice of buzzing other aircraft.

On 10 December, Wagner's squadron had escorted B-17s flying up from Del Monte Field, Mindinao, for a bombing mission on Japanese invasion shipping. No opposition was encountered. That afternoon Japanese bombers attacked an auxiliary field at Del Carmen, 35 miles north of Clark Field. Wagner and his group caught the bombers heading back towards their base at Vigan. Wagner may have shot down two Japanese this day.

In the morning of 12 December 1941, Wagner took off on a solo mission from Clark Field to patrol the Aparri area. Just north of this Jap-held airfield he was bounced by five Zeros (or Ki-27 Nates?). Using an AVG Flying Tiger tried-and-true tactic, he dove his P-40 to wave level and headed ashore. Two Japanese fighters dove and stayed on his tail, nimbly matching any evasive tactic he tried. Becoming desperate, Wagner quickly chopped his throttle, and the surprised enemy fighters over ran the P-40 and became its quarry and then victims. Wagner headed back to Aparri at treetop level and strafed a neatly parked line of 12, destroying five. Low on fuel, he returned to base. Combat narratives of the 17PS credit Wagner with four victories for this day, but the dates seem to be confused in the records, and two victories on the 10th seem to be more logical. The confusion arises because the records held at Maxwell AFB, AL, are incomplete due to the chaos of the evacuation of the Philippines after the fall of Bataan. USAAF Historical Study 85 and researcher Frank Olynyk both credit Wagner with four victories, but Study 85 gives the date as the 13th and Olynyk questions the 12th as "can not be right, folklore?" Despite the confusion in chronology, it seems Wagner did have four victories by the time.

On 16 December, Wagner took off before dawn with Lts. Russell Church and Allison Strauss to attack the Jap airfield at Vigan. The three Kittyhawks, armed with six 30-pound fragmentation bombs, came in low over the sea at daybreak. Strauss provided top cover for the two. Wagner, diving first, had the advantage of surprise and succeeded on his bombing run on two dozen poorly deployed aircraft on the field, causing heavy damage. However,

LtCol. Boyd "Buzz" Wagner was the first American ace in WWII. In the chaos of the Japanese attack on the Philippines during the week after Pearl Harbor, Wagner was flying a P-40E for the 17PS of the Fifth Interceptor Command and downed four Japanese aircraft. On 16 December, Wagner downed his fifth enemy aircraft, a Zero, during a strafing attack on Vigan A/D. Wagner scored eight victories in the war before being KIFA flying a P-40 from Elgin Field, FL. (USAF)

Church, with Japanese AA batteries alerted, had flak hit his engine, setting it on fire. Nonetheless, Church continued his attack, crashing to his death.

Wagner made five strafing runs on the field, destroying ten aircraft and setting the enemy fuel dump on fire. On one of his strafing runs Wagner shot down another Zero (or Nate?) just as it lifted off the ground to score his fifth aerial victory to become America's first ace. For this action Wagner was awarded the DSC.

On 22 December, Wagner and a few remaining serviceable fighters left in the Philippines attacked the Japanese beachhead at Vigan on Lingayan Gulf. An exploding shell hit Wagner's windshield, and he was badly injured in the face and chest by the shattered glass. He was evacuated to Australia aboard one of the last transports to leave the Philippines in early 1942.

After recovering from his wounds, Wagner was assigned to the V Fighter Command as Director of Fighters at Port Moresby, New Guinea. On 30 April 1942 (now a Major), Wagner led 13 P-39s from two squadrons against Japanese positions at Lae and Salamaua. Taking off from Seven Mile Airdrome in the late afternoon, the group climbed to 20,000 feet to clear the Owen Stanley Mountains, which run down the spine of New Guinea. Approaching over Huon Gulf, the planes dropped to treetop level to strafe Lae Airfield. Over Salamaua the P-39s were jumped by 15 to 20 Zeros, which engaged them all the way back to base. Four of the outnumbered and outclassed P-39s were shot down. Wagner downed three Zeros in the chase/retreat to total eight victories for the war, which made him the top American ace of the war at the time.

On 29 November 1942, after returning to America as a light Colonel, Wagner was killed flying a P-40N on a routine flight between Elgin Field, FL, and Maxwell Field, AL.

First USAAF Ace/ETO
Pilot: Capt. Charles London
Unit: 83FS/78FG/8AF Red Flight
Time: 30 July 1943: 1020
Place: Haldern, Germany
Action: By mid-1943, B-17 bombers of the 8AF were venturing across the borders of Germany, escorted by P-47 fighters. The Thunderbolt's range had been extended by the use of 200-gallon impregnated compressed paper drop tanks, which were first used by the 78FG out of Duxford on 30 July 1943.

On that day the 78th was assigned a bomber withdrawal support mission, rendezvousing with the B-17s near Haldern on the German border. Capt. Charles London, Red Flight Leader of the 83FS, climbed to 23,000 feet and 180 mph above the English Channel, jettisoning his drop tank 15 miles off the Dutch coast. Continuing across Holland at 27,000 feet and 180 mph, the 83rd sighted the bomber formation just beyond Haldern, and just as it was about to be attacked by a large mixed group of Me-109s and FW-190s.

At 1020, three FW-190s were positioning themselves for a frontal attack on the bombers when London's flight appeared on the

Capt. Charles London of the 83FS/78FG out of Duxford was the first USAAF ace in the ETO. By mid-1943, the P-47s range had been increased by the use of drop tanks. On 30 July, London led his flight on a bomber withdrawal mission and intercepted a mixed group of Me-109sand Fw-190s over western Germany and downed two –109s to become the first AAF ace. He scored no further victories and was sent back to the States to sell War Bonds. (Author/London)

scene. The Focke Wulfs took no evasive action, as they probably did not expect to find American fighters penetrating so deeply into their territory. As London closed on his first target, a Me-109 pulled up along side his P-47 but did nothing, assuming it to be a FW-190, which had a similar appearance. Despite his unwanted companion, London continued his firing run on the FW, which began to smoke, and one wheel came down. London looked out to find that the escorting Me-109 had vanished and came around to explode the crippled enemy with a short burst.

London climbed above the bomber formation, as German fighter strategy was to concentrate on the bombers and to avoid Allied fighters unless attacked. The Thunderbolts benefited from the German tactic by gaining the altitude advantage, so they could dive on the enemy as he maneuvered to attack the bombers and then could convert the diving speed back to altitude in a climb. London spotted a Me-109 below coming out of a dive and dove on him. Once on the Messerschmitt's tail, London fired from 75 yards, having the German blow up into pieces directly in front of him for his second victory of the mission.

These two victories, along with the FW-190 on 22 June and two Me-109s a week later made London the first ace in the ETO. He scored no further victories and was shipped home at the end of the summer to sell war bonds.

The mission of 30 July saw some other "firsts" besides the first ETO ace and the first mission to use drop tanks. The first "triple" in the ETO was scored by Maj. Eugene Roberts, who shot down two FW-190s and a Me-109. The first strafing attack in the ETO was carried out by Lt. Quince Brown, who shot up a flak emplacement and locomotive west of Rotterdam.

First USN Ace

Pilot: Lt. Edward H. "Butch" O'Hare
Unit: VF-3 Fighting Squadron 3 *Lexington* (CV-2)
Time: 20 February 1942/1705-1740
Place: Off the south coast of Bougainville Island
A/C: F4F-3 Wildcat/"F-15"

Action: In the mid-morning of 20 February 1942, two Japanese Mavis seaplanes out of Rabaul—400 miles to the southwest—discovered an American task force headed by the carrier *Lexington* and supported by a number of cruisers and destroyers. The mission of Task Force 11 was to launch an air strike against shipping in the large Jap roadstead at Rabaul, New Britain, that was the supply hub for New Guinea and the Solomons. Task force commander Vadm. Wilson Brown knew that it would be only a matter of time before the Japanese would launch what would be the first land-based air strike against a carrier in the Pacific. He immediately ordered a CAP of six Wildcats under Lt. Noel Gaylor to the northwest, while six more under Lt. Lt. Cdr. James Thach were readied on deck to relieve or reinforce the CAP. A third group was put on standby.

This third group was led by 28 year old, St. Louis-born Chicago resident Lt. Edward H. "Butch" O'Hare. The son of a wealthy

Lt. Edward "Butch O'Hare of Fighting Squadron 3 off the *Lexington* was the first USN ace of the war. On 20 February 1942, he was flying a F4F Wildcat on CAP over the carrier and shot down five Japanese bombers and disrupted their bombing attack. For this action O'Hare was awarded the CMH. He was MIA on a night mission on 26 November 1943. O'Hare International Airport in Chicago is named in his honor. (USN)

prominent building contractor, O'Hare graduated from the Naval Academy in 1937. He completed flight training at Pensacola in May 1940, being assigned to VF-3 "Felix the Cat" Squadron on the *Saratoga*. The stocky O'Hare carried his childhood nickname "Butch" onto the *Lexington* in 1942.

At 1630, nine dark-green Mitsubishi G4M Betty bombers in three Vs of three were picked up on the *Lex's* CXAM radar some 25 miles to the west at 12,000 feet in a slight dive. Gaylor's six Wildcats were in a landing pattern after being relieved by Thach's men when they were recalled. The 12 F4Fs climbed to meet the fast, unescorted Bettys at 12 miles, and attacked them all the way into the task force's AA defense, downing six bombers. The shipboard gunners downed two Japanese bombers previously damaged by the fighters and drove off the last one smoking toward Rabaul.

Meanwhile, another formation of eight Bettys were belatedly picked up by radar, closing astern to the east. The *Lexington's* decks were in confusion; attempting to launch O'Hare's group and to land Gaylor's fuel-starved first group and another group of anti-torpedo SBDs. Thach's Wildcats were widely scattered from the previous combat. This early radar was unable to determine the attacker's exact course, so O'Hare's six fighters were dispersed in pairs to spread out to intercept the Jap formation. O'Hare and his wingman, Lt (jg) Marion "Duff" Dufilho, were the first to see the Japanese, who were only 12 miles away from the Task Force. The bombers, deployed into two compact Vs of five and three, made shallow fast dives as the two Navy pilots, with a height advantage of several thousand feet, set up their interception at 1715. They approached the Japanese from ahead, allowing the forward left V to pass, and then rolled to attack the right V. O'Hare fired from the beam or quarter position to deny the enemy tail gunners a good target. He attacked the right trailing bomber, hitting the starboard engine and wing root and causing it to smoke and flame. Continuing his run, O'Hare pulled up sharply to avoid a collision with his first victim. He attacked the next bomber in the V, also hitting it in the starboard engine and causing it to leave formation, its engine trailing gasoline and smoking. As O'Hare crossed over to the left of the formation, he checked on his wingman, Dufilho, only to find him missing, as he had to leave combat due to jammed guns, a common, frustrating malady that beset the Wildcat in early 1942.

Now alone to protect his carrier, O'Hare crossed over to the left hand five-plane V, attacking the left three aircraft rear to front. He made a shallow, high side pass, hitting the left engine of his third victim with a short burst and causing it to skid violently and go into a spiraling dive, almost hitting O'Hare. He moved astern to the next bomber in the V, and his .50 caliber bullets hit the port engine,causing it to seize and put it into a steep dive into the sea. O'Hare's third pass on this V, also from the left, was made through task force AA fire, as the enemy formation had come within bombing range of the carrier. Meanwhile, a Japanese bomber (damaged earlier by O'Hare?) joined the formation, and the five bombers made a determined bombing run.

Ignoring the anti-aircraft bursts around him, O'Hare attacked the lead command bomber, hoping to disrupt the bombardier. He hit this bomber from close range, tearing out its port engine. Nevertheless, the mortally wounded aircraft, piloted with skill and courage, aimed itself directly at the *Lexington*, crossing the AA fire of the protecting destroyers and cruisers. The Jap finally crashed just 1,500 yards ahead of the carrier. This near miss was recorded in some of WWII's most famous motion picture combat footage. O'Hare continued his attack, expending his remaining ammunition into the formation and hoping for a lucky hit before it released its bombs. The four bombers released their bombs, and the war correspondents aboard the carrier reported that the bombs missed by the proverbial mile because the Japs were so shaken by O'Hare's attack. But the *Lexington's* battle action commentaries reported a miss of only a 100 feet astern of the carrier. Carrier FDO directed other CAP Wildcats to the retreating enemy, and two more Japanese bombers were shot down.

O'Hare landed back on the carrier amongst great jubilation. His aircraft had only three holes, despite being the target of numerous bomber gunners. His high deflection shooting had kept him out of accurate cones of defensive fire. Ever the professional, he asked for a drink of water and to be rearmed for further combat. Admiral Frederick C. Sherman, skipper of the *Lex*, ordered O'Hare to the bridge. Sherman, who had observed the combat that had taken place directly above the carrier, gave his person congratulations for the five victories. In fact, Sherman was so impressed that he immediately jumped O'Hare two grades to Lt. Commander. Sherman and other senior officers concurred that O'Hare's heroism deserved the Congressional Medal of Honor. Thach enthusiastically agreed and started the ball rolling, much to O'Hare's chagrin. O'Hare would rather face a formation of Zeros than the press.

Over the years historians have disputed O'Hare's five victories. John B. Lundstrom, in his meticulously researched *The First Team: Pacific Naval Air Combat from Pearl Harbor to Midway*, gives O'Hare credit for three victories and two probables. Press releases issued by the Navy claim five victories and one probable, which Frank Olynyk, another careful and respected researcher, confirms. Shipboard observers gave O'Hare credit for six victories. A SBD scout reported a Betty headed back to Rabaul trailing smoke in a slow gliding dive into the sea some 30 miles from the battle scene. This may have been O'Hare's second victim that rejoined the formation during its bombing run. O'Hare claimed five Bettys on his combat report. In any event, America got its hero.

In April, O'Hare returned to the States, a celebrated hero who was ardently pursued by the media. Reunited with his family, he was received in Washington by F.D.R., who watched as O'Hare's wife, Rita, placed the Medal of Honor around her modest husband's neck. He returned to the Pacific as a squadron commander on the *Enterprise* (CV-6). During this tour he developed and trained many future aces. Among his protégés were Richard May (6 victories) and Alex Vraciu (19 victories). As part of Task Force 50, the *Enterprise* took part in the heavy air fighting over the Gilbert and Marshall Islands. O'Hare added two more victories to his total while flying the F6F Hellcat.

During the fighting in the Gilberts, the Japanese, after suffering heavy losses in daylight, began night bombing raids. To counter this threat a few Hellcats under O'Hare's command were to be accompanied by radar-equipped TBF Avengers, which would direct the Hellcats towards night contacts. On the night of 26 November

1943, O'Hare took off, never to return. There are several accounts conjecturing his loss. One theory states that his plane was mistakenly shot down by a nervous TBF rear gunner who misidentified him as a Japanese fighter. Another version speculates he was the victim of a Japanese bomber gunner, as several intruders were lurking in the area. O'Hare's wingman thought he saw O'Hare's Hellcat cross in front of him in a shallow, dive probably with engine trouble (battle damage?), and disappear into the darkness.

The Navy had lost its first great hero, leader, and teacher, whose name was given to Chicago's O'Hare International Airport.

Footnote: If one were to disallow O'Hare's first ace status, then the Navy's first ace would be Lt. Noel Gaylor, who also flew from the *Lexington* with VF-3. During the 2 February "O'Hare" mission, Gaylor scored two shared victories and a full credit over the attacking Bettys. On 19 March 1942, he shot down an open-cockpit Dave recon float biplane on an anti-shipping mission off Lae-Salamaua. Then, on 8 May, during the Battle for the Coral Sea, he became an ace while O'Hare was home receiving the Medal of Honor. Gaylor was escorting torpedo bombers with VF-2 of the *Lexington* when he got a Zero probable and two dive bombers confirmed to give him his fifth and last victory of the war.

First USMC Ace
Pilot: Capt. Marion Carl
Unit: VMF-223
Time: 24 August 1942/1430
Place: Guadalcanal area between Malarta and Florida Islands
A/C: F4F Wildcat
Action: In May 1942, Marion Carl, a tall, affable Marine Corps Captain from Oregon, was trying to gain flying time in his F4F Wildcat for VMF-221 on Midway Island. For months the island was preparing itself for the expected Japanese invasion. At 0600 Midway radar picked up a large formation of Japanese aircraft in-

Capt. Marion Carl of VMF-223 became the first USMC ace on 24 August 1942. Piloting a F4F Wildcat in a running air battle over "The Slot" Carl downed a Betty bomber and then destroyed an escorting Zero over Henderson Field. Carl became America's first double ace and went on to score 18 1/2 career victories. After the war he became a premier test pilot setting world altitude and speed records. Carl is shown receiving the Navy Cross from Adm. Nimitz on Guadalcanal on 1 October 1942. (Author/Carl)

bound from the northwest. As part of a mixed bag of 19 Brewster Buffalos and six Wildcats, Carl dove on the Jap dive-bombers, losing altitude on his firing pass. Several escorting Zeros followed Carl, who rolled and pulled out, heading away from Midway to try to gain valuable altitude, and also losing his pursuers. At 15,000 feet he headed back towards Midway, when he was startled by the noise of bullets striking his Wildcat. Carl reacted with violent evasive maneuvers, but failed to shake the Zero on his tail. He dove into a nearby cloud with the Zero following. He cut his throttle and skidded his fighter into position behind and below the Zero as they exited the cloud. But due to the negative Gs of the dive, all four of his guns jammed and the Jap escaped. Carl circled Midway at 20,000 feet and saw a lone Zero, and he went into a shallow dive, closing unseen, high astern. He hit the Zero, which plunged into the sea for the first of Carl's 18 1/2 victories (16 1/2 in Wildcats).

At the end of June 1942, Carl and two other VMF-221 Midway survivors were transferred to VMF-223 under tough CO Maj. John Smith. During the next month, Carl and his fellow pilots gained valuable flying time and gunnery experience before shipping out on the escort carrier *Long Island* on 2 August. By 20 August, the carrier had reached the southern Solomon Islands, where the Wildcats were catapulted for their 80-minute flight to "Cactus," the code name for Guadalcanal. The Squadron landed at Henderson Field, a former Japanese airstrip that was named after a Marine dive-bomber pilot killed at Midway. During the first three days the Japanese attacked the airfield several times, with the Marines getting five victories (three to Eugene Trowbridge) for one loss.

On 24 August, the Japanese attempted to reinforce the island, with the resulting naval action being the first of four battles for the Eastern Solomons. The Japanese light carrier *Ryujo* (which was sunk later that day) launched 15 dive-bombers and 12 escorting fighters, which were joined by 20 Betty bombers from Rabaul. The Japanese mission was to neutralize Henderson Field so that their troop barges could land reinforcements unopposed. However, VMF-223 was forewarned, and 14 Wildcats led by Smith headed north over the "Slot" at 1410. Ten minutes later, the Jap formation was intercepted between Malaita and Florida Islands. Carl peeled off, making an overhead firing pass on a Betty bomber and destroying it. The air battle soon degenerated into a running gunfight, with Carl pursuing the attackers toward Henderson. He downed another escorting Zero to become the Marine Corps' first ace.

During the battle, the Marines destroyed 16 Japanese aircraft, including six Zeros. That day marked the turning point in Zero dominance—both real and psychological—in American minds. Eugene Trowbridge also downed a Zero and a Betty that day to become an ace, but the records on his early claims are sketchy due to the confusion of the times. During the following weeks Carl and his CO, John Smith, waged a battle for top scorer of VMF-223. On 9 September, a Zero jumped Carl after he had shot down his 13th enemy. His oil lines were hit, causing him to bail out over the sea. He was picked up by natives and returned from the dead to Henderson five days later. During Carl's absence Smith regained the victory lead, which he kept at 19 to 16 1/2 when VMF-223 left Cactus on 12 October. VMF-223 had suffered 43% casualties but scored 110 victories, including 47 Zeros. Smith and Carl shot down more twin-engine bombers (10 and 8, respectively) than any Marine pilots in the war. Smith scored 19 and Carl 18 1/2 career victories to rank as the sixth and seventh highest scoring USMC aces of the war.

CHAPTER 8

USAAF Fighters

First Victories, First Aces, and Top Scorers

U.S. Air Force Fighter Designations

Early World War I American-built fighters bore complex designations indicating aircraft type, manufacturer, company design sequence, engine type, and so on. In September 1920, another designation system was adopted using aircraft type (e.g. P = Pursuit), engine cooling system (e.g. W = water-cooled), number of this type, and version of this number (indicated alphabetically).

In May 1924 the system was simplified, with the aircraft being identified by a single letter signifying its function (e.g. P = Pursuit and B = Bomber). Subsequent designs were given the next number in sequence. This system prevailed until June 1948, when the more accurate F designation was given to Fighters. The first fighter named under this system was the P-1 Curtiss Hawk in 1924. The last P was the P-80 Shooting Star jet fighter, which was redesignated the F-80 after June 1948.

Curtiss P-40 Warhawk

The P-40 was America's first mass-produced single seat fighter, and operated with the USAAF and other Allied Air Forces in every theater of the war. During the first half of the war it and the P-39 made up more than half of USAAC fighter strength. Although not an outstanding fighter aircraft, it was on hand at the time the P-47, P-38, and P-51 were in the early stages of development and production. And so, the P-40 gained a reputation for dependability and ruggedness, and was able to hold its own only when using the validated tactics. The deficiencies of the P-40 could not be blamed on the Donovan Reese Berlin design team at Curtiss, but on the AAC's 1930s concept of bombardment aviation taking precedence over pursuit aviation that repressed American fighter development. The P-40 was built for ruggedness, handling capability, and low altitude performance. The Berlin/Curtiss team had designed the P-36

(Hawk 75A) in 1934, and the P-40 was a direct extension of that design, which was unable to compete with its contemporaries. The prototype XP-40, designated the Hawk-81A by Curtiss, was a converted P-36 airframe with an Allison 1,160hp V-1710-19 liquid-cooled engine, and first flew on 14 October 1938 with Edgar Elliott at the controls. On 27 April 1939 an order for 524 P-40s (there were no P-40As) was placed, and the first production model flew on 4 April 1940. The initial order of 524 was later reduced to 200 to allow Curtiss to run 192 for the French government. These in turn were diverted to the RAF, who named it the Tomahawk I. Because this fighter was only armed with two .30 caliber machine guns and had no protective armor or self-sealing tanks, the British sent them to the Middle East. After the 200th production aircraft, two additional wing-mounted .30 cal. were added, along with some protective armament and self-sealing tanks, and was called the P-40B. The RAF took delivery of 110 as the Tomahawk II, while the USAAF took delivery of 131. One hundred of the RAF order was diverted to supply the American Volunteer Group in China. The P-40C added two more wing guns for six total (two .50s in the cowling and four .30s in the wing). The USAAF received 193 and the RAF 930 as the Tomahawk IIB. The 1,040hp V-1710-33 engine P-40, P-40B, and P-40C were essentially similar, except for armament and some internal differences. The first significant redesign occurred in 1941 in the P-40D, which was powered by a 1,150hp Allison V-1710-39 engine in a shorter nose without the two-.50 caliber nose guns. The four wing guns were upgraded to .50 caliber, and provisions for a fuselage drop tank or 500lb. bomb and six 20lb. underwing bombs were added. Only 22 Ds were delivered to the USAAF and 560 to the RAF as the Kittyhawk I. The P-40E (Kittyhawk IA) had its armament increased to six .50s and was the first large scale production model. Of the 2,.320 built, 820 went to

P-40B F/Ldr. David "Tex" Hill, 2AVG, 13 1/4 P-40 victories (15 1/4 total). (J.W. Gooch/Warbirds Resource Group)

the USAAF and 1,500 to the RAF. It was faster at altitude and better armed, but climb and maneuverability continued to be mediocre. The P-40F exchanged its Allison for a 1,300hp Packard-Merlin 28 engine. Of the 1,311 built, 100 went to the Soviet Union and others to the Free French (FAFL), but the RAF Kittyhawk II was canceled. The RAF took delivery of 21 P-40Ks, 600 P-40Ms (Kittyhawk III), and 586 P-40Ns (Kittyhawk IV). There were 1,300 P-40Ks (increased fin area) produced, 700 P-40Ls (similar to the P-40F, but with only four guns), and 4,219 P-40Ns (four guns and F and L characteristics, along with the 1,360hp V-1710-81 engine). The N was the most numerous model, with 5,216 being built. The P-40R was the conversion of 300+ P-40F and L models from Merlin to Allison engines to be used as advanced trainers. P-40 production ceased in December 1944 when the 13,738th rolled off the production line.

P-40 MTO First Victory in Type
Pilot: 1Lt. William O'Neill
Time: 14 August 1942
Place: North Africa
Unit: 65FS/57FG/Attached to RAF 233 Wing
A/C: P-40F/Me-109
Pilot: 1Lt. William Mount
Time: 9 October 1942
Place: 64FS/57FG/9-12AF
A/C: P-40F/Me-109

British P-40 Tomahawks and Kittyhawks had been successfully operating with the Desert Air Force against Rommel's Afrika Korps, which had driven the British back to El Alamein in May and June 1942. During that summer the Germans tried unsuccessfully to breach the British defensive positions. RAF Air Marshal Arthur Tedder used his outclassed and outnumbered Tomahawks aggressively in both aerial combat and ground support roles. Low level ground attack missions were particularly devastating to the Afrika Korps' supply lines, depots, positions, and armor. In the air the Tomahawks were able to handle the Italian Regia Aeronautica and the air transports which tried to cross the Mediterranean. Against the Me-109 the P-40s were no match, as the record of JG-27 and its 158 victory ace, Hans-Joachim Marseille, attest. However, Australian Wing Commander Clive Caldwell did score 20 victories flying a P-40.

Donovan Berlin designed the Curtiss P-36 (Hawk 75A) in 1934, and the P-40 was a direct extension of that design. (Curtiss)

On 30 July 1942, the pilots and aircraft of the 64th, 65th, and 66th FS of the 57FG arrived at Muqueibila, Palestine, to "acclimatize": to live and learn the facts of life about desert warfare. On their way to North Africa the 57FG became the first American fighter group to take off from an aircraft carrier in land-based aircraft when 72 P-40s safely left the *Ranger* on 19 July 1942. It was the first U.S. fighter group in the MTO, and probably the first to see combat in

P-40K Maj. Edward Nollemeyer, 26FS/51FG, 5 P-40 victories. (J.W. Gooch/Warbirds Resource Group)

either the MTO or ETO. The 31FG had arrived in England in June 1942, but after training did not see action until the Dieppe commando raid of 19 August. The 4FG was activated from RAF Eagle Squadrons in September. The green American pilots learned by flying on RAF operations and were assigned to various British and South African units. The widely dispersed Americans were entirely dependent on the R.A.F. for everything, and were totally integrated into these foreign squadrons. In this three week acclimatization period (to 13 September), the fledgling 57 FG flew 158 sorties, with their first mission occurring on 9 August. The missions were mostly bomber escort, with only two being offensive sweeps. At 0630 on 14 August, the U.S. pilots saw their first combat, as they provided top cover for 12 RAF Bostons bombing Fuka Station. Six U.S. P-40Fs of the 65FS—which was attached to the 233 Wing of the R.A.F.—joined 12 RAF Kittyhawks of the 260 Squadron. The Luftwaffe sent up five Me-109s, and 1Lt. William O'Neill downed a Me-109 for the first American victory in the MTO or ETO. 2Lts. Joseph Shaffer in a P-39 and Elisa Shahan in a P-38 shared a victory two days later over Iceland, but they were part of the AAC at the time and not attached. O'Neill also had another first that day: the first 57FG loss (MTO loss?) when he was hit by AA fire, belly-landed on a calm sea, and drifted and swam 2-3 miles to shore. He was met by two South African soldiers and returned to base.

By 19 August, all 57th personnel had arrived in the Middle East. On 16 September, the entire group was brought together for final acclimatization and training at L.G. 174 near El Alamein, Egypt, under the control of RAF 211 Group. On 19 September, the group began independent combat operations as a reserve unit under RAF 211 Wing. It went on full operations on 7 October and was utilized primarily in a ground attack role. The first independent American victory in the ETO or MTO and in the P-40 was claimed by 1Lt. William Mount of the 64FS while escorting 18 Boston and 6 Baltimore RAF medium bombers to attack Luftwaffe airdrome LG 104. Mount chased a Me-109 out to sea, shooting its tail off.

P-40 MTO First Ace and Most Victories in Type
Pilot: Maj. Levi R. Chase
Time: 15 March 1943
Place: South of Mezzouna
Unit: 58 & 60 FS/33FG/12AF
A/C: P-40L/Mc-202
Victories: 10
Record:

V #	Date	E/A/C
1	12-18-42	FW-190
2	12-22-42	He-111 ?
3	01-31-43	FW-190
4	02-02-43	FW-190
5	03-15-43	Mc-202
6	03-30-43	Me-109
7-8	04-01-43	2 Me-109s
9	10 04-05-43	2 Me-109s

Victories in CBI (2 Commando Group / P-51)

11	03-15-45	Oscar
12	03-26-45	Oscar

The three squadrons (58th, 59th, and 60th) of the 33FG flew its 77 P-40Fs off the deck of the carrier *Chenango* on 10 November 1942 as part of "Operation Torch," the invasion of French-held North Africa two days earlier. The carrier takeoffs were uneventful; however, the landings on the poorly maintained airfields proved treacherous, as 17 fighters were lost or damaged. On its arrival, the group and its CO, Col. William "Spike" Momyer, found that the

1Lt. William Mount (USAF)

Maj. Levi Chase (USAF)

three-day resistance of the Vichy French had subsided. Then the 33ʳᵈ was ordered to donate 30 of their aircraft to the newly repatriated Vichy French pilots to form new Free-French units to fight the Nazis!

The 33ʳᵈ finally saw combat on 6 December as it began to operate out of Thelepte. Newly promoted Captain Levi Chase, a New Yorker flying with the 58FS, scored his first victory on 18 December, downing a FW-190. Four days later he intercepted a He-111 or Ju-88 over Djeba bou Dabouse and destroyed it with his one operable gun.

On the last day of January 1943, and now a major with the 60FS, Chase was flying his second sortie of the day, providing ground support in the Gafsa-Senad area. Chase got a Me-109 and damaged another against the crack Luftwaffe II/JG-77, which claimed two P-40s. Two days later, six P-40s of the 60ᵗʰ flew cover for P-39s of the 154ᵗʰ Observation Squadron over Kairouan. Four FW-190s attacked out of the sun. Chase shot down one, but the 60ᵗʰ lost two more fighters in what had become a war of attrition. The 33ʳᵈ was short on pilots and aircraft, having only 13 of its original P-40s. The Group was pulled from combat after claiming 37 victories. The 33ʳᵈ spent time on R&R and re-equipped with P-40Ls, which was the Packard (Merlin) powered version, rather than the Allison.

After returning to combat on 15 March, 13 P-40s escorted B-25s to attack Mezzouna Airfield. Two Me-109s attacked the 60ᵗʰ at 12,000 feet near Gafsa. The Americans turned into the attack as Axis reinforcements were arriving from the south. Chase shot down an Italian Mc-202 to become the first MTO P-40 ace. Capt. Lyman Middleditch of the 64 FS/57FG/9AF is often credited with being the first MTO ace. Middleditch's fifth victory came on 2 April, when he destroyed a Me-109 during the "Palm Sunday Massacre," which made him the first 9AF ace.

On 30 March, Chase would begin a week in which he would score as many victories as he had in the previous 3 1/2 months. That day he blew a FW-190 into pieces during a B-25 escort mission to La Fauconniere Airfield. On 1 April, 12 P-40s escorted 12 A-20s to El Djem, when they were attacked by four Me-109s before reaching the target. After these attackers were driven off and the group was withdrawing, six to eight Me-109s attacked, and Chase downed one immediately. He got a second Messerschmitt in a running dogfight.

Four days later, 16 P-40s led by Col. Momyer took off after noon on an escort mission to La Fauconniere. On the way home a dozen Me-109s attacked in a running dogfight. Chase got one at once, then continued on the hunt to get a second Me-109 in the Hajeb el Aiouna area. In the combat 1Lt. Harry Henry shot a German off Chase's tail in a diving attack. Chase claims to have damaged or destroyed four more E/A, but never received official credit. The action made him a double ace with ten victories and the top-scoring P-40 ace in the MTO (and ETO).

As a Lt. Colonel, Chase became CO of the 2ⁿᵈ Commando Group, flying P-51s in the CBI, where he shot down two Oscars in March 1945. His victories over the Luftwaffe, Regia Aeronautica and Japanese made him one of three pilots to score victories over three Axis powers. The others were Louis Curdes (82FG and 3ACG),

who was the first (7 February 1945), and Carl Payne (31FG and 413FG).

As the last Axis units in Africa surrendered on 18 May 1943, there were five P-40 groups operational in North Africa (33ʳᵈ, 57ᵗʰ, 79ᵗʰ, 324ᵗʰ, and 325ᵗʰ). Although combat losses in these units were high, the fighter was invaluable in its ground support role and was adequate as an air fighter. With the surrender the P-40 moved on to harass the Axis in Sicily and Italy. In these campaigns the P-40s again did yeoman duty as a ground support weapon, and continued to hold their own against second-line Luftwaffe units in the air. The P-40 would score 592 victories in the MTO

MTO P-40 Aces (14 Aces/82 victories)

Ace Name	Rank	Unit (FG)	P-40 V	Other V
Chase, Levi	LCol	33	10	+2 P-51
Momyer, William	Col	33	8	
Whittaker, Roy	Capt	57	7	
Byrne, Robert	1Lt	57	6	
Taylor, Ralph	Capt	31	6	
Baseler, Robert	Maj	325	5	+1 P-47
Bradley, John	Maj	33	5	
Collins, Frank	Capt	325	5	+4 P-47
Duffy, Richard	2Lt	324	5	
Fenex, James	Capt	324	5	
McArthur, Paul	1Lt	79	5	
Middleditch, Lyman	Capt	57	5	
Overcash, Robert	1Lt	57	5	
Powers, McArthur	2Lt	324	5	+2.5 Spit

P-40 PTO First Victory in Type

Pilot: 2Lt. George Welch
Time: 7 December 1941 / 0815-0845
Place: Ewa, Hawaii
Unit: 47FS/15FG/7AF
A/C: P-40B / Nakajima Type 97 Kate
Action: *See P-40 ETO First Victory in Type*

2Lt. George Welch (USAF)

P-40 PTO First Ace In Type

Pilot: Lt. Col. Boyd D. "Buzz" Wagner
Time: 16 December 1941
Place: Vigan Airfield, Philippines
Unit: 17 PS/V Interceptor Cmd.
A/C: P-40E / Zero ? (Nate)
Action: *See P-40 PTO First Ace AAC*

Wagner and other evacuated airmen would help form the nucleus of the 5AF pilots who would continue the fight against the seemingly unstoppable Japanese advance. Immediately after the fall of the Philippines, the 5AF continued to operate P-40 squadrons: the 3rd, 17th, and 20th PPS in the East Indies Campaign in January and February of 1942; and the 49FG in the defense of Darwin, Australia, in March to August 1942. The East Indies campaign was another no win struggle of attrition and retreat, with the P-40s knocking down 44 Japanese aircraft and sustaining heavy losses before evacuation. The air battles defending Darwin saw the P-40s score 79 victories and suffer fewer aircraft and pilot losses while gaining air superiority.

P-40 PTO Top Scorers in Type

Pilot: Capt. Robert DeHaven
Unit: 7 FS/49FG
Victories:

V#	Date	E/A/C
1	07-14-43	Val
2	10-17-43	Oscar
3-4	10-27-43	Zeke & Tony
5	12-10-43	Tony
6	12-12-43	Oscar
7	01-02-44	Tony
8	01-23-44	Oscar
9	03-15-44	Oscar
10	05-07-44	Judy?

LtCol. Boyd Wagner (USAF)

Capt. Robert DeHaven (Author/DeHaven)

DeHaven left Washington & Lee University after Pearl Harbor and joined the Army Reserves in February 1942. He received his wings as part of Class 43-A, and was graduated from Advanced Training at Luke Field, AZ, in January 1943. He took 40 hours of transitional P-40 training at Pinellas Field, FL, and at Kanoehe, HI, before being posted to the 7FS/49FG at Dobodura, New Guinea, flying the P-40K.

It was not until his 25th combat mission that DeHaven would claim his first victory on 14 July 1943, getting a Val dive bomber over Salamua. On 12 December 1943, now flying P-40Ns, DeHaven's flight was on a routine sweep over Hansa Bay when they were called back to base at Guaan, which was under attack by a mixed group of Zeros, Tonys, and Oscars. The Warhawks intercepted the homeward-bound Japanese near Mandang and were to attack a pair of Oscars, when DeHaven spotted a pair of Tonys about to attack them. He rolled over and got a quick deflection shot on the lead Ki-61 and broke on the second Tony. As he was about to fire he saw a third Tony on his tail and had his right aileron shredded by bullets, and then his ammo boxes blown out. With bullets rattling off his seat armor plate, he tried to evade the Jap, who was no novice, by diving and turning down to 2,500 feet. Suddenly, if for no reason, the Tony turned away, followed by four more Tonys. The Tony looks very much like a P-40, and DeHaven figured that his pursuer thought the four Tonys on his tail were P-40s and the four Tonys in turn thought DeHaven's pursuer was a P-40. With hydraulics shot out and manifold pressure dropping, DeHaven flew back to base and was about to make a belly landing when he saw a C-47 in the opposite direction on final approach. Since his radio was damaged he had no choice but to go around again and belly in the riddled P-40. Upon landing he counted 180 holes in his fighter. DeHaven became a double ace in the P-40 and was also credited with sinking a 2,000 ton tanker in a dive bombing mission on Astrolabe Bay on 20 January 1944. DeHaven flew 222 combat missions (632.5 hours) in the Warhawk before transferring to the P-38 in September 1944. He flew 16 more missions in the P-38, adding four more victories over the Philippines to give him 14 for his tour.

Pilot: Capt. Ernest Harris
Unit: 8 FS/49FG/5AF
Victories:

V#	Date	E/A/C
1-3	01-07-43 3	Zeros
4	03-03 43	Zeke
5	7 04-11-43	2 Zekes & Val
8	9 05-14-43	2 Bettys
10	09-21-43	Hap

The 49FG left Morrison Field, Florida, in January 1942, and sailed for Australia, where it received its recently assembled P-40Es. The group saw action defending Darwin, Australia, between March and August 1942, and gained air superiority for the first time against the Japanese. In September, it moved to Port Moresby, New Guinea, to provide air defense, bomber escort, and ground support. The 8FS was based at Kila Airdrome, the closest of six air bases surrounding Port Moresby. While the 8FS' sister squadron, the 9th of Dick Bong fame, began to receive P-38s, the 8th was relegated to continue flying the P-40. Flying with the 8th was 26 year old 1Lt. Ernest Harris.

On 7 January 1943, 49FG P-40s were sent to attack a Japanese convoy east of Salamaua. These initial attacks crippled the convoy, which limped into Lae. The V FC dispatched 16 P-40s of the 8th FS to strafe the convoy when 20 Zeros bounced. Harris in "*Miss Kat*" was leading a flight of four Warhawks that separated to engage the Zeros and attack the convoy. Harris pressed his firing run on a transport ship, damaging it. As he pulled up, he shot a Zero off the tail of another P-40, flaming it. He went into a firing run on a second Zero, hitting it with three long bursts and causing it to spin out of control into the clouds. As he pulled up, he immediately attacked a third Zero, getting two close-range hits on the cockpit. Following the spiraling Zero under the cloud cover, Harris saw it burning in the water, along with the nearby circular wakes of his other two victims. The 8FS got 12 victories, two probables, and two damaged for the day.

Capt. Ernest Harris (Author/Harris)

Harris' next big day occurred on 11 April, when the Japanese sent a formation of Val dive bombers heavily escorted by Zeros. Harris, now flying out of Dobodura, got two Zeros over Oro Bay. The next month, on the 14th, Harris claimed two of the squadron's 13 victories. He downed two Betty bombers of an escorted formation attacking Port Moresby to give him nine victories. In September, the 8th had received the P-40N and was flying from Tsili Tsili. Harris, now a captain, became a double ace by downing a Hap clipped-wing Zero over Hopoi, New Guinea.

Records and narratives of combat in these early days of the war are sketchy and incomplete. The P-40 served the squadron well and was slowly replaced by the P-38, but it continued to be flown effectively into Spring 1944.

1Lt. Andrew Reynolds, also with the 49FG/9FS, scored six victories with this unit from April to the end of August 1942, and is often credited with 10 victories flying P-40s. Earlier in February 1942, Reynolds flew P-40s over Java with the 20th and 17th PS (Provisional). He downed three Zeros and an unidentified twin-engined bomber. This bomber was shot down with two other pilots and is usually listed as a 1/3 victory (Olynyck and 20PPG history), but some sources (HS 85) credit him with a whole victory

PTO P-40 Aces (27 Aces/185.33)

Ace Name	Rank	Unit (FG)	P-40 V	Other V
DeHaven, Robert	Capt	49	10	+4 P-38
Harris, Ernest	Capt	49	10	
Reynolds, Andrew	1Lt	17P/49	9.33	
Kiser, George	Capt	17P/49	9	
Lisicka, Joseph	Capt	18	9	
White, Robert	Capt	49	9	
Head, Cotesworth	Capt	18	8	+6 P-38
Stanton, Arland	Maj	49	8	
Gaunt, Frank	Capt	18	7	+1 P-38
Hennon, William	Capt	17P/49	7	
Morehead, James	Maj	17P/49	7	+1 P-38
Shuler, Lucien	1Lt	18	7	
Westbrook, Robert	LCol	18/347	7	+13 P-38
Wheadon, Elmer	Capt	18	7	
Hagerstrom, James	1Lt	49	6	
Howard, Robert	1Lt	49	6	
Landers, John	1Lt	49	6	+4 P-38 +4.5 P-51
Meuten, Donald	1Lt	49	6	
West, Richard	Capt	8	6	+8 P-38
Wright, Ellis	Capt	49	6	
Bade, Jack	1Lt	18	5	
Byrnes, Robert	Capt	18	5	
Day, William	1Lt	49	5	
Donalson, I.B.	1Lt	49	5	
Everhardt, Lee	Capt	9	5	+1 P-38
Gladen, Cyrus	Capt	18	5	
Wagner, Boyd	LCol	17P/VFC	5	+3 P-39

Flying the P-40 Warhawk (PTO)
By
Richard West: 6 victory P-40 ace 8FG
14 total victories

I flew the P-40N for six months for the 35th Fighter Squadron of the 8th Fighter Group in late 1943, over New Guinea. Luckily, on my first encounter with the Japanese on 22 September, I was able to shoot down two Hamp fighters and claim a probable near Finschhafen. I did not see another Jap until 15 November, when I shot down two Zekes and two Sallys and got a probable of each.

We were flying the P-40N-5, which was the most improved P-40 model of the time. But these improvements over the M and N series only included a new radio, a better seat, and the addition of external bomb racks. Along with rust and corrosion due to the high New Guinea humidity, my pre-flight checks often showed a number of fluid leaks of various kinds: fuel; hydraulic; coolant, etc. streaking the aircraft.

The cockpit was fairly roomy, but the controls, pedals, and instrument panel could be too far forward for a small pilot, who would require a cushion. I had no problem being 5'10"/175 pounds. For the novice pilot ground handling and taking off in the P-40 was difficult, because it was equipped with a number of late 1930s systems which required four hands to even start the engine. I never had any problems with the P-40 on the ground. Its long cowling and tail-down mode made ground handling difficult. To taxi you had to make S-turns and look through the side panels to navigate. Because of the tropical heat we left the canopy open and hung our heads out the side to taxi, but we then stuck our noses into the exhaust smells and had to hold our breaths. The Allison heated up very quickly, and it was not long before the coolant gauge went into the red. So a quick takeoff was necessary, or you were forced to shutdown. The brakes were effective in turning, but as a novice you had to watch not to apply them too hard and nose over. The tail wheel was effective but stiff. On the takeoff run you steered with the brakes at first until the tail lifted off the ground, then the rudder was used. The Allison's great torque pulled the left wing down, and

to keep the wings level, right stick and hard right foot were required. A major weakness of the aircraft was its agonizingly slow climb to altitude. To gain speed in the climb ASAP it was necessary to use full military power, which in the Allison was about five minutes.

Once in the air the P-40's foibles on takeoff disappeared, and it was normal in all flight characteristics and was easy to fly after some practice. But in green hands it was demanding and unforgiving. The fuel mixture settings were straightforward, and a fuel low warning light flashed a reminder to change tanks. As the fuel was used the CG moved forward and added stability and made the fighter a better gun platform. Trim required some manual dexterity and vigilance. A slight buffeting warned of a stall. Once in a spin, the aircraft would come out of it by itself if the controls were released. To get out of a spin quickly you had to cut the throttle, kick the rudder the opposite direction of the spin, and pull the stick forward. The aircraft did not have enough range or altitude capacity. A supercharger would have made it a dandy fighter. It was reasonably maneuverable due to its extremely responsive ailerons and being easy to roll. The main asset the P-40 had going for it was that it was a great diver and picked up speed quickly in a dive. However, in a dive the normally light ailerons got heavy and you had to stand on the rudder to keep the diving fighter flying straight. Like the Flying Tigers, we used our diving advantage to initiate and leave combat at our choice. The more nimble Japanese fighters could easily best us in a dogfight, but could not catch us in a dive.

The pipper gun sight was ok, although you had to duck down in your seat to see the pipper. It was supplemented with a cowl-mounted ring and bead sight. The sight was used both to shoot and drop bombs. The windscreen would fog up to a point of uselessness going from 15,000 feet to deck. This fogging happened in my first combat, but I managed to get two Japs mainly by luck, and also by flying up their asses. I always felt that a good combat pilot needed to combine good flying and good shooting. I had grown up hunting, so shooting was a given for me. I habitually tried to approach the Jap as close as possible, although I was always scared of Japanese tail gunners. It was important to go over enemy aircraft recognition charts. Once you got within 20-30 yards the effect of six .50 caliber machine guns was awesome.

The P-40 landed like a rock, and the air speed indicator needed to be monitored at all times. When the carburetor scoop came up it blocked the view of the runway. Once on the ground it was necessary to taxi quickly to your destination before the engine overheated. If you overheated you could either shut down or face into the wind to get more air into the radiator.

The P-40 was not as bad as a lot of people would have you think, especially the later models. A good fighter jock could do the job against the Japs anytime.

Capt. Richard West (Author/West)

P-40 CBI First Victory In Type

Pilot: 1Lt. Henry P. Elias
Time: 10 July 1942
Place: Hangkow, China
Unit: 75 FS/23 FG/14AF
A/C: P-40E / Jap Fighter

On 4 July 1942 the contracts of the men of the Flying Tigers expired, and with them the AVG. That same day the 23FG was activated at Kunming with personnel shipped from the U.S. Some 20 AVG pilots volunteered to stay on for two weeks to aid in the transition. Top AVG pilots Tex Hill, Ed Rector, Chuck Older, and Frank Schiel would become Majors on 18 July as permanent members of the group. Early operations were limited by the confusion of transition and lack of fuel and supplies. On 6 July Tex Hill, CO of the 75FS, and departing AVG pilot John Petach each scored a victory over Nates while escorting five B-25s bombing the docks and warehouses at Canton.

On 10 July, four P-40s of the 75FS bombed Japanese-held Liuchwan, which was under attack by the Chinese. John Petach led a bomb run, but his Warhawk was hit by AA fire and went into a spinning crash, losing a wing and killing its pilot, who was to ship home in a week. Arnold Shamblin, another AVG "extendee," was also hit by ground fire and forced to bail out and was taken prisoner. Under this dark cloud, another flight of 75FS P-40s took off to strafe river shipping near Hangkow. 1Lt. Henry Elias, a new stateside arrival, took part on the mission. After successfully bombing the shipping, the flight was bounced by a large formation of Japanese fighters. Elias turned into the attack and downed the Jap with a difficult deflection shot. His victory was the first by USAAF personnel in the CBI and the first by a P-40.

Elias went on to score four victories. On 2 September, he was intercepted by three enemy fighters in the Nangchang area after a strafing run on river traffic in the area. He shot down one, but the other two set his aircraft on fire. Elias bailed out and was machine gunned and killed in his parachute.

Utilizing the tactics and an experienced nucleus of AVG personnel, the 23rd continued the Flying Tiger P-40 tradition.

P-40 CBI First Aces in Type

Pilots: Capt. John F. Hampshire
1Lt. Charles H. Dubois
Time: 27 November 1942 / 0845-1200
Place: Canton Harbor
Unit: 75 FS (Hampshire) 76 FS (Dubois) /23FG/CATF
A/C: P-40K / Hampshire (3 Zeros) Dubois (Nate & Zero)

The 23FG was organized as part of the Chinese Air Task Force (CATF) from the disbanded AVG on 7 July 1942. The 23FG was comprised of the 74FS at Kunming, the 75FS at Kweilin, and the 76FS at Hengyang. The 74th served as an operational training squadron for the inexperienced Air Force pilots coming out of flight schools from the States. Many AVG pilots agreed to extend for two weeks until replacement AAF pilots arrived in number on 18 July. The 23rd found itself with only 34 P-40Es and 18 H-81 export (Chinese) P-40s on hand to cover an area as large as Western Europe. One year later the situation was no better, with only 64 P-40s on hand. Col. Robert Scott, AVG veteran and *God Is My Co-Pilot* author, led the group. The squadron COs were also AVG vets: 74FS-Frank Schiel (4 victories); 75FS-Tex Hill (9 1/2 v.); and 76FS-Ed Rector (4 1/2 v.)

On 25 October 1942, the CATF began an air offensive when 12 B-25s and seven P-40Es led by Scott raided Jap shipping in Victoria Harbor, Hong Kong. The formation took off in the early morning, flying 500 miles to refuel at noon. They arrived at their target—the Kowloon docks—at 1315, with the Mitchells dropping their 500lb. bombs from 17,000 feet. As the formation turned off target, it was attacked by about 20 climbing Zeros and a few Nicks. Flying in the American formation was Capt. John Hampshire of the 75th and 1Lt. Charles Dubois of the 76th. Hampshire shot down the Zero that had shot down the first B-25 in the CBI. Hampshire then got a second Zero. Dubois claimed a Nick and Zero on the return leg of the mission. Dubois got a Zero over Mengtze two days later for his third victory.

On 27 November, the 23FG, now flying P-40Ks, escorted 10 B-25s to Canton harbor. A large mixed group of Zeros, Nicks, and Nates attacked the bombers. Dubois got a Zero and Nate, but was outscored by Hampshire, who got three Zeros. Both pilots became the first AAF P-40 aces in the CBI.

**Capt. John Hampshire
(USAF)**

**1Lt. Charles Dubois (Author/
Dubois)**

P-40 CBI Top Scorers in Type
Pilot: Col. Bruce K. Holloway
Unit: 76FG/23FG & 23FGC/14AF
Victories:

V#	Date	E/A/C
1	11-24-42	Nate
2-3	11-27-42	I-45 & Zero
4	12-14-42	Biplane
5	12-22-42	Biplane
6	04-26-43	Sally
7-8	05-15-43	Zero & Bomber
9	07-23-43	Zero
10	07-24-43	Zero
11	08-20-43	Zero
12	08-21-43	Zero
13	08-24-43	Zero

Pilot: Capt. John F. Hampshire
Unit: 75FS/23FG & 23FGC/14AF

V#	Date	E/A/C
1-2	10-25-42	2 Zeros
3-5	11-27-42	3 Zeros
6	04-01-43	Zero
7-8	04-24-43	Zero & I-45
9-11	04-28-43	2 Zeros/bomber
12-13	05-02-43	2 Zeros

Even though the P-40 was generally considered inferior to contemporary Japanese fighters in the Pacific, it was the only fighter the AAC had in sufficient inventory to counter the Japanese. In the three years it fought in the CBI, it became part of aviation legend and history. It was the backbone of the 23FG, which scored the majority of its 519 victories in the P-40 before switching to the P-51. Against the nimble, fast-climbing Japanese fighters, the P-40 owed its success to its rugged construction, high diving speed, and heavy firepower. Of course, the tactics developed by the Flying Tigers and the better training and leadership of the American pilot gave the P-40 the intangible advantage.

From the time of its activation, the 23FG flew missions which would allow it to engage the Japanese Army Air Force: strafing enemy airfields; escorting bombers; and defending its own airfields. Two 23rd aces were the top P-40 scorers in the war. One was a 1937 West Point graduate named Col. Bruce Holloway, and the other was Capt. John Hampshire, who was the first P-40 and 23FG ace in the CBI. Both men would score 13 career victories, all in the P-40. One pilot's career would end in tragedy, while the other would continue up the chain of command in the post-war Air Force.

On 2 May 1943, the 75FS sent 16 P-40s to attack a reported formation of 47 Zeros approaching their home base. Hampshire, with 11 victories, was flying on the wing of Lt. Col. John Alison at 18,000 feet when a flight of a dozen Zeros crossed the field at 10,000 feet. Hampshire scored a victory, and the squadron continued on to pursue the main enemy formation. Descending to avoid a storm, Hampshire and Alison attacked three Zeros. They missed the leader, but each got a wingman. Alison lost Hampshire in the combat, and

he did not return to base. The Chinese reported an American plane had crash-landed in a lake near Changsha, and its pilot, though rescued, suffered serious chest wounds. Hampshire died of his wounds the next day. Hampshire's death provides an interesting aside. When the clipped-wing Zero was first seen it was thought to be a new fighter type and was code named "Hap" in "honor" of Gen. H. H. "Hap" Arnold, USAAF Commander. Arnold was not at all happy with the accolade, and it was quickly changed to "Hamp" in December 1943. According to a press release issued in April 1944, it was changed to "Hamp" in honor of an air hero in China.

Maj. Holloway was a key participant in the transition of the AVG to the 23FG and CATF. When Gen. Claire Chennault assumed command, he named him his group operations officer. It would not be until 24 November 1942 that Holloway would score his first victory, when he destroyed a Ki-27 Nate. In December he was promoted to Lt. Colonel, and became an ace when he downed two biplanes on the 14th and 27th. He was transferred to Group HQ to begin his second tour in April 1943. In the mornings of 23 and 24 July, the Japanese raided American air bases and he shot a Zero down each day to become a double ace. On 24 August, Col. Holloway led a formation of P-40s from the 16th, 74th, and 76th FS to escort B-24s to Hankow. At 1245, Holloway got a Zero for his thirteenth victory to tie Hampshire for the most AAF P-40 victories. When his tour ended, Holloway was assigned various command positions. After the war he became Group Commander of the 1FG, which was the first jet-equipped tactical unit. He served as Deputy Commander of the 9th and 12th Air Force, Vice Chief of Staff of the Air Force, and retired as a Brig. General in 1972.

To accommodate the inclusion of the 23FG into the Army Air Force, the CATF was disbanded, and in March 1943 the 23rd became part of the 14AF. As part of the CATF the 23rd scored 150 victories in nine months, while losing only 16 P-40s to the Japanese. The P-40 remained the primary American CBI fighter until April 1944, when it began to be superseded by the P-51.

Capt. John Hampshire (USAF)

CBI P-40 Aces (49 Aces/337.4 Victories)				
Ace Name	Rank	Unit (FG)	P-40 V	Other V
Hill, David	Col	2 AVG/23	13.25	+2 P-51
Neale, Robert	F/L	1 AVG	13	
Hampshire, John	Capt	23	13	
Holloway, Bruce	Col	23	13	
Burgard, George	F/L	1 AVG	10	
Little, Robert	F/L	1 AVG	10	
Older, Charles	F/L	3 AVG	10	+8 P-51
Scott, Robert	Col	23	10	
Reed, William	LCol	3 AVG/3P	9	
Smith, Robert T.	W/M	3 AVG	8.9	
Cruickshank, Arthur	Maj	23	8	
McGarry, William	W/M	1 AVG	8	
Richardson, Elmer	Maj	23	8	
Bond, Charles	VS/L	1 AVG	7	
Lawlor, Frank	F/L	2 AVG	7	+2 F6F
Little, James	1Lt	23	7	
Lombard, John	Maj	23	7	
Newkirk, John	S/L	2 AVG	7	
Stewart, John	Capt	23	7	+2 P-51
Turner, William	1Lt	17P/3P	7	+1 P-400
Rector, Edward	Col	2 AVG	6.75	+1 P-51
Alison, John	LCol	23	6	
Callaway, Ray	Maj	3P	6	
Colman, Philip	Capt	5P	6	
DuBois, Charles	1Lt	23	6	
Goss, Edmund	Maj	23	6	
Hedman, Robert	F/L	3 AVG	6	
Lubner, Marvin	Capt	23	6	
Rosbert, Joseph	W/M	1 AVG	6	
Rossi, John	W/M	1 AVG	6	
Vincent, Clinton	Col	23	6	
Williams, James	1Lt	23	6	
Prescott, Robert	W/M	1 AVG	5.5	
Bartlett, Percy	F/L	2 AVG	5	
Bartling, William	F/L	1 AVG	5	
Bonner, Stephen	1Lt	23	5	
Bright, John	Maj	2 AVG/23	5	+1 P-38
Clinger, Dallas	Capt	23	5	
Gordon, Mathew	Capt	23	5	
Grosvenor, William	Capt	23	5	
Jones, Lynn	Capt	23	5	
Liles, Robert	Maj	51	5	
Marshall, Lyndon	1Lt	5P	5	
Nollmeyer, Edward	Maj	5P	5	
Overend, Edmund	W/M	3 AVG	5	+3 F4U
Pryor, Roger	Capt	23	5	
Quigley, Donald	Maj	23	5	
Sandell, Robert	S/L	1 AVG	5	
Smith, Robert H.	W/M	1 AVG	5	

Flying the P-40 Warhawk (CBI)

By
Bruce Holloway:
13 victories 23FG
Second ranked P-40 ace

The Curtiss P-40 was not an extraordinary performer. But, except for some very early models, it was a rugged, simple, and reliable fighter that could take punishment and get home safely more often than any other fighter of its day, with the possible exception of the P-47.

I flew approximately 100 combat missions, with something over 300 hours in the P-40. Most of this was in the E and K models, but I also had passing experience in other models: the "X"; B; M; N; and Q. The first encounter I had with the fighter was the P-40 "X" at Wright Field in the summer of 1941. On the rare occasions it was in commission, I was allowed to fly it. From the firewall back it was identical to the P-36, weighed 2,500 pounds more, was aerodynamically less stable, had half the climb rate, had 7-8,000 feet less service ceiling, and possibly slightly more range and speed. My reaction to the aircraft was "why bother?"

Nearly a year passed before the P-40 and I met again, this time in China with the American Volunteer Group (AVG), or Flying Tigers. We were equipped with the B models, but just before the AVG was amalgamated into the 23rd Fighter Group we received some Es. As I recall, the C and D models were similar to the Bs, but the E was a great improvement. Most of the improvement was in the armament, but it also had more power, better protective armor, and a little more fuel capacity. The basic armament, however, was what made the P-40 a combat aircraft worthy of the name Warhawk. There were three .50 caliber machine guns in each wing, and they performed extremely well. The ammunition load was fairly respectable for those days, and the guns rarely jammed. The E model also incorporated an illuminated reticle gun sight that was, of course, a major improvement over the ring and bead iron sights of the previous series. Bomb rack size was increased, so we could eventually carry a 500-pound bomb. The only really disappointing thing about the E was that it had no improvement in service ceiling and only slightly more speed. Climb performance was infinitesimally better,

Col. Bruce Holloway (Author/Holloway)

but like the small speed increase, it was only achieved because its newer model Allison engines could be operated at considerably higher power settings. To the end of its career, except for the Q model, the significant deficiencies of the P-40 were climb and altitude performance.

In my opinion the P-40K was the best of the series, principally because it was the fastest. Horsepower ratings were then up to 1,350, but the old-style streamlined propeller blades were still used. Subsequent series—the M and N—had a slightly lower wing loading, an extended fuselage, and a paddle blade propeller (ostensibly to improve climb and altitude ratings). These models were better in these regards, but not by much, and certainly not enough to counterbalance a degradation in speed and cruising range at lower altitudes. They also had the annoying habit of nosing over rather easily on the ground.

I was privileged to participate in some comparative operational tests at Elgin in 1945 between the P-400, the P-63 (L?), and the P-47J (which held the world speed record for propeller aircraft at that time). The Q was a delight to fly, and had a performance which made you forget it was a P-40. However, it was strictly a breadboard model, and required several high-priced specialists to keep it in commission. I often wondered why Curtiss and Allison did not do something like this sooner. Curtiss did put a Rolls Royce (Packard-built) Merlin in their F model, but it was an early version and provided essentially the same performance as the Allison-powered Es and Ks. The Q was too late and never caught on, and if it had there was a lot of work to do before it could go into production.

The P-40 in all models was a tough bird, and one of its biggest plus factors was its ruggedness. I have personally seen 450 mph indicated on the gauge in dives and have never heard of one coming apart. The P-40's Allison engine 1710 was just plain sturdy. On one mission I received a hit to the scavenge oil pump and immediately lost all oil pressure. Unbelievably, the engine ran for almost four minutes without oil, which was time enough to get back to friendly territory and set her down pretty much in one piece. Other than from enemy action, I had only a few problems with the Allison 1710. The coolant location in the P-40 was one of the things that

Col. Bruce Holloway

got so many wounded P-40s home and doomed so many P-51s. In the P-40 both engine and oil radiators were up front, with commensurably short interconnecting lines. Almost all small arms ground fire had a tendency not to lead low-flying aircraft enough, so that the hit pattern was usually in the aft section of the aircraft. The P-51, with its aft radiators and thus long connecting lines, was more vulnerable to ground fire. But then the Allison's power output was never raised to anywhere near the levels of the Merlin 1650 in the P-51. Its ruggedness prevented anyone who flew the P-40s in combat from ever damning this airplane, in spite of its rather marked deficiencies in performance.

Curtiss built a long line of successful fighters that saw action all over the world. Although never in a prima ballerina role, they nevertheless performed well in a variety of mission applications. Principally through their close identity with the Shark Mouth of the Flying Tigers did the P-40 achieve immortality in the hearts and minds of all those who loved to fly.

The following is excerpted and adapted from my article "The P-40" (AEROSPACE HISTORIAN: Vol. 25 No. 3/ Fall 1978.) Gen. Bruce Holloway

FLYING TIGERS, the AVG

"Flying Tigers," the name evokes a picture of idealistic young Americans, heroically flying their shark-mouthed P-40s against great odds, humbling the barbaric Japanese Air Forces in China. Books, such as *God is My Co-Pilot*, and movies, such as John Wayne's "Flying Tigers," perpetuate this image, even to this day. So as not to provoke the Japanese in pre-Pearl Harbor 1941, pilot and auxiliary recruitment was made surreptitiously under the auspices of a commercial air operation, Central Aircraft Manufacturing Company (CAMCO). To "manufacture, repair and operate aircraft" pilots were tendered a one year contract offering basic $600 per month flight pay (flight leader $675 and squadron leader $750) to which was to be added a food allowance, travel expenses, free accommodations and a 30 day paid leave at the contracts end. Unwritten in the contract, but interjected in the oral interview was the patriotic appeal that CAMCO would also defend the southern terminus of the Burma Road and the monetary appeal that every confirmed aerial victory would be rewarded with a $500 bonus paid by the Chinese.

Chennault's initial prerequisite for pilot qualification were that the candidate be in his 20's, have three years in fighters and have a minimum of 300 hours flying time. Of the 109 volunteer pilot recruits only a dozen met each of the requirements. But since mid-1937, Chennault had tried to organize a unit of Americans to fight the Japanese and now could not be choosey. In early 1941, the Chinese government had contrived to buy 100 Curtiss P-40's which had originally been consigned to Sweden. President Roosevelt authorized recruitment for these pilots from the active duty ranks of the American armed forces. About half of the pilot recruits had Navy or Marine backgrounds, one-third Air Corps and the remainder were commercial or test pilots or old-fashioned aerial soldiers of fortune. After completion of their contracts, these volunteers would be allowed to rejoin their prior military service without loss of rank or tenure.

A number of motives prompted these men to volunteer but probably the adventure and money along with the desire to avoid the discipline and red tape of the military were the foremost reasons. Most pilots tripled their military pay and the large bonuses for aerial victories would add to that. There was no military hierarchy, only an employer/employee relationship bonded by a contract. Under such an organization, discipline was forever a problem and it was a credit to Chennault's leadership ability that he was able to coalesce such a diverse group of men under trying circumstances. A schedule of fines was spelled out for infractions but the specter of a dishonorable discharge always threatened. In its nearly eight months (December 1941 to July 1942) nearly one-quarter (22 pilots and 43 ground crew) were discharged on disciplinary grounds.

It was Chennault's demanding training regimen and combat doctrine, which gave the Flying Tigers its strength. He required each pilot to master the P-40 in order to utilize its characteristics to advantage. The pilot was taught to use its diving speed to make a pass, to shoot, and then to break away. Under no circumstances were they to engage the nimble Japanese in a dogfight.

When the AVG disbanded on 4 July 1942, they ranked with Churchill's' "Few" of the Battle of Britain, as an aviation legend. The achievements of the Tigers are somewhat confused as without gun cameras and usually being outnumbered in the dive, shoot and run air battles, verification of victories was difficult. The Group was credited with 297 confirmed victories (11 more than the Chinese bonused). It is believed that over 150 "probables" fell, unconfirmed into the Gulf of Martaban or the Burmese jungles while another 200 plus were destroyed on the ground. The AVG and RAF succeeded in keeping the port of Rangoon and the Burma Road open to supplies for more than two months. In early May the Japanese routed the Chinese armies, which retreated through the Salween River Gorge. Continuous bombing and strafing of the Gorge's bridges and Japanese supply convoys stopped the enemy's drive, probably saving China from total collapse. Of course, another plus was the inestimable effect the AVG had on the morale of the Chinese and American people.

P-40 AVG First Victory in Type
Pilots: F/L Fritz E. Wolf (1 AVG)
 W/M Charles R. Bond (1 AVG)
 W/M Edward F. Rector (2 AVG)
Time: 20 December 1941
Place: SE of Kunming
Unit: See above
A/C: P-40Bs/"Type 97" (Ki-48, Lily) Army bomber
100 P-40s modified for export were diverted to the Chinese for use in the newly organized American Volunteer Group (AVG), under Gen. Claire Chennault. With the unstated blessing of the Roosevelt government, American pilots were recruited from the three military services, and also included a few civilian pilots. By June 1941 the pilots and their crated fighters had arrived at Toungoo, Burma, for training. To overcome the apparent superiority of Japanese aircraft and airmen, Chennault's demanding training regimen and combat doctrine would more than equalize the shortcomings of the P-40. He required each pilot to master the P-40 in order to utilize its characteristics to best advantage. The pilot was to use its diving speed to make a pass, shoot, and break away. Under no circumstances were they to engage the nimble Japanese fighters in a dogfight. The AVG was composed of three squadrons: 1st (Adam and Eves); 2nd (Panda Bears); and 3rd (Hell's Angels), of 18 fighters each. Copying the RAF 112 Sqn. that flew P-40s in the Libyan desert, Chennault ordered the shark mouths painted on his P-40s' cowlings. After Pearl Harbor was attacked Chennault deployed the group to Kunming (700 miles to the east) to face the Japanese.

During the first morning at Kunming at 0930, 20 December, the warning network reported that ten bombers were incoming from

F/L Fritz Wolf (Author/Wolf)

W/M Charles Bond (Author/Bond)

W/M Edward Rector (Author/Rector)

Indochina. Sixteen 1 Squadron Tomahawks under Sandy Sandell flew southeast at 15,000 feet and were backed by Jack Newkirk's 2 Squadron. Soon Newkirk saw the ten, unescorted twin-engine bombers (Ki-48 Lilys), which jettisoned their bombs and turned home. Unexplainably, Newkirk also retreated without attacking. The Lillies had to circle near Kunming to find the Iliang rail line, which was to lead them back to Indochina. While circling, the Japanese met the Adam and Eves who were patrolling over Iliang. According to Chennault doctrine, two P-40s were to climb to cover against escorts. The main formation of three flights of four P-40s were to divide, with two flights diving to attack the Japanese bombers out of the sun while the other remained in reserve. But in the heat of combat, Chennault's edicts were forgotten or ignored, and a free-for-all developed, with all the P-40s, except top-cover, getting into the fray. Fortunately, no Japanese fighters appeared.

W/M Charles Bond decided to attack from above and right, and as he dove and squeezed the trigger on the stick nothing happened! In his excitement, while checking and rechecking his gun switch he had turned it off. He broke off and repositioned himself for another attack, which was successful. F/L Fritz Wolf also attacked during this undisciplined melee. He came in from below, exposing himself to the Lily rear gunner. He fired from long range, closing in to finish off his target unscathed.

W/M Ed Rector of the 2AVG was standing down that day, as his P-40 needed 25-hour service. When he saw Newkirk's squadron returning from combat, he could not resist and ordered his fighter be made ready. Seeing the confused combat, Rector utilized his Navy training and Chennault's tactics. He gained altitude and made a long, sweeping firing run, knocking out the rear gunner. The Lily continued to fly on in formation as Rector passed through his run. As he prepared to finish off the wounded bomber, he saw it nose down in flames. After making other runs, he ran out of fuel and was forced to make a wheels up landing, totaling his P-40, but escaping injury.

Since the original AVG combat reports have been lost there are discrepancies concerning this combat. If all individual narratives are to be believed, then more Lillys were shot down than were in the sky! It seems as though the Bond, Wolf, and Rector victories can be substantiated. But Wolf and Bond each claimed another bomber in their narratives, as did Rector. Also in narratives, Sandell claimed one, Louis Hoffman one, and Joe Rosbert one, along with a shared with Ed Liebolt. Einar Michelson has been awarded credit for a victory after the war. It seems fairly certain that a fourth bomber was lost, as three were seen to go down during the battle over Kunming and a fourth was lost on the way back home. The possible reason for the excessive claims was that each American pilot hit the Japanese bombers repeatedly on several runs. Each pilot believed that his Japanese bomber could not possibly withstand his attack and was a victory. The pilots supposedly voted to share 1/15th of the victory among those pilots in the combat: 14/15th to the 1st Squadron and 1/15th to Ed Rector!

P-40 AVG First Aces in Type
Pilots: F/L Charles H. Older
         F/L Robert "Duke" Hedman
Time: 25 December 1941 / 1215
Place: Rangoon, Burma
Unit: 3AVG "Hell's Angels"
A/C: P-40Bs / Hedman (4 Ki-21 Sallys, 1 Model "O")
     / Older (3 Ki-21 Sallys)

The exploits of the Flying Tigers are legend. The group scored 297 victories and boasted 23 aces in its ranks (29 aces, depending on the source and counting ground victories). Over 80% of its pilots were originally trained in the American military air services in the late 1930s. Charles Older had received flight training at Pensacola and served with Marine Fighting Squadron One. In July 1941, he resigned his commission to join 3AVG Squadron. Also joining the 3AVG was a former Air Corps pilot, Robert Hedman. The 3AVG Squadron "Hell's Angels" was led by S/L Arvid E. Olson and was stationed at Mingaladon Air Drome, a RAF base 12 miles from Rangoon. The Burmese capital was the last supply access available for the war in China, and its loss would open India to Japanese invasion.

F/L Charles Older (Left, Author/Olds) and F/L Robert "Duke" Hedman (Right: Author/Hedman)

The Japanese flew recon missions over the city on 21 December in preparation for a full-scale air attack, which came two days later. At 1100, after several early morning false alarms, 48 Ki-27 Sally bombers, escorted by 20 fighters, flew over the Gulf of Martaban, where the formation divided into two. Eighteen bombers were dispatched to bomb Rangoon's docks, while the remainder headed for Mingaladon Airdrome. Communication between British radar stations and control at Mingaladon was ineffective, and the first 18 Sallies hit Rangoon unopposed. The patrolling RAF first warned the 3AVG Brewster Buffalos, and 12 of Olson's P-40s took off to intercept the incoming Japanese. The Americans climbed and split into two flights: one led by F/L Parker Dupouy, who flew to Rangoon; and the other by V/S/L George McMillan, who led his flight to defend the Airdrome.

That day Chuck Older and Ed Overend were on standby and bicycling near the base. They were alerted by the sound of fighter engines and pedaled back to base. Seeing two unmanned P-40s on the flight line, they climbed into the combat. Older homed on a bomber on the left outside of the formation and scored hits, which caused it to begin to smoke from its port engine. He rolled to the left to renew his attack on the wounded Sally, and he closed and hit it with a long burst. It dropped from the formation streaming smoke, rolling over into a vertical dive and out of sight. He continued to attack from below, this time concentrating on the formation leader. His hits flamed, then exploded the bomber.

The battle was costly for both sides. In the confused air battles the Japanese managed to hit Rangoon, causing destruction and pandemonium among the population. The Japanese lost ten bombers and a fighter, along with five probables and ten damaged aircraft. The AVG lost five valuable and irreplaceable P-40s and two pilots, while the British lost five Buffalos and their pilots. Heavy damage and casualties (British and Burmese) were sustained at Mingaladon. P-40 strength dropped to ten aircraft.

On Christmas Day the Japanese crossed into Burma to attack an electric power plant near Rangoon. Olson sent up his P-40s, now numbering 13 thanks to the efforts of AVG ground crews. They again divided into two flights led by McMillan and Dupouy. McMillan patrolled over the oil refinery at Syriam, while Dupouy circled the base. McMillan's flight attacked the Japanese Sallys after their bombing run over Rangoon. F/L "Duke" Hedman climbed up on the rear left Japanese flank during the initial in string attack and kept firing until he closed to 50 yards of his target, which exploded in front of him. He then maneuvered behind the Japanese formation and took on the last bomber from directly astern. His .50 caliber bullets flamed it, causing it to fall out of formation. Charging his guns, he chased the next two Sallys in the formation before half-rolling out of combat. Returning to the fray, he saw three Sallys in a "V" moving away to their port from their formation. Hedman attacked from below and hit the starboard Sally with a short burst at 100 yards, causing it to smoke and roll out of the "V." He then pulled up to fire on the lead bomber, hitting it with a burst from 100 yards and putting it into a precipitous smoking dive. However, a bullet from the gunner of the remaining bomber smashed his canopy and lodged in his headrest. As he half-rolled away he spotted a Model "O" at 500 yards turning away from him, about to attack another P-40. Turning inside the Jap, he closed to 300 yards and fired. The Japanese burst into flame and went into a vertical dive. An ace-in-a-day, Hedman was then chased by a fighter. He half-rolled and went into a 15,000 foot power dive, leveling off at 5,000 feet, and flew in the shelter of a cloud bank until he reached a RAF satellite field almost out of gas.

Meanwhile, in the swirling battle, Chuck Older and his wingman, F/L Thomas Haywood, maintained Chennault's fighter doctrine of fighting in pairs. East of Thongwa, each downed two Sallys. Then Older got a Model "O" over the Gulf of Martaban, which also made him an ace that day.

Again, different sources give different credits on this day. Some sources (Danny Parker: *Flying Tigers*) claim that Hedman suggested that morning that all members of the flight receive credit for any Japanese shot down, or 2 5/6 apiece. Hedman was mistakenly given a victory on 23 December and ended the day with 3 5/6. Likewise, Older was credited with the 2 5/6 to go with his two victories on 23 December, to give him 4.83. Dr. Frank Olynyck credits each with five victories to end the day.

The day was pivotal in the Pacific air war. The 3AVG claimed 24 victories (15 bombers and nine fighters) for a loss of two P-40s and no pilots. Eager for good news after the Pearl Harbor disaster, the press gave extensive coverage to the Flying Tigers and their shark-mouthed P-40s. It was the first time that the invincible Japanese were defeated in the air.

After his spectacular scoring debut, Hedman went on to score only one more victory (two shared halves in April 1942). Older went on to get five more AVG victories to become a double ace. When the Tigers disbanded, he returned to the States and joined the Air Force as a major. In mid-1944 he returned to the CBI with the 23FG, and flying P-51s he scored eight more victories. In an interesting footnote: after the war Older became a Superior Court Judge and became distinguished for presiding over the infamous Charles Manson trials.

P-40 AVG/CBI Highest Scorers in Type
Pilot: LtCol. David "Tex" Hill
Unit: 2AVG/75FS/23FG
Victories: 13 1/2 in P-40 (10 1/2/AVG & 3/23FG)

V#	Date	E/A/C
1	01-03-42	I-97 Fighter 2AVG
2-3	01-23-42	2 I-97
4-5	01-24-42	Bomber & fighter
6	01-29-42	I-97
6 1/2	03-24-42	1/2 Type 98 bomber
7 1/2-8 1/2	04-28-42	2 Model O Fighters
9 1/2	05-05-42	Zero
10 1/2	07-06-42	I-97
11 1/2	07-30-42	I-97 75FS/23FG
12 1/2	09-03-42	I-97
13 1/2	10-25-42	Zero
14 1/2	11-25-43	Oscar (P-51) 23FG/HQ
15 1/2	05-06-44	Hamp (P-51)

David Lee "Tex" Hill was the highest scoring AVG ace with 15 1/2 victories during the war, 10 1/2 in the P-40 with the AVG and three more P-40 victories with the 23FG. Hill was born on 13 July 1915, the son of missionary parents in Kwangju, Korea. After graduating from Austin College in Sherman, TX, in 1938 he entered the Navy, where he graduated from Pensacola as a Naval Aviator. He spent 18 months with Torpedo 3 aboard the *Saratoga* and Scouting 41 aboard the *Ranger* as a torpedo and dive-bomber pilot. He was recruited out of the Navy in 1941 to join the AVG, serving as a Squadron Leader of the Second Squadron ("Panda Bears"). On 3 January 1942, Hill, along with John Newkirk, Jim Howard, and Bert Christman, flew on a mission against the Japanese air base at Tak, 170 miles to the east. The group—minus Christman, who turned back due to engine problems—arrived over the field at 10,000 feet. The Japanese appeared to have been taken by surprise, having rows of aircraft lined up along the runway. Howard immediately dove upon the field for a strafing run, but three Japanese fighters bounced the Tigers, one getting on Howard's tail. Hill quickly moved astern, shooting down the Jap to save Howard. He was soon confronted by a head-on attack, taking several hits that caused his plane to vibrate. Meanwhile, Newkirk downed the other two enemy fighters and Howard destroyed four aircraft on the ground. Before the Tigers disbanded, Hill scored 8 1/2 victories and volunteered to remain in China to serve with Chennault. He was commissioned as a Major and activated the 75FS of the 23FG, where he was the squadron commander. He scored three victories with them in the P-40 before returning to the States in late 1942 to become Group Commander at Elgin Field. In late 1943 he returned to China as 23FG Commander and scored two more victories. When he returned to the States in late 1944 he took over command of the 412FG, America's first jet group, flying the Bell YP-59, and later the P-80.

Pilot: V/S/L Robert H. Neale
Unit: 1 AVG "Adam And Eve" Squadron
Victories: 13 (6 Probables)
Record:

V#	Date	E/A/C
1	01-23-42	Nate
2-3	01-24-42	2 Sallys
4	01-26-42	Fighter
5	02-06-42	Nate
6-9	02-25-42	4 Nates
10-12	02-26-42	3 Nates
13	05-03-42	Recon Bomber

V/S/L Robert Neale, a 28 year old ex-Navy flier from Seattle, had scored four quick victories in four days at the end of February 1942. He downed two Sallys on the 24th for his second and third victories. For these victories he closed to about 35 yards to the rear of the first victim and blew out its starboard engine. He then moved through intense defensive fire and attacked the lead bomber. He closed, in the true meaning of the word, to 50 feet. His machine gun hits caused a huge explosion that turned his fighter upside down, tearing hunks out of his wing and aileron. Limping back to Mingaladon, two Nates pounced and put two holes in his cockpit and shot the microphone off his helmet, nearly ending his life.

On 2 February Neale led a flight against about 20 Japanese Nates, which split into two groups, one high and one low. The Japanese were able to evade Neale's best efforts, getting on his tail and causing him to break combat. He lost the Nates for a while, but regained them 2,000 feet below as they retreated. He surprised the rearmost Nate and opened fire at 100 yards to become an ace.

In late February 1942, the Japanese Army was approaching the last river barrier protecting Rangoon, and by the 22nd the AVG was

S/L and Maj. David "Tex" Hill (Author/Hill)

V/S/L Robert Neale (Author/Neale)

put on one hour's evacuation notice. On the 25th, at 1030, Neale and wingman Bob Prescott took off with four other Adam and Eves to intercept 20 Japanese Nates that were about to sweep the Tiger airfield. Three Tigers immediately got lost, but Neale managed to down two Nates and Prescott one. Later that day a large formation of Japanese Lillys escorted by Nates came again. Neale downed two Nates to put him ahead of Jack Newkirk as the top AVG ace with nine. The next day the AVG was told to evacuate on 1 March; if the British could out that long. Early in the morning Neale led his flight to strafe Moulmein, getting two shared (1/7th) ground victories and three of the AVG's 20 aerial victories.

At sunrise on the 4th of July 1942, the air warning net in the Hengyang area informed the AVG base at Lingling that a dozen Japanese bombers were approaching from Nanchang. Six P-40s of the 2AVG under Maj. Ed Rector were joined by the two 1AVG P-40s of Neale and his wingman, F/L Charles Sawyer. The bombers were discovered to be fighters and were called in as "Zeros." But AVG pilots tended to call all Japanese fighters "Zeros," and these Zeros were, indeed, Army Nakajima Ki-27 Nates. The Japanese were flying at 13,000 feet when they dove on Neale and Sawyer. Rector's unit simultaneously dove on the Japanese, who were silhouetted against a 7,000 foot cloud base. Rector's flyers got three Nates for the last AVG victories of the war. Neale, after claiming a recon bomber on 3 May for his thirteenth and last victory, made two probable claims. As the Tigers disbanded, Neale returned to the States and joined Pan American Airways with $7,776.18 in his pocket for his 13 air victories, six probables, and 3 2/7th ground victories—top AVG and P-40 ace (tied) of the war.

Flying the P-40 Warhawk (AVG)
By
Robert Neale:
13 victories AVG
Second leading P-40 Ace

Like many pilots in the AVG, I was a Navy flyer, having graduated from flight training at Pensacola in 1939. I served aboard the *Saratoga* for two years with VB-3, flying SBCs and SBDs. In 1941, I refused a regular commission and resigned from the Navy, got married in June, and joined the American Volunteer Group. When we arrived in Burma we were introduced to the P-40B Tomahawk,

V/S/L Robert Neale (Author/Neale)

of which we knew nothing, except some rumors on how difficult it was to fly. The P-40s we received were headed for the RAF in North Africa, but the Chinese government was able to purchase them and ship them in crates to Burma to be reassembled. Chennault scheduled flight training and lectures to help us hot shot pilots become proficient in the P-40. We Navy pilots had a difficult time adapting, as we were used to carrier operations. For deck landing we were used to stalling in nose high, three point, and letting the tail hook engage. The landing gear of a Navy fighter could take a lot more punishment than that of the P-40. We banged down hard and bounced along the runway, and had no tail hook to keep us out of trouble at the end of the runway. There were a lot of ground loops, bent props, and worn brakes. I think we lost more P-40s to flying accidents than to the Japanese.

A vivid recollection of my first meeting with the P-40 was its long thin nose, which was in striking contrast to the stubby noses covering our Navy radial engines. On a carrier we did not have to do much taxiing, so it took some practice to S-turn down the taxiways without hitting something. To compound matters the Allison engine would overheat quickly, so we couldn't delay in taking off. The V-1710-33 developed about 1,100 hp with a low growl, a sound one never forgets. The engine's torque pulled the aircraft to the left, so a lot of right rudder was needed, along with the forward pressure on the stick to get the tail up. Once the tail was up the pilot could finally see over the nose. It seemed to take forever for the P-40 to gain altitude, but once over 15,000 feet it wasn't worth much, anyway. There was plenty of warning of a stall, and recovery was quick and easy by dropping the nose and reapplying power. Spins were no problem, either. Compared to the SBD and SBC, it was fun to snap roll, slow roll, chandelle, and loop. While it was fun, I did not try it near a Jap Zero! The P-40's greatest asset was its ability to dive. This advantage, along with Chennault's tactical doctrine, gave us air supremacy over the superior Japanese Zero. Chennault knew that the Zero was built for turning combat, being able to climb faster, turn in a shorter radius, and operate at higher altitudes. The P-40, along with its great diving capability, had a higher top speed and greater firepower (four .30 cal. and two .50 cal. machine guns). Chennault's hard and fast rule of aerial combat was "No dogfighting: Attack and dive away." He stressed gunnery and discipline. When he got done with us, we were married to the P-40.

ACES of the AVG
The Chinese government had spent $8 million on the AVG: $5 million to purchase the P-40s and auxiliary equipment, and $3 million more for salaries, bonuses, and other personnel expenses. The human cost was 13 pilots lost in action: four in air-to-air combat; six by ground fire in bombing and strafing missions; and three in air raids. Two more died in that old bugaboo—flying accidents. Four were made POWs. At no time did the group have more than 55 P-40s serviceable. A breakdown of the 80 P-40s lost shows:

Destroyed in aerial combat:	12
Destroyed by ground fire:	10
Destroyed in air raids:	13
Destroyed in accidents:	23
Destroyed in evacuation:	22

AVG ACES

Name	Rank	Sq	US	V	GV	PV	TV	Notes
Neale, Robert	S/L	1	USN	13	3	15.5	15.5	*
Little, Robert	F/L	1	AAC	10	3	10.5	10.5	KIA 5/22/42
Burgard, George	F/L	1	AAC	10	0.75	10.75	10.75	
Older, Charles	L.Col.	3	USMC	10	0	10.25	10	+7v. 23FG/AAF
Reed, William	L.Col.	3	AAC	9	7	10.5	11.5	+ 6v. 23 FG/AAF
Hill, David	S/L	2	USN	8.75	2	12.25	11.25	+ 6v. 23FG/AAF
Smith, Robert T.	F/L	3	AAC	8 .9	6	8.33	8.33	To 23FG/AAF
McGarry, William	W/M	1	AAC	8	3.25	10.25	10.25	POW 3/24/42
Rector, Edward	VS/L	2	USN	7.75	3.5	6.5	6.5	+ 3v. 23FG/AAF
Bond, Charles	VS/L	1	AAC	7	2.5	8.75	9.25	*
Newkirk, John	S/L	2	USN	7	2	10.5	10.5	KIA 3/24/42
Lawlor, Frank	F/L	2	USN	7	0	8.5	8.5	+2v. VBF-9/USN
Howard, James	S/L	2	USN	6	4	6.33	6.33	+6v. 354FG?AAF
Rosbert, Joseph	W/M	1	USN	6	0.25	4.25	0	
Hedman, Robert	F/L	3	AAC	6	0	4.83	5	
Rossi, John	W/M	1	USN	6	0.25	5.25	6.5	
Prescott, Robert	W/M	1	USN	5.5	3.25	5.25	5.25	
Bright, John	F/L	2	USN	5	2	6	7	+ 23FG/AAF
Overend, Edmund	W/M	3	USMC	5	0	5.83	8	
Bartling, William	F/L	1	USN	5	1	7.25	7.25	*
Smith, Robert H.	W/M	1	AAC	5	0.5	5.25	5.25	KIA 2/7/42
Sandell, Robert	S/L	1	AAC	5	0	5.25	5.25	
Bartlett, Percy	F/L	2	USN	5	2	7	7	Resigned 3/21/42

Possible AVG Aces

Name	Rank	Sq	US	V	GV	PV	TV	Notes
Jernstedt, Kenneth	F/L	3	USMC	3	7	10.5	10.5	
Schiel, Frank	VS/L	2	AAC	4	3	7	7	USAAF
Haywood, Thomas	F/L	3	USMC	4	0	5 1/2	5.25	
Bishop, Lewis	F/L	3/2	USN	4.2	3	5.25	5.2	POW 5/28/42
Laughlin, C.H.	W/M	3	USMC	2.2	5	5.2	5.2	
Wolf, Fritz	F/L	1	USN	4	0	2.25	0	+1v. VBF-3/USN
Raines, Robert	W/M	3	USN	3.2	0	3.2	5	*
Moss, Robert	W/M	3	AAC	2	0	4	7	
Petach, John	F/L	2	USN	4	0	4	5.25	KIA 7/10/42
Boyington, Gregory	F/L	1	USMC	2	2.25	3.5	6	+22v. VMF-214

Legend: Sq = AVG Squadron GV=Ground victories *=stayed 2 weeks after disbandment of AVG
US= Pre-AVG US service PV=Paxton victory list disbandment
V= Olynyk Victory list TV=Toliver victory list

AVG Squadron Victories

Squdron	Squadron Nickname	Victories	Probables	Damaged	#Aces
1	Adam & Eves	98.5	21	5	11
2	Panda Bears	65.5	8	1	4
3	Hell's Angels	68	14	27	3

The AVG ace list varies greatly from source to source. The AVG did not set up a claims board until April 1942, as before this time the RAF handled claims, since AVG squadrons were attached to the RAF. The RAF decided claims on eyewitness reports or wreckage location. Once the RAF decided a claim then the individual AVG squadron would determine how to allot the bonus payment, a procedure that created discrepancies in victory credits. Another cause for inconsistencies occurred, as Chennault requested bonus payments for aircraft destruction on the ground. This procedure was initiated in March 1942. A frequently used source of AVG victory credits comes from George Paxton, the AVG finance officer, who paid the bonuses for claims. However, it appears that some of these victory totals included ground claims. Raymond Toliver and Trevor Constable, co-authors of *Fighter Aces of the USA*, also supply a victory list which seems to credit higher scores, probably because it includes ground victories and possibly "probable/damaged" claims. Researcher Frank Olynyk probably has the most accurate numbers, as he has cross-searched several sources (e.g. bonus claims, Historical Study 85, citations, and most importantly, combat reports).

After the disbandment only five pilots (Hill, Bright, Rector, Schiel, and Sawyer) along with 25 ground crew chose to remain in China with the Army Air Force. Some other pilots, perhaps feeling they could not pass a military physical exam, chose to fly transports for the Chinese National Aviation Corp (CNAC) and Pan American Airways. Most of the other pilots elected to rejoin the services in which they held a commission before joining the Tigers. Four AVG aces went on to become aces again in American units. Chuck Older (10 AVG victories) scored seven victories with the 23FG, Tex Hill (8 1/2 AVG) scored six with the 23FG, and Jim Howard (6 AVG) scored six with the 354FG. The most famous ex-Tiger was the controversial Gregory "Pappy" Boyington, who scored 22 victories while commanding the Black Sheep (VMF-214) as a Marine. Some sources credit Boyington as being an AVG ace, but careful accounting of combat reports limit his claims to two victories, 3 1/2 maximum. Both Boyington and Howard went on to win the Congressional Medal of Honor.

G/C Clive Caldwell of RAF 250 and 112 Squadrons scored 20 1/2 victories to become the leading P-40 ace of the war. (Author)

P-40 Kittyhawk in RAF and Commonwealth Service

During the North African Campaign, which began in January 1942 and ended in May 1943, Kittyhawk squadrons of the RAF, RAAF, RZNAF, and SAAF accounted for 420 German and Italian aircraft and several double aces. The leading squadron was the RAF 112 "Shark" Squadron, with leading scorers S/L Clive Caldwell with 20 1/2 (of 28 1/2 total career victories) P-40 victories to become the leading P-40 ace of the war. S/L Billy Drake with 14 (of 19 total) P-40 victories was the second highest P-40 ace. 3RAAF squadron boasted S/L Robert Gibbes with 11 and S/L Andrew Barr with 12 1/2 victories, while F/O John Waddy of 250 Squadron had 10 1/2 (of 15 1/2 total) and F/L James Edwards of 260 squadron showed 14 (of 16 1/2 total). After their air combat success in North Africa the Kittyhawk squadrons were relegated to a ground support role in Sicily and Italy.

In the Pacific, the RAAF and RNZAF P-405 had minor successes. The RAAF 75 Squadron scored 18 victories over northern New Guinea in spring 1942. The RNZAF operated 297 P-40s during the Pacific war, and were credited with destroying 99 Japanese in aerial combat. F/O Geoffrey Fisken of the 15 Squadron was credited with 5 (of 11 total-he scored 6 in the Brewster Buffalo over Singapore in 1942) and S/L Percival Newton of the 17 Squadron with 5 victories were RNZAF P-40 aces.

Lockheed P-38 Lightning

The P-38 was major player in all combat theaters, performing a wide variety of roles, and it destroyed more Japanese aircraft in the Pacific than any other fighter. Its design was conceived in 1937 at a time when worldwide interest in twin-engine single seat fighter design was revived. It was to become the only twin-engine design from that time to attain mass production and see wide service in WWII. H.L. Hibbard and his protégé, Clarence "Kelly" Johnson, tendered a design in response to a 1936 AAC specification for a twin-engine interceptor that was a radical departure from conventional American fighter development. An inventory of divergence from the conventional were its tricycle landing gear, twin booms, impressive firepower (four .50 caliber machine guns and a 20mm cannon), and its size and power, which were twice that of its contemporaries, making it the largest, heaviest, and fastest American fighter of the time. The Lockheed Model 22 was the winner of the competition, and in June 1937 one XP-38 prototype was ordered to be powered by the new Allison V-1710 engine developed by Norman Golman. It was first flown by Lt. Ben Kelsey on 27 January 1939, but crashed two weeks later. Despite the crash, the Army was so impressed by its performance that it ordered 13 YP-38s. The first YP-38 flew on 16 September 1940 with the more powerful 1,150hp Allison V-1710 engines, the replacement of two of the four .50s by .30s, and the 20mm cannon by the 37mm. The production version of 35 P-38Ds (there were no A, B, or Cs) had the original XP-38 machine gun arrangement, pilot armor, self-sealing fuel tanks, and minor airframe modifications. It was followed by 210 P-38Es that reverted back to the 20mm cannon and carried twice the ammunition. The name Lightning was given by the RAF, which had ordered three Lightning Is and a subsequent order for 524 Lightning Is, which was canceled. The remaining 140 Lightning Is were re-

P-38J Capt. Laurence "Scrappy" Blumer, 393FS/367FG (ETO), 6 P-38 Victories. (J.W. Gooch/Warbirds Research Group)

possessed by the USAAF, which procured the Lightning Is built for England, as well. These Is were converted to the F and G standard. An increase in engine power was the major improvement in the F and G models, which enabled them to carry external fuel tanks and/ or weapons on under wing racks for the first time. A production run of 527 P-38Fs and 1,082 P-38Gs with deliveries during 1942 supplied enough P-38s for deployment in the ETO, North Africa, and the PTO. A further increase in horsepower marked the 601 P-38Hs. The 2,970 P-38Js were the only Lightnings to undergo major external changes, with the introduction of chin air cooler intakes under the prop spinners, a flat panel replaced the curved windscreen, and the radiators located in the booms were enlarged. It was the fastest of the P-38s with a top speed of 420 mph, and its increased internal fuel capacity, along with external tanks, gave it an endurance of 12 hours. The L-model was the most prolific, with 3,810 being produced by Lockheed and a further 2,000 ordered from Vultee, but only 113 were completed before the order was canceled at the end of the war. Two 1,475hp V-1710-111 engines powered the L. As was the case with most long-lived mass produced aircraft, the P-38 was converted for other duties. The 75 P-38Ms (from the L model) were converted into two seat radar-equipped night fighters. The undesignated "Droop Snoot" and pathfinder models were P-38 J and L model conversions fitted with bombardier type Plexiglas

Kelly Johnson, protégée of Chief Lockheed designer, Hal Hibbard, is considered the father of the P-38 (Lockheed)

noses. The P-38 as the F-4 or F-5 was the most numerous photo recon aircraft of WWII, with approximately 1,400 being converted from the P-38E, F, G, H, J, and L. A total of 9,923 Lightnings were produced.

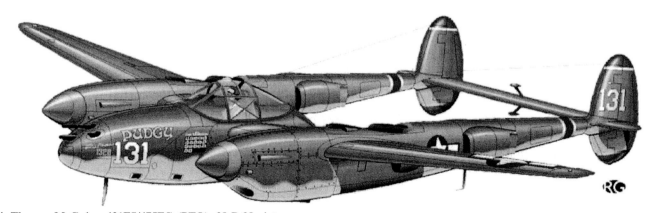

P-38H Maj. Thomas McGuire, 431FS/475FG (PTO), 38 P-38 victories. (J.W. Gooch/Warbirds Research Group)

1Lt. Ben Kelsey, shown here with MGen. Hap Arnold (L) and BGen. Warner Robins (C), first flew the XP-38 on 27 January 1939. (Lockheed)

P-38 CBI First Victory in Type

Pilot: 1Lt. Lewden Enslen
Time: 24 July 43 / 0950-1105
Place: Kweilin, China
Unit: 449 FS/23FG/14AF
A/C: P-38/Zero

Only two squadrons were primarily equipped with the P-38 in the CBI: the 459th and the 449th. The 449th "Lightning Tigers" of the 23FG was organized in July 1943 from aircraft and volunteers who flew with the 1st, 14th, and 82nd FGs in the concluded North African campaign. Former Flying Tiger ace Maj. Ed Goss initially led the group, but soon Capt. Sam Palmer took over. Based at Ling Ling, China, the squadron began operations in late July.

On 24 July the squadron, which arrived the previous day, was operating over Kweilin Airdrome, where 1Lt. Lewden Enslen scored the first P-38 victory in the CBI when he got a Zero. He was credited with another Zero victory and probable on the 26th, and another probable the next day, both over Hengyang. The squadron would not score again until 21 August. In October 1943 the squadron was reassigned to the 51FG. Squadron CO Capt. Enslen was killed in action on 30 October 1943 over Kiukiang on a river shipping strike led by football All-American Tom Harmon. During the disastrous mission four of eight precious P-38s were lost in exchange for four Japanese losses. The squadron would fair better, as it scored 71 1/2 victories and had three aces before it eventually ran out of targets in late 1944.

P-38 CBI First Ace

Pilot: Capt. Hampton E. Boggs
Time: 2 April 44 / 1220
Place: Heho A/D, Burma
Unit: 459 FS/10 AF
A/C: P-38H / Oscar

The P-38 was an afterthought in the makeshift CBI theater, equipping only two squadrons, the 449th of the 14AF and the 459th of the 10AF. As part of the 80FG, the 459th was organized in India in September 1943 and was under the command of Gen. Lewis Brereton. When it was disbanded in Burma after the war it would have the distinction of being the only U.S. unit formed outside the Zone of the Interior (e.g. the States), never to see service within its home country. The 459ers were known as the "Twin Dragons," because each of its P-38 engine nacelles was painted with eyes and an open mouth containing menacing fangs. The squadron's mission was B-24 and B-25 bomber escort and to protect ATC "Hump" cargo planes and their bases, along with doing ground support duties for Gen. Stillwell in North Burma and harassing Japanese airbases.

On 1 December the 459th sent 15 P-38s to escort 7 BG B-24s to the Insein marshaling yards near Rangoon. The 110 P-51s scheduled to assist were late because of refueling delays. Just after noon, 60 Japanese fighters bounced the outnumbered American formation from ahead, out of the sun. The BG leader, his left wingman, and squadron leader were shot down in quick succession. 1Lt. Hampton Boggs, flying his P-38 *Melba Lou,"* jumped into the fray, shooting down a Hamp for his first victory and preventing a further slaughter.

On 25 March 1944 the Dragons took off from Cox Bazaar on a mission to torment the JAAF over its own airfield at Aisakan, Burma. At 1000 hours Lt. Boggs caught two Army Hamps as they were taking off and shot them down. He proceeded to strafe the field, destroying another Hamp. Pulling up, he noticed a Jap fighter in flames behind him; 2Lt. Jim King had shot a Jap off Bogg's tail. Boggs dove back into battle, getting his third Hamp and damaging another.

Capt. Hampton Boggs (USAF)

The 459th continued to supplement its escort missions with aggressive attacks on enemy airfields. On 2 April Boggs became the first CBI P-38 ace by destroying an Oscar over Heho at 1220. Boggs went on to score four more victories to go with four on the ground to become the CBI's second highest-scoring P-38 ace with 9. He was killed in a F-86 flying accident after the war.

P-38 CBI Top-Scorer in Type
Pilot: Capt. Walter F. "Bill" Duke
Unit: 459FS/80FG/10 AF
Victories: 10 (13?) (8 1/2 ground)
Record:

V#	Date	E/A/C
1-2	03-11-44	2 Oscars
2 1/2	03-25-44	1/2 Oscar
3 1/2	04-17-44	Oscar
4	04-23-44	1/2 Tojo
5	04-25-44	Oscar
6	04-29-44	Oscar
7	05-03-44	Oscar
8	05-07-44	Oscar
9	05-19-44	Oscar
10	05-23-44	Oscar
11-13?	06-06-44	3 Oscars

On 4 March 1944 the 459th, after a session of gunnery training with the RAF, moved to Chittagong on the Bay of Bengal, attached to RAF 224 Group. The next week the "Twin Dragon" Squadron would begin an 11 week campaign against the Japanese Army Air Force, which had been building its strength to support Japan's move on Imphal in preparation to invade India.

On 11 March, 12 P-38s led by CO Capt. Verl Luehring attacked the JAAF airfield at Aungban. The early (0800) raid surprised the enemy, who were just taking off as the Lightnings arrived. Thirteen Oscars were claimed that day, including two by 1Lt. Bill Duke of Leonardstown, MD. Flying his P-38 *Miss V,"* Duke originally enlisted in the RCAF in July 1941, finishing service training before

enlisting in the U.S. Air Force in May 1942 and graduating in August. He went overseas with the 80 FG, flying P-40Ns out of India before transferring to the 459th.

On 25 April, Capt. Duke became an ace by shooting down an Oscar over Heho Airfield. A month later he became a double ace, scoring a victory over an Oscar while harassing Meiktila Airfield to become the top CBI P-38 ace of the war.

On 6 June, the squadron split to attack Heho and Meiktila. Maj. Luering led one group, and his exec., Capt. William Broadfoot, led the other, which included Duke. Broadfoot's group, low on fuel and ammo, was bounced from above by a mixed bag of Oscars and Hamps, and scattered attempting to make it back to base. Duke lost his wingman, 2Lt. William Baumeister, and radioed that he had enough fuel to go and look for him. Baumeister, however, returned to base, but Duke became MIA. After the war, Hampton Boggs, Duke's 459th squadronmate, participated in an intelligence mission to Japanese airbases. The investigation discovered that Hamps which were waiting for the lone fighter had ambushed Duke. The interrogation revealed that Duke turned into the overwhelming enemy formation and shot down three of them before going down himself. These three victories have never been officially confirmed or credited to Duke's 10 air victories (in 88 combat missions).

By 26 May, the Dragons had been in combat 58 of 77 days beginning 11 March, and had claimed 61 aerial and 67 ground victories (in the CBI and 8AF ground victories were credited), mainly harassing Japanese airfields. They lost only seven P-38s in the air and six to ground fire. By May the JAAF had fewer than 100 aircraft on strength, and became so depleted that in the next 11 months it would score only 29 more victories.

CBI P-38 Aces (9Aces/62 Victories)

Ace Name	Rank (FS)	Unit	P-38 V
Duke, Walter	Capt	459	13
Boggs, Hampton	Capt	459	9
Glenn, Maxwell	Maj	459	7.5
Gregg, Lee	Capt	449	7
Goodrich, Burdette	1Lt	459	5.5
Beardon, Aaron	2Lt	459	5
Mahon, Keith	1Lt	449	5
Schultz, Robert	Capt	449	5
Webb, Willard	Maj	459	5

P-38 ETO First Victory in Type
Pilots: 2Lt. Elisa E. Shahan 1/2 victory
    (2Lt. Joseph D. Shaffer 1/2 victory in P-39)
Time: 14 August 1942 / 1030
Place: Western Icelandic coast
Unit: 27FS/14FG
Action: See First Victory in Type ETO

Capt. Walter "Bill" Duke (USAF)

P-38 ETO First Ace and Top Scorer

Pilot: Capt. James Morris
Unit: 77 FS / 20 FG / 8 AF
Victories: 7 1/3 (+3 1/3 ground)
Record:

V#	Date	E/A/C
1/3	02/05/44 1/3	He-111
1/3 to 4	1/3 02/08/44	2 Me-109 & 2 FW-190
5	1/3 02/11/44	Me-109
6	1/3 02/24/44	Me-110
7	1/3 07/07/44	Me-410

The higher level of experience of the 55FG saw it receive its P-38s and begin operations first. The 20FG received a few aircraft and rotated its pilots in escort missions accompanying the 55th in the fall of 1943. After three frustrating months, the 20th became a fully equipped combat unit at the end of December. The next three months were to be a time of disappointment and loss for the group, as it lost 54 pilots, many to "unknown" causes (e.g. suspected mechanical), for a trade off of 52 Germans. The high altitude deficiencies and mechanical difficulties of the P-38, along with the lack of combat opportunities caused the group's morale to ebb. It was not until April 1944, with the switch to large-scale strafing missions which increased the group's combat purpose, that its morale and self-esteem was stimulated.

However, on 8 February 1944 1Lt. James Madison Morris of Columbus, Ohio, gave the 20th a morale boost on an otherwise difficult day. The group, led by Lt. Col. Robert Montgomery, took off at 0950 with 50 P-38s to escort B-17s of the Third Bomb Division to Frankfurt. Mechanical problems caused a staggering 14 P-38s to abort early. Morris was leading the second element of Montgomery's flight. While descending to 12,000 feet, the group spotted a Me-109 approaching its base. A P-38 attacked but blew its turbo, and then Montgomery was unable to complete his firing run when his windshield frosted. Morris then slid behind the charmed Me-109, getting hits and blowing off large chunks, which caused the Ger-

Capt. James Morris (Author/Morris)

man to bail out. The mission continued on deck, and a locomotive was destroyed near Saarburg. Near Sedan, Morris encountered two FW-190s that had just taken off and were carrying belly tanks. Morris, dropping his flaps to make a sharp left turn, immediately got a shot during their head on pass. As they went by he dropped his flaps and made another hard left, getting on the Focke Wulf's tail. A 30 degree deflection shot scored hits, and then Morris continued to get hits as he slid dead astern, causing the German to go out of control, cartwheeling along the ground. He then pursued the second through rain clouds, getting two close-in bursts and destroying it. Finding himself alone in bursting light flak near Dena, he spotted a Me-109 coming towards him at 45 degrees. Morris executed a quick, hard 90 degree turn which brought him astern the 109. As the German tried to pull up, Morris' .50 cal. machine guns ripped the cockpit at 200 yards, giving Morris his fourth victory of the day (he had been credited with 1/3 of a He-111 on 5 February).

Three days later, Morris and the 77th found themselves under continuous attack by Luftwaffe fighters while escorting 200 B-17s to targets in Northern France. At 1156 Morris shot down a Me-109 off the tail of a P-38 to become an ace. The mission had dire results for the 20 FG, however, as it lost eight pilots, including its CO, Lt. Col. Montgomery.

On 24 February the 8AF launched a large-scale mission, with over 800 bombers and almost as many fighter escorts participating. The 20th was assigned to escort the second wave of Flying Fortresses. Only one German interceptor was seen (a Me-110), which Morris downed at 1352 over Schweinfurt for his 6 1/3 victory.

In the Spring of 1944, while flying mostly bomber escort missions, the P-38 veterans of the 20th and 55th Fighter Groups found little opposition. The Luftwaffe had ordered its pilots to avoid combat with the American fighters and concentrate on the bombers. Since the large, twin-boomed Lightning was easily recognized by the Germans at long distances they avoided attacks and waited for the bombers. Thus, it was not until 7 July that now Captain Morris was to score his next and last victory of the war. Flying a B-25 escort, the formation was attacked by 50 Me-410s and a mixed bag of about 100 Me-109s and FW-190s. The P-38s dove on the Me-410s, which were about to pounce on the bombers. Morris chased one of the twin-engine interceptors and put a fatal burst into it. However, its barbette guns caught Morris' fighter, forcing him to bail out and be taken prisoner.

Morris would remain the leading P-38 ace in the ETO with 7 1/3 victories in the air and 3 1/3 on the ground. When Gen. James Doolittle took over the 8AF he decided to replace the much maligned P-38 with the P-51. The switch was to create no problems, as the pilots of the 8AF did not want the P-38, while Gen. Kenney of the 5AF in the SWPA and Gen. Twinning in Italy would take all the P-38s available. The 20th and 55th FGs re-equipped with P-51s in mid-July 1944.

The P-38 scored 496 victories in the ETO, but suffered heavy losses, a high abort rate (9-10%), mechanical and maintenance problems, and pilot discomfort due to the cold weather. The aircraft was to vindicate itself as a strafer in the theater.

ETO P-38 Aces (8 Aces/43.83 Victories)

Ace Name	Rank	Unit	V
Morris, James	Capt	20	7 1/3
Blumer, Lawrence	Capt	367	6
Graham, Lindol	Capt	20	5 1/2
Brown, Gerald	Capt	55	5
Buttke, Robert	Capt	55	5 (+ 1 P-51)
Kirkland, Lenton	1Lt	474	5
Milliken, Robert	1Lt	474	5
Olds, Robin	Maj	479	5 (+ 8 P-51, 4 F-4)

Note: Jack Ilfrey (20 FG) scored 2 v. ETO and 6 MTO (12 AF)
Clarence Johnson (479 FG) scored 1 v. ETO and 4 MTO (82 FG)
Joseph Miller (474 FG) scored 1 v. ETO and 4 MTO (14 FG)

P-38 MTO First Victory in Type

Pilot: 1Lt. Carl T. Williams
Time: 21 November 1942
Place: Escort to Tunis
Unit: 48FS/14FG/12-15AF
A/C: P-38 / Me-109

The 48FS of the 14FG arrived in North Africa three days after the "Torch" invasion (8 November), and was based at Maison Blanche on 16 November. That night a Luftwaffe raid damaged seven of their precious P-38s. Two days later the squadron flew its first combat mission, escorting C-47 transports to Constantine.

On 21 November, six Lightnings of the 48th, moving their base to Youks-les-Bain, escorted B-17s to Tunis. As the formation approached the target a flight of four Me-109s attacked. 1Lt. Carl Williams shot down a Messerschmitt in a diving dogfight to score the first MTO P-38 victory.

P-38 First Ace MTO

Pilot: 1Lt. Virgil Smith
Time: 12 December 1942/1345-1645
Place: Gabes A/D
Unit: 94FS/14FG/12AF
A/C: P-38F "Kniption"/FW-190

"Operation Torch," the invasion of North Africa, was the Allies' first major offensive of the war in the West. Victory in this far-flung theater depended on their ability to checkmate the German supply lines across the Mediterranean through effective air power. The 12AF was created for the MTO and equipped with the P-38s of the 1FG and 14FG that had not been committed to combat in the ETO with the 8AF (although both groups did fly a few missions over France before their assignment to the 12AF). The P-38F, despite the primitive conditions of this desert theater, proved itself in multiple roles: bomber escort; high and medium altitude fighter; strafer; ground attacker; and recon aircraft. The priorities of the war relegated MTO P-38 units to utilize the F variant, while other theaters received the newer G and H types. It was not until early 1943 that the Gs arrived, and then the Hs in mid-year. MTO replacement pilots found they were assigned to these Gs and Hs after training in the Js and Ls in the States!

A post war controversy arose over who was the first P-38 ace in the MTO in WWII. The controversy arose when the 12AF changed its method of awarding shared victories after the North African Campaign had been concluded. On 29 November 1Lt. Jack Ilfrey of the 94FS/1FG took off from Youks-le-Bains at 0635. Eight P-38s strafed Gabes Airdrome, and while returning home encountered two Me-109s. Ilfrey scored hits on both Germans, but three other pilots, Capt. Newell Roberts of the 94FS and Capt. Ralph

1Lt. Virgil Smith (Author/Ilfrey)

Capt. Jack Ilfrey (Author/Ilfrey)

Watson and 1Lt. Virgil Smith of the 49FS/14FG, claimed hits, and were initially credited along with Ilfrey with 1/4 victory each. Later the 12AF Victory Assessment Board decided that there were to be no shared victories, only full ones. Ilfrey and Watson were awarded a full victory apiece, leaving Newell and Smith without. Post-war AAF Historical Study 85 (HS-85) gave Watson a full victory, Roberts and Ilfrey a half victory, and Smith none.

On 2 December, Ilfrey participated in an early morning fighter sweep on Luftwaffe Airdromes. Four Me-109s were taking off in line. Ilfrey shot down the second, but the fourth got on his tail at 500 feet. He reversed positions and chased the German across the airdrome, scoring hits that caused it to crash into the ground and winning Ilfrey the DFC.

On 26 December Ilfrey took off in "Happy Jack's Go-Buggy" with 11 other P-38s to escort 18 B-17s that bombed Bizerte from 27,000 feet. After the bombing run, he was ordered to escort a crippled B-17. Ilfrey and his wingman, Lt. Sahl, descended to 15,000 feet to find two of the bomber's crew bailing out and the bomber under attack by seven FW-190s. The two Americans pursued the Germans. One pulled up in front of Ilfrey at 100 yards, who fired and hit it in the belly, causing it to crash into a hillside. Returning to the descending B-17, Ilfrey chased another Focke Wulf off its tail and followed it. He got a long burst at 300 yards, causing it to crash into a lake to win his second DFC. Thus, Ilfrey had 4 1/4 victories at the time, but five in the post campaign 12AF reassessment.

Texan 1Lt. Virgil Smith of the 49FS/14FG downed a Ju-88 on 28 November, a 1/2 Me-110 on 29 November, a Me-109 on 30 November and 3 December, a shared 1/3 Ju-52 on 7 December, and a FW-190 on 12 December for a total of 4.83 victories at that date. On 28 December he claimed a Me-109 to become an ace. When the 12AF reassessed Smith's claims they awarded him a full victory on the Ju-52 on 7 December, which with the 12 December FW-190 victory made him an ace on that date. Ilfrey was an ace on 28 December, but post war HS-85 gave him a 1/2 on 29 November for 4 1/2 victories for the North African campaign. Again, researcher Frank Olynyk has confirmed the Smith/Ilfrey claims and makes Smith the first P-38 WWII and MTO ace.

Ilfrey would become an ace on 3 March 1943 when he downed a Me-109. On 24 May 1944 he got two Me-109s over Germany while flying P-38Js for the 79FS/20FG to give him 7 1/2 victories. Smith got his sixth victory on 28 December. Two days later 12 P-38s escorted 12 Bostons of the 15BS over Gabes Airdrome, and Smith's P-38 "Kniption" was severely damaged in aerial combat. Smith tried to crash-land the P-38, but hit a ditch, causing it to explode and killing him instantly.

The Smith/Ilfrey first ace controversy is further muddled by the probable five victory day by 1Lt. Virgil Lusk of the 49FS/14FG on 24 November 1942. Lusk shot down five Italian Savoia Marchetti transports between Gabes and Sfax. HS-85 credits Lusk with four victories, while Dr. Olynyk acknowledges his fifth claim that day. Lusk was KIFA near NAS San Diego on 9 March 1943.

P-38 MTO Top-Scorer
Pilot: 1Lt. William "Dixie" Sloan
Unit: 96FS/82FG/12AF
Victories: 12
Record:

V#	Date	E/A/C
1	01-07-43	Me-109
2	01-30-43	Me-109
3-4	02-02-43	Me-109 & Do-217
5	02-15-43	Me-109
6-7	05-20-43	Ju-88 & Mc-200
8	06-18 43	Mc-200
9-10	07-05-43	Me-109 & Re-200
11	07-10-43	Mc-200
12	07-22-43	Me-109

In early January 1943 the 14FG was relieved and replaced by the embryonic 82FG, which was to be fleshed out by the P-38s and pilots left behind by the 14FG. Most of the new pilots were recently commissioned staff sergeant pilots with less than 30 hours in the P-38 and no gunnery time. After arriving in the British Isles these pilots trained in Ireland in the fall of 1942, and then flew to their North African base at Telegma in late December 1942.

On 7 January the 82nd saw its first combat when it escorted the 319BG to heavily defended Gabes. 2Lt. William "Dixie" Sloan of the 96FS scored the group's first victory when he shot down one of the six Me-109s that intercepted the Americans over the target. The former "flying sergeant" from Richmond, Virginia, flying P-38 F and Gs nicknamed *Snooks" (I To IV)*, quickly became an ace. On 2 February, 16 P-38s escorted six 319BG B-26s on an anti-shipping raid northeast of Cap Bon. The Luftwaffe sent up 20 fighters to attack the B-26 Marauders. The 96th went into a defensive Lufbery circle, which moved inland towards their base. A Me-109 tried to break into the circle and flying into Sloan's sights, whose machine guns caused a spectacular explosion. As the Lufbery reached the

1Lt. William "Dixie" Sloan (Author/Sloan)

coast the Lightnings scattered, diving toward the deck. A FW-190 got on Sloan's tail, shooting out his right engine, smashing his canopy, and damaging his right stabilizer, so that only the control cables were holding it together. Despite having his goggles covered with hydraulic fluid, he was able to evade his pursuer. He rejoined the B-26 formation for protection, but soon a Do-217 attacked the bombers. Sloan was able to get a tail shot, sending it down in flames.

On 15 February, 24 P-38s escorted B-26s of the 17BG to an airdrome near Kairouan. A mixed group of Me-109s and FW-190s came up to defend, and Sloan became an ace when he flamed a Me-109.

On his second tour, on 20 May the 96th, with Sloan now a 1Lt. and a flight leader, escorted B-25s to Villacidrio Airdrome. German and Italian fighters rose to intercept. Sloan claimed a Ju-88 with a lethal burst from below and behind. He then got an Italian Mc-200 and damaged a pair of Me-109s.

Sloan became a double ace on 5 July during an attack on Gerbini #1 Airdrome, Sicily. He destroyed a Me-109 and Re-200, and the two victories tied him with P-40 pilot Maj. Levi Chase, CO of the 33FG, as top MTO ace. It is interesting to note that day 4 Stormo was led by veteran Italian aces Franco Lucchini (26 victories) and Leonardo Ferrulli (22 victories). Both Italian aces were lost that day, and it is probable Sloan may have been responsible for one.

After downing a Mc-200 on 10 July, Sloan scored his twelfth and last victory of the war on 22 July. He was escorting 310BG B-25s to a railway junction at Battopaglia, Italy. Two Me-109s bounced the bombers, and Sloan and fellow ace Ward Kuentzel took care of them. Sloan finished his tour of 50 combat missions on 27 July and remained the top MTO ace for eight months, until overtaken by Maj. Herschel Green, who scored 18 victories flying P-40s, P-47s, and P-51s. 2Lt. Claude Kinsey, also of the 96FS, was the top P-38 scorer in North Africa with seven victories. Kinsey was shot down and taken prisoner during the famous 5 April "Palm Sunday Massacre" of Luftwaffe transport aircraft flying into North Africa to supply Rommel's Afrika Korps.

Over North Africa, the P-38 was the premier American low altitude fighter, being able to maneuver with both the Me-109 and

FW-190, and was faster than both in level flight. The German fighters could out climb the P-38 initially, but the Lightning could then overtake the Germans. In a dive the Germans were initially faster, but the P-38 was able to dive faster and stay in a dive longer. By the time the Afrika Korps surrendered on 13 May 1943, the P-38 had established its superiority both numerically and operationally.

Pilot: 2Lt. Michael Brezas
Unit: 48FS/14FG/15AF
Record:

V#	Date	E/A/C
1	07-08-44	Me-109
2-4	07-14-44	Me-109 & 2 FW-190s
5	07-19-44	Me-109
6	07-20-44	Me-109
7-8	07-22-44	2 FW-190s
9-10	08-07-44	2 Me-109s
11-12	08-25-44	2 FW-190s

For over half a year the P-38 had dominated Mediterranean skies. By early 1944, the war in the air in the MTO was concentrated to Northern Italy and Southern Europe. The 15AF was formed as a strategic bombing force, and due to it virtually all rail and ground transport had ceased in the MTO. The primary duty of its P-38s was escort. Once the P-38 gained numerical superiority and remedied its mechanical and maintenance problems, the 15AF Lightnings clearly demonstrated their dominance. They gained a victory ratio of 4 2/3 to 1 (608 victories vs. 131 lost). Early mechanical problems were solved so that the P-38's abort and serviceability rates were better than the P-51 in the theater. After Luftwaffe opposition had diminished, the P-38's heavy firepower and load carrying capacity established it as a savage ground attack aircraft.

In early May 1944, 2Lt. Michael Brezas of Bloomfield, NJ, was assigned to the 48 FS of the 14FG. He made his first claim on 8 July on a freelance sweep to Vienna, claiming a Me-109 and damaging another. He scored quickly in the middle of July. On the 14th he scored a triple, getting a Me-109 and a pair of FW-190s on an escort to Budapest. On the 19th he became an ace when he downed a FW-190 on an escort and sweep to Munich. The 22nd saw Brezas' squadron flying top-cover for the 82FG on a strafing mission on Buzua and Zeolisti Airdromes in Romania. A mixed bag of 30 Me-109s and FW-190s bounced the Americans from the rear. Brezas got two FW-190s for eight victories in two weeks.

In August he got two doubles. He shot down two Me-109s on 7 August on a bomber escort to Blechammer, Germany, to become a double ace. Then, on 25 August, he got two FW-190s during a bomber escort to Kurim, Czechoslovakia, to give him a dozen victories. By September, Luftwaffe opposition had all but evaporated, with no E/A being encountered by P-38 units that month (the 14 FG saw none in its 18 missions).

In November 1944 he crash-landed on returning from gunnery practice. He was caught by a crosswind, and his prop dug into the turf. He was hospitalized for two weeks with a wrenched back and cuts. On 2 April 1945 he was MIA during a sweep of Vienna. He was last seen by his wingman heading toward Russian territory with

2Lt. Michael Brezas (R) with Cy Wilson in front of the 48FS scoreboard in August 1944. Brezas would add two more victory symbols before the war ended. (Author)

its right engine and rudder shot out, and the left engine streaming coolant. After crash-landing in Hungary he was captured by the advancing Russians, who treated him poorly as a POW before liberating him on 9 May when the war ended. Brezas died in a flying accident in February 1952 while flying a F-94.

MTO P-38 Aces (12-15AF) (62 Aces/375 Victories)

Ace Name	Rank	Unit (FG/AF)	P-38V MTO	Other V
Sloan, William	1Lt	82/12	12	
Brezas, Michael	1Lt	14/15	12	
Leverette, William	LCol	14/12	11	
Hurlbut, Frank	F/O	82/12	9	
Curdes, Louis	1Lt	82/12	8	+1 P-51
Maloney, Thomas	1Lt	1/15	8	
Tovrea, Philip	1Lt	1/15	8	
Zubarik, Charles	1Lt	82/12	8	
Carroll, Walter	1Lt	82/15	7	
Kinsey, Claude	2Lt	82/12	7	
Kuentzel, Ward	1Lt	82/12	7	
Liebers, Lawrence	2Lt	82/12	7	
Sears, Meldrum	1Lt	1/12	7	
Ross, Herbert	Maj	14/12	7	
Vaughn, Harley	Maj	82/12	7	
Waters, Edward	1Lt	82/12	7	
Adams, Charles	1Lt	82/15	6	
Campbell, Richard	1Lt	14/12	6	
Crawford, Ray	2Lt	82/12	6	
Holloway, James	1Lt	82/15	6	
Ilfrey, Jack	Capt	1/12	6	+2 P-38 ETO
Kienholtz, Donald	1Lt	1/15	6	
MacKay, John	2Lt	1/12	6	
Miller, Armour	1Lt	1/15	6	
Schildt, William	1Lt	82/12	6	
Smith, Virgil	1Lt	14/12	6	
White, Thomas	2Lt	82/12	6	
Anderson, Leslie	1Lt	82/15	5	
Aron, William	1Lt	325/12	5	
Benne, Louis	1Lt	14/15	5	
Cochran, Paul	2Lt	82/12	5	
Fisher, Rodney	1Lt	1/12	5	
Ford, Claud	Maj	82/15	5	
Gardener, Warren	Maj	82/15	5	
Griffith, Robert	1Lt	82/15	5	
Hanna, Harry	2Lt	14/12	5	
Hatch, Herbert	1Lt	1/15	5	
Johnson, Clarence	Capt	82/15 352/8	5	+2 ETO
Jones, Warren	2Lt	14/15	5	
Kennedy, Daniel	1Lt	1/12	5	
Knott, Carroll	1Lt	14/15	5	
Lathrope, Franklin	2Lt	1/15	5	
Lee, Richard	1Lt	1/15	5	
Leikness, Marlow	1Lt	14/15	5	
Lenox, Jack	1Lt	14/15	5	
McArthur, T.H.	Capt	82/12	5	
McGuyrt, John	1Lt	14/15	5	
Osher, Ernest	Capt	82/12	5	
Owens, Joel	Maj	1/12	5	
Roberts, Newell	Capt	1/12	5	
Rounds, Gerald	1Lt	82/12	5	
Seidman, Robert	1Lt	14/15	5	
Taylor, Oliver	Col	14/15	5	
Visscher, Herman	1Lt	82/15	5	
Weatherford, Sidney	Capt	14/12	5	
Welch, Darrell	Capt	1/12	5	
Wilkens, Paul	2Lt	14/15	5	
Wiseman, Lee	Capt	1/12	5	
Wolford, John	1Lt	1/12	5	
Wright, Max	Capt	14/15	5	
Johnson, Clarence	1Lt	82/12	4	+1 P-38 ETO +2 P-51
Miller, Joseph	Capt	14/12	4	+1 P-38 ETO

Flying the P-38 Lightning (MTO/ETO)
By
Jack Ilfrey:
8 victories 20 & 79FG

The biggest thrill of my young life was that December day in 1941 when I checked out in the P-38. I consider myself being born and raised in the P-38, which in my opinion was the greatest fighter produced in WWII. I completed two tours, one in the MTO and the other in the ETO, flying 142 missions and 528 combat hours in the Lightning and getting eight victories.

We fighter pilots to a man had great faith in our crew chiefs. If he said the plane was ready to go, we never doubted him. The cockpit was comfortable for the average-sized pilot (I was 5'10" and 145 pounds). The seat was adjustable and reasonably comfortable for the first five hours of a mission. Cockpit heating was sadly lacking, especially over 30,000 feet. The winter of 1943-44 over Europe was awful, with temperatures of 50 to 60 degrees below zero at altitude. We put on so many clothes that our ground crews joked that we looked like waddling penguins. The heating problem was somewhat solved in the L model. At first there seemed to be a hell of a lot of instruments on the panel, but as time went by it got to be second nature to quickly discover when anything went wrong. The yoke did block the view of several instruments, but a twist of the neck took care of the problem. The earliest P-38 models had somewhat stiff controls, but were manageable in an emergency, such as when a German got on your tail. Adrenaline-boost helped you manhandle the aircraft to get the S.O.B. before he got you. Later, hydraulic boost for the controls and combat dive flaps was introduced. Cockpit visibility was excellent for taxiing, takeoff, and landing. The armor plate behind my seat saved my life on two occasions. One time I felt the thump of a German cannon shell hit behind my head. It tore up the radio and dented the plate. In combat the engine and wing could block out some of your forward and downward visibility, but I could turn the fighter up on one wing tip and take a quick look around. Rearward visibility was good with a slight head twist around the seat back armor plate. Our early radios were full of static. When we got to England in July 1942, we were equipped with the superior RAF VHF system.

In all my combat missions I never had an abort, which says a hell of a lot about the reliability and ruggedness of the Allison engines and the efficiency of my ground crew. The belly tank gave us adequate fuel capacity, but we had to watch fuel consumption in using high manifold pressure for speed. The P-38 had a very good climb rate, and I feel it could out climb anything the Germans had. We could out cruise them if we watched our fuel consumption.

The P-38 had the finest gun platform of any fighter. The cannon and four machine guns fired straight out the nose to get you on target, and were wonderful for ground strafing. In the Spring of 1944 we got the K-14 gyroscopic gun sight, which we called the "no-miss-em" sight. We could carry two 1,000lb. bombs or four 500lb. bombs, as well as several other combinations, including clusters, incendiary, etc.

Maneuverability—a good P-38 pilot could make his fighter talk to him. We could dive, but not Split-S. We knew of the P-38's infamous compressibility problem, and learned the warning signs that you were approaching it, so you backed off. This problem was solved with dive flaps on the J-25 and later models. The P-38 had wonderful zoom. It could climb away from the enemy or up into him. In North Africa, in my F-1 model I got on the tail of a Me-109. I threw down some flaps to tighten my turn and sucked the yoke into my stomach to get the gun sight on him without stalling. You could damage the flaps doing this, but what the hell, I shot him down. The P-38 had excellent stall characteristics because of its reciprocating props.

One of the weaknesses of the P-38 was that its twin booms made it easy to recognize. This allowed the Luftwaffe the choice to take you on or get out of your way. The P-38 was tough. I came home several times with congealed holes in my self-sealing fuel tanks. In North Africa several Lightnings, including my own, limped home with severe battle damage. Thank God for two engines! Landing a one engine turning P-38 was a little tricky. There were a lot of rumors about the dire consequences of bailing out of the P-38 because of its twin tail. I went out of two and am here today, but some are not. The way I looked at it: you know when you have to go, so just do it!

When it came time for our Group to change to P-51s in late July 1944 I was very much against it. I even tried to transfer out so I could stay in a unit which was to continue flying my beloved P-38. But my Group CO wanted to keep me as a Squadron CO, and all his threats and cajoling finally persuaded me to stay. However, after a few reluctant hours in the D model P-51, I realized it too was a great little fighter. But to this day, I have never regretted flying what I consider the best fighter of WWII—the Lockheed P-38 Lightning.

P-38 PTO First Victory in Type
Pilots: 2Lt. Stanley Long
 2Lt. Kenneth Ambrose
Time: 4 August 1942 / 1200
Place: Nazan Bay, Atka Is. Aleutian Is. Alaska
Unit: 54FS/343FG/11AF
A/C: P-38E/Kawanishi 97 "Mavis"

In early June 1942 the Japanese put troops on the Aleutian Islands of Kiska and Attu as a maneuver designed to draw the American fleet, which was decimated at Pearl Harbor except for its carriers, into a decisive battle in the North Pacific. Instead, the Japanese Fleet suffered an irreversible defeat at Midway. To help dislodge the Japanese from their perceived continent-threatening foothold, the 11AF dispatched P-38s of the 54FS to counter enemy four engine, Kawanishi Ki-97 flying boats, which were harassing the American base at Dutch Harbor. A three-plane system consisting of two P-38s and a B-17 was developed to meet the needs of the Aleutian Theater. The B-17 led the fighter pilots, who were inexperienced in navigation and whose aircraft were ill-equipped to contend with the atrocious, fog-plagued weather in the Bering Sea.

After arriving in the Aleutians the 54th spent its time flying training missions and covering Cape Field, Umnak Is., against threatened attack. Once U.S. seaplane tenders were sent to Nazan Bay, Atka Is., squadron P-38s, led by B-17s, were sent to provide CAP beginning 4 August. The first two patrols of that day went without incident. For the third patrol, 2Lt. Stan Long and 2Lt. Ken Ambrose were led by a B-17 piloted by Maj. H. McWilliams to Nazan. As McWilliams flew to his waiting station he spotted three incoming four-engine Japanese Mavises flying in a "V" at 7,000 feet. He radioed a warning, and Long and Ambrose climbed to 22,000 feet to be in position to intercept. Long spotted the Japanese first, and the two lieutenants dove on them. The Japanese also saw the P-38s and broke formation, heading for the cover of a low sea fog that was 1,500 feet above the surface. The two Lightnings quickly caught up with the ponderous seaplanes. Choosing their prey, the Americans, careful not to tangle with the tail-mounted 20mm cannon, made frontal attacks. Long claims to have made the first attack,

Capt. Jack Ilfrey
(Author/Ilfrey)

Left: 2Lt. Stanley Long. Right: 2Lt. Kenneth Ambrose (USAF)

shattering the canopy of his target, which limped off. He then climbed to rejoin Ambrose to attack another Mavis. Ambrose set the left wing on fire, and the stricken seaplane headed into the overcast. Heading toward Kiska, they engaged another Mavis, which frantically attempted to escape. Long made a head-on attack while Ambrose attacked from the side, and both riddled the enemy, which disappeared into the clouds.

The first P-38 kill in the "real" Pacific was by the 13AF. On 13 November 1942, the first P-38s arrived on Guadalcanal's Henderson Field to equip the 13AF's 339FS of the 347FG, which had successfully flown the inadequate P-39 against the Japanese. On 18 November Capt. William Sharpsteen led escort of 11AF B-17s over Tonolei Harbor, on the southern tip of Bougainville. The squadron was attacked by a number of Japanese floatplanes and land-based Zeros. 1Lt. Deltis Fincher and 2Lt. James Obermiller encountered Japanese fighters, and Fincher claimed two Zeros, while Obermiller got one, his only victory of the war. Fincher had shared a P-39 victory over a Zero on 24 August 1942, and later added a floatplane on 19 December 1943 to total 3 1/2 victories. The initial escort missions showed that the P-38 could not maneuver with the Japanese fighters, and the Lightning, when engaged by Japanese fighters, needed to utilize their climbing or diving advantage to escape and then engage on their own terms: speed and firepower.

The first P-38 kill by the 5AF in the SWPA was unusual. On 25 November 1942, five P-38s of the 39FS/35FG left Port Moresby carrying a 500 lb. bomb under one wing and a drop tank under the other. The squadron bombed an airdrome near Lae. Capt. Robert Faurot overshot his target, and his bomb exploded in the water at the end of the runway. The explosion raised a solid wall of water, and a Zero that was taking off flew into it and crashed into the sea. Since Faurot had witnesses and the Zero was in the air, he claimed a victory. When Faurot saw 5AF CO Gen. George Kenney, he asked, tongue in cheek, if he were going to be awarded an Air Medal for this historic victory? To which Kenney replied: "Hell no, I want you to shoot them down, not splash water on them !"

If Faurot's claim for a victory was accepted, then perhaps another unusual, but similar claim should be recognized as the first "kill" in the Pacific. The first P-38s to arrive in the Pacific were the F-4 photo-recon versions assigned to the 8th Photo Recon Squadron "Eight Balls," which came under the command of Maj. Karl "Pop" Polifka in April 1942. The unit did yeoman pioneer photo-recon duty in the theater. Sketchy combat reports credit the squadron with one victory, even though the F-4 was unarmed! Lt. Alex Guerry spotted four Rufe float planes and began to make close, low-level passes at them, forcing them to land. As the last Rufe was landing, Guerry dove so close that his prop wash flipped the Jap on his back. Guerry swung his aircraft around to photograph his inverted victim to establish confirmation of his "kill."

1Lt. Deltis Fincher 339FS/347FG scored the first P-38 victory in the "real" Pacific when he shot down two Zeros on 18 November 1942. (USAF)

P-38 PTO First Ace
Pilot: 1Lt. Hoyt Eason
Time: 31 December 1943/1210-1235
Place: East of Lae Airdrome
Unit: 39FS/35FG/5AF
A/C: P-38F/3 Zeros

During the retreat from the Philippines through the Allied holding action from Australia against the Japanese advance through the SWPA, the 5th AF had just held its own with its inferior P-39s and P-40s and was in dire need of the P-38. However, Gen. George Kenney, 5AF Commander and long-time P-38 advocate, soon found that the Pacific theater would have to take a back seat to the ETO, when Gen. "Hap" Arnold shuttled available P-38s to Britain and on to North Africa. Finally, in August 1942 30 P-38s arrived in Brisbane, Australia. But after all the procurement delays and frustrations, these Lightnings were found to need extensive field work to remedy numerous mechanical faults, especially leaks in fuel tanks and intercoolers. To make matters worse, the ground crews in the theater were not trained in P-38 maintenance.

It was not until 27 December that the first full-scale air battle was engaged using P-38s. A dozen 39FS P-38s left 14-Mile Drome at Port Moresby at 1130 to intercept 12 Val dive bombers escorted by 12 Navy Zeros and 31 Army Oscars, which were on the way to attack the American airfield at Dobodura. At noon, 49FG P-40s radioed the Japanese position to the patrolling P-38s, which were led by veteran P-39 (three victories) pilot Capt. Thomas Lynch. The American formation crossed the Owen Stanley Mountains and spotted the Vals making bomb runs from 6,500 feet. A dozen P-38s split into three flights of four aircraft. Lynch, leading Red Flight, initiated the combat, attacking the escorting Oscars and claiming

two to become an ace. A young, green farm boy from Wisconsin, 2Lt. Richard Bong, scored victories over a Val and Zero for the first of the 40 victories which would make him America's "Ace of Aces."

1Lt. Hoyt Eason, leading the White Flight, arrived over Dobodura with Lynch's flight at 10,000 feet. He spotted three Zeros, which immediately turned into him. One broke right, one left, and the last rolled out of combat. Eason followed the right turner and fired two long bursts from 300 yards and 30 degrees deflection. The second burst shattered the cockpit, and the stricken enemy plunged into Huon Gulf. Continuing a right-hand turn, Eason saw a 49FG P-40 being chased by a Zero. Eason's presence caused the Zero to break combat. Both U.S. fighters pursued the fleeing Japanese, with Eason getting his second victory of the day and then adding a probable.

Four days later, the 39th was escorting bombers on a mission to Lae. Three flights of Zeros intercepted the formation shortly after noon. Lynch led the fighting, immediately downing a Zero. Eason was the unit's top-scorer of the day, claiming three Zeros over Lae to become the first P-38 ace in the Pacific.

On 8 January 1943 Eason got an Oscar victory, probable, and damaged over Lae for his last claims of the war. On 3 March, he was flying topcover for B-17s attacking Japanese shipping in the Battle of the Bismarck Sea. While aiding a harassed B-17, his right engine was hit in a dogfight, and he was forced to pancake his P-38 into the sea, 20 miles from Cape Ward Hunt, New Guinea. He managed to get into the water, floating in his Mae West. He was spotted several times during the day by returning aircraft, but SAR were unable to locate him later and he was listed MIA and later KIA.

P-38 PTO Top Scorer
Pilot: Maj. Richard Bong
Unit: 9FS (TDY 39FS)/49FG/5AF and 5FC/5AF
Victories: 40 victories (8 probables and 7 damaged)
Record:

V#	Date	E/A/C
1-2	12-27-42	Val & Zeke
3-4	01-17-43	2 Oscars
5	01-08-43	Oscar
6	03-03-43	Oscar
7-8	03-11-43	2 Zeros
9	03-29-43	Doris
10	04-14 43	Betty
11	06-12-43	Oscar
12-15	07-26-43	2 Tony & 2 Zero
16	07-28-43	Oscar
17	10-02-42	Dinah
18-19	10-29-43	2 Zekes
20-21	11-05-43	2 Zekes
22	02-15-44	Tony
23-24	03-03-44	2 Sallys
25	04-03 44	Oscar
26-28	04-12-44	3 Oscars
29-30	10-10-44	Oscar & Irving
31	10-27-44	Oscar
32-33	10-28-44	2 Oscars

1Lt. Hoyt Eason
(USAF)

34	11-10-44	Oscar
35-36	11-11-44	2 Zekes
37-38	12 07-44	Sally & Tojo
39	12-15-44	Oscar
40	12-17-44	Oscar
Off Ops 12-29-44		

Of the 70,000 pilots America produced in World War II, Richard Ira Bong was her "Ace of Aces," being credited with 40 victories—all against the Japanese, and all in the P-38. Bong was born on 24 September 1920 in Superior, Wisconsin, but was raised on a farm in Poplar. After attending teacher's college, he enlisted in May 1941 in the AAF Civilian Pilot Training Program, becoming commissioned as a 2Lt. on 9 January 1942. He was not immediately posted to combat, taking an instructor's course before joining the 4PG of the 4 AF, which defended the West Coast. While defending San Francisco, Bong was introduced to the P-38, and soon looped the Golden Gate Bridge and buzzed the waterfront with his hot new fighter. Gen. George Kenney chewed Bong out and transferred him to the 49PS. This move prevented Bong from being posted to North Africa with the 4th.

Finally, in the Fall of 1942, Kenney chose 50 P-38 pilots to aid MacArthur in the defense of Australia. Bong arrived in September and was assigned to the 49th FG, but was put on temporary duty (tdy) with the 39 FS / 35 FG / 5 AF under Maj. George Prentice at 14 Mile Airdrome, New Guinea. Problems with the P-38 delayed effective deployment until late December. On 27 December, 12 P-38s led by Capt. Tom Lynch were scrambled to intercept some 50 incoming Japanese aircraft at 14,000 feet. Bong, flying an aircraft nicknamed *Thumper*," served as Lynch's wingman. In the combat Bong chased a Jap off Lynch's tail, but had his left engine hit. As he dove to escape, he came upon a Val dive bomber and exploded it for his first victory. Soon after he found a Zero in his sights and got

Maj. Richard Bong (USAF)

his second victory of the day, and was awarded the Silver Star.

On 7 January of the new year Bong scored victories over two Oscars, and the following day he became an ace while escorting B-17s bombing Japanese shipping off-landing troops and supplies. The Japanese sent up 20 interceptors, and Bong shot down an Oscar that was attacking 1Lt. Dick Suehr's P-38. This claim made Bong an ace, and Gen. Kenney sent him and Tom Lynch, who had six victories, to Australia for R&R.

Returning to combat in late February 1943, Bong was assigned to the 9FS. With this squadron he scored 16 victories, 5 probables, and 3 damaged over New Guinea before completing his first tour of duty in November. During this time he was promoted from 2Lt. to 1Lt. to Captain. After scoring four victories and winning the DSC in a combat over the Markham Valley on 26 July, Bong become the dominant player in the Pacific Theater ace race. He was sent home in November with 21 victories. Upon his return in February 1944 he was assigned to HQ of the Fifth Fighter Command and renewed his quest to surpass Eddie Rickenbacker's American victory record of 26 established in World War I. His main rivals were Tom Lynch, who now flew with Bong in the VFC, and Neel Kearby, CO of the P-47 equipped 347FG. However, both contenders were lost in combat, and Bong continued to add victories in ones and twos. On 12 April he shot down three Oscars over New Guinea to surpass Rickenbacker's record. Upon reaching this milestone, Kenney took Bong off operations, promoting him to major, and sent him back to the States, where he carried out PR duties, became engaged to the love of his life, Marge, and took a gunnery course. In his public appearances, the shy, unassuming Bong won America's heart as the all-American farm boy pilot.

Bong returned to the Pacific in October to what Kenney thought would be only an advisory capacity, entering combat only in "self-defense." Bong would be credited with 12 more victories in 30 "self-defense" missions flying Lightnings named after Marge. On 12 December he was awarded the Congressional Medal of Honor by Gen. MacArthur, after which he would score two more victories to give him 40, tops for an American fighter pilot. His last victory occurred on 17 December during a sweep over Mindoro when he disintegrated an Oscar. Bong's last challenger, Tom McGuire with 38 victories and flying P-38s with Bong, became so obsessed by the 40 victory standard that he literally flew himself into the ground pursuing it.

Back in America again, Bong married Marge in February 1945 and was assigned to test the P-80 jet at Lockheed's Burbank plant. On 6 August, his P-80's engine failed just after takeoff. Bong frantically tried to find a place to land safely in a heavily populated area. Spotting a nearby airstrip, he tried to bail out just before the jet crashed, but he was too low to have his chute deploy and he was killed. An American fighter had killed Bong where no Japanese could. Thus ended the career of America's Ace of Aces, who was less than a month shy of his 25th birthday.

PTO P-38 Aces (5-13AF) (89 Aces/767 Victories)

Ace Name	Rank	Unit (FG/AF)	P-38V MTO	Other V
Bong, Richard	Maj	49/5	40	
McGuire, Thomas	Maj	475/5	38	
MacDonald, Charles	LCol	475/5	27	
Robbins, Jay	Maj	8/5	22	
Johnson, Gerald R.	LCol	49/5	20	+2 P-47
Lynch, Thomas	LCol	35/5	17	+3 P-400
Harris, Bill	LCol	347/13	16	
Cragg, Edward	Maj	8/5	15	
Homer, Cyril	Capt	8/5	15	
Westbrook, Robert	LCol	347/13	13	+7 P-40
Ladd, Kenneth	Capt	8/5	12	
Roberts, Daniel	Capt	475/5	12	+2 P-400
Lent, Francis	1Lt	475/5	11	
Loisel, John	Maj	475/5	11	
Smith, Cornelius	Capt	8/5	11	
Sparks, Kenneth	1Lt	35/5	11	
Shubin, Murray	1Lt	347/13	11	
Watkins, James	Capt	49/5	11	+1 P-40
Giroux, William	Capt	8/5	10	
Stanch, Paul	Capt	35/5	10	
Summer, Elliott	Capt	475/5	10	
Champlin, Frederick	Capt	475/5	9	
Dahl, Perry	Capt	475/5	9	
Fanning, Grover	1Lt	49/5	9	
Forster, Joseph	1Lt	475/5	9	
Hill, Allen	1Lt	8/5	9	
Smith, Merle	LCol	475/5	9	
Welch, George	Capt	475/5	9	+4 P-40 +3 P-39
Damstrom, Fernley	1Lt	49/5	8	
Harris, Frederick	Capt	475/5	8	
Hart, Kenneth	1Lt	475/5	8	
Jones, John	Capt	8/5	8	
O'Neill, John	1Lt	49/5	8	
West, Richard	Capt	8/5	8	
Aschenbrenner, Robert	Capt	49/5	7	
Dean, Zack	2Lt	8-475/5	7	
Dunaway, John	1Lt	8/5	7	
Elliott, Vincent	1Lt	475/5	7	
Fisk, Jack	Capt	475/5	7	
Lewis, Warren	Maj	475/5	7	
Purdy, John	1Lt	475/5	7	
Smith, Richard	1Lt	35/5	7	
Wire, Calvin	1Lt	475/5	7	
Allen, David	1Lt	475/5	6	+2 P-40
Andrews, Stanley	1Lt	35/5	6	
Czarnecki, Edward	1Lt	475/5	6	
DeGraffenreid, Edwin	2Lt	8/5	6	
Drier, William	Capt	49/5	6	
Eason, Hoyt	1Lt	35/5	6	
Gallup, Charles	1Lt	35/5	6	
Gresham, Billy	1Lt	475/5	6	
Head, Cotesworth	Capt	18/13	6	+6 P-40
Ince, James	1Lt	8-475/5	6	
Jett, Verle	Capt	475/5	6	
Lane, John	1Lt	35/5	6	
Lucas, Paul	Capt	475/5	6	
Meigs, Henry	1Lt	347/13	6	
Murphey, Paul	Capt	8/5	6	
Paris, Joel	Capt	49/5	6	+3 P-40
Pietz, John	1Lt	475/5	6	
Reeves, Horace	1Lt	475/5	6	
Smith, John C.	2Lt	475/5	6	
Walker, Thomas	1Lt	347/13	6	
Adams, Robert	1Lt	8/5	5	
Ambort. Ernest	2Lt	49/5	5	
Barnes, Truman	1Lt	347/13	5	
Brown, Harry	Capt	475/5	5	+2 P-40
Castle, Nial	2Lt	49/5	5	
Chandler, George	Capt	347/13	5	
Cloud, Vivian	1Lt	475/5	5	
Condon, Henry	1Lt	49/5	5	
Curton, Warren	1Lt	49/5	5	
Gupton, Cheatham	1Lt	49/5	5	
Holmes, Besby	1Lt	347/13	5	
Jordan, Wallace	Maj	49/5	5	+1 P-47
King, Charles	Maj	35/5	5	
Kirby, Marion	1Lt	8-475/5	5	
Lanphier, Thomas	Capt	18/13	5	
Lutton, Lowell	1Lt	475/5	5	
Makin, Jack	1Lt	49-475/5	5	
Mathre, Milden	2Lt	49/5	5	
Mitchell, John	Col	347/13	5	+3 P-39 +3 P-51
Monk, Franklin	1Lt	475/5	5	
Morriss, Paul	Capt	475/5	5	
Myles, Jennings	1Lt	8/5	5	
Ray, C.B.	1Lt	8/5	5	
Tilley, John	1Lt	475/5	5	
Wandrey, Ralph	Capt	49/5	5	+1 P-47
Wenige, Arthur	1Lt	475/5	5	+1 P-40

Left: Maj. Thomas McGuire/2nd P-38 ace. (USAF) Right: LtCol. Charles McDonald/3rd P-38 ace. (Author/McDonald)

Flying the P-38 Lightning (PTO)
By
Jay Robbins: 22 victories 8FG
4th ranked P-38 ace

Discussion and Opinion:

PRE-FLIGHT PROCEDURE: The walk around and pre-flight procedure for the P-38 was relatively simple and easy to perform in the SWPA. Climatic conditions were such that extremely adverse weather conditions were uncommon. However, getting onto the wing via a ladder and into the cockpit was not always easy at night, or when high temperatures made the metal very hot.

COCKPIT: The cockpit was roomy compared to other fighters I had flown (P-400 and P-39). The seat could easily be adjusted to accommodate pilots of different heights. The seat and rudder pedals were easily adjusted to suit a pilot of my height, 6"1". Very small pilots needed to use cushions to reach the rudder pedals. Cockpit temperature control was no problem in the SWPA because of the temperate climate and flight operating procedures in this theater. We did not operate at high altitudes, so we had no need for heating. I understand that in the ETO cockpit heating was a problem. The oxygen system was adequate in early models of the P-38 (the F and G), but it was considerably improved in later models (J and on). The instrument layout was fairly simple, with instrument groupings being easy to learn. Instrument flying per se was not difficult, although we tried to maintain VFR whenever possible to simplify formation flying. In fact, the P-38 was very good under instrument conditions due to its inherent stability and lack of torque. Control layout left little to be desired, and was better than most aircraft I have ever flown. Visibility was exceptionally good, both on the ground and in the air, for all phases of operation. As with all fighter aircraft, visibility to the rear and low was limited. Communications were adequate, and any limitations were not peculiar to the P-38. We originally had low frequency radios, which had the advantage of range but whose clarity was, at times, not very good. When the VHF radios were introduced, the range was sacrificed, but clarity improved dramatically.

ENGINE: The two Allison engines were very good in all models, but the later version Allisons were considerably improved. Aborts for engine problems were not excessive, considering the operating environment in New Guinea and on up the ladder of recaptured islands, where maintenance facilities were meager at best. Although I made several one-engine landings, most were combat related. I considered the liquid-cooled Allisons reliable and rugged, although loss of coolant due to enemy action was not uncommon. Radial engines probably enjoyed an advantage in this respect. Having two engines in the SWPA was a distinct plus, since most of our operational flying was either over vast expanses of water or over dense jungles. The confidence factor alone for the pilot was immeasurable. The fact that we had the ability to return to base on a single engine, in case one engine was lost for whatever reason, tended to make the pilots more aggressive in combat.

CLIMBING TO ALTITUDE: The P-38 could take off and climb to altitude better than most other fighters. Performance in this phase was not too important, except in attaining safe airspeed as soon as possible. As Squadron leader I normally operated at reduced power at squadron join-up, and only increased power to desired climb parameters when all aircraft were in proper formation.

CRUISE: I have no significant comments in this regard. Our cruise procedures were dictated by a number of operating factors, and not necessarily by the aircraft's capabilities. Mainly we wanted to conserve fuel. We wanted to avoid adverse weather conditions and early detection by the enemy that would use additional fuel and jeopardize mission accomplishment. During bomber escort we reduced power as much as we could in order to be able to weave back and forth over the bombers until they reached the target.

COMBAT: The extremely long range of the P-38 was one, if not the most important, combat characteristic it possessed. This feature enabled us to escort bombers to Japanese targets at ranges even the Japanese thought impossible. In later models of the aircraft, combat missions in excess of seven hours were not uncommon. Earlier in the war the normal mission time was three to four hours. This was dictated in some measure by the strategic situation and a number of aircraft we had available in the SWPA in the early days of 1942-43. With the prospect of replacement personnel aircraft questionable, it was paramount that we preserve the limited resources we had on hand. Understandably, priority for equipping the Air Force went to the European Theater, with build up in the Pacific taking place later. As our fighter and bomber forces grew and we took the offensive, we operated at longer ranges and struck more diverse targets. The combat range of the P-38 improved significantly after technical representatives, particularly Charles Lindbergh, visited all groups in the theater. Lindbergh's "very high manifold pressure/ low RPM" technique was not well received at first, but was eventually adopted with considerable success. It allowed us to hit deep targets, and utilizing large external tanks, special missions of 11 hours or more were possible.

The concentration of four .50 caliber machine guns and a 20mm cannon in the nose was a highly desirable feature for several reasons. This concentration of firepower insured a shoot down if you were in range and squarely on target. A burst of three to five seconds would bring down most Jap fighters. The concentration of armament in the nose eliminated the need for figuring convergent fire, which was common for fighters with guns in the wings. We had a variety of gunsights depending on the aircraft model. The F and G models had the old 70 mil fixed ring sight (circle and dot). Later models were equipped with the computing sight. I preferred the old fixed sight because that was what I learned on and had confidence in. I had a natural tendency for high angle deflection shooting, since I had done considerable bird shooting as a boy with my father.

Bombing and strafing were relatively simple because of the lack of propeller torque and negative trim problems. Only slight trim was necessary, even when air speed varied greatly. The Lightning was also an excellent dive-bombing platform. I never used rockets in combat.

Maneuverability was limited in the early models, but improved later with the addition of dive and maneuvering flaps. The distinct advantage the P-38 had over most Jap fighters was in high-speed

Maj. Jay Robbins (Author/Robbins)

climbs and shallow dives, which enabled us to engage or disengage almost at will. Even with maneuvering flaps we did not try to get into a turning engagement with most Jap fighters. In the early P-38 models we had to avoid high vertical dives at relatively low altitudes because the aircraft tended to tuck under. We were made well aware of this tendency and knew how to avoid it.

I considered the Lightning to be fairly rugged. Armor plating and self-sealing fuel tanks enabled the aircraft to take a lot of punishment and continue to operate, even with one engine. On one mission, I had one engine shot out, took 189 bullet and cannon hits and was still able to return home.

LANDING: The P-38 was simple to land, and directional control was good. Single engine landings only required that you maintain adequate airspeed and avoid turning into the dead engine. In early models emergency extension of the landing gear was a problem. It took 125 to 150 strokes on a manual pump to lower and lock the gear, and it always seemed to happen after a long and tiring mission when you were very low on fuel. Later models had an emergency electrical pump to extend the gear.

BAILOUT AND DITCHING: I never had to bail out, but we were all well aware of the dangers of hitting the horizontal stabilizer during bailout. I never had to ditch in the water, but did belly in once without difficulty. Although the aircraft was badly damaged, I sustained no injuries. I had turned off all electrical switches prior to impact to prevent the aircraft from catching fire. The cockpit remained basically intact, although the nose section was badly broken.

OVERALL IMPRESSIONS: I always had great confidence in the Lightning and my ability to use it effectively in any combat situation. Compared to most Jap fighters, the P-38 was a superstar in nearly every respect, except in turning, and we learned early on not to get into a turning contest.

Flying the P-38 Lightning (PTO)
By
Bill Harris:
15 1/2 victories 347FG

During training at Muroc Dry Lake (later Edwards AFB) I learned to pre-flight the P-38. With two engines, etc., it did take longer than a single engine fighter, but it was simple to do so. Also, it was my first fighter, and one that I had dreamed of for years to fly, so it was an act of love to check it and just be around it. Later in combat the pre-flight was second nature, and you trusted your CC and ground crew.

The cockpit was about perfect in size for me at 5'8', but some of my taller pilot friends could be a bit cramped. A 6'6" wingman and former B-25 pilot was not able to wear a seat pack parachute when flying—not a good idea. Early cockpit heating was poor. Even in the tropics at altitudes over 25,000 feet the cockpit windows could frost over. Throughout my entire time in the various P-38 models I was never warm enough. The instrument layout was excellent for a twin engine. Every important instrument could be seen with one sweep of the eyes, and any abnormality noticed at once. Cockpit visibility was good, except for the 10 o'clock and 2 o'clock down at a 20-degree angle. The only other blind spot was directly to the rear because of the armor plate, which could easily be looked around if the head moved a little to the side. I preferred this inconvenience to removing the armor plate! Despite the location of the twin engines on either side, visibility around them was good. Ground visibility on takeoff and landing was excellent, as there was no engine in front, and the tricycle landing gear lowered the nose. The controls were well located for use and convenience. They were less tiring than some other fighters. As heavy as the plane was it should have had power assist on the wheel. This was added on the L models, which were heavier and clumsier than the lighter models D to F. The J seemed most balanced to me, however, the L had more power. The communications system was fair, and we had quite a bit of trouble keeping them operating.

Even though they had a bad reputation for reliability and maintenance problems, I liked the two Allison V-1710s. They were powerful, and I never had a dependability issue with them. As I recall I only came back from a mission twice due to engine problems. With two engines it was more likely that one would be shot out, however, the other was enough to come home on. I should know, I did it eight times! Being a twin-engine fighter, the P-38 had no problems with torque, whereas a single-engine fighter at high speeds was constantly battling it and could only turn fast in one direction. In early missions we had to worry about fuel conservation. Eight hundred mile missions with 15 minutes of combat were a stretch, and the last half an hour was used watching the fuel gauge. Col. Charles Lindbergh put out some figures on slowing the engines down and raising the manifold pressure that could double our mileage. Capt. Joe Grunder of the 18FG/13AF did some studies on operating engines at different RPMs and fuel mixture settings, and we were able to lengthen our range to as much as 2,300 miles nonstop in ten hours. We usually used two 165-gallon fuel tanks, but sometimes switched to one 330-gallon fuel tank and a 2,000-pound bomb on anti-shipping sorties, or two 330-gallon napalm tanks on short-range ground support missions.

We could climb at over 4,000 fpm, reaching combat altitude in seven to eight minutes. We had a 400+ mph maximum speed at war emergency power at 25,000 feet. Cruising speed was 230 mph. The Lightning was still a fighting aircraft at 35,000 feet, and had a service ceiling of 44,000 feet. I ran the engines at full war emergency power for 20 minutes one time, because it was really necessary or else. The specs said five minutes was tops, but I never had an engine falter under war emergency power. At low altitude a Jap Zero could out turn the P-38, and at low speeds it could out climb it. But at high speeds it could not out turn or out climb the Lightning.

The P-38 fuselage nose nacelle mounted a 20mm cannon with 150 rounds and four .50 cal. machine guns with 300 to 500 rpg. There was no fighter that could compare to the bullet pattern fired from a P-38. In combat my guns only jammed once and failed to fire. The gun camera was poor, probably due to the damp weather, which ruined the film. In three years of combat I only got one picture of a shoot down.

The P-38 could sustain a lot of damage and still keep on flying. Squadron member Rex Barber had 104 holes in his plane after the Yamamoto mission. I had a hole in my wing over 18 inches in diameter and did noy even realize it until the flight was over. Another time I lost over one quarter of my horizontal stabilizer and the outboard hinge while strafing a destroyer and flew the damaged fighter back 700 miles safely home. In other words, the P-38 was a mighty tough airplane.

In retrospect, I think the P-38 was the best all around airplane in the Pacific once we learned to use it at its full capacity.

Republic P-47 Thunderbolt

In June 1940 the U.S. issued requirements for a fighter based on air combat factors in the early European war. In 1939, Republic Aviation designer Alexander Kartveli created the lightweight XP-47, but before construction could begin he realized that this fighter

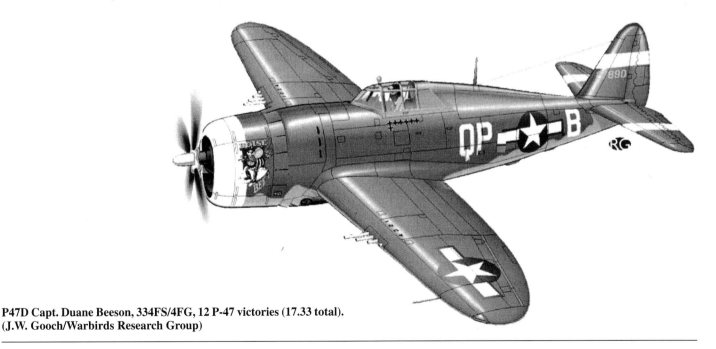

P47D Capt. Duane Beeson, 334FS/4FG, 12 P-47 victories (17.33 total).
(J.W. Gooch/Warbirds Research Group)

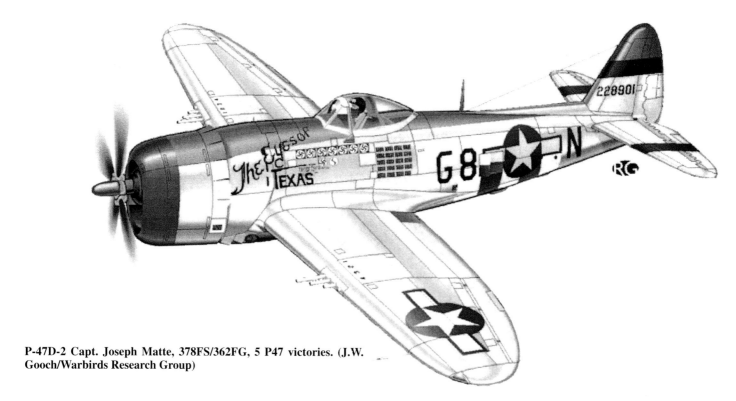

P-47D-2 Capt. Joseph Matte, 378FS/362FG, 5 P47 victories. (J.W. Gooch/Warbirds Research Group)

would not meet the 1940 requirement, so he began again. The result was the XP-47B, and was by far the largest and heaviest single seat fighter at that time at 11,500 pounds. The aircraft was designed and built around the turbo-charger and the new 2,000hp Pratt & Whitney Double Wasp engine. Orders for 171 P-47Bs and 602 Cs were placed in September 1940. The B and C models basically differed only in the slightly longer fuselage of the C, which gave it better maneuverability. The XP-47B was first flown on 6 May 1941 by test pilot Lowry Brabham, but it took one and a half years of testing and redesign to make the huge fighter combat ready, and they entered USAAF service in November. The first Thunderbolts, as they were now called, became operational with the 8AF in April 1943, and in the Pacific with the 348FG in June. When pilots first

flew the fighter they found its weight and size gave it poor climb, zoom, and turning capabilities, mushing in high-speed turns and stalling and snapping into a spin at any speed. But to offset the disadvantages they found that the Thunderbolt had great high altitude performance, and the ability to out-dive any opponent, enabling it to break off combat at will. It was also found to have an extraordinary capacity to absorb punishment, and had a very heavy eight .50 machine gun armament. In mid-October 1941, the first P-47D emerged, which was a refined reversion of the C. It was the most numerous P-47, with 12,602 being built by Republic in four runs and 354 by Curtiss as the P-47G. Variations in the D included external provisions for fuel tanks or bombs and water injection. However, the major modification was the introduction of the bubble

In 1940, Republic designer Alexander Kartveli designed the heaviest single seat fighter at the time, the XP-47B that was built around Pratt & Whitney's 2000hp Double Wasp engine. (Republic)

Lowry Brabham, shown here with Republic VP, Hart Miller, first flew the XP-47B on 6 May 1941. (Republic)

canopy, which replaced the cockpit that blended into the fuselage spine that ran back to the tail and gave the aircraft its "razorback" nickname. The weight saved permitted extra fuel to be carried, but necessitated a dorsal fin fairing to be added to restore stability. A total of 8,179 bubble-canopied P-47s were manufactured. The RAF received 240 Thunderbolt Is (the early P-47D) and 590 MK II (later P-47Ds), with the Soviet Union acquiring 203 under lend-lease and Brazil another 88. The next major model was the M (the intervening E-Ls were various experimental models), which was a D airframe fitted with a 2,800hp R-2800-57 engine. This model (160 built) was an improvisation to counter the German V-1 "Buzz Bomb." They had a speed of 470 mph and needed to be fitted with air brakes to allow them to decelerate after attacking their explosive targets. The final production model (1,816 built) was the N, a long-winged version that was built for long-range escort missions in the Pacific. It was the heaviest P-47 at 21,100lbs., compared to the 12,000lbs of the XP-47B. Beginning as a long-range escort, the Thunderbolt found its niche as a superlative fighter-bomber. P-47 production ended in December 1945 with 15,680 being built, and two-thirds survived the war and flew with many post-war air forces.

P-47 ETO First Victory in Type

Pilot: Maj. Donald J. M. Blakeslee
Time: 15 April 1943/1720
Place: Knocke, Belgium
Unit: 335FS/4FG/8AF
A/C: P-47C/FW-190

The first P-47Cs arrived as deck cargo in Britain on 20 December 1942 and were assigned to the 4FG, which was the only fighter group in the VIII FC at the time. The 4FG, based at Debden, was the continuum of the RAF Eagle Squadrons, American volunteers who flew the Spitfire for the RAF before the United States entered the war. The 4FG pilots, accustomed to the lithe, elegant Spit, found they had difficulties adjusting to the brutish, powerful Thunderbolt. These transitional problems, along with numerous technical problems, delayed the fighter's debut into combat until 10 March 1943. Even though the pilots were becoming accustomed to the Thunderbolt, their first mission, a sweep of 14 aircraft, was uneventful action-wise but a technical disaster. It required another

month for the malfunctioning pieces of equipment to be modified and repaired by field service units of the AAF and manufacturer, Republic Aviation. During this time, two other fighter groups arrived in Great Britain to fly the P-47: the 56FG stationed at Kings Cliffe and the 78FG at Goxhill. By 8 April, 24 serviceable P-47s were drawn from the three groups to bring the fighter operational again in an uneventful sweep over the Straits of Dover. Several subsequent missions failed to result in enemy contact.

On 15 April 1943, a mixed formation of 59 T-Bolts of the three groups was dispatched to carry out sweeps of the Furnes/St. Omer area. Leading the 335FS/4FG was Maj. Don Blakeslee, who had scored four victories with the 133 Eagle Squadron. The 335th took off from Felixstowe at 1700. Soon Blakeslee found his gyro was malfunctioning, but he continued at 29,000 feet over the Channel by compass. Finding himself about 20 miles north of the planned Belgium landfall of Knocke, Blakeslee spotted five condensation trails moving west at 24,000 feet. Blakeslee turned to the port and saw three FW-190s heading southwest. The Germans, knowing they were about to be bounced, turned inland, back towards their base. The American Major took off after the closest Focke Wulf, which had gone into a 15-20 degree dive. Two other P-47s took long-range shots before breaking off their firing passes from opposite directions. Blakeslee trimmed his huge fighter for a steep dive, which allowed him to quickly close on the FW, which increased its dive. He opened fire above and astern at 700 yards and continued to fire to 500 yards. Seeing his tracers miss high, Blakeslee increased his angle of dive, scoring hits in the German cockpit. The stricken fighter lurched sharply and quickly exploded into the ground. Blakeslee pulled out his dive at 300 feet above the city of Ostende, but was not fired upon by flak. He proceeded to mid-Channel on deck before climbing to 3,000 feet to return to base, landing at 1820 with the first P-47 victory of the war.

The 4FG scored two other FW-190 victories and one damaged that day, but they lost three MIA and one damaged. P-47 combat doctrine had been established: if its pilot maintained an altitude advantage and utilized the fighter's high diving speed and considerable firepower of eight .50 caliber machine guns, it could be a match for the FW-190 or Me-109. When Blakeslee was congratulated for demonstrating the P-47's diving qualities in combat he is reported to have replied: "By God, it ought to dive; it certainly can't climb!"

The 4FG never liked the P-47, and it re-equipped with the P-51 Mustang, which was more reminiscent of their beloved Eagle Squadron Spitfires. Blakeslee scored three P-47 victories and went on to score 8 1/2 victories in the P-51 to give him 11 1/2 AAF victories and 15 1/2 wartime.

Maj. Donald Blakeslee (Author/Blakeslee)

P-47 ETO First Ace in Type

Pilot: Capt. Charles P. London
Time: 30 July 1943 / 1020
Place: Haldern, Germany
Unit: 83FS/78FG/8AF/Red Flight
A/C: P-47C/FW-190 & Me-109
See ETO First Ace

The effort to increase the P-47's range to enable it to escort bombers further into Germany until the P-51 became operational was ongoing. Jettisonable external belly-mounted drop tanks evolved from crude, unpressurized compressed paper types into small, pressurized 75 gallon tanks left over from P-39 operations, and on to the British-built pressurized 108 gallon tanks. The introduction of the D model also was a significant advance for two reasons. Besides the many internal modifications which made it a better fighter, it was the addition of two underwing pylons which enabled the fighter to carry two 1,000 lb. bombs or two drop tanks. This new bombing/strafing capability was the antithesis of its designed role as a high altitude fighter. The first strafing attack in the ETO was carried out by 1Lt. Quince Brown, who shot up a flak emplacement and locomotive west of Rotterdam in the 30 July mission, while the first designated ground attack mission took place on 25 November 1943. Once the P-51 came into service, the P-47 became a fearsome ground attack fighter.

P-47 ETO Top Scorer in Type

Pilot: Lt. Col. Francis "Gabby" Gabreski
Unit: 61FS/56FG/8AF
Victories: 28 (1 probable/3 damaged/2 1/2 ground)

V#	Date	E/A/C
1	08-23-43	FW-190
2	09-03-43	FW-190
3	11-05-43	FW-190
4-5	11-26-43	2 Me-110s
6-7	11-29-43	2 Me-109s
8	12-11-43	Me-110
9	01-29-44	Me-110
10-11	01-30-44	Me-110 & Me-410
12-13	02-20-44	2 Me-410s
14	02-22-44	FW-190
15-16	03-16-44	2 FW-190s
17-18	03-27-44	2 Me-109s
19	05-08-44	Me-109
20-22	05-22-44	3 FW-190s
23-24	06-07-44	Me-109 & FW-190
25-26	06-12-44	2 Me-109s
27	06-27-44	Me-109
28	07-05-44	Me-109

Plus 6 1/2 victories in Korea in F-86s

By autumn 1943, the 8FC had deployed six Thunderbolt groups, as the 352nd, 353rd, and 355th joined the 4th, 56th, and 78th. By the end of the year a total of ten P-47 groups were on station in Britain. These reinforcements expanded and changed the role of the fighter. In autumn it provided bomber escort in relays. Different P-47 units

Capt. Charles London (Author/London)

would rendezvous with the bombers at given points during their mission penetration and withdrawal, providing continuous protection. As the P-51 began operations from Britain in late 1943, it assumed the escort duties of the P-47. Instead, the Thunderbolt was sent to areas along the bomber route in which Luftwaffe interception was most probable to do battle. The winter success of the P-51 long-range escort allowed the P-47 to hunt the Luftwaffe in the air and on the ground, along with increasing harassment of the German Wehrmacht and transportation system. In each of its changing roles the P-47 continued to distinguish itself, claiming large numbers of aerial victories and aces.

Francis Stanley Gabreski, a short, stocky pilot of decidedly Polish ancestry, played an important part in formulating, and then implementing the tactics required of the P-47's changing roles. Upon arriving in England with the 56FG he flew a few missions with the RAF Polish squadron. Never a prolific daily scorer like George Preddy or John Meyer, "Gabby" steadily claimed victories in ones and twos. He scored his first victory on 23 August 1943 when he downed a FW-190 near Dreux, France. It would not be until 26 November, when he scored two victories over Me-110s southeast of Oldenburg, that Gabreski became an ace. His best day occurred on 22 May 1944, when his squadron engaged about 20 FW-190s

LtCol. Francis Gabreski (Author/Gabreski)

attempting to land at Hopenhofer airdrome. His 61FS dove to attack, but were driven off by heavy flak. The Focke Wulfs were low on fuel, and their leader fired a green flare, which signaled the German AA to stop firing so they could land. This gave the Americans their opportunity, and Gabreski claimed three victories and a probable for his best career day.

By the end of June 1944 he had 27 victories, and had completed his tour only one victory behind ETO scoring leader Robert Johnson, who also flew the Thunderbolt with the 56th. While waiting to go home, he flew a mission on 5 July, getting his last victory to tie him with Johnson. Subsequently, the post-war USAAF Study 85 would downgrade a Johnson victory claim and make Gabreski the top ETO ace. On his 166th mission on 20 July, he decided to strafe a German airdrome. He came in too low, and his prop hit a knoll, causing him to crash land. He evaded for five days before being captured and spending ten months as a POW at Stalag Luft I. In the Korean War he flew the F-86 Sabre with the 4FIW, totaling 6 1/2 more victories to become one of the seven pilots to become aces in both wars. His 34 1/2 victories made him America's third all-time ace.

During 1944, 8AF fighter groups progressively exchanged their brutish Thunderbolts for the sensitive Mustangs. The 78FG exchanged theirs in December, leaving only the 56th to steadfastly retain their P-47Ms until the end of the war. The 9AF was reactivated in England in October 1943, and of its 20 fighter groups, 15 flew the P-47 some time during their tour. With the 9th the P-47 flew peerlessly in a ground attack role with occasional escort missions. To discuss the relative merits of the P-47 versus the P-51 is much like discussing the B-17 and B-24. In the ETO, the P-47 gained its share of aerial victories (2,685 to 4,238 for the P-51) for a record low lost rate per combat sortie (even though a considerable number of its missions were dangerous ground attack sorties subjected to heavy AA fire). Lacking the pure fighter characteristics of the P-51, it was a steady gun platform, and endeared itself to its pilots for its ability to survive extensive battle damage and fly home safely.

8AF P-47 top-scorers: (L-R): Capt. Robert Johnson (27 v.), Col. Hubert Zemke (15 1/2 v.), Maj. Walker Mahurin (19 1/2 v.). (USAF)

Capt. Frederick Christensen: 21 P-47 victories. (USAF)

Col. David Schilling: 22 1/2 P-47 victories (USAF)

8AF Top scorers
P-47 ETO/Eighth Air Force (61 Aces/575.35 Victories)

Ace Name	Rank	Unit	P-47 V	Total V
Gabreski, Francis	LCol	56	28	28*
Johnson, Robert	Capt	56	27	27
Schilling, David	Col	56	22.5	22.5
Christensen, Frederick	Capt	56	21	21
Mahurin, Walker	Maj	56	19.75	20.75
Duncan, Glenn	Col	353	19.5	19.5
Beckham, Walter	Maj	353	18	18
Johnson, Gerald	Maj	56/356	16.5	16.5
Zemke, Hubert	Col	56/479	15.25	17.75
Powers, Joe	Capt	56	14.25.	14.25
Williamson, Felix	Capt	56	13	13
Brown, Quince	Maj	78	12.3	12.3
Beeson, Duane	Capt	4	12	17.3
Schreiber, Leroy	Maj	56	12	12
Conger, Paul	Maj	56	11.5	11.5
Stewart, James	Maj	56	11.5	11.5
Quirk, Michael	Capt	56	11	11
Gladych, Michael	Maj	56	10	10
Rankin, Robert	1Lt	56	10	10
Gallup, Kenneth	LCol	353	9	9
Jucheim, Alwin	Capt	78	9	9
Maroney, Virgil	Capt	352	9	9
Morrill, Stanley	1Lt	56	9	9
Roberts, Eugene	LCol	78	9	9
Bostwick, George	Maj	56	8	8
Jackson, Michael	Maj	56	8	8
Schlitz, Glen	Capt	56	8	8
Vogt, John W.	Maj	56/356	8	8
Edens, Billy	1Lt	56	7	7
Hockery, John	Capt	78	7	7
Klibbe, Frank	1Lt	56	7	7
Lamb, Robert	Capt	56	7	7
Maguire, William	Capt	353	7	7
Poindexter, James	Capt	353	7	7
Smith, Leslie	Maj	56	7	7
Truluck, James	1Lt	56	7	7
Moseley, Mark	Capt	56	6.5	6.5
Garrison, Vermont	1Lt	4	6.3	7.5
Carter, James	Capt	56	6	6
Cook, Walter	Capt	56	6	6
Hall, George	1Lt	56	6	6
Hart, Cameron	Capt	56	6	6
Keen, Robert	1Lt	56	6	6
Oberhansly, Jack	LCol	78	6	6
Olson, Norman	Capt	355	6	6
Thwaites, David	Capt	356	6	6
Turley, Grant	1Lt	78	6	6
Wilkensen, James	Capt	78	6	6
Bennett, Joseph	Capt	56/4	5.5	5.5
McCauley, Frank	1Lt	56	5.5	5.5
Smith, Donovan	1Lt	56	5.5	5.5
Comstock, Harold	Maj	56	5	5
Egan, Joseph	1Lt	56	5	5
Gerick, Steven	1Lt	56	5	5
Goodson, James	Maj	4	5	12
Icard, Joseph	1Lt	56	5	5
London, Charles	Capt	78	5	5
McMinn, Evan	F/O	56	5	5
Mills, Henry	Maj	4	5	5
Pompetti, Peter	1Lt	78	5	5
Price, Jack	Maj	78	5	5

9AF Top scorers
ETO/Ninth Air Force (12 Aces/68 Victories)

Ace Name	Rank	Unit	P-47 V	Total V
Douglas, Paul	LCol	368	7	7
Fisher, Edwin	Capt	362	7	7
Gray, Rockford	Maj	365/371	6.5	6.5
Coffey, Robert	LCol	365	6	6
Johnson, Robert D.	LCol	50	6	6
Edwards, Edward	1Lt	373	5.5.	5.5
Hendricks, Randall	Maj	368	5	5
Hill, James	Maj	365	5	5
Magoffin, Morton	Col	362	5	5
Matte, Joseph	1Lt	362	5	5
Paisley, Melvin	1Lt	366	5	5
Scherer, Donald	1Lt	358	5	5

Lt.Col. Paul Douglas: 7 P-47 victories (USAF)

Capt. Edwin Fisher: 7 P-47 victories (USAF)

Flying the P-47 Thunderbolt (ETO)
By
Robert Johnson: 27 victories 56FG
Second highest scorer in the ETO

Your immediate reaction to the Thunderbolt is its enormous size for a single seat fighter. The cockpit was so roomy that sitting in it was just like sitting in your favorite chair in your den! There were a dozen pre-flight checks that soon became automatic. The cluttered instrument panel was only satisfactory, and the flight instruments layout could have been better. This deficiency was compensated by the excellent control layout and their ease of use. On taxiing and the start of takeoff the large nose blinded the pilot. "S-ing" or ground crewman direction could help on taxiing. Forward visibility became excellent once the tail lifted on takeoff. Our D-model Razorback Thunderbolt had a 20-degree blind spot from behind, but the closed in back gave the physiological feeling of security from astern enemy attacks. This faired cockpit was replaced by the superior bubble canopy in later models.

A lot of guys are alive today because of the Thunderbolt's Pratt & Whitney engine. The R-2800 radial engine was excellent, as it was rugged and dependable. It had good power-to-weight ratio, but was a gas hog and needed a lot of fuel. The addition of drop tanks helped a great deal in extending our range.

For safety, takeoff was always made with the main fuel tank and the tail wheel locked to prevent swing. The fighter climbed slowly, taking 15 to 20 minutes to reach its best cruising altitude of 20,000 feet, where we would go over to using the drop tanks. The sooner they could be drained and released the sooner we could get rid of their drag. We did not want to go into combat with them. Fuel consumption was always a concern in the Thunderbolt, and often we had to cut way back in order to get back home.

The versatility of the Thunderbolt as a weapons platform was a forerunner of today's large fighters, like the F-15 and F-16. The concentrated firepower of its eight .50s was tremendous. You could see where your bullets were hitting, tearing out pieces of the enemy aircraft. We could carry two 1,000 lb. bombs under the wings and one 500 lb. bomb under the fuselage. In combat the P-47 could out run, out dive, and out roll any WWII plane, but you had to know how to use the aircraft. All controls were good. Laterally it was surprisingly light, but fore and aft control was heavy going. Its superiority in turning against the Germans increased with altitude. It was not wise to try to turn too far with a Me-109 or Fw-190; only a half circle, shoot, and get out! The P-47 had no match in a dive, with 2,200 horses propelling 14,000 lbs. of fighter downward. It was our best advantage for getting to or away from a German. It could zoom up from a dive, but it was not in the pilot's best interest to climb up to the enemy. Water injection drew war emergency power of 15%. The turbo gave the P-47 maximum performance at 27,000 to 30,000 ft.

The P-47 was undoubtedly the toughest fighter in the war. The rugged P & W engine and the huge airframe made the pilot feel safe just sitting in it. It could give and take more punishment than any other fighter of its day. My P-47 caught twenty-one 20mm shells and over 200 .30 caliber bullets on 26 June 1943. I got home, and I'm here to write about it. Another time my aircraft was badly hit and the Razorback canopy was jammed by a 20mm shell, so I could not get out with my chute. I had no choice but to nurse the damaged, but still flying, plane back to England. The aircraft was just plain tough.

Once the runway was clear and lined up the P-47 landed itself. The wide, sturdy undercarriage made the three point landing easy. But once on the runway you had to concentrate until you stopped, because of the poor visibility of the long nose.

The Thunderbolt could out fly any German aircraft, except in a climb. The Me-262 jet was the only German plane able to out run the P-47. The P-47's victory-to-loss ratio was better than the Mustang's. The P-47's ability as an air-to-ground weapon made it more versatile than the P-51, which was more vulnerable to ground fire due its liquid-cooled engine.

Flying the P-47 Tunderbolt (ETO)
By
Gerald Johnson:
16 1/2 victories 56FG

I left college in September 1941 to become an aviation cadet, and after completing flight training and being commissioned as a 2nd Lieutenant I was assigned to the 56th Fighter Group at Mitchell Field (NY). Here we trained in P-36s, P-40s, and P-38s. After a few months we were moved to Bridgeport (CT) and received the first P-47s delivered to a tactical unit. I flew over 100 combat missions in the Thunderbolt and became the first 56th Fighter Group ace, and the second ace in the ETO.

My crew chief and ground crew were highly competent, so pre-flight was pretty simple: while walking around the aircraft I would take a quick look at the maintenance log and have a brief conversation with the CC about anything I should be aware of about

Capt. Robert Johnson
(Author/Johnson)

my fighter. The P-47 was very large for a fighter, and so was the cockpit. The instruments and controls were well-located and easy to use. Visibility was good in flight, but restricted by the large nose in taxiing, takeoff, and landing. The introduction of the bubble canopy was a great improvement over the "Razorback" version, but I only flew the Razorback in WWII. Initially, the heater was adequate for our missions, but once we undertook high altitude bomber escort we needed to dress accordingly. The only communication was the HF radio, which came with all its noise, static, and interference. Understanding pilot communication during combat was difficult, but not always due to the HF. The voice of a scared pilot often sounded strange! The HF was state-of-the-art for that day and age.

The Pratt & Whitney R-2800 radial engine was a real gem, rugged, reliable, and powerful at 2,300 HP in our D-model. We needed all the HP we could to push the 14,000 pound+ aircraft through the sky, especially later in the war when we flew a lot of fighter-bomber missions carrying a huge amount of external ordnance: bombs and rockets, along with drop tanks. Unfortunately, the engine used a lot of fuel. To get as much range as possible external fuel tanks were used for climb and cruise, and then dropped when they were empty or upon engaging in combat. As the war went on this external tankage was increased from 300 gallons (two 150 gallon tanks) to over 400 gallons. The internal tankage was also increased to give us 600-700 miles range in the D-models. The airplane was heavy to begin with, and the three external fuel tanks resulted in increased weight and drag. Usually we would not reach our cruising altitude of 20,000 feet until we reached the coast of France, Belgium, or Holland. Cruise was ok for that time, about 250 mph on lean to about 300 mph.

The eight .50 caliber machine guns were what made the P-47 a great fighter and caused the German pilots to respect it. The guns were staggered in the wing, permitting the ammo belts to feed straight into the guns. Consequently, G-forces had no effect, and very rarely did they fail to feed or jam. If the P-47 pilot learned to estimate his distance to the enemy aircraft and hold his fire when he closed until his sight was filled, the great rate and volume of fire of the armor-piercing ammo would absolutely devastate any enemy aircraft it hit. Eight guns vs. six guns was a 33% increase in firepower, and that is significant. Two fewer guns do not make a fighter faster or more maneuverable. The guns on a P-47 were located exactly in the CG (center of gravity), both laterally and longitudinally. Thus, the only gain in removing two guns and their ammo was a slight percentage decrease in weight in the already heavy 14,000 pound Thunderbolt. This same firepower made the P-47 a great strafing weapon. It was also a great dive-bombing platform, being able to carry a huge load of bombs and/or rockets. It was probably one of the Allies' best fighter-bombers, along with the RAF's Typhoon and Tempest and the USN/USMC's F4U Corsair. The aircraft was rugged and could withstand a great amount of damage from ground fire, which was important in its fighter-bomber role. The day I was shot down by enemy ground fire I crash landed in a rugged and heavily wooded area and suffered only minor cuts and bruises. But my luck ran out, as I was captured and spent the next 13 months in a German Stalag.

After the war I flew the P-47N model for about 100 hours. It was designated for use in the Pacific. It was slightly larger, had no fin, and was fitted with the bubble canopy, which was a great improvement. Another big improvement was that it carried more fuel, both internally and externally, giving it more range, which was important in the Pacific, but we sure could have used that extra fuel in the ETO.

I found the D-model I flew in the ETO was generally an easy plane to fly with no serious faults. In air-to-air combat turning and climbing were not its long suits, but it could catch anything in a dive. In early February 1944, while flying at 23,000 feet over the Ruhr Valley, I spotted a lone Ju-52 transport far below and moving away from me. I went into a screaming 19,000 foot dive, quickly caught it, and blasted it a 4,000 feet. After the introduction of water injection, which boosted war emergency power, and the paddle-blade propeller, which increased prop area, the P-47 could pretty well hold its own against anything the Luftwaffe could offer. I always thought it was the best fighter of WWII. The only thing that kept it from doing better was that it used just too much fuel, which kept it from roaming the skies as the P-51 Mustang was able to do because of its longer range.

P-47 MTO First Victory in Type
Pilot: 1Lt. Harold Monahan
Time: 16 December 1943 / 0900-1200
Place: Trpanj, Yugoslavia
Unit: 65 FS/57FG/12-15AF
A/C: P-47D/Me-109
The 57FG flew the P-40 Warhawk in the North African Campaign, over Sicily, and up the Italian boot in the autumn of 1943, flying close support missions for the British 8th Army. In early December, 12 new P-47s arrived at the group's base at Amendola, Italy, and four each were assigned to its three squadrons. The P-47 was designed as a high-altitude escort, but in Italy their primary function was to serve in a low-altitude, ground support role. Therefore, the group needed to develop new tactics and aircraft modifications to meet this fighter-bomber requirement. The first P-47 mission was an uneventful escort to a Greek airdrome on 14 December. Two days later, the group was assigned to a morning strafing mission

Maj. Gerald Johnson (Author/Johnson)

1Lt. Harold Monahan flew a P-47 such as the one pictured for 65FS/57FG to the first P-47 MTO victory. (USAF)

Capt. Herschel Green
(Author/Green)

along the Yugoslavian coast. 1Lt. Harold Monahan of the 65th squadron encountered a Me-109 in the Trpanj area and shot it down for the first MTO P-47 victory. 1Lt. Alfred Froning, also of the 65th, soon shot down two more Messerschmitts in the same area. Monahan then followed by downing another Me-109 for his second and last victory of the war.

P-47 MTO First Ace and Top Scorer in Type

Pilot: Capt. Herschel L. Green
Time: 30 January 1944/1200
Place: Villaorba, N. Italy
Unit: 317FS/325FG/15AF
A/C: P-47D/Mc-202 after 4 Ju-52s(1145)
Victories: 10 P-47 (+ 3 P-40 and 5 P-51)
Top Scorer
Record:

V#	Date	E/A/C
3	P-40 tour	
4-9	01-30-44	4 Ju-52s, Mc-202 & Do-217
10	03-11-44	Me-109
11	03-18-44	Me-109
12	03-29-44	FW-190
13	04-07-44	Me-110
P-51 tour		

The 325FG ("Checkertail Clan") entered the war on 19 January 1943 when they flew P-40s off the aircraft carrier *Ranger*, which had transported them from Norfolk NAS. The group's five months of P-40 operations in North Africa saw its three squadrons, the 317th, 318th, and 319th, score 135 victories against 35 losses in 3,990 sorties and produce four aces. On 18 September 1943, the 325th turned its P-40s over to the 324FG. The transition period to the huge, Republic-built, radial-engine P-47D Thunderbolt was marked by other changes. The group moved from North Africa to Italy in early December, and transferred from the 12th to 15AF. The mission of the 15AF was to isolate Italy from Germany by destroying the railway

system in Northern Italy. The Checkertails provided escort for heavy bombers and swept Luftwaffe airfields to keep enemy interceptions at a minimum. Beginning 14 December 1944, the group began slowly, scoring just 18 victories in 38 missions in their new Razorbacks.

Maj. Herschel Green, nicknamed "Kentucky" for his home state, had scored three P-40 victories over Me-109s while flying for the 317th FS. He had been off operations for several weeks due to an episode of malaria he had contracted in North Africa. The day Green resumed flying, 30 January 1944, G-2 had discovered that the Luftwaffe fighters were always scrambled a quarter of an hour before the American bombers reached their target. To utilize this intelligence the 325th dispatched 61 P-47s early to surprise the German fighters as they took off. The group flew 300 miles at 50 feet over the Adriatic Sea to avoid radar. Upon reapproaching the mainland they climbed, stacked from 15,000 to 18,000 feet, and arrived over Villaorba at 1145. Their timing was perfect, as the Germans had 60 fighters scrambling to take off. Also, a large number of Ju-52 transports and assorted other aircraft were leaving to escape the impending bombing. Capt. Green flew a P-47D adorned with a comely cowgirl framed in an ace of hearts. He was leading A-Flight, consisting of 1Lt. George Novotny, F/O Cecil Dean, and F/O Edsel Paulk, when they spotted a number of Ju-52s trying to escape. Green's first firing pass was made too fast, and he passed under the formation. He turned back and methodically exploded four Junkers in succession in a climbing firing run. He chased an Italian Mc-202 to the deck and shot it down. Then on the way back to base he chased a fleeing Do-217 at treetop height and claimed it for his sixth victory of the day. The three other pilots of A-Flight got three victories apiece and would subsequently become aces.

In March, Green added three more victories, and the Me-110 he claimed on 7 April made him the leading ace in the Mediterranean at the time with 13 victories (10 P-47), taking the lead from 1Lt. William Sloan, a P-38 pilot of the 82 FG. The 325th flew its first P-51 mission on 27 May, but its six months flying the P-47 were extremely successful. The Checkertails scored 153 victories

(131 single-seat fighters) in 3,626 sorties (97 missions) for a loss of only 18 aircraft. This kill ratio of one victory for every 24 sorties far exceeded the average of one victory per 137 sorties for all P-47 units operating in Europe. The Group had six aces in the P-47 with Green's ten victories leading the way, but 1Lt. Eugene Emmons was a close second with nine. The 325th went on to score 246 Mustang victories against 75 losses in nearly three times the number of sorties (10,596). They had 16 P-51 aces, including Green, who scored five more victories to give him 18 total in the war.

MTO/Fifteenth Air Force (6 Aces/40 Victories)

Ace Name	Rank	Unit	P-47 V	Total V
Green, Herschel	Maj	325	10	18
Emmons, Eugene	1Lt	325	9	9
Chick, Lewis	LCol	325	6	6
Novotny, George	1Lt	325	5	8
Paulk, Edsel	1Lt	325	5	5
Rynne, William	Capt	325	5	5

P-47 PTO First Victory in Type

Pilot: Capt. Max R. Wiecks
Time: 16 August 1943/1500
Place: Marilinan, New Guinea
Unit: 340FS/348FG/5AF
A/C: P-47D/Oscar

Allied global grand strategy consigned the P-47 to join the preferred P-38 in the secondary Pacific Theater, which was compelled to accept ETO air surplus and rejects. As the P-51 was coming online in Europe and the P-47 was being produced in large numbers, a desperate Gen. George Kenney, CO of the 5AF, was able to divert the 348FG from its original European posting. Pilots and crew under the redoubtable Lt. Col. Neel Kearby arrived in Australia in June 1943, followed by their crated fighters in early July. The aircraft were quickly assembled and tested, and all 86 were flown to

Port Moresby, New Guinea, by 20 July. The 348th was scheduled for escort duties, but as in Europe the fighter's huge fuel consumption caused modifications and drop tanks to be improvised in the field. However, this fuel expenditure problem was never really overcome in these early P-47s until proper drop tanks arrived. Using the tried and true P-47 combat tactic of dive-shoot-run and never engage in a dogfight, 348th pilots successfully flew sweeps, escorts, and maritime cover missions.

During the afternoon of 16 August, all three 348th squadrons (340, 341, and 342) were assigned to escort transports over the Huon Valley to advance bases. The 340FS was commanded by Capt. Max Wiecks, who had flown P-40s for the 33PS out of Darwin, Australia, early in the war and had the misfortune to be forced to bail out on his first combat sortie on 19 February 1942. Wieck's Thunderbolts were at 11,000 feet over Marilinan when the controller radioed that a formation of Ki-43 Army Oscars were approaching. Wiecks observed a pair of Oscars moving in from the left to attack the Thunderbolts from the rear. Another Oscar 2,000 feet ahead and below was climbing in an Immelmann. At the end of its maneuver this fighter made a left turn in front of Wiecks, who fired two short ineffective bursts at long range. The American continued to close, firing as the Japanese completed his turn and headed towards him. Wiecks fired a long, 700 round burst that caused the Oscar to fall off on his left wing as the two fighters passed. As the combat continued, another Oscar chased by 1Lt. Charles Allen flew up in front of Wiecks. He fired, scoring hits that caused this target to fall off to the left and burst into flames, spinning into the jungle below for the first P-47 victory in the Pacific. Wiecks went on to score three more victories and a probable during the war.

P-47 PTO First Ace and Top Scorer on Type

Pilot: Lt. Col. Neel E. Kearby - Ace
Time: 11 October 1943 / 1125-1130
Place: Near Boram airstrip, Wewak New Guinea
Unit: 348FG/HQ/5AF
A/C: P-47D-2/6 Oscars
Top Scorer
Victories: 22

V#	Date	E/A/C
1-2	09-04-43	Betty & Oscar
3	09-14-43	Dinah
4-9	10-11-43	2 Zekes, 2 Hamps & 2 Tonys
10	10-16-43	Zeke
11-12	10-19-43	2 Petes
13-15	12-03-43	3 Zekes
16	12-22-43	Zeke
17	12-23-43	Tony
18-19	01-03-44	Sally & Zeke
20-21	01 09-44	2 Tonys
22	03-05-44	Nell

Fifth Air Force Commander Gen. George Kenney felt that the P-47 was too large and heavy to handle the light, nimble, and highly maneuverable Japanese fighters. But in no position to be choosy, he reluctantly accepted the P-47s of the 348FG led by Lt. Col. Neel

Capt. Max Wiecks (USAF)

Kearby, a 32 year old Texan from Wichita Falls. Kearby was confident that the heavily constructed "Jug," with its great speed and heavy armament, was ideally suited for the hit and run tactics pioneered by Chennault's Flying Tigers. The 2,000hp Pratt & Whitney R-2800 radial engine was the world's most powerful aircraft engine and gave the Thunderbolt a great operational ceiling and diving speed. Kearby felt that an undetected high speed diving attack from an altitude advantage would negate Japanese dogfighting superiority. At this stage in the war the Japanese pilots were highly trained and experienced, but their fighters were designed for climbing and maneuverability. Their lack of armor and self-sealing fuel tanks made them vulnerable to being flamed by the P-47's eight .50 cal. machine guns and incendiary ammunition. All the Thunderbolt had to do was maintain altitude.

The initial lack of auxiliary fuel tanks limited the group operationally to the Port Moresby area, which had long been ignored by the Japanese. The group did not see much combat until the drop tank situation was remedied in early September. On 4 September, Kearby was flying air cover for an Australian division landing at Hopoi Beach, near Lae. Protected by his wingman, he dove from a 4,000 foot altitude advantage to explode a Betty bomber from astern and then turn on its Oscar escort, tearing off a wing. At the time of these first victories, 1Lt. Dick Bong had 16 victories and Capt. Tom Lynch 15 in their P-38s; tops in the Pacific.

LtCol. Neel Kearby (USAF)

Ten days later he got a Dinah near Malahang and was promoted to Colonel. During the next several weeks Kearby led the 348th on bomber escort missions, fighter sweeps, and maritime CAP without seeing much action. Things would change on 11 October, when Kearby left Port Moresby at 0730 leading a flight of P-47s. They arrived over Wewak and its nearby Boram airstrip, and in the ensuing air battle (described in Chapter 14: Ace in a Day: Six Victories in a Day and the CMH) Kearby shot down two Zekes, two Hamps, and two Tonys to become an ace in a day and to total nine victories. Later, when Gen. Kenney was informed of the six victories, he recommended to MacArthur that Kearby be nominated for the Congressional Medal of Honor.

In the meantime, Kearby shot down a Zeke on 16 October to become a double ace and was awarded the Silver Star. He then added two Pete floatplanes on a sweep over Wewak three days later. Kearby transferred to the staff of the 5AF Fighter Command in mid-November, but took the desk job with the proviso that he could fly combat. He returned to Wewak on 3 December and spotted 24 Japanese fighters flying in loose formation 4,000 feet below. Kearby opened fire at 500 yards, setting a Zeke on fire, and continued his run. He was intercepted by four Japanese fighters and turned into them, hitting the first and setting it on fire. Instinctively he turned slightly and hit the third Zeke. For this action he was awarded his second Silver Star (Oak Leaf Cluster). He concluded his December scoring by downing a Zeke and Tony on the 22nd and 23rd, respectively, to give him 17 victories. On 3 January he got a Sally and Zeke, and then on the 9th two Tonys, all over the hot Wewak area to give him 21 victories to tie Dick Bong, who had been sent home for 60 days R&R in mid-November. On 24 January 1944 MacArthur presented him the CMH in a ceremony at Brisbane, Australia. On 8 February, Kearby was named CO of the 308 Bomb Wing (H), which curtailed his flying time. Bong returned and got victory #22 on 15 February. Pickings were slim, and neither pilot scored. On 5 March, Kearby prepared to take off in "Firey Ginger IV" when his crew chief informed him the P-47 had oil pump problems. Wanting to catch Bong, Kearby borrowed a P-47 and took off with fellow aces Bill Dunham (16v.) and Sam Blair (7v.) to their favorite hunting ground, Wewak. They arrived at 1710 and patrolled the coast at 22,000 feet. Soon they spotted three Nell bombers approaching Dagau airfield to land. Kearby dove and shot one down and made another pass at another Nell. However, he didn't realize that he had lost Blair and Dunham in the melee, and three Zekes closed on his tail. Blair and Dunham desperately turned into the attackers, each shooting one down, but the third Jap put a long burst into Kearby's cockpit at close range. Kearby was badly wounded, and his P-47 was mortally damaged. He was forced to bail out, but was too low; his chute did not fully deploy, and he crashed into the ground. His broken body was found by local tribesman and buried in a shallow grave. In 1946, Dunham returned to the Wewak area, aided by RAAF search parties, and found the grave and returned the body to the U.S.

Kearby died thinking he had again tied Bong in the ace race, but Bong scored victories over two Sallys that day to never lose his lead for America's top ace.

P-47 PTO/Fifth Air Force (24 Aces/177 Victories)

Ace Name	Rank	Unit	P-47 V	Total V
Kearby, Neel	Col	348	22	22
Dunham, William	LCol	348	16	16
Banks, William	Maj	348	9	9
Benz, Walter	Maj	348	8	8
Grossheusch, Leroy	Capt	348	8	8
Roddy, Edward	Capt	348	8	8
Rowland, Robert	Col	348	8	8
Blair, Samuel	Capt	348	7	7
Davis, George	1Lt	348	7	7
Grant, Marvin	1Lt	348	7	7
Moore, John	Maj	348	7	7
Brown, Meade	Capt	348	6	6
Fleischer, Richard	Capt	348	6	6
Foulis, William	Capt	348	6	6
Mugavero, James	1Lt	35	6	6
Strand, William	Capt	35	6	6
Della, George	1Lt	348	5	5
Ditkovitsky, Michael	1Lt	348	5	5
Gibb, Richard	1Lt	348	5	5
Hnatio, Myron	1Lt	348	5	5
Knapp, Robert	Capt	348	5	5
O'Neill, Lawrence	1Lt	348	5	5
Popek, Edward	Maj	348	5	5
Sutcliffe, Robert	1Lt	348	5	5

P-47 PTO/Seventh Air Force (8 Aces/45 victories)

Ace Name	Rank	Unit	P-47 V	Total V
Stone, Robert	1Lt	318	7	7
Wolfe, Judge	Capt	318	7	9
Lustic, Stanley	1Lt	318	6	6
Anderson, Richard	1lt	318	5	5
Hoyt, Edward	Capt	35*/507	5	5
Mathis, William	1Lt	318	5	5
Perdomo, Oscar	1Lt	507	5	5
Vogt, John E.	Capt	318	5	5

*5AF

Flying the P-47 Thunderbolt (PTO)

By

Walter (Jim) Benz: 8 victories 348FG

Fourth highest P-47 ace PTO

Although I spent all of my nearly 30 years in the Air Force associated with fighter flying activities and loved to fly, I was never very interested in how the aircraft was put together or what made it go. I just got in and went. I flew 330 combat missions, flying 806 combat hours in the P-47 and later the F-80 and F-86 in Korea.

In May 1943, my 348th Fighter Group was the first unit to use the P-47 in the Pacific Theater, and the fighter proved itself to be very effective in combat against Japanese aircraft, and later in the air-to-ground role.

The cockpit was large and comfortable, but at the low altitudes we flew at over New Guinea it was just plain hot! Pacific versions did not have a pressurized cockpit, and above 35,000 feet I frequently got very uncomfortable pains in my joints. The instrument and control layouts were very good. For a good bit of our time in New Guinea our radios were original issue. They had a hard to see dial and were difficult to crank in and tune to desired frequencies. After these were replaced by the push button VHF sets the radio problems were solved.

The radial Pratt & Whitney was a rugged, reliable, and almost indestructible engine. It could take a great deal of combat damage and still bring you home. P&W fuel consumption was something else, and a major concern in the Pacific, where there were long distances over water to the target. Some 25-30 gallons could be used just to warm up and take off. In cruising we used about 100 gallons per hour, and in a dog fight we could use 275 gallons per hour or more. When we learned the Charles Lindbergh method of cruise control; we greatly extended our range. We had 305 internal gallons, to which 75-150 gallon belly auxiliary tanks were first added. Later the addition of two larger wing tanks further increased our range. The P-47 had an adequate, but not great, rate of climb, and with the turbo super charger you could get it up to 39,000 feet and a little more, but this altitude was seldom necessary. The top speed depended on its load configuration, which often was stagger-

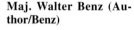

Maj. Walter Benz (Author/Benz)

LtCol. William Dunham (16 v.): second top PTO P-47 scorer. (USAF)

Opposite: F/O Harold Rouse and 1Lt. Albert Frese flew to the first P-47 CBI victory in a 33FG Thunderbolt. (USAF)

ing. Clean, we could do 350 mph at 5,000 feet and 425 at 30,000 feet. Most of the time we were loaded down with external fuel tanks, bombs, rockets, napalm, etc., which greatly affected the fighter's speed and performance until they were jettisoned.

The P-47 was equipped with eight .50 caliber machine guns, probably making it the best armed fighter of WWII. We had a good gunsight and an adequate amount of ammunition. With this heavy firepower, using a combination of tracer, ball, and AP ammo we could blast any Japanese aircraft out of the sky.

The Thunderbolt was a versatile fighter, successfully performing all the missions assigned to it: air-to-air fighter; bomber escort; and fighter-bomber. Against Japanese fighters we were not as maneuverable and could not climb with them, but we had the great advantage of speed in a dive and could stay with them in a turn. In the P-47's ground support/fighter-bomber role it was an outstanding and reliable aircraft. The main reason for this was that it was so rugged and could withstand a lot of battle damage. We used it very effectively as a dive bomber and skip bomber against Japanese shipping. Against enemy airfields and personnel we used rockets, napalm, and machine guns with devastating effect. In the Philippines we saw lots of action, particularly low-level bombing and strafing, in which the Japanese threw up considerable AA and ground fire. In these missions we were thankful we were flying our tough old Thunderbolts.

P-47 CBI First Victory in Type

Pilot: F/O Harold Rouse & 1Lt. Albert Frese
Time: 18 October 1944/1015
Place: Mingladon, Burma
Unit: 58FS/33FG/10-14AF
A/C: P-47D/Oscar
Action: In the CBI, the 10th and 14th Air Forces had three full fighter groups (33rd, 80th, and 81st) and two squadrons of the 2nd Air Commando Group equipped with P-47s. As the primary role of the fighter in the theater was as a fighter-bomber with little aerial opposition, the Thunderbolt only totaled 16 victories in the theater.

The 33FG arrived in Karachi, India, after being pulled from the Italian Campaign in March 1944 and were put under the control of the 10AF. The 58 and 60FS received the P-47D, while the 59th received new P-40Ns. The P-47 squadrons operated out of Moran and flew bombing and patrol missions. F/O Harold Rouse and 1Lt. Albert Frese of the 58 FS/33FG claimed its first victories over a formation of Oscars near Mingladon, Burma. The two squadrons would convert to P-38s in November. Some 40 minutes later, 1Lt. Everett Kelly of the 6 CS/2ACG shot down an Oscar over Rangoon.

P-47 CBI Top Scorer in Type

Pilot: 1Lt. Samuel Hammer
Unit: 90FS/80FG/10AF
Victories: 3
The 80FG began operations in September 1943, flying P-40Ns over Burma. The group scored a total of 44 victories, but only four were in the P-47. The group participated mainly in a ground support role, in which they proved especially proficient.

On 14 December 1944, 1Lt. Samuel Hammer of the 90 FS/80FS/10AF became the top CBI P-47 scorer when he shot down three Tojos south of Bhamo, China. These victories, along with the two Helens he shot down in a P-40 in late May 1944 over Shimobwigyang, made him an ace.

1Lt. Jules Young of the 92FS/81FG had a very busy day on 17 January 1945 when he claimed a probable and five damaged Oscars near Hankow, China, flying the P-47. Three days earlier he got a shared Oscar and another probable, also near Hangkow. The 81FG originally flew P-39s and P-40s in the MTO, where it scored eight victories, and then moved on to China, initially flying P-40s. It was credited with nine more victories in the CBI, seven in the P-47.

1Lt. Samuel Hammer (USAF)

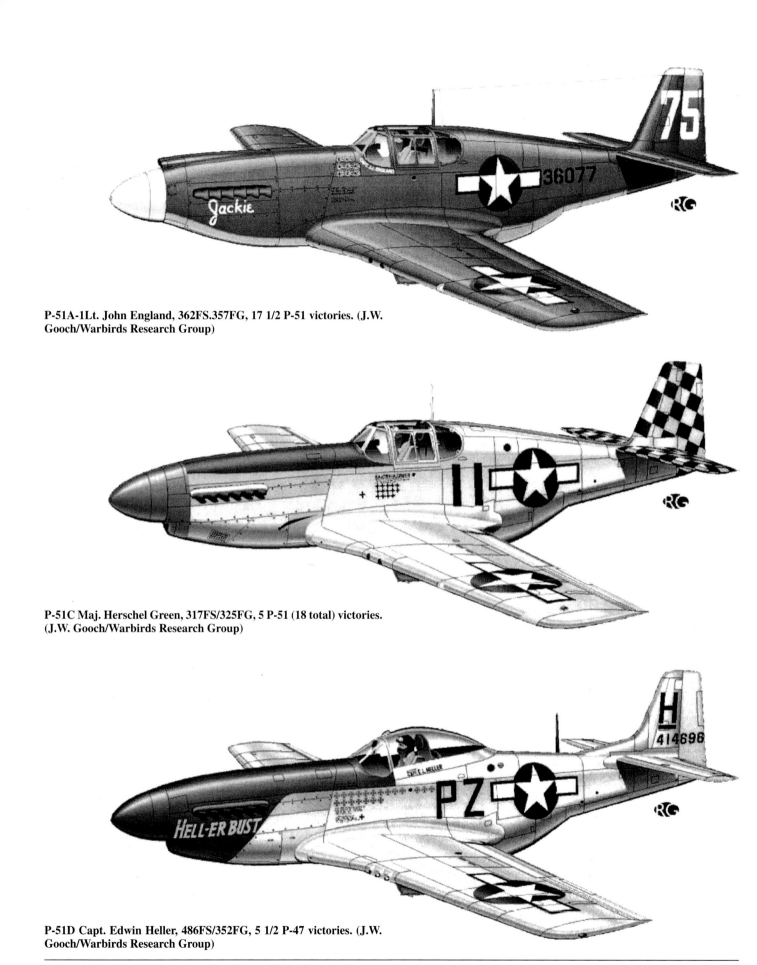

P-51A-1Lt. John England, 362FS.357FG, 17 1/2 P-51 victories. (J.W. Gooch/Warbirds Research Group)

P-51C Maj. Herschel Green, 317FS/325FG, 5 P-51 (18 total) victories. (J.W. Gooch/Warbirds Research Group)

P-51D Capt. Edwin Heller, 486FS/352FG, 5 1/2 P-47 victories. (J.W. Gooch/Warbirds Research Group)

North American P-51 Mustang/F-6

In April 1940 the British approached North American Aviation to build the Curtiss P-40 for the RAF. However, North American had other ideas, and proposed that it would build a better fighter using the P-40 Allison V-1710 engine. The British agreed, stipulating that the prototype be completed in four months. The design team of head designer Raymond Rice and Edgar Schmued completed the NA-73 prototype in 122 days, but the engine was not ready for an additional six weeks. The NP-73 flew for the first time on 26 October 1941, and it demonstrated notable performance due its innovative laminar flow airfoil, which was designated to become the standard for most future high speed fighter designs. The USAAF and test pilot Robert Chilton tested two NA-73s as the XP-51, and were impressed enough to order 150. The RAF ordered 620 as the Mustang I, with deliveries starting in November 1941, and another 150 were ordered as the Mustang II (55 were repossessed by the USAAF to be converted to the F-6A photo recon aircraft). The low altitude Allison engine made the fighter unsuited for air to air combat, which took place at higher altitudes. In England the Rolls Royce Merlin 60 was fitted to the Mustang I airframe, which was to define the Mustang as one of, if not the, elite fighter of the war. In the meantime, the Air Force had accepted 500 Allison-powered A-36s, the ground attack version of the P-51, and 310 Allison-powered P-51As. The RAF received 50 Allison Mustangs as the Mustang II and 35 others to be modified to F-6Bs. The A-36 was briefly named the "Invader," and the first P-51s the "Apache," but the RAF designation "Mustang" was the adopted name for all P-51 models. The first Merlin-powered Mustangs were the P-51B and C (RAF Mustang III). The American-built Merlins were licensed to Packard, and the USAAF ordered 2,200 before its Merlin Mustang had ever flown. The B and C were identical, with the B being built in Inglewood and the C in Dallas, and began operations in December 1943. A combined total of 3,749 (1,999 Bs and 1,750 Cs) were built, of which 910 were shipped to the RAF and 91 were converted to the F-6C (a total of 482 F, or photo recon, versions were completed to F-6A/B/C/D/K from P-51/51A/C/D/K, respectively). The P-51D was the first major design change, and gave the Mus-

tang its classic lines. The fuselage cockpit fairing was cut down to the tail plane to permit the elegant teardrop canopy to be fitted, thus eliminating the blind spot created by the faired cockpit. A dorsal fin was added to compensate for keel loss. The D carried six .50 machine guns instead of four, moved the wing slightly forward, and provided rocket launchers. The D was the most numerous P-51 model with 7,956 being produced, including 876 Mustang IVs for RAF. The 1,337 K models were similar to the Ds. The H was the last production model (555 built) and was the fastest, with a speed of 487 mph. Neither the K or H saw operational service, as the war ended in the Pacific and contracts for an additional 3,000 were canceled. Some 15,367 Mustangs were built and helped to change the course of the war in the ETO, allowing American bombers to penetrate into German-held territory under continuous escort protection.

P-51 ETO First Victory in Type

Pilot: 1Lt. Charles F. Gumm
Time: 16 December 1943/1330
Place: Bremen area, Germany
Unit: 355FS/354FG/9AF ("Pioneer Mustang Group")
A/C: P-51B/Me-109

In the disastrous two-pronged Regensburg/Schweinfurt missions of 17 August 1943, the long-range bombers of the 8AF suffered heavy losses to the Luftwaffe because of the lack of adequate continuous escort by both the P-47 and P-38, and the inability of the bombers to be mutually protective. Allied operational planning for 1944 projected a deep-penetration bombing campaign against the German war machine, particularly the aircraft industry. Tactical leaders of the 8AF were aware of the long-range capabilities of the Rolls Royce Merlin-powered P-51B Mustang. But somewhere in the web of USAAF bureaucracy there remained the belief that this Mustang was a tactical fighter, like its Allison-powered A-36 and P-51A predecessors. Therefore, these new Mustangs were assigned to the 9AF, which was being formed as a tactical air force to support the upcoming invasion. The unit designated to receive them was the 354FG, which originally trained as a P-39 outfit. The VIII

Edgar Schmued (shown) and Raymond Rice completed the NA-73— the P-51 Mustang prototype—in just 122 days. (North American)

Robert Chilton did much of the early testing of the XP-51. (North American)

FC controlled the 354ᵗʰ operationally. After several uneventful missions resulting only in a damaged claim, the Mustang would be blooded on 16 December 1943.

On this day the "Pioneer Mustangs" escorted a mixed group of B-17s and B-24s to Bremen. 1Lt. Charles Gumm and 1Lt. Gilbert Talbot of the 355FS climbed toward their assigned position defending the leading bomber box, when at 1320 they sighted four Me-109s making a run on the box. They climbed after them and closed to 400 yards when the 109s spotted them and dove left. The P-51s pursued, with Gumm dropping slightly behind to cover Talbot's tail. One Messerschmitt dove left, while the other continued towards the bombers. Talbot maneuvered up and right to cover Gumm, who was closing on this second Me-109. Gumm fired at 100 yards without effect. Another three second burst from 100 yards caused the Daimler Benz engine to start smoking. Gumm fired again from very close range, and his fighter was hit by flying debris. The mortally wounded German fell off to the left, its engine smoking heavily. Gumm broke combat to chase another Me-109 off Talbot's tail. In the next two months Gumm shot down an additional five enemy aircraft, along with 2 1/2 probables and eight damaged. On 21 February he became the first ace of the 354ᵗʰ when he shot down a Me-109 over Brunswick at 1430. On 1 March, on his return from a training flight his Mustang's engine malfunctioned near base. In order not to plow into the village of Nayland Gumm did not bail out, but attempted to bank away. He was too low and hit a tree, fatally crashing his aircraft into the ground.

The first Mustang I (Allison-powered) victory by an American was credited to F/O Hollis Hill, an American flying with the RCAF. On 19 August 1942, Hill downed a FW-190 over the Dieppe commando invasion beaches.

The early Mustang experienced numerous nagging technical difficulties. It was underarmed with four .50 cal. machine guns, and the auxiliary fuel tanks were troublesome. Nonetheless, the 354ᵗʰ proved the value of their mount with a 18 victory / no loss mission over Kiel on 5 January, and a 15-0 mission over Oschersleben on 11 January. On 11 February, the second Mustang group (357ᵗʰ) debuted, followed by the 363ʳᵈ on the 22ⁿᵈ, and on the 25ᵗʰ the 4ᵗʰ traded their Thunderbolts.

P-51 ETO First Ace in Type

Pilot: Maj. James H. Howard
Time: 30 January 1944/1215
Place: 50 miles NW of Brunswick
Unit: 356 FS/354FG/9AF
A/C: P-51B/Me-110

By mid-1944, round trips of 1,000 to 1,500 miles by the 300 to 400 Mustangs deployed by the USAAF were commonplace. In early January 1944, Lt. Gen. Jimmy Doolittle assumed command of the 8AF and revoked the tactical edict which coupled the fighter as an escort directly to the bomber formation, thus waiting for the Luftwaffe to attack. The Mustang was now free to roam, attacking the Luftwaffe at will, and consequently, unit and individual scores began to climb. In the Mustang, the hard-pressed Luftwaffe was confronted anywhere over the Reich with a single seat fighter matching the latest versions of the FW-190 and Me-109. The vaunted twin engine "destroyers," such as the Me-110, were particularly vulnerable to the predations of the Mustangs. The Luftwaffe found itself being severely mauled over its homeland, not only by force of numbers, but by superior equipment, tactics, and determination.

James Howard resigned from the Navy to join Chennault's Flying Tigers as a squadron leader for the 2AVG. Howard scored 5 1/3 victories in January 1942, although some reliable sources (Dr. Frank Olynyck) claim some of these may have been air-to-ground victories. He scored his last victory on 4 July, the day before AVG disbandment, when he shot down a I-97 Japanese fighter.

After his tour with the Tigers, Howard returned to the States and joined the 354FG of the 9AF as a Major, and CO of what was then a P-39 unit. The 354ᵗʰ was shipped to Boxted, England, where it was introduced to the P-51B.

On 5 January 1944 Howard, with a ME-109 victory on 20 December, led the group to Kiel on a bomber and target withdrawal escort. A large formation of Me-110s was intercepted as it was lobbing rockets into the B-17 boxes. During the clash 18 Luftwaffe twin-engine fighters were destroyed, and the Germans were reluctant to commit them into future battles.

1Lt. Charles Gumm (USAF)

Maj. James Howard (Author/Howard)

On 11 January, the 354th was assigned to furnish target support over Halberstadt and Oschersleben. Upon rendezvous the Mustangs divided into flights of four, above and laterally to the B-17 formation. This deployment gave them the altitude advantage against enemy interception, and also allowed them free-rein, not tying them to the bombers. At 1140, Luftwaffe fighters engaged the bombers over Halberstadt, and the overzealous Mustangs broke off to attack, leaving Howard alone. He headed toward the forward bomber boxes and saw that one was under strong attack by about 20 Me-109s and 110s. Howard turned *"Ding Hao"* into a twin-engine Me-110 and chased the daylighting night fighter down, firing and watching it crash into the snow-covered ground. Soon he noticed a FW-190 flying below. The Focke Wulf pulled up into the sun to try to escape, but Howard hit him with a short burst that caused the pilot to bail out. Howard found that in these turning firing passes his fire power diminished from four guns to three. Ten minutes into the combat, he saw a Me-109 below and a few hundred yards ahead. The Messerschmitt, detecting his pursuer, chopped his throttle and scissored below, hoping Howard would overrun. Not falling for this venerable combat maneuver, Howard also chopped his throttle and scissored. The two fighters went into a circular dogfight, with the eventual winner being the pilot with the aircraft that could turn the tightest circle. Howard maneuvered inside by dumping 20 degrees flaps, getting on the German's tail as he dove. Howard fired, getting some hits from long range, but did not see the German crash. In this skirmish he lost another gun, leaving him with two in operation. A Me-110 passed in front of him, and he shot it down with a short burst. Regaining altitude, Howard saw a Me-109 and Mustang flying a parallel course, each trying to gain an advantage. The Mustang peeled off after seeing a compatriot coming up from behind, while the Me-109 slowly circled. Howard descended on the German, putting a burst into its fuselage before it flew off smoking. Running low on fuel and with only one gun now operable, Howard broke off combat.

Upon returning to base the bomber crews claimed six victories for Howard, who would only take credit for three, as he could not remember the sequence of events in the heat of battle. However, Commander of the 401BG Howard Bowman, wanting to reward his rescuer contacted 8th AF HQ with the P-51's buzz number. Bowman exclaimed: "For sheer determination and guts it was the greatest exhibition I've ever seen; they can't give that boy a big enough reward." They did give "that boy" a big enough reward—the Congressional Medal of Honor. Howard's modest response to the citation was: "I seen my duty and I done it." Howard's total for the day is variously listed as three or four victories, depending on the source. He went on to score two more victories before the end of his tour, which he finished as a full Colonel. He and John Landers are the only two American pilots to become aces in both Europe and the Pacific. Landers scored six victories with the 49FG of the 5AF, and then 8 1/2 victories with the 78th and 357FG in Europe.

P-51 ETO Top Scorer in Type
Pilot: Maj. George E. Preddy
Unit: 487FS & 328FS/352FG/8AF
Victories: 23 5/6 (P-51) & 3 (P-47)

V#	Date	E/A/C
5	P-47 Tour	
3 1/3	04-22-44	1/3 Ju-88
4 1/3 –5	1/3 05-13-44	2 Me-109s
6 1/3-7 5/6	05-30-44	2 1/2 Me-109s
8 5/6	06-12-44	Me-109
9 5/6-10	1/3 06-20-44	Fw-190 & 1/2 Me-410
11 1/3	06-21-44	Me-109
12 1/3-14 1/3	07-18-44	Me-109 & 2 Ju-88s
14 5/6	07-21-44	1/2 Me-109
15 5/6	07-29-44	Me-109
16 5/6	08-05-44	Me-109
17 5/6-22 5/6	08-06-44 6	Me-109s
23 5/6	11-02-44	Me-109
24 5/6	11-21-44	FW-190
25 5/6-26 5/6	12-25-44 2	Me-109s

In March 1944 the 4FG became the first 8AF group to re-equip with the P-51. By the end of the year all of the 8AF's 15 fighter groups, totaling 42 squadrons were Mustang equipped (with the conspicuous exception of the 56FG, which with good reason loved their P-47s). Once the long range Mustang escorts gained air superiority they were authorized to seek out Luftwaffe airfields and strafe its aircraft on the ground. The introduction of the D model, though having a very slight decrease in performance, offered other improvements that would enhance its role as a ground attack aircraft: the bubble canopy for improved vision from the previous "coffin hood"; six (from four) .50 cal. machine guns; and a strengthened wing, which allowed heavier external loads of fuel and bombs.

Maj. George Preddy (USAF)

George Preddy was a man of determination. After failing three Navy physicals because of his small size, he finally got into the Army's Aviation Cadet Program in the fall of 1940. He served in the Coastal Artillery until April 1941, and received his wings in mid-December. He was shipped to the SWPA, flying P-40s for the 9PS/49PG. He damaged two Japanese aircraft before being severely injured in a mid-air collision that killed a squadronmate. He was hospitalized for three months, and returned to the States in October 1942. He remained unassigned for two months before being reluctantly accepted by John Meyer's 34FS (to become the 487FS) of the 352FG, which was training in P-47s. The 352nd flew its first combat on 9 September 1943, but it was not until 5 December that Preddy would score his first victory. He would score two more victories in the P-47 before the group re-equipped with the P-51 in April 1944. The transition seemed to suit Preddy, who had scored only three victories in the eight previous months and then scored 23 5/6th victories in the next seven and a half months. Preddy scored 5 5/6th victories in P-51B "Cripes A Mighty 2nd," while its P-51D successor "Cripes A Mighty 3rd" got the rest.

Preddy scored steadily in the P-51, having six missions on which he scored multiple victories. His greatest day came on 6 August 1944. He had gotten a Me-109 south of Hamburg by hoisting a few beers in the local pub the day before, and since the weather was predicted to wash out the next day's mission he decided to commemorate the victory. The weather unexpectedly cleared, but Preddy's head did not, and he blearily led his flight of blue-nosed Mustangs on a bomber escort to Brandenburg. He threw up during the flight and hoped the weather would not roll his fighter. His flight observed an unsuspecting Luftwaffe formation of Me-109s, who probably were relying on their top cover for protection. Preddy dove and systematically shot down six as the combat proceeded from 27,000 to 7,000 feet. Upon being told he had set an 8AF record for victories in one day for an individual pilot he replied: "I just kept shooting and they kept falling." The feat earned him the DSC and a Stateside leave.

When he returned to England he was given command of the 328FS, in expectation his leadership would improve its performance. On his first mission as CO on 2 November, he got a Me-109 and the squadron claimed 25 of an 8AF daily record 38 E/A. Lack of Luftwaffe opposition limited his November victory total to two, while December weather shut down the air war over Europe. This poor weather had protected Hitler's surprise Panzer thrust (Battle of the Bulge) from Allied air interdiction. On Christmas day the weather cleared, and Preddy led his squadron against targets in the Bulge. Early in the mission Luftwaffe Me-109s were engaged in the Koblentz area, and Preddy claimed two of the total 11 victories claimed. Quickly the unit was vectored to the Leige area to intercept low-flying enemy fighters. Flying with his wingman, 1Lt. Jim Boudchier, and a 479FG pilot, they were warned of heavy friendly flak, but were told it would be lifted as they entered the area. Southeast of Leige Preddy dove on a low flying FW-190 and chased after it at tree-top level through an area guarded by the 12AA Group. Both Preddy and Bouchier were hit by their AA fire. Bouchier was able to bail out, but Preddy, hit by two .50 cal. bullets, died as he tried to crash land.

Preddy's 23 1/3 victories in the P-51 were the most by any Mustang pilot in the war. In their year and a half of operations over Europe, 8th and 9th Air Force Mustangs dominated the European skies, claiming 4,238 of the 7,505 ETO aerial victories. This 56 1/2% of theater total victories was only exceeded by the 65% P-40 victories in the CBI (where it was virtually the only American fighter in combat throughout the war). The F6F Hellcat scored 43% of all fighter victories in the Pacific.

LtCol. John Meyer: 2nd ranking P-51 ace with 21 victories. (USAF)

Maj. Glenn Eagleston: Top 9AF P-51 ace with 18 1/2 victories. (Author/Eagleston)

ETO P-51 ACES 9AF					ETO P-51 ACES 8AF (160 Aces/1180.6 Victories)				
Ace Name	Rank	Unit	P-51	Other	Ace Name	Rank	UNIT	P-51	Other
		FG	V	V			FG	V	V
Eagleston, Glenn	Maj	354	18.5		Preddy, George	Maj	352	23.83	+3v P-47
Beerbower, Don	Capt	354	15.5		Meyer, John	LCol	352	21	+3v P-47
Bradley, Jack	LCol	354	15		Carson, Leonard	Maj	357	18.5	
Carr, Bruce	1Lt	363/354	15		England, John	Maj	357	17.5	
Emmer, Wallace	Capt	354	14		Wetmore, Ray	Capt	358	17	+4.25 P-47
East, Clyde	Capt	15TRS	13	(in F-6)	Anderson, Clarence	Capt	357	16.25	
Stephens, Robert	Maj	354	13		Gentile, Don	Capt	4	15.5	+2v Spit
Brueland, Lowell	Maj	354	12.5						+4.33v P-47
Dahlberg, Kenneth	Capt	354	11	+3v P-47	Peterson, Richard	Capt	357	15.5	
Frantz, Carl	1Lt	354	11		Foy, Robert	Maj	357	15	
Turner, Richard	Maj	354	11		Whisner, William	Capt	352	14.5	+1v P-47
O'Conner, Frank	Capt	354	10.75		Brown, Henry	Capt	355	14.2	
Overfield. Loyd	1Lt	354	9	+2v P-47	Bochkay, Donald	Maj	357	13.83	
Hoefker, John	Capt	15TRS	8.5	(in F-6)	Godfrey, John	Capt	4	13.83	+2.5 P-47
McDowell, Don	1Lt	354	8.5		Hofer, Ralph	2Lt	4	13	+2v P-47
Lamb, George	Maj	354	7.5		Thornell, John	1Lt	352	13	+4.25 P-47
Lasko, Charles	Capt	354	7.5		Carpenter, George	Maj	4	12.83	+1v P-47
Goodnight, Robert	1Lt	354	7.25		Moran, Glennon	1Lt	352	12	+1v P-47
Anderson, William	1Lt	354	7		Megura, Nicholas	Capt	4	11.83	
Dalglish, James	Maj	354	7	+2v P-47	Kirla, John	1Lt	357	11.5	
Reynolds, Robert	1Lt	354	7		Yeager, Charles	Capt	357	11.5	
Rogers, Felix	Capt	354	7		Hively, Howard	Maj	4	11	+1v P-47
Hunt, Edward	1Lt	354	6.5		Littge, Raymond	Capt	352	10.5	
Koenig, Charles	1lt	354	6.5		Storch, John	LCol	357	10.5	
Rader, Valentine	1Lt	111TRS	6.5	(in F-6)	Strait, Donald	Maj	356	10.5	+3v P-47
Weldon, Robert	1Lt	354	6.25		Glover, Fred	Maj	4	10.33	
Emerson, Warren	Capt	354	6		Blickenstaff, Wayne	LCol	353	10	
Gross, Clayton	Capt	354	6		Jeffrey, Arthur	LCol	479	10	+4v P-38
Gumm, Charles	1Lt	354	6		Lines, Ted	Capt	4	10	
Howard, James	Col	354	6	+3v P-40	Millikan, Willard	Capt	4	10	+3v P-47
Larson, Leland	2Lt	15TRS	6	(in F-6)	Hovde, William	Maj	355	9.5	+1v P-47
Simmons, William	1Lt	354	6		Spencer, Dale	1Lt	361	9.5	
Bickel, Carl	1Lt	354	5.5		Adams, Fletcher	Capt	357	9	
Bickford, Edward	2Lt	354	5.5		Anderson, Charles	1Lt	4	9	+1v P-47
King, William	1Lt	354	5.5						
Long, Maurice	Capt	354	5.5						
Shoup, Robert	1Lt	354	5.5						
Waits, Joe	1Lt	15-62TRS	5.5						
Miller, Thomas	2Lt	354	5.25						
Asbury, Richard	Capt	363/354	5						
Fisk, Harry	Capt	354	5						
Martin, Kenneth	Col	354	5						
Ritchey, Andrew	1Lt	354	5						
Rose, Franklin	1Lt	354	5						
Rudolph, Henry	1Lt	354	5						
Talbot, Gilbert	Maj	354	5						
Warner, Jack	Capt	354	5						
Wise, Kenneth	1Lt	354	5						

Capt. Don Beerbower: 2nd ranking 9AF P-51 ace with 18 1/2 victories. (USAF)

Name	Rank	Group	Score	Notes
Beyer, William	Capt	361	9	
Cueleers, George	LCol	364	9	+1.5 P-38
Bryan, Donald	Capt	352	9	+4.33v P-7
Gleason, George	Capt	479	9	+3v P-38
Goodson, James	Maj	4	9	+5v P-47
Norley, Louis	Maj	4	9	+1.33v P-47
Bankey, Ernest	Capt	364	8.5	+1v P-38
Blakeslee, Donald	Col	4	8.5	+3v Spit +3v P-47
Cesky, Charles	Capt	352	8.5	
Doersch, George	Capt	359	8.5	+2v P-47
Fiebelkorn, Ernest	Capt	20	8.5	+0.5v P-38
Hayes, Thomas	LCol	357	8.5	
Jenkins, Otto	2Lt	357	8.5	
Luksic, Carl	1Lt	352	8.5	
Moats, Sanford	1Lt	352	8.5	
Broadhead, Joseph	Maj	357	8	
Fowle, James	Capt	364	8	
Gerard, Francis	Capt	339	8	
Kinnard, Claiborne	LCol	4/355	8	
Olds, Robin	Maj	479	8	+5v P-38
Shaw, Robert	1Lt	357	8	
Sublett, John	Capt	357	8	
Weaver, Charles	Capt	357	8	
Lang, Joseph	Capt	4	7.83	
Bryan, William	Maj	339	7.5	
Davis, Glendon	Capt	357	7.5	
Halton, William	Maj	352	7.5	+1v P-47
Karger, Dale	1Lt	357	7.5	
McGratten, Bernard	Capt	4	7.5	
McKennon, Pierce	Maj	4	7.5	+2.5v P-47
Miklajcyk, Henry	Capt	352	7.5	
Righetti, Elwyn	LCol	55	7.5	
Schlegal, Albert	Capt	4	7.5	+1v P-47
Andrew, Stephen	Maj	352	7	+1v P-40
Becker, Robert	Capt	357	7	
Browning, James	Capt	357	7	
Carder, John	1Lt	357	7	
Crenshaw, Claude	1Lt	359	7	
Elder, John	Maj	355	7	+1v P-47
Graham, Gordon	LCol	353	7	
Jamison, Gilbert	Capt	364	7	
Lewis, William	Capt	55	7	
Marshall, Bert	Maj	355	7	
O'Brien, Gilbert	1Lt	357	7	
Pierce, Joseph	1Lt	357	7	
Stewart, Everett	Col	352/355	7	+0.83 P-47
Tyler, Gerald	Maj	357	7	
Woody, Robert	Capt	355	7	
Cramer, Darrel	Maj	55	6.5	
Bille, Henry	Maj	355	6	
Brown, Harley	1Lt	20	6	
Candelaria, Richard	1Lt	479	6	
Clark, James	LCol	4	6	+0.5v Spit +4v P-47
Cundy, Arthur	1Lt	353	6	
Drew, Urban	1Lt	361	6	
Evans, Andrew	LCol	357	6	
Haviland, Fred	Capt	355	6	
Howes, Bernard	1Lt	55	6	
Jackson, Willie	LCol	352	6	+1v P-47
Jones, Cyril	1Lt	359	6	
Kemp. William	2Lt	361	6	
Larson, Donald	Maj	339	6	
Pugh, John	Capt	357	6	
Riley, Paul	1Lt	4	6	+0.5v P-47
Roberson, Arval	1Lt	357	6	
Schmanski, Robert	Capt	357	6	
Starck, Walter	Capt	352	6	+1v P-47
Starnes, James	Capt	339	6	
Welch, Robert	Capt	55	6	
Whalen, William	1Lt	4, 2 SF	6	
Amoss, Dudley	1Lt	55	5.5	
Burdick, Clinton	1Lt	356	5.5	
Cummings, Donald	Capt	55	5.5	
Cutler, Frank	Capt	352	5.5	+2v P-47
Fortier, Norman	Capt	355	5.5	+.33v P-47
Gailer, Frank	1Lt	357	5.5	
Hatala, Paul	Capt	357	5.5	
Heller, Edwin	Capt	352	5.5	
Lenfest, Charles	Capt	355	5.5	
Minchew, Leslie	Capt	355	5.5	
O'Brien, William	Capt	357	5.5	
Ruder, LeRoy	1Lt	357	5.5	
VandenHuevel, George	1Lt	361	5.5	
Winks, Robert	1Lt	357	5.5	
Beeson, Duane	Capt	4	5.33	+12v P-47
Allen, William	1Lt	55	5	
Ammon, Robert	1Lt	339	5	
Bank, Raymond	1Lt	357	5	
Beavers, Edward	Capt	339	5	
Bostrom, Ernest	1Lt	352	5	

Maj. Leonard Carson: 3rd ranking 8AF P-51 ace 18 1/2 victories. (USAF)

Carlson, Kendall	Capt	4	5	+1v P-47
Chandler, Van	1Lt	4	5	
Cole, Charles	Capt	20	5	
Coons, Merle	Capt	55	5	
Cox, Ralph	Capt	359	5	
Cranfill, Niven	Maj	359	5	
Culleton, William	1Lt	355	5	
Daniel, J.S.	1Lt	339	5	
Dregne, Irwin	LCol	357	5	
Elder, Robert	Maj	353	5	
Hanseman, Chris	1Lt	339	5	
Harris, Thomas	Capt	357	5	
Hauver, Charles	1Lt	355	5	
Haworth, Russell	1Lt	55	5	
Hiro, Edwin	Maj	357	5	
Howe, David	1Lt	4	5	+1v P-47
Johnson, Evan	Capt	339	5	
Jones, Frank	Capt	4	5	
Lazear, Earl	1Lt	352	5	
Markham, Gene	Capt	353	5	
Marsh, Lester	1Lt	339	5	
Maxwell, Chester	Capt	357	5	
McElroy, James	Capt	355	5	
Pascoe, James	1Lt	364	5	+0.5v P-38
Priest, Royce	1Lt	355	5	
Reese, William	1Lt	357	5	
Scheible, Wilbur	Capt	356	5	+1v P-47
Schuh, Duerr	1Lt	352	5	
Sears, Alexander	1Lt	352	5	
Stengel, William	Capt	352	5	
Stanley, Morris	1Lt	357	5	
Sykes, William	1Lt	361	5	
Waggoner, Horace	1Lt	353	5	
Warren, Jack	Capt	357	5	
Wilson, William	Capt	364	5	
Woods, Sidney	LCol	4	5	+2v P-38
York, Robert	1Lt	359	5	

Flying the P-51 Mustang (ETO)
By
William Whisner: 21 victories (14 1/2 P-51) 352FG
(15 1/2 WWII and 5 1/2 Korea)

I began my combat career flying the P-47 for the 487FS of the 352FG out of Bodney, England. For the first several months I was fortunate to fly for George Preddy, whom I consider the greatest fighter pilot I have ever known. (Preddy went on to become the top Mustang ace with 23 5/6th P-51 victories-ed.)

We exchanged our Thunderbolts for Mustang Bs in April 1944. The P-51 was the better of the two fighters. It was faster, had a smaller turning radius, had better acceleration and rate of climb, far outclassed the P-47 below 25,000 feet, and had a longer combat range. Even in a dive, for which the Thunderbolt was renown, the Mustang could hold its own. In the initial pushover into a dive the Mustang was faster, and thereafter it could keep up with the heavier Thunderbolt, which fell like a rock. The P-47 did have a better rate

**Capt. William Whisner
(Author/Whisner)**

of roll, and with its high altitude supercharger was slightly better at altitudes above 25,000 feet. The P-47 was the more rugged of the two aircraft, with its sturdy construction and radial engine. Although it was more heavily armed with eight .50 caliber machine guns to the Mustang B's four, in aerial combat this was no problem, as most kills were from 10 degrees or less deflection and within 250 yards—can't miss territory. But on ground support missions the two extra pair of guns was nice.

Our first B-models did have some teething problems that needed to be worked out. The Packard Merlin engine that was a license-built Rolls Royce Merlin had numerous difficulties with its coolant, oil, fuel, and electrical systems. Our guns were also a continual source of frustration. Any time we pulled more than 1 1/2 to 2 Gs they would jam, usually because rounds would fail to eject from the belt. Some stopgap measures were undertaken, but the problem was not alleviated until the introduction of the D-models, which had a redesigned gun and belt system. Meanwhile, we had to take our chances with the guns while maneuvering in combat, or confine our firing to straight and level flight! The greenhouse canopy had the disadvantage of restricted visibility, especially to the rear, which was a real problem in combat.

The cockpit was well laid out, with the instruments and controls easy to reach and visible. Ground handling of the aircraft was superb due to its wide landing gear. We were able to taxi without using the brakes by steering with the rudder. The wide gear also made take off and landing easy. The flight characteristics of the Mustang were great. It gave ample warning of a stall, and generally had no severe handling faults. The air-cooled engine was more susceptible to battle damage than a radial engine. Also, the belly scoop made ditching a dicey situation.

We received our D-models in May, which diminished most of our early problems and made the Mustang the best fighter of the war. The D was fitted with a one-piece canopy that gave excellent vision. The gun jamming was worked out, and the number of guns was increased to six and the number of rounds from 1,200 to 1,800. The K-14 gunsight, introduced in the fall of 1944, enabled me to shoot down six (actually seven, but my gun camera film ran out) FW-190s on 21 November 1944. Its range was extended by reinforcing the wings to increase the external fuel. With two external fuel tanks we could escort bombers to any target. The long seven to eight hour escort missions did not seem so bad once you landed back at base.

The D had numerous modifications that made the aircraft heavier without a matching increase in engine power. In my opinion this factor subtly decreased the D's performance compared to the B. Nonetheless, the P-51 was the best fighter in the sky in the fall of 1944. In it I always felt in control of any combat. It was faster, more maneuverable, and had a better rate of climb, turn, and roll than anything the Germans could throw at us in any situation or altitude.

P-51 First MTO Victory
Pilot: Col. Charles McCorkle (HQ)
 Capt. Samuel Brown (307FS)
Time: 17 April 1944/1215-1300
Place: Sofia, Rumania
Unit: See above/31FG/15AF
A/C: P-51B/Me109s
Action: The P-51 (as the A-36 Invader) had been present in the MTO since early spring 1943, flying fighter-bomber missions with the 27th and 86FBG of the 12AF. When the 15AF was activated on 1 April 1944, the 31st and 52FGs traded in their Spitfires for P-51Bs and Cs, in which they achieved distinction during their bomber escort missions. The 31FG went on operations first on 16 April 1944 when they escorted bombers to Rumania. In May, the 52FG went into combat, while late that month the veteran 325FG moved from P-47s to P-51s.

On 16 April 1944 the 31FG flew the first MTO P-51 mission when it escorted B-24s to marshaling yards at Turnu-Severo, in central Italy, under Col. Charles "Sandy" McCorkle, who had earlier become an ace with the group. The next day the 31FG was assigned B-24 escort to Sofia, Rumania. Flying that day with the 307FS was Capt. Samuel Brown, who had served under McCorkle in the Aleutians. Just after noon, Me-109s attacked the Liberator bombers. In a 45-minute battle, McCorkle downed two and Brown got one and damaged another to get the first MTO P-51 victories.

Brown went on to become CO of the 307FS and totaled 15 1/2 victories (one probable and seven damaged) in the next 3 1/2 months. McCorkle claimed six victories in the next 2 1/2 months to give him a wartime total of 11 victories He was one of the few pilots to become an ace in two different fighters.

P-51 MTO First Ace in Type
Pilot: 1Lt. Frederick O. Trafton
Time: 23 April 1944/1300-1345
Place: Lake Balatine, Hungary
Unit: 308 FS/31FG/15AF
A/C : P-51B/2 Mc-200s & 1 Me-109
After enlisting in the Army in 1940 and being discharged, Fred Trafton earned pilot's wings and an officer's rating in the RAF. He flew Spitfire missions out of England with the American Eagle Squadron until October 1942. He transferred to the VIII FC, but got himself assigned to the 308FS/31FG/12AF. With the 308th he flew Spitfires, but did not score a victory in them, as the squadron flew combat across North Africa, over Sicily, and up the Italian boot. In April 1944, the 31st was re-equipped with the P-51B and assigned "long-legged" bomber escort missions over the Balkans, Eastern Europe, and occupied Italy.

Trafton flew uneventful missions on 16 and 17 April, but on the 18th he got his first victory when he shot down a Me-109 over Udine while attacking airdromes in the area. On the 21st, the 308th

Capt. Samuel Brown (Author/Brown)

Col. Charles "Sandy" McCorkle (Author/ McCorkle)

flew bomber escort to the Ploesti oil fields. The mission was recalled by bad weather, but only a handful of the bombers heard the recall and returned. Despite the weather the P-51s managed to rendezvous with the B-24s, which were beginning their bombing runs. About two dozen Me-109s attacked the vulnerable bombers, but the Mustangs intercepted them in the nick of time, allowing the completion of their runs. Trafton's flight attacked 20 Me-109s at 35,000 feet, and he got one and a probable.

On the 23rd, 956 B-17s and B-24s flew to Austria to bomb the Me-109 assembly plant at Wiener-Neustadt. The 308th was assigned to escort 107 B-24s, which unbeknown to the escorts were held back one hour. Trafton was leading yellow flight when just before I.P.—Lake Balatine, Hungary—he found his second element lagging behind and below at 10,000 feet because of oxygen failure. Trafton and his wingman, 2Lt. George Hughes, dropped down to provide cover when they spotted three Me-109s. Trafton half-rolled toward the deck, trying to sucker the Germans into combat. As he did, three Italian Macchi 200s passed line astern in front of Trafton, who fired, getting numerous fuselage hits on all three. He confirmed two crashes before rejoining his neophyte wingman, who had lost his leader. Hughes had come under attack, sustaining a H.E. hit on his cowling. Hughes jettisoned his canopy and bailed out. Trafton circled once but lost sight of the parachute. Soon he spotted a large number of fighters climbing south of the lake towards him. Alone, as the rest of the group flew on, Trafton attacked head on and shot at five or six of the Me-109s, destroying one of them for his third victory of the day and fifth in the P-51. He dove through the gaggle of enemy fighters, leveling off. Low on ammo and fuel, Trafton encountered three more Messerschmitts. A cannon shell tore through his canopy, shattering his instrument panel and putting holes of various sizes in Trafton's P-51. He bailed out at 700 feet, landing in an icy pond. A group of partisans rescued the wounded flyer and hid him in the mountains for two months. After recuperating he

worked behind enemy lines with the British as a cipher for a time. Using his Army training he led a detachment of 14 British and three Americans through Nazi-held Hungary and Austria before being picked up by a DC-3. He was repatriated back to the 308th after three months listed as MIA. Since he had intimate knowledge of the partisan organization he was prevented from further combat in case of capture. He was returned to the Z.I. to serve as an instructor for the duration.

The three victories on the 23rd made Trafton the first MTO P-51 ace. Records show that Trafton scored his victories between 1300 and 1345 on the mission's initial phase. Later, on the same mission but over Wiener-Neustadt, 31 FG CO Col. Charles McCorkle claimed two Me-110 victories at 1400, and then a FW-190 victory and damaged at 1415 for his fifth victory in the Mustang.

P-51 MTO Top Scorer in Type
Pilot: Capt. John J. Voll
Unit: 308FS/31FG/12-15AF
Victories: 21

V#	Date	E/A/C
1	06-23-44	FW-190
2-3	06-26-44	Me-109 & Me-210
4	06-27-44	Me-109
5	07-02-44	Me-109
6	07-18-44	FW-190
7-8	08-17-44	2 Me-109s
9	08-25-44	Fi-156
10	08-29-44	FW-190
11-12	08-31-44	2 Ju-52s
13	09-23-44	Mc-202
14-16	10-17-44	2 Me-109s & Do-21
17	11-06-44	Me-109
18-21	11-16-44	Ju-88, 2Fw-190s & Me-109

1Lt. Frederick Trafton
(Author/Trafton)

Capt. John Voll (Author)

As a 2Lt., John Voll was sent to Italy as a replacement pilot to join the 308FS of the 31 FG. Flying a P-51 named *"American Beauty,"* Voll was a wingman for 20 missions before being assigned to lead an element in June 1944. He scored his initial victory on 23 June while returning from a bomber escort mission to the Ploesti oil fields in Rumania. He downed a Me-109 north of Bucharest, and that same day, Maj. Herschel Green, the leading Mediterranean ace, scored his 15th victory. In June Voll got three more victories over Rumania and was promoted to 1Lt. On 2 July he became an ace by shooting down another Me-109 over Bucharest. Before Voll would get his next victory, Green, with 18 victories, was rotated home. The last two weeks in August were good, as Voll racked up six more victories, including two doubles. On 23 September he shot down one of the last Italian fighters flying for Mussolini, a Macchi-202. On 17 October he had his biggest day to date by downing a Do-217 and two Me-109s near Bratislavia. He then added a Me-109 on 6 November to give him his 17th victory and promotion to Captain. Although he was the leading active ace in the theater, as his tour was coming to an end he remained one victory behind Green.

On 16 November Voll climbed into *"American Beauty"* for his 57th and last combat mission. During the mission he had his radio shot away and was forced to return early. Alone over Northern Italy, he sighted a Ju-88 which turned tail, speeding over the Adriatic towards its base. Near Aviano seven Focke Wulfs dove out of the sun, while another five Me-109s closed on the apparently easy kill. Voll closed rapidly on the Junkers and dispatched it, and then turned into the dozen Germans. In the desperate dogfight Voll shot down two of the FW-190s and a Me-109, and added two probables and two damaged. The mission gave him four victories for the day and 21 for his career—tops in the MTO.

In the year that the Mustang became operational in the Mediterranean, the fighter was credited with 1,063 victories. Deteriorating Luftwaffe aircraft numbers and pilot quality aside, the P-51 was the supreme fighter in this theater, as it had been since the day it was introduced into combat.

MTO P-51 ACES 12-15AF				
Ace Name	Rank	Unit FG	P-51 V	Other V
Voll, John	Capt	31	21	
Varnell, James	Capt	52	17	
Brown, Samuel	Maj	31	15.5	
Brooks, James	1Lt	31	13	
Curtis, Robert	Maj	53	13	+1v Spit
Parker, Harry	Capt	325	13	
Skogsted, Norman	1Lt	31	12	
Goebel, Robert	Capt	31	11	
Lawler, J. Berry	Capt	52	11	
Lowrey, Wayne	1Lt	325	11	
Riddle, Robert	1Lt	31	11	
Goehausen, Walter	Capt	31	10	
Dorsch, Frederick	Capt	31	8.5	
Fiedler, Arthur	Capt	325	8	
Sangermano, Philip	1Lt	325	8	
Warford, Victor	Maj	31	8	
Allen, Calvin	1Lt	52	7	
Brown, Robert	2Lt	325	7	
Franklin, Duane	1Lt	52	7	
McLaughlin, Murray	Capt	31	7	
Shipman, Ernest	1Lt	31	7	
Simmons, John	1Lt	325	7	
Zoerb, Daniel	Capt	52	7	
Hoffman, James	1Lt	52	6.5	
Johnson, Arthur	1Lt	52	6.5	+2v Spit
Ainley, John	1Lt	31	6	
Buck, George	Capt	31	6	
Davis, Barrie	1Lt	325	6	
Dillard, William	Capt	31	6	
Hanes, William	1Lt	52	6	
Karr, Robert	Capt	52	6	
McCorkle, Charles	Col	31	6	+5v Spit
McDaniel, Gordon	1Lt	325	6	
Molland, Leland	Capt	31	6	+5.5v Spit
Tyler, James	Capt	52	6	+2v Spit
Wilhelm, David	Capt	31	6	
Lampe, Richard	1Lt	52	5.5	
Aron, William	1Lt	325	5	
Daniel, William	Col	31	5	
Dorris, Harry	Maj	31	5	
Dunkin, Richard	Capt	325	5	+1v P-40 +3v P-47
Emmert, Benjamin	1Lt	325	5	+1V P-47
Empey, James	2Lt	52	5	
Green, Herschel	Maj	325	5	+3v P-40 +10v P-47
Loving, George	Capt	31	5	
Ohr, Frederick	Capt	52	5	+1v Spit
Russo, Michael	1Lt	27 (12AF)	5	(in A-36)
Smith, Jack	Capt	31	5	
Thompson, Robert	1Lt	31	5	
Trafton, Frederick	1Lt	31	5	

Capt. John Varnell: second ranking P-51 ace in the MTO. (Author)

Flying the P-51 Mustang (MTO)
By
Robert Curtis: 13 P-51 victories 52FG

In April 1943 I was sent to North Africa to join the 52FG. There I took transitional training in the Spitfire and flew combat missions in them with the 2nd Fighter Squadron. I got a victory over a Me-109 in the Spitfire in February 1944, and then converted to the North American P-51 Mustang two months later. We Second Squadron pilots got to compare the Mustang D to the Mark 9 Spitfire. It had the maneuverability of the Spitfire, but had much greater range and diving speed. It could turn with the Spitfire except while climbing, and only then could the much lighter Spitfire out turn the P-51.

I flew the B-model at first, but only for a few missions before getting a D-model in June 1944. In the B-model I had two encounters with German fighters which involved high-speed dives from high altitude, one chasing a FW-190 and the other chasing a Me-109. In both cases I was able to stay with these fighters even though speeds of 550 mph were reached, greatly exceeding the 505 mph red line speed of the P-51.

Once I received my D-model, however, I was never able to stay with these fighters in such high-speed dives. At speeds over 505 mph the aircraft would start to "porpoise" uncontrollably, so I had to slow down to stop this behavior, allowing the enemy aircraft to escape. A North American Tech. Rep. visited our squadron, but was unable to suggest the reason for this behavior, or any way, other than not to dive at such high speeds, to overcome this apparent defect. I test flew a D-model over Madna Airstrip, Italy, in July 1944, and found that the porpoising again started at speeds over 550 mph. I feel that it was somehow caused by the characteristics of the airflow over the new bubble canopy, and then over the horizontal stabilizer and then the elevator. But whatever the reason for this behavior, it made the D-model a less capable fighter plane, because most experienced German pilots would Split-S into a high-speed dive to escape a dangerous situation at high altitude.

Most of our pilots preferred the D-model over the B- and C-models because of the superb visibility afforded the pilot, and because of its six (instead of four) machine guns. However, I felt that four guns seemed entirely adequate for the job. Again, I feel the D-

was not as good because of the porpoising limitation. I am sure that most pilots, because they were reluctant to greatly exceed the red line speed, never experienced porpoising. Although I, like most aces, was reckless, I also had a good "feel" for the behavior of the plane, because I was an instructor for a year and a half before going overseas, and consequently was completely at home in a single-engine aircraft in an ultra high speed dive. When my D-model was retired from combat after I left the squadron, an inspection showed that its wings were slightly sprung. I presume that this condition was caused by my high-speed dives, on one of which I hit compressibility during a dive after a 109 from 38,000 feet. I think in this dive I went through the porpoising phase so rapidly that I did not notice it. I was able to score 12 victories, one probable, and five damaged from the end of May to the end of July 1944, often exceeding the red line while chasing Luftwaffe fighters. Only once did I dive to elude enemy fighters, and then I combined it with rolling, so it was not truly a high-speed dive.

I previously had loved flying the smaller, lighter Spitfire, but once I flew the Mustang I never had the same attitude about it. What did I like best about the Mustang? I have to say it was the great feeling that I was flying a plane fully the equal of the 109 or 190, at least until I encountered the D-model. But the D- damped my Mustang enthusiasm only slightly.

P-51 PTO First Victory in Type
Pilot: Capt. Charles Adams
Time: 14 January 1945/1110-1120
Place: Philippines
Unit: 3FS/3ACG/5AF
A/C: P-51D/Sally

Action: The 3ACG was assigned to the 5AF, and initially saw action over the Philippines in late 1944 flying P-51Ds. Led by ex-Flying Tiger Col. Arvid Olson, its primary function was ground support on Luzon, escort duty to Formosa and the Chinese coast, and sweeps on Formosa's airfields and rail system. After the Japanese abandoned their defense of Luzon the group had little opportunity for air-to-air combat. On 14 January 1945, Maj. Walker Mahurin, of 19 3/4 victory 56FG fame in the ETO, led the 3FS' 10

Maj. Robert Curtis (Author/Curtis)

Capt. Charles Adams (USAF)

Mustangs on a top cover mission to protect a B-25 attack on Aparri, on the north coast of Luzon. After the bombing run the P-51s strafed a local airfield and destroyed four parked aircraft. Before noon, two flights of four returned south down the Cagayan Valley at 10,000 feet when a Sally and Dinah were seen flying north at 5,000 feet at 3 o'clock. Captain Charles Adams, 3FS Operations Officer, and his wingman peeled off and closed directly behind the Jap, and Adams opened fire at point blank range, sending the Sally crashing into a mountain. The Dinah took off in the opposite direction, and Maj. Mahurin jettisoned his drop tanks and took off after the fast twin engine recon aircraft, and after ten minutes caught it. He fired several short bursts, and the enemy rolled over and crashed. Two days later Adams was hit by AA fire while strafing targets on the Negros Islands. He turned his stricken aircraft back out over the sea and bailed out. He was picked up by friendly Filipinos and returned to base the next day by a PBY. Adams was a six-victory ace in the MTO flying P-38s for the 82FG.

P-51 PTO First Ace in Type

Pilot: Maj. James B. Tapp
Time: 12 April 1945/1130-1315
Place: Tokyo area
Unit: 78FS/15FG/7AF
A/C: P-51D *"Margaret"*/Tony
Action: In November 1944, the Marine's conquest of the Mariana's islands of Saipan and Tinian put the Air Force's huge, four-engine B-29 bombers within bombing range of Tokyo. At the time the 3,000 mile round trip to the Japanese capital was out of the range of any American escort fighter. The need for escorted missions became more urgent, as it became apparent that more Kamikazes were tormenting the B-29s. In February 1945, the Marines landed on Iwo Jima, which was 850 miles closer to Tokyo and in range of the P-51. By March the island was nearly secured, and the Japanese airstrip was repaired and the main runway lengthened. The 15FG,

Maj. James Tapp
(Author/Tapp)

consisting of the 45th, 47th, and 78th Fighter Squadrons, arrived and was joined by the 21FG. Their first missions were air defense and local ground support to mop up the stubborn Japanese holdouts on the island. On 27 March the remaining fanatical Japanese staged a desperate Banzai attack, killing 44 7AF personnel and wounding 88 others for a loss of 333 to themselves. On 30 March, both fighter groups flew a non-stop round trip to Saipan to practice for their upcoming Very Long Range (VLR) Empire escort missions.

On 7 April, 108 P-51s took off from Iwo's South Field on their first VLR mission to rendezvous with two formations of XXI BC B-29s. The Superfortresses had been flying for hours from their Mariana's bases towards Tokyo's Nakajima aircraft engine plant before the P-51s even took off. Maj. James Tapp, 78FS operations officer, was leading a flight of P-51Ds that were distinguished by their yellow-tipped wings and tails, which were broken by a black stripe. The Minnesotan was finally flying combat after being based in Hawaii for three long, uneventful years, only interrupted by a few months on Midway. The Mustangs, minus a few aborts and spares, managed to rendezvous with the bombers over Kozu, despite an overcast. The fighters positioned themselves ahead of both bomber formation flanks, staged from 18,000 to 20,000 feet above the B-29s, which were flying at 15,000 feet. The Japanese mainland was crossed ten minutes after rendezvous, and the first of numerous Japanese fighters of all types were encountered at 1045 over Sagami Bay, which was 30-50 miles from the target. The Japanese tried to avoid the Mustangs and concentrate on the bombers with individual uncoordinated head-on and high-side attacks. The P-51s flew in weaving four plane flights, protecting each other and their assigned B-29s, which were ID'd by large black tail markings. A Nick dove on the formation, and Tapp fired a long burst into both engines, flaming one. Then Tapp quickly closed on a rapidly climbing Tony, setting it on fire. As soon as he got back to his escort station, a Dinah began a frontal pass and was confronted by Tapp, who fired a 90 degree shot, damaging it. Escort duty finished, Tapp dropped down to protect a crippled B-29 flying at 14,000 feet attempting to reach the Japanese coast. An Oscar was positioning itself to attack the straggler, but Tapp cut it off and got a long burst into its fuselage, knocking off its canopy and exploding it. Returning to the damaged B-29, Tapp found it being harassed by four Zeros and two Tojos. The American and his wingman broke up the attack, with Tapp blowing off part of the wing of a Tojo for his fourth victory of the day. Running low on fuel, the Mustangs had to break off combat and sweat out this common problem until they reached Iwo safely. This inaugural VLR escort was a great success, with the Mustangs claiming 21 victories for only two losses (one pilot saved).

The next VLR mission was flown on 12 April to Tokyo. Tapp flamed a Tony over Tokyo around noon to become the first Pacific theater Mustang ace. Tapp went on to score three more victories in May to give him eight for the war and place him third in the 7AF. After the war Tapp spent 30 years in the Air Force doing R&D.

P-51 PTO Top Scorer in Type

Pilot: Maj. Robert W. Moore
Unit: 45FS & 78FS/15FG/7AF
Victories: 11 (+1 in P-40)
Record:

V#	Date	E/A/C
1 (P-40)	01-26-44	Zeke
2-3	04-07-45	2 Hamps
4	04-22-45	Oscar
5-6	05-25-45	2 Zekes
7-9	05-29-45	2 Jacks, George
10	06-07-45	Nick
11	06-10-45	Frank
12	08-10-45	Tojo

Action: The P-51 made its debut in the Pacific with the 7AF as a VLR B-29 escort over Japan. During the fighter's first VLR mission on 7 April 1945, Capt. Robert Moore of the 78FS/15FG shot down two Hamps in less than a minute over the Choshi area, near Tokyo. While watching a Superfortress explode, he spotted a line of four Hamps and joined their formation as the fifth man. Moore closed on #4 and exploded it with a short burst aft of the cockpit. Accelerating, he then closed on #3, which was diving on the American bombers. He got hits on the Nakajima's engine, setting it on fire. While Moore was occupied searching for #2, the Japanese leader had turned into him. Moore managed to evade just in time with a full throttle dive to safety.

The P-51's intended VLR escort duties changed as the B-29's strategic bombing role changed. In early March, Gen. Curtis LeMay flew his B-29s on their first night incendiary fire bombing raids. The success of these nightly raids and the lack of effective Japanese night interception diminished the need for the P-51 as an escort. Thus, from mid-April the VII FC Mustangs were allowed to carry out fighter sweeps against Japanese airfields in the Tokyo-Osaka-Nogoya area. Moore got an Oscar over Akenogahara A/F on 22 April, and two Zekes over Kashiwa A/F on 25 May. Soon Moore was transferred to the 45FS of the 15FG, with whom he claimed

Capt. Judge Wolfe: 2nd P-51 ace PTO (USAF)

two Jacks and a George over Atsugi A/F on 29 May, a Nick and Frank in June, and on the 7AF's next to last mission of the war, a Tojo on 10 August. An unusual aspect of his tops in the Pacific Theater (11 Mustang victories) was that eight were against different Japanese fighter types.

The VII FC flew 51 VLR escort and sweep missions in the last 4 1/2 months of the war, boasting nine aces in its ranks with Moore leading with 12 (11 in the P-51, as he scored a P-40 victory in late January 1944). Moore was followed by Capt. Judge Wolfe with nine victories. Three of the Seventh's nine aces scored all their victories in one day: Lt. Richard Anderson (318FG on 25 May 45); Capt. John Vogt (318FG on 28 May 45); and 1Lt. Oscar Perdomo (507FG on 13 August 45).

PTO P-51 ACES 5-7AF

Ace Name	Rank	UNIT FG	P-51 V	Other V
Moore, Robert	Maj	15/7	11	+1v P-40
Shomo, William	Capt	82TRS/5	8	(in F-6)
Tapp, James	Maj	15/7	8	
Crim, Harry	Maj	21/7	6	
Aust, Abner	Capt	506/7	5	

P-51 CBI First Victory in Type

Pilot: 2Lt. Clifton L. Bray
Time: 25 November 1943/1330
Unit: 530FS/311FG/10-14AF
A/C: P-51A "Lil Sophie"/Nick
Action: The Allison-powered P-51A followed the A-36 dive bomber version of the Mustang off the production line. The 311FBG equipped its 528th and 529th squadrons with the A-36A, and its 530FS with the P-51A. The 530th operated as a separate fighter unit from Mohanberi on 17 October, but was transferred to Kurmitola in Bengal on detached duty to the 459FS four days later.

Maj. Robert Moore
(Author/Moore)

2Lt. Clifton Bray (USAF)

In the late fall of 1943, the 10AF detached several bomb groups to cooperate with RAF bombers in attacking Rangoon. These missions were to be the first long range escort missions embarked upon by the PTO Mustangs. To provide for sufficient range for the 830 mile round trip, two 75 gallon drop tanks were carried.

On 25 November 12 P-51s of the 530th, under Col. Harry R. Melton, provided escort for a dozen B-25 Mitchells of the 490BS of the 341BG. Melton, 311FBG CO, led the Mustangs from Kurmitola to refuel at Ramu, leaving at 1040. Malfunctions with the new wing tanks caused three fighters to abort. The Mitchells arrived at the Japanese airdrome at Mingaladon at 1300 and bombed under a 7,000 foot undercast, hitting airfield installations and destroying two aircraft. The Americans were intercepted by 12 Oscars and five Nicks of elite JAAF Sentai groups. 2Lt. Clifton Bray attacked a twin-engine Nick at 8,000 feet at point blank range, exploding its left engine and causing the enemy to spiral into the ground. The P-51 had scored its first Pacific victory. Another Nick and an Oscar were probables, and none of the B-25s were lost. No

P-51s were lost, but Col. Melton was forced to bail out of his flaming aircraft to be taken a POW. The Japanese transport Melton and other POWs were being shipped to Japan in was torpedoed and, in vengeance, the Japanese sank the prisoner's lifeboats, and only one survived to report the incident after the war.

After four escort missions the 530th had lost half its strength to the talented veteran Japanese pilots, and further missions were discontinued. Bray scored two more confirmed victories over Burma on 12 and 14 May 1944, but was shot down by AA on 23 May and was taken prisoner, not being released until May 1945.

P-51 CBI First Ace in Type

Pilot: Capt. James J. England
Time: 27 March 1944/ 1110-1135
Place: East of North Pass, Burma
Unit: 530FS/311FG/10AF
A/C: P-51A "*Jackie*"/2 Oscars, 1 Helen
Action: The 530FS scored 13 victories during bomber escort missions to Rangoon flying their new P-51As in late November 1943 while detached to the RAF. After four strength-deleting missions against a superior enemy the squadron was withdrawn, and scored only three victories over the next four months.

Of the first 13 victories, 1Lt. James England claimed a Nick on 25 November and a Zeke (plus a damaged Zeke) on 27 November. On 27 March 1944 the JAAF concentrated its attacks on airfields in the Ledo area, sending 18 Helens and 20 mixed fighters at an altitude of 19 to 20,000 feet. The Americans countered by sending up 85 fighters, but a 12,000 foot overcast prevented 60 fighters from interception. The remaining American fighters gave good account of themselves, shooting down 11 Helens and getting three probables and two damaged, along with 13 fighters downed, three probables, and two damaged for a loss of three aircraft and two pilots. In 25 minutes of combat Capt. England shot down two Oscars and a Helen and damaged one of each. These victories made England the first P-51 ace in both the CBI and Pacific. He went on to become a double ace with 10 victories in the war.

P-51 CBI Top Scorer in Type

Pilot: Maj. John C. Herbst
Unit: 76FS & 74FS/ 23FG/14AF
Victories: 14 (+4 P-40 +1 RAF)
Record:

V#	Date	E/A/C
1 P-51	06-17-44	Oscar
2-3 P-40	07-15-44	Oscar, Tojo
4-5 P-40	08-06-44	2 Oscars
6-7 P-51	09-08-44	2 Vals
8 P-51	09-05-44	Oscar
9 P-51	09-16-44	Hamp
10 P-51	10-09-44	Tojo
11 P-51	12-18-44	Oscar
12-13 P-51	12-23-44	Oscar, Jake
14-15 P-51	12-27-44	2 Oscars
16-17 P-51	01-16-45	Nell, Tess
18 P-51	01-17-45	Tojo

Capt. James England (USAF)

Maj. John Herbst (USAF)

Action: During 1943 and early 1944, the Japanese Army Air Force was virtually non-existent in China. Thus, the USAAF's 23FG, flying mostly war-weary P-40 Warhawks, found itself in a ground support role for Chinese Nationalist troops. The Allison-powered P-51 Mustang began to replace the P-40s in late 1943. Its longer range, higher speed, maneuverability, and ability to carry two 500 lb. bombs, as well as the newly introduced rockets made the aircraft an ideal ground support weapon. However, it lacked high altitude performance, which put it at a disadvantage in aerial combat.

In mid-1942 John Herbst, although a qualified, licensed pilot, was found to be too old at 32 to join the Air Corp's Cadet Training Program. Herbst went to Canada to enlist in the RCAF, becoming a commissioned Pilot Officer and flying in England as a test and ferry pilot. Finally, he was assigned to the Desert Air Force, flying long-awaited combat in the late stages of the North African Campaign and downing a Me-109.

When America entered the war Herbst transferred, expecting to be assigned to lead a combat squadron, but due to his age he reluctantly flew desks. Perseverance paid off, as Herbst was assigned to the 14AF as a replacement pilot to the 23FG at Kweilin, China, under Col. David "Tex" Hill. Herbst was assigned to the 76FS and was quickly promoted to Major and made CO of the 74FS at Kanchow. The 74th initially flew P-40s and later P-51s.

In the summer of 1944, the Japanese Army began a large-scale offensive to capture American airbases in eastern China. These bases were home for the long-range B-29 bombers that threatened the Japanese homeland. By early August Herbst had become an ace, scoring four P-40 (three Oscars and a Tojo) and a P-51 (Oscar) victory. Herbst's outstanding leadership abilities caused Chennault to utilize him more and more in operational planning (e.g. non-combat). But as the Japanese Army advanced against the exhausted Chinese, every available pilot was needed to blunt their attack, and Herbst was put back into combat.

On 3 September, Herbst led the 74th on a skip-bombing, bridge-busting mission near Poyang Lake. After bombing the railway bridges, two Val dive bombers, attracted by the rising smoke, came out of a 2,000 foot cloud base to investigate. Unseen, the climbing Herbst was able to maneuver astern to the Vals, shooting down one immediately. He had to chase the second nimble bomber, evading the bullets of its rear gunner, before hitting its tail and fuselage. The stricken Val tried to crash-land in a rice paddy, but flipped over on its back.

On 5 September, Herbst was flying a new C-model P-51 named "*Tommy's Dad*," after his son back in southern California. On a flight back to Kweilin for a field modification on his aircraft he spotted two, eight plane flights of Oscars above him at 10,000 feet. He climbed towards the Oscars, who spotted the shining aluminum P-51. The adversaries closed on each other level and head-on. The lead Oscar took hits and began to smoke, while Herbst's Mustang was hit in the windshield. Wounded in the face, the outnumbered American continued his attack on the lead Oscar. Almost blinded and with only one gun functioning, Herbst broke away with a victory, only to find himself under the concerted attack of the other Oscars. When his remaining gun jammed, he desperately dove away to safety.

In early December, the Japanese Army divided China by joining with its forces from Indo China. On 23 December Herbst had two victory claims, and on the 27th he got two more to give him 15 total victories. In the latter combat, he was leading the first U.S. fighter sweep over Canton when he came upon three Oscars that were diving on strafing American fighters. He fired point blank on one Oscar, causing it to crash, while the other two evaded in different directions. Herbst followed one, flaming it with hits on the wings and fuselage. Meanwhile, the surviving Oscar got on "*Tommy's Dad*" tail, but the P-51, with its superior speed, was able to come around and meet the Jap head-on. The Oscar broke, and Herbst swung the Mustang around to get on its tail to score hits for a probable.

In mid-January 1945 Herbst got his last three victories (a double on the 16th) to give him 18 (14 P-51). In February, he was promoted to Lt. Colonel and sent home, the top-scoring ace in the 14AF and in the P-51 for all the Pacific. During an air show in San Diego on Independence Day, 1947, his P-80 Shooting Star jet crashed when its engine malfunctioned at low altitude, killing him.

CBI P-51 ACES 10-14AF

Ace Name	Rank	Unit FG	P-51 V	Other V
Herbst, John	Maj	23	14	+4v P-40
McComas, Edward	LCol	23	14	
England, James	Maj	311	10	
Older, Charles	LCol	23	8	+10v P-40
Arasmith, Lester	1Lt	311	6	
Reeves, Leonard	1Lt	311	6	
Bolyard, John	1Lt	23	5	
Chapman, Philip	Maj	23	5	
Mulhollen, Robert	1Lt	311	5	
Williams, Russell	1Lt	23	5	

LtCol. Edward McComas: second ranking P-51 ace in the CBI with 14 victories. (USAF)

Flying the P-51 Mustang (CBI)
By
Randy Reeves: 6 victories 311FG

I was fortunate to have flown four models of the P-51 (A, B, C, and D models) during my tour with the 530th Fighter Group of the 14th Air Force in the CBI.

The cockpits of all four models were very similar, with changes in successive models generally enhancing pilot safety and comfort. The "A" was smaller, and its heater was a vent into the cockpit from the engine. Since we could only fly at 25,000 feet maximum, the heat output was usually adequate to keep the pilot warm. I wore normal G.I. shoes, and my feet stayed comfortable. Sometimes I wore a flight suit over my Sun-tans in Burma. We would wear a winter uniform under our A-2 (later A-15) jackets in China if the temperature was forecast to be low at our assigned flying altitude. After the late model-D came out with pressurization units we wore anti-G suits over our uniforms and flight suits. I always felt that the instrument locations were great. When we transitioned to the Mustang from the P-40 we took blindfolded tests to check our familiarity with the various instrument positions. Controls were easy to use, and in good position for pilot use. I once broke off a landing gear handle in a "D" model when retracting the gear and had to use my foot to force the handle down to lower the gear. A scary way to end a mission! I don't think I could have flown the F-16 with the control stick on the right side of the cockpit, instead of between my legs. The seats were adjustable, and were as comfortable as a seat could be.

Taxiing was a little hazardous, as the long nose of the P-51 blocked out a frontal view in a three-point position. We had to S-taxi to get a clear frontal view out the side window. Similarly, when landing in a three-point tail low/nose high position, I always made sure the runway was clear with a slight S-turn after touching down. Also, on take off the torque from the prop tended to pull the nose off center before the fighter had picked up enough speed to get its tail up to be rolling on the two main wheels. I always double and triple checked the trim setting on the rudder to counteract the pull of the prop torque. Rearward visibility in combat in the P-51 "A,"

"B," and "C" was very poor, because the fuselage was faired into the canopy. This created a blind spot in the six o'clock position. Wise combat pilots in these models kept their necks on swivel to be sure that their tails were clear. The "D" was equipped with the bubble canopy that eliminated most of the blind spot, but a good pilot always needed a swivel neck to watch his tail.

Communication equipment was not very good, but we didn't know anything different, so we felt comfortable with what we had. We did lose a flight of four 51s coming in from a mission to Peking. Our base was covered by a sand storm, and visibility was next to zero way up to 10,000 feet. We could hear the pilots calling in, but they could not hear us because our transmitter was good only out to 10 to 15 miles. The Mustangs flew until they ran out of fuel, and one-by-one the pilots bailed out. All were saved.

The engines were very reliable, and I never lost an engine in any model. The P-51A engine was not supercharged, giving us a maximum ceiling of 25,000 feet. When we escorted B-24s to Rangoon they wanted to fly at 25,000 feet. We said ok, but told them we could not give them any top cover. The bomber command insisted on this altitude, so we flew along side of the bombers. It was a great relief to us when we saw Jap flak coming up and concentrating on the bombers!

The "B" models were equipped with the outstanding Rolls Royce Merlin engine. I took this model up to 42,000 feet. The "C" was practically the same aircraft as the "B," except it was equipped with the licensed Packard-built Rolls Royce engine. It was also a great engine, but the highest I ever got it was 38,000 feet. Our "D" models had the supercharged Allison engine.

Fuel consumption was very good, and with two 75-gallon wing tanks we could cover a good part of Burma. China was a whole different ball game. The "B" and "C" models had a 65-gallon internal tank located just behind the cockpit. This threw the aircraft out of balance, so the pilot could not make tight turns with his fuel tank full. However, you could make one hell of a snap in the opposite direction! We emptied this fuselage tank for the climb out down to 35 gallons. At this point the fighter would become balanced, and we switched to the wing tanks. We cruised on the wing tanks until we encountered the Japs, and then went back to the internals, dropping the wing tanks. In China we were equipped with two 150-gallon wing tanks, which allowed us to escort B-29s to Manchuria on 7 1/2 hour missions. Some of our fighter sweeps to Tientsen, Peking, and Chinese coastal cities were of the same duration. These were referred to as "Dead End Missions," describing the condition of our butts when we landed. Time to reach altitude was dictated by our external load, which usually was two 500 lb. Bombs or two 500 lb. Depth charges, or external wing tanks. The "A" would cruise at 265 mph clean, which was quite a bit faster than the "B," "C," or "D" models. My crew chief kept my plane (which I named *Dallas Darling*) simonized, which made it slicker and faster than the other "Bs" in the squadron.

The "A," "B," and "C" had two guns in each wing. The armorer could synchronize the guns for 250 (my preference) or 300 yards convergence of fire. This got to be a problem when flying an airplane other than your own. The gunsight on the "A" was fairly primitive, but other models had the ring projected onto the windscreen, which made it easier to get your lead when flying a pursuit curve on the enemy. For every deflection shot you had to calculate the speed of the enemy plane and pull your one, two, or three ring lead on what you guessed the enemy speed to be. That's why we fighter pilots shot so much skeet in training.

When you had to you could safely pull a few more Gs in combat than your body could stand. I had a few black outs and quite a few gray outs when I pulled tight turns to evade a Jap on my tail. We could out dive, out run, and most of the time out climb them. The Jap Zeros had such large ailerons for turning and maneuverability that in a dive, after 300 mph or so, they could only turn with torque. We could dog fight with a Zero until they started to try to turn inside us, then we would Split-S and climb back up to engage them again from altitude.

The Mustangs had self-sealing fuel tanks and armor plating behind the pilot's seat. This armor plating is the reason I got my Purple Heart. The plating stopped a Zero's 20mm cannon shell. Since these shells were not armor piercing they would explode when they hit the plate, spraying shrapnel all over the place, and the concussion would knock you out momentarily. My shoulders and the back of my head were full of shrapnel, and when I came to, I had to pull out of a 500 mph dive!

The in-line engine of the Mustang was extremely vulnerable, and a hit in the wrong place, even by a small caliber slug, could cause you a great deal of trouble. I had a .25 caliber hit in the cooling line, but luckily the increasing heat of the engine congealed the bullet to the hole and stopped too much coolant from leaking. Usually any hit in the radiator, which was located in the air scoop beneath the belly of the P-51, meant that you had two or three minutes before the engine froze. Otherwise the Mustang could sustain a great deal of battle damage and get you back home safely. Once on a long-range mission to Nanking three Tojo fighters got on my tail and shot away three feet of my right horizontal stabilizer. I dove 17,000 feet, first to evade them and then to gain control. By rolling back the horizontal trim she flew pretty good, and I was able to climb back up to 12,000 feet to get over the mountains between

F-6D

home and me. That was a better choice than bailing out, and a heck of a lot better than ditching or a crash landing. Bailing out was no big deal in a Mustang, except that the walk home was usually long and could be hazardous. Crash landing or ditching a P-51 was not recommended, since the large belly radiator scoop would dig in upon touching down, doing great damage.

The good old Mustang had a few shortcomings, but its numerous assets made it the nicest flying fighter of the war.

F-6 ETO First Victory in Type
Pilot: 1Lt. Joseph E. Conklin
Time: 6 June 1944/1225
Place: Dreux A/F, France
Unit: 10PRS
A/C: F-6/FW-190
Action: The "F" prefix designated the photo recon version of a particular aircraft (e.g. F-3 = A-20, F-4/5 = P-38, F-6 = P-51, F-7 = B-24, F-8 = Mosquito, F-9 = B-17, F-10 = B-25, and F-15 = B-29). The primary difference between the fighter and recon version of the Mustang was the installation of cameras. Unlike the unarmed F-5 (P-38), whose camera replaced its nose armament, the F-6 retained its full complement of wingborne armament and carried its cameras in underwing pods, or in the rear fuselage in an area located just under the national insignia. Though fully armed, the TAC

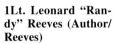

1Lt. Leonard "Randy" Reeves (Author/Reeves)

1Lt. Joseph Conklin (USAF)

R pilot was ordered to avoid combat, but was allowed to "defend" himself against attack.

The visual TAC R sortie was flown in a two aircraft section, with the senior or most experienced pilot designated as the leader. This number one pilot was responsible for navigation and photographing and/or observing the target. The number two man was liable for protecting his leader and to warn him of AA or ground fire. This wingman usually flew 200 yards abreast and down sun so his leader's tail was covered towards the sun, from which most enemy attacks occurred. Visual recce missions flew at 3,500 to 6,000 feet (the visual limit), while TAC R missions operated at somewhat higher altitudes. For more information on TAC R and Photo Recon see chapter 15.

On D-Day, the 15PRS flew 63 visual recce sorties in support of the D-Day landings. Their task was to observe Wehrmacht dispositions on roads and bridges which might be used to reinforce the defense of the beachhead. The 15th, commanded by Lt. Col. George Walker, had been flying since 26 March without any enemy contact. Shortly after noon, 1Lt. Joseph Conklin claimed the first aerial victory on D-Day, and the first for a F-6, when he shot down a FW-190 near Dreux airdrome, west of Paris. This was to be Conklin's only victory of the war.

F-6 ETO First Ace in Type

Pilot: Capt. John Hoefker
Time: 17 December 1944/1510-1545
Place: Griesen-Kirch-Weisbaden
Unit: 15TRS/10TRG/8AF
A/C: F-6D/2 Me-109, 1 FW-190, 1/2 Ju-188
Action: The Germans began their last large-scale offensive in the West on 17 December 1944, under the cover of bad winter weather. The Wehrmacht breakthrough was given the name Battle of the Bulge by the Allies. The confusion of the situation to the surprised Allies gave the Tactical Reconnaissance groups the assignment to locate the disposition of the combatants. The TAC R groups encountered increased Luftwaffe activity in support of the offensive.

During the mid-afternoon of the 17th, Kentuckian Capt. John Hoefker and his wingman, 1Lt. Charles White, were on a routine recce over the highways and railways in the Frankfurt-Griesen-Hanau area. Near Griesen, two Me-109s passed below the pair of F-6s. Hoefker swung around to get on the tail of one Messerschmitt and fired from 150 yards until he reached point blank range, getting numerous hits. The German pilot tried to bail out at 100 feet, but his stricken fighter winged over into the ground before he got clear. The other Me 109 had gotten on Hoefker's tail, but the American turned into the attack and got a short burst from 100 yards at deck level, getting hits on the wing roots and fuselage. The German climbed to 1,500 feet and winged-over to the deck, only to find that this maneuver did not shake the pursuing Mustang, which had closed to 100 feet. Hoefker put a two second burst into his victim, and soon was able to photograph its wreckage. Hoefker and White flew along the autobahn toward Kirch/Gono Airfield and spotted a FW-190 flying below and in the opposite direction. A diving turn closed Hoefker to 50 yards behind the Focke Wulf, whose wings and fuselage took hits. The 190 broke right, and Hoefker broke left in a circling turn, which put him on its tail again. More .50 cal. hits persuaded the German pilot to bail out. Hoefker was then rejoined by wingman White to continue the recon. On their way back to base, a Ju-188 flew into their path northeast of Weisbaden. Hoefker closed on the evading bomber, whose gunners were returning inaccurate fire. He got hits on the bomber's right wing and fuselage with two short bursts, and then set fire to the right engine and wing root with two more short bursts. White followed in with more hits, exploding the right engine. The Ju-188 rolled over in a dive trying to escape, leveling off at 4,000 feet. Hoefker followed, getting additional hits and causing the bomber's four man crew to bail out. The two F-6 pilots shared this victory.

Hoefker had previously scored three victories in June over Me-109s and a fourth in November over a Fw-190. The 3 1/2 victories on 17 December made him the first F-6 ace of the war and won him the Silver Star. Hoefker went on to total 10 1/2 victories to become the second leading F-6 ace behind squadronmate Clyde East, who had 13 victories.

Capt. John Hoefker (USAF)

Capt. Clyde East (Author/East)

F-6 ETO Top Scorer in Type

Pilot: Capt. Clyde B. East
Unit: 15TRS/10PRG/8AF
A/C: F-6C *"Lil Margaret"*
Victories: 13
Record:

V#	Date	E/A/C
1	06-06-44	FW-190
2	12-17-44	Me-109
3	03-15-45	Me-109
4-5	03-24-45	2 Me-109s
6-7	03-27-45	2 Ju-87s
7 1/2-8 1/2	04-04-45	1/2 Ju-188, FW-190
9 1/2-12	04-08-45	2 Ju-87s, 1/2 He-111, Si-204
13	04-13-45	Me-109

Action: In the early Spring of 1945 Patton's Third Army was racing into Germany, and to aid them the 15TAC R Group flew recon missions looking for targets for marauding fighter bombers. It was during this time that a former Virginian, who had joined the RCAF in June 1941, made his mark as the foremost F-6 ace in the war. Capt. Clyde East, after flying a tour with the 414TAC R group of the RCAF flying Mustang Is for five months, transferred to the 15TRS of the 67TRG of the 8AF in January 1944.

East would claim his first victory on D-Day when he and Ernest Schonard were working a late afternoon visual and photo recce of the Laval area, when they came upon a flight of four FW-190s in a landing pattern. East shot down the last German in the pattern, while Schonard got the number three man and added another Focke Wulf as a probable when the two remaining Germans pulled up to attack East.

It would be over six months later when East would score his next victory, as he returned to the U.S. on leave at the end of June and did not return until October. Except for a Me-109 shot down over Gleissen on 12 December during the opening phases of the Battle of the Bulge, East did not score any aerial victories, but ha-rassed German troops and transport in January and February. In less than a month in the Spring of 1945, he would score 11 more victories. On 24 March, after a Me-109 victory nine days earlier, East was flying a mission near Eisnach with wingman 1Lt. Leland Larson when six Me-109s attacked the pair out of the early morning sun. The Americans turned into the attack and put themselves on the German's tails. East's fighter was slightly damaged when his quarry exploded in front of him. Larson's target also exploded as it hit the ground. East then shot a Me-109 off Larson's tail for his fifth victory to make him the 10PRS' second ace after John Hoefker.

In the next three weeks, East would score eight more victories while searching for Wehrmacht Panzers and German rail and road transport. On 4 April, he was credited with 1 1/2 victories. On this mission East and Leland Larson shared a Ju-188, and an hour later East shot down a FW-190 to tie him with John Hoefker, as both had 8 1/2 victories to lead 10TAC R. At 0800, Hoefker shot down a He-111 east of Wettenberg. At the same time, East and Larson encountered three Ju-87 Stukas. East made a firing run on the left dive bomber at 200 yards, crashing it into the ground. Larson destroyed a second with hits in the fuselage and engine. East went after the third German, which had been circling the wreckage of East's victim. A three second burst ended this Stuka's mission. Immediately, East and Larson spotted a circling He-111, and both shared this victory. About an hour later, East got a twin-engine Siebel 204 near Riesa, which gave him 3 1/2 victories for the day and 12 total.

In 13 April, East and wingman 1Lt. William Miekle were bounced out of the sun by two Me-109s near Hof. East's Mustang *"Lil Margaret"* was hit four times, once in the right drop tank. East coolly jettisoned his tanks and turned into his attacker, climbing to get onto its tail to get his 13th and last victory, tops for a F-6 pilot in the war.

East remained in the post-war Air Force, specializing in reconnaissance. He flew RF-51 Mustangs and the RF-80 in Korea, flying 100 missions, and received a DFC for his recce flights during the Cuban Missile Crisis. He retired as a Lt. Colonel in January 1965.

2Lt. Clyde Burrud (USAF)

2Lt. Robert Fenske (2nd Left) (USAF)

F-6 PTO First Victory in Type

Pilot: 2Lt. Robert Fenske
Time: 2 January 1945/AM?
Place: West of Tagudin, Philippines
Unit: 82TRS/71TRG/5AF
A/C: F-6D/Tojo
and
Pilot: 2Lt. John "Pappy" Burrud
Time: 2 January 1945/PM?
Place: West of Viagan, Philippines
Unit: 82TRS/71TRG/5AF
A/C: F-6D/Dinah

In late November 1943, the 71TRG arrived in New Guinea and began operations: armed reconnaissance and strafing missions along the coasts of New Guinea and New Britain. The group had only scored two aerial victories before it received new P-51s and F-6s in November 1944. Moving up to Mindoro in the Philippines, the first Pacific F-6 victories were scored on a recon mission on 2 January 1945. Second lieutenants Robert Fenske and John Burrud claimed a Tojo and Dinah, respectively, on missions that day. Burud was KIA on 5 August 1945 strafing over Kyushu.

F-6 PTO Top Scorer in Type

Pilot: Capt. William A. Shomo
Unit: 82TRS/71TRG/5AF
A/C: F-6K *Flying Undertaker*
Victories: 7 (+1 in P-51)
Record:

V#	Date	E/A/C
1 (P-51)	01-10-45	Val
2-8	01-11-45	1 Betty, 6 Tonys

Action: The 26 year old Shomo was born in Jeanette, PA, and studied Mortuary Science in Cincinnati. He was licensed and served as a funeral director for five years before joining the Air Force and receiving his wings in March 1942. He flew coastal patrol observation before being assigned to the 82nd Tactical Recon Squadron of the 71st TAC RECON Group. He flew P-39 Airacobras ("*Snooks 2nd*") in New Guinea. He transferred to P-40s in November 1943, and to P-51s a year later in the Philippines. The entire 82nd claimed only two Japanese planes during that time. Shomo was promoted to Captain and given command of the 82nd. In December 1944 the group moved to San Jose Airfield, Mindoro, in the Philippines, and was equipped with the F-6K, the camera-carrying version of the P-51D. Unlike other camera recon aircraft, the F-6 carried armament along with its cameras.

During the morning of 10 January, Shomo destroyed his first enemy when he shot down a Val dive-bomber that was preparing to land at Taguegaras Airfield, in Northern Luzon, PI. The next morning Shomo and his wingman, Texan 2Lt. Paul M. Lipscomb, were assigned a visual and photo recon mission over North Luzon, to be followed by a recon and strafing run over Aparri and Laoag Airdromes. Shomo's unpainted, raw metal F-6 had *Flying Undertaker* painted in yellow on the cowling, reflecting his past and present profession. The two pilots took off about 0800 from San Jose and headed north at 200 feet to a point just south of Cabagan Valley, where they were to prepare to a make photo run. In route, east of Clark Field, a strafing attack was made on a train, which was left on fire. At 1000 Shomo looked up to see a number of single engine fighters escorting a single bomber. The Japanese formation was 2,500 feet above and going from the opposite direction. A Betty bomber escorted by 11 Tony fighters and a single Tojo were ID'd. Shomo ignored the Jap's numerical and altitude advantage, feeling that such a large escort for a single bomber indicated the importance of the bomber's passenger. Shomo and Lipscomb climbed above and behind the enemy formation in an Immelmann maneuver that caused them no immediate concern. They maintained their flight integrity for the moment, a large stepped down V composed of three two-plane elements on each wing of the bomber.

Shomo and Lipscomb made a doglegged pass through the left side of the slowly reacting enemy. Shomo attacked the rear element leader and his wingman. He fired on the wingman and flamed him, then moved on the lead Tony, exploding it. He then set the second element's wingman on fire. The Japanese formation finally counterattacked. A Tony crossed in front of Shomo, who destroyed it with a short burst for his fourth victory of the day. Lipscomb, who had never fired a shot in combat and had just checked out in the Mustang, downed two Jap fighters as they crossed in front of the duo. Lipscomb missed the twin engine Betty bomber, which would eventually escape. Shomo dropped to a position below, firing up into the Mitsubishi's fuselage and wing tanks, starting a fire. The Jap pilot tried to make a belly landing but exploded. Lipscomb pulled up to find a Tony closing head on, but quick reflexes and a short burst from the "*Undertaker's*" machine guns exploded the attacker. Shomo climbed in a vertical spiral to clear his tail of a pursuing Tojo and turned toward two fighters that were on deck trying to escape. Shomo dove to pick off one and continued his pass after his seventh victim, which he destroyed with a short burst while he skimmed the deck.

Shomo rejoined Lipscomb, who had destroyed his third Tony. The two pilots photographed the ten burning wrecks and flew the two hours back to Mindoro. Shomo came in low over the field,

Capt. William Shomo (Author/ Shomo)

executing two victory rolls. He proceeded to make five more rolls, causing disbelief and irritation among the brass on the field. Lipscomb landed first and confirmed Shomo's victories, and added that he also had accounted for three more. When Lipscomb was asked why he had not done any victory rolls, he replied that he had just checked out in the P-51 and was not sure he knew how!

For this six minute, seven victory combat Shomo was promoted to Major and awarded the Medal of Honor. He was offered Stateside R&R selling bonds, and to be personally presented the Medal by the President at the White House, but refused, staying in combat. The award ceremony was held at Lingayen Gulf by Gen. Ennis Whitehead, Vice Commander of the FEAF, and was attended by Shomo's squadron. Later Intelligence confirmed that a high-ranking Japanese officer perished in the ill-fated Betty.

Shomo scored no further victories in the war, as he was grounded by the War Department's policy of removing Medal of Honor recipients from combat. He never returned to undertaking, spending 28 1/2 years in the Air Force flying SAC fighters and completing tours with the Air Defense Command NORAD in Labrador and Greenland. He retired in 1971 as a Lt. Colonel.

A-36 (USAF)

A-36 MTO First Victory in Type

Pilot: 1Lt. Tom A. Thomas
Time: 12 July 1943/0940
Place: East of Basacquino, Tunisia
Unit: 524FS/27FBG/12AF
A/C: A-36A/Mc-202

Action: The A-36 became available to the Air Force in October 1942 for training, where it gained the dubious distinction of having the highest accident rate per flying hour of any major aircraft type. The Air Force adopted an official aircraft nicknames policy, and the A-36 was christened the "Apache," but soon the RAF name "Mustang" was approved. The A-36 was unofficially called the "Invader" by the press after its participation in the invasions of Sicily and Italy. However, this name did not endure beyond the spring of 1944.

The 27 FG, equipped with the A-36A, arrived in North Africa in June 1943, joining the 12AF in Algeria. In combat the A-36 demonstrated itself to be an accurate and very capable dive bomber, as well as a very stable and efficient strafing gun platform. These features were complimented by its excellent maintenance record in a difficult theater. German AA defenses took a great toll of A-36s in their dive bombing mode. By the spring of 1944, nearly half of the original force had been lost. Since no replacement aircraft were being manufactured, the group's four squadrons were cut to three. Later, these squadrons became so depleted that the 27th was forced to convert to the inferior P-40.

A-36s did not see much air-to-air combat, as their pilots were advised to jettison their bombs when bounced at high altitudes and escape, because the A-36 was no match for the Luftwaffe fighters there. Combat was to be reluctantly engaged only below 8,000 feet.

The first of the A-36's 67 victories in the MTO (none was scored in the ETO) was achieved two days after the invasion of Sicily. The 524FS of the 27FBG sent 12 Invaders to Marsala at 0940. While patrolling along the Sicilian coast, flight leader 1Lt. Tom Thomas encountered a lone FW-190 at low altitude east of Biscaquino. Thomas followed the enemy down to 500 feet and hit him, causing him to bail out. Thomas' A-36 was hit by AA fire, which hit his cooler and immediately set his aircraft aflame. He managed to trim the aircraft at 250 feet, pop the canopy, pull back hard on the stick, and bail out. He landed behind German lines, badly burned and breaking both legs. He was treated in a German military hospital, and actually met the German pilot he shot down and the AA gunner who had shot him down. He was taken to Palermo airfield to be evacuated to Germany. At this time the Italians were about to surrender and the Germans were trying to evacuate Sicily ASAP, so Allied prisoners took a low priority. He lingered around the airfield for several days, and finally slipped away to join Italian partisans, who hid him until the U.S. 33rd Infantry captured Palermo. He was evacuated to a hospital in North Africa, where he spent three months. Even though at the time it was against the Geneva Convention for ex-POWs to re-enter combat he managed to return to the 27th and fly seven more missions before being relegated back to the U.S. to teach tactics. The victory was his fourth of the war (he scored three P-40 victories with the 58FS/33FG).

A-36 CBI First Victory in Type
Pilot: F/O Hoyt Hensley
Time: 10 December 1943/1135
Place: North of Laza, China
Unit: 529FS/311FG/10AF
A/C: A-36A/Oscar or Zeke
Action: The 311FS was the only A-36 trained group to see combat in the Pacific. Assigned to the 10AF, the group arrived in Nawadih, India, via Australia in mid-September 1943. There were only about 40 A-36s available, so the 528th and 529th were equipped with them, while the 530th received the first P-51As that had followed the A-36 off the North Aviation production lines.

Under Col. Henry Melton the group flew escort missions because of the long range of both the A-36 and P-51. However, during an early C-47 transport escort mission over the Hump, three A-36s were lost, demonstrating that the aircraft was more suited to ground support fighter-bomber activities.

On 10 December 1943, the 529th assigned four A-36s from Dinjan Airfield to fly escort for three C-47s that were to deliver supplies to Fort Hurtz in northern Burma, near the Chinese border. At 1120, as they approached Fort Hurtz they found that the airfield was under attack by four strafing Oscars. Twenty year old F/O Hoyt Hensley, flying wing to Lt. Harold Paige, followed him in an attack on the Oscars, who turned into the diving Americans. Hensley and Paige both scored hits on the first Oscar and were credited with a probable. Minutes later, following the Japs into China, north of Laza, a second Oscar pulled up to get on Paige's tail. This maneuver allowed Hensley a clear shot at the Jap's belly, and he continued to put shells into the Oscar's fuselage. The enemy fighter rolled over and crashed. At low level, and nearly in a stall, Hensley found another Oscar on his tail. Fortunately, 2Lt. Wil McEvoy got behind this attacker, pursuing it in a twisting, low level dogfight, and shot it into the Lashi Hka River.

On 18 January 1944, Hensley shot down a Zeke north of Ukyinkoi to get the second of three total victories scored by the A-36 in the CBI (PTO).

A-36 Ace
Pilot: 1Lt. Michael T. Russo
Unit: 522FS/27FG/12AF
A/C: A-36A *"Pat"*
Victories: 5
Record:

V#	Date	E/A/C
1	09-13-43	FW-190
2	10-24-43	Fi-167
3	12-08-43	Ju-52
4-5	12-30-43	2 Me-109s

Action: The AAF bought 500 A-36s from North American Aviation, which had essentially converted its P-51A into a dive bomber

1Lt. Michael Russo. (Author/Russo)

by adding a set of lattice-work aluminum brake panels to the upper and lower wing borders. Four .50 caliber machine guns were mounted in pairs in the wings, while two fired through the prop. These guns were synchronized to a 200-250 yard point of concentration that would shatter an intended strafing target.

The 27FBG, after fighting in North Africa, reducing the island of Pantelleria, and providing air cover for the invasion of Sicily took part in the invasion at Salerno. The unit received the Distinguished Unit Citation for its harassment of Panzer armor there. On 13 September 1943, 522 CO Maj. Daniel Rathbun's flight happened upon a dozen FW-190 fighter bombers attacking invasion shipping offshore of Salerno. A mustachioed Invader pilot, 2Lt. Mike Russo, was one of four American pilots to score a victory that morning. Russo added a Fiesler 167 seaplane on 24 October and a Ju-52 transport on 8 December to give him three victories.

On 30 December, Russo's olive-colored A-36, named after his wife, Pat, led a dozen dive bombers on marshaling yards at Sezzo, near Rome. Their formation was attacked by 16 Me-109s at 14,000 feet at mid-morning near the target. Following A-36 tactical doctrine, Russo quickly took his group down to 8,000 feet, where his 1,325 hp Allison engine gave the A-36 airframe better performance against the 109. In the combat Russo destroyed two Germans to make him the only A-36 ace of the war.

Mustang I First Victory in Type
Pilot: F/O Hollis Hills
Time: 19 August 1942
Place: Dieppe, France
Unit: 414 Squadron RCAF
A/C: Mustang I/FW-190
Action: Flying Officer Hollis Hills, a Los Angeles resident, flew the Allison-powered Mustang I for the RCAF over the beaches of Dieppe during the commando raid there on 19 August 1943. After a dawn tactical recon mission, the 414th again sent out Flt/Lt F.E.

F/O Hollis Hills (Author/Hills)

Clarke and his weaver (wingman) Hills from Gatwick at 1025 to recon the beaches. TAC R sorties were flown in pairs, with the leader surveying the ground while his weaver covered him from above. Hill's radio malfunctioned over Dieppe, and when three FW-190s bounced them, Hill was unable to warn Clarke of the dilemma. Clarke's engine was hit and seized, forcing him to ditch in the seas off the beach, where a Royal Navy destroyer picked him up. Meanwhile Hills, flying through both British Navy and German Army AA fire, shot the Focke Wulf off Clarke's tail for his first victory and the first Mustang victory for an American in WWII.

On 29 April 1944, Hills shot down three Zekes while flying a F6F for VF-32 off the *Langley*. These three Japanese kills gave Hills victories against both Axis powers, which happened infrequently during WWII. However, these victories, flying for different countries, made Hills unique.

Bell P-39 Airacobra

The Bell Aircraft Company had been in business for less than three years when the XP-39 made its debut on 6 April 1938. The aircraft was a divergence from the conventional, as designer Robert J. Woods installed the 1,150hp Allison V-1710 engine below and behind the cockpit, amidships, near the center of gravity. This placement permitted a smaller nose configuration, afforded better handling and maneuverability, and allowed the placement of the armament in the most advantageous position, the centerline of the fighter. The drawback of the engine placement was that the propeller needed to be connected to the engine via an eight-foot shaft coupled to a gearbox in the nose. Also, engine air-cooling was accomplished through scoops located on the fuselage sides (later, the on the wing leading

P-400 of the 67FS/347FG on Guadalcanal. (USAF)

edge). Other unique features were that it was the first USAAC single engine fighter to employ a tricycle landing gear and automobile type cockpit doors. The first flights were performed with a supercharged engine, giving the prototype a performance of nearly 400mph at 20,000 feet, but these tests revealed that some modifications needed to be made. The usual evaluation lot of 13 YP-39s for service testing was contracted for at the end of April. However, the planes in this order were ordered without superchargers, a decision that would alter the combat future of the P-39. The result was a lower rated engine driving a heavier gross weight aircraft due to the modifications, causing the performance to fall to less than 370 mph at only 13,500 feet. The armament was impressive: two .30 cal. and two .50 cal. machine guns in the nose and a 37 mm cannon, which utilized the space usually occupied by a forward mounted engine. On 10 August 1939 the USAAC placed an order for 80 Bell P-45 Airacobras, but this identification was changed to the P-39C. The Cs were equipped with bullet proof windshields and self-sealing fuel tanks, and further modifications subsequently added to the fighter's weight and denigrated performance. Only 20 Cs were produced, and the remaining 60 were converted to the D. The first contracts were placed by the French government, but were taken over by the British Purchasing Commission in 1940. The first P-39s reached the RAF in July 1941 and became operational in October. Without superchargers these aircraft were limited to ground support duties and withdrawn from service, with the remainder turned over to the USAAF for training purposes. A further 863 Ds were produced and used in a ground support role, as the V-1710-35 engine performed best under 10,000 feet. The D and P-400 (repossessed and rejected RAF Airacobras) in USAAF service saw action in the months after Pearl Harbor. They were found to be totally

Standard Bell factory-issued PR P-39 photo. (Bell)

Robert Woods' design was unusual in that the Allison V-1710 engine was placed behind the cockpit. (Bell)

P-400 Export Airacobra First Victory in Type

Pilot: 1Lt. Thomas Lynch
Time: 20 May 1942/0900
Place: Waigani, New Guinea
Unit: 39FS/35FG/5AF
A/C: P-400/2 Zeros

The P-400 was built by Bell Aircraft of Buffalo, NY, for the RAF, which contracted for 675 as the Airacobra Mk I. The fighter, a politically motivated and perpetuated project, was already obsolete when it was first tested in spring 1938. The RAF testing unit and the 601 Squadron rightfully refused the fighter as not combat-capable in Europe. The remaining Mk Is in England were foisted off on the desperate Russians, and the RAF refused to take delivery of the remainder of their order. Bell, with an excess inventory of Mk Is, shipped over 200 to the Russians, and another 179 were taken by the ACC. These rejected Mk Is were redesignated the P-400, and basically only replaced the RAF roundels with the U.S. stars and bars, while retaining the RAF day fighter camouflage and serials. The principal differences between the P-400 (Mk I) and the P-39D were in the RAF compatible oxygen system, radios, gunsights, and the cannon caliber. The P-400s mounted a 20mm Hispano-Suiza cannon, while the P-39D carried a 37mm American Aircraft Corp. (Oldsmobile) cannon; both of which fired through the nose hub. After their rejection by the RAF a few ACC P-400s were utilized as trainers, but the majority were shipped off to Australia, where the situation was desperate after Pearl Harbor. The 35FG withdrew from the Philippines after the Japanese takeover, then defended Australia, and subsequently went into combat over Java. The attrition of men and aircraft in the South Pacific was high, and replacements were green pilots and second-rate aircraft. In mid-April 1942, the 35th and 36th squadrons of the 35FG were sent to New Guinea, and were reinforced by the 39th and 40FS in early May as conditions worsened.

inadequate in aerial combat, but did yeoman work on the ground, particularly in North Africa and the South Pacific. The D through M models differed mainly in engine power rating and armament: E (3 test models); F (229); G (1,800 to K, L, M, N); J (25); K (210); L (250); M (240); N (2,095); and Q (4,905). There were no H, I, O, or P models. Some 4,758 (200 were lost in route) N and Q models were sent to Russia under Lend-Lease. The N and Q were similarly powered, with the Q somewhat faster and armed with .50s instead of .30s. These aircraft served well on the Eastern Front in a ground support capacity for the Soviets between 1942-45. A total of 9,558 Airacobras were produced, and would give rise to the P-63 Kingcobras (1,725 As and 1,227 Cs built). The P-63s did not see U.S. service.

P-400 Top Scorers

It was not long before 1Lt. Tom Lynch of Hazeltown, PA, found himself flying a 35FS P-400 while on Tdy (temporary duty) from the 39FS. In the morning of 20 May 1942 an assorted group of P-40s, P-39s, and P-400s of the 35th, 36th, and 39th fighter squadrons escorted C-47 transports. The formation was attacked, and Lynch downed two Zeros near Waigani with his 20mm cannon for the first of his 20 victories (17 in the P-38). Six days later he downed another Zero over Mt. Lawson while escorting transports to Wau. Lynch's three P-400 victories made him, along with 1Lt. Donald Green (also of the 39th, who got a Zero on 9 June and two Zeros on 18 June 1942), the top-scoring P-400 pilot. (Capt. Dale Brannon of the 67FS/347FG/13AF claimed 2 1/2 Zeros over Guadalcanal in late August 1942). Flown by capable pilots, the 100 P-400s were able to claim 45 victories before being retired from combat. It was a poor high altitude performer and was easily outclassed by enemy Messerschmitts and Zeros, but served well in an unintended close support and dive bombing role. But all-in-all, the P-400 was rightfully referred to as "a P-40 with a Zero on its tail."

1Lt. Thomas Lynch
(USAF)

P-39 PTO First Victory in Type

Pilot: Maj. Boyd "Buzz" Wagner
Time: 30 April 1942 / PM
Place: Salamaua, New Guinea
Unit: V FC
A/C: P-39D / Zero

In the confusion after the attack on Pearl Harbor, there was a frantic deployment of aircraft and fighter units to the Pacific to stem the Japanese advance. The first unit to have the dubious distinction of flying the P-39 overseas was the 8th PG, which was part of the defense force for New York City in December 1941. The Group arrived at Brisbane, Australia, in early 1942. In early April, the group detached a few pilots and aircraft from Australia to Port Moresby, the major American base in New Guinea. Airacobra units soon came to realize that they were saddled with a difficult-to-maintain and inferior aircraft. They flew from primitive steamy jungle bases with inadequate maps and intelligence over vast stretches of open water, which meant almost no chance of rescue if forced down. On 6 April, two Airacobra pilots scored hits on Japanese aircraft, but full combat operations did not begin until 30 April, when all-out attacks on enemy bomber formations and ground targets began.

Maj. Boyd Wagner was America's first ace of the war when he scored five victories flying P-40Es over the Philippines in December 1941. He was evacuated to Australia with eye, face, and chest wounds caused by an explosive shell that shattered his windshield. After recovering from these wounds he was assigned to the VFC as Director of Fighters at Port Moresby. On 30 April 1942, Wagner led 13 P-39Ds of the 35FS and 36FS of the 8PG against Japanese installations at Lae and Salamua, 180 miles to the north. Taking off from Seven Mile Airdrome in the late afternoon, the American formation climbed to 20,000 feet to clear the Owen Stanley Mountains, which form the spine of New Guinea. Approaching Huon

Gulf, the fighters dropped to the deck to strafe Lae Airfield. Over Salamaua the P-39s were jumped by 15 to 20 Zeros of the elite Tainan Kokutai. The ensuing air combat was fought across New Guinea and back to Port Moresby, as the P-39s withdrew from their strafing mission. In a fierce low-altitude dog fight 30 miles down the coast and back across the mountains, Wagner got three Zeros, while 1Lt. George Green of the 35FS got another. Four P-39s were lost, but all their pilots either bailed out or crash-landed safely. Wagner's three victories were his last of the war and made him the leading U.S. ace at the time, and the first to score a P-39 victory in the war.

Despite facing experienced Japanese pilots, the 8PG claimed 40 victories, 12 probables, and nine damaged in the month it flew P-39s from Port Moresby before being relieved by the 35FG. The 8th had lost 25 P-39s in combat, eight in forced landings, and three on the ground. The P-39 was never a popular fighter, having numerous mechanical and performance shortcomings. However, along with the P-40, in desperate times and despite heavy losses, it helped slow the Japanese aerial onslaught.

P-39 Only Ace

Pilot: 1Lt. William F. Fiedler
Time: 16 June 1943/1415
Place: Fighter I To Koli Point, Guadalcanal
Unit: 68 & 70FS/347FG/13AF
A/C: P-39D, N, K
Record:

V#	Date	E/A/C
1	01-26-43	Zero
2	02-04-43	Zero
3	06-12-43	Zeke
4-5	06-16-43	2 Vals

Maj. Boyd "Buzz" Wagner (USAF)

1Lt. William Fiedler (Left) (USAF)

The first Bell Airacobras that the 347FG of the 13AF received were 46 crated export P-400s still carrying RAF roundels, serials, and camouflage. The group trained at Tonouta, New Caledonia, and was then assigned to Guadalcanal, where it received additional "domestic" P-39s. Over the months they had found that the fighter lacked maneuverability and high altitude performance. However, combat in the Solomons usually involved enemy aircraft covering their naval forces or attacking American positions; all taking place under 10,000 feet. To counter the American build up on "Cactus" (Guadalcanal), the JAAF reinforced Rabaul with aircraft from Malaya.

On 26 January 1943, 2Lt. William Fiedler, flying a P-39D with the 70FS, shot down a Zero over Wagana Island at 0850 for his first victory. On 4 February, the "Tokyo Express" sent 22 destroyers, covered by 25 Zeros, down "The Slot" to evacuate Japanese troops from Guadalcanal, which they considered a lost cause. Led by Capt. James Robinson, the 70th intercepted the Japanese forces at 1610, 200 miles out and just north of Kolombangara. Fiedler got a Zero in the fight. In April Fiedler was transferred to the 68FS.

On 12 June, 50 zeros flew a fighter sweep toward the Russell islands, and the Americans sent up all serviceable fighters (90) to meet the threat. As part of the 31 Japanese aircraft lost that day, Fiedler claimed a Zero for his third victory at 1035, ten miles west of Cape Esperance.

Four days later a coast watcher on Vella Lavella radioed that 38 Zeros, followed by another 30 Zeros escorting 50 Val dive bombers, were on their way at noon from the northwest to attack Navy transports off Guadalcanal. Between 1315 and 1400, the U.S. put 104 aircraft in the air to meet the Japanese over the Russell Islands and to cover shipping off Guadalcanal. The Japanese attacked from two directions, one formation over Beaufort Bay and the other from the north. Both formations were immediately engaged, but about 30 Vals got to the transports. Six P-39s of the 68FS were the last aircraft to take off, being held in reserve to meet a possible threat to the transports that had now materialized. At 1400, the first dogfights took place, running from base (Fighter I) to Koli Point to the east. Fiedler claimed two Vals, the second with his 37mm cannon inoperable and using only his four small .30 cal. wing-mounted machine guns. Fiedler had become an ace, as 97 Japanese were shot down for a loss of only five U.S. aircraft, a barge, and a merchant ship.

In a predawn mission on 30 June, to avoid taxiing Fiedler and his squadron decided to wait on the opposite end of the runway until four flights of P-38s took off. This was made necessary because the P-39 had a bad reputation for overheating during even short taxi times. To get out of the hot cockpit the pilots sat on the wings of their aircraft, watching the P-38s. One of the Lightnings had some kind of problem on takeoff and rolled over at liftoff, crashing into the P-39s and killing Fiedler.

Excluding the 45 P-400 victories, the P-39 would score approximately 113 victories in the Pacific. Through necessity it was to assume a ground attack role, for which it was discovered to be more suited and more successful. So, in the critical months before sufficient numbers of P-38s could come into inventory, the P-39 made an effective contribution to American air power.

P-39 ETO First Victory in Type

Pilot: 2Lt. Joseph Shaffer
Time: 14 August 1942/1030
Place: Icelandic Coast
Unit: 33 FS/Icelandic Base Command
A/C: P-39D/FW –200
Action: *See P-38 ETO: First Victory in Type*

Following the dismal RAF experience with the MK I (P-400) version of the P-39D and its embarrassing withdrawal from British operations in December 1941, the USAAC nonetheless sent a group of P-39s to the ETO. The 31st FG was reorganized with the 307th, 308th, and 309th Fighter Squadrons, and trained in the P-39. Many of its pilots were transferred to Pacific-bound units, and its P-39s lacked sufficient range to complete the trans-Atlantic flights planned for "Operation Bolero" (the build up for a second front in northwest Europe). So, the 31st sailed for Great Britain in June 1942 without their Airacobras, and being equipped with Spitfire Vs on arrival. The other P-39 group sent to England (the 52nd) also arrived without its aircraft. The P-39 saw no combat over continental Europe. The oft-repeated story of the 31st losing six of its 12 Airacobras

Capt. Charles Hoover (USAF)

2Lt. Hugh Dow (Author)

during their first and last ETO combat in July 1942, before quickly replacing their P-39s for Spitfires, seems not to have occurred.

P-39 MTO First Victory in Type

Pilots: 2Lt. Hugh Dow
 Capt. Charles Hoover
Time: 15 February 1943
Place: Thelepte #1, North Africa
Unit: 346FS/350FG/12AF
A/C: P-39Ns/Me-109's

Two 12AF Fighter Groups, the 81st and 350th, flew Russian-diverted P-39s and P-400s in the MTO. These fighters presented spare parts and maintenance problems, which in turn affected pilot training and utilization. The internment of ferried P-39s also affected the deployment of the fighter in this theater. On 15 January 1943, 13 P-39s of the 81st and 11 of the 350th left England led by a navigation bomber. Meeting fierce head winds, the bomber turned back, forcing the fighters to land at Lisbon, where they were interned. So many P-39s were interned by the Portuguese that they were able to form a combat squadron!

Early sorties were limited to convoy escort and airdrome defense. The limited combat ceiling of the P-39 prevented the interception of high-flying Luftwaffe bombers and recon aircraft. The P-39 made its contribution in the MTO in low-level recon and strafing missions, supported by Spitfires or P-40s flying cover.

At dawn, 12 Spitfires of the 309FS/31FG escorted eight P-39Ns of the 346FS/350FG to strafe the Sidi bou Zid area. As the two formations were rendezvousing over Thelepte, six Me-109s of JG-77 attacked the Allied base. The Spitfires intercepted the Germans, shooting down one and damaging another. 2Lt. Hugh Dow, flying *Rowdy II*," shot down one and damaged another, while Capt. Charles Hoover got a Me-109 victory.

Top Scorer P-39 MTO

The 350FG continued to fly P-39 low-level missions over Sardinia, Corsica, Italy, and France, winning a DUC in April 1944 before finally transitioning to P-47s. The P-39 is credited with 25 victories in the MTO, 19 by the 350th and six by the 81st. Dow got another Me-109 on 16 April 1944, which made him the highest MTO P-39 scorer with two.

Flying the P-39 Airacobra
By
Paul Bechtel:
Two P-39 victories 18 FG (5 total)

I had a lot of experience with the P-39, having started my flying career in that type aircraft in February 1941 in the YB-39 at Patterson Field, Ohio. I flew it quite a bit there, doing both Accelerated Service Testing and regular squadron flying. My Squadron, the 39PS, was the first in the AAF to be outfitted with the P-39. After moving to Christmas Island in early 1942, I again flew the P-39, training new pilots with the 12th Squadron of the 18th FG. Of all the fighters I ever flew, I think I liked the P-39 the best insofar as flying, ground handling, visibility, and general handling performance were concerned. Previously, I had flown the P-35 and P-36, so the more

recently designed P-39 had changes that made it more modern. It was faster and performed better in the air and on the ground.

Initially, I was impressed and satisfied with the armament, until I got into combat, where I began to rethink this. The P-39 had six machine guns: two or four .30 caliber free-firing guns in each wing; two .50 caliber machine guns in the fuselage, which were synchronized to fire through the propeller; and a 37mm cannon that fired through the propeller hub. The 37mm never did work right in any of the outfits I was in. It would jam after two or three shots, and usually the jam could not be cleared in the air. We tried to scrounge 20mm guns when we could to replace the 37. A 20mm was the standard in the British P-400 export version of the P-39, and in the P-38 it was a good reliable gun. Once we got into actual combat, I believe that all of us began to realize the importance our gun installations. Our targets were always moving, and when you finally were able to get one in your sights you wanted to throw as much lead as possible in the short time you were "on target." That meant that you wanted to have as many big guns as possible delivering as many rounds as possible. The 37 mm was big, but it was slow and undependable. The .30 caliber free-firing wing guns delivered many more rounds than the .50 caliber prop-synchronized guns per period of firing, but the .50s were much more destructive than the .30s. I think we all began to look forward to flying fighters, such as the P-38, P-47, or P-51, which carried a lot of free-firing .50s. When we got into combat with the Jap Zero we could not maneuver with it because of our heavier wing loading. They had no armor plate and were much lighter, and so were much more maneuverable. The only way you could cope with them in combat was to hit them first and get out, turn around, and try to hit them again.

In our early P-400s, the British export version, we could not go above 10-12,000 feet because its high-pressure oxygen system required equipment we did not have. This limited us to ground support work. When we received our P-39s that altitude limitation went away, but our reputation for this role was established. In my opinion, the .30 caliber machine guns were as effective against ground troops as the .50s, since their rate of fire was faster. But the .50s

Capt. Paul Bechtel (Author/
Bechtel)

were more effective against hard targets, such as vehicles, gun emplacements, shipping, etc. My two P-39 victories over Munda on Christmas eve 1942 were over very cooperative Zeros. They let me join up in their formation like I was one of their own. So I pulled up behind them and wrapped them up. They seemed to turn on my tail instead of the other way around. They didn't do that too often, which was lucky for me.

Overall, the P-39 fought a good war. It did not shoot down a lot of the enemy, but it did its strafing and ground support duties very, very well.

Flying the P-39/P-400 Airacobra
By
Richard Suehr:
One P-400 victory 39 FS (5 total)

The P-39/P-400 was a small, beautiful, streamlined fighter with many modern features for its time, such as the tricycle landing gear, air-cooled inline engine located behind the cockpit, and the heaviest armament on any American fighter of the time.

We entered the cockpit over the right wing through a door that was similar to an automobile door, complete with roll-down windows (editor's note: they were manufactured by the Hudson Motor Car Co.). The throttle quadrant was on the left side of the cockpit, so the real obstacle was to crawl over it. The sturdy cockpit was spacious for a small, 5'5" pilot like me. It was very comfortable, with everything right at my elbows or fingertips. The instruments were easy to see or read, but the gun sight above the panel could rearrange a pilot's face in a crash landing. The visibility was excellent in all directions because the canopy was almost a full bubble, and the aircraft stood on a tricycle gear. Our radio system was the state-of-the-art four channels VHF, but it tended to be crowded.

The 1,150hp Allison engine was located behind the cockpit, and was coupled by a long drive shaft passing under the cockpit to a reduction gearbox that connected it to the prop. When starting the engine all these gears and linkages made a racket and shook the plane until enough revs were reached to smooth things out. The engine and linkages were generally reliable, but were low-altitude rated and condemned the P-39 to low-level combat and ground support duties. As was usual, the combat versions of a fighter become overweight from the prototype versions, and thus become underpowered, as was certainly the case with the P-39.

The tricycle landing gear gave the P-39 very good ground handling characteristics during taxiing, take off, and landing. We tried not to waste too much time on the ground because of the Allison's tendency to overheat. We also had to watch our fuel consumption, which was somewhat more than two hours. We were later equipped with a 75 gallon belly tank that helped extend our range by about an hour. The Airacobra had a high rate of climb from takeoff, but at 12-13,000 feet the plane almost stopped dead in the air. It took forever to climb from there to 20-25,000 feet, where the Japs usually flew. We were hurting when and if we reached this altitude, and would have had trouble catching a Jap fighter, or even a Betty bomber! A turbo supercharger would have been a great help. We had no maneuverability up there, and our main hope was to make one surprise run at them and dive for our lives. The P-39 did have

1Lt. Richard Suehr (Author/Suehr)

beautiful dive characteristics, as it could dive away from the pursuing Jap like a brick! Our best bet in combat was to lure the Jap below 12,000 feet, where we were more maneuverable and had some chance. The plane was good in a shallow climb, but had no ability to pull straight up to gain altitude advantage. But even at these favorable altitudes the quick, maneuverable Japanese aircraft often overmatched us. Fortunately, our small fighter was ruggedly built, with armor plate surrounding the cockpit and bulletproof glass fore and aft of the canopy. The fuel tanks were self-sealing.

The Airacobra was a stable gun platform, and was the most heavily armed American fighter of the time. It was equipped with a 37mm cannon that fired through the propeller hub, two nose mounted, propeller synchronized .50 caliber machine guns, and four wing mounted .30 caliber machine guns. The 39th FS flew a mixed bag of P-39Ds and P-400s (which were RAF rejects). The only difference between the two were the 37mm cannon in the P-39 and the 20mm cannon in the P-400, along with slight engine variations and a different, non-interchangeable oxygen system. The 37mm fired about 30 shells, and its looping trajectory took some time to master. When it worked it could put some good-sized holes in the sides of Japanese ships and barges. It was useless in aerial combat.

The P-39's performance was discouraging to pilots engaging in aerial combat, but its ruggedness and firepower made it a great ground support weapon. Sitting on the ground and in pictures the P-39 looked to be a great fighter, but its performance in the air never matched its great looks. The fondest memories I have about the aircraft are of the people I flew with and who supported us on the ground.

P-39 Airacobra in Soviet Service

More than half (4,924) of the P-39s manufactured were earmarked for service with the Soviet Union as part of the Lend-Lease Program. Although a failure in American and RAF service, the aircraft was ideally suited to Soviet Air Force tactical doctrine, which was designed to support Soviet Arm. In early 1942 the P-39 was welcomed by the Soviets, as their aircraft industry was in a shambles, and the Cobra compared favorably to the best Soviet-built fighters of the time, the MiG-3 and Yak-3. The P-39 possessed excellent low altitude performance, was heavily armed with a 37 or 20mm cannon, and could sustain heavy battle damage. Three Soviet aces scored more victories in the P-39 than any American or RAF ace did in the P-38, P-47, P-51, or Spitfire!

The 153 IAP became the first VVS (Russian Air Force) Cobra unit in June 1942. The unit scored over 130 victories by August 1943 and had four aces with over 17 victories: Aleksej Smirnov, 34 victories; Leonid Bykovets (19 v.); F.M. Mazurin (18 v.); and Anatoli Kislyakov (17 v.). The second unit to receive the P-39 (RAF P-400 cast offs) was the 19 Guards IAP, which downed over 170 German aircraft by the end of 1943 and numbered aces Leonid Galchenko, who scored 24 victories, and Gregory Dmitryuk with 18 victories. The 45 IAP began flying P-39s in October 1942 at the battle for the Kuban River, where it scored 118 victories. It ended the war with 502 aerial victories, mostly in the P-39. Top aces included: the Glinka brothers (Dmitri with 50 and Boris with 30 victories); Ivan Babak, 37 victories; N.Y. Lavitskij, 26 victories; and Pyotr Guchyok, 20 victories, all of whom scored most of their victories in the P-39. The Soviets did not keep accurate records on victories scored by fighter type by their aces, so it is difficult to segregate P-39 victories from total victories. The 55 IAP was probably the most prolific Soviet P-39 unit, downing 697 German aircraft, the majority in the Cobra. The 55 IAP was second to the 5 Guards IAP, scoring 739 victories mainly flying La-5s and 7s. Second-ranking Soviet and Allied ace Alexander Pokryshkin scored 48 of his 59 victories in the P-39 to become the leading P-39 ace of WWII. Pokryshkin was awarded the DFC by U.S. President Roosevelt. Gregory Rechkalov scored 44 of his 56 victories in the Cobra, followed by Alexander Klubov, who scored 24 of 31 victories in the P-39, while V.Y. Bonderenko (24), Andre Trud (24), K.V. Sukhov (22), V.A. Figichev (21), and A.V. Fyodorov (20) scored the majority of their victories in the Cobra.

Alexander Pokryshkin was the leader of the most prolific Soviet P-39 unit, the 55 IAP, and was the leading P-39 ace of WWII with 48 of his 59 total victories in the Cobra. (Author)

Spitfire
Spitfire ETO First Victory in Type
Pilot: 2Lt. Samuel F. Junkin
Time: 19 August 1942/0800-0830 (approx.)
Place: Dieppe, French coast
Unit: 309FS/31FG/8AF
A/C: Spitfire VI/FW-190
Action: *See ETO First Victory USAAF*

Spitfire MTO First Victory in Type
Pilots: 1Lt. Charles C. Kenworthy
       1Lt. Carl W. Payne
       Maj. Harrison R. Thyng
Time: 8 November 1942/1700
Place: Tafaraoui Airdrome
Unit: 309FS/31FG/12-15AF
A/C: Spitfire Vb/Dw-520
Action: On 8 November 1942, America undertook her first amphibious invasion in the West. The Rangers of Lt. Col. William Darby moved ashore on Oran to capture the port city from the balking French. Leaving their original Spitfires in England, the 31st had picked up new "desertized" Spitfires in Gibraltar. These fighters were repainted sand brown with darker brown spots, and with light blue under surfaces. They were fitted with large Vakes air filters to cope with the gritty dry desert sands. The RAF roundels were replaced with the "Stars and Bars" national insignia and appropriate unit codes. When the three pronged invasion began, the troops at the port of Oran met unexpectedly strong French opposition. Gen. Jimmy Doolittle ordered air cover. Since the Spitfires of the 31st were parked to take off before those of the 52nd, two squadrons of the 31st—the 308th and 309th—took off first for Oran. The two squadrons, led by Col. John Hawkins, had to fly around thunder storms and attempted in vain to contact fighter control at Tafaraoui Airdrome, which was located ten miles inland from Oran. They arrived at the airdrome at 1700, and four Sea Hurricane fighters from the Royal Navy carrier *Furious* were scheduled to provide air cover while the Americans landed. The top cover was seen far above as the Americans approached. As Col. Hawkins was landing the covering aircraft dove and opened fire, shooting down Hawkins' wingman, Lt. Joseph Byrd, as he approached, flaps and gear down. After the first pass it was realized that the aircraft were enemy French Dewoitine 520 fighters. Three 309th Spits, led by Maj. Harrison Thyng, retracted their gear and flaps and attacked the French fighters, knocking down three at less than 1,000 feet over the airdrome. Thyng, 1Lt. Carl Payne, and 1Lt. Charles Kenworthy were each credited with a victory in no established sequence, the first for a Mediterranean Spitfire.

After the pilots landed they found that the base had just been captured a few hours earlier by American paratroopers dropped by C-47s flown from England. The 31st ground echelons arrived the next morning with food, but the lack of gasoline and ammunition grounded the Spitfires. The efficient and clever American personnel siphoned gasoline from the C-47s and scrounged ammo from the disabled French aircraft and captured dumps, putting the 31st back online.

Carl Payne went on to have an interesting WWII career by destroying aircraft of all four Axis powers. After he shot down the French Dw-520, he shot down an Italian Mc-202 on 10 June 1943 and then added a German Fw-190 during the invasion of Sicily,

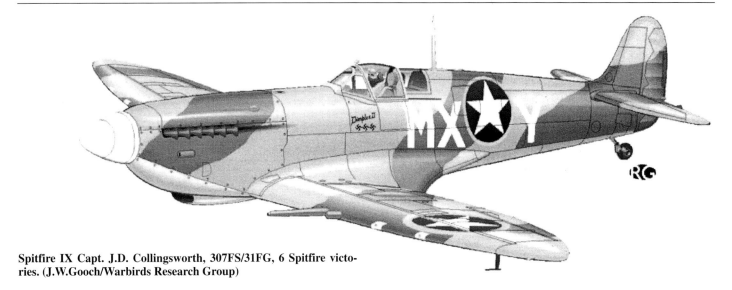

Spitfire IX Capt. J.D. Collingsworth, 307FS/31FG, 6 Spitfire victories. (J.W.Gooch/Warbirds Research Group)

which made him an ace. During the final days of the war in the Pacific Payne was assigned to the 34FS/413FG/7AF, which was led by Col. Harrison Thyng. On 8 August 1945 Payne downed a Japanese Zeke fighter to complete his Axis sweep.

It would not be until 30 November 1943 that a 52FG pilot would score a victory, when Capt. James S. Coward shot down a Me-109 near Bone. James Thyng went on to become an ace with five victories in the MTO, including French, German, and possibly an Italian (misidentified Mc202/Me-109) aircraft. He almost duplicated Payne's feat of four Axis victories when he got a probable on the 8 August mission with Payne. Thyng destroyed five MiG-15s in Korea to become one of seven pilots to become aces in two wars. Kenworthy scored a victory over a Me-109 in February 1943, flying a Spitfire to complete his WWII scoring.

Spitfire MTO First Aces in Type
Pilots: Capt. Norman L. McDonald
          Capt. Arnold E. Vinson
Time: 3 April 1943/1730
Place: S.E. of El Guettar
Unit: 2FS/52FG/12AF
A/C Spitfire Vb/3 Ju-87 McDonald & 1 Ju-87 Vinson
Action: The 52FG followed the 31FG to England in the summer of 1942 as a P-39-trained group. Like the 31st, it received desert-modified Spitfires at Gibraltar in preparation for "Operation Torch," the invasion of North Africa. While the 31FG left on 8 November 1942 to fly to Oran to fight the Vichy French on the day of the invasion, the 52nd left the next day, but was put into reserve, as the Vichy resistance ended.

1Lt. Carl Payne (USAF)

Maj. Harrison Thyng (Author/Thyng)

**Capt. Norman McDonald and Capt. Arnold Vinson
(Author/McDonald)**

After the fall of the port of Bone to the British, the Germans and Italians transferred air units to the area. The 2FS of the 52FG was loaned to the RAF 322 Wing in late November to meet this new Axis air threat. During the period the 2FS was assigned to protect Bone Harbor and Allied lines against enemy air attacks, escort medium and dive bombers, convoy patrol, and perform fighter sweeps and strafing missions. The sustained Axis air offensive on the port in early December led to 10 victories. Capt. Arnold Vinson started, scoring quickly by downing 2 1/3 Luftwaffe in three days, 2-4 December. Vinson claimed a FW-190 on the 2nd during a sweep over Mateur, and the next day shared a FW-190 north of Bone with two RAF pilots of the 81st squadron. On the 4th, the 2FS joined the RAF 81 on a sweep west of Tebourba, where they encountered three Ju-88s and their escorts, and Vinson got a Me-109. This mission saw a 1st Lieutenant from Massachusetts, Capt. Norman McDonald, claim a Me-109 probable and two damaged.

It would not be until 22 March 1943 that 1Lt. McDonald would score his first victory. Italian and Afrika Korps armor were attacking the Allies in the Mereth area, and McDonald got two Ju-88s in quick succession near their base at Mezzouna Airdrome. Meanwhile, Vinson had destroyed a Ju-87 on 2 January 1943, and then got a FW-190 two days after McDonald's first victory to give him 4 1/3 victories.

On 3 April, the Axis was bombing the U.S. II Corps, which was forcing the Afrika Korps into Tunisia after its defeat by the British 8th Army at Mereth. The squadrons flew endless hours of virtually wasted time on daylight patrols. But on that day, Capt. Vinson's flight maintained a low level patrol and intercepted a large number of Ju-87 Stuka dive bombers escorted by Me-109s at 1730 near El Guettar. Of the 13 Stukas claimed that day, McDonald, now a captain, attacked a flight of four Stukas flying in echelon as they were ready to dive. McDonald fired on the top Stuka, hitting it, and then fired on the second, which blew up, colliding with the first. He lined up the third, which like the other two made no attempt to evade, and shot it to pieces. The lead Stuka, however, turned sharply

to port, but McDonald hit him before the German put down his dive brakes, causing the Spitfire to over run. As he tried to pick up the evading Stuka, McDonald saw two Me-109s and attacked, but soon was the prey of the Messerschmitts. Through luck, skill, defensive flying McDonald was able to escape with three victories and one probable to make him an ace. However, Vinson was killed when his Spitfire was shot down by an escorting Messerschmitt after he downed a Stuka to make him an ace.

McDonald went on to score two more victories in the Spitfire to give him 7 1/2 before returning to the States. He requested a return to combat and scored four more victories in the P-51 as CO of the 318FS in the ETO from late May 1944 to V-E Day. The first aces of the 31FG were Capt. Frank A. Hill, who got three Me-109s, and Maj. Harrison R. Thyng, who got a Me-109 on 6 May 1943.

Spitfire MTO Top Scorer in Type
Pilot: 1Lt. Sylvan Feld
Victories: 9
Unit: 4FS/52FG/12AF
Record:

V#	Date	E/A/C
1	03-22-43	Me-109
2	04-01-43	Ju-88
3	04-08-43	Me-109
4	04-09-43	Ju-88
5	04-18-43	FW-190
6-7	04-19-43	FW-190 & Me-109
8	06-03-43	FW-190
9	06-06-43	Me-109

Action: By April 1943, the territory occupied by the Afrika Korps had shrunk to the Tunis/Cap Bon area. Increased Allied fighter and bomber strength had put the Axis air forces on the defensive. To protect their fighters from marauding Allied fighters and fighter bombers, the Axis moved them to Sicily or Pantelleria. Enemy shipping was ravished by U.S. medium bombers and torpedo bombers,

1Lt. Sylvan Feld (USAF)

American Spitfire Aces (12 Aces/71.83 Victories)				
Ace Name	Rank	Unit	Spit V	Total V
Feld, Sylvan	1Lt	52	9	9
McDonald, Norman	Maj	52	7.5	11.5
Hill, Frank	Maj	31	7	7
Collingsworth, J.D.	Capt	31	6	6
Fields, Virgil	Capt	31	6	6
Hurd, Richard	1Lt	31	6	6
Vinson, Arnold	Capt	52	5.33	5.33
Fischette, Charles	1Lt	31	5	5
McCorkle, Charles	Col	31	5	11
Payne, Carl	Maj	31	5	6
Thyng, Harrison	Col	31	5	10
White, John	1Lt	31	5	5

Flying the Supermarine Spitfire
By
Jerry Collingsworth:
6 victories 31FG
Fourth ranked U.S. Spitfire ace

so the Luftwaffe had to dispatch massive fleets of transport aircraft to supply their troops in North Africa. The outnumbered Axis fighter forces were unable to provide adequate escort for the large formations of Ju-52, Sm-82, and the giant Me-323 transports, and huge losses were inflicted on them. The "Palm Sunday Massacre" of 18 April 1943 climaxed the defeat of the Axis Air Forces in North Africa when 77 (including 58 transports) enemy aircraft were destroyed.

1Lt. Sylvan Feld of the 4FS/52FG saw his first combat in late March 1943, and had scored four victories—two over Ju-88s and two over Me-109s—by mid-April. On 18 April he shot down a FW-190 escort southwest of Tunis to become an ace. The next day, he was part of a group of six Spitfires patrolling north of Tunis. The Spitfires spotted four Fw-190s below them, and Feld dove, scoring hits in the cockpit of a Focke Wulf and causing the pilot to bail out. Six Me-109s came on the scene, and 1Lt. Edwin Smith found one on his tail. Feld maneuvered behind this attacker and turned inside him at ground level to explode it with a short burst.

On 3 June, Feld downed a FW-190 near Cap Bon, and on 6 June concluded his scoring by destroying a Me-109 and damaging another in the aerial reduction of the enemy island stronghold of Pantelleria. These victories made Feld the top Spitfire ace with nine victories, followed by Norman McDonald with 7 1/2 and Arnold Vinson with 5 1/3. Top Spitfire scorers for the 31st were Maj. Frank Hill with 6 1/2, followed by four aces with six victories and four with five victories.

For the 52nd and 31st fighter groups the air war in North Africa was not only a war against veteran and lethal Luftwaffe units, but also an existence in constant dust, heat, and insects, which was compounded by life in tents and latrines and eating bad food. The tours in Sicily, Italy, and Corsica saw continued bombing, strafing ground support, and anti-shipping missions, all carried out in primitive conditions. The 31st flew its last Spitfire mission on 29 March 1944, while the 52nd flew its on 6 April, when both groups converted to P-51s. The pilots of the 31st accounted for 189 1/2 victories in their Spitfires, while the 52nd totaled 154 1/2.

Although I flew 125 combat missions and 293 hours in the Spitfire, fifty years is a long time, and some things are a bit hazy after all these years. After training in P-39s and P-40s, our 31st Fighter Group was the first American fighter group to arrive in England in the early summer of 1942. Immediately upon our arrival we were given the Spitfire Mark V.

Our pre-flight check was a rather passive general overall walk-around exterior inspection, checking the tires, freedom of all controls, and then to clean the windshield and glass all around. The cockpit was the smallest fighter cockpit I ever flew in, but did not present any particular problem for someone my size. We entered the Spit through the port access door with the canopy slid back. The seat was molded Bakelite, and was adjustable forward, back, and in height, which was helpful to see over the engine when taxiing. The oxygen system was good, and the radio had the normal amount of problems, but was better than the American low frequency radios. The heater left a lot to be desired. I was part of the fighter escort for the first B-17 raid on the Continent in August 1942. Twelve B-17s bombed Rouen (France) Airdrome from 26,000 feet, and all I remember about it was how cold my feet were. We were shipped to North Africa where, fortunately, the vast majority of our flying was done at medium to low altitude (15,000 feet or less). There were not many instruments to be concerned about in the Spit. The brakes were also new for us. American aircraft had individual brakes on the rudder pedals. Not so on the Spit! Instead, you needed to squeeze a lever on the control column and then push the rudder pedal concerned with the direction you wished to return; i.e. squeeze, left turn, left rudder. We had trouble on checkouts. Push rudder and forget to squeeze (for brake air pressure), or squeeze the lever and forget to push the rudder, and we were quickly in a ground loop. The control column was also different in that it had two parts. The bottom half moved forward and aft, and the top half contained the ring, firing button, and brake lever. This lower portion moved left and right for control of the ailerons. The gear handle was really a new twist. After takeoff the pilot moved his left hand

Capt. J.D. Collingsworth
(Author/Collingsworth)

to the control column to fly the aircraft, while using his right hand to reach down to the right side of his seat to raise the gear handle. Simultaneously he had to be sure the throttle lock was tight. Talk about concentration! Ground visibility was poor, just like the P-40 or P-47. The long nose made you cautious during taxiing. You needed to weave to see in front of you. The visibility was fine once the tail was up in the horizontal position and while flying.

I flew only two Spit V models, the B in England and the C in Africa. The only difference was the "desert" dust filter for use against the blowing sand in North Africa. The Spitfire V was equipped with a Merlin 45 engine delivering 1,470hp, while the IX model was equipped with the Merlin 61 that produced 1,565hp. That does not sound like much of a difference in horsepower, but for some reason it made a tremendous difference in performance. The Me-109 and Fw-190 could out climb, out run, and out dive our Spitfire V models. We could only out turn them, which was our "out" in combat. With the IX model we were able to out climb, out run, and still out turn them, but not out dive them. It changed our entire outlook on the day's activities! The Merlin was reliable, but not rugged. One hit in the glycol tank and you were out of business. Therefore, we did not recommend the Spit in a ground support role where we could be hit by ground fire. It had a very short range, as we only carried only about a 100 Imperial gallons of fuel. During combat we always were concerned with how much fuel we had remaining to engage the Germans and still have enough to get home.

The guns were a deficiency in my view. We had two 20mm cannons with only 60 rounds per gun. Added to this were four .30 caliber machine guns that were inadequate. What we needed were four cannons and four .50 caliber machine guns, or at least more ammo for the two cannons we did have. I carried no bombs or rockets and did no strafing during my tour.

The Spit was not a rugged airplane. It could take relatively little punishment and keep on flying. Also, the armor protection for the pilot was inferior, consisting of two pieces of 1/4 inch steel plate: one for the pilot's head and one behind the seat. I found a wrecked Spit and added its armor to my installed armor to give me

a 1/2 inch of protection. Fortunately, I never had to test my theory, but a fellow pilot was hit and insisted his added armor had saved him. In my opinion the location of the fuel tanks was a disadvantage. They were located in front of the cockpit, which meant any engine fire could have dire consequences, as happened to several RAF pilots in the Battle of Britain.

Landing was easy once you got used to the unique braking system. We were instructed never to ditch the Spitfire, as the radiator would act as a scoop, causing the aircraft to rapidly fill with water and sink. Always bail out!

All in all, the Spitfire was an honest aircraft with no dirty or underhanded characteristics. It got me six FW-190s and got me home safely. That's all you could ask of any fighter.

Flying the Spitfire
By
Frank Hill:
7 victories 31FG
Third ranking U.S. Spitfire ace

I flew the Spitfire Vb and later Marks VIII and IX for the 31st Fighter Group. We had been flying P-39s and P-40s in the States before we sailed for England in May 1942. When we arrived we were equipped with the Spitfire Vb. The experience level of the pilots and ground crews was very high, so it took only about a month of indoctrination before all hands had the Spitfire tamed. However, it did take a little of practice to master the unusual braking system, which utilized not only the rudder pedals, like American fighters, but also a lever on the control column. This lever was similar to a bicycle brake lever and gave a squirt of air pressure to the pedal. We were on operations for about a month, escorting light bombers before we had our first real aerial encounters with the Luftwaffe over the beaches of Dieppe on 19 August 1942. Here Lt. Sam Junkin of the 31st was credited with the first confirmed victory over Europe since World War I.

On alert operations our aircraft were pre-flighted by the ground crews: engine run up; fuel; oxygen; radio; etc. checks. The pilot would recheck everything, including walk-around and Form 1 with the crew chief on duty. On a scramble the crew chief would be waiting on the wing, ready to give the pilot a hand up in getting into the cockpit and buckling up. Meanwhile, the ground crew manned the starter cart, ready to apply power to start the engine. A quick look around, thumbs up, taxi into position, all instruments in the green, and then airborne at full power. Both the pilot and ground crew needed to be sharp and alert to be sure everything was in proper order.

The Spitfire was a great plane to fly, something like an AT-6, only with more power and a quantum leap in maneuverability. The cockpit was small, and a small portside access door made entry easier. The parachute and dinghy were usually ready on the seat, with their snaps arranged for quick buckle-up. The oxygen hose and radio plug-in were set up by the crew chief. Despite its small size, the cockpit was comfortable, with all the instruments and various controls within easy reach and sight. It has been said that the Spitfire became part of the pilot when he was strapped in. You more or less strapped the plane on and flew it instinctively in the direction you pointed it. Its response to the controls was superb. The VHF radio, with its push button selection, was a tremendous improvement over the old coffee grinder-type installed in the P-39 and P-40.

The Rolls Royce Merlin engine was a smooth running package, which gave very little trouble. Our original Spit Vbs were only equipped with 110 Imperial gallon internal fuel tanks. When we were in Tunisia we were always near the front lines, so this fighting range was fine, but we had to watch the fuel gauge in a dogfight. The 30-gallon belly tanks that were added during the invasion of Sicily and Italy continued to provide sufficient range. However, there was a severe range problem when we fought up the Italian boot. It was the primary reason the Group re-equipped with the P-51.

The excellent maneuverability was the greatest asset of the Spitfire, so you could mix it up with the Me-109 and FW-190, which were faster in a climb and dive. With each fighter on level flight below 20-25,000 feet the Spitfire could usually emerge the victor. Because of this the Germans tried to attack from above a Spitfire formation. The Spitfire Marks VIII and IX were really great airplanes, with increased performance due to the more powerful Merlin engines and four bladed propellers. On 6 May 1943, the Spitfire made me the first 31st FG ace when I downed two Me-109s and got probable on another.

Miscellaneous Fighter Types

Boeing P-26 Peashooter
P-26 First Victory in Type
Pilot: Capt. Jesus A. Villamor
Time: 12 December 1941
Place: Bantangas A/F Philippines
Unit: 6PS/PAAF
A/C: P-26A/Nell
The Philippine's National Defense Act of 1935 established a ten year plan for the development of the Philippines Department Air Force, which was under the control of American Army Air Force officers. The years 1936-40 saw the PDAF acquire training, observation, and transport aircraft. By mid-1941, with a Japanese war

Capt. Jesus Villamor (Author)

looming, the PAAF (Philippines Army Air Force, as it was then known) began to reorganize and build up under American 1Lt. Charles Backes. The 35 Boeing P-26s assigned to the USAAC were not only obsolete, but worn out, most having first arrived in the Philippines in the spring of 1937. A Pratt & Whitney R-1340 Wasp, nine cylinder radial, air-cooled engine that was rated at 500hp powered the fighter, which gave it a maximum speed of 234mph. It was armed with two .30 caliber Browning machine guns that fired at 500rpm. As the USAAC began to receive the P-40, twelve P-26s were transferred in July to the Philippine's 6PS at Batangas, which was about 60 miles south of Manila.

After Pearl Harbor, the air war did not reach the 6PS until 10 December. Five P-26s were temporarily stationed at Zablan Field for an air defense briefing when a number of strafing Zeros attacked as a preliminary to a bombing raid. Capt. Jesus Villamor, CO of the 6PS, led three P-26s into the air. The "Peashooter's" worn out engines could barely do 200 mph. Lt. Jose Gozar had his guns jam on his first pass, and he then tried unsuccessfully to ram the enemy bomber out of frustration. No claims were made, but the Filipinos harassment disrupted the Jap attack.

Two days later, the Japanese attacked the 6th at their home base at Batangas with 20 Nell bombers escorted by Zeros. Five P-26s, again led by Villamor, intercepted the second wave of 27 bombers, also escorted by Zeros. In his first firing pass, before the Zero escorts arrived, Villamor shot down a bomber. His aggressive attack caused the Japanese bombers to jettison their bombs haphazardly. Also, no less than six 6PS pilots shared another victory. However, two Peashooters were lost, and thereafter the squadron's role was reduced to reconnaissance duties; their numbers being divided between Clark Field under Gen. Wainwright and Zablan under Gen. Parker. For his role in the battle Villamor was awarded the DSC with Oak Leaf Clusters. By 24 December, the six P-26s that remained were ordered to be destroyed, as the Japanese had landed in full force at Limom Bay. The order was later rescinded, but the

P-26C (USAF)

little fighters had already been destroyed, and the remaining 6PS personnel had retreated to Bataan, where they became known as the "Flying Infantry."

Seversky P-35

P-35 Seversky First Victory in Type
Pilot: 1Lt. Ben S. Brown
Time: 8 December 1941/1250
Place: Over Clark Field, PI
Unit: 34PS/24PG /5AF
A/C: P-35A/Zero

As the prospect of a war with Japan appeared to be imminent, the AAC decided to send precious reinforcements to the Philippines. When the men of the 34PS arrived in the Philippines on 20 November 1941, they expected to be equipped with the new P-40 variant, but instead found themselves flying the obsolete Seversky P-35A. Fifty-seven P-35s had arrived between December 1940 and March 1941, so by November, after nearly constant use in training and gunnery practice, they were in dire need of engine change or overhaul and gun replacement. To add to the squadron's woes, it was based at Del Carmen, an isolated, primitive, dust-choked satellite dirt airstrip connected to Clark Field by radio. Though they did not know at the time, the 35th would only have two weeks of training in the P-35.

When the news of the Japanese attack at Pearl Harbor (Sunday 0800) was received in Manila, it was 0300 Monday morning local time. However, it was not until 0800 that Air Force communications got through to Del Carmen. Squadron CO 1Lt. Sam Marrett was given orders to patrol over Clark for the expected Japanese air attack. They patrolled with no contact until 1100 and returned to base. Shortly after noon, they heard rumbling and saw smoke clouds rise from Clark Field in the north. Without waiting for orders, Marrett and his wingman, 2Lt. Frank Bryant, led three flights into the air to intercept the Japanese. After a dust-shrouded takeoff, Marrett and Bryant were immediately bounced 500 feet off the ground by two Zeros diving through the overcast from 6,000 feet. Luckily, through quick reaction, the two escaped without being hit. Marrett's guns jammed, and he returned to base, leaving command to second flight leader 1Lt. Ben Brown (Class 40-D). Led by the Georgia native,

1Lt. Ben Brown (Author/ Brown)

the Americans proceeded towards Clark Field at only 8,000 feet, as they could go no higher since their aircraft had no oxygen. They approached Clark at the base of the overcast, where six aggressive Zero pilots attacked them disdainfully, flying directly at the inexperienced Americans, who were flying inferior fighters. Brown got a 90 degree deflection shot at a two ship element. He missed the lead aircraft, but got another deflection shot and claimed a Zero. The battle continued, but the American's lack of training, inferior aircraft performance, and firepower (two .50 cal. and two .30 cal. machine guns) were no match for the Zeros. Miraculously no P-35s were lost, though several were hit.

On 10 December, the lack of an early warning system saw a dozen strafing Zeros destroy 12 and damage eight P-35s on the ground at Del Carmen. Earlier in the day Marrett had been killed by debris while flying over an exploding barge he had strafed at Vigan.

Brown's victory was to be the only American P-35 victory of the war. The fighter never had a chance to prove itself in combat because of ground losses, as by 15 December only seven were in service. Also, maintenance and engine problems took their toll. Its good high altitude performance was negated because no oxygen was available. The two .30 and .50 cal. machine guns, besides being too light, often malfunctioned, were worn out, and ammo (especially the heavier .50 cal.) was scarce.

Brown went on to score two more Zero victories on 12 March 1942 while flying P-40s over Cavite, Luzon. The last two P-35s were evacuated from Bataan 8 April 1942, the day before the surrender. The P-35 would never see combat again in American service.

P-35A 97PS Iba Field, Spring 1941. This aircraft was Buzz Wagner's plane. (USAF)

P-36C

Curtiss P-36 Hawk
P-36 First Victory in Type
Pilot: 2Lt Harry W. Brown
Time: 7 December 1941/0850-0930
Place: Near Kaneohe Point, Hawaii
Unit: 46FS/21FG /7AF
A/C: P-36A/Val

The Seversky P-35 and Curtiss P-36 were 1930 designs that represented the initial transition between American biplane and modern monoplane fighters, having an enclosed cockpit and retractable undercarriage. The plane was first test flown in May 1935, deliveries began in Spring 1938, and production ceased for the ACC in May 1939. Throughout 1940 and 1941, the original P-36 units were exchanging their fighters for newer P-40s and P-39s. Meanwhile, their P-36s were equipping newly formed pursuit squadrons, which then usually received P-40s and P-39s themselves in a short time. On 7 December 1941, there were 39 then obsolescent P-36As and P-36Cs based in Hawaii with the 46th and 47PS. It was in the air over Pearl Harbor that the American P-36 was to have its best day of the war.

After its brief combat at Pearl Harbor (*See First AAC Victories/Pearl Harbor*), the P-36 was retained by the 15th PG in Hawaii, but did not again see combat. Elsewhere it was relegated to second line and training responsibilities, but was quickly replaced. It was to have more combat success in the service of other nations as the

2Lt. Harry Brown (Author/Brown)

H75 Hawk, particularly with the French Armee de l'Air and Finland's LeLv 32 Squadron. By Finland's surrender on 4 September 1944, this squadron claimed 190 victories in three years of combat, many by Curtiss 75 Hawks.

Flying the P-26 and P-36
By
Philip Rasmussen:
P-36 victory over Pearl Harbor

When I arrived in Hawaii I was assigned to the 46th Fighter Squadron at Wheeler Field in May 1941. We were equipped with three types of aircraft: the P-26; P-36; and P-40 (which had just arrived). I initially checked out in the P-26, which was an open cockpit, low-wing monoplane. It was an extremely exhilarating plane for a fighter pilot to fly, because it was very acrobatic, and with the wind streaming by the open cockpit it gave a tremendous feeling of speed and excitement. We even wore long scarves like World War I fighter pilots to blow in the slipstream. Even though it was great fun to fly I would have hated to fly it in combat against the Zero, even though it was probably even more maneuverable. The P-26 was outdated at that time and did not have adequate engine or firepower.

The P-36 was the next aircraft I checked out in, and it was the type I spent the most time in prior to December 7th. Compared to the P-26, the P-36 was much larger, all metal, and had an enclosed cockpit. It was more powerful, but only had slightly more firepower. The cockpit was roomy compared to the P-39 we were equipped with after the war began. Of course, in Hawaii we did not have to worry about heating because we did very little high altitude work. When we did fly at altitude we sucked oxygen out of a wooden tube. It was constant flow, and we would often get a sore throat for the rest of the day afterward. The instrument panel was not significantly different from the P-26, maybe it had a few more gauges. The control layout was good. We had normal communications for the time, HF along with the little dit-dah-dit Morse code system. About a month before Pearl Harbor, we had a series of incidents where a number of P-36s had to land wheels up because we could not lower our landing gear. One day, preparing to land, I lowered the gear, but when the right hand wheel went down to 3/4s, the left one would go back up. Commanding General (Howard) Davidson was in the control tower and insisted that I try everything possible not to land wheels up. I pumped the manual gear handle, tried aerobatics, and pulled maximum Gs until I was nearly out of fuel. Nothing happened, so in desperation I pushed the hand pump with my foot. I bent it to the floor to make sure they knew I had attempted everything. I landed wheels up on the grass without a problem. Gen. Davidson was an engineer, and insisted that I had done something wrong. He put the plane up on jacks, climbed into the cockpit, and started to pump the wheels down. And low-and-behold, the left wheel went down, and just as it started to lock the right wheel started down normally! Fortunately for my flying career, the left wheel then started to move back up.

We had one .30 caliber machine gun and one .50 caliber firing through the prop. Firing the guns sounded like a funeral cadence march, as they were very, very slow. We had frequent solenoid problems with the guns. We had a lot of mock combat experience before

1Lt. Philip Rasmussen with P-36 showing some 450+ holes made by "friendly" AA fire. (Author/Rasmussen)

December 7th. We thought the P-36 was a maneuverable aircraft, but we had no idea how it would compare to the Zero, whose maneuverability we had heard so much about. Thank heavens, during the Pearl Harbor attack I did not have the opportunity to turn with the Zero. He flew into my guns, and I just had to lead him a little bit, as he was flying straight and level, and an easy victory. On that day, as I took off I charged my .30 and .50 caliber guns by pulling the charging arm back, feeding the bullet into the chamber and then letting the charging arm slide back, cocking each gun. But my .50 began to fire by itself. To stop it, I had to keep its charging arm pulled fully back towards the rear of the aircraft in the fully cocked position. I assumed that my .30 was ok because it was not firing. But when I began to fire at the Zero, the .30 would not fire, and the only way I could get the .50 to fire was to let the charging arm slide in and let the gun fire by itself again!

The Pratt & Whitney engine was extremely reliable, and no one in our squadron had any problems with it. The large radial engine did block forward vision, so on taxiing we had to make S-turns. Takeoff was normal, not like the P-40 where you had to crank in a lot of rudder to overcome torque. We never really had to worry about fuel, because most of our flights were about an hour. The fighter did not climb to altitude well; the higher you went, the slower it went. It was a dog above 12-15,000 feet. It was very easy to fly, cruised very well, was a stable platform, and was a good aircraft for instrument flying. It was a rugged aircraft. At Pearl Harbor, I suffered two explosive 20mm hits behind the cockpit and 450-500 other assorted holes. My canopy had been shot off, my tail wheel flattened, and my rudder cable and brake line were severed. I landed safely, so I personally can not say enough about the P-36's ruggedness.

I would have hated to have flown the P-36 against the Zero on a daily basis. It was faster, more maneuverable, and had more fire power. At the time it had everything going for it, while the P-36 really had nothing going for it. The P-36 was a bridge to the Army Air Corps' more modern types, which I would fly later: the P-39; P-40; P-38; P-47; P-51; and P-61.

Seversky P-43 Lancer

P-43 Lancer First Victory in Type
Pilots: 1Lt. Philip O'Connell (1/2 victory)
 1Lt. Burrell Barnum (1/4 victory)
Time: 17 August 1942/1005-1040
Place: Kweilin to Canton, China
Unit: 75FS/23FG/14AF
A/C: P-43/Ki-45 "Nick"

The P-43 Lancer arose from the many concepts which Alexander Seversky originated in the P-35, which was built by his company before it was reorganized as Republic Aviation in September 1939. Although an improvement over the P-35, the stout YP-43 version of the fighter was under powered and lightly armed. It was first delivered in any numbers in the Spring of 1941. The rapidly changing technology and tactics of the European air war soon made the Lancer obsolete. Rather than close the Lancer production line and lay off many, difficult to replace, skilled workers who would be needed when the U.S. P-47 would come online, Republic continued to build the P-43A as an advanced trainer. As tool-up for the P-47 lagged and P-43 contract numbers were met more P-43s were built using lend-lease money. The fighter served in secondary units as a trainer, but a quantity found their way to China.

By mid-August 1942, the 75FS of the 23FG was relocating its base from Hengyang to Changyi, stopping at Kweilin on the way. In mid-morning on 17 August, a twin-engine Japanese recon bomber was reported to be approaching Kweilin. A four-plane division was sent up to intercept, two of which were P-43s piloted by 1Lt. Philip O'Connell and 1Lt. Burrell Barnum. O'Connell attacked first, putting a .50 cal. bullet into the Jap's propeller before his guns jammed. O'Connell tried to radio for help, but his radio also malfunctioned. Soon, however, Barnum appeared and chased the snooper, which was ID'd as a Kawasaki Ki-45 Nick. His Lancer gained in climbs but lost ground in dives during the chase. Barnum, in the slower fighter, was forced to take long-range bursts, finally scoring enough hits with his four .50 cal. MGs to bring down the Japanese bomber over its home base at Canton. This shared victory was one of the only three claimed by the P-43 in WWII.

During 1942, the AAF decided to convert all P-43As to recon aircraft as P-43Bs. The Chinese had at least 108 of the leftover A-Models dumped on them, which are said to have seen some unsuccessful combat action.

P-43 Lancer of the 76FS/23FG at Kunming, China 1942. (USAF)

Liaison Aircraft

The liaison aircraft entered active duty in U.S. service with the 25th Liaison Squadron of the 71TRG in New Guinea in fall 1943. By the end of the war there were 28 liaison squadrons, whose multi-faceted roles included observation and reconnaissance, and courier and personnel ferry service. The primary liaison aircraft were the L-series, with the Grasshopper (L-2,-3,-4) being the most common. Because of their small size and because they often flew from grass fields, the L for liaison series were nicknamed Grasshoppers. Taylorcraft built the L-2, Aeronca built the L-3, and Piper, the L-5. The only defense for these aircraft was to dive to the deck, where their low speed and maneuverability kept them out of the sights of enemy fighters. Although liaison pilots carried .45s and an occasional carbine behind the seat, there are no records of an enemy aircraft being shot down from the air.

Capt. Alfred "Dutch" Schultz was the 3rd Infantry Division's Artillery Air Officer during its drive towards Cassino in September 1943. After flying an artillery spotter mission, Schultz' L-4B "Janey" was flying over an American supply convoy traveling through a canyon when he was attacked by a Me-109. German pilots were given incentives for downing the pesky Allied observation planes, and this pilot went after the helpless Cub. Schultz had flown over the area previously and knew there was a low hill and sinking air currents at the end of the canyon. Utilizing the L-4's low speed and short turning radius, he was able to zigzag at treetop level, luring the German at each pass closer to the end of the canyon. Luckily escaping the German's bullets on each of the –109's firing passes, Schultz put "Janey" into a tight turn at the end of the canyon to escape. The Messerschmitt hit the downdraft and exploded into the hill at the end of the canyon. Schultz received credit for a "kill" from the "Cub Air Force." Schultz later served as General Patton's pilot in South France.

Grasshopper vs. Stork

Pilot 1Lt. Duane Francis, and his observer, 2Lt. William Martin of the Fifth Armored Division, were flying their L-4 Piper Cub "Miss Me" in late April 1945 when they spotted a German Fieseler Storch (= Stork). The two Army pilots, brandishing .45 cal. pistols, forced the enemy observation plane to land, capturing its pilot and his observer.

USAAF Fighter Aircraft Comparative Strengths

To determine the comparative strengths of USAAF fighters in WWII, the total number of months each fighter was on active operations with a fighter group was tabulated. Of course, "active" does not differentiate between frontline and backwater combat, and the operational roles assigned the specific fighter. Both factors affected the opportunity for aerial combat and accumulating aerial victories.

In the ETO the P-47 was active 54% of all combat time, followed by the late-arriving P-51 at 33% and the early-excused P-38 at 12%. In the ETO, the P-47, though initially utilized for air combat, was supplanted by the Mustang and then used in a ground support role, as was the inadequate ETO P-38. The air combat-bred P-51 outscored the P-47 in aerial victories by more than 58% (4,239 vs. 2,685) though having 39% less operational time (177 combat months vs. 290).

In the MTO the P-38 was somewhat more active than the P-47 (101 vs. 90 combat months), while the ETO-bound P-51 was active in the Mediterranean only half the time of either the P-38 or P-47 (50 months). Nonetheless, the P-38 only outscored the P-51 (1,431 vs. 1,063), even though after its MTO introduction it joined the P-47 (203 v) in a ground support role, as there was markedly less Luftwaffe activity in the MTO and less opportunity to score aerial victories.

Capt. Alfred "Dutch" Schultz and his L-4 *"Janey."* (USAF)

In the Pacific the P-38 vindicated itself as an air combat fighter, scoring more victories in less active time (1,700v in 108 months) than the P-51, P-47, and P-40 combined (1,654v in 183 active months). The P-38, because of its European inadequacies, was relegated to this theater, where combat conditions were more suited to the twin-engine fighter's strengths.

In the CBI the redoubtable P-40 more than doubled the score of the P-51 (741 vs. 345), while the P-47 scored only 16 victories. All three fighters had similar combat month totals (P-40: 29; P-51: 34; and the P-47: 39), but the P-40 enjoyed the early war opportunities to score against a much more numerous Japanese Air Force. By the time the P-47 and P-51 came online the Japanese Air Forces were a non-entity, and both fighters performed yeoman's ground support duty.

For the entire war, all theaters, the P-47 was active 35% of all combat months, scoring 3,661 victories, while the P-51 with 21% activity scored 5,944 victories, the P-38 with 20% scored 3,785, and the P-40 with 13% scored 1,993 before being phased out of combat before the war ended.

Major USAAF fighter types established their combat niches in the various theaters of the war. As seen, the P-38, failing in the ETO, became the pre-eminent air fighter in the Pacific. The rugged P-47, more than adequate in aerial combat, was probably unsurpassed in its ground attack role. The P-51, after its marriage to the Merlin engine, became the superlative ETO Air Force dog fighter, being placed in a position to score heavily against the Luftwaffe.

USAAF Fighters/Comparative Strengths (in Group/Months*)

	AF	Spit mo	Spit %	P-40 mo	P-40 %	P-39 mo	P-39 %	A-36 mo	A-36 %	P-38 mo	P-38 %	P-47 mo	P-47 %	P-51 mo	P-51 %	Total mo	Total %
ETO	*	10.0	1.8	—	—	—	—	—	—	64.0	11.8	290.0	53.6	177.0	32.8	541.0	100
MTO	*	32.0	8.0	82.2	20.4	20.7	5.2	27.0	6.7	100.7	25.0	89.8	22.3	50.0	12.4	402.4	100
Total		42.0	4.4	82.2	8.7	20.7	2.2	27.0	2.8	164.7	17.5	379.8	40.3	227.0	24.1	943.4	100
PTO	*	—	—	62.5	18.2	52.3	15.3	—	—	107.8	31.4	80.2	23.4	40.1	11.7	342.9	100
CBI	*	—	—	39.9	29.0	—	—	10.7	7.8	14.2	10.3	39.0	28.3	33.8	24.6	137.6	100
Total		—	—	102.4	21.3	52.3	10.9	10.7	2.2	122.0	25.4	119.2	24.8	73.9	15.4	480.5	100
War		42.0	3.0	184.6	13.0	73.0	5.1	37.7	2.7	286.7	20.1	499.0	35.0	300.9	21.1	1423.9	100

*Group/Month = FG on active operations for one month
**AF: ETO>8/9 MTO>12/15 PTO>5/7/11/13 CBI>10/14

CHAPTER 9

USN & USMC Fighter Aircraft

First Victories, First Aces, and Top Scorers

U.S. Navy Fighter Designations

The Navy adopted a system to designate its aircraft according to principal function or functions, the chronological number of that particular aircraft accepted from a particular manufacturer, and the modification of the original model. For instance, the F6F-3 was the third model of the sixth fighter made by Grumman.

By Function			By Manufacturer	
B=	Bomber	*	A=	Brewster
F=	Fighter	*	B=	Boeing
J=	Utility	*	C=	Curtiss
N=	Training	*	D=	Douglas
O=	Observation	*	F=	Grumman
P=	Patrol	*	G=	Goodyear
R=	Transport	*	J=	North American
S=	Scout	*	M=	Eastern
T=	Torpedo	*	M=	Martin
		*	U=	Chance-Vought
		*	V=	Vega
		*	Y=	Consolidated

Aircraft name designations, such as Mustang, Thunderbolt, or Hellcat was to conceal developmental versions, such as the P-51B, C, D, etc. in press releases.

Grumman F4F/General Motors FM-1 and FM-2 Wildcat

The Brewster XF2A Buffalo was selected as the Navy's choice for carrier-based monoplane fighter in a 1935 competition. The Navy was not sold on the monoplane design for carrier work and ordered a backup biplane design from Grumman, the XF4F-1. But by July 1936, the Navy saw that biplane fighter design had peaked and al-

The Grumman design team of William Schwendler (L) and Dick Hutton. (Grumman)

lowed Grumman to develop its own monoplane design. The result was the XF4F-2, which bore the same tubby fuselage that distinguished Grumman biplane fighter designs. Robert Hall first flew the prototype on 2 September 1937. The 900hp, supercharged Pratt & Whitney R-1830 Twin Wasp engine powered the design. The Navy decided to conduct a fly off between the XF2A-1 and the XF4F-2, but the Grumman had problems and the Brewster was selected for production in June 1938; fortunately, Grumman was permitted to continue design improvements. On 12 February 1939, Robert Hall flew the XF4F-3, which was a decidedly different aircraft. It was fitted with a 1,200hp P & W XR-1800, increased wing area and redesigned wing tips and tail assembly, and a speed increase of 50-mph (35-mph faster than the XF2A-1). By August the

F4F-3 LtCdr. Edward "Butch" O'Hare, VF-3, 5 F4F victories (7 total). (J.W. Gooch/Warbirds Research Group)

Grumman test pilot Robert Hall, shown here with Connie Converse in 1943, first flew the XF4F-3 in February 1939 and the XF6F-1 in late June 1942. Converse flew the first XF6F-3 on 30 July 1942. (Grumman)

XF2A-1 was beginning to show deficiencies, and the Navy ordered 78 F4A-3s. The French ordered 81 G-36As (the export designation) that would later serve the Royal Navy after the fall of France as the Martlet. The Marlet had been operational with the FAA for a year before America and the Wildcat entered the war. Eventually 285 F4F-3s were built, and then 95 F4F-3As. The F4F-4 was the first Wildcat to be carrier operational. It featured six .50 cal. machine guns, pilot armor protection, self-sealing fuel tanks, and was the first Wildcat to have folding wings. Grumman built 1,169 F4F-4s and 220 F4F-4Bs as the Wright Cyclone powered Martlet Ivs for the Fleet Air Arm. The Eastern Aircraft Division of General Motors licensed-built 839 four-gun FM-1s for the Navy and 311 for the FAA as the Martlet V. In late 1942, when the new and superior F6F was accepted for production the Long Island Grumman factory converted its production. However, it was evident that the Wildcat had not come to the end of its usefulness. It was suited for use on the many small escort carriers with short flight decks coming into service. General Motors/Eastern Aircraft was put in charge of developing the XF4F-8 prototype. It was built with the 1,350hp Wright Cyclone R-1820 (and taller fin and rudder) to give it enough power for short takeoffs on escort carriers and gave it the nickname "Wilder Wildcat." A total of 4,777 FM-2s were manufactured; 4,407 were allocated to the Navy, and 370 to the Royal Navy, which by then designated it the Wildcat IV instead of the Martlet. The final production version was the 21 F4F-7 fixed wing, unarmed photo reconnaissance Wildcats. A total of 7,493 F4Fs and FM-2s were produced. It was fortunate that the Grumman continued its faith in the tubby fighter after the Navy selected the ill-fated Brewster F2A as its carrier fighter. In the Pacific it was outnumbered and outclassed by the Japanese opposition, and nonetheless it more than held its own during the early and middle stages of the war with almost a 6 to 1 kill ratio.

F4F/USN/ETO First Victory in Type
Pilot: Lt(jg) Charles A.Shields
Time: 8 November 1942/0700-0930
Place: Cazes Airdrome, N. Africa
Unit: VF-41 *Ranger*
A/C: F4F-4/D520
Action: The early November 1942 invasion of North Africa, code named "Operation Torch," was the first large-scale amphibious operation undertaken by the Allies. Its objective was to deal with the Vichy French forces in Africa so that they would not fall into German hands, and to open a second front. Air cover for the invasion Task Force 34 was assumed by the U.S. Navy, which had lost four of its seven pre-war aircraft carriers. Only the *Ranger*, which was unsuited for the Pacific, was available, along with four newly built "Jeep" escort carriers.

Inconceivably, the large invasion fleet was not discovered until its landing craft began to hit the beaches at 0630. The *Ranger* launched VF-9 at 0610, and it was followed at 0700 by the first section of 18 Wildcats of VF-41, led by CO Lt. Cdr. Tom Booth. The remainder of the veteran "Red Rippers," led by Lt. Malcomb "Mac" Wordell, were launched soon after. Booth's section was to attack the airfield at Cazes, while Wordell's section was to provide CAP for the Fedhala beachhead. Booth's first objective was to knock out the French anti-aircraft positions around the airfield, with Lt. G. H. Carter flying top cover. After his first run Booth called down Carter's aircraft to attack the French aircraft on the ground. However, an unseen AA position opened up, and Lt. Charles "Windy" Shields, who was the wingman in the last element of Carter's section, took the full brunt of this flak on his pass. In a determined attack he turned full circle and wiped out the gun position. As he dove on a second gun position, he saw two French Dewoitine fight-

F4F of VF-9 flying off the *Ranger* during *Torch*, 8 November 1942. (USN)

Five future Navy aces scored victories over the Vichy French during "Torch." VF-9 Wildcat pilots, Ens. Louis Menard (A) got 1 victory over North Africa and added 7 with VF-4 and 1 with VBF-12, Ens. Marvin Franger (D), (2 victories) got 7 later with VF-9, Lt(jg) Harold Vita (B), (1 victory) and 5 later wlth VF-12. VF-41 pilot, Ens. Will Taylor (E), (1 victory) claimed 6 later with VF-4. Ens. Bruce Jaques (C) with VGF-29 shot down a Vichy bomber and added 4 1/2 Japanese aircraft in October 1944 with VF-29.

ers ready to make a firing run on his starboard side. Shields chased one Dewoitine, but it was traveling too fast and he overshot it. The French pilot tried to come around on the F4F's tail, but Shields pulled up and maneuvered back over in a quick turn, which turned him towards the enemy. The anxious Shields fired a burst at too long range, but hit the Dewoitine, which fell over to the starboard, diving into the ground in a bouncing crash. Soon, he saw a racing Wildcat being chased low over the airfield by two French Hawk 75s (American-built P-36s) that were scissoring behind him, each taking turns firing. Shields dove full throttle to the rescue, causing one of the attackers to break away. He got on its tail, but the maneuverable fighter escaped. He again contacted a H-75, and in a running fight destroyed it when its pilot went into a climbing turn, giving Shields an easy shot. The Hawk caught fire and went into a spinning crash. Shields found himself alone with a number of French fighters milling around. A Hawk got on his tail and hit the Wildcat's wing with shells, and nothing Shields tried would shake the talented French pilot. Soon other Hawks congregated, and in his life-and-death scramble Shields was able to damage one (uncredited) and incredibly evaded his own destruction. Finding himself again over Cazes Airfield, he strafed an American-built (A-20) Douglas DB-7 bomber in Vichy markings, which blew up on the runway just as he passed over it. In his excitement he did not realize that he still had unused incendiary bombs on his wing racks. He decided to make one last run on the airfield, but as he released his bombs a H-75 dove out of the sun. Shells hit the Wildcat's fuel line and filled the cockpit with fumes. Three more H-75s joined the fray, and Shields tried to turn into his attackers, but had to fly for his life as his port guns were empty. An incendiary bullet hit the Wildcat, starting a fire and causing an immediate bailout. As he was floating down infantry on the ground began to shoot at him but missed, and took him prisoner of war. Three days later when the French surrendered Shields was repatriated.

During the short three day battle 109 Wildcats faced 46 Curtiss-built Hawk 75s and 40 Dewoitine 520s. The Americans claimed 26 Vichy aircraft: eight Hawks; five Dewoitines; seven more fighters (Hawks or 520s); and six bombers and five probables. However, two of these "victories" were probably RAF aircraft. The French claimed nine Wildcats and an OS2U, along with a probable and damaged.

With VF-4, Shields went on to score a victory over a Tony on 25 November 1944 for his only other victory. Five pilots who scored victories in "Torch" went on to become aces later against the Japanese in the Pacific: Ens. Will Taylor of VF-41 (one victory in "Torch") got six more with VF-4 in the Pacific; Ens. Marvin J. Franger, VF-9 (two victories) got seven more with VF-9; Ens. Louis A. Menard, VF-9 (one victory) scored seven with VF-9 and one more with VBF-12; Lt(jg) Harold E. Vita, VF-9 (one victory) downed five more with VF-12; and Ens. Bruce D. Jaques, VGF-29 (one victory) became an ace with four and a half more with VF-29 in October 1944.

Note: The first American-built fighter to destroy an enemy aircraft was a F4F Wildcat. Two Royal Navy 804 squadron Wildcats, called the Martlet by the British, were patrolling over Scapa Flow on 25 December 1940. A Luftwaffe reconnaissance Ju-88 out of Bergen, Norway, was intercepted by Lt. L.V. Carver (RN) and Sub Lt. Parke (RNVR). They shot out one engine, forcing its crew to bail out and be taken prisoner.

F4F/USN/PTO First Victory in Type

Pilot: Lt(jg) Wilmer E. Rawie
Time: 1 February 1942/0704
Place: Taroa Airfield, Maloelap Atoll
Unit: VF-6 (3rd Division) *Enterprise*
A/C: F4F-3/Claude

Action: In late January 1942, Task Force 17 with the *Yorktown* and Task Force 8 with the *Enterprise* were sailing towards the Japanese-held Gilbert and Marshall Islands. The group was to carry out the first counter attack by U.S. forces against the Japanese. SBD dive bombers and TBD torpedo bombers (armed with bombs for horizontal attack) were to hit the enemy stronghold at Kwajalein. On the *Enterprise*, Fighting "6," under Lt. Cdr. Wade McClusky, was assigned to surprise Japanese airfields in the northern Marshalls. VB-6 Third Division, under Lt. James Gray, was to bomb Taroa Airfield on Maloelap Atoll, which was supposedly undefended except for a few seaplanes.

Flying as Grey's wingman was 1938 Naval Academy graduate Lt(jg) Wilmer "Will" Rawie, flying a Grumman F4F-3 Wildcat numbered F-14. Having a longer flight, Gray's division left the carrier first in the dark at 0610 in order to attack at sunrise (0700). Arriving at the Atoll, Gray, followed by Rawie, bombed the wrong island. Realizing his mistake, Gray warned his flyers not to waste their bombs and raced off toward Taroa. The island was far from being undefended, and its defenders were not surprised. The Japanese had earlier discovered U.S. Navy warships offshore ready to bombard Taroa. However, the Japanese had not detected Gray's Wildcats, which came in unmolested to drop their bombs. After his first bombing run with Gray, Rawie climbed to 6,000 feet and raced after his leader, following Gray in another dive-bombing and strafing attack on the atoll. After recovering from his dive, Rawie found himself flying in the same direction as a pair of enemy fighters which had been on CAP. Accelerating, he closed on the starboard

Lt(jg) Wilmer Rawie (USN)

fighter, a Claude Type 96 carrier fighter. He fired a long burst at close range, setting it on fire and causing its pilot to bail out. At 0704, the men on the cruiser *Chester* confirmed Rawie's victory, the first for a Navy fighter in the war.

Rawie continued well on past his victim's wingman, bringing his Wildcat into a sharp 180 degree turn into a head-on attack. Neither pilot deviated from this collision course. Rawie's F4F's belly was hit by the Jap's wing, which was crumpling, destroying its aileron. Rawie's tough Wildcat sustained only dents and a sheared antenna. The Claude limped back home, while Rawie headed back to Taroa to strafe. But there he found that his guns were malfunctioning, and soon a Claude was on his tail. Rawie ducked into a nearby cloud bank and escaped back to the *Enterprise*.

Rawie received the DFC for this action. He subsequently scored only 1/3 shared victory in the war and remained in the post war Navy, retiring in 1962 as a Captain. Rawie's victory was the first fighter victory for the Navy. Lt(jg) Clarence Dickenson and his gunner, William Miller, had downed a Zero during the Pearl Harbor attack while flying a SBD Dauntless dive bomber.

Lt. Edward "Butch" O'Hare (USN)

F4F/USN First Ace in Type

Pilot: Lt. Edward H. O'Hare
Time: 20 February 1942/1705-1740
Place: Off the south coast of Bougainville
Unit: VF-3 *Lexington*
A/C: F4F-3/ 5 Bettys
Action: *See PTO First Ace USN*

F4F/USN Top Scorer in Type

Pilot: Ch/Mach. Donald E. Runyon
Unit: VF-6 *Enterprise*
Victories: 8 (+3 in F6F with VF-18)
Record:

V#	Date	E/A/C
1-2 (F4F)	08-07-42	2 Vals
3-4 (F4F)	08-08-42	Betty, Zero
5-8 (F4F)	08-24-42	3 Vals, Zero
9 (F6F)	11-11-43	Val
10 (F6F)	01-04-44	Jake
11 (F6F)	02-22-44	Betty

Action: The First Marine Division landed 19,000 troops on the north central coast of Guadalcanal on 7 August 1942. The invasion was supported by 99 F4F-4 Wildcats from VF-5 off the *Saratoga*, VF-6 off the *Enterprise*, and VF-7 off the *Wasp*. Flying search, strike, and strafing missions, the stubby fighter destroyed 25 Japanese aircraft in the air and many floatplanes on the ground (sea) this first day.

The first enemy air attack occurred at 1300 by 27 Mitsubishi Betty bombers sortied from Rabaul escorted by 17 Zeros. In the combat the Japanese 25th Air Flotilla lost seven Bettys and two Zeros, while the Navy lost nine Wildcats and a SBD dive bomber. After the attack, six VF-6 Wildcats led by 29 year old Chief Machinist Donald Runyon returned to the *Enterprise* after an uneventful patrol. *Enterprise* Air Group Commander Lt. Louis Bauer selected his squadron leaders on ability, so an enlisted machinist like Runyon was able to lead ensigns and lieutenants in combat. As soon as the six landed they were refueled and launched toward Savo to reinforce the CAP over the destroyer screen protecting the transports there. Runyon, with Ens. Emeral Cook, Ens. Harry March, Mach. Patrick Nagle, AP1 Howard Packard, and Ens. Joseph Shoemaker took off at 1400. As they approached station, AA was spotted over the destroyers. Runyon realized that the Japanese had targeted the vulnerable transports off Guadalcanal's "Red Beach" and skirted the flak bursts to reach the battle. The Japanese had dispatched ten fixed-gear Val dive bombers with the first attack, but due to their slower speed they had arrived an hour after the attack. Runyon made a high side diving run on a Val over Laguna Point, but missed as it dove away, only to be shot down by Packard. Runyon leveled off and spotted the wingman of his escaped Val coming head on. Runyon fired on this Val at the same time that his wingman, "Dutch" Shoemaker, made a beam attack. Their target cartwheeled and exploded into the sea. (Shoemaker later gave Runyon credit for this victory). Runyon saw two Vals at wave top level heading back to Rabaul. He dove, firing at 200 yards for a victory, while Ens. March got the other Val. Seven of ten Vals were shot down, and

Japanese records show the other three did not reach Rabaul because of battle damage and/or lack of fuel. Runyon, Packard, and March just made it back to the carrier on their last gallons of fuel, while Cook, Nagle, and Shoemaker had to land on the *Saratoga*, which was closer.

The following day the *"Big E"* was operating southwest of Guadalcanal, providing CAP for the carrier and cruiser screen located off Savo Island. Japanese R.Adm. Yamada sent his remaining 23 Bettys and nine Vals with a strong Zero escort to destroy the American carriers. The enemy bombers, carrying torpedoes, evaded the primitive U.S. radar by coming in low over the mountains north of the American ships. Runyon led three Wildcats at 17,000 feet when the FDO radioed a warning of the approaching Bettys over the eastern end of Florida Island. Runyon dove and made a flat beam attack on the lead bomber, which he missed. He turned sharply, met a second bomber head on, and made a successful firing pass. Ens. Wildon Rouse got the bomber Runyon missed with a point blank stern attack. While searching for another target Rouse found a Zero on his tail and Shoemaker on the Zero's tail. This Zero turned quickly to port to avoid Shoemaker, only to cross into Runyon's head on fire and crashed into the sea. The Japanese air attack hit the destroyer *Jarvis*, but lost all its aircraft. That evening, V.Adm. Frank Fletcher withdrew his valuable carriers from the Guadalcanal, as a strong enemy cruiser and destroyer force had come on the scene, and also Fletcher had fuel worries.

On 24 August, Fletcher moved Task Force 61, which consisted of the *Enterprise* and *Saratoga* (the *Wasp* was refueling), against V.Adm. Nagumo's carriers *Shokaku* and *Kuikaku*. The ensuing combat was to be the first of two carrier battles off Guadalcanal: the Battles of the Eastern Solomons and Santa Cruz. U.S. carrier radar reported bogies, and all of Fighting 6's 28 Wildcats were launched between 1637 and 1645. Runyon led his division up sun five miles from the carrier. The altitude advantage enabled him to dive onto the Val leader, exploding it at 15,000 feet. Using his diving speed to regain altitude, Runyon positioned himself in the sun. He dove on the Japanese bomber "Vs" and hit another, causing it to burn with a

large plume of smoke into the sea. Runyon again converted speed into altitude and began his third attack when a stream of tracers flashed past him from a Zero high astern. Runyon chopped his throttle, and the speeding Zero passed below; he headed down, giving the Zero a short, fatal burst. His diving attack had put him below the Val formation, but again his speed allowed him to climb quickly to get a belly shot, claiming an easy third victory for the day. An escorting Zero dove on Runyon, who continued to climb, firing on the approaching Jap, who turned away toward home, smoking heavily to become another of the 54 victories the U.S. Navy claimed that day. Runyon had gotten four victories, and the last of eight in 2 1/2 weeks to become the top scoring Navy Wildcat pilot.

Runyon later flew F6F Hellcats as a Lt(jg) off the *Bunker Hill* on VF-18's first tour, claiming three more victories. Runyon's eight victories were the most Navy Wildcat victories, but Lt. Ralph Elliott of VC-27 got nine flying the FM-2, which was an improved Wildcat variant built by General Motors. Lt. Stanley Vejtasa of VF-10 was second in the F4F with 7 1/2 victories, of which seven came in one day (26 October 1942).

By mid-November the crucial phase of the battle for Guadalcanal had passed. The Wildcat's glory days came in its 12 months in the Solomons, where it gained a 3 to 1 victory ratio over the Japanese. The introduction of the F6F Hellcat marked the end of the Wildcat's career, and by September 1943 there were no F4F units operational.

U.S. NAVY F4F Wildcat Aces (23 Aces/134.67 Victories)

Ace Name	Rank	Unit	F4F V	Total V
Runyon, Donald	Ens	VF-6	8	11
Vetjasa, Stanley	Lt	VF-10	7.25	10
Jensen, Hayden	Lt	VF-5	7	7
Register, Francis	Lt(jg)	VF-5, 6	7	7
Brassfield, Arthur	Lt(jg)	VF-42, 3	6.33	6.33
McCusky, Scott	Lt(jg)	VF-42, 3	6.33	13.33
Flatley, James	LCdr	VF-10, 42	6	6
Leonard, William	Lt	VF-42,3,11	6	6
Starkes, Carlton	Lt	VF-5	6	6
Stimpson, Charles	Lt(jg)	VF-11	6	6
Torkelson, Ross	Lt	VGF11,		
VF21			6	6
Thach, John	LCdr	VF-3	6	6
Roach, Thomas	Lt(jg)	VF-21	5.5	5.5
Symmes, John	Lt	VF-21	5.5	5.5
Vorse, Albert	Lt	VF-3,2,6	5.5	11.5
Wrenn, George	Ens.	VF-72	5.25	5.25
Bright, Mark	Lt	VF-5	5	5
Gaylor, Noel	Lt	VF-3, 2	5	5
Graham, Vernon	Lt(jg)	VF-11	5	5
Mankin, Lee	AP/1c	VF-6	5	5
O'Hare, Edward	Lt	VF-3	5	5
Sutherland, John	Lt	VF-8,72,10	5	5
Wesolowski, J.M.	Lt(jg)	VF-5	5	7
Others	——	——	——	——
Haas, Walter	Lt(jg)	VF-42, 3	4.83	4.83
Swope, James	Lt(jg)	VF-11	4.67	9.67

Ch/Mach. Donald Runyon (USMC)

Flying the F4F Wildcat (USN)
By
William Leonard:
6 victories VF-42, -3 & -11

Like all Grumman fighters, the cockpit had plenty of room once the pilot squeezed through its narrow opening. It was well-tailored for the average-sized pilot. The seat was adjustable, if you knew how to use your thigh muscles. The rudder pedals were nicely adjustable for the shorties. The oxygen system was an up-to-date dilution-demand type and worked well. The hand cranked landing gear was a pain to use, but bearable due to its simplicity. The instrument panel had a fair layout, but the magnetic compass was difficult to see. The fuel gauge was wildly inaccurate, and I had to use the clock to keep in touch with my fuel situation. The gun charging was all manual and a chore, but luckily it did not have to be done often. The F4F-3/4 conformed well to USN standards for stability and control. Rudder control at takeoff and low speeds was deficient and caused problems. At high combat speeds the F4F had excellent control and response. Too bad it didn't have enough engine to fly that way and still maintain altitude. During taxiing we had to zigzag due to the nose-high stance. Vision in flight was good, except directly aft, but we had a rear view mirror to help there.

The Pratt & Whitney R-1830 engine was highly reliable and trouble-free. It was rugged, and stood up to the high demands from the airframe and pilots. It had a large weight investment in the 2-speed, 2-stage supercharger, which was underused in 1942, when our fighters found full employment at moderate altitudes. The engine was always willing, and put out without overheat or complaint. It just did not have enough power to pull the heavy Wildcat around the sky. The P&Ws were hard diving and fast rolling, and saved many lives. It was hard to start with the shotgun starter in the humid Pacific conditions. The Curtiss electric prop also had some reliability problems. The Wildcat did not have enough onboard fuel capacity (147 gallons), so it was quite short-legged and short-winded. On Guadalcanal two 58 gallon underwing auxiliary tanks were introduced. While they added range and endurance, they decreased performance and had to be jettisoned before combat. These tanks were ungauged, and along with the deceiving main fuel tank

gauge made fuel-remaining estimation a chronic problem. Climbing to altitude was very slow, and cruising was hot and noisy, and definitely not hands off flying!

The .50 caliber was a good piece, but needed care and understanding. In good hands it was a winner. The F4F-3's mounted 4 x .50 cal. with corresponding ammunition was tolerable, but the F4F-4 with 6 x .50 cal. had less ammunition, and consequently was a poorer battery. They were impressive for strafing. I had a good hit on a Japanese destroyer on 4 May 1942, running him aground. The Mark 8 reflector gun sight was adequate, but poorly mounted and difficult to use on the F4F-3. Although installed somewhat cleaner and easier to use on the F4F-4, it became a threat to the pilot, as it projected into the pilot's face on landing.

Grumman's "Iron Works" had a way of putting together a rugged airframe. When perforated or bashed it still could fly and fight. There was no armored seat, but there were steel plates on the bulkheads ahead and behind the pilot. The main fuel tanks were self-sealing. The auxiliary tanks were inerted with CO_2.

The fighter came in fast and hard, and was difficult to slow down on carrier landings. The average pilot, with some experience, could master well-behaved carrier deck landings. On field landings there was a tendency to ground loop, usually without much harm, except to the pilot ego. Time and experience was the usual remedy. Early Wildcats did not have shoulder straps until the Summer of 1942. On our over water flights we suffered from the dread of having to ditch. The F4F landed fast and sank fast, and the pilot was usually knocked senseless by the gun sight or instrument panel. It was not much better on carrier landings, where our faces jerked toward the gun sight when the arrester hook caught.

When aware of the strengths and weaknesses of the F4F-3/4, a knowledgeable pilot could earn his keep. He needed to remember: do not dogfight, keep speed up, and watch your fuel, then you can tally, come home, and repeat. You could develop an affection for a machine like that!

F4F/USMC First Victory in Type
Pilots: 2Lt. David D. Kliewer
        T/Sgt. William J. Hamilton
Time: 9 December 1941/1145
Place: Wake Island: SE over Peacock Pt.
Unit: VMF-211
A/C: F4F-3/Betty
Action: *See PTO First Victory in Type USMC*

Neither pilot scored again during the heroic struggle for Wake. On 12 December at 1600, Kliewer spotted a surfaced Japanese submarine 25 miles offshore and made an attack, strafing and then dropping two 100lb. bombs, which exploded within 15 feet of the sub. The sub, which was suspected to have been directing Japanese air attacks on the island, was probably sunk. Hamilton, an enlisted man with many years experience, did yeoman's work, salvaging and cannibalizing damaged aircraft and putting them back into combat. VMF-211 lost only two F4Fs in actual combat, while claiming nine victories over Wake. Capt. Henry T. Elrod was credited with downing two Bettys on 10 December despite heavy friendly AA fire. On the 23rd he heroically led the remaining men of VMF-211 on the

Lt. William Leonard (Author/Leonard)

2Lt. David Kliewer and T/Sgt. William Hamilton. (USMC)

ground against the Japanese invasion of the island. He was posthumously awarded the Congressional Medal of Honor for these actions. 2Lt. Robert M. Hanna, who commanded VMF-211 AA units, and his men held out after the surrender with only ten survivors, of which nine were wounded. Meanwhile Lt. Kliewer and a three man detail located at the end of the runway unsuccessfully tried to set off dynamite charges planted under the airstrip. Unfortunately, the generator wires shorted in the previous night's rain. Despite enemy fire they continued to try to explode the charges even after the surrender. Finally, they were forced to surrender.

Wake was a costly victory for the Japanese. During the sixteen days of fighting they lost 820 killed and 333 wounded, while the Americans lost 120 killed and 49 wounded. The POWs were evacuated from Wake on 12 January 1942 on a grueling 12 day voyage to China. After 44 months of harsh treatment and forced labor, moving from China to Korea, and finally to work coal mines on the Japanese mainland, the U.S. 1st Cavalry Division liberated the surviving Wake POWs in mid-September 1945. Of the 1,462 American POWs evacuated from Wake, 231 died in camp, aboard ship, or escaping. Another 98 left on Wake to operate heavy equipment were executed in October 1943.

F4F/USMC First Ace in Type
Pilot: Capt. Marion E. Carl
Time: 24 August 1942/1430
Place: Offshore Guadalcanal area
Unit: VMF-223
A/C: F4F-4/Bettys,2 Kates, Zero
Action: *See PTO First Ace USMC*

Capt. Marion Carl (Author/Carl)

F4F/USMC Top Scorer in Type
Pilot: Capt. Joseph J. Foss
Unit: VMF-121
Victories: 26
Record:

V#	Date	E/A/C
1	10-13-42	Zero
2	10-14-42	Zero
3-5	10-18-42	2 Zeros, Bomber
6-7	10-20-42	2 Zeros
8-11	10-23-42	4 Zeros
12-16	10-25-42	5 Zeros
17-19	11-07-42	2 Petes, Rufe
20-22	11-12-42	2 Bettys, Zero
23	11-15-42	Float plane
24-26	01-15-43	3 Zeros

Action:

Top Marine Corps ace Joseph Foss was born on a South Dakota farm outside Souix Falls on 17 April 1915. After his father was electrocuted, Foss tried to take care of the farm and attend Augustana College in 1934. The pressure made him drop out of school after a year, but he and his younger brother made the farm profitable, and he enrolled part time in Souix Falls College. During this time he became engrossed with flying, and in 1937 soloed using money he earned playing saxophone. In 1939 he went to the University of South Dakota, where he helped start an aviation course, getting over 100 hours flying time. After graduation he hitchhiked to Minneapolis to enlist in the Marine Corps. After spending seven months at Pensacola he was commissioned as a 2Lt., getting his wings at the end of March 1941 an "old" man at 26. He spent time as an instructor, and then was assigned to a photo squadron. Through persistence he managed to become carrier-qualified in the F4F and got himself assigned to VMF-121, which shipped to Guadalcanal in October 1942.

**Capt. Joseph Foss.
(USMC)**

When -121 arrived the Japanese had concentrated their efforts on reinforcing the island. On the night of 11-12 October, the naval battle of Cape Esperance forestalled Japanese attempts to land troops and equipment. The next day the Japanese sent back-to-back air raids to Henderson Field. The first raid came in undetected until the last moment, and heavy damage was sustained to the field. Two hours later, while most Wildcats were refueling, the second wave attacked. Foss led three divisions aloft. He noticed his wingman suddenly peel off and found that he was alone. Looking up, he found the reason his squadronmates had left him; a large number of Zeros were closing in on him. The Jap leader, anxious for a kill, pulled out of his firing pass just in front of Foss, who flicked off a shot and exploded the Zero. Foss was chased back to the field with his engine out and made a harrowing crash landing, safe but much the wiser. Undaunted, he got another Zero the next day.

During the 33 days Foss spent in combat over Guadalcanal he would become a legend. Wearing his faded lucky hunting cap and clenching a cigar between his teeth, he used the years of bird hunting as a boy to become the top-scoring Marine ace. Most of his victories were deflection shots, with pairs of his six guns boresighted at 250, 300, and 350 yards. His next six scoring combats would see him rack up a double, three triples, a quadruple, and an ace-in-a-day for 20 victories total. He would become an ace on his fifth day in combat when he got two Zeros and a bomber. Foss got four Zekes on the 23rd, and then became the first Marine "ace-in-a-day" when he downed two Zeros on a morning sortie and added three more in the afternoon. He would pass John Smith's Marine Corps leading 19 victories on 7 November. On that day –121 located a large formation of float planes 120 miles northwest of Henderson. The maneuverable, little Japanese aircraft were no match for the Wildcats, as eight were destroyed, including two Petes and a Rufe by Foss. On his way back to base he got lost in a series of squall lines and ran out of fuel, ditching off Malaita. He spent the night with a coastwatcher and was rescued by a PBY the next day.

On 12 November the Japanese began a concerted effort to retake Guadalcanal. They sent 25 Bettys and eight escorting Zeros, which were spotted by a coastwatcher, giving Henderson warning. Foss led seven pilots to 29,000 feet, covering USN transports unloading Army reinforcements off Kukum Point. Henderson radar lost the Bettys at 30 miles out because they dove from 20,000 feet to get under American CAP. Instead of the customary horizontal bombing Bettys, these were torpedo bombers heading to take out the transports. Foss spotted the Japanese through some broken cloud and took off after them. However, the precipitous dive caused windscreens to frost, which had to be scratched off with finger nails. The Marines caught the Bettys just as they began their runs. Army P-400s and VMF-112 Wildcats joined the fray. Foss got within 100 yards of the closest bomber and hit its starboard engine. He had to pull up quickly, as the Jap bounced off the water. Foss was chasing a Betty when a Zeke began a firing run on him. In a quick maneuver, Foss snapped off a great deflection shot, exploding the fighter just above the water. He then turned his attention back to the Betty and flamed it. He ended the day as the first American pilot to score 20 or more victories in WWII, and put him only four victories behind Eddie Rickenbacker's American record of 26 set in WWI. Three days later Foss, wracked with malaria and dysentery, got another float plane for his 23rd victory. For the next six weeks he was forced to recuperate in New Zealand.

By the time he returned to combat in January 1943, VMF-121 was flying combat over New Georgia. On the 15th, VMF-121 escorted SBDs in a late afternoon strike against a cargo ship northwest of Munda. In the battle Foss downed three Zeros to tie Rickenbacker. On 25 January, he was returned to the States to receive the Congressional Medal of Honor. When VMF-121 left combat it had scored 132 victories—72 by Foss' "Flying Circus Flight"—for a loss of only 14 pilots.

Foss saw no more combat, but the post war years brought the personable, dry-witted veteran further renown. He was elected Governor of South Dakota, served as President of the American Football League in its difficult early years, and retired from the Air Force Reserve as a Brig. General.

The Wildcat's twenty month combat stint ended in the Northern Solomons in September 1943. The Corsair had proved itself in combat, and the Hellcat was arriving in the Pacific. In their time Wildcat squadrons were credited with 986 victories, 282 carrier-based and 704 land-based, with 497 Navy and 489 Marine. The stubby little aircraft produced 65 aces, 34 Marine Corps and 31 Navy.

Marine aces over Guadalcanal (L-R): Maj. John Smith (19 v./#2 USMC F4F ace); Maj. Robert Galer (14 v./#4); and Capt. Marion Carl 16 1/2 v./#3). (Author/Carl)

U.S. MARINE CORPS F4F-4 Wildcat Aces
(34 Aces/300.5 Victories)

Ace Name	Rank	Unit (VMF)	F4F V.	Total V.
Foss, Joseph	Maj	121	26	26
Smith, John	Maj	223	19	19
Carl, Marion	Capt	221, 223	16.5	18.5
Galer, Robert	Maj	224	14	14
Marontate, William	1Lt	121	13	13
Trowbridge, Eugene	2Lt	223	11	11
Frazier, Kenneth	2Lt	223	12.5	13.5
Bauer, Harold	LCol	223,224,212	10	10
Conger, Jack	1Lt	223, 212	10	10
Everton, Loren	Capt	223, 212	10	12
Mann, Thomas	2Lt	224, 121	9.5	9.5
Loesch, Gregory	Capt	121	8.5	8.5
DeBlanc, Jefferson	1Lt	112	8	9
Hollowell, George	2Lt	224	8	8
Dobbin, John	Maj	224	7.5	7.5
Hamilton, Henry	M/G	223, 212	7	7
Narr, Joseph	2Lt	121	7	7
Swett, James	1Lt	221	7	15.5
Haberman, Roger	2Lt	121	6.5	6.5
Freeman, William	2Lt	121	6	6
Kunz, Charles	2Lt	224	6	8
Pond, Zenneth	2Lt	223	6	6
Stout, Robert	1Lt	224, 212	6	6
Yost, Donald	Capt	121	6	8
Payne, Frederick	Maj	223, 212	5.5	5.5
Davis, Leonard	Maj	121	5	5
Doyle, Cecil	2Lt	121	5	5
Drury, Frank	1Lt	223, 212	5	6
Fontana, Paul	Maj	112	5	5
Kendrick, Charles	2Lt	223	5	5
Percy, James	1Lt	112	5	6
Phillips, Hyde	2Lt	223	5	5
Pierce, Francis	Capt	121	5	5
Ramlo, Orvin	2Lt	223	5	5

Flying the F4F Wildcat (USMC)
By
George Hollowell:
8 victories VMF-224 (land-based)

When I arrived on Guadalcanal in August 1942, I was 21 years old, I had left college after three years, and was overwhelmed by what was going on in my life and the world. I was a 2Lt. with about 300 hours in all types of aircraft, but I had a grand total of 43 hours in the F4F! My unit, VMF-224, had been ferried from Hawaii to Efate in the New Hebrides on the aircraft transport *Kitty Hawk*, which was a converted Sea Trains banana boat with rails in the well deck. Our aircraft were snaked out of the well deck onto the escort carrier *Long Island*, which was moored next to us. We were to be catapulted for a flight to nearby Joe Bauer Airfield on Efate. I had only one actual carrier qualification, and it did not help our confidence when one of the F4F's "fell off" the end of the carrier deck when the black powder catapult did not ignite properly. We stayed overnight at Efate while our Wildcats were fitted with belly tanks, and we RON-ed to the "Canal." We had never been trained for anything like we encountered when we landed at Henderson Field. We had to contend with the Jap Navy coming down the "Slot" to shell us each night, the Jap Air Force overhead day and night, and the situation on the ground not secure, with the sounds of battle going on nearby. Aircraft servicing facilities were very basic, and a determined team effort was needed to get things done. All our fuel was flown in by DC-3s in 55-gallon drums, which had to be manhandled onto jeeps to be taken to the flight line and then hand-pumped through a chamois cloth filter directly into the aircraft. Rearming the guns and bombs was a laborious, backbreaking process. Our crews were super! We had problems greasing our guns. Too much would freeze at high altitudes and too little would mean we would have dirt problems and they would stick. When properly serviced the machine guns worked very well.

We always tried to park in the same spot after each mission to save confusion and time during a scramble. When we first got to Henderson all aircraft took off, landed, parked, refueled, rearmed, and were serviced and repaired there. It had single runway, and there were traffic problems at the best of times, especially during night operations. It was covered by Marsden steel matting, which tended to sink into the chronic mud with all the traffic. After a while the Marine squadrons decided to move to "Fighter One," which was a weed-covered field that we named the "Cow Pasture." This apparent self-imposed hardship turned out to be a smart move, as it allowed us to disperse our precious fighters from the daily Japanese attacks.

The F4F cockpit was small! I was 6'1", and it was very cramped and uncomfortable, and even the movable seat didn't help. But once in combat I was too busy to notice. The instruments were rather primitive, but to a 2Lt. who finished flight school in a F3F biplane with an open cockpit, it seemed almost futuristic. I had one of the two F4Fs in the squadron with a hand wobble pump, while the others had an electric pump. The pump handle was a pistol grip attached to the end of a rod that stuck out of the lower left side of the cockpit dash. The WP was used to maintain fuel pressure to the engine above 10-11,000 feet, where pressure was required to keep the engine running. While working this pump you used up a great amount of oxygen. I don't know if it was my ability or lack of it, because the other hand wobble pump aircraft went to only the enlisted NAPs we had in the squadron to fly.

Takeoff was always fun, turning the 13 full revolutions of the landing gear crank handle with the right hand while flying with the left, hoping you did not catch up with the aircraft that took off just before you. During the time the gear was in transit, you had better not let go of the handle. If the gear made a full descent on its own, its wishbone shape could cause it to be easily broken, which could certainly be a problem on the next landing! So if you had to let go, to stop it you had to put your right leg in front of it and suffer a painful knock on your shin. Once the wheels were up you could shift to flying with your right hand and get into formation. I was under the gun to do so, as I was (squadron CO) Bob Galer's wingman. Takeoff in my case was full throttle, "butterfly," tighten the throttle so there would be no slipping, then with the left hand start "wobbling" (pumping)! The climb to altitude was agonizingly slow. Thanks to the brave and wonderful coast watchers on the islands in Jap Air Force's path towards us, we got some advanced warning by radio. If it weren't for them we would have been in very bad shape, being caught on the ground or at best just climbing up to meet them.

We needed the height advantage to even think about engaging the Japs in combat. We had the most rugged aircraft and could take hits, having cockpit and seat armor and self-sealing fuel tanks. It could come home. We could put the F4F into a dive and not be afraid it would lose its wings in the pull out. I have had a Zero make high sides on me while in a vertical dive, but he could not stay there because he could lose a wing. Our air combat strategy was to have the altitude advantage over the enemy, dive on him, shoot, and then dive away. Never get into a dogfight!

Faster would have been better, but the best thing about the F4F was that it was reliable and rugged and brought you home. Later, I flew the F4U Corsair, which was superior in every way, but that is another story.

Flying the F4F Wildcat (USMC)
By
Jeff DeBlanc:
8 F4F victories VMF-112 (CMH)

I am only 5'9" tall and weighed about 155 pounds back then, so the Wildcat cockpit was very comfortable for me. The seat could easily be moved up and down and fore and aft. The oxygen system left a lot to be desired. We had only nose fitting masks, which were only one step above the mouth insert tube in the earlier fighters we flew in training. Later we were equipped with the full-face mask. To qualify for our flight physical there was the useless requirement that the cadet had to have no overbite so as to fit into this mask, which in reality was no problem. Our heater seldom functioned, but it was rarely needed over the tropical Solomons, and because we rarely flew at high altitudes.

The instrument layout suited me to a tee, as the panel and switches were located at my fingertips. The engine unit gauge and basic flight instruments—needle, ball, and air speed indicator—were very visible and readable. The switches were readily avail-

2Lt. George Hollowell.
(Author/Hollowell)

able by the visual or Braille method. The stick, flaps, and gun chargers were ok. But hand cranking to raise or lower the wheels was a real chore. As a ham radio operator, I found the "coffee grinder" radio was inadequate. I did not appreciate the frequency and the stability of the Arc 5 transmitters and receivers. The VFOs would drift, and fading was a factor. Lee Roy Grumman's carrier fighter designs were known for their outstanding visibility in taxiing, take-offs, and landing. In combat the pilot had to bank for a full view.

The Pratt & Whitney R-1830 was a good engine that could take a lot of punishment and get you home after taking some hits. I did not trust the automatic General Electric propeller pitch control for short takeoffs. The only time I used automatic prop pitch was on long Stateside runways. I saw S/Sgt. Conti takeoff before me from Fighter 2 on Guadalcanal in auto pitch control and crash to his death in the coconut palms at the end of the runway. I always lifted off the runway in manual prop pitch with max manifold pressure until I was airborne during combat tours. The engine generally had the blowers wired open during our flights from that cow pasture called Henderson Field. The range of the Wildcat was short, with an internal gas tank of 180 gallons and a small emergency tank. The external connections for the wing tanks were very unreliable during the "dark days" on the Canal.

The Wildcat used brute force to climb to altitude. One had to get a lot of forward speed (160 kts or better) *before* easing back on the stick to get a clean rate of climb. When you had to switch blowers at 14,000 feet, the engine would often quit or you had an excess of manifold pressure after the blower cut, in which case you had to immediately take off or blow your rate of climb. The Wildcat was a flying brick at cruise, but I did enjoy the soothing and reliable comfort of cruise speed, which made the F4F a good escort fighter.

1Lt. Jefferson DeBlanc (Author/DeBlanc)

I never flew the Wildcat in the 235 hours of cadet training before shipping out. I had less than nine hours in it before I was thrown into the thick of the air fighting over Guadalcanal. I had never fired guns or flown at night until I got there. But to me the fighter was a perfect gun platform to shoot from in terms of the aerodynamics of flight: a mid-wing with square wing tips. In combat, I fought with only four guns, saving two for the return home. Our "coach," Lt.Col. Joe Bauer, told us: "Dogfight the Zeros, they are just paper kites," and I did just that. I did not fear the Zero on a head on run, or even on my tail. Head on he was a dead man. On my tail, I could always rely on skidding and my armor plate to protect me. Over Japanese territory we would have to accept combat with them, but could always use our diving capabilities to break away whenever we wanted. The weakness of the Wildcat was its lack of speed and weight when compared to the Zero.

Landing was the tricky part of flying the land based F4F. Since the distance between the wheels was narrow and made for carrier landings, ground loops were a real problem. The answer to landing was simple once the pilot mastered the technique. After flare out, the pilot had to take his toes *off the brakes* and fishtail the plane to keep it straight *until all flying speed was lost*; *then* gently toe the brakes to keep it going straight.

One topic I am highly qualified to address on the Wildcat is bailout and ditching, as I accomplished both in my career. On a pre-dawn patrol over Guadalcanal my engine seized after an oil line broke. I trimmed the plane to 110 kts and climbed out on the wing three times to bail out, losing my nerve each time. I had seen one of our pilots jump and not have his chute open. I finally strapped back in and went on instruments to glide toward the sea. Luckily, I saw the phosphorescent wakes of our ships below that lit up a beautiful landing field below. Although I did not drop my wing tank, my wheels up landing was perfect in the wake of the *USS Jenkins*. I had time to unbuckle my seat belt and drag out the rubber boat from under the parachute seat pack to inflate and paddle off before the plane sank. Two days after the ditching I was shot down in a wild dogfight. With the plane on fire, this time I had no choice but to bail out. I remembered the bail out instructions from flight school: dive for the trailing edge of the wing. I cleared the tail and floated down through the middle of a dogfight. I managed to avoid being strafed in my chute, but then my problem was landing in the ocean below. In those days I had 20/10 eyesight and could judge distances well. But it was past 1800 hours, and the water was glassy, making things difficult to judge. We were trained to release from our chute just before our feet touched the water to prevent the collapsed chute from covering you. I released at what I thought was 10 feet, but due to the smooth surface it turned out to be closer to 40 feet. Needless to say, I survived.

Although the Wildcat was the only first line fighter we had to fight the Japanese Zero, I felt confident in the cockpit of this little fighter for four reasons:
(1) Foremost in my mind is the outstanding stable gun platform it provided, namely; square-tipped wings supporting six .50 caliber machine guns. This provided less aerodynamic drag and assured stability in all flight positions during the gunnery run.

(2) The pilot's seat was on the plane's center of gravity, which lessened the chance of blackout during the pull of G-forces during combat.

(3) The instrument panel was ideal for all conditions.

(4) Generally, the Wildcat was "Idiot proof." During a pre-dawn emergency scramble, I became airborne and saw the pitot tube cover in position in the light glaring from the wing tip. I had forgotten to remove it in my excitement to take off. Regardless, I flew the entire mission with "zero airspeed" and landed without looking at the airspeed indicator for help. Stability and touch were built into this aircraft.

Eastern FM-2 Wildcat

FM-2 First Victory in Type
Pilots: Lt. John Dinneen
        Ens. Rufus Kirk
Time: 20 March 1944/1700
Place: North of New Ireland
Unit: VC-63/*Natoma Bay*
A/C: FM-2/Tony

Action: In February 1942, the success and increased need for the F4F Wildcat led its manufacturer (Grumman), with War production Board urging, to allow General Motors to establish its Eastern Aircraft Division for the manufacture of the fighter. From its idle Linden, New Jersey, automobile factory, GM converted the facility into a mass-production aircraft factory. The first FM-1s, accepted in September 1942, were identical to the last Grumman F4F-4s, except they had four guns instead of six. In November, the first XF4F-8 was completed. This lighter, more powerful fighter was designated the FM-2, and began production in December 1943 when the FM-1 ceased production. During 1944, almost 2,900 FM-2s were built, which was 40% of all Wildcats produced.

FM-2s were deployed to escort carriers in early 1944. In the reduction of Rabaul, it was decided to bypass the stronghold of Kavieng on north New Ireland and capture the small island of Emirau. In the operation the fast carriers would not be needed, and the CVEs *Manila Bay* and *Natoma Bay* were to provide air support. On 20 March 1944, a Japanese plane closed on TG36.3 and a division of FM-2s was dispatched from each carrier. Finally, after a 50-mile pursuit, the eight Wildcats surrounded a hapless Tony. Two pilots from each carrier made several firing passes before Lt. John Dinneen and Ens. Rufus Kirk off the *Natoma Bay* finally downed the Jap for its only victory of the war, but the first for the FM-2. After this initial victory several more VC squadrons scored sporadic victories leading up to the Battle of Leyte Gulf on 24-25 October 1944, which would become the signature battle for the FM-2s.

FM-2 First Ace in Type
Pilot: Lt. Kenneth G. Hippe
Time: 24 October 1944/0840-0900
Place: Northern Leyte
Unit: VC-*3/ Kalinin Bay*
A/C: FM-2/ 5 Lilys

Action: On 24 October 1944, the Battle of Leyte Gulf began and would spell the death knell for the Imperial Japanese Navy. Six "Jeep" carriers of Task Force 77.4 ("Taffy 1") were assigned to fly CAP over the invasion beaches, providing ground support for MacArthur's newly-landed troops. Division leader of VC-3, Lt. Ken Hippe, was leading four FM-2s on CAP at 10,000 feet. At 0830 radar vectored them towards Leyte Gulf to the northwest. Hippe picked up a lone Ki-48 Lily, made a high-side run on it, and shot it down. The Lily was a decoy intended to lure the Americans away from the main attack force incoming over Lungi Point at 20,000 feet. Radar picked up this Japanese formation and vectored the FM-2s towards them. Since the weather was clear, visual contact was quickly made on "Vs" of 21 Lily kamikazes in a dive directed at the American transports.

At 0900 Hippe and his wingman, Ens. John Buchanan, made a high side run on the formation. As the Japanese were quickly closing on the transports, the Navy pilots realized that there wasn't time to make successive runs and stayed on the Lily's tails. Hippe in his

Natoma Bay

Lt. Kenneth Hippe. (Author/Hippe)

excitement forgot to drop his wing tanks, and waded into a "V" of four Japanese bombers. He attacked the first high astern, flaming it with hits on the wing and fuselage. Continuing on he got the second from below, and then burned the third and fourth, running out of ammunition. As he descended, he followed a lone Lily through friendly AA fire. He considered ramming it, but thought AA would get it, but unfortunately it crashed a LST. In the combat, the astern attacks covered his windshield with oil, which made it difficult to see the landing signal officer on the *Kalinin Bay*. Hippe had to lean out of his cockpit to land safely on the small carrier deck.

For this five or six minute combat, in which he became an "instant ace," Hippe was awarded the Navy Cross. In the combat his division destroyed 12 Lilys and claimed two probables (Buchanan, his wingman, got three). Hippe would never see another Japanese plane in the war, and VC-3 would only score five more victories.

FM-2 Top Scorer in Type
Pilot: Lt. Ralph E. Elliott
Unit: VC-27/ *Savo Island*
A/C: FM-2 "*Baldy*"
Victories: 9
Record:

V#	Date	E/A/C
1-3.5	10-24-44	3 1/2 Frances
4.5 –5.5	10-25-44	2 Tojos
6	10-27-44	1/2 Val
7	12-15-44	Oscar
8-9	01-05-45	1/2 Tony, 1/2 Jack, Jill

Action: Lt. Ralph Elliott flew his FM-2, nicknamed "*Baldy*," with Composite Squadron VC-27 off the jeep carrier *Savo Island*. Elliott, the squadron operations officer, took part in the massive three day Battle of Leyte Gulf (24-26 October 1944), in which the FM-2 would first prove itself. Eighteen escort carriers carrying 228 FM-2s comprised the three tactical units Taffy 1, 2, and 3, which were assigned to TF 77.4. On 24 October, VC-27 "The Saints" of Taffy 2 spotted a large force of Japanese Frances (Sally?) bombers headed for the vulnerable transports anchored off the Leyte invasion beaches. The

FM-2s had the altitude advantage when Elliott and his wingman dove on the leading bomber, making several high side beam firing passes and hitting it to share the victory. Elliott moved behind a second bomber and flamed its starboard engine, spinning the victim into the ocean. He quickly got astern another bomber, blowing off its port wing. The determined Japanese kamikaze formation, despite its heavy losses, continued to close on the transports and prepared to dive to their deaths. Elliott dove after a diving kamikaze, but could not catch it before it hit an LST. Navy anti-aircraft fire drove Elliott out of the area to search for other targets. Soon he saw another Frances starting its dive. This time Elliott was able to catch up and put several rounds in its cockpit for 3 1/2 victories on the day.

The following day V.Adm. Kurita's massive force of four battleships, eight cruisers, and eleven destroyers broke into Leyte Gulf to threaten the transports and troops on the beaches, and thus the entire invasion. The heroic attack by 180 FM-2s and 120 TBMs off the escort carriers helped to save the day in a one-sided battle which will live forever in the annals of naval history. At 1632, Taffy 2 was on CAP and vectored towards a large formation of 18 Vals and a mixed bag of 16-18 Zero and Tojo escorts. Elliott's four plane division made the initial contact, and the outnumbered Americans went into a weave as the escort fighters peeled off to attack. A Tojo crossed in front of Elliott, who exploded its engine. He then broke up a Tojo attack on another FM-2. The enemy pilot tried to split-S, but Elliott, a superb pilot, being a flight instructor in his early war years, put .50 cal. shells into the Jap's wing roots, destroying it to become an ace. Elliott's wingman, Ens. Wilton Stubbs, also got two victories that day. On the 26th and 27th, Elliott got a shared victory and a shared damaged. The momentous air/sea battle ended in a stunning loss for the Japanese, who lost 26 ships and 387 aircraft. The jeep carrier aviators, however, lost 43 pilots KIA or MIA and nine wounded.

Elliott's last victories were scored on 5 January 1945, during the invasion of Luzon at Lingayen Gulf. At 1650, 16 kamikazes

Lt. Ralph Elliott. (Author/Elliott)

with four escorts were headed for R.Adm. Jesse Oldendorf's TG 77.4. Elliott was leading a CAP and shared a Tony and Jack, and then got a Jill for his ninth victory in the FM-2. During the week over Luzon American air forces reduced Japanese air strength to nearly one quarter (150 aircraft to 35).

During its combat career the FM-2 operated solely from escort (CVE) carriers. Despite limited combat opportunities due to their primary roles as ground support, CAP, and anti-sub duties, the FM-2 accounted for 422 Japanese aircraft. This compares to 282 carrier and 704 land-based victories scored by the earlier F4F-4 and 4 Wildcats. Five FM-2 pilots were to become aces.

U.S. NAVY FM-2 Wildcat Aces (5+1* Aces/34.5 Victories+1*)

Ace Name	Rank	Unit	FM-2 V	Total V
Elliott, Ralph	Lt	VC-27	9	9
Funk, Harold	LCdr	VF-26	6	6
Ferko, Leo	Lt	VC-4	5	5
Hippe, Kenneth	Lt	VC-13	5	5
McGraw, James	Ens	VC-10	5	5
Davidson, George	Lt(jg)	VF-21, VC-27	5.5*	5.5*

*Scored 1 F4F victory and 4 1/2 FM-2 victories
Note: Three VC-27 pilots off the *Savo Island* were near aces with 4 1/2 victories: Ens. Thomas Mackie; Ens. Robert Pfeifer; and Wilton Stubbs.

FM-2s on Escort Carriers

The escort carrier was born of necessity in 1940 when Winston Churchill, former Lord of the Admiralty, requested that the U.S. build or convert merchant ships of 6,000 to 8,000 tons to carry aircraft to combat the U-boat threat to Atlantic convoys. Thus, the first of 128 U.S. escort carriers (AVGs) were built (38 were sent to Britain). The original AVG designation—Aircraft Escort Vessel—was changed to ACV (Auxiliary Aircraft Carrier) on 20 August 1942, and was then changed to CVE, or Escort Aircraft Carrier, on 15 July 1943. The CVE designation was translated by their crews as "Combustible, Vulnerable, and Expendable." Their construction was deemed as fragile and unseaworthy. Their low speed, lack of armor protection, and defensive armament made them vulnerable to any confrontation with Japanese naval forces.

Under the Churchill request, 22 *Bogue* class carriers were built as conversions on merchant hulls. Twelve "trade protection carriers" were sent to the Royal Navy, and the ten U.S. carriers were used to ferry aircraft (*Block Island*, *Prince William*, *Copahee*, and *Breton*) and in AS (anti-submarine) duties in the Atlantic (*Card*, *Core*, and *Bogue*). The Casablanca class was the most numerous, with 50 being produced by the Henry Kaiser Company Vancouver Yard in the space of a year. The longest building time was eight months, and the shortest 3 1/2. This class gave rise to the name "Jeep" carrier, because of their small size and quick, automobile assembly line building techniques. The flight deck was 475 feet long and 85 feet wide, with two elevators fore and aft and a port side catapult, and a hangar deck measuring 256 x 56. This compares to the *Essex* class fleet carriers, which had a 862 x 96 foot flight deck, 654 x 70 hangar deck, and carried 36 F6F fighters, 37 SB2C bombers, and 18 TBF torpedo bombers. The usual CVE air contingent consisted of Composite Squadrons (VC) of 12-16 FM-2 Wildcat fighters and 9-12 TBF/TBM Avenger torpedo bombers. The CVL *Independence* class, light carriers, were as small as the CVEs, having flight decks measuring 544 feet long by 73 feet wide (due to being built on narrow cruiser hulls) and hangar decks measuring 320 x 58 feet. The CVLs were built on light cruiser hulls, and were faster and more battle and seaworthy than the CVEs.

As the war progressed, particularly in the Pacific, where some 80 CVEs were deployed, the aircraft of the "Baby Flat Tops" provided CAP and AS duties for the amphibious invasion fleet and the supporting supply vessels, furnished close air support and CAP for ground forces, and spotted naval gun fire. The Composite Squadron was under a single command of the fighters and bombers. As a rule the Composite Squadron Cos flew the TBMs, and the senior pilot led the FM-2s. The small size of the FM-2 Wildcat made it suitable for storage and operations from the small escort carrier decks, and it operated from most U.S. escort carriers.

The FM-2 equipped 38 Composite Squadrons and was credited with 422 victories. The top-scoring FM squadron was VF-27 off the *Savo Island* with 61 1/2 victories. Ralph Elliott got nine, and four other of its pilots got 4 1/2 apiece (see FM-2 Ace table). VF-27 was followed by VF-26 *Santee* with 31, VC-81 *Natoma Bay* with 21, VOC-1 with 20, and eight more squadrons with 16 to 19 victories. VOC-1's 20 victories are remarkable because it flew endless hours as an observation squadron, spotting gunfire for battleships and cruisers during the Philippines, Iwo Jima, and Okinawa campaigns.

Flying the FM-2 Wildcat
By
Ken Hippe:
5 victories VC-3
First FM-2 ace

The FM-2 Wildcat was the Navy's answer to the need for a lighter, more powerful F4F to operate from its small jeep carriers with their shorter decks. Since Grumman was just building the Hellcat, General Motors' Eastern Aircraft unit built the FM-2, which was known as the "Wilder Wildcat."

The cockpit was small but comfortable for the average size pilot, but even more noisy and hotter than the F4F. We had the adjustable seat and sat on our parachute and folded life raft. It was not a comfortable seat for a four or five hour mission. Instrumentation was standard for a prop aircraft, and its controls were responsive and effective. After takeoff you bounced up and down as you cranked up the retractable landing gear 28 times with your right hand while holding the stick with your left. Our four channel VHF radios worked ok most of the time. We had IFF gear. Cockpit visibility was adequate in the air, but not too good on the ground, because in the tail down attitude it was difficult to look over the engine. There was a blind spot to the rear behind the pilot's head due to the cockpit being faired into the fuselage. The plane was difficult to taxi, especially in a crosswind. The narrow landing gear caused the plane to roll from side to side, so you had to use the brakes carefully to keep from ground looping. The lighter weight of the fighter and increased torque of the more powerful engine caused a swing on takeoff, but generally the fighter had good take-off and landing characteristics.

The 1,350hp Wright R-1820-56 Cyclone replaced the 1,200hp Pratt & Whitney Twin Wasp of the F4F-4. A higher vertical rudder and fin were necessary on the FM-2 due to the increased engine power and resultant torque. This increased fin area was helpful in the event we were suddenly waved off during a landing. This happened frequently when attempting to land on the short decks of the escort carriers. The R-1820 was 230 pounds lighter than the P&W because of having forged cylinder heads. The engine was reliable and ran well, and drove a Curtiss constant speed propeller. We had more speed (depending on altitude), better range and climb, and were more maneuverable than the F4F. The engine shook quite a bit at low RPMs, which we often used in order to conserve fuel on CAP. We carried 126 gallons of internal fuel, and could also carry two 58-gallon jettisonable tanks. We burned 30 to 40 gallons per hour, depending on our power settings. The FM-2 was over 500 pounds lighter than the F4F-4, and its more powerful engine gave it much better performance, except at altitude. We had only a single stage supercharger instead of the double used on the F4F-4, so our high altitude performance was not as good. But this did not make any difference, as our missions were usually at low or medium altitudes, such as close air support and anti-sub patrols. We very seldom encountered Jap aircraft from our escort carriers. Our improved climbing and diving abilities and increased acceleration and maneuverability made us a match for the Zeros when we encountered them. We cruised at 165-170 mph, and our top speed at combat altitude was 320 mph, which while better was still not enough. Later models had a ten-minute water injection system. The lateral exhausts located above the wing left dark smudges on the fuselage.

To save weight the FM-2 was armed with four .50 caliber Browning machine guns fed by 1,720 rounds, instead of the six on the F4F-4. We did not often carry bombs, but when we did they were two 250 pounders. We didn't have rocket rails in 1944, as only the last models were equipped with them. The FM-2 was rugged and could sustain a great deal of battle damage. We had self-sealing fuel tanks and an armored seat.

I think I was the first FM-2 ace. We did not get many chances at the Japs, but when I did I was able to shoot down five Lili kamikazes during the Battle of Leyte Gulf.

Grumman F6F Hellcat

The Bureau of Aeronautics requested that Grumman design a successor to the company's F4F Wildcat carrier-borne fighter at a time when the Chance Vought F4U had appeared to have garnered the procurement. As was the case of the F4F Wildcat/F2A Buffalo production debate, the F4U did not become carrier-ready until near the end of the war, and the F6F became the Navy carrier fighter. Designer William Schwendler submitted a proposal which was a logical development of the Wildcat. The primary differences were its low-wing instead of mid-wing, shorter undercarriage which retracted into the central section of the wing instead of the fuselage, better pilot forward visibility, six .50 cal. machine guns instead of four, and a higher 50 mph speed advantage. The XF6F-1 powered by the 1,700hp Wright R-2600 Cyclone was ordered on 30 June 1941 and first flew exactly one year later, piloted by Robert Hall. It was re-engined with the water injected Pratt & Whitney R-2800 Double Wasp to become the XF6F-3 and first flew on 30 July 1942 with Sheldon Converse at the controls. The production F6F-3 was essentially unchanged from the XF6F-3 and was ready for delivery on 4 October 1942. The British Fleet Air Arm accepted 252, first designated as the Gannet and then a short time later as the Hellcat I, and they made their operational debut in July 1943. U.S. Navy F6F-3 production totaled 4,646 aircraft, including 18 F6F-3Es and 205 F6F-3N night fighters, and debuted with the U.S. Navy in mid-January 1943 with VF-9 aboard the *Essex*. The F6F-5 was very similar to the F6F-3, with modifications to the tail, ailerons, engine fairings, and windscreen, and had provisions for bomb and/or rocket attachments on the wing. It was powered by the same P&W R-2800 engine and was the last and most numerous Hellcat. The total

Lt. Kenneth Hippe (Author/Hippe)

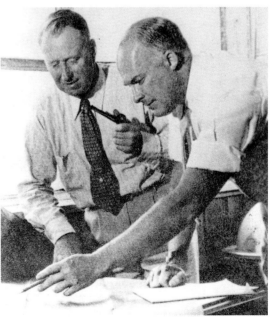

LeRoy Grumman (L) and Bill Schwendler. (Grumman)

F6F-3 Lt(jg) Alexander Vraciu, VF- & VF-16, 19 F6F victories. (J.W. Gooch/Warbirds Research Group)

F6F-5 production was 7,870 aircraft, of which 1,434 were modified into the F6F-5N night fighter, approximately 200 for the F6F-5P photo recon version, and 930 to the Royal Navy as the Hellcat II, with about 75 converted to the –5N night fighter version (all British Hellcats were returned to the U.S. after VJ-Day). When production ceased in November 1945, a total of 12,275 Hellcats were produced, including prototypes and an order for an additional 1,677 was canceled in August 1945. The Hellcat was the first American fighter to master the Japanese Zero; it was better armed, stressed pilot safety (armor protection and self-sealing fuel tanks), was rugged, and out performed it in rate of climb, diving speed, and level speed (except at lower altitudes). From its introduction in January 1943 until the end of the war it was the carrier fighter that stopped the Japanese air forces and then totally crushed them in the Battles

of the Philippines Sea, the Great Marianas Turkey Shoot, and later over Formosa and the Japanese homeland. It was joined, not supplanted, by the F4U Corsair in achieving this air superiority in the Pacific air war.

F6F/USN/PTO First Victory in Type

Pilot: Lt(jg) Richard L. Loesch
Time: 1 September 1943/1314
Place: Over Howland Island
Unit: VF-6 (detached)/*Princeton*
A/C: F6F-3/Emily H8K Flying boat
Action: After its brief North African campaign against the Vichy French in November 1942, VF-9 was slated to be equipped with the F4U Corsair. But due to the slow delivery of the F4U, it became the first Navy F6F Hellcat unit in mid-January 1943. The pilots of this veteran Wildcat unit found the Hellcat to be larger and roomier, better armed, and faster horizontally and vertically than the Wildcat. The Squadron was joined in Hawaii in August by other Navy squadrons for training.

One squadron was VF-6, led by Lt.Cdr. Edward "Butch" O'Hare, who had won the Congressional Medal of Honor in the Wildcat when he downed five Japanese Betty bombers, saving the *Lexington* in February 1942. On 1 September 1943 the light carriers *Princeton* (CVL 23) and *Belleau Wood* (CVL 24), under R.Adm. Arthur Radford, were assigned to provide CAP to cover a small task force landing engineers and base troops on Baker Island to establish an air search and photo recon airstrip.

The *Princeton* carried VF-23 and a detachment of VF-6, both of which had recently been equipped with F6F Hellcats. At noon, a VF-6 division commanded by Lt(jg) Richard Loesch began CAP over Baker Island. The FDO on the destroyer *Trathen* vectored the four Hellcats north to 10,000 feet towards an incoming i/u Japanese aircraft at 7,000 feet. Over Howland Island (the intended land-

Lt(jg) Richard Loesch (VF-6) flies his F6F-3 off the *Princeton*. Loesch scored the first Hellcat victory of the war when he shot down an Emily H8K flying boat on 1 September 1943. (USN)

Lt(jg) Wayne Presley (top, center) was the first pilot to score victories in both the F4F Wildcat (VF-5/*Saratoga*) and the F6F Hellcat (VF-38/land-based/Guadalcanal). (USN)

ing area of Amelia Earhart in 1937 before her disappearance) the bogey was intercepted and identified as a four-engined H8K Emily. At 1314 Loesch and his wingman, Ens. Albert Nyquist, made head-on firing passes on the large flying boat. They opened fire at 500 yards, unleashing over 300 rounds that hit the cockpit and inboard engines. The wounded Japanese aircraft went into a shallow starboard circling dive, exploding into the sea. The victory, credited to Loesch, was the first of 5,164 for the Hellcat in WWII.

On 3 September the *Belleau Wood's* VF-22 got another Emily, and on 8 September two VF-6 Hellcats got a third Emily. These three Makin-based Emilys had been shot down so quickly that they had no time to make radio calls. The Japanese air commander on Makin, according to a captured diary, grounded his remaining Emilys, thinking they had been lost due to mechanical failure.

Loesch is often credited with being the first pilot to score victories in both the Wildcat and Hellcat. However, the victory he claimed in a VF-6 Wildcat in the Battle of the Eastern Solomons was never officially credited to him. It appears that this distinction for "Cat" victories belongs to Lt(jg) Wayne C. Presley. Flying a Wildcat for VF-5 off the *Saratoga* over Guadalcanal, he scored a victory over an Aichi 99 on 24 August 1942. Then, flying a Hellcat for VF-38, a land-based Guadalcanal squadron, he got a Zeke and Tony on 16 September 1943.

F6F/USN First Ace in Type

Pilot: Lt(jg) Hamilton McWhorter III
Time: 18 November 1943/1130
Place: Tarawa
Unit: VF-9
A/C: F6F-3/Pete
Action: When the F6F-3 production models were delivered in early October 1942, the fighter was found to be the ideal carrier fighter, specifically designed to meet the needs of the carrier pilot and the tactical requirements to defeat the Japanese fighters. The success of the Grumman design was demonstrated in the fighter's excellent combat record (5,156 victories vs. 270 combat losses: a 19 to 1 victory ratio!) so that only two major versions, the F6F-3 and F6F-5, needed to be manufactured. Where the Wildcat lacked speed and

rate of climb, the Hellcat was superior to its contemporary Japanese opponents. On 16 January 1943 VF-9 became the first operational squadron to fly the Hellcat.

Georgian Hamilton McWhorter joined VF-9 in March 1942 at Oceana, Virginia. In November he saw his first combat over North Africa in a F4F Wildcat off the *Ranger* on strikes in the Casablanca area during "Operation Torch." Returning to the States, the squadron re-equipped with Hellcats and was assigned to the *Essex* (CV-9) on its first tour. The *Essex* saw its first combat in early October 1943, when Fighting Nine CO Lt.Cdr. Philip Torrey led his new Hellcats during the Wake Island raids. On 5 October, Lt.(jg) McWhorter found himself in an early morning dogfight when a Zeke suddenly appeared in his gunsight. One quick burst exploded the Zeke, earning him the nickname "One Slug." This first raid validated American tactical doctrine against the lighter and more agile Japanese fighters: to maintain high speed and to fight in the vertical, diving and climbing, thus negating the Japanese low-speed turning advantage in the horizontal. Also, the concept of leader/wingman teamwork was stressed.

On 11 November the Navy raided the Japanese stronghold of Rabaul in a two phase attack. A second attack was to be launched only one half hour after the first, hoping to catch the Japanese fighters on the ground being rearmed and refueled. McWhorter and VF-6, part of V.Adm. Alfred Montgomery's TG 50.3, took part in this second attack that was launched after the unsuccessful first attack, which ran into bad weather and also limited Japanese opposition. VF-6's twelve plane formation ran into 60 Zekes in the overcast off Cape St. George at 0900. In a brief dogfight in cloud cover over the mouth of Simpson Harbor, McWhorter shot down two Zekes and got a probable. He returned to base with 11 holes in his aircraft.

On 18 November, McWhorter scored a victory over a Pete—a JNAF short-range observation float biplane—over Tarawa atoll in a pre-invasion raid. The victory was his fifth to make him the first of 311 Hellcat aces. Lt(jg) James Kinsella of VF-33 had actually become the first ace in a Hellcat on 8 November 1943, but two of his victories were scored in a Wildcat.

Lt(jg) Hamilton McWhorter. (USN)

McWhorter went on to get a victory the next day, but had to wait until 29 January to get two Hamps over Roi. He tallied a triple on 17 February over Truk, which made him the first carrier-based double ace. McWhorter got two victories with VF-12 in 1945 off the *Randolph* to give him 12 for the war.

F6F Top Scorer in Type

Pilot: Cdr. David McCampbell
Unit: VF-15/*Essex*
Victories: 34
Record:

V#	Date	E/A/C
1	06-11-44	Zeke
2	06-13-44	Helen
3-9	06-19-44	5 Judys, 2 Zekes
10-10 1/2	06-23-44	1 1/2 Zekes
11 1/2-14 1/2	09-12-44	Dinah, 2 Zekes, Jack
15 1/2 –17 1/2	09-13-44	2 Nates, Oscar
18.5	09-22-44	Dinah
19	09-24-44	1/2 Pete
20-21	10-21-44	Dinah, Nate
22-30	10-24-44	5 Zekes, 2 Oscars, 2 Hamps
31-32	11-05-44	Val, Zeke
33	11-11-44	Oscar
34	11-14-44	Oscar

Action: After a brief stint at Georgia Tech, Floridian David McCampbell was appointed to the Naval Academy, where he graduated in 1933. The Depression caused the government to cut back the Navy's budget, and McCampbell's Class of 1933 was discharged. He tried to join the Army Air Corps, but was rejected because of supposed poor eyesight, and for the next year he worked construction and for Douglas Aircraft Co. In 1934, he was called to active duty as Ensign and assigned to the cruiser *Portland* for three years. In 1937, he passed a second Naval eye test after failing once and was assigned to flight training at NAS Pensacola. In April 1938 he was assigned to Flight Squadron 4 aboard the *Ranger*, where he flew the F3F biplane and F4F Wildcat.

Cdr. David McCampbell.
(USN)

As the war broke out, he was transferred to the *Wasp* as a Landing Signals Officer (LSO), paddling other aviators onto the carrier deck. The *Wasp* participated in Atlantic convoy patrols and delivered Spitfires to Malta before heading to Guadalcanal in June 1943. But McCampbell saw no flying duty before the *Wasp* was sunk by a submarine on 15 September 1942. McCampbell was sent back to the States, where he was promoted to Lieutenant Commander as LSO instructor at NAS Melbourne, Florida. In August 1943 he was ordered to NAS Atlantic City as commanding officer to commission and train a new group, VF-15, which would become known as the "Fabled Fifteen." After training it was assigned to the new *Hornet* and dispatched to Pearl Harbor for advanced training in February 1944. McCampbell was made Air Group Commander (AGC) of AG-15, which included fighters, bombers, and torpedo aircraft.

AG-15 embarked on the *Essex* for its first combat and took part in the Marcus Island raids, where McCampbell's F6F Hellcat sustained damage from anti-aircraft fire. He scored his first victory over the Saipan beachhead, downing a Zeke on 11 June 1944. For the next six months AG-15 was to see almost continuous combat, participating in two legendary air/sea battles, along with attacking shipping and bases in the Western Pacific in support of Marine amphibious operations in the Marianas, Peliliu, Iwo Jima, and Leyte. McCampbell's combat action for this period won him the Congressional Medal of Honor that was awarded to him by F.D.R on 10 January 1945. Its citation sums up his accomplishments:

For conspicuous gallantry and intrepidity at the risk of his life, above and beyond …as Commander AG-15…led his fighter planes against a force of 80 Japanese carrier-based aircraft bearing down on our fleet on 19 June 1944, during the Battle of the Philippine's Sea ("Great Mariana's Turkey Shoot") personally destroyed seven of the hostile planes (five in his first sortie of the day and two in his second) and on 24 October (Battle of Leyte Gulf) Cdr. McCampbell, assisted by but one plane (wingman, Roy Rushing who got six victories and three damaged) intercepted and daringly attacked a formation of 60 hostile land-based aircraft approaching our forces. Fighting desperately but with superb skill he shot down nine Japanese planes (and damaged three)…forced the remainder to abandon the attack before a single aircraft could reach the fleet. (Parentheses are the authors) See Chapter 14: Aces in a Day for a further description of this mission.

The nine victories in one sortie were the most scored by an American pilot during the war, while his seven victories were equaled by only four other American pilots and made him the only American to become an "ace-in-a-day" twice. His nine victory day gave him 30 victories, which briefly tied him for three days with Bong as the leading American ace in the war. McCampbell went on to score four more victories before being removed from operations to give him 34, which made him the Navy's "Ace-of-Aces," but left him behind Air Force aces Richard Bong with 40 victories and Tom McGuire with 38 at the end of the war. McCampbell scored all his victories on one tour, as opposed to Bong and McGuire.

After the war McCampbell progressed through a succession of commands, including CO of the attack carrier *Bon Homme Richard* and a member of the Joint Chiefs of Staff. He retired in 1964 after 31 years of naval service.

The Hellcat scored 5,156 victories in the Pacific (5,060 by the USN and 96 by the USMC). Of these victories 4,939 (one USMC) were carrier-based and 217 (122 USN and 95 USMC) were land-based. The Hellcat boasted 311 (one USMC) aces, for the most of any American fighter in the war. But more valuable than its impres-sive victory totals are the Hellcat's little-known ability as a super-lative bomber escort (probably even more so than the P-51 "Little Friend"). In the period of its duty in the Pacific from 1943 to VJ-Day only 42 American carrier-based bombers were downed by Japa-nese aircraft, and only seven in the last eight months of the war.

Hellcat Top Scorers

Lt. Eugene Valencia (23v.) (USN)

Lt. Cecil Harris (22v.) (USN)

Lt(jg) Alex Vraciu (19v.) and Adm. Marc Mitscher (USN)

Lt. Patrick Fleming (19v.)

Lt(jg) Cornelius Nooy (19v.)

Lt.(jg) Douglas Baker (16.33v.)

Flying the F6F Hellcat
By
David McCampbell:
Top Navy ace 34 victories AG-17

The Hellcat cockpit was entered from the starboard wing. Entry could be difficult when the wing was folded, as there was barely enough room between the wing and fuselage for the pilot to squeeze through. A push button was located just under the windshield and allowed the canopy to be easily slid aft to the open position so the pilot could crawl in. The cockpit was relatively comfortable for even a large pilot. The seat was adjustable about six inches vertically by a control lever at its right side. The shoulder strap harness could be adjusted by a control on the left side of the seat.

The aluminum-framed windshield consisted of a bulletproof front plate surrounded by Plexiglas top and side panels. The Plexiglas canopy could be cranked fully open or closed with 4 1/2 turns on the hand crank, and locked into any open position by a pin mounted on the hand crank. The pilot could execute an emergency quick canopy release by pulling two red rings located at the latches at the front end of the track. The Hellcat's cockpit gave the pilot substantial protection. The bulk of the engine protected the pilot from head on enemy fire. Armor plate was located behind the seat and served as a bulkhead at the rear of the cockpit. The construction of the metal framework and aluminum sheeting around the cockpit area was very strong. Also, the self-sealing fuel tanks under the cockpit could absorb enemy fire.

The main instrument panel was well thought out, simple to use, and easy to reach. It consisted of engine, flight, and navigation instruments. The left side of the cockpit was comprised of engine related controls, while the right side was electrical/radio oriented. Generally, Hellcat instrumentation was stereotypical and similar to the Wildcat, but much more sophisticated. The rudder pedals were hung from a bar under the instruments and length adjustable in four positions. The control stick was standard. It had a pistol grip, gun trigger, and bomb release button.

Cdr. David McCampbell (USN)

The radio equipment was located in the fuselage behind the cockpit. It was a VHF and HF transmitter/receiver and a navigation receiver. The radio equipment was connected to a cockpit controlled explosive charge to prevent it from falling into enemy hands. The Mark 8 electric gun sight was located on the centerline, above the instrument panel. Illuminated cross hairs and deflection rings were projected on the windshield to aim the six machine guns. The oxygen system was locked behind the aft bulkhead and was of the dilute demand type.

The Pratt & Whitney R-2800 Double Wasp was an 18-cylinder air-cooled radial engine developing 2,000hp. The prop was the three blade, 13 foot Hamilton-Standard Hydromatic. It was a constant speed, delivering full horsepower regardless of airspeed or RPMs. There was just over six inches of ground clearance between the prop tips when the fighter was fully-loaded and in the tail up take off position. The R-2800 was a finely crafted, reliable, and rugged engine. Regular carrier-board maintenance was no problem, but its complexity could cause problems beyond basic repair. Internal fuel tankage consisted of two main wing tanks containing 87.5 gallons and a reserve tank under the pilot's seat containing 75 gallons. A drop tank located under the fuselage held 150 gallons, while two additional 100 gallon drop tanks could be attached to the under wing bomb racks.

Armament was six .50 caliber machine guns, three in each outer wing panel. They were fired electrically by the trigger switch on the forward side of the control stick. Each gun was fed by 400 rounds, and the guns were bore sighted—you converge to a point which would be inline with the gun sight. At this 300-foot convergence over 90% of the bullets would hit an area of a three-foot circle, which was lethal to the lightly built Japanese aircraft. Gun heaters were installed to keep them operating freely at high, cold altitudes where lubricants would stiffen. The six machine guns were generally reliable and rarely jammed.

When flying the Hellcat the pilot's comfort was his first requirement, as he had to endure five to seven hour missions. The seat, shoulder harness, rudder pedals, and rear view mirror were adjusted as part of the pre-flight. The crewmen turned the prop 12-15 blades to be certain that there was no residual or oil in the engine's lower cylinders. The pilot went through the pre-start settings and checks. The wings were previously unfolded and locked into position, and the tail wheel unlocked (for carrier take off). The engine was started and settings checked. The rudder trim tab, ailerons, and elevator tabs were set. The pilot taxied to the take off spot as directed by the Launch Officer's hand signals. The pilot applied the brakes, and when he saw the LO circling his flag, he revved his engine to maximum RPMs, lowered his flaps for maximum lift, and put the prop into flat pitch. When the LO signaled, the pilot saluted, released his brakes and, keeping is tail down, left the deck. As soon as the wheels left the deck the gear was retracted immediately to build up air speed more rapidly. A right turn was made to get out of the carrier's path, and then the pilot would regain his heading.

The Hellcat was stable at normal settings and forgiving to mistakes. Stalls were characterized by a drop of the right wing and a forbidding shaking of the aircraft. It was relatively easy to recover from stalls and spins. The fighter could withstand almost every maneuver the pilot could ask of it, but it could fly inverted for only 3-4 seconds due to the oil scavenger pump. A rule of thumb to achieve maximum range was to fly at the lowest RPMs and full mixture practicable.

The landing characteristics of the Hellcat were excellent. One had to remember to: (1) reduce airspeed to 120 knots; (2) open the canopy (to facilitate escape in case the plane landed in water); (3) select the tank with the most fuel; (4) mixture control to auto-rich; (5) supercharger to neutral; (6) cowl flaps to half open; (7) extend the arresting hook; (8) extend the wheels and unlock the tail wheel; and (9) lower flaps. Then, watching the Landing Signals Officer (LSO), chop the throttle, pull the stick back, and stall-in, trying to touch the main wheels first and engage the arrester hook. Once stopped the flaps were raised and cowl flap opened to prevent over heating. Following the hand directions of the taxi directors, the pilot taxied back to his parking position and shut down the engine. The safety lock pins were released in the cockpit so that the wings could be folded manually by the crew. The aircraft was then parked by the plane handlers to be serviced for the next time.

Flying the F6F Hellcat
By
Alex Vraciu:
19 victories VF-6 & VF-16

It will come as no surprise to those familiar with WWII fighters that most carrier pilots would endorse the Grumman F6F Hellcat as being the right fighter at the right time for our war in the Pacific. Some enthusiasts will even claim that it won the war against the Japanese when it took control of the air from the Zero.

In general, the Hellcat was designed to counter the Japanese Zero, the dominant plane early in the war. The Hellcat gave us not only the speed, range, and climb to finally compete successfully against it, but also to dictate the rules of combat. It was the perfect aircraft for newly trained pilots arriving with the fleet. It had few bad habits and many great ones, and was more of a pussycat than a Hellcat in all phases of its carrier operations. What better success could be attributed to the F6F than to acknowledge its 19 to 1 kill-to-loss ratio.

The cockpit was roomy, and the seat and widely spaced pedals were adjustable to accommodate all sizes of pilots. The visibility was great, because the pilot sat at the highest point of the aircraft and actually looked down over the engine in flight. This visibility and the wide undercarriage made taxiing easy, although we did not have to go far on the carrier deck. Takeoff was routine, with the wheels locking up with a loud thump.

The Pratt & Whitney R-2800 (-8 and −10) gave us more than adequate performance, along with incredible ruggedness and dependability. The 250-gallon capacity of the internal tanks and the 150 gallons of external fuel were totally sufficient for operational needs. Fuel consumption was no problem, whether on escort, fighter sweep, or CAP missions.

The Hellcat climbed well up to 20,000 feet, after which its rate of climb slowed. The supercharger gave a service ceiling of 37,000 feet, but over 32,000 the plane became noticeably sluggish. The fighter was stable in all axes, but on the −3 models the controls became heavy at high speeds, but all in all the Hellcat possessed excellent handling characteristics. On the landing approach the F6F was steady, and altitude and speed control was precise, but any nose up attitude decreased visibility and could make landings touchy.

Although the F6F weighed twice as much as the Zero, it could out climb, out dive, and out run the Zero. The Hellcat could not outmaneuver it at low altitudes, but by keeping one's airspeed above 230mph and fighting basically in a vertical plane above 10,000 feet, the F6F could outperform the Zero. It gave us the opportunity to fight aggressive-smart against the enemy. If we found ourselves in tactical difficulty, we could always dive out of trouble. At these higher speeds the Hellcat could match turns with our opponent, since the aerodynamic forces on the Zero's control surfaces, particularly the ailerons, at higher speeds caused them to have stiff control responses.

The six Browning .50 caliber machine guns with the 400 rounds per gun suited us fine. They were sufficient in the amount of ammunition, dependability, and hitting power. The Mark 8 illuminated gun sight was an improvement for the time and gave us the capability for deflection shooting. Later in the war the Hellcat's versatility was further demonstrated when it inherited bomb and rocket duty, as well. After discharging our ordnance we were again pure fighters and could hunt the Japanese, which was more to our liking.

Armored seats and the self-sealing fuel tanks gave us great peace of mind, especially after seeing how quickly the enemy, without self-sealing tanks, caught fire when hit. The Hellcat's airframe was rugged and could withstand an amazing amount of battle damage, especially from ground fire. I was labeled Grumman's "best consumer" after having survived two ditchings and a bailout in their fighter. I can truthfully say that they were a piece of cake in the rugged fighter.

The Hellcat was not the fastest or most maneuverable carrier fighter, but it magnificently carried out its design purpose: specifically, to gain air superiority over the Zero. Once it accomplished this, its versatility allowed it to efficiently assume a fighter-bomber role. It was the most important carrier aircraft of the war, and almost single-handedly turned the tide of the air war.

Lt(jg) Alex Vraciu (Author/Vraciu)

Flying the F6F Hellcat
By
John Strane:
13 victories VF-15

Our squadron pre-flight always included going over as much information as we had available pertaining to our upcoming mission. Distances to and from target and the approach and recovery routes were planned and studied in detail. We tried to learn all geographical and topographical features to and from the target, as well as the layout of the target. We were particularly interested in the number and positions of the defending gun emplacements. In my pre-flight brief, I stressed the importance for each pilot to keep a running log on his chart board. Often this paid dividends in enabling pilots to make a safe return after becoming separated from the group.

Our aircraft pre-flight procedure included the customary kick of the tire ritual, which has been observed by fighter pilots from day one. Among the items we checked for full throw of the ailerons and horizontal stabilizer and complete movement of all moveable surfaces. The oil and fuel tanks were checked for fill and their caps checked for tightness. We made certain that the cover of the pitot tube was removed, which was sometimes hard to remember on night or pre-dawn missions.

The cockpit of the Hellcat was great. It was large enough to be comfortable for the average size pilot. Only one large pilot in our squadron, movie star Wayne Morris, had any trouble fitting into it. The layout was such that all instruments, switches, levers, and knobs were within easy reach and visibility.

Any pilot who has flown a plane equipped with a P&W R-2800 engine will tell you that it rated with the best aircraft engines ever built. Enough said! On our climb to altitude our policy was not to go into high blower until we reached 15,000 feet. We never used water injection until requirements of the mission dictated: to close on a fleeing enemy plane or to open from a pursuing enemy plane.

The Hellcat carried six .50 caliber guns. Although there were times we could have used more than the 2,400 rounds of ammunition we carried, this load was usually adequate to meet our normal mission needs. Our squadron boresighted its guns in pairs from onboard out at 800, 900, and 1,000 feet. Each squadron was free to

make its own decision on boresighting, and I felt that our technique paid off in victories. Our Mark 8 gun sight filled the bill well and made many of us better shots, especially in deflection. We did not receive the 5-inch high velocity rockets until we had been in combat for some time. When we first used them we probably did not use them to their full advantage due to our lack of training and practice. After a while we received good enough instruction and practice and obtained better results. We found that a good steep angle of attack was required when firing rockets on ground targets. We loved the Hellcat for its stability as a gun platform and its ability to serve as a fighter bomber.

Its rugged construction saved numerous pilots. During many a post-mission recovery, we would watch Hellcats make it back to the carrier with unbelievable battle damage. We were thankful for the armor plate, bullet proof glass, and self-sealing fuel tanks.

The Hellcat had great bailout and ditching capabilities. Several of my pilots made successful ditchings, some with flaps down or gear down, and some with both flaps and gear up. I never heard of a pilot being unable to bail out successfully once he made the decision to leave the aircraft. In my own case, I caught my right parachute riser on the canopy locking lever, which was located on the right canopy rail. I had to struggle against the slipstream to reach up and pull the riser free and parachute into the sea.

F6F/ETO First Victory in Type

Pilots: Lt.Cdr. Harry Bass (1/4 v.)
        Lt. Leo Horacek (1/4 v.)
        Lt(jg) Edwin Castanedo (1/4v.)
        Ens. Paul Pavlovich (1/4v.)
Time: 19 August 1944/0805
Place: Rhone river, Southern France
Unit: VF-74/*Kasaan Bay*
A/C: F6F-5/Ju-88

Action: The Navy's F6F Hellcat saw ETO combat action during "Operation Anvil-Dragoon," the invasion of Southern France, on 15 August 1944. As part of Task Force 88 an escort carrier group under Adm. T.H. Troubridge of the Royal Navy stood off the Riviera beaches. The CVEs *Kasaan Bay* and *Tulagi* embarked VF-74 and VOF-1, respectively. VF-74, under CO Lt.Cdr. Harry Bass, flew tactical/recon missions for which they were inadequately trained; having no TAC R or artillery spotting training, and only having fired but a few practice rockets.

On D-Day, VF-74 flew 60 sorties without engaging the Luftwaffe, which did not appear until four days later on the 19th. Early that morning Bass led his division of F6F-5s (Lt. Leo Hornacek, Lt(jg) Edwin Castenado, and Ens. Paul Pavlovich) up the Rhone River Valley looking for transportation targets. A Ju-88 was spotted at 0805 and was attacked by the four Hellcats. The Junkers twin-engine bomber made a few ineffectual evasive maneuvers and was butchered by all four pilots, who shared the quarter victory.

VOF-1 off the *Tulagi* was a specially trained unit used for plotting naval gunfire, providing close support, and executing armed recon patrols. On 19 August VOF-1 encountered a group of He-111s north of Vienne, knocking down three of them: Ens. Alfred

Lt. John Strane. (Author/Strane)

Four pilots on the *Kasaan Bay* shared a Ju-88 victory over Southern France to claim the first Hellcat victory in the ETO. (USN)

Wood was credited with 1 1/2 victories. On the 21st, Lt(jg) Edward Olszewski attacked three Ju-52 transports. He shot the two trailing Germans of the V-formation to make him the top-scoring Navy pilot against the Luftwaffe.

The 13 day air campaign over Southern France was a costly one for the Hellcats of the two CVEs, which lost 11 aircraft (one quarter of their complement); however, none was lost to the Luftwaffe. The Germans lost eight aircraft, of which none were fighters. The Hellcats demonstrated their strike capability by destroying 825 German trucks and vehicles and damaging 334 others, along with hitting 84 locomotives.

F6F/USMC First Victory in Type (Carrier)
Pilot: Lt. Bruce J. Reuter
Time: 3 July 1945/0100
Place: Balikpapan, Borneo
Unit: VMF-511(N)/*Block Island*
A/C: F6F-5N/Jake
See: *Nightfighters*

F6Fs on Escort Carriers
F6Fs served onboard the four escort carriers of the *Sangamon* class. They were larger than the *Bogue* and *Casablanca* class escort carriers, as they were built on oil tanker hulls, and were more seaworthy and had more deck space. They could handle up to 34 aircraft, and the enclosed hangar could accommodate 30 aircraft. F6Fs were assigned to a small number of Escort Carrier Air Groups (CVEG) on these carriers and worked as part of CARDIV 22 in the Pacific.

Top F6F CVE Scorers

Name	Rank	Carrier	Unit	V
Kenyon, Karl	Lt(jg)	*Sangamon*	VF-37	4
Singleton, Royce	Lt(jg)	*Suwannee*	VF-60	3 1/4
Donnelly, Joseph	Ens.	*Sangamon*	VF-37	3
Longino, Walter	LtCdr	*Suwannee*	VF-40	3

Lt(jg) Karl Kenyon's victories were all scored on 24 October 1944 during the Battle of Leyte Gulf. Kenyon became separated from his squadron when he came upon a large formation of Sallys over San Juanico Strait. He shot down four Sallys and claimed three probables and two damaged before turning back to the *Sangamon*. His Hellcat ran out of fuel on the way, and Kenyon put the F6F into the water and was picked up two hours later by a destroyer escort.

VF-60 was the highest scoring Hellcat squadron with 25 victories during its 1943-44 cruise on the *Suwannee*, and was followed by VF-37 with 20 on the *Sangamon* in 1943-44.

Ens. Alfred Wood (L) and Lt(jg) Edward Olszewski (R) of VOF-1 shot down 1 1/2 and 2 He-111s, respectively, to become the top F6F scorers in the ETO. (USN)

#V	Ace Name	Rank	Unit	Carrier
34	McCampbell, David	Cdr	AG-15	*Essex*
23	Valencia, Eugene	Lt	VF-9	*Yorktown*
22	Harris, Cecil	Lt	VF-27	*Land*
			VF-18	*Intrepid*
19	Fleming, Patrick	Lt	VF-80	*Hancock*
19	Nooy, Cornelius	Lt(jg)	VF-31	*Cabot&Bunker Hill*
19	Vraciu, Alexander	Lt(jg)	VF-16	*Intrepid&Lexington*
16.33	Baker, Douglas	Ens	VF-20	*Enterprise*
14	Hawkins, Arthur	Lt(jg)	VF-31	*Cabot*
14	Wirth, John	Lt	VF-31	*Cabot*
13.5	Dunkin, George	LCdr	VF-15	*Essex*
13	Rushing, Roy	Lt(jg)	VF-15	*Essex*
13	Strane, John	Lt	VF-15	*Essex*
13	Twelves, Wendell	Lt(jg)	VF-15	*Essex*
12.5	Shirley, James	Lt	VF-27	*Princeton*
12	Carmichael, Daniel	Lt(jg)	VF-2	*Hornet*
			VBF-12	*Randolph*
12	Kirkwood, Philip	Lt(jg)	VF-10	*Enterprise*
12	McWhorter, Hamilton	Lt	VF-9	*Essex*
			VF-12	*Randolph*
11.75	Craig, Clement	Lt	VF-22	*Cowpens*
11.5	Carr, George	Lt(jg)	VF-15	*Essex*
11	Dean, William	Cdr	VF-2	*Hornet*
11	French, James	Lt(jg)	VF-9	*Lexington*
11	Picken, Harvey	Lt	VF-18	*Intrepid*
11	Reber, James	Ens	VF-30	*Belleau Wood*
11	Rigg, James	LCdr	VF-15	*Essex*
10.5	Beebe, Marshall	LCdr	VF-17	*Hornet*
10.5	Brown, Carl	Lt	VF-27	*Princeton*
10.33	Murray, Robert	Lt	VF-5	*Yorktown*
10	Check, Leonard	LCdr	VF-7	*Hancock*
10	Coleman, Thaddeus	Lt	VF-6	*Belleau Wood*
			VF-83	*Essex*
10	Mallory, Charles	Lt(jg)	VF-18	*Intrepid*
10	Masoner, William	Lt(jg)	VF-19	*Enterprise*
10	Mitchell, Harris	Lt(jg)	VF-9	*Yorktown*
10	Singer, Arthur	Lt(jg)	VF-15	*Essex*
10	Smith, Armisted	Lt	VF-9	*Essex*
			VBF-12	*Randolph*
10	Stambrook, Richard	Lt	VF-27	*Princeton*
10	Stewart, James	Lt	VF-31	*Belleau Wood*
10	Stimpson, Charles	Lt	VF-11	*Hornet*
9.5	Henry, William	Lt	VS-3	*Independence*
			VF-4N	*Independence*
9.33	Coats, Robert	Lt	VF-18	*Bunker Hill*
			VF-17	*Hornet*
9.25	Redmond, Eugene	Lt	VF-10	*Enterprise*
			VF-2	*Hornet*
9	Berree, Norman	Lt(jg)	VF-15	*Essex*
9	Buie, Paul	LCdr	VF-16	*Lexington*
9	Carlson, Robert	Lt(jg)	VF-40	*Land*
			VF-30	*Belleau Wood*
9	Collins, William	Cdr	VF-8	*Bunker Hill*
9	Eastmond, Richard	Lt	VF-4	*Hornet*
9	Franger, Marvin	Lt	VF-9	*Yorktown*
9	Harris, Thomas	Lt(jg)	VF-18	*Bunker Hill*
			VF-17	*Hornet*
9	Hedrick, Roger	LCdr	VF-18	*Hornet*
			VF-84	*Bunker Hill*
9	Rehm, Daniel	Lt(jg)	VF-50	*Bataan*
			VF-8	*Bunker Hill*
9	Van Haren, Arthur	Lt	VF-2	*Hornet*
8.75	Watts, Charles	Lt(jg)	VF-18	*Bunker Hill*
			VF-17	*Hornet*
8.5	Anderson, Robert	Lt	VF-80	*Ticonderroga*
8.5	Banks, John	Lt(jg)	VF-2	*Enterprise*
8.5	Foster, Carl	Ens	VF-30	*Belleau Wood*
8.5	Hargreaves, Everett	Lt(jg)	VF-2	*Hornet*
8.5	Pigman, George	Ens	VF-15	*Essex*
8.5	Plant, Claude	Ens	VF-15	*Essex*
8.5	Prater, Luther	Lt(jg)	VF-19	*Enterprise*
8.5	Self, Larry	Ens	VF-15	*Essex*
8.25	Evenson, Eric	Lt(jg)	VF-30	*Monterey*
8.25	Gray, John	Lt	VF-5	*Yorktown*
8	Barnard, Lloyd	Lt	VF-2	*Hornet*
8	Bonneau, William	Lt	VF-2	*Essex*
8	Cain, James	Lt	VF-45	*San Jacinto*
8	Cormier, Richard	Lt	VF-80	*Hancock*
8	Devine, richard	Lt	VF-10	*Enterprise*
8	Doner, Landis	Lt	VF-2	*Hornet*
8	Gabriel, Francis	Lt(jg)	VF-2	*Hornet*
8	Griffin, Richard	Lt	VF-2	*Hornet*
8	Hadden, Mayo	Lt	VF-9	*Essex*
8	Harris, Leroy	LCdr	VF-18	*Bunker Hill*
			VF-17	*Hornet*
8	Johnson, Byron	Lt(jg)	VF-2	*Hornet*
8	Johnston, John	Lt(jg)	VBF-17	*Hornet*
8	Lindsley, Elvin	Lt	VF-19	*Enterprise*
8	Menard, Louis	Lt(jg)	VBF-12	*Randolph*
8	Miller, Johnie	Ens	VF-30	*Bunker Hill*
8	Mucahy, Douglas	Lt	VF-31	*Cabot*
8	Reiserer, Russell	Lt	VF-10	*Enterprise*
			VF-76N	*Enterprise*
8	Stanley, Gordon	Ens	VF-27	*Princeton*
8	Winters, Theodore	Cdr	VF-19	*Enterprise*
7.5	Bakutis, Frank	Cdr	VF-20	*Enterprise*
7.5	Bardshar, Frederick	LCr	VF-27	*Princeton*
7.5	Berkheimer, Jack	Ens	VF-41N	*Independance*
7.5	Edwards, William	Lt	VF-80	*Hancock*
7.5	Fleming, Francis	Lt(jg)	VF-16	*Lexington*
7.5	Knight, Willaim	Lt	VF-14	*Wasp*
7	Hibbard, Sam	Lt	VF-47	*Bataan*
7	McClelland, Thomas	Lt	VF-5	*Yorktown*
7	Batten, Hugh	Lt(jg)	VF-17	*Hornet*
7	Brocato, Samuel	Lt(jg)	VF-83	*Essex*
7	Burley, Franklin	Lt(jg)	VF-18	*Intrepid*
7	Burdette, Roy	Lt	VF-8	*Intrepid*
7	Clark, Lawrence	Lt(jg)	VF-83	*Essex*

7	Conants, Edwin	Lt	VBF-17	*Hornet*
7	Conroy, Thomas	Ens	VF-27	*Princeton*
7	Dahms, Kenneth	Ens	VF-30	*Bunker Hill*
7	Dear, John	Lt(jg)	VF-76N	*Hornet*
7	Duncan, Robert	Lt(jg)	VF-5	*Yorktown*
7	Dungan, Fred	Lt(jg)	VF-76N	*Hornet*
7	Eckerd, Bert	Lt	VF-9	*Yorktown*
7	Fecke, Alfred	Lt	VF-29	*Cabot*
7	Franks, John	Lt(jg)	VF-9	*Essex*
			VF-12	*Randolph*
7	Galvin, John	Lt(jg)	VF-8	*Bunker Hill*
7	Huffman, Charles	Ens	VF-14	*Wasp*
7	Jennings, Robert	Lt	VF-72	*Land*
			VF-82	*Bennington*
7	Jones, James	Lt(jg)	VF-3	*Hornet*
			VBF-3	*Hornet*
7	Kirk, George	Lt(jg)	VF-18	*Bunker Hill*
7	Manson, Armand	Lt	VF-18	*Intrepid*
			VF-82	*Bennington*
7	Maxwell, William	Lt	VF-51	*San Jacinto*
7	McCormick, William	Ens	VF-50	*Bataan*
			VF-8	*Bunker Hill*
7	McCusky, Elbert	LCdr	VF-8	*Bunker Hill*
7	Morris, Bert	Lt	VF-15	*Essex*
7	Nelson, Robert	Lt	VF-5	*Yorktown*
7	Nobel, Marvin	Lt(jg)	VF-2	*Hornet*
7	Null, Cleveland	Lt(jg)	VF-21	*Wasp*
			VF-21	*Randolph*
7	O'Mara, Paul	Ens	VF-17	*Enterprise*
7	Pope, Albert	Ens	VF-13	*Franklin*
7	Savage, James	Lt	VF-11	*Hornet*
7	Schneider, Frank	Ens	VF-33	*Land*
7	Skon, Warren	Lt(jg)	VF-2	*Hornet*
7	Toaspern, Edward	Lt(jg)	VF-3	*Belleau Wood*
			VF-18	*Intrepid*
7	Troup, Franklin	Ens	VF-29	*Cabot*
7	Truax, Myron	Ens	VF-83	*Essex*
7	Turner, Edward	Lt	VF-14	*Wasp*
7	Voris, Roy	Lt	VF-10	*Enterprise*
			VF-2	*Hornet*
7	Webb, Wilbur	Ens	VF-2	*Hornet*
7	Williams, Bruce	Lt	VF-19	*Enterprise*
7	Wilson, Robert	Lt(jg)	VF-31	*Cabot*
7	Wolf, John	Lt(jg)	VF-2	*Hornet*
7	Wordell, Malcomb	Cdr	VF-44	*Langley*
6.67	Nelson, Robert K.	Ens	VF-20	*Enterprise*
6.5	Blyth, Robert	Ens	VF-27	*Princeton*
6.5	Brewer, Charles	Cdr	VF-15	*Essex*
6.5	Cozzens, Melvin	Lt(jg)	VF-29	*Cabot*
6.5	Drury, Paul	Ens	VF-27	*Princeton*
6.5	Fowler, Richard	Ens	VF-15	*Essex*
6.5	Hamblin, Louis	Lt(jg)	VF-80	*Hancock*
6.5	Hardy, Willis	Lt(jg)	VF-17	*Hornet*
6.5	Haverland, Charles	Ens	VF-20	*Enterprise*
6.5	Lundin, Walter	Lt(jg)	VF-15	*Essex*

6.5	McGown, Edward	Lt	VF-9	*Essex*
6.5	Slack, Albert	Lt(jg)	VF-15	*Essex*
6.5	Stokes, John	Lt(jg)	VF-14	*Wasp*
6.5	Taylor, Ray	Lt(jg)	VF-14	*Wasp*
6.5	Thelen, Robert	Lt(jg)	VF-24	*Belleau Wood*
6.25	Bridges, Johnie	Lt	VF-6	*Saratoga*
			VF-7	*Hancock*
6.2	Scales, Harrell	Lt	VF-31	*Cabot*
6.08	Smith Daniel	Cdr	VF-20	*Enterprise*
6	Baird, Robert	Capt	VMF(N) 533	*USMC Land*
6	Bare, James	Lt(jg)	VF-15	*Essex*
6	Barnes, James	Ens	VF-83	*Essex*
6	Brunmeir, Carland	Lt	VF-44	*Langley*
6	Burckhalter, William	Lt(jg)	VF-16	*Lexington*
6	Byrnes, Matthew	Lt	VF-9	*Essex*
			VBF-12	*Langley*
6	Carroll, Charles	Lt(jg)	VF-2	*Enterprise*
6	Clark, Robert	Ens	VBF-17	*Hornet*
6	Coleman, Wilson	Cdr	VF-13	*Franklin*
6	Copeland, William	Lt(jg)	VF-19	*Enterprise*
6	Cowger, Richard	Lt	VF-17	*Hornet*
6	Cronin, Donald	Lt	VF-8	*Bunker Hill*
6	DeCew, Leslie	Lt	VF-9	*Essex*
6	Denman, Anthony	Lt	VF-18	*Intrepid*
6	Eberts, Byron	Lt(jg)	VBF-17	*Hornet*
6	Fash, Robert	Lt(jg)	VF-50	*Bataan*
			VF-15	*Essex*
6	Frendberg, Alfred	Lt(jg)	VF-16	*Lexington*
6	Gillespie, Roy	Lt	VF-30	*Belleau Wood*
6	Gustafson, Harlan	Lt	VF-8	*Bunker Hill*
6	Hamilton, Robert	Lt(jg)	VF-83	*Essex*
6	Hanks, Eugene	Lt(jg)	VF-16	*Lexington*
6	Harmon, Walter	Lt	VF-10	*Enterprise*
6	Hyde, Frank	Lt(jg)	VF-31	*Cabot*
6	Heinzen, Lloyd	Lt	VF-8	*Bunker Hill*
6	Houck, Herbert	LCdr	VF-9	*Essex*
6	Hurst, Robert	Lt(jg)	VF-18	*Intrepid*
6	Kane, William	Cdr	VF-10	*Enterprise*
6	Kingston, William	Ens	VF-83	*Essex*
6	Lake, Kenneth	Ens	VF-2	*Hornet*
6	Mencin, Adolph	Lt	VF-31	*Cabot*
6	Mitchell, Henry	Lt(jg)	VBF-17	*Hornet*
6	Mollard, Norman	Lt(jg)	VF-45	*San Jacinto*
6	Montapart, John	Lt(jg)	VF-44	*Langley*
6	Moranville, Horace	Lt(jg)	VF-11	*Hornet*
6	Orth, John	Ens	VF-9	*Yorktown*
6	Outlaw, Edward	LCdr	VF-32	*Langley*
6	Parrish, Elbert	Ens	VF-80	*Hancock*
6	Paskoski, John	Lt	VF-19	*Enterprise*
6	Pool, Tilman	Lt(jg)	VF-17	*Hornet*
6	Pound, Ralston	Lt(jg)	VF-16	*Lexington*
6	Rennemo, Thomas	Lt	VF-16	*Intrepid*
6	Rosen, Ralph	Lt(jg)	VF-8	*Bunker Hill*
6	Rossi, Herman	Lt	VF-19	*Enterprise*

Score	Name	Rank	Squadron	Carrier
6	Seckel, Albert	Lt	VF-18	*Enterprise*
6	Silber, Sam	LCdr	VF-18	*Bunker Hill*
6	Smith, Clinton	Lt(jg)	VF-9	*Yorktown*
6	Smith, Nicholas	Ens	VF-13	*Franklin*
6	Sturdivant, Harvey	Lt(jg)	VF-30	*Belleau Wood*
6	Taylor, Will	Lt	VF-41	*Essex*
			VF-4	*Essex*
6	Turner, Charles	Cdr	VF-31	*Cabot*
6	Umphfries, Donald	Lt	VF-83	*Essex*
6	Vineyard, Merriwell	Lt(jg)	VF-2	*Hornet*
6	Vorse, Albert	LCdr	VF-80	*Hancock*
6	Winfield, Murray	Lt(jg)	VF-17	*Hornet*
6	Wolverton, Robert	Lt(jg)	VF-45	*San Jacinto*
6	Yeremian, Harold	Ens	VBF-17	*Hornet*
5.75	Laird, Dean	Lt	VF-4	*Essex*
5.75	Revel, Glenn	Lt	VF-14	*Wasp*
5.5	Anderson, Alexander	Lt	VF-80	*Ticonderoga*
5.5	Davis, Robert	Lt	VF-18	*Intrepid*
5.5	Dewing, Lawrence	Ens	VF-14	*Wasp*
5.5	Keith, Leroy	LCdr	VF-8	*Hancock*
5.5	Sherrill, Hugh	Lt(jg)	VF-81	*Wasp*
5.5	Symmes, John	Lt(jg)	VF-15	*Essex*
5.5	Wendorf, Edward	Ens	VF-16	*Lexington*
5.5	Wood, Walter	Ens	VF-20	*Enterprise*
5.33	Balsinger, Henry	Lt(jg)	VF-29	*Cabot*
5.33	Chambers, Cyrus	Lt(jg)	VF-6	*Intrepid*
			VF-84	*Bunker Hill*
5.33	Dunn, Bernard	Lt(jg)	VF-29	*Cabot*
5.33	Humphrey, Robert	Lt(jg)	VF-17	*Hornet*
5.25	Bryce, James	Lt(jg)	VF-22	*Independence*
5.25	Crosby, John	Lt(jg)	VF-18	*Bunker Hill*
			VF-17	*Hornet*
5.25	Gray, Lester	Lt(jg)	VF-10	*Enterprise*
5.25	Pearce, James	Lt	VF-18	*Bunker Hill*
			VF-17	*Yorktown*
5.25	Prichard, Melvin	Lt(jg)	VF-20	*Enterprise*
5.25	Thomas, Robert	Ens	VF-21	*Bunker Hill*
5	Amsden, Benjamin	Ens	VF-22	*Cowpens*
5	Bailey, Oscar	Lt	VF-28	*Monterey*
5	Barackman, Bruce	Lt	VF-50	*Bataan*
5	Bartol, John	Lt	VF-16	*Lexington*
			VF-16	*Randolph*
5	Beaudry, Paul	Ens	VF-80	*Ticonderoga*
5	Bertelson, Richard	Ens	VF-29	*Cabot*
5	Bishop, Walter	Lt(jg)	VF-29	*Cabot*
5	Blair, William	Lt	VF-10	*Enterprise*
			VF-2	*Hornet*
5	Blydes, Richard	Ens	VF-2	*Hornet*
5	Borley, Clarence	Ens	VF-15	*Essex*
5	Buchanan, Robert	Ens	VF-29	*Cabot*
5	Buldoc, Alfred	Lt	VF-12	*Randolph*
5	Champion, Henry	Lt(jg)	VF-9	*Hornet*
5	Clements, Donald	Lt	VF-28	*Monterey*
5	Clements, Robert	Lt	VF-11	*Hornet*
5	Davies, Clarence	Lt(jg)	VF-8	*Bennington*
5	Denoff, Robert	Lt	VF-9	*Essex*
			VBF-12	*Randolph*
5	Driscoll, Daniel	Lt(jg)	VF-31	*Cabot*
5	Duffy, James	Lt(jg)	VF-15	*Essex*
5	Eder, Willard	LCdr	VF2,3	*Lexington*
			VF-29	*Cabot*
5	Farnsworth, Robert	Ens	VF-19	*Enterprise*
5	Feightner, Edward	Lt	VF-10	*Enterprise*
5	Flinn, Kenneth	Ens	VF-15	*Essex*
5	Foltz, Ralph	Lt(jg)	VF-15	*Essex*
5	Galt, Dwight	Lt(jg)	VF-31	*Cabot*
5	Gordon, Don	Lt	VF-10	*Enterprise*
5	Gregory, Hayden	Lt	VF-82	*Bennington*
5	Hearrell, Frank	Lt	VF-18	*Intrepid*
5	Henderson, Paul	Lt	VF-1	*Yorktown*
5	Hildebrandt, Carlos	Lt	VF-33	*Land*
5	Hill, Harry	Lt	VF-5	*Yorktown*
5	Hoag, John	Ens	VF-82	*Bennington*
5	Hoel, Ronald	LCdr	VF-8	*Bunker Hill*
5	Hudson, Howard	Lt	VF-9	*Essex*
5	Johannsen, Delmar	Ens	VBF-12	*Randolph*
5	Johnson, Wallace	Ens	VF-15	*Essex*
5	Kallin, Joseph	Ens	VF-9	*Lexington*
5	Kidwell, Robert	Ens	VF-45	*San Jacinto*
5	Kostik, William	Ens	VBF-17	*Hornet*
5	Lamb, William	Lt	VF-27	*Princeton*
5	Lamoreaux, William	Lt(jg)	VF-8	*Bunker Hill*
5	Langdon, Ned	Lt	VF-19	*Enterprise*
5	Martin, Albert	Lt(jg)	VF-9	*Essex*
5	May, Richard	Lt	VF-32	*Langley*
5	Mazzocco, Michele	Ens	VF-30	*Bunker Hill*
5	McClure, Edgar	Lt	VBF-9	*Yorktown*
5	McCudden, Leo	Lt	VF-20	*Enterprise*
5	McKinley, Donald	Lt(jg)	VF-25	*Cowpens*
5	McPherson, Donald	Ens	VF-83	*Essex*
5	Michaelis, Frederick	LCdr	VF-12	*Randolph*
5	Milton, Charles	Lt	VF-15	*Essex*
5	Mollenhauer, Arthur	Ens	VF-18	*Intrepid*
5	Moseley, William	Lt	VF-1	*Yorktown*
5	Olson, Austin	Ens	VF-30	*Belleau Wood*
5	Overton, Edward	Lt	VF-15	*Essex*
5	Owen, Edward	LCdr	VF-5	*Yorktown*
5	Philips, David	Ens	VF-30	*Belleau Wood*
5	Phillips, Edward	Ens	VF-20	*Enterprise*
5	Reulet, Joseph	Lt(jg)	VF-10	*Enterprise*
5	Rieger, Vincent	Lt(jg)	VF-31	*Cabot*
5	Robinson, Leroy	Ens	VF-2	*Hornet*
5	Robinson, Ross	Ens	VF-2	*Hornet*
5	Schecter, Gordon	Cdr	VF-45	*San Jacinto*
5	Schell, John	Lt	VF-3	*Yorktown*
5	Shackford, Robert	Lt(jg)	VF-2	*Hornet*
5	Sipes, Lester	Lt(jg)	VF-10	*Enterprise*
			VF-2	*Enterprise*
5	Sistrunk, Frank	Lt(jg)	VF-17	*Hornet*
5	Smith, Kenneth	Lt	VF-90(N)	*Enterprise*

5	Sonner, Irl	Lt(jg)	VF-82	*Bennington*
		Lt(jg)	VF-29	*Cabot*
5	Spitler, Clyde	Lt	VF-2	*Hornet*
5	Stone, Carl	Lt(jg)	VBF-17	*Hornet*
5	Strange, Johnnie	LCdr	VF-50	*Bataan*
5	Swineburne, Harry	Lt(jg)	VF-45	*San Jacinto*
5	Swope, James	Lt	VF-11	*Hornet*
5	Topliff, John	Lt(jg)	VF-8	*Bunker Hill*
5	Townsend, Eugene	Lt	VF-27	*Princeton*
5	Tracey, Frederick	Lt	VF-18	*Intrepid*
5	Ude, Vernon	Lt(jg)	VF-10	*Enterprise*
5	Vander Linden, Peter	Lt(jg)	VF-8	*Bunker Hill*
5	Van Dyke, Rudolph	Lt	VF-18	*Intrepid*
5	Vita, Harold	Lt	VF-12	*Randolph*
5	Ward, Lyttleton	Ens	VF-83	*Essex*
5	Watson, Jack	Lt(jg)	VF-33	*Land*
5	West, Robert	Lt(jg)	VF-14	*Wasp*
5	Wolley, Millard	Lt	VF-18	*Bunker Hill*
			VF-17	*Hornet*
5	Zaeske, Earling	Lt(jg)	VF-2	*Hornet*
5	Zink, John	Lt(jg)	VF-11	*Hornet*
			VF-18	*Intrepid*
			VF-7	*Hancock*

Chance Vought designer Rex Beisel was the father of the F4U. (Chance Vought)

Chance Vought F4U Corsair

Since its inception in 1917, the Vought Company had been active, but not particularly successful, in naval fighter design. In 1936 Vought-Sikorsky chief engineer Rex Beisel began work on a high performance fighter built around the powerful 1,800hp Pratt & Whitney XR-2800 Double Wasp engine. On 1 February 1938 Beisel submitted the V-166B (the V-166A was designed with an alternate engine choice), and on 30 June the prototype was ordered under the designation XF4U-1. Since the Double Wasp required a large diameter propeller, the undercarriage needed to be very high, which was a disadvantage for landing on a carrier. For this reason, after extensive wind tunnel testing, Beisel embraced the inverted gull wing design, which was to characterize the aircraft. Aside from the wing, the fighter was conventional in design, but two years went by before the prototype first flew. The delay was caused by problems P&W experienced in developing the engine, and Vought's move from Hartford into the Sikorsky plant in Stratford, CT. On 29 May 1940 chief test pilot Lyman Bullard took off from Bridgeport airport and completed a very promising maiden flight. Several months later, the XF4U-1 became the first American fighter to break the 400mph barrier. On 28 November the Navy issued a pre-production requirement for Vought to rework the design in order to simplify manufacturing procedures, and also to incorporate pilot armor protection and self-sealing fuel tanks, along with upgrading the armament. On 30 June 1941, the Navy ordered 584 F4U-1s, and the first was flown by Boone Guyton on 25 June 1942. The increase in weight caused by the modifications was offset by the incorporation of the upgraded P&W R-2800-8. The fighter had been called the Corsair after Vought's earlier O2U-1. The first 178 came off the Vought-Sikorsky assembly line in 1942. The seventh was

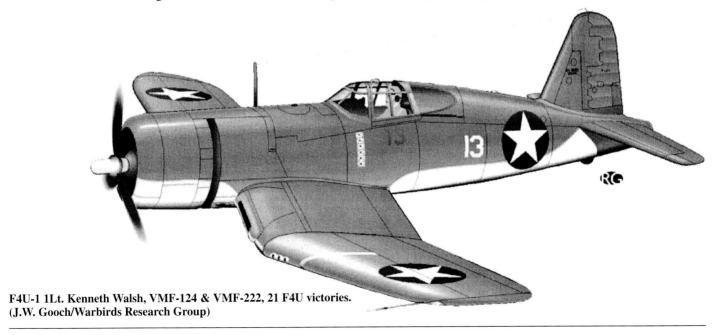

F4U-1 1Lt. Kenneth Walsh, VMF-124 & VMF-222, 21 F4U victories. (J.W. Gooch/Warbirds Research Group)

Boone Guyton flew the first F4U-1 on 25 June 1942. (Chance Vought)

2800 water injected engine. This modified fighter was designated the F4U-1A. The next significant variant was the F4U-1D, which was fitted with under wing bomb racks to give it fighter-bomber potential. About 90% of Corsair wartime production were the basic –1 versions. Brewster production of the F3A-1 ended at 735 in July 1944, Goodyear built 4,014 FG-1s and –1Ds, and Vought built 4,669 F4U-1s and –1Ds. The FAA received 1,927 as the Corsair MKs I-IV and the RNZAF 425. Vought closed F4U-1 production and began to build the F4U-4 powered by the 2,450hp R-2800, but only completed 40 of the 2,357 that it eventually built until production stopped in April 1946. A total of 12,681 Corsairs were built as production continued into the postwar years, and the fighter flew in the Korean War and remained in French inventory until 1964. The Corsair earned the Japanese nickname "Whispering Death" by downing over 2,000 enemy aircraft and delivering lethal fighter-bomber attacks.

used in carrier-suitability trials on the *Sangamon.* The trials were a major disappointment, as the landing gear shock absorbers were ineffective, and the most serious fault was that the pilot was unable to see the carrier deck on approach due to the long nose (engine). The Navy did not carrier qualify the fighter, and land-based Marine squadrons, which were to wait for the Goodyear FG-1, which had non-folding wings, received delivery of the folding wing F4U-1. The FG-1 did not fly until February 1943, and the Brewster-produced land-based F3A-1 was not completed until late April 1943. From the 689th Corsair Vought undertook modifications to carrier qualify the fighter: blown canopy for improved visibility; seating the pilot higher in the cockpit; and fitting the more powerful R-

F4U/USMC First Victory in Type

Pilots: Capt. Joseph Quilty
1Lt. James English
2Lt. Gordon Lyon

Time: 14 February 1943/1000-1300

Place: Kahili Airdrome, Bougainville

Unit: VMF-124 (Land-based)

A/C: F4U-1/Zero

Action: After a series of teething problems and modifications, the F4U-1 was first delivered to Marine Corps VMF-124, which was commissioned in September 1942 under Maj. William Gise. After a hurried training and aircraft preparation period the squadron sailed

Capt. Joseph Quilty (L) and 1Lt. James Lyon (R). (USMC)

1Lt. Kenneth Walsh. (Author/Walsh)

Lt.Col.William Millington (VMF-124) scored the first F4U carrier-based victory off the *Essex* on 3 January 1945. Here he is being congratulated for that victory by RAdm. Frederick Sherman and Capt. C.W. Weiber on the bridge of the *Essex*. (USN)

for Espiritu Santo the first week of 1943. Once in the Pacific VMF-124 had to work out many bugs in its fighter, particularly with the ignition system, before it could go into combat.

The squadron flew combat out of Fighter One Airstrip at Henderson Field on Guadalcanal. It was only two hours after it had arrived there on 12 February 1943 that it was sent out to escort a PBY on a rescue mission. The mission was a success, as two downed Marine fliers were picked up. One was 1Lt. Jefferson DeBlanc of VMF-112, who was to be awarded the Congressional Medal of Honor for earlier shooting down five Japanese on 31 January in a F4F Wildcat.

In the morning of 14 February the squadron's Corsairs were part of a mixed escort for PB4Y Liberators bombing Kahili Airdrome on southern Bougainville. The bombers flew in at 20,000 feet with AAF P-40s ahead and low, the F4Us high and behind, and a P-38 division flying top cover. The alerted Japanese were waiting with 50 Zeros in ambush at altitude. They quickly disposed of all four P-38s on top cover before diving on the P-40s, downing two before breaking through to the bombers. The F4Us met the Zeros, with Capt. Joseph Quilty and 1Lt. James English claiming a Zero each before the Zeros shot down two of the Liberators and two Corsairs for the loss of three Zeros. 2Lt. Gordon Lyon was killed, but credited with a victory when he collided with a Zero. This loss of ten aircraft to the Japanese would become known in history as the "Saint Valentine's Day Massacre," but also marked the first of 2,140 victories for the F4U Corsair.

Note: The first carrier-based Marine Corps F4U victory was scored by Lt. Col. William Millington, CO of VMF-124 off the *Essex* on 3 January 1945. After strafing while on a morning escort of VT-4 TBMs on Kagi Airfield, Formosa, he spotted two twin-engined Nick fighters and got a long burst into one, causing it to spin into the ground.

F4U/USMC First Ace in Type
Pilot: 1Lt. Kenneth A. Walsh
Time: 13 May 1943/1210-1410
Place: East of Russell Islands
Unit: VMF-124 (Land-based)
A/C: F4U-1/ 3 Zeros
Action: When VMF-124 came into the combat in the Solomons in mid-February 1943, it initiated a significant change in the balance of air power in the Pacific. Its powerful, long-ranged Corsairs savaged the once invincible Zero piloted by the last of Japan's talented veteran pilots. On 1 April Admiral Yamamoto launched "I-Operation," which was a large scale attempt to retaliate for the loss of Guadalcanal and to regain air superiority in the SWPA. The Japanese sent down 58 Zeros escorting dive bombing Vals in an attempt to disrupt the construction of the new airfield at Banika. 1Lt. Ken Walsh, who began his career as a private and mechanic, was leading a CAP of seven Corsairs east of the Russell Islands. After two hours on station his flight was relieved by six P-38s. Almost immediately after the F4Us headed back to base, the Lightnings were attacked by the Japanese. Walsh returned, surprising the Japanese. He quickly shot down a Zeke, then another, and finally a Val.

On 10 April Walsh was shot down and rescued by a small boat after ditching in the sea. In one of Japan's last serious raids on Guadalcanal, about two dozen Zekes escorted reconnaissance aircraft down the Slot. VMF-124 CO Bill Gise led 15 VMF-112 and -124 Corsairs on the interception near the Russell Islands. The Marines dropped 15 Zekes for the loss of three F4Us, including Gise. Walsh destroyed three Zekes, but after his last victory tangled with a veteran Japanese pilot. After a hard-turning, harrowing escape, he landed to find two holes in his tail.

Walsh was the first F4U ace, and increased his tally to eight by scoring two victories on 5 June; he then went on R & R in Australia. In mid-August VMF-124 moved to an airstrip under construction on Munda to support the invasion of Vella Lavella. Since the landing beaches were only 90 miles from the Japanese airbase at Kahili, the squadron had ample opportunity for combat. Walsh would score 12 victories in 2 1/2 weeks, becoming a double ace on the 12th. On 30 August, his last scoring mission in the northern Solomons before completing his tour, Walsh would win the Congressional Medal of Honor. After his supercharger quit during a B-24 escort he returned to base and borrowed another Corsair. He was able to catch up to the Libs as they were about to begin their bomb run. At 30,000 feet Walsh found himself above and behind about 50 Zekes and shot down two despite heavy anti-aircraft fire. Escaping from surrounding Zekes, he broke up attacks on the bomber formation until, outnumbered, he was forced to flee by enemy fighters. Hearing another bomber formation call for help, Walsh met another large group of Zekes and shot down two more. But this attack alerted the Japanese, who swarmed to the scene, crippling Walsh's fighter. As the Japanese closed for the kill, a P-40 and another F4U drove them off. Walsh ditched off Vella Lavella and was rescued by See Bees building the airstrip there.

1Lt. Robert Hanson. (USMC)

In November he was awarded the Congressional Medal of Honor by F.D.R. and was assigned as a flight instructor in the States. Captain Walsh was transferred to the Philippines as Ops Officer of VMF-222. On 22 June 1945, the 20 victory ace was able to sneak himself into combat and shoot down a Zero near Okinawa for his last victory. His 21 victories made him the third leading F4U scorer after 1Lt. Robert Hanson (VMF-214 and 215) with 25 and Maj. Gregory Boyington (VMF-214) with 22.

F4U/USMC Top Scorer in Type

Pilot: 1Lt. Robert M. Hanson
Unit: VMF-214 and 215
Victories: 25
Record:

V#	Date	E/A/C
(VMF-214)		
1	08-04-43	Tony
2	08-26-43	Zero
(VMF-215)		
3-5	11-01-43	2 Zeros, Kate
6-10	01-14-44	5 Zeros
11	01-20-44	Zeke
12-14	01-22-44	2 Zeke, Tony
15-18	01-24-44	4 Zekes
19-21	01-26-44	3 Zekes
22-25	01-30-44	Zeke, 2 Tojos, Zero

Action: Robert Hanson was born of Methodist missionary parents in Lucknow, India. He alternated his education between America and India, excelling as an athlete. After graduating from Hamline University in St. Paul, he enlisted in Naval flight training in May 1942. He won his wings and was commissioned as a 2nd Lieutenant at Corpus Christi in February 1943.

In July, he was assigned to VMF-214 as a replacement pilot flying the F4U Corsair. He claimed a Tony over Munda for his first victory on 4 August and went on to claim a Zero on the 26th before completing his first tour.

In October he was transferred to VMF-215 on Vella Lavella as a 1st Lieutenant. On 1 November the squadron was to support the Marine amphibious landings at Empress Augusta Bay on south Bougainville. That day it attacked a formation of 20-30 Japanese bombers and fighter escorts heading towards the navy shipping off the invasion beaches. Without warning Hanson broke off and singly attacked the Kate bomber formation so aggressively that it jettisoned its bombs. He shot down a Kate and two Zeke escorts before they turned back towards their base. Not content, Hanson followed the bombers, only to have a rear gunner hit his engine. He was able to safely ditch and get into his raft. After floating for six hours and nearly being seen by Japanese warships, he spotted an American destroyer and vigorously paddled towards it, singing a popular song of the day as ID. The new ace was picked up and returned to base. He completed his second tour without further scoring. During these tours he gained a reputation for a lack of teamwork, using lone wolf and often fool-hearty individualistic tactics.

Eligible to go home, Hanson elected to continue on to an outstanding third tour, in which he would shoot down 20 Japanese in six combats over only 17 days to earn him the nickname "Butcher Bob." In December 1943, after the fall of Bougainville, the Japanese decided to reinforce their air/sea bastion at Rabaul from their base at Truk. The American response was to move VMF-215 to Torokina airstrip at the tip of Bougainville. some 200 miles closer to Rabaul.

The "Rabaul Combats" began on 14 January when VMF-215 left Vella Lavella at 0605 and landed at Torokina an hour later. After a briefing the squadron left at 1010 to rendezvous with Navy TBF torpedo bombers at 1115 on their way to Rabaul's Simpson Harbor. Over the New Ireland coast, several flights totaling 60 Zekes were encountered. and a continuing battle developed on to the target. Hanson and his wingman, 2Lt. Richard Bowman, escorted the Avengers into Simpson Harbor, where they peeled off to challenge the defending Zeros. The two Marines made an astern attack on a pair of Zeros at 1,500 feet, each pilot getting a victory, but becoming separated. Hanson trailed a Zero into thin cloud and exploded it. He chased Zeros off the tails of two Corsairs and then decided to vacate the area. as enemy fighters were closing. Skipping from cloud to cloud, he climbed and came upon two Zeros at 3,000 feet crossing 500 feet below and in front of him. Hanson dove and got the turning Zero with a great 45 degree deflection shot. Pulling out of his dive and regaining altitude, he found himself on the tail of another Zero and dispatched it. After engaging in a few additional indefinite combats he came upon one last Zero and shot it down to become an ace-in-a-day and a double ace.

On his next Rabaul mission on 20 January, he "only" got one victory, but followed up spectacularly: 22 January he got 3 victories; 24 January-4 victories; 26 January-3 victories; and 30 January-4 victories, to give him 25 victories. Hanson had quickly moved within one victory of America's leading aces, fellow Marine Joe Foss and WWI ace of aces, Eddie Rickenbacker. At this time Richard Bong led the Air Force with 21 victories, the Navy's top ace, Ira Kepford, only had 12, while ETO ace Walt Beckham had 16. Hanson's tour was due to end in a few weeks as he took off on 3 February, the day before his 24th birthday. The mission was to be a sweep of Rabaul, but upon arriving at the target, VMF-215 found it under thick clouds and returned to base. On the way back, Hanson got permission to attack a lighthouse on Cape Alexander on the southern tip of New Ireland. The lighthouse had been used by the Japanese as an early warning outpost and flak tower, and had withstood several previous attempts to knock it out. On his second strafing pass Hanson's Corsair had part of its wing torn off by AA fire. He attempted to ditch in a storm-whipped St. George Channel, but just as the Corsair was to touch down, its wing tip hit the rough water, cartwheeling several times. A search was made for Hanson, but it appears he never escaped the sinking fighter.

VMF-215 received the first Navy Unit Commendation award for shooting down 137 Japs in 18 weeks. Because of the short term of Hanson's furious action, his feats are virtually unknown when compared to the other aces of the time. Seven months later, on 19 August 1944, Hanson's mother accepted her son's posthumous Congressional Medal of Honor.

Top F4U Scorers

Maj. Greg Boyington was the second highest F4U scorer with 22 victories. (USMC)

VMF-215 boasted three top USMC F4U aces (L-R): 1Lt. Robert Hanson (#1/25v.); Capt. Donald Aldrich (#4/20v.); and Capt. Harold Spears (#6/15v.). (USMC)

Flying the F4U Corsair (USMC)
By
Greg "Pappy" Boyington:
22 Corsair victories

As you probably all know I was with the AVG after resigning as a captain from the Marine Corps (in late 1941). When I got to Toungoo (China) I first saw the P-40s painted with the shark's mouth. We got a bunch of them that were headed for England. I had never flown an aircraft with a liquid-cooled engine, and had not flown for over three months before coming to China. I did all right until I tried to land. In the Marines we made three-point carrier landings, but even though I knew in the P-40 I had to touch the main gear first, I didn't. I bounced about ten feet in the air and headed for the weeds. I slammed on the throttle, went around again, and made a proper landing. In China the Japs could outdo us in everything: out run, out turn, out climb and out maneuver, but thank God could not out dive us. When the AVG disbanded I did not want to go into the Army Air Corps and was glad to get to the Corps. (Boyington left the AVG due to disagreements in his claims and in AVG payments, receiving a dishonorable discharge.)

At first I was the CO of VMF-122, which was flying the Grumman Wildcat at Guadalcanal. The F4F was a good little machine, but the Zero could out climb and out run us, and just about all Jap planes could out turn and out maneuver us. You needed to have a wingman around to protect you from attack. If you got into a fight you hoped to God that you had a chance to dive away. It was your only chance other than if he ran out of gas or ammo and let you go. At Cactus (Guadalcanal) we did a lot of escort duty over the "Slot," but didn't see many Japs during the tour.

I got my first look at the Corsair on Espiritu. Compared to the P-40 and Wildcat, what a sweet-flying machine. Now we could go after the Japs and not have to fly by their rules. We could now set the rules. We could climb with the Zero, and we had more speed. We could catch up to them and no longer had to wait for them to attack us. Above 12,000 feet the Corsair could outdo the Jap, and below it we could more than hold our own against just any maneuver the Jap could throw at us. But it still wasn't smart to get into a turning dogfight with them at low altitudes. It had a R-2800 (Pratt & Whitney-ed.) engine, which was a great piece of machinery. It was dependable and fast. Before I could be reassigned I broke my ankle wrestling and was sent to Australia to recuperate. (Boyington, in fact, was relieved as VMF–122 CO when he broke his leg in a drunken bar room brawl.) After it healed I bounced around as a replacement pilot before I could get my chance to form VMF-214, the "Black Sheep," in late 1943.

We (the Marines) got the Corsair because the Navy did not want them. The Navy pilots banged up a bunch of them when they tried to land them on their carriers. They could not get used to their long noses, and a blind spot which was more than a spot. They would have been stuck with them, but the Navy High Brass decided why not pawn them off on the Marines, since we were fighting off land bases. The long nose was a problem in the three-point position, either taxiing or landing. There was a complete blind spot forward. I can see why the Navy guys were not happy about landing it on a short and narrow carrier deck. But our runways were cut out of the jungle and were also very narrow. You had to look straight out the side window, since there was no room to do S-turns to see down the runway. When taking off, taxiing to the end of the runway you had to flick the tail around, look to see if it was clear of the jungle, and kick the aircraft around for the takeoff. You had to continue to look out the side window until the tail came up, when you could finally see out the front, over the nose. When landing, you swung around the end of the runway to check to see if it was clear and then go in. Once down on the runway in a three point position you just had to hope it was still clear. Once flying you had no problems with forward visibility.

Our six .50 machine guns out gunned the Japs 7.7 peashooters, and their 20mm cannon was slow shooting and not very accurate. We could tear up a Zero with a short burst, but he would have to pump us full of 7.7s or get a good hit on us with his cannon to bring us down. They always seemed to burst into flames when we hit them. The people at Chance Vought gave the Corsair a lot of protection for the pilot. This was particularly comforting when you were strafing and every damn Jap was shooting up at you.

On long missions I would bring rubber bands and string along. I would jury rig my own automatic pilot and doze off. After you have flown as long as I had you didn't need to look at the instrument panel to see what was happening. You could tell what was going on by the sound of the engine. I would not even have to open my eyes. A tap on one of the rubber bands or strings would quickly straighten matters out. I had no fear of being bounced by the Japs, as I had a lot of sharp and nervous eyes in my squadron.

I am a nonstop smoker, and you weren't supposed to smoke in the cockpit because of the fire danger. But I smoked anytime I wasn't in combat. When I was about to attack I would crack the canopy open and flip the butt out into the slipstream. My wingman, Bob McClurg, always knew when I was going to go into combat when

Gregory "Pappy" Boyington

he saw this. Another time my windshield oiled up so bad that I could not see out of it. I unbuckled my seat belt and parachute harness and opened my cockpit. I leaned into the howling slipstream and tried to wipe it off. It just smeared it up, and I still couldn't see out of it, so I turned around and went home. Lucky there were no Japs around. I loved the Corsair, and my guys and I got good results flying it.

[Editor: Boyington's appraisal of the Corsair was excerpted from an informal round table discussion during an "Air War in the Pacific" seminar on 12 September 1981 and a discussion with the author at the Tamiami Air Show several years before his death in January 1988. Also, parentheses are the author's].

Flying the F4U Corsair (USMC)
By
Archie Donohue:
12 victories VMF-112 (7v.) & VMF-451 (5v.)
9th ranked F4U ace

To start off, I am a Corsair devotee. I truly love the machine. The Corsair was the best over all WWII fighter! I back my statement with its superb kill-to-loss ratio and its continued production many years after the war. Its history in conflict continued through 1958. My conclusion is further supported by my experience of piloting all U.S. WWII fighters, and even Japan's vaunted A6M2 Zero.

After getting two victories in Grumman's rugged little F4F Wildcat over Guadalcanal in the fall of 1942 I transitioned to the F4U. I found the cockpit of the Corsair spacious and comfortable

Archie Donohue

in comparison. I had no complaints. Everything was good about it: the instrument and control layout; the radio; and the oxygen system. The only thing bad about the plane was the well-documented poor vision. But it was due to the P & W R-2800 engine, which made the Corsair a great fighter. More than a trade off. You had to make S-turns to get a good view when taxiing. However, the visibility was good on takeoff once the tail went up, and in landing before the tail touched down. In flight it was good.

The R-2800 Pratt & Whitney Double Wasp was the best aero engine of the war. They were reliable and rugged, and gave us the performance we needed. Near the end of the war Harry Ellis, of our squadron, had a cylinder shot out on a mission over Tokyo and flew it back over 60 miles to land safely under power on the *Bunker Hill*. Pulled by an enormous 13 foot Hamilton Standard propeller, the F4U had impressive climb characteristics to 20,000 feet. It cruised better than any other fighter at 20-25,000 feet. It was stable in both cruise and high speed, and could be trimmed to hands off flying. Flying a clean aircraft we could do 340 mph at 25,000 feet. Acceleration from cruise into a dive was remarkable. The Corsair possessed relatively light aileron control at high speeds as compared to the Jap Zero. This fact enabled us to either roll away from or turn inside to get at the Zero in combat. The only limitation were the G-forces we had to withstand. The introduction of the G-suit made turns easy. We had 237 gallons of internal fuel and two 62-gallon tanks built in the leading edge of the wing (these were deleted in later models). We could carry one 175-gallon centerline drop tank, or later two 154-gallon tanks hung on the two wing pylons. We could hang at 35 gallons per hour, but guzzled 275 gph in combat. But all in all we generally had enough range for our missions.

We carried six .50 caliber Brownings which were fed by 2,350 rounds (400 rpg in the four inboard guns and 375 rpg in the two outboard guns). Later F4U-1C models were re-equipped with four 20mm cannons, but I preferred the six .50s for both ground support and aerial combat. We could carry two 1,000-pound bombs and six 2-inch rockets on under wing shackles. When I flew Corsairs off the *Bunker Hill* with VMF-451 my Corsair was loaded with a 4,000-pound payload. Of course, this overload greatly decreased the performance of the aircraft until it was dropped.

The primary attribute of an aircraft is the probability of a "round trip." Its dependable engine, airframe strength, great power, maneuverability, and firepower gave the Corsair the maximum probability. No other WWII fighter could handle all facets of combat: air engagement; ground support (strafing, dive bombing, rocket attack); and carrier tactics. It was superlative as a land or carrier based fighter.

USMC F4U Corsair Aces (76 Aces/584.5 victories)

Ace Name	Rank	VMF (Unit)	F4U V.	Total V.
Hanson, Robert	1Lt	214, 215	25	25
Boyington, Gregory	Maj	214	22	24
Walsh, Kenneth	Capt	222	21	21
Aldrich, Donald	Capt	215	20	20
Thomas, Wilbur	Capt	213	18.5	18.5
Spears, Harold	Capt	215	15	15
Shaw, Edward	1Lt	213	14.5.	14.5
Cupp, James	Capt	213	12	12
Donohue, Archie	Maj	112, 451	12	14
Segal, Harold	1Lt	211	12	12
DeLong, Philip	1Lt	212	11.17	11.17
Stapp, Donald	Maj	222	10	10
Magee, Christopher	1Lt	214	9	9
Thomas, Franklin	1Lt	211	9	9
Morgan, John	1Lt	213	8.5	8.5
Snider. William	Capt	221	8.5	11.5
Swett, James	Capt	221	8.5	15.5
Hernan, Edwin	1Lt	215	8	8
Warner, Arthur	Maj	215	8	8
Brown, William	2Lt	311	7	7
Case, William	1Lt	214	7	7
Caswell, Dean	2Lt	221	7	7
Crowe, William	Capt	124	7	7
Jensen, Alvin	1Lt	214	7	7
Long, Herbert	Maj	451	7	10
McClurg, Robert	1Lt	214	7	7
O'Keefe, Jeremiah	1Lt	323	7	7
Owens, Robert	Maj	215	7	7
Ruhsam, John	1Lt	323	7	7
Wade, Robert	1Lt	323	7	7
Williams, Gerard	1Lt	215	7	7
Dillard, Joseph	1Lt	323	6.33	6.33
Durnford, Dewey	2Lt	323	6.33	6.33
Terrell, Francis	1Lt	323	6.17	6.17
Axtell, George	Maj	323	6	6
Bolt, John	1Lt	214	6	6
Chandler, Creighton	1Lt	215	6	6
Conant, Arthur	Capt	215	6	6
Dillow, Eugene	1Lt	221	6	6
Dorroh, Jefferson	Maj	323	6	6
Finn, Howard	Capt	124	6	6
Fisher, Donald	1Lt	214	6	6
Hall, Sheldon	1Lt	213	6	6
Hundley, John	1Lt	211	6	6
Jones, Charles	2Lt	222	6	6
McManus, John	1Lt	221	6	6
Mullen, Paul	1Lt	122,214,112	6	6
Shuman, Perry	Capt	121	6	6
Valentine, Herbert	Capt	312	6	6
Vedder, Milton	1Lt	213	6	6
Hansen, Herman	Maj	122, 112	5.5	5.5
Hood, William	1Lt	323	5.5	5.5
Kirkpatrick, Floyd	Capt	441	5.5	5.5
Ireland, Julius	Maj	211	5.33	5.33
Elwood, Hugh	Maj	212	5.16	5.16
Alley, Stuart	2Lt	323	5	5
Baker, Robert	1Lt	121	5	5
Balch, Donald	Capt	221	5	5
Baldwin, Frank	Capt	221	5	5
Braun, Richard	Capt	215	5	5
Carlton, William	Capt	212	5	5
Drake, Charles	2Lt	323	5	5
Farrell, William	1Lt	312	5	5
Ford, Kenneth	Capt	121	5	5
Hacking, Albert	1Lt	221	5	5
McCartney, Henry	1Lt	121, 124	5	5
McGinty, Selva	1Lt	441	5	5
Olander, Edwin	Capt	214	5	5
Poske, George	Maj	212	5	5
Post, Nathan	Maj	121, 221	5	8
Powell, Ernest	Capt	112	5	5
Reinberg, Joseph	Maj	121, 122	5	5
Scarborough, Hartwell	1Lt	214	5	5
See, Robert	1Lt	321	5	5
Weissenberger, Gregory	Maj	213	5	5
Wells, Albert	1Lt	323	5	5

F4U/USN First Victory in Type
Pilot: 1Lt. Hugh D. O'Neill
Time: 31 October-1 November 1943/2300
Place: SE of Shortland Island
Unit: VF(N)-75
A/C: F4U-2(N)/Betty
See: *First F4U Night Fighter Victory*

F4U/USN First Daytime Victory and Ace in Type
Pilot: Lt. Cdr. John T. Blackburn
First Daytime Victory
Time: 1 November 1943
Place: Empress Augusta Bay, Bougainville
A/C: F4U-1 "Big Hog"/Zero
First Ace
Time: 26 January 1944/1215-1230
Place: Lakunai Airfield, Rabaul
Unit: VF-17 (land-based)
A/C: F4U-1/Zeke
Action: The first production F4U-1 was delivered to the Navy in late July 1942, with the first carrier qualifications being held in late September 1943 on the carrier Sangamon. Various design factors caused serious problems in the adaptation of the F4U for carrier duty. VF-12, the Navy's first Corsair squadron, suffered 14 pilots killed in training. VF-17 became the second Navy Corsair unit and was led by Lt.Cdr. John Thomas Blackburn. Blackburn, who had his name legally changed to Tom in 1977, was born on 24 June 1912 in Annapolis to a distinguished Navy family. He graduated from the Naval Academy in 1933, and after completing the obligatory fleet duty he was accepted for flight training and graduated in 1937. He was CO of VF-29 aboard the Santee during "Operation

LtCdr. John Blackburn (Author/Blackburn)

Torch" in North Africa, 1942. Flying the F4F Wildcat, he ran out of fuel and had to ditch at sea. He returned to the U.S. to take over VF-17.

During land-based training the squadron suffered six fatalities, but Blackburn worked with Corsair manufacturer Vought Aircraft to remedy problems in the field which could be then incorporated on the production line. VF-17 was assigned to the Bunker Hill on its shakedown cruise in summer 1943, and through hard work proved the F4U's viability as a carrier fighter. However, upon reaching Hawaii, the unit found it was to be detached from the Bunker Hill and replaced by the favored F6F Hellcat.

The Squadron was shipped to the Solomons in September 1943, and was based at Ondonga, New Georgia, for land-based ops in late October. Keeping with the Corsair = Pirate theme, the unit called itself the "Skull and Crossbones" Squadron. On 1 November, Allied landings were made at Empress Augusta Bay on Bougainville, and VF-17 was sent up to provide morning fighter cover. Flying at 5,000 feet, they spotted a large number of Jap dive bombers escorted by 40 Zeros. Since his radio was out, Blackburn had to alert his flight by firing his guns and pointing toward the oncoming Japanese. The F4Us dove at high speed, head on, at the Japanese, who had seen the approaching Americans and went into climbing turns. Blackburn got astern of a Zero and exploded it at close range. During the combat he damaged two other Zeros. On the way back to Ondonga, he saw a lone P-40 being pursued by a Zero. Blackburn's F4U "Big Hog" closed, and a stern shot at 100 yards dispatched it for his second victory. The previous evening Lt. Hugh O'Neill of VF(N)-75 got the Navy's first F4U victory of the war.

On 8 November, Blackburn downed a twin-engined bomber over Buka Airfield, Bougainville, and a Tony on the 11th for his fourth victory. Air fighting tailed off as the invasion was secured, and Blackburn saw little action until the squadron moved up to Pive Yoke Airfield on Bougainville on 25 January 1944 to escort bombers to Rabaul. The following day VF-17 went into action escorting SBDs to Rabaul, where shortly after noon Blackburn got a Zero over Lakunai Field to become the Navy's first Corsair ace.

In the next 1 1/2 weeks he would score six more victories, including three Zeros and a Hamp while escorting B-25s over Lakunai on 6 February. Blackburn completed his tour with 11 victories, making him the Navy's second leading F4U ace. Under his command, VF-17 scored 127 victories in 75 days of combat (57 1/

2 from 27 January to 2 February). VF-17 boasted 15 aces in its ranks, including top Navy F4U ace Lt. Ira "Ike" Kepford, who had 16.

F4U/USN Top Scorer in Type

Pilot: Lt(jg) Ira C. "Ike" Kepford
Unit: VF-17
Victories: 16
Record:

#V.	Date	E/A/C
1-4	11-11-43	3 Vals & Kate
5-6	01-27-44	2 Zekes
7-10	01-29-44	4 Zekes
11-12	01-30-44	Tony & Zeke
13	02-03-44	Zeke
14-16	02-19-44	Rufe & 2 Zekes

Action: Ira Kepford was a star back on the Northwestern football team and a member of the Navy ROTC there. He became a Naval Aviation Cadet in late April 1942, getting his wings in November 1942. He was assigned to Lt.Cdr. Tommy Blackburn's VF-17, the first Navy Corsair unit. While training in the U.S. the unit became known as "Blackburn's Irregulars" because of their non-regulation flying escapades over populated areas. VF-17 became carrier qualified on the Bunker Hill, but was bumped by a Hellcat squadron and shipped to the Solomons as a land-based unit on 27 October 1943.

Although the squadron scored a number of victories in early November flying out of Odonga, New Georgia, Ens. "Ike" Kepford would not score until the 11th. On that day, VF-17 was assigned to provide CAP for Task Force carriers, then land aboard a carrier, refuel, and take off to continue patrolling. At dawn, 23 VF-17 F4Us joined 12 F6Fs of VF-33 to begin the patrol over the carriers. Running low on fuel at 0830, Blackburn's Corsairs, ironically, landed on the Bunker Hill to refuel. They took off to continue an uneventful CAP before running low on fuel again and returning to Ondonga. At 1313, FDO reported bogies 120 miles out, and VF-17 and Kepford again returned over the fleet in time to surprise a formation of retreating Val dive bombers. He quickly shot down three and damaged one. Almost immediately the reported bogies attacked, and Kepford returned over the fleet. He spotted a Kate dive bomber

Lt(jg) Ira Kepford (USMC)

just astern the *Bunker Hill* ready to release its torpedo. Kepford ignored friendly AA fire and, buffeted by the Kate's prop wash, closed to within a no-miss 50 feet. The torpedo bomber splashed in the carrier's wake. Nearly out of fuel and ammo, Kepford had to wait for a third Jap attack to subside and was forced to land on the carrier again. His aircraft was replenished, and he was able to take off and land back at base at 1800. For his busy 14 hour day (11 in the air), two carrier landings and takeoffs, and four victories and a damaged, Kepford was awarded the Navy Cross.

Kepford's next claims were made in late January 1944, when VF-17 moved over to Piva Yoke. As a Lt(jg) he got two Zekes and a probable in the Rabaul area on the 29th to become an ace. On the 29th, he flew a two-plane top cover patrol with Lt(jg) Howard Burriss for a SBD attack on Tobera Airfield, which protected Rabaul. Flying at 30,000 feet, they saw 12 Zeros 6,000 feet below. Alternating their attack the duo dove and chandelled, each shooting down four Zeros. The victories made him a double ace and added a gold star to his Navy Cross. The next day he got two more Zekes over Simpson Harbor, Rabaul, to give him 12, which put him ahead of leading Navy ace Lt. Stanley Vejtasa, who had ten since 26 October 1942. On 3 February he got another Zeke over Cape Tawui, New Britain.

On 19 February, 26 F4Us led by VF-17 XO Lt.Cdr. Roger Hedrick joined 48 other mixed fighters escorting Navy bombers to Rabaul. As Kepford's division neared New Ireland Island his wingman, Ens. Don McQueen, returned to base with engine trouble and Kepford followed. On the way back, he saw a lone Rufe floatplane at 1,000 feet off Cape Siar and shot it down. Flying at wave top and low speed, Kepford was seen by over 20 Japanese at 16,000 feet, and four intercepted him in a diving line astern attack. The first diving Zero approached at high speed. To counter, Kepford dropped his flaps to further slow his fighter, causing the Jap to over run. In pulling out of the dive the Zero framed itself fatally in Kepford's gunsights. Menaced by another Zeke and two Tonys, he was forced to head north, away from his base. Using full-throttle

and the newly installed water injection system to get maximum rpm, he managed to pull away from his pursuers over New Ireland. Finally the water for the injectors ran out as the F4U reached the sea on the other side of the island. Traveling in the wrong direction, running low on fuel, and now slowing down to be closed on by the Japanese; Kepford needed to do something. He threw the Corsair into a violent high G port turn at low speed and altitude, having to fight unconsciousness and stalling. The closest Zero tried to cut inside Kepford's turn but caught a wingtip in the water and cartwheeled into disintegration. The two Tony's gave up the chase, as they were too wide in Kepford's turn and fell behind. After four hours, the exhausted Kepford returned his perforated F4U to Bougainville on gas fumes. His three victories gave him 16, which continued him as the highest Navy scorer at the time and eventually made him the fifth highest Navy scorer and top Navy F4U scorer in the war. Kepford ended his tour and returned to the States, and was assigned non-combat duties for the duration.

The air battle of the 19th marked the end of the Japanese fighter defense of Rabaul, as they evacuated most of their remaining aircraft. At the end of its tour VF-17 had established itself as the foremost F4U Squadron. From November through February, it had been credited with 152 victories, 100 of which were collected by 12 aces. Only 24 F4Us were lost (20 in combat), along with 13 pilots (12 in combat). Blackburn's early confidence in the fighter was justified by these overwhelming statistics, and this Squadron primarily proved the fighter's worth.

Of its 2,140 victories, all in the Pacific, 1,620 were scored by the Marines and 520 by the Navy (one Air Force). There were 579 carrier victories: 361 USN and 218 USMC and 1,561 land-based: 1,402 USMC and 159 USN. There were 99 Corsair aces (75 USMC and 24 USN) who scored 761 victories.

Flying the F4U Corsair (USN/Land based)
By
Tom Blackburn: 11 victories
First USN F4U ace
2nd ranked USN F4U ace

Fifty years have passed since I've flown the Corsair, but that great experience remains with me to this day.

The F4U cockpit was strange, but very accommodating. Below the foot troughs, which extended comfortably far back, the fuselage was open. There were two small windows in the bottom to aid in dive-bombing. This space gave me the advantage of being able to dangle my feet, stretch my legs, and ease my butt and back during a long mission. The disadvantage was that it was a catch all, and in negative Gs was apt to promote at least a cloud of dust and an occasional wrench. The heating and oxygen systems were adequate. The placement of the oxygen bottle and storage battery could prove dangerous to the pilot if they were hit. The instrument layout was excellent, and the control layout was straightforward and satisfactory. Much has been written about the dreadful early visibility, and I have little to add except to note the vast improvement with the introduction of the bubble canopy and raised seat in the fall of 1943. The 4-channel VHF radio was satisfactory, but by no means overly reliable.

VF-17 had foremost Navy F4U scorers (L-R) in LtCdr. Roger Hedrick (#2/12v.total- 9v.VF-17), LtCdr. Tom Blackburn (#3/11v.) and 1Lt. Ike Kepford (#1/16v.). (Author/Blackburn)

The Pratt & Whitney R-2800 powering the Corsair, which we received in early '43, was a superb engine, but suffered from some growing pains, which were mostly corrected when we received the next batch of Corsairs, which arrived in August. A lot of the deficiencies in these early Corsairs arose from "over-engineering." There was always significant oil leakage which, coupled with the individual hydraulic cylinders for each cowl flap, made for badly fouled windshields almost immediately after takeoff. We learned early on to seek out clouds to fly through for wash jobs. Generally, the R-2800 was remarkably reliable and rugged. This was a happy contrast to the R-2600s installed in our companion VF-17's SB2Cs, which plagued them with difficult maintenance problems and catastrophic failures. Of course, we had forced landings and ditchings when the R-2800 crapped out, but they were rare, especially when you consider that inexperienced pilots were getting into clutch situations where it appeared that the only way to survive was to firewall the throttle. I have no recollection of any of our pilots beefing about the engine's performance or reliability.

The six .50 caliber machine guns on our F4Us were very reliable with careful, proper maintenance. We found out during our shakedown around Trinidad that any moisture in the gun bays or on the guns themselves was disastrous. Any oil left on the guns was an invitation for stoppages. Our standard practice on combat area flights was to fire ASAP after takeoff, then leave the guns charged and ready to fire, except for the master armament switch. After combat firing we recharged them each time to clear any unfired rounds. On an anti-shipping strafing mission I failed to do this. After attacking some small vessels, I had to pass over the harbor shore AA batteries. To my horror I found I only had one gun firing into the teeth of a ton of AA fire. A 7.7 round went through my left wing tip and then through the top of my canopy, just above my head. We bore sighted the guns to converge with the horizontal line of sight at 200 yards. Since the guns were some six feet below the gunsight this, of course, required some mental adjustments to the point of aim, especially at longer ranges, such as during strafing. Tracers were of significant help, although with air targets they were somewhat de-

ceptive. One was never quite sure of what portion of the bullet's flight was being seen. Our standard belting was armor-piercing/armor-piercing incendiary/tracer.

We found the Corsairs we took into combat to be very responsive and satisfactory in pitch and roll characteristics. The controls did not "heavy up" excessively with very high speeds.

Our Corsairs could and did take a lot of battle damage and still get home and get the pilot on the ground with minimal to zero damage. For example, on one mission Ike Kepford lost a significant portion of his right wing, all of the starboard half of his horizontal tail, and could not extend his landing gear. He bellied in at 150 knots. The plane was totaled, but Ike suffered only complete terror. Several of our aircraft sustained direct hits on the windshield from approximately dead ahead. Whether 7.7 or 20mm, the heavy glass was opaqued but not pierced.

Landing the F4U, particularly the early or "Birdcage" model, especially for the first few times on land and even more so on a carrier was a real experience and pucker producer. We insisted that our pilots make three point landings from the onset. Many Marine squadrons made Air Corps-type high-speed touchdowns tail high. Not infrequently they ran out of runway. At first the F4U oleo struts were stiff and bounce producing, and we had some wild bounces and heart stopping halts sometimes not in the bushes. The oleos were reworked and gave remarkably smooth landings, even with a high sink rate. The forward visibility on takeoff and landing attitudes was approximately zero. The landing approach was made with a fairly tight turn, and we soon learned to keep on the straight and narrow by frequently checking on either side of the long, long nose.

The Corsair was a superb fighting machine, the best of its time. It would rapidly pull away from the Jap fighters in a dive, and matched them in turning situations provided that air speed was high. The gun installation was infinitely superior to that of the Zero. Until the installation of drop tanks on the F4U, the Jap fighters had a wide margin in endurance and combat radius. It was simply a great fighter to fly in combat.

Flying the F4U Corsair (Carrier based)
By
Tom Blackburn:
11 F4U victories VF-17

Although I never flew the Corsair off a carrier in combat, VF-17 did the preliminary work with the newly delivered F4U-1A. After the flight test people at Anacostia did some incomplete carrier work on the X-model we got it about nine months later. We were scared of it, and we did not get any data on flying it and had to start from scratch. During training at Manteo, NC, we lost six pilots in accidents. The airplane was unforgiving to pilot error. Two things in particular—a nasty bounce on landing and no stall warning—made carrier landings a tough proposition.

Our first test work in the spring of 1943 was off the *Charger*, a small jeep carrier converted from a merchantman. The deck was only 50 feet wide, and when I made my first landing approach the Corsair's long nose blocked out my view of the deck. The only thing I could see was "Catwalk" Cummings, our brave LSO (Landing Signals Officer), on his platform over the water, and no deck

LtCdr. Tom Blackburn (Author/Blackburn)

was in sight. I saw Cummings give the "Roger" and then "cut" signals with his paddles. Knowing better I chopped the throttle and quickly pushed the stick forward to see the deck that I so desperately wanted to see. But I set up a sink rate of 30fps, and the aircraft was stressed for 12fps. I hit on three points and bounced up a good 20 feet. Fortunately, before I bounced again I caught the arresting hook with another, even harder jolt, which blew both tires and destroyed the wheels. After a while we perfected our technique and pronounced the F4U a carrier fighter.

In late June, VF-17 transferred to the new *Bunker Hill* for carrier qualifications under the supervision of Captain John Ballentine. We had numerous accidents due to the bad bounce trait, and also because the arresting hook design was defective. The hook would dig into the wooden decking, and when it hit a metal drain it would snap off. The aircraft would continue down the deck, out of control until it was stopped by the barrier cables, where it would flip over on its back. It looked like the Corsair not only would not become carrier qualified, but wouldn't even become accepted as a satisfactory operational fighter. Despite efforts by the Corsair manufacturer (Chance-Vought) to correct the situation, our troubles were not remedied by the end of the qualifying period. It took a lot of talking to convince Captain Ballentine to allow us to take the newly modified aircraft along with him to the West Coast. I bet him we would not blow ten tires in the next 200 landings. To my chagrin I blew a tire on my first landing, but it was only one of five, so I won ten bucks from him and a begrudging acceptance.

We shipped to Pearl Harbor in September, and when we got there we received a directive from the Navy Department. VF-17 was to be detached from the *Bunker Hill* and was ordered to report to the Solomon Islands as a land-based unit. The reason given for this shift was that VF-17 was the only Navy Corsair squadron on carrier duty, and Washington felt that logistical support would be complicated by having one carrier have Corsairs while all the others were Hellcat equipped.

By the end of 1944 the Corsair had finally become a carrier fighter. The first squadrons were Marine Corps, but somewhat later Navy squadrons came aboard. Several of the pilots in my VF-17 squadron flew Corsairs with VF-84 on the *Bunker Hill*. Roger Hedrick was the CO, and other VF-17 alumni were John Smith, John Ellsworth, and Chico Freeman, who died there in a kamikaze hit on the carrier.

USN F4U Corsair Aces (26 Aces/195.5 Victories)

Ace Name	Rank	Unit (VF)	F4U V	Total
Kepford, Ira	Lt(jg)	VF-17	16	16
Hedrick, Roger	LCdr	VF-17	12	12
Blackburn, Tom	LCdr	VF-17	11	11
Reidy, Thomas	Lt	VBF-23	10	10
Smith, John	Lt(jg)	VF-17, 84	10	10
Freeman, Doris	Lt	VF-17, 81	9	9
Gile, Clement	Lt	VF-17	8	8
Kirkwood, Philip	Lt(jg)	VF-10	8	12
May, Earl	Lt(jg)	VF-17	8	8
Burris, Howard	Lt(jg)	VF-17	7.5	7.5
Chenoweth, Oscar	Lt	VF-38	7.5	8.5
Farmer, Charles	Lt(jg)	VF-17	7.25.	7.25
Cordray, Paul	Lt(jg)	VF-17, 10	7	7
Cunningham, Daniel	Lt(jg)	VF-17	7	7
Giddea, John	Lt(jg)	VF-84	7	7
Heath, Horace	Ens	VF-10	7	7
Lerch, Alfred	Ens	VF-10	7	7
Davenport, Merle	Lt	VF-17	6.25	6.25
Mims, Robert	Lt(jg)	VF-17	6	6
Quiel, Norwood	Ens	VF-10	6	6
Godson, Lindsley	Lt	VBF-83	5	5
Kincaid, Robert	Lt	VBF-83	5	5
Laney, Willis	Lt	VF-84	5	5
Maberry, Lewis	Lt(jg)	VF-17	5	5
Schiller, James	Lt(jg)	VF-5	5	5
Streig, Frederick	Lt(jg)	VF-17	5	5

USN Fighters in the Fleet Air Arm

The Fleet Air Arm scored only 455 victories in WWII, and American-built fighters accounted for 171 1/2 of them. The F4F Wildcat was called the Martlet by the British and scored 67 victories during the war, both in the Atlantic and Pacific. The leading squadron was 882 off the *Searcher* with seven kills, four occurring in late March 1945 while escorting an Avenger raid on the Norwegian coast. The leading Martlet scorer was Lt. C.C. Tomkinson with 2 1/2 over Vichy French aircraft over northern Madagascar in May 1942.

The Corsair was the most numerous American-built fighter to see service in the Royal Navy with 2,012. Eight squadrons flew combat, with the 1836 scoring 17 and 1834 12 1/2 victories for the

F2A

USN/USMC Fighter Aerial Combat Data WWII

BASE FIGHTER	Sorties Engaging E/A/C	E/A/C Engaged		E/A/C Destroyed		Own A/C Casualties to E/A/C		Kill Ratio
		Bomber	Fighter	Bomber	Fighter	Lost	Damaged	
Carrier-Based	8799	2800	8696	1930	4327	339	499	18.5
F6F	6582	1878	6888	1387	3568	245	419	20.2
F4U/FG	1042	200	1026	159	419	34	31	17.0
FM	753	305	407	194	228	13	26	32.5
F4F	422	417	375	190	112	47	23	6.4
Land-Based	3373	1222	5062	611	1770	325	334	7.3
F4U/FG	2258	462	3617	319	1241	155	231	10.1
F6F	393	76	482	58	150	25	38	8.3
F4F	704	653	948	228	375	131	62	4.6
F2A	17	31	15	6	4	14	3	0.7

47th Wing off the carrier *HMS Victorious*. The top Corsair II pilot was 47th Wing Leader Ronald Hay, with three victories over Palembang in late January 1945. Hay had scored a Skua victory over Norway in 1940 (801 Squadron/*Ark Royal*) and four+ Fulmar I victories in the Mediterranean as part of "Force H" in 1941 (808 Squadron/*Ark Royal*).

The Hellcat served without the Fleet Air Arm in the Pacific, getting 52 victories, 19 of them over Okinawa. The carrier *Indomitable* got 39 1/2 victories, with 1839 Squadron getting seven and 1844 Squadron accounting for 32 1/2 victories, with Sub-Lt. E.T. Wilson Amos becoming an ace with 4 5/6 victories and SubLt. W.M. Foster getting 4 1/2 victories for 1844.

Brewster F2A Buffalo

The F2A was the Navy's first monoplane fighter to enter service, but that is the only distinction the barrel-like little fighter could claim. An original XF2A-1 design put forward by R.D. McCart and Dayton Brown was basically sound, and in a fly off between the Grumman XF4-1 (a F3F derivative) Brewster was awarded the prototype contract for the Model 139, which the Navy dubbed the F2A. The prototype was completed and first flown in January 1938 (under) powered by the 850hp Wright Cyclone engine. It was an unremarkable but adequate all-metal fuselage, mid-wing monoplane fighter with enclosed cockpit and retractable landing gear. In its test flights there were numerous correctable defects, and the engine was prone to over heating. It exceeded the 300mph criterion the Navy required, but won approval on its good maneuverability, and the Navy ordered 54 Model B-239s in June 1938. The caveat was that the Navy would have the option of reviewing Grumman's XF4F-2 monoplane after its development. Eleven were delivered to Navy carriers, and the remainder released for export to Finland, which increased armament to four machine guns. During 1939, the F2A-2 (B-339) was fitted with a more powerful engine, and export or-

Carrier vs. Land-Based A/C Victories

Aircraft	Service	Carrier Victories	Land-Based Victories
F6F	USN	4946	122
	USMC	1	95
	Total	4947	217
F4U	USN	218	159
	USMC	361	1402
	Total	579	1561
F4F	USN	282	215
	USMC	0	489
	Total	282	704
FM-2	USN	422	0
	USMC	0	0
TBM/TBF	USN	72	26
SBD	USN	106	32
F2A	USMC	0	10
	TOTALS	6408	2550

ders came in 1940: 40 for Belgium; 170 for Great Britain; and 92 for the Netherland East Indies AF. But problems began to appear. Reports from the European skies concluded that the Buffalo could not compete with its contemporaries. Navy carrier landings disclosed that the F2A landing gear was unable to withstand the rigors of carrier landings. Finally, export countries and the Navy requested more pilot armor protection, which further increased the weight of the fighter to a point at which it adversely affected performance. There was no easy fix without total redesign of the entire aircraft. With Grumman's F4F-3 proving itself to be the first Navy fighter to be carrier qualified, the Navy ordered its first 58 of thousands.

U.S. Carrier Fighters vs. Enemy Aircraft

Carrier Type Fighter Type		Total Action Sorties	Enemy Aircraft Destroyed In Combat		Own Losses to E/A/C
			Bombers	Fighters	
CV	Totals	51,821	1271	3169	263
	F6F	41,715	933	2641	185
	F4U (USN)	6488	100	260	18
	F4U (USMC)	2650	53	159	16
	F4F	968	185	109	44
CVL	Totals				
	F6F	15,099	406	876	58
		15,099	406	876	58
CVE	Totals	19,076	263	282	18
	FM	12,925	194	228	13
	F6F (USN)	5426	48	51	2
	F6F (USMC)	146	0	0	0
	F4U (USMC)	443	6	0	0
	F4F	136	5	3	3
Carrier Fighter	**Totals**	85,996	1940	4327	339

CV 4440 E/A for 263 16.9 to 1 ratio
6,267 E/A/C destroyed for 339 U.S. fighters lost to E/A/C 18.5:1 ratio
CVL 1,282 E/A for 58 22.1 to 1 ratio
CVE 545 E/A for 18 33.0 to 1 ratio

	% Action Sorties Flown	E/A/C Destroyed
CV	60.3%	70.8%
CVL	17.6 %	20.5%
CVE	22.1 %	8.7%

USMC/USN Land-based Fighters vs. Enemy Aircraft

SERVICE/YEAR		Total Action Sorties In Combat	Enemy Aircraft Destroyed		Own Losses to E/A/C
			Bombers	Fighters	
USMC		55,597	527	1432	232
	1941-42	923	108	221	74
	1943	2907	106	555	107
	1944	30,717	19	383	37
	1945	21,050	234	273	14
USN		4189	84	338	93
	1941-42	166	25	26	19
	1943	1388	57	162	56
	1944	2514	2	150	18
	1945	121	0	0	0
Land-based Fighter Totals		59,786	611	1770	325

USMC 1,959 E/A/C destroyed for 232 lost 8.4 to 1 kill ratio
USN 422 E/A/C destroyed for 93 lost 4.5 to 1 kill ratio
2,381 E/A/C destroyed for 325 lost 7.3 to 1 kill ratio

USN/USMC Fighter Aircraft vs. Various Japanese Aircraft
(1 September 1944-15 August 1945)

E/A/C	F6F Kills	F6F Lost	F4U/FG Kills	F4U/FG Lost	FM Kills	FM Lost	TOTALS Kills	TOTALS Lost
Zeke/Hamp	1000	75	327	27	87	2	1414	104
Oscar	396	26	46	1	38	3	480	30
Tony	275	11	60	2	29	0	364	13
Tojo	283	9	53	4	17	2	353	15
Frank	114	12	28	4	0	0	142	16
Jack	33	9	9	3	1	0	43	12
George	28	0	7	0	0	0	35	0
Myrt	36	0	19	0	0	0	55	0
Nate	59	1	82	1	1	0	142	2
U/i S/E	90	6	3	0	10	0	103	6
Total Fighters	2314	149	634	42	183	7	3131	198
Val	215	0	187	2	88	0	490	2
Judy	134	1	36	1	5	0	175	2
Kate	26	0	13	0	4	0	43	0
Jill	105	0	23	0	7	0	135	0
Sonia	21	0	7	0	1	0	29	0
Other VB/VT	14	1	5	0	0	0	19	1
Total VB/VT	515	2	271	3	105	0	891	5
Jake	50	0	6	0	7	0	63	0
Pete	18	0	8	0	0	0	26	0
Rufe	15	0	0	0	0	0	15	0
Rex	0	0	6	0	0	0	6	0
Paul	0	0	1	0	0	0	1	0
Dave	0	0	3	0	0	0	3	0
Total F/P	89	0	24	0	7	0	120	0
Betty	185	6	29	1	2	0	216	7
Dinah	48	0	23	0	1	0	72	0
Frances	118	0	7	0	18	0	143	0
Irving	20	0	2	0	0	0	22	0
Nick	46	1	16	0	4	0	66	1
Sally	33	0	5	0	16	0	54	0
Helen	12	0	9	1	0	0	21	0
Lily	27	0	3	0	21	1	51	1
Nell	18	0	1	0	0	0	19	0
Peggy	6	0	4	0	0	0	10	0
U/i T/E	17	1	0	0	9	0	26	1
Total T/E	530	8	98	2	81	1	709	11
Flying Boats	17	0	0	0	0	0	17	0
Transports	36	0	3	0	1	0	40	0
Trainers	17	0	12	1	0	0	29	1
U/I	0	1	0	1	0	1	0	3
TOTAL	3518	160	1042	49	377	9	4937	218

After the fall of Belgium, England received that country's Buffalo allocation of nearly 200. The fighter was rejected for European service by the RAF and FAA and relegated to squadrons in Malaya, but after the fall of Singapore it was withdrawn from operational service. In the Dutch East Indies the fighter was almost annihilated, but did score 55 victories against the Japanese. Meanwhile, Brewster worked on changes on the F2A-3, but introduced so many equipment and structural additions and revisions that the increased gross weight further reduced performance and controllability. The last of the 108 F2A-3s rolled off the production line in March 1941. The Buffalo did somewhat vindicate itself in Finnish service. Flying against inferior Russian fighters it scored numerous victories and had a positive kill ratio until 1944.

F2A First Victory in Type

Pilot: Capt. James L. Neefus
Time: 3 March 1942/Late AM
Place: Southwest of Midway
Unit: VMF-221/USMC
A/C: F2A-3/Mavis

Action: Few American fighters were as controversial or maligned as the stubby F4A Brewster Buffalo. The fighter was beset by manufacturing problems and profiteering scandals within the Brewster company, along with inherent design and performance deficiencies which rendered it obsolete before it ever reached combat.

With the Pacific Fleet, VF-2 was the only Navy squadron to utilize the F2A-3 at the onset of the war, flying scouting missions. VF-2 re-equipped with F4F Wildcats, and the Navy gladly passed the Buffalos on to the Marine Corps. Marine Air used these castoffs as training aircraft for newly formed squadrons. Once trained, these squadrons would convert to Wildcats and pass the Buffaloes on to other new squadrons. However, two operational Marine Corps squadrons were equipped with F2A-3s: VMF-211 based on Palmyra Island, and VMF-221 flying from Midway.

Capt. James Neefus receives the Navy Cross from Adm. Nimitz on 2 May 1942. (USMC)

The Japanese employed large Kawanishi flying boats—the H8K Emily and Ki-97 Mavis—which flew out of Wotje in the Marshall Islands to recon American island bases. The Japanese planned to extend the range of these flying boats by refueling them from large submarines at sea. In the mid-morning of 10 March 1942, during a prototype submarine refueling mission, two Mavis took off from Wotje: one toward Midway, and the other to Johnston Island. They were to rendezvous with the refueling sub at French Frigate Shoal, which lies halfway between Midway and Pearl Harbor. Radar at Midway intercepted one Jap snooper about 45 miles to the southwest. VMF-221 CO Maj. Verne McCaul dispatched a four plane division of Buffaloes under Capt. James Neefus. The interception was made at 10,000 feet, with Neefus making the first pass, setting fire to an engine. The Jap dove to 3,000 feet, with Lts. Francis McCarthy and Charles Somers each making ineffective firing passes. MG Robert Dickey attacked from astern, but had to break off combat when his aircraft was hit by a Jap gunner and he was wounded in the shoulder. Neefus made a second pass, again scoring hits on the seaplane, which crashed into the sea, scattering burning debris. Marine aviation CO on Midway Col. W.J. Wallace rewarded Neefus and his division for their first victory with a bottle of whiskey.

Flying the F2A Brewster Buffalo
By
Charles Kunz: 2 F2A victories VMF-221
8 total victories (6v. F6F)

I arrived at Wake Island in March 1942 with other second lieutenant reinforcements for VMF-221. We had 24 F2A-3s when we arrived, including several additional newer versions. We had lots of time to become familiar with the fighter by June, when the Japanese were threatening to invade the island. The fighter had been an underachiever from its prototype days. It supposedly had been improved and modified to our –3 "combat ready" version, which the Navy had "given" the Marine Corps, as they wanted the F4F Wildcat. We did receive four of the early model Wildcats in June.

The F2A cockpit was fairly comfortable for a fighter. There were adjustments for the rudder pedals, and the seat could be moved up and down. It did not have heat, and the oxygen system was primitive, with a very small, uncomfortable mask. The canopy had clear side Plexiglas panels and inside mounted grab handles to aid in opening the sometimes-stubborn sliding mechanism. The instrument panel layout was standard and generally good. The controls were normal and manageable, though somewhat heavy. Like all tail draggers, the F2A had poor forward visibility for taxiing, so S-turns or ground crew walkouts were necessary. On takeoffs and landings, the pilot scanned, left and right, beyond the wing and engine of the stubby fighter. The visibility on landings needed to be precise, as the F2A was a carrier fighter, but fortunately it was never used as such. The radio and throat mike were primitive but reliable, and adequate for our purposes on Midway. The bulky 28" telescope gun sight was located in the center of the windscreen, and was inadequate when compared to the next generation of electrically projected windscreen sights. The armament of 2 x .30 caliber synchronized in the cowling and 2 x .50 caliber wing guns were only just adequate.

I personally did not like the 1,200hp Wright R-1820-40 engine or the electric prop control. But from personal experience I do have to give it an "A" for ruggedness, as numerous Jap 20mm and 7.7 holes did not stop me from getting back to Midway. The –3 was given 80 extra gallons of fuel, which gave it more than adequate range for our patrols from Midway. There were no provisions for external fuel tanks. The ongoing modifications from the prototype had increased the weight of the –3 so much that it was seriously underpowered and a notoriously slow climber. Most of this increased weight was due to the addition of armor protection (seat plates and backs), increased fuel capacity, self-sealing fuel tanks, and increased ammo capacity. Like the early F4F, it was a poor performer at altitude and had a tendency for high speed stalls. The –3 was probably a few knots faster than the F4F, but overall the F4F was superior to the F2A in performance. When compared to the Jap Zero neither one was in its league. The enemy had the advantage of speed and maneuverability, a winning combination.

In the air battle over Midway on 4 June 1942, I was credited with two victories in the F2A over the Japanese Kate dive-bombers. That morning our division was at 21,000 feet when our CO, Capt. Kirk Armistead, radioed a tally-ho dead ahead and down. We were in ideal position for a high side attack on a large formation of bombers escorted by Zeros. I quickly shot down one surprised bomber and then another, but picked up three Zero attackers after my second victory. I headed back to Midway at 20 feet off the water, and fortunately my pursuers abandoned their attack. I was grazed behind the ear, and my fighter was riddled by Jap 7.7 and 20mm fire. Bleeding and scared, I then had to wait 15-20 minutes until the enemy finished his attack on our airfield before I could land. I was lucky—the squadron lost two-thirds of its F2As. After the battle we survivors suggested that the Buffalo be transferred to the training command (which it was as an advanced fighter trainer). All in all, for the time, the F2A was not so bad, but neither was it very good. I know I was a whole lot happier in the Wildcat.

2Lt. Charles Kunz.
(Author/Kunz)

The F2A Brewster in Foreign Service

In April 1940, one month after the Winter War of 1940 against Russia, the Finnish Air Force Lentolaivue (Fighter Squadron) 24 was re-equipped from its Fokker D.XXIs to the Brewster (as the Finns called them). Four years later, in April 1944, the squadron converted to the Me-109 after scoring 477 confirmed victories, with 13 of 35 Finnish Brewster aces becoming double aces in the obsolesent fighter. Hans Wind was the top Brewster ace with 39 of his 75 victories in it, while top Finnish ace Eino Juutialinen with 94 1/6 victories had 34 in the Brewsters. Before Finland capitulated in September 1944, a further 19 victories were scored by Lentolaivue 26, which inherited the fighter from L.24 for a total of 496.

Miscellaneous Fighters

Douglas SBD Dauntless

The SBD's role in the Pacific war goes beyond its sinking of four Japanese carriers at the Battle of Midway. It was the only American aircraft to engage in all carrier battles from the Coral Sea through the Battle of the Phillippine Sea. The Dauntless is best known as a dive bomber, but it did account for 138 aerial victories. Some USN SBD squadrons were credited with 94 air-to-air victories, mostly in 1942. These victories were divided between the two cowl-mounted .50 caliber machine guns of the pilot and the flexible twin .30s of the rear gunner (five victories were squadron credited). There were 22 USMC SBD victories over Guadalcanal, and another 22 claimed by land-based Marine squadrons over the central and upper Solomons in 1943-44. Of the Marine SBD victories, 35 were credited to gunners, seven to pilots, and three as joint victories.

SBD First Victory in Type

Pilot: Lt. Clarence E. Dickinson
           ARM1/C William C. Miller
Time: 7 December 1941/0825
Place: Off Barber's Point, Pearl Harbor
Unit: VS-6/*Enterprise*
A/C: SBD-2/Zero
Action: On 7 December 1941 the carrier *Enterprise* was 200 miles off the coast of Oahu after delivering planes to Wake Island. Cdr. Howard "Brigham" Young of VS-6 took off from the carrier at 0615 in a SBD-2 Dauntless with Lt.Cdr. Bromfield Nichol riding in the rear seat, carrying a highly classified radio transmitter. Young and his wingman, Ens. Perry Teaff, proceeded to Ford Island, Oahu, followed by 16 other SBDs of Fighting Six led by Lt. Cdr. Hallsted Hopping. Young and his wingman arrived off Barber's Point at 0820, assuming the circling aircraft over Ewa were Army fighters until they were attacked as they landed safely at Ford Island.

Ens. Manuel Gonzalez of VS-6 was probably the first Japanese aerial victory and the first American loss. Upon approaching Oahu, Gonzalez's last radio contact warned: "Please don't shoot! Don't shoot! This an American plane." Then to his rear gunner: "We're on fire, bail out." Gonzalez and his gunner were lost without a trace.

Lt(jg) Clarence E. Dickinson and his wingman, Ens. J.R. McCarthy, were alerted by the smoke and anti-aircraft bursts over Ford Island, but were nonetheless surprised by Zero fighters.

Lt. Clarence Dickinson. (USN)

Dickinson has described this encounter in his book *The Flying Guns "6."* McCarthy flew into Zero bullets intended for Dickinson, his dive bomber bursting into flame and slowly descending. McCarthy climbed out of his cockpit and jumped, but hit the tail assembly, breaking his leg. Fortunately, his parachute opened and he landed safely, but was hospitalized for months afterwards. McCarthy's rear gunner was unable to get clear of the encumbering rear seat/machine gun area and perished in the crash. Meantime, Dickinson found four or five Zeros on his tail. His rear gunner, ARM.1/C William Miller, desperately fired, downing one attacker and expending all six of his ammunition drums. Miller's victory was confirmed by Marines on the ground at Ewa. Miller had been wounded in the initial Zero attack and was mortally wounded in subsequent attacks. Dickinson bailed out at a low altitude and landed at Ewa about 0825. Twelve SBDs landed at Ford despite intense AA fire.

SBD Top Scorer in Type
Pilot: Lt(jg) John A. Leppla
             ARM.3/C John Liska
Unit: VS-2/USN
Victories: 4 (+2 Rear gunner + 1 F4F VF-10)
Record:

V#	Date	E/A/C
1-2 *	05-07-42	Zero, Floatplane
3-4	05-08-42	2 Zeros
5	10-26-42	Zero (F4F/VF-10)
*(Liska) (2 v.)	05-07-42	2 Zeros

Action: John Leppla was an unusual ace in that he scored most of his victories while flying a dive bomber! On his 26th birthday he took part in the Battle of the Coral Sea, 7-8 May 1942. On the 7th, Leppla followed *Lexington* CAG Cdr. William Ault towards the Japanese fleet. The Air Group spotted the carrier *Shoho* escorted by four cruisers and a destroyer, and Scouting Two dove to the attack. Fourth in line, Ens. Leppla began his dive and was followed by two Zeros, which closed quickly astern. Leppla's rear gunner, ARM.3/C John Liska, shot down both with his twin .30 cal. machine guns.

Meantime, another Zero overran Leppla and attacked the number three SBD ahead. Interrupting his dive on the Jap carrier, Leppla got the Zero in his sights and fired his two .50 cal. guns with deadly effect. He continued in his dive on the enemy carrier and scored a near miss with his 500lb. bomb. Returning to the *Lex*, they encountered an enemy floatplane and closed in on it. The Jap turned into Leppla's attack and a dog fight followed. Both adversaries scored hits, but finally Leppla's Douglas got a telling burst and downed it. Leppla landed his damaged bomber back on the carrier, thoroughly holed with 7.7 and 20mm hits.

The next day, Leppla and Liska were back in the air when they were scrambled to intercept Japanese torpedo bombers. Unable to get the Jap bombers that put torpedoes in the *Lexington*, they were attacked by swarms of escorting Zeros. Leppla immediately shot one down. Outnumbered, Leppla turned into each attack and downed another. But soon he found one of his machine guns inoperable, and the other out of ammunition. The SBD had sustained numerous hits, and Leppla needed to nurse it back to the carrier. Seeing an easy target, the Zeros closed for the kill. Leppla maneuvered the SBD to put Liska into firing position. The rear gunner got several hits which drove off these attackers. Upon reaching the Task Force, Leppla had to land on the *Yorktown*, as the *Lexington* had been heavily hit. Gasoline vapors from a broken fuel line inside the *Lex* exploded, and a second explosion two hours later led to the order to aboandon ship, and she was sunk by her own escorts.

Lt.Cdr. James Flatley recruited Leppla into his newly organized F4F Wildcat unit VF-10, the "Grim Reapers." Now a Lt(jg), he was a flight leader on the *Enterprise* off the Solomons. During the Battle of Santa Cruz, 26 October 1942, his squadron escorted VT-10 Avengers. The formation was attacked, and three Avengers were quickly shot down. To save the remaining bombers, Leppla turned his division into the Zeros. The Wildcats were decimated, with Leppla downing a Zero before he died. The victory was confirmed by sole survivor "Chip" Reding, who also reported that he saw Leppla bail out and that his chute did not fully open. In the Battle of Santa Cruz, in which Leppla was KIA, VS-10 got eight victories, while VB-8 and VS-8 off the *Hornet* claimed five Kates.

Leppla's victory record has been questioned by historians and purists. Many sources credit him with one victory during the Battle of the Coral Sea, but researcher Dr. Frank Olynyk, gives him two and Liska two. Postwar victory boards credit the rear gunner's claims

Lt(jg) John Leppla and ARM.3/C John Liska. (USN)

to the plane and pilot, so Leppla could be considered a SBD ace with six victories.

On 7-8 May 1942, the SBD had its greatest day in air-to-air combat during the Battle of the Coral Sea in the strikes against the Japanese fleet and the defense of the *Lexington*. Four SBD squadrons claimed a total of 22 of the 59 Japanese aircraft shot down (eight and one probable on the first day and 14 and one probable on the second day). VS-2 got 13 kills, VS-5 got 4, VB-2 got 3, and VB-5 got 2 for a loss of seven SBDs on the 7th and 13 on the 8th.

In the late morning of the 8th, VS-2 and –5 returned early from an early search and were launched to provide additional low-level anti-torpedo patrol. Lt(jg) Stanley Vejtasa of VS-5 became separated from his division and was attacked by eight Zeros that were escorting torpedo bombers. During the three quarter hour sea level fight Vejtasa determinedly turned into the Japanese attacks. His Dauntless was hit several times, and a piece of metal pierced his leg, but he kept his head, conserved his ammunition, and downed three Zeros. Vejtasa would score 7 1/2 (seven on 26 October 1942) more victories flying the F4F for VF-10 off the *Enterprise*. Lt(jg) William Hall of VS-2 off the *Lexington* intercepted nine Kates and shot down two. As he was coming around for a firing run he was jumped by five escorting Zeros. Hall pushed his SBD into high speed turns, and he was able to get a quick high deflection shot on a Zero, which veered into the sea. Hall's SBD took hits, and he was severely wounded in both feet. Unable to disengage combat, he hit a second Zero whose fate he did not wait to determine and nursed the badly damaged dauntless back to the *Lexington*. In severe pain, Hall managed to land his aircraft safely, but the aircraft was written off and dumped overboard before the carrier was abandoned. Hall was awarded the Medal of Honor for his courageous action.

After the carrier battles of 1942 the SBDs saw little aerial combat. In 1943 they scored 13 victories for two losses, and in 1944, before they left carrier service they claimed five victories for two losses. The star squadron of these late aerial battles was VB-16 under Cdr. Ralph Weymouth off the new *Lexington*. On 4 December 1943, in an attack on Japanese bases at Roi on the Kwajalein Atoll, the squadron scored 7 1/2 victories and two probables. In this battle Lt. Cook Cleland pulled up along side a Betty bomber.

His gunner, ARM2/c Bill Hisler, and the enemy bomber turret gunners traded volleys, much in the tradition of Nelson at Trafalgar. On 20 June 1944 VB-16 carried out the last SBD dive bombing attack of the war. After hitting the Japanese carrier *Hiyo*, the nine remaining VS-16 SBDs were attacked by Zeros. In the running escape Weymouth's SBDs shot down two Zeros and damaged 13 before being rescued by Hellcats.

Top-scoring USN SBD Pilots

Pilot Name	Rank	Unit	V.
Leppla, John	Lt(jg)	VS-2	4
Hall, William	Lt(jg)	VS-2	3
Vejtasa, Stanley	Lt(jg)	VS-5	3
Cleland, Cook	Lt.	VB-16	2
Johnson, William	Lt(jg)	VS-10	2
Neely, R.F.	Ens.	VS-2	2
Zalewski, Chester	Lt(jg)	VS-71	2

Top-scoring USN SBD Gunners

Gunner Name	Rank	Unit	V.
Liska, John	ARM2/c	VS-2,	
VS-10	4		
Colley, W.C.	ARM2/c	VS-10	2

Top-scoring USN SBD Squadrons

Squadron	Carrier	CV	V.
VS-2	*Lexington*	CV-2	13.5
VS-10	*Enterprise*	CV-6	11
VB-16	*Lexington*	CV-16	10.5
VB-2	*Lexington*	CV-2	8
VS-5	*Yorktown*	CV-5	6
VS-6	*Enterprise*	CV-6	6
VS-71	*Wasp*	CV-7	5

Top-Scoring USMC Pilots and Gunners

Name	Rank	VMSB	V.
McGuckin, John *	1Lt.	-132	2
Read, Wallace +	Sgt.	231	3
Byrd, Virgil +	Sgt.	231	2

* = pilot + = gunners

Top-scoring USMC Squadrons

Squadron	Base	V.
VMSB-132	Solomons	6
VMSB-231	Solomons	6
VMSB-236	Solomons	5
VMSB-241	Midway, Solomons	5
VMSB-141	Solomons	4
VMSB-233	Solomons	4

Lt(jg) William Hall receiving the CMH. (USN)

TBF/TBM Top Scorer in Type
Pilot: Lt. Charles E. Henderson
Unit: VT-10 & VT(N)-90
Victories: 4
Record:

V#	Date	E/A/C
1	06-05-44	Jake VT-10
2	06-07-44	Jill VT-10
3	03-19-44	Emily VT(N)-90
4	05-13-45	Rufe VT(N)-90

Action: The heavy, underpowered TBM Avenger manufactured by Grumman and GM was an unheralded and mostly unloved Navy torpedo bomber whose major redeeming feature was as a weapons platform. The aircraft carried an assortment of bombs, rockets, and depth charges in its multiple capacity as a dive and torpedo bomber/day and night bomber. The bomber was armed with three gun positions: dorsal turret (1 x .50 cal.); ventral hatch (1 x .30 cal.); and forward-firing (1 x .30 cal. cowling initially, then 2 x .50 cal wing later). During the war Avenger crews claimed 98 aerial victories (72 from carriers and 26 from land bases). During the Battle of the Eastern Solomons on 24 August 1942, VT-3, a *Saratoga* torpedo squadron flying off the *Enterprise*, encountered a formation of Vals six miles from the carrier. In a time of sketchy record keeping, it appears that gunner ARM3/C C. L. Gibson scored the first TBM victory when he shot down a Val in the late afternoon for VT-3.

One Avenger pilot came within an empty ammo tray and an empty fuel tank of becoming an ace! Lt. Charles Henderson served two tours on the *Enterprise*, his first with VT-10 and second with VT(N)-90. In eight combat contacts he claimed four victories, one probable, and one damaged.

During his first combat mission on 16 February 1944, Henderson had completed a bombing run on Truk Harbor when he spotted a small Japanese seaplane heading back toward base. Pushing the lumbering Avenger to its top speed, Henderson was still

forced to fire two long bursts at extreme range with his two custom-mounted .50 cal. machine guns. The seaplane began to smoke, but Henderson was compelled to break off his attack, as he was being led into enemy AA fire. On his return to the *Enterprise*, he encountered an oblivious Zero that was attacking another Avenger. Unfortunately, his wing guns were empty, so he pulled alongside the vulnerable Jap in order that his rear turret gunner could get a shot. However, the Avenger's rear turret was useless, even at such close range. The American's harmless persistence so irritated the Jap pilot that he broke off his attack on the first Avenger and took off after his new nemesis. Henderson deftly maneuvered to escape five passes by the Zero, which finally ran out of ammo.

During a long-range patrol off Saipan on 5 June, Henderson encountered a Japanese Navy Jake seaplane. By carefully stalking through cloud cover he got close enough to blow up the unsuspecting recon aircraft. Two days later he shot down a JNAF Jill torpedo bomber. These two victories and the damaged wetted his appetite for aerial combat. When VT-10 finished its tour in July, he decided to remain with his CO, Lt.Cdr. William Martin, who was assigned to take over Night Air Group 90 on the *Enterprise*. Martin was a long-time advocate of night carrier operations, and AG(N)-90 was the first night unit to embark on a large fleet carrier, flying F6F Hellcats with VF(N)-90 and Avengers with VT(N)-90.

Relegated again to flying the Avenger did not dampen the enthusiasm of the aspiring fighter pilot and his radar operator, Lt(jg) Edwin Halbach. They spent long hours practicing night air-to-air radar interceptions on friendly aircraft and then fruitless contacts and attempted interceptions on enemy aircraft. Finally, on 19 March 1945, Halbach picked up a bandit on his radar scope, and the two crewmates expertly maneuvered through a misty, rainy night to contact a large Emily flying boat at 12,000 feet. As soon as the Avenger fired the unwieldy Emily tried to evade, but Henderson stayed on its starboard wing, pumping .50 cal. bullets into its wing root and engine. The battle dropped from 12,000 feet to nearly wave top level. Henderson fired one last long burst that set the Jap on fire to crash into the sea.

On 13 May, off Kyushu, Japan, they engaged a George JNAF fighter, and on a perfect gunnery run in the clear pre-dawn, hit the Jap fighter. Probably low on fuel, the Jap did not do the usual—explode—and flew off smoking for a probable. Soon, a Zero Navy Rufe floatplane was contacted, and the Avenger began a long "dogfight." Henderson scored hits by lowering his wheels and dropping his flaps to enable him to turn inside his elusive foe and put it into the sea. After four victories and almost a fifth, Henderson's fantasies of acedom came to an abrupt end when that same day the *Enterprise* was crashed by a kamikaze and retired from combat for the duration.

Lt. Charles Henderson (center). (USN)

CHAPTER 10

Night Fighters

A Brief Background

Unlike the English, the Americans never felt an immediate urgency for a night fighter, and therefore never put a very high priority on its development and production. After America's entry into the war the enemy's nighttime aerial activity and potential posed no real threat to the outcome of the war. Nonetheless, the USAF developed and produced a "pure, from a blank sheet" night fighter, the P-61 Black Widow. The irony of this situation lies in the fact that the RAF, besieged at night during the Battle of Britain, relied on converting existing two-seat aircraft into makeshift night fighters. The Air Ministry believed that a single-seat fighter would prove to be too difficult to fly and to tune the radar simultaneously. Great Britain never took a "pure" night fighter into inventory until after the war.

Of over a dozen night fighter types—mainly single seat—tried during WWII by the U.S., three emerged as the most successful: the Air Force's P-61; and the Marine/Navy's F6F-5N Hellcat and the F4U-2 Corsair.

As early as October 1940, after the British unselfishly disclosed the secrets of their radar, the USAAC formulated specifications for a "from scratch" night fighter. The outcome was the XP-61 design proposal submitted by Northrop. The overdone design was too sophisticated and complex, culminating in the P-61, which was a large, costly, complicated, twin-engine maintenance nightmare. By the time the aircraft was over its teething problems and combat-ready, the tactical situation gave it no purpose, surrender was at hand, and aviation's future was looking toward the jet engine.

Paradoxically, the most successful American night fighter statistically was the Grumman Hellcat, a single-seat day fighter conversion. The F6F was chosen over the F4U as the Navy/Marine night fighter in the Pacific. Both had good visibility and adaptability to the (N)ight radar-carrying configuration. The Corsair had a performance advantage at altitude and a small superiority in speed. But because the Hellcat was easier to land on a carrier and was a better gun platform, it was initially given the nod over the Corsair.

Night Fighter Training

In July 1942 night fighter training began at the Fighter Command School, Night Fighter Division, AAF School of Applied Tactics in Orlando, FL. The radar operators were sent to the Airborne Radar School at Boca Raton, FL. Pilot training was composed of two stages: night flying (78 daylight flying hours and 137 hours of ground school); and night fighting (76 hours of night flying and 30 hours of ground school). Ground school subjects included instrument flying, night navigation airborne radar, aircraft recognition, searchlight coordination, and airborne-ground control radar coordination. Pilots and crew would receive 90 hours of Link trainer flying, 93 hours of instrument flying, 15 hours of night interception, and 10 hours of ground control interceptions. The lack of sufficient training aircraft and radar failures hindered training. In April 1943 the 414th, 415th, 416th, and 417NFS completed training and deployed overseas.

In January 1944 the training program was relocated to Hammer Field, near Fresno, California, under the administration of the 4AF and the 481st Night Fighter Operational Training Group. After initial training the night fighter crews were placed into Overseas Training Units. The OTUs entered three one month phases. Phase One was aircraft familiarization training. Phase Two concentrated on shaping the pilot and R/O into a team, with day and night interceptions practiced. Phase Three was advanced training, with emphasis on night flying. After a two-month period of organizational training the night fighter squadrons were ready for combat. The 481st graduated the 422nd NFS in March 1944 and the 425th and 426th NFS in May 1944. In May the night fighter training scheme again changed. The 319th Wing replaced the 481st and graduated the 427th, 547th, 548th, 549th, and 550th NFS.

The Art and Science of Nightfighting

The basic control unit of the night fighter group was the CGI (Ground Control Intercept Station), which was either ship or land-based. It was managed by a fighter director and was able to operate as an independent radar and control station. "Bogeys" (unidentified night intruders) were to be detected on the GCI radar screen. Once detected, the IFF (Identification, Friend or Foe) homing signal was verified. No reply made the Bogey an enemy, whose speed, altitude, and direction were radioed by VHF (Very High Frequency voice channel) to orbiting fighters on Bat CAP (Bat = radar combat air patrol).

Bat CAP was usually scheduled for two hours, with enough overlap to insure that two fighters were always at altitude. GCI vectored (directed) the fighter to an area as close as possible to the enemy radar contact. The fighter pilot flew toward the enemy and, using his airborne radar set could usually pick it up at two miles. The three-inch diameter indicator scope was mounted at the center of the instrument panel. A parabolic sweep line, looking like a beaded necklace, moved vertically up and down the phosphorescent screen every two seconds. If the target were in range, its echo would appear as two small dots about 3/16th of an inch apart horizontally. A "ghost" was left behind on the screen as the sweep line passed. The target's distance was designated by the vertical position of the dots on the scope. When the bogey was first contacted, its double dot was located at the top of the screen, and as the night fighter closed, the dot moved toward the bottom of the screen. Since the scanner was transmitter and receiver there was a limit on how close the target could be approached. This limit occurred because the detecting echo would come back while the radar was continuing to transmit. This cut off of the echoes would generally occur at 300 yards. On the scope, a target on the left of the line of flight would show up as a pair of dots to the screen's left. If the enemy were above its attacker, the right dot would be above the left dot. Thus, both altitude and bearing were simultaneously represented on one screen.

In making an interception, the pilot would first try to bring the dots to the vertical center of the screen and then, by adjusting his altitude, he would bring the dots side-by-side. The dots would move to the scope's bottom as overtaking speed was increased. The final approach was vital in order that a visual contact could be made while not becoming the target of a rear gunner. The approach speed had to be carefully regulated so as not to overshoot the slower bomber target. Throttling back quickly to avoid overshooting would cause the exhausts to flare past their dampening extensions, threatening detection by the enemy. Pilots usually wore red goggles an hour before takeoff, as night vision, which is not affected by red light, took about three quarters of an hour to peak. All cockpit lighting, except the radar screen, was red, and usually kept on low gain. Once off onboard radar the pilot began to look for the enemy outside his cockpit. The search technique was not to look directly at the point the target should be at, but at a point 15 to 20 degrees away, because the periphery of the eye's retina is more acute and could pick up the dim silhouette more easily. Relative brightness of the night had to be considered when making a visual contact. The general rule was to make the target silhouette and the night fighter not one. The pilot could utilize starlight or moonlight and hide in the darkness below, unless, of course, there were bright clouds below. Or he could use the ambient light of the horizon, especially near dawn or dusk, while hiding in the approaching or retreating daylight. So, depending on lighting conditions, the enemy's silhouette or undampened exhausts could be seen at 100 to 1,000 yards. In the Pacific, before the introduction of IFF into the Navy or Marine Corps, night fighter pilots were required to make positive ID before firing on a possible "friendly." But after IFF introduction in mid-1944, pilots of AI-equipped fighters were authorized to fire upon unseen and/or visually unidentified aircraft. However, in the ETO, Air Force night fighter pilots were required to identify their targets visually under all circumstances. Once visual contact was made, the night fighter closed to get into firing position, usually astern; the clock position, depending on lighting conditions and the enemy's defensive armament. Short bursts were fired, not only to conserve ammunition, but also to assess the damage inflicted and to maintain night vision in the glare of the muzzle flashes.

Night landing was made easier by GCI, which vectored the Bat CAP aircraft back to base. Nonetheless, a night landing was always a scary situation, whether it be on a landing strip, or especially on the narrow 70 foot wide deck of a moving escort carrier.

During the war the USAAF sent 666 night fighter crews overseas, built 706 P-61s, and converted 200 P-70 and P-38s to shoot down 158 enemy aircraft. The contribution of the night fighter was minimal in terms of air victories. However, the enemy could have done much more damage if allowed to roam the night skies unopposed, and was forced to fear withering ground attack both day and night. But the significant contribution of the American night fighter force was to initiate the concept of the 24-hour all weather combat to be used in future wars.

Northrop P-61 Black Widow

In less than two years after its founding, Northrop Aircraft designers John Northrop and Walter Cerny were able to present a design proposal for a USAAF design specification for a large radar-carrying, long range, high performance night fighter. Northrop's reputation led to a contract for two XP-61 prototypes on 11 January 1941. Even before the XP-61's first flight, the necessity for the development of an operational night fighter led to the order of 13 YP-61s on 10 March, 150 more on 1 September, and 410 on 12 February 1942. Finally, on 21 May 1942, test pilot Vance Breese flew the XP-61 on a successful initial flight. The XP-61 was a twin boomed, cantilever mid-wing fighter powered by two Pratt & Whitney R-2800 radial engines and armed with four fixed ventral 20mm cannons and a dorsal GE turret with four .50 cal. machine guns. The twin engines were housed in twin nacelles that tapered towards the vertical tailplanes, which were connected by a horizontal tailplane with control flaps. It was crewed by three: the pilot; the radar operator in the nose; and the observer/gunner situated above the pilot. At 25,000lbs. it was as large as a medium bomber, but had fighter speed and maneuverability. The aileron surfaces were very small and were mounted at the wing tips to give the necessary roll for a turn. A small set of retractable spoilers located forward of the flaps performed as ailerons so the P-61 was able to quickly reverse direction. The test fighters were painted black, and hence the name "Black Widow." The first of 200 P-61As were delivered in Novem-

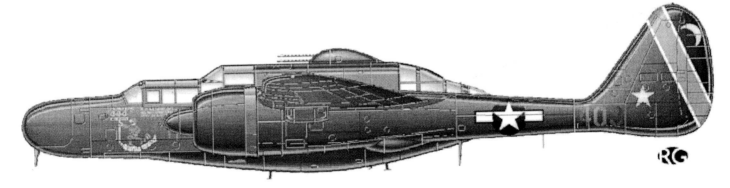

P-61B Maj. Carroll Smith, 418NFS, 5 P-61 victories (7 total). (J.W. Gooch/Warbird Research Group)

P-61 designers (L-R) Walter Cerney and Jack Northrop designed the first American purpose-built night fighter, the P-61 Black Widow. (Northrop)

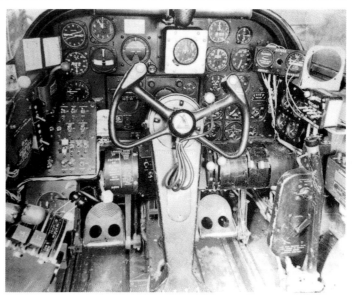

Pilot's radar scope located above the control column. (Northrop)

ber 1943. The first 37 had dorsal turrets, and the remainder were delivered without, as they caused buffeting (the observer/gunner position was deleted). The problem was solved, and all P-61s from 201 onward had the dorsal turret. Throughout its operational life the P-61 maintained its original appearance with little external change. The Pratt & Whitney R-2800 engines were minimally up-graded in the A and B models, and the supercharged –73 increased the maximum speed from 370 to 430 mph in the P-61C models. The first operational P-61s were delivered in the Pacific in early 1944 and in the ETO in May 1944. The P-61 was a successful night fighter design, but it entered service too late to have any serious effect on the outcome of the air war, as neither the Luftwaffe nor Japanese were able to raise any night attacks. Of the 691 Black Widows produced, there were 200 P-61As, 465 P-61Bs, and 517 P-61Cs, of which only 41 were produced before the contract for the remaining 476 was terminated as the Pacific war ended. The P-61 was the forerunner for post war all-weather fighters and remained in front line service until the early 1950s.

R/O position in the P-61B with the azimuth radar scope located in the top center and the horizontal scope below it and the compass in the upper right hand. (Northrup)

1Lt. Raymond Anderson (L) Pilot and 2Lt. John Morris (R) R/O. (USAF)

P-61 ETO First Victory in Type

Pilot: 1Lt. Raymond Anderson
Radar: 2Lt. John U. Morris
Time: 7 August 1944/2330
Place: St. Michel Bay, N. coast of France
Unit: 422NFS/9AF
A/C: P-61A/Ju-88

Action: Although the majority of the P-61 Black Widows were deployed to the Pacific, the 422NFS was shipped to the ETO in March 1944 and was soon followed by the 425NFS. Development and production problems delayed these units from attaining their full complement of P-61s, and also postponed the conversion of the 414, 415, 416, and 417 Squadrons to P-61s until the last month of the war.

Upon their arrival at Charmy Down, England, in early March 1944, the men of the 422nd found themselves without aircraft for the next 2 1/2 months, which were spent in ground training and waiting. It was not until 3 July that the first night mission was flown (without combat, although two friendly Mosquitoes were intercepted). On the 16th the group was assigned V-1 Buzz Bomb ("Anti-Diver") missions. 1Lt. Herman Ernst was credited with the first successful combat when he intercepted a V-1 at 2,500 feet. He closed to 300 yards and destroyed the German guided missile four miles south of Beachy Head. Three more V-1s were shot down before the unit was transferred to a captured German airfield near Cherbourg, France, in late July to protect the Normandy invasion beaches.

On 5 August two intercepts were made, with enemy aircraft being seen falling through the overcast, but only probables were credited. The first confirmed victory was credited on 7 August just before midnight. The team of 1Lt. Raymond Anderson (pilot) and 2Lt. John U. Morris (R/O) intercepted a Ju-88 over the picturesque Bay of St. Michel. Anderson got on the tail of his quarry, hitting him with his 20mm cannons and blowing him up in mid-air.

P-61 ETO First Ace in Type

Pilot: 1Lt. Paul A. Smith
Radar: 1Lt. Robert E. Tierney
Time: 26 December 1944/2210 & 2253
Place: St. Vith (Battle of the Bulge)
Unit: 422NFS/9AF
A/C: P-61A *"Lady Gen"*/2 Ju-188s

Action: 1Lt. Paul Smith and his radar operator, 1Lt. Robert Tierney, had been a successful team in their P-61 *"Lady Gen."* They had been credited with three victories: a Me-410 on 4 October; a He-111 on 27 November (plus a V-1); and a Ju-88 on 25 December.

On the night of 26/27 December, the two took off at 2108 from a Belgian airstrip to patrol the area between the Meuse river and St. Vith-Monachau. After about 40 minutes on patrol, Marmite CGI vectored them towards a bogie at 7,000 feet. AI contact was made, and Tierney guided the interception. Despite violent evasive action, visual contact was made on a Ju-188. While closing between 500-1,000 feet, the Junkers made a hard port turn as Smith put a 60 degree deflection burst into the cockpit. Further hits were made on the starboard wing root. The German bomber fell off its starboard wing, hitting the ground in an explosion.

After a GCI bogie vector which turned out to be a B-17, *"Lady Gen"* was alerted to another Bogie. AI contact was secured at four miles. Tierney obtained a visual on another Ju-188, which took evasive action. Another P-61 had been vectored to the area and fired an errant deflection shot, causing the German to peel off starboard and then split "S" to port. A chase took place from 9,000 to 500 feet, during which visuals were lost three times, but Tierney regained them through AI. Smith closed and fired at a slight deflection, striking the fuselagea and setting it on fire. A second burst was fired from 300 feet dead astern, exploding the engine and causing the end of the wing to break off. The bomber spiraled off to port and hit the ground in a violent explosion. The two victories made Smith and Tierney the first American night fighter aces of WWII. They were just three days ahead of another Smith, Maj. Carroll (and R/O 1Lt. Philip Porter) of the 418NFS in the Pacific, who shot down four Japanese in two sorties 29/30 December to give them seven victories.

1Lt. Robert Tierney (L) R/O and 1Lt. Paul Smith (R) Pilot. (USAF)

P-61 ETO Top Scorers in Type

Pilots-R/O: 1Lt. Paul A. Smith/1Lt. Robert E. Tierney
                1Lt. Herman E. Ernst/1Lt. Edward H. Kopsel
                1Lt. Eugene D. Axtell/3 different R/Os

Unit: All 422NFS/9AF

Victories: 5

1Lt. Paul Smith (5v./1p./0d. –Ace on 26 December1944)

V#	Date	R/O	EA/C
1	10-04-44	2Lt. Robert Tierney	Me-410
2	11-27-44	"	He-111
3	12-25-44	"	Ju-88
4	12-26-44	"	Ju-188
5	12-26-44	"	Ju-188

Smith and Tierney scored two victories over Ju-188s on 26 December to become the first American night fighter aces.

#327 1Lt.Herman Ernst (L) Pilot and 1Lt. Edward Kopsel (R) R/O. (Author/Ernst)

1Lt. Eugene Axtell (USAF)

1Lt. Herman Ernst (5v./0p./2d.—Ace on 2 March 1945)

V#	Date	R/O	EA/C
1	11-27-44	2Lt. Edward Kopsel	Me-110
2	12-17-44	"	Ju-87
3	12-27-44	"	Ju-188
4	03-02-45	"	Ju-87
5	03-02-45	"	Ju-87

The Luftwaffe was noticeably absent at night in January and February 1945, with the 422nd getting only one kill for the period. On 2 March, Ernst and his R/O Kopsel were on a low level mission over the front lines along the Rhine River. On the sortie they damaged a Me-110 at 0450 and then quickly dispatched two Ju-87 Stuka dive bombers in nine minutes, which made the duo the 422FS' second aces. Upon returning to base they found that their P-61 had been damaged by AA and Stuka rear gunners.

1Lt. Eugene Axtell (5v./2p./0d.—Ace on 11 April 1945

V#	Date	R/O	EA/C
1	12-27-44	2Lt. Bernard Orzel	Ju-88
2	12-27-44	"	Ju-188
3	01-01-45	2Lt. John Morris	Ju-188
4	04-11-45	1Lt. Creel Morrison	Ju-52
5	04-11-45	"	Ju-52

On 11 April 1945 the Germans were attempting to evacuate vital personnel from an encircled pocket in Western Germany using lumbering Ju-52 transports. After midnight Marmite GCI vectored Axtell and his R/O, Creel Morrison, towards a slow, low-flying Ju-52 in the Holzminden-Kassel area. Morrison could not pick up the German on his airborne AI radar set. But the GCI had done a good job, and Axtell made a visual and dropped the Ju-52. Axtell and Morrison made a second sortie that night and were again vectored to the Kassel area, where they again downed a Ju-52, making Axtell the third and last ETO P-61 and night ace.

Note: 1Lt. Robert Elmore (pilot) and 1Lt. Leonard Maple (R/O) of the 422nd were credited with four manned aircraft and one unmanned V-1, which was not considered a victory.

In its ten months of combat, the 422nd flew 1,576 sorties, destroying 43 Luftwaffe aircraft with five probables and five damaged to go along with five V-1 (buzz bomb) victories. The group improved their efficiency over the last half of their tour, even though they had only a quarter of the contacts. They made 51% visuals from GCI vectors versus 39% in the first half. Of course, many of their GCI vectors ended in visuals of "friendlies," which made for good practice.

P-61 Intruder Missions

As interceptions came to nil American night fighters over Continental Europe and Italy diverted to night intruder missions. Since day strafers wreaked havoc on the German transportation system the enemy was forced to move troops and supplies in the cover of darkness. In its 1,576 sorties in the ETO, the 422NFS destroyed 448 trucks, 50 locomotives, and 476 railroad cars. During the Battle of the Bulge, the 422nd and 425th NFS were the only American aircraft to be able to fly in the bad weather covering the German attack. The two squadrons claimed 115 trucks, three locomotives, and 16 railroad cars attempting to supply the Wehrmacht.

Flying the P-61 Black Widow (ETO)
By
Herman Ernst:
5 victories 422 NFS
Top ETO P-61 ace

Our 422nd Night Fighter Squadron was the first unit to be equipped and trained in the P-61 A model Black Widow in the States. It took us over 2 1/2 months to get our aircraft after we arrived in England in early March 1944. When we received them they came without the top .50 caliber turret, so we had to transfer our turret gunners to bomber units. After a round of Mosquito vs. Black Widow night fighter controversy we finally got to fly the P-61 as part of the 9th Air Force.

Before a mission we performed the standard pre-flight check and entered the cockpit via a folding ladder through the nose wheel well. The radio/radar operator entered his compartment through a door under the tail cone. The instrument panel was well laid out, with everything easy to reach and see. The seat was adjustable on tracks and rollers to accommodate most pilots. The controls were adjustable, well harmonized, and easy to use. The Lucite canopy was framed by aluminum and gave good visibility in most directions. The oxygen and heating systems were never a problem, but the four-channel radio left a lot to be desired, especially in wet weather. The pilot, R/O (radar operator), and ammo storage boxes were well protected by armor plate, deflection plate, and bullet proof glass.

I loved the Pratt & Whitney R-2800 engines, which only caused me a problem on one mission. With one engine out we could retain control even if fully loaded. In spite of its large size, the P-61 was very easy to fly, and its flight characteristics were excellent. I used to feel very fast on chases and confident to take on any German. Of course, every pilot wanted more speed and better climb when chasing the enemy. I believed I could stay with and out maneuver anything in the air. The spoiler-type aileron was an innovation, which allowed us to use near full span flaps and make very fast, tight turns for an aircraft our size. We were able to cut off the smaller, supposedly more agile, Luftwaffe fighters who tried to turn inside of us. They also increased the plane's speed and range and allowed us to take off from short fields, which was an advantage, as we moved to the Continent after D-Day. The P-61 could easily cruise at 160mph and reach over 350mph in combat. We had to be careful about fuel, as we did not receive auxiliary tanks for some time.

The P-61 was rugged, and many returned to base in pretty rough shape. On 15 July 1944 my R/O, Ed Kopsel, and I were assigned to our first combat mission, an Anti-diver patrol that was to chase V-1 Buzz Bombs. We were vectored by GCI (Ground Control Intercept) to intercept incoming V-1s approaching the English Coast. To gain enough speed to catch them we had to go into a dive. As we dove through the clouds on instruments Ed was yelling something over the radio that I could not understand. It seems the tail cone collapsed and disintegrated. I finally figured out what the problem was and aborted the mission without difficulty. The damaged tail cone section was replaced with a flat piece of Plexiglas, and we went out the next night and shot down a V-1.

We were armed with four 20mm cannons in the belly, which carried 600 to 800 rounds. The key to our successes was the SCR 720 radar set, which was derived from the British design. The early sets were a constant maintenance headache, breaking down before and during too many missions. The radar set was very sensitive, so any aerobatic or snap maneuvers were prohibited. After a while the bugs were worked out and the radar could be relied on in combat. It took practice to develop pilot-R/O teamwork after the GCI vector was received. Despite the lack of Luftwaffe opposition, Ed and I were fortunate to make the most of our opportunities and score five night victories.

First USAAF Night Fighter/P-61 Victory
Crew: 2Lt. Dale Haberman (pilot)
          F/O Raymond Mooney (R/O)
Time: 30 June 1944/2045-2230
Place: East of Saipan
Unit: 6 NFS/7 & 13 AF
A/C: P-61A "Moon Happy" vs. Betty

Action: The 6 FS was activated as the 6 NFS on 9 January 1944, receiving P-61A Black Widows as soon as they were off the assembly line. The squadron gained operational status training in Hawaii. It was sent with six P-61s to be attached to the 7th Air Force on Isley Airfield, Saipan, to protect the B-29s stationed there.

On 27 June 1944, 2Lt. Dale Haberman and his radar operator, F/O Raymond Mooney, were patrolling in their P-61A "Moon Happy" north of Rota when they intercepted a Kate intruder and claimed a probable.

Three days later, the orbiting duo was vectored by GCI to a bogie at 7,000 feet. Mooney picked up two aircraft on his scope and instructed Haberman to chase them up to 23,000 feet before getting a visual. Above them was a Betty escorted by a Zero.

1Lt. Herman Ernst.
(Author/Ernst)

2Lt. Dale Haberman (standing with arm raised) and F/O Raymond Mooney (under radar array) applying kill decal on their P-61, "Times A Wastin." (USAF)

Haberman pulled his fighter up on the Betty's tail and hit it in the port engine, dooming it. The Zero then dove on the stalling P-61, getting on its tail. Haberman put the heavy fighter into a twisting evasive redline dive. The straining P-61 left the Zero far behind as Haberman pulled the plunging aircraft out at 1,000 feet, living to claim the first AAF and P-61 victory of the war. Haberman and Mooney went on to score three more night victories, all against Betty bombers, and two on Christmas Eve 1944.

P-61 PTO First Ace and Top American Night Fighter Ace Scorer

Pilot: Maj. Carroll C. Smith
Radar: 1Lt. Philip B. Porter (P-61/5 victories)
Victories: 7 (2v. in P-38J and 5v. in p-61)
Unit: 418NFS
Record:

V#	Date	E/A/C
1 (P-38)	01-13-44	Val
2 (P-61)	10-07-44	Dinah
3 (P-38)	11-28-44	Betty
4-7(P-61)	12-29/30-44	2 Irvings, Rufe & Frank

Action: Carroll Smith's night fighting career in the Pacific parallels the evolution of the Air Force's night aircraft and tactics there. While with the 418NFS he flew the P-70, P-38, and P-61 at night.

In early 1943 air cadets gathered at Williams Field, Arizona, for night fighter training in the RP-322 and P-70 twin-engine aircraft. The RP-322 was a stripped down early RAF P-38 Lightning reject, while the P-70 Nighthawk was a Douglas A-20 conversion. The two represented a makeshift night fighter force made necessary by the slow development of the P-61.

The 418NFS was activated on 1 April 1943 at Orlando, Florida, and assigned to the Air Force School of Applied Tactics. The squadron was shipped to Guadalcanal and then to Milne Bay, New Guinea, in early November under its CO, Maj. Carroll Smith. The 418th was equipped with the P-70, whose limited numbers were supplemented with P-38s, both of which were 6NFS castoffs. The mixture of P-38s and P-70s required the squadron to develop new tactics to ac-

commodate the performance and equipment of these aircraft. For instance, Japanese *bombers* could outrun and out climb the P-70! Despite numerous efforts to improve the P-70 its deficiencies were never remedied. The night P-38s were conventional daylight versions without radar or other night fighting aids. The P-38 pilots would patrol over base and wait for the Japanese to fly into searchlight beams, a method tried with mixed success by both the RAF and Luftwaffe ("Wild Sow"). This tactic subjected the P-38 pilot to its own AA fire and that of gunners on enemy aircraft. Later GCI vectored the Lightnings by VHF towards the targets, but again without much success. On 13 January 1944, Smith destroyed a Val dive bomber over Alexishafen in a P-38J to give the 418th its first victory and only one for nine months, as there was little air activity during patrols over the Solomons New Guinea.

In late September the group was given some P-61As to replace the P-70s and to complement its P-38s. While on patrol in a new Black Widow over their base at Morotai, Smith and his able R/O, 2Lt. Philip Porter, were vectored to a target at 12 miles. With Porter relaying instructions and Smith flying by his instruments, an airborne radar intercept was promptly made on a twin-engine Dinah on a course towards the P-61 base at 8,000 feet. Using his water injection, Smith quickly closed for a visual contact, 2,000 feet ahead. The Jap also saw his attacker and took evasive action by climbing. The P-61 climbed faster and caught the Dinah at 17,500 feet. Smith's first several firing bursts failed to hit or damage the bomber. As the Widow pulled to within 40 yards of the Jap's port wing, Smith put a full-deflection burst into it as it flew past, tearing off chunks and setting it on fire to record the squadron's first P-61 victory.

Back in a P-38 Smith claimed a twin-engine Betty on 28 November for his third victory. In December the group was stationed at San Jose, Mindoro, P.I., and received P-61B versions. Smith named his aircraft *"Time's A Wastin'"* and adorned the horizontal stabilizers with the squadron's white crescent moon and star markings.

On 29 December the 418th was assigned shipping convoy escort duty off Mindoro under the direction of shipboard GCI. Smith and Porter took off just before dusk, and an hour later GCI alerted

Maj. Carroll Smith (R) Pilot and 2Lt. Philip Porter (L) R/O. (Author/ Smith)

Porter to an incoming E/A/C at 8,000 feet and 12-15 miles out. Using his airborne radar set, Porter guided Smith on a two mile course to a visual contact with an Irving. After a seven minute chase through the clouds, Smith was able to make a diving firing run, getting hits on the twin-engine recon bomber's wing root. The burning enemy dove away and crashed into the sea at 1910.

Smith returned to patrolling altitude, and Porter soon found another incoming Irving at their altitude. Not having time to maneuver to a more favorable astern attack position because of the Jap's vicinity to the convoy, Smith made a full-throttle head-on attack and dove to intercept the Jap before he was able to initiate a bomb run. At about 300 yards he fired his 20mm cannons, getting hits on the canopy and fuel tanks and setting the enemy on fire, causing it to crash into the sea.

After briefly resting and refueling, *"Time's A Wastin"* went back into station on its second patrol. After 30 minutes, GCI vectored Smith and Porter to a Rufe floatplane flying three miles out at sea level. The slow and maneuverable JNAF plane was a difficult target for the P-61, escaping using low, tight turns. Smith partially lowered his flaps to cut his speed and was able to put a short, devastating burst of cannon shells into the fragile Rufe.

Two hours later, the Americans were again vectored towards an incoming aircraft, which was identified as a speedy Frank fighter. Utilizing surprise, Porter maneuvered the P-61 to 25 yards, where his cannons again had deadly effect, disintegrating the Frank for their fourth kill of the night. The four victories made Smith and Porter the top PTO P-61 aces and made Smith America's top night fighter ace with seven of 418NFS' 20 victories.

Flying the P-61 Black Widow (PTO)
By
Carroll Smith:
7 Victories (5 P-61) 418NFS
Top American Night Fighter Ace

The heavy, box-like P-61 looked more like a bomber than a fighter, but indeed, it was one and more. The P-61 was hindered by problems getting into production, and thus its late start prevented it from becoming one of the best fighters of the war.

Our pre-flight procedure was a normal walk-around checking for general safety, such as tires, the gun load, landing gear, fuel (we drained off a bit of fuel for water residue), and so forth. One thing we did not have to check, though, since our missions were night flights, were the lights, as to use them was inviting trouble. The cockpit was entered through the nose wheel well, and it was about as comfortable as any other WWII aircraft. The Lucite canopy hatches were always checked, as they were unreliable. We always checked our instrument panel lights, as they were vital in our night operations. Everything had to be usable by feel, for we used a minimum of light to better retain our night vision. The instrument panel layout was good for the time. The tricycle landing gear made the fighter good to taxi, take off, and land. The main gear was the same as the B-25, but was reversed in its trunions. Our communications consisted of two SCR-522 four channel VHF sets for air-to-air and air-to-ground communications. They functioned reasonably well, although we had some problems with mountain interference. We had a tail-warning radar set and a SCR-695 IFF (Identification Friend or Foe) transponder, which was known as "parrot" because it squawked.

I can't say enough about the Pratt & Whitney 2800 radial engine. It was simply a great engine, and probably one of the most rugged, efficient, and reliable aircraft engines ever built. It kept running when by all rights it should not have, and was an excellent confidence builder. Our aircraft had four internal fuel tanks, two in the engine nacelles (205 gallons each) and two in the inner wing (118 gallons each). This fuel load gave us about 3 1/2 hours of normal cruising, but our endurance could be stretched out quite a bit through judicious flying. One time I extended my flight to 5 1/2 hours and had 60 gallons left. This was possible by using only 1,500rpm or less and a very lean mixture (this did not seem to damage the engines). The next series were equipped with four wing-mounted drop tanks, which extended the range significantly.

The P-61 had four 20mm cannons in the belly and four .50 caliber machines guns in the remote dorsal turret, which was installed in the early models. We discarded this turret and saved 1,100 pounds, dropped a crew member, and greatly reduced drag. The loss of this turret was more than compensated for by the increase in performance, and the remaining four 20mms with their 600 rounds gave us enough firepower. Our gun sight was adequate, as most of our work was done at close range. We were ordered to identify any aircraft we shot at, so we had to be at quite close range.

The P-61's climb rate was very good for the time, and it could out climb most of the Japanese aircraft we were up against. The P-61 was the most maneuverable I ever flew, and I flew 58 types in my career. You could stall one at 500 feet and not worry. I could turn with any aircraft when climbing, diving, or in level flight. The unique spoiler aileron system Northrop used was very effective in combat. The aircraft had no bad characteristics, and was a pleasure

**Maj. Carroll Smith.
(Author/Smith)**

to fly. The Widow was tough; we were shot up but not shot down. I do not know of a P-61 that was shot down by an enemy fighter. Our main concern was anti-aircraft fire, sometimes from our own nervous ground troops! I am familiar with only one bailout from the Widow. Hit by AA the pilot slowed the aircraft down, walked out on the wing, and stepped off with no problems. No problems, at least until he got to the ground, where had to demonstrate his .45 pistol to some unfriendly natives. The P-61 was simple to land, with no bad habits. We rarely used landing lights for safety reasons, and if we did, it was only for a few seconds.

As I said, I flew 58 aircraft types during my career, and I consider the P-61 my favorite. It made me an ace and got me home safely.

The P-61 in the CBI

Two P-61 night fighter squadrons, the 426th and 427th, served with the 14AF in the CBI, with the 426th scoring all five CBI P-61 victories.

On 27 October 1944, the 426th initiated operations based in Kunming, China, to protect B-29 bases from night attacks. Their first victory was claimed during the night of 29 October by pilot Capt. Robert Scott and radarman F/O Charles Phillips. On patrol in *"Merry Widow"* at 5,000 feet, they were vectored by CGI towards a Japanese aircraft inbound, 40 miles away. Scott flew at full throttle in a gentle climb to 11,000 feet, where Phillips made an AI contact at 2-3 miles away. Visual contact was made at 1,000 feet on a twin-engine Ki-48 Lily bomber, which was climbing in easy turns. Scott closed to 500 feet and fired just as the alerted enemy plane took a sharp diving turn to the left. In the climbing, turning, and diving dogfight, at 4,000 feet the P-61 finally dove at high speed to close and fire, getting hits on the starboard wing and engine, starting a fire and blowing off small pieces. Fearing an explosion, Scott broke off combat and climbed up from 3,000 feet with the first P-61 victory in the CBI.

Capt. Robert Scott, shown here with Col. Winston Kratz, scored the first CBI night victory with F/O Charles Phillips (R/O) on 27 October 1944. (USAF)

Capt. Carl Absmeier (R) Pilot and 2Lt. James Smith (L) R/O of the 426NFS were the top CBI night scorers with 2 victories. (USAF)

1Lt. Robert Graham (L) had five victories as a back seat ace with the 422NFS. He led 1Lt. Robert Bolinder to 4 victories and Capt. Raymond Anderson to one victory. (Author)

Capt. Carl Absmeier (pilot) and 2Lt. James Smith (R/O), flying their P-61 *"Jing-Bow Joy-Ride"* of the 426NFS, downed Lily bombers on the nights of 27 and 30 January 1945 while based at Loaokow to qualify as the top CBI P-61 scorers.

From early 1945, Japanese night fighter opposition disappeared. Abandoned by the broken Imperial Navy, the Japanese troops in China were left with insufficient reinforcement and supplies. The two P-61 squadrons flew day and night intruder missions over Burma with great success against Japanese communications, motor, and rail transportation, leading the way to their ultimate defeat.

Grumman manufactured 1434 F6F-5N Hellcats, installing the AN/APE-4 and –6 radar. Many of the "Bateye" Hellcats were armed with two 20mm cannons and four .50 cal. machine guns. Except for the radar and armament the N variants were basically similar to the standard day F6F. Shown are F6F-5(N)s of VMF(N)-541, the "Bateyes," on Falaop Island, May 1944. (USMC)

The pilot radar scope for the AN/APS-6 radar installation on the F6F-5N. (Grumman)

Grumman F6F(N) Night Hellcat
F6F(N)/USN First Victory in Type
Pilot: Ens. George L. Tarleton
Time: 20 June 1944/0350
Place: Agana Airfield, Guam
Unit: VF(N)-77
A/C: F6F-3N/ Val

Action: The U.S. Navy began its night fighter program "Project Affirm," in late 1942, using both the Hellcat and Corsair. Though there was little difference between the two fighters, the Hellcat was ultimately chosen because it was easier to land on a carrier and a better gun platform. Radar-equipped F6F-3Ns of VF-76(N) and –77(N) were assigned to fleet carriers in late 1943 and early 1944. The first night victory scored by a F6F-N was by Ens. George L. Tarleton of VF(N)-77 on 20 June 1944 at 0350 when he downed a Val over Agana Airfield, Guam. Over the Marianas, VF(N)-76 Hellcats had scored a victory on 15 June, and eight more (including

Ens. George Tarleton scored the first F6F-3N for VF(N)-77. (USN)

five Vals by Lt. Russell Reiserer) on 20 June, but all were scored in the daylight. During the first half of 1944 night Hellcat operations were minimal, as carrier captains did not wish to disturb their nightly pattern by having to cope with the difficulty of launching and re-covering nighttime CAPs ("Batcaps").

Top USN/F6F(N) Night Ace
Pilot: Lt. William E. Henry
Unit: VF(N)-41/ *Independence*
Victories: 6 1/2-night/3-day
A/C: F6F-5N

Bill Henry was born in Bakersfield, CA, on 20 January 1920. In 1940 he completed Naval Flight Training at Pensacola and was as-signed fleet duty in 1941 with VS-3 on the carrier *Saratoga*. Like many other future fighter aircraft leaders (Stanley Vejtasa, seven victories in a day, and Gus Widhelm, leader of the Navy's first night fighter unit, VF(N)-75), Henry initially flew the SBD Dauntless dive-bomber. On the *Saratoga*, Henry took part in the Battle of the Eastern Solomons, 24 August 1942. Upon returning to the carrier that day, his Scouting Three flight encountered two small groups of Vals, which turned away but were engaged by other SBDs, frustrat-ing the future ace.

After the *Saratoga* was torpedoed off the Solomons on 31 Au-gust, VS-3 was transferred to RAdm. Slew McCain's command in the South Pacific, where it operated for five weeks with the Ma-rines. After his combat tour, Henry returned to the States and taught dive bombing in 1943, then joined VF(N)-79, a fledgling Navy night fighter squadron. The squadron was led by Lt.Cdr. Turner Caldwell, another SBD pilot of VS-5 on the *Enterprise* who had won three Navy Crosses over Guadalcanal. VF(N)-79 was commissioned on 20 January 1944 at Quonset Point and moved to Charlestown, RI. Caldwell named three former SBD pilots as the nucleus of his unit and appointed Henry as his XO. The enthusiastic Caldwell managed to convince light carrier *Independence* skipper Capt. E.C. Ewen to take his squadron aboard. VF(N)-79 was disbanded and reorganized as VF(N)-41 with 14 F6F-5Ns and five F6F-5s. The *Independence* left Eniwetok on 29 August 1944 with Task Force 38 to engage the Japanese over the Philippines.

Soon the squadron found themselves operating their aircraft in the conventional daylight functions of CAPs, fighter sweeps, and "heckler" missions. Frustration and disappointment set in, as the highly trained pilots and ground radar support personnel felt they were being misused. Finally, on 12 September, Henry was returning with his division from a dusk CAP when *Independence* radar made a contact and vectored four Hellcats towards it. The intruder closed on the fleet, which fired its AA and caused it to turn and climb towards Leyte. Henry was vectored for pursuit, picking up the Jap on airborne radar over Samar at 21,000 feet. Observing the visual ID requirement, Henry found himself on top of a Dinah twin-engine Army Ki-46 recon bomber. Dropping back astern, he fired, as did Ens. Jack Berkheimer on his wing. The bomber was set on fire when Henry finished it off with another short burst. Both Henry and Berkheimer were credited with a shared victory.

September's combats for VF(N)-41 were of the conventional daylight variety. On the 21st, Henry scored a probable over an Oscar fighter in a mid-morning sweep over Clark Field to Mt. Arayat, in the Philippines. The next day he downed two Vals in the early morning on another sweep over Luzon. All of VF(N)-41's ten monthly victories were in the sunshine.

In October, the invasion of the Philippines and air strikes on Formosa gave VF(N)-41 the chance to use their night training, as ten of their twelve confirmed victories were in the night. On 12 October, Bill Henry had his best night in the air. He was leading four Hellcat –5Ns back from a dusk CAP off Formosa. As things were quiet, the *Independence* launched only two more Hellcats to replace Henry's flight for night CAP. Henry entered the landing pattern and was down wind with his wheels and tail hook down when CIC on the carrier gave him a vector towards a bogie low and close to the fleet. As he passed over a DD screening the fleet, he was given a target location of two miles crossing port to starboard.

At 500 feet, in low clouds and light rain, he picked up the target on his radar and followed around to a visual at 300 feet distance, a Betty bomber that was about to make a torpedo attack on the fleet. Short bursts hit the bomber in both wing roots, flaming it and causing it to crash into the sea and explode. Immediately, the controller vectored him to two more Bettys, which were astern. A 360-degree turn put Henry and his wingman, Ens. Jim Barnett, astern of the bombers, where they made radar contact. They closed to a visual of the two bombers, which were flying in loose formation at 200 feet above the water. A short burst by each Hellcat's machine guns credited each pilot with a victory. The Task Force AA was firing, so the controller sent them away from the screen to orbit. The two recently launched night CAP Hellcats of Ensigns G.W. Obenour and J.F. Moore joined Henry and Barnett, but lost radio contact and vanished to continue their CAP. Finally, the *Independence* landed the remaining four Hellcats on its narrow 70-foot wooden deck just as a Japanese snooper dropped a flare, depriving Henry of another chance at combat.

Three days later, Henry was sitting in the dark in his Hellcat on the carrier catapult on Condition Two watch when an enemy contact was made. At 0245, he was propelled into the darkness and almost immediately contacted the target three miles ahead on his radar. The enemy flew into a rain cloud, and Henry countered by tuning down his radar, which became flooded from the rain. As the bogie left the cloud, it was picked up again by retuning the set. As Henry closed to 700 feet, a visual was made, detecting the large, four-engine flying boat coded "Emily." Henry fired into the left wing, and carrier personnel who saw the victim crash into the sea confirmed his victory, making Henry an ace.

In November VF(N)-41 scored eight nocturnal and one daylight victories. On the 6th, Henry downed a Topsy, a twin-engine Ki-57 transport over Clark Field, just before dawn. Then, on the 19th, the squadron had a good night, claiming four enemy aircraft. Henry became a night ace when he shot down another Emily over Luzon at 0205. On 24 December Henry scored his last night victory, claiming yet another Emily at 0415. On 16 January he downed an Oscar fighter in a daylight raid over Canton, China, to give him 10 1/2 victories in the war.

VF(N)-41 finished its five month tour at the end of January 1945, claiming ten more Japanese that month and giving it 46 total and 26 at night, the high for any Navy night fighter unit. Bill Henry was credited with 6 1/2, Ens. Jack Berkheimer with 5 1/2, Ens. Wallace "Bill" Miller with 4 1/6, Ens. James Barnett with 3 1/3, and Ens. Emmett Edwards with 3. Ten of the unit's 35 pilots were lost, six to enemy action (including Berkheimer, who either collided with an intended victim or succumbed to enemy AA over Manila), and only three to operational accidents. This record was about average for daylight fighters, and vindicated the Navy's belief in night fighting.

Besides Henry, the Navy had three other night aces: Lt(jg). John Orth with six victories, no day VF-9 (*Yorktown* and *Lexington*); Ens. Jack S. Berkheimer with 5 1/2, plus two day VF(N)-41 (*Independence*); and Lt. Robert J. Humphrey with 5, plus 1/3 day, VF-17 (*Hornet*). On 13 August 1945 Ens. Philip T. McDonald of VF(N)-91 off the *Bon Homme Richard* knocked down four JAAF

Lt. William Henry. (Author/Henry)

twin-engine Nick bombers in one sortie, which was an American nighttime record.

Flying the F6F (N) Hellcat
By
William Henry:
6 1/2 victories VF(N)-41
Top USN night fighter ace

After a tour flying SBDs with VS-3 off the *Saratoga* and land-based from Guadalcanal, I volunteered to join one of the Navy's first night and all weather squadrons. In December 1943 I joined VF(N)-79, headed by Lt.Cdr. T.F. Caldwell, another former Dauntless pilot. We trained at NAAF Charleston in F6F-3Ns equipped with AN/APS-6 radar during the winter and spring of 1944. We flew from 10 AM to 6 PM, six days a week. The winter weather gave us plenty of opportunity to develop our instrument flying skills. One week we flew up to Norfolk and practiced landings on the *Charger*. Besides hours of instrument flying, we spent hours learning to use the AN/APS-6 radar. The set was quite good for its time, with a single scope in the instrument panel and a single scanner in the pod mounted on the outer right wing. The radar had search, intercept, and gun aim modes. The search mode gave us a single dash that showed the range, while the intercept mode gave two dots, indicating the range and position of the target above and below your aircraft. We did not use the gun mode, since in most cases the target could be seen at close range and a sure hit could be made using the regular gun sight. A lot of training was necessary to fly instruments, watch the radar scope, change range scales, and get a visual on the target. Then, of course, we also had to retrain in night carrier landings.

One of the Hellcat's primary virtues was its versatility, so its adaptation to the night fighter role was easy. Not so easy was convincing the Brass to use us in this new role. The "Night Hellcat" had the same outstanding flight characteristics as the day version. The fiberglass radome's weight and drag was adjusted for and had no meaningful effect on the aircraft's performance. The forward visibility from the cockpit was exceptional, which was vital in night fighting to achieve a visual contact from the radar chase.

Lt. William Henry. (Author/ Henry)

After the early reluctance to utilize our skills we were assigned night CAP missions. With our extensive training we became proficient in our nighttime role: coordinating shipboard control and our radar to attain visual contact and attack. VF(N)-41 got a total of 26 nighttime victories, the highest of any Navy night unit of the war. I scored 6 1/2 night victories (9 1/2 total-ed.), and my good friend, Jack Berkheimer, who was KIA in December 1944, also became a night ace with 5 1/2 victories.

Maj. Norman Mitchell scored the first USMC land-based F6F-5N victory for VMF(N)-541. (USMC)

F6F(N)/USMC First Victory in Type/Land based
Pilot: Maj. Norman L. Mitchell
Time: 31 October 1944/1945
Place: Schonian Harbor, Peleliu
Unit: VMF(N)-541
A/C: F6F-5N/Jake
Action: VMF(N)-541, "Bat Eyes" squadron, was the first Marine night squadron to see combat and was commanded by RAF-trained CO Maj. Peter Lambrecht. It was initially land-based in the Palaus Islands, which at the time the war had passed. The squadron spent its time flying barge sweeps in the Palaus and nightly CAPs. On 31 October 1944, Maj. Norman Mitchell shot down a two-seat JNAF recon floatplane over Schonian Harbor, Peleliu, for the unit's first and only victory in the area in 461 night CAPs.

F6F(N)/USMC First Victory in Type/Carrier
Pilot: Lt. Bruce J. Reuter
Time: 3 July 1945/0100
Place: Balikpapan, Borneo
Unit: VMF-511 (N)/*Block Island*
A/C: F6F-5Ns/Jake
Action: Four Marine Corps escort carriers saw combat. The first Marine carrier squadron, VMF-511 off the *Block Island* (CVE-106), was the only Marine carrier squadron equipped with Hellcats. The unit, under Maj. Robert C. Maze, consisted of eight F6F-5Ns, two F6F-5Ps, and eight F4U-1D Corsairs. The squadron flew strike and ground support missions on Okinawa and Formosa during May and June 1945.

Lt. Bruce Reuter. (USN)

Capt. Robert Baird. (Author/ Baird)

MacArthur proposed three landings by Australian troops on Borneo in May and June. Three escort carriers (*Suwannee*, *Gilbert Island*, and *Block Island*) were assigned to R.Adm. William Sample's TU 78.4.1. The Japanese had few aircraft in the area, and ground support became the fighter's main task. Before midnight on 2 July, 1Lt. Bruce Reuter took off from the *Block Island* for a night CAP. Shortly after midnight carrier radar showed a bogey about 50 miles out. FDO vectored Reuter, who picked up the u/i on his radar scope and closed to find an oblivious JNAF two-seat reconnaissance Jake seaplane. The Marine pilot steadily closed and hit the plane's fuselage, setting it on fire and into the sea. This victory was the only USMC Hellcat victory of the war.

F6F(N) Top Scorer and First USMC F6F(N) Ace
Pilot: Capt. Robert Baird
Unit: VMF(N)-533 "The Crystal Gazers"
Victories: 6 (all night)
A/C: F6F-5N

Californian Bob Baird was born on 29 November 1921 in Los Angeles. While attending Crompton Junior College in April 1942 he joined the Navy's Flight Training Program. After completing flight training he was assigned to the Marine Corps' first single-seat night fighter squadron. VMF(N)-532 was commissioned at MCAS Cherry Point, NC, on 3 April 1943, and was commanded by Maj. Everett H. Vaughn. It was not until August that the Naval Aircraft Factory (NAF) delivered its first completely modified and radar-equipped F4U-2 Corsair. By 10 December the squadron had received its 12 combat-ready Corsairs (plus three spares) and left Cherry Point for Ella Island in the Tarawa Atoll, via San Diego and Hawaii on the carrier *White Plains*, arriving on 14 January 1944.

The squadron saw little action, and it was not until the night of 13/14 April that the Marine Corp's first successful "Bat eye" interception was made by 1Lt. Edward Sovik when he shot down a Betty bomber at 0111 near Engebi, Eniwetok. The same night Capt. William Bollman scored the only other victory of VMF(N)-532's eight-month tour, downing another Betty (see USMC F4U Night fighter victories). During the summer of 1944, the squadron flew night

CAP over Kwajelein Atoll, the Marianas, and the Marshalls, along with selected bombing and strafing missions. On 21 September it was ordered to secure flight ops. It boarded air transports for the States two days later to retrain in the new F7F Tigercat night fighter. Baird had flown his entire eight-month tour without spotting a single enemy aircraft.

After a short six-month stay in the Z.I. Baird managed to become reassigned to VMF(N)-533 under Lt.Col. Marion "Mac" Magruder flying the F6F-5N Hellcat. The unit, nicknamed "The Crystal Gazers," had spent a year on Eniwetok Atoll without one enemy contact. Baird joined them in May 1945 at Yonton airbase on Okinawa.

On 16 May, 1Lt. Robert Wilhide scored the squadron's first victory by shooting down a Betty. Then, two days later the unit downed a nocturnal record five enemy aircraft (three by 1Lt. Robert Wellwood and two by 1Lt. Ed LeFaivre). The squadron ended the month with 15 victories, but Baird was shut out.

Finally, on 9 June at 1430 and 60 miles north of Point Mike, Baird got his long-awaited first victory, shooting down a Jake, Aichi Navy recon seaplane. A week later, on the 16th, Baird began to make up for lost time. Patrolling at 10,000 feet over his new base at Ie Shima, Baird received a vector from "Arsenic" control. Climbing to 23,000 feet Baird was able to close within a half mile by utilizing his airborne radar. He was ordered away as the Betty bomber began to make its bombing run, entering the AA firing zone. Baird radioed a request to continue his pursuit, as he had a solid contact. AA fire was withheld, and he closed to 100 yards astern, verifying the ID and then opening fire. He found that only half of his six machine guns would fire and had to press on to fire several more times to finish off the Betty at 0350. Baird continued his patrol, and about an hour later ground radar vectored him above a Nell, Navy G3M attack bomber. Using his radarscope, Baird decreased his speed by dropping his landing gear and descended 3,000 feet to 18,000. At one and a half miles, Baird moved to the western side of his target in order to silhouette it against the dawning eastern horizon and was able to make visual contact. Slowing down even more, he dropped astern and fired at 100 yards, flaming the starboard engine with his only two operable guns.

The night of 22 June saw –533 score five more victories and another double for Baird. Taking off after midnight he flew night CAP northwest of Ie Shima at 17,000 feet under the ground control of "Ringtail." Soon the GCI vectored him towards a bogie, which he quickly closed on and identified as a Frances, P1Y1 twin-engine night fighter. The Hellcat's machine guns, all functioning, blew the tail off the Jap, which exploded, showering its pursuer with oil and debris. Baird settled in from his fourth night victory flying his Hellcat FN4 (Fox-Nan-Four) on CAP when "Ringtail" vectored him to 19,000 feet, where his airborne radar made contact with another bogie two miles away and 1,000 feet above, executing S-turns. He made visual contact at 100 yards astern and attempted ID by skidding from side to side to glimpse the enemy's silhouette. The u/i aircraft was a Betty bomber, and Baird attacked it from 5 o'clock, setting it into a spiral with its right engine on fire. Baird followed with a one-turn spin, which quickly terminated when muzzle flashes were observed coming from the enemy's port side. The Hellcat maneuvered into a dive at 6 o'clock. Another two-second burst set the Betty's fuselage on fire, but the bomber put the flames out at 12,000 feet by continuing the dive. Following, Baird managed another short burst, but contact was lost as his windscreen was smeared with oil from his previous victim. Baird circled and observed explosions after the Betty disappeared into the 6,000 foot overcast. GCI confirmed the kill at 0233, making Baird an ace.

On 8 July, the –533 moved to Chimu as XO Maj. Sam Folsum relieved Magruder. On 13/14 July Baird was to make his sixth and last kill of the war. At the time tests were being conducted using both the 20mm cannon, along with .50 caliber machine guns. The new –5N night fighters came equipped with two 20mm cannons and four .50 machine guns, but the 20mms were soon removed, as their muzzle flash suppressers had never been installed. Nighttime firing of the 20mm cannons without flash suppressers would destroy the pilot's night vision. The shielded cannons were reinstalled in Baird's Hellcat, which was tested for week before they operated without stoppages or other problems.

On the night of 13/14 July, Baird got his chance to try the new armament. Vectored by "Baywood" GCI, he climbed to 18,000 feet and chased an inbound contact until he closed astern. The Jap made evasive S-turns, which gave Baird no problems following on his airborne radar. A positive "Betty" ID was made at 0441. He closed under the bomber to 100 feet and fired a three second mixed 20mm and .50 burst that hit both engines, causing the bomber to burn vigorously and then dive and break up. With Bruce Porter, Baird became one of two Marines to score victories with mixed gunnery.

VMF(N)-533 scored only four more victories in the war to give it 35, which was as many as the other two night Marine squadrons on Okinawa combined (VMF-542/18 kills and VMF-543/16 kills). The top four scoring Marine pilots over Okinawa came from –533: Baird-6; and 1Lt. Albert Dellamans, 1Lt. Robert Hemsted and 1Lt. Robert Wellwood had three victories each.

Baird remained in the Marine Corps after the war. During his Korean duty he flew night interdiction and close support missions in the F7F-3N Tigercat with VMF(N)-542 and-513. In Vietnam he managed to get away from a desk job to fly a few combat missions in the A-4 Skyhawk. He retired as a Colonel in July 1971.

Chance Vought F4U(N) Corsair

First USN and F4U Night Fighter Victory (Land-based)
Pilot: 1Lt. Hugh D. O'Neill
Time: 31 October/1 November 1943/0400
Place: SE of Shortland Island
Unit: VF(N)-75
A/C: F4U-2(N) vs. Betty
Action: Commissioned in April 1943, VF(N)-75 was not only the Navy's first single-engine night fighter squadron, but also its first operational F4U Corsair squadron. Led by Lt. Cdr. W.J. "Gus" Widhelm, it was formed at NAS Quonset Point, RI, as part of the Navy's aerial radar program "Project Affirm." The unit received extensive night training before it received its greatly modified F4U-2 for additional training. By mid-September, the first contingent of six Corsairs shipped to Munda, New Georgia, via Espiritu Santo. After equipment setup and testing, the squadron flew its first night patrol on 2 October 1943. During the first two weeks of October the Japanese sent 15 night intruders over Munda, but the unit was unable to make any successful interceptions due to inexperience and technical difficulties.

On the night of 31 October/1 November 1943, seven contacts were attempted. Five were by AI, but all were lost due to equipment failure on the final target approach. The other two were visual with one escaping. Lt. Hugh D. "Danny" O'Neill, squadron XO, took off at 2310 and 90 minutes later was vectored by GCI towards a bogey off the northwest tip of Vella Lavella, 15 miles away at 10,000 feet. AI contact was made at 2 1/2 miles head-on, but the contact was immediately lost, as the bogie passed 2,000 feet below in the opposite direction. GCI again vectored the Corsair to the bogie, and a visual contact was readily made at 4,000 feet and 3,000 feet above, as the bogey had no exhaust dampers. O'Neill closed and set the bogie's port engine on fire with a short burst, but he overshot and had to make a 360 to again come astern. The bogey's engine fire had gone out, and O'Neill closed at 7,500 feet altitude, identifying it as a Betty bomber. He closed dead astern and squeezed

1Lt. Hugh O'Neill (L) is seen here with Lt. Thomas Hunt (2L), VF9(N)-75 FDO and LtCdr. William "Gus" Widhelm (R), CO. Widhelm was known as the "Father of USN night fighting" as he led "Project Affirm" at NAS Quonset Point in April 1943. (USN)

F4U-2(N) of VF(N)-101 off the *Enterprise*. (USN)

out a killing burst. American searchlights followed the falling victim as it crashed into the sea. This was both the first Navy F4U and only Navy night fighter victory of the war. About nine hours later, LtCdr. Tom Blackburn shot down two Zekes for the F4U's first of many daylight victories.

First USN F4U Night Fighter Victory (Carrier-based)

Pilot: LtCdr. Richard Harmer
Time: 24 October 1944/2010
Place: Off Hollandia, New Guinea
Unit: VF(N)-101
A/C: F4U-2(N)/Betty (Sally?)
Action: The *Enterprise* was supporting the invasion of Hollandia as part of TF 58 on 22 April 1944. Two days later the Japanese sent two Betty bombers to locate and illuminate the fleet in advance of a dozen torpedo bombers. Just before sunset *Enterprise* radar picked up the snoopers, and LtCdr. "Chick" Harmer and his wingman, Lt(jg) Robert Holden, were catapulted for the interception. Harmer had flown F4Fs for VF-5 off the Enterprise and was credited with a dive bomber over Guadalcanal. The F4U had its problems in carrier operations and night landings were too much for the young ensigns to handle, so Harmer and Holden flew the night patrols. The Bettys stayed out of range until the sun set, but a half hour later Harmer made radar contact on a solitary Betty about 30 miles be-

hind the task force. Harmer closed to within a half mile and saw a twin engine aircraft silhouetted against the fading light in the western sky. Harmer lost altitude to attack the Jap from below and closed, but was greeted by fire from the Betty's 20mm tail gun. He moved off laterally and fired as the Betty dove toward the sea. Harmer s-turned and followed, trying to clear his jammed .50s. His Corsair was again fired on by the Jap's tail gun and dorsal turret. Harmer hit the port engine just as the bomber released its torpedo and then dropped back to fire a long burst into the bomber at only 100 feet above the water. The Betty made a crash-landing into the water, floated for a while, and then sank. Harmer was vectored to the main Betty formation, joined up with five of them, and attacked his first target. He put a short burst into its belly before his guns jammed completely and he was forced to return to his carrier.

Top USN F4U Night Scorers

On 28 June 1944, Harmer and Holden were waiting in their Corsairs to be catapulted toward bogies picked up by AIA radar sets. Holden had shot down an unsuspecting Sally the night before and was launched first at 1940 toward a bogie 56 miles out. Holden searched for 40 minutes before obtaining a radar contact at maximum range. He closed to 300 yards before he made visual contact on a Betty. He closed to 75 yards and opened fire with a short burst from dead astern, exploding his unaware target. Holden made a second contact an hour and a quarter later and closed. This time the bomber took evasive action, but Holden set it on fire to crash into the sea for his third F4U night victory, best for a Navy pilot. Harmer was launched when Holden returned and dispatched another Betty for his second night victory. In seven months, VF-101(N) was credited with five night victories, a probable, and three damaged, all by either Harmer or Holden. The squadron's night Corsairs were left in Hawaii for use in night fighter school, and Harmer was sent to Florida as an instructor and on staff duty.

USMC F4U Night Fighters

The only Marine night fighter squadron to be equipped with the F4U-2(N) was VMF-532(N), which had trained at Cherry Point under Maj. Everett Vaughn. The unit was to score its first and only victories just after midnight on 14 April 1944 when 12 Betty bomb-

LtCdr. Richard Harmer. (USN)

1Lt. Edward Slovik of VMF-532(N) scored the first of the only two night victories scored by USMC F4U-2(N)s. (USMC)

ers attacked their base at Engebi. Five Corsairs took off to intercept the Japanese. 1Lt. Joel Bonner was vectored to a contact at 20,000 feet and opened fire, only to find his two starboard guns operating. He charged his port guns and continued to fire, getting hits, but the Jap tail gunner hit Bonner's Corsair and he was forced to bail out. He spent the night drifting in his raft and was rescued by a destroyer the next morning. At 0045 1Lt. Donald Spatz was sent out, but radar control put him out of range and he failed to return to base. 1Lt. Frank Lang was next, but the Japanese dropped metal chaff and he lost his targets. 1Lt. Edward Slovik was vectored west and orbited at 20,000 feet. He was vectored to a bogey at 23,000 feet and closed to 300 yards and began firing. In his excitement he had armed only three of his guns, but nonetheless exploded the Betty. Capt. Howard Bollman was the fifth F4U to take off, and was quickly sent to a contact at 22,000 feet and fired two quick bursts before almost colliding with the enemy bomber. He rolled away and renewed his attack, and cut the bomber in two for the second and last F4U Marine night victory. The unit engaged in 28 night raids on Wotje in the Marshall Islands. However, pickings were slim for the squadron, as it moved from Engebi to Roi, and finally Saipan and Guam.

P-38 Night Lightning

In June 1943 the 6NFS received two P-38Gs to replace their inadequate P-70s. The P-38s and their pilots (detached from the 339FS), known as "Project X" as part of the 6NFS, would cooperate in a night fighter-searchlight team. This team began to function when enemy aircraft were scoped by GCI, and the P-38 was scrambled and vectored into orbit. Here it waited until the radar-controlled searchlight batteries illuminated the enemy. Friendly AA was instructed to hold its fire until the Japanese bombers reached their bomb drop point, or until informed to shoot by the P-38 pilot. This was the theory, but American AA had difficulties holding their fire. However, they also had problems in downing the large, slow Japanese bombers, so P-38 pilots thought they were relatively safe in

A converted P-38 of Detachment A used for searchlight cooperation night missions. (Author)

1Lt. Henry Meigs of Detachment B (13AF) flew a modified P-38 on searchlight cooperation missions. On night CAP, Meigs shot down a Betty bomber on 15 August 1943 and then added two more on 21 September. He later added 3 more daylight victories to become an ace. (Author/Meigs)

pursuing the enemy into the "no-fly" zone. The first searchlight team victory occurred on 12 July 1943 when 1Lt. Ralph Tuttle shot down a Betty that was caught by a half dozen searchlights. Subsequently, three more Betty bombers were shot down (two by 1Lt. James Harrell) before "Project X" became independent of the 6NFS in September and was designated as Detachment B as part of the 13AF. Their only victories came on 21 September when 1Lt. Henry Meigs (who got a Betty on 15 August) was scrambled to meet a large number of Betty bombers. Meigs attacked a searchlight lit Betty, but his elevator was hit by fire from the rear gunner. He continued his attack and sent it down in flames. He proceeded to pursue a second Betty, whose gunners also hit Meigs' Lightning. Again he pressed his assault and set fire to the Jap, who crashed into the sea. Detachment B was disbanded on 15 December. Some personnel were transferred to the newly arrived 419NFS, while Meigs and others were sent back to their original units. Meigs went on to score three more daylight P-38 victories with the 339FS in February 1944 to become an ace. The P-38 searchlight teams scored seven victories in its short stint over Guadalcanal without a loss, even to friendly AA.

The USAAF tried some field conversions of the standard P-38 into a true night fighter capacity. In October 1943 the 6NFS on New Guinea refitted two of its P-38Gs by using two SCR-540 airborne intercept (AI) radar units taken from P-70s and installing them in modified drop tanks. The radio equipment behind the pilot's seat was removed to make room for a radar operator and his equipment. The aircraft HF and VHF radio equipment was then moved to a belly tank. Testing was just started when the 418NFS arrived, and the 6NFS were disbanded.

When the 418NFS arrived in Dobodura, New Guinea, in January 1944 it had a "strength" of ten P-70s and six war-weary P-38F and Gs. The unit participated in searchlight cooperation missions and dusk fighter sweeps. On 13 January, Maj. Carroll Smith and 1Lt. Harold Whittern were patrolling in the Alexishafen area when Smith saw a Val dive bomber heading for its air strip, and Smith closed to point blank range and let go three bursts of fire to give the 418th its first and only victory in its nine months. There was little Japanese air activity in the area, but the unit did engage in night intruder missions, which was not only destructive, but very unnerving to the enemy soldier on the ground. The 418th was re-equipped with the P-61 on its second tour in late Fall 1944, but still had several P-38s on hand for searchlight cooperation over their base at Morotai. On 11 November Maj. Smith was orbiting at 25,000 feet when he spotted a Betty caught by the searchlights at 14-16,000 feet. Smith went into a steep dive, and when he tried to pull back on the wheel, the Lightning did not respond. Smith remembered something about compressibility and the P-38, and he throttled back and let the engine go to full RPM. The fighter responded, and as he came out of the dive he was on the Betty and shot it down. The P-38 Night Lightning had scored nine night victories in the Pacific before giving way to the P-61.

Lockheed PV-1 Ventura

Following the Navy's lead, the Marine Corps formed its first night fighter squadron, VMF(N)-531, at Cherry Point MCAS, NC, in November 1942. The selection of the night fighter aircraft proved problematical for the Marine Corps planners. The Army's P-61 would not be ready until June 1943, while the F4U was scheduled for January 1943. Since the Army and Navy had embarked on separate night fighter programs, and because Marine Corps aviation had been looked upon as a stepchild, the Corps was forced to accept the Ventura. This twin-engine light bomber, designated the PV-1 by the Navy, was operated by a three-man crew: the pilot; a combined radio/radar operator; and a top turret gunner manning twin .50s. The PV-1 had sufficient speed, maneuverability, and firepower to qualify as an adequate night fighter, but it possessed a low service ceiling, precluding interceptions at the anticipated 25,000 foot combat altitudes in the PTO. In actual combat, however, the Japanese did operate within the Ventura's ceiling. It was later found that its inability to slow down quickly, causing it to overrun or lose its target, would be its primary combat liability.

PV-1 of VMF(N)-531.

VMF(N)-531 was under the command of Lt. Col. Frank H. Schwable, who had been trained in night fighting techniques by the British and his XO, Maj. John D. Harshberger. The unit experienced numerous problems in training with its personnel, aircraft, and radar sets. In December 1942, nightly Japanese nuisance raids over Guadalcanal were lowering the combat efficiency of U.S. troops, and Adm. Halsey urged that night fighters be sent ASAP. So, in the next six months in training the pressure was on Schwable. The PV-1 continued to be merely a makeshift night fighter, and the radar averaged one in three sets operable at any one time. In late June, VMF(N)-531 was ordered to San Diego to sail to Espiritu Santo, where the men and radar equipment arrived on 30 July. On 31 July, six PV-1s were loaded on the carrier *Long Island* and shipped to Pearl Harbor, where they were flown in hops to the Russell Islands, arriving at Banika on 11 September. It was not until 23 September that the men, radar, and aircraft were reunited at Munda. However, VMF(N)-531's CGI was not allowed to operate with its own aircraft as a combat unit, and the group had to utilize whatever other controllers were available. This situation caused a lack of coordination and loss of enemy contacts. Also, the PV-1s were often vectored away from the target area, so that the ineffective but morale-building (for the infantry below) AA guns could blast away. During N-531's stay in the Solomons, Schwable had difficulty convincing Navy brass of the potential of night fighting and received little cooperation. Added to these troubles were the constant problems with CGI stations, the radar units, and communications. It was found that its major combat liability was its inability to slow down quickly, which caused it to overrun or lose its target. Schwable's entire undertaking operated on the proverbial shoe string,

(L-R) LtCol. John Harshberger, LtCol. Frank Schwable and 1Lt. Duane Jenkins at Banika, Russell, Islands. Each of these pilots scored two night victories in the PV-1 for VMF(N)-531, tops for the type. Jenkins scored the first PV-1 night victory on 13 November 1943.

having minimal personnel, spare parts, and supplies. His six PV-1s were replaceable only from the United States.

The night Corsairs of VF(N)-75 joined the squadron several weeks after its arrival. The faster F4U-2s had a higher operating ceiling and often flew high-cover patrols, while the Venturas flew medium and low-level sorties.

PV-1 First Victory in Type
Pilot: Capt. Duane R. Jenkins
Time: 13 November 1943/0420
Place: 50 miles SW Bougainville
Unit: VMF(N)-531
A/C: PV-1/Betty
Action: Schwable's Venturas flew often during October and November, covering landings at Bougainville and Treasury Islands. It was not until 13 November that the Marines would get their first night victory of the war. At 0400, Capt. Duane Jenkins, his radio/radar operator Sgt. Thomas Glennon, and gunner T/Sgt. Charles Stout were vectored by a FDO (fighter director) in the task force offshore to a point 50 miles to the west of Torokina Point. In this area Jenkins intercepted a formation of five Betty bombers headed for the American task force. In the bright moonlight the PV-1 moved in dangerously close from a position below and astern to one somewhat laterally, in order to take advantage of the existing light so visual contact and a sure kill could be made. Once positive visual ID was made, Jenkins set up his firing pass from below, climbing up until the bomber's silhouette filled the dimly lit gunsight. He fired the four .50 cal. MGs mounted under the nose AI/IV radar unit, downing the Betty. On 3 December Jenkins shot down an u/i with his nose guns over Empress Augusta Bay, but were MIA during the mission for the unit's first loss.

PV-1 Top Scorers in Type
Victories: 2 each
> Col. Frank H. Schwable (pilot) and
> T/Sgt. Walter E. Tiedeman (gunner)
> Lt.Col. John D. Harshberger (pilot) and
> Sgt. William J. Fletcher (gunner)
> Lt. Duane R. Jenkins (pilot)

When VMF(N)-531 was replaced in June 1944, it had scored 12 confirmed victories for a loss of seven Venturas to all causes. Four victories were scored in Venturas piloted by Col. Schwable and Lt.Col. Harshberger. In each of their eight victories the credit was shared by the gunners and their pilots, even though the gunners

Mosquito 416NFS. Although only one victory was scored by a Mosquito in American service, three Americans became night aces in the aircraft with the RAF. (USAF)

alone shot down the enemy aircraft. So officially, each had four half victories to total two each. Capt. Duane Jenkins, who scored the first victory, got another u/i Japanese aircraft with his nose guns to give him two victories as a pilot. VMF(N)-531, called the "Gray Ghosts," returned to the U.S. and began to train in the twin engine Grumman F7F Tigercat, which would have been the optimal night fighter had the war continued.

DeHaviland Mosquito
Mosquito First and Only Victory in Type
Pilot: Capt. Lawrence E. Englert
Radar: 2Lt. Earl R. Dickey
Time: 28 February 1945/2307
Place: NW of Villafranca di Verona
Unit: 416NFS/12AF
A/C: Mosquito XXX/Ju-188
Action: American interest in the Mosquito centered on its utilization for reconnaissance; however, the shortage of P-61s moved the AAF to borrow seven Mosquitoes for night fighter duties. These fighters were assigned to the 425NFS at Etain, France, in early 1945 and were transferred to the 416 NFS, temporarily stationed at Etain. The 416th converted from their Beaufighters in January to the Mosquitoes, since P-61s continued to be in short supply. The squadron had about a dozen Mosquitoes on strength at Pisa, Italy, during February and March 1945.

At 2154 hours on 28 February 1945, GCI picked up a hostile aircraft on its radar scope and scrambled a Mosquito crewed by Capt. Lawrence Englert and 2Lt. Earl Dickey from Pontedera Airfield in Italy. After losing the contact, for the next hour the Mosquito was handed from one GCI to another. Finally, Dickey made AI radar contact and directed Englert to a visual on a Ju-188. Since the moon was behind and ID was easily made, Englert maneuvered to 125 yards directly astern the Junkers and gave it a two second burst, hitting the tail and causing the enemy to go into a shallow dive. Another two second burst missed, but a third hit the German's fuselage. A final salvo knocked off a large chunk of fuselage and set the aircraft on fire, resulting in an explosion. This was to be the only American Mosquito victory of the war. The Mosquito flew through the smoke and debris. Several minutes later its starboard engine caught fire and was feathered, and the starboard wheel dropped permanently. To make matters worse the instrument panel went dead. The Mosquito continually lost altitude and was unresponsive to control. Realizing that it would be impossible to land the aircraft, the crew bailed out, landing safely.

Mosquito: Top American Night Fighter Ace (RAF)
Pilot: Lt. Archibald A. Harrington
Maj. Carroll Smith of the 5 AF/418 NFS is generally credited as being the top scoring American night fighter ace with seven victories. However, the name of the most productive American night fighter ace is not found on the roster of American night fighter aces, even though he was born in Zanesville, Ohio, and was an officer in the USAAF. This unknown ace is A.A. (Archibald A.) Harrington, who eventually retired as a Lt. Colonel in the USAF!

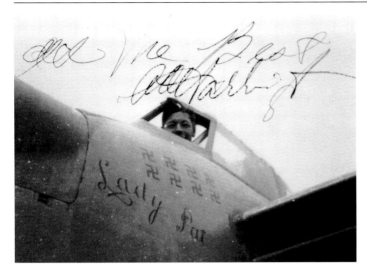

Lt. Archibald Harrington. (Author/Harrington)

After the Battle of Britain, Harrington went to Canada to enlist in the RCAF and was accepted in early March 1941 as AC2 (Aircraftman Second Class), the lowest grade possible. Although he had over 2,000 hours in the air, he was required to complete flight school, A to Z, finally winning his wings as a Pilot Officer (2Lt. equivalent) in late December 1941. He became a Chief Flying Instructor at a station near Ottawa, where he courted and married the mayor's daughter. In October 1942 he was promoted to Flying Officer (1Lt. equivalent) and was shipped to England for training on twin-engine fighters. He was assigned to the 410 Squadron in late June 1943 and soon transferred to the USAAF. He remained with the 410th as an attached officer, and thus filed his combat reports with the RCAF/RAF and not with the USAAF, which used their combat reports as the basis for U.S. official ace lists.

The 410 was flying the Mosquito II night fighter (equipped with AI radar) mainly on defensive sorties against Luftwaffe night intruders. It was not until 15 September 1943 that Harrington flew his first combat mission by blowing up a munitions train in Rennes, France, and almost ending his flying career at the same time in the

Lt. Archibald Harrington. (Author/Harrington)

debris and fire of the explosion. He was sent off for additional schooling, and it was not until February 1944 that he and the 410 were in a position to enter combat, as the Luftwaffe began its "Little Blitz" against London. During this time Harrington received the Mosquito XIII and was joined by his radar operator, F/O Dennis Tongue. Harrington already had over 1,000 hours of operational flying and had yet to score his first victory.

At 2110 on the night of 14/15 March 1944, English radar detected 150 German bombers crossing the Channel, heading towards London. At 2200 Harrington and Tongue were scrambled and ordered to patrol over a radio beacon. After circling for over an hour they noticed searchlights probing for a bomber that had dropped incendiaries. Soon Tongue got a radar contact four miles ahead, and Harrington closed but overshot on his first pass. The German bomber dropped "window"—shredded aluminum strips—which obliterated the bomber's image on the Mosquito's radarscope. Harrington waited and regained contact visually on the enemy that he identified as a twin-engine Ju-188 bomber. Closing to within a "no-miss" 100 feet, the Mosquito's four 20mm cannon set the Junkers on fire, causing it to explode. Harrington insists in his log that he destroyed two enemy aircraft that night, and there is some evidence in British records for the night to validate his claim.

After the "Little Blitz" ended in early April, the 410 trained for long-range patrol missions in preparation for patrols over the Allied invasion beaches. Harrington saw action from D-Day +1, but it was not until the night of 18/19 June that he was to score again. He chased and caught his first contact, which he visually ID'd as another Mosquito. GCI vectored him towards a Ju-88 carrying external bombs or torpedoes. He closed to 75 yards, exploding the bomber, tearing off its wing and showering his Mosquito with debris.

Harrington was not to score for another three months, even though he flew regularly in the superlative Mosquito XXX, the last wartime variant. It was outfitted with the Mark X AI radar set, which had been developed in the United States. In late September 410 moved to the Continent and was stationed in Glisy. On the night of 26/27 September, he downed a Ju-87 Stuka in a low speed, turning combat over Aachen. On 29 October he got his fourth victim, a FW-190.

On the 81st and final mission of his combat tour on 25 November, the 30-year-old Harrington took off in the early evening and began patrolling between 10,000 and 15,000 feet. After two hours GCI vectored him toward u/i aircraft, and Tongue made radar contact four miles ahead. At 1,200 yards Harrington picked up a Ju-88G night fighter that he hit with a cannon burst at 200 yards, and watched it until it exploded as it hit the ground. After assuming patrol altitude, Tongue made another contact, which Harrington visually identified as another Ju-88G. The Junkers and Mossie went into a ten mile chase before Harrington managed to put a short burst into the German's cockpit, sending it into an inverted spin and crash. Moving back to patrol altitude again, GCI vectored him towards two enemy planes flying a parallel course five miles apart. Harrington chose one and closed. Tongue observed the battle on his radarscope, watching his aircraft close on one German while the other was closing on their Mosquito! The visual disclosed an-

1Lt. Clarence Jaspar (Author/Jaspar) and 1Lt. John Luma (USAF)

other Ju-88G. The unsuspecting German took 20mm hits in the cockpit and port wing roots, catching fire. Harrington quickly went into a steep dive to shake his pursuer and headed for base with three victories in one night.

Harrington flew no further combat missions and was sent back to the States, where he taught night fighter tactics with the 450th Night Fighter Combat Crew Training Unit. He would remain in the USAF after the war, retiring as a Lt. Colonel in 1963.

Other American Mosquito Night Fighter Aces in the RAF
Pilots: 1Lt. John F. Luma (C.G. Finlayson R.O./N)
           1Lt. Clarence M. Jasper (O.A. Martin R.O./N)
Victories: 5 each
Unit: 418 Squadron RCAF "City of Edmonton"
A/C: Mosquito
The two Americans joined the RCAF in 1941 to train as night fighter pilots. They were posted to the 418 "City of Edmonton" Squadron to fly Mosquitoes on intruder interception missions. When the United States entered the war they were transferred to the USAAF, but remained with the 418th as attached officers.

Luma shot down five German aircraft in the air and destroyed five on the ground between late January and April 1944, when he finished his tour. Jasper shot down five, destroyed three on the ground, and added three V-1s between March and August 1944.

Bristol Beaufighter
Beaufighter First Victory in Type
Pilot: Capt. Nathaniel H. Lindsay
Radar: F/O Austin G. Petry
Time: 24 July 1943/0730
Place: Tyrrhenian Sea
Unit: 415NFS/12AF
A/C: Beaufighter VI/HE-111
Action: In the spring of 1943, four independent USAAF night fighter squadrons (the 414th, 415th, 416th, and 417th) arrived in Great Britain to train with RAF units on Beaufighters for eventual deployment with the 12AF/NAAF (Northwest African Air Force) in the MTO. The aircraft used were assigned to the RAF, and the training of inexperienced American pilots produced numerous prangs in these borrowed twin-engine fighters. The four squadrons completed train-

Beaufighter of the 415NFS. Four USAF Beaufighter squadrons scored 37 victories for 48 lost to all causes. The 414NFS scored 13 victories and the 415NFS 11. (USAF)

Capt. Nathaniel Lindsay. (USAF)

ing at various times between early July and early September 1943 and were shipped to North Africa. Once there, they were equipped with war-weary Beaufighter MK VIs scrounged from RAF maintenance units and equipped with British MK IV radar. Twelve aircraft were the normal squadron complement.

The 415NFS arrived in Tunisia on 3 July 1943, flew its first operational sortie on the 5th, and lost its first crew on the 10th. On the 24th, the 415th was assigned to begin "Operation Panther," the destruction of enemy transport aircraft over the Tyrrhenian Sea. Pilot Capt. Nathaniel Lindsay and radar operator F/O Austin Petry spotted a Luftwaffe He-115 floatplane at 0725 about 45 miles east of Olbia. Lindsay made a pass on the Heinkel, setting its right engine on fire. A Beaufighter of the 414NFS made a pass as the German went into a fatal dive and was seen breaking up in the sea for the Beaufighter's first American victory.

Beaufighter Top Scorers

On 18 March 1944, Lindsay and Petry downed a Ju-88 just after midnight for their second Beaufighter victory. 2Lt. William Henderson (pilot) and 2Lt. Rayford Jefferies (radar) also claimed two Beaufighter MTO victories: 2 February and 28 March 1944, both over Ju-88s.

The four American Beaufighter Squadrons had furnished night defense for the 12AF in North Africa, then Sicily, and Italy. The 415th and 416NFS later operated out of France. The 415th got six victories there, three by 1Lt. Edward Schlueter (pilot) and 2Lt. Donald Meiers (radar): two on 29 December 1944 (a He-111 and a Ju-88 near Nancy), and a Ju-88 on 1 January 1945. These three victories made Schlueter the top American Beaufighter scorer. Capt. Harold F. Augspurger (pilot) and 2Lt. Austin Petry (radar) shot down a FW-190 on 28 September 1944, and a He-111 two days later. These two victories and his two with Lindsay made Petry the top scoring Beaufighter R/O with four. 2Lt. Donald J. Meiers, as mentioned above, scored three R/O victories with Schlueter.

The Beaufighter's MK IV airborne radar sets picked up excessive ground clutter and were unreliable. The lack of replacement parts and maintenance problems on both the aircraft and the radar equipment led to further difficulties. The 414th converted to the P-61 in December 1944, while the 416th received Mosquitoes to supplement their Beaus in late 1944. The British stopped building Beaufighters in January 1944, so the 415th and 417th kept their weary Beaufighters (some of which had seen service in the Battle of Britain!) until spring 1945. Over 100 Beaufighters served with the USAAF, claiming 37 victories (30 MTO and 7 ETO) in the war: 414NFS-13v.; 415NFS-4v. (MTO) and 7v. (ETO); 416NFS-4v.; and 417NFS-9v, and losing 48 Beaufighters from all causes.

Douglas P-70 Nighthawk

P-70 First Victory in Type
Pilot: Capt. Earl C. Bennett
Radar: Corp. Edwin E. Tomlinson
Time: 19 April 1943/0430
Place: Off Tulagi, Solomon Is.
Unit: 6NFS/7AF
A/C: P-70B-2/Betty
Action: American interest in the conversion of the A-20 low-level attack bomber into a night fighter arose from the need for an interim measure until the P-61 Black Widow, plagued with development and production problems, could be brought into inventory. Since the British had already converted the DB-7, the export version of the A-20, into a night fighter (the Havoc series), the A-20 seemed to be a logical night fighter adaptation.

The 6FS received 25 P-70B-2s and began an unenthusiastic Hawaiian training session in September 1942. In February 1943, six crews and maintenance personnel were sent to Guadalcanal to counter nightly Japanese bombing raids designed for aggravation rather than destruction. By 25 March, the six P-70s began nightly alerts from Carney Field. GCI would send the Nighthawk to intercept the Japanese intruder in a designated area extending 50 to 10

Naming the A-20 the "Nighthawk" and adding a radar set could not convert the slow, low altitude medium bomber into a fast-climbing, high altitude night interceptor. (USAF)

miles from a "gun-defended" zone. The P-70 was not authorized in this area, because if it had not made the interception by that time, the E/A/C was either too fast or too high and too close, and the best defense was AA fire. Also, since American AA command operated separately from night fighter command, often "friendly" AA fired into the darkness without regard for friend or foe.

On 19 April, Capt. Earl Bennett and his R/O, T/Sgt. Raymond Mooney, were flying a midnight to 6 AM patrol. GCI picked up Japanese raiders that were headed for Guadalcanal at 22,000 feet. The enemy reached the gun-defended area before the P-70 could intercept. The anti-aircraft batteries were also unsuccessful, and as the Japanese were about to leave the searchlight beams, Bennett decided to attack. Ignoring exploding flak bursts and while thousands of troops watched from the ground, Bennett's tracers exploded a Betty bomber, which burned until it crashed. Bennett had just accounted for the first and half of the P-70's total victories.

Other P-70 Scorers

On 15 May, 2Lt. Burnell W. Adams (pilot) and F/O Paul DiLabbio (R/O) were on alert out of Port Moresby. Their P-70 struggled to 22,000 feet on its patrol and was given a ground control vector at 18,000 feet and behind. DiLabbio picked up the bogey on his scope and directed Adams into a dive, which put the Nighthawk in visual contact behind the Sally bomber. The rear gunner opened fire but missed, and Adams fired a burst which silenced the gunner and probably wounded the pilot, as the Japanese bomber went into a shallow dive. Adams fired again, setting the enemy on fire. A third burst exploded the enemy at 2005 for the only New Guinea P-70 victory. Adams later went on to score six additional victories in P-38 day fighters with the 80FS/8FG. Capt. Samuel Blair flew for the 6NFS and later scored seven P-47 victories for the 348FG.

The Japanese discovered the P-70's performance limitations at altitudes over 20,000 feet and came in higher. Also at these altitudes its radar equipment functioned intermittently or failed completely. Naming the A-20 the "Nighthawk" and adding a radar set could not convert the slow, low-altitude bomber into a fast-climbing, high-altitude night interceptor. Fortunately, the P-61, a purpose-built night fighter, would finally come online in the SWPA.

Note: Some sources credit a P-70 victory in the MTO to 1Lt. Robert Walber and his radar operator, F/O Emmett Faison, of the 415 NFS over a Cant 1007 over Tunis-Bizerte on 16 August 1943. However, the squadron's records reveal that it was flying the British Beaufighter VI at the time.

Flying the P-70 Nighthawk
By
Carroll Smith:
Top U.S. night fighter ace

In August 1942, we pilots and crews of the 418NFS were sent to AAFSAT, Orlando, Florida, to begin night fighter training. We trained in the P-70, which was essentially a modified A-20 bomber. The forward crew compartment and guns were replaced with radar equipment, and a ventral gun pack was installed in the bomb bay or mounted on the side of the fuselage. A R/O compartment was placed in the rear of the former gunner's position.

The pilot entered the cockpit by climbing up to and crossing the wing, and then stepping onto a deck leading down to the pilot's seat through a hinged canopy. The seat was adjustable only for height. The flight controls were the conventional wheel-column-pedal type, and were nothing out of the ordinary. The radio operator's compartment in the rear had the necessary flight controls for emergency operation of the aircraft. A low-pressure oxygen was installed, and was adequate for the altitudes we were to operate. Four 20mm fixed forward-firing cannon were mounted in a compartment projecting below the lower surface of the fuselage. The complete gun installation was removable as a single unit. A firing switch was located on the control wheel. A gun selector switch allowed the pilot to fire the inboard, outboard, or all four cannons in salvo. The gun sight was a type N-2A mounted in an adjustable frame on the centerline of the windshield.

Everything the Air Force knew about night fighter tactics, which was not much at the time, was learned from British experience. There was a lot of emphasis on instrument training. The aircraft was easy to fly and had no vices. The tricycle landing gear was particularly suited for night operations, facilitating ground handling, take offs, and landings. The twin Wright double R-2600 Cyclones were designed for the A-20, which was a low-level attack bomber. For that job the A-20 was maneuverable and possessed sufficient speed and altitude capabilities. But painting it black and calling it a night fighter did not make it one, as we found out when we deployed to New Guinea in early 1944. In the SWPA our crews found that, besides being unable to climb to the altitudes the Japanese

Maj. Carroll Smith. (Author/Smith)

were operating at, they wee often out run by the speedier Jap bombers! There was little Jap air activity in the area until we received our P-61s in the fall of 1944.

Backseat Aces

It is obvious that teamwork was instrumental for a multi-place night fighter crew to be successful. The pilot had to rely on his navigator/radar operator to locate and then close on the enemy so that the pilot could make visual contact. The RAF only recognized the pilot when awarding a night victory. The U.S., a latecomer in multi-place night fighter aircraft with its "pure night" design (P-61 Black Widow), had only a handful of aces in the type. The Air Force, always "unofficial" on aces, only recognized the night fighter pilot during the war. However, USAF Historical Study 85 began in 1959 with its "Preliminary List of USAF Aces 1917-53" gave full victory credit to all crewmembers of a multi-seat aircraft.

Under these criteria, the following Black Widow Radar Operators were "Backseat Aces" (listed as to date they became aces):

R/O Name and Rank	Unit	Date Ace	Pilot Name and Rank
Tierney, 1Lt. Robert	422NFS	12/26/44	Smith, 1Lt. Paul
Porter, 1Lt. Philip	418NFS	12/30/44	Smith, Maj. Carroll
Kopsel, 1Lt. Edward	422NFS	3/2/45	Ernst, 1Lt. Herman
Graham, 1Lt. Robert	422NFS	3/21/45	Bolinder, 1Lt. Robert (4v.)
			Anderson, Capt. Raymond (1v.)

An interesting footnote: the original Vietnam Preliminary Ace List of October 1971 divided victories between crew members. But in August 1972, with the entry of the multi-seat F4 fighter into Southeast Asian operations, each crew was awarded a full victory for the destruction of an enemy aircraft, making the American Ace list consistent.

CHAPTER 11

Aces in Multiple Aircraft

Aces in Two Different Aircraft

America's introduction of improved, second-generation fighters afforded a few pilots the opportunity to become aces in two or different aircraft. The venerable Navy/Marine F4F Wildcat in the early Pacific War and the AAC P-40 Warhawk in all early theaters were the primary front-line fighters. The Wildcat was replaced by F6F Hellcats and F4U Corsairs, while the Warhawk units were re-equipped with P-38 Lightnings and P-47 Thunderbolts, which were in turn succeeded by the P-51 Mustang. A large number of skilled pilots scored victories in two or more tours in two different aircraft.

Of the aces who scored ten or more victories in WWII, 14 scored five or more victories in two different fighters. In the Pacific the Navy flew the F4F Wildcat over the Solomons to stop the Japanese advance on Australia. Scott McCusky scored 6 1/2 victories with VF-42 and VF-3, Charles Stimpson 6 victories with VF-11, John Symmes 5 1/2 with VF-21, and Albert Vorse 5 1/2 with VF-3, 2, and 6. In their next combat tours they transitioned to the F6F Hellcat and became double aces in that fighter. McCusky got 7 Japanese with VF-8, Stimpson 10 again with VF-11 (5 victories occurred on 14 October 1944), Symmes 5 1/2 with VF-15, and Vorse 6 with VF-80.

James Howard and Charles Older scored 7 1/3 and 10 victories, respectively, in the shark-mouthed P-40s of the Flying Tigers (AVG). Older claimed 8 victories in the P-51 after the disbandment of the AVG, as he continued on with the 14 Air Force's 23FG in the CBI. Howard transferred to the 356th and 354th Fighter Groups of the 8AF flying the P-51 in the ETO. Howard got 6 more victories and the Congressional Medal of Honor. He and John Landers are the only two pilots to become aces in the Pacific and European Theaters.

In the Pacific, two 13AF P-40 aces later became P-38 aces. Robert Westbrook scored 7 victories in 44FS' P-40s, while squadron mate Cotesworth Head scored 8. Westbrook became an ace in the P-38 by shooting down 13 Japanese to become the top ace in the 13AF with 20 victories before being killed in action in November 1944 by AA fire over Makasser Strait. Head tallied 6 P-38 victories before he was KIA in mid-January 1944 over Rabaul. Richard West of the 5FG of the 5AF scored 6 P-40 victories in his first two combat missions. He then went on to get 8 more P-38 victories in his next 173 missions.

In the ETO, 4FG ace James Goodson of the 336FS got 5 P-47 victories, while fellow 4FG ace Duane Beeson of the 334FS was a double ace with a dozen Luftwaffe claims. Goodson recorded 2 MTO P-51 victories while detached to the 31FG, and then scored 7 more P-51 victories again with the 336 before being taken POW in mid-June 1944 after being shot down by flak over Neubrandenberg

Airdrome. Beeson totaled 5 1/3 victories in the P-51 before being shot down by AA over Brandenberg, and also becoming a POW in early 1944. Robin Olds accounted for 5 P-38 victories for the 479FG/434FS and then 8 in the P-51. Twenty-three years later, at 45 years old, he nearly became America's only ace in three different fighters when he participated in 4 F-4 Phantom victories over Vietnam with the 8TFW.

In the Mediterranean, Herschel Green of the 325FG, after getting 3 victories in the P-40, scored 10 in the P-47. Green claimed 5 in the P-51 over Italy. Charles McCorkle of the 31FG had 5 Spitfire victories over North Africa, and when the Group re-equipped with Mustangs he got 6 victories over Italy in that fighter.

The Korean War produced 40 aces, and 7 of these were also aces in WWII. All flew F-86 Sabres in Korea. Francis "Gabby" Gabreski had 28 P-47 victories with the 56FG in WWII and 5 1/2 in the Sabre over Korea, while Vermont Garrison had 7 victories in 4FG P-47s and 10 victories with the 4FIW over Korea. In the Pacific, 5AF ace George Davis got 7 victories in the P-47s of the 49FG, and in the Korean War had 14 Communist aircraft with the 4FIW. William Whisner of the 352FG/8AF scored 15 1/2 Mustang victories in the ETO and 5 1/2 with the 51FIW over Korea. James Hagerstrom of the 49FG/5AF scored 6 P-40 Pacific victories and 8 1/2 Sabre victories over Korea with the 18FIW. Harrison Thyng had 5 in the Spitfire with the 31FG over North Africa and 5 jet victories with the 4FIW. Marine Corps ace John Bolt got 6 F4U victories with VMF-214 and scored his 6 Korean victories as a Marine attached to the 51FIW.

Aces with Victories in Three Fighter Types

Twenty-nine aces, all Air Force, scored victories in three different fighter types. Of the 29, seven scored F-86 jet victories in Korea and victories in two fighter types in WWII. Robin Olds had 5 P-38 and 8 P-51 WWII victories, and in the Vietnam War got 4 credits in the F-4 Phantom. Four aces claimed Spitfire acehood while flying as volunteers with the RAF and RCAF previous to transferring to the USAAF.

Of the 17 aces who scored victories in three fighter types in WWII, Maj. Paul Bechtel probably had the most unusual record. He was transferred to the Pacific flying the obsolete P-39 as CO of the 12FS/13AF over Guadalcanal. His Cobra victories came over Munda when he shot down two Zeros on Christmas Eve 1942. During the first week of April 1943 he got two Zekes while flying the P-38. Bechtel later served as Air Op Officer for the 13FC with COMAIRSOL at Guadalcanal and Munda. In this position he was able to fly combat sorties in P-38s, P-39s, P-40s, F6Fs, and F4Us. On 2 September 1943 he was flying a borrowed Marine F4U from

Aces in Two Different Aircraft in WWII

Pilot Name	A/C#1	V#	Units	A/C#2	V#	Units
Beeson, Duane	P-47	12	4FG	P-51	5.3	4FG
Goodson, James	P-47	5	4FG	P-51	9	31, 336FG
Green, Herschel	P-47	10	325FG	P-51	5	325FG
Head, Cotesworth	P-40	8	44FS	P-38	6	44FS
Howard, James	P-40	7.3	AVG	P-51	6	356,354FG
McCorkle, Charles	Spitfire	5	31FG	P-51	5	31FG
McCusky, Scott	F4F	6.5	VF-42, 3	F6F	7	VF-8
Older, Charles	P-40	10	AVG	P-51	8	23FG
Olds, Robin	P-38	5	479FG	P-51	8	479FG
Stimpson, Charles	F4F	6	VF-11	F6F	10	VF-11
Symmes, John	F4F	5.5	VF-21	F6F	5.5	VF-15
Vorse, Albert	F4F	5.5	VF-3,2,6	F6F	6	VF-80
West, Richard	P-40	6	5FG	P-38	8	5FG
Westbrook, Robert	P-40	7	44FS	P-38	13	44FS

Footnote: See WWII/Korean War Aces

Aces in Two Fighters

Duane Beeson: P-47 (12v.)/P-51 (5.3v.) (USAF)

Left: James Goodson: P-47 (5v.)/P-51 (9v.) (Author/Goodson)

Right: Herschel Green: P-47 (10v.)/P-51 (5v.) (Author/Green)

Cotesworth Head: P-40 (8v.)/P-38 (6v.) (USAF)

James Howard: P-40 (7.3v.)/P-51 (6v.) (Author/Howard)

Scott McCusky: F4F (6.5v.)/F6F (7v.) (USN)

Charles McCorkle: Spitfire (5v.)/P-51 (5v.) (Author/McCorkle)

Charles Older: P-40 (10v.)/P-51 (8v.) (Author/Older)

John Symmes: F4F (5.5v.)/F6F (5.5v.) (USN)

Robin Olds: P-38 (5v.)/P-51 (8v.) (Author/Olds)

Albert Vorse: F4F (5.5v.)/F6F (6v.) (USN)

Charles Stimpson: F4F (6v.)/F6F (10v.) (USN)

Richard West: P-40 (6v.)/P-38 (8v.) (Author/West)

Right: Robert Westbrook: P-40 (7v.)/P-38 (13v.) (USAF)

John Landers almost became an ace in three different fighters. He was a 6 victory ace in the P-40 in the Pacific (seen here). He transferred to the ETO and went on to score 4 1/2 victories in the P-51 and 4 in the P-38. (Author/Landers)

Herschel Green spent his career with the 325FG which flew in three different fighters in the MTO. Green scored 3 victories in the P-40 (seen here), 10 in the P-47 and then 5 in the P-51. (Author/Green)

VMF-124 on a late afternoon bomber escort mission over Kilili, Bougainville. He was credited with shooting a Zeke off the tail of eight victory Marine ace Don Yost.

Maj. Walker "Bud" Mahurin was the only ace to score victories in Europe, the Pacific, and Korea. Flying a P-47 for the 56FG, he scored 19 2/3 victories before being shot down and evading back to England. He transferred to the Third Commando Group, getting a Zero over the Philippines in a P-51. During the Korean War he claimed 3 1/2 victories in the F-86 Sabre Jet before being taken POW.

Seven aces scored P-40 victories early in the Pacific War. The seven were promoted and transferred to the ETO, scoring more victories there. But John Landers did them one better. He claimed 6 Japanese in the P-40 with the 49FG in the Pacific. He was later transferred to the 8AF in various CO positions as a Lt. Colonel. He flew P-38s for the 78FG, getting 4 P-38 victories, and P-51s for the 357Fg, getting 4 1/2 victories. The 6 Pacific and 8 ETO victories made Landers one of two American two theater aces (the other was James Howard in two fighter types).

In a special category is Texan Albert "Ajax" Baumler, who scored 5 1/2 victories in the Spanish Civil War flying Russian-built fighters, the Polikarpov I-15 (3 1/2 victories) and the I-16 (2 victories), to become an ace. He then joined the AVG Flying Tigers and scored a victory in a P-40, and afterward went on to score 4 (3 1/2?) victories, also in the P-40, with the USAAF (23FG/75FS) to become a two war ace.

Aces with Victories in Four Different Fighter Types
Col. John Mitchell

V#	Date	A/C	E/A/C
1	10/09/42	P-39	Float
2	10/23/42	P-39	Zero
3	11/07/42	P-39	Rufe
4	01/05/43	P-38	Float Zero
5-6	01/27/43	P-38	2 Zero
7	01/29/43	P-38	Type 97 TE bomber
8	02/02/43	P-38	Float Zero
9	06/26/45	P-51	Zeke
10-11	07/16/45	P-51	2 George
12	01/21/53	F-86	MiG-15
13	03/09/53	F-86	MiG-15
14	04/11/53	F-86	MiG-15
15	05/15/53	F-86	MiG-15

Col. John Mitchell (R), shown here with Thomas Lanphier (L) after the famous "Get Yamamoto" mission, claimed victories in 4 different fighters. Mitchell got 3 victories in the P-39, 5 in the P-38, 3 in the P-51 and then 4 in the F-86 over Korea to give him 15 career victories. (Author/Mitchell)

Aces Scoring Victories in Three Different Fighters

Pilot Name	Units	A/C 1	V #	A/C 2	V#	A/C 3	V#
Adkins, Frank*	35&50FG	P-40	2	P-400	1	P-51	2+
Andrew, Stephen*	49&35FG	P-40	1	P-47	1+	P-51	7+
Baker. Royal	31&78FG&4FIW	Spitfire	3	P-47	0.5	F-86	13
Bechtel. Paul	18FG &VMF-124	P-39	2	P-38	2	F4U	1
Blakeslee. Donald	401RAF&133RCAF &4FG	Spitfire	2	P-47	3	P-51	8.5
Clark, James	4FG	Spitfire	0.5	P-47	4	P-51	6
Dean, Cecil	325FG	Spitfire	1	P-47	3	P-51	2
Dunkin, Richard	325FG	P-40	1	P-47	3	P-51	2
Emmert, Ben	325FG & 4FIW	P-40	1	P-51	5	F-86	1
Evans, Roy	4FG & 359FG	Spitfire	1	P-47	4	P-51	1
Garrison, Vermont	4FG & 4FIW	P-47	6.3	P-51	1	F-86	6
Gentile, Don	133RAF & 4FG	Spitfire	1.3	P-47	4	P-51	16.5
Green, Herschel	325FG	P-40	3	P-47	10	P-51	5
Herbst, John	??RAF& 23FG	Spitfire	1	P-40	4	P-51	10
Hogg, Roy	325FG	P-40	2	P-47	2	P-51	2
Hovde, William	355FG & 4FIW	P-47	1	P-51	9.5	F-86	1
Johnson, Jerry	Aleutian HQ&49FG	P-39	2?	P-47	2?	P-38	20
Kruzel, Joseph	17PPS & 361FG	P-40	3	P-47	1.5+	P-51	2+
Landers, John*	49FG & 78FG	P-40	6	P-38	4+	P-51	4.5+
Mahurin, Walker#	56FG, 3Cdo, 51FIW	P-47	19.7	P-51	1	F-86	3.5
McGee, Donald*	8FG & 357FG	P-39	3	P-38	2	P-51	1+
McKeon, Joseph*	8FG, 475FG&20FG	P-39	1	P-38	4	P-51	1+
Meyer, John	353FG & 4FIW	P-47	3	P-51	21	F-86	2
Murphy, John*	353FG & 343FG	P-40	0.5	P-47	1.8+	P-51	4.5+
Olds, Robin	479FG & 8TFW@	P-38	5	P-51	8	F-6	4@
Troxell, Clifton	8FG	P-39	2	P-38	2	P-40	1
Welch, George	47PS & 80FG	P-40	4	P-39	3	P-38	9
Whisner, William	352FG & 4FIW	P-47	1	P-51	14.5	F-86	5.5
Wynn, Vasseur	??RAF & 4FG	Spitfire	2.5	P-47	12	P-51	1

* = PTO to ETO # = ETO to PTO + = ETO victories @=Vietnam
Footnote: The Air Force had 58 aces, the Navy 15, and the Marines 13 who became aces with victories in two different aircraft.

America's top aces—Bong USAAF (40), McCampbell USN (34), and Foss USMC (26)—scored all their victories flying one aircraft type. A number of pilots scored victories in three different fighters, but only one ace scored victories in four different aircraft; Col. John Mitchell, a brilliant leader and pilot in two wars.

Mississippian Mitchell graduated from the AAC Flying School in July 1940 and was assigned to the 20FG to fly the P-36, P-39, and P-40. In January 1942 he was sent to the 347FG/339FS/13AF as the squadron CO flying the P-39 Airacobra from Henderson Field on Guadalcanal as part of the "Cactus Air Force." In the early morning of 9 October 1942, Capt. Mitchell led seven P-39s from Henderson escorting SBD bombers of VS-71 in search of Japanese shipping that attacked the island the night before. Six Japanese warships were sighted, and the SBDs dove into their attack, scoring several hits. Five Zeros and five float biplanes attacked the Airacobras. Mitchell dove on a floatplane, getting astern and tearing it to pieces with the Cobra's 37mm cannon. However, the cannon jammed and he was forced to leave combat. During these Guadalcanal days, Mitchell and the 339th flew many ground support and anti-shipping missions, giving good account of themselves and their mediocre fighter. Mitchell scored two additional victories in the Bell fighter: a Zero on 23 October and a Rufe on 7 November. In early November Mitchell and his men were relieved and sent to Tontouta for R&R and transitioned to the P-38.

The unit returned to action in the Solomons in early 1943, with Mitchell soon downing a float Zero on 5 January over Tonolei Harbor for his first Lightning victory. During the week of 27 January-2 February, Mitchell would score four more victories to make him an ace (and a P-38 ace) and give him eight victories in the war. It was during this P-38 period (18 April 1943) that he would gain everlasting fame as the leader of the brilliantly executed interception and killing of Japanese Admiral Yamamoto, head of the combined Japanese Fleet.

After the "Get Yamamoto" mission Mitchell returned to the States and was assigned to flying America's first jet fighter, the Bell P-59 Airacomet. He became the first man to fly a jet cross-country, from the Bell Factory in Buffalo, NY, to Murac Lake, CA.

In mid-1945, Lt. Col. Mitchell became commander of the 15FG/7AF, flying P-51Ds off Iwo Jima escorting B-29s over the Japanese homeland. During this time he scored 3 victories: a Zeke on 26 June (with the 78FG) and 2 Georges on 19 July (with the 15FG) to finish the war with 11 victories.

In June 1952, Col. Mitchell took over as commander of the 51FIW from WWII top ETO scorer Gabby Gabreski, who had scored 6 1/2 Korean victories. Mitchell flew the F-86 Sabre Jet to score 4 MiG victories in the first half of 1953 to give him 15 career victories in four fighter types.

Rudy Augarten

V#	EA/C	Date	A/C
1-2	2 Me-109s	10/3/44	P-47
3	Spitfire	10/16/48	Avia (Me-109)
4	Spitfire	10/21/48	Spitfire
5	Dakota	11/4/48	P-51
6	Mc205	12/22/48	Spitfire

Of American aces, Rudy Augarten has probably the most unusual record. He was credited with shooting down a C-47 Dakota while flying a P-51 Mustang, shooting down a Spitfire while flying a Spitfire, and to top this he shot down a Spitfire while flying a Me-109! All this from a pilot who claimed only six victories.

Philadelphian Augarten enlisted in the U.S. Army in January 1941 and transferred to the ACC in 1942, and was assigned as an instructor after getting his wings in March 1943. He was eventually released to P-47 training and was posted to the 403FS/371FG of the 9AF, which was primarily a ground support outfit. He damaged a Me-109 on 8 June 1944, but two days later was hit by flak patrolling over the Normandy beachhead during his twelfth mission. He bailed out and was hidden by a French farmer for several weeks before trying to work his way back through German lines. He was captured by a German sentry and imprisoned in a stable. That same night he and his fellow prisoners cut through the ceiling with a

Rudy Augarten also had victories in four very different fighters. Flying for the USAAF he got two Me-109s in a P-47 in WW-2. He volunteered to fly for the Israeli AF in the 1948 War for Independence. There he got a victory over a Egyptian-flown Spitfire flying a Czech-built Me-109 derivative, shot down a Spitfire flying a Spitfire, shot down a DC-3 flying a P-51 and finally downing an Italian-built MC.205 while flying a Spitfire. (Author/Augarten)

kitchen knife and escaped. Dressed as a farmer Augarten was stopped by a Wehrmacht soldier and replied in poor French to the challenge. Fortunately the German, who spoke even poorer French, was fooled, and let him go on his way. Later, he joined a Resistance group of Senegalese soldiers waiting in the thick hedgerows in ambush. An intimidating tank came along, followed by soldiers, and a premature shot was fired. One of the tank soldiers dove into a ditch below Augarten, who was prepared to fire until he heard a voice whisper "For Christ's sake, McCarthy, get off my foot." After evading for 63 days he directly rejoined his unit so he could continue flying. On 3 October, he shot down two Me-109s over Rupt sur Marne at 1630.

After flying 103 missions he separated from the Air Force as a Captain in July 1945 and entered LSU in December on the GI Bill, and then transferred to Harvard. He joined the Zionist club and was recruited by Abba Eban to fly for the new Israeli state after his exams in 1948. The War for Independence against Egypt began in May 1948, and Augarten, who had not flown for three years, went to Czechoslovakia. He was put into an Arado trainer for two hours and then in a two-place Me-109 (Avia S-199) for another 4 1/2 hours before being shipped to Israel on 4 July. The Avia was an inferior post war Czech-built derivative of the Me-109, which was the only fighter the Israelis could buy due to the British post war arms embargo. The dismantled Avia S-199s were reassembled, and the Israeli Defense Force/Air Force (IDF/AF) was born. Initially, he flew the Avia S-199, and there were usually no more than four serviceable at any one time for the 20 pilots. Fortunately, there were truces in May and June, and the Israelis were able to acquire or rebuild scrapped Spitfires (the first was a shot down Egyptian Spitfire!). At that time they had about 30 fighters, but only 13 S-199s and four Spitfires were available. On 16 October 1948, flying a S-199 for 101 Squadron (the only Israeli squadron) he shot down a REAF Egyptian Spitfire. In June, Israel was able to purchase 50 Spitfire IXs flown by RAF Czech pilots to Czechoslovakia after WWII. These were not delivered until mid-September. On 21 October, Augarten, in a Spitfire IX, shot down an Egyptian Spitfire which was protecting a supply drop over the Ashqelon pocket, where the Israelis had 5,000 Egyptians surrounded, including Gamal Abdul Nassar. On 4 November, Augarten was flying a re-built P-51D (one of four) and shot down a C-47 Dakota near El Arish A/F on the Sinai. Back to flying the Spitfire, Augarten damaged a REAF Spitfire (which was dragged back to base later for parts) on 17 November. Finally, on 22 December on a recce mission he was flying on deck to avoid heavy AA when he shot down an Italian-built Macchi 205, or Fiat, which was in the El Arish landing pattern with its wheels down on final. This gave him four victories, which would make him the top scoring Israeli pilot for the next 19 years. When the war ended on 7 January 1949 he remained in Egypt to train two classes of fighter pilots. He returned to Harvard, and after graduation went back to Israel to command a fighter base. In 1952 he returned to the U.S. to go on to mechanical engineering degree from Drexel and work for Rockwell before retiring after 27 years.

The IAF scored 23 aerial victories, 15 by Spitfire, six by Avias, and two by Mustangs for a loss of 15, mainly through accidents rather than combat. Ten other Americans flew in the War for Independence, but none are credited with an aerial victory over the REAF. Probably the most well known was Christopher Magee, who joined the RCAF in 1941 but transferred to Greg Boyington's VMF-214. Magee seemed to be a maverick in the Boyington mold, earning his nickname "Wildman." He flew two tours and was only second to Boyington, scoring nine victories with the Black Sheep. After the war he became involved in what he has described as an "underground black market smuggling operation in New York and Europe." He joined the IAF, but did not score any victories, as he flew mainly ground support missions. After his Israeli sojourn he got into pre-New Age spiritualism, but had undisclosed problems with the government and spent time at Leavenworth and Atlanta, where he edited the prison magazine and self-educated at the university level. After his release he edited several community publications and became a poet.

Another interesting American volunteer was Chalmers "Slick" Goodlin, who flew Spitfires for the RAF and then transferred to the U.S. Navy. As a post-war test pilot, Goodlin made the first powered Bell X-15 test flight. He lost his chance to fly through the sound barrier when his demands for a $100,000 fee were bypassed by using a USAF test pilot, Chuck Yeager. Goodlin went on to fly for the IAF for much, much less money. On 6 January 1949 the Israelis had driven into Egyptian territory, and the British called for a withdrawal before the armistice the next day. Four RAF Spitfires on recce to check on compliance were met by two IAF Spits, one piloted by Goodlin, who shot down one of the four RAF Spitfires shot down.

Maj. George Laven is thought to be the only Jewish ace in the USAAF. He scored four victories with the 54FS/343FG over the Aleutians in 1942. He got his fifth victory with the 49FG as the group's victory last of the war on 26 April 1945 when he shot down a Emily flying boat over Formosa.

Flying Multiple Aircraft
Flying the P-39/P-40/P-47/P-51: An Appraisal
By
James Tapp:
8 victories 15 FG (PTO)

Although I scored all my eight victories flying the P-51D for the 15th Fighter Group of the 7th Air Force in the Pacific in April and May 1945, I had more hours in other Air Force fighters. Through the end of the war I flew 33 hours in the P-39, 788 in the P-40, 267 in the P-47D, 218 in the P-51D, and even one hour in the P-38L.

One thing a pilot cares about is cockpit comfort, especially one measuring 6'2". I would rank the P-51 first, the P-47 second, the P-40 third, and the P-39 dead last. The P-51 had plenty of leg and head room, which was important on our 7 1/2 hour missions. I found the closeness of the rudder pedals and the higher seat in the P-47 less desirable than the P-51 or the P-40. The P-39 was something else again. It was made for a 5'6" pilot, so it was hard for me to find a place for my other eight inches. Thank God its short range would not allow me to stay up too long in it. Its car door cockpit was small, and I'm sure I would have had a problem getting out in a hurry. The design of the P-51, having started a little later than the other fighters, was influenced by more operational feedback and additional technology. It was quite superior to the P-40 or P-47. All knobs, handles, and switches seemed to be logically located and handy. The P-51 was equipped with the SCR 522 four button VHF radio. This was not as good as the later eight button AN/ARC-3, but was a tremendous step up from the manually tuned HF radios that we had in the P-40s. One of the greatest inventions for use in the P-51 was the AN/ARA-8 homing adapter, which could home on any other VHF signal that was on any of our four channels. This permitted rendezvous with other aircraft and rescue aircraft and finding home base. The most important instrument in the cockpit for the fighter pilot was his gun sight. The P-51 was far superior in this respect. The N-9 gun sight was placed behind a single bullet proof glass windshield and had good clearance over the nose. The P-40 I flew had the older ring and bead sight. The P-47 suffered from the V windshield, which had a separate bullet proof glass inside it. The sight was mounted low on the cowl, and with the big nose it was difficult or impossible to make high deflection shots or accurate dive bombing runs. The pilot, of course, was not bothered by a big engine sticking out in front of the P-38 or P-39. By the end of May 1945, replacement aircraft began to arrive equipped with the K-14 computing gun sight installed. Very scrimpy information was supplied with this sight on its use, and we had little opportunity to train with it. On the job training was the order of the day. Fortunately, it had a fixed sight mode which we could use until we figured it out. Once we did figure it out it made the average pilot a great shot.

Like all tail draggers, the P-51 required essing while taxiing, but it wasn't as bad as the P-40 or P-47 due to its lower engine profile. The P-39 and P-38 were the best when taxiing, as they had a tricycle nose wheel gear. The addition of the bubble canopy in the P-47 and P–51 gave these fighters excellent visibility once the tail came off the ground. This was a great improvement over the P-40 and the "Razorback" P-47, as well as early canopy to fuselage Mustangs. The nose wheel landings and taxiing with the P-38 and P-39 were easy, but with all the experience I had with non-nose wheel aircraft, poorer visibility on landing was (mainly after touchdown) an accepted fact of life that you got used to. I recall only one taxiing incident, and that was where a P-47 ran over another on the runway.

Maj. James Tapp. (Author/Tapp)

The Packard-built Rolls Royce V-1650 engine installed on the P-51D was the best engine I flew. Generally, the basic engine (*without* considering the coolant system) was the better performer, more reliant, and as rugged as the V-1710 Allison or R-2800 Pratt & Whitney. The P-51 airframe, in combination with the RR engine and increased fuel capacity, gave the fighter excellent long range, which was important in our theater's long-range escort operations. The P-51 had the best climb characteristics when compared to the others. The P-40 (Allison engine versions) and the P-39 had single stage blowers, and their rate of climb dropped off drastically from 15,000 feet up. The P-40 service ceiling was around 25,000 feet depending on the model. The P-47D, with its turbo supercharger, was still climbing well at that altitude (near 1,000 feet /minute vs. the P-51's 1,500/minute). When we transitioned to the P-51Ds, I was making claims about its superiority over the P-47s we were still flying. The purpose was to get the air and ground crews enthused about our new fighter. An argument arose: "Yeah, but the P-47 can outperform the –51 above 30,000 feet." The Republican (P-47) tech was particularly sensitive about this. Our engineering officer, based on what I was claiming, bet the tech that the P-51 could outrun the P-47 above 30,000 feet. The Group CO, Lt.Col. Jim Beckwith, had a P-47D28 with a bubble canopy specially readied to race the Mustang. The Thunderbolt's wing racks were removed, and it looked as though it had been waxed. The P-47 was flown by vice CO Maj. Emmett Kearney, while I went out to the line and jumped into one of the Mustangs there and taxied out behind Kearney. I flew on his wing and had to hold back the P-51 while we climbed to 30,000. After we reached altitude and leveled off, he signaled that he was going full power. I stayed with him for a while and asked, "Is that all you have?," to which has nodded. I then pushed the throttle full forward to 3,000 RPM and ran off and left him. To rub it in, I dove for base, knowing that because of the P-47's compressibility problem she could not follow. I landed, grabbed a coke and folding chair, and waited for him to taxi in.

The P-51 was a "cruiser," due to its low drag, efficient airframe and engine, and increased internal fuel capacity. The P-40 and P-47 flew at relatively low cruise air speeds. I suppose it is academic to try to compare the P-51 to the others, as they were inherently short range fighters (except the P-38). The N model P-47, which came on line in late July 1945 with the 414th Fighter Group, was modified to extend its range. It had more wing area, clipped wings, reduced load limit factor, and increased internal fuel. But, as a consequence, the "N" lost the legendary ruggedness of its forerunners. Their cruise speed for long range missions was 185 mph at 10,000 feet versus the P-51's 210 mph. We were able to take off after them, spend more time over the target area, and then beat them home. They did have the advantage of an autopilot and folding rudder pedals, which allowed their pilots to stretch out their legs for a more comfortable but not faster ride home.

In the category of flight characteristics (stability, control, compressibility, and load factor), all AAF fighters had problems of some sort; some more serious than others. The static and dynamic stability of the P-51 about all axes was excellent when the fuselage tank was down to 25 gallons. Unfortunately, on our long range missions we entered the combat area with a fuselage tank that had been used

only for take off, and then we had to switch to the external drop tanks, which we did not want to have hanging on during combat. This led to a stick reversal situation that the elevator control system bob could not compensate. The pilot's manual says that the aircraft should not be flown with more than 65 gallons in the fuselage tanks, and that accelerated maneuvers should not be attempted until that tank was down to 25 gallons. In practice we had to ignore that precept. At redline (505 mph) the fighter would become unstable in pitch. This created the "JC maneuver" situation: when you tried to make corrections in pitch you would aggravate a tendency for the plane to porpoise. The P-40 had a similar problem when flying with a full fuselage tank, particularly with the heavier models, such as the K. I don't recall any stability problems with the P-47. The P-51D had superior control characteristics compared to the P-39, P-40, P-47, and unboosted P-38. It trimmed well, and trim did not change with air speed as it did with others, particularly the P-40. The controls remained light and responsive at all speeds, perhaps too much so in pitch. The others stiffened up quite a bit as the speed increased. With the P-40 it was primarily the rudder that took considerable attention and strength to keep the ball centered in a dive bombing run, for instance. We lost some pilots and aircraft to the snap roll that resulted when the pilots tried to do a high G out with the aircraft out of trim. The P-47D was probably the worst in this respect. At high speed it took considerable effort to move the ailerons and elevator. When we transitioned from the P-47 to the P-51, I picked up a new Mustang at the depot and was buzzing the field at low altitude, inverted, and tried to do a crisp snap roll to level flight, right side up. I more than succeeded, as I did a half snap roll. I manhandled the aileron and rudder as I would have in the P-47 and got a beautiful, but heart-stopping, result. I accepted praise for the maneuver for a long time before I admitted what really happened. All these aircraft reported unusual stall and spin characteristics. I had the philosophy that a fighter pilot should be very familiar with stalls and spins if he wanted to survive. In one-on-one combat situations you had to push your aircraft beyond it limits, and if you did you had to be able to get out of it quickly. I had no problems with either the P-51 or P-47 in a spin. The P-40 had to be nursed out of a bad spin, particularly if the aircraft had not been trimmed. The P-39 also gave me a few hairy moments when I was practicing high power stalls, as none of the conventional recovery techniques worked. Somehow I was able to analyze and correct the situation before crashing into the ground. One of the faults that continually plagued us was the introduction of new equipment without proper training or manuals. When the P-47 arrived in our theater, they came without this necessary precautionary information. On one of the initial flights one of the pilots stalled in a tight turn at 35,000 feet. Rather than just roll it back, right side up, he thought he would pull it through. The next thing he knew was he was headed straight down, and nothing would stop the dive. He pulled back on the throttle, and that just seemed to make the aircraft want to tuck under. Nothing happened when he rolled full trim on the elevator. At about 12,000 feet the aircraft started a very high G recovery because of full trim. The pilot blacked out and came to in the low 2,000s, just as he was about to stall out. He managed to recover and gingerly brought the damaged aircraft home. The wrinkled aircraft had to be

Class 26'd, as the techs figured it must have had 13 Gs put on it. Soon after another P-47 dove sans wings. Then a TWX from the States arrived describing something called compressibility. It seems that in a high speed dive, shock waves formed on the stabilizer and blocked out the air flow over the elevator, making it ineffective. When the aircraft reached the lower, warmer, and more dense air and the higher speed of sound, the shock waves would disappear and the aircraft would be able to recover. This was not a problem with the P-39 or P-40, as they never got high enough or fast enough to get into trouble. The P-38 also had this same problem, and it was even more difficult for it to recover. I never experienced the problem in the P-51.

Based on air-to-air and air-to-ground experience, I strongly felt that we needed bigger guns with explosive projectiles, which would be incorporated into a reliable weapons system. The Germans concluded the same in an in depth operations analysis during the war. As a consequence, the Me-262 jet fighter showed up with four MK 108 30 mm cannons. With six .50 caliber machine guns and 367 rounds per gun for four of the guns and 420 for the other two, the P-51D was adequately armed, considering the weapons options available at that time. The early P-40s had two .50 caliber guns in the cockpit firing through the propeller and two .30 calibers in each wing. Starting with the D model, the P-40 went to six .50 wing guns, a set up similar to the P-51. The P-39 had the same configuration, but in early models had a 37mm Browning cannon firing through the prop hub. Because of serious ammunition feed problems this gun was replaced by the 20mm Hispano-Suiza cannon that had a very reliable attached magazine. The P-47 was our most heavily armed fighter, with eight .50 caliber wing mounted machine guns which were fed by 425 rounds each. Due to the lack of a bomb sight none of these fighters was an accurate bomber. The P-51 was as good as any, or perhaps a little better, as it had better visibility over the nose than the P-40 or P-47 and was more stable in a dive. With three racks the P-47 gave more weapons flexibility. The P-51 bomb release system was all electric, with the bombs being released by a button on top of the stick grip. The P-47 pilot,

on the other hand, was required to reach down on the left side of the seat and find the three mechanical bomb release handles. The P-51 and P-47 were good strafing platforms, but the P-51 was more vulnerable to ground fire because of its liquid-cooled engine. Our "fifties" were fairly effective against aircraft, especially if they were loaded with fuel. However, against larger targets, such as ships and locomotives, being equipped with larger weapons would have been more effective. In any discussion of ruggedness the P-51 never fares well because of its liquid-cooled engine The durability of the P-47 is legendary, and the safety of twin engines gives the P-38 the nod over the Mustang. However, in air-to-air combat this was not a big problem to a good pilot, since he could use the attributes of the P-51 to keep it from taking any rounds. Air-to-ground combat was a different story, because the pilot had less control of the variables (the number and location of enemy AA guns, amount of ground fire, etc.). This could be somewhat minimized using good tactics, surprise, and good intelligence information.

The P-47 was the easiest to land due to its wide gear, while the P-51 was relatively easy to land as tail draggers go. The P-40 had a narrow gear and was tricky to three point. Cross winds from the right were a particular problem. The left wing would drop, and if you applied power disaster could result, as this procedure only worsened the situation.

Overall, I would rate the P-51 as the best and my favorite fighter of World War II.

Flying the Mustang and Spitfire: An Appraisal
By
Richard "Dixie" Alexander:
4 Spitfire victories 133 Sq. RAF (2)/52FG (2)
2 Mustang victories 52 FG

During WWII I got to fly the Spitfire and Mustang, both of which were powered by the Rolls Royce Merlin engine. I flew the Spitfire early in the war with the American-manned RAF Eagle Squadron, and again later in the Mediterranean with the USAAF's 2FS of the 52FG, then later the 52nd transitioned to the P-51.

1Lt. Richard "Dixie" Alexander. (Author/Alexander)

Anyone who was lucky enough to fly the Spitfire would agree that it had to be the most enjoyable aircraft they ever flew. It was completely stable with no bad habits. Took off easily, landed slowly, and was easy to control. I liked the hand brake and 20mm cannon. It could out climb and out turn a P-51, but not by much. The –51 could out dive the Spit and probably out run it on the straight and level, but again not by much. These comparisons are made between the Merlin 63 powered Spitfire IX and the Mustang D. The great advantage of the –51 was its Davis wing, which gave it the ability to carry a far greater fuel load, extending its range significantly. Many Mustang pilots claimed to prefer its six .50 caliber machine guns, but then they never fired the 20mm cannons at the Luftwaffe.

You could call this comparison a toss up but, of course, each pilot has his own personal preferences in evaluating an aircraft. For just plain pleasure I liked the Spitfire. In short range and defensive situations I would also prefer it. However, with its greater range, firepower, and capacity for carrying larger bomb loads I would take the Mustang

Flying the P-40 in the PTO and the P-38 in the ETO
By
James Morehead:
7 P-40 victories 17PPS (PTO)
1 P-38 victory 1FG (ETO)

I was one of the few pilots to fly in both the Pacific and in Europe. On Pearl Harbor Day I was scheduled to board a transport ship in San Francisco, headed for the Pacific. I flew P-40s over Java and Australia and scored seven victories. After R&R in the States I was sent to Italy to join the 1st Fighter Group in 1944. There I flew the P-38, mostly on strafing missions, but got a Me-109 in June.

Comparing the two planes is difficult, because our grim situation in the early war in the Pacific was entirely different from that in the Mediterranean, where we had air superiority. The P-40 I flew in the Pacific was a primitive aircraft compared to the P-38 I flew in Italy. The P-40 had a lot of 1930s engineering and was much more difficult to fly. Early communications in the P-40 was very poor, but by the time I got to the P-38 there had been a huge improvement. We had a lot of trouble with the early .50 caliber ma-

chine guns in the P-40. Often one or more, and sometimes all six would not fire. This problem was pretty much solved by the time I left Australia. The arrangement of the six .50s on the P-40 was ok, but its convergence was poor. The P-38, with all its firepower mounted in the nose, had no convergence problems and delivered withering fire, both in aerial combat and strafing. The cross hair sight on the P-40 was right out of a WWI movie. Even though I considered myself a good skeet shooter I was better with the later ring and bead sight in the later P-40s. The gyroscopic computing sight we had in Italy made shooting easy. Both fighters were powered by Allison engines, but there was a big difference between the early series V-1710 and later models. Also, there was a big difference between having one or two engines, and I'm not talking about performance. I felt much safer in the P-38, especially with one engine out! The P-38 had a least a 50 mph advantage in top speeds and cruising speeds over my P-40. The P-38 could climb to 20,000 feet much faster, and even when the P-40 got there it wasn't good for anything. Fuel always seemed to be a problem in the P-40, while the 300 gallons in the P-38L belly tanks would let you fly much farther. In fact, it would let you go too far, as ten hours is a long time to sit anywhere. Early on we knew nothing about low RPMs, and so we had little cruise time in the P-40. In the P-38, using low RPMs, I was able to cruise smoothly practically forever. The P-40 was notorious for its overheating while taxiing and would load up, so you had to sweat it out if there were any delays. The only thing a P-40 could really do better than a P-38 was dive. It could out dive the Jap anytime, and thank God for that, as the Japs could out climb and outmaneuver us, and our only salvation was to get the hell out of there. The German could do the same against the P-38, and would dive away from us when he was in trouble. Except in a dive, I felt the P-38 with its supercharger, combat flaps, and firepower was more than a match for any German I fought against. The visibility in the P-40, being a tail-dragger, was poor, and you had to go essing down the runway to see. Once in the air the long nose and rear cockpit fairing got in the way. The view from the tricycle gear P-38 was gorgeous, and it took off and landed better, although the engines mounted on the booms could get in the way of downward vision.

Maj. James Morehead. (Author/Morehead)

Lt. James Billo. (Author/Billo)

All in all I felt total confidence in the P-38 in fighting anything the Luftwaffe could fly against us. But I knew the Jap could whip me anytime in the P-40. Lucky it could dive!

Flying the F4F and F6F: An Appraisal
By
Henry Billo:
5 victories VF-10 & VF-18

I flew the F4F for VF-10 under the legendary Jimmy Flatley off the *Enterprise* and the F6F for VF-18 under Sam Silber off the *Bunker Hill*. (Billo downed a Zero on his first tour in the F4F and three Zeros and a Betty in the F6F on his second tour-ed.). Both the Wildcat and the Hellcat possessed good carrier qualities: visibility; low speed handling; ruggedness, etc. The F6F was the natural evolution of the F4F and required little transitional experience for a pilot moving from one to the other. The really nice thing about moving to the Hellcat from the Wildcat was that the pilot no longer had to crank up the landing gear by hand after takeoff. Both were much less maneuverable than the competition, but could out climb and out dive them and were much more rugged.

Opportunity was always the primary factor in determining who scored a victory. Many great pilots never became aces because they never happened to be in the right place at the right time. The type of fighter flown was not that important for success, if the number of victories scored measured success. Most combats were over quickly, and victory usually went to the pilot who initiated the combat. But I describe success as the ability to get home, and the qualities of both Grumman cats got us home much more often than not.

In a head-to-head encounter with a Zero with both fighters firing at each other, the Zero usually would lose to either the F4F or F6F because of its lack of firepower and lack of protection for the pilot and fuel and oil systems. In a maneuvering situation, which put both Cats at a disadvantage, we got out of combat by utilizing our superior diving capabilities, or we had to depend on our wingmen attempting to place the enemy in his sights. On both my first and second tours I was fortunate to have wingmen who became aces by protecting me. My wingman on my first tour was Bill Blair (5 victories-ed.), and my second tour wingman was Ted Crosby (5 1/2 victories-ed.) In combat it was essential to always have your wingman nearby. I feel good training and teamwork was as important as flying a good aircraft.

CHAPTER 12

Multiple War Aces

American Ace in Two Wars: Albert Baumler

"Ajax" Baumler is unique in fighter pilot annuals, as not only was he an ace for two different nations, but also scored victories against all major Axis powers: Germany; Italy; and Japan.

A Texan from Denison, Albert John Baumler washed out of Army Air Corps Advanced fighter training at Kelly Field, San Antonio, TX, for: "Failing to show proper flying proficiency." Cadet Baumler forgot to switch a fuel tank on a twin-engine bomber and was forced to crash land.

In 1937 he saw the Spanish Civil War as an opportunity to continue his passion for flying and adventure. Baumler joined the Republicans (Loyalists) in their battle against Franco's Nationalists. who were aided by Fascist Germany and Italy. About 30 Americans volunteered to fly for the Republicans. but only 17 flew in combat. The most successful of these pilots served with the Lacalle Squadron. which was led by top Loyalist ace Maj. Andres Garcia Lacalle. who was credited with 11 Nationalist aircraft. The squadron included Americans Baumler, Frank G. Tinker, Harold "Whitey" Dahl. and Chang Selles. Tinker attained eight victories, including two against the new German Condor Legion's Me-109. When Tinker returned to the United States his passport was seized. and he tried to rejoin the Navy—his previous service—but was denied. He subsequently wrote a successful biography *Some Still Live,* but committed suicide in 1939. Dahl claimed four victories, but Loyalist propaganda insisted he scored five. Records fail to confirm his ace status. He became a prisoner and was condemned to death, but was reprieved by Franco after Dahl's wife made a personal appeal to the Nationalist Leader. After the war he became an instructor in the RCAF in Canada. Selles was executed for allegedly spying for the Japanese government against the Russian aviation units in Spain.

The Lacalle Squadron was equipped with the little Russian-built Polikarpov I-15, gull-winged biplane, nicknamed "Chato" (Seagull) in early 1937. On Baumler's first mission, the engine of his aircraft failed as he was pursuing an Italian CR-32 biplane, and he needed to make a forced landing. Soon, he downed two of the Fiat-built CR-32s and a Heinkel He-51, with a third CR-32 shared victory and a He-51 probable.

The Squadron transitioned to the faster, stumpy I-16 monoplane, which was nicknamed "Mosca" ("the Little Fly") by its pilots, but "Rata" ("the Rat") by its opponents. On an early mission, a He-51 got on his tail and put several explosive shells into Baumler's cockpit. Shrapnel hit him in the back, but it was slowed by his armored seat back and he suffered only superficial wounds and was soon back into combat. Flying Moscas, Baumler claimed an additional two victories and a probable to give him 5 1/2 victories. Some sources give him eight. Baumler was hospitalized with a chronic swollen throat and returned to the United States.

America was heading towards war, and Baumler became one of the last pilots to sign with Gen. Claire Chennault's Flying Tigers, the AVG (American Volunteer Group). Baumler was on his way to join the AVG in China aboard Boeing's China Clipper when upon reaching Wake Island, the crew learned of the Japanese attack on Pearl Harbor. The flying boat refueled and retreated back to California with its passengers. Baumler returned to active duty with the AAC and was assigned to the 23FG of the 10AF under Chennault. Capt. Baumler arrived in China just prior to the disbandonment of the AVG and scored his first victory on 22 June 1942 over a Jap I-97 fighter while flying a P-40 Warhawk. It is possible that Baumler scored additional victories with the AVG, since he was ACC, temporarily assigned to the AVG, and its war diaries did not reflect claims made by non-AVG personnel. Upon AVG disbandonment on Independence Day 1942, Baumler joined the 75FS/23FG as a Major. On many nights the group suffered unopposed enemy bombing attacks on its base at Hengyang. Looking up at the raiders, which were betrayed by their engine exhausts, Maj. John Alison, deputy CO, and Tex Hill decided to do something about them. The next night an efficient telephone warning system alerted Hengyang of an impending air raid. Alison and Baumler took off first, followed by several other pairs of P-40s. Climbing in the darkness to 1,200 feet Alison spotted six twin-engine bombers and attacked. He downed one and damaged another. Baumler closed in on the bomber damaged by Alison and set it on fire. He then chased after a fleeing Jap and exploded it for his second victory. Both he and Alison were awarded the DSC for this first successful American night interception of the war.

Albert "Ajax" Baumler had 5 1/2 victories flying the Russian-built I-15 and I-16 biplanes for the Republican Air Force in the Spanish Civil War. He joined the AVG and became an ace for the second time flying the P-40. (Author)

American pilots flying for the Republicans in the Spanish Civil War (L-R sitting): Frank Tinker, Chang Selles, Harold "Whitey" Dahl and 3 Spanish mechanics (standing). Tinker scored 8 victories, including 2 against the German Condor Legion. Dahl is credited with 4 or 5 victories. A Polikarpov I-15 Chato fighter is seen in the background. (Author)

The next morning the Japs sent 40 Zeros to wipe the P-40s out of the sky but lost four; one to Baumler's guns. In the morning of 3 September, Baumler scored a victory over a Zero south of Hengyang to become an ace for the second time. (Note: USAF Historical Study 85 gives him credit for this victory, while other historians, such as Frank Olynyk and Cornelius & Short in *Ding Hoa*, give a shared credit with Tex Hill).

In a footnote on the Spanish Civil War aces. Of the 26 German Condor aces five went on to score over 100+ victories with the Luftwaffe in WWII: Herbert Ihlefeld (9 Spain/123 WWII); Walter Oesau (8 and 115); Werner Molders (14 and 101); Gunter Lutzow (9 and 103); and Raymond Seiler (9 and 100). Russian Vladimir Bobrov scored 13 victories for the Republicans and 30 more on the Eastern Front in WWII. Angel Sales Larrazabal of the Nationalists scored 16 1/3, and then seven more while fighting with Germans against the Russians.

American Aces in WWII and Korea

On Sunday, 25 June 1950, at 0600, the North Korean People's Army invaded South Korea, bringing war to a world that had seen peace for less than five years. The North Korean Air Force (NKAF) consisted of 150 obsolete Russian aircraft that were quickly and efficiently decimated by the Far East Air Force (FEAF), so that by late July there was no North Korean Air Force. On 1 November, six Russian-built MiG-15 jet fighters attacked four P-51s over Namsidong, and the air war over Korea started up again. Air combat had entered the jet age. The USAF countered the MiG challenge by sending their North American F-86 Sabre Jets into the battle. The air battle was invariably restricted to a singular scenario during the 32 months from November 1959 to July 1953. The MiGs were based in a politically established "sanctuary" just north of the Yalu River in Manchuria. The F-86s would fly into northern Korea, patrolling the famous "MiG Alley" corridor and trying to draw the often-reluctant MiGs into combat. Many times the frustrated Americans gazed across the Yalu at the hundreds of MiGs riveted on the airfields the Communists contemptuously built just inside their border. Thus, because of the unique political guidelines of the war and the character of jet warfare, the air battles were remarkable for their vertical depth and great speed. In combat the F-86 was slower and could be easily out climbed by the MiG. The F-86 was dependable, rugged, maneuverable, and equipped with a radar ranging gun sight. At the armistice in July 1953, the bottom line showed 802 MiGs destroyed to 56 Sabre Jets—a 14 to 1 kill ratio. Why? The USAF destroyed the enemy using the traditional air-to-air combat tactics it developed in WWII, only at sonic speeds. Once in combat it was pilot skill, both cognitive and physical, that translated the new technology of the jet age into basic stick and rudder operation, allowing the pilot to close "to stick it up his exhaust."

During the Korean War 40 pilots became aces, and of these seven had been aces in WWII.

WWII Aces/Korean Aces

Pilot Name	Service	WWII victories	WWII Unit	Korean Victories	Korean Unit	Total Victories
Bolt, John F.	USMC	6	VMF-214	6	VMF-215 51 FIW	12
Davis, George A.	USAF	7	348FG	14	4FIW	21
Gabreski, Francis S.	USAF	28	56FG	6 1/2	4&51FIW	34 1/2
Garrison, Vermont	USAF	7 1/3	4FG	10	4FIW	17 1/3
Hagerstrom, James P.	USAF	6	49FG	8 1/2	18FIW	14 1/2
Thyng, Harrison R.	USAF	5	31FG	5	4FIW	10
Whisner, William T.	USAF	15 1/2	352FG	5 1/2	51FIW	21

George Davis (USAF)

Harrison Thyng (Author/Thyng)

William Whisner (Author/Whisner)

John Bolt (USMC)

Francis Gabreski (USAF)

James Hagerstrom (USAF)

Vermont Garrison
(Author/Garrison)

John Bolt was the Marine Corps' only ace in Korea. Flying F4Us for VMF-214 "Blacksheep" off the carrier *Block Island*, he was credited with six Japanese Zeros. In Korea he flew 92 missions with VMF-215 in F9Fs. He then flew 42 missions on an exchange tour with 51FIW. He flew with top Korean War ace Joe McConnell (16 victories) and commanded McConnell's flight when he left combat. On 10 July 1953 Bolt shot down two MiGs to score his fifth and sixth victories to give him 12 lifetime.

Texan George Davis flew P-47s for the 348FG of the 5AF. He downed two Japanese aircraft on 10 December 1944 and three more on 20 December over the Philippines, ending the war with seven victories. In October 1951 he flew F-86s for the 4FIW and became CO of the 334FS. He scored his first two victories on 27 November, and three days later he downed three TU-2 piston bombers and a MiG escort to become an ace. He became the first double ace in Korea, scoring four more victories on 13 December 1951 and giving him 12 total. On 2 February 1952 Davis and his wingman attacked about a dozen MiGs. Davis shot down two and damaged a third before succumbing to a MiG and crashing into a mountainside. Davis was awarded the Congressional Medal of Honor for this action. Davis had 14 victories in Korea to be the fourth ranking ace there.

"Gabby" Gabreski was the top ace in the ETO with 28 victories, but he finished the war as a POW in a German stalag after being shot down on a strafing run. After the war he joined the Douglas Aircraft Corporation, but soon returned to the Air Force as a Lt. Colonel to become CO of the 55FS. As the Communists sent MiG jets into battle, Gabreski was posted as the deputy commander of the 4th Fighter Interceptor Wing, which was the first unit to fly the F-86A in combat. He destroyed three MiGs before he was promoted to full Colonel and given command of the 51FIW, which was converting from the P-80 Shooting Star to the F-86E in November 1951. Gabreski scored his fourth victory in January and became the eighth ace in Korea on 1 April 1952. He scored his sixth victory on 13 April and ended the war with 34 1/2 career victories to place him third on the all-time list after Dick Bong (40) and Tommy Maguire (38), and a half ahead of David McCampbell.

Vermont Garrison transferred from the RAF in 1943 to the 4FG, downing 7 1/3 Germans before being captured and held as a POW. During the Korean War he joined the 4FIW, commanding the 335FS. He was a double ace, scoring ten victories and giving him a lifetime total of 17 1/3. He also held the distinction of being the oldest Korean War ace at 37 years old.

James Hagerstrom flew P-40s for 8FS of the 49FG (5AF) in the SWPA, downing six Japanese. In the Korean War he was credited with an additional 8 1/2 enemy aircraft while flying with the 334 and 67FS.

Harrison Thyng has the unique distinction of not only being a WWII/Korean and piston/jet ace, but also of hitting the aircraft of five different enemies. In WWII he scored MTO victories over six German, one French, and one Italian aircraft (?) while flying with the 31FG. In the Pacific he got a Japanese fighter while escorting B-29s out of Ie Shima, which is listed as a probable. In Korea he commanded the 4FIW, scoring five victories to give him a career total of 14. However, the Italian victory may have been a mis-identified Me-109.

William Whisner of the 352FG concluded his WWII total by downing four German fighters during the Battle of the Bulge, giving him 15 1/2. He left the Air Force briefly after the war, but rejoined as a Major, flying sorties for the 334FS of the 4FIW. He scored his first and second Korean victories on 8 and 9 November 1951. He transferred to the 25FS of Gabreski's 51FIW. With them he scored two more victories in early January 1952. On a mission on 2 February, Gabreski's flight intercepted a group of MiGs. Gabreski attacked the last MiG and hit it, causing it to smoke. As they crossed the Yalu Gabreski broke off, but Whisner followed it into Manchuria to confirm the victory. But the smoking MiG continued to fly, and as his fuel was getting low Whisner decided to finish off the MiG himself. Back at base Gabreski claimed a probable, but Whisner gallantly confirmed Gabreski's victory. Since both pilots had four victories at the time, one more would make either an ace. Gabreski telephoned Whisner, demanding that he unconfirm his victory and make his own claim. Whisner declined, and Gabreski hung up in anger. Minutes later Gabreski called back suggesting that they share the victory. Three days later Whisner got another MiG to become the war's seventh ace, giving him 21 career victories.

In Korea, 17 other WWII aces increased their totals by scoring additional victories, including top WWII aces John Meyer (24 WWII + 2 Korea), Bud Mahurin (20 3/4 + 3 1/2), and Glenn Eagleston (18 1/2 + 2). Seven pilots who scored victories in WWII scored additional victories in Korea to become aces (see chart), including the war's second leading ace James Jabara (1/2 WWII and 15 Korea) and fifth Korean ace Royal Baker (3 1/2 +13). Also, four pilots scored victories in each war to become lifetime aces: John Andre (USMC) (4 WWII + 1 Korea at night); Brooks Liles (1 WWII + 4 Korea); Conrad Mattson (1 WWII + 4 Korea); and Howard Price (4 WWII + 1 Korea).

Despite the 802 enemy aircraft destroyed and the arrival of the jet age, Korea was primarily a theater of ground-support missions. The venerable P-51 Mustang was found to be without a peer in its fighter-bomber role, but it required the F-86 to protect it from the MiG. Without this protective cover, the Mustang and other ground support aircraft would have been unable to deliver the deadly blows to the hoards of North Korean and Chinese troops which swarmed United Nation's troops without regard to mass sacrifice. Thus, the ground war could have turned impossibly costly to the West, which held human life dear.

Other WWII Aces with Korean Victories*

Name	WWII	Korea	Total
Brueland, Lowell	12	2	14.5
Chandler, Van	5	3	8
Colman. Philip	5	4	9
Delong. Philip (USMC)	11.16	2	13.16
Durnford, Dewey (USMC)	6.33	0.5	6.83
Eagleston, Glen	18.5	2	20.5
Emmert, Benjamin	6	1	7
Heller, Edwin	5.5	3.5	9
Hockery, John	7	1	8
Hovde, William	10.5	1	11.5
Lamb, William (USN)	6	1	7
Little, James	7	1	8
Mahurin, Walker	20.75	3.5	25.25
Meyer, John	24	2	26
Mitchell, John	11	4	15
Visscher, Herman	5	1	6
Wade, Robert	7	1	8

Plus Korean Aces with Victories in WWII

Name	Korea	WWII	Total
Adams, Donald	6.5	4	10.5
Baker, Royal	13	3.5	16.5
Bettinger, Stephen	5	1	6
Creighton, Richard	5	2	7
Jabara, James	15	0.5	15.5
Johnson. James	10	1	11
Ruddell, George	8	2.5	10.5

WWII and Korean Victories to Become an Ace

Name	WWII	Korea	Total
Andre, John (USMC)	4	1	5
Liles, Brooks	1	4	5
Mattson, Conrad	1	4	5
Price, Howard	4	2	6

WWII Aces to Die in the Korean War

1Lt. Ernest "Red" Fiebelkorn was the top-scoring ace for the 20FG/9AF with nine victories (8 1/2 in P-51s). He is credited with downing 258 victory Luftwaffe ace Walter Nowotny, who was flying a Me-262 jet near Achmet airdrome on 8 November 1944.

Shortly after the North Koreans invaded the South in June 1950, the 51FIW was flying night intruder missions out of Japan. On 6 July 1950, Fiebelkorn was flying a F-82G for the 4FS. He and his observer crashed into the hills south of Seoul to become the first WWII ace to die in that conflict. He was MIA for 2 1/2 years until the crash was found by U.S. troops. He is now buried in Arlington Cemetery.

WWII Aces to Die in Korea

Name	V#	WWII Unit	Fate	Date
Brezas, Michael	12	56FG5 56FG	KIFA	02/06/52
Brown, Meade	6	348FG	KIA	08/24/50
Brown, William	7	VMF-311	KIA	02/24/52
Davis, George	7	348FG	KIA	02/10/52
Fiebelkorn, Ernest	9	20FG	KIA	07/06/52
Gibb, Robert	5	352FG	KIA	12/31/53
Halton, William	10.5	352FG	KIA	?/?/52
Hernan, Edwin	8	VMF-215	MIA	07/19/51
Molland, Leland	10.5	31FG	KIA	?/?/51
Powers, Joseph	14.5	56FG	KIA	01/16/51
Schlitz. Glen	8	56FG	KIA/MIA	?/?/?

Three-Decade Ace: Robin Olds

Robin Olds was born in Honolulu on 14 July 1922, the son of Maj.Gen. Robert Olds. He spent his childhood in Hampton, VA. He entered West Point 1 July 1940, receiving flight training as a cadet. He took primary training at the Spartan School of Aviation in Tulsa, OK, and basic and advanced instruction at Stewart Field, NY. During this training period he was West Point football captain and an All-American. He received his wings on 30 May 1943 and graduated from the Military Academy two days later. Olds spent the next nine months in fighter tactical training. He was then assigned to the 434FS, a newly activated P-38 unit, and received additional instruction in the type. The 434th was shipped to England aboard the *USS Argentina* in May 1944 and was stationed at RAF Watisham under the command of the redoubtable Hub Zemke. It was not until 14 August 1944 that Olds scored, downing two FW-190s over Montmirail at 0700. These victories were followed eleven days later by Olds' best day in the air. Flying his P-38 *"Scat II"* over Rostock just before noon, the squadron broke up a large formation of Me-109s, which headed toward the deck. Olds dove and quickly shot down two of the Messerschmitts. While diving, Olds saw a Mustang being pursued by another Me-109. Rolling over to go to the aid of the P-51, Olds' P-38, already at minimum altitude and near compressibility, responded to the pull out by losing its

Maj. Robin Olds scored 13 air and 11 1/2 ground victories in WWII flying the P-38 in which he got five victories and the P-51 in which he was again an ace with eight victories. (Author/Olds)

canopy and side panel, and scaring the life out of the pilot as it shuttered toward the ground before pulling up. On his way back to base, Olds was bounced from astern by a –109, which closed to 75 yards. The P-38 responded sluggishly to Olds' left break and high-speed stall. This maneuver caused the German to overshoot, putting itself in Olds' gun sight for his third victory of the day. His next victories were scored in the P-51 Mustang, finishing the war in *"Scat VII."* Olds flew 107 missions, scoring 13 victories in the air and 11 1/2 on the ground.

After the war he flew the P-80 jet fighter with the 412FG at March AFB and was part of the Air Force's first aerobatic team. He finished second in the 1946 Thompson Jet Trophy Race at the Nationals. He was assigned to fly Meteor IV jets with the RAF at Tangmere, commanding No.1 Squadron. Much to Olds' chagrin he was stationed stateside with the 71FIS, missing the Korean War. After that, he variously spent time in Germany as CO of the 86FG, organized Wheelis AFB as a weapons center, was assigned to the Pentagon, commanded the 81 FG, spent time at 9AF HQ, and married movie actress Ella Raines.

Finally, as a full Colonel and at the age of 44, in September 1966 he was assigned to fly the F-4C Phantom with the 555TFS of the 8TFW out of Ubon, Thailand. In December he was given command of "Operation Bolo," which was a plan to draw the newly committed MiG-21 into combat. On 2 January 1967 the plan was put into effect. Olds and his radar man, 1Lt. Charles Clifton, scored a victory, as they put a Side Winder (AIM-9) missile into a MiG. Altogether, Olds and the 8TFW "Wolf Pack" knocked down seven of the 15 MiG "Fishbeds" the North Vietnamese had on station.

On 4 May he downed another MiG-21 with a Sidewinder, but his biggest day came on 20 May, while escorting F-105s that were bombing railway yards. Ten or 12 MiG-17s attacked the –105s, but were intercepted by Olds' F-4s. The MiGs went into a large defensive wheel. Olds, now in the backseat, and his pilot, 1Lt. Steve Croker, fired two Sparrow (AIM-7) missiles, one of which exploded near a MiG, flaming it. They continued to try to break up the circular MiG defense, but had to head home, low on fuel. They encountered a lone enemy fighter, and in a deck level dogfight exploded a Sidewinder near it for his fourth victory. This made him the top Vietnam pilot, until Randy Cunningham (USN) and Steve Ritchie (USAF) became aces.

After his combat tour Olds trained pilots and was the Commandant of Cadets at the Air Force Academy. He retired as a Brigadier General in 1973.

Twenty-two years later, Col. Robin Olds is seen applying a North Vietnamese victory marking to his F-4 Phantom. Olds scored four MIG victories over Vietnam to give him a career total of 17. (Author/Olds)

Olds, at 45 years old, had scored victories in two wars, 23 years apart. For the Luftwaffe, several WWI pilots flew for Hitler. Maj. Harry von Bulow-Both Kamp scored six victories in WWI and then, at 42 years old, scored 18 victories in WWII flying night fighters for the Luftwaffe Nachtjager. Alexander von Winterfeldt scored nine victories for SG2 and SG77 after flying but not scoring in the Great War. Klaus Mietusch of JG26 scored three victories in WWI and 72 in WWII. Probably the most well known German two-war ace was Theo Osterkamp, who scored 32 victories in WWI to become the German Navy's top-scorer. Then, at 48 years old and 22 years between victories in 1940, he was Kommodore of JG51 and scored six victories in the Me-109. After retiring from combat he assumed staff assignments, becoming a Lt. General in the Luftwaffe.

The Allies also had pilots who scored in both world wars. French pilot Marius Abrogi was credited with 14 victories in WWI flying with ESC507 and SPA90. Then, as deputy commander of GC I/8 he shot down a German Ju-52 in May 1940. Eduard Corninglion-Moinier scored eight WWI victories and four or five with GC 111/2 Squadron. Lionel de Marmier scored eight victories with ESC SPA 81 and 176, and then three more in 1940 as commander of ESC Polonais.

The only British pilot to claim victories in both wars was AVM Stanley Vincent with No. 60 Squadron in 1916-17. As a Group Captain for No. 229 Squadron he gained two victories in 1940, flying Hurricanes to become a career ace.

CHAPTER 13

Victories Over Axis Aircraft

Of course, Dick Bong with 40 victories over the Japanese Air Forces and Gabby Gabreski with 28 over the Luftwaffe were the top-scorers over the major Axis powers.

Top-scorer over the Italian Regia Aeronautics was 2Lt. Lawrence Liebers and 1Lt. Virgil Lusk. Liebers flew P-38s for the 96FS/82FG/12AF, and in May and June 1943 he shot down four Mc.202s (damaged three others) and a Mc.205 in four combats over the Mediterranean. P-38 pilot Lusk, of the 49FS/14FG/12 and 15AF, became an instant ace on one mission when he shot down five Savoia-Marchetti transports between Gabes and Sfax on 24 November 1942. Lusk's squadronmate, 1Lt. James Butler, got four more of the S-M transports on the same day. 1Lt. William Sloan counted three MC-200s and a RE-2001 fighter among his 12 MTO victories while flying P-38s for the 96FS/82FG/12AF in the first seven months of 1943.

Surprisingly, the top-scorers against the Vichy French Air Force were U.S. Navy pilots flying F4F Wildcats for VF-41 off the *Ranger*. The *Ranger* was joined by the *Suwannee* and *Sangamon* in the support of the Allied amphibious landings on North Africa ("Operation Torch") on 8 November 1942. Lt(jg) Charles August originally claimed three American-manufactured Curtiss 75 Hawk fighters, but was later officially credited with two. In the battle over Cazes Air Drome, three other VF-41 pilots got double victories: Lt. Maynard Furney (two D.520s or D.75s); Lt(jg) Boyd Mayhew (two D.520s or D.75s); and Lt(jg) Charles Shields (D.520 and D.75). The next day Lt.Cdr. John Raby (VF 9) got a D.75 confirmed and a probable inland of Fedala to go with his LEO-45 of the previous day. Lt. Ernest Wood got a D.520 and another D.520 the previous day.

Lt(jg) Bruce Laird, VF-4 Wildcat pilot, shared a quarter victory over a German He-115 and a half Ju-88 off the *Ranger* over Bvodo Harbor, Norway on 4 October 1943. Lt. "Diz" Laird later got 5 Japanese to become the only Navy ace to score victories over both the Germans and Japanese. (USN)

Ensigns Marvin Franger and Louis Menard and Lt(jg) Harold Vita of VF-9 also got a Curtiss Hawk each on the 9th. Later, in the Pacific, the trio scored victories against the Japanese to become Navy aces who got victory credits against two Axis powers.

Lt(jg) Boyd Mayhew, having French victories also scored against the Germans. On 4 October 1943, the *Ranger* was assigned to join the Royal Navy and Home Fleet to strike Bvodo Harbor, Norway. While flying CAP at 1430 FDO vectored F4Fs from VF-4 towards a target. Mayhew spotted a Ju-88 in the clouds some 3,000 feet below and dove, hitting the twin-engine bomber with a deflection shot and smoking the port engine. Following Mayhew's firing run was Lt(jg) Dean Laird, who also hit Mayhew's German as it disappeared into the clouds and then crashed into the sea. Several minutes later FDO discovered another e/a, and four F4Fs pounced on a He-115 flying through a rainstorm at 200 feet. The twin-engine twin floatplane was no match for the Navy pilots, who gained a quarter victory apiece: Lt(jg) Earle Craig; Ens. Laurence Hensley; and Mayhew and Laird. VF-4 "Fighting-Four" was transferred to the Pacific in late 1944 and was posted to the *Essex* flying F6F Hellcats. Lt. "Diz" Laird went on to score five victories against the Japanese to become the Navy's only ace to score victories against both the Germans and Japanese.

During "Operation Dragoon"—the invasion of Southern France, 15 August 1944—Task Force 88, the escort carrier group under Adm. T.H. Troubridge of the Royal Navy, stood off the Riviera beaches. In the task force were nine CVEs, including the American *Tulagi* and *Kasaan Bay*, but none of their air groups saw air-to-air combat until 19 August. VOF-1 of the *Tulagi* was a specially trained unit used for plotting naval gunfire, providing close support, and executing armed recon patrols. On 19 August, VOF-1 encountered a group of He-111s north of Vienne and knocked down three of them. Ens. Alfred Wood was credited with 1 1/2 victories. On the 21st, Lt(jg) Edward Olszewski attacked three Ju-52 transports. He shot down the two trailing Germans of the V-formation to make him the top-scoring Navy pilot against the Luftwaffe.

Victories Over All Axis Powers
Carl Payne USAAF
America undertook her first amphibious invasion on 8 November 1942 as "Operation Torch." The Rangers of Lt.Col. William Darby moved onshore to Oran to capture the port city from the vacillating French. Spitfire Vbs of the 309FS/31FG and Seafires from the British carrier *Furious* flew air support over the battlefield. In the late afternoon, the French sent up Dewoitines 520 fighters to intercept. The American-flown Spitfires, led by Maj. Harrison Thyng over Tafaraoui Airdrome, which lay ten miles inland, shot three down. One pilot scoring that day was 2lt. Carl Payne, a Salem, Ohio, resi-

dent who had flown in the Dieppe raid and escorted U.S. bombers on their initial bombing raids in 1942.

In the next several months, Payne claimed several damaged and a probable and two, half shared victories before getting a solo claim over a German Me-109 on 6 May 1943.

Payne added his third Axis Air Force credit on 10 June 1943 as the 31FG was escorting 12th and 15th Air Force bombers in their aerial reduction of Pantellaria Islands off the Italian boot. In the dusk, Payne downed a Macchi 202 Folgore fighter five miles off the beleaguered island. Then, covering the invasion of Sicily, Payne added a FW-190 to become an ace and leave combat with five victories, one probable, and four damaged.

During the final days of the war Payne was assigned to the 34FS/413FG/7AF, which was led by, now Colonel, Harrison Thyng. The group was stationed at Yonton, Okinawa, flying P-47Ns after training in late 1944 for very long-range escort missions. After flying bombing and strafing sorties, the group flew its first and only escort mission on 8 August 1945. Covering B-29s over Yawata, Japan, Payne shot down a Zeke at 1018 to complete his Axis cycle: French; German; Italian; and Japanese in 253 missions. On the return from this mission the flight was blinded by an intense white flash which penetrated the overcast in a huge tapering cloud miles across. A map check showed the clouds approximately to be near Nagasaki.

Harrison Thyng often receives credit for scoring victories over all Axis powers. Researching Thyng's career record shows he scored over a French D.520 with Payne on 8 November 1943. He scored a probable and two damaged in the ETO in August and September 1942, and got three Me-109s and a FW-190 in the MTO from May to November 1943. Italian-marked Me-109s did not appear until June 1943, although one of the Me-109s could have been a misidentified Italian Mc 202. It appears probable that Thyng did not score against the Regia Aeronautica. As mentioned Thyng flew combat in the Pacific as commander of the 413FG. On the 8 August Yawata mission he scored a probable over a Japanese Oscar fighter. In the Korean War, he commanded the F-86 Sabre Jet-equipped 4FIW and added five MiG-15s to his career total to become one of seven WWII aces to become aces over Korea.

Louis Curdes USAF

In the spring and summer of 1943, the Germans were trying to supply their retreating Afrika Korps Armies in North Africa. Large numbers of Luftwaffe transports and their fighter escorts fell prey to the P-38 Lightning pilots of the 82FG. 2Lt. Louis Curdes was flying an anti-shipping, skip-bombing sortie off Cape Bon on 29 April when the unit was attacked by a dozen Me-109s. In the battle Curdes shot down three Messerschmitts, but ran out of fuel and made a forced landing in a riverbed. Engineers were brought in and laid 1,500 feet of steel mat, enabling Curdes to fly back to base several days later. On 24 June, he shot down an Italian Macchi 202 Folgore over the Aranci Gulf, Sardinia. Curdes also scored two doubles over the Luftwaffe on 19 May and 27 August, and all his victims were Me-109s. In his last battle his P-38 was hit, destroying his armament and an engine. While limping back to base at San Pancrazio, Sicily, accurate AA fire over Naples put out the other engine, forcing him to land on an Italian beach. He set his fighter on fire and was captured. He managed to escape and was returned to the States. He was transferred to the 3rd Air Commando Group in the Pacific in January 1945. He was given a P-51D and assigned to the 4FS at Mangalden, Luzon. The primary duty of the group was ground support and armed reconnaissance. On 7 February Curdes, flying in "*Bad Angel*," shot down a twin-engine Dinah Army recon bomber 30 SW of Formosa. The victory completed his sweep of three Axis powers, the first American to do so.

But Curdes had another victory flag to add to the side of his cockpit—an American flag! On 10 February 1945, Curdes' flight left Luzon on a recon sweep over Bataan Island. While strafing a Japanese airstrip, one of the Mustangs was hit and the pilot was

Carl Payne. (USAF)

Louis Curdes. (Author/Curdes)

forced to bail out into the Pacific. Curdes circled over the island until a PBY rescue amphibian could arrive. Soon Curdes noticed a twin-engine transport carrying full American Army Air Force markings approaching the Jap airstrip for a landing. The Japanese had copied the American P-47 transport, which was code-named "Tabby." Whatever the case, Curdes had to make a decision. He fired a volley across the transport's nose, but it continued its landing approach, ignoring this warning. Curdes then shot out the port and starboard engines on two gunnery runs, forcing the P-47 to belly land into the ocean. The passengers and crew got onto a large life raft before their aircraft sunk. Upon returning to base, Curdes learned that the C-47 was American, far off course, lost, and ready to land anywhere. The next day the downed P-51 pilot and the 13 on the C-47, including two nurses, were picked up by a PBY and saved from capture by the Japanese. For his action Curdes was awarded the DFC, probably the only U.S. pilot to win the award for shooting down a friendly aircraft.

Levi Chase. (USAF)

Levi Chase USAAF

Capt. Levi Chase, a Cortland, NY, native, was the top P-40 ace in the ETO, flying for the 58th and 60th Fighter Squadrons of the 33FG of the 12AF and 10AF in the Mediterranean area. As soon as the North African airfields at Oran were captured on 10 November 1942, two days after D-Day for "Torch," the 33FG flew its 70 P-40Fs off the carrier *Chenango* to these fields. Chase was assigned to the 58FS, but made no claims there. The squadron was posted at Thelepte, Tunisia, and Chase shot down a FW-190 near the field on 18 December for his first victory. Four days later, Chase intercepted a Ju-88 (or HS-129) and shot it down with only one gun operating. Promoted to Major and made CO of the 60FS, Chase downed two more Germans, a Me-109 on 31 January 1943 and a FW-190 on 2 February. On March 15th, the 60th escorted B-25s to Mezzouna and south of the target were attacked by Italian MC-202s. In a running dogfight Chase claimed an Italian fighter for his fifth victory to become an ace. He went on to score five victories over Me-109s in six days (30 March to 5 April) to become a double ace. In July, Chase returned to the States, where he remained for a year.

As a Lt.Colonel Chase was deployed to the CBI, flying P-51s for the 2nd Air Commando Group of the 10AF. On 15 March 1945 he shot an Oscar down over Don Muang Airfield, Bangkok, followed eleven days later when he shot down another Oscar north of Rangoon for his twelfth and last victory, and at least one over Germany, Italy, and Japan.

Victories Over Both Axis Powers Flying for Two Nations
Pilot: Hollis B. Hills
Victories: 19 August 1942 RCAF (414 Squadron)
Mustang I vs. FW-190
29 April 1944 USN (VF-32) F6F vs. Zeke
Time: 19 August 1942
Action: Flying Officer Hollis Hills, a Los Angeles resident, had joined the Royal Canadian Air Force and flew his first combat in an Allison-powered Mustang I over the pre-invasion beaches at Dieppe. After a dawn tactical recon mission, the 414th RCAF Squadron again sent out Flt/Lt. F.E. Clarke and his "weaver" (wingman) Hills from Gatwick at 1025 to recon the beaches. Tac R missions were flown in pairs, the leader surveying the ground while his weaver covered him from above. Over Dieppe Hills' radio broke down, and when three FW-190s bounced them he was unable to warn Clarke. Clarke's engine was hit and seized, forcing him to ditch in the sea off the beaches to be picked up by a Royal Navy destroyer. Meanwhile, Hills was flying through both Royal Navy and German AA fire to shoot the FW off Clarke's tail for his first victory, and the first victory for an American in a Mustang in WWII.

Action: 29 April 1944
After America's entry in the war, Hills transferred to the U.S. Navy, flying F6F Hellcats for VF-32 off the carrier *Langley*. On 29 April 1944, VF-32 was flying an eight-plane fighter sweep at 10,000 feet over Truk's airfields, which had been reinforced after a series of damaging raids two weeks earlier. Lt.Cdr. Edward Outlaw's two divisions of fighter-bombers were alerted to a large Japanese formation of approximately 30 Zeros by Hills, who was his second division leader. The enemy was about eight miles away at 6,000 feet, flying in three plane Vs. Leaving Hills' division for top cover

F/O Hollis Hills RAF. (Author/Hills) and Lt. Hollis Hills. (USN)

duties, Outlaw dove on the Japanese, who went into poorly disciplined defensive Luftbury circles. Lt(jg)s Richard May and Donald Reeves each downed three Japanese apiece. Outlaw became an ace-in-a-day by downing five Japanese in this single combat. Once the air battle was initiated, Hills was released from top cover and dove into the battle. He fired a short burst into a Zeke's cockpit, killing the pilot. Hills proceeded to follow Outlaw, knocking one more Zeke off his tail. Hills claimed a probable later. With three claims, Hills had victories against both Axis powers, which happened infrequently during WWII, but these victories flying for different countries made Hills unique. Later in his tour, Hills' F6F was hit by AA on a strafing run and water-landed in the middle of Manila Bay. He was incredibly picked up by a surfacing Navy submarine and returned to the *Langley*.

Two Theater Aces

Pilot: John D. Landers
PTO: April 1942 to January 1943
      9PS/49FG/5AF P-40 *"Texas Longhorn"* & *"Skeeter"*
      6 victories
ETO: June-July 1944
      38FS/78FG/8AF P-38
      4 victories
ETO: November 1944 to January 1945
      357FS/357FG/8AF P-51 *"Big Beautiful Doll"*
      1 victory
ETO: 66FW/78FG/8AF P-51 *"Big Beautiful Doll"*
      3 1/2 victories

John Landers was born in Wilson, OK, on 23 August 1920 and spent his childhood in Joshua, TX. He attended Texas A&M and Arkansas State Universities, leaving only one semester short of graduation to enter the Army Air Corps in March 1941. He took his

Maj. Landers transferred to the 55FG as CO of the 38FS in summer 1944 flying the P-38 and claimed four victories. (Author/Landers)

cadet training in California and graduated in Class 41-I. The new Second Lieutenant was shipped to Darwin, Australia, to fly P-40s with the Fifth Air Force's 9FS/49FG. On 4 April 1942, flying the *"Texas Longhorn,"* Landers attacked a formation of Betty bombers and shot down two for his first confirmed victories, and he damaged several others for probables. When he returned to base, Landers did a few victory rolls, only to be greeted by AA from trigger-happy gunners who had been strafed by enemy Zeros only a few minutes earlier.

Landers' last big day in the Pacific came on the day after Christmas, 1942. Eleven Zeros came in to strafe Dobodura Airfield on New Guinea and were met by 12 49FG P-40s out of Port Moresby. Four Japanese were shot down, two by 1Lt. Landers, one of which was the Group's 100th victory. Landers was shot down and bailed

2Lt. John Landers got six victories over the Japanese over Darwin and New Guinea in 1942 flying P-40s named *"Skeeter"* and *"Texas Longhorn"* for the 49FG. (Author/Landers)

LtCol. Landers transferred to the 357FG as XO and got a victory in the P-51 in November 1944 and returned to the US. In March 1945 he was named CO of the 78FG and got three and half more P-51 victories in the *"Big Beautiful Doll."* (Author/Landers)

out over the jungle. He walked out a week later as an ace with six PTO victories.

Landers was shipped ZI to train P-38 pilots, after which he returned to combat at Northampsted, England, as CO of the 38FS/78FG. He scored a triple on 7 July 1944. Leading a flight of four Lightnings over Bernberg, Landers engaged about 20 Me-110s, and in 20 minutes he accounted for three and his flight damaged four others. In mid-August, Landers took off to accompany B-17s on a pre-target shuttle mission. His engine acted up during take off, and he radioed base to prepare another aircraft. He landed and took off again, rejoining his group to assume his lead. After this short stint with the 38FS, Landers was transferred as XO and acting CO of the 357FG in the fall of 1944. He flew a P-51 "*Big Beautiful Doll*," for the 357th and claimed a Me-109 on 18 November, completing his second tour, and returned stateside for R&R in December. This was his fifth ETO victory, to make him an ace in this theater, also.

Soon he was back in combat as CO of the 78FG based at Duxford, again flying a P-51 nicknamed "*Big Beautiful Doll*." He downed two Me-109s on 2 March 1945 over Burg Airdrome. On 19 March he shot down a Me-109 near Osnabruck, and on 30 March he shared a Me-262 jet victory with a pilot of the 84FS, which was his last claim of the war, giving him 14 1/2. However, he was still to see considerable combat. On 10 April 1945 Lt.Col. Landers led the 78th to gain 52 victories and 43 damaged, claiming eight ground victories for himself. But this day was far surpassed six days later when he led the 78th to the biggest day enjoyed by any Group in the 8AF when they destroyed 125 German aircraft on the ground. At war's end, Landers had scored over 20 ground victories. After V-E Day he became CO of the 361FG in charge of preparing it for Pacific combat. The Japanese surrendered before the Group was shipped out.

Landers ended the war as a full Colonel at 24 years old, making him the second youngest bird Colonel after Chesley Peterson. Landers was almost an ace in three separate fighter aircraft: P-40 (6); P-38 (4); and P-51 (4 1/2). By scoring six in the Pacific and eight and a half in Europe, he shared with Lt.Col. James Howard the distinction of being America's two theater ace.

P-40/P-38/P-51: An Appraisal
By
John Landers:
14 1/2 victories/Two theater ace
P-40 (6v.)/P-38 (4v.)/P-51 (4 1/2 v.)

Comparing these aircraft is difficult, because I flew them in different combat situations, in different theaters, and during various phases of the war.

I had just graduated with Class 41-I when I was sent to Australia to join the 49th Fighter Group. I delivered a P-40 to Darwin in early April 1942, and I think this flight gave me a grand total of 10 hours in the aircraft. The next afternoon the squadron was scrambled, and I was thrown into my first combat. Luckily I was able to shoot down two Japanese bombers, even though my P-40 was having engine problems and I was left alone to be shot up by Zeros. In the Pacific the Japanese were on the offensive, and most of my flying was defensive over Darwin and Port Moresby. The Warhawk was a good fighter, but it had to be used right, as it was no match for the Zero in a dogfight. As General Chennault had shown with the Flying Tigers in China, you had to get the altitude advantage, dive, shoot, and get out. Its strong points were its diving speed, six .50 caliber machine guns, and its ruggedness. After my last two victories the day after Christmas, 1942, my P-40 was hit by a bunch of Zeros. The fighter held together, and I was able to bail out into the jungle and walk out.

After my Pacific tour I was able to spend a lot of time in the States as an instructor training P-38 pilots. I finally got back into combat as CO of the 38th Fighter Squadron of the 55th Fighter Group in mid-1944. In the winter of 1943, the P-38 had its share of problems as a high altitude escort. At the time I joined the 55th, the 8th and 9th Air Forces were in the process of gaining air superiority over the Luftwaffe and knocking out tactical targets in preparation for D-Day. Our role was to seek out German fighters, both in the air and on the ground, and destroy transportation targets. The P-38 was better suited for these missions, as they were conducted at lower altitudes at which the Lightning was more efficient. The P-38 was very good in the fighter-bomber role, being a stable gun platform and having tremendous punch with its guns and ability to carry a large payload. Also, at lower altitudes we were able to hold our own against the German fighters.

Headquarters had long decided to gradually phase out the P-38 in favor of the Mustang by the fall of 1944. I was assigned as acting CO of the 357th Fighter Group, which flew Mustangs. I scored my first Mustang victory over a Me-109 in November to end my second tour. I then joined the 78th Fighter Group, which also flew Mustangs, as their CO in early January 1945, and we continued to attack the Germans on the ground, harassing their transportation and communication systems, along with their airdromes. The P-51 was the best all-around fighter I flew in the war. It could do everything well, at high or low altitudes and at the longest ranges of any fighter of WWII. The Merlin engine was vulnerable to ground fire, but I was able to score 17 stafing victories in two missions in April 1945. In the air at this time we had it pretty much our way, as the Luftwaffe was low on fuel and experienced pilots. It was a time of easy pickings for the Mustangs, which roamed everywhere over Germany.

V/S/L James Howard flew P-40s for the 2AVG Squadron between January and August 1942 and claimed 6.33 victories. (Author/Howard)

Pilot: James H. Howard
AVG: January to August 1942
     2nd Squadron/P-40 B&E
     6 1/3 victories
ETO: December 1943 to May 1944
     354FS/354FG/9AF P-51 "*Ding Hao*"
     6 victories
For Howard's ETO victories: *See P-51 ETO First Ace in Type*
James Howell Howard was born in Canton, China, on April 1913 of medical missionary parents. His family returned to America when he was 14. He received a B.A. degree from Pomona College, and in 1938 was commissioned as a Naval fighter pilot on the carrier *Enterprise*. In 1941, he resigned from the Navy to join Chennault's Flying Tigers in the China Burma India Theater. He was a Squadron Leader of the Second AVG Squadron, where he scored 5 1/3 victories in January 1942. However, some reliable sources (Frank Olynyk) claim that four of these victories were air-to-ground victories. On 4 July, he downed his last Jap I-97 fighter. While with the AVG, Howard had several close calls. While strafing a Jap airfield in Thailand his Warhawk was hit by ground fire and crash-landed near the field. The long-legged (6'2") Howard took off and reached an inlet, and that night borrowed a fishing boat and contacted friendly Chinese troops, who returned him to base. On 10 January, over Tak airdrome, his aircraft's electrical system failed, causing his engine to quit while he was firing on a Jap that was landing. The Jap quickly turned the tables on Howard, who was busy trying to get his engine restarted. Fortunately, Tex Hill shot the Ki-27 off Howard's tail as his dead engine came back to life.

Howard returned to the States, joining the 354FG/9AF in Oregon, where he had become a Major and CO of a P-39 squadron. The Group was shipped to Boxted, England, where it was introduced to the P-51B. This Mustang featured the Rolls-Royce Merlin engine, which gave the fighter superior performance over Luftwaffe fighters for the first time and extended its range, allowing it to continuously escort American bombers. The "Pioneer Mustang" Group, as it was called, scored its first victory on 16 December 1943 and ended the war with the greatest number of victories of any American fighter in the war.

Maj. Howard flew his P-51 "*Ding Hoa*" for the 356FS/354FG. On 11 January 1944 he shot down three Germans and damaged two others to drive off a concerted Luftwaffe attack on B-17s. For this action he was awarded the CMH. (Author/Howard)

Capt. Don Willis of the 335FS/4FG wore the uniforms of four nations during his WWII career. (USAF)

Flying for Four Nations

Capt. Donald Willis, op officer for the 335FS/4FG, wore the uniforms of four nations during his career. He was a graduate of the Finnish Military Academy and then served with the Norwegians. He joined RAF 121 Squadron and then transferred to the 4 FG when the Americans entered the war. On 10 April 1944, he participated in the first P-38 Droop Snoop mission, in which his aircraft was hit and he was forced to bail out and was taken prisoner.

Close Encounters of an Odd Kind
P-38 vs. P-51

On 29 October 1944, the 95FS of the 82FG was flying home from a bomber escort mission to Munich which never materialized, as they failed to rendezvous due to heavy cloud cover. On the way back they hunted locomotives, and Lt. William Hawthorne needed to be covered, as he lost one of his engines to AA fire. The flight had seen an olive drab P-51 Mustang B or C tailing them for a while, and about 30 miles southeast of Linz, Austria, the Mustang made a pass at the flight. It wasn't an unusual occurrence for pilots of other units to playfully, and sometimes even aggressively make passes at their fellow pilots. 2Lt. Eldon Coulson turned into the Mustang, who opened fire at about 4,000 feet and continued to fire. The anxious Coulson fired a short burst and hit the P-51 in its engine and canopy. It rolled over and dove into a mountain.

At debriefing, Coulson and his squadron mates reported the Mustang attack. The Mustang did not appear to have any national markings, or the red spinner which identified 15AF P-51s. The victim was probably a captured P-51, as other 15AF P-51 units flying over Italy that day were contacted and all were accounted for. Coulson was officially awarded a victory credited.

Lt. John Blumer was credited with one of three Soviet Yak fighters downed in the unfortunate air battle of 7 November 1944 by P-38 pilots of the 82FG over Yugoslavia. (USAF)

Yak vs. Lightning: Soviet-U.S. Air Battle

The 82FG was again to have another strange encounter on 7 November 1944. The 95th and 97th Fighter Squadrons of the 82FG/15AF out of Foggia, under Group CO Col. Clarence "Curly" Edwinson, were to attack transport and German troops retreating from Greece. The 95FS strafed and destroyed a locomotive, and then flew on to attack a truck convoy. It was not before inflicting considerable damage that they discovered that they were over the wrong road and had attacked Russian trucks and troops. As they were pulling up from the deck, their top cover (97FS) cautioned

Lt. Philip Brewer (R) and 2Lt. Eldon Coulson (L) were victims of the Soviet Yaks. The week before, Coulson had been attacked by a P-51 Mustang and shot it down. It was probably a captured P-51 in Luftwaffe service as no American Mustangs were missing that day. Coulson was given credit for a victory. (USAF)

them that "bogeys" were taking off from a field in front of them. The Russians had scrambled Yak fighters under Capt. A.I. Koldunov to protect the convoy. The P-38s and Yaks both climbed for altitude, but a Yak pulled up its nose and fired on the last P-38, piloted by Lt. Philip Brewer, who crashed and exploded. Lt. Kenneth Katschke, flying top cover at 7,000 feet, dove on the "enemy" and shot it down at about 4,000 feet. Katschke only saw the red stars as the fighter was about to crash. A bogey crossed in front of Lt. Thomas Urton, who was leading the 95FS medium cover, and then broke toward him. The four P-38s and six Yaks engaged in a dogfight. Urton finally identified the fighters as Soviet Yaks and called the information to his flight. Just as he did he was warned to break, and he looked back to see a Yak on his tail, shooting at close range. Urton was rescued by Lt. John Blumer, who flamed the Soviet. The other Yaks continued to press the attack, and a second was hit by Urton and was seen to spiral, smoking towards the ground (probable). Urton chased and hit a third Yak that was on the tail of another P-38 and chased it off (damaged). 2Lt. Eldon Coulson's P-38 was hit and seen to crash and burn. The fighters finally separated, and when Urton waggled his wings the Yaks did likewise and allowed the P-38s to withdraw.

In the mean time, a Yak attacked Edwinson's flight head on and the P-38s broke, and after two or three passes Lt. William Blurock got on its tail, got a few hits, and caused it to pour smoke and partially drop its wheels (probable). The Russian waggled his wings and Edwinson replied, and the unfortunate battle ended with two P-38s and two Yaks destroyed and two Yak probables and one damaged.

The air battle ended, but the incident caused diplomatic repercussions, as one of the dead in the strafing attack was a Soviet Lieutenant General, along with two officers and three enlisted men and 20 vehicles. The Russians demanded an immediate investigation from Gen. Ira Eaker and the Joint Chiefs of Staff and the discipline of those responsible. Gun camera film concluded that the Russians were indeed strafed and the target road was 55 miles (10 minutes) away. On 25 November 1944, a seven-page report was sent to the War Department and Joint Chiefs of Staff. The JCS sent a message to the Red Army General Staff saying that the P-38s had made a navigational error and attacked a Red Army column by mistake. It went on to state that the P-38s were "justifiably attacked by Soviet fighters defending their column" and "the Soviet flight Leader courageously closed into formation with the U.S. Flight Leader, and mutual identification was confirmed." The message concluded: "Please accept my heartfelt regrets and be assured that every precaution has been taken to prevent such errors in the future." Edwinson was relieved of his command on 20 November and awarded the DFC the next day, and on the 22nd was on his way to the States to explain the "incident."

P-38 Downs a B-17, Wolf in Sheep's Clothing

On 12 June 1943, a green American pilot blundered and landed his P-38G on the Italian A/F at Capoterra. The captured Lightning was flown to the Regia Aeronautica Test and Research Center at Guidonia, where the fighter was examined by engineers and test flown by Colonello Angelo Tondi.

The P-38 remained in its olive drab paint scheme, but had white Italian crosses painted on both sides of each of its twin tails, however, Tondi did not repaint the red spinners that identified AF fighters. Because of its unique twin-boom tail configuration, Tondi felt he could fly the P-38 close to American bomber formations before being discovered. On 11 August, Tondi and several escorting Macchi 202s attacked a formation of 12AF B-17s near Torvajanica. He attacked the last bomber in the formation from 5 o'clock, and the Lightning's .50 cal. machine gun rounds and 20mm cannon shells hit the right side of the bomber. The cockpit was hit, and the co-pilot was killed and a fire was started. The B-17 crashed into the sea, but several survivors were able to inflate their life raft and were rescued the next day.

The crew debriefed that they were shot down by an outlaw P-38, and Group Intelligence instructed lone P-38 pilots to no longer continue the practice of joining bomber formations and advised bomber gunners to fire on lone P-38s until further notified. Tondi flew several more of his wolf in sheep's clothing missions without success. Ultimately, low octane Italian aviation fuel caused damage to the Lightning's Allison engines, grounding it.

Strange Enemies: American Beaufighter vs. German B-17

An interesting victory occurred on 3 March 1945 when 415NFS Beaufighter crew 1Lt. Henry Gablin and 2Lt. Walter Cleary were vectored to a bogey they ID'd as a FW-200. The four engine bomber's rear gunner fired, but the Beau hit it with cannon and machine gun fire in the two starboard engines, which caught fire, and the German was seen to crash. Investigation of the wreck showed it to be a B-17, and six of its occupants survived. The occupants were Germans, who upon interrogation disclosed that the bomber was one of several B-17s used by the top secret German KG-200 to drop agents behind the lines. The B-17 had operated in Russia and had been recently transferred. The B-17 had taken off from Stuttgart-Euchterdingen at 2308 and crossed the Rhine north of Basel, flying at low level. It carried 11 crew, nine agents, and three supply containers. The first two agents jumped at 0200, and at 0300 three others and the supply containers were dropped. At 0320 three men and a woman were dropped. The B-17 became lost, was picked up by

Captured B-17 in German markings. This B-17 was the *"Wulf Hund"* of the 303BG that was shot down on 12 June 1943 and captured in tact. It was used at the Experimental and Test Center at Rechlin for tests and then went to the KG-200 and took part in covert operations. (USAF)

Jerry Johnson shot down 22 aircraft with the 49FG but here he shows another victory. On 15 November 1943 he shot down a RAAF Wirraway recon aircraft by mistake. (USAF)

Allied ground radar, and was intercepted and shot down by Gablin and Cleary. Six of the 11 crew bailed out, but five perished in the crash. The Germans admitted that they had dropped nine agents that night just before being intercepted, and that the pilot had ordered his crew to bail out. Unfortunately for the interrogators, only the pilot and observer, who perished in the crash, knew the location of the agent drops. The Germans lacked a long range aircraft for use in these operations, and captured B-17s had the range and had the advantage of being able to fly over enemy territory without too many problems. Since KG-200 was a top secret unit, little information was available on it after the war.

P-38 vs. Wirraway

On 15 November 1943, Capt. Gerald Johnson, 22-victory ace and future CO of the 49FG, was flying his P-38 *"Jerry"* on a routine patrol over New Guinea to check out reports of Japanese fighters lurking in the area when he encountered a bogey. Johnson approached the bogey head on and shot it down. As he flew past his victim he saw to his dismay it was an Australian RAAF Wirraway A-46. The Wirraway had been a two-seat trainer that was converted by No. 4 Squadron to a recon/artillery spotter aircraft. During a head on attack it looked much like a Zero. The pilot, F/O R.M. Stewart, managed to crash land near his base and escaped with minor injuries. Johnson met the Australian later, who accepted his apology when Johnson explained that he had been advised that the RAAF had left the area.

CHAPTER 14

Aces in a Day

"Ace in a Day," the destruction of five or more enemy aircraft in a day—the fantasy of every fighter pilot. A total of 159, two of whom accomplished the feat twice, joined this elite group: 59 (two twice) from the Navy; 90 from the Air Force; and 10 from the Marine Corps. Of the 159 Pilots, 44 scored their first five (or six) victories of the war, and of these 24 scored all their victories of the war in one day to become "instant aces." Ens. Alfred Lerch (VF-10 off the carrier *Independence*) scored seven victories on 21 September 1945, while Maj. Jefferson Dorroh (VMF-323) scored six victories on 11 April 1945. Each man got no further victories during his tour.

The top-scoring daily ace was Cdr. David McCampbell of the Navy (VF-15/*Essex*), who was one of two fighter pilots to score five or more victories in a day on two occasions. McCampbell claimed seven victories in two sorties during the "Great Marianas Turkey Shoot" on 19 June 1944. On 24 October 1944, during the Battle of Leyte Gulf, he collected nine victories in one mission, tops for an American pilot in WWII. Of his 34 victories—tops for the Navy—16 were attained in two days. Nineteen victory ace Lt. Patrick Fleming was the other American pilot to score five victories in a day twice. On 14 December 1944 he got four Zeros and an Oscar while flying a F6F-5 Hellcat of VF-80 off the *Ticonderoga*. On 16 February 1945 flying for VBF-80 off the *Hancock* Fleming got five Zekes. The next day he shot down four Nates to nearly have a record three fives in a day. Five other pilots claimed seven victories in a day:

Lt. Eugene Vejtasa (VF-10/*Enterprise*) 26 October 1942
1Lt. James Swett (VMF-221/Solomons) 7 April 1943
Maj. William Leverette (14FG/12AF/MTO) 9 October 1943
Capt. William Shomo (82TRS/5AF/Luzon) 11 January 1945
Ens. Alfred Lerch (VF-10/*Independence*) 16 April 1945

Nine Victories in a Day: Top U.S. Total
Pilot: Cdr. David McCampbell
Unit: VF-15 "Fabled 15" *Essex* Task Group TG 38.3
A/C: F6F-5 Hellcat "*Minsi II*"
Date: 24 October 1944/0835-1000
Place: Battle of Leyte Gulf
Action: After the June invasion of the Marianas and the disastrous Battle of the Philippine Seas ("Marianas Turkey Shoot"), the Japanese High Command spent the summer of 1944 planning for their next and inevitable clash with the U.S. Navy. They needed to strike U.S. amphibious invasion forces as soon as they landed somewhere on the Japan-Ryukyus (Okinawa)-Formosa-Philippines defensive perimeter. A plan code-named "Sho-Go C" ("Operation Victory") was formulated involving three separate naval task forces converging on the invasion forces from three different directions.

MacArthur's "return" to Leyte on 20 October prompted the Japanese to put "Sho-Go" into action. Alerted to the movement of the Japanese fleet by U.S. submarines, Task Group 38.3 moved towards the Philippine coast to protect their invasion sea and land forces, and to meet the three incoming Japanese task forces.

In the morning of 24 October, Adm. Frederick Sherman's group lay to the north off Luzon, conducting searches and air strikes on Japanese airfields there. At 0750, radar on several of Sherman's carriers simultaneously picked up large numbers of Japanese aircraft in two formations at 75 miles. Sherman sent up 12 fighters each from the *Princeton* and *Langley* and seven from the *Essex* to meet the threat. Several minutes later an even larger third force of about 60 bogies was reported 60 miles to the west.

On the *Essex*, her Air Group Commander (AGC), David McCampbell, was waiting in the ready room. McCampbell, the "elderly" 34 year old, had 21 victories and was the hero of the "Marianas Turkey Shoot" four months earlier, scoring seven victories in one day. His Hellcat "*Minsi II*" (named after a Milwaukee girlfriend, Mary Blatz) was spotted on the port catapult to be fueled for an air strike against Adm. Kurita's task force. When the third incoming Japanese air strike was discovered, the Kurita air strike was scrubbed, and all *Essex* pilots were ordered to their aircraft. All except McCampbell, who Adm. Sherman thought too valuable as a leader to be put in jeopardy. McCampbell called the Air Offices and asked if he could go since his plane was already on the catapult. He was told "OK," and then "No." *Essex* captain Carlos Wieber, finding that only seven pilots were available to meet the Japanese attack, gave his permission for his AGC to fly. The contradiction of orders confused McCampbell's plane handlers, who filled his external drop tanks first and then under-filled the wing tanks. Since

Cdr. David McCampbell. (Author/McCampbell)

the drop tanks were jettisoned upon entering combat, McCampbell tried to delay in order to get more fuel in his wing tanks, but was threatened with having his aircraft sent below if he did not launch immediately. *"Minsi II"* was catapulted, followed by two divisions, but the section leader was unable to launch, giving the defenders only seven fighters to face the 60 incoming Japanese. As the Hellcats climbed to 6,000 feet, *Essex* FDO Lt(jg) John Connally (future Texas Governor, U.S. Secretary of State, and Presidential candidate) vectored them to a radar plot 38 miles north. Soon the American saw a large formation at 25 miles. At first it appeared to be a returning "friendly" TG 38.3 strike force, but quickly it was identified as "60 rats, hawks, and fish." As they closed at 14,000 feet, the majority of the Japanese fighters ("rats") had the altitude advantage, protecting the dive bombers ("hawks") and torpedo bombers ("fish") below. At this point McCampbell wanted to lead his four-plane division against the fighters above and send his three-plane division against the bombers below. A snafu in radio frequency changes sent five Hellcats diving through the overcast towards the bombers, leaving only McCampbell and his wingman, Lt. Roy Rushing, alone to engage about 40 fighters, which were mainly bomb-carrying Zekes (IJAAF Zeros) and a few escorting Oscars (IJAAF)) and Hamps (IJNAF Zeros). Loaded with bombs and without adequate escorts, the Japanese formation went into a large, orderly Lufbery Circle. This defensive maneuver requires each plane to protect the tail of the plane ahead, so that any attacker going astern of any aircraft in this circle would come under fire from the one following. The disadvantage of this defense was that altitude was gradually lost, and sufficient fuel was needed to hold out against a prolonged attack. The two Hellcats made three or four careful, but unsuccessful, probes at the circle. McCampbell decided to wait, circling above the Lufbery, reasoning that the Japanese, having flown from Manila and needing to fly back, would soon have to worry about their fuel situation. In about 10 to 15 minutes McCampbell's hunch paid off, and the Lufbery dispersed and headed back toward the Philippine mainland. Using similar tactics to those of the U.S. Navy, the Japs kept good formation, scissoring and weaving. But McCampbell and Rushing remained patient, maintained altitude, and did not expose themselves. Soon a Japanese fighter straggled or went too wide in a weave or climbed out of formation, and was picked off by a diving Hellcat, which then converted its diving speed back to altitude. The *Essex* was radioed for help, but all her fighters were launched to meet the other Japanese formations. Lt(jg) Albert Slack, one of McCampbell's second section who had dove on the bombers, rejoined and pressed the attack, knocking down three planes in each of their next two passes. Slack got four Zeros and an Oscar probable before running out of ammo and returning to the carrier.

The McCampbell/Rushing tandem had made 18-20 passes before being forced to disengage, as they ran were running low on fuel and ammo. McCampbell had downed five Zeros, two Hamps, and two Oscars, and a further Zeke and Oscar as probables. His nine victories were the most scored by an American in one day

during the war and tied him briefly with Dick Bong for top American ace with 30 victories. Rushing raised his victory total from six to twelve, claiming four Zekes, an Oscar, and a Hamp, along with two damaged Zekes. These claims were only those seen by either Rushing or McCampbell to flame or explode. Several were observed with engines smoking or diving away (two spiraling towards the water were claimed as probables). The furious action prevented the two from recording types and angles of attack for the action report. In fact, it was not until they had downed five that McCampbell decided to keep score on his instrument panel with a pencil. The only damage to the Hellcats were dents and scratches from the debris from exploding Japanese aircraft.

As they flew back to the *Essex*, McCampbell, with a fuel short-fill at the start of the mission, began to worry about his fuel situation. As they approached the TF 38.3 perimeter they were fired on by the *Hornet*, forcing them to dive to the deck, where the *Hornet's* CAP prepared to make firing passes on them before ID was established. McCampbell contacted the *Essex* ops and got permission to land. As they closed they found the carrier decks filled with aircraft returned from the second strike, forcing them to circle. McCampbell's fuel gauge read almost empty, so Adm. Sherman sent him to the *Langley*, whose decks were lined with TBFs. The torpedo bombers were quickly cleared, and Sherman's valuable AGC landed. As he came to a stop, he accelerated the engine to take it out of gear but it just stopped, out of gasoline.

When the fighter was rearmed it was found to have only six unspent rounds, all jammed in one gun. McCampbell realized that he was in Sherman's doghouse when he was given orders directly from Sherman to leave the *Langley* on a humble "low patrol" to protect the fleet against torpedo aircraft. As he landed back on the *Essex* he was summoned directly to Sherman's quarters and chastised for disobeying direct orders not to fly. McCampbell tried to explain the mysterious "fly-grounded-fly, and then catapult or else" orders he received over the intercom. But in the end it probably was McCampbell's nine victories which caused Sherman to relent.

The Battle for Leyte Gulf continued for several more days. Adm. Ozawa's carriers *Zuikaku*, *Zuiho*, *Chiyoda*, and *Chitose*, and their total complement of 116 aircraft (80 fighters) were annihilated. The Japanese lost 26 of 60 warships: four carriers; three battleships; ten cruisers; and nine destroyers. Only two of their warships were undamaged. The U.S. Fleet lost six warships. A total of 517 Japanese aircraft were lost (270 on 24 October). Besides McCampbell (9v.) and Rushing (6v.), the Navy had seven other aces in a day.

In early November, McCampbell scored four more victories to make him the top Navy ace with 34 victories, to go along with 20 strafing ground victories. On 10 January 1945 he was awarded the Congressional Medal of Honor by F.D.R for his seven victories in the Marianas and nine in the Philippines. He joined the legendary "Butch" O'Hare as one of the two Navy pilots to be awarded the CMH in WWII.

Seven Victories in a Day

Pilot: Lt. Stanley Vejtasa
Unit: VF-10 "Grim Reapers" Red 7/*Enterprise*
A/C: F4F Wildcat
Date: 26 October 1942/0910-1100
Place: Santa Cruz Islands
Action: From the initial Marine Corps landings on Guadalcanal on 7 August 1942, the situation on the island remained critical into fall. It was obvious to U.S. Navy Commander of the Pacific Fleet Adm. Chester Nimitz that the island could only be held if it could be reinforced. However, reinforcement meant the risk of engaging superior Japanese naval forces. On 18 October, Nimitz appointed the aggressive William "Bull" Halsey to command two task forces. Task Force 16 under R.Adm. Thomas Kinkaid was centered around the carrier *Enterprise*, while Task Force 17 under R.Adm. George Murray focused around the carrier *Hornet*. The strategy was for the two task forces to rendezvous, and to be in a position to intercept any Japanese naval units approaching Guadalcanal.

In the early morning of 26 October, U.S. scout planes contacted elements of a Japanese force under Vice Admirals Kondo and Nugamo. The superior Japanese force included four carriers and four battleships. At 0600, Halsey radioed the message "Attack-repeat-attack" to his command, and the complex and often confused Battle of Santa Cruz began.

Stubby F4F Wildcat fighters of VF-10, the "Grim Reapers," under the redoubtable Lt.Cdr. Jim Flatley, were scrambled to meet the oncoming Japanese. "Red 7," a Reaper division led by Lt. Stanley Vejtasa, joined Flatley on CAP. Vejtasa, a 28 year old Montana Swede, had joined the Navy out of college in 1937. He graduated from Pensacola and joined Scouting Squadron 5 on the *Yorktown* as a SBD dive bomber pilot.

During the Battle of the Coral Sea he put a bomb into the Jap carrier *Shoho's* deck, helping to sink her. A day later, he lost contact with his VS-5 formation and was attacked by eight Zeros. Expertly handling his Dauntless and utilizing their ammunition judiciously, Vejtasa and his rear gunner fought off the Japanese in a half hour struggle at wave top level. Despite receiving several hits and being wounded in the leg he downed three Zeros. The action earned him a stateside ticket to retrain as a F4F fighter pilot with VF-10.

At 0900, to supplement a dozen Wildcats on CAP, Vejtasa and his wingman, Lt. Leroy "Tex" Harris, and second section leader Lt. Stan Reuhlow and his wingman, Ens. William Leder, climbed to intercept a reported contact at five miles and 12,000 feet. Soon a loose formation of incoming Aichi D3A1 Type 99 dive bombers, dubbed Val, appeared overhead. A Val dove from the group and passed in front of Vejtasa, who shot it down in a high side run before it menaced the *Hornet*. Losing altitude, the big Swede destroyed a fleeing Japanese bomber, while his #4, Ens. Leder, got another. Climbing to gain altitude, Vejtasa's engine sputtered and stopped. His fuel pressure gauge registered zero as his drop tank emptied. Troublesome drop tank connectors caused him to disengage combat in order to force the toggle with both hands to jettison the external tank.

At 0940, the second wave of Japanese attackers approached. It consisted of two formations: 20 Vals from the carrier *Zuikaku*, closely followed by 11 Nakajima B5N1 "Kate" torpedo bombers from the *Shokaku*. Both formations were supported by Zero escorts. Confusion reigned as aircraft "friends" returning and "foes" attacking converged at all altitudes, flak bursting and clouds obscuring the aerial battlefield. Below the *Hornet* lay dead in the water, listing with three bomb hits, two torpedo strikes, and an island destroyed by a crashed Val. Most returning Wildcat pilots were out of ammo and helpless to defend the *Enterprise*, which now became the object of the Japanese attack.

Vejtasa's second section under Reuhlow had separated at 13,000 feet. Wingman Leder saw 11 Kates 6,000 feet below in three Vics of three aircraft with a single two plane section all headed toward the *Enterprise*. Vejtasa and Harris angled into a steep high speed dive, intercepting the Japs in a high speed pass, with each pilot downing a Kate and causing the Japanese formation to scatter. Vejtasa again climbed to regain lost altitude, but lost his wingman, Harris, in the clouds. He intercepted a three plane V in heavy clouds at 2,000 feet. Closing astern, he exploded the left leg of the V with two short .50 caliber bursts. Then, sliding to the right, he concentrated on the leader, blowing off his rudder, which flew up over Vejtasa's cockpit. Fire broke out on the enemy torpedo bomber, causing it to spiral into the sea. A long burst finished the third aircraft in the V, giving Vejtasa his sixth victory of the day. He spotted another Kate closing on the fleet and made a low-side pass, missing badly. The Japanese pilot, too close to release his torpedo, then crashed his aircraft into the forward turret of the destroyer *Smith*, causing heavy casualties. "Friendly" AA fire caused Vejtasa to prudently standoff. As he circled two more Kates appeared through the haze and smoke at water level. Joined by another Wildcat that came on the scene, Vejtasa emptied his remaining ammo on the Jap bomber, causing it to crash into the sea for his seventh kill of the mission.

The *Enterprise*, damaged by two bomb hits and facing the possibility of further attacks, was forced to discontinue flight operations, so Vejtasa and other fellow pilots had to circle for 60 minutes until the *Enterprise* was able to take on her pilots and those of the floundering *Hornet*.

Lt. Stanley Vetjasa. (USN)

Added to his three victories in the Dauntless at the Battle of the Coral Sea, Vejtasa was the top American ace at the time with ten victories. His commanding officer, Jim Flatley, recommended Vejtasa for the Congressional Medal of Honor, but he was eventually awarded the Navy Cross instead. Vejtasa added a 1/2 victory in November 1942, but scored no further victories while commanding several fighter squadrons in the Pacific, Atlantic, and Mediterranean.

The Battle of Santa Cruz cost the Japanese 49 confirmed aircraft lost and 27 probable against the Navy's loss of 27 Wildcats. The Japanese had two carriers, two cruisers, and two destroyers damaged. The U.S. lost the *Hornet* and a destroyer, along with having the battleship *South Dakota*, carrier *Enterprise*, cruiser *San Juan*, and a destroyer sustain damage. Though a tactical defeat for the U.S., the battle prevented the Japanese from gaining control of the seas around Guadalcanal, thus insuring the success of the Marine efforts on the ground.

Pilot: 1Lt. James E. "Zeke" Swett
Unit: VMF-221
A/C: F4F Wildcat No.77 *"Melvin Massacre"*
Date: 7 April 1943/1455-1655
Place: Tulagi-Solomons Islands
Action: After their final evacuations from Guadalcanal on 7/8 February 1943, the Japanese High Command initiated plans to avenge the humiliating defeat. Admiral Yamamoto arrived in Rabaul in March to take personal charge of the undertaking that was coded "I Operation." Yamamoto's presence was to be his undoing, as on 18 April he would be killed when his Betty bomber was shot down in the famous "Get Yamamoto" mission led by John Mitchell and executed by Rex Barber.

Yamamoto flew 96 fighters, 65 dive bombers, and a small number of torpedo bombers from his carrier force to Rabaul. There, they would join 86 fighters, 27 dive bombers, and a few more tor-

1Lt. James "Zeke" Swett. (Author/Swett)

pedo bombers of the 11th Air Fleet. The initial phase of the attack concentrated on Guadalcanal. On 6 April, F-5 (P-38) photo recon planes discovered the large overnight buildup of aircraft on Jap-held islands in the Northern Solomons (Kihili went from 40 to 114 aircraft, and Ballale from none to 95). In the early afternoon of the 7th, the coast watching network reported a large formation, estimated at 160 Zero fighters and Val dive bombers, forming over Bougainville and heading for Guadalcanal. Among the 76 American airmen sent to intercept was 23 year old 1Lt. James "Zeke" Swett. The Seattle native had attended San Mateo Junior College in California, but quit as a sophomore to join the Marines in August 1941. He graduated from naval flight training at Corpus Christi on 15 April 1942 as a 2nd Lieutenant in the Marine Corps. After additional training he was shipped to Guadalcanal on 1 December 1942 to join VMF-221.

In the early morning of 7 April 1943, Swett arose at 0430 to lead a four plane patrol at dawn. He flew a F4F Wildcat (no. 77) named *"Melvin Massacre"* after an Al Capp "Li'l Abner" comic strip incident. The patrol was uneventful and returned to Henderson Field three hours later for breakfast. At 1130, the division again patrolled and again sighted nothing. But as they were set down, the FDO picked up a flight of Japanese aircraft approaching from the south towards Tulagi Anchorage. Grabbing a quick lunch of D-ration chocolate, Swett waited in the ready tent while his fighter was refueled to meet the "very condition red." As he took off at 1455, his armorer informed him that he had added an additional 15 .50 rounds to each gun pan. Zeke was the leader of the second division of four, five plane divisions. The FDO vectored them over Sea Lark Channel, where at 1530 they should intercept the large Japanese formation that was heading through thin cloud cover towards American shipping in Tulagi Harbor. Swett's Wildcats were jumped by Zeros, but nonetheless raced towards the Jap dive bombers, which were menacing shipping.

At 15,000 feet, 15 Vals were intercepted as they were about to dive. Swinging astern, Swett moved into the Val formation. He hit the rear Val in the fuselage with a short burst of only a few rounds, causing it to jettison its bombs prematurely and explode into flame. He then skidded and mushed to the right, getting behind the second Val and exploding it with another very short burst. Swett was unable to swing across fast enough to intercept the next Val forward, but took off after the Val above him. He had difficulty getting the third dive bomber in his sights as he dove. Following the Val down through increasingly "friendly" AA fire, Swett fired and hit it at 800 feet, destroying it. As he pulled out, a 40mm shell hit his left wing, putting a hole in it and disabling one of the two guns. He disengaged combat, heading at tree-top level over Florida Island towards a protective rain storm to check the damage to his aircraft. Satisfied that the damage was minor, he emerged from the clouds, spotting five more Vals. The Japs were retiring to the north in line astern ("Indian file"), spread very wide at about half mile intervals. He attacked the rear two bombers from below at low deflection in order to keep away from the fire of their rear gunners. The destruction of these two bombers made him an ace. The next unsuspecting Val was about a half mile ahead. Closing the gap, Swett was too eager and became buffeted in his slipstream. He eased off and was able to sight and destroy it. The seventh victim presented the perfect textbook beam deflection shot, and Swett led his quarry like a duck hunter and bagged it. By this time the remaining Val of the five was alerted to the danger. In order to set up this firing pass, he had to cross the firing radius of the rear gunner. The gunner's 7.7mm rounds smashed into his engine block and shattered his cockpit glass, severely gashing his nose and causing him to overshoot his target and not to fire. With his vision blurred from his bleeding nose and his ammo running low, Swett carefully approached the Val. He killed the rear gunner and scored several hits before his ammo ran out. The dive bomber escaped, smoking, into the clouds for a probable. Alone and trailing a two mile stream of oil, he headed back towards Henderson Field. Over Tulagi Harbor, his oil-starved engine gave out, forcing him to turn out to sea to attempt a water landing. As he turned over Tanambogo, another "friendly" AA battery fired on him as he glided downward. He hit the water hard, breaking his already damaged nose on the stick. The F4F began to sink as Swett struggled with his hung up parachute harness. Just as the fighter sank he was able to free himself. Dazed and bloody, he inflated his life raft and was soon approached by a patrol boat. Looking over he saw the crew pointing machine guns and rifles at him.

"You an American?" asked the mistrusting Coxswain.

"You God damn right I am" Swett shouted back.

"Oh, one of them Marines" the Coxswain replied, "OK, Pick him up."

VMF-221 accounted for 17 of 29 Jap losses. In his first contact with the enemy, Swett knocked down seven, which was the WWII best for Marine Corps aviators. He went on to get 8 1/2 more during his tour for a total of 15 1/2. For this action he was awarded the Medal of Honor. His feat was well-documented in the state-side media, which gave rise to the popular phrase of the time "Do a Jimmy Swett," and was a watch word for aspiring Marine pilots.

Pilot: Maj. William L. Leverette
Unit: 37FS/14FG/ 12AF
A/C: P-38 *"Stingeree"*
Date: 9 October 1943/1217
Place: Aegean Sea: off the coast of Rhodes
Action: Leverette was born in Palatka, Florida, 5 September 1913, and graduated in engineering from Clemson in 1934. He entered the Army Reserve as a 2Lt. in the Infantry. Entering the AAF, he earned his wings with Class 40-A, and subsequently was assigned to the 31PS. He spent the next two years teaching fighter tactics for the 53rd and 338th Fighter Groups in Tallahassee. By the time he was transferred to North Africa with the 14FG he had more than 1,000 hours in fighters.

At this time the English were about to invade the Greek Dodecanese Islands off the Turkish Coast. These islands were held by unenthusiastic Italian troops, and Churchill felt if the islands could be captured before the Germans could reinforce them he could persuade the neutral Turks into the Allied camp. The Turks would then open the Dardanelles Straits into the Black Sea so the Russians could be supplied. But since the Italian Campaign was a drain on Allied resources, on 4 October the 1st and 14th Fighter Groups were reluctantly transferred from Ste. Marie-du Zi, Tunisia, further

east to a RAF strip known as Gambut 2. The long-range P-38s were to provide air cover for the Royal Navy and to attack German convoys headed towards the Dodecanese.

On 9 October, the 30-year-old Leverette, CO of the 37FS, led a flight of eight P-38s on a mission to cover a Royal Navy flotilla of a cruiser and several destroyers off the island of Rhodes. As they reached the area, a mixed formation of approximately 25 Ju-87 Stuka dive bombers covered by Ju-88 twin engine bombers was about to attack the British ships. Leverette left three fighters for top cover and attacked the ungainly Stukas, which carried two wing-mounted 7.92mm MG 17 machine guns and a rear gunner manning a 7.92mm flexible MG 15 machine gun. Leverette was leading a group of inexperienced pilots, and with so many targets he warned his men to close and to make every round count. The Lightnings closed on the unsuspecting dive bombers, with Leverette getting two before the Germans could react. On his next pass he killed the rear gunner and forced the pilot to bail out of his stricken aircraft. His fourth victory was scored on a 30 degree deflection shot from 200 yards, followed by another deflection shot victory. His sixth victim fired in defense, but was quickly dispatched with a burst to the belly. Leverette was closing quickly when the Stuka, its prop shot off, nosed straight down, almost causing a collision, and Leverette's left propeller nicked the Stuka. The American's last victory came as he closed on a Stuka, only to have it turn into him. He went into an abrupt bank and fired from an almost inverted posture, destroying his seventh victim.

Meanwhile, 2Lt. Harry Hanna also became an instant ace by scoring five victories, while Leverette's wingman, Lt. Homer Spinkle, got three. 2Lts. Wayne Blue and Robert Argison scored top cover victories over a Ju-88 and another Ju-87. In 15 minutes, 16 Stukas and a Ju-88 were downed by the 37FS, which was to go on to score 105 aerial victories, largely under Leverette's leadership.

Commander of the 14FG Col. Oliver B. Taylor recommended Leverette for the Medal of Honor, especially since he pursued the attack to the point of ramming. However, decorations in the MTO

Maj. William Leverette
(Author/Leverette)

were doled out more conservatively than in other theaters, and Leverette received the Distinguished Service Cross, America's second highest award. He went on to claim four more single victories, two each over Me-109s and Me-110s to bring his career total to 11.

After the war, he received a MS in aeronautical engineering from Princeton in 1948 and went on to serve in engineering assignments with the Air Force until his retirement as a Colonel.

Pilot: Cdr. David McCampbell

Unit: VF-15 *Essex*/Task Force 58
A/C: F6F-5 *"Minsi II"*
Date: 19 June 1944
Place: Battle of Philippines Sea: "Great Marianas Turkey Shoot"
Mission I: 1139: 45 miles 245 degrees from Task Force 58
Mission II: 1515: over Orote Field/Guam

Action: In June 1944, the Marine landings on the key Marianas island of Saipan prodded the Japanese Naval High Command to send out its carriers for the first time since the Battle of Santa Cruz in October 1942. The Marianas were vital to the Japanese, as their loss would expose the Homeland to the bombs of the Air Force's new long-range B-29 bombers. On 19 June, the Imperial Navy sent nine carriers against Task Force 58's fifteen carriers, hoping that their land-based aircraft in the Marianas would equalize the disparity in carriers.

In this scenario, Cdr. David McCampbell, an old man at 34, would finally enter combat. He graduated from the Naval Academy in 1933, only to have his class dismissed because the Depression-plagued country could not afford a navy. He was recalled in 1934 and applied for naval aviation, graduating from Pensacola in 1937. As America entered the war he was stationed on the carrier *Wasp*. He saw no combat in the carrier's Atlantic cruises, and was torpedoed while aboard her during a routine patrol of Guadalcanal in October 1942. He was sent back to the States and given command of VF-15, which was being organized in the summer of 1943. After months of training the squadron was assigned to the *Essex*. McCampbell was given command of the entire *Essex* air group:

Cdr. David McCampbell (USN)

fighters; dive-bombers; and torpedo bombers—everything that flew. The carrier steamed to the Marianas to participate in the invasion. On 11 June he scored his first victory, shooting down a Zero over Saipan, and two days later he added a Helen. Then on 19 June, after fending off the initial Japanese air attack, the *Essex* dispatched ten McCampbell-led Hellcats to meet the second attack. The newest Japanese carrier, the *Taiho*, launched 128 aircraft under Lt.Cdr. Tarui. The mission soon ran into problems. Eight aircraft aborted due to mechanical difficulties, while two were shot down and eight damaged as Tarui led them over the trigger-happy forward Japanese carrier and battleship area. Nonetheless, with over 100 aircraft the Japanese pressed onward, closing on the American task force at 1100. Because his pilots were inexperienced, Tarui needed time to get them organized and into position to attack. This interlude gave McCampbell time to gain the altitude advantage. Climbing to 25,000 feet, two Hellcats developed engine problems and were sent back to circle the *Essex* in CAP. Once at altitude, VF-15 was vectored to intercept two large amalgamated formations that were stacked 1,500 feet deep on three-plane sections of a nine-plane division at about 45 miles from the task force.

Leaving four planes for top cover, McCampbell's Hellcats dove from their 5,000-foot height advantage to hit the Japanese formation on its left flank with a high-side attack. This high-side tactic was a favorite of Navy pilots. Beginning at a higher altitude, the Hellcat pilot would begin a smooth nose high turn. Then, dropping the nose to keep the enemy in sight, he would begin a banking turn in the opposite direction to reverse the turn, making sure to lead his victim.

McCampbell chose a Judy dive-bomber at the mid-left side of the formation, planning to fire and pass under the formation to then engage another plane on the right side. However, the Judy exploded directly in front of him, causing an abrupt change in his strategy. He was forced to pull up and fly across and above the entire formation, exposing himself to the bomber formation's rear gunners. He escaped to the right unscathed and attacked another Judy from above and astern, hitting it with a long burst and flaming it. He then dove below the formation, working his way forward and firing on another Judy, who left the formation smoking. McCampbell claimed it a probable. Pulling up and to the side, the Hellcat was in position to attack the Japanese formation leader and his wingman. McCampbell's run on the Jap leader was ineffective, and as he pulled up to the left he found himself above and astern the left Jap wingman. A burst from *"Minsi's"* .50 cal. machine guns exploded the dive bomber for his third victory.

Breaking down and to the left, McCampbell put himself below and astern the Jap leader. Firing a long burst, he caused the Jap plane to burn violently and spin out of control. During this run McCampbell's guns suffered stoppages, and he disengaged combat to recharge them. Returning to combat, he found the enemy formation ravaged, but its survivors pressing the attack on the task force. He overtook the leader of the lower formation, but upon firing on it the Hellcat went into a violent skid, as only his starboard guns were operating. Breaking off the attack, he recharged his guns twice as his quarry dove away, gaining speed. McCampbell pursued form astern, firing only short bursts so as not to skid. The guns scored enough hits before again stopping to cause the Judy to wing over and dive into the sea. It was a good morning for the AGC, with five victories. McCampbell tried to clear his guns to no avail. Deciding that he was nearly out of ammo anyhow, he decided to head back to the *Essex*, taking care not to get in the range of the nervous, trigger-happy American fleet. He landed at 1226.

That afternoon, while VF-15 was down being rearmed and re-fueled, TF 58 radar picked up Jap carrier aircraft from the previous attack landing at Orote Airfield on Guam for rearming and refueling. Fighter planes from the *Cowpens* (12), *Hornet* (19), *Enterprise* (8), *San Jacinto* (4), *Princeton* (4), and McCampbell's dozen from the *Essex* were ordered to Guam to sink this land-based "carrier."

Reaching 24,000 feet at 1515, the "Fabled 15" dove through scattered clouds towards the enemy aircraft. McCampbell and wingman Ens. R.L. Nall attacked the leading two Zeros of a four-plane division. On his pass Nall damaged the Jap wingman, who left the formation, while McCampbell exploded his target. In the face of two remaining experienced Jap pilots, their attack left the two Hellcats without the all-important speed and altitude advantage. The Japanese turned into the Americans, who were unable to break away. Nall's elevator was shot away, causing him to lose speed and maneuverability. A 20mm and six 7.7mm shells hit McCampbell's fighter. Finally breaking away, the two went into a Thach Weave; weaving in and out in a continuous series of turns so that no opening would be offered to the Japs to make an unopposed attack. The damage to Nall's fighter caused him to straggle, leaving him vulnerable to the two stalking Zeros. McCampbell scissored, moving sideways, enabling him to destroy the leading Zero. Nall headed back to the *Essex*, while McCampbell chased the other Zero, which split-essed toward Orote. He maneuvered astern, and the Zero countered with a slow roll. McCampbell was able to follow and fired, causing the Zero to smoke. At this point he found himself alone and surrounded by Zeros, and very prudently decided not to follow and finish off the wounded Zero.

Looking for the safety of other friendly aircraft, he spotted two SOC floatplanes picking up downed pilots. Two *Enterprise* F4U pilots were circling protectively above the rescue. Soon, Lt.Cdr. G.C. Duncan and his wingman, W.V. Twelves, of the *Essex* joined the mixed group helping fend off Zeros for half an hour so the floatplanes could taxi out of danger. By this time fuel and ammunition was running low, and many Navy fighters were rendezvousing in the area. McCampbell was unable to score, but Duncan got three and Twelves two. Thus ended what popular history was to call "The Great Marianas Turkey Shoot," and for good reason, as the Japanese lost 380 aircraft for a loss of 16 Hellcat and 13 pilots for the Navy. Air Group 15 accounted for 104 aerial victories and 136 Japanese aircraft destroyed on the ground. As a reward the Air Group was given a two-week rest at Eniwetok before supporting the invasion of Palau on 29 August.

Capt. William Shomo: Here Shomo (R) and his wingman, 2Lt. Paul Lipscomb, are congratulated by Gen. Ennis Whitehead. (Author/Shomo)

Seven Victories in a Day

Pilot: Capt. William A. Shomo
Unit: 82 TAC R Squadron/71 TAC R Group
A/C: F-6K *"Flying Undertaker"*
Date: 11 January 1945/1010
Place: Between Cabagan and Mali, N. Luzon, P.I.
See F-6 Top-Scorer PTO

Pilot: Ens. Alfred Lerch
Unit: VF-10/*Intrepid*
A/C: F6F-1D
Date: 16 April 1945/0730-0930
Place: NW of Okinawa
Action: From 1 April 1945 (L-Day, the first day of "Operation Iceberg," the invasion of Okinawa) the Japanese launched ten major kikusui, or kamikaze attacks. On 16 April, the Japanese launched the third kikusui, unleashing 165 aircraft. VF-10, aboard the *In-*

Ens. Alfred Lerch. (USN)

trepid, was a Navy unit equipped with F4U Corsairs. Early that morning, three divisions were flying CAP. Lt(jg) Phillip Kirkwood led one of these divisions, which was comprised of Ensigns Alfred Lerch, Horace Heath, and Norwal Quiel. The Corsairs had been in orbit at 10,000 feet for about 20 minutes when the FDO vectored them to intercept two individual groups of six to eight Vals and several Nates. Kirkwood ordered his division to separate, with he and Heath remaining below the clouds and Lerch and Quiel staying above. Flying at 5,000 feet, Lerch identified the Vals at 2,000 feet above him and about 4-5 miles away. Joined by Kirkwood and Heath, the four climbed and attacked a three plane section of two Vals and a Nate from the rear. Lerch and Kirkwood each got a Val, while Quiel finished off the Nate. Heath became separated from the division during the dogfight and chased a couple of Vals into the clouds, shooting one down before linking up with Lerch and going into CAP orbit.

Kirkwood and Quiel were heading back to orbit when they received a call for help from a destroyer picket which had been hit by a kamikaze. They ran into a group of seven low-flying Japanese aircraft, Vals and Nates. Ignoring the destroyer's AA fire, Kirkwood downed a Val and a Nate, while Quiel got two Nates to drive off the attack. During the next hour they defended the damaged destroyer against the determined attack of the remaining three Japs. Kirkwood became an ace in a day by shooting down two more Nates, and Quiel got the last Nate for his fourth victory. While returning back to the CAP orbit, Kirkwood and Quiel saw the AA fire from another group of picket destroyers and went on the attack. Kirkwood took off after a Nate Kamikaze that was going into a death dive from 4,000 feet and caught it with three short bursts as it was about to crash the destroyer for his sixth victory of the day.

When Lerch and Heath again arrived at CAP they saw a large formation of bomb-carrying Nates in ten three plane Vs northwest of Okinawa. The two dove on the surprised formation, and each got a Nate before the Japanese dispersed by diving towards the ocean. The poorly trained Japanese pilots, who had apparently lost their leader, flew aimlessly, and Lerch took advantage by downing three with easy no deflection runs. He then pursued three Nates heading along the northern tip of the island. As he got into a gunnery run on a Nate it exploded in front of him as Heath attacked from above. In the confusion one of the Nates escaped, but Lerch caught the third one and exploded it. The two took off after a hapless Nate, and Lerch got there first and set it on fire with a short burst for his seventh victory of the day.

Nine Navy Aces in a Day: 24 October 1944 Battle of Leyte Gulf
Pilots:
Cdr. David McCampbell (9)
Lt. Roy Rushing (6)
Lt(jg) William Masoner (6)
Lt. Thomas Conroy (6)
Lt. Cdr. Harold Funk (6)
Lt. Ken Hippe (6)
Lt. Eugene Townsend (5)
Lt. James Shirley (5)
Lt. Carl Brown (5)

McCampbell's F6F "Minsi" (9v.). (Author/McCampbell)

Lt. Roy Rushing (6v.). (Author/Rushing)

Lt(jg) William Masoner (6v.). (USN)

Lt. Thomas Conroy (6v.). (USN)

The Battle of Leyte Gulf, 24 October 1944, produced nine aces in a day. As previously chronicled, *Essex* ACG David McCampbell downed an American record nine, while his wingman, Lt. Roy Rushing, got six. The other stars of this battle were Lt.Cdr. Frederick Bardshar's VF-27 from the *Princeton*, which counted four daily aces in its ranks. RAdm. Frederick Sherman's TG 38.3, which included the carriers *Essex, Lexington, Langley,* and *Princeton*, was stationed 100 miles east of Luzon and bore the brunt of the air battle. Three divisions from the *Princeton* were on CAP, including those of Lts. James "Red" Shirley and Carl Brown. FDO gave Shirley two radar vectors to track Japanese search planes. At 0800 Shirley downed a twin engine Army Nick snooper. Brown was also vectored twice, but each time met false alarms, American TBF Avenger torpedo bombers with their IFF shut down. Soon the FDO gave Brown's division (stationed at 10,000 feet) and Shirley's (at 20,000 feet) the same vector for a large group of bogies flying at 20,000 to 23,000 feet. As Brown's division reached 20,000, Shirley had already downed two Tojo, Ki-44 Army fighters. The two divisions closed up, and they spotted the large Japanese formation numbering upwards of 80 aircraft. Brown and Shirley radioed the *Princeton* "Hatchet Base" of the incoming enemy and then led their men into the fray. Shirley used up his ammunition downing another Tojo and a Zeke, giving him five victories for the day and 12 1/2 for the war. Carl Brown, climbing into the formation, found his Hellcat at a speed and altitude disadvantage and was hit numerous times, suffering leg wounds. Nonetheless, he downed five Zekes and had to shake four from his tail with an intense, plane-rattling maneuver to save himself. As he returned to the *Princeton*, Brown found his instrument panel damaged, the cockpit floor pooled with gasoline, and his tail hook unable to extend for landing. Then, to make matters worse, the *Princeton's* decks were filled, and then *Langley* and *Lexington* refused him because of his tail hook situation. As he prepared to ditch, the *Essex* volunteered to take him. As he landed the stuck tail hook shook loose and grabbed the arresting wire. Brown had scored all his victories of the war.

During the battle two other VF-27 divisions joined Shirley and Brown. Ens. Thomas Conroy shot down three Tojos and three Zekes that gave him his final total of seven victories. Lt(jg) Gene Townsend shot down five Tojos to give him all the victories he would get in the war.

Lt(jg) William Masoner, of VF-19 off the *Lexington*, took off shortly after 0600 on a search mission. At 0730 his section encountered 20 twin-engine bombers formed into four groups. In the ensuing combat he downed a Betty, a Dinah, and four Nells, and damaged another Nell for six victories on the mission to give him 11 total, to which he added a Zeke two weeks later.

Lt. Ken Hippe was flying CAP for VC-3 of the *Kalinin Bay*, which was a CVE escort carrier of Task Force 774, when he scored all his WWII victories (five). He was flying a FM-2, which was an upgraded version of the F4F Wildcat, when he spotted a lone twin engine Lily bomber over northern Luzon. Getting above and behind the bomber, he hit it in the wing root, causing it to roll over and crash just offshore. After another contact which escaped, Hippe's division was vectored at about 0900 toward a formation of 21 Lilys stacked in a V of Vs. Maneuvering to get into position for the Navy's favorite mode of attack, the high-side pass, Hippe and his wingman, Ens. John Buchanan, closed. Hippe attacked a group of four bombers, while Buchanan chose a group of three. Hippe, coming high astern on the slowly diving bombers, attacked the first, flaming it with wing and fuselage hits. Continuing his run, he got a second from below, and then burned the third and fourth. In less than ten minutes Hippe became an ace.

Another "Baby flat-top" aviator of TF 77.4, Lt.Cdr. Harold Funk, leader of VF-26 off the *Santee* also scored as an ace in a day on 24 October. Leaving at 0510, Funk led a group of three FM-2s (one plane crashed on take off, killing the pilot) to patrol off Leyte Gulf. The FDO vectored them over San Jacinto Strait. At 0920 four Sally, Army heavy bombers were spotted 2,000 feet above at 13,000 feet. Climbing, Funk made an ineffective head on pass on the lead bomber. On his second firing run he downed a Sally. The FDO directed Funk and his section to rendezvous and climb. At 15,000 feet they encountered 30 plus bombers in widespread waves of four abreast, escorted by fighters. Funk's trio made a head on pass, with Funk getting his second bomber of the day. His wingman, Ens. H.V. Shulz, was nearly rammed by Funk's victim, and in trying to evade it a Zeke get on his tail. Funk came to the rescue and claimed his third victory. The group reorganized and attacked a new wave of Jap Sally bombers. Funk went into an overhead pass, turning in a stern attack. His four .50 caliber machine guns hit the bomber in the wing, setting it on fire and causing the fuel tank to explode, shattering the wing and leaving the stricken bomber to spin into the ocean. Another Sally came into the area and Funk shot it down in two passes for his fifth victory, while also spending all his ammunition. On a later mission that day at 1750, he downed a Navy twin engine Irving recon bomber for his sixth victory of the day (6 1/2 for the war).

Seven Navy Aces in a Day: 19 June 1944 Marianas Turkey Shoot
Pilots:
Cdr. David McCampbell (7)
Lt. Alex Vraciu (6)
Lt. Wilbur Webb (6)
Lt. Cdr. Charles Brewer (5)
Lt. Russell Reiserer (5)
Lt. George Carr (5)
Lt. William Lamb (5)

The Battle of the Philippines Sea, 19 June 1944, produced seven aces in a day. In 13 hours the Japanese lost a staggering 380 aircraft (Olynyk). During a debriefing session on the *Lexington* after the battle, Lt. Cdr. Paul Buie of VF-16 listened to one of his pilots describe the lopsided battle as "an old-time turkey shoot." Buie passed the remark on to Adm. Marc Mitscher, and whether the story is genuine or not, the battle will forever be known in U.S. Naval history as "The Great Marianas Turkey Shoot." Navy fighters participated in over 400 sorties, of which 290 made contact with Japanese. Squadrons VF-1, 2, 15, 16, and 27 had pilots score five or more victories that day.

VF-15, under Cdr. David McCampbell, had three pilots score five or more victories. The redoubtable McCampbell, as described previously, scored seven (five and two) in two sorties. Cdr. Charles Brewer, skipper of VF-15 encountered 16 Judy dive-bombers at 18,000 feet escorted by four Zeros on each flank. He quickly exploded two Judys and got a Zero at the edge of the formation. A Zero got on his tail, but a quick turn reversed the situation, and after a running dogfight he downed his skillful opponent, which made him an ace with 5 1/2 total victories when added to his 1 1/2 previous victories. Later that afternoon at 1825 he shot down a Zero landing on Orote Airfield, Guam. His firing run caused him to lose speed and altitude, and he and his wingman were bounced and killed by Zeros. Lt. George Carr was the leader of Brewer's second section encountering the same Japanese formation. He attacked a Judy that exploded in front of his Hellcat, disorienting him. Climbing back into battle he surprised another Judy, splashing it, but found a Zero on his tail. A 90-degree high-speed dive followed by an aileron roll to the right shook the Zero, but another Zero came directly at him. Both aircraft fired, the Zero was flamed, and Carr's windshield was hit and "snowed." He got on the tail of a Zero and set it on fire, and quickly shifted to a second Jap and fired on it, causing it to smoke and lose altitude and explode to make Carr an instant ace.

Lt(jg) Alex Vraciu of VF-16 *Lexington*, a student of the redoubtable "Butch" O'Hare, was part of standby groups of 12 fighters launched to supplement the CAP already aloft. Vraciu led Cdr. Paul Buie's second division. Soon two Hellcats were stranded when first division leader Buie and his wingman aborted due to mechanical problems joined him. (Buie ditched and was fortunate to be found and picked up by a destroyer 12 hours later). Vraciu discovered that his supercharger would not shift into high blower, and his engine was throwing oil on his windshield. When he reported this

Cdr. David McCampbell (7v.). (Author/McCampbell)

Lt. Alex Vraciu (6v.). (Author/Vraciu)

Lt. Wilbur Webb (6v.). (USN)

problem to the *Lexington* FDO, Vraciu was told he was needed to lead his division to circle at 20,000 feet. But soon the FDO vectored Vraciu to 265 degrees, which led them 35 miles to a rambling formation of over 50 Japs, 2,000 feet below, portside and closing. Peering through his oil-blurred windshield, he began a firing run on a straggling Judy dive-bomber, but was almost blindsided by another attacking Hellcat and was forced to abort his run. Vraciu closed on another Judy astern, flaming it. He pulled up quickly and closed on two more Judys flying in a loose wing. He moved astern, shooting down one and then, dipping the Hellcat's wing, slid over, getting the second on the same pass. The Japanese formation continued to fly toward the fleet. When a Judy broke formation Vraciu slid astern, getting a short burst into its wing root and causing it to burn and spin into the sea. By the time the Jill torpedo bombers were beginning their runs the Judys were also about to peel off to dive bomb the fleet. Vraciu closed on a column of three Judys that had penetrated the destroyer screen. Ignoring "friendly" AA fire, he torched a diving Judy with a short burst. Continuing on, he hit another Judy that exploded so violently that he could feel the heat in his cockpit. Vraciu used only 360 rounds to shoot down six enemy aircraft, probably because he needed to get in close to see through his oil-streaked windshield to fire. He added a Zero the next day to give him 19 victories, making him the Navy's top-scoring ace for the next three months.

Lt(jg) W.B. "Spider" Webb of the *Hornet's* VF-2 "Rippers" was assigned to a late afternoon strike against some new targets in the Agana Town area on Guam. Webb was tail end Charlie of a high cover division of fighters. As the division passed over the Orote Peninsula, Webb spotted a Navy pilot on a raft about 100 yards from the Jap-held shore. Webb dropped down to cover the downed pilot, while his section leader tried to get the attention of an OS2U Kingfisher rescuing another downed flyer about three miles away. Webb circled, dropping dye markers when he noticed a long line of 40 to 50 aircraft, some with landing gear down, approaching the Orote Airfield. He then radioed his famous call: "Any American fighter near Orote Airfield, I have 40 Jap planes surrounded and need a little help." Webb moved into the Japanese traffic pattern and slipped behind three Vals. He exploded the left one with a short burst and then hit the leader in the left wing root, exploding it. Webb then skidded behind the right Val, hitting it in the right wing root and also exploding it. He moved behind another three-plane Val section at 300 feet with only four guns operable, but he was able to hit the rear gunner and pilot and flame the Val. Sliding close behind the center Val, Webb's shells exploded it with debris flying around him. His five Vals were all destroyed in 12 to 15 minutes at a close-in range of 30 to 100 feet behind and all below 1,000 feet altitude. In order to stay in close behind his victims, Webb had to constantly use flaps and power to prevent collisions. Webb's guns stopped, and he left the Jap landing pattern. When he managed to recharge four of his guns he returned to combat, where he followed a Val turning into its final landing approach. His .50 cal. rounds flamed the bomber, which crashed onto the rocks below. At only 300 feet

he moved behind two Vals, hitting the leading Val with a short burst into the wing and rear seat. Webb had to quickly break combat to avoid hitting the ground and did not see his target crash, so he was awarded a probable. He chased a Val attempting to land, and at 200 feet altitude made a firing pass that caused the Jap to smoke and go into a roll. Again Webb did not see the aircraft go in. His gun cameras malfunctioned after his sixth victory, so he was awarded two probables. When he returned to the *Hornet*, his landing gear had been shot out, his canopy shattered, and his goggles shot off his helmet. There were 147 holes in his Hellcat, which was subsequently written off for spare parts. Adm. Marc Mitscher recommended him for the Medal of Honor, but he was awarded the Navy Cross instead.

Lt. Russ Reiserer of VF(N)-76, a night fighter squadron, was assigned to the *Hornet* and flew the new F6F-3N Hellcat, which carried airborne radar. During the air battles of the Turkey Shoot, VF(N)-76 was set down, as their specialized training made them too valuable to risk in daylight combat. Finally, late in the afternoon, after it appeared that the Japanese had been annihilated, four of the squadron's pilots were allowed to escort a group of SB2C Helldivers to destroy Japanese AA positions operating on Orote Airfield on Guam. However, they were not to fly their night fighters, but flew VF-2 daylight Hellcats. The four escorts made two long strafing runs during the SB2C dive-bombing attacks. As he pulled up from his second run, Reiserer spotted a U.S. Navy cruiser floatplane picking up a downed pilot near Orote. As they circled the rescue, a large number of aircraft, first thought to be another U.S. carrier strike, approached. As the formation closed they were identified as 65 to 70 Japanese wanting to land at Orote. The four pilots joined the Jap landing pattern and quickly separated into individual dogfights. Reiserer fired on some Zeros, and then turned his attention to a group of six Vals that were trying to escape. He chased them across the island, picking them off one by one, and was able to knock down four Vals. During the earlier strafing he had emptied his four outboard guns and had only two inboard guns remaining to use on these four Vals. He emptied these guns, but pursued the remaining, a Val which maneuvered at treetop level trying to lose him before turning out to sea. Unable to summon help due to radio malfunction, he continued to harass the Val, dropping his wheels, flaps, and tail hook to avoid over running the slow bomber. Reiserer faked hitting the Val's tail with his prop several times, so discouraging the Jap that he turned into the wind and made a water landing to get away from the exasperating Hellcat. So Reiserer scored his fifth victory of the day without firing a shot. He totaled only one more victory during the war.

Lt. William Lamb, VF-27 executive officer, scored two victories over Kate dive-bombers at 1030 before heading his Hellcat back to the *Princeton* to refuel and rearm. At 1242 he spotted 12 Jill torpedo bombers about 40 miles out. As he was alone he kept out of combat, reporting his position before engaging. Lamb had to make repeated passes on the formation due to gun stoppages. Nonetheless, he managed to down three more Japs to give him five victories: all he was to score during his tour.

The Other Turkey Shoot: Japan 16 February 1945:
Pilots:
Lt. Patrick Fleming VBF-80 (5)
Cdr. Leroy Keith VF-80 (5)
Lt. William Edwards VF-80 (5)
Lt. Alexander Anderson VF-80 (5)
Cdr. Gordon Schecter VF-45 (5)
Ens. Robert Kidwell VF-45 (5)

New York City resident Patrick Fleming graduated from the Naval Academy in 1941 and was assigned to the cruiser *Cincinnati*, where he served until he was attached to flight school. He served as a flight instructor at NAS Atlantic City from December 1943 to March 1944. He was posted with VF-80 off the *Ticonderoga* flying F6F-5 Hellcats. In November 1944 he scored three victories in two combats. On 14 December, VF-80 attacked Japanese airfields in preparation for the invasion of Luzon. On the way to the target the Hellcats spotted a number of unsuspecting Zekes and Oscars and jettisoned their bombs and rockets to attack. The U.S. Navy gives Fleming credit for four Zekes for the day. Diligent aerial victory researcher Dr. Frank Olynyk gives Fleming credit for an additional Oscar that day to make him an ace in a day. Meanwhile, Lt. Robert Anderson got five Zekes and an Oscar and Capt. Richard "Zeke" Cormier got four Zekes and an Oscar to also become aces in a day.

Fleming downed a Tojo and two Oscars (or Zekes?) on 3 January 1945. On 10 January, VF-80 was divided into two, VF-80 and VBF-80, with Fleming becoming Exec of VBF-80. On 21 January, the *Ticonderoga* was hit and sunk by two kamikazes, and CAG-80 transferred to the *Hancock*. On 16 February Fleming led nine F6Fs on an afternoon mission to attack Japanese airfields on the Chiba Peninsula. This was the first raid on Tokyo since the Doolittle raid on 18 April 1942. This raid followed a successful morning VF-80 mission in which VF-80 CO Cdr. Leroy "Pete" Keith and his second section leader, Lt. William Edwards, each shot down five Japanese aircraft (Keith: 2 Oscars, a Zeke, a Nate, and a Val; Edwards: 2 Nates, 2 Zekes, and an Oscar). Fleming's men dropped their ord-

nance on Mobara Airfield and got hits on its hangars and buildings. After their run Fleming spotted Zekes flying north of the field at a high altitude. The flight caught the Japs just as they were trying to escape into the cloud base. He quickly downed two Zekes from astern, and then got two more in a chase down to ground level. He claimed a fifth as a probable, but it was confirmed later to make him an ace-in-a-day for possibly a second time. In another VF-80 raid at the same time Lt. Alexander Anderson got five (2 Oscars, a Zeke, a Tony, and Tojo) over Imba Airfield to give the *Hancock* four aces in a day and 73 victories that day.

During the running air battle over Japan that day two pilots from VF-45 off the *San Jacinto* also became aces in a day. Cdr. Gordon Schecter, Squadron CO, and Ens. Robert Kidwell became aces in a day, each in two missions. In the morning mission running from Ktori to Mobara Schecter got half a Dinah, half a Claude, three Zekes, and a Zeke probable, while Kidwell claimed a Zeke, a Tony, and a Claude. Then, in a late afternoon sortie from Nakajima Oto to north of Chosi Point, Schecter got an Oscar for his fifth victory and a Tojo probable, while Kidwell got two Tonys for five victories. (Note: Schecter was killed by AA fire over Okinawa on 18 March 1945). A total of 270 Japanese aircraft were destroyed that day.

Still another Turkey Shoot: Okinawa 6 April 1945 Invasion
Pilots:
Ens. Carl Foster VF-30 (6)
Ens. Kenneth Dahms VF-30 (5 1/2)
Ens. Johnnie Miller VF-30 (5)
Lt(jg) Willis Hardy VF-17 (5)

On 6 April 1945 the Japanese launched their first of ten massed Kikusui Kamikaze attacks on U.S. shipping off Okinawa. It was to be their largest attack, composed of 355 aircraft. The Japanese pilots acted strangely, not returning fire or taking any evasive action, but instead headed directly towards shipping at wave top level. This was to be the first time American pilots met determined massed Kamikaze suicide attacks.

In the afternoon 15 F6Fs from the *Belleau Wood* OD were on CAP defending the newly secured beach head when late into the CAP a mixed formation of 20 Vals, Zekes, and Tojos carrying one or two 200kg bombs were intercepted at sea level. True to Kamikaze tactics, the bombers flew directly towards the fleet without taking any evasive action. The Hellcat pilots easily picked off the Jap bombers. Ens. Carl Foster got 3 Vals, 2 Tojos, and a Zeke; Ens. Kenneth Dahms got 3 Vals, 2 Zekes, and shared an Oscar; while Ens. Johnnie Miller claimed 3 Vals, a Zeke, and a Tojo. VF-30 was credited with 32 Japanese aircraft.

That same afternoon F6Fs from VF-17 off the *Hornet* were on CAP when large numbers of Kamikazes closed on the shipping. At the beginning of their patrol, Lt(jg) Willis Hardy and Lt(jg) Harrison Morgan were vectored to a Zeke and a Judy flying in close formation at 2,500 feet. In diving stern attacks, Hardy got the Zeke, and Morgan, the Judy. Pulling up from the attack they saw four Vals heading away from them at 2,500 feet towards a picket. The Hellcats executed a climbing turn and were able to gain the altitude advan-

Lt. Patrick Fleming (5v.). (USN)

Ens. Carl Foster (6 v.).
(USN)

tage, diving from astern. Hardy and Morgen added 2 Vals apiece in this attack. The two pilots chased a lone Judy and attacked. When Morgan opened fire he found that he was out of ammo. Hardy closed to 300 feet astern and fired a three second burst into the cockpit, setting it on fire. The Jap pilot rose from his seat to bail out, but appeared to be hung up on something and got back in. He regained control of the bomber, but not in time, as the Judy hit the water and exploded. Hardy's fifth victory was unusual. A Judy, thinking the Hellcats were friendly, turned to join the formation. Morgan, out of ammo, got on one side, and Hardy, with only one gun operating, got the other side of the Judy, boxing it in. Morgan turned into the Judy, who reflexively turned toward Hardy, who fired a short burst, but then had to recharge his gun. The two Navy pilots did this maneuver several times without much luck. Finally, Hardy, while charging his gun, lowered his flaps, turning inside the Judy, and was able to get a long burst at short range, hitting the cockpit and causing it to crash into the ocean. During the air battle that day Navy pilots scored 257 victories with minimal losses.

Three Marine Aces in a Day: 22 April 1945
Pilots:
Major Jeffrson Dorroh (6)
Major George Axtell (5)
1Lt. Jerry O'Keefe (5)

By April 1945, the American qualitative and quantitative superiority in the air was undeniable, but nevertheless did not properly reflect the effectiveness of Japanese tactics. The principal task of the Japanese fighters was not to engage in dogfights for air superiority, but to herd the Kamikazes and other dive and torpedo bombers to their intended victims. So, while it is true that the Japanese suffered grievous losses on every mission, one has to examine the results of these raids. Thousands of American seamen were killed and wounded, and major material damage was done to the ships of the fleet. In this perspective the Japanese could justify their strategy.

The most proficient of all Marine squadrons in gaining lopsided victory totals was VMF-323. In less than two months over Okinawa the F4U-D Corsairs of the "Death Rattlers" scored 124 1/2 victories without a single combat loss. On 22 April, three VMF-323 Marines who had never scored an aerial victory became aces. Maj. George Axtell, Squadron CO, Maj. Jeff Dorroh, and 1Lt. Jerry O'Keefe had waited over two years in training for their chance to get at the Japs. Axtell assumed command of VMF-323 in May 1943 and was the youngest CO in the Marine Corps at 23. In April 1945, the squadron was transferred to Okinawa via escort carrier to become part of the Marine land-based fighter contingent stationed there.

At 1800 on 22 April 1945, after an uneventful day two "Death Rattler" CAP elements were vectored westward to the destroyer picket line, 40 miles to the north of Aguni Shima in the East China Sea. About 35 low-flying Japanese Navy Vals were closing on the harassed little picket destroyers in scattered to heavy clouds with occasional showers. Axtell led one three-plane element (one aborted in route due to engine problems). At 1830, the seven F4U-Ds intercepted the slow, but very maneuverable Japanese dive bombers, which split up and took evasive action. Axtell attacked with beam runs from slightly above with 10-45 degree deflection shots, and 15 minutes later had claimed five down and three damaged.

It was now Jerry O'Keefe's turn. Dropping full flaps to remain in firing position, O'Keefe attacked the Vals methodically, knocking down four from a point blank 6 o'clock position. He was scissoring with a fifth Val and made a head on run. The Val kept coming, looking as though he was going to ram the Marine. O'Keefe pressed the trigger until the bomber fell off on one wing at 50 feet and crashed into the ocean. O'Keefe had to pull up violently to avoid collision. He left combat with ammo in only two guns. After the battle he said, "It was one of the most exhilarating, brief moments of my life."

Top scorer of the combat was Jeff Dorroh, who was flying his ninth mission of the war. Dorroh's three plane section located the same Val formation that Axtell encountered. Upon seeing the large

Three Death Rattler aces in a day are congratulated by Gen. Alexander Vandegrift (2L), and Gen. Francis Mulcahy (center). The VMF-323 aces are Maj. George Axtell (5v.) (R), Maj. Jefferson Dorroh (6v.) (2L) and 1Lt. Jerry O'Keefe (5v.) (L). (USMC/O'Keefe)

number of enemy aircraft he switched off two of his guns. He had to drop his wheels and flaps to stay behind the first Val, which made a sharp turn. He hit the bomber from astern, killing the pilot. In the next twenty minutes Dorroh made wide deflection gunnery runs on six other Vals, hitting each. Two burning Vals were seen but not confirmed, giving him five victories. On the way back to base at Kadena, he joined 2Lt. Charlie Allen of Axtell's element. They spotted a fleeing Val, and Dorroh urged Allen to go after it. But Allen was out of ammo, so Dorroh set it on fire with another deflection shot to gain his sixth victory of the day.

All three pilots began the battle without a victory and came back "instant aces." In his next 24 missions Dorroh did not score, while Axtell and O'Keefe downed one and two Nates, respectively, on the same mission six days later, and would get no more claims during their tours. Axtell and Dorroh received the Navy Cross, while O'Keefe received the DFC for their action on 22 April. The seven – 323 pilots returned to base with 24 3/4 victories, the highest daily total for any air squadron during the Okinawa campaign.

Six Victories in a Day and the CMH
Pilot: Lt.Col. Neel Kearby
Unit: 348FG/HQ/5AF
A/C: P-47D *"Firey Ginger"*
Date: 11 October 1943/1125-1130
Place: 30-mile radius of Borum Airstrip, Wewak, New Guinea.
Action: The Allies' decision "Europe first" forced the U.S. Air Force in the Pacific to cope with their outclassed P-40 Warhawks and P-39 Airacobras throughout 1942 and into 1943. So it was out of necessity that the huge Republic Thunderbolt came to the Pacific. Actually, the sleek, twin engine P-38 Lightning, which was more or less a European outcast itself, was the preferred choice of Fifth Air Force Commander Gen. George Kenney. The P-47, he felt, was just too large and heavy to handle the nimble and highly maneuverable Japanese fighters. But being in no position to be choosy, Kenney reluctantly accepted the P-47s of the 348FG, which were led by a 32-year-old Texan from Wichita Falls, Lt.Col. Neel Kearby. Kearby

**LtCol. Neel Kearby.
(USAF)**

was confident that the "Jug," with its great speed and heavy armament was ideally suited for the hit and run tactics pioneered by Gen. Claire Chennault's AVG Flying Tigers. The 2,000hp Pratt & Whitney R-2800 radial engine was the world's most powerful, and gave the Thunderbolt a great operational ceiling and diving speed. Kearby felt that undetected high speed from an altitude advantage would negate the Japanese dog fighters. At that stage of the war Japanese pilots were highly trained and skilled. But Japanese fighters were designed for climbing and maneuverability, lacking armor and self-sealing fuel tanks and making them vulnerable to being set on fire by the P-47's .50 caliber machine guns and incendiary ammunition.

On 20 June 1943, the three squadrons (340th, 341st, and 342nd) of the 348FG arrived at Brisbane, Australia. By mid-July, its aircraft were assembled and tested, and its pilots acquainted with air fighting tactics in the SWPA Theater. A month later the Group left Australia and flew 1,200 miles, arriving at Port Moresby to begin operations. A lack of auxiliary fuel tanks caused the group to be limited operationally to the Moresby area, which had been long ignored by the Japanese, and thus they did not see combat for some time. Finally, on 4 September, the drop tank situation was remedied, and Kearby's pilots were able to go to the enemy. Kearby dove from a 4,000-foot height advantage to knock down a Betty bomber and an Oscar escort for his first victories. During the next several weeks Kearby led the 348th on bomber escort missions, fighter sweeps, and protective cover missions for shipping without seeing much combat. Things were to change on 11 October.

Kearby left Port Moresby at 0730, leading P-47s of Captains William Dunham and John Moore and Major Raymond Gallagher. The foursome landed at the newly completed forward airfield at Tsili Tsili at 0915 for refueling. Once refueled, the P-47s climbed to 28,000 feet, arriving over Wewak and its nearby Borum Airfield. The weather was unusual, clear with only scattered clouds between 2,000 and 8,000 feet. The empty belly tanks were jettisoned at 1115, as a lone Zeke fighter was tally ho'd at 8 o'clock low and 20,000 feet. Kearby dove from 7 o'clock high, opening fire from 300 yards and obviously surprising the Jap pilot, who took no evasive action and was hit, catching fire and crashing into the sea. Kearby led the four P-47s up to 26,000 feet and immediately to the east spotted a mixed group of 36 Zeke, Hap, and Tonys at 10 to 12,000 feet escorting a dozen unidentified bombers flying at 5,000 feet. In spite of the Japanese numerical superiority, the 348th dove on the large and unsuspecting formation. Kearby closed on a Zeke, opening fire at 500 yards and flaming it, as it took no evasive action. Sliding to the left, closing from 7 o'clock, and firing a short burst from 500 yards, he flamed a Hamp that also took no evasive action. As he looked up he saw a Hamp turning at 8 o'clock. A quick burst flamed the Jap fighter for his fourth career victory. Running low on fuel and ammo and outnumbered by a now alerted enemy, Kearby put *"Fiery Ginger"* into a full power climb. Leveling off at 20,000 feet he was joined by Dunham's P-47, and the two set off for Lae. At once they saw a P-47 below with two Tonys closing astern. The two pilots dove to help, with Dunham acting as wingman, protecting his CO's tail. Kearby's Thunderbolt, hitting 500mph in its dive, came on the tail of the rear Tony. He fired at 500 yards on the un-

Two aces in a day. Good friends Neel Kearby (L) and wife, Virginia, and Bill Leverette (R) and wife, Frances, have dinner before each left for his tour of duty. On 9 October 1943, Leverette downed 7 Ju-87 Stuka dive bombers over North Africa and two days later, Kearby got 6 Japanese in the Pacific and was awarded the CMH for the combat. (Author/Leverette)

suspecting Jap, flaming it. The second Tony, now alerted to the attack, dove to escape. Firing from 2,000 feet, Kearby's shells hit the Tony at this long range, tearing off pieces of wing and fuselage. Later, back at base, Dunham confirmed the victory, Kearby's sixth of the day. It is interesting to note that all six victims caught fire due to their vulnerability to incendiary ammunition. This allowed the Pacific P-47 pilot to open fire at twice the range of his ETO counterpart. Also, the large size of the Thunderbolt made it a very stable firing platform, even with eight machine guns firing.

Dunham and Kearby headed back to Wewak and encountered an escaping Tony, but Kearby made a poorly calculated deflection shot, using most of his remaining ammo. Another Tony got on his tail, and he had to dive into nearby clouds to escape. As he came out of the protecting clouds, Kearby saw the battle was over and radioed his P-47s to regroup and head to Lae for refueling, and then to continue on back to Port Moresby.

Capt. John Moore was credited with two Tonys, while Dunham got one. When Kenney was informed of Kearby's six victories he recommended to MacArthur that he be nominated for the Medal of Honor. On 24 January 1944, MacArthur presented the CMH to Kearby in a ceremony in Brisbane.

On 5 March 1944, Kearby was shot down and killed leading his P-47s over Wewak. He had shot down a Japanese bomber for his 22nd victory, breaking a tie with Dick Bong for top American ace. When Kearby turned to attack another bomber he was jumped by three Oscars from above and behind. His wingmen managed to knock down a Jap each during their head on attacks, but the third got a long burst into Kearby's *"Fiery Ginger IV,"* which dove into the ground. Dick Bong scored two victories that day to become the leading ace in the Pacific, never to be surpassed.

Lt. Cdr. Conny Nooy-Multiple Daily Scorer

Lt(jg) Cornelius Nooy could have easily been America's top multiple ace in a day. The VF-31 Hellcat pilot had five claims in four different combats. In early 1944, while flying off the *Cabot* he scored three victories in two missions. On Independence Day 1944 Nooy downed four Zekes and got a smoking probable on a sweep over the Bonin Islands to win the Navy Cross.

In September the *Cabot* moved up to the Philippines, and on the 13th Nooy claimed three victories and two damaged over Oscars near the Negros Islands. Eight days later VF-31 attacked Clark Field on Luzon. On a bombing mission Nooy engaged a large group of Japanese fighters. Instead of dropping his 500lb bombs he went after them and downed two Zekes and two Tojos. After bombing his target and out of ammunition, he flew a fifth victim, a Tony, into the ground to become an ace in a day and win his second Navy Cross.

Nooy flew his second tour for VF-31 off the *Belleau Wood* in July 1945. Navy carriers were launching large strikes against airfields on the Japanese Homeland. Now a Lt. Commander, the 24 year old New Yorker led a flight on a strafing run over Yokaichi Airfield on 25 July. His Hellcats were bounced by a large enemy formation, and he turned into the attack and shot down two Franks. Rejoining the division, he came into combat again, claiming two more Franks and having another get away as a probable. The previous day he hit a Japanese battleship in Kure Harbor with a 500lb bomb. For these final actions he became one of the few men to be awarded the Navy Cross three times.

Nooy was credited with 19 victories during the war, tying him as the fourth highest scoring Navy ace with Pat Fleming and Alex Vraciu. Of his victories, he scored 16 victories, two probables, and damaged in only four combats, almost becoming an ace in a day four times.

LtCdr. Cornelius Nooy. (USN)

Rank	Pilot Name	Fgtr Grp	Date	#V	#P	#D	Victory Numbers	Career Victories
1Lt	Allen, William	55	09/05/44	5	0	0	1-5	5
1Lt	Anderson, Richard	318	05/25/45	5	0	0	1-5	5
1Lt	Archibald, David	368	12/22/44	5	0	1	1-5	5
Capt	Bankey, Ernest	364	12/27/44	5.5	0	0	3-7.5	9.5
1Lt	Beyer, William	361	09/27/44	5	0	0	2-6	9
LCol	Blickenstaff, Wayne	353	03/24/45	5	0	0	6-10	10
Capt	Blumer, Lawrence	367	08/25/44	5	0	0	1-5	6
Capt	Bryan, Donald	352	11/02/44	5	0	2	7-11	13.5
1Lt	Carr, Bruce	353	04/02/45	5	0	1	9-13	15
Capt	Carson, Leonard	357	11/27/44	5	0	0	7.5-11.5	18.5
Capt	Christianson, Fred	56	07/07/44	6	0	0	16.5-21.5	21.5
2Lt	Cleaveland, Art	57	04/18/43	5	0	0	1-5	5
1Lt	Daniell, J.S.	339	11/26/44	5	0	0	1-5	5
2Lt	Duffy, Richard	57	04/18/43	5	0	1	1-5	5
Maj	Elder, Robert	353	03/24/45	5	0	1	1-5	5
Capt	Green, Herschel	325	01/30/44	6	0	0	4-9	18
2Lt	Hanna, H.T.	14	10/09/43	5	0	1	1-5	5
2Lt	Hatch, Herbert	1	06/10/44	5	1	1	1-5	5
Maj	Hovde, William	355	12/05/44	5.5	0	0	6-10.5	10.5
Col	Kearby, Neel	348	10/11/43	6	0	0	4-9	22
1Lt	Lesicka, Joseph	18	07/15/43	5	0	0	4-8	9
Maj	Leverette, William	14	10/09/43	7	0	2	1-7	11
1Lt	Lewis, William	55	09/05/44	5	0	0	1-5	7
1Lt	Luksic, Carl	352	05/08/44	5	0	0	3-7	8.5
1Lt	Lusk, Virgil	49	11/24/42	5	0	0	1-5	5
LCol	McComas, Edward	23	12/23/44	5	0	0	9-13	14
1Lt	McDaniel, Gordon	325	03/14/45	5	0	0	2-6	6
1Lt	Olson, Paul	368	12/22/44	5	0	0	1-5	5
1Lt	Perdomo, Paul	507	08/13/45	5	0	0	1-5	5
2Lt	Powers, McArthur	324	04/18/43	5	0	0	1-5	5
Maj	Preddy, George	352	08/06/44	6	0	0	17.8-22.8	26.8
1Lt	Rankin, Robert	56	05/12/44	5	0	0	0.25-5.25	5.25
Col	Schilling, David	56	12/23/44	5	0	0	18.5-22.5	22.5
Capt	Shomo, William	82R	01/11/45	7	0	0	2-8	8
2Lt	Shubin, Murray	347	06/16/43	5	1	0	3-7	11
1Lt	Skogsted, Norman	31	03/25/45	5	0	0	8-12	12
Capt	Vogt, John	318	05/28/45	5	1	0	1-5	5
Capt	Voll, John	31	11/16/44	5	0	0	17-21	21
1Lt	Wheadon, Elmer	18	07/01/44	5	0	0	2-6	7
Capt	Whisner, William	352	11/21/44	6	2	0	5.5-10.5	15.5
Capt	Willaimson, Felix	56	01/14/45	5	0	0	7-11	13
LCol	Woods, Sidney	4	03/22/45	5	0	0	1-5	5
1Lt	Woody, Robert	355	04/24/45	5	0	1	3.5-7.5	7.5
1Lt	Yeager, Charles	357	10/12/44	5	0	0	2.5-6.5	11.5

Rank	Pilot Name	Squad VF/VC	Date	#V	#P	#D	Victory Numbers	Career Victories
Lt	Anderson, Alex	80	02/16/45	5	1	1	0.5-5.5	5.5
Lt	Anderson, Robert	80	12/14/44	6	0	0	2-7	8.5
Cdr	Barnard, Lloyd	2	06/15/44	5	0	0	1-5	5
Cdr	Beebe, Marshall	17	03/18/45	5	0	0	2.5-6.5	10.5
LCdr	Brewer, Charles	15	06/19/44	5	0	0	2.5-6.5	6.5
Lt	Brown, Carl	27	10/24/44	5	0	0	6.5-10.5	10.5
Lt	Buchanan, Robert	29	10/16/44	5	0	0	1-5	5
Lt(jg)	Carr, George	15	06/19/44	5	0	0	1-5	11.5
Lt	Coats, Robert	17	03/18/45	5	0	0	4-8	9.33
Lt	Collins, William	8	10/12/44	5	0	0	5-9	9
Lt	Conroy, Thomas	27	10/24/44	6	0	0	2-7	7
Lt	Cormier, Richard	80	12/14/44	5	0	0	1-5	8
Lt	Craig, Clement	22	01/21/45	5	0	0	7.75-11.75	11.75
Lt(jg)	Crosby, John	17	04/16/45	5	0	0	0.25-5.25	5.25
Ens	Dahms, Ken	30	04/06/45	5.5	0	0	1-6.5	7
Lt	Eckhard, Bert	9	05/11/45	5	0	0	3-7	7
Lt	Edwards, William	80	02/16/45	5	0	1	3.5-7.5	7.5
Lt	Fecke, Alfred	29	10/16/44	5	0	0	2-6	7
Lt	Fleming, Patrick	80	12/14/44	5	0	0	4-8	19
Lt	Fleming, Patrick	80	02/16/45	5	0	0	11-15	19
Lt	Foster, Carl	30	04/06/45	6	0	0	2-7	8.5
LCdr	Funk, Harold	26	10/24/44	6	0	0	0.5-6.5	6.5
Lt	Graham, Vernon	11	06/12/43	5	0	0	1-5	5
Lt(jg)	Hanks, Eugene	16	11/23/43	5	1	0	1-5	6
Lt(jg)	Hardy, Willis	17	04/06/45	5	0	0	1-5	6.5
Lt(jg)	Hargreaves, Everett	2	06/24/44	5	1	0	1-5	8.5
Lt(jg)	Harman, Walter	10	02/17/44	5	0	0	1-5	6
Lt(jg)	Hawkins, Arthur	31	09/13/44	5	0	0	6-10	14
Lt	Hippe, Kenneth	CS3	10/24/44	5	0	0	1-5	5
LCdr	Keith Leroy	80	02/16/45	5	2	0	0.5-5.5	5.5
Lt(jg)	Kidwell, Robert	45	02/16/45	5	0	0	1-5	5
Lt(jg)	Kirkwood, Philip	10	04/16/45	6	0	0	7-12	12
Lt	Lamb, William	27	06/19/45	5	0	0	1-5	6
Ens	Lerch, Alfred	10	04/16/45	7	0	0	1-7	7
Lt(jg)	Mallory, Charles	18	09/21/44	5	0	0	1-5	10
Lt(jg)	Masoner, William	19	10/24/44	6	0	1	6-11	12
Cdr	McCampbell, David	15	06/10/44	7	1	0	3-9	34
Cdr	McCampbell, David	15	10/24/44	9	2	0	22-30	34
Lt(jg)	McCusky, Elbert	3	06/04/42	5	0	3	2.5-6.5	15.5
Ens.	Miller, John	30	04/06/45	5	0	0	3-7	8
Lt(jg)	Mitchell, Henry	VBF17	03/21/45	5	0	0	2-6	6
Ens	Mollenhauer, Art	18	10/12/44	5	0	0	1-5	5
Lt(jg)	Murray, Robert	29	10/16/44	5	0	0	2.33-6.33	10.33
Lt(jg)	Nooy, Cornelius	31	09/21/44	5	0	0	11-15	19
LCdr	O'Hare, Edward	3	02/20/42	5	1	0	1-5	7
LCdr	Outlaw, Edward	32	04/29/44	5	1	0	1-5	6
Lt	Picken, Harvey	18	09/21/44	5	0	0	3-7	11
Lt(jg)	Reiserer, Russell	76(N)	06/19/44	5	0	0	2-6	9
LCdr	Riggs, James	15	09/12/44	5	0	1	6-10	11
Lt(jg)	Rushing, Roy	15	10/24/44	6	0	3	7-12	13
Cdr	Schecter, Gordon	45	02/16/45	5	2	0	1-5	5
Lt	Shirley, James	27	10/24/44	5	0	0	8.5-12.5	12.5

Lt	Stimpson, Charles	11	10/14/44	5	2	0	7-11	16
Lt(jg)	Townsend, Eugene	27	10/27/44	5	0	0	1-5	5
Ens	Truax, Myron	83	05/05/45	5	0	0	3-7	7
Lt	Turner, Edward	14	10/18/44	5	0	0	3-7	7
Lt	Valencia, Eugene	9	04/17/45	6	1	1	10.5-15.5	23
Lt	Vejtasa, Eugene	10	10/26/42	7	1	0	4-10	10.25
Lt(jg)	Vraciu, Alexander	16	06/19/44	6	0	0	13-18	19
Ens	Webb, Wilbur	2	06/19/44	6	2	0	1-6	7
Ens	Wrenn, George	72	10/26/42	5	0	0	0.25-5.25.	5.25

USMC Aces in a Day

Rank	Pilot Name	Unit VMF	Date	#V	#P	#D	Victory Numbers	Career Victories
Maj	Axtell ,George	323	04/22/45	5	0	3	1-5	6
Maj	Boyington, Gregory	214	09/16/43	5	0	0	1-5	22
1Lt	DeBlanc, Jefferson	112	01/31/43	5	0	0	4-8	9
Maj	Donohue, Archie	451	04/12/45	5	0	0	11-14	14
Maj	Dorroh, Jefferson	323	04/22/45	6	2	0	1-6	6
Capt	Foss, Joseph	121	10/25/42	5	0	0	12-16	26
1Lt	Hanson, Robert	215	01/14/44	5	0	0	5-10	25
1Lt	O'Keefe, Jeremiah	323	04/22/45	5	0	0	1-5	7
1Lt	Swett, James	221	04/07/43	7	1	0	1-7	15.5
Capt	Valentine, Herbert	312	05/25/45	5	1	0	2-6	6

Top Axis and Allied Aces in a Day

The beleaguered pilots of the Luftwaffe tallied the most daily victories in WWII, primarily on multiple sorties over Russia. Former Lufthansa pilot Emil "Bully" Lang (JG 54/173 victories) seems to be the highest scorer in a day when he claimed 18 victories during multiple missions in a day over Russia in November 1944. Three weeks earlier he got 12 victories in a day. The formidable Hans Joachim Marseille (JG 27/158 victories) tirelessly worked on his shooting proficiency until he was able to shoot down a number of British aircraft in a row. On 3 June 1942, he got six kills in 11 minutes, and two weeks later improved that feat by getting six in seven minutes. On 1 September 1942, he got 17 victories over RAF fighters in three missions over the North African desert (he got eight fighters in 10 minutes on one mission). Two weeks before his death on 30 September 1942, he got seven fighters in 11 minutes to become an ace in a day for the fourth time. August Lambert (SG 2, 151 and 77/116 victories) also got 17 victories in multiple missions over the Russians in the Crimea in Spring 1944. Lambert also scored 12 and 14 victories in a day in the Crimea. Erich Rudorffer (JG 2 and 54/ 222 victories) downed 11 Russians in one mission on 6 November 1943, and again on 28 October 1944. Rudorffer was an ace in a day two other times with eight victories on 9 February 1943 and seven more six days later. In a three and a half month period in mid-June Walter Nowotny (JG 54/250 victories) became

Emil "Bully" Lang who scored 173 victories for JG 54 over Russia claimed 18 victories during multiple missions in November 1944. (Author/West)

The formidable Hans Joachim Marseille, 158 victories with JG 27. was a quick and proficient shooter. He claimed 17 RAF fighters in three missions (eight in 10 minutes on one mission) over the North African Desert on 1 September 1942. (Author/West)

Walter Nowotny, 250 victories with JG 54, became an ace in a day five times over Russia. Nowotny is seen here celebrating the group's 300ᵗʰ victory. (Author/West)

W/O Hiromichi Shinohara of the Japanese Army Air Force was the leading IJAAF ace with 58 victories including 11 on 27 July 1939 during the Mongolian border skirmish, tops for a Japanese pilot in WWII. (Author)

an ace in a day no less than five times. He downed 10 on 24 June, nine on 13 August, seven on 21 August, 10 on 1 September, and eight on 9 October. The Luftwaffe had 43 "Aces in a Night." Among these night aces was Hauptmann Heinrich Prinz zu Sayn-Wittgenstein, who was an ace in a night three times. On 24/25 July 1943 he got six Soviet bombers on the Eastern Front. On 1 January 1944 he celebrated his promotion to Kommodore of NJG 2 by shooting down six RAF Lancaster bombers. Three weeks later, on 21 January he shot down five RAF bombers, but his Ju-88 was shot down, and he died as the leading German night fighter at the time with 83 victories in 170 sorties. Hauptmann Martin Becker, I/NJG 6, also was a triple ace in a night. On 22/23 March 1944 he claimed six victories, and eight days later got seven in a night. On 14/15 March he shot down six, while his gunner/radio/radar operator claimed three more. Becker had 57 victories. Top scoring Luftwaffe night ace was Oberleutnant Heinz-Wolfgang Schnaufer, NJG 1, who scored 121 night victories in just 164 sorties. He was the top ace in a night with nine victories on 21 February 1945. He downed two RAF Lancasters in the early morning hours, and then that evening he got seven more Lancasters in 17 minutes. Previously (24/25 May 1944) he had downed five RAF bombers. Hauptmann Wilhelm Herget, Kommandeur of I./NJG 4, on the night of 20/21 December 1943 shot down eight RAF four engine bombers in 45 minutes during a raid on Frankfurt. Herget was shot down three times and survived four crash-landings on his way to 57 victories. Hauptmann Alois Lechner of NJG 100 was credited with 43 total

victories. He was the top ace in a night on the Eastern Front with seven victories on 27/28 October 1943. Three further Luftwaffe night fliers were aces in a night twice: Hauptmann Helmut Bergmann (36 victories/NJG 4); Maj. Martin Drewes (47 v./NJG 1); and Hauptmann Gerhard Rath (58 v./NJG 2). A total of 33 German pilots surpassed McCampbell's nine victories in a day.

The top Japanese ace in a day was W/O Hiromichi Shinohara of the Japanese Army Air Force, who was the leading IJAAF ace

Heintz-Wolfgang Schnaufer, the world's top night fighter ace with 121 victories for NJG 1 became one of 46 Night Luftwaffe aces. (Author/West)

with 58 victories. On 27 July 1939, Shinohara was flying a Ki-27 Nate for the 11th Sentai against Soviet-Mongolian forces during the Mongolian border skirmish. He was credited with 11 victories over Tam-Bulak that day.

The top RAF daily total is seven by C.H. Dyson of 33 Squadron. On 11 December 1942 he shot down six Italian CR42 biplanes, one of which collided with a SM79 bomber, causing it to crash into the Libyan Desert.

Lt. Aleksandr Gorovets (11 total victories) was the leading Soviet ace in a day flying a La-5 for 88 GIAP. Gorovets shot down 9 Ju-87 Stukas on 6 July 1943 during the Battle of Kursk. During the combat over Vladimiroka-Olkhovatha he was bounced by four FW 190s and shot down. He was awarded the Hero of the Soviet Union Medal for this action.

C.H. Dyson of 33 Squadron shot down six Italian CR42 biplanes and SM79 bomber on 11 December 1942 over the Libyan Desert, tops for the RAF in WWII. (Author/Dyson)

CHAPTER 15

The Fighter Bomber and
TAC R and Photo REC Units

Fighter Bomber

Strafing

Background

The German Army Air Corps in the First World War, using their Junkers and Fokkers to attack Allied troops in their trenches, had first practiced strafing. The technique derived its name from the German verb "strafe," meaning "to punish." The Allies soon entered the word into their aviation vocabulary attacking Ludendorff's troops. The word and technique was resurrected by the 4FG, flying Spitfires in the fall and winter of 1942-43. The 4ᵗʰ engaged in low-level harassing attacks, called "rhubarb" missions, against targets of opportunity. However, when the group was re-equipped with P-47s, it was assigned to high altitude bomber escort duties.

On 30 July 1943, the P-47s of the 78FG crossed the German border to rendezvous with returning B-17s near Haldern. The group's P-47s had been using belly auxiliary fuel tanks for a short time and found them to be cumbersome and leaky, often refusing to draw fuel and at times to unrepentantly fall off! On this mission the 78ᵗʰ surprised the Luftwaffe, as they were able to penetrate into German territory more miles than usual. After engaging German fighters, lLt. Quince L. Brown of the 84FS lost altitude and was heading back to England on deck west of Rotterdam. On the way Brown expended his remaining ammunition on a locomotive and assorted gun positions. Brown's attack was the first strafing attack in the

ETO since the early rhubarb missions. Ironically, on 6 September 1944 his P-47 "*Okie*" was shot down by flak while strafing near Schleiden. After bailing out a SS officer, prodded by irate German citizens, murdered Brown. Strafing was done only sporadically, and usually for the fun of it in the ETO for the remainder of 1943.

In early 1944, the Luftwaffe was reluctant to engage the fighters of the VIII Fighter Command, as it was saving its aircraft for advantageous tactical situations. Gen. H.H. "Hap" Arnold's 1944 New Year's message had emphasized the importance of defeating the Luftwaffe both "in the air, and on the ground." Engineering

In early 1944, the Luftwaffe was reluctant to engage U.S. fighters in the air. After being released from escort duty, Gen. Hap Arnold authorized his fighters to engage in attacking ground targets. On 22 February 1944, Col. Glenn Duncan led his 353FS P-51s against an airdrome near Ostheim. (USAF)

1Lt. Quince Brown of the 84FS/78FG is given credit for making the first strafing attack in the ETO. On 30 July 1943, after engaging Luftwaffe fighters, he dropped to the deck and expended his remaining ammo on a train and assorted gun positions. (USAF)

advances, such as water injection and the installation of paddle blade propellers enhanced the low-altitude performance of the P-47. The introduction of drop tanks increased its range, making it more suited for ground strafing duties. 8AF Lt. Gen. James Doolittle had commanded the 12AF in North Africa and had seen the fruitful results of ground strafing in the MTO. Doolittle and Maj. Gen. Carl "Tooey" Spaatz were instrumental in the decision to have the VIIIFC move from a defensive to offensive posture against the Luftwaffe. The decision was made to allow withdrawing escort fighters to attack German airdromes (A/D) on the way back to base. To encourage pilots to engage in this dangerous endeavor, the 8AF decided to credit ground victories towards total victories. This practice was also accepted by the 10th and 14th Air Forces in the CBI Theater.

On 22 February 1944, the 353FS, after being released from bomber escort duty, was led by Col. Glenn Duncan on a strafing run on Ostheim A/D. Following Duncan, Walt Beckham led the next flight in. The second strafing attack was always more dangerous, as the enemy AA defenses were alerted. The gunners hit Beckham's P-47 *Little Demon,* forcing him to pull up and bail out. The leading ace in the ETO at the time was captured and made a POW for the duration.

The first planned pure strafing mission was flown on 11 March, when the 353FG conducted a low-level sweep over Luftwaffe A/D in the Pas de Calais area. Small arms and light flak claimed two P-47s, while a third crashed on its return to base. These losses were unacceptable, and Duncan, wanting to maximize the rewards and minimize the risks of strafing, presented Maj.Gen. William Kepner, CG of the VIIIFC, with the idea of organizing a unit of strafing specialists. Kepner agreed to the concept, and four pilots each from the 353, 355, 359, and 361 Fighter Groups volunteered, forming a unit to be known as "Bill's Buzz Boys," named after Kepner.

On 15 March, the 16 pilots began training, equipped with the rugged P-47s all fitted with paddle blade propellers, which greatly enhanced its low altitude capabilities. The first mission flown by the unit came on the afternoon of 26 March, when 12 P-47s, each carrying four M-4 fragmentation cluster bombs, strafed four German A/Ds. Ground claims were made for one aircraft destroyed, one probable, and four damaged, along with the damage to the A/D's facilities. One P-47 pilot was shot down and taken prisoner, and three aircraft were damaged. The mission determined that the P-47's .50 caliber machine guns were more destructive than the fragmentation bombs, but that these bombs did tend to discourage enemy AA gunners.

The mission on 29 March, was probably the unit's most successful, when Duncan led 12 P-47s against four airfields in northwest Germany. The group preceded a bombing mission and found ideal 6/10-8/10, 5,000 foot cloud layer. Duncan's flight of four dove from 10,000 feet out of the sun to deck level about two miles from the airdrome. At the edge of the field they pulled up to 150 feet looking to strafe parked e/a, but found none. A flak tower at the corner of the field put out a lot of ammo, but was unable to get proper deflection on the low-flying 400mph Thunderbolts. The group passed over the end of the field, pulled up to 5,000 feet, and watched as Duncan attacked Vechhta A/D, which was loaded with

parked aircraft. Duncan lined up two twin-engine aircraft, hitting them. He then proceeded on to a line of fighters, putting a few rounds into each and avoiding some flak. Following Duncan in, the group knocked out the flak positions that had revealed themselves on Duncan's run and destroyed more parked aircraft. A crash landed B-17 was intact in an open field, and Duncan deprived the Germans of their trophy by setting it on fire. The group reassembled at 5,000 feet to attack another A/D. Four P-47s flying line abreast destroyed more parked aircraft there, along with a speeding staff car. Targets of opportunity were harassed on the return to base. Total claims were 7/5/9 aircraft on the ground and 8/3 locomotives, in addition to damage to hangars, flak towers, and river barges. One P-47 was lost and four received minor damage.

A total of eight were flown (two uneventful) in which 90 P-47s were dispatched, with 83 making effective sorties. Three aircraft and two pilots were lost, and 13 were damaged. Claims were 14/6/14 aircraft on the ground, one air probable, 9 hangars, 15/3 locomotives, and 9 barges.

On 12 April Kepner disbanded the group, thanking them for their work and returning them to their stations. Their mission resulted in the formulation of basic strafing tenants:

1 Preparation: Obtaining as many photographs and information about an A/D in preplanned attacks allowed the unit leader to plan the approach, the attack, and the withdrawal using all the local terrain features to his advantage. For impromptu attacks a quick assessment, based on the skills learned in prepared missions, was a requirement for the mission's safety and success.
2 Surprise! Attack and knockout the German before he can react.
3 Plan one pass: Always go into a strafing pass considering the target to be heavily defended. Pick a target. High speed/stay low. Make every round count. Get out low and quickly.
4 Consider risk/reward. A parked enemy aircraft destroyed is not worth our fighter *and* its pilot. How many trucks equal a fighter? In equal numbers ground attack was found to be four times more dangerous than air-to-air combat.

Strafing continued to take its toll. Gabby Gabreski, the topscorer in the ETO and finished with his combat tour, decided to fly one last hurrah mission. After strafing an A/D west of Frankfurt, Gabreski decided to make a second pass. He saw his P-47's rounds were overshooting a parked He-111 and dropped a little lower, but his prop hit a hump and forced him to belly land, after which he spent the remainder of the war as a POW.

Strafing was not only taking its toll on aces in Europe, but also in the Pacific. Lt(jg) Alex Vraciu had talked his way into serving a second tour with VF-20 after getting 19 victories with VF-17. On 14 December 1944, Vraciu was shot down on his second mission of the day while strafing near Clark Field in the Philippines. He parachuted to safety and joined USAFFE guerrillas. He was given the honorary rank of brevet major and command of 180 men. They eluded the Japanese for five weeks and linked up with MacArthur's advancing troops. Vraciu was a strafing ace with 21 ground victories at a cost of two crash landings and two bail outs.

Europe

By the end of 1943 the worth of close air support had been firmly demonstrated by both the Germans and Russians on the Eastern Front, and by the Allies over North Africa. In November 1943, the Allies established tactical air forces for the impending invasion of Europe. The RAF established the 2nd Tactical Air Force from experienced personnel from the Mediterranean. The USAAF transferred the entire 9AF HQ from the MTO to England. However, initially the 9AF operated under the control of Fighter Command in a fighter escort role. It was not until April 1944 that two Tactical Air Commands were instituted to support the two U.S. Armies slated to take part in the D-Day invasion. The IX TAC (7 P-47 groups/21 squadrons and 3 P-38 groups/9 squadrons) was to support the 1st U.S. Army, while the XIX TAC (5 P-47 groups/15 squadrons and 2 P-38 groups/6 squadrons) was to support the 3rd U.S. Army. In early October 1944 the XXIX TAC was established from the merger of the 303FW and 84FW in the 9AF. During the same month the First TAC Air Force (Provisional) was established to provide tactical air support for the Franco-American Army group over the southern ETO. The mission of these TAC Air Forces was threefold:

1 Gain air superiority by attacking enemy airfields, with destruction of E/A on the ground and in the air.
2 Isolate the battlefield by cutting rails and bridges, destroying his motor and rail transportation, and attacking enemy supply depots and troop concentrations in the rear to prevent or delay their movement to the battlefront.
3 Give direct support to ground forces by hitting troop concentrations, strong points, and tanks and gun positions.

TAC and 1st TACAF UNIT ASSIGNMENTS

IX TAC	XIX TAC	XXIX TAC	1ST TACAF
365FG	354FG	36FG	50FG
366FG	358FG*	48FG	324FG+
367FG	362FG	373FG	371FG
368FG	405FG	404FG	415NFS+
370FG	406FG		
474FG	425NFS		
422NFS			

67TRG	10PRG	363TRG	PRG
107TRS	12TRS	160TRS	111TRS+
109TRS	15TRS	161TRS	162TRS
30PRS	31PRS	33PRS	34PRS
	155PSN		

* to 1st TAF(P) on 15 Nov 1944   + = units from 12AF

Note:

1945 9AF composition:	1945 1st TACAF composition:
43% fighter/fighter bombers	50% fighter/fighter bombers
43% light/medium bombers	29% light/medium bombers
2% night fighters	4% night fighters
12% recon a/c	17% recon a/c

Pacific

In the Pacific, close air support was carried out by U.S. Navy carrier aircraft in support of amphibious invasions, and by the U.S. Marine Corps land-based fighter and dive bomber units once an airfield had been secured (particularly on Guadalcanal, the Solomons, and Okinawa). In the SWPA, Gen. Kenney's 5AF fighters were often too busy with air combat to be used as fighter bombers. As the war wound out, Japanese fighter opposition lessened and the 5AF fighter could be used as a fighter bomber. In the Philippines its fighter-bombers and USMC land-based fighters carried out close air support once the invasion beaches were secured. In early 1945, the latest versions of the P-38 and P-51 became available in quantity, and the 5AF used them extensively in the fighter bomber capacity in the Philippines and over Formosa. The F4U Corsair became one of WWII's great fighter bombers in the Pacific. It carried six .50 machine guns, and like all U.S. Navy fighters it was designed with bomb load in mind. Initially, the F4U could carry a 500 or 1000lb bomb on its center line pylon, and the later F4U-1D could carry two 500 or 1000lb bombs on two pylons, and this was increased to a pair of 2000lb bombs.

Fighter-bomber Adaptability

In addition to its strafing/ground attack role, the adaptable fighter-bomber was able to carry out of a number of tasks: light and medium bomber escort; short and long range interdiction missions; short and long range fighter sweeps; and anti-shipping sorties. In contrast to light and medium bombers, the fighter-bombers were mission-adaptable and not confined to one target. They could go from an interdiction target and proceed to a ground support target on the same mission. The fighter-bomber could be rearmed, refueled, and its pilot briefed more quickly than a bomber crew, which enabled fighter-bomber units to carry out three or four missions per day, as compared to the usual two for light and medium bombers. The fighter-bomber boasted imposing firepower and ordnance, and compared to bombers could deliver more ordnance per day and

CG of the VIII FC, MGen. William Kepner shown here with Don Blakeslee, organized a unit of strafing specialists known as "Bill's Buzz Boys." (USAF)

inflict more damage for effort expended. The fighter-bomber was able to attack targets with more precision than bombers, with the exception of targets requiring pattern bombing, such as extensively prepared positions or gun areas. Being able to deliver their ordnance at lower altitudes they were less vulnerable to heavy enemy AA than the higher flying bombers. Enemy fighters were of little consequence at this stage of the war, but small-caliber flak was a major concern, as it was effective to 3,000 feet and not visible. The major shortcoming for the fighter-bomber was its lack of combat range. With 2x500lb bombs (thus unable to carry external fuel tanks) the P-38 and P-47 had a combat range of 260 miles, while the P-51 had a range of 325 miles. This factor necessitated that airfields be located near the battlefront.

Strafing Attack/General Tenants
Every scheduled strafing attack required thorough planning, requiring the pilots to become totally familiar with the geography of the target area and the layout of the target itself, particularly the location of AA guns. Landmarks in a five-mile radius of the target needed to be memorized and the best approach and withdrawal routes selected.

For attacks to be effective, visibility needed to be at least 6,000 feet, and the cloud base no lower than 5,000 feet for bombing and 3,000 feet for strafing. For rocket attacks and dive bombing the wind could impose the direction of approach. Enemy AA concentration and disposition needed to be determined, as it would dictate tactics on route to the target and during the attack.

An altitude of 15,000 feet was maintained on the way to the target area. The leader located the target and dropped to the deck. The formation then turned 180 degrees, setting course on target, flights dropping line astern in about 1,000 yard intervals. The approach was made at normal cruising speed at as low altitude as possible, trying to use a road or other landmark to stay on target. About one mile from target the first flight pulled up to 100 feet, correcting their heading if necessary, and gave full rpm and throttle. The flight and element leaders concentrated on shooting up the target itself, while the wingmen acted as "anti-flak" aircraft, picking out gun positions and knocking them out. It was important to pick an aimed target, rather than "hosing" the area. The pilot had to have his aircraft properly trimmed and set his gunsight to fire at correct range, putting as many rounds into the target while on it. Succeeding flights utilized similar tactics. Once past the target all aircraft stayed on deck until the formation leader gave the signal to climb, usually five to ten miles away.

Another method of attack had the formation come around on the target at 4,000 feet, dive at high speed, shoot up the target, stay low, and get away. It was a matter of the leader's preference as to which method was to be used, but the on deck method was most common.

The guns of the fighter were harmonized for rounds to converge at a point ahead of the aircraft where the rounds would impact the target together. The harmonization point was set for air to air combat at 250 yards, which was acceptable when strafing individual targets, such as soft or armored vehicles. Low-level strafing attacks at this harmonization were risky to the pilot, as apart from

AA and small arms fire, a small miscalculation or target-fixation could cause the fighter to crash into the target, or into nearby trees or obstructions. If the target were carrying ammunition or explosives it could explode in the path of the attacker. The most accurate of all fighter bomber armament was the machine gun or cannon, as the great number of rounds fired assured more hits in an area, but the striking power of each round inflicted much less damage to the target than a rocket or bomb. Many pilots felt tracers gave a false sense of direction and range. When the steel cores of the .50 slug hit they caused sparks, which looked like blinking lights. It was advised that pilots save about 50 rounds per gun during strafing missions. In the P-51, a pilot could expend all the ammo in his outboard guns and have enough left in the two inboard guns to engage in combat, if necessary.

If heavy AA fire was encountered only one pass was made, but if the target were undefended the formation leader detailed at least one flight to fly top cover while the remainder of the formation flew another pass on the target. Top cover circled at 2,000 feet above the target in the opposite direction to the attacking aircraft to be able to intercede, if necessary, without delay. The formation often was disrupted after the first pass, and all aircraft had to beware of other aircraft and stay out of their fire. A minimum airspeed of 250 mph was advised because of the constant possibility of passing over unexpected AA positions while on deck, and the possibility of being bounced.

Airdromes
Planned airdrome attacks had the primary objective of surprise. They were flown by four aircraft in line abreast within flights and flights in close trail, each weaving and skidding and firing individually. No more than two eight-ship sections were considered safe for these attacks. The sections were to make their passes from different directions and timed as close together as possible. If a pilot did not have a target in front of him he was discouraged from turning toward another target, as that interfered with another pilot's run and was dangerous for both. Because valuable airdromes were usually heavily defended by flak the flights stayed as close to the deck as possible. Well-defended airdromes were often attacked by an anti-flak flight detailed to attack ground defenses before the actual attack. The flight opened fire at 300 to 400 yards and fired as long as possible. Pilots were urged not to cross the middle of the airdrome. Flying close to the edges was safer, because the gun positions were situated there. By flying close to the guns the aircraft presented a target moving at a high angular speed that made it difficult for the gunners to track. Also, the hangars where enemy aircraft were most likely to be found were located close to the perimeter of the field. On withdrawal evasive action was continued on deck, skidding and keeping up airspeed for five to ten miles beyond target when altitude was regained and sections reformed.

A/D attacks as targets of opportunity after an escort mission had the disadvantage of having airdromes in line with the bomber's track being alerted as to the possibility of attack from withdrawing escort fighters strafing. The impromptu A/D mission in mid-1944 had the group's squadrons separated by a few miles. They flew at 12-15,000 feet in order to detect enemy aircraft parked on the airfields and moving transport, such as trucks, trains, etc. Once a target was spotted part of the squadron was left out of the target's sight for top cover, while the remainder flew 10 to 20 miles beyond the objective, appearing to be headed home. The fighters would descend in a shallow 180-degree dive back toward the target. The direction of the approach was sometimes determined by wind direction and strength. Attacking down wind was desirable so that smoke from the targets damaged in the first pass would not conceal targets for the next strafers. Also, attacking across a strong wind could cause the aircraft to drift and influence accuracy. A low morning or afternoon sun in a clear, revealing sky or cloud cover could be used to conceal the attack. Each flight attacked line abreast, or staggered line astern. The line abreast formation exposed all attackers at once for a short period of time, while the line astern exposed each flight in turn to all the defensive fire. The staggered astern mode required 1,000 yard intervals to prevent ricochet damage to the flight ahead from those following. The line astern mode did allow the trailing aircraft to spot ground AA positions firing at those ahead and to then attack these AA positions. A reference several miles from the A/D was chosen while at altitude to aid navigation to the target once on deck. The lead flight(s) came in at 300-350mph, as higher speeds interfered with gunnery. If heavy AA fire were encountered the leader would radio off the remainder of his unit. If opposition were light then the next wave of attackers was able to come in at lower speeds, improving their accuracy. The approach was made on deck with a bounce up to 30 to 70 feet on sighting the objective, with each member of the flight selecting a target on his run. About 500 to 750 yards from the target, with a slight pull on the control column to correct for bullet drop (e.g. G-pull on the fired round), long, two to three second firing bursts were made again. It was important for the pilot to have his aircraft properly trimmed and know the characteristics of his gun sight. The fighter continued to fly low once beyond the end of the A/D for a half mile or more to escape airfield defenses. But if no flak were encountered then a climbing turn could be made and a textbook

The strafing of German airdromes was probably the most dangerous ground attack undertaking as they were usually heavily defended by AA positions. Here a P-47 attacks a sitting Potez bomber. (USAF)

flying school gunnery pattern would be initiated on the following passes. In the vicinity of the airdrome, the safety of minimum altitude and high speeds was maintained at all times. If the A/D was heavily defended a preplanned strafing attack could be carried out in conjunction with medium bombers. The bombing units would fly at medium altitude, followed by the strafers. About 20 miles from target the bomber squadron leader would waggle his wings. Acting on this signal, the strafers turned 360, losing altitude to ground level on the original course and speed. This maneuver allowed the strafers to arrive at the A/D shortly after the bombers struck, which caused the base to be in a state of confusion and the AA gunners under cover.

Airdrome strafing was the most hazardous form of ground attack. Permanent German air bases were usually well defended. The impromptu solo attack on the way home was especially dangerous. A bored pilot, seeing no combat and having a full load of ammunition, would inevitably be tempted to go on deck to carry out an exhilarating high speed sweep of an airfield, often with disastrous consequences, as Glenn Duncan was to find on 7 July 1944. After escort penetration, Duncan led the 351FS on Wesendorf A/D, getting a parked He-111 on his first pass. Duncan decided on another injudicious run, and flak hit his oil line, causing his engine to overheat on the way home. A quarter hour later, he was forced to belly land, and after setting his fighter on fire became an evader. After spending nine months with the Dutch Underground, he returned to England in April 1945. Along with Duncan, the list of pilots lost on strafing missions reads like an ace's who's who: Beeson; Beckham; Gerald Johnson; Jucheim; Andrew; Hofer; Goodson; Schreiber; Millikan; Carpenter; Mahurin; Gabreski; and on and on….

As the Third Reich was shrunk by the onslaught of Allied troops in 1945, the Luftwaffe was able to concentrate AA guns around its shrinking number of bases. The Luftwaffe wanted to divert the attention of manruding Allied fighter bombers from vital targets, and large numbers of non-operational aircraft were lined up on heavily defended airfields. As a result, enemy gunners were constantly on the alert for the inevitable strafer who had no foe in the air. Without the element of surprise losses to strafers mounted. In January 1945, Bill Cullerton with 21 strafing victories was taken prisoner, and on 16 April Elwyn Righetti, top ETO strafer with 27, crash landed his damaged P-51, and the next day the second leading strafing ace, Joe Thury with 25 1/2 ground claims, barely limped back to base in his damaged P-51.

The 56FG strafing mission of 13 April 1945 was one of the war's great strafing missions on an airdrome to that time. The 56FG had been selected to combat-test the new T-48 .50 caliber ammunition that had a higher muzzle velocity and more incendiary material to ignite the lower octane fuels used by the German jets. The Group, consisting of the 61st, 62nd, and 63rd Fighter Squadrons flying 49 P-47Ms, was on a free lance bomber support mission when it swept Eggebeck A/D. They encountered an estimated 150-200 aircraft of all types scattered on it and its two satellite fields. The 63rd orbited at 5,000 feet with the 62nd flying top cover at 15,000 feet, while the 61st waited at 10,000. The 63rd went first to primarily silence AA positions. It made 140 passes, firing 31,148 rounds and destroying 43 aircraft. The 61st then came in making 94 passes, firing 22,243 rounds and claiming 25 aircraft, and was followed by the 63rd, which made 105 passes expending 24,682 rounds to destroy 26 aircraft. The Group made 339 individual passes, destroying 94 aircraft and damaging 95 others using 78,073 rounds for a loss of one fighter. The 56FG was observing the second anniversary of its first mission and had destroyed its 1,000[th] German aircraft that day. For the day P-47s destroyed 137 and damaged 83 over the ETO.

On 16 April, this number was far surpassed as P-47s claimed 228 destroyed/109 damaged on the ground, P-51s claimed 86/66 when released from bomber escort, while freelance bomber support P-51s claimed an astounding 410/198 on the ground. The ground total for the day was a truly grand total of 724/373. After this day the fighters of the 8AF ran out of targets, and three weeks later the war ended.

In the estimated 8,000+ ground victories scored in the ETO/ MTO, P-51s scored 4,000+ victories, P-47s 3,000+, and the P-38 750+. P-38 units flew far fewer strafing missions than the P-47 or P-51, but did have some notatable days. In the ETO, Capt. John Hollingsworth of the 479FG destroyed six enemy aircraft on the ground strafing Ettinghausen Airdrome on 5 September 1944, which may be the best P-38 ground score in one day. The 479FG, during a six week period beginning mid-August 1944, claimed 29 in the air and 60 on the ground. On 8 August 1944, the 20FG, led by CO Col. Harold Rau, got seven Luftwaffe aircraft in the air and 21 on the ground on a sweep over Salzwedel on 8 April 1944. On 25 August 1944, the 392FS of the 367FG "Dynamite Gang" found 16 Ju 52 transports sitting on an airfield near Dijon waiting to evacuate high ranking German personnel back to Germany after the invasion of South France. All 16 were destroyed, five by CO Maj. Robert "Buck" Rogers on two passes.

On 25 August 1943, the 82FG joined the 1FG from bases in North Africa for a concerted attack on the Luftwaffe satellite airfields, which were concentrated on the Foggia area on the central East Coast. The 82FG claimed 21 aircraft destroyed on the ground and 34 damaged, while the 1FG destroyed 43 and damaged 52 others. Nearly three quarters of the Luftwaffe aircraft were bombers, mostly Ju-88s. 2Lt. Joseph Solko of the 95FS/82FG claimed nine Ju-88s, which was probably the highest one-day MTO total. As the Allied armies invaded Italy and moved up the boot, the Luftwaffe withdrew its aircraft from bases there to protect them from marauding tactical fighters.

Trains/Road Convoys and the Transport System

As Allied strafing attacks increased in 1944, the Germans armed their trains with flak cars. To minimize the risk from these guns the strafing attacks were made at 90 degrees in line abreast to the target and in a 20 to 30 degree dive from 500 to 2,000 feet, concentrating fire. Little or no firing lead was necessary, and trains were considered a stationary target. The locomotive was the primary target to stop the train and make it an easier target. Attacks on the engine were made from 90 degrees by the No. 1 and, if necessary, No. 2 of the flight. Once the train was stopped 10 to 15 degree deflection passes were made by Nos. 2, 3, and 4 to destroy as many cars as possible with a minimum number of attacks. Long, methodical bursts

caused the most damage and kept return AA and small arms fire down.

In strafing road convoys a flight would attack in line abreast, perpendicular to the road. Each pilot should choose a target and concentrate on it. The most vulnerable area of a truck was the fuel tank or radiator, and since trucks and half-tracks carried their own fuel supply they often exploded when hit. In attacking a road convoy the front and rear vehicles were taken out first to immobilize the convoy and make it an easier target on succeeding attacks.

If a target had the possibility of exploding, pilots fired a short burst from a distance away, aiming high in an attempt to explode it. If this failed, a long burst was fired somewhat high. The pilot watched for hits and then led fire into the target. The attack was to be broken off at a distance to insure safety from an explosion, but all too often strafing fighters were lost to explosions.

The unrelenting attacks and destruction of forward rail facilities (railheads, bridges, and crossing points) increased the demand for motor vehicles, which increased the demand for fuel, which itself was under attack and in turn needed replenishing by rail. The further back the railheads were pushed, the motor columns used more fuel on the longer runs, exposed themselves to attacks for longer periods, and increased the delay in deliveries to the front. The fact that regular railway traffic all but ceased in 1945 caused the whole burden of transport to fall on road vehicles, which had to travel at night. The maneuverability of the Wehrmacht in the field was largely dependent upon motor transport. The damage or destruction of the motor transport system had immediate and direct effect on the battlefront in terms of casualties and ground lost.

From D-Day to the end of the war, the three 9AF TACs destroyed 53,811 motor vehicles destroyed and 22,546 damaged for loss of 1,374 P-47s. There are no records available as to the loss of locomotives, but German records indicate that between August 1944 and the end of that year an average of 600 per month were lost. However, in 1945 the Allies increased their attacks, and in January 800 were lost, and in February 1,700 were lost.

Allied fighter bombers were so effective attacking German railways that by 1945 regular rail traffic had all but ceased and the burden of transport fell on road vehicles that had to travel at night. (USAF)

The U.S. did not develop an aircraft or airborne gun specifically designed for the anti-tank role. The development of effective dive-bombing techniques and rockets proved this decision to be correct. The P-47 was the AAF anti-tank aircraft of choice. Here a StuGIII was destroyed by P-47s outside Daleiden, Germany, in February 1945. (US Army)

Tank Busting

The Allies decided to depend on fighter bombers for ground support and not develop an aircraft or airborne gun specifically designed to combat enemy tanks. The development of effective dive bombing techniques and airborne rockets in an anti-tank role confirmed this decision to be correct. Operating with eight .50 caliber machine guns, a 500lb GP bomb, and two 260lb fragmentation bombs the P-47 fighter bomber was more accurate and effective than long range heavy artillery.

The P-47 was the American anti-tank fighter of choice, but on D-Day there were no Thunderbolts carrying RPs (rocket projectiles) and RAF 2TAC Typhoons were the primary Allied tank busters. The first U.S. tank busting operation occurred on 11 July when 366FG P-47s attacked 32 tanks of the Panzer Lehr Division and knocked out 20 of them. Though RPs were used to great effect by RAF Typhoons, P-47 pilots did not like the drag caused by the launchers and their poor accuracy. Therefore, many P-47 groups had their rocket apparatus removed, and dive bombing was the preferred anti-tank method. P-47 pilots could set fire to and destroy German armored vehicles with the .50 caliber API ammunition if used at low altitudes from the rear, hitting the engine compartment.

One of the 9AF top tank-busting units was the 406FBG, which had the only rocket armed tank buster unit in the 9AF, the 513FS "Bashers." Their P-47s became operational in July 1944, carrying 5-inch HVARs that they delivered in low-level attacks, releasing them at 600-1,000 yards or from a 30 degree dive at 1,000 yards or more. By September, the squadron had flown 323 sorties, firing 1,117 rockets along with .50 caliber ammunition to destroy 114 tanks, 16 armored cars, and 187 motor vehicles. Despite this success the 9AF never adopted the rocket on any large scale. During the Battle of the Bulge the 406FBG flew support for the besieged defenders at Bastogne. During the period 23-27 December, its three squadrons flew 81 missions (529 sorties), operating from sunrise to sunset and destroying 194 German tanks and armored vehicles, 610

motor vehicles, 226 gun positions, and damaged or destroyed 14 Luftwaffe aircraft.

One of the most impressive missions enjoyed by a 9AF Fighter Bomber Group occurred on 13 August 1944 when 37 P-47 pilots of the 36FBG encountered 800 to 1,000 German vehicles in the Falaise Pocket west of Argentan trying to escape the advancing American and British pincers. The Thunderbolts attacked until they ran out of ordnance, disabling 400 to 500 vehicles in the next hour. However, the brunt of the Falaise fighter bomber attacks were carried out by British 2TAF Typhoons, which caused such carnage that the area was named the "Corridor of Death."

From D-Day to VE-Day the 9AF placed German armored and motor vehicles as their priority target. The three TACs under its command claimed 4,509 tanks and other armored vehicles destroyed and 3,751 damaged.

Necessity on the Russian Front motivated the Germans into perfecting tank busting into an art form. The greatest tank buster of all time was Hans-Ulrich Rudel, who flew a mind-boggling 2,530 missions in the Ju-87 Stuka on the Eastern front from 22 June to VE-Day. He destroyed 519 tanks (17 on 22 March 1944 and 12 on 8 February 1945); 800 vehicles; four armored trains; 150 artillery; anti-tank and AA positions; one battleship (*Marat*), a cruiser, a destroyer, and 70 landing craft. He was also an air ace with nine victories, but was shot down 30 times by ground fire and wounded five times, losing a leg on 8 February 1945. Leading Soviet tank buster was A. N. Yefimov, who flew 222 missions in the Shturmovik Il-2, knocking out 126 tanks and 85 Luftwaffe aircraft on the ground.

Troops

The recommended method for attacking ground troops was to fly abreast and fire simultaneously. The German soldier was well-trained in small arms anti-aircraft defense. It was best to combine bombing/rocket and gunnery runs in attacking troops. Allied air supremacy had a distinct effect on the morale of German ground troops from the High Command to the lowest private. A number of German commanders, including Gen. Erwin Rommel, were killed

The diaries of German soldiers were dominated by fears of attacks by Allied Jabos which ruled the skies. Here a P-51 is fitted with 12x30lb. anti-personnel fragmentation bombs which were utilized at the end of the war. (USAF)

or wounded by strafing attacks on staff cars and headquarters. The diaries of German soldiers were dominated by the fears of Allied Jabos, which had gained air supremacy over the battlefront. After D-Day Allied air power had an overwhelming and completely paralyzing influence on German conduct of the battlefront. Whenever the weather permitted, Allied fighter bombers appeared from sunrise to sunset over the front lines to a depth of 10 to 12 miles. Anything that moved was attacked with rockets and machine guns. Men and vehicles were hidden in dense vegetation or in barns. No one dared to show himself in the open, and the skies were constantly searched.

Flak Towers
Pilots were hesitant to attack flak towers, as they could outgun and out range the fighters. The only time they were attacked was if they were causing a problem to attacks in the area. Also, many towers reported as flak towers were actually water towers!

Dive Bombing
Dive bombing tactics were determined by target type, AA concentration, and the weather and wind. High-level dive bombing attacks were made at steep angles, usually between 60 and 70 degrees, which were imperative for accuracy. It was difficult for the pilot to

Although this photo is spectacular, flak towers were generally off limits as they could outgun and out range the attacking fighters. (USAF)

Dive-bombing tactics were determined by target type. Here a 373FG P-47 is framed by 500lb. bomb storage racks. (USAF)

see straight down to the target without tipping the wing. Target identification needed to be precise but was difficult, and often the leader would use the R/T to ID the target to his pilots. As he was about to dive the leader would R/T "Bomb switches on," followed by "Diving in 10 seconds" and "Diving now." The dive was braked by dropping the main gear, whose fairing acted as a dive brake. This would allow the pilot time to line up the target before releasing his bombs. Following their leader into the attack, the pilots released their bombs at 2 to 3,000 feet. After releasing the bombs an intense evasive turn was made in a predetermined direction before reforming line abreast. If the target were heavily defended, the attack would be made out of the sun and/or from two directions in order to reduce AA proficiency.

Low level attacks were usually at 20 to 30 degrees, with the bombs being released at 800 feet at high speed and short range in order to evade small arms and light flak, as well as the burst and debris from their bomb explosions.

Glide bombing was a high speed, accelerating attack delivered at 30 to 55 degrees without the use of dive brakes. The initial element of surprise and the built up speed made the attacker a difficult target going in and out.

Rocket Attacks
The airborne rocket was developed to fill the need for an aerial weapon falling between the machine gun/cannon and the bomb. Aerial rockets could be launched without adverse recoil effect on the aircraft, were lightweight without having the dead weight of the large, cumbersome cannon, and did not reduce the fighter's number of machine guns, bomb load, or drop tanks. They were comparatively light, causing a small decrease in speed, and if necessary both the rockets and their launching devices could be jettisoned.

The standard American rocket was the 5-inch HVAR (High Velocity Aerial Rocket), which had five-inch warheads mounted on high velocity bodies. They were initially mounted on four zero length launchers mounted on each outer wing panel. Later the rocket was launched from two streamlined posts or studs, one at the front end and the other at the rear end of the rocket. These studs sup-

Rocket attacks were utilized more in the Pacific than the ETO and MTO. Here a VMF-323 Corsair fires a rocket salvo on Japanese positions on Okinawa in May 1945. (Author/Brandon)

ported the six-foot projectile parallel to the aircraft's line of flight. The rocket was very simple in construction and employment. Because the rocket motor caused no recoil, the warhead could be much heavier and of a larger caliber than the airborne cannon shell. They could be fired singly or in salvo. With practice a salvo of rockets could insure a hit. Since the rocket was driven by the powerful thrust of the propellant its impact was far greater than a bomb's, and its detonation would occur ahead of the aircraft, not under it, as was the case with a bomb.

As with dive bombing, rocket tactics were determined by target type, AA concentration, and weather/wind. The HVAR had the explosive effect of a 155mm shell. A rule of thumb for rocket targets stated that any target suitable for artillery fire was a suitable rocket target. It was estimated that a salvo of all eight rockets was equal to the destructive power of a broadside from a naval destroyer.

Against heavily defended targets pilots were advised to make a steep 60 degree dive at 7-8,000 feet and fire all rockets in salvo at about 4,000 feet at a range of 5,000 feet. On these strongly defended targets, doctrine stated that they should only be attacked once. If the target were lightly defended, the pilots were to make a shallow dive of 20-30 degrees at 3-4,000 feet and to fire them in pairs from 1,500 feet at a range of 3,000 feet. However, in practice the pilots disregarded the prescribed tactics and developed their own tactics.

In the MTO and ETO U.S. fighter bombers never adopted rockets on a large scale. The 9AF utilized only 13,959 during the war as compared to 222,515 used by the RAF 2TAF.

First Victory Using a Rocket
Pilot: Capt. Judge E. Wolfe
Unit: 333FS/318FG/7AF
A/C: P-47 vs. Zeke
Date: 6 June 1945/1145-1530
Place: Kyushu, Japan
Action: Capt. Judge Wolfe added a new dimension to air combat while leading a P-47 flight at 21,000 feet over Kyushu, Japan. In a mid-afternoon mission on 6 June 1945, seven Zekes lurking at

25,000 feet bounced the Thunderbolts. The Americans turned into the attack of the onrushing Japanese. Wolfe had two rockets remaining under wing and salvoed them at the lead attacker. One rocket hit the enemy fighter, disintegrating it in a huge explosion. Wolfe flew through the debris and shot down another Zeke by conventional means. Wolfe went on to claim nine victories in the war, but none more unusual than his rocket victory.

Napalm
Napalm is a powder that thickens gasoline to a gel. It was named so because it is made from the aluminum salts of *na*phennic and *palm*itic acids. Napalm was ignited by a white phosphorous igniter. A 150 gallon tank could burn out a 90x150 foot area and was extremely difficult to extinguish. A fighter bomber could carry three napalm tanks: 160 gallon on the center line pylon and two 150 gallon on each wing pylon. Initially napalm was considered most effective for the incineration of enemy troops entrenched in pill boxes and caves, but it was also used to destroy enemy camouflage prior to rocket attacks. For this reason napalm tank(s) were mixed with bombs or rockets. The nose cowl was used as a sighting device.

Napalm tanks were used in the MTO/ETO, and more extensively in the PTO. In hilly terrain the tanks were dropped in a shallow dive, while against targets on more or less level terrain they were dropped in level flight from minimum altitude so as to produce long swathes of fire that enveloped the target.

Conclusion
The increasing effectiveness of 9AF TACs can be illustrated by comparing the *monthly* (June 1944) performance figures to a *one day* figure (25 March 1945) when the Allies pushed across the Rhine.

TARGET (Destroyed/Damaged)	June 1944	25 March 1945
E/A Air	180/96	3/0
E/A Ground	33/15	15/26
Locomotives	91/55	76/26
RR Cars	427/513	858/1351
Tanks/Armored Vehicles	22/24	118/76
Motor Transport	1288/583	742/649
Guns	14/10	27/16

Napalm was used more extensively in the Pacific than the ETO or MTO. Here a Corsair with wheels down to slow diving speed drops a napalm tank on Bloody Nose Ridge on Peleliu. (USMC)

CLAIMS	392			393			394		
	DESTROYED	PROBABLE	DAMAGED	DESTROYED	PROBABLE	DAMAGED	DESTROYED	PROBABLE	DAMAGED
AIRCRAFT	142	10	121	144½	3	83	145	15	140
AMUNITION DUMP	14	2	6	.26	0	0	18	0	0
BRIDGES	11	4	18	18	0	11	1	7	19
BUILDINGS	244	9	165	345	81	103	173	18	152
GUN EMPLACEMENTS	125	2	7	130	2	14	51	1	39
HIGHWAYS	17	1	4	31	3	0	26	0	7
LOCOMOTIVES	134	5	27	127	0	57	118	19	36
MOTOR VEHICLES	1094	3	274	1176	10	404	955	30	769
MARSHALLING YARDS	32	0	0	39	0	0	55	0	0
RAILROAD CARS	718	37	1111	1314	10	1733	1123	137	2289
RAILROAD TRACKS	262	5	19	405	0	9	221	0	0
TANKS	23	4	8	134	0	33	39	0	21
SORTIES	4558			4807			4810		

The 367FG kept a meticulous score board for its three squadrons. (USAF)

Maj. Joseph Thury followed as the second most prolific ETO strafer with 25 1/2 ground (2 1/2 air) victories as CO of the 505FS/339FG. (USAF)

Strafing Units and Aces

The Units

The week of 10-17 April 1945 saw the utter decimation of the Luftwaffe on the ground. On 10 April, the 56FG got 45 destroyed to put its air-ground total at 911 for the war and put it ahead of the rival 4FG, which only had five to give it 893 in the race to reach 1,000. Roving P-51s claimed 309 ground victories and 235 damaged. Thury's 339FG got 105 and Lander's 78FG got 52. The daily total surpassed the high of 177 scored on 5 September 1944. On 11 April, a field order was issued banning strafing, as Patton's Armies were advancing rapidly and might be endangered by the eager strafers. On 13 April the ban was lifted, and 285 e/a were destroyed and 220 damaged on the ground. It was becoming more difficult for a fighter pilot to gain a ground victory, as the parked aircraft were left there as they had no fuel in their tanks. With no fuel in their tanks they would not catch fire when hit and could not be seen burning on the gun camera films. The 56th made a fighter sweep on Eggebeck A/D near Kiel in north Germany. Its P-47s met virtually no resistance and destroyed 95 aircraft. These victories put the Wolf Pack over 1,000 aircraft, much to the chagrin of the 4FG, which could only destroy a few moored seaplanes off the coast of Denmark. Lt. Randal Murphy set a record by destroying ten aircraft on the ground in one location. On the 14th and 15th there were no fighter escorts as the bombers attacked strong points on the French Atlantic coast and needed no escorts for these "milk runs." On 16 April, fighters escorted bombers to the Regensburg area, while others freelanced against airfields in Czechoslovakia. The daily totals were record-setting: 724 e/a were destroyed and 373 were damaged on the ground. Landers' 78 FG got 125 destroyed and 86 damaged in the Prague-Pilsen area for the most strafing victories in a day for any fighter group. Thury's 339th got 118, with 1Lt. Robert Ammon of its 503FS breaking Murphy's record, claiming 11 destroyed for the mission. The 353FG, Glen Duncan's former group, now led by Col. Ben Rimmerman, got 110 near Munich. The 352nd got 68. The 4FG got 61 freelancing over Prague and 44 from its escorts strafing Gablingen A/D to put it over 1,000 victories. 1Lt. Douglas Pedersen

LtCol. Elwyn Righetti was the top-scoring strafing in the ETO with 27 ground victories to go with his 7 1/2 aerial victories. He was shot down and killed on 16 April 1945 after destroying nine Me-109s near Dresden. (USAF)

1Lt. Bill Cullerton of the 357FS/355FG preferred strafing and had 21 ground claims to go with his five air victories. In April 1945, Cullerton's "Miss Steve" was shot down and he was a POW until the end of the war. (Author/Cullerton)

1Lt. Randal Murphy of the 56FG scored 10 strafing victories on 13 April 1945 for the highest one day individual ground total to that date. (USAAF)

Four 8AF pilots claimed 20 or more ground strafing victories. The top ETO strafer was Lt.Col. Elwyn Righetti of the 338FS/55Fg with 27. The energetic and personable leader made the 55FG a leading 8AF group, taking the headlines away from the 4th and 56th fighter groups in early 1945. The aggressive Righetti had a headline day on 16 April. After relinquishing B-17 escort to another P-51 group, Righetti's unit searched for targets to strafe near Dresden. Accompanied by wingman 1Lt. Carroll Henry, Righetti dropped down and strafed a row of Me-109s, destroying three. On his second run he got four more 109s, but his P-51 "*Katydid*" was hit and began to lose oil pressure. Despite knowing he would not make it back to base but could make another run, Righetti made another pass, destroying two more Messerschmitts to give him nine for the day. He crash-landed soon after the attack, but his fate remains unknown, as his aircraft went down in Soviet-occupied territory. Speculation is that German civilians killed him.

The second leading ground ace in the 8AF was Maj. Joseph Thury, CO of the 505FS/339FG, with 25 1/2. Thury's best days also came in mid-April 1945. While searching for targets in southern Germany after escort duty, the group discovered a large camouflaged airfield that was using the autobahn as a runway. Thury's eight Mustangs separated into two, four ship flights and strafed the field. Thury's P-51 "*Pauline*" destroyed a Me-109 and made a second run to silence an anti-aircraft gun. He got a Me-262 jet on his next pass. Returning to base, he was informed that his group was scheduled to return the next day to finish the job. The next day the group was to fly to target at the end of a bomber formation heading into Germany. Using the autobahn as a navigation reference, Thury led his flight to the familiar target. Thury's first run met surprisingly weak opposition, and he was able to shoot up a FW-190. Thury made his second pass accompanied by three other top cover flights. As they approached, a German flare signaled their waiting AA gunners to open fire on the unsuspecting P-51s. To escape the ricocheting strafing rounds the Germans had built platforms in the trees surrounding the airfield. The German fire took a heavy toll on the attackers, and one shell put a hole in Thury's right wing. Thury ordered the Mustangs to concentrate on knocking out the gun positions on their second pass and then again on their third pass. It took four passes to make the area safe for strafing the many-parked aircraft on the field. On his fifth pass, Thury's guns set fire to a Me-262 jet, while his next passes exploded a Me-109, followed by a pass that added two Fw-190s to his score. Thury had only enough ammo for one more pass, and he tempted fate. A 20mm shell ripped open the leading edge of his right wing. His P-51 struggled to 3,000 feet, and protected by 1Lt. James Starnes headed across Europe. The P-51 began to run hot as it neared the North Sea. Thury tried all the tricks to cool the Merlin down, but by finally lowering the flaps he diverted enough cold air to cool the engine down. After six hours Thury was able to nurse the fighter to a landing. The 505th had gotten 39 e/a to total 59 in two days. The 505th was able to claim more squadron victories, air and ground, in one year than any other 8AF squadron. Thury added seven claims to his totals and was awarded the Silver Star.

got eight victories. A total of 31 pilots were MIA after the raids, including Group Leader Lt.Col. Sid Woods and Joe Thury. On the 17th, the fighters escorted bomber groups over Dresden and then returned to finish off the airdromes attacked on the previous day. They again had great success, scoring 286 destroyed and 113 damaged, but lost 17, including Righetti. The four missions of the 10th, 13th, 16th, and 17th claimed 1,604 destroyed and 941 damaged for a MIA count of 64 fighters. The 4FG flew its last mission on 20 April, and its rival, the 56th, flew for the last time the following day. The 361FG quit on the 20th, the 505th on the 21st, and the 78th on the 25th.

Ground Victories in the CBI

Gen. Claire Chennault, Air Commander of the CBI Air Forces stated: "I don't care if we get them in the air or on the ground, as long as we get them. It's better to get the enemy on the ground before he has a chance to cause any damage." While leading the AVG, Chennault allowed bonus payments for strafed aircraft destroyed on the ground. So it is not surprising that the 10AF and 14AF under his command allowed strafing victories as part of a pilot's victory total.

1Lt. Robert Ammon 503FS/339FG scored 11 ground victories on 16 April 1945 for the highest one day total of the war. (USAF)

Many pilots found strafing more exciting and rewarding than aerial combat. One of them was William Cullerton of the 357FS/355FG, who was a legitimate ace with five aerial victories, but also had 21 ground victories. Some sources credit him with 13 on the ground, but he was adamant about the 21 throughout his career. On 2 November 1944 Cullerton's squadron was escorting B–17s, and on the mission he shot down a Me-109 while it was landing. The squadron proceeded to strafe the same field, destroying 26 Luftwaffe aircraft, of which Cullerton accounted for six. In April 1945, Cullerton's P-51 "*Miss Steve*" was shot down while strafing. He was taken prisoner but survived the war.

Lt.Col. John Landers probably had one of the most varied scoring records of any pilot in the war. He was an ace in the Pacific with six victories, and then an ace in the ETO with 8 1/2. He scored victories in three different aircraft: P-40 (6); P-38 (4); and P-51 (4 1/2). Landers' 20 ground victories made him the fourth highest ETO strafing ace. On 10 April 1945 Landers, the new CO of the 78FG, got eight ground victories.

Top WWII/CBI Strafing Ace
Maj. Thomas Reynolds
The top-strafing ace of the war was Maj. Thomas Reynolds, who flew for the little-known Chinese American Composite Wing (CACW) of the 14AF. The Wing was under the command of Brig. Gen. Clinton D. "Casey" Vincent, who the cartoonist Milt Caniff modeled his comic strip character Col. Vince Casey. Reynolds flew P-40s and was credited with 38 1/2 ground victories and four aerial victories while leading the Fifth Fighter "The Bloody Hatchet" Group. On two consecutive missions in July 1944 he led strafing runs on the Pauilichi A/D near Hangkow, China. The fields were packed with Japanese aircraft ready to aid the Japanese Ichigo ground campaign to capture 14AF bases in China. These two missions added greatly to his score and were confirmed by his CO, Col. Virdenn. On 11 November, Reynolds led ten P-40s on a surprise attack on Hengyeng Airfield. There were about 25 aircraft on the field. The P-40s dropped fragmentation bombs and made 37 strafing runs. The 7FS destroyed 17 aircraft on the ground, and Reynolds was awarded the Silver Star. In a series of three raids on airfields near Hangkow in January 1945, 71 Japanese aircraft were destroyed and 57 damaged. Reynolds, flying a P-51, destroyed 12 enemy on the ground for a record for one raid. On 10 February, far-ranging Mustangs flew six hours to coastal Tsingtao, where they found crowded Japanese airfields. Reynolds and 1Lt. James Moore each destroyed ten Kates (Sonyas?). Soon after, Reynolds rotated home.

Medal of Honor Strafing Ace
Pilot: 1Lt. Raymond L. Knight
Unit: 346FS/350FG/12AF
Time: 24-25 April 1945
Place: Northern Po Valley
A/C: P-47 "*Oh Johnnie*"
Action: Texan 1Lt. Raymond Knight joined the 346FS "Checkerboard" of the 350FG on 7 December 1944. The Group's three top aerial scorers only had three victories each. During its entire tour the Group had 50 aerial and 108 ground victories. Knight had flown 82 missions without having an aerial claim.

On the morning of 24 April 1945, Knight volunteered to lead two P-47s to the Luftwaffe airdrome at Ghedi. Once over the target he risked heavy AA fire to recon the field, discovering eight cam-

Maj. Thomas Reynolds of the CACW was the top American strafing ace of the war with 38 1/2 in the CBI. (USAF)

After leading multiple strafing raids on 24-25 April 1945 in the Po Valley, 1Lt. Raymond Knight of the 346FS/350FG was hit on the 24th and managed to bring his fighter back to base. The next day his P-47 was hit again and he refused to leave his valuable aircraft. Knight tried to nurse his badly damaged fighter back to base but crashed into the Appennine Mountains. For his bravery he was awarded the CMH. (USAF)

ouflaged aircraft. Leading a strafing run he claimed five and his wingman two. After returning to base, Knight again volunteered to lead a flight to the airfield at Bergamo, which was in the same area as Ghedi. Approaching the target, heavy flak damaged his aircraft, but he pressed on and discovered camouflaged enemy aircraft and led the flight into battle. He made ten passes and was hit twice more. He was credited with destroying six fully loaded twin-engine bombers and two fighters, while his flight got four other TE bombers and a fighter. Knight was able to bring his damaged fighter back to base.

The next morning Knight led another flight to Bergamo. He destroyed three more TE bombers, but his aircraft was badly damaged. His Medal of Honor citation reads: "Realizing the critical need for aircraft in his unit, he declined to parachute to safety over friendly territory and unhesitating attempt to return his shattered plane to his home field. With great skill and strength, he flew homeward until caught by treacherous air conditions in the Appennines Mountains, where he crashed and was killed."

These missions helped the Allies maintain a bridgehead across the Po River at a critical time during which German air interdiction may have made a difference. Knight's wife accepted his posthumous award.

Strafing Aces

Judgment of ground victory claims as either destroyed or damaged was determined by gun camera evidence. "Destroyed" was an aircraft left burning or exploded, while a "damaged" was an e/a holed by machine gun fire. Combat film confirmation was subjective, much like football instant replays, and there was a lot of give and take between group and wing assessments

8th Air Force Strafing Aces

Pilot Name	Rank	Aerial Victories	Ground Victories
Righetti Elwyn	Lt. Col.	27	7.5
Thury, Joseph	Lt.Col.	25.5	2.5
Cullerton, William	1Lt.	21	6
Landers, John	Lt.Col.	20	8.5 (6)
Godfrey, John	Capt.	18	18
Tower, Archie	Maj.	18	11.5
Kinnard, Claiborne	Col.	17	8
McKennon, Pierce	Maj.	16.5	5.5
Heller, Edwin	Capt.	16.5	5.5
Everson, Kirke	Capt.	16	1.5
Crompton, Gordon	Maj.	15	6.5
Stewart, David	1Lt.	15	0
Preddy, George	Maj.	14.5	26.83
Brown, Henry	Capt.	14.5	17.5
Montgomery, Gerald	Maj.	14.5	3
Hightshow, Melville	1Lt.	14.5	0
Kolb, Herbert	Capt.	14.5	0
Hofer, Ralph	1Lt.	14	16.5
Meyer, John	Lt.Col.	13	24
Johnson, Gerald	Capt.	13	15
Goodson, James	Maj.	13	15
Littage, Raymond	Capt.	13	10.5
Elder, John	Lt.Col.	13	8
Glover, Frederick	Maj.	12.5	10.33
Boone, Walker	Maj.	12.17	2.67
Welch, Robert	Capt.	12	6
Biggs, Oscar	1Lt.	11.5	0.5
Olds, Robin	Maj.	11	12
Ammon, Robert	Capt.	11	5
Corey, Harry	Capt.	11	1
Lanove, Roland	1Lt.	11	1
Miller, Gerald	2Lt.	11	0
Schilling, David	Col.	10.5	22.5
Gustice, Richard	F/O	10.5	0
Cueleers, George	Lt.Col.	10.5	0
Morris, Ray	1Lt.	10	3.5
Murphy, Randall	2Lt.	10	2
Pattillo, Charles	1Lt.	10	1
Burch, Harold	1Lt.	10	0
McMullen, Joseph	1Lt.	10	0
Blickenstaff, Wayne	1Lt.	10	0
Broadhead, Joseph	Maj.	10	0
Lines, Ted	1Lt.	10	0
Meroney, Virgil	Capt.	10	0
Rankin, Robert	1Lt.	10	0
McKinnon, Pierce	Maj.	9.67	12
Graham, Gordon	Lt.Col.	9.5	7
Gilbert, Olin	Lt.Col.	9.5	2
Olson, Thomas	1Lt.	9.5	1
Lowell, John	Lt.Col.	9	7.5
Duffy, James	Capt.	9	5.2
Anderson, Woodrow	Capt.	9	4.5
Johnson, Martin	Capt.	9	1
McCormick, Arthur	Capt.	9	1
Greenwood, Ray	1Lt.	9	0
Orcutt, Leon	1Lt.	9	0
Taylor, Clyde	2Lt.	9	0
Rimmerman, Ben	Lt.Col.	8.5	7
Duffy, Claire	Maj.	8.5	3
Pierce, Don	Capt.	8.5	0
Zemke, Hub	Col.	8	19.5
Bankey, Ernest	Capt.	8	9.5
Harrington. Francis	1Lt.	8	4
Mellen, Joseph	Capt.	8	2
Real, Joseph	Capt.	8	2
Clark, William	Lt.Col.	8	1
Hermansen, Cephas	1Lt.	8	0
Josey, Danford	2Lt.	8	0
Jurgens, Fred	F/O	8	0
MacClarence, Wm.	1Lt.	8	0
Messinger, Richard	1Lt.	8	0
Palson, Richard	2Lt.	8	0
Duncan, Glenn	Col.	7.8	19
Waggoner, Horace	Capt.	7.5	5
Munson, Norman	Maj.	7.5	0

Gentile, Don	Capt.	7	21.83	Smith, Robert	Capt.	6	1
Luksic, Carl	1Lt.	7	8.5	Jones, Thomas	1Lt.	6	0.5
Malmoten, Donald	Capt.	7	3.5	Barger, Clarence	2Lt.	6	0.33
Mansker, Joseph	1Lt.	7	3	Apple, George	2Lt.	6	0
Waldron. Karl	1Lt.	7	3	Robert, Blizzard	1Lt.	6	0
Cunnick, John	1Lt.	7	2	Bowers, Arthur	2Lt.	6	0
Emory, Frank	Capt.	7	2	Chenez, Gordon	1Lt.	6	0
Gevorkian. Sam	Capt.	7	2	Clifton, Frank	1Lt.	6	0
Kier, Edward	1Lt.	7	2	Deanda, Louis	2Lt.	6	0
Kyler, Russell	1Lt.	7	2	DeVilliers, Don	1Lt.	6	0
Slack, Henry	1Lt.	7	1.5	Einhaus, Lowell	Capt.	6	0
Ayers, James	1Lt.	7	1	Frisch, Robert	1Lt.	6	0
Zettler, Vincent	1Lt.	7	1	Frum. Rollin	F/O	6	0
Antonides, William	2Lt.	7	0	Gordon, Ray	1Lt.	6	0
Caywood, Herbert	1Lt.	7	0	Herner, Kenneth	1Lt.	6	0
Chin, Claude	1Lt.	7	0	Lenvings, Loton	1Lt.	6	0
Elmgren, Charles	1Lt.	7	0	Peterson, Douglas	1Lt.	6	0
Hepner, Neal	2Lt.	7	0	Pogue, Charles	1Lt.	6	0
Hollingsworth, Jas.	Capt.	7	0	Paul, Robert	1Lt.	6	0
Hopcraft, Ernest	1Lt.	7	0	Snope, Herbert	1Lt.	6	0
Kulik, Edward	Capt.	7	0	Tracey, Richard	Capt.	6	0
Mahaney, Howard	2Lt.	7	0	Uttenweiler, ?	Capt.	6	0
Murphy, Jerome	1Lt.	7	0	Williams, Gene	Capt.	6	0
Weber, Carl	1Lt.	7	0	Woolery, James	1Lt.	6	0
Witzell, George	1Lt.	7	0	Anderson. Charles	1Lt.	5.5	10.5
Andrew, Stephen	Maj.	6 1/2	8	Johnson, Michael	Maj.	5.5	8
Starnes, James	Capt.	6 1/2	6	Miklajiyk, Henry	Capt.	5.5	7.5
Sowerby, Theodore	Capt.	6 1/2	2	Dregne, Irwin	Col.	5.5	7
Swift, Ben	1Lt.	6.5	1	Fortier, Norman	Maj.	5.5	5.83
Falvey, Harold	F/O	6.5	1	Jones, Frank	Capt.	5.5	5
Boring, Lloyd	1Lt.	6.5	0.5	Malstrom, Einer	Col.	5.5	1
Leslie, Charles	Capt.	6.5	0	Golden, John	1Lt.	5.5	1
Truett, Jesse	Capt.	6.5	0	McMahan, Bruce	2Lt.	5.5	0.5
Jucheim, Alwyn	Capt.	6	10	Bell, Thomas	Capt.	5.5	0
Haviland, Fred	Capt.	6	9	Bledsol, Norman	Capt.	5.5	0
Bostwick, George	Maj.	6	9	Cooper, Randolph	2Lt.	5.5	0
Dade, Luian	Lt.Col.	6	6	Quick, Michael	Maj.	5	12
Biel, Hippolitus	1Lt.	6	5.33	Norley, Louis	Maj.	5	11.33
McElroy, James	Capt.	6	5	Schlegal, Albert	Capt.	5	10
Merritt, George	Maj.	6	5	Jones, Cyril	1Lt.	5	6
Jacobson, Gail	1Lt.	6	4.5	Sykes, William	1Lt.	5	5
Duncan, John	1Lt.	6	4	McDuffie, Duncan	1Lt.	5	4
Kirk, John	1Lt.	6	4	Visconte, Romildo	Capt.	5	4
Cole, Charles	Capt.	6	3	Webb, Roy	Lt.Col.	5	4
Giller, Edward	Maj.	6	3	Alfred, Carl	Capt.	5	3
Halter, Robert	1Lt.	6	3	Jones, Repo	1Lt.	5	3
Hunter, John	Capt.	6	3	Farmer, Owen	Capt.	5	2
Johnson, Clarence	Capt.	6	3	Jones, william	1Lt.	5	2
Alexander, Frederick	1Lt.	6	3	Kier, Edward	Capt	5	2
Flag, Walter	Capt.	6	3	Shupe, Joseph	1Lt.	5	2
McGinnis, Keith	1Lt.	6	3	Henry, Carroll	Capt.	5	1.5
Mudge, William	1Lt.	6	3	Olander, Richard	Capt.	5	1.5
Chetneky, Steve	1Lt.	6	1	Rich, George	Capt.	5	1.5
Diamond, Brack	1Lt.	6	1	Bosworth, Richard	1Lt.	5	1
Silva, Stanley	Capt.	6	1	Brasher, G.E.	1Lt.	5	1

Colletti, Anthony	1Lt.	5	1
Dissette, Lawrence	Capt.	5	1
Gould, Clifford	1Lt.	5	1
Irion, Robert	1Lt.	5	1
Kirby, Henry	Maj.	5	1
Nelson, Robert	1Lt.	5	1
Reynolds, Garth	Maj.	5	1
Speer, Frank	2Lt.	5	1
Whinnen, Donald	1Lt.	5	0.5
Carter, Joseph	1Lt.	5	0.5
Kurtz, Robert	Capt.	5	0.5
Loveless, Philip	Capt.	5	0.5
Morgan, Frank	Capt.	5	0.5
Peel, Eugene	1Lt.	5	0.5
Ramm, Albert	Capt.	5	0.5
Baugh, Donald	F/O	5	0
Birtcul. Frank	Capt.	5	0
Biddgett, Burton	1Lt.	5	0
Byers, John	1Lt.	5	0
Denson, Gordon	2Lt.	5	0
Demars, R.E.	1Lt.	5	0
Dewitt, Charles	Capt.	5	0
Dickson, Melvin	1Lt.	5	0
Doss, Gene	1Lt.	5	0
Fletcher, Jack	1Lt.	5	0
Fussell, Roscoe	1Lt.	5	0
Guyton, William	1Lt.	5	0
Hanson, Kenneth	1Lt.	5	0
Helfrecht, Kenneth	1Lt.	5	0
Hendrickson, Robert	1Lt.	5	0
Hunt, Harlan	1Lt.	5	0
Jackson, Boyd	1Lt.	5	0
John, Leedom	1Lt.	5	0
Kerr, Warren	Capt.	5	0
Kesler, Gilbert	1Lt.	5	0
Kissell, William	1Lt.	5	0
Lynch, William	2Lt.	5	0
MacKean, Robert	Capt.	5	0
Marsh, Halbert	2Lt.	5	0
McClure, James	1Lt.	5	0
McCollom, Frances	1Lt.	5	0
McFadden, Jack	1Lt.	5	0
McHugh, Philip	1Lt.	5	0
Peterburs, Joseph	1Lt.	5	0
Phaneuf, Richard	1Lt.	5	0
Pryor, Thomas	1Lt.	5	0
Queen, Thomas	2Lt.	5	0
Reinhardt, Edwin	1Lt.	5	0
Rose, Robert	1Lt.	5	0
Rich, John	F/O	5	0
Shane, Presson	Capt.	5	0
Smigel, Alfred	1Lt.	5	0
Smith, Vernon	2Lt.	5	0
Sweat, Dale	1Lt.	5	0
Sykes, Henry	1Lt.	5	0
Vickery, Daran	1Lt.	5	0

CBI Strafing Aces

Pilot Name	Rank	Unit (FG)	Ground Victories	Aerial Victories
Reynolds, Thomas	Maj.	5CACW	38.5	4
Moore, James	Capt.	?	17	0
Chapman, Philip	Maj.	23	16	7
Reed, Robert	1Lt.	311	14	2
Brown, Robert	Capt.	23	13	2
Terry, Wade	1Lt.	23	13	2
Finberg, Floyd	Maj.	23	11	1
Binkley, Ira	1Lt.	23	11	1
Witzenberger, Edw.	Maj.	?	10	0
Glenn, Maxwell	Maj.	459	9.5	7.5
Pearson, Wesley	1Lt.	23	9	2
Swetland, Paul	1Lt.	23	9	2
Muenster, Les	1Lt.	23	9	1
Wells, Robert	1Lt.	23	9	1
Conn, John	1Lt.	?	9	0
Howard, Lauren	1Lt.	?	9	0
Duke, Walter	1Lt.	459	8.5	10
Wyatt, Walter	1Lt.	3	8	1.5
Anderson, Louis	1Lt.	23	8	1
Branz, John	1Lt.	23	7	1
Harrison, James	2Lt.	8	7	0
Kosa, Silvan	1Lt.	23	7	0
Watson, George	1Lt.	3	6	1.5
Slocomb, Clyde	Maj.	23	6	1
Copenberger, Chas.	1Lt.	?	6	0
Corfman, Leslie	1Lt.	?	6	0
Long, Nimrod	1Lt.	23	6	0
Field, Warren	1Lt.	311	5.5	4
Rector, Edward	Lt.Col.	23	5	7.75
Paxton, Haywood	1Lt.	3CACW	5	6.5
Mahon, Keith	Capt.	51	5	5
Brink, Thomas	1Lt.	5CACW	5	3
Denney, Chester	Capt.	23	5	3
Westermark, Robert	1Lt.	311	5	3
Cole, Heston	1Lt.	23	5	1
Honeycutt, John	1Lt.	?	5	1
Loosey, Hobert	1Lt.	311	5	1
Mahony, Grant	Maj.	1Cdo	5	1
Colleps, Carl	1Lt.	?	5	0
Everest, Frank	1Lt.	5CACW	5	0
Miller, John	1Lt.	5	5	0
Perelka, Charles	1Lt.	3	5	0
Ray, Edgar	2Lt.	?	5	0
Spann, Robert	1Lt.	1Cdo.	5	0

TAC R and Photo Reconnaissance

They were described as unarmed, unafraid, and unsung. The photo reconnaissance pilot could gather more vital information in less time than any other means of military intelligence. In WWI aircraft production emphasized the reconnaissance aircraft over the pursuit aircraft (fighter) and bomber. In WWII, of all the aircraft in the American inventory none was specifically designed for reconnaissance. The modification of standard combat models, fighters, and bombers led to the "F" prefix series of photo reconnaissance aircraft:

F-3	A-20	F-8	Mosquito
F-4	P-38	F-9	B-17
F-5	P-38	F-10	B-25
F-6	P-51	F-13	B-29
F-7	B-24		

Modifications to reconnaissance aircraft were completed by the manufacturer or in modification centers, and in some cases in the field. These modifications took place throughout the war because tactical conditions changed faster than the manufacturers could change their production lines. The P-39 and P-40 were tried as photo recon aircraft early in the war, but both were found wanting. The P-39 was a total failure due to its short range, low speed, and poor maneuverability, and suffered high losses. The P-40 was somewhat better, but lacked sufficient range that led the AAC to look to the P-38, which had a longer range and much better performance.

The P-38 Photo Variants: The F-4 and F-5s

In mid-1941 the success of the twin-engine British Mosquito led the USAAC to consider their new P-38 for its photo reconnaissance niche as the redesignated F-4. The F-4, adopted in July 1942, was to be unarmed, depending on its speed, altitude, and range to accomplish its new role and elude the enemy. The F-4 was a P-38E (the F-4A was a P-38F) with all armament removed from the large nose and replaced with a variety of camera installations that made operation and maintenance easy. The placement of the camera ap-

A camera being unloaded for film processing from an F-5 Lightning of the 8PRG at Lingling, China. The F-5 was unarmed and the most numerous of the US photo recon aircraft. Its large gun bay in the nose made for a variety of camera installations and made operation and maintenance easy. (USAF)

A pair of K-17 cameras being installed into the nose of a F-5. A pair of K-18 cameras that were exchanged sit on the scaffold. Cameras were replaced to meet mission requirements. (USAF)

paratus in front of the pilot made it simple for him to aim them correctly, even during difficult low altitude, high-speed runs using high oblique cameras. In the early war the F-4 had sufficient speed, range, and altitude for combat recce. However, in the Pacific the need for increased range added fuel, and in turn weight, which decreased its speed and altitude capabilities. However, by early 1943 the F-4 no longer had the speed to outrun improved enemy fighters and gave way to the F-5 series: F-5A/B=P-38G; F-5C=P-38H; F-5E/F=P-38J; and F-5E/G=P-38L.

The successful F-4 configuration was used in this next P-38 photo reconnaissance generation, which were adopted in November 1943. The F-5A was a P-38G, and the series ran up to the P-38L conversion to the F-5G. The F-5 variations were the most numerous U.S. recon aircraft of the war, with over 1,200 being specifically built or converted at modification centers. At its inception the F-5A was an excellent photo recon aircraft due to its service ceiling, speed at altitude, rate of climb, and range, which was extended from 450 miles to 2,250 miles by the addition of two external wing tanks. But it was the exceptional flexibility of camera installation and ease of use in the F-5s that kept it in operations. The F-5A at 20,000 feet could photograph a 40-mile area, and at 200mph it could photograph 8,000 square miles per hour. At 30,000 feet it was able to photograph six square miles with photos so sharp they could detect barbed wire. Operating the camera was easy, all the pilot had to do was to push a button and the camera worked automatically. However, when and where to push the button necessitated extensive training. But by mid-1944 F-5 performance in Europe made it vulnerable to enemy interceptors, especially the Luftwaffe's fuel-injected FW-190s and Me-262 jets. The F-5s required fighter escort, particularly on deep penetrations. They only continued in any large scale use because of these escorts and because Luftwaffe fighters concentrated on Allied bombers. It excelled at photomapping, but was eventually withdrawn from fundamental photo recon re-

F-6 camera ports were located at the posterior bar of the National Insignia. The larger port was for the left looking high oblique camera and the smaller port immediately below housed the left trimetrogon camera. Just under this camera and forward of the tail wheel doors was the collar that surrounded the vertical camera window. (USAF)

A 15TRG F-6C with Plexiglas bubble oblique camera port behind the cockpit. The F-6s were armed and accounted for 220 victories and seven aces. (USAF)

F-24 oblique camera mounted behind the pilot in a F-6. (USAF)

sponsibilities. In the Pacific its performance was adequate against Japanese fighters to remain on operations throughout the war.

The P-51 Photo Variant: The F-6

The requirement for a photo P-51 was established in June 1942 and mandated a three camera installation, which was difficult in the small Mustang. Arguments were also made that the installation of cameras in the P-51 would change its center of gravity and reduce performance. But the three-camera requirement was reduced to two, the performance concerns were unfounded, and production began in August 1942. These first F-6s were unarmed, or armed only for defense, but a few F-5s in North Africa kept their original four or six gun armament and were used in attack and photo and visual reconnaissance. The F-6 surpassed the F-5 in maximum speed climb and service ceiling, and had equivalent range with external drop tanks. The forte of the photo Mustangs was close troop support reconnaissance over the Continent from D-Day to VE-Day. Ten of the twelve F-6 TAC R squadrons were based in the ETO, one in the western Pacific, and one in the CBI. The F-6 variants were: F-6B=P-51A; F-6C=P-51B/C; F-6D=P-51D; and F-6K=P-51K. For more information on the F-6 see Chapter 8/P-51.

U.S. Navy Photo Reconnaissance Fighter Conversions

When the war broke out the Navy had no reconnaissance aircraft. In 1931 the U.S. Army and Navy agreed that all Army aircraft would operate over land and coastal areas, and Navy aircraft would operate in conjunction with the fleet. Since mapping (of land) was the primary function of photo reconnaissance at that time, the Navy did not actively pursue it, except for some hand-held cameras. Before 1942, only a handful of carrier aircraft, usually the outdated SBDs, had fixed camera mounts, and these were given the "P" suffix. After Pearl Harbor several inadequate F2A Brewster Buffaloes were also tried in the reconnaissance role. The SBD and F2A were tried in this role because "good" fighters were needed to fight the Japanese. However, they were found as inadequate in this role, as

A F-5 on a dicing mission over pre-D-Day beaches. The photo points out gun emplacements located in the cliffs above the beach. Note the shadow of the F-5 on the water. (USAF)

1Lt. Joe Waits scored 2 victories for the 15 TRS and got 3 1/2 more with the 162 TRS working to support the Third Army. (Author)

they were as combat aircraft. The F4U-1P Corsair was considered, but its problems adapting to carriers led to the switch to the F6F. The F6F-3P and the more numerous F6F-5P were in use from early 1944, but the TBF-3P Avenger was the Navy's recon aircraft of choice, as it was reliable and rugged. It was a stable camera platform with plenty of room for the cameras, making it an easy reconnaissance conversion. At that time in the Pacific war Japanese air power was definitely on the wane, and the TBF was adequate for the task. Also, USAAF reconnaissance was well established and widespread, and the necessity for a large USN reconnaissance arm was not required.

Photo Reconnaissance Mission

The photo reconnaissance mission was probably one of the most dangerous and demanding of all combat missions. Alone and unarmed, the F-5s normally roved 100-150 miles from their bases on front line and pinpoint missions and from 250-300 miles on bomb damage assessment. Photo recce missions included:

Front line coverage: Daily missions to photograph in detail the front line region to detect enemy defenses, such as troop, armor, and artillery deployment.

Strips and Mosaics: Photography of the entire battle zone, including areas of impending action, lines of communications, and transport into the area.

Dicing Missions: A technique used when close-up photos were needed. Several F-5s would make high-speed, low-level passes in quick succession (50 feet apart) before enemy AA could react. "Dicing" was derived from the RAF slang for a very dangerous mission, as in rolling the dice against death. The nose and oblique cameras would film simultaneously to provide overlapping coverage.

Pinpoints: Photography of defined targets, such as airfields, roads, bridges, railheads, artillery position and strong points, and HQ and command posts.

Bomb Damage Assessment: Photography of targets that had been recently bombed.

TAC R Missions

TAC R missions involved a two-plane section in which the no.1 (leader) was responsible for navigation and observing and/or photographing the target, and the No.2 was to provide protection against surprise air attack and to warn against AA fire. No.2 flew about 200 yards to the flank of the leader and down sun so that the no.1's tail was always covered toward the sun. Most of the TAC R missions were visual, and usually were flown between 3,500 and 6,000 feet maximum (above which ground details could not be seen in detail). Often it was necessary to fly in close to obtain detailed observations, which could be very dangerous. TAC R missions included:

Area Search: This mission was intended to provide army HQ immediate intelligence on the disposition and movement of enemy troops to a depth of 100 miles beyond the front lines. This large area was divided into smaller sectors of 650 square miles, which could be covered in about one hour by a recce section.

Route Recce: A visual reconnaissance of road and rail lines to a depth of 200 behind enemy lines to determine enemy logistics, supply routes, and troop deployment and movement.

Capt. Clyde East of 15TRS/10PRG was the top-scoring F-6 ace with 13 victories in the F-6. (Author/East)

Capt. John Hoefker also of the 15TRS/10PRG was second to East with 8 1/2 victories in the F-6. (USAF)

Artillery Adjustment: This mission involved TAC R pilots surveying the fire of long range artillery (155mm to 8-inch howitzers) and calling adjustments when it was too dangerous for light aircraft (L-4s or L-5s) to operate safely. These missions were either planned with a thorough briefing or impromptu by request.

Merton Oblique Photo Cover: Missions requested by an artillery commander to provide gridded photos to be used in planning fields of fire.

Photo Recce Missions: In conditions where F-5s could not operate effectively, 4,000 feet or less ceilings, and long range missions.

The armed TAC R F-6s encountered enemy aircraft during their missions, scoring 287 victories/42 probables/94 damaged and claiming 8 aces in their ranks.

LtCol. Edward McComas was the leading TacR ace with 14 victories with 118TRS in the CBI but his missions were flown in the P-51C and the F-6. (USAF)

TAC R Groups and Squadrons

Group/Squadron		V	P	D	Aces
10PRG		87	14	25	
	10TRS	0	0	0	
	12TRS	22	3	12	
	15TRS	65	11	13	East 13, Hoefker 8 1/2 , Larson 6, Waits 2 (5 1/2)
67TRG		15	3	4	
107TRG		4	2	1	
109TRG		11	0	3	
68 TRG		40	8	16	
	111TRS	39	8	16	Rader 6 1/2
	154TRS	1	0	0	
71TRG		38	2	1	
	82TRS	18	0	0	Shomo 8
	110TRS	20	2	1	
363TRG		39	5	19	
	160TRS	8	1	5	
	161TRS	12	0	1	
	162TRS	19	4	13	Waits 3 1/2 (5 1/2)
14AF					
	20TRS	1	0	0	
	118TRS	52	11	25	McComas 14, Waits 5

CHAPTER 16

Pistons vs. Jets

Me-262

In late July 1944, during the first operational sightings of Luftwaffe jet aircraft, 359FG Mustangs reported Me-163s. The revelation came as no surprise to Allied Intelligence, which had followed German jet development even before the outbreak of the war in 1939. Four days before Hitler invaded Poland (27 August 1939), Capt. Erich Warsitz flew the He-178, the world's first true jet aircraft. Luftwaffe rocket and jet aircraft development progressed rapidly, with the first operations-ready jet fighter, the twin engine Me-262, flying in July 1942. This initial jet superiority was to be impeded by the subordinate position of the Luftwaffe in the German war machine, the difficulties in getting the Jumo 004 engine into production, and Hitler's well-documented insistence on using the Me-262 as a fighter bomber, rather than as a pure fighter to counter Allied bombers and fighters, as Luftwaffe General of the Fighters, Adolf Galland, had recommended. So it was on D-Day that only 30 Me-262/converted fighter bombers had been delivered, with neither aircraft nor pilots combat-ready. By 20 July 1944, nine Me-262s of Erprobungs-Kommando *Schenk*, led by bomber ace Maj. Wolfgang Schenk, were ready for combat. The unit began sporadic fighter bomber operations, moving its bases as the Wehrmacht retreated.

A Me-262 in the gun camera film of an attacking P-47. Another Thunderbolt can be seen in the upper left-hand side of the film frame. The German jets were particularly vulnerable in taking off and in their landing patterns near their airfields as they guzzled fuel and needed to land. A total of 145 Me-262s were shot down, 127 1/2 by P-51s and 17 1/2 by P-47s. (USAF)

The advantages of the Me-262 were its speed, acceleration, and climbing ability. These attributes enabled it to gain the tactical advantage of altitude and, thus, surprise, allowing it to accept or refuse combat at will. The inherent disadvantage of early jets were their large turning radii, lack of maneuverability, and lack of range due to their voracious Jumo jet engines. American fighters found they could turn inside the Me-262, putting them into position to attack the jet head on or to be in firing position if the jet over ran its attack. Luftwaffe "Experten," aces who had run up large numbers of victories in maneuverable Me-109s and FW-190s, had to refrain from dog fighting while flying the Me-262.

American fighters, especially the aggressive P-51 Mustangs, were able to score a few jet victories by bouncing the Me-262s as they flew at low altitudes searching for U.S. bombers silhouetted against high clouds. The German jets were at their most vulnerable upon take off and landing. On take off the Jumo 004 engines were underpowered, causing take off to be very long, with slow acceleration once the fighter became airborne. Alerted by recon to imminent Me-262 deployment, the waiting P-51s would swoop to strafe the taxiing and waiting jets. The runways and facilities were bombed and strafed, rendering them unserviceable. The Jumos also gobbled huge amounts of fuel, shortening the jet's combat endurance. Concentration and precision were required on landing the jet, or a go-around was necessitated, and many crashes occurred during this time. Again, American fighters were positioned near known jet bases, attacking the vulnerable jets when they were committed to their landing patterns. The Luftwaffe countered by providing cover with piston-powered fighters to divert American attacks on the jets. The tactic was welcomed by the aggressive American fighter pilots, who were eager to increase their victory totals.

First Me-262 Downed

Pilots: Maj. Joseph Myers/2Lt. Manford Croy
Unit: 82FS/78FG/8AF
A/C: P-47s
Date: 28 August 1944/1915
Place: Tremonde west of Brussels
Action: On 28 August 1944, Maj. Joseph Myers of 82FS/78FG was leading a flight of P-47s, flying top cover for other units attacking ground targets. Myers was at 11,000 feet, west of Brussels, when he spotted what he thought was a B-26 heading south at 500 feet. He dove at a 45 degree angle at 450mph to investigate. At 4,500 feet the target began small evasive maneuvers, and Myers saw it was a Messerschmitt jet (of 1/KG(J)51). The jet's turning radius was large, and Myers' high IAS easily enabled him to cut off the jet, causing it to change direction. At full throttle, 2,000 feet above and astern, Myers closed 500 yards astern. As he was about to fire

The first Me-262 was destroyed by Maj. Joseph Myers in a P-47 of the 82FS/78FG on 28 August 1944. Myers, seen here with his crew chief, flew the jet into the ground and then destroyed it in his strafing run. (USAF)

the jet slowed and crashed into a plowed field. As the enemy hit the ground, Myers opened fire, hitting the cockpit and engines. The pilot, Ofw. Hieronymous Lauer, escaped as Myers' wingman, 2Lt. Manford Croy, shared the victory in a strafing attack.

First Me-262 Victory (?)

Pilot: 1Lt. Valmore Beaudrault
Unit: 387FS/365FG/9AF
A/C: P-47
Date: 2 October 1944/1530
Place: 20 miles NE Dusseldorf
Action: 1Lt. Valmore Beaudrault of the 387FS/365FG/9AF is sometimes credited with the first air-to-air victory over a Me-262 (KG-51) on 2 October 1944, while leading a recon mission in the Munster-Dusseldorg area at 9,000 feet. Suddenly a jet streaked through the American's flight into the clouds, and Beaudrault's P-47 dove in pursuit, but was quickly outdistanced. The jet's superior speed en-

On 2 October 1944, 1Lt. Valmore Beaudrault of the 387FS/365FG in his P-47 chased a jet which was probably low on fuel. The jet crashed into the ground before Beuadrault could fire. (USAF)

abled it to gain firing position on the Thunderbolt. Beaudrault swung into a tight turn inside to escape, and the maneuver was repeated down to the deck as the jet continued to attack. The jet slowed, probably out of fuel, or flamed out, allowing the P-47 to get on the gliding jet's tail. The German side-slipped, trying to evade .50 caliber hits. Just as he was about to fire the jet's wing hit the ground and exploded. The unfortunate pilot was again Ofw. Lauer, the victim of the 28 August combat, who was injured in this combat. Because he did not fire, Beaudrault was not officially credited with the victory, but was awarded the DFC for the action.

Maj. Richard Conner of the 82FS/78FG finally got the first all-aerial victory over the Me-262 on 7 October 1944. The jet, urgently low on fuel and wheels down, was hit in the air by Conner's 90 degree deflection shot and crashed on its base. (USAF)

First Me-262 Victory

Pilot: Maj. Richard Conner
Unit: 82FS/78FG
A/C: P 47
Date: 7 October 1944/1220
Place: Osnabruck area
Action: Flying at 24,000 feet, Conner, CO of the 82FS, and two other P-47s of his flight spotted two bogies at 12-14,000 feet. They dove after the Germans, but when they could not close they realized they were chasing jets. They continued the pursuit, and their persistence paid off, as the jets ran low on fuel and circled an airfield to land. Conner closed, but the jet turned into him on a head-on pass. Conner easily turned inside the jet and fired a 90 degree deflection shot. The jet urgently headed to land and lowered its gear. Conner closed and fired a long burst, heavily hitting the fighter and causing it to crash on the airfield for the first credited Me-262 victory.

Me-262 Daily Double Victories

The Me-262s based at Achmer were led by 250 victory ace Walter Nowotny, and were thus designated *Kommando Nowotny*. Since the heat from the twin jet engines would melt conventional Luftwaffe asphalt runways, bases with concrete runways were required. On the unit's first day of operations, 7 October, 1Lt. Urban "Ben" Drew (375FS/361FG) observed two Me-262s taxiing for takeoff. Once

1Lt. Urban Drew, flying a P-51 for the 375FS/361FG downed two, just airborne after takeoff, Me-262s on 7 October 1944. Drew would not receive confirmation of these victories until 1983! (Author/Drew)

they were airborne, Drew rolled from 15,000 feet in a 450mph dive, catching one slowly accelerating jet which was at 1,000 feet. Drew got hits at 400 yards, 30 degrees deflection, exploding a fuel tank. The second jet was 500 yards ahead and beginning to climb to port. Drew's speed from the dive was at 400 mph, and he hauled back on the stick to get a 400 yard, 60 degree firing pass to get a double jet victory. An interesting note on these victories is that they were not credited until 1983! Drew thought his wingman, 2Lt Robert McCandliss, would confirm them, but he had flown off to attack some flak batteries and was shot down and bailed out to become a POW. In 1983, Georg-Peter Eder, 78 victory Luftwaffe ace, an eye witness to the combat, confirmed the two jet victories. Capt. Don Cummings (38FS/55FG) would also score a double Me-262 jet victory over just airborne jets taking off from Giebelstadt Airdrome on 25 February 1945. That day was a black day for 1 and 2/JG (J) 54, as it lost six Me-262s, two pilots killed, three bailed out and were wounded, and another Me-262 crash landed. To cap the day

Capt. Don Cummings, 38FS/55FG, was one of six pilots to score two victories over the –262. On 25 February 1945, Cummings P-51 destroyed two jets as they were in the airborne. The other four double jet victors scored on their kills on separate days. (Author/Cummings)

off, that afternoon four more jets were destroyed on the ground during strafing attacks, and two more were lost to accidents.

Other Me-262 Combats

On 8 November 1944 Walter Nowotny was shot down either by marauding Mustangs, or more likely German anti-aircraft fire while attempting to get back to Achmer. *Kommando Nowotny* had scored 22 victories in five weeks, but was disbanded and its pilots were transferred to form the core of the first jet fighter wing, JG7 under 200 victory ace Theo Weissenberger. Only a few jets were encountered as 1944 closed. Over 500 had been completed, but many were destroyed in transit in the chaotic German rail system, and those which were delivered were destroyed on the ground. Organization and training took up more valuable time. The Me-262 fighter-bomber version was flown by KG-51 in February. On the 25th the jets suffered one of their worst losses of the war, losing eight with 14 others sustaining damage from Mustangs loitering around their airfields. The 55FG, under Elwyn Righetti, got seven jet victories, the highest daily total for any fighter group of the war.

On 2 March, 1Lt. Ted Sedvert (353FS/354FG/9AF) had one of the most unusual Me-262 encounters of the war. Sedvert observed a Me-262 fighter-bomber drop a bomb on Osthofen. The P-51 dove on the surprised German, getting hits on its tail and fuselage. The jet lost power and slowed as Sedvert emptied his guns, but to no apparent effect. Looking across into the jet's cockpit, Sedvert saw the German pilot thumb his nose at him. Pulling his cockpit back the angry American unholstered his .45 and emptied it at the jet, again to no consequence. Finally, as they flew along, the jet began to smoke from the previous hits and the German bailed out.

In late February, Lt. Gen. Adolf Galland formed JG44, an elite jet unit made up of such Knight's Cross holding experten as Gerhard Barkhorn (301v.), Heinz Baer (220v.), Walter Krupinski (197v.), and Johannes Steinhoff (176v.). The unit became quite successful against bomber boxes, but the German pilots converting to the Me-262 during March and April had little opportunity for training and were thrown into battle. On 4 April, the Luftwaffe put up 47 jets, lost nine, and 14 were damaged (two AR-234 jet bombers were also lost). Even though over 1,200 Me-262s had been accepted by April 1945, no more than 200 were operational at any one time. On 10 April, the jet war climaxed as the Luftwaffe put up 55 jet sorties to counter 1,100 American bombers heavily escorted by fighters. The German jets claimed ten bombers, but lost 19 and had 13 more damaged for their largest daily losses of the war.

After the losses of the 10th, Me-262 operations declined as Germany shrunk, due to the Ally advances from both the east and west. Airfields were overrun, and jet units disbanded and dispersed to safer areas. By 26 April, the last jet airfield was overrun and Capt. Herbert Philo, flying a P-47 for the 522FS/27FG/12AF, shot down the last Me-262 near Munich.

Despite Hitler's meddling and engine production difficulties, the overriding reason that the Me-262 never reached its potential was that only a small percentage of those produced ever went into combat. American fighters were able to control the jet situation through their superior numbers and harassment of jet airfields. The Me-262s claimed about 150 Allied aircraft for an operational loss of 145 destroyed, 21 probable, and 210 damaged. These are U.S. claims and do not include German training and flying accidents. P-51s scored 127 1/2 victories, while P-47s, which got the first and last Me-262 victories of the war, accounted for 17 1/2. P-38s destroyed no Me-262s, but damaged six.

Me-163

The Me-163 *Komet* was the first manned rocket powered fighter. It made its first powered flight on 13 August 1941 and first operational flight on 13 May 1944. The aircraft proved to be more hazardous to its pilot than the enemy, as many exploded on the highly volatile peroxide/alcohol fuel mixture. In January 1944, JG1 was authorized to become operational with 12 fighters. It would not be until 13 May that the first combat sortie was carried out, but the flight was inauspicious. The 163's rocket motor stopped, and when it was restarted, its pilot lost control due to its excessive speed and he had to terminate the flight. JG1 was redesignated I/JG400, but lack of numbers and technical problems precluded any serious combat. It was not until 16 August that the first Me-163 victory would be claimed by an American pilot.

First Me-163 Victory

Pilots: 2Lt. Cyril James and Lt.Col. John Murphy
Unit: 357FS/359FG/8AF
A/C: P-51
Date: 16 August 1944/1030
Place: SE Leipzig
Action: In late June 1944, Maj.Gen. William Kepner, Commander of the 8FC, issued a communication notifying his command of the possibility of encountering the short range Me-163 defending oil refineries and industrial areas. The first victories over the rocket were scored on 16 August when Lt.Col. John Murphy and his wingman, 2Lt. Cyril James, of the 357FS/359FG/8AF were flying escort for the 305BG southeast of Leipzig at 27,000 feet. As they noticed a contrail climbing astern, the two dove to the aid of a lone,

LtCol. John Murphy (L) and 2Lt. Cyril James (R) shared a Me-163 victory as the Luftwaffe rocket fighter was gliding back to base. Shortly afterward, Murphy hit and exploded another unpowered "jettie" on its way back to base. (USAF)

straggling B-17 when a Me-163 (of JG 400) arrived from its rapid, steep climb and leveled off. Murphy and Jones went into a diving turn and closed on the unsuspecting gliding rocket fighter. Murphy opened fire at 350 yards, getting a few hits along the enemy's tail and fuselage before overrunning. Jones then attacked the German and missed with his first shots, but continued after the rocket as it half-rolled on its back. Jones obtained hits on the canopy to claim the victory. While attempting to follow the rocket in its dive, Jones blacked out after being hit by his victim's backwash but survived.

Meanwhile, Murphy had completed a steep climbing turn to 25,000 feet when he spotted another "Jettie" in a turn about a mile ahead and a mile below. He closed at 400 IAS, following the homeward-bound, now unpowered, gliding rocket to 8,000 feet before overtaking it. He fired a long burst at 750 yards, hitting the fuselage and causing a large explosion. (This aircraft may have been a Me-163 that had been shot down by a B-17 tail gunner and vacated by its pilot.)

Capt. Arthur Jeffery of the 479FG flying a P-38 is sometimes credited with the first Me-163 victory on 29 July while escorting B-17s of the 100BG at 11,000 feet over Wessermunde. A lone Me-163 attacked the formation in a shallow dive and Jeffrey followed, getting hits, but the German reignited its engine, climbing to 15,000 feet. Jeffery was able to turn inside and follow when the 163 went into a near-vertical dive, getting a few more hits before he had to concentrate on pulling out of his own dive. He came out at 1,500 feet and blacked out. Jeffrey claimed a destroyed or probable and was given the kill by the FC Victories Credits Board. After the war JG-400 records showed no losses that day and claim was recredited as a damaged.

The Me-163 scored its first victory on 5 August 1944 when a 1/JG400 rocket fighter shot down three Mustangs, but this action is undocumented. The first authenticated victory occurred on 24 August when Fw. Siegfried Schubert shot down a B-17 of the 92BG. The Me-163 scored 16 verified victories, while it lost six to American fighters, all P-51s. The 370FS/359FG/8AF was credited with three Me-163 victories.

A rocket-powered Me-163 goes into a spin after being hit in the tail by marauding P-47. The Me-163 used all its fuel getting to altitude and after their attack glided back to their base which left them susceptible to attack. Six Me-163s were shot down, all by P-51s. (USAF)

The twin-engine AR-234 was the world's first operational jet bomber. A total of 14 were shot down, 11 by P-51s and three by P-47s. (Author)

AR-234

The world's first operational jet bomber was the Arado 234, which began development in early 1941 and first flew in late July 1943. On 2 August 1944, the prototypes were fitted with cameras and flew recon missions. The first bombing mission took place on 24 December 1944 over Leige, Belgium, during the Battle of the Bulge. It was not until 11 February 1945 that an Arado jet was shot down. S/C David Fairbanks, an American citizen flying Tempests for 274 Squadron of the RCAF, shot down a lone bomber approaching Rheine Airdrome for a landing.

First AR-234 Victory

Pilots: 1Lt. Eugene Murphy and 1Lt. Richard White
Unit: 385FS/364FG/8AF
A/C: P-51
Date: 25 February 1945/1100-1115
Place: Over Steinhuder Lake.
Action: 1Lt. Eugene Murphy was flying at 5,000 feet and spotted a German twin engine jet bomber 2,000 feet below. The German began a medium port turn, and Murphy caught the bomber in about a quarter of his turn and opened fire at 800 yards before the jet accelerated away. Following through the turn Murphy hit the port engine and then fired a long burst into the wings and fuselage when he expended his ammo. 1Lt. Richard White got on the jet's tail when it cut its power. White chopped his throttle but still passed 50

yards behind its tail, firing and ending up on its port wing about 30 feet away with power cut and 40 degrees flap. The German pilot tried to go into a starboard turn, but did a half-roll only 30 feet above the deck, exploding into the ground.

A total of 14 Ar-234s were recorded as destroyed by U.S. fighters: 11 by P-51s and three by P-47s.

U.S. Jet Claims
U.S. Claims by Type Over German Jet Types

Jet Type	US A/C	Victories	Probable	Damaged
Me-262	P-51	127 1/2	16	157
	P-47	17 1/2	5	47
	P-38	0	0	6
Totals		145	21	210
Me-163	P-51	6	0	2
AR-234	P-51	11	0	1
	P-47	3	0	0
Totals		165	21	213

Total Jet claims by U.S. Type

US Type	Victories	Probable	Damaged
P-51	144 1/2	16	160
P-47	20 1/2	5	47
P-38	0	0	6
Totals	165	21	213

Top-Scoring U.S. Fighter Groups vs. Jets

FG	AF	A/C	Victories	Probable	Damaged	Notes
357	8	P-51	19 1/2	0	19	
55	8	P-51	16	0	7	
78	8	P-51	14	2	2	2 AR-234s
339	8	P-51	13	2	18	1 AR-234
364	8	P-51	9	1	17	1 Me-164 & 1 AR-234
361	8	P-51	8	0	14	
354	8	P-51	7	0	6	
31	12/15	P-51	7	0	9	
353	8	P-51	7	0	4	
4	8	P-51	6	2	4	2 Me-163s
359	8	P-51	3	0	0	3 Me-163s

Note: 363FS/357FG and 82FS/78FG each had 8 victories to be the top squadrons

1Lts. Eugene Murphy and Richard White flying P-51s for the 385FS/364FG shared the first USAAF victory over an AR-234 on 25 February 1945 over Steinhuder Lake, Germany. (USAF)

Rank	Pilot Name	FG	Jet Type	Dates	Yr.
Capt.	Bochkay, Donald	357	2 Me-262	9 Feb. & 18 Apr.	45
Capt.	Compton, Gordon	353	2 Me-262	22 Feb. & 10 Apr.	45
Capt.	Cummings, Donald	55	2 Me-262	Both 25 Feb.	45
1Lt.	Drew, Urban	361	2 Me-262	Both 7 Oct.	45
Capt.	Fifield, Robert	357	2 Me-262	19 Mar. & 19 Apr.	45
1Lt.	Thompson, Hilton	479	1 Me-262	7 Apr.	45
			1 AR-234	25 Apr.	45

Note: All P-51 pilots

V-1 Buzz Bombs

As a footnote on jet hunting, the Germans began to launch the V-1 (Fi-103) in June 1944 from sites along the French coast between Dieppe and Calais. Dubbed "Buzz Bombs" (noise of their engines), "Doodlebugs" (odd insect-like buzzing and appearance), or "Divers" (dive into their target) by the press, the new weapon was a small, pilotless monoplane (22 feet long with a 17 foot wingspan) powered by a pulse-jet engine mounted above the rear fuselage. It flew at 300-375 mph at 8,000 feet carrying about two tons of HE that was delivered when the fuel was expended, causing the "guided" bomb to crash onto its target, intended or not.

The initial fighter response to the V-1 was conducted by specialized RAF squadrons flying "clean" versions of the Tempest, Spitfire, Mustang, and Mosquito (night fighter). Heavy and light AA guns and balloons supplemented the fighters. August 1944 saw 15 day and six night RAF fighter units engaging the Buzz Bombs. When Allied armies overran the launching sites, thus ending the threat, 3,957 of the 7,488 reaching landfall had been destroyed, 1,847 by RAF fighters (638 Tempest V, 428 Mosquito, 303 Spitfire, and 232 Mustang). S/L Joseph Berry of the FIU flying a Tempest claimed 60 V-1s, while another 159 RAF pilots claimed five or more V-1s. Among these "V-1 aces" were three Americans flying in RAF service:

#V	Name	Rank	Squadron	Aircraft
10.25	Feldman, Seymour	P/O	3 Squadron	Tempest V
9.00*	Miller, B.F.	F/O	FIU/	Mosquito(1v)
			501 Squadron	Tempest V (8v)
7.25*	Whitman, G.A.	F/Lt	3 Squadron	Tempest V

*plus 1 aerial victory

Since units of the RAF were specifically allocated to V-1 patrol, while other units were officially forbidden to intercept the Buzz Bombs so as not to interfere, and thus few USAAF units launched specific anti V-1 sorties. The Germans launched V-1s at night, as their launch platforms needed to be camouflaged in the daytime to protect them from marauding fighter-bombers. In the tactical anti-V-1 scheme, the night air was the province of RAF night fighter Mosquito units. However, the USAAF 422 Night Fighter Squadron, flying Black Widows, claimed a total of five from 15 to 27

American born RAF Buzz bomb "ace" P/O Seymour "Buck" Feldman, is seen receiving the DFC from King George VI. Feldman is credited with 10 1/2 V-1 victories flying the Tempest V for 3 Squadron. (Author)

In addition to his 7 aerial victories Capt. Edwin Fisher of the 377FS/362FG flying his P-47, *"Shirley Jane,"* perhaps was the leading USAAF V-1 killer with three. Fisher also destroyed 25 trucks, 5 locomotives, participated in 40 bombing missions, 25 dive bombing missions, 15 sweeps. (Author/Fisher)

1Lt. Lewis Powers (R) of the 355FS/353FG claimed 2 1/2 V-1 victories on a nighttime sortie in late June 1944. (USAF)

July 1944 while flying assigned anti-Diver patrols. P-61 ace 1Lt. Paul Smith with R/O 2Lt. Robert Tierney scored the first V-1 victory, and 1Lt. Herman Ernst and R/O 2Lt. Edward Kopsel the last. On the 20th Capt. Tadas Spelis and 2Lt. Elutherious Eleftherion, known as "Lefty," had a scary V-1 kill. The accepted method of destroying a V-1 was to allow it to pass on one side and then loose a long deflection burst in order to stay out of range of the resulting violent explosion. Five recorded Allied fighters were lost to these explosions, along with yards of burnt fabric and blistered paint. However, Spelis and Eleftherion closed and hit the V-1 in its explosive-laden fuselage from behind at 450 feet. They flew through the explosion, which jolted the large fighter out of control, and Spelis was barely able to gain control. Upon their return to base, they found that the fabric on the left rudder was burned away, along with half of that on the left elevator, while the fuselage paint was scorched and the left and right ailerons were badly damaged. In August, the 425 NFS got one V-1 each of four nights, 5-8 August, with the team of 1Lt. Garth Peterson and 2Lt. John Howe (R/O) claiming one on the 5th and 6th.

After D-Day, the 354FG was stationed at Cirqueville, France, and found its base under the flight path of just-launched V-1s. On 17 June 1944, 1Lt. William Y. Anderson of the 353FS probably became the first American V-1 victor when he encountered one on his way out to a dive bombing mission. Anderson got behind a Buzz Bomb and fired and almost became a victim himself when the warhead exploded. 1Lt. Lewis Powers of the 355FS claimed 2 1/2 V-1s on one nighttime sortie in late June for the highest one sortie total. The leading USAF buzz bomb killer probably was Capt. Edwin Fisher of the 377FS/362FG who, in addition to his seven German aircraft victories, downed three V-1s.

Japanese Ohka /Baka Rocket Suicide Aircraft

Unlike the German V-1, the Japanese Ohka was a piloted suicide rocket bomb. The Ohka, meaning Cherry Blossom in Japanese, was a simple expendable, twin-tailed rocket-propelled kamikaze aircraft which was carried to the target under the belly of a modified G4M2 Betty bomber. It measured 19.9 feet long with a 16.8-foot wingspan and could carry 3,500lbs. of explosive. The three posterior rockets gave an 8-10 second burst, which could propel the aircraft to 400+mph after drop.

Japanese homeland-based formations of Ohka-carrying Bettys with fighter escort were to approach within 30 miles of the target at 16 to 18,000 feet, whereupon the Betty was to release the Ohka and return to base. Usually the Japanese tried to take advantage of diminishing lighting conditions of dawn, dusk, or moonlight. After release the Ohka pilot could either glide towards the target or ignite his three rockets simultaneously to increase speed or singly to increase range. However, in combat over Okinawa, ideal tactics could not be implemented as USN and USMC CAPs ranging from 50 to 100 miles from the fleet would cause the Ohka-encumbered and extremely vulnerable Betty to release its ward prematurely. It is for this reason that most Ohka targets were outlying destroyer radar picket ships.

There are no records of an Ohka being shot down, but a large percentage of the carrying Bettys were destroyed by AA or CAP, or merely prematurely dropped their Ohkas and escaped home. On 12 April 1945, eight Betty/Ohka combinations escorted by 100 fighters, flying low over the water to escape radar detection, managed to release their Ohkas without success and the loss of seven of the escaping Bettys, two by AA fire. Navy pilots accounted for four of these Bettys. VF-84 pilots Lt(jg) John Gildea got one Betty and Ens. George Triplett and Lt(jg) Edward Peck shared another. VF-17 pilots Lt(jg) Eldridge Courrage and Lt. Joseph Stenstrom got one apiece. Marine pilots of VMF-323 1Lt. Del Davis, 2Lt. Dewey Durnford, and 1Lt. Charles Spangler downed the other hapless Betty. On the 14th all seven attacking Betty/Ohkas were destroyed by pilots of VBF-9 (Lt. Charles Arthur, Lt(jg)s Leonard Walker and Charles Hall), VF-30 (Ens. James Noel, Keith Curry, Robert Rhodes), and VF-10 (Ens. Horace Heath), achieving no hits. On

The Japanese Ohka was a piloted suicide rocket bomb carried to 30 miles of its intended target by a G4M2 Betty bomber. The Ohka was nicknamed the "Baka" which translates as "fool" in English. There are no records of a Baka being shot down but many of their vulnerable Betty mother bombers fell victim. (Author)

the 16th five of six Betty/Ohkas were destroyed, but one hit the picket destroyer *Mannert L. Abele*, killing 79 and wounding 35. USN pilots Lt(jg) Lawrence Grossman, VF-45, and Ens. John Tice, VBF-9, destroyed two. USMC pilots 2Lts. Merlin O'Neil and James Sharp of VMF-312 shared one, while 2Lt. William Eldridge of VMF-441 and 2Lt. Dewey Durnford of VMF-323 got another. Durnford was so surprised when the Betty he was firing at released its Ohka that he exclaimed over his radio: "It was carrying a papoose!" The next large scale Ohka attack took place on 29 April, which had no success except that all four Bettys appear to have escaped. On 22 June, six Betty/Ohkas attacked the fleet; two were unable to release their Ohkas and turned back to base, and a third Ohka crashed as it over flew the fleet. The Marines harassed the remaining four Bettys. 2Lt. H..L. Pierce caused a Betty to release its Ohka, which crashed into the sea. 1Lts. John Leaper and William Milne of VMF-314 each destroyed an empty Betty, and two other Marine Corsair pilots claimed damage to two Bettys. One of these Bettys may have been destroyed by 1Lt. Ewart Dick of VMF-113 as it escaped up the Okinawa coast. Leaper also destroyed two escorting Zekes that day, one by ramming it with his fuel tank (as described elsewhere).

Maj. Bruce Porter was CO of VMF(N)-531 flying the F6F-5N from Yonton, Okinawa. Porter had flown F4Us for VMF-121 in mid-1943 where he scored three Zero victories. On 22 June 1945, as he was vectored toward a bogey he ID'd as a Ki-45 Nick. Porter had installed 20mm cannons on his fighter to give it more punch and dispatched the Jap at 2118. He was vectored to another bogey that he identified as a Betty, and as he closed in to fire he saw it was carrying a Baka. The Betty and its passenger blew up in a large explosion at 2225, which the radar GCI controller saw was much larger on his screen than Porter's first victory. As Porter dove away he wondered if he would get credit for two aircraft. He did not, but he still was an ace.

On 16 April 1945, 2Lt. Dewey Durnford flying a F4U for VMF-323 against Kamikaze attacks over Okinawa shot down a Betty bomber. Durnford was so surprised when his target released its Baka he exclaimed over his radio: "It was carrying a papoose!" (Author/Brandon)

After the capture of Okinawa by the U.S. the full force of U.S. Naval airpower was able to concentrate on the Japanese mainland airfields. Consequently, Ohka attacks fell to nil as their Betty bomber "mothers" were destroyed on the ground. Japanese propaganda claimed 300 Ohka attacks against Allied shipping, but the exact number is difficult to determine, as most attacks were launched at dusk, dawn, or in moonlight, and the confusion of combat caused distortions in identification. The *Mannert L. Abele* was definitely sunk, and three other destroyers were damaged by Ohkas, for a 1.3% success ratio. The U.S. nickname "Baka," Japanese for "fool," appears to be appropriate. Admiral J.J. Clark, with tongue in cheek, accessed the Ohka: "The Baka failed because it was a one-shot deal—the pilots never got any practice."

CHAPTER 17

Lasts

Last Air Battles

ETO/MTO: 8 May 1945

The beginning of April 1945 found the Luftwaffe confined to a small area of central Germany surrounded by Allied and Russian Air Forces. Goering's once proud Luftwaffe had its chain of command in dissolution and its units in disintegration. Conventional fighters flew their last meaningful mission on 7 April, when 120 fighters took part in ramming sorties against American bombers. By mid-April Luftwaffe single engine fighter strength had declined by over 1,000 due to strafing, disbanding of units, and the overrunning of airfields. By the beginning of May what remained of the German air strength was concentrated in northern Austria and Czechoslovakia. The majority of USAAF sorties were armed recon flights. The unconditional surrender had been signed in Reims on 7 May and was scheduled to take effect at 0001, 9 May.

On 8 May, TAC R pilots spent most of the day gathering surrendering German aircraft and escorting them to American-held airfields. The 162 TAC R historian wrote: "Tuesday, May 8, 1945, was by all means the strangest day in 17 months. The whole German Air Force went out to return to its bases and give up to the Yanks." At 0715, 1Lt. Manuel Geiger and 2Lt. Stan Newman (who was to fly three missions that day) approached a group of six FW-190s near Bischofteinitz, Czechoslovakia, hoping to force them to land at a captured base, but the Germans reacted by jumping the

On 8 May 1945, at 1945 hours, 2Lt. Robert Little of the 12TRS was patrolling over the Danube in his F-6D.when he and his wingman were attacked by five FW-190s. Little shot down one for what at the time was considered the last ETO victory of the war as post-war research showed that 2Lt. Kenneth Swift of the 474FG shot down a Si-204 several minutes later. (USAF)

Americans. After a rolling and turning chase each shot down a FW-190. However, most of the day's missions were relatively uneventful, such as one led by Lt. Col. David Lewis. A Feisler-Storch was encountered by Lewis, who chased the agile observation/liaison aircraft across the landscape in his P-38. Finally, after several passes Lewis forced it to land in a field occupied by American troops, where the pilot and passenger surrendered. Lewis then encountered a German He-111 acting as a transport heading west away from the onrushing Russians. Lewis fired a few shots across the nose of the Heinkel, which set down near American troops. The ten passengers, waving white handkerchiefs, jumped out of the downed transport to gladly surrender.

However, not all Germans wished to surrender peaceably. When 15TAC R pilots Bob Jeffrey and Julian Biniewski tried to escort a Me-109 to the base at Furst, the German pilot turned into the Americans and made a pass at Jeffrey, who responded and hit the German with a deflection shot. Biniewski closed and finished it off.

In the early evening four more German aircraft fell to pilots of the 12th, 15th, and 162nd TAC R. On 15TRS' last mission Leland Larson and George Schroeder came upon two FW-190s near Radwitz and indicated that they were to be escorted to Furst. The Focke Wulfs fired off short bursts and hit Schroeder's wing, and then quickly turned to escape. Schroeder followed one to the deck and pursued it until it crashed into a stand of trees. Larson dove after the other German, who tried a tight turn at 500 feet but went into a spin and hit the ground. It was Larson's sixth victory of the war. At 1945 hours, 2Lt. Robert Little and 2Lt. Fred Mitchell of the 12TRS were patrolling F-6 Mustangs over the Danube. Little's flight was attacked by five FW-190s, which broke out of the clouds 2,000 feet above them at 10 o'clock. As the five Germans came in the Mustangs banked sharply left, making the German attack almost head on. No shots were fired, and the Americans went into a high speed climb and the Germans turned and followed. Climbing about 2,000 feet Little and Mitchell peeled off and came sharply around. The maneuver put Little on the tail of a FW, and he shot him down. The slogan of the day for the 10PRG, which got six victories that day, was: "First on D-Day, Last on VE Day," as Lt. Joseph Conklin of the 15TRS had scored the first aerial victory on D-Day. However, the slogan was not to be, as post-war research has credited the ETO's last victory to P-38 pilot 2Lt. Kenneth Swift of the 429FS/474FG/9AF, who downed a lowly Si-204 twin engine liaison/communications bomber near Rodach at 2005 for the last of the AAF's 7,504 victories.

The last MTO American claims were on 26 April, as Luftwaffe opposition had disappeared. At noon, 2Lt. Thomas Jefferson of the 310FS/332FG and squadron mate 1Lt. Jimmy Lanham got a double and single Me-109s, respectively, flying P-51s. At 1310, 2Lt. Roland

Lee flying a P-47 of the 68FS/71FG got a Me-109 for the last of 3,764 victories over the MTO.

PTO: 15 August 1945

Even before the two Atomic Bombs in early August 1945, Japanese air resistance was on the wane. The U.S. Navy recorded only 23 victories in the six weeks beginning 1 June, and American pilots were beset by rumors of a last-ditch Japanese Banzai En Mass defense of the Homeland. In mid-August the weather cleared, and strikes against airfields near Tokyo again made the American pilots acutely aware of the war and their mortality. On 13 August, 250 Japanese aircraft were destroyed on the ground, while 22 bogies, usually single Judys or Jills, were splashed by Navy CAP as the Japanese approached the Task Force.

The Marine Corps knocked down 40 Japanese aircraft over Okinawa on 22 June 1945 when the Japanese made one last aerial assault, but after that day they claimed only 31 victories, 18 of these by F6F(N)-5 night fighters. During this period the Japanese would send nightly intruders or lone kamikazes to harrass Okinawa. On 7 August 2Lt. Thomas Danaher of VMF(N)-543 shot down a Betty at 2331. On 8 August VMF(N)-542 dispatched 2Lt. William Jennings from Yonton to intercept a bogie off the west coast of the island. At 0308, Jennings shot down a Tony for the last Marine Corps victory of WWII.

In the early morning of 15 August the Navy sent air strikes to hit Tokahaski and Atsugi Airfields. The first victory of the day was scored by Lt. Thomas Reidy of VBF-83 off the *Essex*, who became a double ace with ten victories. On their way to the target, F6F pilots of VF-31 *Belleau Wood* shot down six Japs. Two of these victories were claimed by Lt(jg) Edward Toaspern, which gave him seven victories for the war. A short while later *San Jacinto* pilots of VF-31 got seven victories, three probables, and two damaged over a formation of Zeros over Mita.

VF-49 Forty-Niners attacked Mito A/F at 0620 and had four pilots shoot down seven Zeros, along with two probables and three

Ens. William Harris became the last Navy ace of the war when he shot down a Jill on 28 July. However, Harris also became the last ace KIA when, on 9 August 1945, a 1000lb. bomb he was carrying exploded on route to target. (USN)

damaged west of Mito. Lt. Jack Gibson, Lt(jg) George Williams, and Lt(jg) Elwood MacDonald claimed two each for the second highest squadron total that day.

As the first strikes were about to commence at 0645, Fleet HQ radioed their air groups to cease hostilities, as the war had ended. As the six Hellcat fighter bombers of VF-88, led by Lt. Howard Harrison, headed back to the *Yorktown* they were bounced at 8,000 feet astern over Atsugi A/F by a mixed formation of 17 Jack and

1Lt. Oscar Perdomo flying a P-47N for the 464FS/507FG became America's last ace when he downed four Oscars and a Willow trainer on 13 August 1945 near Seoul, Korea. Perdomo is shown here after the mission with Frank Parker, Republic Aviation chief test pilot. (USAF)

At 0645 six Hellcat fighter-bombers of VF-88 engaged in one of the Navy's last air battles. Lt(jg) Maurice Procter (R) got three Japanese fighters but the mission claimed America's last (four) air casualties. Among these casualties were Lt(jg) Joseph Sahloff (L) and mission leader, Howard Harrison (C). (Author/Blake)

At 1300, 15 August 1945, Ens. Ora Myers of VBF-86/WASP shot down a Zero and a hour later Ens. Clarence Moore of VF-31 off the *Belleau Wood* got the Navy's 6826th and last victory of the war. (Author)

Capt. Joseph Miller, 429FS/474F, became the last Lightning ace in the MTO/ETO when he shot down a FW-190 on 13 March 1945. (USAF)

Frank fighters that had not heard the cease fire order. In the battle the Navy pilots claimed nine Japanese, three by Lt(jg) Maurice Proctor, whose wingman, Lt(jg) Ted Hansen, got two Franks. Unfortunately these pilots must have been Japan's last experienced pilots, as Ensigns Wright Hobbs and Eugene Mandeberg, Lt(jg) Joseph Sahloff, and mission leader Howard Harrison became America's last air casualties. VF-88 claimed the highest total for squadron on the last day of the war with nine, and its VBF contingent scored three more.

By mid-morning the last of the strike forces had returned, but Adm. Halsey ordered CAP to "investigate and shoot down all snoopers in a friendly sort of way" (a statement later claimed by AG6 commander H.L. Miller). Five Japanese aircraft were destroyed after cease-fire that day.

LtCdr. Charles Gunnell of VBF-87 sent four F6Fs to attack targets of opportunity through low cloud cover. The Hellcats were

in their dives when the recall order was issued to the Task Force, but they completed their attack rather than expose themselves to anti-aircraft fire. Lt(jg) John McNabb is thought to be the last pilot to bomb Japan.

A VBF-6 F4U pilot off the *Hancock*, Ens. E. Robert Farnsworth, shot down a Kate kamikaze at 1122 as it was diving on the Royal Navy carrier *Indefatigable*. At 1200 Ens. Falvey Sandidge of VBF-85 shot down a Judy over a destroyer picket line. At 1300 Ens. Ora Myers got a Zeke, and two others shared a Judy for VF-86. The 34th victory of the day, the last victory of the war, and the Navy's 6,826th victory was apparently scored by Ens. Clarence Moore of VF-31 off *Belleau Wood*. At 1400 Moore shot down a Judy which was closing on the Task Force.

At 0845 on the 14th, five P-38s of the 35FG out of Ie Shima, Okinawa, under Capt. Raymond Meyers, rendezvoused with a PBY attacking a Japanese lugger on the Inland Sea. The circling P-38s

1Lt. Horace Reeves, 431FG/475FG, became the last P-38 ace in the PTO when he shot down four Hamps on 28 March 1945. (Author/Reeves)

1Lt. Philip Colman, 26PS/5PG, became the last P-40 ace of the war when he downed a Hamp on 21 September 1944. (USAF/Colman)

Lasts **339**

2Lt. Melvin Paisley, 390FS/366FG, became the last P-47 ace in the ETO when he shared a FW-190 victory on 20 April 1945. (Author/Paisley)

1Lt. Eugene Emmons, 317FS/325FG, became the last Thunderbolt ace in the MTO when he shot down a Me-109 on 6 April 1945. (USAF)

were surprised by eight Frank fighters coming out of the sun. The P-38s broke immediately upon seeing the Japanese cannon shell tracers and escaped the initial attack and took the initiative. Capt. William Moore and Leiutenants Dwight Hollister and George Stevens each downed a Frank, while Capt. Meyer got two Franks for his only victories of the war. The AAF had scored 3,713 victories in the Pacific. In the battle Lt. Duane Keiffer was the Air Force's last casualty of WWII when he overshot a Ki-84 and fell victim to it as he was hit in the left tail boom and engine. Keiffer's canopy was jettisoned just before he hit the water, but he went down in the sinking fighter.

Last Ace of WWII
Pilot: 1Lt Oscar Perdomo
Date: 13 August 1945: 1410-141
Place: Keijo (Seoul), Korea
Unit: 464FS/507FG
A/C: P-47N "*Lil Meatie's MEAT CHOPPER*"/4 Oscars(?)/Willow
Action: In the aftermath of the two atomic bomb drops on Japan it was anticipated that there would be a surrender forthcoming. On 13 August, the VII FC dispatched 53 P-47Ns of the 507FG to sweep Korea in search of the remnants of the JAAF. The group took off from Ie Shima on Okinawa, four hours away. They arrived over Keijo, modern day Seoul, to find over 50 Japanese aircraft wandering around at 8,000 feet. One of the first to score was Capt. Edward "Judge" Hoyt, flying "*Hoyt's Hoss*" of the 465FS. Hoyt shot down a Betty to become the 507th's first ace. After being WIA and out of action for three months in November 1943 he had scored four Oscar victories in March 1944 over Wewak, New Guinea, while flying P-47Ds for the 41FS/35FG.

Meanwhile, 464FS CO Maj. James Jarman led his flight on a group of Oscars and was followed by 1Lt. Oscar Perdomo, who was about to see his first combat against Japanese aircraft. The Japanese were flying in a loose V, and Perdomo hit the last one in the cockpit and exploded the engine. Perdomo moved immediately to

a second Oscar at 30 degrees deflection and tore off parts from the bottom of the cowling, causing the fighter to roll over and dive into the ground. Perdomo quickly found another Jap in a spiraling turn and fired a leading burst, chasing it to the deck. The Jap hit a high speed stall that snapped it into the ground, where it exploded in a fireball. Climbing back toward Keijo he came on two Yokosuka K5Y1 Willow JNAF biplane trainers. The slow, unsuspecting trainer had no chance, as Perdomo crossed his controls and put his Thunderbolt into a skid. He fired and apparently killed the pilot, as the biplane went into a tight spiral and dove into the ground. The second Willow made use of his wingman's plight to escape. Perdomo again headed toward Keijo, and as he was breaking through overcast he spotted three or four Oscars above him to the right. At a tactical disadvantage, Perdomo turned immediately into them and went into a dive, which the heavy P-47 did quite well. He put his fighter into water injection and headed for a cloud, getting ahead

1Lt/ Oscar Perdomo (R), 464FS/507FG, became the last P-47 ace in the PTO when he downed four Oscars and a Willow on 13 August 1945. (USAF)

1Lt. Andrew Ritchey, 353FS/354FG, became the last P-51 ace in the ETO when he was credited with two Me-109s on 20 April 1945. (Author/Ritchey)

Capt. Abner Aust, 457FS/506FG, became the last P-51 ace in the PTO when he claimed two Zekes on 10 August 1945. (USAF)

and above his pursuers who had broken, three to the left and one to the right. He went after the single Jap who went into ineffective evasive turns, but Perdomo exploded him to become America's last WWII fighter ace and ace in a day.

The 507th claimed 20 destroyed and two probables for a loss of one P-47 and was awarded the DUC, the only one awarded to a P-47 Group in the Pacific, including Neel Kearby's 348FG. Post war research showed Perdomo's Ki-43 Oscars to be Ki-84 Franks.

Last Ace KIA

William Harris had a varied naval career. After graduating from Yale, he enlisted in the Navy and flew crew with Patrol Wing 5. He became a naval aviator and joined VB-17 aboard the *Bunker Hill* in a SB2C Helldiver. On 11 November 1943 he shot down a Val in the vicinity of the task force to become the only ace to get a victory in the SB2C. Retraining in the F4U, he scored four more victories with VBF-83 off the *Essex* in Spring 1945. At 1720 Harris scored a victory over a Jill on 28 July to become the last Navy ace of the war. On 9 August, a 1,000lb. bomb Harris was carrying exploded en route to target, making him the last ace to die in the war.

1Lt. William Aron, 318FS/325FG, became the last Mustang ace in the MTO when he shot down a Ju-88 on 10 April 1945. (USAF)

Lt(jg) George Davidson, VC-27 (*Savo Island*), became the last USN ace in the F4F/FM-2 when he shared an Irving on 5 January 1945. This is the only known photo of Davidson. (USN)

1Lt. Eugene Dillow, VMF-221 (Land-based), became the last USMC ace in the F4F/FM-2 when he shot down a Zero on 17 July 1943. (USMC)

Lt. Cleveland Null, VF-16 (*Randolph*), became the last USN ace in the Hellcat when he downed three Franks on 28 July 1945. (USN)

Capt. Robert Baird, VMF(N)-533 (Land-based), became the last USMC ace in the F6F when he destroyed a Betty on 22 June 1945. Baird is shown with shown with MGen. Lewis Woods, CO 2MAW on Okinawa. (Author/Baird)

Capt. Joseph Lynch, VMF-224 (Land-based), became the last USMC Corsair ace when he destroyed two Tonys on 2 July 1945. (USMC)

Last Ace V	Theater	Date	Rank	Pilot Name Aircraft	Unit FS/FG	E/A Destroyed
				P-38		
Ace	PTO	03-28-45	1Lt.	Reeves, Horace	431/475	4 Hamps
V	PTO	08-15-45	Capt.	Meyer, Raymond	35/8	2 Franks
Ace	MTO 4v ETO 1v	03-13-45	Capt.	Miller, Joseph	429/474	FW-190
V	ETO	05-08-45	2Lt.	Swift, Kenneth	429/474	Si-204
V	MTO	04-15-45	1Lt.	Danielson, Warren	27/1	FW-190
				P-40		
Ace	MTO	03-29-44	Capt.	Fenex, James	316/324	FW-190
V	MTO	05-13-44	2Lt.	Dealy, J.P.	316/324	Me-109
			1Lt.	King, W.		Me-109
			1Lt.	Schweiwe, W.		Me-109
Ace	PTO	09-21-44	1Lt.	Colman, Philip	26P/5P	Hamp
V	PTO	12-18-44	1Lt.	Silver, James	32P/5P	Lily
V	PTO	2-18-45	Lt.	Wei, S-K (Chinese)	26P/5P	Topsy
				P-47		
Ace	ETO	04-20-45	2Lt.	Paisley, Melvin	390/366	1/2 FW-190
V	ETO	05-04-45	2Lt.	Sides, J.P.	511/405	Ju-88
Ace	MTO	04-06-45	1Lt.	Emmons, Eugene	317/325	Me-109
V	MTO	04-26-45	2Lt.	Lee, Roland	66/71	Me-109
Ace	PTO	08-13-45	1Lt.	Perdomo, Oscar	464/507	4 Oscars/1Willow
V	PTO	08-14-45	1Lt.	Shaw, Richard	1/413	Frank
				P-51		
Ace	ETO	04-20-45	1Lt.	Ritchey, Andrew	353/354	2 Me-109s
V	ETO	05-08-45	1Lt.	Schroeder, George	5TRS/	FW-190
	(F-6)		2Lt.	Larson, Leland	10PRS	FW-190
Ace	MTO	04-10-45	1Lt.	Aron, William	318/325	Ju-88
V	MTO	04-28-45	2Lt.	Jefferson, Thomas	301/332	Me-109s
			2Lt.	Simons. Richard	100/332	Me-109
				Lanham, Jimmy	301/332	Me-109
Ace	PTO	08-10-45	Capt.	Aust, Abner	457/506	2 Zekes
V	PTO	08-14-45	1Lt.	Johnson, Herman	110TRS/71TRS	Oscar
	(F-6)					
				P-61		
Ace	ETO	04-11-45	1Lt.	Axtell, Eugene (P)	422NFS	Ju-52
				Morrison, C.H. (R)		
V	ETO	04-24-45	1Lt.	Slayton, Jack (P)		Ju-188
			1Lt.	Robinson, Jack (R)	425NFS	
Ace	PTO	12-30-44	Maj.	Smith, Carroll (P)	418NFS	Frank
			1Lt.	Porter, Philip (R)		
V	PTO	08-07-45	2Lt.	Griffitts, Curtiss (P)		
			2Lt.	Bigler, Myron (R)	418NFS	Betty

USN & USMC Aircraft Lasts/Last Aces and Victories

Last Ace V	Service	Date	Rank	Pilot Name	Unit Aircraft	E/A Destroyed
				F4F/FM		
Ace	USN	01-05-45	Lt(jg)	Davidson, George	VC-27 (*Savo Is.*)	1/2 Irving
V	USN	08-05-45	Lt.	Beckwith, Eugene	VC-98 (*Laguna Pt.*)	Frances
Ace	USMC	07-17-43	1Lt.	Dillow, Eugene	VMF-221 (Land)	Zero
V	USMC	08-06-43	1Lt.	Dillow, Eugene	VMF-221 (Land)	Zero
			1Lt.	Segal, Harold	VMF-221 (Land)	Zero
				F6F		
Ace	USN	07-28-45	Lt.	Null, Cleveland	VF-16 (*Randolph*)	2 Franks
			Lt.	Hatch, Leonel	VF-16 (*Randolph*)	
V	USN	08-15-45	Ens.	Moore, Clarence	VF-31(*Belleau Wood*)	Judy
Ace	USMC	06-22-45	Capt.	Baird, Robert	VMF(N)-533 (Land)	Betty
V	USMC	08-08-45	2Lt.	Jennings, William	VMF(N)-542 (Land)	Tony
				F4U		
Ace	USN	07-28-45	Lt.	Harris, William	VBF-83 (*Essex*)	Jill
V	USN	08-16-45	Ens.	Sandidge, Falvey	VBF-85 (*Shangri-La*)	Judy
Ace	USMC	07-02-45	Capt.	Lynch, Joseph	VMF-224 (Land)	2 Tonys
V	USMC	08-05-45	LCol.	Yost, Donald	VMF-351 (*Cape Glouster*)	Frances

CHAPTER 18

Top Fighter Units

Top USAAF Fighter Groups

Unit pride ran high, especially in the ETO, where Air Force fighter groups were often based in close proximity in England. An ardent rivalry developed between the 4th and 56th Fighter Groups of the 8AF abetted by the press, who helped to create the rivalry as a good story line. The commanding officers of these two groups, Don Blakeslee of the 4th and Hubert "Hub" Zemke of the 56th, were two of the great air combat leaders and tacticians of WWII, and their abilities and enthusiasm were imbued into their men. The 4FG was one of the first American fighter groups to see action. It was founded from the RAF's three Eagle Squadrons, whose nuclei were American volunteers. By the end of September 1942, the Eagle Squadrons and their 73 1/2 victories were transferred to the VIII Fighter Command of the USAAF at Debden. The 56FG came on board during the first week of April 1943, flying out of Horsham St. Faith. Both groups flew the P-47 Thunderbolt, but the pilots of the 4th disliked the seven ton Jug after flying the svelte, nimble Spitfire as Eagles. The 4th, being operational first, took an early victory lead, but it wasn't long before Zemke's "Wolfpack" could claim twice as many victories as Blakeslee's "Debden Gangsters," as they were called by Joseph Goebbels' Nazi propaganda machine. By 6 March 1944, the 56th claimed the top two aces in the ETO, Walker "Bud" Mahurin and Bob Johnson, each with 17 victories. It also counted Francis "Gabby" Gabreski and Jerry Johnson with 14 victories, Zemke with 11, and Dave Schilling with 10. The only 4th P-47 pilot

to enter this select list was Duane Beeson with 14 victories. When the 4th re-equipped with the P-51 in spring 1944, its missions and fortunes changed. The 4th undertook bomber escort missions in late March and claimed over 100 kills, while the 56th was relegated to ground support mission and scored only 10 kills, putting the 4th back into the spotlight. The 56th lost Zemke when he was transferred to the 479FG. Blakeslee rotated out after three years and several duty tours, but the rivalry continued on, encouraged by the press, who kept tabs and encouraged it.

The 8AF's allowance of ground strafing claims enabled the 56FG ground strafers to again catch up to the 4FG bomber escorters, who saw less Luftwaffe opposition in the air. But strafing claims complicated the scoring race even months after V-E Day. Returning POWs provided new information on the claims, while captured Luftwaffe airfields were reassessed for strafing claims. At the war's end the 4FG had been credited with 1,002 ground and aerial victories, but was edged out by the 56th 1,005 1/2. Shortly, the figures were changed in the 4th's favor 1,011 to 1,003 1/2, but by September 1945 the VIII Fighter Commands' final figures gave the 4FG 1,052 1/2, and the 4th reduced the 56th's to 985 1/2. The 56th had the highest total of aerial victories with 664 1/2 to 555 for the 4th. While the 56FG remained the top FG in aerial victories in the ETO, the 4th was surpassed by the 354FG/9AF, the Pioneer Mustang Group, which scored 637 victories, featuring such aces as Glenn Eagleston (18 1/2), Don Beerbower (15 1/2), and Jack Bradley (15). The

The 49FG/5AF tied the 56FG for most victories for a group with 664 victories. The photo shows 49th pilots (Back L-R) George Lavan (1v.), LtCol. Jerry Johnson (22v.) and LtCol. Clay Tice (2v.) (Front L-R) Capt. Robert DeHaven (14v.), 1Lt. Wayne Jorda (4v.) and Capt. James Watkins (12v.). Dick Bong scored 21 of his 40 victories with the 49th. (USAF)

Zemke's Wolfpack, the 56FG/8AF also had 664 victories. (L-R) Capt. Walter Cook (6v.), 1Lt.Stanley Morrill (9v.), 1Lt. John Bryant (2 v.), 1Lt. John Truluck (7 v.), Capt. Walker Mahurin (19 3/4 v.), 1Lt. Harold Comstock (5 v.), LtCol. David Schilling (22 1/2 v.), Maj. Francis Gabreski (28 v.), Capt. Ralph Johnson (3 v.), Maj. James Stewart (11 1/2 v.), 2Lt. Frank Klibbe 7 v.), 1Lt. Jack Brown (1 v.), Capt. Eugene O'Neill (4 1/2 v.), Lt. Raymond Petty (0 v.), F/O. Irvin Valenta (2 v.) and 1Lt. Anthony Carcione (3 1/2 v.) (USAF)

The 31FG/12-15AF got 582 victories to be the top group in the MTO. (L-R) 1Lt. Robert Riddle (307 FS) 11 victories, Capt. Walter Goehausen (308) 10, Capt. Leland Molland (308) 10 1/2, Col. Charles McCorkle (HQ) 11, Capt. Murray McLaughlin (309) 7 and Capt. John Voll (308) 21. (USAF)

The 354FG/9AF was the third highest group with 637 victories. Aces (Clockwise LR #5): Capt. Don Beerbower (353FS) 15 1/2 v., Capt. Wallace Emmer (353) 14, 1Lt. Robert Goodnight (356) 7 1/4, Capt. Frank O'Conner (356) 10 3/4, Capt. Lowell Bruland (355) 12 1/2, 1Lt. Carl Frantz (353) 11, 1Lt. Edward Hunt (353) 6 1/2, Capt. Richard Turner (356) 11, Capt. Robert Stephens (355) 13, Capt. Glenn Eagleston (353) 18 1/2 and Capt. Jack Bradley (353) 15. (USAF)

357FG/8AF flew P-51s and scored 595 1/2 victories, with Leonard Carson (18 1/2), John England (17 1/2), Bud Anderson (16 1/4), and Bud Peterson (15 1/2) contributing victories. The 31FG/12-15AF flew P-40s, Spitfires, and P-51s to 582 victories. John Voll (21), Sam Brown (15 1/2), and Jim Brooks (13) were the leading aces.

However, the point became mute, as the air war in the Pacific continued after VE-Day. Group scoring was less well documented as a news story there, and the 49FG of the 5AF, which featured Dick Bong, tied the 56th; 664 to 664, without much fanfare or reassessments.

The 357FG/8AF scored 595 1/2 victories to make it fourth. These 4 aces added 67 3/4 victories to the group's total (L-R) Capt. Bud Peterson (364 Squadron) 15 1/2 victories, Capt. Leonard Carson (362) 18 1/2, Capt. John England (362) 17 1/2 and Capt. Bud Anderson (363) 16 1/4. (USAF)

The 4FG got most of the publicity in the ETO but ended up sixth in group victories. (L-R/336FS) 1Lt. John Godfrey 16 1/3 victories, Capt. Don Gentile 21 5/6, 1Lt. Peter Lehman 0, Maj. James Goodson 14, and 1Lt. Willard Milliken 13. (USAF)

Top USAAF Fighter Groups (450+ Victories)

FG/AF	Victories*	Aces**	HQ Victories/Aces	Squadron Victories/Aces	Squadron Victories/Aces	Squadron Victories/Aces
49/5	664	32	25/2	7FS 178/7	8FS 207/13	9FS 254/12
56/8	664	39	39.25/2	61FS 230/18	62FS 221.5/11	63FS 173.25/10
354/9	637	43*	15/1	353FS 295/20	355FS 142.2/10	356FS 184.8/11
357/8	595.5	41*	30/2	362FS 198/12	363FS 155.5/8	364FS 211.5/17
31/12-15	582	33*	20/1	307FS 194/8	308FS 186/8	309FS 182/12
4/8	550	32	20.4/3	334FS 200.7/10	335FS 162.2/10	336FS 166.7/9
82/12-15	553	24*	5/0	95FS 198/7	96FS 201/10	97FS 149/6
475/5	552	34	43/2	431FS 221/16	432FS 167/10	433FS 121/6
325/12-15	540	27	21/1	317FS 212/15	318FS 180/8	319FS 127/2
352/8	504.5	26	12/1	328FS 143/5	486FS 114/7	487FS 235.5/13
23/14	467	27*	47/4	74FS 135/5	75FS 162/9	76FS 123/4
8/5	453	25*	16/0	35FS 130/5	36FS 94/2	80FS 213/15

*Victories are based on Dr. Frank Olynyk studies.

**Pilots scoring 5+ victories while in the group. Some pilots scored a total of 5+ victories while in two of the group squadrons. Some pilots scored 4 or less victories in the group or other groups and became aces while in the group, or while in other groups, and are not included.

Top USAAF Scoring Fighter Squadrons

By far the top scoring USAAF squadron was the 353FS of the 354FG/9AF. The 353rd flew combat from December 1942 until the end of the war, mainly in the P-51. The squadron had the most pilots (20) to score five or more victories while flying for it, with eight pilots scoring double-digit victories. Glenn Eagleston (18 1/2), Don Beerbower (15 1/2), and Jack Bradley (15) were the squadron's leaders.

The 9FS, the Flying Knights of the 49FG/5AF, was second in squadron scoring with 254 victories flying the P-40 initially in New Guinea, and then re-equipping with the P-38, in which it scored the majority of its victories over New Guinea and then the Philippines. It had 12 aces, including Dick Bong with 16 of his 40 victories, while Jerry Johnson got 11 of his 22 and James Watkins got 11 of his 12 while with the unit. The 8FS of the 49th were not far behind the 9th with 207 victories and 13 aces. Bob Aschenbrenner and Ernie

Left: VF-17 narrowly outscored VF-15 313 to 310 victories but needed two tours to do so. The first tour was led by LtCdr. Tom Blackburn and scored 152 victories and the second was led by LtCdr. Marshall Beebe and scored 161 victories. (Author/Blackburn)

Harris each scored 10 victories to lead the Black Sheep.

The 56FG also had two squadrons scoring over 200 victories in their P-47s. The 61FS had 230 victories and 18 aces, including Gabby Gabreski (28) and Bob Johnson (25), who were to be the leading two aces in the ETO, and Joe Powers (12) and Jim Stewart (11 1/2). The 62FS had 221 victories and 11 aces, including Fred Christensen (21 1/2), Felix Williamson (13), and Mike Quirk (11).

Top USAAF Fighter Squadrons (200+ Victories)

FS	FG/AF	Victories	Aces*
353	354/9	295	20
9	49/5	254	12
61	56/8	230	18
62	56/9	221.5	11
431	475/5	221.	16
80	8/5	213	15
317	325/12-15	212	15
364	357/8	211.5	17
8	49/5	207	13
96	82/12-15	201	10
334	4/8	200.7	10

*Only includes pilots who scored 5+ victories while with the squadron.

Top USN Squadrons

VF-17 narrowly outscored VF-15 in the Pacific 313 to 310, but needed two tours to accomplish its victory. VF-17 was led on its first tour by LtCdr. John "Tom" Blackburn and flew land-based F4U-1s. Based on Ondonga, New Georgia, from 27 October to 1 December 1943, the Jolly Rogers claimed 47 1/2 victories before going on R&R. Returning to action on Piva Yoke, Bougainville, the squadron scored 106 1/2 victories from 25 January to 4 March 1943. Ike Kepford led the unit's 12 aces with 16 victories, followed by Blackburn with 11. VF-17 was re-formed as a F6F-5 Hellcat unit on the *Hornet* in mid-April 1944 under the command of LtCdr. Marshall Beebe. In January VF-17 was halved, and VBF-17 was

VF-15, posing in late 1944 in front of CO David McCampbell's *"Minsi"*, got all its 310 victories in one tour. (USN)

VF-2, led by LtCdr. William Dean (with a squadron-leading 11 victories), was the third Navy squadron with 262 victories (245 in its second tour). 27 pilots in this mid-1943 photo were aces. (USN)

formed from it. On this tour VF-17 scored 161 victories and had 12 aces, led by Beebe with 10 1/2. VBF-17 was the top-scoring VBF unit with 121 victories and 8 aces.

VF-15 served only one tour lasting from 30 April to 17 November 1944, flying F6Fs off the *Essex*. Initially, LtCdr. Charles Brewer, who was MIA over Guam on 19 June, led the squadron. LtCdr. James Rigg succeeded him. The unit rolled up large victory totals during the strikes on the Marcus and Wake Islands on 14-26 May, the Battle of the Philippine Sea on 6 June to 6 July, and the Battle of Leyte Gulf on 6-30 October. It had 310 victories and 26 aces, led by David McCampbell with 34, followed by George Duncan with 13 1/2, and Roy Rushing, James Strane, and Wendell Twelves with 13.

VF-2 was the third highest-scoring VF squadron with 262 victories scored in two tours. The first tour, the Chiefs, flew F4Fs off the *Lexington* during the Battle of the Coral Sea and scored 17 victories, but had no aces. The second tour, the Red Rippers, was led by LtCdr. William Dean and flew the F6Fs off the *Hornet*. In a period from 11 June to 3 July 1944, it scored 201 (of 245) victories.

VF-9 scored 120 victories on its second tour and 130.8 on its third. The third tour had 8 aces and was made famous by "Valencia's Flying Circus". (L-R) Lt(jg) Harris Mitchell (10 v.), Lt. A. B. "Chick" Smith (6 plus 4 later victories), Lt(jg) James French (11 v.) and Lt. Eugene Valencia (15 1/2 plus 7 1/2 previous victories). (USN)

VF-18 (#5 USN victories) scored 176 1/2 of its 250 1/2 victories on its second tour on the *Intrepid*. The squadron was led in victories by 13 aces led by Lt(jg) Charles Mallory (L) with 10 victories and Lt. Cecil Harris with 22 of his 24 victories. (USN)

The unit boosted 27 aces, the most for any Navy squadron during one tour. Dean was the top ace with 11 victories, followed by Dan Carmichael and Art Van Haren with 9.

VF-9 scored 256 3/4 victories in three tours. The first tour, flying F4Fs, was off the *Ranger* during the North African Invasion and accounted for 6 victories. The second tour flew F6Fs off the *Essex* and scored 120 victories, with 10 aces led by Hamilton McWhorter with 10. VF-9 was re-formed for its third tour and was split into VFB-9 in January 1945. It served aboard the *Lexington* from 3 February to 6 March 1945, and then on the *Yorktown* from 6 March to 16 June when the carrier was attacked. The squadron had 130 3/4 victories and 8 aces led by Eugene Valencia's "Mowing Machine": Gene Valencia 15 1/2 victories; Jim French 11; Harris Mitchell 10; and Clinton Smith with 6. VBF-9 scored 51 victories and had one ace (Edgar McClure 5).

VB-18 was the fifth Navy squadron to exceed 250 victories. It scored 74 F6F victories off the *Bunker Hill* in early 1944 and had no aces before it was decommissioned. The second tour served aboard the *Intrepid* in late 1944 and took part in the Battle of Leyte Gulf, scoring 176 1/2 victories before the *Intrepid* was put out of action on 25 November. It had 13 aces led by Cecil Harris with 22, and followed by Henry Picken with 11 and Charles Mallory with 10.

Top USN Squadrons (250 victories)

VF (VBF)	V	Aces*	1st Tour V	1st Tour Aces	2nd Tour V	2nd Tour Aces	3rd Tour V	3rd Tour Aces
VF-17	313	24/5	152	12/3	161	12/2	———	———
+(VBF-17)	(125)	(8/0)	(121)	(8/0)	———	———	———	———
VF-15	310	26/1	310	26/1	———	———	———	———
VF-2	262	27/4	17	0/3	245	27/1	———	———
VF-9	256.8	18/14	6	0/3	120	10/5	130.8	8/6
+(VBF-9)	(51)	(1/2)	(51)	(1/2)	———	———	———	———
VF-18	250.5	14/16	74	1/12	176.5	13/4	———	———
VF-10	217	10/18	43	1/9	88	5/6	86	4/3
+(VBF-10)	(15)	(0/1)	(15)	(0/1)	———	———	———	———
VF-5	186.5	11/9	79	5/4	93.5	6/2	14	0/3
VF-31	165.6	13/5	146.5	13/2	19	0/3	———	———
VF-30	159.8	9/6	49.8	1/3	110	8/3	———	———
VF-80	159.5	11/1	159.5	11/1	———	———	———	———
VF-20	158.2	9/3	158.2	9/3	———	———	———	———
VF-11	157	7/7	55	2/4	102	5/3	———	———
VF-8	156	13/3	5	0/1	151	13/2	———	———
VF-19	155	11/0	155	11/0	———	———	———	———
VF-16	154.5	7/7	136.5	7/4	18	0/3	———	———
+(VBF-16)	(1)	(0/0)	(1)	(0/0)	———	———	———	———

* Pilots with 5+ victories in squadron/pilots with less than 5 victories in squadron but had additional victories with other squadrons to become aces.

Top USMC Squadrons

VMF-121 was the highest scoring Marine squadron with 205 1/2 victories. The squadron relieved VMF-221 on Guadalcanal in January 1943, where it scored the majority of its victories in F4Fs under Joe Foss. The squadron boasted 15 aces, led by Foss, who scored 26 victories, and followed by Bill Marontate with 13 and Greg Loesch with 8 1/2. VMF-121 was deployed again in late 1944 as a F4U unit, but only achieved one victory.

VMF-221 was second in Marine scoring, needing three deployments. The first deployment was to relieve Wake Island in April-May 1942, where it scored 12 F4F and F2A victories. The second deployment was sent to Guadalcanal, where it served two tours, and then a third tour on Vella Lavella flying the Wildcat. It scored 77 victories and had 7 aces, led by Zeke Swett with 14 1/2 and Harold Segal with 10. The squadron was reorganized in January 1944 and flew F4Us off the *Bunker Hill* December 1944 to 11 May 1945, when the carrier was put out of action. The unit scored 66 victories and had 3 aces, led by Dean Caswell with 7.

VMF-112 scored 144 victories in two deployments. The Wolfpack flew the F4F over Guadalcanal and the Solomons from November 1942 to August 1943 on its first deployment. It scored 90 victories and had six aces, led by Archie Donohue with 9 and Jeff DeBlanc with 8. The second deployment flew F4Us off the *Bennington* from December 1944 to mid-June 1945. This deployment totaled 54 victories, but had no aces.

VMF-215, the Fighting Corsairs, had two deployments, but did all its scoring during the first over the Solomons, especially the Bougainville operations. It claimed 135 1/2 victories and had 10 aces, including Bob Hanson with 23, Don Aldrich with 20, and Harold Spears with 15.

VMF-223 gained fame over Guadalcanal where it scored 126 1/2 victories and had seven aces in F4Fs. John Smith was the leading ace with 19 victories, followed by Marion Carl with 15 1/2 and Ken Frazier with 11 1/2. The squadron flew land-based F4Us on its second deployment, scoring 21 victories and no aces.

VMF-112 was third with 144 victories in two deployments (90 in the first and 54 in the second). (USMC)

The most famous Marine squadron was the "Black Sheep," VMF-214, led by Pappy Boyington but was seventh with 126 victories, 96 in its second (Boyington) deployment. (USMC)

VMF-121 was the top Marine squadron with 204 1/2 victories, all but one on its first deployment at Guadalcanal. The squadron boasted 15 aces, lead by Joe Foss with 26. (USMC)

VMF-323, the "Death Rattlers," had 124 1/2 victories (#7) but had 12 aces in its 6 week battle over Okinawa. (L-R) Maj. George Axtell (6 victories), Maj. Jeff Dorroh (6), 2Lt. Stuart Alley (5), 1Lt. Al Wells (5), 1Lt. Francis Terrill (6 1/6), 2Lt. Bill Drake (5), 1Lt. Joe Dillard (6 1/3), 1Lt. Jerry O'Keefe (7), 2Lt. Dewey Durnford (6 1/3), 1Lt. Bill Hood (5 1/2). 1Lt. John Ruhsam (7) and 1Lt. Robert Wade (7) are not pictured. (Author/O'Keefe)

VMF-212 also flew F4Fs over Guadalcanal and got 56 1/2 victories and had 7 aces, including 11 victories by CO Henry Bauer and 10 each by Jack Conger and Doc Everton. The second deployment was in land-based F4Us over the Northern Solomons, where it claimed 70 victories and 3 aces, led by Phil DeLong with 12.2 victories.

The most well known Marine squadron was VMF-214, made famous by its CO, Pappy Boyington. On its first deployment (without Boyington) it scored 30 victories and had two aces flying F4Us in the Russell Islands. The Black Sheep tour at Munda scored 96 victories and had 8 aces, including Boyington with 22 and Chris McGee with 9.

VMF-323, the Death Rattlers, scored 124 1/2 victories in its only deployment, six weeks over Okinawa flying F4Us. It had 12 aces, the second most for one squadron and for one tour.

Top USMC Squadrons (125+ Victories)

VMF	Vict.	Aces	1st Deploy Vict.	1st Deploy. Aces	2nd Deploy. Vict.	2nd Deploy. Aces	3rd Deploy. Vict.	3rd Deploy. Aces
121	205.5	15/6	204.5	15/6	1	0/0	——	——
221	155	10/7	12	0/2	77	7/2	66	3/3
112	144	6/8	90	6/6	54	0/2	——	——
215	135.5	10/0	135.5	10/0	0	0/0	——	——
223	132	8/5	125.5	8/2	21	0/3	——	——
212	126.5	7/1	56.5	3/1	70	4/0	——	——
214	126	10/2	30	2/1	96	8/1	——	——
323	124.5	12/0	124.5	12/0	——	——	——	——

CHAPTER 19

Aircraft Vulnerability and Personnel Losses

Background

The two major causes for aircraft lost or damaged in combat are:

1 Air-to-air combat (enemy aircraft fire)
2 Ground-to-air (anti-aircraft fire)

The primary factors affecting loss and damage to an aircraft are:

1 Aircraft susceptibility to enemy action by type and make
2 Characteristics of enemy opposition
3 Mission and combat conditions/theater of operations

A lost aircraft is defined as one that fails to return to base, while a damaged aircraft is one that does return to base after being hit.

In 1950, the "Think Tank" at the Rand Corporation of Santa Monica, California, conducted an extensive investigation of aircraft vulnerability (*RM 402: Aircraft Vulnerability in WWII*) for Air Force and Navy aircraft in WWI using the above determinates.

Vulnerability by Aircraft Type

USAAF

Three principal fighter types were studied: P-47; P-38; and P-51. The P-47 mounted an air-cooled Pratt & Whitney engine. The P-38 was powered by twin Allison liquid-cooled engines. The Mustang initially was equipped with an Allison engine, but later became a great fighter when it converted to the liquid-cooled Packard/Rolls Royce. The engines of the P-38 and P-51 were liquid-cooled and caught fire when damaged, while the air-cooled Pratt & Whitney of the P-47 was less vulnerable to damage. The ruggedness of the P-47 airframe and engine during the war is legend. Approximately eight of ten P-47s that were hit returned, as compared to seven of ten P-38s and six of ten P-51s.

Because a fighter was able to continue flying after it had been damaged, distance to base became a major factor. Holed oil or coolant systems would allow about 10 to 20 minutes flight time. If friendly territory were within this radius, the aircraft returned as damaged, or otherwise it was lost. The P-51 had the longest range of the three and was used as a long-range bomber escort. This assignment contributed to the Mustang's higher loss rate when hit far from base. The P-47, because of its lesser fuel capacity, was assigned shorter missions that would tend to reduce its loss rate. Contrary to the belief that the second engine of the P-38 increased its chances to return safely, less than 10% of damaged P-38s returned to base on one engine; the disablement of one engine generally led to the loss of the fighter. Thus, the second engine of the P-38 probably increased its vulnerability. A rough measure of the degree of exposure to enemy action is the number of claims vs. enemy aircraft. While the loss rate for the P-51 was three times that of the P-47 per 1,000 sorties, its claim rate was approximately four times that of the P-47. In contrast, the P-38 loss rate was about the same as the P-51, but its claim rate was lower than both the P-51 and P-47. In the latter stages of the war the Luftwaffe was decimated, and anti-aircraft fire became the major cause for damage and loss. With no air opposition the Air Force concentrated on flak-intensive ground support and strafing sorties. An interesting finding was that bombers hit by enemy aircraft fire were about ten times more likely to be lost as those hit by AA fire, whereas fighters hit by enemy aircraft fire were only two times as likely to be lost as those hit by AA fire. Almost all AA fire causing loss to bombers was of large caliber (75mm to 120mm), large fragmentation type fired to the high altitudes in which bombers operated. However, for fighters most of

The ruggedness of the P-47 was legend. Here a T-bolt of the 367FG demonstrates its ability to take punishment.(USAF)

The liquid-cooled Packard Rolls Royce V-1650 was very vulnerable. A small arms bullet hit the coolant system of this 355FG P-51D causing its engine to seize. (USAF)

The twin engines of the P-38 were thought to give the Lightning an advantage but suffered the worst loss rate of any front-line American fighter. Here a P-38H of the 364FG made a successful—for the pilot, anyway—wheels up landing. (USAF)

The FM-2 was called the "Wilder Wildcat" and was the offspring of the F4F. The landing gear of this VC-83 *Sergeant Bay* FM-2 failed but the fighter was repaired and flew again. (USN)

the hits from AA weapons were small caliber, consisting of armor-piercing, incendiary, and cannon shells. These types of hits were sustained mostly on strafing missions. Comparing hits from enemy aerial machine guns and cannon showed the following. Hits from .50 caliber were about 2.4 times as lethal as .30 caliber, while 20mm cannon hits were 5.4 times more lethal as .30 caliber and 2.2 times as .50 caliber.

Anti-Aircraft Vulnerability
(A/C lost:A/C hit)

A/C	%	A/C	%
P-51	29%	F4U	26%
P-38	25%	F6F	25%
P-47	10%	F4F	22%

F4F includes FM-2

Enemy Aircraft Vulnerability
(A/C lost:A/C hit)

A/C	%	A/C	%
P-38	49%	F4U	46%
P-51	46%	F6F	36%
P-47	37%	F4F	25%

F4F includes FM-2

Between August 1943 and May 1944, the Eighth Fighter Command recorded a summary of the causes for damaged (1,330 A/C) and lost (659 A/C).

Causes of Damaged and Lost Aircraft

Cause	% Damaged	% Lost
AA Fire	63%	27%
E/A Fire	22%	39%
Unknown	6%	12%
Collision (with ground or A/C)	7%	6%
Mechanical failure	1%	12%
Others	1%	4%

Causes of Damaged and Lost Aircraft

A/C	*****Damaged*****			+++++ Lost++++++		
	E/A	AA	Other	E/A	AA	Other
P-47	22%	63%	15%	40%	20%	40%
P-38	16%	70%	14%	40%	28%	32%
P-51	25%	59%	16%	37%	35%	28%

The Evaluation Section, Air Branch, Office of Naval Intelligence studied 1,202 Navy aircraft lost to AA fire and 234 lost to enemy aircraft. The study determined the aircraft component that was damaged, causing the loss.

The Grumman fighters were solidly built and their radial, air-cooled Pratt & Whitney engines were tough. Here the tail hook of a F6F-5 of VF-33 *Sangamon* fails to catch the first arresting wires and the Cat collides heavily with a barrier. Both the pilot and fighter flew again. (USN)

Component Damage

Component	AA Fire	E/A Fire
Engine	23%	16%
Flight controls	8%}>	6%}>
Pilot	4%} >25%	2%} > 34%
Pilot or flight controls	13%}>	26%}>
Fuel system	16%	12%
Oil system	13%	11%
Airframe	13%	13%
Hydraulic system	7%	11%
Other	3%	3%

The Navy study also determined how often a component, when hit, failed and caused the aircraft to be lost:

Component	AA Fire	E/A Fire
Oil system	74%	85%
Engine	70%	62%
Pilot &/or Flight controls	67%	76%
Fuel system	61%	80%
Hydraulic system	44%	60%
Airframe	7%	12%

Of the aircraft that went down immediately, 54% were due to hits on the pilot and/or flight controls, and 25% to hits to the fuel system. Hits on the engine or oil system caused the loss of 68% of those aircraft forced to make a controlled water landing or bailout near target. Damaged airframe and hydraulic systems accounted for 73% of the aircraft that were able to make a landing at base, but were written off.

The aircraft component hit by enemy fire causing damage to a returning aircraft was:

By AA Fire	Airframe	60%	Surface Controls	14%
By E/A Fire	Airframe	60%	Surface Controls	10%

The VIII Fighter Command conducted a study assessing damage and loss as to mission type due to the changing character of the war.

Loss Rate of Fighters Hit by Enemy Fire

A/C	Avg.Hrs/ Sortie	A/C Damaged/ 1000 Sorties	A/C Lost/ 1000 Sorties	% A/C Lost/Hit
	8/24/43	to	5/31/44	
P-47	3.2	18	6	25%
P-38	4.2	22	17	44%
P-51	4.4	27	19	41%
	6/1/44	to	8/31/44	
P-47	3.7	28	7	19%
P-38	3.9	16	7	30%
P-51	4.3	16	11	41%

Damage/Loss by Mission Type

Mission Type	# Sorties	A/C Damaged /1000 Sorties	A/C Lost/ 1000 Sorties	% A/C Lost/Hit
MARCH	APRIL	MAY	1944	
Bomber Support	31,688	23	10	30%
Sweeps	1999	35	13	27%
Strafing	1723	80	36	31%
Fighter-bombing	1722	49	9	16%
JUNE	JULY	AUGUST	1944	
Bomber Support	39.675	13	6	35%
Strafing, sweeps	17,488	34	14	29%
Fighter-bombing	1669	32	16	33%
Fighter-bomber escort	370	24	3	11%

Escort of bombers in both periods was the safest mission for fighters (despite the high loss/hit ratio due to the long distances involved), with only 16.5 and 9.5 hits/1,000 missions, respectively. Fighter-bombing became similar to sweeps and strafing in the latter period because of low level bombing of tactical targets during the period before and after D-Day. While the loss and damage rates for this type of mission was very high in the first period compared to the second (37 avg./1,000 sorties vs. 20.5 avg./1,000 sorties), the return rates if hit in each period were similar when looking at the % A/C lost figures. Fighter-bombers in the earlier period tried to remain above the light AA fire that is reflected in the 16% to 33% figures in the two periods.

Changing Character of Operations

Period	Damaged % Due to AA	Damaged % Due to E/A	Lost % Due to AA	Lost % Due to E/A
8/43-5/44	63%	21%	27%	39%
6/44-5/45	69%*	5%	32%	13%

* Includes 14% small arms and ground fire

The decreased and selective Luftwaffe fighter opposition after mid-1944 is shown in the decreased losses due to E/A (1/4 fewer damaged and 1/3 fewer lost). AA fire continued to be the dominant cause for loss and steadily increased form 2.5 to 5.5 to 1 times the losses due to E/A by February 1945, despite the contribution of flak maps to fighter pilots in August 1944 to aid them in avoiding known AA concentrations.

In a paper prepared for the Secretary of Defense and Institute of Defense Analysis in 1966, Joseph Reinberg researched in part a quantitative comparison of various American fighter types in Europe and the Pacific.

Fighter Comparison by Type
ETO & PTO USAAF

A/C Type	Sorties A/T/A	Sorties A/T/G	Loss % E/A	Losses % AA	Losses % Ops	Loss % All
****	******	*6 April*	*to*	*5 June*	*1944*	******
P-51	24,000		.66		.15	.48
	6000	.25	.83	.32	1.53	
P-47	25,000		.53		.11	.24
	25,000	.17	.38	.14	.70	
P-38	19,000		.41		.36	.77
	1000	.90	1.50	.90	3.30	
****	******	*6 June*	*to*	*5 Sept.*	*1944*	******
P-51	59,200		.29	.02	.22	.53
	2000	.74	4.74	.40	5.88	
P-47	41,900		.11	.02	.22	.35
	72,300	.09	.25	.23	.57	
P-38	13,600		.41	.03	.25	.69
	1600	.31	4.18	.31	4.80	
P-61	26,200		.02	.02	.10	.14
****	******	*6 Sept.*	*1944*	*to*	*7 May*	*1945*
P-51	152,100		.26	.06	.12	.44
	16,500	.49	1.87	1.19	3.55	
P-47	140,000		.32	.11	.12	.55
	113,500	.14	1.90	.12	2.15	
P-38	9300		.77	.11	.42	1.29
P-61	38,200		.04	.05	.25	.34

(A/T/A = Air-to-air A/T/G = Air-to-ground)

ETO Summary:

In all operational periods surveyed of air-to-air combat the sturdy P-47 had the lowest loss rate, followed by the P-51, and then in a poor third place was the P-38. The P-61 night fighter had a very low loss rate because it was virtually unopposed. In all operational periods surveyed of air-to-ground sorties the legendary ruggedness of the P-47 again proved itself, as it far surpassed the P-51 and P-38 in this dangerous undertaking, primarily due to its air-cooled Pratt & Whitney engine and sturdy airframe. Approximately 8 out of 10 Thunderbolts that were hit returned, as compared to 7 of 10 Lightnings and 6 of 10 Mustangs. Of course, the type of mission also determined loss ratio. The P-51 primarily flew long-range bomber escort missions where a hit to the oil or coolant system meant only 10 to 20 minutes flying time and almost certain loss. The P-47 mainly flew shorter range strafing and ground support missions, which in case of a hit to its more rugged air cooled engine was more than likely to allow it to return to friendly territory, which was usually nearby. But then the P-47 strafing missions were very much more dangerous than the P-51 escort missions, which as the war went on did not meet determined Luftwaffe opposition. Later, because of this decreased air opposition, the Mustangs were released from the bombers and allowed to engage in ground strafing missions and sustained higher losses.

A/C Type	A/T/A Sorties	% Losses % A/T/A Battle	% Losses % Ops of the	% Losses Total % Coral Sea
5/8/42				
F4F 208	5.3	2.4	7.7	
6/4-6/42		*Battle*	of	*Midway*
F4F 90	6.7	1.1	7.8	
2/1/42	to	8/31/42	New	Guinea
P-39	600	14.0	23.5	35.7
P-40	1300	7.4	13.1	20.5
9/1/42	to	6/30/43	New Guinea	New Britain
P-38	1800	1.9	2.3	4.2
P-39	3000	1.4	2.1	3.2
P-40	3800	1.2	1,7	2.9
8/7/42	to	2/7/43	Guadalcanal	
F4F 1526	1.1	3.7	4.8	
P-38	98	3.1	6.1	9.2
P-39	83	6.0	9.6	15.7
P-40	52	7.7	17.3	25.0
10/1/43	to	2/17/44	Rabaul	
F4U3300	2.1	1.9	4.0	
F6F 920	1.7	2.1	3.8	
P-38	475	2.3	3.0	5.3
P-40	650	2.3	2.8	5.1

LOSSES

Battle Casualties All USAAF Officers/All Theaters

Year	Total Casualties	Died	Wounded, Evacuated	Missing, Interned, Captured
TOTAL	50,415	17,021	6442	26,952
1941*	79	49	29	1
1942	1840	987	149	704
1943	3999	1213	3669	13,631
1944	29,790	9481	3705	16,604
1945**	9325	2413	1290	5622

Battle Casualties All USAAF Enlisted Personnel /All Theaters

Year	Total Casualties	Died	Wounded, Evacuated	Missing, Interned, Captured
TOTAL	71,452	23,040	11,796	36,616
1941*	649	266	372	11
1942	6948	2490	320	4138
1943	13,631	6003	2968	4660
1944	38,827	11,591	6252	20,984
1945+	10,235	2187	1756	6292

* December 1941

\+ January to August 1945

USAAF FIGHTER AIRCRAFT LOSSES by THEATER and TYPE of LOSS

Theater & Type of Loss	Total	1941*	1942	1943	1944	1945**
All Theaters						
Total Losses	19,568	310	1085	3240	9400	5551
1st Line Losses***	17,839	211	1035	3219	8800	4574
2nd Line Losses	1747	99	50	21	600	977
ETO						
Total Losses	7421	——	68	301	4897	2155
1st Line Losses	7124	——	68	301	4758	1997
2nd Line Losses	297	——	——	——	139	158
MTO						
Total Losses	5107	——	138	1689	2231	1049
1st Line Losses	4572	——	138	1678	2150	606
2nd Line Losses	535	——	——	11	81	443
PTO ****						
Total Losses	5414	310	809	1000	1545	1750
1st Line Losses	4664	211	765	990	1226	1472
2nd Line Losses	750	99	44	10	319	278
CBI						
Total Losses	1644	——	70	250	727	597
1st Line Losses	1479	——	64	250	666	499
2nd Line Losses	165	——	6	——	61	98

* December 1941

** January through August 1945

*** 1st Line Losses are combat and accident losses

****PTO includes Pacific Ocean Area, Far East AF, XX AF, Alaska and miscellaneous areas

USAAF FIGHTER COMBAT LOSSES by THEATER and CAUSE

Fighter Combat Losses Theater/Cause of Loss	Total	1942	1943	1944	1945
ETO		*			*
Total Losses	5324	10	178	3765	1371
Enemy Aircraft	1691	10	161	1293	227
Anti-aircraft Fire	2449	——	1	1611	837
Other Causes	1184	——	16	861	307
MTO		**			**
Total Losses	3157	54	1088	1571	444
Enemy Aircraft	1357	46	816	441	24
Anti-aircraft Fire	822	8	115	493	206
Other Causes	1008	——	157	637	214
PTO +		***			***
Total Losses	1695	199	310	513	673
Enemy Aircraft	636	192	244	141	59
Anti-aircraft Fire	300	1	9	100	190
Other Causes	759	6	57	272	424
CBI	****				
Total Losses	774	24	146	371	233
Enemy Aircraft	295	20	94	157	24
Anti-aircraft Fire	208	——	10	86	112
Other Causes	271	4	42	128	97

* August-December 1942 & January-May 1945
** June-December 1942 & January-May 1945
***January-December 1942 & January-August 1945

**** April-December 1942 & January-August 1945
+ PTO includes Pacific Ocean Area, Far East AF, XX AF, Alaska and Miscellaneous Areas

On 19 March 1945, the *Franklin* took two bombs through its flight deck suffering 1,100 casualties. AG-5 sustained 124 KIAs which with the 17 losses on board the *Yorktown* on its first cruise was the highest loss rate endured by any USN air group. (USN)

Due to its long nose, large prop and poor forward visibility the F4U had its problems in earlier carrier qualifications and gave way to the F6F Hellcat as the Navy's carrier fighter of choice. A F4U-1 of VF-17 comes to grief during its initial carrier qualifications aboard the *Ranger*. (USN)

USN CARRIER FIGHTER LOSSES

Carrier Type Fighter Type	Total Action Sorties	To Enemy AA	USN Fighter Losses ——On Action Sorties——	——Non-combat——		
			To Enemy A/C	Oper-ational	Other Flights	On Ship
CV Totals	51,821	510	263	303	775	366
F6F	41,715	366	185	212	509	233
F4U (USN)	6488	93	18	48	182	76
F4U (USMC)	2650	40	16	21	42	37
F4F	968	11	44	22	42	20
CVL Totals	15,099	128	58	91	279	122
F6F	15,099	128	58	91	279	122
CVE Totals	19,076	118	16	102	344	122
FM	12,925	62	13	75	283	71
F6F (USN)	5426	44	2	18	41	48
F6F (USMC)	146	2	0	0	8	0
F4U (USMC)	443	4	0	0	5	1
F4F	136	6	3	9	7	2
Carrier Fighter Totals	85,996	756	337	496	1398	610

1589 fighters lost on action sorties
2008 fighters lost on other non-combat flights and on shipboard
3597 fighters lost total

USN/USMC LAND-BASED FIGHTER LOSSES

SERVICE/YEAR	Total Action Sorties	To Enemy AA	OWN FIGHTER LOSSES ——On Action Sorties——	——Non-combat——		
			To Enemy A/C	Oper-ational	Other Flights	On Ground
USMC	55,597	216	232	171	519	79
1941-42	923	3	74	11	19	26
1943	2907	15	107	26	100	5
1944	30,717	109	37	63	133	31
1945	21,050	89	14	71	267	31
USN	4189	19	93	27	55	25
1941-42	166	0	19	2	5	19
1943	1388	9	56	11	32	2
1944	2514	5	18	14	16	2
1945	121	2	0	0	2	2

USMC   619 lost on action sorties
        598 lost on non-combat
USN   139 lost on action sorties
        80 lost on non-combat

The *Bunker Hill* took 137 KIAs among its five squadrons on board during a kamikaze attack on 11 May 1945. These were the most fatalities suffered by a USN carrier in WWII. (USN)

Top P-38 scorer in the MTO, 1Lt. Michael Brezas, crash-landed in Russian-held territory and was captured by the Soviets and was treated very poorly by them. (Author)

An example of losses sustained by a group is demonstrated by 56FG statistics. This group had the best overall ETO claims to losses ratio of approximately eight per cent from all causes and about five per cent in the air. Of the 128 Thunderbolts it lost, almost two-thirds were lost on ground attack missions. Of these 128 pilots, 84 were KIA, 36 survived as POWs, and eight evaded capture. A total of 48 pilots were KIFA, 34 in the ETO, 12 in training in the U.S., and two more in England after the war ended.

On 19 March 1945 the *Franklin* took two bombs through the flight deck, suffering 1,100 casualties, including 124 KIA in AG-5, which with the 17 losses suffered on the *Yorktown* on its first cruise was the highest suffered by a Navy Air Group in the war. The *Bunker Hill* took 137 KIAs among the five squadrons on board in a kamikaze attack on 11 May 1945, which was the most suffered by a USN carrier in a single action. On 11 May 1945, at 1002, Marine Corps Medal of Honor fighter pilot Maj. James Swett of VMF-221 spotted two Japanese Kamikaze aircraft diving on Adm. Marc Mitscher's flag carrier *Bunker Hill*, and alerted CIC on the carrier. The first Zero dropped a bomb through the flight deck, from where it skidded through the hull and exploded. The Zero crashed on the flight deck that held a flight of manned and armed F6F Hellcats. The Zero continued bouncing across the *Hill's* deck, spreading fiery gasoline among the waiting Navy fighters, and finally plunged over the side. As the carrier's crew raced out to aid the wounded and to put out the fires, the second Zero Kamikaze attacked with a 500lb, hitting the flight deck amidships and exploding the gallery

1Lt. Fletcher Adams (9v/357FG) was murdered by the Chief of the German Home Guard after bailing out safely. (Author)

Maj. John Bright had a varied flying career involving several hair-raising experiences. He was involved in a training collision flying for the AVG but bailed out but the other pilot died. He was shot down in January 1942 but safely bailed out. As CO of the 37FG/14FG his fighter engine failure and he became a POW of the Italians but escaped. With the CACW in May 1945 he crash-landed but was aided by Chinese troops in returning to base. (Author)

Capt. Robert Goebel had 11 victories with the 308FS/31FG. These photos were carried on missions to aid in the fabrication of false ID papers in case of capture. When the photos were taken the same suit coat, tie and shirt were used by all Group members. (Author/Goebel)

Lt(jg) Horace "Rabbit" Moranville's (VF-11) Hellcat was hit by AA fire over Indo-China and he was captured by the Vichy French. His adventures during the next two and a half months were out of Hollywood films. (Author/Moranville)

deck. Instantly this Jap aircraft hit the carrier's island nearby Adm. Mitscher. Gasoline fires raged on the deck, while ammunition and gasoline tanks exploded in the hangar decks just below. A total of 402 officers and men perished, and 264 were wounded. Pilots of VF-84 had been waiting below deck in the ready room and were trapped and asphyxiated. Among the dead were three aces of VF-84: Lt(jg) Doris Freeman (9 v.); Lt(jg) John Gildea (7 v.); and Ens. John Sargent (7 1/2 v.).

Aces Lost

A total of 171 aces, or one in seven, were killed in action or in flying accidents during the war. An additional 84 were taken prisoner, and 57 were shot down and evaded and returned. A total of 313 aces, or one in four, were lost.

Maj. Bert Marshall, CO of the 354FS, crash-landed his wounded P-51 near the German border and 1Lt. Royce Priest landed and rescued his CO. (USAF)

1Lt. George Green (on lap) landed in a field near Berlin to rescue his 335FS CO, Maj. Pierce McKennon, who was hit by AA fire and bailed out. To fit into the cockpit the smaller Green had to sit on McKennon's lap for the long ride back to England. (USAF)

The Blood Chit was a screened fabric insignia worn by AVG pilots sewn on the back of their leather flight jackets. It stated in Chinese that if the life of the downed pilot were saved, a reward would be given. (Author's Collection)

Pilot Name	Rank	Unit	Date	Theater/Cause
Adams, Fletcher	Capt	357	5/30/44	ETO /Combat (*1)
Adams, Robert	1Lt	8	9/2/43	PTO/MIA
Anderson, Charles	Capt	4	4/19/44	ETO/??
Aron, William	1Lt	325	5/22/45	MTO/AA
Baker, Douglas	Lt(jg)	VF20	12/14/44	PTO/Combat
Bauer, Harold	LCol	VMF 212	11/14/42	PTO/Combat
Beavers, Edward	Capt	339	11/27/44	ETO/AA
Beerbower, Donald	Capt	354	8/9/44	ETO/AA
Beeson, Duane	Capt	4	4/5/44	ETO/AA
Berkheimer, Jack	Ens	VF41	12/16/44	PTO/??
Biel, Hipolitus	1Lt	4	4/24/44	ETO/Combat
Bishop, Walter	Lt(jg)	VF29	12/14/44	PTO/Collision
Brewer, Charles	Cdr	VF15	6/19/44	PTO/Combat
Bright, Mark	Lt	VF16	6/17/44	PTO/AA
Brown, Quince	Maj	348	9/6/44	ETO/AA (*2)
Browning, James	Capt	357	2/9/45	ETO/??
Burckhalter, William	Lt(jg)	VF16	6/11/44	PTO/AA
Burriss, Howard	Lt(jg)	VF17	1/31/44	PTO/Combat
Chapman, Philip	Maj	23	3/28/45	CBI/AA
Check, Leonard	LCdr	VF7	1/4/45	PTO/Collision
Condon, Henry	Lt	475	1/2/45	PTO/Target explosion
Cragg, Edward	Maj	8	12/26/43	PTO/Combat
Cundy, Arthur	1Lt	353	3/11/45	ETO/??
Cutler, Frank	Capt	352	5/13/44	ETO/Collision
Dorsch, Frederick	Capt	31	10/29/44	MTO/??
Doyle, Cecil	2Lt	VMF 121	11/7/42	PTO/Collision
Duke, Walter	Capt	459	6/6/44	CBI/??
Eason, Hoyt	1Lt	35	3/3/43	PTO/??
Egan, Joseph	1Lt	56	7/19/44	ETO/AA
Everhart, Lee	Capt	8	10/12/44	PTO/AA
Fields, Virgil	Maj	31	2/6/44	MTO/Combat
Formanek, George	Lt	VF30	4/23/44	PTO/ Strafing crash
Freeman, Doris	Lt	VF84	5/11/45	PTO/ Kamikaze crash (*3)
Fryer, Earl	Capt	55	11/8/44	ETO/AA
Gildea, John	Lt(jg)	VF84	4/11/45	PTO/Kamikaze crash (*3)
Graham, Lindol	Capt	20	3/18/44	ETO/Strafing crash
Griffith, Robert	1Lt	82	7/26/44	MTO/Combat
Hamilton, Henry	M/G	VMF 212	10/21/42	PTO/Combat
Hampshire, John	Capt	23	5/3/43	CBI/Combat (DoW)
Hanseman, Christopher	1Lt	339	7/29/44	ETO /Strafing crash
Hanson, Robert	1Lt	VMF 215	2/3/44	PTO/AA
Harris, William	Lt	VF17	8/9/45	PTO/Own bomb exploded
Hayde, Frank	Lt(jg)	VF31	7/15/45	PTO/Weather
Head, Cotesworth	Capt	18	1/18/44	PTO/Combat
Henderson, Paul	Lt	VF1	6/15/44	PTO/Combat
Hiro, Edwin	Maj	357	9/19/44	ETO/??
Hofer, Ralph	1Lt	4	7/2/44	ETO/Combat
Holloway, James	1Lt	82	6/18/45	ETO/Weather
Hunt, Edward	1Lt	354	11/8/44	ETO/AA
Icard, Joe	2Lt	56	3/8/44	ETO/AA?
Johnson, Clarence	Capt	352	9/23/44	ETO/Combat
Johnson, Paul	FLt	RAF	7/18/44	ETO/Hit tree
Jones. Frank	Capt	4	8/8/44	ETO/AA

Jones, Ripley	FLt	RAF	10/17/42	ETO/Collision
Kearby, Neel	Col	348	3/5/44	PTO/ Combat
Kendrick, Charles	2Lt	VMF 223	10/2/42	PTO/Combat
Kirkland, Lenton	1Lt	474	12/24/44	ETO/AA
Knight, William	Lt	VF14	11/5/44	PTO/??
Kuentzel, Ward	2Lt	82	6/19/44	MTO/Weather?
Ladd, Kenneth	Capt	8	10/14/44	PTO/Combat
Lang, Leo	Capt	4	10/14/44	ETO/Combat
Larson, Donald	Maj	339	8/4/44	ETO/Strafing collision
Leppla, John	Lt(jg)	VF10	10/26/42	PTO/??
Little, Robert	F/L	AVG	5/22/42	CBI/AA
Lucas, Paul	Capt	475	1/15/45	PTO/??
Lutton, Lowell	1Lt	475	11/2/43	PTO/Fuel?
Lynch, Thomas	LCol	35	3/8/44	PTO/AA
Mahony, Grant	LCol	1Cdo	1/3/45	CBI/AA
Marontate, William	1Lt	VMF 121	1/15/43	PTO/Combat
McDowell, Don	1Lt	35	5/28/44	ETO/??
McGrattan, Bernard	Capt	4	6/6/44	ETO/Combat
McGuire, Thomas	Maj	475	7/7/45	PTO/Combat
McMillan, George	LCol	51	6/24/44	CBI/AA
McMinn, Evan	2Lt	56	6/6/44	ETO/AA?
McPharlin, Michael	Maj	4	6/6/44	ETO/Engine?
Merritt, George	Maj	361	6/7/44	ETO/ AA?
Meuten, Donald	1Lt	49	5/7/44	PTO/??
Miklajcyk, Henry	Capt	352	11/2/44	ETO/??
Mitchell, Henry	Lt(jg)	VBF 17	4/3/45	PTO/AA
Mollenhauer, Arthur	Ens	VF18	10/29/44	PTO/Combat
Moore, John	Maj	348	10/6/44	ETO/AA?
Morgan, John	1Lt	VMF 213	3/28/45	PTO/AA
Morrill, Stanley	1Lt	56	3/29/44	ETO/ Bomb explosion on base
Moseley, William	Lt	VF1	7/4/44	PTO/AA
Murphy, Alva	Capt	357	3/2/45	ETO/AA
Myers, Jennings	1Lt	8	12/22/43	PTO/??
Narr, Joseph	2Lt	VMF 121	11/11/42	PTO/Combat
Nelson, Robert	Ens	VF20	11/19/44	PTO/Combat
Newkirk, John	S/L	AVG	3/24/42	CBI/AA
O'Hare, Edward	LCdr	VF6	11/26/43	PTO/Combat
Olson, Norman	Capt	355	4/8/44	ETO/AA
Ostrom, Charles	Cdr	VF21	11/24/43	PTO/??
Parker, Harry	Capt	325	4/2/45	MTO/??
Pierce, Joseph	1Lt	357	5/21/44	ETO/AA
Plant, Claude	Ens	VF15	9/12/44	PTO/Combat
Pond. Zenneth	2Lt	VMF 223	9/10/42	PTO/Combat
Powell, Ernest	Capt	VMF 122	7/18/43	PTO/??
Preddy, George	Maj	352	12/25/44	ETO/AA (by US)
Reed, William	LCol	3(P)	12/19/44	CBI/Fuel
Reese, William	1Lt	357	5/21/44	ETO/AA
Righetti, Elwyn	LCol	55	4/17/45	ETO/AA
Roach, Thomas	Lt(jg)	VF21	7/25/43	PTO/Combat
Roberts, Daniel	Capt	475	11/9/43	PTO/Collision
Rynne, William	Capt	325	3/28/44	MTO/Combat
Sangermano, Philip	1Lt	325	12/9/44	MTO/??
Sargent, John	Lt(jg)	VF84	5/11/45	PTO/Kamikaze crash (*3)
Schecter, Gordon	Cdr	VF45	3/18/45	PTO/AA

Schlegel, Albert	Capt	4	8/28/44	ETO/AA
Schneider, Frank	Lt(jg)	VF33	1/9/44	PTO/AA
Schreiber, Leroy	Maj	56	4/15/44	ETO/AA
Seidman, Robert	1Lt	14	5/14/44	MTO/AA
Simmons, William	1Lt	354	4/25/44	ETO/AA
Smith, John	2Lt	475	11/9/43	PTO/Combat
Smith, Merle	LCol	475	12/7/44	PTO/Combat
Smith, Robert	Maj	367	6/22/44	CBI/AA
Smith, Virgil	1Lt	14	12/30/42	MTO/Combat
Stout, Robert	1Lt	VMF 212	3/4/45	PTO/AA
Thorne, James	P/O	RAF	9/10/44	ETO/AA
Torkelson, Ross	Lt	VF21	7/22/43	PTO/AA
Turley, Grant	2Lt	78	3/6/44	ETO/Combat
Vedder, Milton	1Lt	VMF 213	2/11/44	PTO/Illness
Vinson, Arnold	Capt	52	4/3/43	MTO/Combat
Warren, Jack	Capt	357	3/18/44	ETO/AA?
Weaver, Claude	P/O	RAF	1/28/44	MTO/??
Westbrook, Robert	LCol	347	11/22/44	PTO/AA
Wolford, John	1Lt	14	5/19/43	MTO/??
Wood, Walter	Ens	VF20	10/18/44	PTO/Combat

1   Murdered by Chief of German Home Guard after bailing out
2   Murdered by SS officer after bailing out
3   See Three aces die in *Bunker Hill* kamikaze attack

KIFA (46)

Pilot Name	Rank	Unit	Date	Location
Ackerman, Fred	Ens	VF80	9/15/45	US
Adkins, Frank	LCol	50	2/23/45	US
Barnes, James	Lt(jg)	VF83	7/2/45	PTO (??)
Bong, Richard	Maj	49	8/6/45	US (test pilot)
Boyle, Gerald	Lt	VF20	10/31/44	PTO (crash)
Bryce, James	Lt(jg)	VF22	4/10/45	US (take off)
Carroll, Walter	1Lt	82	1/20/45	US
Damstrom, Fernley	1Lt	49	4/11/45	PTO (take off)
Deakins, Richard	1Lt	325	11/24/44	MTO (crash)
Dibb, Robert	Lt	Det.	8/29/44	US (crash)
Dillow, Eugene	1Lt	VMF 221	4/4/44	US
Dunaway, John	1Lt	8	11/22/44	MTO (??)
Fiedler, William	1Lt	347	6/30/43	PTO (Collision takeoff)
Fraser, Robert	Maj	VMF 112	6/18/45	US
Gordon, Mathew	Capt	23	8/10/45	CBI (*1)
Gray, Rockford	Maj	371	9/4/44	ETO (Crash)
Gresham, Billy	1Lt	475	10/2/44	PTO/(Parachute failed)
Gumm, Charles	1Lt	354	3/1/44	ETO/ (Crash)
Harris, Frederick	Capt	475	10/31/43	PTO/(Crash)
Heath, Horace	Ens	VF10	7/8/45	US (Hawaii)/Crash
Heinzen, Lloyd	Lt	VF8	11/11/45	US (Weather)
Hennon, William	Capt	49	3/31/43	US/??
Jenkins, Otto	2Lt	357	3/24/45	England/??
Johnson, Gerald	LCol	49	10/7/45	PTO/Weather
Laird, Wayne	1Lt	VMF 112	4/30/43	PTO/Test flight
Lent, Francis	1Lt	475	12/1/44	PTO/Crash
Loesch, Gregory	Capt	VMF 121	12/27/43	PTO/Collision
Lombard, John	Maj	23	6/30/43	CBI/??

Lusk, Virgil	Capt	14	3/8/43	US
Maguire, William	Capt	353	8/11/45	England/Weather
McArthur, T.H.	Capt	82	5/3/43	England/??
McDonough, William	Maj	35	4/22/44	PTO/parachute failure
Owen, Donald	Capt	VMF 112	5/26/45	PTO/Carrier takeoff
Poindexter, James	Capt	353	1/3/45	England/Crash
Register, Francis	Lt(jg)	VF3	5/16/44	PTO/Crash
Rimerman, Ben	LCol	353	8/11/45	England/Weather
Sandell, Robert	S/L	AVG	2/7/42	CBI/Test flight
Schiel, Frank	Maj	23	12/5/42	CBI/??
Shaw, Edward	1Lt	VMF 213	7/31/44	PTO/??
Sonner, Irl	Lt(jg)	VF29	3/22/45	PTO/Crash carrier landing
Sparks, Kenneth	1Lt	35	9/5/44	US (Instructor)
Spears, Harold	Capt	VMF 215	12/6/44	US (Crash)
Varnell, James	Capt	52	4/9/45	US
Wade, Lance	S/L	RAF	1/12/44	MTO/Crash
Wagner, Boyd	LCol	24PG	11/29/42	US/Crash
Wainwright, John	2Lt	404	7/5/45	ETO/Crash
White, John	1Lt	31	11/5/45	US
Wilkinson, James	Capt	78	6/4/44	England
Wirth, John	Lt	VF31	4/13/45	US

1   Was killed while flying a L-5B attempting his second rescue of a pilot behind enemy lines that day.

POW (84)

Pilot Name	Rank	Unit	Date	Theater/Cause
Alexander, Richard	1Lt	52	5/30/44	ETO/Combat (by B-24?)
Amoss, Dudley	2Lt	55	3/21/45	ETO/AA
Andrew, Stephen	Maj	352	7/2/44	ETO/Engine
Archibald, David	1Lt	359	12/18/44	ETO/Combat
Aron, William	1Lt	325	4/22/45	MTO/AA
Bank, Raymond	1Lt	357	3/2/45	ETO/AA
Bearden, Aaron	2Lt	459	9/3/44	PTO/Collision
Beckham, Walter	Maj	353	2/22/44	ETO/AA
Benne, Louis	1Lt	14	6/14/44	MTO/Combat
Bennett, Joseph	Capt	4	5/25/44	ETO/Collision
Booth, Robert	1Lt	359	6/8/44	ETO/AA
Boyington, Gregory	Maj	VMF 214	1/3/44	PTO/Combat
Brezas, Michael	1Lt	14	4/2/45	MTO/AA (By Russians) (*1)
Bright, John	Maj	14	8/30/43	MTO/AC failure (escaped)
Brown, Henry	Capt	355	10/3/44	ETO/AA
Candelaria, Richard	1Lt	479	4/13/45	MTO/AA
Carder, John	1Lt	357	5/12/44	ETO/Combat
Care, Raymond	Capt	4	4/15/44	ETO/AA
Carlson, Kendall	Capt	4	2/25/45	ETO/AA
Carpenter, George	Maj	4	4/18/44	ETO/Combat
Cole, Charles	Capt	20	2/25/45	ETO/Combat
Collins, Frank	Capt	325	7/10/45	PTO/AA
Cullerton, William	1Lt	355	4/8/45	ETO/AA
Curdes, Louis	2Lt	82	8/27/43	MTO/Mechanical (escaped)
Dahlberg, Kenneth	Capt	354	1/14/45	ETO/??
Dean, Cecil	2Lt	325	7/2/44	MTO/Collision
Edens, Billy	2Lt	56	9/10/44	ETO/AA
Edner, Seldon	FLt	RAF	3/8/44	ETO/?? (*2)
Emmer, Wallace	Capt	354	8/9/44	ETO/AA (*3)
Emmert, Benjamin	1Lt	325	9/1/44	MTO/AA

Evans, Roy	Maj	359	2/14/45	ETO/Combat
Fairbanks, David	S/L	RAF	2/28/45	ETO/Combat
Feld, Sylvan	1Lt	52	8/13/44	MTO/AA (*4)
Fisk, Harry	Capt	354	1/13/45	ETO/??
Flinn, Kenneth	Ens	VF15	10/13/44	PTO/Combat (*5)
Gabreski, Francis	Col	56	7/20/45	ETO/AA
Gailer, Frank	1Lt	357	11/27/44	ETO/??
Garrison, Vermont	1Lt	4	3/3/44	ETO/AA
Gimbel, Edward	Capt	RAF	4/16/45	ETO/AA (*6)
Godfrey, John	Maj	4	8/24/44	ETO/AA
Goodrich, Burdette	1Lt	459	6/6/44	CBI/Combat (Died a POW 1/1/45)
Goodson, James	Maj	31	6/20/44	ETO/AA
Harris, Thomas	1Lt	357	5/27/44	ETO/Collision
Hillman, Donald	LCol	365	10/7/44	ETO/AA
Hockery, John	Capt	78	11/26/44	ETO/Combat
Howes, Bernard	1Lt	55	3/3/45	ETO/Crash takeoff
Hubbard, Mark	LCol	20	3/18/45	ETO/??
Johnson, Gerald W.	Maj	356	3/27/44	ETO/AA
Juchheim, Alwin	Capt	78	5/28/44	ETO/Collision
Kinsey, Claude	2Lt	82	4/5/43	MTO/Combat (Escaped)
Koralski, Walter	Capt	355	4/15/44	ETO/Engine
Lenfest, Charles	Capt	355	10/3/44	ETO/Rescue (*7)
Liles, Brooks	Capt	55	3/3/45	ETO/AA
Lowry, Wayne	1Lt	325	10/7/44	ETO/Fuel
Luksic, Carl	1Lt	352	5/24/44	ETO/??
Magoffin, Morton	Col	32	8/10/44	ETO/AA
Mahon, Jackson	Capt	RAF	8/10/42	ETO/Combat (Dieppe)
Martin, Kenneth	Col	354	2/11/44	ETO/Collision
McKeon, Joseph	Capt	20	10/7/44	ETO/Collision
Megura, Nicholas	Capt	4	5/22/44	ETO/Combat (by P-38?) Interned Sweden 6/28/44
Meroney, Virgil	Capt	352	4/8/44	ETO/AA
Miller, Thomas	2Lt	354	9/7/44	ETO/AA?
Millikan, Willard	Capt	4	5/30/44	ETO/Collision
Mills, Henry	Maj	4	3/6/44	ETO/??
Morris, James	Capt	20	7/7/44	ETO/Combat
O'Conner, Frank	Capt	354	11/5/44	ETO/AA
Pieri, Donald	FLt	RAF	5/3/45	ETO/Strafing ricochets
Pompetti, Peter	1Lt	78	3/17/44	ETO/AA
Pryor, Roger	Capt	23	3/26/45	CBI/AA
Quigley, Donald	Maj	23	8/10/44	CBI/AA
Quirk, Michael	Capt	56	9/10/44	ETO/AA
Reynolds, Robert	1Lt	354	12/12/44	ETO/Combat
Riley, Paul	1Lt	4	4/24/44	ETO/AA
Shipman, Ernest	1Lt	31	7/31/44	ETO/Combat (by P-38)
Shoup, Robert	1Lt	354	5/12/44	ETO/??
Smith, Kenneth	Capt	4	3/21/44	ETO/??
Starck, Walter	Capt	352	11/27/44	ETO/Debris
Sykes, William	1Lt	361	12/24/44	ETO/Combat
Trafton, Frederick	Capt	31	4/23/44	MTO/Combat/Escaped
Warford, Victor	Maj	31	10/11/44	MTO/AA
Woods, Sidney	LCol	4	4/16/45	PTO/AA
Wynn, Vasseure	Capt	4	4/13/44	ETO/Combat
Zemke, Hubert	Col	479	10/30/44	ETO/Engine
Zubarik, Charles	1Lt	82	5/24/43	MTO/Combat

1 Crashlanded in Russian territory and captured by the Soviets, who treated him very poorly, after which he held a lifelong grudge against the Russians.
2 Was shot down by ground fire from Greek Communist guerrillas on 21 January 1949 and murdered.
3 Died in POW camp of myocarditis 2/15/45.
4 Died of wounds sustained in a U.S. bombing attack 8/21/44.
5 Died of malnutrition in a POW camp in Japan 7/25/45.
6 Shot down and evaded 4/43, WIA and crashed 3/45, shot down by flak and taken POW 4/45.
7 Was taken prisoner when he landed behind enemy lines and got stuck in the mud attempting to rescue Henry Brown, who had been downed by flak.

E&E (57)

Pilot Name	Rank	Unit	Date	Theater/Cause/Returned
Aschenbrenner, Robert	Capt	40	6/10/44	PTO/AA/ 1/17/45
Augarten, Rudolph	2Lt	371	6/10/44	ETO/AA/ 8/14/45 (*1)
Barber, Rex	1Lt	347	4/29/44	PTO/ Combat/ 6/7/44
Bright, John	Maj	14	8/30/43	MTO/AC failure/ 11/12/43 (*2)
Bright, John	Maj	CACW	3/31/45	CBI/Fuel/ 5/26/45 (*2)
Brown, Gerald	Capt	55	9/5/44	ETO/Engine/ 9/6/44 (*3)
Carl, Marion	Capt	VMF 223	9/9/42	PTO/Combat/ 9/15/42
Coen, Oscar	P/O	RAF	10/20/41	ETO/Target explosion/ 12/41
Coffey, Robert	LCol	365	7/11/44	ETO/AA/ 8/6/44
Copeland, William	Lt(jg)	VF-19	11/6/44	PTO/AA 12/1/44
Curry, John	FLt	RAF	3/2/44	ETO/AA/ 5/44
Czarnecki, Edward	1Lt	475	10/23/43	PTO/Combat/ 2/44
Dahl, Perry	Capt	475	11/10/44	PTO/Collision/ 12/10/44
Dahlberg, Kenneth	1Lt	354	8/16/44	ETO/Combat/ ?/44 (*4)
Davis, Clayton	Capt	352	8/17/44	ETO/??/ 9/4/44
Davis, Glennon	Capt	357	4/28/44	ETO/Engine/ 11/44 (*5)
Dent, Elliott	Capt	49	11/1/44	PTO/AA/ 11/15/44
Duncan, Glenn	Col	353	7/7/44	ETO/AA/ 4/14/45
Felts, Marion	1Lt	49	11/2/44	PTO/Combat/ 12/10/44
Flack, Nelson	Capt	49	2/14/44	ETO/Combat/ 3/12/44
Gimbel, Edward	Capt	RAF	4/4/43	ETO/Combat/ ?/?/? (*6)
Giroux, William	Capt	8	12/25/44	ETO/AA/ 1/45
Glover, Fred	Maj	4	4/30/44	ETO/AA/ 5/28/44
Gregg, Lee	1Lt	51	5/6/44	CBI/Combat/ ?/?/?
Hills, Hollis	Lt	VF32	9/22/44	PTO/AA (rescued SS *HADDO)*
Hoelscher, William	1Lt	4	4/25/45	ETO/??/ 5/7/45
Ilfrey, Jack	Capt	20	6/13/44	ETO/AA/?? (*7)
King, Benjamin	Capt	347	7/17/43	PTO/Combat/9/17/43
Landers, John	LCol	49	12/26/42	PTO/Combat/ 1/2/43
Lathrope, Franklin	2Lt	1	5/10/44	MTO/Combat/ 5/31/44
Mahurin, Walker	Capt	56	3/27/44	ETO/Combat/5/7/44 (*8)
Maloney, Thomas	Capt	1	8/19/44	ETO?Target explosion (*9)
Marshall, Bert	Maj	355	8/18/44	ETO/AA/ (*10)
McArthur, Paul	1Lt	79	6/10/43	ETO/Combat/ Rescue (Walrus)
McKennon, Nicholas	1Lt	4	8/28/44	ETO/AA/ 9/22/44
Meguera, Pierce	Maj	4	3/18/45	ETO/AA/ (*11)
Moranville, Horace	Lt(jg)	VF11	1/12/45	PTO/AA/(*12)
Overfield, Loyd	1Lt	354	8/7/44	ETO/Combat/ 8/12/44
Parham, Forrest	Capt	23	4/2/45	CBI/AA/ 4/25/45
Paxton, Heywood	1Lt	3(P)	1/14/45	CBI/1/27/45

Peterson, Chesley	LCol	4	4/15/43	ETO/Engine (Rescue Walrus)
Pierce, Sammy	1Lt	49	10/13/43	PTO/Weather/ 10/21/43
Pissanos, Spiros	1Lt	4	3/5/44	ETO/Engine/ 9/9/44
Purdy, John	1Lt	475	12/11/44	PTO/Fuel/ 12/11/44
Purdy, John	11Lt	475	1/9/45	PTO/AA/1/24/450
Sargent, John	Lt(jg)	VF84	4/4/45	PTO/AA/ 4/4/45
Segal, Harold	1Lt	VMF 211	7/11/43	PTO/Combat/ 7/11/45 (Rescued)
Segal, Harold	1Lt	VMF 211	1/26/44	PTO/Engine/ 1/26/44 (Rescued)
Segura, Wiltz	Capt	23	8/7/44	CBI/AA/??
Slocumb, Clyde	Capt	23	4/2/45	CBI/Engine/ 4/25/45
Smith, John	2Lt	475	9/2/43	PTO/Fuel/ 9/21/43
Suehr, Richard	1Lt	35	1/1/45	PTO/Hit sea/ 1/4/45
Sullivan, Charles	Capt	35	9/18/43	PTO/Combat/ 10/13/43
Vraciu, Alexander	Lt(jg)	VF20	12/14/44	PTO/AA/ 12/14/44
West, Richard	Capt	8	11/44	PTO/??
Williams, James	1Lt	23	9/10/43	CBI/AA/??
Williams, James	1Lt	23	12/1/43	CBI/Combat/ 12/17/43
Yeager, Charles	Capt	357	3/5/44	ETO/Combat

(1) Scored 2 victories as P-47 pilot 371FG and four flying for Israel in 1948

(2) Bright was involved in a training collision flying for the AVG and bailed out (the other pilot was killed). He was shot down in January 1942 but bailed out. As CO of the 37FS/14FG he became in POW in North Africa but escaped from an Italian POW camp when Italy surrendered in September 1943. In May 1945, he crash-landed and was aided by Chinese troops in returning to base.

(3) Brown as a POW in Korea 11/50 when he was shot down by AA and released in 1953.

(4) Dahlberg was also shot down by AA on 12/26/44 but landed in Allied territory.

(5) Davis was KIA in Korea 2/10/52 in combat after scoring 14 victories to go with his 7 in WWII.

(6) Jack Ilfrey came close to being interned. On 9 November 1942, the 1FG was flying from England to Oran, North Africa. On the way one of his two 150 gallon belly tanks fell off. Ilfrey decided to stay with the flight to Gibraltar but ran into thunderstorms which he had to dodge. He was running low on fuel and headed for Lisbon, Portugal and landed on an airdrome on the outskirts. He was greeted by armed horsemen and taken into custody. He agreed to a demostration of the then top secret P-38 which, of course needed fuel. During the demonstration another P-38 on one engine came in for a landing and all but one of his captors left to watch it. Ilfrey quickly advanced the throttles for taxiing and the Lightning's quick acceleration cleared the onlooker off the wing and onto the ground. Ilfrey was able to take off and escape, hoping the Portuguese had put in enough fuel for the 400 mile trip to Gibraltar which they did. Ilfrey went on to score 7 1/2 victories.

(7) Mahurin was a POW in Korea after being shot down on 5/13/52 by AA and released in 9/53 after being "brain-washed" into admitting U.S. germ warfare use.

(8) Maloney was badly wounded when he crash-landed in a mine field and spent 3 1/2 years in the hospital.

(9) Marshall's P-51 crash-landed near the German border and 1Lt Royce Priest rescued his 354FS CO.

(10) McKennon was rescued by 1Lt George Green who landed behind the lines to rescue his 335FS CO. McKennon was forced to bail out when his Mustang was hit by AA fire and landed in a field about 40 miles north of Berlin. As he landed two men and a German Shepard approached but were driven off by strafing squadronmates. Green landed near McKennon who released the P-51's drop tanks while Green detached his parachute. Since Green was smaller he sat on McKennon's lap for the 550 mile flight back to base, sharing the oxygen mask when bad weather forced to a higher altitude.

(11) On a mission to Kiel, 1Lt. Nicholas Megura shared a Me-109 with a P-38 pilot but the same P-38 then shot up Megura's P-51. His glycol tank was hit and his flight escorted him back toward England. But over Denmark he realized he would not make it and headed toward neutral Sweden. He managed to nurse his damaged P-51 to Kalmar where he crashlanded and was interned from 22 May until 28 June 1944. He returned to Debden but was not allowed to reenter combat.

(12) Moranville was picked up by the Vichy French in Indo-China and held in a Saigon prison with 5 other US airmen. When the Japanese closed in, they were marched 13 days to Dien Bien Phu with 200 French Foreign Legionnaires and were ambushed suffering 75% losses. On 28 March they were flown out to safety.

313 Aces Lost

Footnote: Col.Oliver "Obie" Taylor, five victory ace and CO of the 14FG, was invalided back to the U.S. in July 1944 when he contracted polio.

CHAPTER 20

Americans in Foreign Service, Foreigners in American Service, and Others

Americans in the RAF/RCAF

During the two years before Pearl Harbor, 240 odd volunteer American pilots flew with the RAF/RCAF in three squadrons that were to become immortalized as the Eagle Squadrons. These men were young and inexperienced, and their early performance was so mediocre that the RAF considered demobilizing the Eagles and returning them to the United States. There never was any doubt as to their courage, and in time they matured into a cohesive and effective fighting unit. The Eagles who survived went on to form the matrix on which USAAF fighter units in Europe were built.

The first Eagle Squadron victories were scored on 2 July 1941 when twelve 71 squadron Hurricanes under S/C Paddy Woodhouse escorted twelve Blenheim bombers to Lille, France, on a mid-day raid. As the bombers released their bombs they were attacked by 25-30 Me-109s. P/O William Dunn, flying wing to Woodhouse, dove on a Messerschmitt, firing from the port quarter and followed it down, firing three more bursts, and recorded the first American Eagle victory. Five minutes later, P/O Gus Daymond went after two Me-109s attacking the Blenheims at 8,000 feet. Daymond went after the second German, who turned and fired on him, getting hits on the Hurricane. The German erred by changing direction, allowing Daymond to get on his tail. He chased him down to 3,000 feet and fired two bursts at 100 yards, blowing its canopy off, and the pilot bailed out. British radio news credited Daymond with the Eagle's first victory, which ignited an intense scoring rivalry between the two. Four days later, Dunn shared a Me-109 with a 306

Squadron Polish pilot, while Daymond downed a Me-109. On 21 July Dunn got a Me-109, and on 3 August Daymond got a Do-17 bomber. Dunn took the scoring lead 3 1/2 to 3 by destroying a Me-109 on 9 August. On 27 August Dunn, now converted to Spitfires, was escorting Blenheims attacking the steel works at Lillie when 71 Squadron was bounced by three staffeln of Me-109s from above. Dunn dove on a Me-109 passing through the formation and fired from 150 yards and closing, then fired again at 50 yards, flaming the German. Dunn saw tracers pass his cockpit and pulled back the throttle, dropped his flaps, and skidded to slow his Spitfire. The German overshot, and Dunn put a lethal three second burst into the -109, causing it to catch fire and roll over with its tail section braking off to become the Eagle's first ace. Dunn hit another Messerschmitt, but explosions ripped his cockpit, smashing his instrument panel and wounding his right leg and head. Dunn gained control of his damaged fighter, released his shoulder harness, and prepared to bail out, but reconsidered. After assessing the damage to the Spit and himself, he decided to try to make it back across the Channel to England. With blood seeping from two machine gun bullet wounds in his leg and from a bullet crease on the back of his head, Dunn fought off unconsciousness to land safely. While Dunn spent the next three months recuperating, Daymond shot down his fourth German on 4 September, and became an ace 15 days later when he shot down a Me-109. RAF press releases credited Daymond with being the Eagle's first ace, while there was no one to promote Dunn's victories on the 27th. King George officially presented the DFC to Daymond for becoming the Eagle's first ace, while Dunn, with part of his foot amputated, taught gunnery in Florida. Eventually, Dunn somehow talked himself back into combat, flying P-47s with the 406FG flying D-Day support missions, downing one more German in the air and 12 on the ground, and also adding a German troop ship sunk in Brest Harbor. After finishing his ETO tour he was transferred to the CBI. It was not until 1965 when Dunn donated his logbook to the Air Force Museum in Dayton, Ohio, that Col. William Curry, Museum Director, ran an inquiry with RAF records to confirm Dunn's status as the first Eagle and American ace.

The Eagle Squadrons numbered six aces in its ranks (Carroll McColpin 8, Gus Daymond 7, Chesley Peterson 6, Bill Dunn 5.5, Seldon Edner 5, and Jackson Mahon 5). The leading ace was S/L Carroll "Red" McColpin of Los Angeles, who scored eight victories and became CO of the 133 Squadron before its transfer to the 4FG. Col. McColpin scored three unconfirmed FW-190 victories flying P-47s for the 404FG on 27 August 1944. Three high-scoring 4FG aces also flew with the Eagles. P/O Don Gentile claimed two of his 19.83 with 133 Squadron, and great leader and tactician F/Lt Don Blakeslee scored four of his 15.5 victories with 133 Squadron.

P/O William Dunn of the 71 Eagle Squadron was the first American ace in WW-2. Gregory "Gus" Daymond was considered the first American ace until 1965 when further examination of RAF records gave the honor to Dunn. Dunn scored 3 1/2 Hurricane and 2 Spitfire victories and then added a P-47 victory with the 406FG in January 1944. (Author)

S/L Carroll "Red" McColpin, was the top Eagle Squadron ace with 8 Spitfire victories. McColpin scored an additional 3 victories in the P-47 with the 404FG in August 1944. (Author)

S/L Chesley Peterson scored six victories with 71 Squadron, and added a P-47 victory over a FW-190 on 15 April 1943. He became the youngest squadron commander in the RAF at 21, and at 23 became the youngest full colonel in the USAAF. Also, while not scoring with the Eagles, Duane Beeson (17 1/3v) and George Carpenter (13 5/6v) both joined the RCAF and posted to the 71 and 121 Squadrons, respectively, before transferring to the 4FG.

By 29 September 1942, when the Eagles were transferred to the 4FG of the VIII Fighter Command, they had scored 73.5 victories (71 Squadron: 41v., 121 Squadron: 18v., and 133 Squadron: 14.5v.). But they lost nearly one third of their number killed on active duty, and many more were lost in other units in the years after their transfer to the USAAF in late 1942. The seasoned Eagle veterans were to lead the younger pilots of the 4FG, making it the top-scoring group in the USAAF, a legacy that continued into the Korean War. After their transfer to the USAAF, many proud Eagles

retained their English heritage, wearing their Air Force wings on the left side and their RAF wings on the right side.

Besides the Eagle Squadrons, other Americans fought for the RAF or RCAF. The first victory scored by an American is problematical. F/Lt James Davies was born of British parents in New Jersey to technically become an American citizen. He fought over France and the Channel with 79 Squadron. On 21 November, he may have been the first American to score a victory when he shared a half credit over a weather recon Do-17 in a Hurricane I. He went on to score seven more victories, but was KIA on 29 October 1942. While flying for 234 Squadron he was bounced by four FW-190s near the Isle de Batz and bailed out, but was never found. F/O Cyril "Pussy" Palmer, a Cleveland, Ohio, native, joined the RAF before the war. He was serving with 1 Squadron equipped with Hurricanes and was shipped to France, where he shared a one third victory over a Do-17 on 23 November 1939. He scored 2 1/2 more victories in May 1940 and was KIA on 27 October 1942.

A Battle of Britain media-made martyr was William Meade Lindsley Fiske, a rich 29-year old New York society bobsled and sports car racer. When the war broke out he was accepted into the RAF, and after training and commissioning as a Flying Officer joined the 601 "Millionaire's" Squadron at Tangmere in July 1940. On 15 August, two days after the Luftwaffe initiated the Battle of Britain, Fiske, out of ammunition, claimed a victory by forcing a straggling German aircraft into the Portsmouth balloon barrage. The following day Fiske's Hurricane was set on fire, and despite severe burns to his face and limbs, he belly-landed the valuable fighter so that it could fly again. Two days later Fiske died of his wounds, and was lionized by the presses in England and America. A bronze plaque at St. Pauls Cathedral immortalizes Fiske's deed: "An American Citizen Who Died that England Might Live."

By Spring 1942 there were so many American-born pilots posted to the besieged island of Malta that an all-American flight was formed in 126 squadron. Berkeley, California, native James Peck, who joined the RCAF in 1941, flew a Spitfire off a carrier *Eagle* to Malta in March 1942. He subsequently was named flight

S/L Chesley Peterson, shown here with Gregory Daymond (below), scored six victories with 71 Squadron and was the youngest squadron commander in the RAF at 21 and the youngest full Colonel in the USAAF at 23. (Author/Daymond)

Top scoring American ace in the RAF was Texan, F/O Lance Wade, who scored 23 victories, 13 in the Hurricane and 10 in the Spitfire, 21 over North Africa and 2 over Sicily. (Author)

commander of 126 Squadron's American flight and just missed becoming an ace with 4 1/2 victories, but also had 4 probables and 9 1/2 damaged. After his Malta stint Peck joined the 52FG, but was KIFA in England in April 1944. Another Californian, John Lynch, was posted to 249 Squadron on Malta in November 1942 after scoring two shared victories with 71 Eagle Squadron. S/L Lynch scored 13 victories over German (10) and Italian (3) aircraft, including the RAF's 1,000[th] victory over Malta (a Ju-52 on 28 April 1943). In July 1943 Lynch transferred to the USAAF as a Lt. Colonel, but scored no further victories. Claude Weaver of Oklahoma City joined the RCAF before he graduated from high school and was posted to 185 Squadron on Malta. He scored 10,1/2 victories there from July to August 1942. On 9 September 1942 he crash landed on Sicily after claiming his last victory on Malta and was held a POW there. He escaped within days of the Italian surrender and returned to Allied lines on 9 September 1943, a year after his capture. He joined 403 Squadron in England and scored two more victories in late 1943-early 1944 before being KIA over Amiens on 28 January 1944.

The top scoring American in the RAF was Lance Wade of Broaddus, Texas, where he was an avid pilot, flying at 17 and owning an aircraft at 20. Wade joined the RAF in late 1940 and became a P/O flying the out-classed Hurricane I for 33 Squadron out of Egypt supporting the British Eighth Army in the Western Desert. He scored his first victories on 18 November 1941 over two Italian Cr.42 biplanes during a strafing sortie over El Eng A/F. During missions on 22 and 24 November he added three victories to become an ace. On 5 December Wade made a strafing run on an Italian airfield at Agedabia, setting three Caproni bombers on fire. Turning away, Wade spotted a SM-79 bomber flying very low and closed astern, but Wade's Hurricane was hit by AA fire. He was able to nurse his aircraft to a belly landing 25 miles behind enemy lines and walked until he was picked up the next day. He began his second combat tour in April 1942 and added eight victories, including his 12th and 33 Squadron's 200th on 11 September. Wade had a close call before he was evacuated in mid-September. He was returning from a solo recon mission when he was bounced by a skillful Mc

202 pilot who hit Wade's Hurricane twice, the first time he was hit. Wade was assigned to the RAF delegation in Washington, DC, and was loaned to the USAAF touring training centers, testing U.S. aircraft from mid-October to the end of December. "Wildcat" Wade arrived back in Egypt in January and was assigned to 145 Squadron, which was chasing the Afrika Korps across North Africa in the Tunisian Campaign. He was promoted to S/L and made squadron CO. Flying the Spitfire IX he scored eight victories in March and April to run his score to 21. He experienced hits on his fighter in several combats but was not wounded. In October and November he led the squadron over Sicily and Italy, adding two FW-190s on 2 October to bring his total to 23. The day before his tour ended he damaged three FW-190s on 3 November and left as the top MTO ace. He was promoted to A/W/C in mid-November and posted to HQ DAF, joining AVM Harry Broadhurst's staff. On 12 January 1944 he was KIFA when his Auster liaison aircraft went into a spin and crashed near Foggia, Italy. Wade was posthumously awarded England's second highest decoration, the DSO.

The highest scoring American ace of the RCAF was Ithaca, New York, resident David Fairbanks, the son of a Cornell University professor. Fairbanks grew up loving aviation, and ran away from home to join the RCAF, but Canadian border officials turned the 19-year-old back, as he had only 20 cents in his pocket. A month later he persuaded his widowed mother to allow him to enlist, and he received his wings in November 1941. He served as an instructor in Canada until April 1943 and was sent to England for advanced and operational training. Finally, F/Lt Fairbanks was assigned to 501 Squadron in mid-January 1944 flying Spitfire Vs. On 8 June he destroyed a Me-109 over the Normandy invasion beaches for his first victory. In August he was transferred to 274 squadron, which was equipped with powerful Hawker Tempest V on anti-Diver patrol, and shot down two V-1s. In November the squadron moved to the Continent as part of the 2TAF and was assigned to attack ground targets. During an attack on locomotives his Tempest was hit by AA fire, but he managed to gain control of the burning, inverted fighter and landed safely. On 17 December he downed two Me-109s and damaged another to gain the unit's first air victories. He was transferred to the 3 Squadron in January 1945. On the 4th he claimed a FW-190, and on the 14th he became an ace when he shot down a Me-190 near Paderborn, and five minutes later added a FW-190. On 8 February he returned to 274 Squadron as a S/L and its CO. His first victory with 274 was over a Me-262 jet on a landing approach to Rheine A/D on 11 February. He got two Me-109s on the 16th, two FW-190s on the 22nd, and a FW-190 on the 24th to make him the top Tempest ace. On the 28th he led six Tempests to the Onasbruck area on an armed reconnaissance against ground transport. After regrouping after a strafing run they were attacked by a mixed group of 40 FW-190s and Me-109s. After dropping his auxiliary fuel tanks, Fairbanks was shot down during a wild dogfight and claimed an uncredited FW-190 victory. He was made a POW and was repatriated at the end of the war. After the war he graduated in mechanical engineering from Cornell and became a Canadian citizen. He flew as a test pilot for Avro and DeHavilland of Canada and became Manager of Flight Operations of the latter.

In the air war at night, A.A. Harrington of 419 Squadron shot down seven Germans while flying the Mosquito night fighter to become the highest scoring American night fighter ace of any service. More on Harrington's career can be found in Chapter 10: Night Fighter /Mosquito.

So it was that young Americans left their homes and families to fight the Germans. Some fought for freedom and ideals, while others for adventure and the pure love of flying. But no matter the reason, these men won the gratitude and respect of the British for their courage, accomplishments, and sacrifice.

Americans Who Became Aces in the RAF/RCAF

Name	Rank	RAF Unit (Sq)	A/C	#V	Notes
Wade, Lance	F/O	33, 145	Hurr 13) Spit (10)	23	KIFA 1/2/44
Lynch, John	S/L	71, 249	Spit	13	Malta
Fairbanks, David	S/L	501, 274, 3 (RCAF)	Spit (1) Temp (11.5)	12.5	POW 2/28/45
Weaver, Claude	F/O	185, 403 (RCAF)	Spit	12.5	KIA 1/2/44
McColpin, Carroll	S/L	71,121	Spit	8	+3 USAAF (P-47)
Jones, Ripley	F/Lt	126	Spit	7.7	Malta KIA 1017/42
Curry, John	S/L	601 (RCAF)	Spit	7.33	N. Africa Ev 3-5/44
Daymond, Gregory	S/L	71	Hurr (3) Spit (4)	7	
Harrington, A.A.	Lt	410 (RCAF)	Mosq	7	Night
Tilley, Reade	F/O	121, 601, 126	Spit	7	
Edinger, Charles	F/Lt	410 (RCAF)	Mosq	6	
Peterson, Chesley	S/L	71	Spit	6	+1 USAAF (P-47)
Dunn, William	P/O	71	Hurr (3.5) Spit (2)	5.5	+1 USAAF (P-47)
Barrick, John	F/L	17	Hurr	5	CBI
Campbell, John	P/O	258	Spit	5	
Edner, Seldon	F/Lt	121	Spit	5	
Gimbel. Edward	F/Lt	401, 403, 421 (RCAF)	Spit	5	Ev 4/43POW 4/16/45
Jasper, Clarence	F/Lt	418 (RCAF)	Mosq	5	
Johnson, Paul	F/Lt	421 (RCAF)	Spit	5	KIA 7/18/44
Luma, John	Lt	418 (RCAF)	Mosq	5	
Mahon, Jackson	F/Lt	121	Spit	5	POW 8/19/42
Zary, Henry	S/L	421, 403 (RCAF)	Spit	5	
Thorne, James	P/O	64, 122, 504, 401	Spit (1.83) Must (3)	4.83	KIA 9/10/44
Peck, James	F/Lt	126 (RCAF)	Spit	4.5	Malta KIFA 4/12/44

Poles "On Loan" to the 8AF

After the invasion and fall of their country in 1939, Polish airmen flew courageously, albeit with vengeance for various Allied air forces. The RAF formed entire squadrons made up of Poles, such as the 303 Squadron that was the top-scoring squadron in the Battle of Britain with 117 1/2 victories. When the 2TAF was formed prior to D-Day, RAF units, including 30 Polish officers, were assigned to the 8AF to study AAF tactics and organization. Capt. Francis Gabreski, a second generation Polish-American, had been detached from the 56FG upon its arrival in Great Britain and assigned to the 315 Polish RAF Squadron to train them. Later, as a Lt. Colonel and commander of the 61FS of the 56FG, Gabreski was instrumental in the assignment of Polish pilots to his squadron. The first of these pilots to arrive in early February included F/Lt Bolek Gladych and W/C Aleksander Gabszewicz, who was soon recalled to the PAF. F/Lt Tadeusz Andersz joined in mid-March, while S/L Kazimierz Rutkowski, S/L Tadeusz Sawicz, F/Lt Zbigniew Janicki, and P/O Witold Lanowski joined at the end of April.

Bolek Michael Gladych was already a legend among his countrymen when he joined the 56FG. The 34-year-old Gladych was born on a farm near Warsaw in 1910. He joined the Polish Air Force (PAF) and flew an outdated PZL fighter for the Bomber Escort Wing, shooting down "several" Luftwaffe aircraft in September 1939 as the Germans invaded Poland. After Poland was overrun he escaped to France via Rumania, escaping from a Rumanian internment camp. According to Gladych's flamboyant biography he was captured in France and tortured by the Gestapo. He killed a Gestapo agent in hand-to-hand combat, but the shock of the experience caused him to lose his eyesight and to enter an asylum, where his eyesight returned. He escaped and joined the Armee de l' Air G.C. 1/145 "Group Finois," flying the new but ineffective Caudron 714, which was to take part in the Soviet-Finnish War. The expedition to aid Finland was never realized, and he claimed to have scored several more victories over central France during the May Blitzkreig before escaping to England. Gladych asserts to have not kept records on

Bolek "Mad Mike" Gladych was a legend among his countrymen when he joined the 56FG. Gladych had scored 8 victories flying Spitfires for the Polish RAF squadrons and then became a double ace with 10 victories with 56FG. (Author)

these victories to protect relatives living in Poland from reprisals, but there is no evidence in either Polish or French records of any victories for him in their service. In England special Polish units were formed as the Free Polish Air Force as part of the RAF. Gladych attended 57 OTU, and then went on to 303 Squadron, flying the Spitfire II in October 1940. On 23 June, Gladych got his first victory for the RAF when he downed a Me-109 over St. Omer in an afternoon mission. In a late afternoon sortie that day he shot down two Me-109s, and then rammed a third near Desvres. He crash landed his damaged Spitfire at Manston and was hospitalized until October, when he returned to combat. On the 24th he downed 303's first FW-190 to become an ace. He would not score again until June 1942 when he got a FW-190 on the 5th. He began a second tour with 302 Squadron as a flight commander, getting a FW-190 in both April and May, but had to wait until September to score his next victory, a Me-109. His scoring drought was due to flying the short-ranged Spitfire V, which gave him little chance for combat, since in late 1943 it was centered over the Continent or on bomber escort duty. There is a story that in the fall of 1943 Gladych mistakenly shot down an aircraft carrying Winston Churchill, and as punishment the High Command decided to punish him by grounding him. To remedy the situation he got himself posted to Gabreski's American 56FG, which was seeing a lot of action, being the first U.S. fighter group to score 100 victories.

Six Poles formed a special Polish flight within the 61FS flying P-47s, with each man alternating as leader. Now known as Mike

Gabreski's Poles (L-R): F/Lt. Bolek Gladych, S/L Tadeusz Sawicz, LtCol. Francis Gabreski, F/Lt. Zbigniew Janicki, F/Lt. Tadeusz Andersz, and P/O Witold Lanowski. (USAF)

Withold Urbanowicz scored his first victory in 1936 shooting down a Russian recce plane that had violated Polish airspace. He scored 15 victories, as the CO of the Polish RAF 303 Squadron, during the Battle of Britain. He managed to "visit" the 23FG in China and shot down two Japanese Zeros in December 1943 and collected nine ground victories and the US Air Medal from Gen. Chennault (shown here). (Author/Urbanowicz)

among the Americans, he scored his first victory on 21 February 1944 when he downed two Me-109s over the Zuider Zee. The Poles flew the Berlin escort missions in March, with Gladych shooting down two more Luftwaffe fighters and being awarded the Silver Star for his action on 8 March. The Silver Star citation reads that during this mission, although outnumbered, he engaged and drove off German fighters attacking the B-17 formations. He shot down a FW-190 and was pursued by a pair of Focke-Wulfs, which he eluded until they ran out of ammo. On his way home he strafed a German A/D, destroying three refueling aircraft. Running low on fuel he was escorted by an ASR plane and bailed out near the English coast and was rescued. Gladych's version of the story has him being forced by the three Focke Wulfs to land at the German airfield. He extended his landing gear to pretend to do so, and when the Germans overshot he shot down one of them and proceeded to strafe the airfield, destroying three other FW-190s. He added that suspicious English soldiers interrogated the parachutist with the foreign accent before releasing him. During the D-Day invasion, Gladych got Me-109s on the 6th to become an ace in American service. The next day he added another Me-109, followed by another on 7 July and a Ju-88 on 12 August. Four Polish pilots left the unit in late June 1944 to return to the PAF, but Gladych and Lanowski stayed on, ignoring a PAF ultimatum to return to Polish service, and were dismissed. "Mad Mike" became a double U.S. ace on 21 September when he downed his final two FW-190s near Arnhem. These last victories gave him 18 RAF/USAAF victories. He claims to have downed a Me-262 jet fighter while flying a P-51 for another U.S. fighter group, but there are no records concerning this claim. As the war was ending Gladych alleges to have rescued his brother from a German POW camp that had been liberated from the Russians in 1945. After the war Gladych remained unofficially attached

to U.S. units in England and engaged in "clandestine, if not illegal, activities," according to his biography. Gladych emigrated to the U.S., studied aeronautical engineering, and received a Ph.D. in philosophy. He wrote many extravagant articles about his wartime exploits, which did not endear him to his countrymen.

Before the war Witold Lanowski trained for the 1940 Olympics, and also learned to fly. He flew with 121 Eskadra of the Polish Air Force in September 1939. After Poland surrendered he escaped to France, where he flew for 1/145 French Squadron, but had to escape again and joined the RAF. He was posted to 308 Squadron in December 1941, and subsequently with 317 and 302 Squadrons. In 1944 he was posted to the USAAF 354FG/355FS as an intelligence officer. He was then posted to the 56FG Polish unit and scored four victories in two tours, and was commissioned in the USAAF as a Captain. Of the other Poles, Andersz scored a Me-109 victory while on an escort mission to Kiel on 9 April. Janicki got a damaged and a probable before he was killed on 16 June when his engine was hit by ground fire and he crashed.

Polish RAF ace S/L Antoni Glowacki had scored 8 1/3 victories during the Battle of Britain with the 501 and 303 Squadrons in 1940, but had been instructing or behind a desk since. He used his influence in March 1944 to become attached to the 354FG/356FS of the 9AF, flying P-51s mainly in a ground support role and scoring no aerial victories. He was recalled to the PAF/RAF or else, and left the 354th. Five and a half victory ace Czeslaw Glowzynski decided to "study logistics" with the 366FG and would fly P-47s as part of his curriculum, without scoring an aerial victory.

Another Pole in this interesting cast of characters to serve with the USAAF was Witold Urbanowicz, who joined the Polish Air Force in 1930 and received his wings two years later. In 1936 he scored his first victory flying a PZL P.11c for Eskadra 111 by shooting down a Russian recce plane which had violated airspace in Eastern Poland. At the outbreak of the war he was serving as a fighter instructor at Deblin, and escaped with 50 cadets through Rumania to France, and finally to England. He joined the RAF in January 1940 and was posted to 145 Squadron on 4 August flying the Hurricane I. On 8 and 12 August he shot down a Me-109 and Ju-88, respectively, before being named flight commander of the Polish 303 Squadron on the 21st, the youngest in the RAF. He was named its CO on 6 September, and the 303 was to distinguish itself during the Battle of Britain, becoming the top-scoring squadron with 117 1/2 victories. Urbanowicz scored 15 victories between 6 and 30 September, including four on both 27 and 30 September, getting a pair of victories on each of two sorties on each day. In October he was taken out of combat and posted to HQ of the 11 Group. Between June 1941 and July 1942 he came to the U.S., first to recruit descendants of Polish immigrants for the RAF, and after the U.S. entered the war to lecture combat tactics to the USAAC. He returned to England in a training role, but returned to the U.S. in November as Assistant Polish Air Attaché. In Washington he met Gen. Claire Chennault and was able to wangle a "visit" to the U.S. 14AF in China. He paid his own salary, and arrived at Kunming in his PAF uniform on 23 October 1943. Here he flew the P-40 in 34 missions for the 23FG/75FS and shot down two Zekes (Oscars) on 11 December 1943 over Nanchung. He added nine ground victo-

Waclaw Sobanski was born in New York City while his mother was visiting from Poland. He spent his childhood in Poland and when the war broke out he made his way to America and won his wings with the RCAF. He joined the 56FG and became CO of the 334FS. (USAF)

ries while visiting, and was awarded the U.S. Air Medal. His 18 victories made him and Mike Gladych the second highest WWII Polish aces after Stanislaw Skalski, who has been variously credited with between 19 and 21 victories. He returned to Washington and served out the war as Polish Air Attaché. In 1946 he returned to Poland, but was soon arrested by the Communists; he was freed, and he decided to leave Poland for the U.S.

Waclaw Michal Sobanski was born in New York City while his mother was visiting her sister on 29 July 1919. He returned to Warsaw and served in the Polish infantry when the war broke out, and was wounded when Stuka dive bombers attacked the train in which he was being transported to the front. As the Germans entered Warsaw he left the hospital hobbled by a leg injury and made his way home. He found his American birth certificate and made his way to his aunt in New York via Czechoslovakia, Hungary, Rumania, and Istanbul. His uncle, Harry Bruno, was influential in aviation circles, having written the classic book *Wings Over America*. Bruno's influence got Mike Sobanski an appointment in the RCAF, but his deficiency in English hampered his training, and he almost washed out. Bruno's friendship with the great Canadian WWI ace Billy Bishop gave Mike a second chance. After he won his wings, he spent a brief period with the RAF in the 132 and 164 Polish squadrons. He confirmed his American citizenship, transferred to the 4FG, and became the CO of the 334FS in mid-April 1944. He scored a shared victory on 1 January 1944 flying a P-47, and got an additional damage and probable claim. When the 334FS transitioned to P-51s he got three damaged before getting a FW-190 victory on 13 April, and then shared a one third fraction of a Me-110 and destroyed a Me-109 on 28 May. On D-Day, 6 June, Sobanski led a flight on a strafing run on a train. On his first run he hit electrical cables, but pressed home his attack, flying through heavy flak and small arms fire. He attacked a second train, again through heavy AA and small arms fire, sustaining hits to his fighter. He and his wingman pressed another attack, but were bounced by Luftwaffe fighters. Sobanski's Mustang was heavily damaged, and it was reported that he crashed his mortally damaged P-51 into the German train.

CACW-Chinese American Composite Wing
American and Chinese Aces of the USAAF

The CACW (Chinese American Composite Wing) was a little-known unit which fought a backwater, low-priority war which, nonetheless, ultimately helped keep the Chinese in the war. The CACW was under the command of the 14AF that was to provide equipment, technicians, and officers to complement the Chinese personnel. The "Composite" designation derived not from its Chinese and American personnel, but from fighter and bomber components. There were two fighter groups, the 3ʳᵈ and 5ᵗʰ, which were made up of four fighter squadrons each:

3FG: 7FS, 8FS, 28FS and 32FS
5FG: 17FS, 26FS, 27FS and 29FS

Each fighter squadron consisted of nine U.S. officers and 20 enlisted men. Five U.S. pilots (a commander and four flight leaders) each had a Chinese counterpart, along with as many as 20 additional Chinese pilots and 50 enlisted men. The purpose of the American contingent was to train the Chinese to a level where they could function independently, allowing the Americans to withdraw. But this never transpired, as the number of American pilots actually increased in subsequent years, as the Chinese often left the combat flying to the American pilots. The Chinese were divided into veterans and recently trained cadets. The latter group had been sent to Arizona to train at Luke and Thunderbird Fields. The language barrier was a constant problem. The younger pilots, who were the cream of Chinese youth, translated for the non-English speaking veterans. A series of hand signals was invented for communication between aircraft in flight. In combat the English speaking Chinese pilots would repeat messages in Chinese to confirm orders. The Chinese pilots were notoriously hard on their aircraft, and their maintenance was mediocre at best. Initially, the wing was equipped with tired ex-AVG P-40s and P-40Ks flown in North Africa by the 51FG. Later a number of P-51s trickled in to re-equip several squadrons, but the American pilots had first pick on them.

The CACW became operational on 1 December 1943. Like the rest of the CBI, the CACW suffered from equipment and gasoline shortages, bad weather, poor living conditions, and low morale. Initially, CACW units attacked Japanese installations and shipping along the Yangtze and China Sea and supported Chinese armies. During the war in this role they killed over 13,000 Japanese troops, destroyed 1,956 vessels, and damaged another 6,765 others.

On 6 December 1943, four CAWC B-25s attacked Changteh escorted by a flight of P-40s led by 1Lt. Clifford Boyle. As the B-25s reached the target they were jumped head-on by six Ki-44 Tojos. The P-40s flying top cover dove on the Japanese, and Boyle scored the first CACW victory and added a probable. On a similar escort mission to Changteh that afternoon Boyle was KIA, but got another probable. The first victory registered by a Chinese pilot occurred on 23 December. The 32FS escorted 308BG B-24s over Canton when 1Lt. P. C. Chen got a Tojo. During its history the CACW scored 194 1/2 victories, of which Chinese pilots scored 115. Eight aces—five American and three Chinese—were numbered in its ranks:

Maj. William Turner (L) talks with 1Lt Heywood Paxton, dressed in Chinese peasant garb. Paxton had just returned from being shot down and evading and had scored his last victory to make him the top scoring American ace in the CACW with 6 1/2. Turner was also an ace with 5 victories. (Author/Paxton)

Name	Rank	Unit	#V	A/C (V)
American				
Paxton, Heywood	1Lt	3FG/7FS	6.5	P-40 (2.5)
				& P-51 (4)
Callaway, Raymond	Maj	3FG/8FS	6	P-40 (6)
Colman, Philip	1Lt	5FG/26FS	6	P-40 (6)
Reed, William	LCol	3FG/7FS	6	P-40 (6)
				+3v. AVG
Turner, William	Maj	3FG/32FS	5	P-40 (5)
				+3v. SWPA
Chinese				
Kuang-Fu Wang	1Lt	3FG/7FS	8.5	P-40 (5.5)
				& P-51 (3)
His-Lan Tsang	1Lt	3FG/8FS	6	P-40 (6)
Kun-Tan	1Lt	3FG/7&32FS	5	P-40 (5)

Aces of the CACW

Heywood Paxton, operations officer of the 7FS, scored 2 1/2 Oscars over Kingman A/D on 27 October 1944. On 3 January (flying a P-40) and 4 January (flying a P-51) 1945, Paxton got an Oscar victory on each day. The next day, he led a P-51 top cover mission over Hankow and attacked 30-40 Oscars and Tojos, and shot down a Tojo and damaged an Oscar. On 14 January, Paxton's P-51 was carrying 100 lb bombs on a mission to Hankow. Paxton's flight had to jettison their bombs when they ran into 25-30 Japanese defenders. Paxton got an Oscar confirmed and a damaged to make him the top American CACW ace with 6 1/2 victories. In the battle Paxton's Mustang had been hit, and he had to crash land, suffering a leg injury. He joined up with another downed CACW pilot, and they evaded for two weeks before returning to base. Paxton was invalided home and flew no more combat.

Capt. Raymond Callaway, who was naturally nicknamed "Cab," had served in the 56th and 80th Fighter Groups, and then became an instructor with the 326FG. Tired of Stateside duty, he joined CACW, initially instructing Chinese pilots and then moving to the 8FS/3FG as Operations Officer. He got his first claims (an Oscar destroyed and another probable) on 9 June, and followed with another Oscar

and Tojo damaged two weeks later. On 8 August he downed a Hamp and Oscar covering a fighter sweep along the Yangtze River. He became an ace on 22 August when the unit strafed four boats on the Yangtze when 12-16 Oscars intercepted them and he shot one down. On 16 and 17 September he shared a Nick and Oscar to conclude his scoring at six victories. In September he was named as CO of the 32FS, where he served until January 1945 when he returned to the States.

1Lt. Philip Colman flew for the 26FS/5FG and got six victories, two probables, and seven damaged in the P-40. On 12 September he got an Oscar, a Hamp probable, and two damaged Oscars over Sinshih. On 21 September he had his best day on a strafing and bombing mission on warehouses and targets of opportunity. Flying in a top cover flight, Colman bounced a number of Japanese fighters, claiming an Oscar and Hamp and damaging two more Oscars and another Oscar as a probable. The victories made him the only 5FG ace. He scored another victory on 14 January 1945 and went on to down four MiG-15s flying F-86s for the 4FIW over Korea.

LtCol. William Reed scored three air and eight ground victories with the 3AVG. After his AVG tour he returned home and reentered the USAAF in January 1943. After a stint in a training capacity he joined the 7FS/3FG(P) in mid-1944. On a morning mission to destroy a downed Chinese P-40 before it could be captured, Reed shared a victory over a Val. Later that day Reed went out again to search for the missing P-40 and shared an Oscar, and downed a Val and Tojo to win the DFC. He added two Oscars in August and finished with a Lily on 27 October to give him nine victories. Reed became a LtCol. and the CO of the 3FG. After dusk on 19 December 1944 his flight arrived over their base at Liangshan, which was under three-ball alert and blacked out. With his fuel running low he was forced to bail out and plunged to his death. When his body was found the next day it appeared that his head had struck the tail plane, and he was unable to pull the ripcord.

Lt.Col. William Reed had scored 3 victories with the AVG and then another 6 with the CACW. Reed was KIA when bailing out on 19 December 1944 when his head hit the tail plane and he was unable to pull his ripcord. (USAF)

Maj. Raymond Callaway scored 6 victories with the 8FS/3FG and was the CO for the 32FS. (Author/Callaway)

Maj. William Turner joined the 17FS/24PG and scored two victories over Java flying P-40s in February 1942. In August 1942 he got a Zero victory flying a P-400 with the 41FS/35FG. Capt. Turner was recruited in the U.S. as the 32FS CO in October 1943. Turner got his first CACW victory on 23 December 1943 and became an ace on 11 February 1944 when he shot down a Japanese fighter during a B-25 escort mission to bomb Kai Tak A/D. Maj. Turner ran his victory total to eight (five in the CACW) on 25 August during a recon and sweep mission on rail targets in the Loyang area. On 19 December, while flying with Reed, Turner's fighter also ran out of gas, and he was forced to bail out. He broke his leg on landing and was carried back to base by Chinese peasants the next morning. Turner was promoted to LtCol. and, unable to fly because of his leg, was made XO. In March he was sent home for gunnery training.

1Lt. Kuang-Fu Wang originally joined the Chinese Air Force in March 1936. He flew the Curtiss Hawk III, Vultee P-66, and the Russian-built I-15 and I-16, but little is known of this period of his career. He joined the 3FG/7FS in late 1943 as a flight leader. He scored his first victory on 25 June 1944, and in July in three combats shot down a Tojo and damaged five others. Wang would become the second CACW Chinese ace on 27 October during a sweep of the railway between Hankow and Puchi. Led by Capt. Armit "Bill" Lewis, the 7FS flew top cover for the strafers. After covering a successful strafing run the unit headed for the Japanese airdrome at Kingman, where they ran into nine Lily bombers and 8-10 Oscar escorts that were staging for a night raid on CACW bases. In the melee that followed, Wang shot down 2 1/2 Oscars and a Lily of

the 16 Japanese destroyed in the air that day (four were destroyed on the ground). Wang would score a victory in a P-51 on 7 March 1945 and two more after he became the CO of the 7FS to make him the highest scoring Chinese ace with 8 1/2 victories.

1Lt. Hsi-Lan Tsang joined the 75FS/23FG from the Chinese Air Force and shot down a Zero on 31 May 1943. He transferred to the 8FS/3FG of the CACW in late 1943. On 2 June 1944 he scored his first victories, claiming a Tojo and Zero and adding an Oscar on 23 July. Tsang became CO of the 8FS from June to September 1944. On 23 August the 8FS flew top cover for a B-25 mission against a railway bridge west of Kaifang. The attack was met by 7-8 Tojos and Oscars, and Tsang knocked down two and damaged another to become the CACW's first Chinese ace. In the skirmish, Tsang's P-40 was hit and he crash-landed, and later returned to the squadron. Tsang would score no further victories, but became Staff Operations Officer in September. On 1 January 1945 he transferred to 3FG HQ. When the Communists took over China Tsang fled to Formosa (Taiwan) with the Nationalist government. He served in the Nationalist Air Force and retired as a General.

1Lt. Kun-Tan 7FS/3FG was the third and last Chinese ace of the CACW. He scored his first two victories (Oscars) on 11 May 1944 while providing top cover for a strafing attack against rail targets along the Yellow River. He was shot down on 16 May 1944 and evaded to return to combat. He added an Oscar and damaged another on 29 August, but had to wait until 5 January 1945 to become an ace. While flying afternoon top cover the unit was jumped by a mixed gaggle of 30-40 Tojos and Oscars coming out of the overcast at 10,000 feet above Hankow. Tan destroyed an Oscar and Tojo for his fourth and fifth victories.

In addition to these aces, Maj Thomas Reynolds of the 7FS/3FG scored three aerial and 38 1/2 ground victories, which was tops for WWII strafer victories. Reynolds was also one of the many Stateside fighter pilot gunnery instructors who were itching to get into combat. He transferred from two years as 338FG gunnery instructor to become part of the original CACW pilot contingent that sailed to China aboard the carrier *Mission Bay* in early 1944. One

1Lt. Kuang-Fu Wang was the leading Chinese ace (of three) in the CACW flying for the 7FS and credited with 5 1/2 P-40 victories and 3 P-51 victories. (Author/Wang)

of Reynolds's best days as a strafer occurred on 11 November 1944, when he planned and led a surprise strafing attack against Hengyang Air Base. His pilots dropped 18 fragmentation clusters and made 37 strafing runs. In six passes Reynolds accounted for four Oscars destroyed and three damaged before moving up to provide top cover. He was bounced by an Oscar and was hit, but luckily was saved when a fellow pilot hit and drove off the attacker. Reynolds was awarded the Silver Star for his actions that day. The aggressive strafer became the CO of the 7FS in January 1945 and was re-equipped with P-51s. On 8 February he led an attack against the airfields at Tsingtao. Reynolds made six passes and estimated that he destroyed ten and damaged 13 more Japanese aircraft parked there.

Towards the end of the war the Chinese were reluctant to use pilots and aircraft, which would be needed for the forthcoming battles against the Chinese Communists. On 21 September 1945 the CACW was disbanded, and the groups were reformed using the same designations under Chinese Air Force Command. All equipment was transferred to the CAF, which began its battle against the Communists. However, the Nationalist leadership was ineffective in utilizing its air force against the Communists and were forced to retreat towards Formosa (Taiwan). Once on Formosa in 1949, the Nationalist Air Force stabilized and reapplied the air combat concepts learned in the CACW to good advantage.

Addenda: Shui-Tin (Arthur) Chin is an unusual "American" ace. His father was from China, his mother from Peru, and he was born in Portland, OR. He was one of 15 Chinese-Americans to start flying in the U.S. in the 1930s. After primary training they volunteered for the Cantonese Air Force, and Chin became a Warrant Probationary Pilot, and then 2Lt. in late February 1933. He completed his training in Germany in 1937 and returned to China. On 16 August 1937, flying a Curtiss III Hawk with 5 Group/28 Squadron of the Chinese Air Force, he shot down a G3M Japanese bomber. In mid-1938 he was flying Gloster Gladiators as the CO of the 28 Squadron and scored three victories, including the ramming of a A5M. On 27 December 1940, as Vice Commander of the 5 Group he downed two A5Ms and shared another to total 6 1/2 victories,

but was badly burned when his Gladiator was hit and spent the rest of the war in various hospitals. He was in Hong Kong when the Japanese invaded, but was able to escape and eventually returned to the U.S. for treatment.

Black Pilots in WWII

In the era of "separate but equal," the 1939 Congress established the first AAC Negro training units. The initial unit was the 99FS, which was comprised of carefully selected cadets who had college training and a mechanical background. The unit trained at Tuskegee, Alabama. Col. Benjamin O. Davis was assigned to command the squadron, as it was sent to the MTO to operate with the 33 and 79FS. The 99th flew its first mission in P-40s on 2 June 1943, but did not score a victory until a month later. On 2 July six P-40s were on an early morning mission, escorting 16 B-25s to Castelvetrano A/F on the Sicilian coast. 1Lt. Charles B. Hall saw two FW-190s closing in on the Mitchell bombers and turned his P-40 *Buster* inside the attackers. He scored a long burst on the second FW and followed it until it crashed into the ground for the first Negro air victory of WWII.

While the 99th was in combat, the 332FG, all-Negro fighter group was being trained at Tuskegee. The group, called the "Red Tails" because of their tail plane color, was made up of the 100FS, 301FS, and 302 FS, and was assigned to the 12AF. The squadrons were equipped with P-47 Thunderbolts as they entered combat out of Montecorvino, Italy, during the first week of February 1944. The group flew missions, but encountered limited enemy contact until it was assigned to the 15AF for bomber escort duty. On 9 June, the 301st and 302nd claimed its first victories: five Me-109s over Udine. The 99th transferred to the 332 FG on 3 July, and the entire group re-equipped with P-51s.

During the war, Negro squadrons had 75 pilots claim 112 aerial victories, including three Me-262 jets and four of the last five air victories in the MTO. The group's 450 pilots scored 150 ground victories, numerous transport claims, and even a destroyer in 1,578 missions/15,533 sorties. One in seven, or 66 pilots lost their lives. The statistic the group was most proud of was that none of the bomb-

The war weary P-40s of the CACW were traded for P-51Bs in 1945. The American pilots had first choice and left the Chinese pilots with the Warhawks. (Author)

Probably the most notable member of the 332FG was its leader, Benjamin O. Davis. He was the first Negro to graduate from West Point in 47 years, the first to command a fighter squadron and a fighter group, the first to command a military base, was chief of staff for the UN Command in Korea and commanded the 13AF in 1967. He retired as a three star general in 1970. (USAF)

Capt. Joseph Elsbery of the 301FS also scored 4 victories only after 3 were credited in the 1990s by researcher, Dr. Frank Olynyk. (USAF)

2Lt. Lee Archer of the 302FS was credited with 4 victories while flying the P-51. He retired from the Air Force as a Lt. Colonel in 1970. (USAF)

ers it escorted was lost to enemy fighters. The top-scorer was 2Lt. Lee Archer of the 302FS, who was credited with four victories, including three Me-109s on 1 October 1944 (the book *Tuskegee Airmen* credits him with five victories, but Frank Olynyk can not find documentation for a 20th July victory). He flew a P-51 named "*Ina the Macon Belle*." He retired from the Air Force as a Lt. Colonel in 1970. Capt. Joseph Elsbery of the 301FS also scored four victories, but three were belated, as in the 1990s Frank Olynyk's research confirmed three victories and a probable he got on 12 July 1944 to go along with the victory he got on 20 July 1944.

Probably the most notable member of the 332FG was its leader, Benjamin O. Davis. In 1936 Davis was the first Negro to graduate from West Point in 47 years. He was the first CO of the 99FS, and

was recalled to the U.S. to assume command of the 332FG. He was the first Black to command a military base. He was chief of staff for the UN Command in Korea, and later commanded the 13AF in August 1967. He retired as a three star general in February 1970.

332 Fighter Group Top Scorers

Squadron	V	P	D	Top Scorer	V
99	31	8	11	Capt. Charles Hall	3
				Capt. Ed Toppins	3
				2Lt. Leonard Jackson	3
100	22	4	4	2Lt. Charles Lester	3
301	31	2	7	Capt. Joseph Elsbery	4
302	28	1	2	2Lt. Lee Archer	4
Total	112	15	24		

CHAPTER 21

Personal Markings of the Aces

Broads, Swastikas, and Meatballs

The PR photo of the ace posing under the gaudily decorated nose of his fighter was standard wartime copy. The concept of nose art dates back to the knights of the Middle Ages, who adorned their shields with individual identifying symbols. Warships throughout history have been given names: Horatio Nelson's *Victory*; John Paul Jones' *Bonhomme Richard*; the *Monitor*; and the *Merrimac*. The Wright brothers named the world's first successful airplane the *"Flyer."* Wiley Post flew the *"Winnie Mae,"* and Charles Lindbergh crossed the Atlantic in the *"Spirit of St. Louis."* WWII aircraft art was a painting and/or a name, usually on the nose of the fighter. WWII aircraft art became a morale-builder and an extension of the pilot's personality

The Air Force artists who painted nose art were inspired by *Esquire* magazine pin-up illustrators, first by George Petty, and then

Arthur De Costa who was a cook with the 355FG did this *"Miss Thunder"* pin up nose art on Walter Koraleski's (5 1/3 victories/354FS/355FG) Thunderbolt. Fighter nose art was often done on the engine cowling which could be removed and done sitting down and out of the weather. Painted cowlings could also be transferred when the fighter was replaced. Bomber nose art needed to be painted outdoors and standing on a ladder. (Author/Koral)

in late 1941 by Alberto Vargas and his Varga Girl (the "s" was dropped, as the magazine trademarked the artist's name). Also during the war a multitude of pin-up pictures and calendars wallpapered billets in every theater. Those of artist Gil Elvgren were particularly cherished. Artistic ground crew personnel became entrepreneurs, being sought after by entire squadrons and bases to create or duplicate the pin-ups. Most of the artists were unknown, creating their works during off-duty hours. Don Allen, a crew chief of the 4FG, and Arthur De Costa, a cook from the 355FG were among the most talented of the ETO artists. Allen was a graduate of the Cleveland School of Art, while De Costa was unschooled. Allen's best known works included Steve Pissano's *"Miss Plainfield,"* Howard Hively's *"Deacon,"* Ralph Hofer's *"Salem Representative,"* and Duane Beeson's *"Boise Bee."*

When eminent *Time-Life* artist Tom Lea saw De Costa's 355th Officer's Club mural and pilot portraits, he recommended that De Costa become the unit's full time artist. Fighter nose art was often done on the engine cowling, which could be detached and more comfortably done propped up in front of the artist, who could sit in front of it. This was easier than doing bomber art, which had to be done standing on a ladder. Also, the fighter cowling could be transferred when the fighter was replaced. Paint was a problem, as colors were limited to Army stock: black; red; white; blue; khaki; and zinc chromate primer. Allen got $35 for painted nose art (which was about one third of his monthly pay), $20 for lettering only, and $13 for leather patches. Soon artists expanded into painting leather A-2 jackets. The going rate for aircraft painting and lettering, of course, depended on quality and ranged from $10 up to $35 for an early Allen or De Costa. Today original painted A-2 jackets are priceless.

After the war Allen joined an art studio as a commercial artist, and eventually became its president. DeCosta used the GI Bill to graduate from the Pennsylvania Academy of Fine Arts, and became a renown illustrator for medical texts and journals.

At the time America entered the war in December 1941, Disney was a small cartoon studio in Burbank, but its characters, such as Mickey Mouse and Donald Duck, had become well known among both children and adults. Walt Disney, an ambulance driver in WWI, was very generous in giving his approval for use of his characters by the military without charge. By the end of the war his artists had designed over 1,200 squadron emblems and unit markings for the military, including those of the American RAF Eagle Squadron and the Flying Tigers. The Flying Tiger emblem was commissioned to Walt Disney Studios by the AVG supply contingent in Washington, DC. It is said Walt Disney personally designed the overly cute Bengal tiger flying, claws outstretched, on almost fairy-like wings. The design appeared on the fuselage of the P-40s, patches, and beauti-

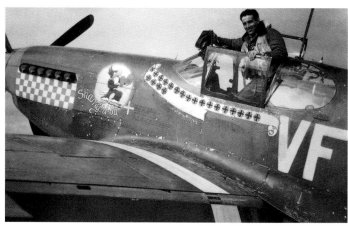

Capt. Don Gentile flew his P-51, *"Shangri-la"*, to 21 5/6 victories for the 336FS/4FG. This photo was taken near the end of his tour as 21 Maltese Crosses are displayed on the unusual banner under the cockpit. (USAF)

Don Allen, a crew chief of the 4FG, had graduated from the Cleveland School of Art. Allen and other artists did their entrepreneurial work off-hours. Allen is shown here with his work on "Deacon" Hiveley's P-51. The 4FG displayed some of the best nose art in the ETO as shown by the art work on Don Gentile's and Pierce McKennon's and Red Norley's P-51s. These artists expanded into painting the backs of A-2 flight jackets that are a priceless commodity today. (USAF)

ful enamel pins. Although the AVG did not like the design at the time, today original pins and cloth emblems are worth a fortune. After the AVG disbanded, the Flying Tiger emblem evolved into a tiger on a lightning bolt for the 23FG. Later the tiger was leaping through a V-for-Victory hoop with a shredded Japanese flag clutched in its outstretched claws. The tiger design was further changed for the 14AF insignia. The Disney Studios also produced numerous training films and light-hearted cartoon propaganda.

Other cartoonists and comic strip artists, such as Al Capp ("Li'l Abner"), Milt Caniff ("Terry and the Pirates"), and George Baker ("Sad Sack") donated their talents to the cause. Al Capp's Dogpatch characters found their way to entire fighter and bomber units. The 56FG had a number of Dogpatch creations, including Col. David Schilling's *"Hairless Joe."* The 47FS/15FG was known as the "Dogpatchers," as they decorated their 7AF P-51s with Capp's characters. Milt Caniff created "Terry and the Pirates" character Col. Vince Casey from real life, six victory CBI ace Col. Clinton "Casey"

1Lt. Pierce McKennon of the 335FS/4FG had one of the most ornate fighters in the ETO. *"Ridge Runner"* was named for the razor back hogs of his native Arkansas. McKennon's victory totals were painted under the exhaust stacks instead of under the cockpit. (USAF)

Author holding a replica aluminum panel of Gentile's P-51 *"Shangri-la"* hand-painted by Gary Velasco (www.fightingcolors.com). Velasco Enterprises fabricates and sells beautiful fighter ace and bomber nose art. (Author)

John Landers' Mustang *"Big Beautiful Doll"* was certainly well named with its black and white checkerboard nose of the 78FG and bold black script. There are 31 Swastikas which includes Landers' ground victories and six Rising Suns for his victories in the SWPA. (USAF)

Maj. Louis "Red Dog" Norley of the 336FS/4FG flew P-47s and P-51. The P-51D shown is named *"Red Dog XII"* and has 16+ swastika victory totals running along the canopy frame. Since Norley had 10 1/3 aerial victories the extra swastikas represent strafing claims which were recognized by the 8AF. (USAF)

Vincent. Many of the strip's characters, such as the Dragon Lady and Madame Shoo Shoo, appeared as nose art.

Generally fighter nose art did not become too lascivious, displaying the nude female and suggestive phraseology, which was reserved for the bomber units, especially those in the Pacific. In the more conservative 1940s, much of the nose art and names were considered "X-rated," as much of it had strong pictorial and verbal emphasis on "healthy" females. A survey of 500 personal markings of fighter aces showed:

48% Female names or references (usually wives, girlfriends, or generic female)
10% Male names (usually sons, or the pilot's own name)
8% Animal names or references
34% Miscellaneous (often home state or city, mottos, aphorisms, Jap/Hun bashing)

Initially the tone of the names and art were left to good taste, but it seems that the more remote and distant from Headquarters and civilization, the more bold and indiscreet the nose art became. This is evident when comparing fighter nose art of the ETO in very proper England and that in the "uncivilized and amoral" Pacific islands. As the war went on there were occasional outcries and movements to eliminate or, at least, control personal markings, mostly initiated by civilian visitors to the front, the base clergy, and PR-conscious HQ brass. Photos of aircraft nose art made their way into Stateside publications, also causing a hue and cry amongst the righteous. In June 1944, Charles Lindbergh accompanied Gen. Paul Wurtsmith to Topline Airstrip in New Guinea. In his *Wartime Journals* he wrote the following: "The cheapness of the emblems and names painted on the bombers and fighters nauseates me at times—mostly naked women or 'Donald Ducks'—names such as *"Fertile*

Arval Roberson 362FS/357FG probably had one of the most risque fighter nose art renderings in the ETO. His P-51, *"Passion Wagon"*, was decorated with a reclining nude. Since the ETO was covered extensively by the media and the local English may have been offended, ETO fighter nose art tended to be more subdued when compared to those in the Pacific. But then, PTO fighter nose art was tame when compared to that found on Pacific bombers. (Author/Roberson)

The P-40s of the 49FG were painted with ornate nose art. Maj. Sid Woods of the 9FS, born (TX) and schooled (University of Arizona) in rattlesnake country stands by a coiled rattler which was painted on both sides of the cowling. (USAF)

Maj. Harry Crim (R) of the 531FS/21FG and his CC pose before his P-51. Crim scored 6 aerial victories (one Rising Sun not painted in), 6 damaged and 24 bomber escort missions (these were silhouettes of a bomber flanked by two fighters). (Author/Crim)

This 90 PRS F-5 shows camera silhouettes denoting 37 photo recon missions over North Africa. (USAF)

Myrtle" under a large and badly painted figure of a reclining nude." In 1943, renowned novelist and champion of the "illustrated literature on aircraft fuselages" John Steinbeck defended the practice in the following to the *New York Tribune*: "The names must not be changed. There is enough dullness in war as it is." But "boys will be boys," and the markings became increasingly more risqué, especially in the Pacific.

In August 1944, the Air Force issued Regulation (35-22) that stated in part:

3 *Policy:*

The custom of decorating organizational equipment of the Army Air Force with individual characteristic design is authorized by the Secretary of War and is encouraged as a means of increasing morale.

4 *Definitions:*

a) "Equipment" as used herein means operating equipment, i.e. airplanes.

b) "Design" or "Organizational Design" as used herein refers to the markings applied to organizational equipment and does not refer to group or other unit coat of arms not to uniform insignia or shoulder or sleeve insignia.

This double speak placated military and civilian protesters, but made no dictates on the type or method of nose art in the field. Generally, nothing changed, unless there was to be an official inspection. At that time indecent female figures had clothing painted over offending areas, and particularly offensive verbiage was deleted (all temporarily). Some thought provoking nose art/names included:

"Reckless Prostitute" Jack Bade P-40
"Dirty Old Man" Walter Benz P-47
"Prune Face" Henry Bille P-51
"Taxpayer's Delight" John Carder P-51
"Pregnant Polecat" Glendon Davis P-51
"Goat Nose" Milden Mathre P-38

LtCol. Cy Wilson, CO of the 55FS/20FG, took part in 31 top cover missions (top hats), 10 escort missions (umbrellas), 9 bombing missions (bombs) and 7 sweeps (brooms). (USAF)

Crew Chief and ground crew were routinely listed under the pilot's name on the aircraft. Here Walt Beckham, early in his 18 victory career (October 1943) with the 351FS/353FG, sits in his P-47 which was serviced by ground crew, S/Sgt. H. Bush and Sgt. M. Eichsteadt. (USAF)

"Nick Nicholas Nip Nippers" Frank Nichols P-38

".50 Caliber Concerto" Robert Reynolds P-51

"Christian Maker" Fred Trafton P-51

"Holdin' My Own" Dallas Clinger P-40 (depicting a young boy in a cowboy suit peeing on the Rising Sun)

"Passion Wagon" Arval Roberson P-51 (accompanied by a reclining nude which had been ordered to be clad in a painted bathing suit until Gen. Jimmy Doolittle, liking the previous nude, intervened).

Many pilots lovingly adorned their second loves with the names of their first loves, their wives. Chuck Yeager, who was an 11 1/2 victory ace in WWII, flew a Mustang named *"Glamorous Glen,"* after wife Glennis. When he piloted the Bell XS-1 through the sound barrier for the first time to Mach 1.06 on 14 October 1947, the rocket was named *"Glamorous Glennis."* Twenty-two victory P-38 ace Jay Robbins named his Lightning *"Jandina"* (a combination of *Jay and* wife, *Ina*), while Jerry Johnson's P-38 had wife *"Barbara,"* painted on his fighter (after having *"Jerry"* on an earlier P-38). Top Pacific P-47 ace Neel Kearby (22 v.) named his Thunderbolt *"Fiery Ginger"* after his wife. Tom McGuire, America's second top ace (38 v.), lovingly named his P-38 *"Pudgy"* (I through V) after his wife, Marilynn, who must have been thrilled, as she was quite thin and pretty. McGuire was killed on 7 January 1945 while flying Fred Champlain's *"Eilene,"* as *"Pudgy V"* was unavailable for combat that day.

American cities would donate funds to build an aircraft, which shipped to combat as a presentation fighter for PR purposes. These aircraft would be ceremoniously presented to aces, with the photos and news stories appearing Stateside. Walker "Bud" Mahurin (19 1/2 P-47 v.), who had never used personal markings, was given *"Spirit of Atlantic City,"* while Dave Schilling (22 1/2 v. P-47) was presented *"Howlett-Woodmere L.I."* (he normally flew a T-bolt named *"Whack"*).

Pierce McKennon of the 4FG probably flew the most ornate fighter in the ETO. Today the models of his P-51 are among the most sought after of American fighters. His cowling became completely covered with air art as he ran up his victory totals (11 aerial and 9 strafing). *"Ridge Runner"* was named after the razor-backed hogs of his native Arkansas. A stylized red hog in a black frame was painted on the cowling, and forward to it (not under the cockpit, as usual) the increasing number of Iron Cross victory symbols were painted on *"Ridge Runners I"* through *"III."* Another unusual feature on McKinnon's P-51 was the addition of two small parachutes above the hog denoting that he had bailed out twice.

In the last days of the war, a number of especially suggestive B-29s returned to the States from the Pacific. Their voluptuous, larger-than-life female fuselage paintings aroused such ire that a committee was formed to set guidelines to regulate nose art. Subsequently, nose art was banned, and naturally wound down after the war. When the Korean War broke out, nose art returned, more blatant and revealing than ever.

The inherent competitive nature of men has led to the scoreboard, batting and pitching averages, and notches on the six-shooter handle or bedpost. Even in these days of the "Top Gun" automated electronic jet fighter jockey, boys go to the video game arcade dreaming of becoming an ace. "Air Ace," the twentieth century's equivalent of the medieval knight in armor, is the *unofficial* designation bestowed on the military pilot who *officially* shot down five or more aircraft in aerial combat. WWI lent itself to the glorification of air warfare, as airmen fought chivalrously, man-against-man, pitting individual expertise against individual expertise in clean, clear skies, far above the impersonal, muddy battlefields which had produced indescribable carnage. In wartime, both the military and public crave heroes, so when French morale was at an ebb, their Escadrilles provided these heroes. "L'as," the French word for the highest card in a suit, was initially used as a casual title for a pilot of superior skill and courage. Soon certain pilots became proficient in killing, and those scoring ten or more kills were designated as "L'as." When America belatedly entered the Great War, its Press arbitrarily set its "ace total" at five rather than ten, in order to catch up to the French and British, who had a head start. During WWI American pilots accounted for 776 German aircraft and 72 balloons for a loss of 289 aircraft. A product of these victories were 111 aces. In 1920, a policy statement by the U.S. Air Service affirmed: "The USAS does not use the title 'ace' in referring to those who are credited officially with five or more victories over enemy aircraft. It is not the policy of the Air Service to glorify one particular branch of aeronautics, aviation or aerostation at the expense of another." This statement went on to state that bombardment and observation aviation was considered equally dangerous as pursuit aviation and received no recognition. A research paper issued in 1975 by the USAAF's Albert E. Simpson Historical Research Center at Maxwell AFB reiterated the 1920 stand on aces in WWII and Korea, stating: "(that) ….as far as the Air Force was concerned, there are no aces…. These men have been applauded and feted and acclaimed by the public as heroes; but from the Air Force they have no special reward, not even in a medal, a ribbon, or badge to signify that they are aces. Nonetheless, people persist in using the title. The Air Force never has prohibited, or even discouraged, the informal or unofficial use of the title within its own organization." The American Air services shied away from creating individual heroes, stressing teamwork and squadron performance in WWII and Korea. *Stars & Stripes* and *Yank*, the armed services weeklies, emphasized group over individual accomplishments. However, the Press was able to create aces and ace races from the extensive official air statistics collected by the various services.

In addition to names and nose art, victory and mission markings were usually stenciled and sometimes hand-painted on aircraft. Air Force victories were usually carried on the left side of the fuselage, just below and forward of the cockpit. There were variations in this application, with 8AF P-51 aces Louis "Red" Norley displaying his totals on the canopy frame, while Pierce McKennon ran his totals as Knight's Crosses across the top of his cowling from the propeller, under the exhaust stacks to windscreen. Gabby Gabreski and Robert Johnson's P-47s displayed their victory totals under the cockpit, with each aircraft shot down labeled by type. These victory markings, applied from front to rear, were variations on the swastika or rising sun, and denoted enemy aircraft destroyed in the air (and/or on the ground in the 8th and 14th Air Forces). Also, crew chief (and ground crew) names were carried in this area.

The most common ETO victory symbols were swastika modifications: a simple solid black swastika on a white circle with a red flag background; swastikas of various colors surrounded by or in a circle or square; or merely a plain swastika. The other most common symbol was a variation on the Knight's Cross/Maltese Cross: a black German Knight's Cross; a Knight's Cross outlined in white to conform with the German national insignia; or a stylized WWI type Maltese Cross. To reward tactical missions, fighter aircraft carried success symbols as silhouettes of these missions: locomotive; tank; truck; ship; etc. To denote mission types: brooms were for fighter sweeps; bombs for dive-bombing; umbrellas for fighter top cover; top hat and cane for fighter escort; cameras for recon; and aircraft silhouettes for routine, non-eventful sorties.

In the Pacific AAF kill markings varied widely in design and application. The most common was a red sun on a white flag with radiating rays to the edges, followed by the "meatball," which had a plain white flag with a red sun in the center. Some groups used the rising sun naval ensign to differentiate victories over Japanese fighters or bombers.

At the onset of the war it was the Marine Corps and Navy's official policy to prohibit victory markings and personal markings of any kind. Land-based Navy pilots usually had their own assigned fighters and usually flew that plane when it was available for that mission. Carrier-based pilots seldom flew the same fighter during a tour. This occurred because fighters returning to the carrier did not land in the order they were launched. When aircraft were spotted for the next take off, it was not practical to spot individual aircraft in the order that pilots were listed for take off, as they were closely packed in random order in the hangar deck. Thomas "Tex" Harris of VF-18 states that in 34 missions off the *Bunker Hill* in late 1943 to early 1944 he flew a total of 21 different aircraft, and the same one on no more than three missions. The only exceptions were the Air Group Commanders, whose aircraft were scheduled to take off first.

Towards the end of 1942, the Navy eased its strict prohibition on any personal markings, but those which did appear were monochromatic, functional, and without personality. As a means to instill pride, an aircraft was assigned to each pilot, and his name was stenciled on the cockpit rim. Some squadrons were allowed a small insignia just below the right front cockpit window (e.g. VF-10's "Grim Reaper"). Victory symbols were unofficially allowed but were not widely used. When a pilot scored a victory while flying another aircraft, his assigned aircraft had the victory symbol stenciled on it. The Navy applied victory markings from top to bottom under both sides of the cockpit. The most common style Navy marking was the Japanese flag, with a red rising sun in the left center with rays extending to all four corners (the rays could extend into the sun, or the sun could be separate). The other, lesser used, style was the red "meatball," which was used more often by the AAF. Mission markings, small white bombs stenciled in rows from front to rear below the port cockpit fuselage, were applied mainly on torpedo bombers.

In some Navy units, victory markings on a fighter were those victories scored by all pilots flying that particular aircraft. This procedure was designed to boost the morale of maintenance crews as-

signed to that aircraft. Capt. Robert Winston, ACG of AG-31 on the *Cabot* utilized this method and achieved the highest serviceability rate in the fleet.

Close examination of wartime Navy publicity stills of aces of the same squadron disclose that the same fighter was used as a backdrop for all photos, as the aircraft number is identical in each photo. Necessary changes were made to the number of victory markings on the fuselage as each new pilot stepped up to be photographed. The Navy often used removable stickers instead of painted stencils for victory markings. For PR purposes, a few of the top Navy aces were allowed personal names on their aircraft, usually in small letters just forward of the cockpit. Cdr. David McCampbell, top Navy ace with 34 victories, had many wartime publicity photos taken with Japanese victory symbols evident. His first Hellcat was named *"Monsoon Maiden"* by his plane captain, E.E. Caroll, and was exchanged when it was hit in a raid over the Marcus islands. His next F6F was *"The Minsi"* after a Milwaukee girlfriend, Mary Blatz, but he did not score in that aircraft. *"Minsi II,"* his next Hellcat, got 10 1/2 kills, including the seven on 19 June 1944. Its engine cut out twice at high altitude, and he was able to get the balky engine restarted, but had to ask for clearance for emergency landings. His crew was unable to find the cause, and he asked for a new aircraft. *"Minsi III"* was his last Hellcat, in which he scored the remainder of his 34 victories, including his nine on 24 October 1944. McCampbell had "CAG" painted in black to the white tail band on this aircraft. It never carried markings for the final four November victories. The name and victory markings were painted on both sides of the cockpit, as they were on all his aircraft. There was a *"Minsi IV"* that displayed all 34 victories. McCampbell flew it when he returned to the United States and toured 23 Naval Air Stations in January 1945. The *IV* was later repainted to *III*. Top FM-2 Wildcat ace Ralph Elliott flew *"Baldy,"* while 19-victory ace Alex Vraciu flew a F6F named *"Gadget."*

Bougainville-based VF-17 "Jolly Rogers," under Tom Blackburn, possessed some of the Navy's better-known personal markings. Not only did all its F4U Corsairs have the famous skull and cross bones black flag on the engine cowling, but victory markings were stenciled just forward of the cockpit. Also, several pilots put personal names on the forward section of both sides of the horizontal stabilizer. Commander Blackburn (11 victories) flew *"Big Hog,"* Los Angeles native Doris "Chico" Freeman (9 v.) inscribed *"L.A. City Limits,"* while the Corsair of Merl Davenport (6 v.) was named the *"Lonesome Polecat.*

Several FM-2 Wildcats of VC-14, flying off the jeep carrier *Hoggett Bay* , carried small personal names on the lower half of their cowlings, and one even possessed a small, scantily-clad female. The most blatant breach of Navy markings regs was by VF-27 aboard the *Princeton*. Little is known about this distinctive unit, because all written and photographic history was lost when a Kamikaze bomb sank the carrier on 24 October 1944. Carl Brown, 10-victory ace and gunnery officer of VF-27, has provided me with information on these markings. Brown, Robert Burnell, and Dick Stambrook devised schemes during training in Hawaii in spring 1944. A Flying Tiger-type shark's mouth was rejected, as it did not look right on the large cowling of the F6F-3 Hellcat's large radial engine. By the time the Air Group arrived on the *Princeton* a design was finalized: a "Hellcat" with large bloodshot eyes and a growling, multiple fanged red mouth, dripping blood. Robert Burnell hand-painted most of the 24 Hellcats with help from the individual F6F pilots. Paul Drury (6 1/2 v.) told me that he also had the name *"Paoli Local"* stenciled on his fighter. The TBM contingent of VF-27 was unadorned. A close camaraderie was developed with the flight deck crew, who put in extra effort to allow VF-27 pilots to often fly their personal aircraft. On 24 October, Brown was flying Burnell's Hellcat *"Paper Doll"* when he shot down five Zekes. This was the same day the *Princeton* was hit by a kamikaze, and Brown was forced to land on the *Essex*. When the *Princeton* was sunk, nine of its F6Fs were forced to land aboard other carriers. Within a few days all non-reg markings were painted the standard sea blue.

VF-83 flew F6F-5s off the *Essex* under Cdr. James "Pug" Southerland, who had scored two victories with VF-5 over Gaudalcanal, two more with VF-83, and another with VF-23. A F6F named *"Death and Destruction"* was flown in the Okinawa campaign by Ensign aces: Donald McPherson (5v.); William Kingston (6v.); and Lyttleton Ward (5v.). Kingston was shot down by AA fire on 15 July 1945 and was picked up by the submarine *Trepang* and spent three weeks on patrol. Ward was shot down by AA fire on 16 April 1945 and was picked up from his one man life raft after four hours by a PBM.

Almost all of the Marine Corps night fighter squadrons named their F6F(N)-5 Hellcats and added pictures to the engine cowling. Five victory ace Maj. Bruce Porter named his F6F *"Black Death,"* with a Schenley whiskey bottle painted below it on the cowling. VMF(N)-533 CO Lt Col. Marion "Black Mac" Magruder called his *"Little Mac"* after his son. The squadron was called "Black Mac's Killers," with a devil holding a flashlight and machine gun on its emblem.

Richard Bong was America's top ace with 40 victories, flying P-38 Lightnings in the Pacific. He completed three tours of combat flying the F, G, H, J, and L models. Veteran pilots were assigned personal aircraft, but often flew other aircraft when theirs were being serviced or repaired. Also, when a pilot was not flying a mission others flew his fighter. As a rookie pilot, Bong scored his first victories in a P-38F named *"Thumper,"* which was assigned to Lt. John "Shady" Lane (6 v.). Bong's log for his next 16 victories in G models during his first tour are sketchy concerning the specific P-38 he flew on a specific mission—not an unusual omission by fighter pilots.

The P-38 which Bong is most commonly associated with is *"Marge,"* a J-15-LO model. Bong flew this P-38 during his second tour (mid-February to mid-April 1944) and scored several (4?) victories in it. Marge was Bong's fiancée, Marge Vattendahl, who had recently graduated from Superior state Teacher's College. Being in love, he decided to decorate his personal P-38 with a picture of her. Using a small graduation photo of the very pretty Marge, he had intelligence officer Capt. Jim Nichols enlarge it to 20x24" and tinted. The print was glued directly to the nose and heavily varnished. The name *"Marge"* in script and 25 Japanese victory flags completed the creation. After Bong scored four victories in the aircraft he went

on leave. It was used by Lt. Tom Malone on a weather recon mission on 24 March, and was lost when he was forced to bail out when the fighter lost its left engine and electrical system. Bong broke Eddie Rickenbacker's American victory record of 26 on 12 April when he downed three Oscars while flying *"Down Beat,"* which was assigned to William Caldwell. There is some confusion about this aircraft, as Bong had a PR photo done after the historic mission standing in front of another natural metal P-38 with 27 flags.

On his third tour, mid-October to mid-December, Bong scored 12 victories in L-model aircraft. He flew in an unadorned personal P-38 (s/n 44-23964) to seven victories before it was lost while being flown by another 49FG pilot. His last four career victories were scored in a P-38I-1 borrowed from archrival Tom McGuire's 475FG.

Bong went on a U.S. PR/war bond drive after his combat tour flying specially marked P-38s. One recreated the "Marge" motif without any victory markings, and another only displayed 40 victory markings.

Pappy Boyington biographer Bruce Gamble, in his book *Black Sheep One* resolves a popular misconception about the name *"Lulubelle"* on "his" Corsair. In a PR photo session on Espiritu Santo Island on 26 November 1943, a photo shows Boyington sitting in a generic F4U that was being used for the session. The F4U had 20 Japanese victory flags hastily "pasted on" (some backward!) in front of the cockpit, the name, Gregory Boyington, Maj. USMC, directly under the cockpit, and the large number 86 under that. But most interestingly, the name *"Lulubelle"* is partially obscured as *Lu—belle* by the arm of Chance-Vought representative Ray De Leva, standing on the wing. Before he left on his first USMC combat tour Boyington was having an affair with a married woman named Lucy Malcolmson. Boyington naively named her to take care of paying off his debts and the child support of his older children through his pay allotments. Unknown to him, she did neither while he was away, but kept the money. After the war when Boyington was returned as a POW, he again took up with Malcolmson, who was driving across country to meet him in Reno to get a divorce from her husband and marry him. While Lucy was on her way, Boyington met blond would-be actress Frances Baker, and an embarrassing and sordid public scandal ensued. Frances became Mrs. Boyington, but Lucy had his money. So, in later years when he was asked about the name in the photo, Boyington claimed the name to be *"Lulubelle"* rather than *"Lucybelle."*

Top ETO ace Gabby Gabreski (28 v.), except for the brief use of *"Little Miss Kay,"* used no personal markings on his P-47, but did name his F-86 Sabre Jet in the Korean War *"Lady Frances,"* after his wife. ETO runner up (27 v.) Robert Johnson used five different names for his P-47s: *"Half Pint"*; *"Penrod and Sam"* (after his crew chief, J.C. Penrod, and himself, Robert Sam Johnson); *"Lucky"* (the name was accompanied by a hand with an extended middle finger pictorial); *"All Hell"*; and *"Double Lucky."* Top 8AF P-47 aces George Preddy (26 v.) and John Meyer (24 v.) named their fighters *"Cripes A'Mighty"* (1-2-3) and *"Lambie"* and *"Petie"* (1-2), respectively.

The following tables tabulate the nicknames adorning the fighters of America's aces:

Pilot Name	Rank	Unit	V.	A/C	Aircraft Name
Bong, Richard	Maj	49FG	40	P-38	*Thumper, Marge, Down Beat*
McGuire. Tom	Maj	475FG	38	P-38	*Pudgy*
McCampbell, David	Cdr	VF15	34	F6F	*Minsi*
Gabreski, Francis	LCol	56FG	28	P-47	*Little Miss Kay*
Johnson, Robert	Capt	56FG	27	P-47	*Half Pint, Penrod & Sam, Lucky*
Double Lucky					
MacDonald, Charles	Col	475FG	27	P-38	*Putt-Putt Maru*
Preddy, George	Maj	352FG	26+	P-40	*Tarheel*
				P-47	Cripes A'Mighty
				P-51	
Foss, Joseph	Capt.	VMF121	26	F4F	*NPM*
Hanson, Robert	1Lt	VMF215	25	F4U	*NPM*
Boyington, Gregory	Maj	AVG	24	P-40	*NPM*
				F4U	*Lulu Belle*
Meyer, John	LCol	56FG	24	P-47	*Lambie, Petie*
Valencia, Eugene	Lt	VF9	23	F6F	*NPM*
Harris, Cecil	Lt	VF18/27	23	F6F	*NPM*
Schilling, David	LCol	56FG	22 1/2	P-47	*Whack!*
					Howlett-Woodmere LI
Robbins, Jay	Maj	8FG	22	P-38	*"J", Jandina*
Johnson, Gerald R.	LCol	49FG	22	P-38	*Jerry, Barbara*
Kearby, Neel	Col	348FG	22	P-47	*Fiery Ginger*
Gentile, Donald	Capt	RAF	21+	Spit	*Shangri-La, Don, Donnie*
		4FG		P-51	*Buckeye Don*
Christensen, Fred	Capt	56FG	21 1/2	P-47	*Rozzi-Geth, Miss Fire*
Wetmore, Raymond	Capt	359FG	21 1/2	P-47	*Daddy's Girl*
				P-51	
Walsh, Kenneth	Capt	VMF124	21	F4U	*NPM*
Voll, John	Capt	31FG	21	P-51	*American Beauty*
Mahurin, Walker	Maj	56FG	20+	P-47	*NPM (except presentation A/C Spirit of Atlantic City)*
				P-51	*NPM*
Aldrich, Donald	Capt	VMF215	20	F4U	*NPM*
Lynch, Thomas	LCol	35FG	20	P-39	*NPM*
				P-38	*NPM*
Westbrook, Robert	LCol	18/347FG	20	P-40	*Princess Pat, Florida Thrush*
				P-38	

15 to 19 Victories (AAF Aces only)

Pilot Name	Rank	Unit	V.	A/C	Aircraft Name
Beeson, Duane	Capt	RAF	19+	Spit	*Bee, Boise Bee*
		4FG		P-47	
				P-51	
Duncan, Glenn	Col	353FG	19	P-47	*Dove of Peace*
Carson, Leonard	Maj	357FG	18 1/2	P-51	*Nooky Booky*
Eagleston, Glenn	Maj	354FG	18 1/2	P-51	*No name, eagle painting*
Hill, David	Col	AVG	18 1/2	P-40	*NPM*
		23FG		P-51	
Thomas, Wilbur	Capt	VMF 213	18 1/2	F4U	*Gus' Gopher*
Beckham, Walter	Maj	353FG	18	P-47	*Little Demon*
Green, Herschel	Maj	325FG	18	P-40	*NPM*
				P-47	*NPM*
				P-51	*NPM*
Herbst, John	Maj	23FG	18	P-40	*Tommy's Dad*
				P-51	
Older, Charles	LCol	23FG	18	P-40	*NPM*
				P-51	*NPM*
Zemke, Hubert	Col	56FG	17+	P-47	*Mo TOBAP I (= May Tavarish)*
		479FG		P-51	*Oregon Britannia*
England, James	Maj	357FG	17 1/2	P-51	*U've Had It, Missouri Armada Jackie*
Thornell, John	1Lt	352FG	17 1/2	P-47	*Pattie Ann*
				P-51	
Varnell, John	Capt	52FG	17	P-51	*NPM (except "Sully Varnell" under cockpit)*
Johnson, Gerald W	Maj	56FG	16 1/2	P-38	*In the Mood*
				P-47	

Godfrey, John	Capt	4FG	16+	P-47	*Reggie's Reply*
				P-51	
Anderson, Clarence	Capt	357FG	16 1/2	P-51	*Old Crow*
Dunham, William	LCol	348FG	16	P-47	*Bonnie*
				P-51	
Welch, George	Capt	47PS	16	P-40	*NPM*
		8FG		P-39	*Miss Helen the Flying Jenny*
				P-38	*Snatcher (?)*
Beerbower, Donald	Capt	354FG	15 1/2	P-51	*Bonnie Bee*
Brown, Samuel	Maj	31FG	15 1/2	P-51	*NPM*
Peterson, Richard	Capt	357FG	15 1/2	P-51	*Hurry Home Honey*
Whisner, William	Capt	352FG	15 1/2	P-47	*Moonbeam McSwine,*
				P-51	*Gee Whiz, Beverly,*
					Princess Elizabeth
Bradley, Jack	LCol	354FG	15	P-51	*M forMargie, Margie M, Margie Maru, Edgewood's Entry*
Carr, Bruce	1Lt	354FG	15	P-51	*Angel's Playmate*
Cragg, Edward	Maj	8FG	15	P-38	*Porky*
Foy, Robert	Maj	357FG	15	P-51	*Reluctant Rebel, Little Shrimp*
Hofer, Ralph	2Lt	4FG	15	P-47	*Missouri Kid, Show Me*
Salem Representative					
Homer, Cyril	Capt	8FG	15	P-38	*Cotton Duster, Uncle Cy's Angel*

Other Aces' Personal Markings

A

Abernathy, Robert	Capt	352	5	P-47	*Lady Gwen*
				P-51	*Lady Gwen II*
Adams, Charles	1Lt	82	6	P-38	*Judy Ann*
Adams, Fletcher	Capt	357	9	P-51	*Southern Bell*
Alexander, Richard	Capt	52	6	Spit	*Chappie, Dixie MK IV*
				P-39	*S.L. Abortion, Dixie MK V*
				P-51	*Dixie MK VI*
Allen, William	1Lt	55	5	P-51	*Pretty Pattie*
Ambort, Ernest	2Lt	49	5	P-38	*Flying Knight*
Ammon, Robert	1Lt	339	5	P-51	*Annie May*
Andersen, Leslie	1Lt	82	5	P-38	*Pugnacious Peggy*
Anderson, Charles	1Lt	4	10	P-51	*Paul, Hell's Belle*
Anderson, W.Y.	1Lt	20	7	P-51	*Steed, Swede's Steed*
Anderson, Wyman	1Lt	79	6	P-40	*Hokus Pokus*
Andrews, Stan	1Lt	35	6	P-38	*Lil' Women*
Andrew, Steve	Maj	49	9	P-40	*NPM*
				P-47	*Spirit of Los Angeles City College* *
Arasmith, Lester	1Lt	311	6	P-51	*Penny*
Aron, William	1Lt	325	5	P-51	*Big Mike, Texas Jesse*
Asbury, Richard	Capt	363	5	P-51	*Queenie*
Aschenbrenner, R.	Maj	49	10	P-38	*Maj. R.W. Aschenbrenner*

B

Baccus, Donald	LCol	356	5	P-47	*Bloody Shaft*
				P-51	*NPM*
Bade, Jack	1Lt	18	5	P-40	*Reckless Prostitute*
Bank, Raymond	Capt	357	5	P-51	*Fireball*
Bankey, Ernest	Capt	364	9	P-38	*Lucky Lady*
				P-51	*Lucky Lady*
Banks, William	Maj	348	9	P-47	*Sunshine*
Barber, Rex	Capt	347/23	5	P-38	*Diablo*
Barkey, Robert	1Lt	325	5	P-47	*Thuinderbolt Lad No. 90*
				P-51	*Dorothy*
Barnard, Lloyd	Lt	VF-2	8	F6F	*Mom Chung's fair Haired Bastard*
Baseler, Robert	Lcol	325	6	P-40	*Stud, Mortimer Snerd*
				P-47	*Big Stud*
				P-51	*Little Stud*
Beaver, Edward	Capt	339	5	P-51	*Joanie*
Becker, Robert	Capt	357	7	P-51	*Sebastian, Sebastian Jr.*
Bennett, Joseph	Capt	56	6.5	P-47	*Lucky Ann, Ann*
Benz, Walter	Maj	348	8	P-47	*Dirty Old Man*
Bickel, Carl	Capt	354	5.5	P-51	*Bonnie Bee, Z Hub*

Bickford, Edward	2Lt	354	5.5	P-51	*Alice Marie*
Bille, Henry	Maj	355	6	P-51	*Prune Face*
Blackburn, Tom	LCdr	VF17	11	F4U	*Big Hog*
Blair, Samuel	Capt	348	7	P-47	*Frankie*
Blickerstaff, Wayne	LCol	353	10	P-47	*Betty E*
				P-51	*Pvt Betty Mae*
Blumer, Larry	Capt	353	6	P-38	*Scrap Iron*
Bochkay, Donald	Capt	357	13.83	P-51	*Alice in Wonderland, Speedball Alice, (Winged ace of clubs)*
Boggs, Hampton	Capt	80	9	P-38	*Melba Lou*
Booth, Robert	1Lt	359	8	P-47	*Oily Boid*
				P-51	*NPM*
Bostrom, Ernest	1Lt	352	5	P-51	*Little Margie*
Bostwick, George	Maj	56	8	P-47	*Ugly Duckling*
Bright, John	Maj	AVG,23, 14	6	P-40	*NPM*
				P-38	*Josephine*
Broadhead, Joseph	Maj	357	8	P-51	*Lady Ester, Baby Mike, Master Mike*
Brooks, James	1Lt	31	13	P-51	*La Mort*
Brown, Carl	Lt.	VF-27	10.5	F6F	*Paper Doll (Robert Burnell a/c)*
Brown, Harley	1Lt	20	6	P-51	*Be Good, Brownie's Ballroom*
Brown, Harry	Capt	475	6	P-40	*Sylvia*
				P-38	*Florence*
Brown, Robert	F/O	325	7	P-51	*Little Brown Jug, How I Love Thee*
Brown, Henry	Capt	355	14.5	P-51	*Baby, Hun Hunter From Texas*
Brown, Quince	Maj	78	12.33	P-47	*Okie*
Browning, James	Capt	357	7	P-51	*Gentleman Jim*
Brueland, Lowell	Maj	354	12.5	P-47	*Wee Speck*
				P-51	*Grim Reape/ Wee Speck*
Bryan, Donald	Capt	352	13.5	P-47	*Little One*
				P-51	*Little One II-III*
Bryan, William	Maj	339	7.5	P-51	*Big Noise*
Burdick, Clinton	1Lt	356	5.5	P-51	*DoDo*
Buttke, Robert	Capt	56	5.5	P-38	*Lovenia*
				P-51	*Beautiful Lovenia*
Byrne, Robert	1Lt	57	6	P-40	*Sweetie Face*

C

Candelaria, Richard	1Lt	479	6	P-51	*My Pride & Joy*
Callaway, Ray	Maj	CWAC	6	P-40	*Shirley*
Campbell, Richard	1Lt	14	6	P-38	*Earthquake McGoon*
Carder, John	Capt	357	5	P-51	*Taxpayer's Delight*
Care, Raymond	Capt	4	6	Spit	*Calamity Jane*
				P-47	*NPM*
				P-51	*NPM*
Carlson, Kendall	Capt	4	6	P-47	*The Duchess*
				P-51	*The Duchess*
Carpenter, George	Maj	4	13.5	P-51	*Virginia*
Cesky, Charles	Capt	352	8.5	P-51	*Diann Ruth*
Ceuleers, George	LCol	364	10.5	P-38	*Constance, Connie & Butch Inc.*
				P-51	*NPM*
Champlin, Fred	Capt	475	9	P-38	*Buffalo Blitz/We Dood It, Buffalo Blitz Eileen Ann, Eileen*
Chandler, George	Capt	347	5	P-38	*Barbara Ann*
Chandler, Van	1Lt	4	5	P-51	*Wheezy*
Chick, William	LCol	325	6	P-47	*Rocky*
Clinger, Dallas	Capt	23/51	5	P-40	*Holdin' My Own (on tail)*
Coffey, Robert	LCol	365	6	P-47	*Coffey's Pot*
Collingsworth, J.D.	Capt	31	6	Spit	*Dimples*
Compton, Gordon	Capt	353	5.5	P-47	*NPM*
				P-51	*Little Bouncer*
Comstock, Harold	Maj	56	5	P-47	*Happy Warrior*
Condon, Henry	Capt	475	5	P-38	*Condon Cans*
Conger, Paul	Maj	56	11.5	P-47	*Hollywood High Hatter, Bernyce, Dream Baby, Redondo Beach California**
Cook, Walter	Capt	56	6	P-47	*Little Cookie*
Coons, Merle	Capt	55	5	P-51	*Worry Bird*
Cramer, Darrell	Maj	55	6.5	P-51	*Mick*

Cranfill, Nevil	Maj	359	5	P-47	*Deviless*
				P-51	*Deviless 2nd-3rd*
Crawford, Ray	2Lt	82	6	P-38	*Dirty Gertie*
Crenshaw, Claude	1Lt	359	7	P-51	*Louisiana Heatwave, Heatwave*
Crim, Harry	Maj	21	6	P-51	*My Action*
Cullerton, William	1Lt	355	5	P-51	*Fickle Fanny, Miss Stone*
Cummings, Donald	Capt	55	6.5	P-51	*NPM*
Cundy, Arthur	1Lt	353	5	P-51	*Alabama Rammer Jammer*
Cupp, James	Capt	VMF 213	12.5	F4U	*Daphne C.*
Curdes, Louis	1Lt	82, 3CDO	9	P-38	*NPM*
				P-51	*Bad Angel*
Curtis, Robert	Maj	52	14	P-51	*Julie*
Cutler, Frank	Capt	352	7.5	P-51	*Soldier'sVote*

D

Dahl, Perry	Capt	475	9	P-38	*Skidoo*
Dahlberg, Kenneth	Capt	354	14	P-51	*Dahlberg's Dilemma*
				P-47	*NPM*
Dalglish, James	Maj	354, 363	9	P-47	*NPM*
				P-51	*Pvt. Betty Mae*
Daniel, William	1Lt	31	5	P-51	*Tempus Fugit*
Daniell, J.S.	1Lt	339	5	P-51	*Sweet N Low Down*
Davis, Barrie	1Lt	325	6	P-51	*Bee, Honey Bee*
Davis, Clayton	Capt	352	5	P-47	*Marjorie*
				P-51	*Marjorie II*
Davis, Glendon	Capt	357	7.5	P-51	*Pregnant Polecat*
Davis, George	Capt	4	7	P-47	*Inky's Dinky*
Day, William	1Lt	8	5	P-38	*Jerry*
Dean, Cecil	2Lt	325	6	P-40	*Sawtooth Apache,Howling Wolf (emblem)*
				P-47	*NPM*
				P-51	*NPM*
DeHaven, Robert	Capt	49	14	P-38	*Personal name emblem orchid (emblem)*
Della, George	1Lt	348	5	P-47	*Nadine*
Dent, Elliott	Capt	49	6	P-40	*Ann theB'Ham Special, Grade A*
Dick, Frederick	Capt	49	5	P-40	*NPM*
				P-38	*My Marie*
Dikovitsky, Michael	1Lt	348	5	P-47	*Josie/Cleveland Cleaver, Josie II*
Doersch, George	Capt	359	10.5	P-47	*NPM*
				P-51	*Ole Goat*
Donalson, I.B.	1Lt	49	5	P-40	*Mauree*
Dregne, Irwin	LCol	357	6	P-51	*Ah Fung Goo/ Bobby Jeanne*
Drew, Urban	1Lt	361	6	P-51	*Detroit Miss*
Drier, William	Capt	49	6	P-38	*Little Maggie*
Drury, Paul	Ens	VF27	6.5	F6F	*Paoli Local*
Duffy, James	Capt	355	5.5	P-47	*NPM*
				P-51	*Dragon Wagon*
Duke, Walter	Capt	10AF	10	P-38	*Miss V*
Dunkin, Richard	Capt	325	9	P-51	*Thisizit*
Dunn, William	LCol	RAF 406	5	Spit	*Ceylon*
				P-47	*Posterius Ferrous*

E

East, Clyde	Capt	10	13	F-6	*Lil Margaret*
Egan, Joseph	1Lt	56	5	P-47	*Holy Joe(w/skull & crossbones emblem)*
Elder, John	Maj	355	8	P-51	*Moon*
Elder, Robert	Maj	353	5	P-51	*Miss Gamble*
Elliott, Ralph	Capt	VC27	9	FM-2	*Baldy*
Elliott, Vincent	1Lt	475	7	P-38	*Miss Fru-Fru*
Emmer, Wallace	Capt	354	14	P-51	*Arson's Reward*
Emmons, Eugene	1Lt	325	9	P-47	*Hun Hunter*
Empey, James	2Lt	52	5	P-51	*Little Ambassador*
England, James	Maj	311	10	P-51	*Jackie*
Ernst, Herman	1Lt	422	5	P-61	*Borrowed Time*
Evans, Andrew	LCol	357	6	P-51	*Little Sweetie, Little Joe*
Evans, Roy	Maj	359	6	P-47	*Thunderbird emblem*
				P-51	

F

Fiebelkorn, Ernest	1Lt	20	9	P-38	*NPM*
				P-51	*June Nite, Miss Miami*
Fiedler, Arthur	1Lt	315	8	P-51	*Helen*
Fisher, Edwin	Capt	362	7	P-47	*Shirley Jane*
Fischette, Charles	1Lt	31	5	Spit	*Little Mary Martin*
Fisk, Harry	Capt	354	5	P-51	*Duration Plus*
Flack, Nelson	Capt	49	5	P-40	*Ana May*
Forster, Joseph	1Lt	475	9	P-38	*Florida Cracker*
Fowle, James	Capt	364	8	P-51	*Terry Claire*
Frantz, Carl	1Lt	354	11	P-51	*Joy*
Frey, Royal	1Lt	20	2	P-51	*Stardust (became an ace in Korea)*
Froning, Alfred	1Lt	57	6	P-40	*Carole*
				P-47	*Carole*

G

Gailer, Frank	1Lt	357	5.5	P-51	*Expectant*
Galer, Robert	Maj	VMF-224	13	F4F	*Barbara Jane*
Gallup, Ken	LCol	353	9	P-51	*Rat A Dat*
Gaunt, Frank	Capt	18	8	P-40	*Twerp!*
				P-51	*Twerp!*
Gaylor, Robert	Maj	VMF-224	14	F4F	*Barbara Jane*
Gerard, Francis	Capt	339	8	P-51	*Yi-Yi, Twinkle Toes*
Gerick, Steven	2Lt	56	5	P-47	*Tally-Ho Chaps*
Gimbel, Edward	P/O	RCAF	5	Spit	*Hard Luck!*
Giroux, William	Capt	8	10	P-38	*Whilma.Deadeye Daisy*
Gladych, Mike	S/L	56	10	Spit	*Pengie*
				P-47	*Pengie II-III*
Gleason, George	Capt	479	12	P-51	*Hot Toddy*
Glenn, Maxwell	Maj	80	7.5	P-38	*Sluggo*
Glover, Fred	Maj	4	10.33	P-51	*Dolly, Rebel Queen*
Goebel, Robert	Capt	31	11	P-51	*Flying Dutchman*
Goehausen, Walter	Capt	31	10	P-51	*Miss Mimi*
Goodnight, Robert	1Lt	354	7.4	P-51	*Mary Anne*
Graham, Gordon	LCol	356	7	P-51	*Down for Double, Bodacious*
Graham, Lindol	Capt	20	5.5	P-38	*Susie*
Grant, Marvin	1Lt	348	7	P-47	*Sylvia, Racine Belle*
Gresham, William	1Lt	475	6	P-38	*Black Market Babe*
Griffin, Joseph	Maj	23,357	7	P-40	*Hellsapoppin*
				P-38	*Hellsapoppin II*
Gross, Clayton	Capt	354	6	P-51	*Live Bait, Peggy*
Grosvenor, William	Capt	23	5	P-40	*NPM*
				P-51	*Earth Quake McGoon*
Gumm, Charles	1Lt	354	6	P-51	*Toni*

H

Hagerstrom, James	1Lt	49	6	P-40	*Hag & Hag*
Hall, Charles	1Lt	339	+	P-40	*Buster (+1ˢᵗ Afro-American victory)*
Halton, William	Maj	352	10.5	P-47	*Slender, Tender & Tall/ Bugs*
				P-51	*Slender, Tender & Tall*
Hanseman, Chris	1Lt	339	5	P-51	*Eleanore*
Harrington, A.A.	LCol	RCAF/AAF	8	Mosq	*Lady Pat*
Harris, Ernest	Capt	49	10	P-40	*Miss Kat*
Harris, Leroy	LCdr	VF-10,12	9.25	F4F	*NPM*
				F6F	*Mom Chung's Fair Haired Bastard*
Harris, Thomas	Capt	357	5	P-51	*Lil' Red's Rocket*
Hart, Kenneth	1Lt	475	8	P-38	*Pee Wee*
Hartley, Ray	Capt	325/353	5	P-47	*NPM*
				P-51	*Ku*
Hatala, Paul	Capt	357	5.5	P-51	*Jeanne*
Hatch, Herbert	1Lt	1	5	P-38	*Mon Amy*
Hauver, Charles	1Lt	355	5	P-51	*Princess Pat, Patricia*
Haviland, Fred	Capt	355	6	P-51	*The Iowa Beaut, Barbara*
Hawkins, Arthur	Lt(jg)	VF-31	14	F6F	*Lt(jg)Ray Hawkins (script)*
Haworth, Russell,	1Lt	55	5	P-51	*Krazy Kid*
Hayes, Thomas	LCol	357	8.5	P-51	*Frenesi*

Heller, Edwin	Capt	352	5.5	P-51	*Hell-er-Bust*	
Hildebrandt, Carlos	Cdr	VF33	5	F6F	*My Own Joan*	
Hill, Allen	Capt	8	9	P-38	*Hill's Angel*	
Hiro, Edwin	Maj	357	5	P-51	*Horse's Itch*	
Hively, Howard	Maj	4	12	P-47	*The Deacon*	
				P-51	*The Deacon*	
Hogg, Roy	Capt	325	6	P-40		
				P-47	*NPM*	
				P-51	*Thunderbolt Lad, Penrod*	
Holmes, Besby	1Lt	347	5	P-38	*Ole 100*	
Hopkins, Wallace	LCol	361	5	P-51	*Ferocious Frankie*	
Hovde, William	Maj	355	10.5	P-51	*Ole, My Butch*	
Howard, James	LCol	354	6	P-51	*Ding Hoa*	
Howes, Bernard	1Lt	55	6	P-51	*My Lil' Honey*	
Hoyt, Edward	Capt	35	5	P-47	*Hoyt's Horse*	
Hunt, Edward	1Lt	354	6.5	P-51	*Smoldering Boulder, Ready Eddie*	
Hunter, Alvaro	Capt	35	5	P-39	*My Baby*	
				P-40	*My Baby*	
I						
Ilfrey, Jack	Capt	20	7.5	P-38	*TexasTerror, Happy Jack's Go Buggy*	
				P-51	*Happy Jack's Go Buggy*	
Ince, James	1Lt	475	6	P-38	*Impossible Ince*	
Isaacson, Clayton	Capt	82	5	P-38	*Almost "A"Dragon, Kittie*	
J						
Jackson, Michael	Maj	56	8	P-47	*Teddy*	
Jackson, Willie	LCol	352	7	P-47	*NPM*	
				P-51	*Hot Stuff*	
Jamison, Gilbert	Capt	364	7	P-51	*Etta Jane*	
Jaspar, Merle	F/Lt	RAF	5	Mosq	*Earthquake McGoon*	
Jeffrey, Arthur	LCol	479	14	P-38	*Boomerang*	
				P-51	*Boomerang Jr.*	
Jenkins, Otto	2Lt	357	5	P-51	*Toolin' Fools Revenge, Joan Floogie*	
Johnson, Arthur	1Lt	52	8.5	Spit	*LT. ARTHUR JOHNSON*	
				P-51		
Johnson, Clarence	Capt	352	7	P-51	*Bula B*	
Johnson, Evan	Capt	339	5	P-51	*The Comet*	
Jones, Cyril	1Lt	359	6	P-51	*Dora Dee*	
Jones, John	Capt	80	8	P-39	*Panic*	
				P-38	*Panic*	
K						
Karger, Dale	1Lt	357	7.5	P-51	*Cathy Mae/Karger's Dolly, Cathy Mae*	
Kemp, William	2Lt	361	6	P-51	*Betty Lee*	
Kienholtz, Donald	1Lt	1	6	P-38	*Billie Jo/NASA Serbska Sloboda! BarFly*	
King, Ben	Capt	359	7	P-38	*NPM*	
				P-51	*Matilda*	
King, Charles	Maj	35	5	P-38	*King*	
King, William	1Lt	354	5.5	P-51	*Atlanta Peach*	
Kinnard, Claiborne	Lcol	4	8	P-51	*Man O' War*	
Kinsella, James	Lt(jg)	VF-72/VF-33	5	F4F	*NPM*	
				F6F	*good deed Dotty*	
Kirby, Marion	1Lt	8,475	5	P-38	*Maiden Head Hunter*	
Kirkpatrick, Floyd	Capt	VMF 411	5.5	F4U	*Palpitating Pauli*	
Kirla, John	1Lt	357	11.5	P-51	*Spook*	
Kiser, George	Capt	24,49	9	P-40	*Lion with Zero Pliot (emblem)*	
Klibbe, Frank	2Lt	56	7	P-47	*Little Chief*	
Koenig, Charles	1Lt	354	6.5	P-51	*Little Horse(La Petite Chaval)*	
Koralski, Walter	Capt	355	5.5	P-47	*Miss Thunder*	
				P-51	*Miss Thunder, Misstang*	
Kruzel, Ward	LCol	17/361	6.5	P-40	*NPM*	
				P-51	*Vi*	
L						
Ladd, Kenneth	Capt	8	12	P-38	*X Virgin, Windy City Ruthie*	
Lamb, Robert	Capt	56	7	P-47	*Jackie*	
Lamb, George	Maj	354	7.5	P-51	*Uno Who*	
Lampe, Richard	1Lt	52	5.5	P-51	*Betty*	

Lane, John	1Lt	35	6	P-38	*Thumper*
Landers, John	LCol	49	14.5	P-40	*Skeeter*
				P-38	*Big Beautiful Doll*
				P-51	*Big Beautiful Doll*
Lanphier, Thomas	Capt	347	6	P-38	*Phoebe*
Larson, Donald	Maj	39	6	P-51	*Mary Queen of Scots*
Larson, Leland	2Lt	10	6	F-6	*Nancy*
Lasko, Charles	Capt	354	7.5	P-51	*Suga, Buster*
Lavan, George	Capt	49	5	P-38	*Itsy Bitsy*
Lawler, John	Capt	52	11	P-51	*Cathy*
Lazear, Earl	1Lt	352	5	P-51	*Penny's Earl*
Lenfest, Charles	Capt	55	5.5	P-47	*Lorie I-II*
				P-51	*Lorie III-IV*
Lenox, Jack	2Lt	14	5	P-38	*Snookie*
Lent, Francis	1Lt	475	11	P-38	*Trigger Mortis*
Leverette, William	LCol	14	11	P-38	*Stingeree*
Liles, Robert	Maj	51	5	P-40	*Duke*
Lines. Ted	Capt	4	10	P-51	*Thunderbird*
Littge, Raymond	Capt	352	10.5	P-51	*Silver Dollar, E. Pluribus Unum, Helen*
Loisel, John	Maj	475	11	P-38	*Screamin' Kid*
London, Charles	Capt	78	5	P-47	*El Jeepo*
Long, Maurice	Capt	354	5.5	P-51	*Mary Pat*
Lopez, Don	1Lt	23	5	P-40	*Lope's Hope*
				P-51	*Lope's Hope 3rd*
Lowell, John	LCol	364	7.5	P-38	*NPM*
				P-51	*Penny*
Lowery, Wayne	1Lt	325	11	P-51	*My Gal Sal*
Lubner, Marvin	Capt	23	6	P-40	*Barfly*
Luksic, Carl	1Lt	352	8.5	P-47	*Lucky Boy*
				P-51	*Ellie's Lucky Boy*
Luma, James	1Lt	RCAF	5	Mosq	*Moonbean McSwine*
Lustic, Stanley	1Lt	318	6	P-47	*Stanley's Steamer*

M

MacKay, John	2Lt	1	6	P-38	*Shoot, You're Faded*
MaGuire, William	Capt	353	7	P-47	*Boston Bull*
				P-51	*Boston Bull*
Mahon, Barry	Flt/Lt	RAF	5	Spit	*Barry*
Maloney, Thomas	1Lt	1	8	P-38	*Maloney's Pony*
Markham, Gene	Capt	353	5	P-51	*Mr. Gray*
Marshall, Bert	Maj	355	7	P-51	*Jane*
Mason, Joe	Col	352	5	P-47	*Gena/THIS IS IT,*
				P-51	*THIIS IS IT*
Mathis, Willaim	1Lt	318	5	P-47	*Bottoms Up, Joey*
Mathre, Milden	2Lt	49	5	P-38	*Goat Nose*
Maxwell, Chester	Capt	357	5	P-51	*Lady Ester*
McArthur, Paul	1Lt	79	5	P-40	*Spring*
McCauley, Frank	1Lt	56	5.5	P-47	*Rat Racer*
McComas, Edward	LCol	23	14	P-51	*Kansas Reaper*
McCorkle, Charles	Col	31	11	Spit	*NPM*
				P-51	*Betty Jane*
McDaniel, Gordon	1Lt	325	6	P-51	*Mary Mac*
McDonough, Wm.	Maj	35	5	P-39	*Emblem-Fighting Donald Duck*
McDonald, Norman	Maj	52/325	11.5	Spit	*NPM*
				P-51	*Chuck-O*
McDowell, Donald	1Lt	354	8.5	P-51	*Ho-Tel*
McElroy, James	Capt	355	5	P-51	*Big Stoop/Ridge Runner*
McGee, Donald	Capt	8	6	P-38	*Statten Island or Bust*
McGinn, John	LCol	5	6	P-38	*NPM*
				P-51	*Da Quake*
McGraw, Bruce	1Lt.	VC-10	5	FM-2	*Mah Baby* (VF-10 3v./VC-80 2v.)
McKeon, Joseph	Capt	475/20	6	P-38	*Regina Coeli*
				P 51	*Regina Coeli II-III*
McKennon, Pierce	Maj	4	11	P-47	*NPM*

				P-51	Yippi Joe, Ridge Runner
Megura, Nicholas	Capt	4	11.8	P-51	Hot Pants, Ill Wind
Merritt, George	Maj	361	5	P-47	Dr. I.P. Daily
Merony, Virgil	Capt	4	9	P-47	Sweet louise/Hedy, Sweet Louise
Merritt, George	Maj	361	5	P-47	Dr. I.P. Daily
Miklajcyk, Henry	Capt	352	7.5	P-47	The Syracusan
				P-51	Syracusan the 3rd
Miller, Armour	1Lt	1	6	P-38	Jinx
Miller, Joseph	Capt	374	5	P-38	Marg
Miller, Thomas	2Lt	354	5.25	P-51	Gnomee
Millikan, Willand	Capt	4	13	P-47	Missouri Mauler
				P-51	Missouri Mauler
Milliken, Robert	1Lt	474	5	P-38	Swat
Moats, Sanford	1Lt	352	8.5	P-51	Kay
Molland, LeLand	Capt	31	11	P-51	Fargo Express
Monk, Franklin	1Lt	474	5	P-38	Petty Pretty
Moore, Robert	Maj	15	12	P-40	Stinger
				P-51	Stinger II-IV
Moran, Glennon	LCol	352	15	P-51	Stubbles, Little Ann
Morehead, James	Maj	49	24,49	P-40	L'Ace
				P-38	NPM
Morrill, Stanley	1Lt	56	9	P-47	FATS Btfsplk
Morris, James	Capt	20	7.33	P-38	Black Barney, My Dad/Til We Meet Again
Morriss, Paul	Capt	475	5	P-38	Hold Something
Moseley, Mark	Capt	56	6.5	P-47	Sylvia
Mugavero, James	1Lt	35	6	P-47	Pat
Murphey, Paul	Capt	8	6	P-38	Sweet Sue
Murphy, Alva	Capt	357	6	P-51	Bite Me
Myers, Joseph	Maj	55, 78	5	P-38	Journey's End

N

Nichols, Frank	Capt	49/475	5	P-40	Nick Nichols Nip Nippers
				P-38	NPM
Norley, Louis	Maj	4	10.5	P-47	Red Dog
				P-51	Red Dog II-XII
Novotny, George	1Lt	325	8	P-40	NPM
				P-47	Ruthless Ruthie/Ladie Jane, Pittsburgh Pattie

O

Oberhansley, Jack	LCol	78	6	P-47	Iron Ass
O'Brien, Gilbert	Maj	357	7	P-51	Shanty Irish
O'Brien, William	Capt	357	5.5	P-51	Billie's Bitch
O'Conner, Frank	Capt	355	10.75	P-51	The Verna Q./Stinky, Stars Look Down
Ohr, Fred	Capt	52	6	Spit	NPM
				P-51	Marie
Olander, Edwin	1Lt.	VMF-214	5	F4U	Marine's Dream
Olds, Robin	Maj	479	13	P-38	Scat I-III
				P-51	Scat IV-VII
Olson, Norman	Capt	355	6	P-47	Ma Fran
Olson, Paul	1Lt	359	5	P-51	Mari-Helen, Supermouse
O'Neill, Eugene	Capt	56	5	P-47	Jessie-O
O'Neill, John	1Lt	49	8	P-38	Beautiful Lass, Elsie
O'Neill, Lawrence	Flt/Lt	348	6	P-47	Cathy, Kathy/Veni, Vedi, Vici
Osher, Ernest	Capt	82	5	P-38	Sad Sack
Owens, Joel	Maj	1/14	5	P-38	Daisy Mae/Rum Head

P

Paisley, Melvyn	1Lt	366	5	P-47	La Mort
Pascoe, James	1Lt	364	5.5	P-51	Green Eyes
Parham, Forrest	Capt	23	5	P-40	Little Jeep
				P-51	Little Jeep
Paris, Joel	Capt	49	9	P-40	Lizzy, Rusty,
				P-38	Georgia Belle
Pascoe, James	1Lt	364	5.5	P-51	Green Eyes, Desert Rat
Paulk, Edsel	2Lt	325	5	P-47	Littlr Sir Echo

Perdomo, Oscar	1Lt	507	5	P-47	*Lil' Meatie's Meat Chopper*
Pierce, Sammy	1Lt	49	9	P-40	*Kay the Strawberry Blond*
				P-38	*Kay the Strawberry Blond/Hialeah, Wolf*
Pietz, John	1Lt	475	6	P-38	*Vickie, Pattie P.*
Pissanos, Spiros	1Lt	4	5	P-47	*Miss Plainfiield*
				P-51	*Miss Plainfiield*
Pompetti, Peter	F/O	78	5	P-47	*Axe the Axis, Darkie*
Poindexter, James	Capt	353	7	P-47	*Honey*
Popek, Edward	Maj	348	7	P-47	*Little Bess*
				P-51	*The Rolicking Rogue*
Porter, Bruce	Maj	VMF(N)-542	5	F6F	*Black Death*
Powers, Joseph	Capt	56	14.5	P-47	*Power's Girl*
Powers, MacArthur	2Lt	324	7.5	Spit	*Jessy*
Price, Jack	Maj	78	5	P-47	*Feather Merchant*
Pugh, John	Capt	357	6	P-51	*Geronimo*
Priest, Royce	1Lt	355	5	P-51	*Eagle Beak, Weepin' Deacon*
Pryor, Roger	Capt	23	5	P-40	*Weak Eyes Yokum*
Purdy, John	1Lt	475	7	P-38	*Lizzie*

Q

Quigley, Donald	Maj	23	5	P-40	*Reni, the Queen*

R

Rankin, Robert	1Lt	56	10	P-47	*Wicked Wackie Weegie*
Ray, Charles	1Lt	8	5	P-38	*San Antonio Rose*
Reed, William	LCol	AVG/CACW	9	P-40	*Boss Hoss*
Reese, William	1Lt	357	5	P-51	*Bear River Betsy*
Reeves, Horace	1Lt	475	6	P-38	*El Tornado*
Reeves, Leonard	1Lt	311	6	P-51	*My Texas Darling, My Dallas Darli'*
Reynolds, Andrew	1Lt	49	10	P-40	*Star Dust, Oklahoma Kid*
Reynolds. Robert	1Lt	354	7	P-51	*.50 Caliber Concerto*
Riddle, Robert	1Lt	31	11	P-51	*Angel*
Righetti, Elwin	LCol	338	7.5	P-51	*Kadydid*
Riley, Paul	1Lt	4	6.5	P-47	*NPM*
				P-51	*NPM*
Roberson, Arval	1Lt	357	6	P-51	*Passion Wagon*
Roberts, Eugene	LCol	78	9	P-47	*Spokane Chief, Jimmie the First*
Roddy, Edward	Capt	348	8	P-47	*Babs*
Rogers, Felix	Capt	354	7	P-51	*Beantown Banshee*
Ross, Herbert	Maj	14	7	P-38	*Teresa R, Little Carl*
Rounds, Gerald	1Lt	82	5	P-38	*Cadiz Eagle, Chicken Dit*
Rowland, Robert	Col	348	8	P-47	*Miss Mutt/Pride of Lodi, Ohio**
Ruder, LeRoy	1Lt	357	5.5	P-51	*Linda Lu*
Rynne, William	Capt	325	5	P-47	*Ginger*

S

Sangermano, Philip	1Lt	325	8	P-51	*Mary Norris*
Schank, Thomas	1Lt	55	5	P-38	*Stinger, Rocky Mountain Canary*
Schriber, Louis	Capt	8	5	P-38	*Screwy Looie*
Schuh, Duerr	1Lt	352	5	P-51	*Dutchess*
Schultz, Robert	Capt	459	5	P-38	*Golden Eagle*
Sears, Alexander	1Lt	352	5	P-51	*Sheepherder*
Shomo, William	Capt	71	8	P-39	*Snooks*
				F-6	*Flying Undertaker*
Shoup, Robert	1Lt	354	5.5	P-51	*Fer De Lance*
Shubin, Murray	1Lt	347	11	P-38	*Oriole*
Simmons, John	1Lt	325	7	P-51	*Devastating Dottie*
Sloan, William	1Lt	82	12	P-38	*Snooks*
Smith, Carroll	Maj	547	8	P-38	*Swing Shift Skipper*
				P-61	*Time's A Wastin'*
Smith, Cornelius	Capt	8	11	P-38	*Corky, Corky Jr., Dottie from Brooklyn*
Smith, Donavan	1Lt	56	5.5	P-47	*Ole Cock, PJ, Hun Hunter*
Smith, Leslie	Maj	56	7	P-47	*Silver Lady*
Smith, Paul	1Lt	422	5	P-61	*Lady Gen*
Smith, Richard	1Lt	35	6	P-38	*Japanese Sandman*
Smith, Virgil	1Lt	14	6	P-38	*Kniption*

Spencer, Dale	1Lt	361	9.5	P-47	*NPM*
				P-51	*Little Luke*
Stangel, Willaim	Capt	352	5	P-51	*Stinky*
Stanton, Arland	Maj	49	8	P-40	*Empty Saddle, Revenge Side, Keystone Katie*
Starck, Walter	Capt	352	7	P-47	*Lucia*
				P-51	*Starck Mad, Even Stevens*
Starnes, James	Capt	39	6	P-51	*Tar Heel*
Stephens, Robert	Maj	354	13	P-51	*Killer*
Stewert, Everett	Col	4	5	P-47	*Sunny*
				P-51	*Sunny*
Storch, John	LCol	357	10.5	P-51	*The Shillelagh*
Strait, John	Maj	356	13.5	P-47	*Jersey Jerk*
				P-51	*Jersey Jerk*
Sublett, John	Capt	357	8	P-51	*Lady Oxella*
Suehr, Richard	1Lt	35	5	P-39	*NPM*
				P-38	*Regina*
Summer, Elliott	Capt	475	10	P-38	*Blood & Guts, Stiff Action*
Sutcliff, Robert	1Lt	348	5	P-47	*Brown Eyes*
Swett, James	Capt	VMF 221	15.5	F4F	*Melvin's Massacre*
				F4U	
Sykes, William	1Lt	361	5	P-51	*Wilma Lee*

T

Talbot, Gilbert	Maj	354	5	P-51	*Peggy, Deacon*
Tanner, William	Capt	353	5.5	P-47	*Prudence*
				P-51	*Prudence*
Taylor, Oliver	Capt	14	5	P-38	*Pat*
Taylor, Ralph	Capt	325	6	P-40	*Duchess of Durham/My Gal Sal*
Thury, Joseph	LCol	339	2.5	P-51	*Pauline (top ETO strafing ace)*
Thyng, Harrison	Col	31/413	10	Spit	*Mary & James*
				P-47	*Mary-James*
Thwaites, David	Capt	356	6	P-47	*Polly*
Tilley, John	1Lt	475	5	P-38	*Ranooki MaruBette Ann*
Tordorff, Harrison	Capt	353	5	P-47	*Anne, Upupa epops*
				P-51	*Upupa epops*
Tovrea, Philip	1Lt	14	15	P-38	*La Muneca Plata*
Trafton, Fred	1Lt	31	5	Spit	*Christian Maker*
				P-51	*Puddleduck Prostitute*
Truluck, Richard	1Lt	56	7	P-47	*Lady Jane*
Turley, Grant	2Lt	78	6	P-47	*Kitty/Sundown Ranch*
Turner, Richard	Maj	361	11	P-51	*Short Fuse Sallee*
Tyler, Gerald	Maj	357	7	P-51	*Little Duckfoot*
Tyler, James	Capt	54	8	Spit	*Meg*
				P-51	*Meg*

V

Vanden Hueval, G.	1Lt	361	5.5	P-51	*Mary Mine*
Vaught, Robert	Capt	49	5	P-40	*Bob's Robin*
				P-38	
Vincent, Casey	Col	CACW	6	P-40	*Peggy*
Vogt, John E.	Capt	318	5	P-47	*Big Squaw, Drinkin' Sister*
Vogt, John W.	Maj	356	8	P-47	*Jersey Mosquito*
Vraciu, Alexander	Lt(jg)	VF6	19	F6F	*Gadget*

W

Waggoner, Horace	1Lt	353	5	P-47	*Miss Illini*
				P-51	
Wandry, Ralph	Capt	49	6	P-47	*Pin up photos on cowling*
				P-38	
Warner, Jack	1Lt	354	5	P-51	*Chicago's Own, Lady Jane*
Watkins, James	Capt	49	11	P-40	*Duck Butt*
				P-38	*Charlcie Jeanne*
Webb, Willard	Capt	459	5	P-38	*My Ranger*
Welch, Darrell	Capt	1	5	P-38	*Sky Ranger*
Welch, Robert	Capt	55	6	P-51	*Miss Marilyn, Wings of the Morning*
Welden, Robert	1Lt	354	6.25	P-51	*Maekie*

West, Richard	Capt	8	14	P-40	*NPM*
				P-38	*Heart flush (emblem)*
Whalen, William	1Lt	4	6	P-51	*Hi Nell*
Wicker, Samuel	Maj	364	7	P-38	*Betty Jo*
				P-51	*Betty Jo*
Wilkinson, James	Capt	78	7	P-47	*Miss Behave*
Wilson, William	Capt	364	5	P-51	*NPM*
Winks, Robert	1Lt	357	5.5	P-51	*Trusty Rusty*
Winters, Hugh	Capt	VF19	8	F6F	*Hanger Lily*
Wire, Calvin	1Lt	475	7	P-38	*Little Eva*
Wise, Kenneth	1Lt	354	5	P-51	*Wano*
Witt, Lynn	Capt	8	6	P-40	*Home Sick*
				P-38	*Home Sick*
Woods, Sidney	LCol	49/4	7	P-40	*Arizona*
				P-38	*Kip*
Woody, Robert	Capt	355	7	P-40	*NPM*
				P-51	*Woody's Maytag*

Y

Yeager, Robert	Capt	40	5	P-47	*Noisy*
Yeager, Charles	Capt	357	11.5	P-51	*Glamorous Glen*
York, Robert	1Lt	359	5	P-51	*Rudy*

Z

| Zoerb, Daniel | Capt | 52 | 7 | P-51 | *Hey Rube* |
| Zubarik, Charles | 1Lt | 82 | 8 | P-38 | *Pearl* |

Gallery of Victory Symbols

Two aces of the 31FG/308FS, Capt. Robert Goebel (11v.) and Capt. Walter Goehausen (10v.) pose by their P-51Ds. Note that the script for the pilot and ground crew names is the same but the German victory markings differ: Swastika and Iron Cross. (Author/Goebel & Goehausen)

The two top ETO and 56FG aces, Capt. Robert Johnson and LtCol. Francis Gabreski had similar victory scoreboards under their cockpits. Each stenciled Iron Cross had the type of Luftwaffe aircraft stenciled above it. (USAAF)

Capt. Leonard "Kit" Carson of the 362FS/357FG flew his P-51 to 18 1/2 victories. The victory symbols (24, which included strafing victories) are unusual: black swastikas inside black circles. (USAF)

1Lt. Henry Brown of the 354FS/355FG shows some of the victory markings on his P-51, *"Hun Hunter from Texas,"* which would total 14 by the end of his tour. Browns's markings were black swastikas superimposed on white circles. (USAF)

Maj. Levi Chase (60FS/ 33FG) shows off the Italian victory symbol on his P-40 he earned by downing a Mc.202 on 15 March 1943. Chase would number a further 9 Luftwaffe aircraft and then 2 Japanese Oscars while flying for the 1(Prov)FG. (USAF)

Col. John Meyer (487FS/352FG/26v.) shows two different types of victory markings (above left, above). The 4 Maltese Crosses are on his P-47 named *"Lambie"* while the shadowed swastikas and cartoon of *"Petie"* are displayed on his P-51D late in his tour. Note the name of his crew chief, S/Sgt. W.F. Conklin , under his name which was a standard procedure by fighter pilots. (USAF)

Aces were associated with air victories and rarely posted their fighter bomber missions. Maj. William Dunham of the 348FG is shown in his P-47, *"Bonnie,"* displaying 15 victories (he got #16 flying a P-51 late in the war), 30 bombing missions and 2 Japanese ships he sunk. (Author/ Dunham)

The P-47 of Capt. Edwin Heller, 352FG ace (5 1/2 v.), flourished an elaborate scoreboard. Each of his air and ground victories were categorized by type, he had 3 V-1 claims, 20 vehicles and 5 trains destroyed, 40 bomber escort missions, 25 dive bombing missions and 15 fighter sweeps. (Author/Heller)

Lt. John Wirth (VF-31/14 victories) is seen here in a PR shot aboard the *Cabot* after his 4 victory day on 21 September 1944. The standard Rising Sun victory symbols are supplemented by 9 bombing mission symbols. (USN)

1Lt. Kenneth Walsh and his crew chief pose on the wing of his F4U-1 which displays 20 of Walsh's eventual 21 victories. The weather-beaten Rising Suns were the standard for the Pacific. (Author/Walsh)

This is a page from the 1945 CVG-83/*Essex* Cruise Book. For the pilot photos the same F6F, #205, was used. Removable decals were used to indicate each pilot's score. (USN)

A beautiful shot of VF-17 Corsairs which are weather beaten and combat weary. VF-17 was known as the Jolly Rogers, and the Skull & Crossbones insignia can be seen on the engine cowling. The Rising Suns were placed in vertical rows which was the Marine Corps method of positioning victory markings. Pilots were: #29 Ike Kepford, #8 Hal Jackson, #3 Jim Streig and #28 Wilbert Popp. (USMC)

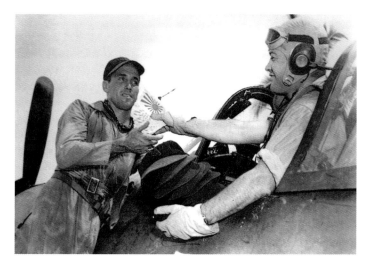

A PR photo of VMF-214 second ranking ace, 1Lt. Chris McGee (9v.), handing his CO, Pappy Boyington, victory decals and baseball caps after a successful mission. The baseball caps were part of an exchange with the 1943 World Series Champs, the St. Louis Cardinals, one cap for every Jap shot down, the Cards did not send enough caps! (USMC)

Opposite: The official policy of the Navy and Marine Corps was to prohibit any personal markings as pilots, especially on carriers, rarely flew the same fighter. A VMF-323 F4U is shown with 10 victory flags when the top scorers for the squadron, Robert Wade, John Ruhsam and Jerry O'Keefe, had 7 victories each. (Author/O'Keefe)

The "meatball" victory symbol was rarely used but early in the war they were quick and easy to paint. Here Maj. William Turner displays 3 kills made in 1942. He would score 5 more as CO of the 32FS/3FG/CACW. (USAF)

Dick Bong broke Eddie Rickenbacker's WW-1 American victory record of 26 in his P-38 named *"Marge."* Bong used a small teacher's college graduation picture of his fiancee, March Vattendahl that was blown up to 20x24 and tinted. The photo was glue directly to the nose and heavily varnished. (USAF)

Dick and Marge after he returned to the States as America's Ace of Aces on his whirlwind War Bond drive. (USAF)

Tom McGuire may have rivaled Bong in victories but in the romance department he lagged far behind. He lovingly named his P-38 *"Pudgy"* which must have thrilled his wife, Marilyn. (USAF)

Twenty-two victory ace Jay Robbins named his P-38 *"Jandina,"* a combination on Jay and wife, Ina. (USAF)

Jerry Johnson had *"Barbara"* painted on his P-38 after having used *"Jerry"* on an earlier Lightning. (USAF)

Leading PTO P-47 ace, Neel Kearby, named his Thunderbolt *"Fiery Ginger"* after his wife. (USAF)

In the most widely publicized Navy ace was its leading ace, Cdr. David McCampbell, who had his share of publicity sessions. He named his Hellcats *"Minsi"* after his Milwaukee girlfriend, Mary Blatz. (USN)

Shark Mouths, Dragons, and Other Fearsome Creatures

The shark mouth motif has been around as long as fighter combat. The design had its first widespread use by the Germans in WWI on the Roland C.11 *Walfisch*. The Luftwaffe, after some sporadic use in 1939, employed the design at unit level with II/ZG 76, the *Haifisch (Shark) Gruppe*. The unit flew the Me-110 against RAF 112 Squadron Gladiators over Greece. 112 was impressed with the design, and when they transitioned to the Curtiss P-40 Tomahawk over North Africa's Western Desert in 1941, it found the P-40 well suited for displaying the shark's face. The long, slim engine cowling for the head and radiator air scoop under the propeller for the open mouth was the ideal canvas.

The most well known use of the shark mouth was by the American Volunteer Group, the Flying Tigers. Soon after the first pilots arrived in Rangoon in mid-November 1941, pilot Erik Schilling was reading the *India Illustrated Weekly* and saw a photograph of a

"Pappy Boyington always seemed to be in trouble. In this photo the name on the F4U seems to be "Lulubelle" which all post war model airplanes and even museum exhibits reflect. However, the Republic factory rep's arm covers part of the name that in recent post war research reveals to be *"Lucybelle,"* the name of the married woman he was romancing. (USMC)

The most famous sharksmouth markings were found on the P-40s of the AVG. (National Archives)

The sharksmouth appeared over Guadalcanal. The P-400 in the photo is from the 67FS/347FG. (USAF)

Capt. Curran Jones, who scored 5 victories for the 39FS/35FG, stands by his sharksmouth P-38. (USAF)

RAF 112 Squadron shark mouth Tomahawk. The next day, Schilling and two other pilots, Lacy Mangleburg and Ken Merritt, sketched a chalk shark's face on a P-40. They asked AVG CO Col. Claire Chennault for permission to use it for their squadron insignia, but Chennault was so impressed he decided to use it for the group symbol.

Each AVG squadron chose a nickname and emblem. The 1st Squadron, "The Adam and Eves," chose an apple with a superimposed naked Eve chasing a uniformed Adam (man's first pursuit). The 2nd Squadron "Panda Bears" had a panda that was the characteristic of China. The 3rd Squadron "The Hell's Angels" had a red nude angel looking like Jean Harlow, who starred in the 1930 WWI film classic about the air war on the Western Front.

On 20 December 1941 ten Japanese Ki-43 Lilys attacked Kunming and four were shot down for the first victories over the Japanese Air Forces. Henry Luce, the editor of *Time* magazine, had been born in China and had visited Generalissimo and Madame Chiang Kai-shek in May 1941. Though the story of these four AVG victories was insignificant in the scheme of the war, Luce had a political agenda and needed a catchy title for the *Time* story. Luce called it "Blood for the Tigers," and the name Flying Tigers was picked up by the American press and public.

The success of the AVG and the shark mouth and other designs continued in the CBI and was passed on into the Pacific. These fearsome designs were intended to spook the superstitious Oriental enemy. When the AVG disbanded in July 1942, its aircraft were inherited by its successor, the 23FG/14AF, which carried on the shark mouth tradition, as did the Chinese-American Composite Wing (CACW) when it was formed by the 14AF and given the P-40. The 15FS/51FG/10AF flew shark mouth P-40Es over Assam, India, and retired them to the Chinese Air Force when they re-equipped with P-51s. The 25FS called their squadron "Our Assam Draggins," after their saber-toothed dragon-adorned P-40s, which were designed by a Disney artist who had become a pilot in the unit. Elsewhere in the CBI the 80FG/10AF flew P-40Ns over Burma and Assam with large white skulls, the exhaust stacks protruding rearward from the eye socket. The P-38s of the 459FS/80FG Twin Dragon Squadron displayed a dragon with large fangs and an arrow-tipped tongue on

The 80FG which flew in he CBI adorned its P-40s with skulls in the fall of 1943. (USAF)

The 25FS/51FG, *"Our Assam Draggins,"* flew these fearsome blue-lipped fanged P-40s over China. (USAF)

The 459FS, the "Twin-tailed Dragons", displayed a fanged dragon on each engine cowling with the tail extending along the Lightning's tail boom. *"Miss-V"* is the P-38J of leading CBI ace, Capt. Walter Duke who scored 10 victories. (USAF)

each engine cowling, and a tail that ran along each tail boom to the horizontal stabilizer.

When Chennault's son, LtCol. John "Jack," became the CO of the 343FG/11AF in the Aleutians he painted his 11FS P-40s with a Bengal tiger and 54FS P-38s with twin shark mouths.

Over the Solomons in 1942-43, the 347FG/67FS/13AF had P-400s and P-39Ds adorned with the shark mouth, as did the 8 and 35FG/5AF in the SWPA. The 347FG flew P-38Fs with the shark mouth off Henderson Field, Guadalcanal, as did the 39FS/35FG.

Milt Caniff and Al Capp/Disney

The 56FG had a number of Al Capp's characters on its P-47s. Capt. Eugene O'Neill (5 v.) is shown posing with the cartoon strip's leading character. (USAF)

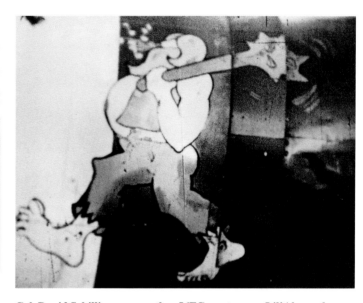

Col. David Schilling was another 56FG ace to use a Lil' Abner character *"Hairless Joe"* on his P-47. (USAF)

Walt Disney was personally supposed to have designed the "Flying Tiger" symbol, which was thought to be too cute by many of the AVG pilots and crew. (Author/Disney)

Col. Clinton "Casey" Vincent was the inspiration for Col. Vincent Casey in Milt Caniff's cartoon strip "Terry and the Pirates." Vincent was as large in life as in the comics. He was a 6-victory ace and at 29 became the second youngest general since the Civil War. (Author)

CHAPTER 22

Some Trivia

All in the Family

America has one father-son team who were aces. In WW1, 1Lt. Howard Burdick of Brooklyn flew a Sopwith Camel for the 17th Aero Squadron, which was initially attached to the RFC and subsequently to the USAS in September 1918. The elder Burdick scored eight victories from mid-September to late October 1918. Son 2Lt. Clinton D. flew P-51s with the 356FG/361FS/8AF. Young Burdick scored his first victory on 5 December 1944 and became an ace when he destroyed 2 1/2 Fi-156 German Army cooperation aircraft on 20 January 1945. He ended the war with 5 1/2 victories and three damaged.

Another father-son tandem was the Harold E. Hartneys, senior and junior. Hartney Sr. scored six victories with the RFC before being shot down. After recovering from his wounds, Maj. Hartney transferred to the USAS and became CO of the 27th Aero Squadron, which flew Sopwith Camels and scored an additional 1 1/2 victories in June 1918. Lt. Col. Hartney became CO of the 1st Pursuit Group in late August 1918. His son was a 2Lt. with the 56FG/62FS/8AF. He was credited with damaging a FW-190 on 8 May 1944 on a Ramrod mission over Berlin, on which he was KIA on 13 May when his fighter was hit by AA fire on an escort mission to Tutow and Politz.

Lt(jg) James French scored 11 victories with VF-9 off the carrier *Lexington* in WWII, while his father, Harold S. French, flew for the USAS with no claims and having survived being shot down.

Brig.Gen. Robin Olds was an ace in WWII with 13 victories and added four more in Vietnam. He was the son of Maj.Gen. Robert Olds, who commanded the first B-17 group, the 2BG, in mid-1937. The elder Olds developed a training system for the bomber and prepared it for its role as a strategic weapon over Germany.

There were many American brother combinations during WWII, but there were none in which both became aces. The Luftwaffe had several famous brother/ace combinations: the Galland

Harold Hartney Sr. scored 6 victories with the RFC before being wounded. He joined the USAS as the CO of the 27th Aero Squadron and destroyed an additional 1 1/2 victories in June 1918. His son, Harold Jr., was a 2Lt. with the 62FS/56FG and was credited for damaging a FW-190 before being KIA on 13 May 1944. (Author)

brothers, Adolf (103 v.), Wilhelm (55 v.), and Paul (17 v.); and the Moulders, Werner (115 v.) and Victor (17 v.). Maj. George Preddy was credited with 26 5/6 victories in the ETO for the 352FG before being KIA by friendly AA fire on Christmas Day 1944. His brother, William, flew for the 339FG/503FS. On 2 March 1945 he shot down a FW-190 and got a Me-109 probable. On 17 April he was last seen chasing a Me-262 jet near Prague. Both brothers were interred at the military cemetery at St. Avold, France.

On 12 January 1945 TF 38 was launching attacks against combined Vichy French and Japanese forces in Saigon, Indo China. VC-11 off the escort carrier *Nehenta Bay* (CVE-74) was flying CAP about 350 miles off the coast when a bogey approached the CVE.

The Burdicks were the only father-son team to become aces. 1Lt. Howard Sr. flew a Sopwith Camel for the 17th Aero Squadron and got 8 victories in September-October 1918. Son, 2Lt. Clinton, flew P-51s with the 361FS/356FG and is credited with 5 1/2 victories. (Author)

Lt(jg) James French scored 11 victories with VF-9 in WWII. His father, Harold, flew for the USAS with no claims and survived being shot down. (Author/French)

Brothers Lt(jg)s Grant and Alton Donnelly intercepted a Jake floatplane 13 miles from the carrier. The Jake, 2,000 feet above them, tried to dive away, but the brothers bracketed the hapless Jap and shared the victory, the only one for VC-11 in the war, and the only one by Navy brothers in the war.

Three sets of twins did some damage to enemy aircraft. 2Lt. Hugh Dow flew for the 350FG/346FS/12AF, flying a P-39 "*Rowdy II.*" Dow scored his group's first victory, downing a Me-109 and damaging another on 15 February 1943 over North Africa. Later, flying P-39s out of Sardinia, he destroyed another Me-109 over Italy on 6 April 1944. Meanwhile, twin brother Glenn was a B-24 co-pilot for the 464BG/15AF. After flying nine bomber missions and transferring to fighters he was scheduled to join Hugh, who was now flying P-47s. Hugh became a 22 year old major and squadron commander flying 247 missions. However, Hugh was shot down while strafing in Italy on 22 January 1945 and taken prisoner. Glenn joined the squadron several days later and checked out in the Thunderbolt. Glenn flew 51 missions, mostly in a ground support role. He was wounded in the leg on his 22nd mission by AA fire, but was flying again in two days. While in the Moosburg POW Camp, Hugh was joined there by other 350FG POWs and followed Glenn's ca-

The three Gallands were the most prolific brother combination in fighter history. Adolf (with trademark cigar) scored 103 victories and became the Luftwaffe's General of the Fighters. His brothers, Wilhelm (L) and Paul (R) scored 55 and 17 victories, respectively, for JG-26. (Author/West)

BGen. Robin Olds was an ace in WWII with 13 victories and added 4 more in Vietnam. He was the son of MGen. Robert Olds who commanded the first B-17 group and developed a training system for the bomber and prepared it for its role as strategic air weapon. The elder Olds is seen here with Gen. George C. Marshall in February 1938 as Olds was about to take a B-17 flight to Buenas Aires on a good will flight. (Author/Olds)

George Preddy was credited with 26 5/6 victories in the ETO for the 352FG before being KIA by friendly AA fire on Christmas Day 1944. His brother, William, flew for the 503FS/339FG and was credited with a FW-190 destroyed before he was MIA chasing a Me-262 near Prague on 2 March 1945. (USAF)

The Dow twins, Glenn (L) and Hugh (R). Hugh was credited with two victories and Glenn was a B-24 pilot before transferring to fighters. He was scheduled to join Hugh with the 350FG but Hugh was shot down and taken prisoner. Glenn was WIA and after recuperating joined his liberated POW brother on the last day of the war. They were headed for the Pacific in August 1945 when the war ended. (Author/ Blake)

reer. POW Hugh was liberated by Patton on 29 April and rejoined Glenn on 8 May, the last day of the war in Europe. On 1 August, they shipped out of Naples with the 350FG and headed for the Pacific, but on V-J Day they were passing through the Panama Canal.

The Pattilo twins, Charles ("Buck") and Cuthbert ("Bill"), joined the 352FG on 10 March 1945 as twenty year old 2nd Lieutenant replacement pilots. On 10 April Bill, flying for the 487FS, shot down a Me-262 jet. (researcher Steve Blake informs me that HS85 credits the victory to the wrong twin). On a strafing mission on 16 April, Bill was credited with six ground victories, while Buck got five. During the sortie, Bill's P-51 was hit by AA fire, and he was forced to crash land and was taken prisoner. Bill, thought to be dead by his brother, was repatriated and rejoined his brother on 17 May. After the war they remained in the Air Force and managed to be stationed together or nearby. They became members of the USAFE aerobatic team the "Skyblazers," and later organized and flew with the "Thunderbirds." They commanded fighter wings in

The Pattilo twins, Cuthbert ("Bill") on the wing and Charles ("Buck") in the cockpit, scored ground victories with the 352FG. Post war they flew for the USAFE aerobatic teams, the "Skyblazers" and organized and flew for the "Thunderbirds. Buck retired from the AF as a Lt. General and Bill as a Maj. General. (USAF)

The parents of 2Lt. Thomas White may have had a premonition as they gave him the middle name, Ace. He scored 6 P-38 victories for 97FS/82FG. (USAF)

F/O Robert Magel (L) destroyed a Me-109 for the 63FS/56FG but was shot down by AA fire and taken POW. Robert's twin brother, 2Lt. David (R), joined the 63FS/56FG and damaged a Me-109 before he was KIA in February 1945. (Author)

The McNickle twins, Marvin (top) and Melvin (R), held CO positions. LtCol. Marvin was CO of the 350FG and LtCol. Melvin was CO of the 78FG. (Author)

the SEA, and Buck retired as a Lt. General and Bill as a Maj. General.

F/O Robert Magel joined the 56FG/63FS in April 1944 and had a Me-109 victory on 4 July 1944. On 7 August he was shot down by AA fire and made a POW. The next day twin brother 2Lt. David joined the 63rd as a replacement pilot. He damaged a Me-109 on 2 December, but was KIA on a sweep by a Me-109 near Berlin on 3 February 1945. 63FS CO and 11 1/2 ace Maj. Paul Conger then shot down the Me-109.

A set of twins who made no claims but held fighter group CO positions were the McNickles brothers. Lt.Col. Marvin was CO of the 350FG (March-October 1943), and Lt.Col. Melvin became 78FG CO on 3 July 1943, but was shot down and made a POW on 30 July.

There were 11 fighter aces named Brown. The top-scoring Brown was Samuel J. (USAAF) with 15 1/2 victories in P-51s in the MTO. Of course, the Smiths were the most numerous, with 20 aces. Col. John Smith (USMC) was the top scoring Smith with 19 victories in F4Fs over Guadalcanal.

P-38 pilot Thomas White of the 97FS/82FG scored six victories in the MTO. White's parents must have had a premonition of their son's future, as they gave him the middle name, Ace.

Gray Beard, No Beard: Oldest and Youngest American Fighter Aces and Pilots

The cliched depiction of the fighter pilot is either of the seasoned veteran ("the old man") or the hotshot youngster ("the kid"). After Pearl Harbor the veteran career aviator bore the brunt of combat, fighting an experienced enemy who flew superior aircraft. The next generation of fighter pilot had attended or graduated from college as a requirement of acceptance to aviation cadet training. As American industry produced more and more aircraft and her involvement in the war expanded, the demand for pilots also increased. To meet this demand, educational and physical requirements were lowered, and the pilots were thus younger. They entered combat against an

The oldest USAF ace was nicknamed "Pappy." Lt. Col. John Herbst of 74FS/23FG became an ace on 6 August 1944 when he shot down two Oscars over China at 35 years, 11 months, 19 days. (Author/USAF)

LtCdr. Jimmy Thach (USNA 1927) of VF-3 off the *Lexington* was the oldest American ace. He scored four victories on 4 June 1944 to become an ace at 37 years, 1 month. (Author/USN)

enemy who had lost many of its skilled veteran pilots and were able to score quick, easy victories over younger, hastily trained enemy pilots flying aircraft which were now inferior to new American designs.

At least 12 Navy aces were over 30 years old when they scored their fifth victory. Of the top-scoring aces, most were graduated from or attended college for two or three years, including a number from the Naval Academy. Most of the early Navy aces, such as Jim Thach and Butch O'Hare, were career Navy. Future aces who enlisted after 1941 often encountered processing problems, and then faced an average of 15 months of training before being assigned to an operational squadron. Then it could easily be six months or more before the squadron saw combat. Thus, a great number of post-

Pearl Harbor enlistees would not become aces until the large naval battles beginning in the spring of 1944. It was unusual to find Navy aces under 22. The average age of the top navy aces was 26 years and one month. The youngest of these top aces was Arthur Hawkins, who was 21 years eight months, while top Navy ace David McCampbell was 34 1/2 when he became an ace. Another reason Navy aces tended to be older was that the more experienced (e.g. older) became air unit leaders, who did most of the shooting.

The oldest American ace was the formidable Lt.Cdr. John Thach (USNA 1927) of VF-3, off the *Lexington*. Thach was recognized as a great leader and tactician, developing the weaving beam defensive maneuver, which became known as the "Thach Weave." Born in Pine Bluff, AR, on 19 April 1905, Thach scored four victories on

MG Henry Hamilton flew F4Fs for VMF-223 and 212 and became an ace on 18 October 1942 at 34 years, 5 months, 20 days. Three days after becoming an ace, Hamilton was MIA over Guadalcanal. (Author/USMC)

Right: Charles Lindbergh flew in the Pacific as a civilian advisor to teach range extension. During this period he flew some 50 missions and at 42 years, 5 1/2 months claimed a Sonia to become the oldest American pilot, though unofficial one, to score a victory in WWII. Lindbergh is shown here with 38-victory ace Tom McGuire, in Hollandia, June 1944. (Author/USAF)

The world's oldest ace was probably Germany's Theo Osterkamp. "Uncle Theo" scored 32 victories for the German Imperial Navy in WWI and scored six more as CO of JG-51 in 1940 at the age of 48. (Author/West)

1Lt. Van Chandler (L) of the 336FS/4FG was the youngest ace in US service at 19 years, 10 months, 4 days on 7 January 1945. Chandler later claimed three more victories over Korea flying F-86s for the 51FIW. (Author)

4 June 1942 to become an ace at 37 years, one month, and 15 days. McCampbell (USNA 1933) was 34 years, six months when he downed five Judys and two Zekes on 19 June 1944 during the Marianas Turkey Shoot. Cdr. Daniel Smith (USNA 1932) with 6 1/2 victories with VF-20 was 34 1/2 when he became an ace by shooting down a Tony over Manila on 14 November 1944.

The Marine Corps aces were Navy-trained, but because they were in combat over Guadalcanal in late 1942 they were somewhat younger on average than the Navy aces at slightly over 25 years. Capt. Joe Foss (VMF-121), highest-ranking USMC ace with 26 victories, was nearly 31, 1Lt. Ken Walsh (VMF-124), 21 victories, was 26 1/2, Capt. Don Aldrich (VMF-215), 20 victories, was nearly 26, Capt. John Smith (VMF-223), 19 victories, was nearly 31, and Capt. Marion Carl (VMF-223), 18 1/2 victories, was almost 27. But 1Lt. Bob Hanson (VMF-215), 25 victories, was 23 years, 8 months, 1Lt. Wilbur "Gus" Thomas (VMF-211), 18 1/2 victories, was 22 years, 8 months, and 1Lt. Ed Shaw (VMF-213), 14 1/2 vic-

tories, was 23 years, 5 months. The oldest Marine ace was MG Henry Hamilton of VMF-223 and 212. While flying a F4F Wildcat he downed two Zeros on 18 October 1942 to become an ace. Born in Bremand, TX, on 29 May 1908, he was 34 years, five months, and 20 days old when he became an ace. Three days later he was MIA over Guadalcanal. Lt.Col. Joe Bauer, CO of VMF-212, 11 victories, was 34 years, 21 days when he became an ace on 3 October 1942 when he shot down four Zeros over Guadalcanal. He was KIA on 14 November 1942 and received a posthumous Medal of Honor for his one and a half months of combat there.

The Air Force's top aces were the youngest of the three services at 24 years, 7 months. Its top pilot/leaders, the "old men" Maj. Don Blakeslee (4FG-14 1/2 victories) and Col. "Hub" Zemke (56FG and 479FG-17 3/4 victories) were relatively young at 29 years, 6 1/2 months and 26 years, 4 months, respectively. The top four AAF aces: Dick Bong (49FG-40 victories) and Maj. Tommy McGuire (475FG-38 victories) in the Pacific; and Col. "Gabby"

1Lt. Chris Hanseman (C) of the 505FS/339FG was the first USAAF teen age ace and second youngest at 19 years, 10 months, 23 days on 21 May 1944. Hanseman was KIA on 9 July 1944 was strafing. (USAF)

1Lt. Dale Karger (R) of the 364FS/364FG has often been considered the youngest ace but was the third ranking teenage ace at 19 years, 11 months and 25 days on 20 January 1945. (Author/Karger)

The youngest Navy ace was Ens. Jack Berkheimer of VF(N)-41 off the *Independence* when he became an ace on 24 October 1944, at 20 years, 2 months, 24 days. Berkheimer was killed in a mid-air collision on 6 December 1944. ((Author/AFAA)

The youngest American ace did not fly for his country. P/O Claude Weaver flew Spitfire Vs over Malta for the RCAF. On 23 July 1942, he became an ace at 18 years, 10 months, 5 days. Weaver scored 12 1/2 victories before being KIA in late January 1945. (Author/RCAF)

Gabreski (56FG-28 victories) and 1Lt/ Bob Johnson (56FG-27 victories) in the ETO, were all in their 23rd year when they became aces. The "old" aces in the ETO, Maj. George Preddy (352FG-26 5/6 victories), Lt.Col. John Meyers (352FG-26 victories), and Lt.Col. Dave Schilling (56FG-22 1/2 victories) were all in their 25th year.

The Air Force's oldest ace was Lt.Col. John "Pappy" Herbst, who joined the RCAF, where he earned his wings. He was sent to the United Kingdom, and when America entered the war he was transferred to the USAAF, where he served as a flight instructor. He finally entered combat at the end of May 1944 when he was assigned to the 23FG/74FS in the CBI, where he flew P-40s and P-51s. On 6 August 1944 he became an ace when he shot down two Oscars over Hengyang, China, at the age of 35 years, 11 months, and 19 days. Col. Robert Scott of *God Is My Co-Pilot* fame graduated from West Point in 1932, and by Pearl Harbor he was considered too old at 33 to become a fighter pilot. He managed to meet Gen. Claire Chennault in Burma and flew "guest missions" with

the Flying Tigers. When the AVG disbanded on 4 July 1942, Scott became CO of its offspring, the 23FG. On 25 September 1942 he became an ace when he shot down an I-45 fighter at the age of 34 years, 5 months, and 13 days.

Col. Edward Anderson was 39 when he shot down two Me-109s (his only victories) for the 4FG on 28 July 1943. Lt.Cdr. LeRoy Simpler of VF-5 off the *Yorktown* was also 39 when he scored his only victory of the war, a Zero, in October 1942. Flying Tiger Wingman Louis Hoffman, of 1 AVG Squadron, was the "old man" at 43 when he flew combat for Chennault and damaged a Japanese aircraft in December 1941.

Charles Lindbergh flew in the Pacific as a civilian advisor in the late Spring and through the summer of 1944. He had been contracted by the War Department to teach range extension by utilizing proper cruise control. On one mission it was noted that he was straggling behind because he had not retracted his landing gear. Radio silence was finally broken with: "OK, Lindy, that's not the *Spirit of St. Louis*" you're flying. Get that gear up!" During this period Lindbergh flew along on some 50 combat missions in AAF P-38s and Marine Corps F4Us. Most of the missions were uncontested strafing and escort missions. On 27 July 1944, he engaged in aerial combat while flying P-38s with the 475FG under 27-victory ace Charles McDonald. At 42 years, 5 1/2 months Lindbergh claimed a Sonia to become the oldest American pilot, though an unofficial one, to score a victory in WWII.

Capt. Henry Cook was an ace in WWI with seven victories (four balloons) while flying with Eddie Rickenbacker's 94th "Hat-in-the-Ring" Squadron. He was a pioneer airmail pilot in the 1920s, and was in the Army Air Corps until 1928. He was recalled to active duty in 1942 as a colonel. There is no record of Cook flying combat before he was killed in a crash on 25 March 1943 while flying a P-40 over New Zealand at the age of 50+.

West Point graduate (1943) Maj. Robin Olds became an ace one month after his 22nd birthday when he shot down three Me-109s while flying a P-38 on 25 August 1944. He went on to score eight more victories in WWII for the 479FG. Twenty-three years later Col. Olds was flying F-4 Phantoms over Vietnam for the 8TWF.

1Lt. Bill Hood (VMF-323) was the youngest Marine Corps aces when he shot down two Vals over Okinawa on 28 April 1945, just nine days short of his twenty-first birthday. (Author/Brandon)

In 1967, at the age of 45, Olds added two separate MIG-17 victories (2 January and 4 May) and a double on 20 May.

The oldest ace was probably Germany's Theo Osterkamp—"Uncle Theo"—who was born in April 1892. He scored 32 victories with the Imperial German Navy in WWI and won the Pour le Merite. Twenty-two years later, at the age of 48, he scored six more victories in 1940 as CO of JG-51. The most successful "old" Luftwaffe ace was Maj. Peter Werfft, who scored his first victories in the Battle of Britain with JG-27 at the age of 37. He continued to fly (and live) to the end of the war, scoring 26 victories (12 four engine) despite being wounded on six occasions. Oberst Johann Schalk of ZG-26 scored 21 victories (10 in the West) while in his late 30s and early 40s. Lt. Alexander von Winterfeldt was an ace with nine victories at 43 years old. Oberst Friedrich Vollbracht scored two victories in WWI and two more in WWII as a 43-year old Zerstorer pilot.

As previously discussed, in early WWII because of the more rigid physical and educational entrance requirements and more demanding training regimen, most pilots entering operations were in the 22 to 24 year old range. However, as the war intensified many young men just out of high school became eligible for pilot training. Due to accelerated processing, and to a lesser extent facilitated training, these new pilots entered combat sooner than their predecessors did. Being assigned to newly formed units or being replacement pilots also moved them into combat earlier. Operationally, there were more opportunities to engage and score against an enemy who was now less skilled and flew in inferior aircraft.

The youngest ace in U.S. service was 1Lt. Van Chandler, who was born on 5 March 1925. He became pilot-rated in early January 1944. He was assigned to the 4FG/336FS flying P-51s, scoring his first victory on 12 September. He became an ace on 7 January 1945 when he shot down a Me-109 over Ulzen. He was 19 years, 10 months, and 4 days. Maj. Chandler went on to claim three more victories flying F-86s for the 51FIW in Korea. While Chandler was the youngest pilot to become an ace, he was the third teenager to become an ace.

1Lt. Chris Hanseman was born on 2 August 1924. He became commissioned and pilot-rated in November 1943. He was assigned to the 339FG/505FS and made his first claims on 21 May 1944 when he scored 2 1/2 victories. He became an ace at 19 years, 10 months, and 23 days when he shot down a Me-109 on 10 June 1944 to become the first teenage ace and second youngest. He was KIA on 9 July 1944, hitting the ground while strafing.

1Lt. Dale Karger was born on 14 February 1925 and is sometimes credited with being the only or youngest teenage ace (e.g. *Fighter Aces of the USA*, Toliver and Constable). He was commissioned in early February 1944, and by September was flying P-51 bomber escort missions with the 364FG/364FS in the ETO. He scored his first victory on 5 December over a FW 190 near Berlin. On 20 January 1945 Karger flew a bomber escort mission to Munich, and while strafing a Luftwaffe airdrome he shot down a Me-262 jet. He was America's third teenage ace at 19 years, 11 months, and 25 days.

The youngest American ace did not fly for America. P/O Claude Weaver was born on 18 August 1923 in Oklahoma City, OK. Before he finished high school he enlisted in the RCAF on 13 February 1941 and received his wings on 10 October 1941. He was assigned to the 185 squadron, which flew Spitfire Vs defending Malta. He became an ace within a week after scoring his first victory. On 23 July 1942 he shot down two Me-109s. He was 18 years, 10 months, and 5 days at the time. After 10 1/2 victories over Malta, on 9 September 1942 he was forced down on Sicily and held prisoner by the Italians. One year later he escaped and returned to combat with the 403 Squadron in England. He claimed two additional victories before he was KIA on 28 January 1945.

Ens. Jack Berkheimer was a F6F Hellcat pilot with the Navy's VF(N)-41 night fighter squadron off the *Independence*. He shot down his first enemy aircraft on 12 September 1944, only 43 days after his twentieth birthday. He scored his fifth victory on 24 October at 20 years, 2 months, and 24 days to become the Navy's youngest ace. Berkheimer had 7 1/2 victories when he was killed in a mid-air collision on 6 December 1944.

1Lt. William Hood of VMF-323 became the Marine Corps' youngest ace on 28 April 1945 by shooting down two Vals over Izena Shima during the hectic air fighting over Okinawa to give him 5 1/2 victories for the war. He was just nine days short of his twenty-first birthday.

A remarkable teenage pilot was Luftwaffe ace, Lt. Hans Strelow, who was born on 26 March 1922. He joined II/JG-51 in the Spring of 1941 just as he turned 19. He shot down his first enemy over Russia, a DB-3 bomber, on 25 June 1941, and by his twentieth birthday had been credited with 66 victories. He was the youngest Knight's Cross of the Iron Cross recipient, and two days short of his twentieth birthday was awarded Oak Leaves to the Knight's Cross. He went off operations for a short time, but returned as CO of 5 Staffel. On 22 May 1942 he shot down a Pe-2 for his 68th victory, but was forced down behind Russian lines. He reportedly committed suicide rather than be captured by the Russians.

The Japanese used many teenage pilots at the end of the war, but the majority were ill-trained kamikaze pilots. It is possible that some teenage Japanese pilots scored victories or became aces, but Japanese records were mostly sketchy or destroyed.

Lt. Hans Strelow joined II/JG-51 in Spring 1941 as he just turned 19. By his 20th birthday he had scored 66 victories and was the youngest recipient of Oak Leaves to his Knight's Cross. (Author/West)

Navy ace and Hollywood star Wayne Morris, as Lt. Bert (his given name) Morris scored 7 victories flying a F6F for VF-15. (USN)

Matinee idol Robert Taylor, seen here in 1944 at NAS Livermore in a Navy recruiting shot, became fighter qualified but spent the war in a PR capacity. (USN)

Movie Star Ace Wayne Morris

Clark Gable's stint as a B-17 aerial gunner on a few 351BG missions was well publicized during the war. Jimmy Stewart piloted B-24s for the 2nd Air Division in England. Robert Taylor trained as a Navy fighter pilot, but did PR and film work, notably the narration for the award-winning aircraft carrier documentary "Fighting Lady." But an ace in the true Hollywood tradition was Wayne Morris, born Bert DeWayne Morris. He debuted in 1936 in "China Clipper" and had his big hit the next year in "Kid Gallahad," with Edward G. Robinson and Bette Davis. By mid-1941 Morris had 27 film credits when he was commissioned in the Navy. After doing initial PR work Morris went to flight school, joining VF-15, which was commanded by Morris' wife's uncle, Cdr. David McCampbell, who was to become the top Navy ace.

VF-15 was assigned to the *Essex*, where Lt. Morris scored his first victory over a Mavis flying boat on 11 June 1944 while on CAP over the Marianas. During the first carrier strikes on the Philippines in September, Morris had accumulated four victories. On a

Actor Wayne Morris and his squadron man their planes in the Battle of Midway sequence in the Warner Brothers film "Task Force," which starred Gary Cooper. Here the *Antietam* substitutes for the *Yorktown*. (Warner Brothers)

mid-day sweep on 10 October over Yonton A/D, Okinawa, Morris became an ace by downing a Tony. During the Battle of Leyte Gulf, Morris led two Hellcat divisions to intercept Japanese bombers heading toward the Task Force. In the ensuing battle Morris got his final victories of the war, two Zekes. He was awarded three DFCs and two Air Medals and left the Navy as a Lt. Commander to resume his Hollywood career.

After the war Morris returned to Hollywood, making 33 movies and a number of TV appearances. In 1949 Morris starred with Gary Cooper in the Warner Brother's film "Task Force," which followed the naval career of Jonathan Scott (Cooper) from fledgling aviator aboard the *Langley* to Captain of the *Franklin*. Morris played Cooper's right hand man (McKinney) in the air group. The film was critically reviewed as one of the most authentic war films ever made, and became one of the highest grossing war films. In his last film in 1958 he appeared as the villain in the critically acclaimed WWI film "Paths of Glory."

In mid-September 1959 Morris sailed on the carrier *Bon Homme Richard*, commanded by Captain David McCampbell, to observe maneuvers. While on the bridge he suffered a massive heart attack, dying at the age of 45.

Aces Attack the Sound Barrier

Chuck Yeager

Of aviation's icons, Chuck Yeager ranks with Jimmy Doolittle and Charles Lindburgh. Yeager became a legend as the test pilot who became the first to break the sound barrier in the Bell X-1. Two days before the record breaking flight, Yeager and his wife went to Pancho Barnes ranch for dinner and horseback riding afterward. On their return from their ride Yeager hit the locked corral gate at full gallop and was thrown off. The next morning, in severe pain, knowing that a military doctor might ground him, he visited a civilian doctor. The doctor found that he had broken two ribs and taped them. The next day, 14 October 1947, Yeager painfully dropped down into the Bell X-1 he named *"Glamorous Glennis"* after his wife. At 1036 the rocket aircraft was dropped from the bomb bay of

Chuck Yeager was an 11 1/2 victory ace flying a P-51 for the 363FS/357FG and is seen here with the Bell X-1, named *"Glamorous Glennis"* after his wife. On 14 October 1947, the rocket-powered X-1 hit Mach 1.06 to break the sound barrier for the first time. (USAF)

a B-29 over California's Mojave desert, and several minutes into the 14 minute flight, at 43,000 feet, the rocket aircraft hit mach 1.06 (700mph) for 20.5 seconds. On the ground, observers heard the double sonic boom marking the landmark, but in the *"Glamorous Glennis"* there was none of the expected violent buffeting or battering of the pilot, and the actual event was somewhat anti-climatic.

However, the Yeager legend began several years before in a P-51 over Europe. The West Virginia farm boy who could shoot a squirrel between the eyes joined the Army Reserves in mid-September 1941 and received his wings as a F/O on 10 March 1943 at Luke Field, AZ. He went to England with the 363FS/357FG at the end of December 1943. He scored his first victory on 4 March 1944 over a Me-109 and damaged a He-111. The next day he was bounced by a FW-190 and shot down over Wittenburg. He was picked up by the French Underground and evaded over the snow-covered Pyrennes Mountains into Spain, and returned to his unit on 27 May. Normally, a pilot who evaded would not be allowed to return to combat so as not to compromise his escape route and underground members. However, Yeager appealed directly to Gen. Eisenhower and was able to return to combat as the area of his escape was recaptured. He scored a half victory over a Me-109 on 13 September. On a bomber escort on 12 October he spotted 22 Me-109s and, having the sun advantage, became an ace in a day when he downed five Me-109s in a running air battle from Steinhuder Lake to Hanover. On 6 November he attacked three Me-262 jet fighters coming in for a landing at 500 feet. Using high deflection shots he damaged two and destroyed another. Yeager concluded his WWII scoring in a big way on 27 November. During a bomber escort to Madgeburg he shot down four FW-190s to claim 11 1/2 victories for the war.

Marion Carl

Unlike Chuck Yeager, Marion Carl was more well known as a WWII ace than as a post war test pilot. Flying with VMF-221 over Mid-

way he shot down a Zero and damaged two others on 4 June 1942. He joined John Smith's VMF-223 on Guadalcanal in August 1942. Flying the F4F Wildcat, he became the first USMC ace on 24 August 1942 when he shot down a Zero and three Japanese bombers. Before his tour ended in October he had scored 16 1/2 victories there. In December 1943 he took command of VMF-223 and flew F4U Corsairs, and claimed two more victories during the reduction of Rabaul to give him 18 1/2 victories.

It was after the war that Carl became the consummate American aviator, a record-setting test pilot who flew more than 260 different aircraft types, including 30 different X (experimental) models, logging 14,000 hours over four decades. He flew the first Marine helicopter, was instrumental in forming the Marines' first jet squadrons and carrying out the first jet carrier operations, and later led the first jet aerobatic teams. He spent 5 1/2 years as a test pilot and four years as the Chief test pilot for all carrier types. On 25 August 1947 he flew the Douglas Skystreak to a world speed record of 650.6 mph. On 21 August 1953 he flew the Douglas Skyrocket (D-558-2) to a world altitude record of 83,235 feet. He retired as the Inspector General of the Marine Corps. Carl died as he lived. At 83 years old, he confronted a drug addled intruder who had kicked in the door of his home. Carl was shot in the head and killed trying to protect his wife, who was also shot, but survived.

Marion Carl was better known as an 18 1/2 victory Marine ace than a post war test pilot. Carl flew more than 260 aircraft types including 30 X-planes logging 14,000 hours. He flew the Douglas Skystreak to a world speed record on August 1947 and the Douglas Skyrocket to a world altitude in 1953. (Author/Carl)

George Welch got the first US victory of WW-2 over Pearl Harbor and went on to score 16 victories. He was a test pilot in the XP-86/F-86 program and became the second man through the sound barrier and the first from take off to landing. He was killed in 1954 testing the F-100 Super Sabre. (USAF)

George Welch

George Welch scored America's first victories over Pearl Harbor when he downed four Japanese aircraft flying the P-40. He scored three P-39 victories for the 36FS/8FG and then nine more in the P-38 for the 8FG to give him 16 victories for the war.

In 1944 he joined North American Aviation as chief test pilot and flew the first test of the P-82B Twin Mustang at the end of October 1945. In October 1947 Welch was assigned to the F-86 Sabre jet program. Designated the XP-86, Welch flew the first of three prototypes on 1 October 1947 when the nose landing gear failed to extend fully on the landing approach. On touching down, Welch was able to keep the nose high and bounce the gear to full extension and land safely. On 26 April 1948 Welch dove the XP-86 past Mach 1 to make it the second aircraft to pass through the sound barrier and the first aircraft to go through it from ground take off to landing. It was the first Western combat aircraft to exceed Mach 1.

After American Ace of Aces, Richard Bong, returned home he joined Lockheed to test their troubled P-80 jet fighter. On 6 August 1945, the fighter experienced mechanical problems and crashed after take off. The photo shows the wide spread wreckage. (Lockheed)

In December 1949 Welch test flew the YF-86D prototypes that would lead to the F-86D, which set a number of successive world speed records just exceeding 700mph.

On 25 January 1950 Welch initially flight-tested the YF-93A, which was dead-ended by the Pentagon. He then moved back to the YF-100A Super Sabre program, which was a continuation of the F-86 program. On 25 May 1953 Welch flew the TF-100 prototype and hit Mach 1.1 on the first flight. Although supersonic speed was not unusual at this time, it was for level flight. On 12 October 1954, Welch was test flying the ninth production F-100A Super Sabre and dove from 45,000 feet to check a tail design problem. The aircraft suddenly sideslipped during a rolling pull out from Mach 1.5. The extremely powerful maneuver caused the aircraft to disintegrate, killing Welch, who did eject but was fatally injured.

Dick Bong

After American Ace of Aces Richard Bong was pulled from combat after scoring 40 victories and winning the Congressional Medal of Honor he returned to the U.S. on New Year's Day 1945. He married his long time sweetheart, Marge Vattendahl, on 10 February. and after a California honeymoon he joined the Air Technical Service Command at Wright Field to complete ground school on jet flight for two months. He joined Lockheed Aircraft as a test pilot on their troubled P-80 jet fighter program. Between 7 July and 6 August he flew 11 test flights for four hours flight time. At 1430, 6 August, he took off from Lockheed Air Terminal on a routine acceptance flight. As the aircraft rose to 300-400 feet the engine cut out and then cut back in. Bong tried to turn the P-80. but the Allison J33 cut out again. The fighter went into a steep dive and crashed in a flaming collision into the ground. Some witnesses claimed that Bong tried to get out of the cockpit before contact with the ground. and even that he steered the aircraft away from nearby houses. The cause of the accident has been attributed to pilot error in engine or control settings. but officially to have been caused by engine failure.

Frank Everest

1Lt. Frank Everest flew 96 P-40 missions in the MTO with the 314FS/324FG/9AF. On 18 April 1943, a large fleet of Ju-52s were on a supply mission to Rommel's Afrika Korps in North Africa when they were intercepted over the Gulf of Tunis. Everest shot down two Ju-52 transports and damaged another as part of the 22 Ju-52s destroyed by the 314th that day. Everest then served another combat tour in the CBI in the P-40 and then the P-51 as the CO of the 29FS/5FG/CACW. He did not score any victories. but was a strafing ace with five ground victories. On 15 May 1945 his fighter was hit by ground fire while strafing boats on the Yangtze River. Everest bailed out and evaded for a time before he was taken prisoner and sent to Peiping. where he was freed when the war ended.

After the war Everest was selected to attend test pilot school and spent some time at Wright Field and Muroc. In the spring of 1949 Everest was part of a team assigned to explore the Bell X-1's high altitude capabilities and flew 10 test flights. On 25 July he took the X-1 to a record 66,846 feet, and then to another record at 71,902 feet on 8 August. On 25 August the X-1 lost pressure, and

Although not an ace, Frank Everest did score two victories in the MTO with the 324FG and was a strafing ace with the CACW. After the war Everest set altitude and speed records in the Bell X-1. (Bell)

the first emergency use of a partial suit saved his life. On 22 August 1951, while testing the Bell X-1D he was forced to eject when an explosion struck the aircraft's tail. In 1952, Everest was named the Chief Test Pilot for the Bell X-2 program. He took the aircraft through its glide trials and first powered flights. On 23 July 1956 he set a world's unofficial speed record of mach 2.87 (1,900 mph). Everest also served on the X-3 (two flights), X-4 (four flights), and X-5 (six flights) programs.

"For Bravery," U.S. WWII Aviation Decorations

The Military Aviator's Badge, which recognized "courage and ability to complete hazardous qualification tests in military aviation," was the first decoration for military pilots, being authorized on 27 May 1913. The 14kt. gold medal was awarded to 14 officers who were then on duty with the Signal Corps. One of these officers was to become the Commanding General of the AAF in WWII, Gen. (then Lt.) H.H. "Hap" Arnold.

Acts of notable valor, military achievement in action, wounds received in action, and honorable service over a period of years were recognized by the President who, through the War Department, awarded appropriate decorations. Units, organizations and detachments, as well as individual airmen were cited for outstanding accomplishments. When a unit was cited, all members wore the award on the right breast pocket. Two awards were bestowed specifically for valor in air combat: the Distinguished Flying Cross and Air Medal. None of the decorations could be issued more than once to any one person, except the posthumous award of the Purple Heart. No one could receive more than one Medal of Honor, Distinguished Service Cross, Silver Star, Distinguished Flying Cross, or Air Medal. But in the AAF, for each succeeding act to justify the same award a bronze oak leaf cluster was given. One silver oak leaf was authorized for wear instead of five bronze oak leaf clusters. In the Navy, a gold star worn on a ribbon attached to the medal marked multiple awards.

Relative ranking of service awards (date authorized and date revised):

ARMY AIR FORCE	Year	NAVY/MARINE CORPS	Year
Medal of Honor	1862	Medal of Honor	1862
(CMH)	1904		1904
	1944		1944
Distinguished Service Cross (DSC)	1918	Navy Cross Marine Corps Brevet Medal	1919
Silver Star (SS)	1918	Silver Star	1918
	1932		
	1932		
Distinguished Flying Cross (DFC)	1926	Distinguished Flying Cross	1926
Air Medal (AM)	1942	Air Medal	1942
Purple Heart (PH)	1782	Purple Heart	1782
	1932		1932
	1942		1942
Distinguished Service Medal (DSM)	1918	Distinguished Service Medal	1918
Legion of Merit (LM)	1944	Legion of Merit	1944
Bronze Star (BS)	1944	Navy & Marine Medal	1942
Presidential Unit Citation (PUC)	1942	Presidential Unit Citation	1942

Congressional Medal of Honor (CMH)

The Congressional Medal of Honor was established during the Civil War (1862) with the 1904 design worn in WWII either as a breast medal or hung by the neck ribbon. In 1944, a redesigned neck ribbon version was authorized. The medal was awarded in the name of Congress, often by the President, to an officer or enlisted man "who in actual conflict with the enemy, distinguished himself conspicuously by gallantry and intrepidity at the risk of his life above and beyond the call of duty."

Apart from the great honor which the CMH imparted on the recipient, he was entitled to free available military air transport on or off active duty. Enlisted recipients were given $2 a month extra pay, and upon reaching 65 the medal holder received an extra $10 per month. However, many recipients were awarded their medal posthumously.

Fighter pilots who received the CMH in WWII were:
Lt.Col. Harold Bauer (USMC) * 1Lt. Raymond Knight (AAF) *
Maj. Richard Bong (AAF) * Cdr. David McCampbell (USN)
Maj. Gregory Boyington (USMC) Maj. Thomas McGuire (AAF) *
Capt. Jefferson DeBlanc (USMC) Lt. Edward O'Hare (USN) *
Capt. Joseph Foss (USMC) Maj. William Shomo (AAF)
Maj. Robert Galer (USMC) Maj. John Smith (USMC)
1Lt. Robert Hanson (USMC) * 1Lt. James Swett (USMC)
Lt.Col. James Howard (AAF) 1Lt. Ken Walsh (USMC)
(* died in WWII)

Medal of Honor (CMH)

LtCol. Joseph Bauer (USMC/posthumous) on 11 May 1946. (USMC)

Maj. Richard Bong (USAF) from Gen. Douglas MacArthur on 12 December 1944. (USAF)

Maj. Gregory Boyington (USMC) from President Harry Truman after release from Japanese POW camp, 5 October 1945. (USMC)

1Lt. Jefferson DeBlanc (Author/DeBlanc) with wife from President Harry Truman on 6 December 1946. (USMC)

Capt. Joseph Foss (USMC) from FDR with mother on 18 May 1943. (USMC)

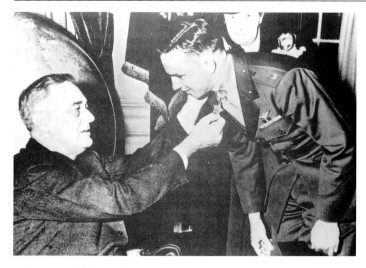

Maj. Robert Galer (USMC) from FDR on 24 March 1943. (USMC)

Col. Neel Kearby (USAF), shown here with Gen. George Kenney, was awarded the CMH on 20 January 1944 by Gen. Douglas MacArthur. (USAF)

1Lt. Robert Hanson (USMC/ posthumous) to mother on 1 November 1943 by MGen. Lewis Merritt. (USMC)

Cdr. David McCampbell (USN) from FDR with mother on 10 January 1945. (USN)

Col. James Howard (USAF) awarded the CMH by Gen. Carl Spaatz on 11 January 1944. (USAF/Howard)

Maj. Thomas McGuire (USAF), seen in an earlier awards ceremony, was awarded the CMH posthumously by Gen. George Kenney on 8 May 1946. (USAF)

LtCdr. Edward "Butch" O'Hare (USN) with wife by FDR on 21 April 1942. (USN)

Maj. William Shomo from Gen. Ennis Whitehead on 3 April 1945. (Author/Shomo)

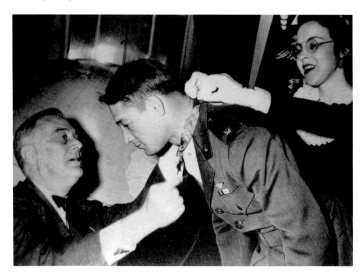

Col. John Smith (USMC) with wife from FDR on 24 February 1943. (USMC)

1Lt. Kenneth Walsh with wife from FDR on 8 February 1944. (Author/Walsh)

Capt. James Swett (USMC) from Gen. Ralph Mitchell, CO Marine Corps Aviation, on 9 October 1943. (Author/Swett)

Ken Walsh Congressional of Medal of Honor Society Membership card. (Author/Walsh)

Distinguished Service Cross/Army.
(DSC)

2Lt. George Welch receives the first DSC of WWII from FDR at the White House on 25 May 1942. Welch was recommended for the CMH for his four victories over Pearl Harbor but was denied as he took off without orders! (USAF)

Distinguished Service Cross (DSC)

The Distinguished Service Cross (DSC), authorized in 1918, was the Air Force's second highest award for valor involving extraordinary risk to one's life while in action with the enemy. The first aviator recipient of the DSC was 1Lt. George Welch of the 47 PS, who won both the DSC and DFC for his four victories over Pearl Harbor. Lts. Ken Taylor and Gordon Sterling (posthumously) were both awarded the DSC for the same action.

Navy Cross

The Navy Cross, established in 1919, was the Navy's second highest decoration awarded to Navy pilots for bravery. The first Navy Cross winner in WWII was Lt. Clarence Dickenson, who downed a Zero and carried out scouting patrols over Pearl Harbor in a SBD for VS-6. Lt(jg) Perry Teaff also won the Navy Cross that day carrying out a search mission in a damaged aircraft.

Silver Star

The Silver Star was authorized in 1918 and revised in 1932 for acts of distinguished gallantry in combat not warranting the CMH, DSC, or Navy Cross.

Distinguished Flying Cross (DFC)

The Distinguished Flying Cross was authorized in 1926 and awarded retroactively to 1917. It could be awarded for heroic acts or meritorious achievements in flight, not necessarily in combat.

Distinguished Service
Cross/Navy. (DSC)

Silver Star (SS)

Navy Cross (NC) and Distinguished Flying Cross (DFC)

Air Medal (AM)

The Air Medal was created in 1932 and was awarded for valor, and in the first 18 months of the war for meritorious achievement in an aerial fight.

The DFC and AM

The DFC was authorized in 1926 and the AM in 1932, and in the first year and a half of the war were awarded automatically following the completion of a specified number of operational sorties and/ or air victories. On 29 November 1942 the following crireria were set:

For Aerial Victories Award

1st E/A Destroyed	AM
2nd E/A Destroyed	OLC (worn on AM Ribbon)
3rd E/A Destroyed	2nd OLC (worn on AM Ribbon)
4th E/A Destroyed	3rd OLC (worn on AM Ribbon)
5th E/A Destroyed	DFC
10th E/A Destroyed	OLC (worn on DFC Ribbon)
15th E/A Destroyed	2nd OLC (worn on DFC Ribbon)

For Sorties Completed Award

10 Sorties	AM
20 Sorties	OLC (worn on AM Ribbon)
50 Sorties	DFC

Gen. H.H. Arnold was reportedly unhappy with the system of awarding the DFC and AM. From 14 August 1943 he ordered a change in the award criteria for the DFC, in particular so that it must be "evidenced by voluntary action in the face of great danger above and beyond the call of duty in aerial flight. The results of achievement while participating in aerial flight was so exceptional and outstanding so as to clearly set the perpetrator apart from other aircrew who have not been so recognized." Subsequently, the DFC was awarded after recommendation (not nomination) for "extraordinary achievements or acts of heroism." The AM generally continued to be awarded (issued) primarily for individual acts or sustained operational activities not warranting the DFCs. The AM was awarded about ten times more frequently than the DFC. Capt. Clyde East, F-6 recon pilot for 5TRS with 13 victories, was awarded a record 42 AMs, along with four DFCs and a SS in his career in the Air Force ending in 1965. Maj. James Hill, five victory P-47 ace of the 365FG, had 39 AMs, four DFCs, and a PH before retiring in 1980. Col. Francis Gabreski, 28 victory ace in WWII and 6 1/2 victory ace in Korea, was awarded 13 DFCs, two SS, and seven AMs in his career.

Purple Heart

George Washington originally established the Purple Heart in 1782 for valor. The inactive medal was resurrected in 1932 as an award for meritorious service, and in 1942 it was decreed that the medal be given to any personnel (civilians were eligible) wounded in action against the enemy, or as the result of acts of the enemy provided such wound necessitates treatment by a medical officer. Oak Leaf clusters were awarded for wounds. The Purple Heart could be awarded posthumously.

Capt. Clyde East was awarded a record 42 Air Medals in his Air Force career that ended in 1965. (Author)

During WWII 506,000 Purple Hearts were struck. Because of the great losses sustained on Iwo Jima and Okinawa the greatest production occurred in 1945 prior to the anticipated invasion of Japan, which was expected to cause not only huge American, but also Japanese military and civilian casualties. In 1942, the Navy had ordered 135,000 Purple Hearts for the entire war, but needed 25,000 more in October 1944 and 50,000 more in spring 1945. The mint was unable to fulfill their 1945 request, and the Navy needed to borrow 60,000 from the Army. Many additional Purple Hearts were immediately ordered to be struck to satisfy the needs of the looming invasion of the Japanese Homeland. When the war was unexpectedly ended by the Atomic Bombs dropped on Hiroshima and Nagasaki there was a wonderful surplus of 495,000 Purple Hearts. Despite 49,051 American dead and wounded, 110,000 Japanese, and 150,000 civilians dead on Okinawa, post war revisionists need to represent the Japanese as victims of an unnecessary atomic massacre. They point out that American politicians and military hierarchy, as an excuse for dropping the Atomic Bombs, fabricated the enormous projected casualty figures for the invasion after the war. But these projected casualty figures were determined long before the very top secret A-bombs were dropped, as the unused 495,000 Purple Hearts testify.

Bronze Star (BSM)

The Bronze Star was created in 1944 by the AAF for heroic or meritorious achievement *not* involving aerial combat and not warranting the Silver Star or Legion of Honor, but must have been achieved in direct combat or in support of combat *on the ground*. The Navy or Marine Medals, established in 1942, were awarded for heroism in *non-combat* action only.

Distinguished Service Cross (DSC)/Legion of Merit (LM)

The Distinguished Service Cross, authorized in 1918, was the highest medal given for exceptional meritorious service to the government and was almost exclusively awarded to General Officers. The Legion of Merit, authorized in 1942, was the second highest award for meritorious conduct or the performance of outstanding service by officers and enlisted men. It was also awarded to foreign personnel in several different degrees unavailable to U.S. citizens.

Distinguished Service Medal (DSM)

The Distinguished Service Medal, authorized in 1918, was awarded to persons in any capacity who distinguished themselves by exceptional meritorious service to the Government in a duty of great responsibility.

The Distinguished Unit Citation (DUC)

The DUC was awarded to USAAF groups or squadrons that demonstrated acts of extraordinary heroism which were deemed to be equivalent to acts which would warrant the award of the DSC to an individual. Members of the unit at the time of the action would be allowed to permanently wear the DUC, but members joining later could only wear it during their tour with that unit.

Maj. James Hill earned 39 Air Medals in his Air force career that ended in 1980. (Author/Hill)

Presidential Unit Citation (PUC)

The Presidential Unit Citation was authorized in 1942 to be awarded in the name of the President for extraordinary heroism in action by a specific group retroactive to 7 December 1941.

Ribbons

Campaign ribbons and medals were created for participation in three war theaters: American Campaign; Asiatic-Pacific Campaign; and the European African Mid Eastern Campaign. All three ribbons had colored stripes representing the U.S., while their other colored stripes represented the Axis (e.g. German: black and white, Japan: red and white, Italy: green, white, and red). The Campaign Medals were hung from ribbons and had engravings depicting combat in the area.

The Good Conduct Ribbon and Medal was authorized in 1941 and was awarded to enlisted men for "efficiency, honor and fidelity for each three-year period of service."

Wings, the symbol of flight, were the coveted reward for aviation qualification by fledgling aviation cadets. The AAF badge was basically the shield of the U.S. without stars centered in a pair of wings. The Navy and Marine wings had the starless U.S. shield centered by a winged fouled anchor.

As a footnote to awards and decorations, F4U #122 of VMF-111 was the only recorded fighter aircraft to receive an official citation. The Corsair had flown 400 hours in 100 missions in the Marshall Island area without an abort or mechanical failure.

Only aircraft to be awarded an official citation was F4U #122 of VMF-111. (USMC)

Service Academy Aces

32 U.S. Naval Academy Aces (WWII)

Pilot's Name USNA	Rank Notes	# V	Grad.	
Bakutis, Frederick	Radm	7.5	1935	
Bardshar, Frederick	Vadm	7.5	1938	
Bauer, Harold	LCol	11	1930	KIA 11/44
USMC				
Blackburn, John	Capt	11	1933	
Brewer, Charles	Cdr	6.5	1934	KIA 6/44
Buie, Paul	Radm	9	1933	
Clements, Robert	Capt	5	1940	
Coleman, Thaddeus	Capt	10	1934	
Collins, William	Capt	9	1934	
Dean, William	Capt	11	1934	
Duncan, George	Capt	13.5	1939	
Flatley, James	VAdm	6	1929	
Fleming, Patrick	Col	19	1941	Post-war transferred to USAF
Gayler, Noel	Adm	5	1935	
Gray, James	Capt	6	1936	
Harris, Leroy	Capt	10	1939	
Kane, William	Capt	6	1933	KIFA 2/57
Lamb, William	Capt	6	1940	
Leonard, William	Radm	6	1938	
Lusk, Virgil	Capt*	5*	+	+Attended 1936-38
*USAAF KIFA 3/43				
McCampbell, David	Capt	34	1933	CMH, Top USN Ace
Mehle, Roger	Radm	5.66	1937	
Michaelis, Frederick	Adm	5	1940	
O'Hare, Edward	LCdr	7	1937	KIA 11/43 CMH
Ostrum, Charles	Cdr	?	1930	? May be an ace
Outlaw, Edward	Radm	6	1935	
Schecter, Gordon	Cdr	5	1935	KIA 3/45
Smith, Daniel	Radm	6.08	1932	
Southerland, James	Cdr	5	1936	KIFA 10/49
Thach, James	Adm	6	1927	
Tinker, Frank	——	8	1933	Spanish Civil War
Vorse, Albert	Radm	11.5	1937	
Winters, T.Hugh	Capt	8	1935	
Wordell, Malcomb	Capt	7	1935	

9 US Military Academy Aces (WWII)

Pilot Name	Rank	#V	Grad.	USMA Notes
Buck, George	Col	6	1942	
Evans, Andrew	Mgen	6	1941	POW Korea
Holloway, Bruce	Gen	13	1937	
Hovde, William	Col	11.5	1943	+1 v. Korea
Lenfest, Charles	Bgen	5.5	1943	POW
Magoffin, Morton	Col	5	1937	POW/WIA
McCorkle, Charles	Mgen	11	1936	
Olds, Robin	Bgen	17	1943	+4 v. Vietnam
Vincent, Clinton	BGen	6	1936	

On 13 April 1944, Don Gentile had surpassed Eddie Rickenbacker's WWI record of 26 victories as the 8AF included ground victories in its totals. The press and military brass had been alerted and Gentile came in roaring over the field at low level and hit a small rise with this disastrous result. (USAF)

Victory Rolls and Buzz Jobs

Sitting in the Saturday matinee, American boys loved the WWI flying epics. When the victorious on-screen pilot returned to base the aspiring future aces rose from their theater seats when they saw the traditional victory roll, which looked so awesome on the big screen. But, in fact the victory roll was seldom used in WWI, as pilot exhaustion and the relief to be back to base, along with the fragile nature of the fighter dictated otherwise.

The victory roll was a low altitude slow or barrel roll directly over one's base; one roll for each victory. The buzz job was another exhilarating staple of the victorious pilot; a high speed, as-low-as-you-can-go run over the base or its control tower. The improved construction and performance of the WWII fighter and the inbred need to celebrate led to the increased use of the victory roll and buzz job. But the maneuvers, carried out so close to the ground, required superior flying and acrobatic skills, especially to perform the multiple rolls which denoted multiple victories. Many pilots became aces because of their gunnery expertise, rather than their flying ability, and so, tragically, crashed into the ground in front of their friends and ground crew.

Don Gentile executed one of the more well known buzz jobs upon the completion of a mission on 13 April 1944. The military and civilian press had been alerted that Gentile had surpassed Eddie Rickenbacker's WWI victory record (the 8AF counted ground strafing victories). Gentile came in low at grass-top level over Debden, straight toward the cameras. Not having his depth perception back after flying for long hours at high altitude, Gentile's P-51 "Shangri-La" hit a small rise. The Mustang headed for the on lookers, bounced back into the air over the scrambling crowd, and skidded to a stop to end up written off for scrap. Col. Don Blakeslee, enraged to the point of court martial, pulled Gentile from combat instead and shipped him back to the States to become a test pilot.

CHAPTER 23

Appendices

American Aces of WWII by Service

U.S. Marine Corps Aces WWII

Ace's Name	Rank	VMF	A/C	V.	P.	D.	Notes
A							
Aldrich, Donald	Capt	215	F4U	20	6	0	
Alley, Stuart	2Lt	323	F4U	5	0	0	
Axtell, George	Maj	323	F4U	6	0	3	
B							
Baird, Robert	Capt	533N	F6F	6	0	0	
Baker, Robert	1Lt	121	F4U	5	1	0	
Balch, Donald	Capt	221	F4F	2	0	2	
			F4U	3	1	0	
Baldwin, Frank	Capt	221	F4F	3	1	1	
			F4U	2	0	0.5	
Bate, Oscar	Capt	121	F4F	4	0	0	
			F4U	1	0	0	
Bauer, Harold	LCol	212	F4F	10	1	0	KIA 11/14/42
Bolt, John	1Lt	214	F4U	6	0	0	+6 v. Korea
Boyington, Gregory	Maj	214	F4U	22	4	0	+2 v. AVG (P-40) POW
Braun, Richard	Capt	215	F4U	5	2	1	
Brown, William	2Lt	311	F4U	7	0	0	
C							
Carl, Marion	Maj	221/223	F4F	16.5	0	2	
			F4U	2	0	1	
Carlton, William	Capt	212	F4U	5	2	1	
Case, William	1Lt	112/214	F4F	1	0	0	
			F4U	7	1	0	
Caswell, Dean	2Lt	221	F4U	7	1	0	
Chandler, Creighton	1Lt	215	F4U	6	0	0	
Conant, Arthur	Capt	215	F4U	6	3	0	
Conger, Jack	1Lt	212	F4F	10	0	0	
Crowe, William	Capt	124	F4U	7	1	1	
Cupp, James	Capt	213	F4U	12	2	0	
D							
Davis, Leonard	Maj	121	F4F	5	0	0	
DeBlanc, Jefferson	Capt	112/422	F4F	3	1	0	
			F4U	6	0	0	
DeLong, Philip	1Lt	212	F4U	11.83	1	2	+ 2 v. Korea
Dillard, Joseph	1Lt	323	F4U	6.33	0	0	
Dillow, Eugene	1Lt	221	F4U	6	2	1	KIFA 4/4/44
Dobbin, John	Maj	224	F4F	7.5	1	0	
Donohue, Archie	Maj	112/451	F4F	6	1	0	
			F4U	8	0	0	
Dorroh, Jefferson	Maj	323	F4U	6	2	0	
Doyle, Cecil	2Lt	121	F4F	5	0	0	KIA 11/7/42
Drury, Frank	Capt	212/113	F4F	5	0	0	
			F4U	1	0	0	
Durnford, Dewey	2Lt	323	F4U	6.33	0	0	+ 0.5 v. Korea
E							
Elwood, Hugh	Maj	212	F4U	5.83	2	0	
Everton, Loren	Maj	212/113	F4F	10	0	0	
			F4U	2	1	0	
F							
Farrell, William	1Lt	312	F4U	5	1	0	
Finn, Howard	Capt	124	F4U	6	0	0.5	
Fisher, Donald	1Lt	214	F4U	6	1	0	
Fontana, Paul	Maj	112	F4F	5	0	0	
Ford, Kenneth	Capt	121	F4U	5	1	0	
Foss, Joseph	Capt	121	F4F	26	0	0	

Fraser, Robert	Maj	112	F4F	4	0	0	
			F4U	2	0	2	
Frazier, Kenneth	2Lt	223	F4F	12.5	0	0	
			F4U	1	0	0	
Freeman, William	1Lt	121	F4F	6	0	0	
G							
Galer, Robert	Maj	224	F4F	14	3	0	
Gutt, Fred	Capt	223	F4F	4	0	0	
			F4U	4	0	1	
H							
Haberman, Roger	2Lt	121	F4F	6.5	0	0	
Hacking, Albert	1Lt	221	F4U	5	0	0	
Hall, Sheldon	1Lt	213	F4U	6	0	0	
Hamilton, Henry	MG	212/223	F4F	7	0	0	KIA 10/21/42
Hansen, Herman	Maj	122 112	F4U	5.5	0	2.5	
Hanson, Robert	1Lt	214/215	F4U	25	2	0	KIA 2/3/44
Hernan, Edwin	1Lt	215	F4U	8	1	0	
Hollowell, George	1Lt	224	F4F	8	0	0	
Hood, William	1Lt	323	F4U	5.5	0	0	
Hundley, John	1Lt	211	F4U	6	1	0	
I							
Ireland, Julius	Maj	211	F4U	5.33	2	0	
J							
Jensen, Alvin	1Lt	214	F4U	7	1	0	
Jones, Charles	2Lt	222	F4U	6	1	1	
K							
Kendrick, Charles	2Lt	223	F4F	5	0	0	KIA 10/2/42
Kunz, Charles	2Lt	221/224	F2A	2	0	0	
			F4U	6	0	0	
L							
Loesch, Gregory	Capt	121	F4F	8.5	0	0	
Long, Herbert	Maj	121/451	F4F	3	0	0	
			F4U	7	0	0	
Lynch, Joseph	Capt	112/224	F4F	3.5	0	0	
			F4U	2	0	0	
M							
Maas, John	Maj	322	F4F	4	1	0	
			F4U	1.5	0	0	
Magee, Christopher	1Lt	214	F4U	9	2	0	
Mann, Thomas	2Lt	121	F4F	9	0	0	
Marontate, William	1Lt	121	F4F	13	0	0	
McCartney, Henry	1Lt	251/214	F4U	5	2.5	0	KIA 1/15/43
McClurg, Robert	1Lt	214	F4U	7	2	0	
McGinty, Selva	1Lt	221	F4U	6	0	0	
McManus, John	1Lt	221	F4U	6	0	0	
Morgan, John	1Lt	213	F4U	8.5	0	0	KIA 3/28/45
Mullen, Paul	1Lt	122/112/214	F4U	6.5	0	0	
N							
Narr, Joseph	2Lt	121	F4F	7	0	0	KIA 11/11/42
O							
O'Keefe, Jeremiah	1Lt	323	F4U	7	0	0	
Olander, Edwin	Capt	214	F4U	5	4	0	
Overend, Edmund	Maj	314	F4U	8*	0	0	* 5 v. AVG (P-40)
Owen, Donald	Capt	314/112	F4U	2.5	0	0	
			F4U	2.5	0	0	KIFA 5/26/45
Owens, Robert	Maj	215	F4U	7	4	0	
P							
Payne, Frederick	Maj	223/212	F4F	5.5	0	0	
Percy, James	1Lt	112	F4F	5	0	0	
			F4U	1	0	1	
Phillips, Hyde	2Lt	223	F4F	5	0	0	
Pierce, Francis	Capt	121	F4F	5	1	0	
			F4U	1	0	0	
Pittman, Jack	2Lt	221	F4F	2	0	0	
			F4U	3	2	0	
Pond, Zenneth	2Lt	223	F4F	6	0	0	KIA 8/10/42

Porter, Robert	Maj	121/542N	F4U	3	1	1	
			F6F	2	0	0	
Poske, George	Maj	212	F4U	5	1	0	
Post, Nathan	Maj	122/221	F4U	8	0	0	
Powell, Ernest	Capt	122	F4U	5	0	0	KIA 7/18/43

R

Ramlo, Orvin	2Lt	*223	SBD	0.5	0	0	
			F4F	5	0	0	* shared w/gunner VMSB241
Reinberg, Hunter	Maj	121/122	F4F	2	0	0	
			F4U	5	0	0	
Ruhsam, John	1Lt	323	F4U	7	0	3	

S

Sapp, Donald	Maj	222	F4U	10	4	2	(Stapp/name change)
Scarborough, Hartwell	1Lt	214	F4U	5	0	0	
See, Robert	1Lt	321	F4U	5	0	0	
Segal, Harold	1Lt	211	F4U	12	1	0	
Shaw, Edward	1Lt	213	F4U	14.5	1	0	KIFA 7/31/45 (US)
Shuman, Perry	Capt	121	F4U	6	1	1	
Sigler, Wallace	Capt	112/542N	F4F	4	1	0	
			F6F	1	0	0	
Smith, John	Maj	223	F4F	19	0	0	
Snider, William	Capt	221	F4F	3	1	0	
			F4U	8.5	0	0	
Spears, Harold	Capt	215	F4U	15	3	0	
Stout, Robert	1Lt	212	F4F	6	0	0	
Swett, James	Capt	221	F4F	7	0	1	
			F4U	8.5	3	0.25	
Synar, Stanley	1Lt	112	F4F	2	0	0	
			F4U	3	0	0	

T

Terrill. Francis	1Lt	323	F4U	6.83	0	4	
Thomas, Franklin	1Lt	221	F4U	9	2.5	4	
Thomas, Wilbur	Capt	213	F4U	18.5	3.33	3	
Trowbridge, Eugene	2Lt	223	F4F	13	0	0	

V

Valentine, Herbert	Capt	312	F4U	6	1	0	
Vedder, Milton	1Lt	213	F4U	6	0	0	

W

Wade, Robert	1Lt	323	F4U	7	0	3	+ 1 v. Korea
Walsh, Kenneth	Capt	124	F4U	21	2	1	
Warner, Arthur	Maj	215	F4U	8	2	0	
Weissenberger, Greg	Maj	213	F4U	5	0	0	
Wells, Albert	1Lt	323	F4U	5	0	0	
Williams, Gerard	1Lt	215	F4U	7	2	0	

Y

Yost, Donald	LCol	121/351	F4F	6	0	0	
			F4U	2	0	0	
Yunck, Michael	Maj	251*/311	F4F	2	0	0	
			F4U	3	0	0	* VMO

Ace in Two Wars:

Andre, John	T/Sgt	541N/513N	F4U	4	0	0	
			F7F	1	0	0	Korea

U.S. Navy Aces in WWII

Ace's Name	Rank	VF	Base	A/C	V.	P.	D.	Notes
A								
Amsden, Benjamin	Ens	22	*Cowpens*	F6F	5	0	0	
Anderson, Alexander	Lt	80	*Ticon*	F6F	5.5	1	1	
Anderson, Robert	Lt	80	*Ticon*	F6F	8.5	0	0	
B								
Bailey, Oscar	Lt	28	*Mont*	F6F	5	0	0	
Baker, Douglas	Ens	20	*Ent*	F6F	16.33	0	1	
Bakutis, Frederick	Cdr	20	*Ent*	F6F	7.5	0	2	USNA '35
Balsinger, Henry	Lt(jg)	29	*Cabot*	F6F	5.33	0	1	
Banks, John	Lt(jg)	2	*Ent*	F6F	8.5	2	0	
Barackman, Bruce	Lt	59	*Bataan*	F6F	5	0	0	

Bardshar, Frederick	LCdr	27	Prince	F6F	7.5	0	0	USNA '38
Bare, James	Lt(jg)	15	Essex	F6F	6	0	0	
Barnard, Lloyd	Lt	2	Hornet	F6F	8	1	0	
Barnes, James	Ens	83	Essex	F6F	6	0	0	KIFA 7/2/45
Bertol, John	Lt	16	Lex/Rand	F6F	5	0	3	
Batten, Hugh	Lt(jg)	83	Essex	F6F	5	1	0	
Beaudry, Paul	Ens	80	Ticon	F6F	5	1	0	
Beebe, Marshall	LCdr	17	Hornet	F6F	10.5	0	2	
Berkheimer, Jack	Ens	41N	Ind	F6F	7.5	0	0	KIA 12/16/44
Berree, Norman	Lt(jg)	15	Essex	F6F	9	0	0	
Bertelson, Richard	Ens	29	Cabot	F6F	5	0	0	
Bishop, Walter	Lt(jg)	29	Cabot	F6F	5	0	0	KIA 12/14/44
Blackburn, John	LCdr	17	Land	F4U	11	5	3	USNA '39
Blair, William	Lt	10/2	Ent	F4F	0	1	0	
			Hornet	F6F	5	1	0	
Blaydes, Richard	Ens	2	Hornet	F6F	5	1	0	
Blyth, Robert	Ens	27	Prince	F6F	6.5	0	0	
Bolduc, Alfred	Lt	12*	Rand	F6F	5	0	1	*VBF
Bonneau, William	Lt	9	Essex	F6F	8	0	4	
Borley, Clarence	Ens	15	Essex	F6F	5	0	0	
Boyle, Gerald	Lt	21/20	Land	F4F	3	0	0	
			Ent	F6F	2.5	0	0	KIFA 10/31/44
Brassfield, Arthur	Lt(jg)	43/3	York	F4F	6.33	0	2	
Brewer, Charles	Cdr	15	Essex	F6F	6.5	0	0	
Bridges, Johnie	Lt	16/17	Sara	F6F	6.25	0	2	
			Hancock	F6F	0	0	0	
Bright, Mark	Lt	15/16	Land	F4F	5	0	0	
			Essex	F6F	4	0	0	KIA 5/17/44
Brocato, Samuel	Lt(jg)	83	Essex	F6F	7	0	0	
Brown, Carl	Lt	27	Prince	F6F	10.5	0	0	
Brunmeir, Carland	Lt	44	Lang	F6F	6	0	1	
Bryce, James	Lt(jg)	22	Ind	F6F	5.25	1	0	KIFA 4/10/45 (US)
Buchanan, Robert	Ens	29	Cabot	F6F	5	0	0	
Buie, Paul	LCdr	16	Lex	F6F	9	1	0	USNA
Burckhalter, William	Lt(jg)	16	Lex	F6F	6	0	0	KIA 6/11/44
Burley, Franklin	Lt(jg)	18	Int	F6F	7	1	0	
Burnett, Roy	Lt	18	Int	F6F	7	0	0	
Burris, Howard	Lt(jg)	17	Land	F4U	7.5	0	0	KIA 1/31/44
Byrnes, Matthew	Lt	9/12*	Essex	F6F	6	0	3	
			Rand	F6F	0	0	0	
C								
Cain, James	Lt	45	San J	F6F	8	0	0	
Carey, Henry	Lt	72/30	Land	F4F	3	0	0	
			Mont	F6F	4	0	0	
Carlson, Robert	Lt(jg)	40/30	Land	F6F	9	1.5	1	
			B. Wood	F6F	0	0	0	
Carmichael, Daniel	Lt(jg)	2/12*	Hornet	F6F	12	0	0	* VBF
			Rand	F6F	0	0	0	
Carr, George	Lt(jg)	15	Essex	F6F	11.5	0	0	
Carroll, Charles	Lt(jg)	2	Ent	F6F	6	1	0	
Chambers, Cyrus	Lt(jg)	6/84	Int	F6F	5.33	1	0	
			B. Hill	F6F	0	0	0	
Champion, Henry	Lt(jg)	9	York	F6F	5	2	5	
Check, Leonard	LCdr	7	Hancock	F6F	10	1	1	KIFA 1/4/45
Chenoweth, Oscar	Lt	17/38	Land	F4U	8.5	2	0	
Clark, Lawrence	Lt(jg)	83	Essex	F6F	7	0	0	
Clark, Robert	Ens	17*	Hornet	F6F	6	0	0	* VBF
Clarke, Walter	LCdr	5/10	Land	F4F	3	0	0	
			Int	F6F	5	0	0	
Clements, Donald	Lt	28	Mont	F6F	5	0	0	
Clements, Robert	Lt	11	Hornet	F6F	5	0	0	USNA '40
Coats, Robert	Lt	18/17	B. Hill	F6F	9.33	3	0	
			Hornet	F6F	0	0	0	
Coleman, Thaddeus	Lt	6/83	B. Wood	F6F	10	0	0	
			Essex	F6F	0	0	0	
Coleman, Wilson	Cdr	13	Frank	F6F	6	1	0	USNA '34
Collins, William	Cdr	8	B. Hill	F6F	9	0	0	

Name	Rank	Squadron	Ship	Aircraft				Notes
Conant, Edwin	Lt	17*	Hornet	F6F	7	1	1	* VBF (aka John Perry)
Conroy, Thomas	Ens	27	Prince	F6F	7	0	0	
Copeland, William	Lt(jg)	19	Ent	F6F	6	1	0	
Cordray, Paul	Lt(jg)	17/10*	Land	F4U	7	1	3	*VBF
			Ind	F6F	0	0	0	
Cormier, Richard	Lt	80	Hancock	F6F	8	1	0	
Cowger, Richard	Lt	17	Hornet	F6F	6	1	1	
Cozzens, Melvin	Lt(jg)	29	Cabot	F6F	6.5	0	1	
Craig, Clement	Lt	22	Cowpens	F6F	11.75	1	0	
Cronin, Donald	Lt	8	B.Hill	F6F	6	1	0	
Crosby, John	Lt(jg)	19/17	B.Hill	F6F	5.25	0	1.5	
			Hornet	F6F	0	0	0	
Cunningham, Daniel	Lt(jg)	17	Land	F4U	7	0	1.5	
D								
Dahms, Kenneth	Ens	30	B. Wood	F6F	7	0	0	
Davenport, Merle	Lt	17	Land	F4U	6.5	0	0	
Davidson, George	Lt(jg)	21/27*	Land	F4F	1	0	0	* VC
			Savo Is.	FM2	4.25-	0	0	
Davies, Clarence	Lt(jg)	82	Benn	F6F	5	0	0	
Davis, Robert	Lt	18	Int	F6F	5.5	0	0	
Dean, William	Cdr	2	Hornet	F6F	11	0	0	USNA '34
Dear, John	Lt(jg)	76N	Hornet	F6F	7	0	0	
DeCew, Leslie	Lt	9	Essex	F6F	6	0	2	
Denman, Anthony	Lt	18	Int	F6F	6	0	0	
Denoff, Reuben	Lt	9/12*	Rand	F6F	6	0	0	* VBF
			Essex	F6F	0	0	0	
Devine, Richard	Lt	10	Ent	F6F	8	0	0	
Dewing, Laurence	Ens	14	Wasp	F6F	5.5	1	0	
Dibb, Robert	Lt	3/6/18	York	F4F	3	0	1	
			Land	F4F	0	4	0	
			B. Hill	F6F	0	0	0	
Doner, Landis	Lt	2	Hornet	F6F	8	0	0	
Driscoll, Daniel	Lt(jg)	31	Cabot	F6F	5	1	0	
Drury, Paul	Ens	27	Prince	F6F	6.5	0	0	
Duffy, James	Lt(jg)	15	Essex	F6F	5	0	0	
Duncan, George	Lt(jg)	15	Essex	F6F	13.5	1	1	USNA '39
Duncan, Robert	Lt(jg)	5	York	F6F	7	0	0	
Dungan, Fred	Lt(jg)	76N	Hornet	F6F	7	1	0	
Dunn, Bernard	Lt(jg)	29	Cabot	F6F	5.33	0	3	
E								
Eastmond, Richard	Lt	1	York	F6F	9	1	0	
Eberts. Byron	Lt(jg)	17*	Hornet	F6F	6	0.5	0	*VBF
Eckard, Bert	Lt	9	York	F6F	7	0	1	
Eder, Willard	LCdr	3/2/29	Lex	F4F	1.5	1	0	
			Cabot	F6F	5	0	2	
Edwards, William	Lt	80	Hancock	F6F	7.5	0	2	
Elliott, Ralph	Lt	27*	Savo Is	FM2	9	0	0.5	* VC
Evenson, Eric	Lt(jg)	30	Mont	F6F	8.25	1	0.33	
F								
Farmer,George	Lt(jg)	10	Int	F4U	7.25	0	0	
Farnsworth, Robert	Ens	19	Ent	F6F	5	0	0	
Fash, Robert	Lt(jg)	50/15	Bataan	F6F	6	0	0	
			Essex	F6F	0	0	0	
Fecke, Alfred	Lt	29	Cabot	F6F	7	0	0	
Feightner, Edward	Lt	10/8	Ent	F4F	4	1	0	
			B. Hill	F6F	5	1	0	
Ferko, Leo	Lt	4*/20	W. Plains	F4F	5	0	0	* VC
			Kad. Bay	FM2	0	0	0	
Flatley, James	LCdr	42/10	York	F4F	6	0	2	
			Ent	F4F	0	0	0	
Fleming, Francis	Lt(jg)	16	Lex	F6F	7.5	2	0	
Fleming, Patrick	Lt	80	Hancock	F6F	19	0	0	USNA '41
Flinn, Kenneth	Ens	15	Essex	F6F	5	0	0	POW 11/13/44 Died as POW
Foltz, Ralph	Lt(jg)	15	Essex	F6F	5	0	1	
Formanek, George	Lt	8/72/30	Hornet	F4F	3	0	1	
			Mont	F6F	2	0	0	KIA 4/23/44
Foster, Carl	Ens	30	B.Wood	F6F	8.5	0	0	

Name	Rank	Squadron	Carrier	Aircraft				Notes
Fowler, Richard	Ens	15	*Essex*	F6F	6.5	0	0	
Franger, Marvin	Lt	9	*Yorktown*	F6F	9	1	1	
Franks, John	Lt(jg)	19/12	*Essex*	F6F	7	0	2	
			Rand	F6F	0	0	0	
Freeman, Doris	Lt	17/84	*Land*	F4U	9	0	2	
			B. Hill	F6F	0	0	0	KIA 5/11/45
French, James	Lt(jg)	9	*Lex*	F6F	11	0	0	
Frendberg, Arthur	Lt(jg)	16	*Lex*	F6F	6	0	1	
Funk, Harold	LCdr	23/26	*Prince*	F6F	0.5	0	0	
			Santee	F6F	6	0	0	
G								
Gabriel, Franklin	Lt(jg)	2	*Hornet*	F6F	8	1	0	
Galt, Dwight	Lt(jg)	31	*Cabot*	F6F	5	0	2	
Galvin, John	Lt(jg)	8	*B.Hill*	F6F	7	0	2	
Gaylor, Noel	Lt	3/2	*York*	F4F	5	1	0	
			Lex		0	0	0	USNA '35
Gildea, John	Lt(jg)	84	*B.Hill*	F6F	7	1	2	KIA 5/11/45
Gile, Clement	Lt	17	*Land*	F4U	8	0	0.5	
Gillespie, Roy	Lt	30	*B.Hill*	F6F	6	0	0	
Godson, Lindley	Lt	83*	*Essex*	F6F	5	0	0	* VBF
Gordon, Donald	Lt	10	*Ent*	F6F	5	1	1	
Graham, Vernon	Lt(jg)	11	*Land*	F4F	5	0	0	
Gray, James	Cdr	6/78N/20	*Land*	F4F	3	0	0	USNA '36
			Int	F6F	3	0	0	
			Ent	F6F	0	1	0	
Gray, John	Lt	5	*York*	F6F	8.5	0	0	
Gray, Lester	Lt(jg)	10	*Ent*	F6F	5.25	0	0	
Gregory, Hayden	Lt	82	*Benn*	F6F	5	0	0	
Griffin, Richard	Lt	2	*Hornet*	F6F	8	1	0	
Gustafson, Harlan	Lt	8	*B.Hill*	F6F	6	0	2	
H								
Hadden, Mayo	Lt	9	*Essex*	F6F	8	0	0	
Hamblin, Louis	Lt(jg)	80	*Hancock*	F6F	8.5	0	1	
Hamilton, Robert	Ltjg)	83	*Essex*	F6F	6	0	0	
Hanks, Eugene	Lt(jg)	16	*Lex*	F6F	6	2	0	
Hardy, Willis	Lt(jg)	17	*Hornet*	F6F	6.5	1	1.5	
Hargreaves, Everett	Lt(jg)	2	*Hornet*	F6F	8.5	2	0	
Harmon, Walter	Lt	10	*Ent*	F6F	6	0	1	
Harris, Cecil	Lt	27/18	*Land*	F4F	1	0	0	
			Int	F6F	22	1	0	
Harris, Leroy	LCdr	10/2	*Ent*	F4F	1.25	1	0	USNA '39
			Hornet	F6F	8	1	0	
Harris, Thomas	Lt(jg)	18/17	*B.Hill*	F6F	9	1	1.5	
			Hornet	F6F	0	0	0	
Harris, William	Lt	17/83*	*Hornet*	SB2C	1	0	1	* VBF, KIA 8/9/45
			Essex	F4U	4	0	1	
Haverland, Charles	Ens	20	*Ent*	F6F	6.5	1	0	
Hawkins, Arthur	Lt(jg)	31	*Cabot*	F6F	14	0	4	
Hayde, Frank	Lt(jg)	31	*Cabot*	F6F	6	0	0	KIA 7/15/44
Hearrell, Frank	Lt	18	*Int*	F6F	5	0	0	
Heath, Horace	Ens	10	*Int*	F4U	7	0	0	KIFA 7/8/45
Hedrick, Roger	LCdr	17/84	*Hornet*	F6F	9	0	3	
			B.Hill	F4U	3	0	1	
Heinzen, Lloyd	Lt	8	*B.Hill*	F6F	6	0	1	
Henderson, Paul	Lt	1	*York*	F6F	5	0	0	KIA 7/8/45
Henry, William	Lt	3*/41N	*Ind*	SBD	3	0	0	*VS
				F6F	9.5	1	0	
Hibbard, Samuel	Lt	47	*Bataan*	F6F	7.33	0	0	
Hildebrandt, Carlos	Lt	38	*Land*	F6F	5	0	0	
Hill, Harley	Lt	5	*York*	F6F	7	0	0	
Hills, Hollis	Lt	414/32	*RCAF*	P-51	1	0	0	
			Lang	F6F	4	0	0	
Hippe, Kenneth	Lt	3	*Kal.Bay*	FM2	5	0	0	
Hoeg, John	Ens	82	*Benn*	F6F	5	3	1	
Houck, Herbert	LCdr	9	*Essex*	F6F	6	1	0	
Hudson, Howard	Lt	14	*Essex*	F6F	5	0	5	
Huffman, Charles	Ens	14	*Wasp*	F6F	7	0	0	

Humphrey, Robert	Lt(jg)	17	*Hornet*	F6F	5.33	0	0	
Hust, Robert	Lt(jg)	18	*Int*	F6F	6	0	0	
J								
Jacques, Bruce	Lt	29*/29	*Santee*	F4F	1	0	0	*VGF
			Cabot	F6F	4.5	0	0	
Jennings, Robert	Lt	72/82	*Land*	F4F	2.5	1	0	
			Benn	F6F	7	0	1	
Jensen, Hayden	Lt	5	*Land*	F4F	7	1	0	
Johannsen, Delmar	Ens	12*	*Rand*	F6F	5	0	0	*VBF
Johnson, Byron	Lt(jg)	2	*Hornet*	F6F	8	0	0	
Johnson, Wallace	Ens	15	*Essex*	F6F	5	1	0	
Johnston, John	Lt(jg)	17*	*Hornet*	F6F	8	0	3	*VBF
Jones, James	Lt(jg)	3/3*	*York*	F6F	7	0.5	0	
			York	F6F	0	0	0	*VBF
K								
Kaelin, Joseph	Ens	9	*Lex*	F6F	5	2	3	
Kane, William	Cdr	10	*Ent*	F6F	6	1	1	USNA '33
Keith, Leroy	LCdr	80	*Hancock*	F6F	5.5	2	0	
Kepford, Ira	Lt(jg)	17	*Land*	F4U	16	1	1	
Kidwell, Robert	Ens	45	*San J*	F6F	5	0.2	0.15	
Kincaid, Robert	Lt	83*	*B.Hill*	F4U	5	0	0	* VBF
Kingston, William	Ens	83	*Essex*	F6F	6	0	0	
Kinsella, James	Lt(jg)	72/33	*Land*	F4F	2	0	0	
			Land	F6F	3	1	0	
Kirk, George	Lt(jg)	8	*B.Hill*	F6F	7	0	1	
Kirkwood, Philip	Lt(jg)	10	*Ent*	F6F	12	1	0	
Knight, William	Lt	14	*Wasp*	F6F	7.5	0	3	KIA 11/5/44
Kostik, William	Ens	17*	*Hornet*	F6F	5	0	0	* VBF
L								
Laird, Dean	Lt	4	*Essex*	F6F	5.75	0	1	
Lake, Kenneth	Ens	2	*Hornet*	F6F	6	0	0	
Lamb, William	Lt	27	*Prince*	F6F	5	1	0	USNA '40
Lamoreux, William	Lt(jg)	8	*B.Hill*	F6F	5	2	0	
Laney, Willis	Lt	84	*B.Hill*	F4U	5	2	1	
Langdon, Ned	Lt	18/17	*B.Hill*	F6F	5	2	0	
			Hornet	F6F	0	0	0	
Leonard, William	Lt	42/3/11	*York*	F4F	6	1	0	USNA '38
			Land		0	0	0	
Leppla, John	Ens	2*/10	*Ent*	F4F	5	0	0	*VS, KIA 10/26/42
			Ent	F4F	0	0	0	
Lerch, Alfred	Ens	10	*Int*	F4U	7	0	0	
Lindsley, Elvin	Lt	19	*Ent*	F6F	8	2	0	
Lundin, Walter	Lt(jg)	15	*Essex*	F6F	6.5	1	0	
M								
Maberry, Lewin	Lt(jg)	84	*B.Hill*	F4U	5	0	0	
Mallory, Charles	Lt(jg)	18	*Ent*	F6F	10	3	4	
Mankin, Lee	AP/1c	6/5	*Land*	F4F	5	1	3	
			Land	F4F	0	0	0	
Manson, Armand	Lt	18/82	*Intrepid*	F6F	7	1	0	
			Benn	F6F	0	0	0	
March, Harry	Lt	6/17	*Land*	F4F	2	0	0	
			Land	F4U	3	0	0	
Martin, Albert	Lt(jg)	9	*Essex*	F6F	5	0	0	
Masoner, William	Lt(jg)	11/19	*Land*	F4F	2	0	0	
			Ent	F6F	10	0	0	
Maxwell, William	Lt	51	*San J*	F6F	7	1	0	
May, Earl	Lt(jg)	17	*Land*	F4U	8	0	0	
May, Richard	Lt	32	*Lang*	F6F	5	0	1	
Mazzocco, Michele	Ens	30	*B.Wood*	F6F	5	0	0	
McCampbell, David	Cdr	15	*Essex*	F6F	34	5	1	USNA '34
McClelland, Thomas	Lt	5	*York*	F6F	7.33	1	0	
McClure, Edgar	Lt	9*	*York*	F6F	5	0	0	*VBF
McCormick, William	Ens	50/8	*Bataan*	F6F	7	1	0	
			B.Hill	F6F	0	0	0	
McCudden,Leo	Lt	20	*Ent*	F6F	5	0	0	
McCuskey, Elbert	LCdr	42/3/8	*York*	F4F	6.5	0	3	
			B.Hill	F6F	7	0	2	

McGown, Edward	Lt	9	*Essex*	F6F	6.5	0	3.5	
McGraw, Joseph	Ens	10*/80*	*GamBay* *ManBay*	FM2	5	0	1	*VC
McKinley, Donald	Lt(jg)	25	*Cowpens*	F6F	5	0	0.5	
McPherson, Donald	Ens	83	*Essex*	F6F	5	0	0	
McWhorter, Hamilton	Lt	19/12	*Essex* *Rand*	F6F	12	2	0	
Mehle, Roger	LCdr	6/28	*Land* *Mont*	F4F	1.67	0.67	0	USNA 37
Menard, Louis	Lt(jg)	9/12*	*Ranger* *Rand*	F4F F6F	1 8	1 1	0 0	*VBF
Mencin, Adolph	Lt	31	*Cabot*	F6F	6	2	0	
Michaelis, Frederick	LCdr	12	*Rand*	F6F	5	0	0	USNA 40
Miller, Johnie	Ens	30	*B.Wood*	F6F	8	0	2	
Milton, Charles	Lt	15	*Essex*	F6F	5	0	1	
Mims, Robert	Ens	17	*Land*	F4U	6	3	0	
Mitchell, Harris	Lt(jg)	9	*York*	F6F	10	1	0	
Mitchell, Henry	Lt(jg)	17*	*Hornet*	F6F	6	0	0	KIA 4/3/45 *VBF
Mollard, Norman	Lt(jg)	45	*San J*	F6F	6	0	0	
Mollenhauer, Arthur	Ens	18	*Int*	F6F	5	0	0	KIA 10/29/44
Montapert, John	Lt(jg)	44	*Lang*	F6F	6	0	0	
Moranville, Horace	Lt(jg)	11	*Hornet*	F6F	6	0	0	POW 1/12/45
Morris, Bert	Lt	15	*Essex*	F6F	7	1	0	
Moseley, William	Lt	1	*York*	F6F	5	1	0	
Mulcahy, Douglas	Lt	31	*Cabot*	F6F	8	0	1	
Murray, Robert	Lt(jg)	29	*Cabot*	F6F	10.33	0	1	
N								
Nelson, Robert J.	Lt	5	*York*	F6F	7	1	0	
Nelson, Robert K.	Ens	20	*Ent*	F6F	6.33	0	0	KIA 11/19/44
Noble, Myrvin	Lt(jg)	2	*Hornet*	F6F	7	2	0	
Nooy, Cornelius	Lt(jg)	31/31	*Cabot* *B.Wood*	F6F	19	3	2	
Null, Cleaveland	Lt(jg)	16	*Lex/Rand*	F6F	7	1	0	
O								
O'Hare, Edward	LCdr	3/6	*York* *Ind*	F4F F6F	5 2	1 0	0 0	USNA 37, KIA 11/26/43
Olson, Austin	Ens	30	*B.Wood*	F6F	5	0	0	
O'Mara, Paul	Ens	19	*Ent*	F6F	7	0	0	
Orth, John	Ens	9	*York*	F6F	6	0	0	
Outlaw. Edward	LCdr	32	*Lang*	F6f	6	1	0	USNA 35
Overton, Edward	Lt	15	*Essex*	F6F	5	1	0	
Owen, Edward	LCdr	5	*York*	F6F	5	3	0	
P								
Parrish, Elbert	Ens	80	*Hancock*	F6F	6	0	0	
Paskowski, John	Lt	19	*Ent*	F6F	6	0	0	
Pearce, James	Lt	18/17	*B.Hill* *Hornet*	F6F	5.5	0	0	
Philips, David	Ens	30	*B.Wood*	F6F	5	0	0	
Phillips, Edward	Ens	20	*Ent*	F6F	5	0	0	
Picken, Henry	Lt	18	*Ent*	F6F	11	0	0	
Pigman, George	Ens	15	*Essex*	F6F	8.5	0	0	
Plant, Claude	Ens	15	*Essex*	F6F	8.5	0	0	KIA 9/12/44
Pool, Tilman	Lt(jg)	17	*Hornet*	F6F	6	1	1	
Popr, Albert	Ens	13	*Frank*	F6F	7	0	0	
Pound, Ralston	Lt(jg)	16	*Lex*	F6F	6	1	0	
Prater, Luther	Lt(jg)	19	*Ent*	F6F	8.5	1	2	
Pritchard, Melvin	Lt(jg)	20	*Ent*	F6F	5.25	0	0	
Q								
Quiel, Norwood	Ens	19	*Int*	F4U	6	0	0	
R								
Reber, James	Ens	30	*B.Wood*	F6F	110	0	0	
Redmond, Eugene	Lt(jg)	10/2	*Ent* *Hornet*	F6F	9.25	2	0	
Register, Francis	Lt(jg)	6/5	*Land*	F4F	7	1	0	
Rehm, Daniel	Lt(jg)	50/8	*Bataan* *B. Hill*	F6F	9	0	0	
Reidy, Thomas	Lt	83*	*Essex*	F6F	10	0	0	*VBF

Name	Rank		Ship	Aircraft				Notes
Reiserer, Russell	Lt	10/76(N)	*Ent*	F4F	1	0	0	
			Hornet	F6F	8	0	0	
Rennemo, Thomas	Lt	18	*Ent*	F6F	6	0	0	
Reulet, Joseph	Lt(jg)	10	*Ent*	F6F	5	1	0	
Revel, Glenn	Lt	14	*Wasp*	F6F	5.75	0	2	
Reiger, Vincent	Lt(jg)	31	*Cabot*	F6F	5	0	1	
Rigg, James	LCdr	15	*Essex*	F6F	11	5	5	
Roach, Thomas	Lt(jg)	21	*Land*	F4F	5.5	0	0	KIA 7/25/43
Robbins, Joseph	Ens	6/85	*Ent*	F6F	2	0	0	
			Shang	F4U	3	0	1	
Robinson, Leroy	Ens	2	*Hornet*	F6F	5	0	0	
Robinson, Ross	Ens	2	*Hornet*	F6F	5	2	0	
Rosen, Ralph	Lt(jg)	8	*B.Hill*	F6F	6	0	1	
Rossi, Herman	Lt	19	*Ent*	F6F	6	0	0	
Runyan, Donald	Lt(jg)	6/8	*Land*	F4F	8	0	0	
			B.Hill	F6F	3	0	0	
Rushing, Roy	Lt(jg)	15	*Essex*	F6F	13	1	4	

S

Name	Rank		Ship	Aircraft				Notes
Sargent, John	Ens	18/64	*B.Hill*	F6F	4.25	0	0	KIA 5/11/45
			B.Hill	F4U	1	0	0	
Savage, Jimmie	Lt	11	*Hornet*	F6F	7	1	0	
Scales,Harrell	Lt	31	*Cabot*	F6F	6.2	0	0	
Schecter, Gordon	Cdr	45	*San J*	F6F	5	2.2	0	USNA 35, KIA 3/16/45
Schell, John	Lt	3	*York*	F6F	5	0	0	
Schiller, James	Lt(jg)	5	*Frank*	F4U	5	1	0	
Schneider, Frank	Ens	33	*Land*	F6F	7	2	0	KIA 1/9/44
Seckle, Albert	Lt	19	*Ent*	F6F	6	0	0	
Self, Larry	Ens	15	*Essex*	F6F	8.5	0	0	
Shackford, Robert	Ens	2	*Hornet*	F6F	5	1	0	
Sherrill, Hugh	Lt(jg)	81	*Wasp*	F6F	5.5	2	0	
Shirley, James	Lt	27	*Prince*	F6F	12.5	0	0	
Silber, Sam	LCdr	27/18	*Land*	F4F	1	0	0	
			B.Hill	F6F	6	1	0	
Singer, Arthur	Lt(jg)	15	*Essex*	F6F	10	3	0	
Sipes, Lester	Lt(jg)	10/2	*Ent*	F6F	5	0	1	
Sistrunk, Frank	Lt(jg)	17	*Honet*	F6F	5	0.5	1.5	KIA Korea
Skon, Warren	Lt(jg)	2	*Hornet*	F6F	7	1	2	
Slack, Albert	Lt(jg)	15	*Essex*	F6f	6.5	2	0	
Smith, Armisted	Lt	9	*Essex*	F6F	10	0	0.33	
Smith, Clinton	Lt(jg)	9	*York*	F6F	6	1	0	
Smith, Daniel	Cdr	20	*Ent*	F6F	6.1	0	0	USNA 32
Smith, John	Lt(jg)	17/84	*Land*	F4U	10	3	1	
			B.Hill	F4U				
Smith, Kenneth	Lt	90N/82	*Ent*	F6F	5	0	1	
			Benn					
Smith, Nicholas	Ens	13	*Frank*	F6F	6	0	0	
Sonner, Irl	Lt(jg)	29	*Cabot*	F6F	5	0	0	KIFA 3/22/45
Southerland. James	Cdr	5/83/33	*Land*	F4F	2	0	0	USNA 36
			Essex					
			Lang					
Spitler, Clyde	Lt	2	*Hornet*	F6F	5	0	0	
Stambrook, Richard	Lt	27	*Prince*	F6F	10	0	0	
Stanley, Gordon	Ens	27	*Prince*	F6F	8	2	0	
Starkes, Carlton	Lt(jg)	5	*Land*	F4F	6	0	0	
Stewart, James	Lt	31	*B.Wood*	F6F	10	0	1	
Stimpson, Charles	Lt	11	*Hornet*	F4F	6	0	0	
				F6F	10	2	0	
Stokes, John	Lt(jg)	14	*Wasp*	F6F	6.5	0	1	
Stone, Carl	Lt(jg)	17*	*Hornet*	F6F	5	0	1.5	*VBF
Strane, John	Lt	15	*Essex*	F6F	13	0	0	
Strange, Johnnie	LCdr	50	*Bataan*	F6F	5	0	0	
Streig, Frederick	Lt(jg)	17	*Essex*	F4U	5	0	2	
Sturdivant, Harvey	Lt(jg)	30	*B.Wood*	F6F	6	1	1	
Sutherland, John	Lt	72/10	*Land*	F4F	5	0	0	
			Ent					
Swineburne, Harry	Lt(jg)	45	*San J*	F6F	5	0	0	

Swope, James	Lt	11/11	*Land*	F4F	4.67	0	0	
			Hornet	F6F	5	2	0	
Symmes, John	Lt(jg)	21/15	*Land*	F4F	5.5	1	1	
			Essex	F6F	5.5	1	0	
T								
Taylor, Roy	Lt(jg)	14	*Wasp*	F6F	6.5	0	4	
Taylor, Will	Lt	41/4	*Wasp*	F4F	1	0	0	
			Essex	F6F	5	0	0	
Thach, John	LCdr	3	*York*	F4F	6	1	0	USNA 27
Thelen, Robert	Lt(jg)	24	*B.Wood*	F6F	6.25	0	0	
Thomas. Robert	Ens	21	*B.Wood*	F6F	5.25	0	0	
Toaspern, Edward	Lt(jg)	31/18	*B.Wood*	F6F	7	0	2	
			Int					
Topliff, John	Lt(jg)	8	*B.Hill*	F6F	5	0	2	
Torkelson, Ross	Lt	11*/21	*Land*	F4F	6	1	0	*VGF, KIFA 7/22/43
			Land					
Townsend, Eugene	Lt(jg)	27	*Prince*	F6F	5	0	0	
Tracy, Frederick	Lt	18	*Int*	F6F	5	1	1	
Troup, Frank	Ens	29	*Cabot*	F6F	7	0	0	
Truax, Myron	Ens	83	*Essex*	F6F	7	0	0	
Turner, Charles	Cdr	31	*Cabot*	F6F	6	2	0	
Turner, Edward	Lt	14	*Wasp*	F6F	7	0	2	
Twelves, Wendell	Lt(jg)	15	*Essex*	F6F	13	1	0	
U								
Ude, Vernon	Lt(jg)	10	*Ent*	F6F	5	0	1	
Umphries, Donald	Lt	83	*Essex*	F6F	6	0	0	
V								
Valencia, , Eugene	Lt	9	*York*	F6F	23	2	2	
Van Der Linden, Peter	Lt(jg)	8	*B.Hill*	F6F	5	1	0	
Van Dyke, Rudolph	Lt	18	*Int*	F6F	5	0	0	
Van Haren, Arthur	Lt	2	*Hornet*	F6F	9	0	0	
Vejtasa, Stanley	Lt	5*/10	*York*	SBD	3	0	0	* V.S
			Ent	F4F	7.25	1	0	
Vineyard, Merriwell	Lt(jg)	2	*Hornet*	F6F	6	0	0	
Vita, Harold	Lt	9/12	*Ranger*	F4F	1	0	0	
			Rand	F6F	5	0	0	
Voris, Roy	Lt	10/2	*Ent*	F6F	7	1	0	
			Hornet					
Vorse, Albert	Cdr	3/2/6/80	*Land*	F4F	5.5	0	0	USNA 37
			Hornet					
			Land					
			Hancock	F6F	6	0	1	
Vraciu, Alexander	Lt(jg)	6/10	*Int*	F6F	19	0	1	
			Lex					
W								
Ward, Lyttleton	Ens	83	*Essex*	F6F	5	0	0	
Watson, Jack	Lt(jg)	33	*Land*	F6F	5	1	0	
Watts, Charles	Lt(jg)	18	*B.Hill*	F6F	8.75	0	0	
Webb, Wilbur	Ens	2	*Hornet*	F6F	7	2	0	
Wesolowski, John	Lt	5/9*	*Land*	F4F	5	0	0	
			York	F6F	2	0	0	*VBF
West, Robert	Lt(jg)	14	*Wasp*	F6F	5	0	1	
White, Henry	Lt	11	*Land*	F4F	5	0	0	
Williams, Bruce	Lt	19	*Ent*	F6F	7	0	0	
Wilson, Robet	Lt(jg)	31	*Cabot*	F6F	7	0	2	
Winfield, Murray	L(jg)	17	*Hornet*	F6F	6	0	1.5	
Winters, Theodore	Cdr	19	*Ent*	F6F	8	1	0	USNA 35
Wirth, John	Lt	31	*Cabot*	F6F	14	2	1	KIFA 4/13/45
Wolf, John	Lt	2	*Hornet*	F6F	7	2	0	
Wood, Walter	Ens	20	*Ent*	F6F	5.5	0	1	KIA 10/18/44
Wooley, Millard	Lt	18/17	*B.Hill*	F6F	5	0	1	
			Hornet					
Woolverton, Robert	Lt(jg)	45	*San J*	F6F	6	0.2	0	
Wordell, Malcolm	Cdr	44	*Land*	F6F	7	0	1	USNA 35
Wrenn, George	Ens	72	*Land*	F4F	5.25	0	0	

Yeremian, Harold	Ens	17*	*Hornet*	F6F	6	0	2	*VBF
Zaeske, Farling	Lt(jg)	2	*Hornet*	F6F	5	0	0	
Zink, John	Lt(jg)	11/18/7	*Hornet* *Int* *Hancock*	F6F	5	0	0	

Legend

Benn=Bennington	GamBay=Gambier Bay	Lang=Langley	Rand=Randolph
B.Hill=Bunker Hill	Int=Intrepid	Lex=Lexington	San J=San Jancinto
BWood=Belleau Wood	KadBay=Kadinin Bay	ManBay=Manila Bay	Sara=Saratoga
Ent=Enterprise	KalBay=Kalinin Bay	Mont=Monterrey	Ticon=Ticonderoga
Frank=Franklin	Land=Land based	Prince=Princeton	York=Yorktown

U.S. Air Force Aces in WWII

Ace Name	**Rank**	FS/FG	Theater	A/C	V.	P.	D.	Notes
A								
Abernathy, Robert	Capt	350/363	ETO	P-47	1	0	0	
				P-51	4	0	0	
Adams, Burnell	Capt	6N/-80/8	PTO	P-70	1	0	0	
				P-38	6	0	0	
Adams, Charles	1Lt	95/82	MTO	P-38	6	0	0	
Adams, Fletcher	Capt	362/357	ETO	P-51	9	0	0	KIA 5/30/44
Adams. Robert	1Lt	80/8	PTO	P-38	5	1	1	KIA 9/2/43
Adkins, Frank	LCol	17P/-39/35	PTO	P-40	2	0	0	KIFA 2/23/45
		313/50	PTO	P-400	1	2	0	
			ETO	P-51	0	0	0	
Ainley, John	1Lt	309/31	MTO	Spit	2	1	1	
				P-51	6	2	2	
Alexander, Richard	Capt	133RAF	ETO	Spit	3	0	0	POW 5/30/44
		27/52	MTO	Spit	2	1	0	
			ETO	P-51	0	0	0	
Alison, John	LCol	75/23	CBI	P-40	6	1	0	
Allen, Calvin	1Lt	5/52	MTO	P-51	7	0	1	
Allen, David	1Lt	7/49	PTO	P-40	2	0	0	
		431/475	PTO	P-38	6	0	0	
Allen, William	1Lt	343/55	ETO	P-51	5	0	0	
Ambort, Ernest	2Lt	9/49	PTO	P-38	5	0	0	
Ammon, Robert	1Lt	503/339	ETO	P-51	5	0	2	
Amoss, Dudley	2Lt	38/55	ETO	P-51	5.5	0	0	POW 3/21/45
Anderson, Charles	1Lt	335/4	ETO	P-47	1	.5	1	KIA 4/19/44
				P-51	9	0	1	
Anderson, Clarence	Capt	363/357	ETO	P-52	16.5	2	2	
Anderson, Leslie	1Lt	96/82	MTO	P-38	5	1	0	
Anderson, Richard	1Lt	18/318	PTO	P-47	5	0	0	
Anderson, William	1Lt	353/354	ETO	P-51	7	0	0	
Andrew, Stephen	Maj	7/49	PTO	P-40	1	0	1	
		486/352	ETO	P-47	1	7	0	POW 7/2/44
				P-51	0	0	0	
Andrews, Stanley	1Lt	39/35	PTO	P-38	6	3	0	
Arasmith, Lester	1Lt	530/311	CBI	P-51	6	0	1	
Archibald, David	1Lt	368/359	ETO	P-51	5	0	1	POW 12/18/44
Aron, William	1Lt	318/325	MTO	P-38	5	0	1	KIA 4/22/45
Asbury, Richard	Capt	382/363 356/354	ETO	P-51	5	0	3	
Aschenbrenner, Robert	Capt	8/49	PTO	P-40	3	0	0	
				P-38	7	0	1	
Aust, Abner	Capt	457/506	PTO	P-51	5	0	0	
Axtell, Eugene	1Lt	422N/—	ETO	P-61	5	2	0	
B								
Baccus, Donald	LCol	359/356	ETO	P-47	2	0	2	
				P-51	3	0	0	
Bade, Jack	1Lt	44/18	PTO	P-40	5	0	1	
Baker, Ellis	1Lt	40/35	PTO	P-47	3	0	0	
				P-51	3	0	0	
Bank, Raymond	1Lt	364/357	ETO	P-51	5	0	0	POW 3/2/45
Bankey, Ernest	Capt	383/364	ETO	P-38	1	1	0	
		GHQ		P-51	8.5	1	0	

Name	Rank	Unit	Theater	Aircraft				Notes
Banks, William	Maj	342/348	PTO	P-47	9	0	1	
		GHQ	PTO					
Barber, Rex	1Lt	70/18		P-39	1	0	0	
		339/347		P-38	4	0	0	
		449/23		P-38	2	0	1	
Barkey, Robert	1Lt	319/325	MTO	P-47	4	1	0	
				P-51	1	0	0	
Barnes, Truman	1Lt	339/347	PTO	P-38	5	0	0	
Beseler, Robert	LCol	—/357	MTO	P-40	5	0	0	
				P-47	1	0	0	
Baumler, Albert	Capt	75/23	CBI	P-40	5	0	0	+ 8 v. Spain
Beardon, Aaron	2Lt	459/—	CBI	P-38	5	0	0	POW 9/3/44
Beavers, Edward	Capt	503/339	ETO	P-51	5	0	0	KIA 11/27/44
Bechtel, Paul	Maj	12/18	PTO	P-39	2	1	0	
		VMF-124		P-38	2	1	0	
				F4U	0	0	0	
Becker, Robert	Capt	362/357	ETO	P-51	7	0	0	
Beckham, Walter	Maj	351/353	ETO	P-47	18	2	4	POW 2/22/44
Beerbower, Donald	Capt	353/354	ETO	P-51	15.5	.5	11.3	KIA 8/9/44
Beeson, Duane	Capt	334/4	ETO	P-47	12	1	3	POW 4/5/44
				P-51	5.33	0	0	
Beene, Louis	1Lt	49/14	MTO	P-38	5	0	1	POW 6/14/44
Bennett, Joseph	Capt	360/56	ETO	P-47	5.5	1	2	POW 5/25/44
		61/56		P-51	3	3	1	
		336/56						
Benz, Walter	Maj	342/348	PTO	P-47	8	1	0	
Beyer, William	Capt	367/361	ETO	P-51	9	0	0	
Bichel, Craig	1Lt	353/354	ETO	P-51	5.5	2	1	
Bickford, Edward	2Lt	356/354	ETO	P-51	5.5	0	0	
Biel, Hipolitus	1Lt	334/4	ETO	P-47	2	0	1	KIA 4/24/44
				P-51	3.33	0	1	
Bille, Henry	Maj	357/355	ETO	P-51	6	4	0	
Blair, Samuel	Capt	341/348	PTO	P-47	7	0	0	
Blakeslee, Donald	Col.	401/RCAF	ETO	Spit	1	2	3	
		133/RAF		Spit	1	3	8.5	
		335/4		P-47	1	0	0	
				P-51	3	0	3	
Blickerstaff, Wayne	LCol	350/353	ETO	P-47	0	1	2	
				P-51	10	0	0	
Blumer, Laurence	Capt	393/353	ETO	P-38	6	0	0	
Bochkay, Donald	Capt	363/357	ETO	P-51	13.83	0	1	
Boggs, Hampton	Capt	459/—	CBI	P-38	9	0	8	
Bolyard. John	1Lt	74/23	CBI	P-51	5	0	1	
Bong, Richard	Maj	9/49	PTO	P-38	40	8	7	KIFA 8/6/45 (US)
		VFC						
Bonner, Steven	1Lt	76/23	CBI	P-40	5	4	0	
				P-51	0	1	1	
Booth, Robert	1Lt	369/359	ETO	P-47	4	0	0	
				P-51	4	0	0	
Bostrum, Ernest	1Lt	486/352	ETO	P-51	5	0	0	
Bostwick, George	Maj	62-63/56	ETO	P-47	8	0	2	
Bradley, Jack	LCol	353/354	ETO	P-51	15	3	12.3	
Bradley, John	Maj	58-59/354	MTO	P-40	5	0	2	
Brezas, Michael	1Lt	48/14	MTO	P-38	12	0	4	Ev 4-5/45
Bright, John	Maj	2AVG	CBI	P-40	3	1	0	
		37/14	MTO	P-38	1	2	0	
		75/23	CBI	P-40	2	0	0	
Broadhead, Joseph	Maj	362/357	ETO	P-51	8	0	1	
Brooks, James	1Lt	307/31	MTO	P-51	13	1	2	
Brown, Gerald	Capt	38/55	ETO	P-38	5	0	1	
Brown, Harley	1Lt	55/20	ETO	P-51	6	0	1	
Brown, Harry	Capt	47/15	PTO	P-40	1	0	1	
		9/49		P-38	5	1	0	
		431/475						
Brown, Henry	Capt	354/355	ETO	P-51	14.2	0	3	POW 10/3/44
Brown, Meade	Capt	340/348	PTO	P-47	6	1	0	
Brown, Quince	Maj	84/78	ETO	P-47	12.33	0	0	KIA 9/6/44

Name	Rank	Group	Theater	Aircraft	Air	Damaged	Ground	Notes
Brown, Robert	2Lt	318/325	MTO	P-51	7	1	1	
Brown, Samuel	Maj	307-309/31	MTO	P-51	15.5	1	7	
Browning, James	Capt	363/357	ETO	P-51	7	2	1	KIA 2/9/45
Bruland, Lowell	Maj	355/354	ETO	P-51	12.5	3	6	+2v Korea
Bryan, Donald	Capt	328/352	ETO	P-47	4.33	0	0	
				P-51	9	0	4	
Bryan, William	Maj	503/339	ETO	P-51	7.5	.5	1	
Buck, George	Capt	307-309/31	MTO	P-51	6	0	0	
Burdick, Clinton	1Lt	361/356	ETO	P-51	5.5	0	3	
Burnett, Robert	1Lt	4/52	MTO	Spit	2	.5	0	
				P-51	3	0	1	
Buttke, Robert	Capt	343/52	ETO	P-38	5	0	2	
				P-51	0.5	0	0	
Byrne, Robert	1Lt	64/57	MTO	P-40	6	0	1	
Byrnes, Robert	Capt	44/18	PTO	P-40	5	1	0	
C								
Callaway, Raymond	Maj	8P/3P	CBI	P-40	6	1	0	
Campbell. Richard	1Lt	37/14	MTO	P-38	6	1	2	
Candelaria, Richard	1Lt	435/47	ETO	P-51	6	1	0	POW 4/13/45
Carder, John	1Lt	364/357	ETO	P-51	7	0	1	
Care, Raymond	Capt	334/4	ETO	P-51	6	1	0	POW 4/15/44
Carlson, Kendall	Capt	336/4	ETO	P-47	1	0	1	POW 2/25/45
				P-51	5	0	2	
Carpenter, George	Maj	335/4	ETO	P-47	1	0	5	POW 4/18/44
				P-51	12.83	1	3	
Carr, Bruce	1Lt	380/363353/354	ETO	P-51	15	1	2	
Carroll, Walter	1Lt	96/82	MTO	P-38	7	1	0	KIFA 1945 US
Carlson, Leonard	Maj	362/357	ETO	P-51	18.5	0	3	
Carter, James	Capt	61/56	ETO	P-47	6	3	3	
Castle, Nial	2Lt	8/49	PTO	P-38	5	0	0	
Cesky, Charles	Capt	328/352	PTO	P-51	8.5	0	0	
Ceullers, George	LCol	383/364	ETO	P-38	.5	0	0	
				P-51	9	0	2	
Champlin, Frederick	Capt	431/475	PTO	P-38	9	0	0	
Chandler, George	Capt	339/347	PTO	P-38	5	0	0	
Chandler, Van	1Lt	336/4	ETO	P-51	5	0	1	+3v Korea
Chapman, Philip	Maj	74/23	CBI	P-51	7	0	0	KIA 3/28/45
Chase, Levi	LCol	58-60/33	MTO	P-40	10	0	1	
		2Cdo CBI		P-51	2	0	0	
Chick, Lewis	LCol	317/325	MTO	P-47	6	0	0	
Christensen, Fred	Capt	62/56	ETO	P-47	21.5	0	2	
Clark, James	LCol	334/4	ETO	Spit	.5	0	0	
		GHQ		P-47	4	6	0	
				P-51	0	2	0	
Cleaveland, Arthur	2Lt	66/57	MTO	P-47	5	0	0	
Clinger, Dallas	Capt	74/23	CBI	P-40	5	3	0	
		16/51						
Cloud, Vivian	1Lt	432/475	PTO	P-38	5	1	0	
Cochrane, Paul	2Lt	49/14	MTO	P-38	5	0	0	
		96/82						
Coffey, Robert	LCol	—/365	ETO	P-47	6	0	1	
Cole, Charles	Capt	77-55/20	ETO	P-51	5	0	0	
Collins, Frank	Capt	319/325	MTO	P-40	5	0	0	POW 1945
			PTO	P-47	4	1	1	
Collingsworth, J.D.	Capt	307/31	MTO	Spit	6	1.25	1	
Colman, Philip	Capt	26P/5P	CBI	P-40	6	2	7	+4v Korea
Compton, Gordon	Capt	351/353	ETO	P-47	2.5	0	1	
				P-51	3	0	0	
Comstock, Harold,	Maj	63/56	ETO	P-47	5	1	6	
Condon, Harry	Capt	432/475	PTO	P-38	5	0	0	KIA 1/5/45
Conger, Paul	Maj	61-63/56	ETO	P-47	11.5	0	0	
Cook, Walter	Capt	62/56	ETO	P-47	6	0	0	
Coons, Merle	Capt	38/55	ETO	P-51	5	1	0	
Cox, Ralph	Capt	370/359	ETO	P-51	5	0	0	
		369/359						
Cragg, Edward	Maj	80/8	PTO	P-38	15	4	0	KIA 12/26/43

Name	Rank	Unit	Theater	Aircraft				Notes
Cramer, Darrell	Maj	339/347	PTO	P-38	.5	1	0	
		338/55	ETO	P-51	6.5	0	1	
Cranfill, Niven	Maj	369/358	ETO	P-47	0	0	1	
		368/358		P-51	5	.5	1	
Crawford, Ray	2Lt	97/82	MTO	P-38	6	1	0	
Crenshaw, Claude	1Lt	369/359	ETO	P-51	7	1	0	
Crim, Harry	Maj	531/21	PTO	P-51	6	0	.25	
Cruickshank, Arthur	Maj	74/23	CBI	P-40	8	6	0	
Cullerton, William	1Lt	357/355	ETO	P-51	5	0	0	POW 4/8/45
Cummings, Donald	Capt	523/27	MTO	A-36	1	0	0	
				P-51	5.5	0	0	
Cundy, Arthur	1Lt	352/353	ETO	P-51	6	0	0	
Curdes, Louis	1Lt	95/82	MTO	P-38	8	0	0	POW 8/27/43 (Escapee/ETO)
		4Cdo	PTO	P-51	1	0	0	
Curtis, Robert	Maj	2/52	MTO	Spit	1	0	0	
				P-51	13	1	5	
Curton, Warren	1Lt	9/49	PTO	P-38	5	1	0	
Cutler, Frank	Capt	486/352	ETO	P-47	2	0	0	KIA 5/13/44
				P-51	5.5	0	0	
Czernecki, Edward	1Lt	431/475	PTO	P-38	6	1	0	

D

Name	Rank	Unit	Theater	Aircraft				Notes
Dahl, Perry	Capt	432/475	PTO	P-38	9	0	1	
Dahlberg, Kenneth	Capt	353/354	ETO	P-51	3	0	1	POW 2/14/45
				P-47	2	0	0	
Dalglish, James	Capt	355-	ETO	P-51	7	0	4.5	
		353/354		P-47	2	0	1	
		381/363						
Damstrom, Fernley	1Lt	7/49	PTO	P-38	8	0	0	KIFA 4/11/45
Daniel, William	Col	2/31	MTO	P-51	5	0	0	
Daniell, J.S.	1Lt	505/339	ETO	P-51	5	0	0	
Davis, Barry	1Lt	317/325	MTO	P-51	6	0	0	
Davis, Clayton	Capt	487/352	ETO	P-47	1	0	0	
				P-51	4	0	0	
Davis, George	1Lt	8/49	PTO	P-47	7	0	0	+14 v Korea
Davis, Glennon	Capt	364/357	ETO	P-51	7.5	0	0	
Day, Wlliam	1Lt	8/49	PTO	P-40	5	0	0	
Deakins, Richard	1Lt	318/325	MTO	P-47	3	0	0	
				P-51	3	0	0	
Dean, Cecil	2Lt	317/325	MTO	P-40	1	0	0	POW 7/2/44
				P-47	3	2	0	
				P-51	0	0	0	
Dean, Zack	2Lt	80/8	PTO	P-38	7	1	0	
		432/475						
Degraffenreid, Edwin	2Lt	80/8	PTO	P-38	6	2	1	
DeHaven, Robert	Capt	7/49	PTO	P-40	10	0	0	
				P-38	4	0	0	
Della, George	1Lt	341-460/348	PTO	P-47	5	0	0	
Dent, Elliott	Capt	7/49	PTO	P-40	3	0	0	
				P-38	3	0	0	
Dick, Frederick	Capt	7/49	PTO	P-40	2	1	0	
				P-38	3	0	0	
Dikovitsky, Michael	1Lt	340/348	PTO	P-47	5	0	0	
Dillard, William	Capt	307/31	MTO	Spit	0	0	1	
				P-51	6	3	2	
Doersch, George	Capt	370/359	ETO	P-47	2	0	1	
		368/459		P-51	8.5	0	2	
Donalson, I.B.	1Lt	21P/24P	PTO	P-40	5	0	0	
		9/49						
Dorris, Harry	Maj	308/31	MTO	P-51	5	0	4	
Dorsh, Frederick	Capt	309/31	MTO	P-51	8.5	0	2	KIA 10/29/44
Douglas, Paul	LCol	396/368	ETO	P-47	7	1	1	
		GHQ						
Dregne, Louis	LCol	—/357	ETO	P-51	5	0	3	
Drew, Urban	1Lt	375/361	ETO	P-51	6	0	1	
Drier, William	Capt	8/49	PTO	P-38	6	0	0	

Name	Rank	Group	Theater	Aircraft				Notes
Dubisher, Francis	Capt	41/35	PTO	P-400	1	0	0	
				P-39	3	1	0	
				P-47	0	0	0	
Dubois,Charles	1Lt	75-76/23	CBI	P-40	6	0	0	
Duffy, James	Capt	354/355	ETO	P-47	1	0	0	
				P-51	4.2	0	0	
Duffy, Richard	2Lt	314/324	MTO	P-40	5	0	0	
Duke, Walter	Capt	459/—	CBI	P-38	10	2	5	KIA 6/6/44
Dunaway, John	1Lt	36/8	PTO	P-38	7	0	0	
Duncan, Glenn	Col	—/353	ETO	P-47	19.5	1	7	Ev 7/44-4/45
Dunham, William	Maj	342-460/348	PTO	P-47	15	0	0	
		GHQ		P-51	1	0	0	
Dunkin, Richard	Capt	317/325	MTO	P-40	1	0	0	
				P-47	3	5	0	
				P-51	1	0	0	
E								
Eagleston, Glenn	Maj	353/354	ETO	P-51	18.5	2	9	+2 v Korea
Eason, Hoyt	1Lt	39/35	PTO	P-38	6	2	1	KIA 3/3/43
East, Clyde	Capt	15TRS/10PRG	ETO	F-6	13	0	0	
Edens, Billy	2Lt	62/56	ETO	P-47	7	0	0	POW 9/10/44
Edwards, Edward	1Lt	411/373	ETO	P-47	5.5	0	0	
Egan, Joseph	1Lt	63/56	ETO	P-47	5	0	0	KIA 3/3/44
Elder, John	Maj	357/355	ETO	P-47	1	0	0	
				P-51	7	0	0	
Elder, Robert	Maj	—/353	ETO	P-51	5	0	1	
Elliott, Vincent	2Lt	431/475	PTO	P-38	7	0	1	
Emerson, Warren	Capt	355/354	ETO	P-51	6	1	3	
Emmer, Wallace	Capt	353/354	ETO	P-51	14	1	0	KIA (as POW)
Emmert, Benjamin	1Lt	318/325	MTO	P-47	1	1	0	+ 1 v Korea
				P-51	5	0	5	
Emmons, Eugene	1Lt	317/325	MTO	P-47	9	0	0	
				P-51	0	0	1	
Empey, James	2Lt	5/52	MTO	P-51	5	0	0	
England, James	Maj	230/311	CBI	P-51	10	1	3	
England, John	Maj	362/357	ETO	P-51	17.5	0	1	
Ernst, Herman	1Lt	422NFS	ETO	P-61	5	0	2	
Evans, Andy	LCol	335/4	ETO	Spit	1	0	0	POW 2/14/45
		—/359		P-47	4	1	0	
				P-51	0	1	0	
Everhart, Lee	Capt	35/8	PTO	P-40	5	0	0	
				P-38	1	0	0	
F								
Fanning, Grover	1Lt	9/49	PTO	P-38	9	2	0	
Faxon, Richard	1Lt	309/31	MTO	Spit	1	0	1	
				P-51	4	0	3	
Feld, Sylvan	1Lt	4/52	MTO	Spit	9	0	1	POW 6/13/44
Felts, Marion	1Lt	8/49	PTO	P-40	3	0	0	
				P-38	2	0	0	
Fenex, James	Capt	316/324	MTO	P-40	5	1	2	
Fiebelkorn, Ernest	1Lt	17/20	ETO	P-38	.5	0	0	KIA Korea
				P-51	8.5	0	1	
Fiedler, Arthur	1Lt	317/325	MTO	P-51	8	1	0	
Fiedler, William	1Lt	70-68/347	PTO	P-39	5	0	0	KIFA 6/30/43
Fields, Virgil	Capt	307/31	MTO	Spit	6	0	2	KIA 2/6/44
Fischette, Charles	1Lt	307/31	MTO	Spit	5	.5	1	
Fisher, Edwin	Capt	377/362	ETO	P-47	7	0	0	
Fisher, Rodney	1Lt	71/1	MTO	P-38	5	0	1	
Fisk, Harry	Capt	356/354	ETO	P-51	5	1	1	POW 1/13/45
Fisk, Jack	Capt	433/475	PTO	P-38	7	0	0	
Flack, Nelson	Capt	8/49	PTO	P-40	2	1	0	
				P-38	3	0	0	
Fleischer, Richard	Cat	340/348	PTO	P-47	6	0	0	
Ford, Claud	Maj	95-97/82	MTO	P-38	5	1	1.5	
Forster, Joseph	1Lt	432/475	PTO	P-38	9	3	1	
Fortier, Norman	Capt	—/354	ETO	P-47	0.33	0	0	
				P-38	5.5	0	2	
Foulis, William	Capt	341/348	PTO	P-47	6	1	0	

Fowle, James	Capt	384/364	ETO	P-51	8	0	1	
Foy, Robert	Maj	—/357	ETO	P-51	15	0	2	
Franklin, Dwaine	1Lt	5/52	MTO	P-51	7	1	0	
Frantz, Carl	1Lt	353/354	ETO	P-51	11	0	3	
Froning, Alfred	1Lt	65/57	MTO	P-40	3	1	0	
				P-47	3	0	0	
G								
Grebreski, Francis	LCol	61/56	ETO	P-47	28	1	3	POW 7/20/44, + 6 v Korea
Gailer, Frank	1Lt	363/357	ETO	P-51	5.5	0	0	
Gallup, Charles	1Lt	39/35	PTO	P-38	6	2	0	
Gallup, Kenneth	LCol	350/353	ETO	P-47	9	1	0	
Gardner, Warner	Capt	35/8	MTO	P-40	4	0	0	
				P-38	4	0	0	
Garrison, Vermont	1Lt	336/4	ETO	P-47	6.33	0	2	POW 3/3/44, + 6 v Korea
				P-51	1	1	0	
Guant, Frank	Capt	44/18	PTO	P-40	7	1	1	
				P-38	1	0	0	
Gentile, Don	Capt	RAF	ETO	Spit	2	0	0	
		336/4		Spit	0	3	0	
				P-47	16.5	0	0	
				P-51	1	1	2	
Gerard, Francis	Capt	503/339	ETO	P-51	8	0	2	
Gerick, Steven	2Lt	61/56	ETO	P-51	5	0	9	
Gholson, Grover	1Lt	36/8	PTO	P-39	1	0	0	
		432/475		P-38	4	0	0	
Gibb, Robert	1Lt	342/348	PTO	P-47	5	0	1	
Giroux, William	Capt	36/8	PTO	P-47	0	3	0	
				P-38	10	0	0	
Gladen, Cyrus	1Lt	44/18	PTO	P-40	5	0	0	
Gleason, George	Capt	434/479	ETO	P-38	3	0	1	
				P-51	9	0	1	
Glenn, Maxwell	Maj	459/—	CBI	P-38	7.5	1	3	
Glover, Frederick	Maj	336/4	ETO	P-51	10.33	1	0	
Godfrey, John	Capt	336/4	ETO	P-47	2.5	1	1	POW 8/24/44
				P-51	13.83	1	3	
Goebel, Robert	Capt	308/31	MTO	P-51	11	1	0	
Goehausen, Walter	Capt	308/31	MTO	P-51	10	0	0	
Goodnight, Robert	1Lt	356/354	ETO	P-51	7.25	1	2	
Goodrich, Burdette	1Lt	459/—	CBI	P-38	5.5	0	2	KIA 6/6/44
Goodson, James	Maj	307/31	MTO	P-51	2	0	0	POW 6/20/44
		336/4	ETO	P-47	5	7	1	
				P-51	0	1	0	
Gordon, Matthew	Capt	75/23	CBI	P-40	5	3	0	
Goss, Edmund	Maj	75/23	CBI	P-40	6	1	0	
		16-449./51		P-38	0	1	0	
Graham, Gordon	LCol	354/355	ETO	P-51	7	1	1	
Graham, Lindol	Capt	79/20	ETO	P-38	5.5	0	2	KIA 3/18/44
Grant, Marvin	1Lt	342/348	PTO	P-47	7	0	0	
Grey, Rockford	Maj	369/371	ETO	P-47	6.5	0	3	KIFA 9/4/44
Green, Herschel	Maj	317/325	MTO	P-40	3	1	0	
				P-47	10	5	0	
				P-51	0	0	6	
Gregg, Lee	2Lt	71/1	MTO	P-38	1	0	0	
		449-52/23		P-38	6	2	1	
		CBI						
Gresham, Billy	1:Lt	432/475	PTO	P-38	6	1	0	KIFA 10/2/44
Griffin, Joseph	Maj	75/23	CBI	P-40	3	0	0	
		393-392/367	ETO	P-38	4	0	0	
Griffith, Robert	1Lt	97/82	MTO	P-38	5	1	2	KIA 7/26/44
Gross, Clayton	Capt	355/354	ETO	P-51	6	.5	3	
Grosshuesch, Leroy	Capt	39/35	PTO	P-47	7	0	0	
				P-51	1	0	0	
Grosvenor, William	Capt	75/23	CBI	P-40	5	3	3	
Gumm, Charles	1Lt	355/354	ETO	P-51	6	2.5	8	
Gupton, Cheatam	1Lt	9/49	PTO	P-38	5	0	0	

H

Name	Rank	Unit	Theater	Aircraft				Notes
Hagerstrom, James	1Lt	8/49	PTO	P-40	6	0	0	+ 6 v Korea
Hall, George	1Lt	63/56	ETO	P-47	6	1	2	
Halton, William	Maj	328/352	ETO	P-47	1	0	0	
		487/352		P-51	7.5	0	0	
Hammer, Samuel	F/O	90/80	CBI	P-40	2	0	0	
				P-47	3	0	0	
Hampshire, John	Capt	74/23	CBI	P-40	13	3	0	
Hanes, William	1Lt	4/52	MTO	P-51	6	0	1	
Hanna, Harry	2Lt	37/14	MTO	P-38	5	0	1	
Hanseman, Chris	1Lt	505/339	ETO	P-51	5	0	0	KIA 7/29/44
Harmeyer, Raymond	1Lt	309/31	MTO	Spit	2	0	1	
				P-51	4	1	3	
Harris, Bill	Capt	364/357	ETO	P-51	5	1	0	POW
Hart, Cameron	Capt	63/56	ETO	P-47	6	1	2	
Hart, Kenneth	1Lt	431/475	PTO	P-38	8	1	0	
Hartley, Raymond	Capt	319/325	MTO	P-47	2	0	0	
				P-51	0	0	0	
		350/353	ETO	P-51	3	0	1	
Hatala, Paul	Capt	364/357	ETO	P-51	5.5	0	0	
Hatch, Herbert	1Lt	71/1	MTO	P-38	5	1.5	3	
Hauver, Charles	1Lt	354/355	ETO	P-51	5	0	1	
Havliand, Frederick	Capt	357/355	ETO	P-51	6	0	2	
Haworth, Russell	1Lt	338/55	ETO	P-51	5	0	1	
Hayes, Thomas	LCol	364/357	ETO	P-51	8.5	1	0	
Head, Cotesworth	Capt	44/18	PTO	P-40	8	0	1	KIA 1/18/44
				P-38	6	1	0	
Heller, Edwin	Capt	486/352	ETO	P-51	5.5	0	1	3.5v Korea
Hennon, William	Capt	17/49/7/49	PTO	P-40	7	0	1	
Hendricks, Randall	Maj	397/368	ETO	P-47	5	0	2	
Herbst, John	Maj	76/23/74/23	CBI	P-40	4	0	1	1v. RAF?
				P-51	14	1	2	
Hill, Allen	Capt	80&36/8	PTO	P-38	9	1	0	
Hill, David	S/L	AVG	CBI	P-40	10.75	0	0	
	Col	75/23	CBI	P-40	2.5	0	3	
				P-51	2	0	2	
Hill, Frank	Maj	308/31	MTO	Spit	7	1	4	
		309/31	ETO	Spit	0	1	0	
Hill, James	Maj	388/365	ETO	P-47	5	0	0	
Hiro, Edwin	Maj	363/357	ETO	P-51	5	2	2	KIA 9/19/44
Hively, Howard	Maj	334/4	ETO	P-47	1	0	0	
				P-51	11	1	1	
Hnatio, Myron	1Lt	340/348	PTO	P-47	5	0	0	
Hockery, John	Capt	82/78	ETO	P-47	7	1	0	1v. Korea
Hodges, William	Capt	370/359	ETO	P-47	2	1	0	
				P-51	3	1	1	
Hoefker, John	Capt	15TRS/10PRG	ETO	F-6	8.5	0	0	
Hofer, Ralph	2Lt	334/4	ETO	P-47	2	0	0	KIA 7/2/44
				P-51	13	0	2	
Hoffman, Cullen	1Lt	317/325	MTO	P-47	4	0	0	
				P-51	1	0	0	
Hoffman, James	1Lt	2/52	MTO	P-51	6.5	2	1	
Hogg, Roy	Capt	318/325	MTO	P-40	2	0	0	
				P-47	2	2	0	
				P-51	0	1	0	
Holloway, Bruce	Col	76/23	CBI	P-40	13	4	0	
Holloway, James	1Lt	95/82	MTO	P-38	6	0	1	
Holmes, Besby	1Lt	339/347	PTO	P-38	5	4	0	
Homer, Cyril	Capt	80/8	PTO	P-38	15	5	4	
Horne, Francis	1Lt	328/352	ETO	P-47	2.5	0	0	
				P-51	3	0	0	
Hovde, William	Maj	358/356	ETO	P-47	1	0	1	+ 1 v Korea
				P-51	9.5	0	0	
Howard, James	LCol	2AVG	CBI	P-40	6.33	0	0	
		356/354	ETO	P-51	6	1	0	
Howard, Robert	1Lt	8/49	PTO	P-40	6	3	2	

Name	Rank	Unit	Theater	Aircraft				Notes
Howe, David	1Lt	334/4	ETO	P-47	1	0	0	POW 3/3/45
				P-51	5	0	0	
Howes, Bernard	1Lt	343/55	ETO	P-51	6	0	0	
Hoyt, Edward	Capt	41/35	PTO	P-47	5	0	0	
		465/507						
Hubbard, Mark	LCol	59/33	MTO	P-40	4	0	0	POW 3/18/44
		—/20	ETO	P-38	2.5	1	0	
Hunt, Edward	1Lt	353/354	ETO	P-51	6.5	2	3	KIA 11/8/44
Hunter, Alvaro	Capt	40/35	PTO	P-39	2	0	0	
				P-40	3	0	0	
Hurd, Richard	1Lt	308/31	MTO	Spit	6	1	2	
Hurlbut, Frank	F/O	96/82	MTO	P-38	9	1	4	
I								
Icard, Joseph	2Lt	62/56	ETO	P-47	5	0	1	
Ilfrey, Jack	Capt	94/33	MTO	P-38	5.5	0	2	
		79/20	ETO	P-38	2	0	0	
Ince, Janes	1Lt	80/8	PTO	P-38	6	1	0	
		432/475						
J								
Jackson, Michael	Maj	62/56	ETO	P-47	8	0	2	
Jackson, Willie	LCol	486/352	ETO	P-47	1	1	1	
		328/352		P-51	6	0	2	
Jamison, Gilbert	Capt	386/364	ETO	P-51	7	0	1	
Jeffrey, Arthur	LCol	434/479	ETO	P-38	4	0	0	
				P-51	10	0	2	
Jenkins, Otto	2:Lt	362/357	ETO	P-51	8.5	0	0	KIFA 3/24/45
Jett, Verl	Capt	36/8	PTO	P-39	1	0	0	
		431/475		P-38	6	0	1	
Johnson, Arthur	1Lt	2/52	MTO	Spit	2	0	1	
				P-51	6.5	0	0	
Johnson, Clarence	Capt	2/52	MTO	P-38	1	3	1	KIA 9/23/44
		436-487.352	ETO	P-38	4	2	0	
				P-51	0	0	0	
Johnson, Evan	Capt	505/339	ETO	P-51	5	0	1	
Johnson, Gerald R.	LCol	9/49	PTO	P-38	20	2	0	KIFA 10/7/45
				P-47	2	0-	0	
Johnson, Gerald W.	Maj	61-360/56	ETO	P-47	16.5	1	4.5	POW 3/27/44
		63/56						
Johnson, Robert	Capt	61/56	ETO	P-47	27	0	3	
Johnston, Robert	LCol	81/50	ETO	P-47	6	0	0	
Jones, Curren	Capt	39/35	PTO	P-400	1	0	0	
				P-38	4	2	0	
Jones, Cyril	1Lt	370/369	ETO	P-51	6	0	1	KIA 9/12/44
Jones, Frank	Capt	335/4	ETO	P-51	5	1	3	KIA 8/8/44
Jones, John	Capt	80/8	PTO	P-38	8	2	0	
Jones, Lynn	Capt	74/23	CBI	P-40	5	3	1	
Jones, Warren	2Lt	49/14	MTO	P-38	5	0	2	
Jordan, Wallace	Maj	9/49	MTO	P-38	5	1	0	
				P-47	1	0	0	
Juchheim, Alwin	Maj	83/78	ETO	P-47	9	2	2	POW 5/28/44
Julian, William	Maj	83/78	ETO	P-47	3	0	1	
				P-51	2	0	1	
K								
Karger, Dale	1Lt	364/357	ETO	P-51	7.5	0	0	
Karr, Robert	Capt	5/52	MTO	P-51	6	0	2	
Kearby, Neel	Col	—/348	PTO	P-47	22	0	1	KIA 3/5/44
Keen, Robert	1Lt	61/56	ETO	P-47	6	1	1	
Kemp, Willaim	2Lt	375/361	ETO	P-51	6	0	1	
Kennedy, Daniel	1Lt	27/1	MTO	P-38	5	0	2	
Keinholtz, Donald	1Lt	94/1	MTO	P-38	6	0	1	
King, Benjamin	Capt	368/359	ETO	P-51	4	0	0	
		339/347	PTO	P-38	3	0	0	
King, Charles	Maj	39/35	PTO	P-38	5	3	4	
King, David	1Lt	382/363	ETO	P-51	1	1	1	
		412/373		P-47	4	0	0	

Name	Rank	Unit	Theater	Aircraft				Remarks
King, William	1Lt	355/354	ETO	P-51	5.5	0	2	
Kinnard, Claibourne	LCol	354/4 355	ETO	P-51	8	0	1	
Kinsey, Claude	2Lt	96/82	MTO	P-38	7	2	1	POW 4-11/43
Kirby, Marion	1Lt	80/8 431/475	PTO	P-38	5	1	0	
Kirkland, Lenton	1Lt	429/474	ETO	P-38	5	0	2	KIA 12/24/44
Kirla, John	1Lt	362/357	ETO	P-51	11.5	0	0	
Kiser, George	Capt	17P-8/49	PTO	P-40	9	0	0	
Klibbe, Frank	Capt	61/56	ETO	P-47	7	0	0	
Knapp, Robert	Capt	342/348	PTO	P-47	6	1	0	
Knott, Carroll	1Lt	49/14	MTO	P-38	5	0	0	
Koenig, Charles	1Lt	353/354	ETO	P-51	6.5	1	2	
Koralski, Walter,	Capt	354/355	ETO	P-47	2.33	0	0	
				P-51	3.4	0	0	
Kruzel, Joseph	LCol	17P/—	PTO	P-40	3	0	0	
		376/361	ETO	P-47	1.5	2	0	
		HQ		P-51	0	1	0	
Kuentzel, Ward	1Lt	96/82	MTO	P-38	7	0	5	KIA 6/18/44
L								
Ladd, Kenneth	Capt	80-86/8	PTO	P-38	12	2	1	KIA 10/14/44
Lamb, George	Maj	356/354	ETO	P-51	7	1	1.5	
Lamb, Robert	Capt	61/56	ETO	P-47	7	1	1	
Lampe, Richard	1Lt	2/52	MTO	P-51	5.5	0	1	
Landers, Jon	LCol	9/49	PTO	P-40	6	0	0	
		38/78	ETO	P-38	4	4.5	0	
		—/357		P-51	0	1	0	
Lane, John	1Lt	39/35	PTO	P-38	6	2	2	
Lang, Joseph	1Lt	334/4	ETO	P-51	7.83	0	1	KIA 10/14/44
Lanphier, Thomas	Capt	70/18	PTO	P-39	1	0	0	
				P-38	5	0	0	
Larson, Donald	Maj	505/339	ETO	P-51	6	1	1	KIA 8/4/44
Larson, Leland	2Lt	15TRS /10PRG	ETO	F-6	6	0	1	
Lasko, Charles	Capt	355/354	ETO	P-51	7.5	0	5.5	
Lathrope, Franklin	2Lt	94/1	MTO	P-38	5	0	1	
Lawler, John	Capt	2/52	MTO	P-51	11	2	3	
Lazear, Earl	1Lt	486/352	ETO	P-51	5	0	1	
Lee, Richard	1Lt	94/1	MTO	P-38	5	1	0	
Leikness, Marlow	1Lt	49/14	MTO	P-38	5	0	0	
Lenfest, Charles	Capt	354-357/ 355	ETO	P-51	5.5	0	1	POW 10/3/44
Lenox, Jack	2Lt	49/14	MTO	P-38	5	1	3	
Lent, Francis	1Lt	431/475	PTO	P-38	11	1	0	KIFA 12/1/44
Lesicka, Joseph	Capt	44/18 HQ	PTO	P-40	9	0	0	
				P-38	0	0	0	
Leverette, William	LCol	37/14	MTO	P-38	11	0	2	
Lewis, Warren	Maj	431-433/ 475	PTO	P-38	7	5	3	
Lewis, William	Capt	343/55	ETO	P-51	7	0	1	
Lieber, Lawrence	2Lt	96/82	ETO	P-38	7	0	5	
Liles, Robert	Maj	16/23	CBI	P-40	5	5	2	
Lines, Ted	Capt	335/4	ETO	P-51	10	0	0	
Littge, Raymond	Capt	487/352	ETO	P-51	10.5	0	0	
Little, James	1Lt	75/23	CBI	P-40	7	0	0	+ 1 V Korea
Loisel, John	Maj	432/475	PTO	P-38	11	0	1	
Lombard, John	Maj	16/51 74/23	CBI	P-40	7	1	0	KIFA 6/30/43
London, Charles	Capt	83/78	ETO	P-47	5	1	2	
Long, Maurice	Capt	355/354	ETO	P-51	5.5	0	0	
Lopez, Donald	1Lt	73/23	CBI	P-40	4	0	4	
				P-51	1	0	1	
Loving, George	Capt	309/31	MTO	P-51	5	0	2	
Lowell, John	LCol	384/364	ETO	P-38	3	0	1	
				P-51	4.5	0	1	
Lowry, Wayne	1Lt	317/325	MTO	P-47	0	1	0	
				P-51	11	1	0	

Name	Rank	Unit	Theater	Aircraft				Notes
Lubner, Marvin	Capt	76/23	CBI	P-40	6	3	0	
Lucas, Paul	Capt	432/475	PTO	P-38	6	1	0	
Luksic, Stanley	1Lt	487/352	ETO	P-51	8.5	0	0	
Lusk, Virgil	1Lt	49/14	MTO	P-38	5	0	1	
Lustic, Stanley	1Lt	19/318	PTO	P-47	6	0	0	
Lutton, Lowell	1Lt	431/475	PTO	P-38	5	0	0	KIA 11/2/43
Lynch, Thomas	LCol	39/35	PTO	P-400	3	0	0	KIA 3/7/44
				P-38	17	1	4	
M								
MacDonald, Charles	LCol	—/475	PTO	P-38	27	2	2.5	
MacKay, John	2Lt	27/1	MTO	P-38	6	1	0	
Magoffin, Morton	Col	—/362	ETO	P-47	5	0	1	POW 8/10/44
McGuire, William	Capt	351/353	ETO	P-47	5	0	2	
				P-51	2	0	0	
Mahon, Keith	1Lt	449-451/23	CBI	P-38	5	0	2	
Mahony, Grant	Capt	3P-17P/24P	PTO	P-40	4	3	0	KIA 1/3/45
				P-51	1	0	1	
Mahurin, Walker	Maj	63/56	ETO	P-47	19.75	3	1	Ev 3-5/44, + 3 v Korea
		3 Cdo	PTO	P-51	1	0	0	
Maloney, Thomas,	1Lt	27/1	MTO	P-38	8	1	3	Ev 8/44
Mankin, Jack	1Lt	9/49	PTO	P-38	5	0	0	
		431/475						
Markham, Gene	Capt	351/353	ETO	P-51	5	0	2.5	
Marsh, Lester	1Lt	503/339	ETO	P-51	5	1	1	
Marshall, Bert	Maj	354/355	ETO	P-51	7	0	1	
Marshall, Lyndon	1Lt	26P/5P	CBI	P-40	5	1	1	
Martin, Kenneth	LCol	—/354	ETO	P-51	5	0	1	POW 2/11/44
Mason, Joe	Col	—/352	ETO	P-47	1	0	0	
				P-51	4	0	2	
Mathis, William	1Lt	19/318	PTO	P-47	5	0	0	
Mathre, Milden	2Lt	7/49	PTO	P-38	5	0	0	
Matte, Joseph	1Lt	378/362	ETO	P-47	5	0	0	
Maxwell, Chester	Capt	364/357	ETO	P-51	5	0	0	
McArthur, Paul	1Lt	87/79	MTO	P-40	5	.5	.5	
McArthur, T.H.	Capt	95/82	MTO	P-38	5	1	0	
McCauley, Frank	1Lt	61/56	ETO	P-47	5.5	1	1	
McComas, Edward	LCol	118TR/23	CBI	P-51	14	1	1	
McCorkle, Charles	Col	—/31	MTO	Spit	5	0	0	
				P-51	6	0	0	
McDaniel, Gordon	1Lt	318/325	MTO	P-51	6	0	0	
McDonald, Norman	Maj	2/52	MTO	Spit	7.5	2	4	
		318/325		P-51	4	0	0	
McDonough, William	Maj	40/35	PTO	P-39	2	1	0	KIFA????
		35/8		P-47	3	0	0	
McDowell, Donald	1Lt	352/354	ETO	P-51	8.5	0	.5	KIA 5/28/44
McElroy, James	1Lt	358/355	ETO	P-51	5	0	6	
McGee, Donald	Capt	36-80/8	PTO	P-39	3	1	0	
		363/357		P-38	2	1	0	
				P-51	0	0	0	
McGinn, John	LCol	339/347	PTO	P-38	3	1	0	
		338/55	ETO	P-51	2	0	2	
McGratten, Bernard	Capt	335/4	ETO	P-47	1	0	0	KIA 6/6/44
				P-51	7.5	0	0	
McGuire, Thomas	Maj	431/475	PTO	P-38	38	3	2	KIA 1/7/45
McGuyrt, John	1Lt	48/14	MTO	P-38	5	2	0	
McKennon, Pierce	Maj	335/4	ETO	P-47	3.5	0	1	Ev 8-9/44
				P-51	7.5	0	1	
McKeon, Joseph	Capt	35/8	PTO	P-39	1	0	0	POW 10/7/44
		433/475	ETO	P-38	4	1	0	
		77/20		P-51	0	1	1	
McLaughlin, Murray	Capt	309/31	MTO	Spit	0	0	1	
				P-51	7	1	5	
McMillan, George	LCol	3 AVG	CBI	P-40	4.5	0	0	KIA 6/24/44
		449-23/513		P-51	4	0	0	
McMinn, Evan	F/O	61/56	ETO	P-47	5	0	2	KIA 6/6/44
Megura, Nicholas	Capt	334/4	ETO	P-51	11.83	0	6	POW 5/2/44
Meigs, Henry	1Lt	334/347	PTO	P-38	6	3	0	

Name	Rank	Unit	Theater	Aircraft				Notes
		6NFS						
Meroney, Virgil	Capt	387/352	ETO	P-47	9	0	1	POW 4/8/44
Merritt, George	Maj	375/361	ETO	P-47	3	0	0	
				P-51	2	0	0	
Meuten, Donald	1Lt	8/49	PTO	P-40	6	0	0	KIA 5/7/44
Meyer, John	Col	487/352	ETO	P-47	3	1	0	+ 2 v Korea
		328		P-51	21	0	2	
Middleditch, Lyman	Capt	64/57	MTO	P-40	5	0	0	
Miklajcyk, Henry	Capt	486/352	ETO	P-51	7.5	0	0	KIA 11/2/44
Miller, Armour	1Lt	27/1	MTO	P-38	6	0	2	
Miller, Joseph	Capt	48/14	MTO	P-38	4	0	1	
		429/474	ETO	P-38	1	0	0	
Miller. Thomas	2Lt	356/354	ETO	P-51	5.25	1	1	POW 8/7/44
Millikan, Willard	Capt	336/4	ETO	P-47	3	0	0	POW 5/30/44
				P-51	10	0	0	
Milliken, Robert	1Lt	429/474	ETO	P-38	5	0	0	
Mills, Henry	Maj	334/4	ETO	P-47	5	2	1	POW 3/6/44
				P-51	1	0	0	
Minchew, Leslie	Capt	354/355	ETO	P-51	5.5	0	4	
		357						
Mitchell, John	LCol	339/347	PTO	P-39	3	0	0	+ 4 v Korea
		78/15		P-38	5	3	0	
		HQ		P-51	0	0	0	
Moats, Sanford	1Lt	487/352	ETO	P-51	8.5	0	1	
Mollard, Leland	1Lt	308/31	MTO	Spit	4.5	1	0	
				P-5	6	0	0	
Momyer, William	Col	—/33	MTO	P-40	8	0	0	
Monk, Franklin	1Lt	431/475	PTO	P-38	5	0	0	
Moore, John	Maj	341/475	PTO	P-47	7	0	0	
Moore, Robert	Maj	45/15	PTO	P-40	1	0	0	
		78		P-51	11	0	1	
Moran, Glennon	1Lt	478/352	ETO	P-47	1	0	1	
				P-51	12	0	2	
Morehead, James	Maj	17/8-49	PTO	P-40	7	0	0	
		71/1	MTO	P-38	1	0	1	
Morrill, Stanley	1Lt	62/56	ETO	P-47	9	0	4	KIA
Morris, James	Capt	77/20	ETO	P-38	7.33	0	0	POW 7/7/44
Morriss, Paul	Capt	431/475	PTO	P-38	5	0	0	
Moseley, Mark	Capt	62/56	ETO	P-47	6.5	0	2	
Mugavero, James	1Lt	41/35	PTO	P-47	6	0	0	
Mulhollem, Robert	1Lt	530/31	CBI	P-51	5	2	2	
Murphey, Paul	Capt	80/8	PTO	P-38	6	3	2	
Murphy, Alva	Capt	362-364/	ETO	P-51	6	0	0	KIA 3/2/45
		357/						
Murphy, John	LCol	11/343	PTO	P-40	.5	0	0	
		370/359	ETO	P-47	1.75	4.5	1	
				P-51	0	1	0	
Myers, Jennings	1Lt	80/8	PTO	P-38	5	0	0	
N								
Nichols, Frank	Capt	7/49	PTO	P-40	4	1	1	
		431/475		P-38	1	0	0	
Nollmeyer, Edward	Maj	26P/5P	CBI	P-40	5	4	1	
Norley, Louis	Maj	336-335/4	ETO	P-47	1.33	0	0	
				P-51	9	0	0	
Novotny, George	1Lt	317/325	MTO	P-40	3	0	0	
				P-47	6	0	2	
O								
Oberhansley, Jack	LCol	82/78	ETO	P-47	6	2	1	
O'Brien, Gilbert	1Lt	362/357	ETO	P-51	7	0	2.5	
O'Brien, William	Capt	363/357	ETO	P-51	5.5	2	1	
O'Conner, Frank	Capt	356/355	ETO	P-51	10.75	2	3	
Ohr, Fred	Capt	2/52	MTO	Spit	1	0	0	
				P-51	5	0	0	
Older, Charles	LCol	3 AVG	CBI	P-40	10	0	0	
		76/23		P-51	8	0	0	
Olds, Robin	Maj	434/479	ETO	P-38	5	0	0	+ 4 v Vietnam
				P-51	8	0	0	

Name	Rank	Unit	Theater	Aircraft				Notes
Olson, Norman	Capt	357/355	ETO	P-47	6	0	2	KIA 4/2/44
Olson, Paul	1Lt	368/359	ETO	P-51	5	0	0	POW 12/18/44
O'Neill, John	1Lt	9/49	PTO	P-38	8	0	0	
O'Neill, Lawrence	1Lt	342/348	PTO	P-47	5	0	0	
Osher, Ernest	Capt	95/82	MTO	P-38	5	0	2	
Overcash, Robert	1Lt	64/57	MTO	P-40	5	0	.5	
Overfeld, Loyd	1Lt	353/354	ETO	P-51	9	0	0	
				P-47	2	0	0	
Owens, Joel	Maj	27/1-14	MTO	P-38	5	1	1	
P								
Paisley, Melvin	1Lt	390/366	ETO	P-47	5	0	0	
Parham, Forrest	Capt	75/23	CBI	P-40	4	2	3	
				P-51	1	0	2	
Paris, Joel	Capt	7/49	PTO	P-40	3	0	0	
				P-38	6	0	0	
Parker, Harry	1Lt	318/325	MTO	P-51	13	0	7	KIA 4/22/45
Pascoe, James	1Lt	385/364	ETO	P-38	.5	1	0	
				P-51	5	0	1	
Paulk, Edsel	F/O	317/325	MTO	P-47	5	0	0	
Paxton, Heyworth	1Lt	7P/3P	CBI	P-40	3	0	0	
				P-51	3.5	0	2	
Payne, Carl	Maj	309/31	MTO	Spit	5	1	4	
		34/413	ETO	Spit	0	1	0	
			PTO	P-47	0	.33	0	
Perdomo, Oscar	1Lt	464/507	PTO	P-47	5	0	0	
Peterson, Richard	Capt	364/357	ETO	P-51	15.5	1	2	
Pierce, Joseph	1Lt	363/357	ETO	P-51	7	0	1	
Pierce, Sammy	1Lt	8/49	PTO	P-40	3	0	0	
				P-38	4	1	0	
Pietz, John	1Lt	431/475	PTO	P-38	6	0	0	
Pissanos, Spiros	1Lt	334/4	ETO	P-47	3	0	1	
				P-51	2	0	0	
Poindexter, James	Capt	352/353	ETO	P-47	7	0	1	
Pompetti, Peter	F/O	84/78	ETO	P-47	5	0	3.5	POW 3/17/44
Pool, Kenneth	1Lt	35/8	PTO	P-40	2	0	0	
				P-38	3	0	0	
Popek, Edward	Maj	342/348	PTO	P-47	5	0	0	
				P-51	2	0	0	
Powers, Joseph	Capt	61/61-56	ETO	P-47	14.5	0	5	
Powers, McArthur	2Lt	314/324	MTO	P-40	5	0	0	
Preddy, George	Maj	487/352	ETO	P-47	3	3	4	KIA 12/25/44
		328/352		P-51	26.83	0	0	
Price, Jack	Maj	84/78	ETO	P-47	5	0	0	
Priest, Royce	1Lt	354/355	ETO	P-51	5	0	0	
Pryor, Roger	Capt	74/23	CBI	P-40	5	3	0	POW 3/26/45
Pugh, John	Capt	362/357	ETO	P-51	6	0	0	
Purdy, Jack	1Lt	433/475	PTO	P-38	7	0	1	
Q								
Quigley, Donald	Maj	75/23	CBI	P-40	5	3	5	
Quirk, Michael	Capt	62/56	ETO	P-47	11	1	1	POW 9/18/44
R								
Rader, Valentine	1Lt	111TR/ 67TR	ETO	F-6	6.5	0	0	
Rankin, Robert	1Lt	61/56	ETO	P-47	10	1	2	
Ray, C.B.	1Lt	80/8	PTO	P-38	5	0	1	
Reed, William	LCol	3 AVG	CBI	P-40	3	0	0	
		7P/3P		P-40	6	0	3	
Reese, William	1Lt	364/357	ETO	P-51	5	0	0	KIA 5/21/44
Reeves, Horace	1Lt	431/475	PTO	P-38	8	0	0	
Reeves, Leonard	1Lt	530/311	CBI	P-51	6	0	2	
Reynolds, Andy	1Lt	20P/17P 9/49	PTO	P-40	9.33	1	0	
Reynolds, Robert	1Lt	353/354	ETO	P-51	7	0	1	POW 9/12/44
Richardson, Elmer	Maj	75/23HHQ	CBI	P-40	8	0	0	
Riddle, Robert	1Lt	307/31	MTO	P-51	11	1	2	
Righetti, Elwyn	LCol	338/55 GHQ	ETO	P-51	7.5	1	2	KIA 4/17/45

Name	Rank	Unit	Theater	Aircraft				Notes
Riley, Paul	1Lt	335/4	ETO	P-47	.5	1	2	POW 4/24/44
				P-51	6	2	2	
Ritchey, Andrew	1Lt	353/354	ETO	P-47	0	0	0	
				P-51	5	0	2	
Robbins, Jay	Maj	80/8	PTO	P-39	0	2	0	
		GHQ		P-38	22	4	4	
Roberson, Arval	1Lt	362/357	ETO	P-51	6	1	0	
Roberts, Daniel	Capt	80/8	PTO	P-400	2	0	1	KIA 11/9/43
		432/475		P-38	12	1	0	
Roberts, Eugene	LCol	84/78	ETO	P-47	9	1	0	
Roberts Newell	Capt	94/1	MTO	P-38	5	1	1	
Roddy, Edward	Capt	342/348	PTO	P-47	8	0	0	
Rogers, Felix	Capt	353/354	ETO	P-51	7	0	2	
Rose, Franklin	1Lt	353/354	ETO	P-51	5	0	1	
Ross, Herbert	Maj	48/14	MTO	P-38	7	1	1	
Rounds, Gerald	1Lt	97/82	MTO	P-38	5	1	2	
Rowland, Robert	Col	—/348	PTO	P-47	8	0	0	
Ruder, Leroy	1Lt	364/357	ETO	P-51	5.5	0	0	KIA 6/6/????
Rudolph, Henry	1Lt	353/354	ETO	P-51	5	1	0	
Russo, Michael	1Lt	522/27	MTO	A-36	5	0	0	
Rynne, William	Capt	317/325	MTO	P-47	5	1	0	
S								
Sangermano, Philip	1Lt	318/325	MTO	P-51	8	0	1	
Schank, Thomas	1Lt	38/55	ETO	P-38	1	0	0	
				P-5	4	0	3	
Scheible, Wilbur	Capt	361/356	ETO	P-47	1	0	0	
				P-51	5	0	2	
Scherer, Donald	1Lt	366/358	ETO	P-47	5	0	0	
Schildt, William	1Lt	95/82	MTO	P-38	6	0	2	
Schilling, Donald	Col	—/56	ETO	P-47	22.5	0	6	
Schlitz, Glenn	Capt	63/56	ETO	P-47	11	0	3	
Schimanski, Robert	Capt	364/357	ETO	P-51	6	0	1	
Schlegal, Albert	Capt	335/4	ETO	P-47	1	2	1	KIA 8/28/44
				P-51	7.5	1	.5	
Schreiber, Leroy	Maj	61/62/56	ETO	P-47	12	1	4	KIA 4/15/44
Schriber, Louis	Capt	80/8	PTO	P-38	5	6	1	
Schuh, Duerr	1Lt	367/352	ETO	P-51	5	0	0	
Schultz, Robert	Capt	449-451/ 23	CBI	P-38	5	1	1	AKA Schoals
Scott, Robert	Col	—/23	CBI	P-40	10	5	3	
Sears, Alexander	1Lt	487/352	ETO	P-51	5	0	0	
Sears, Meldrum	1Lt	71/1	MTO	P-38	7	0	0	
Seidman, Robert	1Lt	49/14	MTO	P-38	5	0	1	
Shafer, Dale	LCol	309/31	MTO	Spit	4	0	1	
		503/339	ETO	P-51	8	1	2	
Shaw, Robert	1Lt	364/357	ETO	P-51	8	1	3	
Shipman, Ernest	1Lt	307/31	MTO	P-51	7	1	3	POW 7/31/44
Shomo, William	Capt	80/71TR	PTO	P-51	1	0	0	
				F-6	7	0	0	
Shoup, William	1Lt	356/354	ETO	P-51	5.5	0	0	POW 5/12/44
Shubin, Murray	1Lt	339/347	PTO	P-38	11	1	0	
Shuler, Lucien	1Lt	44/18	PTO	P-40	7	0	0	
Simmons, John	1Lt	317/325	MTO	P-51	7	0	0	
Simmons, William	1Lt	355/354	ETO	P-51	6	.5	5	
Skogsted, Norman	1Lt	307/31	MTO	P-51	12	0	0	
Sloan, William	1Lt	96/82	MTO	P-38	12	0	5	
Smith, Carroll	Maj	418NFS	PTO	P-38	2	2	0	
				P-61	5	0	0	
Smith, Cornelius	Capt	80/8	PTO	P-38	11	2	1	
Smith, Donovan	1Lt	61/56	ETO	P-47	5.5	1	2	
Smith, Jack	Capt	308/31	MTO	P-51	5	0	0	
Smith, John	2Lt	433/475	PTO	P-38	6	1	0	KIA 1/9/43
Smith, Kenneth	Capt	335/4	ETO	P-47	1	0	0	
				P-51	4	0	1	
Smith, Leslie	Maj	61-62/ 56	ETO	P-47	7	0	3	
Smith, Meryl	LCol	—/475	PTO	P-38	9	0	0	POW 12/7/44
Smith, Paul	1Lt	422NFS	ETO	P-61	5	1	0	

Smith, Richard	1Lt	39/35	PTO	P-38	7	0	1	
Smith, Virgil	1Lt	48/14	MTO	P-38	6	0	0	KIA 12/30/43
Sparks, Kenneth	1Lt	39/35	PTO	P-38	11	2	3	KIFA 3/44 US
Spencer, Dale	1 Lt	376/361	ETO	P-51	9.5	0	1	
Stanch, Paul	Capt	39/35	PTO	P-38	10	1	2	
Stangel, William	Capt	328/352	ETO	P-51	5	0	0	
Stanley, Morris	1Lt	364/35	ETO	P-51	5	0	0	
Stanton, Arlen	Maj	7/49	PTO	P-40	8	0	1	
Starck, Walter	Capt	487/352	ETO	P-47	1	0	0	POW 11/27/44
				P-51	6	1	2	
Starnes James	Capt	505/339	ETO	P-51	6	0	0	
Stephens, Robert	Maj	355/354	ETO	P-51	13	0	1	
Stewart, Everett	Col	328/352	ETO	P-47	1.83	0	0	
		354-355/4		P-51	6	1	3	
Stewart, James	Maj	61/56	ETO	P-47	11.5	1	3	
Stewart, John	Capt	76/23	CBI	P-40	7	3	1	
				P-51	2	1	1	
Stone, Robert	2Lt	333/318	PTO	P-47	7	0	0	
Storch, John	LCol	364/357	ETO	P-51	10.5	0	1	
Strait, Donald	Maj	361/356	ETO	P-47	3	0	0	
				P-51	10.5	0	0	
Strand, William	Capt	40/35	PTO	P-39	1	1	0	
				P-47	6	0	1	
Sublett, John	Capt	362/357	ETO	P-51	8	0	0	
Suehr, Richard	1Lt	39/35	PTO	P-400	1	0	0	
				P-38	4	1	1	
Sullivan, Charles	Capt	39/35	PTO	P-400	1	0	0	Later O'Sullivan
				P-38	4	1	2	
Summer, Elliott	Capt	432/475	PTO	P-38	10	0	1	
Sutcliff, Robert	1Lt	342/475	PTO	P-47	5	1	0	
Sykes, William	1Lt	376/361	ETO	P-51	5	2	0	POW 1224/44
T								
Talbot, Gilbert	Maj	355/354	ETO	P-51	5	0	2	
Tanner. William	Capt	350/353	ETO	P-47	4.5	0	0	
				P-51	1	0	1	
Tapp, James	Maj	78/15	PTO	P-51	8	0	2	
Taylor, Oliver	Col	—/14	MTO	P-38	5	2	2	
Taylor, Ralph	Capt	317/31	MTO	P-40	6	0	0	
Thompson, Robert	1Lt	309/31	MTO	P-51	5	0	3	
Thornell, John	1Lt	328/352	ETO	P-47	4.25	0	1	
				P-51	13	0	1	
Thyng, Harrison	Col	—/31	ETO	Spit	0	1	2	+ 5 v Korea
		309/31	MTO	Spit	5	0	1	
		—/413	ETO	P-47	1	1	0	
Thwaites, David	Capt	361/356	ETO	P-47	6	0	3	
Tilley, John	1Lt	431/475	PTO	P-38	5	0	1	
Tordoff, Harrison	Capt	352/353	ETO	P-47	3	0	0	
				P-51	2	0	0	
Tovrea, Philip	1Lt	27/1	MTO	P-38	8	1	3	
Trafton, Frederick	1Lt	308/31	MTO	Spit	0	0	1	POW 4/23/44
				P-51	5	1	1	
Troxell, Clifford	Capt	35/8	PTO	P-39	2	1	0	
				P-38	2	1	0	
				P-40	0	0	0	
Truluck. John	1Lt	63/56	ETO	P-47	7	0	3	
Turley, Grant	2Lt	82/354	ETO	P-47	6	0	0	KIA 3/6/44
Turner, William	1Lt	20P/17P	PTO	P-40	2	0	0	
		41/35		P-400	1	5	0	
		—/32		P-40	0	1	1	
Tyler, Gerald	Maj	356/357	ETO	P-51	11	0	8	
Tyler, James	Capt	5/52	MTO	Spit	2	0	0	
				P-51	6	0	1	
V								
Vanden Hueval, Geo.	1Lt	376/361	ETO	P-51	5.5	0	0	
Varnell, James	Capt	2/52	MTO	P-51	17	0	2	KIFA 4/8/45
Vaughn, Harley	Maj	96/82	MTO	P-38	7	1	0	

Vaught, Robert	Capt	9/49	PTO	P-40	2	0	0	
				P-38	3	0	0	
Vincent, Clinton	Col	—/23	CBI	P-40	6	4	1	
Vinson, Arnold	Capt	2/52	MTO	Spit	5.33	1	1.5	KIA 4/3/43
Visscher, Herman	1Lt	97/82	MTO	P-38	5	2	0	+1 v Korea
Vogt, John E.	Capt	19/318	PTO	P-47	5	1	0	
Vogt, John W.	Maj	63/56	ETO	P-47	8	0	0	
		360/356						
Voll, John	Capt	308/31	MTO	P-51	21	4	3	
W								
Waggoner, Horace	1Lt	352/353	ETO	P-51	5	0	0	
Wagner, Boyd	LCol	—/17P	PTO	P-40	5	0	0	
		V FC		P-39	3	0	0	
Waits, Joe	1Lt	15/10TR	ETO	F-6	5.5	0	2	
Walker, Thomas	1Lt	339.347	PTO	P-38	6	0	0	
Walker, Walter	1Lt	317/325	MTO	P-38	5	0	0	
Wanderly, Ralph	Capt	9/49	PTO	P-38	5	2	0	
				P-47	1	0	0	
Warford, Victor	Maj	309/31	MTO	P-51	8	1	1	
Warner, Jack	Capt	356/354	ETO	P-51	5	0	1	
Warren, Jack	Capt	364/357	ETO	P-51	5	0	0	KIA 3/18/44
Waters, Edward	1Lt	96/82	MTO	P-38	7	0	1	
Watkins, James	Capt	9/49 HQ	PTO	P-38	11	0	0	
Watson, Ralph	Maj	48/14	MTO	P-38	3	1	2	
		2/52		P-51	2	0	1	
Watts, Oran	1Lt	118TR/23	CBI	P-51	4	0	1	
				P-40	1	0	0	
Weatherford, Sidney	Capt	48/14	MTO	P-38	5	0	0	
Weaver, Charles	Capt	362/347	ETO	P-51	8	1	1	
Webb, Willard	Maj	459/—	CBI	P-38	5	2	0	
Welch, George	Capt	47P/15	PTO	P-40	4	0	0	
		—/15		P-39	3	9	0	
		8/80		P-38	1	0	0	
Welch, Robert	Capt	343/55	ETO	P-51	6	0	1	
Weldon, Robert	1Lt	356/354	ETO	P-51	6.25	0	1	
Wenige, Arthur	1Lt	9/49	PTO	P-40	1	1	0	
		431/475		P-38	5	1	0	
West, Richard	Capt	35/8	PTO	P-40	6	3	0	
				P-38	8	0	0	
Westbrook, Robert	LCol	44/347	PTO	P-40	7	1	0	KIA 11/22/44
		GHQ		P-38	13	.5	1	
Wetmore, Raymond	Capt	370/359	ETO	P-47	4.25	0	1	
				P-51	17	6	0	
Whalen, William	1Lt	324/4	ETO	P-51	6	1	0	
Wheadon, Elmer	Capt	44/18	PTO	P-40	7	1	0	
Whisner, William	Capt	487/352	ETO	P-47	1	0	0	+ 5 V Korea
				P-51	14.5	2	0	
White, John	1Lt	307/31	ETO	Spit	0	.5	0	
			MTO	Spit	5	.25	1	
White, Robert	Capt	8/49	PTO	P-40	9	1	0	
White, Thomas	2Lt	97/82	MTO	P-38	6	1	0	
Whittaker, Roy	Capt	65/57	MTO	P-40	7	2	4	
Wicker, Samuel	Maj	383/364	ETO	P-38	2	0	0	
				P-51	5	0	0	
Wilhelm, David	Capt	309/31	MTO	P-51	6	1	3	
Wilkens, Paul	2Lt	37/14	MTO	P-38	5	1	1	
Wilkenson, James	Capt	82/78	ETO	P-47	6	0	1	KIFA 6/5/44
Williams, James	1Lt	76/23	CBI	P-40	6	2	1	
Williams, Russell	1Lt	118TR/23	CBI	P-51	5	0	1	
Williamson, Felix	Capt	62/56	ETO	P-47	13	0	1	
Wilson, William	Capt	385/364	ETO	P-51	5	0	1	
Winks, Robert	1Lt	364/357	ETO	P-51	5.5	0	0	
Wire, Calvin	1Lt	43/475	PTO	P-38	7	2	1	
Wire, Ralph	Capt	9/49	PTO	P-38	3	3	0	
		—/51	CBI	P-38	2	0	0	
Wiseman, Lee	Capt	71/1	MTO	P-40	5	0	0	

Witt, Lynn	Capt	35/8	PTO	P-40	4	0	0	
				P-38	2	0	0	
Wolfe, Judge	Capt	333/318	PTO	P-38	2	0	0	
				P-47	7	0	0	
Wolford, John	1Lt	27/1	MTO	P-38	5	0	2	KIA 5/19/43
		49/14						
Woods, Sidney	LCol	9/49	PTO	P-38	2	1	0	POW 4/16/45
		—/4	ETO-	P-51	5	0	0	
Woody, Robert	Capt	354/355	ETO	P-51	7	1	1	
Wright, Ellis	Capt	—/49	PTO	P-40	6	0	0	
Wright, Max	Capt	48/14	MTO	P-38	5	1	0	
Wynn, Vasseure	1Lt	RAF	ETO	Spit	2.5	0	0	POW 4/13/44
		334/4		P-47	1.5	1	0	
				P-51	0	0	0	

Y

Yeager, Charles	Capt	363/357	ETO	P-51	11.5	0	3	
Yeager, Robert	Capt	40/35	PTO	P-39	2	0	0	
				P-47	3	0	0	
York, Robert	1Lt	370/359	ETO	P-51	5	1	0	

Z

Zemke, Hubert	Col	—/56	ETO	P-47	15.25	2	7	POW 10/30/44
		—/479		P-51	2.5	0	1	
Zoerb, Daniel	Capt	2/52	MTO	P-51	7	0	0	
Zubarik, Charles	1Lt	96/82	MTO	P-38	8	0	1	POW 5/24/43

Aces/Victories by Fighter Type

P-40 Warhawk Aces
(90 Aces/604.73 Victories)
CBI (49Aces/337.4 Victories)
MTO (14 Aces/82 Victories)
PTO (27 Aces/185.33 Victories)

P-38 Lightning Aces
(168 Aces/1247 Victories)
ETO 8-9AF (8 Aces/43.33 Victories)
MTO 12-25AF (63 Aces/375 Victories)
CBI (9Aces/62 Victories)
PTO 5-13AF (89 Aces/767 Victories)

P-47 Thunderbolt Aces
(111 Aces/905.35 Victories)
ETO 8AF (61 Aces/575.35 Victories)
ETO 9AF (12 Aces/68 Victories)
MTO 15AF (6 Aces/40 Victories)
PTO 5AF (24 Aces/177 Victories)
PTO 7AF (8Aces/45 Victories)

P-51 Mustang Aces
(273 Aces/2078.6 Victories)
ETO 8AF (160 Aces/1180 Victories)
ETO 9AF (48 Aces/382.6 Victories)
MTO 12-15AF (50 Aces/399.5 Victories)
CBI 10-14AF (10 Aces/78 Victories)
PTO 5-7AF (5 Aces/38 Victories)

P-61 Black Widow Aces
(4 Aces/20 Victories)
ETO (3 Aces/15 Victories)
PTO (1 Ace/5 Victories)

Spitfire Aces
(12 Aces/71.83 Victories)

F4F/FM-2 Wildcat
(63 Aces/461.67 Victories)
USN/F4F (23 Aces/134.67 Victories)
USMC/F4F (34 Aces/300.5 Victories)
USN/FM-2 (5 Aces+1*/34.5+1*)
• George Davidson: 1 F4F victory+4.5 FM-2

F6F Hellcat Aces
(311 Aces/2201.82 Victories)
F4U CORSAIR ACES
(102 Aces/782 Victories)
USMC (76 Aces/584.5 Victories)
USN (26 Aces/197.5 Victories)

Equivalent Ranks

Allies

USAAF/USMC	USN	RAF
General (5 Star)	Admiral of the Navy	Marshall of the RAF
General (4 Star)	Admiral	Air Chief Marshall
Lt. General	Vice Admiral	Air Marshall
Maj. General	Rear Admiral	Air Vice Marshall
Brig. General	Commodore	Air Commodore
Colonel	Captain	Group Captain
Lt. Colonel	Commander	Wing Commander
Major	Lt. Commander	Squadron Leader
Captain	Lieutenant	Flight Lieutenant
1st Lieutenant	Lieutenant (jg)	Flying Officer
2nd Lieutenant	Ensign	Pilot Officer
Chief Warrant Officer	Chief Warrant Officer	
Warrant Officer	Warrant Officer	Warrant Officer
Master Sergeant	Chief Petty Officer	Flight Sergeant
Technical Sergeant	Petty Officer (1st Class)	Sergeant
Staff Sergeant	Petty Officer (2nd Class)	Corporal
Sergeant	Petty Officer (3rd Class)	
Corporal	Seaman (1st Class)	Leading Aircraftsman
Private 1st Class	Seaman (2nd Class)	Aircraftsman (1st Class)
Private	Apprentice Seaman	Aircraftsman (2nd Class)

Axis

Luftwaffe	Japanese Navy/Army		Regia Aeronautica
Generalfeldmarshal	Gensui*		Maresciello dell'Aria
Generaloberst	Taisho*		Generale di Armele
General der Flieger	Chujo*		Generale di Squadre
Generalleutnant	Shosho*		Generale di Divisions
Generalmajor			Generale di Brigade
Oberst	Taisa*		Colonnello
Oberstleutnant	Chusa*		Tenente Colonnello
Major	Shosa*		Maggiore
Hauptmann	Taii*		Capitano
Oberleutnant	Chui*		Tenente
Leutnant	IJNAF	IJAAF	Suttotenente
Stabsfeldwebel	Hiko Heisocho	Juni	
Oberfeldwebel	Juto Hiko	Heiso Socho	Sergente Maggiore
Feldwebel	Itto Hiko	Heiso Gunso	
Unterfeldwebel			
Unteroffizier	Nito Hiko	Heiso Gocho	
Hauptgefreiter			Sergente
Obergefreiter	Hiko Heicho	Heicho	Primo Aviera
Gefreiter	Itto Hikohei	Ittohei	
Flieger	Nito Hikohei	Nitohei	Aviera

•IJNAF and IJAAF nomenclature equivalent for officers except prefixes indicating services and branches

Japanese Aircraft Code Designations

Early in 1942 Army officer Capt. Frank McCoy of the Technical Air Intelligence Unit (TAIU) devised a system of nomenclature to help identify the expanding number of Japanese aircraft for intelligence and communication purposes. Since McCoy was from Tennessee and had a hillbilly name, the first selections were names like Zeke, Nate, Rufe, and Jake. Feminine names were assigned to bombers, while masculine names were reserved for fighters and observation aircraft. When hillbilly names were expended, TAIU personnel used the names of wives and family. McCoy used his first name, Frank, and then those of his two assistants, Francis (T.Sgt. Williams) and Joe (Corp. Gratten). McCoy's wife, Louise, and daughter, June, were honored, etc., etc. The abundant Mark II Zeke was originally named the Hap as a courtesy to Air Force Chief Gen. Henry A. "Hap" Arnold. But during a headquarters intelligence briefing Arnold heard of all the Haps being destroyed in the Pacific and became furious. Very soon the Hap was redesignated the Hamp after CBI ace John Hampshire, who had been KIA.

Allied Code Name	Service	Manufacturer	Designation Type	Description
Ann Army	Mitsubishi	Ki-30 Type 97	2 place SE light bomber	
Betty	Navy	Mitsubishi	G4M	7 place TE bomber
Claude	Navy	Mitsubishi	A5M Type 96	1 place SE carrier fighter
Dinah	Army	Mitsubishi	Ki-46	2 place TE night/recon fighter
Emily	Navy	Kawanishi	H8K	9 place 4E recon flying boat
Frank	Army	Nakajima	Ki-84 Type 4	1 place SE fighter/FB
George	Navy	Kawanishi	N1K2-J	1 place SE fighter
Grace	Navy	Aichi	B7A	2 place carrier torpedo/DB
Jack Navy	Mitsubishi	J2M3	1 place SE fighter (land)	
Kate Navy	Nakajima	B5N	3 place SE carrier bomber	
Lily Army	Kawasaki	Ki-48 Type 99	4 place TE Light bomber	
Nate Army	Nakajima	Ki-27 Type 97	1 place SE fighter/FB	
Nell Navy	Mitsubishi	G3M	5 place TE bomber	
Nick Army	Kawasaki	Ki-45 Type 2	2 place TE FB/night fighter	
Oscar	Army	Nakajima	Ki-43 Type 2	1 place SE fighter
Peggy	Both	Mitsubishi	Ki-67 Type 4	6-8 place TE bomber
Sally *	Army	Mitsubishi	Ki-21 Type 97	5 place TE bomber
Tabby	Navy	Showa	L2D	3-5 place TE transport
Tojo Army	Nakajima	Ki-44 Type 2	1 place SE fighter	
Tony	Army	Kawasaki	Ki-61 Type 3	1 place SE fighter
Val Navy	Aichi	D3A Type 99	2 place SE carrier DB	
Zeke **	Navy	Mitsubishi	A6M Type 0	place SE carrier fighter

*also Jane   ** also Zero, Hap, Hamp

An early 1942 Army officer, Capt. Frank McCoy of the Technical Air Intelligence Unit devised a system to identify Japanese aircraft. Since McCoy was from Tennessee and had a hillbilly name, the first selections were names like Zeke, Rufe and Nate. (USAF)

Glossary and Abbreviations

A-1	Personnel Officer or Section
A-2	Intelligence Officer or Section
A-3	Operations or Training Officer of Section
A-4	Supply Officer or Section
AAF	Army Air Force
AA	Anti-aircraft
Abort	Turn back from a mission due to mechanical problems or weather
A/C	Aircraft
ACC	Assistant crew chief
ACG	Air Commando group
A/D	Airdrome
AF	Air Force
A/F	Air Field
AFB	Air Force base
AFC	Air Force Cross
AFM	Air Force Medal
Aileron	Hinged or movable portion on the trailing edge of the wing which function is to cause roll
Airdale	Enlisted Flight Deck Crewman
Airfoil	Any surface(e.g. wing, aileron, rudder) designed to effect a reaction from the air through which it moves
Air Group (AG)	Unit with two or more squadrons
Air Scoop	a scoop or hood designed to catch air and maintain air pressure usually to the engine
Angels	One thousand feet altitude
AP	Armor-piercing ammunition
API	Armor-piercing incendiary ammunition
Armor	Bullet proof or bullet deflecting metal plating shielding the pilot or essential aircraft parts from enemy fire
Armorer (Arm)	Ground crewman who repairs, loads, handles a/c armament and bombs
Arresting Gear	A device incorporated into the tail of an aircraft (hook) and in the landing area to facilitate landing in a limited space.
Attitude	The position of an aircraft in reference to the earth.
AVG	American Volunteer Group "Flying Tigers"
BC	Bomber Command
B/F	Bomber Force
Baby	Drop Tank
Bandit	Enemy aircraft
Bank	To incline an aircraft laterally as in rotating it around its longitudinal axis.
BB	Battleship
Beat up	Thorough buzz job, strafing run, ground attack
Belly-in	To land wheels up
BG	Bomb Group
Big Friends	Allied bombers
Bird	Airplane
Bogey	Unidentified aircraft
Bounce	Attack on an enemy aircraft usually from above
Briefing	Pre-take off instruction session
Browned off	Become angry or upset
BS	Bomb Squadron (M=Medium)
BSM	Bronze Star Medal
BuAer	Bureau of Aeronautics
BuOrd	Bureau of Ordnance
Bug	Cluster to a decoration
Buttoned Up	Ready to go, fly.
Buzz	Fly low over the ground especially the base
BW	Bomb Wing (M= Medium/H= Heavy)
CA	Heavy cruiser
CAG	Commander, Air Group
CAP	Combat air Patrol
Cat	Catapult

CATF	Chinese Air Task Force
CBI	China Burma India Theater
CC	Crew Chief
Ceiling	Maximum altitude for flying (or base of cloud cover)
CG	Aircraft center of gravity
Chattanooga	Railway strafing in a specific area
CinCPac	Commander in Chief Pacific Fleet
CMH	Congressional Medal of Honor
Circus	Large bomber escort formation
CL	Light Cruiser
CO	Commanding Officer
CominCH	Commander in Chief US Fleet
Combat box	Bomber defensive formation
Control stick	Vertical lever that operates the longitudinal and lateral control surfaces of the aircraft. The elevator is operated by the fore and aft movement of the stick while the ailerons are controlled by the side to side movement.
Control Surface	A movable airfoil designed to be rotated or otherwise moved by the pilot in order to change the attitude of the aircraft
Cowling	Removable cover as around an engine
Cowl flap	Controllable louver for regulating airflow through the engine.
CNO	Chief Naval Operations
CP	Command Pilot
CTF	Commander, Task Force
CTG	Commander, Task Group
CTU	Commander, Task Unit
CV	Aircraft Carrier
CVE	Escort Carrier
CVG	Carrier Air Group
CVL	Light Carrier
CWO	Chief Warrant Officer
CQ	Carrier Qualificaton
D	Died
Damaged (D)	Claim in air combat in which an aircraft is partially destroyed but returns to base and is repairable
DB	Dive Bomber
DD	Destroyer
DE	Destroyer Escort
Deck	The ground or flying just above the ground
Deflection	Shooting at the target from an angle
DFC	Distinguished Flying Cross
Dihedral	The angle the wing rises from perpendicular from the fuselage
Dispersal	Squadron huts on edges of airfields used for dress
Ditch	To force land in the water with the intention of abandoning the aircraft
Division	A unit of four to nine aircraft
DO	Donier-built Luftwaffe aircraft
DOW	Died of Wounds
Driving the train	Leading two squadrons into battle
DSC	Distinguished Service Cross
DUC	Distinguished Unit Citation
Duff	Bad or unreliable
E/A	Enemy Aircraft
E&E	Escape and evasion
Eager	Pilot volunteering for combat missions
Element	Two aircraft, leader and wingman
Elevator	A movable airfoil hinged to the stabilizer, which causes pitch
ETO	European Theater of Operations
FBG	Fighter Bomber Group
FBW	Fighter Bomber Wing
FCLP	Field Carrier Landing Practice

FEW	Fighter Escort Wing	Peel off	Diving away from a formation to make an attack or land.
FD	Fighter Director	PG	Pursuit Group
FDO	Fighter Director Officer	Pitch	The angle of motion from the lateral axis
FG	Fighter Group	Port	Left side
Firewall	To accelerate (e.g. push stick forward toward firewall)	POW	Prisoner of War
Flak	Anti-aircraft guns and fire	PPS	Pursuit Squadron (Provisional)
Flap	A hinged or pivoted airfoil forming the rear portion of an airfoil (e.g. wing)	PS	Pursuit Squadron
		Prang	Wreck an aircraft
Flap	Any excitement, action	PRG	Photo Reconnaissance Squadron
Flat Out	Full speed	Probable (P)	A combat claim in which it was not known if the aircraft crashed but was so badly damaged as to make a crash probable
Flight	Eight fighters made up in two sections (A,B, C and D)		
FS	Fighter Squadron		
FS(P)	Fighter Squadron (Provisional)	PRO	Public Relations Officer
FW	Focke Wulf-built Luftwaffe aircraft	PRU	Photo Recon Unit
GAF	German Air Force, Luftwaffe	PTO	Pacific Theater of Operations
Gaggle	A group of aircraft	Rack	To make a sudden violent maneuver
Gen	Information, usually rumor or hearsay	RAF	Royal Air Force
Gong	Decoration or medal	Ramrod	Bomber escort mission
Group	48 and later 72 fighters = 3 squadrons (bomber groups = 4 squadrons)	Rat	Enemy aircraft
		Recce	Reconnaissance
		Red Line	Red mark on the air speed indicator showing safe maximum speed
Hedge hop	Low flying following the contour of the ground		
He	Heinkel-built Luftwaffe aircraft	Rhubarb	Low-level strafing attack by a few fighter aircraft
HQ	Headquarters	Rudder	A hinged or movable auxiliary airfoil which causes yaw.
HVAR	High Velocity Aerial Rocket		
IAS	Indicated air speed	Rudder bar or pedals	Foot bar by which the control cables leading to the rudder are operated.
IFF	Identification, Friend or foe		
IO	Intelligence Officer	RP	Rocket projectile
IP	Initial Point the start of a bomber's run to target	R/T	Radio Telephone
Jackpot	Airdrome strafing in a predetermined area	RV	Rendezvous
KIA	Killed in Action	Salvo	Dropping bombs or firing rockets simultaneously.
KIFA	Killed in Flying Accident	SE (S/E)	Single engine aircraft
Kite	Aircraft	Scramble	Hurried launch of fighter aircraft
Knot	Velocity of one nautical mile per hour.	Section	Four aircraft made up into two elements (coded by colors)
Kriegie	Prisoner of war		
Let down	Gentle reduction of altitude as opposed to a dive	Service Ceiling	The height above sea level under standard air conditions and normal rated load that an aircraft in unable to climb faster than a specified rate (i.e. 100 feet per minute).
Little Friend	Fighter escort		
LM	Legion of Merit		
LSO	Landing Signals Officer		
MAG	Marine Air Group	Show	Mission
MAW	Marine Air Wing	Slip stream	The current of air driven aft by a propeller.
MACS	Marine Corps Air Station	Slow time	Engine breaking in period
Maneuverability	Quality in an aircraft that determines the rate at which its attitude and direction of flight can be changed.	Sortie	A single aircraft on one mission
		Spinner	A fairing covering the propeller hub
		Squadron	12 to 20 fighter aircraft out of 25 on base (AAF), 18 to 36 fighters (USN)
May Day	Warning of imminent bail out, please plot position		
Me	Messerschmitt-built aircraft	SS	Silver Star
MIA	Missing In Action	SS	Submarine
Monocoque	A fuselage construction which relies on the strength of the skin or shell mounted on vertical bulkheads for its strength.	Stabilizer	Any airfoil whose primary function is to increase the stability of an aircraft. It refers to the horizontal tail surface and the vertical tail surface.
MTO	Mediterranean Theater of Operations		
NAF	Naval Air Field	Starboard	Right side
NATC	Naval Air Test Center	Strattle	Bracketing a target with near hits without scoring a hit.
NAS	Naval Air Station	Stream	Large formation of bombers
NC	Naval Cross	Strafe	To fire on a ground target
NFS	Night Fighter Squadron	Supercharger	A pump for supplying the engine with a more air than prevailing atmospheric pressure.
NMF	Natural Metal Finish		
NYR	Not Yet Returned	Tab	A small airfoil attached to the control surface for the purpose of reducing the control force or trimming of an aircraft.
OCS	Officer Candidate School		
O/D	Olive Drab (color)		
OD	Officer of the Day, 24-hour duty in charge of station	TAC	Tactical Air Command
OLC	Oak Leaf Cluster	TAF	Tactical Air Force
Oleo	Shock absorbing, telescopic landing gear strut	Tally-ho	Making enemy contact
Ops	Operations, active duty	Tailend Charlie	Last plane in formation
OS	Observation Squadron	TDY	Temporary Duty
OTU	Operational Training Unit	TE (T/E)	Twin engine aircraft
Overshoot	To fly over or past the enemy when following through the attack	10/10	Cloud Completely overcast. Percentage of overcast expressed in 1/10th of the obscured by cloud.

TF	Task Force	
TFS	Tactical Fighter Squadron	
TFW	Tactical Fighter Wing	
TG	Task Group	
Tour	Specified time or course of duty at a given assignment or place	
Tracer	Visible bullets (every 3rd or 4th bullet)	
Tractor	Aircraft with propeller(s) forward of the main supporting surfaces	
Trim	The level attitude of the wings and fuselage with all controls neutral.	
TRS	Tactical Reconnaissance Squadron	
TRW	Tactical Reconnaissance Wing	
TU	Task Unit	
T/O	Take Off	
U/I	Unidentified	
USAAC	United States Army Air Corps	
USAAF	United States Army Air Force	
USMC	United States Marine Corps	
USN	United States Navy	
VB	Dive bomber squadron (Navy)	
VBF	Fighter bomber squadron (Navy)	
VC	Composite Squadron (Navy)	
Vector	Direct to area (on a magnetic heading)	
VF	Fighting squadron (fighter USN)	
Vic	A V-formation of 3 aircraft	

Victory (V)	A plane that is seen descending completely enveloped in flames or disintegrates in the air or whose tail or wing assembly is shot away from the fuselage or if a single seat a/c whose pilot bails out
VMF	Fighting Squadron (fighter USMC)
VMSB	Scouting Bombing Squadron (USMC)
VMTB	Torpedo Bombing Squadron (USMC)
VFSB	Scouting Squadron (USMC)
VOS	Observation float plane
VP	Patrol squadron (USN)
VS	Scouting squadron (USN usually DB)
VBS	Scouting bomber squadron ((USN)
VT	Torpedo squadron (USN)
W/A	Wounded in Action
Water	The injection of water into a combustible mixture of an engine to injection improve combustion or to improve cooling.
WIA	Wounded in action
Wing Loading	The aircraft gross weight divided by the wing area
Wingover	A climbing turn to the brink of a stall, the nose is allowed to drop, followed by a diving half roll but returning to normal flight after the dive in the reverse direction.
Wingroot	Area where the wing joins the fuselage
Write off	Total wreck, beyond repair
XO	Executive Officer
Yaw	Movement of an aircraft around its vertical axis..
ZI	Zone of the Interior, the USA
Zootsuiter	Japanese Kamikaze suicide aircraft

Index

(Includes names listed in text and **photo captions** only, not lists)

A

Abrogi, Marius (*French*): 281
Absmeier, Capt. Carl: 249, **249**
Adams, 2Lt. Burnell: 262
Adams, Capt. Charles: 165, **165**, 166
Adams, 1Lt. Fletcher: **359**
Aldrich, Capt. Donald: 75, **225**, 350, 409
Alexander, 1Lt. Richard (Dixie): 273, **273**
Allen, 2Lt. Charles: 303
Ammon, 1Lt. Robert: 319, **320**
Amos, S/Lt. E.T. (*English*): 233
Anderson, Lt. Alexander: 301
Anderson, Capt. Clarence (Bud): 346, **346**
Anderson, Col. Edward: 410
Anderson, 1Lt. Raymond: 244, **244**, 249
Anderson, 1Lt. Richard: 167
Anderson, 1Lt. Stanley: 77
Anderson, 1Lt. William: 335
Anderz, F/Ly. Tadeuz (*Pole*): 372, **372**
Andre, Capt. John: 279
Andrew, Maj. Stephen: 314
Alison, LtCol. John: 116
Allen, 1Lt. Charles: 150
Allen, Don: 379, **380**
Alley, 2Lt. Stuart: **350**
Allison, James: 35, **35**
Ambrose, 2Lt. Kenneth: 134, **135**
Archer, 2Lt. Lee: 378, **378**
Armisted, Capt. Kirk: 237
Argison, 2Lt. Robert: 294
Arnold, Gen. H.H.: 13, 80, 116, **127**, 136, 310, 415, 420, 451
Aron, 1Lt. William: **341**
Arthur, Lt. Charles: 335
Aschenbrenner, Capt. Robert: 347
Ault, Cdr. William: 238
Augarten, Capt. Rudolph: 270, **270**, 367
Augspurger, Capt. Harold: 261
August, Lt(jg) Charles: 282
Aust, Capt. Abner: **341**
Auston, Maj.: 97
Axtell, 1Lt. Eugene: 245, **245**
Axtell, Maj. George: 302, **302**, 350

B

Babak, Ivan (*Soviet*): 183
Baer, Heinz (*German*): 331
Bade, 1Lt. Jack: 382
Baird, Capt. Robert: 253, **253**, **342**
Baker, Frances: 385
Baker, 1Lt. George: **380**
Baker, Capt. Royal: 279
Baltimore, S/Sgt. George: 59
Ballentine, Capt John: 232
Barber, 1Lt. Rex: 141, 293
Bardshar, LtCdr. Frederick: 298
Barkhorn, Gerd (*German*): **74**, 75, 76, 331
Barnes, Pancho: 412

Barnes, S/Sgt. J.: 59
Barnett, Ens. James: 251
Barnum, 1Lt. Burrell: 191
Barr, Andrew (*Australian*):124
Bass, LtCdr. Harry: 216
Bauer, LtCol. Joseph: 351, 409, 415, **416**
Baumeister, 2Lt. William: 128
Baumler, Capt. Albert (Ajax): 268, 276, **276**
Bechtel, Capt. Paul: 181, **181**, 264
Becker, Martin (*German*); 308
Beckwith, LtCol. James: 272
Beebe, LtCdr. Marshall: 347, 348
Beerbower, Capt. Donald: 75, **159**, 345, **346**, 347
Beeson, Capt. Duane: 63, 77, 79, 80, 141, 264, **265**, 314, 345, 369, 379
Beckham, Maj. Walter: 59, 63, 77, **77**, 79, 225, 311, 314, **382**
Bennett, Capt. Earl: 261, 262
Benz, Maj. Walter (Jim): 152, **152**, 382
Bergman, Helmut (*German*): 308
Berkheimer, Ens. Jack: 251, 252, **410**, 411
Berlin, Donovan R.: 108, **109**
Berry, Joseph (*English*): 334
Beaudrault, 1Lt. Valmore: 330, **330**
Biesel, Rex; 221, **221**
Bille, Maj. Henry: 382
Billo, Lt. Henry: **274**, 275
Biniewski, 1Lt. Julian: 337
Bishop, Billy (*Canada*): 374
Bishop, 1Lt. Sam: 98, 100
Blackburn, LtCdr. John (Tom): 75, 88, 228, 229, **229**, **230**, 230, 231, **231**, 232, 255, **347**, 348, 384
Blair, Capt. Samuel: 151,
Blakeslee, Capt. Donald: 52, 53, **54**, 77, 101, **143**, 143, **312**, 342, 368, 409
Blatz, Mary: 290, 384
Blue, 2Lt. Wayne: 294
Blumer, Lt. John: 288
Blumer, Capt. Laurence: 126, **127**, 127
Bobrov, Vladimir (*Soviet*): 277
Boggs, Capt. Hampton: 75, 127, **127**, 128,
Bolinder, 1Lt. Robert: **249**
Bollman, Capt. William: 253, 256, 256
Bolt, 1Lt. John: 264, **278**, 279
Bond, W/M Charles: **119**, 119, 120
Bonderenko, V.Y. (*Soviet*): 183
Bong, Maj. Richard: 74, 75, 76, 81, 85, 86, 87, **87**, **88**, 89, 136, 137, **137**, 151, 212, 225, 269, 279, 291, 304, 345, 347, 385, **400**, 409, 414, **414**, 415, **416**
Bonner, 1Lt. Joel; 256
Booth, LtCdr. Thomas: 195
Boudchier, 1Lt. Jim: 158
Bowman, Howard: 157
Bowman, 2Lt. Richard: 86
Boyington, Col. Gregory (Pappy): **72**, 86, 87, 124, **225. 226**, 226, 271, 350, 351, 385, 399, **401**, 415, **416**
Boyle, 1Lt. Clifford: 374
Bradley, Maj. John (Jack): 345, **346, 347**
Bray, 2Lt. Clifton: 167, **168**
Brabham, Lowry: 142, **142**
Brannon, Capt. Dale: 178

Brereton, Gen. Lewis: 127
Breese, Vance: 242
Brewer, LtCdr. Charles: 299, 348
Brewer, Lt. Philip: 288, **288**
Brezas, 1Lt. Michael: 78, **132**, 132, **359**, 366
Bright, Maj. John: **359**, 367
Broadfoot, Capt. William: 128
Broadhurst, Harry (*English*): 370
Brooks, 1Lt. James: 346
Brown, 1Lt. Benjamin: 189, **189**
Brown, Lt. Carl: 297, 298, 384
Brown, Capt. Gerald: 367
Brown, 2Lt. Harry: **97**, 97, 98, 100, 190, **190,**
Brown, 1Lt. Henry: **397**
Brown, 1Lt. Jack: **345**
Brown, 1Lt. Quince: 103, 310, **310**
Brown, Maj. Samuel: 78, 162, **162**, 346, 407
Brueland, Capt. Lowell: **346**
Bryant, 2Lt. Frank: 189
Bryant, 1Lt. John: **345**
Buie, LtCdr. Paul: 299
Bruno, Harry: 374
Bullard, Lyman: 221
Bulow-Both Kamp, Harry von (*German*): 281
Burdick, 1Lt. Howard: 404, **404**
Burdick, 2 Lt. Clinton: 404, **404**
Burnell, 1Lt. Robert: 383
Burris, Lt(jg) Howard: 230
Burrud, 2Lt. Clyde: **173**, 174
Bush, S/Sgt. H.: 59, 382
Bykovets, Leonid (*Soviet*): 183
Byrd, Lt. Joseph: 183

C
Caldwell, Clive (*Australian*): 78, 109, **124**, 124
Caldwell, LtCdr. Turner: 250, 252
Caldwell, William: 385
Callaway, Maj. Raymond: 375, **376**
Caniff, Milt: 380, 403
Capp. Al: 293, 380, 403
Carcione, 1Lt. Anthony: **345**
Carder, Lt. John: 382
Carl, MajGen. Marion: 9, **9**, 51, 73, 77, **83**, 83, **106**, 106, 201, **201**, **203**, 350, 409, 413, **413**
Carmichael, Lt(jg) Daniel: 349
Carpenter, Maj. George: 314, 369
Carr, Lt. George: 299
Carson, Maj. Leonard (Kit): **160**, 346, **346**, **397**(a/c)
Castanedo, Lt(jg) Edwin: 216
Caswell, 2Lt. Dean: 350
Cerney, Walter: 242, **243**
Champlin, Capt. Frederick: 383
Chandler, 1Lt. Van: **409**, 411
Chase, Maj. Levi: 78, **110**, 110, 111, 132, 284, **284**, **396**
Chennault, Gen. Claire: 51, 52, 116, 118, 119, 124, 276, 287, 303, 320, 373, 373, 403
Chennault, Col. John: 403
Chiang-Kai-shek (*Chinese*): 402
Chilton, Robert: 155, **155**
Chin, Shui-Tin (Arthur) (*Chinese*): 377
Christensen, Capt. Frederick: 77, **145**, 348
Christman, F/L Bert: 122
Christiansen, 2Lt. Hans: 98, 100

Church, Lt. Russell: 103
Clark, David: 48
Clark, Adm. J.J.: 336
Clarke, F/L F.E.: 177, 284
Cleary, 2Lt. Walter: 289
Cleland, Lt. Cook: 239
Clifton, 1Lt. Charles: 281
Clinger, Capt. Dallas: 383
Closterman, Pierre (*English*): 76
Collingsworth, Capt. J.D.: 186, **187**
Colman, 1Lt. Philip: **339**, 375
Conklin, 1Lt. Joseph: 171, **171**
Cooner, Maj. Richard: 330, **330**
Comstock, 1Lt. Harold: **345**
Conger, 1Lt. Jack: 351
Conroy, Lt. Thomas: 297, 298, **298,**
Coulson, 2Lt. Eldon: 287, **288**
Connally, Lt(jg) John: 291
Converse, Sheldon (Connie): **195**, 209
Cook, Ens. Emeral: 198
Cook, Capt. Henry: 410
Cook, Capt. Walter: **76, 345**
Cooper, Gary: 412
Corninglion-Moinier (*French*): 281
Courrage, Lt(jg) Eldridge: 335
Coward, Capt. James: 184
Craig, Lt(jg) Earle: 282
Crim, Maj. Harry: **382**
Croker, 1Lt. Steven: 281
Croy, 2Lt. Manford: 329, 330
Cullerton, 1Lt. William: 314, **319**, 321
Cunningham, Lt. Randall: 281
Cummins, Capt. Donald: 331, **331**
Curdes, 1Lt. Louis: 111, 282, **283**
Curry, Ens. Keith: 335
Curry, Col. William: 368
Curtis, Maj. Robert: **165**, 165

D
Dahl, Harold (Whitey): 276, **277**
Dahlberg, 1Lt. Kenneth: 367
Dahms, Ens. Kenneth: 301
Dains, 1Lt. John: 97, 99, 100
Danahar, 2Lt. Thomas: 338
Darby, LtCol. William: 183, 282
Davenport, Lt. Merle: 384
Davidson, Lt(jg) George: **341**
Davies, F/Lt. James: 369
Davis, Gen. Benjamin: **377**, 378
Davis, Betty: 412
Davis, 1Lt. Del: 335
Davis, Maj. Duke: 84
Davis, 1Lt. George: 264, **278**, 279, 367
Davis, Capt. Glennon: 382
Davis, Capt. John: 89
Daymond, P/O Gus: 368, **369**
Deacon, Ens. E.C.: 97, 100
Dean, F/O Cecil: 149
Dean, LtCdr. William: 348
DeBlanc, Capt. Jefferson: 204, **205**, 350, 415, **416**
De Costa, Arthur: 379, **379**
DeHaven, Capt. Robert: **112**, 112, 345
Dellamans, 1Lt. Albert: 254

DeLeva, Ray: 385
DeLong, 1Lt. Philip: 351
Dick, 1Lt. Ewart: 336
Dickinson, Lt(jg) C.E.: 96, 97, **98**, 100, 198, 237, **238**
Dickey, 2Lt. Earl: 258
Dicky, Mach. Robert: 236
DiLabbio, F/O Paul: 262
Dillard, 1Lt. Joseph: **350**
Dillow, 1Lt. Eugene: **342**
Dineen, Lt. John: 206
Disney, Walt: 403
Dmitryuk, Gregory (*Soviet*): 183
Donnelly, Lt(jg), Alton: 405
Donnelly, Lt(jg), Grant: 405
Donohue, Maj. Archie: 227, **227** 350
Doolittle, Gen. James: 129, 156, 311
Dorroh, Maj. Jefferson: 290, 302, **302**, **350**
Douglas, LtCol. Paul: **146**
Dow, 2Lt. Hugh: **180**, 181, 405, **406**
Dow, 1Lt. Glenn: 405, **406**
Drake, 2Lt. Charles (Bill): **350**
Drake, William (*English*): 124
Drew, 1Lt. Urban (Ben): 330, **331**,
Drewes, Martin (*German*): 308
Drury, Ens. Paul: 385
Dubois, 1Lt. Charles: **115**, 115
Dufilho, Lt(jg) Marion: 105
Duke, Capt. Walter (Bill): **128**, 128, **403**
Duncan, LtCdr. George: 296, 348
Duncan, Col. Glenn: 77, 79, 82, **310**, 311, 314, 319
Dunham, Maj. William: 151, **152**, 303, 304, **398**
Dunn, P/O William: 368, **368**
Dupouy, F/L Parker: 121
Durnford, 2Lt. Dewey: 335, **336**, 336, **350**
Dyson, C.H. (*English*): 309, **309**

E
Eagleston, Maj. Glenn: 75, 158, 279, 345, 346, 347
Eaker, Gen. Ira: 288
Eason, 1Lt. Hoyt: 136, 136
East, Capt. Clyde: 172, 172, **173**, 327, **420**, 420
Edner, Seldon (*English*): 366, 368
Edwards, James (*English*): 124
Edwards, Ens. Emmett: 251
Edwards, Lt. William: 301
Edwinson, Col. Clarence: 288
Eichsteadt, Sgt. M.: 382
Elder, Georg-Peter (*German*): 331
Eldridge, 2Lt. William: 336
Eleftherious, 2Lt. Eleftherion: 335
Elias, 1Lt. Henry: 115
Elliott, Lt. Ralph: 207, 207, **384**
Ellsworth, Lt(jg) John: 232
Elmore, Robert: 245
Elrod, Capt. Henry: 200
Elsbery, Capt. Joseph: 378, 378
Elvgren, Gil: 379
Emmer, Capt. Wallace: 346, 366
Emmons, 1Lt. Eugene: 340
England, Capt. James: 168, 168
England, 1Lt. John: 154, 346, 346
Englert, Capt. Lawrence: 258
English, 1Lt. James: 222

Enslen, 1Lt. Lewden: 127
Ernst, 1Lt. Herman: 244, 245, 245, **246**, 246, **335**
Everest, 1Lt. Frank: 414, 415
Everton, Maj. Loren (Doc): 351
Ewen, Capt. E.C.: 251

F
Fairbanks, S/L Douglas: 370, 370
Faison, F/O Emmett: 262
Farnsworth, Ens. E. Robert: 339
Faurot, Capt. Robert: 135
Fiebelkorn, 1Lt. Ernest (Red): 280
Flatley, LtCdr. James: 52, 52
Feld, 1Lt. Sylvan: 78, 185, 186, **366**
Feldman, Seymour (Buck): 334, 334
Fenske, 2Lt. Robert: 173, 174
Ferrulli, Leonardo (*Italian*): 132
Fiedler, 1Lt. William 179, 179
Figichev, V. A. (*Soviet*): 183
Fincher, 1Lt. Deltis: 135, 135
Fischer, Capt. Edwin: 146, 334, 335
Fiske, F/O William: 369
Fisken, Geoffrey (*New Zealand*): 124
Flatley, Cdr. James: 52, 52, **238, 274, 292**
Fleming, Lt. Patrick: 213, 301, 301, **304**
Fletcher, VAdm. Frank: 199
Fletcher, Sgt. William: 258
Flinn, Ens. Kenneth: 366
Folsom, Maj. Samuel: 254
Foss, Capt. Joseph: 51, 76, 77, 84, 84, 202, 202, 226, 269, 350, 409, 415,
416
Foster, Ens. Carl: 301, 302
Foster, W.M. (*English*): 233
Francis, 1Lt. Duane: 192
Franger, Ens. Marvin: 196, 197, 282
Franks, W/C William: 48
Frantz, 1Lt. Carl: 346
Frazier, 2Lt. Kenneth: 350
Freeman, Lt. Doris (Chico): 232, 360, 384
French, Lt(jg) James: 348, 349, 404, 405
French, Harold: 404
Frese, 1Lt. Albert: 153
Froning, 1Lt. Alfred: 149
Fuchida, Mitsuo (*Japan*): 96
Funk, LtCdr. Harold: 297, 298
Furney, Lt. Maynard: 282
Fyodorov, A.V. (*Soviet*): 183

G
Gablin, 1Lt. Henry: 289
Gabreski, Lt. Col. Francis (Gabby): 39, 59, 63, 76, 76, 77, 78, 80, 81,
100, 144, **264, 270**, 278, **279**, 311, 314, **345**, 345, **348, 372**, 372, **383,**
385, 396, 409, 420
Gabszewicz, Aleksander (*Pole*): 302
Galchenko, Leonid (*Soviet*): 183
Galer, Maj. Robert: 83, 203, 204, 415, 417
Gallagher, Maj. Raymond: 303
Galland, Adolf (*German*): 329, 331, 404, 405
Galland, Paul (*German*): 404, 405
Galland, Wilhelm (*German*): 404, 405
Garrison, 1Lt. Vermont: 264, 278, 279,
Gaylor, Lt. Noel: 105, 106

Geiger, 1Lt. Manuel: 337
Geiger, BrigGen. Roy: 83
Gentile, Capt. Don: 77, 80, 102, 346, **368**, **380**, 380
Gerrick, 2Lt. Steven: 75
Gibbes, Robert (*Australian*): 124
Gibson, ARM3/c C.L.: 240
Gibson, Lt. Jack: 338
Gildea, Lt(jg) John; 335, 360
Gimbel, Capt. Edward: 366
Gise, Maj. William: 222
Gladych, F/Lt. Bolek (Mike) (*Pole*): 372, 372
Glennon, Sgt. Thomas: 258
Glinka, Dmitri (*Soviet*): 183
Glinka, Boris (*Soviet*): 183
Glowacki, S/L Anoni (*Pole*): 373
Glowzynski, Czeslaw (*Pole*): 373
Godfrey, Capt. John: 63, 77, 80, 346
Goebel, Capt. Robert: 360, 396
Goehausen, Capt. Walter: 346, 396
Golman, Norman: 124
Goss, Maj. Edward: 127
Gonzalez, Ens. Manuel: 96, 98, 100, 237
Goodlin, Chalmers (Slick): 271
Goodnight, 1Lt. Robert: 346
Goodson, Maj. James: 63, 77, **264**, 265, **314**, 346
Gould, S/Sgt. Ernest: 59
Govovets, Aleksandr (*Soviet*): 309
Graf, Hermann (*German*): 76
Graham, 1Lt. Robert: 249
Gratten, Corp. Joe: 450
Gray, Lt. James: 197
Green, 1Lt. Donald: 178
Green, 1Lt. George: 360, 367
Green, Maj. Herschel: 78, 79, **132**, **149**, 149, **154**, **164**, **264**, 265, 268
Grossman, Lt(jg) Lawrence: 336
Grunder, Capt. Joseph: 141
Grumman, LeRoy: 209
Guchyok, Ivan (*Soviet*): 183
Gumm, 1Lt. Charles: **155**, 156
Gunnell, LtCdr. Charles: 339
Guyton, Boone: **221**, 222

H
Haas, Lt(jg) Walter: 75
Haberman, 2Lt. Dale: **246**, 247
Hagerstrom, 1Lt. James: **264**, **278**, **279**
Halbach, Lt(jg) Edwin: 240
Hall, Lt(jg) Charles: 335
Hall, 1Lt. Charles B.: 377
Hall, Robert: **194**, 195, **209**,
Hall, Lt(jg) William: **239**, 239
Halsey, Adm. Chester (Bull): 292, 339
Haney, Lt. Bill: 99, 100
Hanna, 2Lt. Harry: 294
Hanna, 2Lt. Robert: 200
Hanseman, 1Lt. Chris: **409**, **411**
Hamilton, MG Henry: 408, **409**
Hamilton, T/Sgt. William: 101, 200, 210,
Hammer, 1Lt. Samuel: **153**, 153
Hampshire, Capt. John: **116**, 116, 451
Hardy, Lt(jg) Willis: 301
Hanson 1Lt. Robert: 76, 86, **224**, 224, 225, **350**, **409**, **415**, 417
Hanson, Lt(jg) Theodore: 339

Harmer, LtCdr. Richard: **255**, 255
Harmon, Capt. Tom: 127
Harrell, 1Lt. James: 256
Harrington, Lt. Archibald: **258**, **259**, 259, **371**
Harris, Lt. Cecil: 213, **349**, 349
Harris, Capt. Ernest: 113, **113**, 348
Harris, LtCdr. Leroy (Tex): 292
Harris, Lt(jg) Thomas; 384
Harris, Capt. William: 140
Harris, Ens. William: **338**, 338, **341**
Harrison, Lt. Howard: **338**, 338, 339
Harshberger, LtCol. John: **257**, 257, 258
Hartmann, Erich (*German*): 74, 75, 76
Hartney Sr., Harold: **404**, 404
Hartney Jr., Harold: **404**, 404
Hay, W/L Ronald (FAA): 233
Hawkins, Lt(jg) Arthur: 408
Hawkins, Col. John: 183
Hawthorne, Lt. William: 287
Head, Capt. Cotesworth: **264**, 266
Heath, Ens. Horace: **297**, 335
Hedman, F/L Robert (Duke): **120**, 120, 121
Hedrick, LtCdr. Roger: 230, **230**, 232
Heller, Capt. Edwin: **154**, 398
Hemsted, 1Lt. Robert: 254
Henderson, Lt. Charles: **240**, 240
Henderson, 2Lt. William: 261
Henry, 1Lt. Carroll: 320
Henry, Lt. William: 250, 251, **252**, 252
Hensley, F/O Hoyt: 176
Hensley, Ens. Laurence: 282
Herbst, Maj. John (Pappy): 168, 169, 408, **410**
Herget, Wilhelm (*German*): 308
Hibbard, H. L.: 124
Hill, LtCol.. David (Tex): 108, 115, 122,**122**,**124**, 169, 287
Hill, Capt. Frank: **185**, **186**, **187**, 187
Hill, Maj. James: **420**, 421
Hills, F/O Hollis: 176, 177, **284**, 284
Hippe, Lt. Kenneth: 206, 207, **208**, 209, **297**, **298**
Hisler, ARM2/c William: 239
Ilivcly, Maj. Howard: **379**, 380
Hobbs, Luke: 34
Hobbs, Ens. Wright: 339
Hoefker, Capt. John: 172, 172, **173**, 327,
Hofer, 2Lt. Ralph (Kid): 77, **314**, 379
Hoffman, F/L Louis: 120
Holden, Lt(jg) Robert: 255
Holleman, S/Sgt. Jack: 59
Hollister, 1Lt. Dwight: 340
Holloway, Col. Bruce: 116, 117, **117**, 118
Hollowell, 1Lt. George: 73, **203**, 204,
Hopping, LtCdr. Halstead: 96, 237
Hood, 1Lt. William: 350, 410, **411**
Hoover, Capt. Charles: **180**, 181
Horacek, Lt. Leo: 216
Howard, Col. James: 122, 124, **156**, 156, **264**, 266, **268**, **286**, **287**, 287, **415**, 417
Howe, 2Lt. John: 335
Hoyt, Capt. Edward: 340
Hudson, Lt. Howard: 75
Hughes, 2Lt. George: 163
Humphrey, Lt. Robert: 251
Hunt, 1Lt. Edward: 346
Hunt, Lt. Thomas: 254
Hutton, Dick: 194

I

Ilfrey, Capt. Jack: 130, **130, 133**, 134, 367
Ihlefeld, Herbert (*German*): 277
Immelmann, Max (*German*): 54

J

Jabara, Capt. James: 279
James, 2Lt. Cyril: **332**, 332
Janicki, F/Lt. Zbigniew (*Pole*): **373**, 372
Jarman, Maj. James: 340
Jaspar, 1Lt. Clarence: **260**, 260
Jaques, Ens. Bruce: **196, 197**
Jefferies, 2Lt. Rayford: 261
Jefferson, 2Lt. Thomas: 337
Jeffrey, Capt. Arthur: 332
Jeffrey, 2Lt. Robert: 337
Jenkins, 1Lt. Duane: **257**, 257, **258**
Jennings, 2Lt. William: 338
Johnson, Barbara: 383
Johnson, Clarence (Kelly): **124**, 126
Johnson, Capt. Gerald W.: **59, 63, 64, 77, 79, 80, 147, 148, 314, 345**
Johnson, LtCol. Gerald R.: **79**, 289, **289, 345, 347, 383, 400**
Johnson, Johnny (*English*): **75, 76**
Johnson, Capt. Ralph A.: **81**, 345
Johnson, Capt. Robert: 57, **59**, 76, **77, 78, 79, 80, 81**, 145, **147, 148, 345,
348, 383, 385, 396, 410**
Jones, Capt. Curren: 402
Jorda, 1Lt. Wayne: 345
Juchheim, Maj. Alwin: 314
Junkin, 2Lt. Samuel: **77, 101**, 101, **183**
Juutialinen, Eino (*Finn*): 237

K

Karger, 1Lt. Dale; 409, **411**
Kartveli, Alexander: **141**, 142,
Kearby, Col. Neel: 85, 86, 87, **137, 150, 151, 303**, 303, **304**, 304, **340,
383, 401, 417**
Kearby, Virginia: **303, 383**
Kearney, Maj. Emmett: 272
Keith, Cdr. Leroy: 310
Kelsey, Lt. Ben: **124**, 127
Kenney, Gen. George: **87, 89, 129, 135, 136, 137, 150, 151, 303, 312**,
417
Kenworthy, 1Lt. Charles: 183
Kenyon, Lt(jg) Karl: 217
Kepford, Ens. Ira (Ike): **88, 225, 229**, 229, **230, 231**, 399(a/c)
Kepner, Gen. William: **80, 311**, 311, **332**
Kerr, Lt(jg) Leslie: 75
Kidwell, Ens. Robert: 301
Kiefer, Lt. Duane: 340
King, 2Lt. James: 127
Kingston, Ens. William: 385
Kinkaid, RAdm. Thomas: 292
Kinsella, Lt(jg) James: 211
Kinsey, 2Lt. Claude: 132
Kirk, Ens. Rufus: 206
Kirkwood, Lt(jg) Phillip: 297
Kiser, 1Lt. George: **83**,
Kislyakov, Anali (*Soviet*): 183
Kittle, Otto (*German*): 76
Klibbe, 2Lt. Frank: 345
Kliewer, 2Lt. David: **102, 200**, 201
Knight, 1Lt. Raymond: **321**, 321, 322, **415**

Koldunov, Capt. A.I. (*Soviet*): 288
Kopsel, 1Lt. Edward: **245**, 245, **246, 335**
Koralski, Capt. Walter: 379
Kozedub, Ivan (*Soviet*): 76
Kratschke, Lt. Kenneth: 288
Kratz, Col. Winston: 249
Krupinski, Walter (*German*): 331
Kublov, Alexander (*Soviet*): 183
Kun-Tang, 1Lt.: 376
Kunz, 2Lt. Charles: **236**, 237

L

Lacalle, Maj. Garcia (*Spain*): 276
Lacy, James (Ginger) (*English*): 76
Laird, Lt(jg) Bruce: **281, 282**
Lamb, Lt. William: 300
Lambert, August (*German*): 307
Lambrecht, Maj. Peter: 252
Landers, Col. John: **157, 268**, 268, **285**, 285 (3), **286, 319, 321**, 381(a/c)
Landry, 1Lt. Robert: 76,
Lane, 1Lt. John (Shady): 385
Lang, Emil (*German*): **307**, 307
Lang, 1Lt. Frank: 256
Lanham, 1Lt. James: 337
Lankowski, P/O Witold (*Pole*): **372**, 372, **373**
Lanphier, Capt. Thomas: 268
Larrazabal, Angel Sales (*Spain*): 277
Larson 2Lt. Leland: **173, 337**
Latvitskij, N.Y. (*Soviet*): 183
Lauer, Hieronymous (*German*): 330
Laven, Maj. George: **271**, 345
Lea, Tom: 379
Leaper, 1Lt. John: **45, 336**
Lechner, Alois (*German*): 308
Leder, Ens. William: 292
Lee, 2Lt. Richard: 338
Lee, Theopholis: 13
LeFaivre, 1Lt. Edward: 253
Lehman, 1Lt. Peter: 346
LeMay, Gen. Curtis: 167
Lenfest, Capt. Charles: 366
Leonard, Lt. William: **200**, 200
Leppla, Lt(jg) John: **238**, 238
Lerch, Ens, Alfred: **290, 296**, 296, **297**
Leverette, Maj. William: **290, 294**, 294, 304
Leverette, Francis: 304
Lewis, Capt. Armit (Bill): 376
Lewis, LtCol. David: 337
Liebers, 2Lt. Lawrence: 282
Liebolt, F/L Edward: 120
Liles, Capt. Brooks: 279
Lindbergh, Charles: **140, 141, 381, 408, 410, 412**
Lindsay, Capt. Nathaniel: **260**, 261
Lipscomb, 2Lt. Paul: **174, 296**
Liska, ARM.3/C John: **238**, 238
Little, 2Lt. Robert: **337**, 337
Loesch, Lt(jg) Richard: **210**, 210, **350**
London Capt. Charles: 77, **78**, 103, **103, 144**,
Long, 2Lt. Stanley: **134**, 135
Lucchini, Franco (*Italian*): 132
Luce, Henry: 402
Lufbery, Raoul: 55
Luehring, Capt. Vernon: 128
Luma, 1Lt. John: **260**, 260

Lunn, S/Sgt. Lou; 59
Lusk, 1Lt. Virgil: 78, 131, 282
Lutzow, Gunter (German): 277
Lynch, S/L John: 370, 370
Lynch, Capt. Joseph: 342
Lynch, LtCol. Thomas: 85, 86, 87, 136, 137, 151, 178, 178,
Lyon, 2Lt. Gordon: 222, 222

M
MacArthur, Gen. Douglas: 87, 89, 137, 151, 253, 416
MacDonald, Lt(jg) Elwood: 338
Magee, 1Lt. Christopher, 271, 351, 399
Magel, 2Lt. David: 407
Magel, F/O Robert: 407
Magruder, LtCol. Marion: 253, 254, 385
Mahon, F/Lt. Jackson: 368
Mahurin, Capt. Walker (Bud): 59, 76, 77, 77, 78, 79, 145, 165, 268, 279,
    314, 345, 345, 367, 383
Malcolmson, Lucy: 385
Mallory, Lt(jg) Charles: 349
Maloney, Capt. Thomas: 367
Mallory, Lt(jg) Charles: 349
Mandeberg, Ens. Eugene: 339
Magleberg, W/M Lacy: 402
Marmier, Lionel de (French): 281
Marontate, 1Lt. William: 85, 350
Marseille, Joachim (German): 307, 307
Marshall, Maj. Bert: 360, 367
Marshall, Gen. George C.: 405
Masoner, Lt(jg) William: 297, 297, 298
Mathre, 2Lt. Milden: 382
Mattson, Capt. Conrad: 279
Mayhew, Lt(jg) Boyd: 282
Maple, 1Lt. Leonard: 245
March, Ens. Harry: 198
Marritt, 1Lt. Samuel: 189
Marseille, Hans-Joachim (German): 109
Martin, 2Lt. William: 191
Martin, LtCdr. William: 240
May, Lt(jg) Richard: 285
Maze, Maj. Robert: 252
Mazerin, F.M. (Soviet): 183
McCain, RAdm. Slew: 250
McCampbell, Cdr. David: 75, 86, 88, 89, 212, 212, 214, 214, 269, 279,
    290, 290, 295, 295, 297, 298, 299, 299, 308, 348, 384, 401(a/c), 408,
    410, 412, 415, 417
McCandliss, 2Lt. Robert: 331
McCarthy, Lt. Francis: 236
McCarthy, Ens. J.R.: 96, 97, 237
McCaul, Maj. Verne: 236
McClure, Lt. Edgar: 349
McClurg, 1Lt. Robert: 226
McColpin, S/L Carroll (Red): 368, 369
McComas, LtCol. Edward: 170, 328,
McCorkle, Col. Charles (Sandy): 162, 162, 163, 264, 266, 346
McCoy, Maj. Frank: 451, 451
McCusky, LtCdr. Wade: 197, 264, 265
McDonald, LtCol. Charles: 139, 410
McDonald, Capt. Norman: 184, 185, 186
McDonald, Ens. Philip: 251
McEvoy, 2Lt. Wil: 176
McGuire, Marilyn: 383

McGuire, Maj. Thomas: 75, 87, 87, 89, 126, 137, 139, 212, 279, 383,
    385, 400(a/c), 408, 409, 415, 417
McKennon, Maj. Pierce: 360, 367, 380, 383
McLaughlin, Capt. Murray: 346
McMillan, V/SL George: 121
McNabb, Lt(jg) John: 339
McNickle, LtCol. Marvin: 407, 407
McNickle, LtCol. Melvin: 407, 407
McPherson, Ens. Donald: 385
McQueen, Ens. Donald: 230
McWhorter, Lt(jg) Hamilton: 211, 211, 349
McWilliams, Maj. H.: 134
Megura, 1Lt. Nicholas: 367
Meiers, 2Lt. Donald: 261
Meigs, 1Lt. Henry: 256, 256
Melton, Col. Henry: 176
Menard, Ens. Louis: 196, 197, 282
Merritt, W/M Kenneth: 402
Merritt, MajGen. Lewis: 86, 417
Merony, Capt. Virgil: 50
Meyer, Col. John: 77, 82, 158, 158, 279, 385, 397(2), 410
Meyer, Sgt. Sol: 71
Meyers, Capt. Raymond: 339
Michelson, F/L Einar: 120
Middleditch, Capt. Lyman: 111
Miekle, 1Lt. William: 173
Mietusch, Klaus (German): 281
Miller, Glenn: 57
Miller, Hart: 142
Miller, Ens. Johnnie: 301
Miller, Capt. Joseph: 339
Miller, Ens. Wallace: 251
Miller, Arm1/c. William: 97, 198, 237, 238
Milliken, Capt. Willard: 314, 346
Millington, LtCol. William: 223, 223
Milne, 1Lt. William: 45, 336
Mitchell, Col. John: 268, 269, 293
Mitchell, 2Lt. Frederick: 337
Mitchell, Lt(jg) Harris: 348, 349
Mitchell, Maj. Norman: 252
Mitscher, Adm. Marc: 67, 213, 299, 359, 360
Molders, Werner (German): 277, 404
Molders, Victor (German): 404
Molland, Capt. Leland: 346
Montgomery, VAdm. Alfred: 211
Momyer, Col. William (Spike): 110, 111
Monahan, 1Lt. Harold: 148
Mooney, F/O Raymond: 246, 247, 262
Moore, Ens. Clarence: 339
Moore, Ens. J.F.: 251
Moore, Capt. John: 303, 304
Moore, 2Lt. Malcomb (Mike): 97, 98, 100
Moore, Maj. Robert: 167, 167
Moore, Capt. William: 340
Moranville, Lt(jg) Horace (Rabbit): 360, 367
Morgan, Lt(jg) Harrison: 301
Moreland, Maj. James: 274, 274
Morrill, 1Lt. Stanley: 345
Morris, Capt. James: 129, 129
Morris, 2Lt. John: 244, 244
Morris, Lt. Bert (Wayne): 412, 412
Morrison, 1Lt. Creel: 245
Moseley, C.C.: 13

Mount, 1Lt. William: **109**, 110
Murphy, 1Lt. Eugene: **333**, 333
Murphy, LtCol. John: **332**, 332
Murphy, 1Lt. Randal: **319**, 320,
Murray, RAdm. George: **292**
Myers, Maj. Joseph: **329**, **330**, 330
Myers, Ens. Ora: **339**, 339

N
Nagle, Mach. Patrick: **198**
Nall, Ens. R.L.: **296**
Neale, V/SL Robert: 122, **122**, 123, **123**
Neefus, Capt. James: **236**, 236
Newkirk, S/L John: 122, **123**
Newman, 2Lt. Stanley: **337**
Newton, Percival (*New Zealand*): **124**
Nichol, LtCdr. Broomfield: **96**, **237**
Nichols, Capt. Frank: **383**
Nichols, Capt. James: **385**
Nimitz, Adm. Chester: 106, 236, **292**
Noel, Ens. James: **335**
Nollemeyer, Maj. Edward: **109**
Nooy, Lt(jg) Cornelius: 213, **304**, 304,
Norley, Maj. Louis: **381**, **383**
Norris, Lt.: **98**
Northrop, Jack: **242**, 243
Novotny, 1Lt. George: **149**
Nowotny, Walter (*German*): **307**, 308, **329**, **330**
Null, Lt. Cleveland: 342

O
Obenour, Ens. G.W.: **251**
Obermiller, 2Lt. James: **135**
O'Connell, 1Lt. Philip: **191**
O'Conner, Capt. Frank: **346**
O'Hare, LtCdr. Edward (Butch): 77, 83, 88, 105, **105**, **106**, 194, **198**, 198, **210**, **291**, **299**, **408**, **415**, 418
O'Hare, Rita: **106**
O'Keefe, 1Lt. Jerry: **302**, 302, 350, **399**
Older, LtCol. Charles: 115, 120, **120**, **121**, 124, **264**, 266
Olds, MajGen. Robert: **280**, **404**, 405
Olds, Maj. Robin: **264**, 267, **280**, 280, **281**, **404**, **405**, **410**
Olson, Col. Arvid: **165**
Olszewski, Lt(jg) Edward: **217**, 217, 282
O'Neil, 2Lt. Merlin: **336**
O'Neill, Capt. Eugene: **345**, 403
O'Neill, 1Lt. Hugh (Danny): **228**, **229**, **254**, 254
O'Neill, 1Lt. William: **109**, 110
Orth, Lt(jg) John: **251**
Orzel, 2Lt. Bernard: **245**
Oesau, Walter (*German*): **277**
Osterkamp, Theo (*German*): **281**, 409, **411**
Outlaw, LtCdr. Edward: **284**
Overend, W/M Edward; **121**

P
Packard, AP1 Howard: **198**
Paisley, 2Lt. Melvin: 340
Palmer, F/O Cyril: **369**
Palmer, Capt. Samuel: **127**

Parker, Frank: **338**
Parks, Oliver: 13
Pattilo, 2Lt. Charles (Buck); **406**, 406
Pattilo, 2Lt. Cuthbert (Bill): **406**, 406
Pattle, Marmaduke (Pat) (*South Africa*): **75**
Paulk, F/O Edsel: **149**
Pavlovich, Ens. Paul: **216**
Paxton, George: **124**
Paxton, 1Lt. Heywood: **375**, 375
Payne, Maj. Carl: **111**, **183**, 184, **282**, 283
Peck, Lt(jg) Edward: **335**
Peck, F/Lt. James: **369**
Penrod, S/Sgt. J.C.: 57, 59
Perdomo, 1Lt. Oscar: **167**, 338, **339**, **340**, 340
Peterson, Col. Chesley: **286**, **368**, **369**, 369
Peterson, 1Lt. Douglas: **319**
Peterson, 1Lt. Garth: **335**
Peterson, Capt. Richard (Bud): **346**, 346
Petry, F/O Austin: **260**, 261
Petty, George: **379**
Petty, Lt. Raymond: **345**
Phillips, F/O Charles: **249**
Philo, Capt. Herbert: **331**
Picken, Lt. Henry: **349**
Pierce, 2Lt. H.L.: **336**
Pissano, 1Lt. Spiro (Steve): **379**
Pokryshkin, Alexander (*Soviet*): **76**, **183**, 183
Porter, Maj. Bruce: **254**, **336**, **385**
Porter, 2Lt. Philip: **247**, 247
Powers, Capt. Joseph: **348**
Powers, 1Lt. Lewis: **335**, 335
Preddy, Capt. George: 59, 62, 63, 77, 82, 157, 157, **385**, **404**, 406, **410**
Preddy, 1Lt. William: **404**, 406
Prescott, W/M Robert: **123**
Presley, Lt(jg) Wayne: 211, **211**
Price, Capt. Howard: **279**
Priest, 1Lt. Royce: 360
Procter, Lt(jg) Maurice: 338,
Putnam, Maj. Paul: **102**

Q
Quiel, Ens. Norwal: **297**
Quirk, Capt. Michael: **348**
Quilty, Capt. Joseph: **222**, 222

R
Raby, LtCdr. John: **282**
Radford, RAdm. Arthur: **210**
Raines, Ella: **281**
Rall, Gunter (*German*): **76**
Rath, Gerhard (*German*): 308
Rathbun, Maj. Daniel: **176**
Rasmussen, 1Lt. Philip: 97, **97**, **98**, **100**, **190**, 190,
Rawie, Lt(jg) Wilmer: **197**. 197
Rechkalov, Gregori (*Soviet*): **76**, 183
Rector, VS/L Edward: 115, 119, 11, **120**, 123
Reding, Chip: **238**
Reed, LtCol. William: **375**, 375, **376**
Reeves, Lt(jg) Donald: **285**
Reeves, 1Lt. Horace: **339**
Reeves, 1Lt. Leonard (Randy): **170**, 171,

Reidy, Lt. Thomas: 338
Reiserer, Lt. Russell: 250, 300
Rentschler, Frederick: 32, 34
Reuhlow, Lt. Stanley: 292
Reuter, Lt. Bruce: 217, 252, 253
Reynolds, 2Lt. Andrew: 83, 113
Reynolds, 1Lt. Robert: 383
Reynolds, Maj. Thomas: 321, 321, 376
Rhodes, Ens. Robert: 335
Rickenbacker, Capt. Edward (WWI record): 76, 77, 80, 84, 86, 87, 87, 137, 202, 225, 385
Riddle, 1Lt. Robert: 346
Rigg, LtCdr. James: 75, 348
Righetti, Col. Elwyn: 63, 314, 319, 320, 331
Rimmerman, Col. Benjamin: 319
Ritchey, 1Lt. Andrew: 341
Ritchie, Capt. Steven: 281
Robbins, Maj. Jay: 129, 140,
Robbins, Ina: 383
Robbins, Maj. Jay: 383, 400
Robins, Gen. Warner: 127
Roberson, 1Lt. Arval: 381(a/c), 383
Roberts, Maj. Eugene: 75, 78, 79, 103
Roberts, Capt. Newell: 130
Robinson, Edward G.: 412
Rogers, CO Robert: 97, 99, 100
Rooseveldt, President Franklin D.: 84, 106, 118, 212, 291, 416, 417, 418, 419
Rosbert, F/L Joseph: 120
Rosie the Riveter: 32, 32
Rouse, F/O Harold: 153
Royce, Sir Henry: 36, 37
Rudorffer, Erich (German) 76, 307
Runyon, Ch/Mach. Donald: 198, 199
Ruhsam, 1Lt. John: 350, 399
Rushing, Lt(jg) Roy: 88, 212, 291, 297, 297, 298, 348
Russo, 1Lt. Michael: 176, 176
Rutkowski, S/L Kazimierz (Pole): 372

S
Safford, S/Sgt. Ralph: 59
Sahl, Lt.: 121
Sahloff, Lt(jg) Joseph: 338, 339
Sandell, S/L Robert: 120
Sanders, 1Lt. Lewis: 97, 97, 98
Sandidge, Ens. Falvey: 339
Sargent, Ens. John: 360
Sawicz, S/L Tadeuz (Pole): 372, 372
Sawyer, F/L Charles: 123
Sayn-Wittenstein, Heinrich zu (German): 308
Scott, Capt. Robert: 249, 249, 410
Schalk, Johann (German): 411
Schecter, Cdr. Gordon: 301
Schenk, Wolfgang (German); 329
Schiel, VS/L Frank: 115
Schilling, Capt. David: 58, 59, 76, 77, 79, 80, 82, 145, 345, 345, 380, 383, 403(a/c), 410
Schilling, F/L Erik: 402
Schlueter, 1Lt. Edward: 261

Schmued, Edgar: 155, 155
Schnaufer, Heinz-Wilhelm (German): 308, 308,
Schroeder, 1Lt.George: 337
Schubert, Siegfried (German); 332
Schultz, Capt. Alfred: 192, 192
Schwable, LtCol. Frank: 257, 257, 258
Schwendler, William: 194, 209, 209
Scott, Col. Robert: 115
Sedaker, Lt. Thomas: 75
Sedvert, 1Lt. Theodore: 331
Segal, 1Lt. Harold: 350
Shirley, Lt. James: 297, 298
Seiler, Raymond (German): 277
Selles, Chang: 276, 277
Shaffer, 2Lt. Joseph: 77, 100, 101, 110, 128, 180
Shahan, 2Lt. Elza: 77, 100, 101, 101, 110, 128
Sharp, 2Lt. James: 336
Sharpsteen, Capt. William: 135
Shaw, 1Lt. Edward: 409
Sherman, Adm. Frederick: 106, 223, 290, 291
Shiazaki, Shigekazu (Japan): 97
Shields, Lt(jg) Charles: 195, 282
Shindo, Suburo (Japan): 97
Shonohara, Hiromichi (Japan): 308, 308,
Shoema, Ens. Joseph: 198ker,
Shomo, Capt. William: 174. 174, 290, 296, 296, 415, 418
Shukov, K.V. (Soviet): 183
Slack, Lt(jg) Albert: 291
Sloan, 1Lt. William (Dixie): 78, 131, 131, 149,
Slovik, 1Lt. Edward: 253, 254, 256
Smith, Maj. Carroll: 242, 247, 247, 248, 248, 256, 262, 262
Smith, Lt(jg) Clinton: 348, 349
Smith, Cdr. Daniel (Dog): 75, 409
Smith, 1Lt. Edwin: 186
Smith, 2Lt. James: 249, 249
Smith, Lt(jg) John: 232
Smith, Capt. John: 51, 77, 83, 83, 84, 107, 202, 203, 350, 407, 409, 415, 418
Smith, 1Lt. Paul: 244, 244, 245, 335
Smith, 1Lt. Virgil: 78, 130, 130
Smirnov, Aleksej (Soviet): 183
Sobanski, Capt. Waclaw (Mike): 374, 374
Somers, Lt. Charles: 236
Southerland, Cdr. James (Pug): 385
Spaatz, Brig. Gen. Carl: 10, 417
Spangler, 1Lt. Charles: 335
Spatz, 1Lt. Donald: 256
Spears, Capt. Harold: 225, 350
Spelis, Capt. Tadas: 335
Sprinkle, Lt. Homer: 294
Stambrook, Lt. Richard: 384
Starnes, 1Lt. James: 320
Steinhoff, Johannes (German): 331
Stenstrom, Lt. Joseph: 335
Stephens, Capt. Robert: 346
Sterling, 2Lt. Gordon: 98, 100
Stevens, 1Lt. George: 340
Stewart, Maj. James: 345, 348
Stewart, R.M. (Australia): 289
Stillwell, Gen. Joseph: 127

Stimpson, Lt. Charles: 264, **267,**
Strane, Lt. John: 216, **216**, 348
Strauss, Lt. Allison: 103
Stout, T/Sgt. Charles: 258
Strelow, Hans (*German*): 411, **411**
Stubbs, Ens. Wilton: 207
Suehr, 1Lt. Richard: 182, **182**
Swett, 1Lt. James: 290, 293, **293**, 350, 359, 415, **418**
Swift, 2Lt. Kenneth: 337
Swisher, Ens. Lee: 75
Symmes, Lt(jg) John: 264, **267**

T
Takahashi, Kakuichi (*Japan*): 96
Talbot, 1Lt. Gilbert: 156
Tapp, Maj. James: 271, **271**
Tarleton, Ens, George: 250
Tapp, Maj. James: 166, **166,**
Taylor, 2Lt. Kenneth: **96, 97**, 97, 98, 100
Taylor, Col. Oliver: 294, 367
Taylor, Lt(jg) Robert: **412**
Taylor, Ens. Will: **196**, 197
Teaff, Ens. Perry: 96, 237
Terrill, 1Lt. Francis: 75, **350**
Thach, LtCdr. John (Jimmy): **53**, 55, 77, 105, 408, **408**
Thacker, 1Lt. John: 98, 100
Tinker, Frank: 276, **277**
Thomas, 1Lt. Franklin: 75
Thomas, 1Lt. Tom: **175**, 175
Thomas, Capt. Wilbur: 409
Thury, Maj. Joseph: 314, 319, **319**, 320
Thyng, Maj. Harrison: 102, **184**, 185, 264, **278**, 279, 282, 283
Tice, LtCol. Clay: **345**
Tice, Ens. John: 336
Tiedeman, T/Sgt. Walter: 258
Tierney, 1Lt. Robert: 244, **244**, 245, 335
Toaspern, Lt(jg) Edward: 338
Tomlinson, Corp. Edwin: 261
Tondi, Angelo (*Italian*): 288
Tokyo Rose: 66
Townsend, Lt. Eugene: 297, 298
Trafton, 1Lt. Frederick: 162, **163**, 383
Tripp, LSO Dick: **68**
Triplett, Ens. George: 335
Troubridge, T.H. (*England*): 282
Trowbridge, 2Lt. Eugene: 107
Trud, Andre (*Soviet*): 183
Truluck, 1Lt. John: **345**
Truman, President Harry S.: **416**
Tsang, 1Lt. His-Lan (*Chinese*): 376
Turner, Adm. Kelly: 84
Turner, Capt. Richard: **346**
Turner, Maj. William: 375, **375**, 376, 399
Tuttle, 1Lt. Ralph: 256
Twelves, Lt(jg) Wendell: 296, 348
Twinning, Gen. Nathan: 129
Tyler, Maj. Gerald: 75

U
Urbanowicz, Col. Witold (*Pole*): 373, **373**
Urton, Lt. Thomas: 288

V
Valencia, Lt. Eugene: **213**, 349
Valenta, F/O Irvin: **345**
Van Haren, Lt. Arthur: 349
Vargas, Alberto: 379
Varnell, Capt. James: 78, **164,**
Vattendahl, Margorie (Bong): 86, 137, 385, **400**
Vaughn, Maj. Everett: 253, 255
Vejtasa, Lt. Stanley: 88, 199, 239, 250, 290, 292, **292**
Valencia, Lt. Eugene: **348**, 349
Villamor, Jesus (*Philippines*): 188, **188**
Vincent, B.Gen. Clinton (Casey): 321, 380, **403**
Vincent, Stanley (*England*): 281
Vinson, Capt. Arnold: 184, **185**, 186
Virdenn, Col.: 321
Vita, Lt(jg) Harold: **196**, 197, 282
Vogt. Ens. John: 96, 100
Vogt, Capt. John: 167
Voll, Capt. John: 78, **80, 163**, 163, 346, **346**
Vollbracht, Friderich (*German*): 411
Vorse, Cdr. Albert: 264, **267,**
Vraciu, Cdr. Alexander: **70**, 88, 210, **213**, 215, **215**, 299, **299**, 304, 311, 384

V
Waddy, Robert (*Australian*): 124
Wade, F/O Lance: 369, 370
Wade, 2Lt. Robert: 350. 399
Wagner, LtCol. Boyd (Buzz): 82, 83, 103, **103**, 112,**112, 179**, 179
Wainwright, Gen. Jonathon : 188
Waits, 1Lt. Joe: 327
Walber, 1Lt. Robert: 262
Walker, Lt. Col. George: 172
Walker, Lt(jg) Leonard: 335
Wallace, Col. W.J.: 236
Walsh, 1Lt. Kenneth: 223, 223, 398, **409, 415**, 418
Wang, 1Lt. Kuang-Fu (*Chinese*): 376, 376
Ward, Ens. Lyttleton: 384
Washington, President George: 420
Warsitz, Erich (*German*): 329
Watkins, Capt. James: 345, 347
Watson, Capt. Ralph: 131
Weaver, F/O Claude: 370, 410, **411**
Weaver, Capt. Edwin: 89
Webb, Lt. Wilbur: 299, 300
Webster, 2Lt. John: 97, 100
Weiber, Capt. C.W.: 223, 290
Weissenberger, Theo (*German*): 331
Welch, Capt. George: 82, 96, 97, **97, 98, 99, 100**, 111, **111**, 112, **414**, 414, 419
Wells, 1Lt. Albert: 350
Wellwood, 1Lt. Robert: 253, 254

Welsh, Brig. Gen. W.W.: 11
Welter, Kurt (*German*): 76
Weltman, Maj. John: 100, **101**, 101
Werff, Peter (*German*): 411
West, Capt. Richard: **264**, 267
Westbrook, Lt. Col. Robert: **264**, 267
Wetmore, Capt. Raymond: **75, 82,**
Weymouth, Cdr. Ralph: 239
Whisner, Capt. William: 77, **161**, 161, **264, 278, 279**
White, 1Lt. Charles: 172
White, 1Lt. Eugene: **333**, 333
White, 2Lt. Thomas Ace: 406, **407**
Whitehead, Gen. Ennis: **175, 296,** 418
Whiteman, 2Lt. George: 98, 100
Whittern, 1Lt. Harold: 256
Widhelm, LtCdr. William (Gus): **250**, 254
Wiecks, Capt. Max: **150**, 150,
Wilhide, 1Lt. Robert: 253
Williams, 1Lt. Carl: 130
Williams, T/Sgt. Francis: 451
Williams, Lt(jg) George; 338
Williamson, Capt. Felix: 348
Williamson, LtCol. Herbert: 86
Willis, Capt. Donald: **287**, 287
Wilson, Maj. Cy: 382
Wind, Hans (*Finn*): 237

Wingate, Gen. Orde: 80
Winston, Capt. Robert: 384
Winterfeld, Alexander von (*German*): **281, 411**
Wirth, Lt. John: 398
Wolf, F/L Fritz: 119, **119, 120**
Wolfe, Capt. Judge: **167, 318**
Wood, Alfred: **217,** 217, **282**
Wood, Lt. Ernest: 282
Woodhouse, Patty (*English*):368
Woods, MajGen. Lewis: 342
Woods, Robert: **177,** 178
Woods, LtCol. Sidney: **320, 381**
Wordell, Lt. Malcomb (Mac): 195
Wurtsmith, Gen. Paul: 381

Y
Yamamoto, Iroki: 293
Yeager, Capt. Charles: **383, 412, 413,** 413
Yeager, Glennis: 383
Yost, Col. Donald: 268
Young, Cdr. Howard (Brigham): **96, 237**
Young, 1Lt. Jules: 153

Z
Zemke, Col. Hubert (Hub): **53,** 54, **77, 80, 81, 82, 145, 280, 345**